THE NAVAL GENERAL SERVICE MEDAL ROLL 1793–1840

THE NAVAL GENERAL SERVICE MEDAL ROLL 1793-1840

GUNNER THOMAS HAINES R.N.

His seven clasp medal, one of three earned with this supreme number of clasps, illustrates awards for participation in Fleet (Gold Medal), Squadron, Frigate and Army co-operation actions covering a span of fourteen years. The award also offers some examples of the deviations from perfection which can occur with these historic medals; explained at greater length in the text.

The clasp 'POMPEE 17 June 1809' commemorates an engagement fought on 17 April 1809; the mistake stemming from a printing error in the 'Medal Action List'. Its place in the tray of clasps should be between 'MARTINIQUE' (24 Feb 1809) and 'GUADALOUPE' (5 Feb 1810); an error on the 'Mint List' or by an artisan. Only five of his seven claims were entered on the 'Clasp Lists' due to lax recording of a clerk. The service history of Haines proves his presence in H.M.Ships SOUTHAMPTON and POMPEE at the time of the actions, but even more telling is the proof provided by his photograph (circa 1850). This studio portrait is on glass (daguerrotype) with the medal fashionably painted; the use of a bright light clearly reveals an image of seven separate bars. The details of his rank on the edge of his medal have been vainly(?) altered. The title 'Gunner' has been erased and his assumed rank of 'Lieut' substituted in engraved style alongside his original machine indented naming details.

The handiwork of the stitched button-hole and silver buckle add those finishing nostalgic touches to disclose a deservedly proud 'Old Salt'.

THE NAVAL GENERAL SERVICE MEDAL ROLL

1793–1840

KENNETH DOUGLAS-MORRIS

Printed and bound in Great Britain by Antony Rowe Ltd, Eastbourne

CONTENTS

Dedication to His Royal Highness, The Prince of Wales .... *page* ix

Frontispiece: Gunner Haines' 7-clasp medal iii

List of subscribers x

Sources and acknowledgements xi

Foreword xiii

The History of The Naval General Service Medal xv

Statistics and survival notes xlv

The Medal Roll 1

Abbreviations 400

Index 401

To

His Royal Highness

Charles Philip Arthur George

The Prince of Wales

K.G., K.T., G.C.B., A.K.

Patron

The Orders and Medals Research Society

The Society of Friends Royal Naval Museum,
Portsmouth

Etc

This

Work containing the History and Roll of
recipients of the
Naval General Service Medal 1793-1840

is

by his gracious permission
respectfully dedicated
by his Royal Highness' most obedient servant
The Author

SOURCES AND ACKNOWLEDGMENTS

SOURCES

The Royal Archives at Windsor Castle, reproduced by the most gracious permission of Her Majesty the Queen: extracts from documents RA E 35/25, RA E 35/29, RA E 35/33.

The Public Record Office: Crown copyright reserved, published by permission of the Controller of Her Majesty's Stationery Office. Class/Piece references, ADM 171/1-8. 1/5599. 36/- & 37/- series. ADM 73/94 (G.H.Roll). W.O. 1/598-600. 6/127. MINT 1/40.6/128.21/5.

Hansard: extracts from House of Lords and House of Commons debates.

London Gazettes: (author's own library, 1776-1976)

Coat of Arms of H.R.H. The Prince of Wales is copyright of Sir A. Wagner, J. Brooke-Little and R.O. Dennys.

ACKNOWLEDGMENTS

First and foremost to the staff at the Public Record Office for their many kindnesses, and also to Nicholas Cox, Principal Assistant Keeper, who so courteously consented to write the Foreword.

The history of the award would have been less than its present completeness but for the enthusiasm and expert help so generously provided by Major Charles E.C. Townsend.

My co-author of 'Gunfire in Barbary', Roger Perkins, has subtly made changes to the text of an editorial character, for which it is hard to express my true gratitude.

Private publishers of books need professional friends. It has been my boundless good fortune to be advised and assisted by just such men as Chris Reed, Christopher Steele, Christopher Bradshaw, John Maw, Peter Spurrier, Colin White, Michael Naxton, Alf Flatow and John Tamplin, and for very especial reasons my sincere thanks go to Henry Pownall, Q.C. and John Clarke.

The photographs appearing on the frontispiece were produced by my talented numismatic colleague, Bob Scarlett. The medal and portrait are in the author's collection on permanent display at the Royal Naval Museum, Portsmouth.

The trust, practical aid and moral encouragment of the subscribers has provided a most heart warming experience.

Chris Buckland deserves great credit for being the catalyst in the discussive process which led to the production of this book at this time and to this standard.

But for this tome, I presume some 3,000 hours might have been devoted to my Peggy. Her illustrious part in this work is that she never begrudged me more than a few minutes of this period of selfish indulgence.

FOREWORD

The twenty years of naval War against Revolutionary France and the Napoleonic Empire were the earliest series of maritime engagements for which this country gave recognition to every man who served regardless of his rank or station. The Naval General Service Medal was the mark of that recognition. The fascination which the medal has excercised over naval historians and students of medals for this very reason is demonstrated by the copious published literature concerning it and by much painstaking research in the unwieldy records relating to it.

The medal was first issued thirty-three years after the end of the war and over half a century after the earliest naval action for which it could be claimed. The Committee of flag officers set up by the Admiralty in 1847 to consider the first claims transacted its business and submitted a first report in just over two months. And in the three years before the final report was made, the Committee dealt with over 23,000 letters and proved almost 21,000 claims. It is no wonder that the records of these transactions are unwieldy and that the later nineteenth century Admiralty, faced with their bulk, treated them with the same robustness with which it treated so many of its detailed papers of this period, so that much of the particular information that the historian of the medal would now wish to have available has perished.

Captain Douglas-Morris tells the tale of the seven years of campaigning to have the medal issued, and weaves his way through the intricacies of the procedures that the Admiralty and the Medal Committee laid down for making and settling the vast number of claims. Like his predecessors, who have studied the medal and published concerning it, he remarks with regret on the many serious inaccuracies in the records resulting from the speed of the Committee's work, and the number of claims they had to verify. Many of these inaccuracies have been perpetuated by a curious accident of archival history. When the records of the medal were transferred to the Public Record Office in 1961, included with them was a volume (ADM 171/8) which is not a contemporary record at all, but a roll of the medal's recipients compiled early in this century by Colonel D.A. Hailes, R.M. Although the Hailes Roll has been of considerable value, based as it was on detailed work including use of some original records which have disappeared between 1912 and now, it incorporated many of the old errors of the original records and also, unfortunately, added not a few new ones. Its inclusion in a class of original nineteenth century records has given it an appearance of authenticity which it does not really deserve. It is to be hoped that this new published Medal Roll, based on a dozen or more years of work by its editor will now be seen to replace Hailes. Those who use the records of the Naval General Service Medal in the Public Record Office will have every reason to be grateful to Captain Douglas-Morris for the results of his long efforts.

Nicholas Cox
Public Record Office, 1982

THE HISTORY OF THE NAVAL GENERAL SERVICE MEDAL
(1793–1840)

Soon after its inception in 1847, a clerk employed at the Royal Mint made reference to this historic award as the 'Naval Peninsular Medal'. To the present day student of medallic history this was nothing more than a quaint misnomer, but in fact his chosen title describes exactly the circumstances surrounding its origins.

The inception of the 'Naval War Medal' (for this became its common title until the 'Naval General Service Medal' was introduced in 1915) was only coincidentally connected with the long discussions which initiated the army's 'Peninsular Medal'.

But for the tenacity of certain army officers, old campaigners from the Peninsular War who sought some form of medallic recognition for their past military endeavours, the need for this naval medal roll would never have arisen. It is therefore right and proper that the detailed story of the introduction of the 'Naval War Medal', with its two hundred and thirty-one different clasps, should be preceded by the more general story of the intense struggle to obtain what is now called the 'Military General Service Medal' (1801–1814).

After the end of that 'late Great War', a term used until the end of the 19th century to describe the two decades of conflict with France, there were constant rumblings of discontent, voiced in Service circles and ventilated in military journals and the Press, by men who had received no reward or recognition. Gold medals had been awarded to senior officers in both the army and navy for certain prestigious victories on land and at sea during the period of the war. Then the battle of Waterloo led to the issue of the first campaign medal for any armed forces of the Crown. Every officer and man who participated in that battle, '... Field Marshal or drum-boy ...', received a silver medal of identical design and with his name and regiment impressed upon the outer rim. From that time onwards, there was a persistent but uncoordinated campaign of pleas for similar treatment to commemorate earlier military successes. After twenty-five years of such criticism there commenced a collective approach to the problem, culminating a few years later in justice being accorded to surviving personnel who had fought in battles up to half a century earlier.

In 1840 a number of not so young ex-Peninsular officers placed a memorial before the Duke of Wellington on the subject of their outstanding just desserts as '... undecorated officers ...'. The Duke later explained his stand and reasons for his opposition to this preliminary approach in a letter (10 December 1846) to Lord John Russell: '... Some years have elapsed since the officers who had served in the Peninsular addressed a letter to me in which they expressed the desire that I would apply, and recommend, that a medal should be struck and one granted to each of them in commemoration of their services. In answer to this letter I again recognized their merits and their services but declined to make the desired application and recommendation ...'

His reasons for such a stolid refusal to help his fellow officers were voiced even more succinctly in a House of Lords debate (21 July 1845): '... I stated (to the petitioners) that as to the rewards to the army, these were matters to which I could otherwise make no reference – that they were acts which were confined to the Sovereign, and to the advisers of the Sovereign – and that in this light I had never presumed to interfere in any manner, excepting when called upon to give my opinion, or to carry into execution the orders of the Sovereign to recommend persons for honourable marks of distinction. My Lords, I then recommended those Gentlemen to make their representation to the Sovereign through the proper channel . . . I have inquired whether any application has since been made; and I can not only find no trace of such application but I cannot find any account of such an application having been ever made . . .'

The memorialists did not indeed choose to approach their young and newly married Queen, especially without the background aid of such a dominant advisor as the Duke of Wellington. They had to wait four years before they could find someone to champion their personal cause in the chamber of the House of Commons.

By then (1844) the issue of campaign medals was no longer a novelty confined to former veterans of Waterloo. More and more servicemen, and the public in general, were becoming aware that successful campaigns were being honoured by the presentation of a breast worn emblem. Foreign, Colonial and national governments had approved many different campaign medals since 1840 when the Duke had been first collectively approached.

Following the conclusion of the Syrian campaign in 1840 (a predominantly naval affair), the Sultan of Turkey had caused a medal to be struck to reward the services of his Allies. In making this gesture of respect he was following the precedent of a former Sultan who had awarded gold medals of varying size to British officers of differing ranks, both naval and military, engaged in the Egyptian campaign of 1801. The new Turkish Syrian medal, the 'Jean D'Acre' award, had a far wider distribution to participants. From 26 March 1842, the Admiralty was able to distribute these medals, delivered from overseas, to each and every man who had served aboard vessels employed along the war torn coast of Syria and in the blockade of the port of Alexandria. Senior officers received diamond studded gold medals. Other recipients, depending upon their rank or rate, were presented with similar sized medals in gold, silver or bronze. All received rewards, from Admiral to Boy Third Class. Naval personnel could now wear their first officially approved campaign award, albeit of foreign presentation, for duty performed as British subjects acting in the name of the Crown.

By the year 1844 the East India Company had given approval for several different medals to be struck to commemorate various military actions in the sub-continent and the Queen was pleased to permit these to be presented and worn by eligible European and native servicemen. The military forays so honoured were at GHUZNEE (1839), CANDAHAR – GHUZNEE – CABUL (1841–42), JELLALABAD (1842) and the defence of KELAT-I-GHILZIE in 1842.

Late in 1842 it was announced that the government of India intended to present silver medals to the officers and soldiers of the Army of India who had served in China during the Opium War. Making a clean break with the past, the young Queen (most likely at the behest of her Consort) directed instead that the achievements in China be honoured by her Home government in London. The following passage, in a reply to the Chairman of the East India Company, places this particular campaign medal in historic perspective, as the first awarded on an inter-service basis by the British government: '. . . the Governor-General of India will, I am convinced, share with you and with me in the satisfaction which we feel that the reward, intended by the Govt of India for the naval and military forces of the Company serving with Her Majesty's fleet and army in China, is now to be derived from the highest fountain of honour . . .'

The Duke of Wellington was informed in early January 1843 '. . . that Her Majesty has been pleased to give directions that a medal should be prepared for the purpose of commemorating the signal successes of Her Majesty's naval and military forces upon the coast and in the interior of the Empire of China . . .' The criteria for award were then set out for him in detail. Men would be eligible who had served at any one of thirteen different actions in China during 1841 and 1842. Some of these actions bore little resemblance, in severity of fighting, with the unrewarded Gold Medal actions of the Peninsular War or the major and minor sea-battles of the conflict between 1793 and 1815.

It was against the background of this more enlightened and egalitarian approach by the authorities that the army petitioners heard their case brought up in the House of Commons. The proposer was Sir Andrew L. Hay in a debate (16 April 1844) earning the heading in Hansard of 'Officers who served in the Peninsular War', where he too had served (1808–1814) as A.D.C. to General Sir James Leith.

His Motion was '... to call upon the House to address the Crown praying Her Majesty to be graciously pleased to confer an honorary distinction on the surviving officers of the Peninsular army'. This narrowly drawn submission, to reward only some officers and only in one particular theatre of conflict, was opposed by the Secretary-at-War, General Sir Henry Hardinge, who instanced other areas such as America, India and Egypt where '... brilliant services were performed by our troops'. Captain Sir Charles Napier, R.N., speaking in support of the Motion, stated that he '... could not agree to the principle, that because justice had been delayed for 34 years, it was too late now to grant that reward to the officers and men who had served their country in those battles ... it was never too late to do a good thing ...'. Although he never mentioned an extension of the principle to commemorate naval successes, he did speak strongly in favour of letting the medals be given only to *surviving* officers and men retrospectively for *all* past famous army victories throughout the globe.

Admiral Sir George Cockburn was against the Motion on the basis that 'he had witnessed gallant actions in various parts of the world, and he thought that it would be a great injustice to distinguish the officers of the Peninsular alone ... If it had been the practice to give medals in the early part of the war, those who were present at the Battle of Trafalgar, at the action on the 1st of June and at the battle of Copenhagen, would all have been entitled to medals?'. It is interesting to note that he coupled Copenhagen (1801), which was not a Gold Medal Action, with two that were so honoured.

The Admiral ended his short speech somewhat negatively but nevertheless most prophetically by saying '... if they went back to bestow medals upon the officers and men who had been engaged in all the great battles of the last war, they must go back to a period of more than half a century. The question was, would the government be justified in going back so far?' He thought that an assent to the Motion 'would be attended with very great difficulty'. Sir A.L. Hay then withdrew the Motion '... being conscious of the impossibility of succeeding'. It is interesting to note that, despite the presumed 'very great difficulty', the gallant Admiral Cockburn later received, in 1849, his Naval War Medal with five clasps. The earliest clasp related to his services on 14 March 1795, fifty four years earlier!

A little over a year after the 'cause' had been abortively debated in the Lower Chamber, the Duke of Richmond presented the same Petition for debate in the House of Lords on 21 July 1845. Whilst this airing of the subject in the Upper House achieved nothing tangible, it did introduce to the scene a proposer who was to prove the real champion of the principle of retrospective awards. It was the Duke of Richmond, by his consistent and ardent advocacy, who was to win a belated recognition for the ageing veterans. As the Earl of March he had been A.D.C. to the Duke of Wellington 1810–1814, and later to The Prince of Orange at Waterloo.

In this debate the Duke of Wellington spoke at length, opposing the Motion. Referring later to the content of his speech, he wrote: '... these officers and soldiers subsequently petitioned the House of Lords upon the subject, the object being that the House should interfere to obtain from the Sovereign some mark of distinction for their services. I was at the time in the Queen's Service and was charged with the duty of superintending the conduct of the business of Her Majesty's government in the House of Lords. It was my duty to object to taking notice of the Petition on the ground that such notice would be an interference with the prerogative of the Crown.' Furthermore, he said he had pointed out '... the necessity that care should be taken not to create a precedent which might have an influence in deciding upon similar applications from other armies and fleets employed in the service of the country in bygone periods of time, possibly 50 or 60 years distant, instead of 40.'

Hansard records that, upon naval matters, he voiced opinions which were to prove as rhetorically negative and yet as unintentionally prescient as the views expressed the year previous by Admiral Cockburn. It is with the gift of hindsight that naval medal collectors today may smile upon these next remarks, made by the Iron Duke when opposing the issue of marks of commemorative distinction: '... but I would beg your Lordships to recollect that this is not the only successful army which has served this country: Your Lordships must not forget the army of Egypt, you must not forget the army that fought in Calabria. And when you recollect these services, I would beg your Lordships also not to forget the fleets. Did anyone ever hear of a general medal for a fleet? And yet there have been great naval victories acquired, such as the battle of the 1st of June, the battle of Cape St Vincent, and the Battle of the Nile. Did anyone ever hear of a general medal worn by everybody for those services? Surely if the Peninsular army is to have a grant of this description, and an address is presented by your Lordships for that object, it is impossible that your Lordships should not notice these other occasions. Then there is another circumstance which I beg you to recollect in favour of the navy: I mean those long winter campaigns, if I may so venture to call them, in the blockade of the coast of France, and in the Bay of Biscay. Month after month, week after week, and night after night, that blockade was persevered in through the skill of the officers and seamen in the ships of war of the Sovereign of this Country. Are these services not to be rewarded equally with continued campaigns on shore for six years in winter and summer? Certainly they must be. If you take the step now, you must take others; and it would be impossible that you should not carry the measure to the full extent of giving a general brevet, in fact to everybody who ever served during the whole of the war, as well of the French Revolution as in the Peninsula.'

The Duke was remiss in his homework, for he is hardly fair to two private patrons of the Navy who, from their own pockets, funded medals to every member of the fleets at the Nile (Davison's Medal) and off Cape Trafalgar (Boulton's Medal). A man of great distinction, who often had performed seemingly 'impossible' feats with his army, he was later in this story to find himself in the position of having to compromise the opinions expressed in this speech.

J.H. Mayo, in his erudite set of histories concerning medal awards ('Medals and Decorations of the British Army and Navy', published in 1897) would appear to have been unaware of this important debate (as were many succeeding plagiarisers of his scholastic work).

Twelve months passed before yet another apparently barren public debate took place on a more widely drawn idea for awards. But behind the scenes there were other more persuasive forces at work, and these added to a marginally different approach in Parliament may well have tipped the balance towards ultimate success.

In the House of Commons on 19 August 1846, Sir De Lacy Evans moved several Motions dealing with army pay, promotion and purchase of commissions under the generic title of 'Claims of the Army', adding *inter alia* one extra proposal on the need for retrospective awards for both army and naval personnel. His approach to the subject differed from earlier proposers. He was no doubt influenced by the announcement, one month earlier, that the 14,000 China War (1842) Medals, all of similar design and minted in silver, were ready for issue to every participating soldier, sailor or marine (whatever his exalted rank or lowly rate). His Motion, hidden amongst others, was no repetitious claim for honours solely to Peninsular officers. A short passage on this subject, spoken by De Lacy Evans (who had served as a cavalry subaltern in the Peninsular War for two years and who subsequently commanded the 'British Auxiliary Legion' in the

Carlist War of 1835–40) bears repetition, since it caught the mood of a mounting swell of public opinion in favour of awards for long past but not forgotten battles: '... it appeared very strange that one battle or two should be considered sufficient on a recent occasion to entitle those engaged in them to a medal; and that six years' constant fighting in the Peninsula should not be considered sufficient to establish a claim either to a medal or a ribbon. When they had seen medals recently given for so many shorter periods of service, it appeared inconsistent to refuse that mark of distinction to those who fought at Trafalgar or in the Peninsula. He trusted, therefore, that Government would consent to grant to them the same boon which it had already conferred upon others'.

Whilst a few Members supported the concept, the Prime Minister, Lord John Russell, and the Secretary-at-War, Mr Fox Maule, both opposed his proposals on the simple and oft used basis in former debates '... that it was now too late to make any recommendation to the Sovereign on such a subject...'. De Lacy Evans withdrew his Motion with the caveat that he would bring it again before the House early next session. But his plan was soon overtaken by intervention from 'the highest fountain of honour'.

The Sovereign has so far stayed her hand on this subject, even though, in the Spring of 1846, she had received from the Duke of Richmond a copy of the same memorial which had been presented earlier to both Houses by officers of the Peninsular Army. Now, only a few months after the debate in August and with the words of the memorial well analysed, the Queen was to wipe away all trivial opposition to her veteran soldiers and sailors receiving a medallic memento for their former services.

In this letter from the Queen to the Duke of Wellington, drafted personally by H.R.H. Prince Albert and dated 25 November 1846, the classic and historic Military and Naval General Service medals were conceived, albeit the reference here was only to the military award: 'The Queen has learned from various quarters that there still exists a great anxiety amongst the officers and men who served under the Duke of Wellington's orders in the Peninsula to receive and wear a medal as a testimony that they assisted the Duke in his great undertaking. The Queen not only thinks their wish very reasonable, considering that for recent exploits of infinitely inferior importance such distinctions have been granted by her, but she would feel personally a great satisfaction in being enabled publicly to mark in this way her sense of the great service the Duke of Wellington has rendered to his country and to empower many a brave soldier to wear this token in remembrance of the Duke.'

The Duke of Wellington, no doubt highly flattered by the terms of the Queen's letter, soon produced a mode of carrying the Royal command into execution. Those Peninsular army actions for which Gold Medals had been struck and presented to senior officers would be now commemorated by a new silver medal. On 17 December 1846, Earl Grey (Secretary of State for War and Colonies) informed the Duke that his plan of execution has received the Queen's approval. The Sovereign had consequently directed that a medal, to be called the Peninsular Medal, '... should be struck to record the services of the British army in the Peninsular War, and should be conferred upon the general officers, officers, non commissioned officers and soldiers who were present at the battles and sieges most worthy of commemoration which took place during that war...'. Furthermore, the Duke was informed that '... it is intended that the representatives (being direct descendants of officers and soldiers who, if they had survived would have been entitled to medals) should also be allowed to receive them'. Whilst the former rules restricting awards to the Peninsula area were later expanded to cover other theatres, the latter suffered the practical necessity of limiting awards only to survivors.

There was, however, still no approval for a naval commemorative equivalent, despite the helpful fact that the Duke of Wellington had forwarded (5 December 1846) to Prince Albert his 'means of execution' for the introduction of the Peninsular Medal allied with a covering statement: '... its principle can be applied, if such application should be necessary, to the services performed by the navy at the same or even at a more early period, equally recognised at the time by the grant of a medal (Large and/or Small

Naval Gold Medal) according to the Regulations of those days...'. He also offered the possibility of widening the army actions to include the Gold Medal successes at Maida and during the war in North America.

During the next five months some unrecorded negotiations took place which were to bring the navy into line with the army, with the most likely advocate in Royal circles being the Duke of Richmond. He had received, on 18 December 1846, a copy of a letter from Sir George Grey (Home Secretary) which authorised the institution of the Peninsular Medal, and upon which the Duke wrote the laconic and historic comment: 'The navy should have it'. This is exactly what happened in late May 1847, more than five months after Royal assent was given for the army's Peninsular Medal.

The red letter day for the sailors of long ago (and for modern naval medal students) was 27 May 1847. On this day the Earl Grey informed the Duke of Wellington that Royal approval had just been granted for the introduction (for Gold Medal actions only) of the reward we now call 'The Naval General Service Medal (1793-1840)'. He wrote: '... I have now to acquaint your Grace that Her Majesty has since (my letter 17 Decr 1846) been graciously pleased to command that the intended token of distinction should not be confined to those who served in the Peninsula, but that a Military and also a Naval Medal should be struck, one of which is to be conferred upon every officer, non commissioned officer, Petty Officer, seaman and soldier and of the army and navy who was present in any action, engagement or battle from the commencement of the war in 1793 down to the peace of 1814 for which medals have been given to the superior officers, but for which none have been granted to the inferior ranks of the two Services ... It is considered by H.M. Government that the grant of these medals should be strictly limited to the surviving officers, non commissioned officers, Petty Officers, seamen and soldiers of both Services who shall apply for it...'.

The separate General Orders issued from Horse Guards and from the Admiralty, dated 1st June 1847, which gave details of the introduction of the retrospective awards (later to become known as the Military General Service Medal and the Naval General Service Medal), were advertised to the general public in the London Gazette. These simultaneously dated announcements have masked, in some former histories on this subject, the fact that the issue of the naval reward had lain in the balance for months, as had recognition of army actions fought not only in the Iberian Peninsula but in other parts of the world.

During the seven years of struggle to obtain tangible recognition for veterans of the late Great War, it is obvious that opposition to the concept stemmed from one man, the Duke of Wellington. He stood a square head and shoulders above any other senior military or naval officer of his day. It was his stature and reputation which made the army the senior service.* The only comparable naval officer to utter words on the subject was the First Sea Lord, Vice Admiral Sir George Cockburn, and his negative approach did little to enhance the claims of his junior service. Some mystery still sur-

---

*On the question of the precedence of the Royal Navy, or for that matter the date when the 'Royal Navy' as a formalised title emerged from 'His/Her Britannic Majesty's Navy', little has been formerly written. Notice of the need to regularise this matter arose some twenty years after these medals were introduced, although most people today probably think that the navy's status as the 'Senior Service' stemmed from the days of Lord Nelson's great victories, or even earlier. But t'was not so!

At a Review ceremony to celebrate Lord Napier's taking of Magdala in April 1868, the position of the Naval Rocket Brigade amongst the troops assembled was to be 'on the right of all dismounted branches of the Services'. The cavalry took the prestigious position, as the senior Corps, to the right of the whole parade. Four years later, in 1872, when Captain Tryon (later Admiral, and of fame for the loss of H.M.S. VICTORIA) was Private Secretary to the First Lord of the Admiralty, he fought consistently for the navy to participate in Court favours and honours, previously lavished almost exclusively upon the sister service. His implacable struggle reached its goal and zenith when, against the most strenuous of opposition, he succeeded in agreement to the positioning of a brigade of seamen '... in the place of honour, on the right of the line at St Pauls, as the senior service ...' at the public thanksgiving for the recovery from a serious illness of the Prince of Wales. This new position, with Jack Tars taking precedence over all other servicemen, also reflected the love the public now had for them. They had gained the affectionate nickname of 'Handymen'.

rounds the all important part played by the Duke of Richmond. He seems to be the individual who convinced and won over the Queen and Prince Albert to his constructive ideas for the initiation of these two medals.

The motives of the Duke of Wellington, his dogged earlier opposition to the principle of these awards, his *volte face,* and his subsequent helpful submissions on the mode of execution, are enigmatically described in his own short biographical critique of this whole affair: 'It thus appears that I had objected to the grant of a medal and had stated strong reasons against making it, until informed that it was the wish of the Sovereign and Her Ministers that it would be made.

I then eagerly adopted the plan and suggested means to facilitate its execution to render it satisfactory and to preclude the evil consequences which I had apprehended might result from it.

This course is quite consistent with that which I have followed upon this subject since my first discussion in writing with the officers. I there leave it but I confess that I am anxious that there should be no misrepresentations upon this subject, nor grounds for such as that I had altered my opinion, or my course, with a view to obtaining a distinction or mark of approbation for myself.'

Students of the Duke of Wellington will recall the very different opinion expressed in his letter (dated 28 June 1815) to the Duke of York (Commander in Chief) wherein he stated that; 'I beg leave to suggest to your Royal Highness the expediency of giving the non commissioned officers and soldiers engaged in the Battle of Waterloo a medal. I am convinced it would have the best effect on the Army, and if that Battle should settle our concerns they will deserve it.' A humbler approach exuding sympathetic consideration without thoughts of any 'evil consequences' stemming from his momentously novel approach to rewards!

Turning back now to the 5th Duke of Richmond, the real esteem in which he was held by grateful recipients of their commemorative breast adornments has most recently come to light. In Goodwood House there stands a tall silver trophy of magnificent design and proportions, a glorious example of the silversmith's craft. Four feet in height, it bears a statuette of the Duke at its apex, with some twenty beautifully modelled figures of army and navy officers and men in their distinctive uniforms around but above its base, on which four illustrative plaques in silver depict sea and land battles.

The two side panels list those naval and military engagements considered of greatest importance, with the frontal inscription reading:

PRESENTED on June 21 1851 The Thirtyeighth Anniversary of the Battle of Vittoria To His Grace The Duke of Richmond Lennox and D'Aubigné K.G. by the Recipients of the War Medal in grateful remembrance of his long and unwearied exertions in their behalf. As a Token of Admiration, Respect and Esteem from his humbler Brethren in Arms who successfully aided in defending Their Island Home throughout a long and sanguinary war in which they gained a series of resplendent victories that led to the capture of MADRID, PARIS and WASHINGTON and finally to an honourable and lasting peace.

The subscribers to this superb table monument, '... a piece of the value of fifteen hundred guineas ...', would appear to have been in no doubt as to whom thanks should be given for their much smaller silver rewards.

THE NAVAL GENERAL SERVICE MEDAL ROLL 1793–1840
Rules for claimants of the Naval War Medal

Commencing in June 1847, and spreading over the ensuing three and a half years, five separate and different 'Advertisements' on this subject were published in the London Gazette. It was from these 'Advertisements' that elderly sea-dogs, tarpaulins, tars and jollies gradually learnt of their full entitlement to the medal and clasps. Each successive publication increased the scope for award as officialdom gradually accepted that some types of action were equally as deserving of medallic reward as those initially listed.

Before description is given in detail of the 'Advertisements', and of the discussion leading to each change, it is important to show the broad outline of the commemorative purpose for all but the last of the five publications:

June 1847: Gold Medal actions
June 1848: army co-operation and actions post 1815
January 1849: actions which resulted in the promotion of a First Lieutenant, and Boat Service actions
February 1850: Egypt

The first 'Naval Advertisement' for rewards was based on precepts laid down by the Duke of Wellington in his 'means of execution' letter, dated 5 December 1846, and his covering note which stated that the principle of commemorating Peninsula Gold Medal actions could be applied, if necessary, '... to the services performed by the Navy at the same or even at a more early period ...'

Unfortunately this first 'Advertisement', which appeared in the London Gazette dated 1st June 1847 (p.2044), contained mistakes. In the 'List of Actions', some British and enemy ships' names had become transposed in error, thus giving the impression that the enemy ship had been victorious! A revised edition of this anomalous 'Advertisement' was published three days later, on 4th June 1847, as follows:

"   LONDON GAZETTE.   4th JUNE 1847.   (*Page 2051-2*)
(For the Notice dated "Admiralty" in the Gazette of the 1st June 1847, page 2044, the following is substituted.)
Admiralty, 1st June 1847.

Her Majesty having been graciously pleased to command that a Medal should be struck to record the services of Her Fleets and Armies, during the Wars commencing in 1793 and ending in 1815, and that one should be conferred on every Officer, Non Commissioned Officer, Petty Officer, Soldier, Seaman, and Marine, who was present in any Action, naval or military, to commemorate which medals have been struck by Command of Her Majesty's Royal Predecessors, and distributed to Superior Officers, according to the rules of the Service at that time in force.

All Officers, Petty Officers, Seamen, and Marines, who consider that they are entitled to receive this mark of their Sovereign's gracious recollection of their services, and of Her desire to record the same, are to send in writing the statement of their claims, addressed to the Secretary of the Admiralty, Whitehall, London, specifying for what Action, and at what period of time the claim is preferred, and the names of the persons or the titles of the documents by which it can be established.

A Board of Officers will be appointed to take into consideration the facts stated in these applications and to report upon the same to the Lords Commissioners of the Admiralty, for the information of Her Majesty, so as to enable those commanded by Her Majesty to deliver to the claimants the medals accordingly.

The names of all those, who may apply for the Naval Medal will be classed alphabetically, and to each name will be appended the Actions at which the claimant may have been present, proof of which must be given to the entire satisfaction of the Board.

The occasions for which Medals have been granted by the Sovereign are specified below, for general information and guidance.

THE HISTORY OF THE NAVAL GENERAL SERVICE MEDAL (1793–1840)

By Command of the Lord Commissioners, etc. etc.

Gold Medals (To Flag Officers and Captains) were issued by the Admiralty for the Actions undermentioned:

Lord Howe's action, of the 1st June 1794.
Lord St. Vincent's action, off Cape St. Vincent, 14th February 1797.
Lord Duncan's battle off Camperdown, 11th October 1797.
Lord Nelson's battle of the Nile, 1st August 1798.
Captain Sir Edward Hamilton, H.M's ship Surprise, recapture of the Hermione, 25th October 1799.
Lord Nelson's battle of Trafalgar, 21st October 1805.
Sir Richard Strachan's action, 4th November 1805.
Sir John Duckworth's action, off St. Domingo, 6th February 1806.
Captain Brisbane, H.M's ship Arethusa with H.M's ships Anson, Fisgard and Latona, capture of the island of Curacoa, 1st January 1807.
Captain Michael Seymour, H.M's ship Amethyst, capture of Thetis, 10th November 1808.
Captain Stewart, H.M's ship Seahorse, capture of Badere Zaffer, 6th July 1808.
Captain Mounsey, H.M's sloop Bonne Citoyenne, capture of Furieuse, 6th July 1809.
Captain William Hoste, H.M's ship Amphion, with H.M's ships Cerberus, Active and Volage, action off Lissa, 13th March 1811.
Captain Christopher Cole, H.M's ship Caroline, capture of Banda Neira, 9th August 1810.
Captain Talbot, H.M's ship Victorious, capture of Rivoli, 22nd February 1812.
Captain Broke, H.M's ship Shannon, capture of Chesapeake, 1st June 1813.
Captain E. Palmer, H.M's ship Hebrus, capture of L'Etoile, 27th March 1814.
Captain H. Hope, H.M's ship Endymion, action with President, 15th January 1815. "

From now on the appointed Board of Flag Officers, referred to in this Gazette, was to take charge of the evolution of the award. In so doing it changed the medal's original and special but somewhat narrow historic purpose. The medal became the most ubiquitous of rewards, covering every aspect of naval endeavour and success throughout that 'Great War' and at certain subsequent maritime encounters. In short, the committee created a naval medal for general service. Commentary on how this was achieved is best left at this stage to two official pieces of correspondence which succinctly convey the thoughts and language of those days.

LETTER TO ADM. SIR BYAM MARTIN, G.C.B., CONTAINING THE INSTRUCTIONS OF THE LORDS COMMISSIONERS OF THE ADMIRALTY TO THE COMMITTEE.

Admiralty, June 14th 1847

Sir

Having laid before my Lords Commissioners of the Admiralty your letter of the   instant, I am commanded by their Lordships to convey to you the expression of their satisfaction at your ready compliance with their wish that you should be at the head of a Committee of Naval Officers, to inquire into the claims of medals as signified in the "Gazette" of the 4th inst., and to inform you, that in consequence of the numerous claims already preferred, it is very desirable that the Committee should meet as soon as possible. For this purpose, and for the readier means of reference, a room will be appropriated for the Committee at Somerset House; and my Lords would beg to be informed how soon it would be convenient for the Committee to meet there; when such further arrangements would be made, and assistance afforded, as might be found to be required. With the notice in the "Gazette" herewith enclosed, my Lords scarcely deem it necessary to issue any special instructions for the guidance of the Committee in considering the claims as they come before you. Your long acquaintance with the Service, and with the names of the officers and ships engaged with the enemy, will supply you with the ready means of determining on the greater number of the questions you will have to consider; but it will doubtless be quickly apparent that there are cases not mentioned in the above "Gazette" which must, doubtless, appear to those personally interested in them as intended to be included in the scheme of distinction. To such applications it will be necessary that the Committee should give their attention; and should it appear that they are such as to deserve special consideration, you are invited to represent the same to my Lords, together with such observations and remarks as you may think it desirable to submit to their Lordships.

My Lords request you will communicate the purport of these instructions to Adm. Sir William Gage, Vice-Adm. Sir Bladen Capel and Rear-Adm. Sir James Gordon, who have been appointed to act with you on this Committee, and of which you are to take the chair.

REPORT OF THE UNDERSIGNED FLAG OFFICERS, APPOINTED TO CONSIDER THE CLAIMS TO A MEDAL, FOR SERVICES DURING THE WAR COMMENCING IN 1793 AND ENDING IN 1815.

Admiralty, Somerset House, Aug. 27th 1847

Sir,

We request you will submit to the Lords Commissioners of the Admiralty, the following observations and suggestions, which we offer, with reference to their Lordships' instructions contained in your letter of the 14th of June.

Their Lordships direct our attention specially to the "Gazette" of the 1st of June last, wherein the Queen has signified her gracious intention "to record the services of her Fleets during the war commencing in 1793 and ending in 1815, by conferring a medal on the officers, seamen and marines who were present in any action for which medals were struck by command of Her Majesty's Royal predecessors, and distributed according to the rules of the service at that time in force."

THE QUEEN'S ORDER FULLY CARRIED OUT. In dutiful compliance with this act of grace, which points out for our guidance the particular services for which a medal shall be granted, it has been necessary only to verify the several claims now put before us, for those services, by examining the muster book of the ship to which each applicant respectively belonged, in order to prove actual presence in the battle for which the claim is made.

CREWS OF FRIGATES &c. INCLUDED. We have, perhaps, gone further than a strict construction of the words in the "Gazette" may warrant for it was contrary "to the rules of the Service at that time in force" to bestow a medal on the Captains of frigates and sloops of war associated with the Fleets in great and successful actions; but it would leave Her Majesty's evident intention incomplete, if we did not include in the list for a medal, all the officers, seamen, and marines of such vessels, although their Captains did not, according to the former rule, receive that distinction.

DESCRIPTION OF RETURNS. The book No. 1, sent herewith, will place before their Lordships every action, whether of Fleets or single ships, to which the "Gazette" refers, specifying the names of the ships.

Under the name of each ship follows, in alphabetical order, a list of those persons whose claims have been sent in, and there is a mark corresponding to the number of the applicant's letter, in case at any time it may be necessary to refer to the original document, and to our minute upon it.

A space is left under each ship for such other applications as may hereafter be received. There is a column for the observations of the Committee upon any case that may require comment; another column for desertions from the Service, to which we allude with great satisfaction, on account of their infrequency; but in every such we have noted the individual as unworthy of a medal.

CONJOINT OPERATIONS OF ARMY AND NAVY. The "Gazette" so couples the two professions, Naval and Military, that our intention has naturally been drawn to the claims of the officers, seamen and marines, who had a share in any conjoint operation from which the "Gazette" points out that medals were bestowed upon the Army.

Maida	.. ..	1806.
Martinique	.. ..	1809.
Guadeloupe	.. ..	1810.
Java	.. ..	1811.
St. Sebastian	.. ..	1813.

To this point we now request their Lordship's consideration. The Navy took a part, more or less as circumstances would permit, in all the services mentioned above.

Those officers, seamen, and marines, who have put in claims, in consequence of being landed from the Fleet, and thus, for a time, formed part of the Army, have an unquestionable right to share in the honours, as they did in the perils, of the campaign, in common with the troops.

This claim is readily admitted by the Duke of Wellington, as we are informed by a letter from

THE HISTORY OF THE NAVAL GENERAL SERVICE MEDAL (1793-1840)

Lieut.-Gen. Sir Charles Dalbiac, the Chairman of the Board of General Officers, in reply to a question from us, as to the course intended to be taken by the Military Board in such cases, as we were desirous to guard against the issue of medals by both Services to the same persons.

As such an arrangement will be attended with very little, if any inconvenience, it seems highly desirable that those officers, seamen and marines, who served with the Army should have the gratification of wearing a Military medal. It will carry with it an additional value as a memorial of the harmony with which the two professions always united on such occasions. In like manner we have informed the Board of General Officers of the satisfaction we shall have in receiving and placing on our list for a Naval Medal, the officers, non-commissioned officers, and soldiers of the land Service who were embarked in the ships and served in several actions for which medals were given to the superior officers of the Fleet.

As regards the ships employed in conjoint operations, there appeared to us a necessity for further inquiry as to the nature and degree of their co-operation, in order to see if the crews had such a share in the proceedings against the enemy as to entitle them to the same commemorative notice as was so well earned, and so justly bestowed, on the Military branch of the Service on the occasions before mentioned.

In all these instances strong acknowledgment of the useful, and in some cases, the effective co-operation of the Fleet are to be traced in the public despatches of the Generals.

Perhaps the occasion in which the Navy had the least power to take a share was during the spirited attack upon the enemy at Maida. The General (Sir John Stewart) says,

"The scene of action was too far from the sea to derive any direct co-operation from the Navy; "but Adm. Sir Sydney Smith directed such a disposition of the ships and gun-boats as would have "greatly favoured us had events obliged us to retire."

"The solicitude, however, of every part of the Navy to be of use to us, the promptitude with "which the seamen hastened on shore with our supplies, their anxiety to assist our wounded, and "the tenderness with which they treated them, would have been an affecting circumstance even to "the most indifferent; to me it was particularly so."

Such an acknowledgment is very strong, and cannot fail to be gratifying to the profession at large, as well as to the individuals to whom the compliment is addressed.

That everything was done by the Navy that could be done, no one will doubt; and, in event of adverse circumstances on the battle-ground, the ships would have been everything to a retreating Army. But neither seamen nor marines were present in the action of Maida, or in a position to afford any direct assistance at the moment; we cannot therefore countenance the applications that have been received from some of the survivors of the Squadron, claiming a "medal of distinction" as if participators in that memorable event. It would be repugnant to the feelings of the Service, and offensive to the memory of the high-minded officer who commanded the Squadron, to support questionable claims; but if it shall hereafter appear that any persons belonging to the Fleet were present, and assisting in the action the proof of such service may be submitted to the Military department.

Much may be said, and truly said of the intimidating effect of a Fleet upon an enemy, even at a distance from the scene of operations; and if such a case were to be argued as a claim to prize money, a jury might be led to a different conclusion to that which we arrived in discussing claims to honorary awards.

It may be thought we make no nice distinctions; but when dealing with claims of this nature it is highly desirable to mark out some clearly defined course of service, not of law; and we beg particularly to recommend the subject to the consideration of the Admiralty, as well for the present decision as for future guidance.

We will now for a moment refer to the operations on the coast of America, for which there are also some claims; but we bring it under review more on account of the practical example it affords of what appears to constitute a proper distinction between those belonging to the Fleet, who may fairly claim a participation in honours conferred on the Army, and those who can have no such pretension.

Rear-Admiral Sir George Cockburn was sent by the Com.-in-Chief of the Fleet with a strong party of seamen and marines, in boats forming a large flotilla to act in conjunction with the Army under General Ross. After destroying the opposite flotilla of the enemy, this sea battalion, if we may call it, landed, and united with the Army in a daring, well-executed enterprise, not likely to be out of the recollection of anyone. We are not, however, going to propose that this dashing exploit should, at such a distance of time, receive any mark of distinction beyond what it may have obtained at the moment; but, had this been noticed in the "Gazette" as one of the events commemorated by a Military Medal, we should have said—Give to Sir George Cockburn, and his followers on that occasion, a full share in the honours granted to their gallant companions; but do not include in the compliment seven or eight thousand men in a distant Fleet, ready and willing to share in the attack, but unable to do so from the nature of the coast and the distance of the hostile operations.

This observation and opinion applies with full force to the officers, seamen and marines of the distant Fleet on the coast, at the time of the attack upon the enemy at Maida.

WEST INDIA ISLANDS, JAVA, &c. In the operations carried on against the West India Islands in 1809 and 1810, and Java in 1811 the Fleet was more fortunately circumstanced, and was enabled to act directly and effectually with the Army. General Beckwith, the Commander-in-Chief, says "The co-operation of the Navy (expressed in detail in my despatch No. 6) has been incessant and effectual; and without such exertions, a service of this description, if at all practicable, must have been drawn into great length.

The Navy, on these occasions, attacked the sea defences of the enemy; stormed and took some of the forts; landed seamen and marines to man the batteries; guarded every point to prevent throwing in reinforcements; and kept up the supplies of provisions and ammunition for the besiegers. The Admiral joined with the General in dictating the terms of capitulation, to which his signature is attached. The Navy partook of the thanks of Parliament, and shared in the distribution of prize-money.

We mention these circumstances to show how completely the Services were united and acted together on these occasions, and to warrant a recommendation that medals be granted to the surviving officers, seamen and marines of the ships acting with the Army at Martinique, Guadaloupe, and Java.

The services of the ships acting with the Army at St. Sebastian appear to be entitled to the same distinction.

In book No. 1 will be found the names of all ships at the taking of these islands (Martinique 1809; Guadaloupe 1810; Java 1811.); and in order to guard against any intrusive or undue claims, we obtained from the Admiralty a statement of the Admiral's distribution of his ships during the operations at each place; and as still further evidence of admitted participation in the duties of the enterprise, we procured, most promptly, from the well-regulated Prize Office, the names of each ship which shared in the capture of the islands.

The Admiral's statement is confirmed by the prize list but the latter, in some instances includes some vessels not mentioned in the Admiral's disposition of his Fleet; we, however, insert in our list for medals all which, upon examination of these official documents and the log book, are proved to have been present, and taken part in the operations.

RECAPITULATION. Their Lordships will perceive that what we heretofore have said has reference chiefly to the places named in the "Gazette" being those services for which it appears that the Army, and not the co-operating Fleets, received medals—an omission proper to be corrected at the present time.

What we propose, under this first section of our subject, may be briefly summed up as following:—

1. We recommend that medals be granted to the survivors of the crews of the frigates and smaller vessels present in any general and successful action, for which medals were bestowed on the Captains of ships of the line.

2. We submit for consideration the claims made by some who were in ships associated in the expedition which led to the battle of Maida, and our opinion adverse to the claim.

3. We propose that the officers, seamen and marines of the ships co-operating in the capture of the West India Islands, Java and St. Sebastian be recommended for a medal.

The total number of ships included in the medal list for the foregoing services will be as follows (leaving Maida out for further consideration):—

Total ships of the line engaged in the great actions alluded to in the "Gazette"	109
Frigates, sloops of war, and smaller vessels attending on the Fleets, and present in the actions, recommended to be included	43
Other actions referred to in the "Gazette"	20
	172
Ships co-operating with the Army at the capture of the islands, proposed by the Committee to be included, viz:—	
Martinique	42
Guadaloupe	50
Java	25
St. Sebastian	45
	162
	334

A MORE GENERAL VIEW OF THE SUBJECT. Having in the foregoing sheets stated our proceedings as far as relates to the "Gazette", we come now to the paragraph in your letter, which leaves us free to take the subject more generally, and invites us to offer such observations as we may think desirable.

We have not only well considered the whole bearing of the question before us, but we have examined each individual statement; and this has been done with a constant recollection of their Lordships' considerate regard for those "who may think themselves personally interested and intended to be included in the scheme of distribution," but we dare not hope to realise all such expectations, although we have to submit so large a measure of "medal distinction" as will recognise the claims of all the officers, seamen and marines who were in any action which, at the time it occurred, obtained the marked appreciation of the Admiralty.

To occupy ourselves, as some of the applicants seem to expect, in tracing squadron actions, the single actions, and the spirited operations along the coast of the enemy, throughout a period of 23 years, in order to say which appeared to us most deserving of Royal notice, would be an invidious task, which we feel assured it was never designed we should undertake—for if undertaken it would only aggravate the disappointment against which their Lordships are desirous to guard. It would, indeed, be impracticable to go through such a retrospective examination, as must be evident when it is considered that the glorious result of the actions of the war was the capture or destruction of 156 sail of line-of-battle ships, 382 frigates, 662 corvettes, and, in all 2,506 vessels of war.

To avoid so great a difficulty, and at the same time to meet the expectations of so many of those "who may think themselves intended to be included in the scheme of distinction," we sought some known general principle for our guidance; something done at the same time to stamp with official approbation and reward actions of conspicuous merit; and in this view no better criterion could possibly offer than the rule which prevailed throughout the war.

It was then the practice to mark well fought successful actions by the promotion of the First Lieutenants, or in small vessels the promotion of the officer in command; and this was regarded as a special compliment to the ship, though only beneficial to the individual; except that it gave to all a feeling of pride and perfect satisfaction that their services were so noticed.

This mode of conveying the complimentary approbation of the Admiralty at once enables us to recommend for a "Medal distinction," all officers, seamen, marines and soldiers serving as marines, who took part in any successful action for which the First Lieutenant was promoted; but this condition will not be fulfilled unless the minute of the Board of Admiralty shall be found to connect the promotion of the officer with the event for which the claim was made; or, that the date of his commission shall fully warrant inference that the action was the immediate cause of his advanced rank. Much time must often have elapsed before an action fought on a distant station could be reported to the Admiralty; but if a compliment was intended, it was usual to carry the date of the commission back to the time of the action; and regard to this practice is desirable on the receipt of future applications, as we have found it to be in our investigation of some of the claims. We, however, refer to the rule, without wishing to shut out an indulgent consideration of circumstances tending to prove the validity of claims, although the dates of the action, and of the commission, may not so exactly tally as might be wished.

If this one single rule be adopted, it will extend the scheme of distinction to a vast number of cases; it will include Lord Nelson's battle of Copenhagen in 1801, which though worthy of being classed with the other important actions of the war, has hitherto remained unmarked, except by the promotions of the First Lieutenants.

It is true, a just tribute of Royal approbation and gratitude was bestowed upon the great man who commanded the attack, and upon his second; but the distinction which commemorates other brilliant actions has not been conferred on this, though scarcely inferior to any of those which give such lustre to his Lordship's professional career.

It is not necessary, nor would it be becoming in us to attempt any explanation of this omission; the fact is as we state, and the time has now arrived when that hard fought action may take its due place in the record of Naval rewards.

We repeat that the promotion of the First Lieutenants marked every Fleet or single action deemed worthy of special distinction, whether fought by a cutter or first rate; it was the conduct and intrepidity of the act, not its magnitude, that earned the compliment, and we the more readily propose it to be taken up as the rule for extending the honours now, because its comprehensive operation includes also the occasions for which the Navy separately obtained the thanks of Parliament.

Applications for medals have come in from persons who served in the Fleet under Lord Howe at the time of the occupation of Toulon in 1793; and from some who were in the fleet under Lord Keith employed landing Sir Ralph Abercromby's army in Egypt in 1801; from those who were in the ships at Copenhagen, under Admiral Gambier in 1807; also from some who served in other squadrons, and for services in the lakes in Canada; but as neither the Army nor Navy had medals bestowed upon them on these occasions, their claims cannot now be admitted without going into an examination of all the transactions of the war, to see what other services may be equally entitled to the compliment—a proceeding we have before stated to be impracticable of being carried out without leading to endless disputes and much discontent. The introduction of any one action, hitherto unmarked by any special distinction, however meritorious, must in justice, open the claims to every battle of the 23 years' war service; we therefore deprecate any such measure.

If any services was performed by particular ships of these Fleets, for which the First Lieutenants were promoted as a marked compliment to the occasion, such ships will of course, have the medal, if our proposal be approved, but the "Gazette" gives no sanction to a claim on account of the general services of these Fleets, although important in their way, and known to have been executed in a manner to reflect great credit on the service.

The book No. 2, which we send herewith contains a full list of all the actions for which promotion was given to the First Lieutenants, or officer commanding, as far as we can bring them to recollection (exclusive of the Fleet actions and ships acting with the Army, already stated in book No. 1), and to prevent doubt or mistake, we mention in each case the name of the Lieutenant promoted.

Under each ship follows alphabetically the names of those whose claims have come before us, for services which obtained this mark of approbation, and in all cases, in both books, we leave under each ship's name a space for future applications.

BOAT ACTIONS. There is another class of claimants, by no means to be overlooked in a review of those achievements of the war, which at the time obtained special notice of the Admiralty; namely boat actions in boarding the vessels of the enemy.

Some of these are conspicuous in our naval history as acts of daring intrepidity well worthy of remembrance.

We, therefore, recommend that all successful boat actions, which were complimented at the time by promotion of the officer conducting the enterprise, shall entitle the present survivors, to a medal; but not to include the ships from which they were detached. Several applications for this description of service have already come before us, and will be found registered in book 3, under its proper head.

But we must here claim, and, doubtless through our report, allowance for undesigned omissions, of which no doubt the Admiralty will hereafter be reminded by application from those who have been overlooked.

In book 3 are also included the names of parties whose claims we have not been able to recommend.

PROPOSAL TO US TO RECOMMEND MEDALS FOR ALL WHO SERVED IN THE WAR. Perhaps, foreseeing the difficulty of attempting the comparisons of any one battle with another, in order to select cases for particular notice, may have prompted a proposal we have received to give a medal indiscriminately to every man who served during the war. We think what we have recommended in the foregoing sheets puts an end to the imagined difficulty in finding cases of special merit; they are in fact clearly pointed out to us by the Admiralty at the time they took place; and if what we recommend be approved, the services which obtained distinction will then be the rule for extended distinction now. This will be found so abounding in professional compliment, as to leave no reasonable expectation unsatisfied. We can in no way concur in a proposition which if adopted, would put an end to all the just influence which honours flowing from the Sovereign, and given with strict discrimination, are calculated to produce. If honours be given promiscuously, and become common to all, where shall we trace the distinction of merit.

Lord Nelson, whose saying on the subject, as on other occasions, ought ever to be cherished by the profession, tells us who he thinks ought to receive the meed of Military distinction—"Palmam qui meruit ferat." This was his motto, and if lost sight of so just a definition of what is designed by Military honours, they will cease to have their proper value. It is by making Military and Naval distinctions precious, and not too easily obtained, that they become worthy of the highest efforts of ambition; though this report may be inconsistent with such an opinion, when the sum of our suggestions shall be presently seen to be so large.

In expressing our unqualified objection to an indiscriminate mode of conferring honours, we know and acknowledge that its rejection must shut out many excellent and gallant officers, who earnestly sought out opportunities of distinction, but were denied them by the ever-varying circumstances which give to Naval pursuits so adventitious a character.

We object to this sweeping measure on principle; not on account of the inconvenience it would occasion to the current duties of the Admiralty at Somerset House, though necessarily very great, in tracing out and verifying the claims of 147,000 men including 33,000 Marines, borne on the books of the Fleet during the latter years of the war, and also the survivors of the thousands yearly entered to keep up the numbers.

CLAIMS FROM THE FAMILIES OF OFFICERS AND MEN. Applications have been sent in, by the representatives of those, who had they lived, would on the present occasion be entitled to a medal. This of course would include all the deceased officers and men of the large numbers of ships now proposed for medals, making an enormous aggregate, which we cannot venture to estimate even by conjecture; quite enough, however, to render the claims inadmissable, if it were not objectionable on other grounds.

But we feel assured there will be no disposition to concede the point in favour of the widow, or eldest surviving son, or parent, as the case may be, of any officer, seaman, or marine slain in battle, provided proof of marriage be shown by a duly certified extract from the church register, but on no account to be allowed if not accompanied by such a document.

The three books sent herewith afford such ample information bearing upon every service, and the claim of every man, that it is unnecessary to lengthen our report by any further observations; but it may be convenient shortly to state the number of ships which will come within the scheme of distinction, if our proposal be accepted:—

viz.

Number mentioned in Book No. 1 by Her Majesty's command including frigates	172
Numbers for Islands of Martinique, Guadaloupe, Java, and St. Sebastian, recommended by the Committee	162
Number of ships of which First Lieutenants were promoted, recommended by the Committee	219
Total	553*

(*Considerable additions were made to these numbers, before the list was finally closed.)

We have traced forty-five successful boat actions for which the officer in command was promoted; but the number of boats on each occasion cannot be ascertained.

We beg in conclusion to remark, that the lists we send show the frequent occurrence of several claims by the same individuals, to which it seems proper to call their Lordships' attention, although we are not required to offer any suggestion, whether such claims may be best marked by a medal in each case, or whether plurality of honours, shall be indicated by a difference in the description of the medal.

We are sir, your humble servants
T. BYAM MARTIN. *ADMIRAL.*
W.H. GAGE. *ADMIRAL.*
THOS. BLADEN CAPEL. *ADMIRAL.*
JAMES A. GORDON. *REAR ADMIRAL.*

Henry G. Ward Esq., M.P. &c. &c. Admiralty.

It seems probable that ideas for these considerable extensions to the number of actions to be rewarded by this medal derived mainly from a well attended debate on 'Medals for Naval Services' in the House of Lords on 8 July 1847. Captain The Earl of Hardwicke, R.N. moved the Motion;

'That an Address be presented to Her Majesty, praying Her Majesty to be graciously pleased to direct that the Order of the Admiralty dated the 1st June, directed to all persons serving on board any ship of war engaged with the enemy between the years 1793 and 1815, the Captain of which ship shall have received a medal for any action during that period, be directed to all persons serving on board any ship of war engaged with the enemy between the Years 1793 and 1846, the Captain of which Ship shall have received a medal, or where the fleet, squadron or ship shall have received the Thanks of both Houses of Parliament, or where the commander in chief shall have been created a peer, or received a step in the Peerage for any action with the enemy during that period.'

The new ingredient in this flatulently phrased Motion was the suggestion that the period to be considered by the Board of Flag Officers should be extended from 1815 to 1846. The original vague concept of a 'Peninsular Medal' for the navy, honouring primarily the men who had fought against France and her satellites, was evolving swiftly into a comprehensive general service award. The speakers in the debate ranged their criticisms across some glorious actions not mentioned in the London Gazette advertisement. The Earl of Ellenborough, lately First Lord of the Admiralty, spoke of '. . . the careless manner in which the original Order of the 1st June (1847) was drawn up . . .' The actions specifically mentioned in the House, and deemed deserving of reward, were Cornwallis' Retreat in 1797, Captain Seymour in HMS THETIS, Captain Stewart in HMS SEAHORSE, and the battles of Algiers (1816) and Navarino (1827). Government spokesmen were unsympathetic, and the debate ended when the Earl withdrew his Motion. Seven weeks later the Medal Committee published its Report (dated 25 August 1847) in which the more positive mood of the debate was comprehended, and indeed enlarged upon by its more professionally equitable proposals to include all major and minor engagements previously recognised as battles of conspicuous merit leading to promotions, but the Report made no mention of any actions fought after 1815. The Earl of Hardwicke's concept of using the medal generally to reward these later battles went beyond the terms of reference of the Committee, who loyally kept their discussions within the original directive to assess medallic recognition for the 'late Great War'.

The Report was approved by the Admiralty on 20 November 1847, except for the paragraph which suggested that a medal might be allowed to the widow, eldest son, or parent of officers, seamen, and marines slain in battle. The First Lord of the Admiralty had stated a strong and well founded objection '. . . on the ground of great inconvenience, more particularly if extended to the Military department'.

In the ordinary course of events, one would now expect to find that the Report, bearing the Admiralty's endorsement, was submitted to the Queen for her approval, and that an appropriately worded 'Advertisement' would have appeared shortly afterwards in the London Gazette. In the event, there were no further public announcements until June of the following year. No documentary evidence has survived, but it is evident that some finely balanced discussions were taking place concerning the wisdom of extending the period covered by the 'Naval War Medal'. Apart from the admirals and the politicians, the officials of the Treasury must also have had their say. Any extension to the original terms of the award, resulting in increased administrative, production and distribution costs, would inevitably increase the burden to be borne by the Exchequer.

It is clear that all of these arguments had been settled by late May, 1848, more than six months after the Admiralty had first endorsed the committee's Report. On 1 June a letter was despatched to Queen Victoria by the First Lord of the Admiralty, Lord Auckland, which finally laid to rest the original concept of a 'Naval War Medal' restricted in its application to the period 1793-1815:

'. . . humbly submits to your Majesty the following propositions in regard to the proposed distribution of medals to officers, seamen and marines of your Majesty's Navy.

Representations have been made to the Government that the rule of distribution as signified in the Gazette of the 4th June 1847, would exclude from this distribution many who in the late War had rendered conspicuous service and the subject was referred to a Committee consisting of Admirals Sir Byam Martin, Sir Wm Gage, Sir Bladen Capel & Sir James Gordon – and Lord Auckland humbly proposes with your Majesty's consent to adopt with some modifications the substance of their Report.

It has been further represented that medals will now have been granted for service rendered by the Navy not only in the War 1793, and also in the late War with China, and that in the interval the attack on Algiers, the Battle of Navarino and the operations on the coast of Syria have taken place, and that the services rendered on these occasions should not remain undistinguished. Lord Auckland, also with the assent of Lord John Russell and Earl Grey, humbly proposes to your Majesty that the distribution of medals should be extended to those who were engaged in these affairs.

The Burmese War might fairly have been classed with the operations last-mentioned, but the services rendered in that War by the Navy can only be regarded in connection with the services rendered by the Indian Army, a measure in regard to which is still under discussion with the Directors of the East India Company. . . .'

This letter, which presumably reflected the wishes not only of the Admiralty and the government but also of the Medal Committee, received the immediate approval of the Queen. One week later, on 9th June 1848, the London Gazette carried an 'Advertisement' which not only invited applications for (unlisted) Boat Service actions, and engagements which led to the promotion of a First Lieutenant, but also for the three major naval engagements fought after 1815: Algiers, Navarino and Syria.

" LONDON GAZETTE.   9th JUNE 1848.   PAGE 2185-6.
ADMIRALTY, 7th June 1848.

The Lords Commissioners of the Admiralty having referred to a Committee of Flag Officers the consideration of the Naval Actions for which Medals should be granted, in accordance with the spirit of the Queen's most gracious intentions, as signified in the Gazette of the 4th June 1847; and Her Majesty having been pleased to approve of several of the suggestions submitted by the said Committee, the following notice is issued for the information and guidance of those who may have claims to this honourable distinction:

1st. The rule, directed by Her Majesty to be observed in extending this mark of Her Royal favour is so comprehensive as to bring within its scope all Officers, seamen and marines (and soldiers who served as marines) who were present in any Action which at the time received the special approbation of the Lords Commissioners of the Admiralty.

2ndly. From the commencement of the War in 1793, it was the practice of the Board of Admiralty to notice Battles of conspicuous merit by the promotion of the First Lieutenant of the ship or ships, or the promotion of the Commander if the Action was fought by a small-vessel; and conformably with this practice, it is Her Majesty's pleasure that persons of every rank who were present in such Actions, during the Wars commencing in 1793 and ending in 1815, and now living, shall receive a Medal commemorative of their meritorious services; and they are required forthwith to state their claims for each Action in which they may have been engaged, according to Form (A) hereunto annexed, and transmit the same to the Secretary of the Committee of Flag Officers, Admiralty, London.

3rdly. Her Majesty has also been pleased to take into Her gracious consideration the many instances of gallantry displayed by Officers, seamen and marines in Boat Actions during the same period, and to direct that such services, if distinguished by the promotion of the Officer conducting the enterprize, shall entitle those who were present, and now living, to a Medal, provided the answers to be given in the Form (B), shall enable the Committee to ascertain that the claim is well founded. But the Officers, seamen and marines of the ships from which the boats were detached, are not to participate in a distinction which only properly belongs to those personally engaged.

4th. It is also ordered that services in the Frigates and smaller vessels, which were actually present in any of the great Fleet Actions mentioned in the Gazette of 4th June 1847, for which the Captains of the Ships of the Line received Medals, shall entitle those surviving of the crews of such vessels to a Medal.

And all surviving Officers, seamen and marines belonging to ships actually co-operating and present during the siege and capture of

     Martinique in 1809 Java in 1811
     Guadaloupe in 1810 St. Sebastian in 1813

for which the Army had Medals, will be entitled to a similar distinction according to Form (A), shall enable the Committee to trace the presence and co-operation of the ships to which the applicants belonged.

And 5th. Her Majesty, having taken into Her most gracious consideration the circumstance, that Medals have been granted by Her Majesty for services rendered by the Navy, not only in the Wars commencing in 1793 and ending in 1815, but also for services rendered in the late war in China, whilst the intermediate general Actions, viz:

The Attack upon Algiers in 1816
The Battle of Navarino in 1827, and
The operations on the coast of Syria in 1840

are unmarked by any such distinction, has been pleased to direct, that the surviving Officers, seamen and marines engaged in those Actions shall also receive a similar mark of their Sovereign's gracious recollection of their services, and of Her desire to record the same; and all such Officers, seamen and marines are, therefore, hereby called upon to transmit their claims to such distinction according to the annexed Form (A), and addressed to the Secretary of the Committee of Flag Officers, Admiralty, London.

The following Flag Officers have been directed to re-assemble, as a Committee for the investigation and adjudication of all claims sent in according to the printed forms, viz.

Admiral Sir T. Byam Martin, G.C.B.
Admiral Sir W. Hall Gage, G.C.H.
Admiral the Honourable Sir Thomas Bladen Capel, K.C.B.
Vice Admiral Sir James A. Gordon, K.C.B.

       By Command of the Lords Commissioners etc. etc. etc."

The direct consequence of this 'Advertisement' was to increase dramatically the number of officers and men eligible to claim a medal. It was evident that many of the seamen who had served, for example, under Captain Edward Pellew, RN, when he fought and captured the French frigate NYMPHE in June 1793, had since died. Hence there could be very few applicants from that early period. The campaign along the coast of Syria, on the other hand, had occurred just eight years before the decision to issue a clasp was made, and most of the men engaged were not only alive but possibly still serving in uniform and therefore keenly interested in obtaining a British medal to pair with their earlier Turkish award. It is not surprising, therefore, that nearly half (9,448) of the total number of clasps awarded (20,933) were for Algiers, Navarino and Syria. It is ironic that the 'Naval General Service Medal' was not only created as an afterthought to the 'Peninsular War Medal', but that the clasps most frequently encountered today are themselves the result of a very tardy reversal of policy by the authorities!

Events were now gathering pace. Immediately after the publication of the new (second) 'Advertisement' on 9th June 1848, the London Gazette re-published the first 'Gold Medals Action Advertisement' dated 4th June 1847. Even in an age when communications were poor and when much of the population was illiterate, news of the medal and its availability was now reaching even the most distant former sailors and marines. Letters of application continued to pour in.

The Flag Officers' Committee had been dissolved on 27 August 1847 (the day its Report was despatched), but now Admiral Byam Martin was ordered to re-assemble his committee and to begin the immense task of sifting and adjudicating the thousands of claims. Extra clerical assistance had been already obtained in late June 1847, for the laborious task of examining Ships' Muster Books and to confirm the physical presence of each applicant so that his claim might be verified. The committee re-commenced work on 19 June 1848.

The third 'Advertisement', published in January 1849, contained a large appendix which gave the date, the names of ships proved present, and a précis of the 'action for which a medal is granted', for all Boat Service actions and actions so meritorious that a First Lieutenant had been promoted as a direct consequence of his services in the engagement. The actions listed in the appendix ranged in scale from the Battle of Copenhagen, 1801, down to ten minor single-ship or small boat actions for which no applications for award were ever received. This completed the series of clasps which could be awarded, with the sole exception of the 'army co-operation clasp' covering Egypt, 1801. This same edition of the Gazette also gave notice that some medals were now ready for distribution:

" LONDON GAZETTE. 1849. Page 236.
Admiralty Office, 25th January, 1849.

The Naval Medals prepared according to Her Majesty's gracious commands being now ready for distribution, Claimants, whether Officers, or Seamen or Marines, and soldiers serving as Marines, and others who served in any of the Ships hereafter named, and in the Actions specified, may give their names to the Staff Officers of Pensioners in the different Districts of the United Kingdom in which they reside, who will forward to the Admiralty Lists of such applicants on the 1st and 15th of every month, (Sundays excepted) when their respective Medals will be remitted to the Staff Officers for distribution. Officers may apply at the Admiralty, Whitehall for their Medals, either personally, or by any known Navy Agent or Banker, on or after the 15th February, between the hours of 12 and 3 o'clock.

It will be required of all applicants to make it clear to the Issuing Officer that they do not personate deceased Seamen, Marines, etc.

N.B.—The Medals awarded under the Gazette Notice of 1st June 1847, and for which the claims were preferred in the same year, will be the first issued.

By Command of Their Lordships, etc. etc.

We deliver the following Lists specifying the Ships and Battles for which, according to Her Majesty's gracious commands, and in compliance with the instructions of the Lords Commissioners of the Admiralty, Medals have been awarded to surviving Officers, Seamen and Marines (And soldiers who served as Marines) who were present in any successful Action which at the time received the marked approbation of the Admiralty, as shown by the official records of the promotion granted in compliment to each occasion.
Signed. T. Byam Martin, Admiral
T. Bladen Capel. Admiral
James A. Gordon, Rear Admiral.

NAVAL MEDALS' SHIPS
(The Lists of Actions and Details followed) "

The adjudicating committee soon found itself under pressure to alter the strict rules under which rewards could be approved. The members made plain their position in a memorandum dated 20 February 1849:

'There is an evident misapprehension prevailing as to the duties and the power of the Committee of Flag Officers, which it is desirable to correct.

Several letters recently received make it clear that some of the applicants are under an impression that the Committee can set aside the decisions of the Admiralty, and award Medals according as they (the Committee) may estimate the merits of an action. It is not so. The Admiralty of the day with all the circumstances fresh and officially before them, decided upon these victories which they considered entitled to a mark of their special approbation, and the Committee have only to ascertain that applications as they come in, are for successful battles, for which the Admiralty bestowed special promotion.

According to the instructions under which the Committee act, no Naval Medal is allowed for conjoint operations with the Army, except on those occasions when such a compliment was bestowed on that branch of the Service.

T.B.M. J.A.G. '

It took two further 'Advertisements' to explain all the conditions under which the final additional clasp, that for Egypt, would be awarded to applicants;—

"   LONDON GAZETTE.   15th FEBRUARY 1850.   PAGE 396.
                    Admiralty, February 11, 1850.

With reference to Her Majesty's gracious intentions, as signified in the Gazette of 1st and 7th June 1847, that a Medal should be struck to record the services of Her Fleets and Armies during the Wars, commencing in 1793 and ending in 1815; Her Majesty has further been graciously pleased to grant the Military Medal to the surviving Officers, non commissioned officers and soldiers of the Army who served in the Expedition to Egypt; and Her Majesty having signified Her pleasure to the Lords Commissioners of the Admiralty that measures be taken for granting the Naval Medal, or a clasp in lieu thereof, to the surviving officers and seamen of the Royal Navy who served in that expedition.

All Officers, Petty Officers, seamen and marines who consider that they are entitled to receive this mark of their Sovereign's gracious recollection of their services, and of Her desire to record the same, are to send in writing the statement of their claim to the above-named Medal or Clasp, addressed to the Secretary of the Admiralty, Whitehall, London, specifying the names of the persons, or the titles of the documents by which it can be established.

Such officer, seaman or marine, as shall have already received the Naval Medal for other services, shall receive, instead of a new additional Medal, a Clasp with the word "EGYPT" engraven thereon.

                    By Command etc. etc. etc.   "

This was followed a month later by a further publication, in which was listed all the names of the Ships from which claims would be entertained for the "Egypt" clasp. This second Notice on the subject had this following heading:—

"   LONDON GAZETTE.   YEAR 1850.   PAGE 791.
                    Admiralty, 15th March 1850.

The Naval Medals for which claims have been preferred to the 1st December 1849, being now ready for issue, all persons entitled to the same are hereby required to make application at the Admiralty, either in person or through an authorised friend or agent, or by letter containing full particulars of the claim, or through the Staff Office of Pensioners in the District in which they reside.

Personal applications must be made between 12 and 3 o'clock daily, on and after Monday, 18th March 1850.

The subjoined list contains the names of ships, service in which on the Coast of Egypt between 8th March and 2nd September 1801, entitles the surviving Officers, Seamen and Marines to the Medal granted by Her Majesty, and notified in the London Gazette of the 15 February 1850.
           (There followed the complete list of ships on Page 792).   "

It now remained only for the Flag Officers' Committee to plough through the many new claims for the 'Egypt' clasp and the relatively few late applications resulting from earlier 'Advertisements'. In late 1850 the members wrote a further Report on their historic work, wherein they also sought to bring their business to a close. Their words duplicate, in part, some of their earlier remarks. However, the Report is reproduced here in its completeness because it has the full flavour of a bygone century:

      Sir,   Committee Room, Admiralty, November 1850.

It is now nearly three years and a half since the Committee of Flag Officers assembled, in order to decide upon the validity of claims to a Naval Medal, on the principle laid down by the Queen's gracious command in the Gazette of the 7th (sic) of June 1847, and other subsequent notifications of Her Majesty's pleasure.

After so long a notice the time must be considered ample for claims to come in from every quarter of the globe, and if the Lords Commissioners of the Admiralty shall be of opinion that the object of our Commission has been fully carried out, we submit that it may be desirable to give public notice of the termination of our sittings, on such day as their Lordships may think fit to name. It will however be necessary to give our secretary, and his one assistant, until the middle of

January to arrange the vast accumulation of papers brought before us during so lengthened an investigation.

In proposing to bring our business to a close it is right we should place before their Lordships a summary of our proceedings in a duty so novel in its character, and one coming so home to the feelings of those whose claims to a medal have not, in our opinion, fallen within the rules taken for our guidance.

It may be convenient for their Lordships to have at hand a brief statement of this nature in case it should be a question hereafter, whether the Committee has done all that was due to the service by giving full effect to Her Majesty's gracious intentions.

We trust the facts we have to state will make it clear that everything has been done to give the utmost scope to the distinction of which a medal for particular services is susceptible.

The compliment has been carried to the greatest extent short of an indiscriminate grant to all who served in the war. A measure which would deprive the medal of its value, and take from merit what is alone merit's due.

In their Lordships' order constituting the Committee, we were encouraged to suggest some mode of applying the principle laid down in the Gazette to other battles than those specially referred to. Their Lordships say, "it will be quickly apparent to you that there are cases not mentioned in the Gazette, which must doubtless appear to those personally interested in them as intended to be included in the scheme of distinction. To such applications it will be necessary that the Committee should give their attention, and should it appear that they are such as deserve special consideration, you are invited to represent the same to my Lords, together with such observations and remarks as you may think it desirable to submit to their Lordships."

If the Navy has not fully profited by this intimation of their Lordships' considerate and liberal view of the question, the fault is undoubtedly with the Committee.

In the Gazette beforementioned, the grant of a medal was confined to the surviving officers, seamen, and marines who served in the particular battles therein stated, and in the ships the captains of which were honoured with a gold medal by Her Majesty's Royal predecessors.

This limitation, taken strictly, excluded the frigates and smaller vessels attending on the fleets in the great actions, and extended only to 126 ships for the whole war, commencing 1793, and spreading over a period of 23 years.

The Committee was of opinion that, consistently with Her Majesty's gracious design, the compliment might with propriety include every description of vessel present on such occasions, and this has given the medal to the surviving officers, seamen, and marines of 43 more ships than the Gazette referred to.

In our Report of the 27th of August 1847, allusion was made to the grant of a medal to the troops employed at the capture of Martinique in 1809; Guadaloupe, 1810; Java, 1811, and St. Sebastian, 1813. The generals acknowledged the full share taken by the officers, seamen, and marines of the fleet on shore as well as at sea, and as both services shared alike in the distribution of the prize money, and both equally honoured by the thanks of Parliament, we deemed it our duty to claim for the Navy a participation in the honorary distinction conferred on their gallant associates.

This, under Her Majesty's sanction, gave the medal to the crews of 131 ships.

We next occupied ourselves in considering how their Lordships desire to give a greater scope to the medal distinction than was at first intended, might be carried out in a manner suitable to a wish which left the Committee so entirely unrestricted.

It was quite clear that any stinted measure would disappoint the expectations of the service, and come short of the feeling which prompted this larger view of the subject.

Something was necessary to be done on a large scale, and calculated to bring to remembrance every well-fought successful battle of the war, so that all who had a share in such actions should be included in the medal distinction. We therefore fell back on precedent established by the Board of Admiralty as a mode of acknowledging their sense of the merits of each battle.

The rule of the Board was to notice every well-conducted successful action by the promotion of the First Lieutenant, and this benefit conferred on the executive officer of the ship, was always regarded as a compliment, alike to the captain, and to all on board. It was a new and popular way of noticing meritorious services, one unknown in former wars; for even Lord Rodney's action of the 12th of April 1782, though so important in its consequences as to procure a general peace, was not so favoured. It was first adopted on the breaking out of the war in 1793, on the capture of the "Cleopatra" by the "Nymphe," and thenceforth became so strictly the practice as to afford, on the present occasion, an unerring guide in giving the widest possible range to the medal distinction.

Following this rule and assisted by the well-regulated records of the Admiralty, we have traced the names of 324 ships, whose crews are entitled to a medal.

Extensive as the scheme had thus been made, there remained another claim in no way inferior to those before noticed. The spirited and daring enterprise of British seamen has never been more conspicuous than in boat actions. Other achievements have been of higher public importance, but the conduct of the young officers of the fleet in leading their men on such occasions, will bear comparison with the most heroic deeds on record.

It was therefore proposed that in every case of the promotion of the officer conducting the enterprise, he, and his gallant followers, should have a medal, but not those on board the ships from which they were detached.

It has been difficult to find out the successful expeditions of this sort; there are however 54 of them clearly traced, and reckoning only 10 boats employed on each occasion, we have an aggregate of 540, the crews of which are entitled to a medal.

The following statement shows the general result of the whole scheme:

The number of ships, the crews of which are allowed a medal according to the Gazette of the 7th of June 1847, by Her Majesty's command	126	
Subsequently granted for services on the Coast of Egypt in 1801	117	
For Algiers, Navarino and Acre	63	
	306	
Added, on the recommendation of the Committee, for vessels in attendance on the fleets in general actions		43
By ditto, for ships co-operating with the army at Martinique, Guadaloupe, Java, and St. Sebastian		131
By ditto, for ships entitled on account of the promotion of the First Lieutenants		324
		498
Total number acording to Gazette	306	
Recommended by the Committee	498	
TOTAL Number of Ships	804	

Total number of ships named, 804; besides the crews of 540 boats.

That all this will be gratifying to the service at large there can be no doubt; but there are cases of individual dissatisfaction which it is understood have been laid before the Admiralty by persons who consider themselves aggrieved by the rejection of their claims to a medal, which in the opinion of the Committee did not come within the prescribed rules.

In reviewing the circumstances connected with such appeals, it will be necessary to bear in mind that any departure from the clear course it was our duty to follow, would have thrown us open to an imputation of partiality, and would also have given rise to endless claims founded on each individual's estimate of his own pretensions.

We would gladly have avoided any decision painful to the feelings of men of unquestioned merit, but we cannot regret a rigid adherence to a principle derived from a precedent established by the Board of Admiralty, and so well known to the service throughout the war.

The number of proved claims amount at this date to 20,900, including 3,082 clasps.

The disallowed claims in consequence of not coming within the prescribed rules, not being found on the ships' books, or being marked as deserters, amount to 428.

Several applications have been made for the medal by the representatives of officers who have died since the promulgation of the Queen's order in the Gazette of the 7th (sic) of June 1847.

The medal was then given in unqualified terms to the officers, seamen, and marines at that time living, who had served in any action for which a medal was to be allowed. In point of fact the medal belonged to each individual the moment Her Majesty's pleasure was signified, and death intervening between the date of the Gazette and the issue of the medal from the Mint, could not annul so clearly a vested right. We therefore allowed the medal to pass to the widow, or representative of the deceased.

We have received upwards of 23,000 letters, and each had its due consideration, but we do not presume to suppose that out of such a multitude of cases we have been altogether free from error in our conclusions, and it is a great satisfaction to us that our adjudication is open to their Lordships' overruling correction.

It is scarcely necessary to say how great has been the load of business to be executed by our secretary, Mr. Edward Giffard, but we are glad of the opportunity to acknowledge how comparatively light our duties have been made by his unceasing assiduity, and the efficiency with which he has gone through duties requiring such great research.

We are, &c.

(signed) *T. Byam Martin,* Admiral of the Fleet.
W. H. Gage, Admiral.
T. Bladen Capel, Admiral.
James A. Gordon, Rear-Admiral.

The Secretary of the Admiralty.

This Report led directly to the fifth and final 'Advertisement' on the subject of the 'Naval War Medal'. It dealt with the 'deadline date' beyond which no further claims would be accepted. In the event, hundreds more were received for which medals were awarded after the deadline, but not all the names of these late applicants seem to appear in the Rolls available today. This last Notice read;

" LONDON GAZETTE.   28th January 1851.   Page 209.
ADMIRALTY. 25th January 1851.

Three years and seven months have now elapsed since notice was first issued by Command of Her Majesty, in the Gazette of 1st June 1847, requiring all persons to make application who should consider themselves qualified to receive a Medal for their services during the late Wars, as therein specified.

Although above 17,000 Officers, seamen and marines and soldiers serving as marines, have, after investigation, been declared qualified, it is supposed that some claims may be outstanding;—My Lords Commissioners of the Admiralty therefore direct, that all remaining claims, under the Gazette Notices of 1st June 1847, 1st June 1848 and 11th February 1850 be brought forward without loss of time – and notice is hereby given that no claim will be taken into consideration unless it is submitted before 1st May 1851. "

Accuracy of the Medal Action Lists

The manner in which the 'Medal Action Lists' were drawn up and approved made it inevitable that they would be vulnerable to persistent criticism. Several generations of naval historian have come and gone since the 'Naval War Medal' was first introduced and many have published their views regarding various aspects of the award. Three names in particular are still familiar to us: Clowes, Hailes and Rowbotham. For the moment we may set aside the published findings of Colonel Hailes because they are devoted exclusively to his compilation of a Roll of medal recipients.

It was Sir William Laird Clowes who levelled the most authoritative criticisms at the work of the Medal Committee. In 1901 he published Volume VI of his comprehensive 'The Royal Navy, a History' and, on page 213, he commented adversely upon the committee's apparently inconsistent selection of actions thought worthy of reward, also on errors in their printed list of medal actions.

Thirty years later his strictures attracted the attention of a renowned and most able naval researcher, Commander W. B. Rowbotham RN, who believed that Clowes' condemnation was unfair. Rowbotham therefore set his hand to the task of investigating the whole story from original source material. The Commander soon found, to his surprise, that the number of errors '... was distinctly greater than a casual reader of Laird Clowes would imply'. It was this revelation which led Rowbotham to '... investigate the whole medal action list afresh'. He published a general article on his findings in the 'Mariner's Mirror' in July 1937 (Vol XXIII No 3). This same article appeared subsequently as the Foreword to his privately produced book on the subject.

Rowbotham's type-script book, entitled 'The Naval General Service Medal 1793–1840 – Officers present in Fleet Medal Actions 1794–1811', covers in great detail every one of the actions for which clasps were approved by the committee. His investigation covered the correct spelling of ships' names, the precise date of each action, where the engagements took place, the names of the commanding officers and those promoted, and other points such as army units serving aboard H.M. Ships as Marines. A copy of this excellent reference work is held on a shelf in the Reference Room of the Public Record Office, Kew.

Rowbotham's erudite comments on some of the mistakes to be found in the London Gazette 'Medal Action List' (26 January 1849), and its subsequent re-publication in Quarterly Navy Lists from 1849 to 1869, cannot be bettered:

'Unfortunately this list contains a great many errors. The date (in the later *Navy Lists*, more particularly) is very often incorrectly given, and the same applies sometimes to the name of the captain. This latter can be ascribed to several reasons: the ships and their respective captains have been transposed; another ship of the same name has been noted, which, of course, makes the captain's name wrong; and in some instances the captain quoted had died, or had already left the ship, before the date of the action in question. Then again, there are a few cases of ships having been awarded the medal which were never present on the date specified; and in a few actions it will be found that the same officer has been shown as commanding two separate ships. The details of the actions in column iii of the *Gazette* list are also incomplete in a number of cases, the name of the captured ship being omitted; and the names of ships and captains are misspelled in not a few instances. With regard to the incorrect spelling of names, and also to the dating of actions, an inspection of the medal roll shows that many of these mistakes were due to a copying clerk or to the printers; the data in the original MS. were entered up correctly, though this was not invariably the case.

The *London Gazette* and the first few numbers of the *Quarterly Navy List* contain one or two ships which were omitted from later numbers; their original inclusion was due to clerical errors. When going through the list it will be noticed that, for some actions, ships which are well known to have been present have not been awarded the medal. This may be partly explained by pointing out that column ii of the *Gazette* list is headed "Names of ships for which claims have been proved"; the inference being that there were no survivors in 1847 from the ships omitted, or that if there were they did not trouble to put in a claim. There is also another reason. Claims were normally disallowed in the case of those ships where no promotion was made, although they were present; the Admiralty, however, usually on the recommendation of the Committee, sometimes extended the grant in such cases. Ships which were present, but which took only a very small part in an action, were usually refused the medal; the underlying idea being not to make the medal too cheap, and to impress on everyone that it had to be properly earned. And, as has already been stated, there are a few actions included for which no claims were put in.

In getting out their list of actions for which a medal was recommended to be granted, the Committee appear, in a few instances, to have departed somewhat from their rule as to what constituted an appropriate action to be rewarded. In the case of boat actions the officer who conducted the enterprise was not invariably promoted, but one or more of the junior officers who also went away in the boats, did, on those occasions, receive a step in rank. Similarly for single-ship actions; the lieutenant in command, in the case of a small vessel, was not always singled out at the time for special promotion, although one of his juniors obtained promotion or confirmation in his acting rank. And instances occur where an action was disallowed, but which appears in the printed lists; these may have been due to clerical errors, but there is always the possibility that the Admiralty overruled the Committee's decisions in such cases. There are also a few cases where an approved action was inadvertently omitted from the *Gazette* list, or was approved at a later date; these duly appear in the later *Navy Lists*.

There is no satisfactory explanation available as to why certain ships, which were awarded the medal, have been included. Their logs prove that they were definitely elsewhere at the time of the action in question. In some cases there was more than one ship of the same name shown in the list of the Navy, and the wrong one was picked on; in others there is always the possibility of there having been a vessel of that name which had been taken up locally on the Station, or was a hired vessel, but which was never registered officially. Logs and muster books for these latter have not always been preserved, and so their identity cannot be verified; and as, for boat actions, the name of the captain is not given, it is not possible to trace them with any degree of certainty. The Committee state in their report that they consulted the prize lists, dispatches, logs and muster books, for the purpose of verifying the claims sent in; but the results of their checking, as given in the final list, show that they were not infallible in this respect.'

In his book, Rowbotham recorded all the 'true dates' of the actions where they differed from those printed in the 'Medal List'. It was the inaccuracy of some of the dates shown in the 'Medal List' which led directly to the inaccuracies which appeared later on a few commemorative clasps. He refers to his research in this manner:

'Owing to the fact that, prior to October 1805, ships' logs were written up from noon to noon, i.e. nautical time, there is occasionally some discrepancy between the dates given in the *Gazette* and those in the logs. In the dispatches sometimes nautical time has been used and sometimes civil time, and the only way to check this is by referring to the logs; it will sometimes happen, therefore, that a "p.m." date in the *Gazette* will be a day in advance of the date when adjusted to civil time. *Gazette* times of incidents, involving a change of date when the action or chase was continued after midnight, do not always agree with the statements in the log, which accounts in several cases for an incorrect date having been inserted in column i of the *Gazette* list of actions. I should be inclined to take the log time in preference to that in the dispatch published in the *Gazette*, and to date the actions as from when fire was first opened and not from the time of the surrender; and in the case of cutting-out operations, when the attack developed and not when the boats shoved off from the ships. Occasionally the *Gazette* accounts will be found to contain misprints in respect to times of incidents; these are only to be discovered by referring to the original dispatches. In most cases the captain's letter, reporting an action, is dated the same day as the action, but sometimes the date of the letter is one or more days later; some of the mistakes in column i of the *Gazette* list have been dué to taking the date of the letter as the date of action without verifying the fact.

It is not known how the Committee arrived at some of their dates. For convenience they may have made use of James's *Naval History;* but the author—who did not have access to all the official records, but only to a certain number of logs—is responsible for many errors, and later historians have frequently copied him without checking his statements. Some can be explained by the fact that a dispatch would begin by quoting a date one or more days prior to the action—part of the letter of proceedings—and the Committee took this earlier date as the date of the actual action.'

Of equal interest to surviving claimants at the time, and to students today, were those Actions for which no clasp was approved. Rowbotham expands on this subject in his Article with the following remarks:—
'The publication of the list of medal actions (No.20,939 of 26 January 1849) occasioned in the Press a crop of leading articles and letters to the Editor.
The burden of their song was: "Why has the Committee omitted such and such an action? What can they be thinking of? If action *X* is rewarded, why has action *Y*, which was equally or even more meritorious, been disregarded? etc." Among other periodicals which threw their columns open to the airing of these complaints were the *Naval and Military Gazette* and the *United Service Magazine*. Generally speaking, with one or two minor exceptions, the Admiralty were unmoved by these protests, but at last one pressed-for series of operations was added to the list. This was for the campaign in Egypt in 1801, recognition of which had also been witheld by the military authorities. . . .
The Committee devote fourteen pages (in their Book 3 – Boat Service Clasp Roll) to a list of the actions which they disallowed, in most cases giving full reasons for their decisions. Some of these decisions appear to be inconsistent, and it is now impossible to say upon what grounds they were based. To take a few examples. On 21 October 1794, the *Artois* (Captain Edmund Nagle)

captured the French frigate *Révolutionnaire,* in compliment of which the captain was knighted and the first lieutenant, Robert Dudley Oliver, was promoted. This is merely marked "No". Another action was that of the attack on St Paul, Bourbon (Réunion), on 21 September 1809, when the French frigate *Caroline* and several other vessels were captured and the defences of the place were destroyed. Claims for the medal were allowed, but for some unknown reason (probably due to a clerical error) this action does not appear in any of the official printed lists, and so is not accounted a medal action. Also at 3 a.m. on 4 August 1798, the boats of the *Melpomene* and the *Childers* cut out the French brig *Adventurier* (called *Adventurer* in the medal roll and dated 3 August), in compliment of which Lieutenant Thomas George Shortland was promoted. The action, which is entered up among the boat actions, is marked as having been "Ex^d", but as no claims to the medal were put in it never appeared as a medal action in the printed lists. Other actions, however, for which no claims were put in either, have been included in the medal action list.

Several claims were turned down on the grounds that "the English [were] greatly superior; not a service to constitute a claim". In one case the medal was awarded for a British defeat, but the decision is one that no one will cavil at. This was the case of the capture by two large French frigates of the *Arrow* sloop (Commander Richard Budd Vincent) and the *Archeron* bomb (Commander Arthur Farquhar), while in defence of a convoy. The Committee's notation reads: "Unsuccessful action and not allowed, the English ships captured. But the defence was so meritorious that both Commanders were made Captains; it is one of the cases worthy of favourable consideration." There are also a few instances of additions, either as a complete action or of individual ships to an already recorded action, which were approved after the publication of the list in the *Gazette;* these appear in the later numbers of the *Navy Lists,* but sometimes are only to be found in the index and not in the text.'

From all of this, the reader will understand the problems faced by the present author in attempting to publish a Roll containing the minimum permissible number of errors. To verify the date of a naval engagement should be, in theory, a relatively simple matter, but Commander Rowbotham devoted several years of careful research to the subject before he felt able to publish his findings. The problems become worse compounded when one attempts to verify the medal entitlement of every single officer and rating present at those actions.

Limitations on the construction of a Medal Roll

Even if all the letters, books and associated material used by the Medal Committee had survived, it would have still remained a difficult task to re-assemble the facts into a format for a 'Medal Roll' acceptable to users today.

Since only a fraction of the immense number of these records has been preserved, the chance of any compiler producing a wholly perfect Roll is extremely remote, if not impossible. The reason for this sad state of affairs is best illustrated by indicating the administrative method most probably adopted by the Medal Committee's team, and *inter alia* exposing the only part of their procedure for which records still remain.

On receipt of an applicant's letter, the details of the claim for one or more action clasps were logged against the claimant's surname listed alphabetically in an 'Application Book' (or books), and an application reference number appended. Not one of the 23,000 application letters has survived, and the 'Application Books' have also suffered the same fate of being 'weeded'.

The Committee's next function was that of validating each action clasp claim. To do this they created initially three books, with specially printed pages on which each individual clasp claim taken from the 'Application Book' was then registered under a hand written detailed heading for every approved action.

The information concerning each claim in these 'Clasp List' volumes was then verified by a clerk from muster books, logs and prize lists. His findings were entered as a 'Yes' or 'No' in the relevant column. In addition to the claimant's name, rank or rate, and the ship served in at the time of the engagement, his application reference number was entered also in the 'Clasp List'. These three 'Clasp List' volumes are the only records to have been preserved. They are the Books numbered 1, 2 and 3 referred to in that first Report made by the Flag Officers' Committee. The contents of these books are now on micro-film at the Public Record Office, Kew, under Class/Piece numbers ADM 171/1-3. There was also a Book number 4, created as the clasp list for the 'Egypt' claims, but this has not been preserved.

The 'Yes' or 'No' affirmation in the 'Clasp List' for each clasp claim was then noted in the 'Application Book'. When the time came for the medals to be ordered from the Royal Mint, lists were sent to that establishment, each containing large numbers of individual entries giving precise details of the recipient's name (and rank where applicable) and the type of clasp or clasps to be attached to his reward. Not one of these informative lists has escaped the weeder's hand.

It may be now easier to comprehend the problems of constructing a 'Medal Roll' solely from 'Clasp Lists' which were created (by the Medal Committee) for a different purpose. The Committee possessed an 'Application Book' which showed the totality of clasps to which each applicant was entitled, but these books have sadly been destroyed. The only cross-reference in the 'Clasp Lists' for a claimant to two or more clasps was his application reference number, placed there by the clerk to aid him in finding where to register the 'Yes' or 'No' back in the 'Application Book'. This number today provides useful corroborative (but passive) evidence that two separate clasp claims relate to the same man, but it never actively points the way to where another claim (or claims) by the applicant might be found.

To add to the difficulties, research by the author has shown that very often, when former applicants re-applied for additional clasps, as and when succeeding 'Advertisements' widened the scope for awards, these much embattled veterans were given a new and different reference number. In a few instances they even received two separate medals. Furthermore, experience gained from a study of extant awards of impeccable provenance has shown that, in some cases, the clerks were lax in their duty. They transferred only a part of the number of clasp claims by multiple clasp applicants from the 'Application Book' to the verification 'Clasp List' volumes (see, for example, Gunner Thomas Haines' seven clasp medal on the Frontispiece, and the note in the Roll on Lieutenant W. H. B. Tremlett R.N. under 'LION 15 July 1798'). The fact that all of the one thousand claims from Greenwich Hospital for the pensioners were given the reference of 'G.H.', and that some claims were amalgamated in a single list under a common reference number, does nothing to aid a compiler in finding multiple clasp medals from the only remaining records, the 'Clasp Lists'.

This paucity of source material concerning the 'Naval War Medal' has been the situation since 1961, when the three 'Clasp Lists' were formally lodged at the Public Record Office for manifest gaze and use. The situation regarding archives was obviously better when (Circa 1912) Lieutenant Colonel D. A. Hailes R.M. produced his Roll. For all its faults, nothing can detract from the immense contribution the Colonel made in providing a reference book which has met most of the needs of collectors, historians and genealogists over a period of seventy years.

It is known for certain that 'Book 4', covering claims for the 'Egypt' clasp, existed in 1912. It was also sighted by Commander Rowbotham in the mid-thirties. The present author, having lived so close to this re-construction problem for so long and knowing the hours needed to prove each multiple clasp award from single clasp details, is of the opinion that Colonel Hailes must have had private access to other archives ('Application Books' and/or 'Mint Lists') which were still extant within the Medal Branch of the Admiralty. They have since disappeared.

In preparing this new Roll, each and every detail concerning all claimants contained in the old 'Clasp Lists' has been cross-checked. This scrutiny alone disclosed some thousands of errors in the areas of misspelt surnames and forenames, incorrect initials, incorrect transcriptions of ships' names, ranks and rates, and names omitted (among which were two complete pages for 'G' and 'H' claimants for the Syria clasp). Many of these cases arose from a former misreading of the rank/rate on the right-hand side of a wide page where the name of the men appeared on the left margin of a bent line entry on unruled folios. It has to be added and remembered that the spelling of the names on this new Roll stems from the entry on the 'Clasp Lists', which may or may not have the same spelling as that shown on the 'Mint List'. It was this list which was sent to the Royal Mint where the medals were manufactured and where the names of the recipients were mechanically impressed upon the lower rims.

The new Roll can be reasonably guaranteed now to be an accurate reflection of single clasp validations, but regrettably it is bound to fall short of perfection in disclosing those cases where separate single clasp awards are in fact an award of a multiple clasp medal to one man only. Nor can the Roll compensate in all instances for the failures of the 19th century clerks who frequently neglected to enter all of the clasp claims by multiple clasp applicants in the 'Clasp Lists'.

To try to overcome some of the faults of the clerks, the immediate service histories of all such men awarded a Frigate action or Boat Service action clasp have been sought in the relevant ships' Muster Books. This has led to a large number of extra entries on the new Roll with the notation 'Verified Aboard. Not on Roll', for what may or may not have been additional claims.

There are certainly many known cases of men failing to apply for their full eligible quota of clasps, and in some instances this may be accounted for by their death soon after 1 June 1847. Their executors or families may have been unaware of the rules prevailing for awards announced in later 'Advertisements' whereby relatives could apply for the *additional* clasps of 'Great War' survivors who died after 1 June 1847.

An archive which has survived, and which Hailes seems not to have used, is the application list forwarded by the Greenwich Hospital authorities on behalf of their thousand or so eligible 'In Pensioners'. To facilitate future research, and to add a new dimension to the former active careers of these old sailors and marines, the new Roll shows the Greenwich Hospital number of each such applicant.

From old privately published books on celebrated medal collections, from auction catalogues commencing in 1880, from dealers lists and from museum records, the author has amassed records on 2,300 N.G.S. medals and the clasps attached to them (Syria excepted). These records, plus further research, have resulted in many corrections and additions to the 'Hailes Roll'. A typical error revealed would be two similarly named entries, each with a single clasp notation now found to be the same man eligible for a two clasp award.

From sight of so many rare clasps illustrated pictorially in old auction catalogues, and from the fine displays of so many different clasps at the National Maritime Museum, Greenwich, and at the Royal Naval Museum, Portsmouth, the opportunity has been taken to mirror the exact title on each clasp in every written description on the new Roll. Few reference works, if any, have previously noted the clasp 'Seahorse Wh Badere Zaffere' (Zaffer with an 'e'), nor have these earlier publications shown the inconsistent manner in which the abbreviation for September appears on clasps as 'Sept', 'Septr' or 'Sepr'.

To aid collectors in general, and those readers who are particularly interested in the various parts of the world where the conflicts took place, every clasp list heading now includes the geographical location of the engagement where it is not self-evident in the clasp title. Where applicable, the 'true date' of the action has been included also.

The 'Naval General Service Medal 1793–1840' is by far the most complex award to have been issued to the fighting men of any nation. This book encompasses twelve years of research into the eligibility of the individual recipients, but this is only one aspect of an even larger story. It is regretted that lack of space precludes any possibility of describing the naval careers of each man. Similarly, the book cannot dwell upon the story of William Wyon's vital role in designing this beautiful medal. Much more must await publication elsewhere: the design and production of the famous blue and white ribbon, unrecorded late applications, unlisted Boat Service clasps for valid actions, medals awarded to smugglers, convicts and poachers, applications received from seafaring women, and other stories connected with this historic medal.

Attention has been given, however, to the provision of some illuminating statistics. The appendix includes a complete breakdown for each clasp awarded and how it is distributed between medals with one to seven clasps. The appendix also contains information which will assist collectors seeking to establish the relative scarcity of each clasp type. The sad epilogue is that of all these hard earned and personally cherished commemorative awards, only one in five of their original total has survived as a reminder of the sailors and marines who forged so much of our maritime history.

STATISTICS

ITEMISED STATISTICAL TABLE
SHOWING THE NUMBER OF MEDALS
AND CLASPS AWARDED.

Clasp Title	Clasps awarded	On medals bearing these number of clasps						
		1	2	3	4	5	6	7
Syria	6978	6777	183	13	3	1	1	
Trafalgar	1613	1201	278	96	26	9	2	1
Algiers	1328	1114	159	39	11	5		
Navarino	1142	925	201	12	3	1		
Java	665	468	138	41	11	4	2	1
Egypt	618	387	159	50	16	4	2	
Copenhagen 1801	555	383	110	43	15	4		
1 June 1794	540	303	141	70	16	8	1	1
Basque Roads 1809	529	336	137	44	8	2	1	1
Martinique	486	217	159	87	14	7	1	1
Guadaloupe	483	223	144	96	13	5	1	1
St Domingo	396	236	105	39	11	2	2	1
St Vincent	348	167	99	57	15	6	2	2
Nile	326	137	108	57	16	6	—	2
Camperdown	298	190	78	19	10	1		
4 Novr 1805	296	191	77	20	6	2		
St Sebastian	293	230	49	11	3			
B.S. 14 Dec. 1814	205	136	51	11	5	2		
23rd June 1795	182	55	75	31	14	6	—	1
Gut of Gibraltar 12 July 1801	144	87	37	11	3	4	—	2
Lissa	124	62	36	18	5	2	—	1
B.S. 1 Nov 1809	110	83	20	6	—	1		
The Potomac 17 Aug 1814	108	66	30	5	5	1	—	1
14 March 1795	97	52	24	12	7	1	1	
Gaieta 24 July 1815	89	64	17	6	2			
Off Tamatave 20 May 1811	87	43	16	20	6	1	1	
12 Octr 1798	78	37	19	13	8	1		
Pelagosa 29 Novr 1811	74	22	35	12	2	2	—	1
Banda Neira	68	33	27	6	2			
Victorious with Rivoli	67	46	19	2				
Northumberland 22 May 1812	63	53	7	1	1	1		

THE NAVAL GENERAL SERVICE MEDAL ROLL 1793–1840

Clasp Title	Clasps awarded	On medals bearing these number of clasps						
		1	2	3	4	5	6	7
Curacoa	62	22	26	8	3	3		
Endymion Wh President	58	48	7	1	—	2		
B.S. Ap & May 1813	57	38	11	7	—	—	1	
B.S. 16 July 1806	52	20	21	11				
Anse La Barque 18 Decr 1809	52	2	24	22	3	1		
Acre 30 May 1799	51	8	30	10	2	1		
17 June 1795	49	8	29	7	2	1	1	1
B.S. 2 May 1813	48	31	12	3	1	1		
Pompee. 17 June 1809	47	1	2	39	3	1	—	1
Off Mardoe. 6 July 1812	47	40	4	3				
Implacable. 26 Augt 1808	44	18	19	3	1	3		
Gluckstadt. 5 Jany 1814	44	32	8	2	2			
Centaur. 26 Augt 1808	42	28	6	7	1			
B.S. 23 Novr 1810	42	28	12	2				
Shannon Wh Chesapeake	42	31	7	4				
Venerable. 16 Jany 1814	42	34	6	1	1			
Anholt. 27 March 1811	40	29	9	2				
Hebrus with L'Etoile	40	32	7	1				
Phoebe. 28 March 1814	36	11	7	11	4	2	1	
B.S. 25 July 1809	36	23	9	3	1			
B.S. 27 Sep 1810	36	9	14	11	2			
B.S. 7 July 1809	35	12	19	2	1	1		
Seahorse Wh Bader Zaffere	32	26	6					
Eurotas. 25 Feby 1814	32	28	2	2				
Stately. 22 March 1808	31	15	11	5				
Nassau. 22 March 1808	31	24	5	2				
Amethyst Wh Thetis	31	9	18	3	1			
Amazon. 13 March 1806	30	19	8	3				
Spartan. 3 May 1810	30	27	3					
Phoenix. 10 Augt 1805	29	2	22	5				
B.S. 17 March 1794	29	21	4	3	—	1		
London. 13 March 1806	27	15	7	4	—	1		
Amethyst. 5 April 1809	27	3	21	2	1			
Mars. 21 April 1798	26	5	18	2	1			
B.S. 28 June 1810	26	—	3	16	6	1		
B.S. 29 Sep 1812	25	20	3	1	—	1		
B.S. 29 Aug 1800	25	10	10	3	2			
B.S. 6 Jan 1813	25	1	13	8	3			
B.S. 8 April 1814	24	13	8	1	—	2		
Capture of the Desiree	24	12	9	2	1			
Lion. 15 July 1798	23	18	3	2				
Amanthea. 25 July 1812	23	14	5	1	3			
Blanche. 19 July 1806	22	18	2	2				
Virginie. 19 May 1808	21	19	1	1				
B.S. 1 & 18 Sep 1812	21	—	11	7	3			
Sirius. 17 April 1806	20	2	16	2				
B.S. 13 Feb 1810	20	12	5	3				
Off Rota. 4 April 1808	19	10	6	1	2			
B.S. 4 Dec 1811	19	16	2	—	1			
Malaga. 29 April 1812	19	14	2	2	1			

STATISTICS

Clasp Title	Clasps awarded	On medals bearing these number of clasps						
		1	2	3	4	5	6	7
San Fiorenzo. 8 March 1808	18	6	11	—	1			
B.S. 11 Aug 1808	17	13	2	2				
Arethusa. 23rd Aug 1806	17	—	15	—	2			
Off the Pearl Rock. 13 Dec 1808	16	2	11	3				
B.S. 1 May 1810	15	12	2	—	1			
Boadicea. 18 Sepr 1810	15	12	2	—	1			
B.S. 28 Aug 1809	15	2	3	7	3			
San Fiorenzo. 14 Feby 1805	13	2	10	—	1			
Horatio. 10 Feby 1809	13	12	1					
Castor. 17 June 1809	13	3	—	9	1			
B.S. 24 May 1814	12	10	—	2				
Bonne Citoyenne Wh Furieuse	12	11	1					
Hydra. 6 Augt 1807	12	7	4	1				
Centurion. 18 Sept 1804	12	3	3	5	1			
Sybille. 28 Feby 1799	12	10	2					
Crescent. 20 Octr 1793	12	2	3	1	4	2		
Penelope. 30 March 1800	11	3	3	3	2			
B.S. 17 Sept 1812	11	6	5					
B.S. 29 July 1809	11	9	2					
Anson. 23 Aug 1806	11	—	3	5	1	2		
Indefatigable. 13 Jany 1797	10	1	4	4	1			
B.S. 4 June 1805	10	3	3	3	1			
B.S. 4 Feby 1804	10	4	—	6				
Emerald. 13 March 1808	10	—	7	3				
Comus. 15 Aug 1807	10	6	—	2	2			
B.S. 27 July 1809	10	6	—	2	1	1		
B.S. 4 May 1811	10	6	4					
Thunder. 9 Octr 1813	9	3	6					
B.S. 13 Decr 1809	9	—	2	4	2	—	1	
B.S. 2 Aug 1811	9	7	1	1				
Schiermonnikoog. 12 Aug 1799	9	6	2	—	1			
Fisgard. 20 Octr 1798	9	4	2	3				
Indefatigable. 20 April 1796	8	—	3	4	1			
Southampton. 9 June 1796	8	—	4	2	—	1	—	1
San Fiorenzo. 8 March 1797	8	5	3					
Arrow. 3 Feby 1805	8	7	1					
Pique. 26 March 1806	8	5	—	2	—	1		
Confiance. 14 Jany 1809	8	6	1	1				
Diana. 11 Septr 1809	8	3	4	1				
Scorpion. 12 Jan 1810	8	—	3	4	—	1		
Otter. 18 Sepr 1810	8	7	—	1				
Weazel. 22 April 1813	8	1	5	1	1			
B.S. 21 Jan 1807	8	6	2					
B.S. 10 July 1808	8	6	2					
Surprise Wh Hermione	7	6	—	1				
Seine. 20 Augt 1800	7	5	1	1				
Speedy. 6 May 1801	7	3	3	1				
Grasshopper. 24 April 1808	7	3	1	1	2			
Redwing. 7 May 1808	7	—	3	3	—	1		

THE NAVAL GENERAL SERVICE MEDAL ROLL 1793–1840

Clasp Title	Clasps awarded	On medals bearing these number of clasps						
		1	2	3	4	5	6	7
Redwing. 31 May 1808	7	—	3	3	—	1		
Recruit. 17 June 1809	7	—	5	1	1			
Rosario. 27 March 1812	7	6	—	1				
Cyane. 16 Jan 1814	7	5	—	1	—	1		
Cherub. 28 March 1814	7	3	1	2	1			
B.S. 21 July 1801	7	2	2	3				
B.S. 14 July 1809	7	3	3	—	—	1		
B.S. 24 Dec 1810	6	—	5	1				
B.S. 20 Sept 1811	6	6						
Lively. 13 March 1795	6	—	3	3				
Lowestoffe. 24 June 1795	6	—	3	2	1			
Dryad. 13 June 1796	6	3	2	1				
Amazon. 13 Jany 1797	6	1	4	—	1			
Phoebe. 19 Feby 1801	6	1	3	1	—	—	1	
Hawke. 18 Aug 1811	6	4	1	1				
Weazel. 22 Feby 1812	6	—	3	2	1			
Blanche. 4 Jan 1795	5	2	2	1				
Nymphe. 8 March 1797	5	1	3	1				
Phoebe. 21 Decr 1797	5	1	2	1	—	—	1	
B.S. 27 Octr 1800	5	3	—	2				
B.S. 27 June 1803	5	2	2	—	1			
Onyx. 1 Jan 1809	5	4	1					
Cyane. 25 & 27 June 1809	5	5						
L'Espoir. 25 & 27 June 1809	5	3	2					
Nymphe. 18 June 1793	4	2	—	1	1			
Port Spergui. 17 March 1796	4	1	1	2				
Unicorn. 8 June 1796	4	3	1					
Minerve. 19 Decr 1796	4	—	—	2	1	—	1	
Blanche. 19 Decr 1796	4	1	2	1				
Fairy. 5 Feby 1800	4	3	—	1				
Harpy. 5 Feby 1800	4	1	1	2				
Pasley. 28 Octr 1801	4	3	1					
Scorpion. 31 March 1804	4	—	—	3	—	1		
Sappho. 2 March 1808	4	3	1					
Childers. 14 March 1808	4	2	—	2				
Comet. 11 Aug 1808	4	1	3					
Cruizer. 1 Novr 1808	4	4						
Cherokee. 10 Jan 1810	4	4						
Skylark. 11 Novr 1811	4	2	1	—	1			
Sealark. 21 July 1812	4	2	2					
Royalist. 29 Decr 1812	4	2	1	1				
Pelican. 14 Aug 1813	4	3	1					
B.S. 9 June 1799	4	4						
B.S. 29 July 1800	4	1	2	1				
B.S. 30 July 1811	4	—	3	1				
B.S. 4 April 1812	4	2	2					
Thetis. 17 May 1795	3	2	—	1				
Santa Margaritta. 8 June 1796	3	1	—	2				
Terpsichore. 13 Octr 1796	3	3						

STATISTICS

Clasp Title	Clasps awarded	On medals bearing these number of clasps						
		1	2	3	4	5	6	7
Isle St Marcou. 6 May 1798	3	2	1					
Speedy. 6 Novr 1799	3	1	2					
Courier. 22 Novr 1799	3	—	2	—	1			
B.S. 29 May 1797	3	—	1	1	1			
B.S. 20 Decr 1799	3	1	1	1				
B.S. 2 Jan 1807	3	2	—	—	—	1		
Royalist. May & June 1810	3	3						
Griffon. 27 March 1812	3	1	—	1	—	1		
B.S. 21 March 1813	3	2	1					
Peterel. 21 March 1800	2	—	2					
Vinciego. 30 March 1800	2	—	—	2				
Romney. 17 June 1794	2	1	1					
Astraea. 10 April 1795	2	—	1	1				
Lapwing. 3 Decr 1796	2	2						
Arrow. 13 Sepr 1799	2	1	1					
Viper. 26 Decr 1799	2	1	1					
Zebra. 17 March 1794	2	2						
Sylph. 28 Sepr 1801	2	—	—	1	—	1		
Acheron. 3 Feby 1805	2	1	1					
Pickle. 3 Jan 1807	2	—	2					
B.S. 13 Feby 1808	2	1	1					
B.S. 28 Novr 1808	2	1	—	1				
Staunch. 18 Sepr 1810	2	1	1					
Briseis. 14 Octr 1810	2	—	—	2				
Locust. 11 Novr 1811	2	2						
B.S. 29 April 1813	2	2						
B.S. 15 March 1793	1	—	—	—	1			
Hussar. 17 May 1795	1	1						
Dido. 24 June 1795	1	1						
Spider. 25 Aug 1795	1	1						
Espoir. 7 Aug 1798	1	1						
B.S. 4 Novr 1803	1	—	1					
Louisa. 28 Octr 1807	1	—	—	1				
Carrier. 4 Novr 1807	1	—	1					
Rapid. 24 April 1808	1	1						
Superieure. 10 Feby 1809	1	—	—	—	1			
Surly. 24 April 1810	1	1						
Firm. 24 April 1810	1	1						
Sylvia. 26 April 1810	1	—	1					
B.S. 4 Novr 1810	1	1						
Growler. 22 May 1812	1	1						
B.S. 3 & 6 Sept 1814	1	1						

No applicants for the following clasps:

Carysfort. 29 May 1794
Mosquito. 9 June 1795
Telegraph. 18 March 1799
Wolverine. 13 Sepr 1799
Beaver. 31 March 1804

B.S. 19 April 1807
Ann. 24 Novr 1807
B.S. 25 July 1809
Thistle. 10 Feby 1810
Arrow. 6 April 1811

THE NAVAL GENERAL SERVICE MEDAL ROLL 1793–1840

OVERALL ANALYSIS OF MEDALS & CLASPS AWARDED

For	Entries on Roll	Number of medals awarded
1 Clasp	15,577	15,577
2 Clasps	3,496	1,748
3 Clasps	1,338	446
4 Clasps	352	88
5 Clasps	125	25
6 Clasps	24	4
7 Clasps	21	3
TOTAL	20,933	17,891
	Clasps awarded	Medals awarded

EXAMPLE SURVIVAL RATES

Medal collecting began to develop as a recognised hobby during the latter part of the 19th century. By 1900 there were perhaps a few dozen collectors who were actively seeking and purchasing. They had an immense volume of material from which to choose and, understandably, they dismissed as 'uncollectable' many items which today would command great interest. Those early enthusiasts concentrated their attention upon medals awarded to famous men, to officers, and to members of their own families. Even more pertinently, they collected medals characterised by their numismatic rarity. They had little interest in the 'common' types such as the NGS with clasp 'SYRIA', or examples having only one clasp and awarded in relatively large numbers.

During the first half of the 20th century there was a gradual increase in the number of active collectors, but still they numbered only a few hundred and still they had a wide field of choice. With the passing decades the truly rare medals were traced, purchased and included in private or museum collections. The 'unsaleable common types' disappeared, all too often into the bullion melting pot. Today, therefore, we find a paradox. The clasps awarded originally in the largest numbers have suffered the greatest rate of loss, the clasps issued in the smallest numbers have survived almost intact. It is important that this phenomena should be borne in mind by the collector who is seeking to establish the relative desirability of a medal. All is not what it seems to be!

The following brief table of random examples demonstrates the principle ('TRAFALGAR' has been included, but is not truly representative because it has always been collected for its historic connotations rather than its numismatic rarity):

'TRAFALGAR'   409 clasps known of 1613 awarded = 25%

'ALGIERS'   308 .... 1328......... = 23%

'JAVA'   156 .... 665......... = 23%

'CAMPERDOWN'   87 .... 298 .... = 29%

'GAIETA 24 July 1815' 30 .... 89 .... = 34%

'COMUS 15 Aug 1807'   5 .... 10 .... = 50%

Since some of these clasps share a place with other clasps on multiple clasp medals, the precise survival rate for medals may differ. In round terms, however, it appears that about 20% of single clasp medals ('SYRIA' excepted) have survived, this figure increasing to 35% for two clasp awards and advancing further to the point of 100% for the three medals with seven clasps.

If the survival percentage is assumed to be 10% for 'SYRIA' clasp awards (say 700 medals) this would lead to an overall preservation of NGS medals numbering 3,400, less than one in five of those issued.

(1) 15 MAR BOAT SERVICE 1793

Successful attack on the French trenches before WILLEMSTADT by boats of SYREN and other gun-boats.

AYLMER, Hon Frederick W.	Midshipman	SYREN	
	Lieut. R.N.	SWIFTSURE	*Nile*
	Lieut. R.N.	SWIFTSURE	*Egypt*
	Captain R.N.	SEVERN	*Algiers*

(4) NYMPHE 18 JUNE 1793

Capture of the French frigate CLEOPATRE, off Start Point, Devon.
(Real date 19 June 1793)

GAZE, John	Quarter Master	NYMPHE	
	Midshipman	INDEFATIGABLE	*Indefatigable. 20 April 1796*
			(Vfd Abd. Not On Roll)
	Midshipman	INDIFATIGABLE	*Indefatigable. 13 Jany 1797*
	Master	QUEEN CHARLOTTE	*Algiers*

(It appears probable that the claimant received four single clasp Medals for these 4 actions, and that one was changed to an unofficial clasp of "ARETHUSA 23 Aug 1806" possibly to match an incorrect "Medal Roll". He was never aboard ARETHUSA in 1806, nor on that Roll.)

KELLY, John	Cpl. R.M.	NYMPHE	
SIMPSON, Joseph	Gunner's Crew	NYMPHE	
	A.B.	INDEFATIGABLE	*Indefatigable. 20 April 1796*
			(Vfd Abd. Not on Roll)
	A.B.	INDEFATIGABLE	*Indefatigable. 13 Jany 1797*
			(Vfd Abd. Not on Roll)
SMART, John	Captain's Servant	NYMPHE	*(Deserted 16 Feby 1795)*

(12) CRESCENT 20 OCTR 1793

Capture of the French frigate REUNION, off Cherbourg.

DE PAGE, John	A.B.	CRESCENT	*(M.L. as LE PAGE)*
	A.B.	ORION	*23rd June 1795*
	A.B.	ORION	*St Vincent*
	A.B.	ORION	*Nile*
HANDFORD, Thomas	A.B.	CRESCENT	
JEUNE, Richard	A.B.	CRESCENT*	*(M.L. as JEUNES)*
			Joined ship after ACTION
	Carpenter's Crew	ORION	*23rd June 1795*
JONES, John	Captain's Servant	CRESCENT	
KITT, Joseph	A.B.	CRESCENT	
	A.B.	ORION	*23rd June 1795*
	A.B.	ORION	*St Vincent*
	A.B.	ORION	*Nile*
MADGE, William	Quarter Gunner	CRESCENT	
	Quarter Gunner	ORION	*St Vincent*
	M.A.A.	ORION	*Nile*
MANSELL, Thomas	Midshipman	CRESCENT	
	Midshipman	ORION	*23rd June 1795*
	Master's Mate	ORION	*St Vincent*
	Midshipman	ORION	*Nile*
MARRETT, Joseph	Midshipman	CRESCENT	
	Midshipman	ORION	*23rd June 1795*
			(Vfd Abd. Not on Roll)
	Midshipman	ORION	*St Vincent*
	Midshipman	ORION	*Nile*
	Lieut. R.N.	MARTIAL	*Basque Roads. 1809*
PARKER, George	Lieut. R.N.	CRESCENT	
	Captain R.N.	STATELY	*Stately 22 March 1808*
RYE, Peter	Lieut. R.N.	CRESCENT	
	Lieut. R.N.	ORION	*23rd June 1795*
SOAMES, John	A.B.	CRESCENT	
	Quarter Gunner	ORION	*23rd June 1795*
	Bosun's Mate	ORION	*St Vincent*
	Bosun's Mate	ORION	*Nile*

CRESCENT 20 OCTR 1793

TANCOCK, John	Master's Mate	CRESCENT	
	Master's Mate	ORION	23rd June 1795
	Master's Mate	ORION	St Vincent
	Actg Lt. R.N.	ORION	Nile
	Lieut. R.N.	CAESAR	Gut of Gibraltar. 12 July 1801

(2)   # ZEBRA 17 MARCH 1794

H.M.S. ZEBRA ran alongside the bastion of Fort Royal, Martinique, and stormed and captured the fort.
(Real date 20 March 1794)

BASS, Joseph	Carpenter's Crew	ZEBRA
HILL, Henry	Lieut. R.N.	ZEBRA

(29)   # 17 MAR BOAT SERVICE 1794

Boarding and capturing the French frigate BIENVENUE in Fort Royal Bay, Martinique.

BAKER, William	Ord	VETERAN	
BATH, James	A.B.	BOYNE	
CARSTAIRS, John	Carpenter's Crew	QUEBEC	
CONNOLLY, John.B.	Lieut. R.N.	DROMEDARY	
DOUGHTY, William	Carpenter's Mate	VESUVIUS	
ELDERSHAW, John	Ord	BLONDE	
FARTHING, George	A.B.	IRRESISTIBLE	G.H. 1,391
HALL, Charles.James	Ord or Purser's Steward	ULYSSES	Only HALL, James (1) & (2) found on M.L.
HALLS, Thomas	2nd Lt. R.M.	IRRESISTIBLE	
HOSKEN, James	Gunner	IRRESISTIBLE	
	Gunner	LONDON	23rd June 1795
	Gunner	IRRESISTIBLE	St Vincent
JOHNSON, Edward	A.B.	BOYNE	
	Master's Mate	St GEORGE	Copenhagen 1801
	Lieut. R.N.	LONDON	London 13 March 1806
LUNN, James	A.B.	EXPERIMENT	(M.L. as LOWN)
MATTEN, George	A.B.	VETERAN	
McKENZIE, Charles	A.B.	QUEBEC	
MEADLEY, William	A.B.	BOYNE	(Roll maybe MEDGLEY)
MILWARD, Clement	Midshipman	ALARM	
	Lieut. R.N.	POMPEE	Martinique
OSBORN, John	A.B.	IRRESISTIBLE	
	Master's Mate	VINCIEGO	Vinciego. 30 March 1800
	Master's Mate	VIRAGO	Egypt
PIKE, John	Pte. R.M.	QUEBEC	G.H. 9,617
POLLARD, Thomas	Ord	BOYNE	
PRICE, Francis	Ord	VETERAN	
SAVAGE, William	Ord	VENGEANCE	
	A.B.	ZEALOUS	Nile
SMITH, James	Ord	VENGEANCE	
	A.B.	AMAZON	Amazon. 13 March 1806
STOVE, John.L.	A.B.	ASSURANCE	Alias LISK, John. (M.L. as LESK)
	Boatswain	HUSSAR	Java
SUTHERLAND, Robert	A.B.	ASSURANCE	
THOMAS, Richard	Master's Mate	NAUTILUS	
	Lieut. R.N.	EXCELLENT	St Vincent
TRUEMAN, John.C.	A.B.	VETERAN	
WARDEN, Thomas	L.M.	VETERAN	
WHINYATES, Thomas	Capt's Servant	VETERAN	
	Midshipman	ROBUST	23rd June 1795
	Master's Mate	ROBUST	12 Octr 1798
	Commander	FROLIC	Martinique
	Commander	FROLIC	Guadaloupe
WIGHT, John	Midshipman	ROSE	

No Applicants   # CARYSFORT 29 MAY 1794

Capture of the ex-British frigate CASTOR on 28 May 1794, off Newfoundland.

1 JUNE 1794

(540)   **G.M.**

Defeat of the French Fleet; capture of six sail of the line, and one sunk.

Name	Rating	Ship	Notes
ADAM, Charles	Midshipman	GLORY	
ADAMS, James	Quarter Gunner	IMPREGNABLE	
ALEXANDER, James	Yeoman of Sheets	TREMENDOUS	
ALLEN, Paul	A.B.	BARFLEUR	G.H. 8,378
ALLEN, Robert	Qtr Gnr	PEGASUS	
	Midshipman	AQUILON	23rd June 1795 (? Rating)
ANDERSON, George	Ord	TREMENDOUS	
ANDERSON, John	A.B.	LEVIATHAN	
	A.B.	LEVIATHAN	23rd June 1795
ANDREWS, Philip	A.B.	MARLBOROUGH	
APPLEBY, Young	Bosun's Servant	ALFRED	
	Midshipman	BLENHEIM	St Vincent
ARTHURS, Nicholas	L.M.	BRUNSWICK	
	L.M.	ROBUST	23rd June 1795
	L.M.	ROBUST	12 Octr 1798
ASHLEY, Benjamin	A.B.	INVINCIBLE	
AXFORD, Robert	Ord	MAJESTIC	
AYLMER, Charles	Master's Mate	THUNDERER	
BAILEY, John	L.M.	BELLEROPHON	G.H. 5,823
BAIN, Alexander	Quartermaster	CULLODEN	
	Midshipman	CULLODEN	St Vincent
	Midshipman	CULLODEN	Nile (? Rating)
BAKER, James	Capt's Servant	RUSSELL	
BAKER, John	Capt's Servant	MONTAGU	
BAKER, Richard	L.M.	BELLEROPHON	G.H. 6,240
	A.B.	BELLEROPHON	Nile
BAKER, Richard	L.M.	LEVIATHAN	G.H. 8,188
BAMFORD, Stephen.R.	Pte. 29th Regt	GLORY	(Medal to widow Jan 1851)
BARNES, John	Qtr Gnr	MAJESTIC	
	Q.M.'s Mate	MAJESTIC	Nile
BARRELL, Justinian	Capt's Servant	BRUNSWICK	
	Midshipman	RUSSELL	23rd June 1795
BARREY, Richard	A.B.	MAJESTIC	G.H. 5,563 as BARRY
BASSETT, Joseph	A.B.	LEVIATHAN	
BATCHELOR, James	Servant	RAMILLIES	G.H. 5,336
BATES, Joseph	A.B.	LEVIATHAN	
BEADLE, William	Servant	BARFLEUR	
	Boy 2nd Cl	GOLIATH	St Vincent
	Boy 2nd Cl	GOLIATH	Nile
BEAUFORT, Francis	Master's Mate	AQUILON	(Of "Beaufort Wind Scale")
	Master's Mate	PHAETON	17 June 1795
	Lieut. R.N.	PHAETON (P)	B.S. 27 Oct 1800
BEER, William	Pte. R.M.	CULLODEN	
	Pte. R.M.	CULLODEN	St Vincent
	Pte. R.M.	CULLODEN	Nile
BELL, Josiah	L.M.	DEFENCE	G.H. 9,857 as Joseph
BELL, William	L.M.	ALFRED	G.H. 7,753
	A.B.	BLENHEIM	St Vincent
BELLAMY, George	Actg Surgeon	RANGER	
	Surgeon	BELLEROPHON	Nile
BENNILL, Richard	L.M.	BELLEROPHON	(Alias BONNEY)
BENNIWORTH, William	A.B.	THUNDERER	
BERRY, George	Capt's Servant	QUEEN	(? Rating)
BETTY, Christopher.W.	Midshipman	MAJESTIC	
	Midshipman	MARS	Mars. 21 April 1798
	Lieut. R.N.	DREADNOUGHT	Trafalgar
BEVAN, James	A.B.	CAESAR	
BEVERIDGE, James	Carpenter's Crew	RUSSELL	
BIGGINS, Robert	A.B.	ALFRED	
	A.B.	BLENHEIM	St Vincent
	A.B.	URANIE	B.S. 21 July 1801
BIGNELL, William	A.B.	LATONA	
BLACK, George	L.M.	QUEEN CHARLOTTE	G.H. 5,003
BLAKE, Martin	Lieut's Servant	QUEEN CHARLOTTE	(Rating) G.H. 7,448
BLOYE, Robert	Midshipman	MARLBOROUGH	
	Commander	LYRA (P).	St Sebastian
BOARDMAN, Thomas	L.M.	GIBRALTAR	
BODAH, Elias	A.B.	ORION	
	A.B.	VETERAN	Camperdown
	A.B.	VETERAN	Copenhagen 1801
BOOTE, Henry	Servant	ROYAL GEORGE	
BORAM, Joseph	Bosun's Servant	ROYAL GEORGE	(Rating) G.H. 4,899
BOULK, Thomas	L.M.	INVINCIBLE	
BOULTON, Samuel	A.B.	QUEEN CHARLOTTE	
	Yeoman Sheets	QUEEN CHARLOTTE	23rd June 1795
BOWEN, William	Pte. R.M.	RAMILLIES	
BOYLE, Alexander	A.B.	THUNDERER	G.H. 4,645
BRENHAM, John	A.B.	CULLODEN	
	A.B.	CULLODEN	St Vincent
	A.B.	CULLODEN	Nile

1 JUNE 1794

Name	Rank	Ship	Notes
BRENNAN, Daniel	L.M.	ROYAL GEORGE	
	Ord	BELLEISLE	Trafalgar
	Boatswain	BARRACOUTA	Banda Neira
	Boatswain	BARRACOUTA	Java
BRETT, William	L.M.	MARLBOROUGH	G.H. 5,177
BREWER, George	L.M.	CAESAR	
	A.B.	ROBUST	12 Octr 1798
BREWER, Henry	A.B.	ROYAL GEORGE	
	L.M.	ROYAL GEORGE	23rd June 1795
BRIAN, William	Ord	QUEEN	
	Ord	QUEEN	23rd June 1795
BROOKS, William	Capt's Servant	BARFLEUR	(Rating)
BROWN, David	A.B.	AUDACIOUS	
BROWN, John	A.B.	ROYAL GEORGE	G.H. 8,796
BROWN, Samuel	Pte. R.M.	ORION	G.H. 5,867
BRUFF, Samuel	L.M.	TREMENDOUS	
BRYAN, John	A.B.	QUEEN	
BRYDEN, Edward	A.B.	CULLODEN	
	Q.M's Mate	CULLODEN	St Vincent
	Q.M.'s Mate	CULLODEN	Nile
BUCKINGHAM, Henry	Servant	CULLODEN	(Alias TINK) G.H. 6885.
	Pte. R.M.	MARS	Trafalgar
BUCKINGHAM, Joseph	Midshipman	ROYAL SOVEREIGN	
BUCKLE, Matthew	Lieut. R.N.	ROYAL SOVEREIGN	
BUCKSTEN, William	A.B.	ROYAL GEORGE	G.H. 7537 as BLACKSTONE
BULLEN, Charles	Lieut. R.N.	RAMILLIES	
	Lieut. R.N.	MONMOUTH	Camperdown
			(Rcd Gold Medal—Trafalgar)
BURBRIDGE, William.C.	Capt's Servant	ALFRED	
	Midshipman	BLENHEIM	St Vincent
	Midshipman	NASSAU	Nassau. 22 March 1808
BURCHLEY, Thomas	Pte 25th Regt	GIBRALTAR	
BURGESS, Samuel	Midshipman	IMPREGNABLE	
	Lieut. R.N.	SYLPH	Sylph. 28 Sepr 1801
	Lieut. R.N.	PRINCE	Trafalgar
	Lieut. R.N.	PINCHER	B.S. 27 July 1809
	Flag Lt. R.N.	QUEEN CHARLOTTE (P)	Algiers
BURGOYNE, Frederick.W.	Midshipman	MONTAGU	
	Master's Mate	NYMPHE	23rd June 1795
	Actg Lieut. R.N.	BRITANNIA	St Vincent
BURK, Robert	L.M.	ROYAL GEORGE	
BURK, William	A.B.	ROYAL GEORGE	
	Q.M's Mate	ROYAL GEORGE	23rd June 1795
BURT, Edward	Ord	ROYAL GEORGE	
	A.B.	ROYAL GEORGE	23rd June 1795
BUTCHER, Joseph	Ord	RUSSELL	
BUTCHER, Samuel	Midshipman	QUEEN	
	Lieut. R.N.	AQUILON	23rd June 1795
BUTT, James	Ord	CAESAR	
BYERLEE, George	A.B.	RAMILLIES	
	Yeoman of Signals	RUSSELL	Copenhagen 1801
	Boatswain	CONFIANCE	Confiance. 14 July 1809
CAMPBELL, William	Ord	BRUNSWICK	
CAMPION, William	Servant	AUDACIOUS	
	Ord	AUDACIOUS	Nile
CARDEN, John.S.	Master's Mate	MARLBOROUGH	
	Lieut. R.N.	FISGARD (P)	Fisgard. 20 Octr 1798
	Commander	SHEERNESS	Egypt
CARNE, Robert	Pte. R.M.	CAESAR	
CARNEY, James	Ord	IMPREGNABLE	G.H. 1,648
CARPENTER, John.C.	Master's Mate	DEFENCE	
CARRUTHERS, Robert	Actg Surgeon	COMET	
CARTER, Thomas	A.B.	CAESAR	G.H. 1,615
CARTER, William	Capt's Servant	ROYAL SOVEREIGN	G.H. 8,951 (Rating)
CENTER, Joseph	A.B.	VENUS	(M.L. as KINTER) G.H. 3363.
	Capt After Guard	SHANNON	Shannon Wh Chesapeake
CHALLENOR, Robert	A.B.	DEFENCE	G.H. 7,626 as CHANDLER
	A.B.	DEFENCE	Nile
CHALMERS, James	L.M.	ROYAL SOVEREIGN	(M.L. as SIMPSON)
	Ord	ROYAL SOVEREIGN	17 June 1795
CHAMBERS, George	A.B.	QUEEN	G.H. 7,792
CHAMBERS, John	A.B.	TREMENDOUS	
CHAMBERS, Robert	L.M.	MAJESTIC	
	L.M.	MAJESTIC	Nile
CHUBB, George.J.	Capt's Servant	CHARON	
	Midshipman	ETHALION	12 Octr 1798
CHURCHILL, Charles	L.M.	IMPREGNABLE	
	Ord	MONARCH	Camperdown
	Ord	MONARCH	Copenhagen 1801

CLARKE, James	Pte. R.M.	LATONA	
	Pte. R.M.	SOUTHAMPTON	*St Vincent*
	Pte. R.M.	SWIFTSURE	*Nile*
COCKET, John	Lieut's Servant	QUEEN CHARLOTTE	*(Rating)*
CODRINGTON, Edward	Lieut. R.N.	QUEEN CHARLOTTE	
	Commander	BABET	*23rd June 1795*
	Captain R.N.	ORION	*Trafalgar*
	Vice Admiral	ASIA	*Navarino (as Sir Edward)*
COLEMAN, John	Carp's Crew	GIBRALTAR	*G.H. 5,742*
COLEPACK, John	Capt's Servant	QUEEN CHARLOTTE	
	Boy 3rd Cl	QUEEN CHARLOTTE	*23rd June 1795*
	Vol 1st Cl	BONNE CITOYENNE	*St Vincent*
	Ord	BONNE CITOYENNE	*Egypt*
COLES, William	L.M.	ROYAL SOVEREIGN	
CONNIN, Francis	Surgeon	QUEEN	
	Surgeon	QUEEN	*23rd June 1795*
CONNELLY, Henry	L.M.	CULLODEN	
CONSITT, Thomas	Midshipman	DEFENCE	
	Master's Mate	DEFENCE	*Nile*
COOK, Robert	Cpl. 29th Regt	ALFRED	*(Applied as "Capt")*
COOK, Thomas	Capt's Servant	INVINCIBLE	
COOKE, John	A.B.	BARFLEUR	*(Entitled to 23rd June '95)*
	A.B.	BARFLEUR	*St Vincent*
COOMBE, James	Ord	CAESAR	
	Ord	SYBILLE	*Sybille. 28 Feby 1799*
COOPER, James.A.	Surgeon's Svnt	ALFRED	*(? Rating)*
COOPER, William	Ord	BARFLEUR	
	Ord	BARFLEUR	*23rd June 1795*
	A.B.	BARFLEUR	*St Vincent*
CORNELIUS, William	L.M.	ROYAL GEORGE	
	L.M.	ROYAL GEORGE	*23rd June 1795*
	A.B.	PRINCE	*Trafalgar*
CORNISH, Richard	Ord	PEGASUS	
CORNWALL, Peter	Capt's Servant	BRUNSWICK	*(? Rating)*
COX, Henry	2nd Lt. R.M.	VALIANT	
	1st Lt. R.M.	ROMNEY	*Egypt*
	Captain R.M.	DEFENCE	*Trafalgar*
CRADDOCK, Henry	A.B.	QUEEN CHARLOTTE	
CRAMPTON, John	A.B.	RUSSELL	
CREAGH, Richard	L.M.	ORION	
	L.M.	VETERAN	*Camperdown*
	Qtr Gunner	VETERAN	*Copenhagen 1801*
CREMENE, John	L.M.	ORION	*Spelt 3 different ways on Roll. CREMMERN & CREMERN*
	A.B.	LEVIATHAN	*23rd June 1795*
	A.B.	VETERAN	*Camperdown*
	A.B.	VETERAN	*Copenhagen 1801*
CROKER, William	L.M.	ORION	
CULLEN, Daniel	L.M.	BRUNSWICK	*(M.L. as CULLINS)*
	L.M.	ROBUST	*23rd June 1795*
	Ord	ROBUST	*12 Octr 1798*
	L.M.	ROYAL SOVEREIGN	*Trafalgar*
CULLEN, Edward	L.M.	VALIANT	
CUMMINGS, James	A.B.	AUDACIOUS	
	A.B.	AUDACIOUS	*Nile*
DADD, James	L.M.	MARLBOROUGH	
DALLIMORE, James	Pte. R.M.	SOUTHAMPTON	
	Pte. R.M.	SOUTHAMPTON	*Southampton. 9 June 1796*
	Pte. R.M.	SOUTHAMPTON	*St Vincent*
DALRYMPLE, James	Midshipman	GLORY	
DARLINGTON, Joseph	Servant	CULLODEN	
	Boy	CULLODEN	*St Vincent*
	Ord	CULLODEN	*Nile*
DASHWOOD, Charles	Lieut. R.N.	IMPREGNABLE	
	Lieut. R.N.	MAGNANIME	*12 Octr 1798 (Vfd Abd. Not on Roll)*
	Commander	SYLPH (P)	*Sylph. 28 Sepr 1801*
DAVIES, Henry.T.	Capt's Servant	GLORY	
	Lieut. R.N.	WINCHELSEA	*Egypt*
	Lieut. R.N.	BLANCHE (P)	*Blanche. 19 July 1806*
DAVIES, John	L.M.	SOUTHAMPTON	
	Ord	SOUTHAMPTON	*Southampton. 9 June 1796 (Vfd Abd. Not on Roll)*
	Ord	SOUTHAMPTON	*St Vincent*
	A.B.	SUPERB	*Gut of Gibraltar. 12 July 1801*
	A.B.	SUPERB	*St Domingo*

1 JUNE 1794

Name	Rank	Ship	Notes
DAVIS, James	A.B.	RUSSELL	
DAVIS, John	Yeoman Powder Rm	ALFRED	(Alias SMITH, Thomas)
DAWSON, John	Ship's Corporal	MONTAGU	(M.L. as LAWSON)
DAY, John	Boy 3rd Cl	MONTAGU	
DEBENHAM, John	A.B.	GLORY	
	Midshipman	PRINCE OF WALES	23rd June 1795
DELAISTRE, William	Capt's Servant	COMET	
DELAMAINE, Robert	A.B.	DEFENCE	(M.L. alias STEVERENS)
DEW, Andrew	Pte R.M.	TREMENDOUS	
	Cpl. R.M.	REVOLUTIONNAIRE	St Sebastian
DICK, Daniel	L.M.	TREMENDOUS	
	A.B.	ROYAL SOVEREIGN	Trafalgar
DICKSON, William.H.	Lieut's Servant	CAESAR	(Commander 1815)
DILLON, William.H.	Midshipman	DEFENCE	
	Midshipman	PRINCE GEORGE	23rd June 1795
	Commander	CHILDERS	Childers. 14 March 1808
DINELEY, William	Surg's Servant	THUNDERER	
DOWN, Edward.A.	Midshipman	BARFLEUR	
	Master's Mate	EXCELLENT	St Vincent
	Master's Mate	VINCIEGO	Vinciego. 30 March 1800
DONTON, William	Pte. R.M.	MONTAGU	
DRAYTON, Edward	A.B.	CAESAR	
DREDGE, Thomas	Ord	GIBRALTAR	
DREW, James	A.B.	QUEEN CHARLOTTE	
	A.B.	QUEEN CHARLOTTE	23rd June 1795
DUNCAN, David	A.B.	RUSSELL	
DUNCAN, Robert	A.B.	PHAETON	(M.L. as DONKIN)
DUNN, Archibald	Ship's Corporal	IMPREGNABLE	
DWYER, Mathias	L.M.	DEFENCE	
	L.M.	BRITANNIA	St Vincent
DYER, Thomas	L.M.	QUEEN CHARLOTTE	
EDWARDS, Henry	L.M.	DEFENCE	
	A.B.	DEFENCE	Nile
EGERTON, B.	Lieut, 29th Regt	THUNDERER	(Applied as Gen & Col of 89th Regiment)
EGGLISTONE, Francis	A.B.	BELLEROPHON	
	Quarter Gunner	BELLEROPNON	Nile
	Sailmaker's Crew	PEGASUS	Egypt
ELDER, John	A.B.	LEVIATHAN	
ELLIS, Alexander	Midshipman	LEVIATHAN	
ELLIS, Francis	A.B.	ALFRED	
	A.B.	BLENHEIM	St Vincent
ELLIS, Thomas	Capt's Servant	PEGASUS	G.H. 10,081 (Rating)
	Boy 3rd Cl	AQUILON	23rd June 1795
	Ord	SPENCER	Gut of Gibraltar. 12 July 1801
ENDELL, Stephen	A.B.	QUEEN	
	A.B.	QUEEN	23rd June 1795
ENGLISH, William	Gunner's Mate	TREMENDOUS	
EUSTACE, Philip	L.M.	QUEEN	(M.L. as EASTON)
EYRES, George	A.B.	LEVIATHAN	G.H. 2,240
FERGUSON, William	Capt's Servant	QUEEN	(? Rating)
FERNANDES, Donald	Midshipman	THUNDERER	
	Master's Mate	THUNDERER	23rd June 1795
	Lieut. R.N.	BLENHEIM	St Vincent
FITZGERALD, John	A.B.	LATONA	
FITZGERALD, Joseph	L.M.	MAJESTIC	
FITZROY, William	Capt's Servant	PHAETON	
	Midshipman	SANS PAREIL	23rd June 1795 (Vfd Abd. Not on Roll)
	Lieut. R.N.	PENELOPE	Egypt
	Captain. R.N.	AEOLUS	4 Novr 1805
	Captain. R.N.	AEOLUS	Martinique
FLETCHER, Emanuel	L.M.	ROYAL GEORGE	G.H. 7,594
FLYNN, Robert	Lieut's Servant	TREMENDOUS	G.H. 4.577
FOLEY, Andrew	Pte. R.M.	ROYAL SOVEREIGN	
FORD, Elias	Bosun's Mate	IMPREGNABLE	
FOSS, George	L.M.	VALIANT	
FOX, Samuel	Ord	MARLBOROUGH	
FRASER, William	A.B.	PEGASUS	
	A.B.	AQUILON	23rd June 1795
FREEMAN, William	Capt's Servant	MARLBOROUGH	(Rating)
GADD, Thomas	L.M.	LATONA	
GALE, John	Carp's Crew	BELLEROPHON	
	Carp's Crew	BELLEROPHON	17 June 1795
	A.B.	BELLEROPHON	Nile
	Carp's Mate	SPENCER	Gut of Gibraltar. 12 July 1801
	Carpenter	NORTHUMBERLAND	Northumberland. 22 May 1812
GALE, John	L.M.	CULLODEN	
	A.B.	CULLODEN	Nile

GALE, Stephen	L.M.	DEFENCE	
GARDNER, James	Bosun's Servant	ROYAL GEORGE	G.H. 1,244
GARRETT, John	Ord	DEFENCE	
	A.B.	DEFENCE	Nile
GARRETT, Thomas	Capt's Servant	MARLBOROUGH	(Rating)
GIBBONS, George	A.B.	VENUS	
GIBSON, John	Capt's Servant	ROYAL SOVEREIGN	(Rating)
GILES, Samuel	Midshipman	CULLODEN	
	Purser	ASTRAEA	Egypt
	Purser	ULYSSES	Martinique
GLYNN, Henry.R.	Lieut. R.N.	ROYAL GEORGE	
	Lieut. R.N.	ROYAL GEORGE	23rd June 1795
GOFF, Richard	A.B.	BRUNSWICK	
	A.B.	ACASTA	St Domingo
GOLDSMITH, John	Clerk	THUNDERER	
	Purser	AMAZON	Copenhagen 1801
	Purser	SUPERB	Algiers
GOODENOUGH, George	Quarter Gunner	DEFENCE	
	Gunner's Mate	DEFENCE	Nile
	Q.M's Mate	POLYPHEMUS	Copenhagen 1801
GOSSELIN, Thomas le M.	Commander	KINGFISHER*	This vessel was incorrectly included as an admissable ship. Was "Moored in Downes" on 1 June 1794.
	(As an Admiral of the Red, this Officer applied for, and received this Medal!)		
GRAY, Gabriel	Ord	VENUS	G.H. 3,420
GREENSLADE, John	L.M.	ROYAL GEORGE	G.H. 9,820
	L.M.	PRINCE	Trafalgar
GREER, John.M.	Capt's Servant	INVINCIBLE	(Rtd Cdr in 1840)
GRIST, William	A.B.	AQUILON	
GUSWELL, Richard	A.B.	BRUNSWICK	(M.L. as GOSSWELL)
GWYNNE, Lawrence	Schoolmaster	RAMILLIES	
HAINES, John	Pte. R.M.	TREMENDOUS	
HAINSSELIN, Dennis.F.	A.B.	ROYAL GEORGE	
	A.B.	ROYAL GEORGE	23rd June 1795
HALL, William	Pte. R.M.	MONTAGU	
	Pte. R.M.	MAJESTIC	Nile
HALLORAN, Nicholas	Not Given	GLORY	
HAMOND, Graham.E.	Midshipman	QUEEN CHARLOTTE	
	Captain R.N.	BLANCHE	Copenhagen 1801
HAMSHIRE, James	Capt's Servant	DEFENCE	
	Boy	DEFENCE	Nile
	Ord	DEFENCE	Copenhagen 1801
HANNAH, James	Capt's Servant	QUEEN CHARLOTTE	(Rating)
HANLON, Christopher	A.B.	INVINCIBLE	
HARDINGHAM, Nicholas	A.B.	ALFRED	
HARDIS, Andrew	Ord	LEVIATHAN	
HART, James	A.B.	RUSSELL	
HART, William	A.B.	CAESAR	
	A.B.	AJAX	Egypt
HARVEY, Charles	Pte. R.M.	MONTAGU	G.H. 9093
	Pte. R.M.	MAJESTIC	Nile
HARVEY, James	Caulker	IMPREGNABLE	
HARVEY, Thomas	Capt's Servant	LEVIATHAN	(? Rating)
HASLING, Charles	Q.M.	MONTAGU	
HASWELL, William.H.	Capt's Servant	LEVIATHAN*	"On the books only". Too young to be present.
	Midshipman	PHOEBE	Trafalgar. (Lieut in 1809)
HATTON, John	Pte. R.M.	BELLEROPHON	
	Pte. R.M.	BELLEROPHON	17 June 1795
	Pte. R.M.	BELLEROPHON	Nile
	Cpl. R.M.	SPENCER	Gut of Gibraltar. 12 July 1801
HAVILAND, Henry	L.M.	GLORY	
	Midshipman	PRINCE OF WALES	23rd June 1795
HAWES, William.J.	Capt's Servant	AUDACIOUS	
	Vol 1st Cl	AUDACIOUS	Nile
	Ord	CONQUEROR	Trafalgar
HAWTAYNE, Charles.S.J.	Midshipman	DEFENCE	
	Lieut. R.N.	GREYHOUND	Egypt
HAYDON, William	Capt's Servant	NIGER	(Capt. RN. 1841)
HEALY, John	L.M.	VALIANT	
	L.M.	VALIANT	23rd June 1795
HENDERSON, John	Secretary	ROYAL GEORGE	
	Secretary	ROYAL GEORGE	23rd June 1795
HERANTE, John	L.M.	BRUNSWICK	(May read HERAULE on Roll)
HEWETT, Thomas	A.B.	BRUNSWICK	
	A.B.	ROBUST	12 Octr 1798
	Q.M.	CENTAUR	Centaur. 26 Augt 1808
	Q.M.	IMPREGNABLE	Algiers
HEWETT, James or HEWITT	Ord	ALFRED	G.H. 283
	A.B.	BLENHEIM	St Vincent
	Q.M's Mate	NAIAD	Trafalgar

1 JUNE 1794

HEXT, William	Capt's Servant	RUSSELL	
	Midshipman	RUSSELL	*23rd June 1795*
	Lieut. R.N.	SANTA MARGARITA	*4 Novr 1805*
HIGGINS, Richard	Carp's Crew	QUEEN	
	Carp's Crew	QUEEN	*23rd June 1795*
HILL, James	L.M.	ROYAL SOVEREIGN	
HILL, Samuel	Ord	ROYAL GEORGE	
HILL, Thomas	L.M.	RAMILLIES	
HILLIER, George	Capt's Servant	ALFRED	
	Midshipman	ARDENT	*Camperdown*
	Lieut. R.N.	ALLIANCE	*Acre. 30 May 1799*
	Lieut. R.N.	TIGRE	*Egypt*
HILLIER, John.P.	Capt's Servant	ALFRED	*(Never a Lieut. R.N.)*
HILLIER, William.C.	Midshipman	ALFRED	
	Midshipman	BLENHEIM	*St Vincent*
	Master's Mate	POMPEE	*Gut of Gibraltar. 12 July 1801*
	Purser	COMUS	*Comus. 15 Augt 1807*
HILLMAN, Richard	Ord	CULLODEN	
	A.B.	CULLODEN	*St Vincent*
	A.B.	CULLODEN	*Nile*
HINDMARSH, John	Capt's Servant	BELLEROPHON	
	Vol 1st Cl	BELLEROPHON	*17 June 1795*
	Midshipman	BELLEROPHON	*Nile*
	Midshipman	SPENCER	*Gut of Gibraltar. 12 July 1801*
	Lieut. R.N.	PHOEBE	*Trafalgar*
	Lieut. R.N.	BEAGLE	*Basque Roads. 1809*
	Lieut. R.N.	NISUS	*Java*
HODGE, William	Capt's Servant	ALFRED	
	Boy 3rd Cl	BLENHEIM	*St Vincent*
HOLDEN, William.R.	A.B.	NIGER	
HOLLOWAY, John	L.M.	ROYAL GEORGE	
HOMEWOOD, Isaac	L.M.	LATONA	*G.H. 4,638*
HONE, John	A.B.	RAMILLIES	
HOTCHKIS, John	Master's Mate	GIBRALTAR	
HOUGHTON, William	L.M.	DEFENCE	
	A.B.	EXCELLENT	*St Vincent*
HOWELLS, John	L.M.	ROYAL GEORGE	
	L.M.	ROYAL GEORGE	*23rd June 1795*
HUDSON, Joseph	Clerk	CHARON	
HUGHES, James	Capt's Cook	INVINCIBLE	
HURDIS, George.C.	Midshipman	NIGER	
HUTCHINGS, John	L.M.	VALIANT	
INCH, John	Pte. R.M.	LEVIATHAN	
	Pte. R.M.	LEVIATHAN	*23rd June 1795*
	Sgt. R.M.	DORIS	*B.S. 21 July 1801*
JAMES, Thomas	Pte. R.M.	ORION	
	Cpl. R.M.	ALEXANDER	*Nile*
	Sgt. R.M.	MARS	*Trafalgar*
JAMES, William	A.B.	RAMILLIES	
	A.B.	RAMILLIES	*Copenhagen. 1801*
JEFFERY, Roger	Ord	ROYAL SOVEREIGN	
JOB, William	Pte. R.M.	CULLODEN	
	Pte. R.M.	CULLODEN	*St Vincent*
	Pte. R.M.	CULLODEN	*Nile*
JOHNSON, Ralph	A.B.	ROYAL GEORGE	
JONES, Charles.T.	A.B.	LEVIATHAN	*(Kt in 1809 & Captain 1819)*
	A.B.	LEVIATHAN	*23rd June 1795*
JONES, Edward	L.M.	GLORY	*G.H. 6,608*
JONES, George	2nd Lt. R.M.	VALIANT	
	1st Lt. R.M.	REVOLUTIONNAIRE	*23rd June 1795*
JONES, William	L.M.	AUDACIOUS	
JOY, Benjamin	A.B.	LEVIATHAN	*G.H. 1,418*
	A.B.	LEVIATHAN	*23rd June 1795*
JUDD, Robert.H.	Midshipman	QUEEN	
KELLY, John	Ord	ROYAL SOVEREIGN	
	A.B.	ROYAL SOVEREIGN	*17 June 1795*
KEMPTON, James	A.B.	PHAETON	*G.H. 1,238*
	A.B.	AKBAR	*Java*
KENNEDY, James	Ord	IMPREGNABLE	
KENNEDY, Walter	L.M.	IMPREGNABLE	
KENNETT, Isaac	A.B.	RATTLER	
KILGROVE, James	Pte. 29th Regt	GLORY	
KING, Daniel	Lieut's Servant	ORION	*(Rating)*
KING, Edward.D.	Master's Mate	BARFLEUR	
	Lieut. R.N.	DRYAD (P)	*Dryad. 13 June 1796*
KINSALE, Michael	L.M.	VALIANT	
	L.M.	VALIANT	*23rd June 1795*

KITCHEN, James	Capt's Servant	TREMENDOUS	(? Rating)
KITE, James	Ord	CULLODEN	
	A.B.	CULLODEN	St Vincent
	A.B.	CULLODEN	Nile
KNAPMAN, William	Capt's Clerk	PEGASUS	
KNIGHT, Thomas	Capt's Servant	CULLODEN	
	Boy 3rd Cl	CULLODEN	St Vincent
	Boy 3rd Cl	CULLODEN	Nile
LADLE, Edward	A.B.	BARFLEUR	
LAKE, John	L.M.	CULLODEN	
	Purser's Steward	CULLODEN	St Vincent
	Purser's Steward	NEPTUNE	Trafalgar
LANE, Joseph	Retinue	QUEEN	
	Retinue	QUEEN	23rd June 1795
LANGFORD, William	L.M.	GLORY	
LANGLEY, William	L.M.	MARLBOROUGH	G.H. 6,703
LAWLER, John	L.M.	ROYAL SOVEREIGN	
LAURIE, Robert	Lieut. R.N.	QUEEN	
LAZARUS, William	Capt's Servant	VALIANT	(Rating)
LECKEY, Robert	Ord	CULLODEN	
	A.B.	CULLODEN	St Vincent
	A.B.	CULLODEN	Nile
	A.B.	PIQUE	Egypt
LEE, George.S.	A.B.	RATTLER	
LENARD, Joseph	Ord	CULLODEN	
	Ord	CULLODEN	St Vincent
	Ord	CULLODEN	Nile
	Yeoman of Sheets	NAIAD	Trafalgar
LEROUX, Frederick.J.	Capt's Servant	CHARON	Also entitled to "12 Octr 1798" & "Egypt". On display at Royal Naval Museum, Portsmouth. Only known Medal complete with Box of issue, Ribbon and tissue paper sewn to ribbon to protect clasp(s) when wrapped around. Rtd Cdr 1830.
LEVERTON, Richard	A.B.	ORION	G.H. 709
	A.B.	VETERAN	Camperdown
	Gunner's Mate	TEMERAIRE	Trafalgar
	Yeoman Powder Rm	ANSON	Anson. 23 Augt 1806 (Vfd Abd. Not on Roll)
	Yeoman Powder Rm	ANSON	Curacoa
LEVITT, John	A.B.	QUEEN CHARLOTTE	
LEWIS, Charles	L.M.	INVINCIBLE	
LINDSAY, John	Capt's Servant	VALIANT	G.H. 7,819 (Rating)
LITTLE, Simon	Clerk	AUDACIOUS	
	Purser	MONTAGU	Camperdown
LLEWELLYN, Thomas	A.B.	IMPREGNABLE	
LOCK, James	Capt's Servant	QUEEN CHARLOTTE	(A domestic aged 10 years)
	Ord	MINDEN	Algiers
LONEY, John.J.	Capt's Servant	LATONA	(Lieut. R.N. in 1807)
LONG, Miles	L.M.	VALIANT	
LOVELL, Jeremiah	A.B.	TREMENDOUS	
LOWRIE, Richard	A.B.	LEVIATHAN	
	Carp's Crew	LEVIATHAN	23rd June 1795
LOWTHIAN, Robert	A.B.	ROYAL GEORGE	(Promoted to Cdr in 1813)
	A.B.	ROYAL GEORGE	23rd June 1795
LUCAS, Charles	A.B.	TREMENDOUS	
	Q.M.	DONEGAL	St Domingo
MACEY, Joseph	A.B.	QUEEN	
MACKENZIE, Alexander	1st Lt. R.M.	INVINCIBLE	
	1st Lt. R.M.	ELEPHANT	Copenhagen 1801
MADDEN, Thomas	A.B.	LEVIATHAN	
MAITLAND, James	Ord	BELLEROPHON	Never a Lieut. R.N.
	Midshipman	BELLEROPHON	Nile (Probably Mid Ship Man)
MAJESTIC, Joseph	A.B.	LEVIATHAN	
	A.B.	BELLONA	Copenhagen 1801
MASON, Francis	Midshipman	RUSSELL	
	Midshipman	RUSSELL	23rd June 1795
	Captain. R.N.	PRESIDENT	St Sebastian
MASTERS, Thomas	A.B.	VALIANT	
MATHEWSON, Daniel	Servant	NIGER	
	A.B.	STATELY	Egypt
MATHEWSON, James	Cooper	ALFRED	
MAY, John	A.B.	BRUNSWICK	
McAUSLAND, Peter	A.B.	MONTAGU	
	Gunner's Mate	IRRESISTIBLE	23rd June 1795
	Bosun's Mate	IRRESISTIBLE	St Vincent
	Gunner	PETEREL	Egypt
	Gunner	IMPLACABLE	Implacable. 26 Augt 1808

1 JUNE 1794

McCALLUM, George	Surgeon	VALIANT	
McDONALD, Colin	Midshipman	SOUTHAMPTON	
	Midshipman	DRYAD	*Dryad. 13 June 1796 (Vfd. Abd. Not on Roll)*
McDONALD, James	A.B.	ROYAL SOVEREIGN	
McFARLAND, James	Lieut. R.N.	QUEEN CHARLOTTE	
	Lieut. R.N.	QUEEN CHARLOTTE	*23rd June 1795*
McGEE, George	L.M.	QUEEN CHARLOTTE	
McGENNIS, James	L.M.	QUEEN CHARLOTTE	
	Ord	NEPTUNE	*Trafalgar*
McGWIRE, William	Lieut. R.N.	INVINCIBLE	
McKENZIE, Daniel Tremendous	BABY	TREMENDOUS	*HISTORICALLY UNIQUE*
McLAUGHLAN, James	Ord	BELLEROPHON	
	A.B.	BELLEROPHON	*Nile*
	A.B.	THUNDERER	*Trafalgar*
McLELLAN, John	Yeoman of Sheets	LATONA	
McNICHOL, James	A.B.	GLORY	
MERRITT, William	L.M.	ORION	
	L.M.	VETERAN	*Camperdown*
MILLAR, John	A.B.	MAJESTIC	
MILLETT, Thomas	L.M.	IMPREGNABLE	
MILLINOUX, Alfred	Capt's Servant	AUDACIOUS	*Rating. (M.L. as MOLLINEUX)*
MITCHELL, James	A.B.	GLORY	
	A.B.	BARFLEUR	*23rd June 1795*
	A.B.	BARFLEUR	*St Vincent*
MORGAN, James	L.M.	BRUNSWICK	
	Ord	ROBUST	*23rd June 1795*
	Ord	ROBUST	*12 Octr 1798*
	Ord	SPENCER	*St Domingo*
MORGAN, Thomas. Rev.	Chaplain	ALFRED	
	Chaplain	MARS	*Mars. 21 April 1798*
MORLEY, William	Pte. R.M.	QUEEN	
MORRIS, George	Midshipman	AUDACIOUS	
	Lieut. R.N.	ARDENT	*Camperdown*
MORRIS, John.R.	Master's Mate	ALFRED	
MORRIS, William (I)	A.B.	ROYAL GEORGE	*G.H. 4,507*
	A.B.	CAPTAIN	*14 March 1795*
	A.B.	CAPTAIN	*St Vincent*
MORRISH, Nicholas	Drummer. RM	ROYAL SOVEREIGN	
	Drummer. R.M.	VETERAN	*Camperdown*
	Drummer. R.M.	VETERAN	*Copenhagen 1801*
MUGFORD, George	A.B.	CAESAR	
MUIR, Thomas	Master's Mate	MAJESTIC	
MULLAY, John	Drummer. R.M.	ROYAL SOVEREIGN	*G.H. 9,081*
MURWOOD, William	A.B.	BRUNSWICK	
	A.B.	ROBUST	*23rd June 1795*
NANCARROW, Walter	L.M.	QUEEN CHARLOTTE	
	Ord	QUEEN CHARLOTTE	*23rd June 1795*
NICHOLLS, John	Capt's Servant	VALIANT	*(Rating)*
NICKLIN, Benjamin	Pte. R.M.	IMPREGNABLE	
	Pte. R.M.	DEFIANCE	*Copenhagen 1801*
NIPPER, James	Capt's Servant	MARLBOROUGH	
	A.B.	VICTORY	*Trafalgar*
	A.B.	AMAZON	*Amazon. 13 March 1806 (Vfd Abd. Not on Roll)*
NORTHEY, L.A.	Ensign. 29th Foot	ALFRED	
NUGENT, John	Capt's Servant	INVINCIBLE	
	Lieut. R.N.	PHOENIX	*Egypt*
OATES, William	Drummer. R.M.	VENUS	
O'BRIEN, Cornelius	Capt's Servant	MARLBOROUGH	
OSBORNE, Henry	Asst Surg's Mate	VENUS	
OSBORNE, William	L.M.	IMPREGNABLE	
	Carp's Crew	REVENGE	*Trafalgar*
OWEN, William.F.	Midshipman	CULLODEN	
	Commander	BARRACOUTA	*Java*
PADDINGTON, George	A.B.	BRUNSWICK	
PAINE, Thomas	A.B.	QUEEN CHARLOTTE	
	A.B.	QUEEN CHARLOTTE	*23rd June 1795*
PALMER, John	Admiral's Servant	ROYAL GEORGE	
	Admiral's Servant	ROYAL GEORGE	*23rd June 1795*
PARDOE, William	Master's Mate	MARLBOROUGH	
PARDY, John	Ord	BELLEROPHON	
	Ord	BELLEROPHON	*Nile*
PARK, Henry	A.B.	ROYAL SOVEREIGN	
PARKER, William	Midshipman	ORION	
	Captain. R.N.	AMAZON	*Amazon. 13 March 1806*
PARKES, Peter	L.M.	BELLEROPHON	
PARTRIDGE, William	L.M.	MARLBOROUGH	

PAYNE, Charles.F.	Midshipman	CULLODEN	
	Midshipman	LONDON	23rd June 1795. (Not on Roll but statement found "Claims also 23 June 1795") Vfd Abd.
PAYNE, William	Midshipman	PHAETON	
	Master's Mate	QUEEN CHARLOTTE	23rd June 1795
PEACOCK, William	Ord	MONTAGU	
	Ord	MADRAS	Egypt
PEADON, James	Ord	RAMILLIES	
& Antonio	Ord	RAMILLIES	Copenhagen 1801
PEARSON, Thomas	L.M.	INVINCIBLE	
PEDRICK, Francis	Servant	IMPREGNABLE	
PEEK, William	Capt's Servant	THUNDERER	(M.L. as PEAK) Rating.
PEMBRIDGE, Samuel	A.B.	ROYAL GEORGE	
	A.B.	ROYAL GEORGE	23rd June 1795
PETERSON, John	A.B.	QUEEN CHARLOTTE	
	A.B.	MONARCH	Copenhagen 1801
PETTITT, John	A.B.	LATONA	G.H. 9,865
PIKE, Thomas	Capt's Servant	VALIANT	To Rtd Cdr 1847
PILKINGTON, A.	Lieut. 2nd Queens	ROYAL GEORGE	Applied as Lt General.
PIPER, Henry	A.B.	INVINCIBLE	
PLUMMER, Edward	Capt's Servant	TREMENDOUS	Rating
POLLARD, Thomas	Sailmaker	GIBRALTAR	
POULTON, Benjamin	Pte. R.M.	IMPREGNABLE	
POWER, John	Capt's Servant	GLORY	Rating
PRATTON, James	Drummer. R.M.	CAESAR	G.H. 9,832
PRYOR, John	L.M.	MAJESTIC	
	A.B.	MAJESTIC	Nile
PUMMELL, Samuel	A.B.	RUSSELL	
	A.B.	RUSSELL	23rd June 1795
	Ord	DONEGAL	St Domingo
	Not Given	Not Given	Basque Roads 1809. 171/2/69.
PUNCHER, John	Carp's Crew	BARFLEUR	
RABBICH, Henry	A.B.	BRUNSWICK	
	A.B.	ROBUST	23rd June 1795
	A.B.	ROBUST	12 Octr 1798
RAMSAY, Robert	Midshipman	BELLEROPHON	
RANN, John	Carp's Crew	CHARON	(M.L. as RAND)
	Carp's Crew	SWIFTSURE	Nile
RATSEY, Edward	Midshipman	DEFENCE	
RAYLEY, Charles	Midshipman	AUDACIOUS	
READING, William	Coxswain	ALFRED	
REID, Thomas	Ord	TREMENDOUS	
REIKIE, William	Midshipman	BELLEROPHON	
RENWICK, Thomas	Midshipman	BRUNSWICK	
	Lieut. R.N.	St FIORENZO	San Fiorenzo. 8 Mar 1797
RIBOULEAU, Peter	Lieut. R.N.	GLORY	
RICHARDSON, Charles	Master's Mate	ROYAL GEORGE	
	Lieut. R.N.	CIRCE	Camperdown
	Lieut. R.N.	KENT	Egypt
	Captain. R.N.	CAESAR	Basque Roads 1809
RICHARDSON, John	A.B.	QUEEN	(Medal sent c/o Coast Guard)
	A.B.	QUEEN	23rd June 1795
RICHARDSON, William	Capt's Servant	ALFRED	
	Midshipman	PRINCE GEORGE	St Vincent
RICKETT, Thomas	Pte. R.M.	IMPREGNABLE	
RIDETT, William	L.M.	DEFENCE	
	Quarter Gunner	DEFENCE	Nile
	Purser	GLATTON	Copenhagen 1801
RIDLEY, Thomas	A.B.	LEVIATHAN	
	A.B.	LEVIATHAN	23rd June 1795
ROBERTS, William	A.B.	TREMENDOUS	
	A.B.	CULLODEN	St Vincent
	A.B.	CULLODEN	Nile
ROBBINSON, John	A.B.	ROYAL SOVEREIGN	
ROBINSON, William	Pte. 29th Regt	THUNDERER	
ROBSON, Thomas	Pte. 29th Regt	BRUNSWICK	(Awd MGS 4 Clasp)
ROSE, Israel	Servant	GLORY	
ROSE, James	Servant	AQUILON	G.H. 2,855
ROSE, John	L.M.	ROYAL GEORGE	
	L.M.	ROYAL GEORGE	23rd June 1795
ROWLAND, James	L.M.	ROYAL GEORGE	
SALTER, George.E.	Lieut's Servant	ROYAL SOVEREIGN	(? Rating)
SALTER, John	Pte. R.M.	CULLODEN	
	Pte. R.M.	CULLODEN	St Vincent
	Pte. R.M.	MUTINE	Nile
SANDERS, George	A.B.	ORION	
SANDERSON, William	L.M.	ROYAL GEORGE	
SAUL, George	L.M.	CAESAR	G.H. 295
SAUNDERS, John	L.M.	MARLBOROUGH	
SAVER, George	A.B.	PHAETON	G.H. 7,360

1 JUNE 1794

SCARLETT, Robert	L.M.	ROYAL GEORGE	
SCOTLAND, Andrew	Ord	DEFENCE	
SEDEWAY, James	Midshipman	CULLODEN	G.H. 9,099
	Midshipman	CULLODEN	St Vincent
	Midshipman	CULLODEN	Nile
			(Old Rate of Mid Ship Man)
SEEDS, Robert	A.B.	BRUNSWICK	
	Cook	VESTAL	Egypt
SELBY, Thomas	A.B.	CULLODEN	(M.L. as SELVIE)
	A.B.	CULLODEN	St Vincent
	A.B.	CULLODEN	Nile
SHARP, John	L.M.	ROYAL GEORGE	
SHAW, James	A.B.	ROYAL GEORGE	(M.L. as Thomas SHAW)
SHAW, William	Pte. R.M.	QUEEN CHARLOTTE	G.H. 6,945
SHAW, William	L.M.	GLORY	
SHAW, William	Not Given	VALIANT	
SHAW, William	Servant	CHARON	G.H. 9,435
SHELLSHEAR, Hugh	A.B.	PHAETON	
	A.B.	PHAETON	17 June 1795
	Gunner	SCIPION	Java
SHEPHERD, John	Midshipman	RAMILLIES	
SHERRARD, John	Pte. R.M.	PHAETON	
	A.B.	PHAETON	17 June 1795
SHOWAN, Elijah	Capt's Servant	QUEEN	(M.L. as SHOWEN.)
	Boy 2nd Cl	QUEEN	23rd June 1795
	Gunner's Mate	CALEDONIA	Basque Roads 1809
SHUTE, Thomas	Lieut's Servant	ROYAL GEORGE	G.H. 8,251. Rating
SIMMONS, John	Cook's Servant	ROYAL GEORGE	
	Cook's Servant	ROYAL GEORGE	23rd June 1795
SIMONS, Simon	Gunner's Servant	ROYAL SOVEREIGN	
	A.B.	SULTAN	B.S. 4 Dec 1811
SIMPSON, George	Ord	GLORY	
SIMPSON, George	A.B.	RUSSELL	
	A.B.	RUSSELL	23rd June 1795 (as John)
SIMPSON, John	A.B.	INVINCIBLE	
SINGLETON, David	Cpl. R.M.	VALIANT	
	Pte. R.M.	NEPTUNE	Trafalgar
SISON, Thomas	Pte. R.M.	AQUILON	
SKUCE, William	L.M.	DEFENCE	
	L.M.	DEFENCE	Nile
	L.M.	DEFIANCE	Copenhagen 1801
SLOANE, John	L.M.	MONTAGU	
SMITH, Gilbert	A.B.	ROYAL SOVEREIGN	
	A.B.	ROYAL SOVEREIGN	17 June 1795
SMITH, James	A.B.	CULLODEN	
	A.B.	CULLODEN	St Vincent
	A.B.	CULLODEN	Nile
SMITH, John	Three A.Bs borne	ALFRED	
	Three A.Bs borne	ALFRED	St Vincent
SMITH, John	A.B.	ROYAL SOVEREIGN	
SMITH, John	Capt's Servant	IMPREGNABLE	
	Midshipman	MARTIN	Camperdown
SMITH, John.T.	A.B.	AUDACIOUS	
SMITH, Joseph	Ord	CAESAR	G.H. 3,236
SMITH, Robert	Capt's Servant	IMPREGNABLE	
	Midshipman	BELLONA	Copenhagen 1801
SMITH, Thomas	Pte. 29th Regt	ALFRED	
SMITH, Thomas	A.B.	BRUNSWICK	
	Midshipman	ROBUST	23rd June 1795
SMITH, William	Midshipman	GIBRALTAR	
SNELL, John	Ord	CAESAR	
SONNEY, Constance	Ord	GIBRALTAR	
	A.B.	AJAX	Trafalgar
SOPER, Richard	Cook's Servant	GLORY	(M.L. as SOAPER)
SORTHON, William	Pte. R.M.	PHAETON	
	Sgt. R.M.	SWIFTSURE	Trafalgar
SOUTHCOTT, Henry	L.M.	QUEEN CHARLOTTE	
	A.B.	QUEEN CHARLOTTE	23rd June 1795
	A.B.	MONARCH	Camperdown
	Quarter Gunner	VETERAN	Copenhagen 1801
SPRATT, Alexander	Ord	IMPREGNABLE	
STAFFORD, Matthew	Ord	PHAETON	
STANTON, James	Quarter Gunner	QUEEN CHARLOTTE	
STARKEY, John	L.M.	MAJESTIC	
	A.B.	MAJESTIC	Nile
STARLING, Samuel	A.B.	BARFLEUR	G.H. 4,172
	A.B.	MONARCH	Camperdown
STEBBING, Henry	A.B.	QUEEN	
	A.B.	QUEEN	23rd June 1795
STILES, William	Ord	MONTAGU	

THE NAVAL GENERAL SERVICE MEDAL ROLL 1793-1840

STODDART, Pringle	Midshipman	VALIANT	
	A.B.	QUEEN CHARLOTTE	23rd June 1795
	Lieut. R.N.	KENT	Egypt
STONE, James	Ord	IMPREGNABLE	(Promoted Lieut.RN 1800)
STONE, Simon	L.M.	ROYAL GEORGE	
	A.B.	ROYAL GEORGE	23rd June 1795
STONE, William	Servant	RUSSELL	G.H. 5,771
STOPFORD, Robert	Captain. R.N.	AQUILON	
	Captain. R.N.	PHAETON	17 June 1795
	Captain. R.N.	SPENCER	St Domingo
	Captain. R.N.	CAESAR	Basque Roads 1809
	Rear Admiral	SCIPION	Java
	Admiral	PRINCESS CHARLOTTE	Syria (G.C.B., G.C.M.G.) (His awards are on display at The National Maritime Museum)
STRACHAN, James	L.M.	SOUTHAMPTON	
	Yeoman B.S.Room	SOUTHAMPTON	Southampton. 9 June 1796
	Yeoman B.S.Room	SOUTHAMPTON	St Vincent (B.S. = Bosun's Store)
STRACHEY, Christopher	A.B.	QUEEN CHARLOTTE	(Promoted Capt R.N. 1814)
STREET, Henry	A.B.	MARLBOROUGH	
STRETTON, Samuel	Pte. R.M.	ROYAL SOVEREIGN	
SUMMERS, Edward	Ord	AUDACIOUS	
	A.B.	AUDACIOUS	Nile
SWEENY, Francis	L.M.	ROYAL GEORGE	G.H. 8,246
SWEET, James	Armourer's Mate	CULLODEN	
	Armourer's Mate	CULLODEN	St Vincent
	Armourer's Mate	CULLODEN	Nile
	Armourer's Mate	TEMERAIRE	Trafalgar
	Armourer	LONDON	London. 13 March 1806
SYKES, John	Midshipman	CHARON	
SYKES, William	L.M.	RAMILLIES	
TARRELL, William	A.B.	ORION	
TATTON, William	Ord	BARFLEUR	
TAYLOR, George	A.B.	VALIANT	
	A.B.	VALIANT	23rd June 1795
TAYLOR, Nathaniel	A.B.	VALIANT	
	A.B.	VALIANT	23rd June 1795
	Gunner's Mate	AMAZON	Copenhagen 1801
THAYYERS, Luke	Pte. 25th Regt	GIBRALTAR	
THOMAS, Richard	A.B.	PEGASUS	
	A.B.	AQUILON	23rd June 1795
THOMPSON, Thomas	A.B.	ORION	G.H. 8,953
	A.B.	ORION	St Vincent
	A.B.	ORION	Nile
THOMSON, David	L.M.	TREMENDOUS	
	Quarter Gunner	CAMELION	Egypt
THORN, John	Ord	ALFRED	G.H. 3,564
	Ord	BLENHEIM	St Vincent
THORN, Michael	Capt's Servant	THUNDERER	
	Boy	THUNDERER	23rd June 1795
THORNTON, John	Capt's Servant	ROYAL GEORGE	
	Midshipman	ROYAL GEORGE	23rd June 1795
TOLLETT, Frederick	A.B.	ALFRED	
TOZER, John	Quarter Gunner	ROYAL GEORGE	
	Quarter Gunner	ROYAL GEORGE	23rd June 1795
	Yeo Powder Room	BELLEISLE	Trafalgar
TRACEY, Andrew	L.M.	AUDACIOUS	
	A.B.	AUDACIOUS	Nile
TREMLETT, George.N.	Midshipman	QUEEN	
	Lieut. R.N.	THALIA	23rd June 1795 (Vfd Abd. Not on Roll)
	Lieut. R.N.	FOUDROYANT	12 Octr 1798 (Vfd Abd. Not on Roll)
TREMLETT, W.H.B.	Midshipman	ROYAL SOVEREIGN	
	Midshipman	ROYAL SOVEREIGN	17 June 1795
	Lieut. R.N.	LION	Lion. 15 July 1798 (Vfd Abd. Not on Roll. See "Note" under LION clasp)
TRIST, Thomas	Admiral's Servt	ROYAL SOVEREIGN	(Rating)
TRUNCHEON, William	A.B.	RUSSELL	(M.L. as JONES, John)
	A.B.	RUSSELL	23rd June 1795
TRUSSLER, John	Ord	GIBRALTAR	
TUCKER, Thomas	Ord	BELLEROPHON	
	A.B.	BELLEROPHON	Nile
UNDERDOWN, Henry	Trumpeter/A.B.	RAMILLIES	G.H. 6,908 in TRIUMPH?

1 JUNE 1794

USSHER, Thomas	Midshipman	INVINCIBLE	
	Commander	REDWING (P)	*Redwing. 7 May 1808*
	Captain. R.N.	REDWING	*Redwing. 31 May 1808*
	Captain. R.N.	HYACINTH	*Malaga. 29 April 1812*
	Captain. R.N.	UNDAUNTED	*B.S. 2 May 1813*
VINEY, John	Ord	BRUNSWICK	*G.H. 7,121*
WADE, G.	Ord	CAESAR	
WADE, William	L.M.	IMPREGNABLE	
WAFF, James	Capt's Servant	VALIANT	*(On One Medal)*
	Boy	VALIANT	*23rd June 1795 (As single clasp on 2nd Medal)*
WAGLIN, Edward	L.M.	MONTAGU	*G.H. 7,051*
WAINWRIGHT, David	Sgt 2nd Queens Regt	RUSSELL	
WAKLEY, Thomas	Ord	MAJESTIC	
WALKER, John	Quarter Gunner	CAESAR	*G.H. 6,739*
WATERS, John	Gunner's Servant	LEVIATHAN	
WATSON, John	L.M.	IMPREGNABLE	
WATTLER, Stephen	A.B.	BARFLEUR	*G.H. 6,710*
	Quarter Gunner	BARFLEUR	*St Vincent*
WATTS, William	Ord	BELLEROPHON	
	A.B.	BELLEROPHON	*Nile*
WEBB, John	Two Ords borne	BARFLEUR	
	A.B.	BARFLEUR	*St Vincent*
WEBB, John	Two Ords borne	BELLEROPHON	
WEBBER, William	Pte. R.M.	INVINCIBLE	
	Pte. R.M.	HEBE	*Egypt*
WELLS, Henry	Clerk	RUSSELL	
	Clerk	RUSSELL	*23rd June 1795*
	Purser	THUNDERER	*Trafalgar*
WENDT, Richard	Ord	GLORY	
WEST, James	L.M.	MONTAGU	
WEST, John	Lieut. R.N.	ROYAL GEORGE	
	Lieut. R.N.	ROYAL GEORGE	*23rd June 1795*
WHARTON, Francis	Midshipman	GIBRALTAR	*(Navy List John Francis W')*
	Lieut. R.N.	GOOD DESIGN	*Egypt*
			(V'fd received Gold Medal)
WHEELER, James	Ord	QUEEN CHARLOTTE	
WHEELER, James	L.M.	PEGASUS	*(Confirmed on Roll) A second clasp was probably issued, either 14 March 1795, or 23rd June 1795, — name appears on both Rolls. Ship shown as BOYNE, not present at either, but was present for "B.S. 14 March 1794".*
WHIPPLE, John	Midshipman	GIBRALTAR	
	Lieut. R.N.	ALEXANDER	*Nile*
WHITE, John	L.M.	ROYAL GEORGE	*G.H. 9,962*
	A.B.	ROYAL GEORGE	*23rd June 1795*
WHITE, Peter	Bosun's Servant	LATONA	*(Aged 9. Born 1 Augt 1785)*
	Ord	DEFENCE	*Nile*
	Midshipman	DEFENCE	*Copenhagen 1801*
	Master's Mate	SULTAN (P)	*B.S. 4 Dec 1811*
WHITE, William	Ord	GLORY	
WICKSTEAD, Edward	Capt's Servant	TREMENDOUS	*(Rating)*
WILES, Samuel	A.B.	CULLODEN	
	A.B.	CULLODEN	*St Vincent*
	A.B.	CULLODEN	*Nile*
WILLIAMS, John	Ord	DEFENCE	
WILLIAMS, Robert	Pte. R.M.	INVINCIBLE	
WILLIAMS, Samuel	A.B.	BARFLEUR	
	A.B.	PRINCE OF WALES	*23rd June 1795*
WILLIAMS, William	A.B.	BELLEROPHON	
	A.B.	BELLEROPHON	*Nile*
WILLOUGHBY, Digby	Lieut's Servant	CULLODEN	*(? Rating)*
WILMOT, George	L.M.	TREMENDOUS	
WILSON, Allan	A.B.	GIBRALTAR	
WILSON, John	Midshipman	GLORY	
WILSON, Robert	Pte. R.M.	NIGER	
WITTY, John	Quarter Gunner	BELLEROPHON	
WOOD, James	Midshipman	BELLEROPHON	*(? Rate of Mid Ship Man)*
	A.B.	BELLEROPHON	*Nile (Never a Lieut R.N.)*
WOOD, John	Ord	ALFRED	*(M.L. as HOOD)*
	Ord	BLENHEIM	*St Vincent*
WOODCOCK, James	Ord	ROYAL GEORGE	
WOODWARD, Henry	Lieut's Servant	CHARON	*G.H. 9,938*
WOLF, John	A.B.	GIBRALTAR	*G.H. 9,293*
WRIGHT, Jonathan	Quarter Gunner	MAJESTIC	
WRIGHT, Richard	L.M.	ROYAL SOVEREIGN	
YEOMAN, William	L.M.	ROYAL SOVEREIGN	
YOUNG, Benjamin	Servant	RAMILLIES	

(2) ROMNEY 17 JUNE 1794

Capture of the French frigate SIBYLLE at Greek Island, Mykonos.

DIXON, Manly	Midshipman	ROMNEY	
	Midshipman	BELLEROPHON	17 June 1795
WOODLEY, Charles	Midshipman	ROMNEY	

(5) BLANCHE 4 JANY 1795

Capture of the French frigate PIQUE, off Grande-terre, Guadaloupe.

(Real date 5 January 1795)

CLARK, Joseph	Boy 3rd Cl	BLANCHE	(M.L. as CLARKE)
	Vol 1st Cl	BLANCHE	Blanche. 19 Decr 1796
	A.B.	MINOTAUR	Trafalgar
EVANS, Thomas	A.B.	BLANCHE	
	A.B.	BLANCHE	Blanch. 19 Decr 1796 (Vfd Abd. Not on Roll)
GREELY, Henry	A.B.	BLANCHE	G.H. 2,636
	A.B.	BLANCHE	Blanche. 19 Decr 1796 (Vfd Abd. Not on Roll)
PRESCOTT, Thomas.L.	Midshipman	BLANCHE	
WATKINS, Frederick	Lieut. R.N.	BLANCHE (P)	

(6) LIVELY 13 MARCH 1795

Capture of the French frigate TOURTERELLE, off Ushant.

BUCKMASTER, Ishmael	A.B.	LIVELY	(Vfd Abd. Not on Roll)
	A.B.	LIVELY	St Vincent
	A.B.	AUDACIOUS	Nile
GROVES, John	Midshipman	LIVELY	
	A.B.	LIVELY	St Vincent
HOLLAND, Thomas	A.B.	LIVELY	(Vfd Abd. Not on Roll)
	A.B.	LIVELY	St Vincent. G.H. 6284
	A.B.	ALEXANDER	Nile
LAVERTON, William	Pte. R.M.	LIVELY	(Vfd Abd. Not on Roll)
	Pte. R.M.	LIVELY	St Vincent
SIMPSON, Benjamin	Vol 1st Cl	LIVELY	
	Vol 1st Cl	LIVELY	St Vincent
WILLCOX, Robert	Boy 3rd Cl	LIVELY	
	Ord	LIVELY	St Vincent
	Midshipman	SUPERB	Gut of Gibraltar. 12 July 1801

(97) 14 MARCH 1795

Admiral Hotham's Action with the French Fleet; capture of two sail of the line, off Genoa.

ALLEN, Thomas	A.B.	MELEAGER	
APPLIN, Peter	L.M.	ILLUSTRIOUS	
ARMSTRONG, Thomas	A.B.	WINDSOR CASTLE	
	Master	FALMOUTH Lighter	Algiers
BAKER, William	Pte. R.M.	ILLUSTRIOUS	
BENNETT, William	Carp's Crew	BRITANNIA	
	Carp's Crew	BRITANNIA	St Vincent
BINDON, John.R.	Midshipman	CAPTAIN	
BLOMFIELD, Joseph	Ord	COURAGEUX	
BRIDGER, Henry	A.B.	EGMONT	(M.L. as BRIDGES)
	Q.M's Mate	EGMONT	St Vincent
BRIGGS, Thomas	Midshipman	DIADEM	
	Commander	SALAMINE	Egypt
BROWN, Peter	A.B.	POULETTE	
BURNETT, John	Boy	BEDFORD	
BUSSELL, Rev J.G.	Chaplain	ILLUSTRIOUS	
CAMERON, John	A.B.	CAPTAIN	
	A.B.	CAPTAIN	St Vincent
CHAPMAN, James	A.B.	WINDSOR CASTLE	
CHETHAM, Edward	Midshipman	AGAMEMNON	
(STRODE, Edward.C.)	Lieut. R.N.	SEINE	Seine. 20 Augt 1800
	Captain R.N.	LEANDER	Algiers
CHEVERALL, John	Boy 3rd Cl	St GEORGE	
	Ord	STATELY	Stately. 22 March 1808
	A.B.	PCSS CAROLINE	B.S. 25 July 1809
CHURCHILL, Edward	Carpenter	COURAGEUX	

14 MARCH 1795

CHUTE, Caleb	Captain. 69th Regt	BRITANNIA	
	Capt. 69th Regt	BRITANNIA	St Vincent
CLARK, John	2 Borne.AB & Ord	St GEORGE	
CLARKE, John	Ord	St GEORGE	
	2 Borne.AB & Ord	CANADA	12 Octr 1798
COCKBURN, George	Captain R.N.	MELEAGER	
	Captain R.N.	MINERVE	Minerve. 19 Decr 1796
	Captain R.N.	MINERVE	St Vincent
	Captain R.N.	MINERVE	Egypt
	Commodore	POMPEE	Martinique
	Rear Admiral	MARLBOROUGH	B.S. Ap & May 1813
DAVIS, Thomas	Ord	WINDSOR CASTLE	
DAVIS, William	L.M.	BRITANNIA	
DICK, Thomas	Midshipman	BEDFORD	
DRAKE, William.E.	Midshipman	PCSS ROYAL	
DYER, Thomas.S.	Lieut. R.N.	EGMONT	
EVANS, Roger	Master's Mate	BEDFORD	
	Lieut. R.N.	SOUTHAMPTON	St Vincent
EVANS, William	A.B.	St GEORGE	
FERRIS, William	Drummer. R.M.	WINDSOR CASTLE	
FORREST, Robert	A.B.	PCSS ROYAL	
FRY, Humphrey	A.B.	DIADEM	
	A.B.	DIADEM	St Vincent
	A.B.	DIADEM	Egypt
GAGE, William.H.	Midshipman	PCSS ROYAL	
	Lieut. R.N.	MINERVE	Minerve. 19 Decr 1796
	Lieut. R.N.	MINERVE	St Vincent
	Lieut. R.N.	MINERVE	B.S. 29 May 1797
GIBSON, William	Boy 2nd Cl	LOWESTOFFE	
	Boy 2nd Cl	LOWESTOFFE	Lowestoffe. 24 June 1795
	Midshipman	DIADEM	St Vincent
GREEN, Andrew.P.	Midshipman	ILLUSTRIOUS	(Vfd Abd. Not on Roll)
	Lieut. R.N.	GANGES	Copenhagen 1801
	Lieut. R.N.	NEPTUNE	Trafalgar
	Supn Commander	ELBE gun-boat Flotilla	Gluckstadt. 5 Jany 1814
GRIFFITHS, George	Boy	St GEORGE	G.H. 3750
	L.M.	MONMOUTH	Egypt
HARTLEY, William	A.B.	BEDFORD	
HEATHCOTE, Henry	Midshipman	PCSS ROYAL	
	Captain. R.N.	LION	Java
HEWSON, George	Midshipman	BRITANNIA	
	Lieut. R.N.	DREADNOUGHT	Trafalgar
HODGE, Edward	A.B.	DIADEM	
	Quarter Gunner	DIADEM	St Vincent
HOLLAND, John	Boy 2nd Cl	TERRIBLE	
HONYMAN, Robert	Lieut. R.N.	St GEORGE	
HUTCHINSON, Edward	Lieut. R.N.	INCONSTANT	
JOHNSON, John	A.B.	BRITANNIA	
	A.B.	BRITANNIA	St Vincent
	A.B.	GOLIATH	Nile
	A.B.	ELEPHANT	Copenhagen 1801
	Yeoman of Sheets	CORNELIA	Java
JONES, Thomas	A.B.	MOSELLE	
KEMP, Thomas	A.B.	LOWESTOFFE	
	A.B.	LOWESTOFFE	Lowestoffe. 24 June 1795
KINGSTON, William	Pte. R.M.	ROMULUS	
LAROCHE, Christopher	Lieut. R.N.	St GEORGE	
LAWRENCE, John	Midshipman	WINDSOR CASTLE	
	Commander	FANTOME	B.S. Ap & May 1813
	Captain. R.N.	HASTINGS	Syria
LIBBY, Edward	Midshipman	LOWESTOFFE	
	Midshipman	LOWESTOFFE	Lowestoffe. 24 June 1795
	Actg Lieut. R.N.	BLENHEIM	St Vincent
	Lieut. R.N.	NAMUR	4 Novr 1805
LIPSON, Thomas	Vol 1st Cl	WINDSOR CASTLE	
	Vol 1st Cl	BEDFORD	Camperdown
	Vol 1st Cl	FOUDROYANT	12 Octr 1798
LORING, John.W.	Lieut. R.N.	St GEORGE	
LUTON, William	L.M.	ILLUSTRIOUS	
LYONS, William	Boy	St GEORGE	
MARSHALL, John	Ord	EGMONT	(Appld as Rtd Cdr)
	A.B.	EGMONT	St Vincent
MATSON, Richard	Lieut. R.N.	BEDFORD	

MATTERS, Charles	Boy	St GEORGE	G.H. 4412
MAXWELL, Digby	Lieut 30th Foot	PCSS ROYAL	
McMILLANE, Allan	Boy	BEDFORD	
	A.B.	BEDFORD	Camperdown
	Midshipman	FOUDROYANT	12 Octr 1798
McQUIN, Hugh	Ord	DIADEM	
	A.B.	DIADEM	St Vincent
	Quarter Gunner	DIADEM	Egypt
MERRYWEATHER, Richard	L.M.	ILLUSTRIOUS	
	A.B.	PRINCE GEORGE	St Vincent
MINCE, Thomas	Pte. R.M.	WINDSOR CASTLE	
McNAMARA, Robert	Ord	PCSS ROYAL	
MORGAN, Thomas	A.B.	CAPTAIN	
	A.B.	CAPTAIN	St Vincent
MORRIS, Claud	Ord	TERRIBLE	
MORRIS, William	A.B.	CAPTAIN	G.H. 4507
	A.B.	ROYAL GEORGE	1 June 1794
	A.B.	CAPTAIN	St Vincent
MORRIS, Gaymer	A.B.	BEDFORD	
MOUBRAY, George	Lieut. R.N.	MOSELLE	
	Lieut. R.N.	POLYPHEMUS	Trafalgar
NEWMAN, William	L.M.	TERRIBLE	G.H. 2727
PARKER, William	Midshipman	St GEORGE	
	Midshipman	BRITANNIA	St Vincent
	Midshipman	GOLIATH	Nile
	Lieut. R.N.	DRUID	Egypt (This clasp awarded on separate medal)
PATEY, Charles	Lieut. R.N.	TERRIBLE	
PATTERSON, Francis	Ord	PCSS ROYAL	
	A.B.	RUSSELL	Camperdown
	A.B.	RUSSELL	Copenhagen 1801
	A.B.	CANOPUS	St Domingo
PILE, Thomas	A.B.	CAPTAIN	
	A.B.	CAPTAIN	St Vincent
POTTER, Joseph	A.B.	BRITANNIA	G.H. 7631
	A.B.	BRITANNIA	St Vincent
REID, Robert	L.M.	INCONSTANT	
REYNOLDS, John	Surgeon	ILLUSTRIOUS/ AGAMEMNON	
RIDER, William.B.	Lieut. R.N.	DIADEM	
	Lieut. R.N.	DIADEM	St Vincent
ROBERTS, Thomas	Midshipman	BEDFORD	
ROBERTS, William	A.B.	WINDSOR CASTLE	
	A.B.	BEDFORD	Camperdown
	A.B.	FOUDROYANT	12 Octr 1798
SALVEDORE, George	A.B.	LOWESTOFFE	
	A.B.	LOWESTOFFE	Lowestoffe. 24 June 1795
	A.B.	SCORPION	Scorpion. 31 March 1804 (Vfd Abd. Not on Roll)
SANDBROOKE, Thomas	Boy	EGMONT	(May read SANDBROOK)
	Boy	EGMONT	St Vincent
SAUNDERS, Walter	A.B.	CAPTAIN	
	A.B.	CAPTAIN	St Vincent
SHAW, Isaac	Midshipman	ROMULUS	(Vfd Abd. Not on Roll)
	Midshipman	BARFLEUR	St Vincent
	Lieut. R.N.	NEPTUNE	Trafalgar
	Lieut. R.N.	VOLONTAIRE (P)	B.S. 2 May 1813
SHIRLEY, George	A.B.	St GEORGE	
	Q.M's Mate	VANGUARD	Nile
	Q.M's Mate	FOUDROYANT	Egypt
	Gunner	CLEOPATRA	Martinique
SMITH, John	A.B.	LOWESTOFFE	
	A.B.	LOWESTOFFE	Lowestoffe. 24 June 1795
SPENCER, William	A.B.	INCONSTANT	
	Quarter Gunner	TONNANT	Trafalgar
	Gunner's Mate	GLASGOW	Algiers
STRODE, see CHETHAM			
SYM, William	L.M.	ILLUSTRIOUS	
TERRY, Thomas	Pte. R.M.	WINDSOR CASTLE	
VEALE, William	A.B.	BEDFORD	
WALLER, William	Boy 3rd Cl	DIADEM	
or WALKER	A.B.	DIADEM	St Vincent
WARD, John	Sgt. 25th Foot	St GEORGE	
WELD, Daniel	Midshipman	PCSS ROYAL	
WHITE, James	L.M.	FORTITUDE	
WHYLAND, Nicholas	L.M.	ILLUSTRIOUS	
WILLIAMS, Edward	A.B.	INCONSTANT	
WILLIAMS, Joseph	Midshipman	WINDSOR CASTLE	

14 MARCH 1795

WOODMASON, Andrew	Purser's Steward	St GEORGE	
WRIGHT, Andrew	A.B.	BEDFORD	
	Q.M.	CAESAR	*Gut of Gibraltar. 12 July 1801*

ASTRAEA 10 APRIL 1795
(2)

Capture of the French frigate GLOIRE, off Brest.

MAINLAND, William	Ord	ASTRAEA	
	Ord	ASTRAEA	*23rd June 1795*
	A.B.	VICTORY	*Trafalgar*
TALBOT, John	Lieut. R.N.	ASTRAEA (P)	
	Captain. R.N.	VICTORIOUS	*Victorious Wh Rivoli (Small Naval Gold Medal)*

THETIS 17 MAY 1795
(3)

Action with five French ships, capture of PREVOYANTE and RAISON, in Chesapeake Bay, U.S.A.

(Real date 16 May 1795)

COCHRANE, Thomas. Lord.	Lieut. R.N.	THETIS	*Later Earl of Dundonald (Vfd Abd. Not on Roll)*
	Commander	SPEEDY (P)	*Speedy 6 May 1801*
	Captain. R.N.	IMPERIEUSE	*Basque Roads 1809 (Vfd Abd. Not on Roll)*
HUME, Robert	Surg's 1st Mate	THETIS	
MAUDE, William.G.	Midshipman	THETIS	

HUSSAR 17 MAY 1795
(1)

Action with five French ships, capture of PREVOYANTE and RAISON, in Chesapeake Bay, U.S.A.

(Real date 16 May 1795)

READ, James	Vol 1st Class	HUSSAR

MOSQUITO 9 JUNE 1795
No Applicants

Capture of the French privateer NATIONAL RAZOR by Schooner MOSQUITO, on Jamaica Station.

(Real date 24 May 1795)

(49) 17 JUNE 1795
Brilliant repulse of a Fleet four times superior in force, off Ushant.
(Cornwallis' Retreat)

Name	Rank	Ship	Notes
ARTHUR, Robert	L.M.	MARS	(Vfd Abd. Not on Roll)
	Ord	MARS	Mars. 21 April 1798.
ATKINSON, William	Ord	PALLAS	
	A.B.	ACHILLE	Trafalgar
BACCHUS, Robert	Boy 3rd Cl	MARS	(Vfd Abd. Not on Roll)
	Boy 3rd Cl	MARS	Mars. 21 April 1798
BADCOCK, Squire	Boy 2nd Cl	MARS	
	Boy 2nd Cl	MARS	Mars. 21 April 1798
BEAUFORT, Francis	Master's Mate	PHAETON	
	Master's Mate	AQUILON	1 June 1794
	Lieut. R.N.	PHAETON (P)	B.S. 27 Oct 1800
BLACKBURN, Christopher	Ord	MARS	
BOLTON, Francis.L.	Boy 2nd Cl	MARS	
	Ord	MARS	Mars. 21 April 1798
BOWKER, John	Lieut. R.N.	MARS	(Vfd Abd. Not on Roll)
	Lieut. R.N.	MARS	Mars. 21 April 1798
BROOM, John	L.M.	MARS	(Vfd Abd. Not on Roll)
	L.M.	MARS	Mars. 21 April 1798
CHALMERS, James	Ord	ROYAL SOVEREIGN	(M.L. as SIMPSON, James)
	L.M.	ROYAL SOVEREIGN	1 June 1794
COLLINSON, Robert	Quarter Gunner	PALLAS	
	Q.M.	BELLEISLE	Trafalgar
	Q.M.	LONDON	London. 13 March 1806
DENISON, Edward	A.B.	MARS	
	Midshipman	MARS	Mars. 21 April 1798
DIXON, Manly	Midshipman	BELLEROPHON	
	Midshipman	ROMNEY	Romney. 17 June 1794
DUNCAN, John	Ord	ROYAL SOVEREIGN	G.H. 132
EVANS, Thomas	Q.M.	TRIUMPH	
	Bosun's Mate	TRIUMPH	Camperdown
GALE, John	Carp's Crew	BELLEROPHON	
	Carp's Crew	BELLEROPHON	1 June 1794
	A.B.	BELLEROPHON	Nile
	Carp's Mate	SPENCER	Gut of Gibraltar. 12 July 1801
	Carpenter	NORTHUMBERLAND	Northumberland. 22 May 1812
GALPIN, Thomas	L.M.	BRUNSWICK	
GARRETT, James	Ord	MARS	
	A.B.	MARS	Mars. 21 April 1798
HAMLET, William	Q.M.	TRIUMPH	
	Q.M.	TRIUMPH	Camperdown
HATTON, John	Pte. R.M.	BELLEROPHON	
	Pte. R.M.	BELLEROPHON	1 June 1794
	Pte. R.M.	BELLEROPHON	Nile
	Cpl. R.M.	SPENCER	Gut of Gibraltar. 12 July 1801
HENDERSON, Alexander.	A.B.	TRIUMPH	
	A.B.	TRIUMPH	Camperdown
HINDMARSH, John	Vol 1st Cl	BELLEROPHON	
	Capt's Servant	BELLEROPHON	1 June 1794
	Midshipman	BELLEROPHON	Nile
	Midshipman	SPENCER	Gut of Gibraltar. 12 July 1801
	Lieut. R.N.	PHOEBE	Trafalgar
	Lieut. R.N.	BEAGLE	Basque Roads 1809
	Lieut. R.N.	NISUS	Java
HOCKINGS, Robert	Master's Mate	PALLAS	
	Lieut. R.N.	CALEDONIA	Basque Roads. 1809
HOWARTH, William	Ord	MARS	
	A.B.	MARS	Mars. 21 April 1798
JOHNSON, Thomas	L.M.	MARS	GH 8382 or 3382
JOHNSTON, John	Ord	TRIUMPH	
	A.B.	TRIUMPH	Camperdown
KELLY, John	A.B.	ROYAL SOVEREIGN	
	Ord	ROYAL SOVEREIGN	1 June 1794
LITTLE, John	Boy	PHAETON	
LOWE, Abraham	Lieut. R.N.	TRIUMPH	
	Lieut. R.N.	THAMES	Gut of Gibraltar. 12 July 1801
MONTGOMERY, John	A.B.	MARS	
	A.B.	MARS	Mars. 21 April 1798
MOSER, Peter	A.B.	BRUNSWICK	Alias REYNOLDS, Peter G.H. 1695
	A.B.	SPENCER	Gut of Gibraltar. 12 July 1801
	A.B.	VICTORY	Trafalgar
PRITCHARD, Samuel.P.	Master's Servant	ROYAL SOVEREIGN	Became Vice Admiral and awarded China 1842 medal.

17 JUNE 1795

SAUNDERS, Thomas	Ord	MARS	(Vfd Abd. Not on Roll)
	Ord	MARS	Mars. 21 April 1798
	L.M.	COMUS	Comus 15 Augt 1807
SAXBY, Francis	A.B.	MARS	
	A.B.	MARS	Mars. 21 April 1798
SHELLSHEAR, Hugh	A.B.	PHAETON	
	A.B.	PHAETON	1 June 1794
	Gunner	SCIPION	Java
SHERRARD, John	A.B.	PHAETON	
	Pte. R.M.	PHAETON	1 June 1794
(SIMPSON see CHALMERS)			
SLAUGHTER, William	Vol 1st Cl	TRIUMPH	
	Vol 1st Cl	TRIUMPH	Camperdown
	Lieut. R.N.	AMPHION	B.S. 28 Aug 1809
	Lieut. R.N.	AMPHION	B.S. 28 June 1810
SMITH, Gilbert	A.B.	ROYAL SOVEREIGN	
	A.B.	ROYAL SOVEREIGN	1 June 1794
STEVENS, Richard	L.M.	MARS	
	Barber	MARS	Mars. 21 April 1798
STIRLING, Alexander.G.	Midshipman	BELLEROPHON	
STOPFORD, Robert	Captain. R.N.	PHAETON	
	Captain. R.N.	AQUILON	1 June 1794
	Captain. R.N.	SPENCER	St Domingo
	Captain. R.N.	CAESAR	Basque Roads 1809
	Rear Admiral	SCIPION	Java
	Admiral	PCSS CHARLOTTE	Syria (GCB.GCMG)
TAYLOR, Richard	Boy 2nd Cl	MARS	
	Ord	MARS	Mars. 21 April 1798
TILLEY, James	Boy 3rd Cl	PALLAS	
TOWNSEND, John	L.M.	TRIUMPH	
	L.M.	TRIUMPH	Camperdown
TREMLETT, W.H.B.	Midshipman	ROYAL SOVEREIGN	
	Midshipman	ROYAL SOVEREIGN	1 June 1794
	Lieut. R.N.	LION	Lion. 15 July 1798
			(Vfd Abd. Not on Roll. See "Note" under LION clasp)
TROLLOPE, George.B.	Master's Mate	TRIUMPH	(Vfd Abd. Not on Roll)
	Lieut. R.N.	TRIUMPH	Camperdown
	Commander	GRIFFON	Griffon. 27 March 1812
TUCKER, William	Ord	MARS	G.H.9101.
	Ord	MARS	Mars. 21 April 1798
TURNER, John	A.B.	TRIUMPH	
	A.B.	TRIUMPH	Camperdown
WEST, John	L.M.	MARS	(Vfd Abd. Not on Roll)
	Ord	MARS	Mars 21 April 1798

23rd JUNE 1795

(182)

Action with the French Fleet; capture of three sail of the line, off Isle de Groix, Brittany. (Bridport's Action).

ALLEN, Francis	L.M.	ROYAL GEORGE	
ALLEN, Robert	Midshipman	AQUILON	(? as rating Mid Ship Man)
	Quarter Gunner	PEGASUS	1 June 1794
ANDERSON, John	A.B.	LEVIATHAN	
	A.B.	LEVIATHAN	1 June 1794
ARTHURS, Nicholas	L.M.	ROBUST	
	L.M.	BRUNSWICK	1 June 1794
	L.M.	ROBUST	12 Octr 1798
ASH, James	A.B.	ROBUST	
	Quarter Gunner	ROBUST	12 Octr 1798
ATKINS, James	Boy 3rd Cl	NYMPHE	
ATKINS, William	Boy	LONDON	
	Boy	LONDON	Copenhagen 1801
ATWELL, Robert	A.B.	IRRESISTIBLE	
	A.B.	RUSSELL	Camperdown
	Yeoman of Sheets	RAMILLIES	Copenhagen 1801
	Yeoman of Sheets	PRINCE	Trafalgar
BARRELL, Justinian	Midshipman	RUSSELL	
	Capt's Servant	BRUNSWICK	1 June 1794
BIRMINGHAM, Henry	L.M.	REVOLUTIONNAIRE	(M.L. as BRIMICOMBE)
BOULTON, Samuel	Yeoman Sheets	QUEEN CHARLOTTE	
	A.B.	QUEEN CHARLOTTE	1 June 1794

BREWER, Henry	L.M.	ROYAL GEORGE	
	A.B.	ROYAL GEORGE	1 June 1794
BRIAN, William	Ord	QUEEN	
	Ord	QUEEN	1 June 1794
BRIGGS, Joseph	Boy 2nd Cl	BARFLEUR	
BROWELL, William	Captain (of ?)	SANSPAREIL	(Appld as "Late Captain")
BROWN, Thomas	2 Borne AB & Ord	SANSPAREIL	
BURGOYNE, Frederick.W.	Master's Mate	NYMPHE	
	Midshipman	MONTAGU	1 June 1794
	Actg Lieut. RN.	BRITANNIA	St Vincent
BURK, William	Q.M's Mate	ROYAL GEORGE	
	A.B.	ROYAL GEORGE	1 June 1794
BURT, Edward	A.B.	ROYAL GEORGE	
	Ord	ROYAL GEORGE	1 June 1794
BUTCHER, Samuel	Lieut. R.N.	AQUILON	
	Midshipman	QUEEN	1 June 1794
CAPEL, Thomas Bladen	Midshipman	SANSPAREIL	
	Lieut. R.N.	VANGUARD	Nile
	Captain. R.N.	PHOEBE	Trafalgar
CARRINGTON, William.H.	1st Lt. R.M.	GALATEA	
CARTER, John	L.M.	QUEEN	
CLARK, John	Midshipman	RUSSELL	
	Lieut. R.N.	THUNDERER	Trafalgar
CLARKE, David	Boy	COLOSSUS	
CODRINGTON, Edward	Commander	BABET	
	Lieut. R.N.	QUEEN CHARLOTTE	1 June 1794
	Captain. R.N.	ORION	Trafalgar
	Vice Admiral	ASIA	Navarino (as Sir Edward)
COLE, Rev Samuel	Chaplain	LONDON	
COLEPACK, John	Boy 3rd Cl	QUEEN CHARLOTTE	
	Capt's Servant	QUEEN CHARLOTTE	1 June 1794
	Vol 1st Cl	BONNE CITOYENNE	St Vincent
	Ord	BONNE CITOYENNE	Egypt
CONNIN, Francis	Surgeon	QUEEN	
	Surgeon	QUEEN	1 June 1794
COOPER, William	Ord	BARFLEUR	
	Ord	BARFLEUR	1 June 1794
	A.B.	BARFLEUR	St Vincent
COOTE, William	Midshipman	ROYAL GEORGE	
	Midshipman	EDGAR	Copenhagen 1801 (Vfd Abd. NOR)
	Lieut. R.N.	AGAMEMNON	Trafalgar
	Lieut. R.N.	AGAMEMNON	St Domingo
	Lieut. R.N.	CERBERUS (P)	B.S. 2 Jan 1807
CORNELIUS, William	L.M.	ROYAL GEORGE	
	L.M.	ROYAL GEORGE	1 June 1794
	A.B.	PRINCE	Trafalgar
COX, John	Ord	COLOSSUS	G.H. 9,522
CREMENE, John	A.B.	LEVIATHAN	
	L.M.	ORION	1 June 1794
	A.B.	VETERAN	Camperdown
	A.B.	VETERAN	Copenhagen 1801
CULLEN, Daniel	L.M.	ROBUST	(M.L. as CULLINS)
	L.M.	BRUNSWICK	1 June 1794
	Ord	ROBUST	12 Octr 1798
	L.M.	ROYAL SOVEREIGN	Trafalgar
DEBENHAM, John	Midshipman	PRINCE OF WALES	
	A.B.	GLORY	1 June 1794
DE PAGE, John	A.B.	ORION	(M.L. as LE PAGE)
	A.B.	CRESCENT	Crescent. 20 Octr 1793
	A.B.	ORION	St Vincent
	A.B.	ORION	Nile
DILLON, William.H.	Midshipman	PRINCE GEORGE	
	Midshipman	DEFENCE	1 June 1794
	Commander	CHILDERS	Childers. 14 March 1808
DOWN, James	Ord	STANDARD	
DREW, James	A.B.	QUEEN CHARLOTTE	
	A.B.	QUEEN CHARLOTTE	1 June 1794
ELITHORNE, Miles	Boy	THALIA	
ELLIS, Thomas	Boy 3rd Cl	AQUILON	G.H. 10,081
	Capt's Servant	PEGASUS	1 June 1794
	Ord	SPENCER	Gut of Gibraltar. 12 July 1801
ENDELL, Stephen	A.B.	QUEEN	
	A.B.	QUEEN	1 June 1794

23rd JUNE 1795

FALLICK, William	L.M.	ORION	
	L.M.	ORION	*St Vincent*
	Ord	ORION	*Nile*
FARRINGTON, William	Master's Mate	AQUILON	*(Navy List as FFARINGTON)*
FERNANDES, Donald	Master's Mate	THUNDERER	
	Midshipman	THUNDERER	*1 June 1794*
	Lieut. R.N.	BLENHEIM	*St Vincent*
FERRIS, Abel	Master's Mate	IRRESISTIBLE	
	Master's Mate	COLOSSUS	*St Vincent*
	Lieut. R.N.	PRINCE	*Trafalgar*
FITZROY, William	Midshipman	SANS PAREIL	*(Vfd Abd. Not on Roll)*
	Capt's Servant	PHAETON	*1 June 1794*
	Lieut. R.N.	PENELOPE	*Egypt*
	Captain. R.N.	AEOLUS	*4 Novr 1805*
	Captain. R.N.	AEOLUS	*Martinique*
FLACK, Henry	L.M.	PRINCE GEORGE	
FRASER, William	A.B.	AQUILON	
	A.B.	PEGASUS	*1 June 1794*
GALE, John	Boy 3rd Cl	SANSPAREIL	
GIFFARD, John	Lieut. R.N.	QUEEN CHARLOTTE	
GLADSTONE, William	Surgeon's Mate	SANSPAREIL	
GLYNN, Henry.R.	Lieut. R.N.	ROYAL GEORGE	
	Lieut. R.N.	ROYAL GEORGE	*1 June 1794*
GORDON, James.A.	Midshipman	REVOLUTIONNAIRE	
	Midshipman	NAMUR	*St Vincent*
	Midshipman	GOLIATH	*Nile*
	Captain. R.N.	MERCURY	*Off Rota. 4 April 1808*
	Captain. R.N.	ACTIVE	*Lissa*
	Captain. R.N.	ACTIVE	*Pelagosa. 29 Novr 1811*
	Captain. R.N.	SEAHORSE	*The Potomac. 17 Aug 1814.*
GRANT, Lewis	Lieut. R.M.	ORION	
HAINSSELIN, Dennis.F.	A.B.	ROYAL GEORGE	
	A.B.	ROYAL GEORGE	*1 June 1794*
HAMILTON, Thomas	Carpenter	BABET	
HARLEY, James	L.M.	PRINCE GEORGE	
HART, Richard	Pte. R.M.	IRRESISTIBLE	
	Pte. R.M.	VANGUARD	*Nile*
HAVILAND, Henry	Midshipman	PRINCE OF WALES	
	L.M.	GLORY	*1 June 1794*
HAZARD, William	A.B.	CHARON	
	Q.M.	CHARON	*Egypt*
HEALY, John	L.M.	VALIANT	
	L.M.	VALIANT	*1 June 1794*
HENDERSON, John	Secretary	ROYAL GEORGE	
	Secretary	ROYAL GEORGE	*1 June 1794*
HEXT, William	Midshipman	RUSSELL	
	Capt's Servant	RUSSELL	*1 June 1794*
	Lieut. R.N.	SANTA MARGARITA	*4 Novr 1805*
HIGGINS, Richard	Carpenter's Crew	QUEEN	
	Carpenter's Crew	QUEEN	*1 June 1794*
HIGMAN, Henry	A.B.	CHARON	*(This Roll as Henry.G.)*
	Master's Mate	TRIUMPH	*Campderdown*
	Lieut. R.N.	ARETHUSA	*Arethusa. 23 Augt 1806*
	Lieut. R.N.	ARETHUSA	*Curacoa*
HOARE, Edward.W.	Midshipman	LONDON	
	Lieut. R.N.	NORTHUMBERLAND	*Egypt*
	Captain. R.N.	MINDEN	*Java*
HOBBINS, Thomas	Drummer. R.M.	SANSPAREIL	
HOLMAN, William	Midshipman	ROYAL GEORGE	
	Lieut. R.N.	LONDON	*Copenhagen. 1801*
HOLMES, William	A.B.	COLOSSUS	
HOSKEN, James	Gunner	LONDON	*(? in IRRESISTIBLE)*
	Gunner	IRRESISTIBLE	*B.S. 17 Mar 1794*
	Gunner	IRRESISTIBLE	*St Vincent*
HOWELLS, John	L.M.	ROYAL GEORGE	
	L.M.	ROYAL GEORGE	*1 June 1794*
HUGH, George	L.M.	ROYAL GEORGE	
HUISH, William	L.M.	QUEEN	
INCH, John	Pte. R.M.	LEVIATHAN	
	Pte. R.M.	LEVIATHAN	*1 June 1794*
	Sgt. R.M.	DORIS	*B.S. 21 July 1801*
JAMES, James	A.B.	QUEEN CHARLOTTE	
JEUNE, Richard	Carp's Crew	ORION	
	A.B.	CRESCENT	*Crescent. 20 Octr 1793*
JOHNSTONE, William	A.B.	IRRESISTIBLE	*(M.L. as JOHNSON)*
	Ord	IRRESISTIBLE	*St Vincent*

JONES, Charles.T.	A.B.	LEVIATHAN	(Captain. R.N. in 1819)
	A.B.	LEVIATHAN	1 June 1794
JONES, George	1st Lt R.M.	REVOLUTIONNAIRE	
	2nd Lt R.M.	VALIANT	1 June 1794
JONES, John	(Alias. See TRUNCHEON, William)		
JOY, Benjamin	A.B.	LEVIATHAN	G.H. 1,418
	A.B.	LEVIATHAN	1 June 1794
KELLY, William	A.B.	IRRESISTIBLE	
	L.M.	IRRESISTIBLE	St Vincent
KINGDOM, Arthur	A.B.	COLOSSUS	
KINGWILL, Robert	L.M.	ROYAL GEORGE	
KINSALE, Michael	L.M.	VALIANT	
	L.M.	VALIANT	1 June 1794
KITT, Joseph	A.B.	ORION	
	A.B.	CRESCENT	Crescent. 20 Octr 1793
	A.B.	ORION	St Vincent
	A.B.	ORION	Nile
KNIGHT, John	A.B. or Carp's Crew	IRRESISTIBLE	
	L.M.	IRRESISTIBLE	St Vincent
LAITHWAITE, George	Ord	PRINCE GEORGE	
LANE, Joseph	Retinue	QUEEN	
	Retinue	QUEEN	1 June 1794
LOGIE, William	Pte. R.M.	COLOSSUS	
	Pte. R.M.	BRILLIANT	B.S. 29 Aug 1800
	Pte. R.M.	DONEGAL	St Domingo
LONG, John	Quarter Gunner	THALIA	
	Quarter Gunner	BLANCHE	Copenhagen 1801
LOWE, John	A.B.	ROYAL GEORGE	
LOWRIE, Richard	Carp's Crew	LEVIATHAN	
	A.B.	LEVIATHAN	1 June 1794
LOWTHIAN, Robert	A.B.	ROYAL GEORGE	(To Commander in 1813)
	A.B.	ROYAL GEORGE	1 June 1794
LUTWIDGE, Henry.T.	Midshipman	BARFLEUR	
	Midshipman	BARFLEUR	St Vincent
MAINLAND, William	Ord	ASTRAEA	
	Ord	ASTRAEA	Astraea. 10 April 1795
	A.B.	VICTORY	Trafalgar
MANSELL, Thomas	Midshipman	ORION	
	Midshipman	CRESCENT	Crescent. 20 Octr 1793
	Master's Mate	ORION	St Vincent
	Midshipman	ORION	Nile
MARRETT, Joseph	Midshipman	ORION	(Vfd Abd. Not on Roll)
	Midshipman	CRESCENT	Crescent 20 Octr 1793
	Midshipman	ORION	St Vincent
	Midshipman	ORION	Nile
	Lieut. R.N. Cmdg	MARTIAL	Basque Roads 1809
MASON, Francis	Midshipman	RUSSELL	
	Midshipman	RUSSELL	1 June 1794
	Captain. R.N.	PRESIDENT	St Sebastian
MATTOCKS, George	Pte. R.M.	BABET	(M.L. as MATTOX)
McAUSLAND, Peter	Gunner's Mate	IRRESISTIBLE	
	A.B.	MONTAGU	1 June 1794
	Bosun's Mate	IRRESISTIBLE	St Vincent
	Gunner	PETEREL	Egypt
	Gunner	IMPLACABLE	Implacable. 26 Augt 1808
McCARTHY, James	Boy	STANDARD	(M.L. as CARTHY)
McFARLAND, James	Lieut. R.N.	QUEEN CHARLOTTE	
	Lieut. R.N.	QUEEN CHARLOTTE	1 June 1794
McKENZIE, Andrew	Private Soldier	BARFLEUR	
MILLS, William	Cpl. R.M.	QUEEN	
	Sgt. R.M.	COLOSSUS	St Vincent
	Sgt. R.M.	BELLONA	Copenhagen 1801
MITCHELL, James	A.B.	BARFLEUR	
	A.B.	GLORY	1 June 1794
	A.B.	BARFLEUR	St Vincent
MORGAN, James	Ord	ROBUST	
	L.M.	BRUNSWICK	1 June 1794
	Ord	ROBUST	12 Octr 1798
	Ord	SPENCER	St Domingo
MORR, William	Boy 2nd Cl	ORION	(M.L. as MOORE)
	L.M.	IRRESISTIBLE	St Vincent
MORSE, B.	A.B.	ROBUST	
MURWOOD, William	A.B.	ROBUST	
	A.B.	BRUNSWICK	1 June 1794
NANCARROW, Walter	Ord	QUEEN CHARLOTTE	
	L.M.	QUEEN CHARLOTTE	1 June 1794

23rd JUNE 1795

Name	Rating	Ship	Notes
NOBBS, J.W.	Midshipman	ROYAL GEORGE	*(Became Paymaster & Purser)*
NORIE, Evelyn	Ord	PRINCE OF WALES	*(POW. Made Rtd Cdr 1840)*
OMMANNEY, John.A.	Lieut. R.N.	QUEEN CHARLOTTE	
	Captain. R.N.	ALBION	*Navarino*
ORCHARD, Benjamin	Carp's Crew	THALIA	
	A.B.	NORTHUMBERLAND	*Egypt*
ORMISTON, John	L.M.	IRRESISTIBLE	
	L.M.	IRRESISTIBLE	*St Vincent*
	A.B.	AJAX	*Egypt*
PAINE, Thomas	A.B.	QUEEN CHARLOTTE	
	A.B.	QUEEN CHARLOTTE	*1 June 1794*
PALMER, John	Admiral's Servant	ROYAL GEORGE	
	Admiral's Servant	ROYAL GEORGE	*1 June 1794*
PACKMAN, John	A.B.	ROBUST	
	Midshipman	ROBUST	*12 Octr 1798*
PAUL, James	Ord	LONDON	*G.H. 3,908*
PAYNE, Charles.F.	Midshipman	LONDON	*(Vfd Abd. See Note 1-6-1794)*
	Midshipman	CULLODEN	*1 June 1794*
PAYNE, William	Master's Mate	QUEEN CHARLOTTE	
	Midshipman	PHAETON	*1 June 1794*
PEARSON, George	Ord	ORION	
	L.M.	ORION	*St Vincent*
	Ord	ORION	*Nile*
PEMBRIDGE, Samuel	A.B.	ROYAL GEORGE	
	A.B.	ROYAL GEORGE	*1 June 1794*
PENDERGRASS, James	Midshipman	QUEEN CHARLOTTE	
POPE, William	Boy	ROBUST	
	Boy	ROBUST	*12 Octr 1798*
PORTER, Robert	Pte. R.M.	STANDARD	
PRATT, Benjamin	Pte. R.M.	LONDON	
PUMMELL, Samuel	A.B.	RUSSELL	
	A.B.	RUSSELL	*1 June 1794*
	Ord	DONEGAL	*St Domingo*
	Not Given	Not Given	*Basque Roads 1809. 171/2/69*
RABBICH, Henry	A.B.	ROBUST	
	A.B.	BRUNSWICK	*1 June 1794*
	A.B.	ROBUST	*12 Octr 1798*
RICHARDSON, John	A.B.	QUEEN	
	A.B.	QUEEN	*1 June 1794*
RIDLEY, Thomas	A.B.	LEVIATHAN	
	A.B.	LEVIATHAN	*1 June 1794*
ROBINSON, Scott	A.B.	COLOSSUS	*G.H. 9,217*
RORIE, John James	Midshipman	STANDARD	
	Lt. RN Cmmdg	MORNE FORTUNEE	*Curacoa*
	Lt. RN Cmmdg	MORNE FORTUNEE	*Off the Pearl Rock. 13 Dec 1808 (Vfd Abd. Not on Roll)*
ROSE, John	L.M.	ROYAL GEORGE	
	L.M.	ROYAL GEORGE	*1 June 1794*
RYE, Peter	Lieut. R.N.	ORION	
	Lieut. R.N.	CRESCENT	*Crescent. 20 Octr 1793*
SALMON, Joseph	Not Given	SANSPAREIL	
SALTER, Thomas	A.B.	COLOSSUS	
SHOWAN, Elijah	Boy 2nd Cl	QUEEN	*(M.L. as SHOWEN)*
	Captain's Servant	QUEEN	*1 June 1794*
	Gunner's Mate	CALEDONIA	*Basque Roads 1809*
SIMMONS, John	Cook's Servant	ROYAL GEORGE	
	Cook's Servant	ROYAL GEORGE	*1 June 1794*
SIMPSON, George	A.B.	RUSSELL	*(Roll as ? John)*
	A.B.	RUSSELL	*1 June 1794*
SIMPSON, Thomas	L.M.	Gun-Boat TEAZER	
	L.M.	ADAMANT	*Camperdown*
SKINNER, Joseph	Admiral's Servant	QUEEN	*G.H. 977*
SMITH, Abraham	L.M.	COLOSSUS	
SMITH, John	L.M.	ROYAL GEORGE	
SMITH, Thomas	Midshipman	ROBUST	
	A.B.	BRUNSWICK	*1 June 1794*
SOAMES, John	Quarter Gunner	ORION	
	A.B.	CRESCENT	*Crescent. 20 Octr 1793*
	Bosun's Mate	ORION	*St Vincent*
	Bosun's Mate	ORION	*Nile*
SOUTHCOTT, Henry	A.B.	QUEEN CHARLOTTE	
	L.M.	QUEEN CHARLOTTE	*1 June 1794*
	A.B.	MONARCH	*Camperdown*
	Quarter Gunner	VETERAN	*Copenhagen 1801*
STEBBING, Henry	A.B.	QUEEN	
	A.B.	QUEEN	*1 June 1794*
STODDART, Pringle	A.B.	QUEEN CHARLOTTE	
	Midshipman	VALIANT	*1 June 1794*
	Lieut. R.N.	KENT	*Egypt*

STONE, Simon	A.B.	ROYAL GEORGE	
	L.M.	ROYAL GEORGE	*1 June 1794*
SYMONDS, William	Midshipman	LONDON	
TANCOCK, John	Master's Mate	ORION	
	Master's Mate	CRESCENT	*Crescent. 20 Octr 1793*
	Master's Mate	ORION	*St Vincent*
	Actg Lieut. R.N.	ORION	*Nile*
	Lieut. R.N.	CAESAR	*Gut of Gibraltar. 12 July 1801*
TAYLOR, George	A.B.	VALIANT	
	A.B.	VALIANT	*1 June 1794*
TAYLOR, Nathaniel	A.B.	VALIANT	
	A.B.	VALIANT	*1 June 1794*
	Gunner's Mate	AMAZON	*Copenhagen 1801*
THOMAS, Richard	A.B.	AQUILON	
	A.B.	PEGASUS	*1 June 1794*
THOMAS, Thomas.P.	Boy	BARFLEUR	
THORN, Michael	Boy	THUNDERER	
	Capt's Servant	THUNDERER	*1 June 1794*
THORNTON, John	Midshipman	ROYAL GEORGE	
	Capt's Servant	ROYAL GEORGE	*1 June 1794*
TIDMARSH, William	Boy	PRINCE GEORGE	*G.H. 5,719*
TOWNSEND, James	Midshipman	SANSPAREIL	
	Lieut. R.N.	ATLAS	*St Domingo*
TOZER, John	Quarter Gunner	ROYAL GEORGE	
	Quarter Gunner	ROYAL GEORGE	*1 June 1794*
	Yeo Powder Room	BELLEISLE	*Trafalgar*
TREMLETT, George.N.	Lieut. R.N.	THALIA	*(Vfd Abd. Not on Roll)*
	Midshipman	QUEEN	*1 June 1794*
	Lieut. R.N.	FOUDROYANT	*12 Octr 1798*
			(Vfd Abd. Not on Roll)
TRUNCHEON, William	A.B.	RUSSELL	*(M.L. as JONES, John)*
	A.B.	RUSSELL	*1 June 1794*
TURNEY, Samuel	Pte. R.M.	QUEEN	
	Pte. R.M.	BARFLEUR	*St Vincent*
TURPINS, John	L.M.	ORION	
	L.M.	ORION	*St Vincent*
	Ord	ORION	*Nile*
	Ord	GANGES	*Copenhagen 1801*
WAFF, James	Boy	VALIANT	*(On one Medal)*
	Capt's Servant	VALIANT	*1 June 1794. (As single clasp on 2nd Medal)*
WARD, William	Midshipman	BARFLEUR	*(Vfd Abd. Not on Roll)*
	Midshipman	BARFLEUR	*St Vincent*
	Lieut. R.N.	PIQUE	*Pique. 26 March 1806*
WELCH, Robert	Vol 1st Cl	GALATEA	
	Midshipman	FOUDROYANT	*12 Octr 1798*
			(Vfd Abd. Not on Roll)
	Actg Lieut. R.N.	EXPERIMENT	*Egypt*
WEALE, George	Midshipman	ORION	
WELLS, Henry	Clerk	RUSSELL	
	Clerk	RUSSELL	*1 June 1794*
	Purser	THUNDERER	*Trafalgar*
WEST, John	Lieut. R.N.	ROYAL GEORGE	
	Lieut. R.N.	ROYAL GEORGE	*1 June 1794*
WHEELER, James	(A.B.)	(BOYNE. Not Present)	*See Note in "1 June 1794"*
WHINYATES, Thomas	Midshipman	ROBUST	
	Capt's Servant	VETERAN	*B.S. 17 Mar 1794*
	Master's Mate	ROBUST	*12 Octr 1798*
	Commander	FROLIC	*Martinique*
	Commander	FROLIC	*Guadaloupe*
WHITE, John	A.B.	ROYAL GEORGE	*G.H. 9,962*
	L.M.	ROYAL GEORGE	*1 June 1794*
WICKATT, Thomas	L.M.	ROYAL GEORGE	
WILCOX, Thomas	L.M.	PRINCE	*G.H. 9,959*
WILLERY, James	L.M.	RUSSELL	
WILLIAMS, Samuel	A.B.	PRINCE OF WALES	
	A.B.	BARFLEUR	*1 June 1794*
WILLIAMS, Richard.P.	Surgeon's Mate	REVOLUTIONNAIRE	
WILLIAMSON, Bartholomew	Ord	THALIA	
	A.B.	BLANCHE	*Copenhagen 1801*
YATES, Robert.B.	Vol 1st Cl	SANSPAREIL	

(1) DIDO 24 JUNE 1795

Action with the French frigates, MINERVE and ARTEMISE — the former captured by DIDO and LOWESTOFFE, off Toulon.

LEDDITT, Charles	Ord	DIDO	*(M.L. as LUDDITT)*

(6) LOWESTOFFE 24 JUNE 1795

Action with the French frigates MINERVE and ARTEMISE — the former captured by DIDO and LOWESTOFFE, off Toulon.

GIBSON, William	Boy 2nd Cl	LOWESTOFFE	
	Boy 2nd Cl	LOWESTOFFE	*14 March 1795*
	Midshipman	DIADEM	*St Vincent*
KEMP, Thomas	A.B.	LOWESTOFFE	
	A.B.	LOWESTOFFE	*14 March 1795*
LIBBY, Edward	Midshipman	LOWESTOFFE	
	Midshipman	LOWESTOFFE	*14 March 1795*
	Actg Lieut. R.N.	BLENHEIM	*St Vincent*
	Lieut. R.N.	NAMUR	*4 Novr 1805*
SALVEDORE, George	A.B.	LOWESTOFFE	
	A.B.	LOWESTOFFE	*14 March 1795*
	A.B.	SCORPION	*Scorpion. 31 March 1804* *(Vfd Abd. Not on Roll)*
SMITH, John	A.B.	LOWESTOFFE	
	A.B.	LOWESTOFFE	*14 March 1795*
WHITE, Gilbert	A.B.	LOWESTOFFE	
	A.B.	FOUDROYANT	*Egypt*

(1) SPIDER 25 AUGT 1795

Capture of the French brig VICTORIEUSE by H.M.Lugger SPIDER in the North Sea.

LEAN, John	A.B.	SPIDER	*(In Los Angeles Museum)*

(4) PORT SPERGUI 17 MARCH 1796

Destroying the battery at PORT ERQUI, Britanny, and burning the French corvette ETOURDIE, four brigs, two sloops and one lugger.

BOXER, James	Midshipman	DIAMOND	
	Midshipman	TIGRE	*Acre. 30 May 1799*
	Lieut. R.N.	TIGRE	*Egypt*
	Commander	SKYLARK	*Skylark. 11 Novr 1811*
CARROLL, William.F.	Vol 1st Cl	DIAMOND	
	Lieut. R.N.	CENTURION	*Centurion. 18 Sept 1804*
	Lieut. R.N. (P)	GIBRALTAR FLOTILLA	*B.S. 23 Nov 1810*
McARTHUR, Duncan	Surgeon	DIAMOND	
McKINLEY, George	Lieut. R.N.	LIBERTY	
	Commander	OTTER	*Copenhagen. 1801.*

(8) INDEFATIGABLE 20 APRIL 1796

Capture of the French frigate VIRGINIE in the English Channel, off Ushant.

(Real date 21 April 1796)

CADOGAN, The Hon George.	Vol 1st Cl	INDEFATIGABLE	
	Vol 1st Cl	INDEFATIGABLE	*Indefatigable. 13 Jany 1797*
	Master's Mate	IMPETUEUX	*B.S. 29 Aug 1800*
GAZE, John	Midshipman	INDEFATIGABLE	*(Vfd Abd. Not on Roll)*
	Quarter Master	NYMPHE	*Nymphe. 18 June 1793*
	Midshipman	INDEFATIGABLE	*Indefatigable. 13 Jany 1797*
	Master	QUEEN CHARLOTTE	*Algiers (See Note under NYMPHE)*
GROUBE, Thomas	Master's Mate	INDEFATIGABLE	
	Master's Mate	INDEFATIGABLE	*Indefatigable. 13 Jany 1797*
HARRY, John	Vol 1st Cl	INDEFATIGABLE	
	Vol 1st Cl	INDEFATIGABLE	*Indefatigable. 13 Jany 1797*
JONES, John	A.B.	INDEFATIGABLE	
	A.B.	INDEFATIGABLE	*Indefatigable. 13 Jany 1797*
			(Vfd Abd. Not on Roll)
McKERLIE, John	Quarter Gunner	INDEFATIGABLE	
	Schoolmaster	INDEFATIGABLE	*Indefatigable. 13 Jany 1797*
	Lieut. R.N.	SPARTIATE	*Trafalgar*
PATESHALL, Nicholas.L.	Midshipman	INDEFATIGABLE	
	Midshipman	INDEFATIGABLE	*Indefatigable. 13 Jany 1797*
	Master's Mate	IMPETEUX	*B.S. 29 July 1800*
SIMPSON, Joseph	A.B.	INDEFATIGABLE	*(Vfd Abd. Not on Roll)*
	Gunner's Crew	NYMPHE	*Nymphe. 18 June 1793*
	A.B.	INDEFATIGABLE	*Indefatigable. 13 Jany 1797*
			(Vfd Abd. Not on Roll)

(4) UNICORN 8 JUNE 1796

Capture of the French frigates TRIBUNE and TAMISE — the former by UNICORN, off the Scilly Islands.

AUSTEN, Charles.J.	Midshipman	UNICORN	
	Captain R.N.	BELLEROPHON	*Syria*
DEXTER, William	Ord	UNICORN	
GREEN, John	Pte. R.M.	UNICORN	*G.H. 704*
MATHER, James	Surgeon's Mate	UNICORN	

(3) SANTA MARGARITTA 8 JUNE 1796

Capture of the French frigates TAMISE and TRIBUNE — the former by SANTA MARGARITA (as spelt in Navy List), off the Scilly Islands.

BULLEN, Joseph	Not Given	SANTA MARGARITA	*(Not found on M.L.)*
MARTIN, Thomas.B.	Captain R.N.	SANTA MARGARITA	
	Captain R.N.	FISGARD	*Fisgard. 20 Octr 1798*
	Captain R.N.	IMPLACABLE	*Implacable. 26 Augt 1808 (Chairman of Flag Officer's Committee which introduced N.G.S. Medal & Clasps) In compiler's collection at R.N. Museum, Portsmouth*
PRICE, Thomas	Q.M's Mate	SANTA MARGARITA	
	Yeoman of Sheets	FISGARD	*Fisgard. 20 Octr 1798*
	Boatswain	EUROTAS	*Eurotas. 25 Feby 1814*

SOUTHAMPTON 9 JUNE 1796
(8)

Capture of the French frigate UTILE, off Toulon.

DALLIMORE, James	Pte. R.M.	SOUTHAMPTON	
	Pte. R.M.	SOUTHAMPTON	*1 June 1794*
	Pte. R.M.	SOUTHAMPTON	*St Vincent*
DAVIES, John	Ord	SOUTHAMPTON	*(Vfd Abd. Not on Roll)*
	L.M.	SOUTHAMPTON	*1 June 1794*
	Ord	SOUTHAMPTON	*St Vincent*
	A.B.	SUPERB	*Gut of Gibraltar 12 July 1801*
	A.B.	SUPERB	*St Domingo*
GOODALL, Joseph	L.M.	SOUTHAMPTON	*(M.L. alias HIGGINS, Joseph)*
	L.M.	SOUTHAMPTON	*St Vincent*
GRIFFITHS, David	Pte R.M.	SOUTHAMPTON	*(Vfd Abd. Not on Roll)*
	Pte R.M.	SOUTHAMPTON	*St Vincent*
HAINES, Thomas	Ord	SOUTHAMPTON	*(Vfd Abd. Not on Roll)*
	Ord	SOUTHAMPTON	*St Vincent*
	Coxswain	SUPERB	*Gut of Gibraltar 12 July 1801*
	Coxswain	SUPERB	*St Domingo*
	Gunner	ACASTA	*Martinique*
	Gunner	POMPEE	*Pompee. 17 June 1809*
	Gunner	POMPEE	*(Vfd Abd. Not on Roll)*
			Guadaloupe
SPILL, Samuel	Pte. R.M.	SOUTHAMPTON	
	Pte. R.M.	SOUTHAMPTON	*St Vincent*
STRACHAN, James	Yeoman.B.S.Rm	SOUTHAMPTON	*(Vfd Abd. Not on Roll)* (B.S.=Boatswain's Store)
	L.M.	SOUTHAMPTON	*1 June 1794*
	Yeoman.B.S.Rm	SOUTHAMPTON	*St Vincent*
WAKEHAM, John	A.B.	SOUTHAMPTON	*(Vfd Abd. Not on Roll)*
	A.B.	SOUTHAMPTON	*St Vincent G.H. 5341*

DRYAD 13 JUNE 1796
(6)

Capture of the French frigate PROSPERPINE, off Cape Clear, Britanny.

ALLEN, John	Ord	DRYAD	
KING, Edward.D.	Lieut. R.N.	DRYAD (P)	
	Master's Mate	BARFLEUR	*1 June 1794*
McDONALD, Colin	Midshipman	DRYAD	*(Vfd Abd. Not on Roll)*
	Midshipman	SOUTHAMPTON	*1 June 1794*
PUSEY, John	L.M.	DRYAD	
SHERMAN, Thomas	2nd Lt R.M.	DRYAD	
	Captain. R.M.	CALEDONIA	*Basque Roads 1809*
			(Vfd Abd. Not on Roll)
	Captain. R.M.	CALEDONIA	*B.S. 27 Sep 1810*
VERLING, Edward	Not Given	DRYAD	*Not found on M.L. Possibly a 2 clasp Medal.*

TERPSICHORE 13 OCTR 1796
(3)

Capture of the Spanish frigate MAHONESA, off Cartagena, Spain.

ASHFORD, Thomas	Pte. R.M.	TERPSICHORE	*(M.L. as AXFORD)*
BEAUTYMAN, Thomas	Ord	TERPSICHORE	*(M.L. as BEAUTIMAN)*
PATERSON, William.L.	Vol 1st Cl	TERPSICHORE	

LAPWING 3 DECR 1796
(2)

Capture of the French frigate DECIUS, and destruction of brig VAILLANTE, off Anguilla, Leeward Islands.

LEVEY, William	L.M.	LAPWING
MORROD, Thomas	A.B.	LAPWING

MINERVE 19 DECR 1796
Capture of the Spanish frigate SABINA, off Island of Elba.
(4)

BLACKMORE, Samuel	A.B.	MINERVE	
	A.B.	MINERVE	St Vincent
	A.B.	MINERVE	B.S. 29 May 1797
BROWN, Peter	A.B.	MINERVE	
	A.B.	MINERVE	St Vincent
	A.B.	MINERVE	Egypt
COCKBURN, George	Captain R.N.	MINERVE	
	Captain R.N.	MELEAGER	14 March 1795
	Captain R.N.	MINERVE	St Vincent
	Captain R.N.	MINERVE	Egypt
	Commodore	POMPEE	Martinique
	Rear Admiral	MARLBOROUGH	B.S. Ap & May 1813
GAGE, William.H.	Lieut. R.N.	MINERVE	
	Midshipman	PCSS ROYAL	14 March 1795
	Lieut. R.N.	MINERVE	St Vincent
	Lieut. R.N.	MINERVE	B.S. 29 May 1797

BLANCHE 19 DECR 1796
Action with Spanish frigate CERES, off Island of Elba.
(4)

CLARK, Joseph	Vol 1st Cl	BLANCHE	
	Boy 3rd Cl	BLANCHE	Blanche. 4 Jany 1795
	A.B.	MINOTAUR	Trafalgar
EVANS, Thomas	A.B.	BLANCHE	(Vfd Abd. Not on Roll)
	A.B.	BLANCHE	Blanche. 4 Jany 1795
GREELY, Henry	A.B.	BLANCHE	(Vfd Abd. Not on Roll)
	A.B.	BLANCHE	Blanche. 4 Jany 1795
PRIDHAM, Richard	Midshipman	BLANCHE	

INDEFATIGABLE 13 JANY 1797
Destruction of the French "74", DROITS DE L'HOMME, on Penmarch Rocks, Finistere.
(10)

CADOGAN, The Hon George	Vol 1st Cl	INDEFATIGABLE	
	Vol 1st Cl	INDEFATIGABLE	Indefatigable. 20 April 1796
	Master's Mate	IMPETUEUX	B.S. 29 Aug 1800
GAZE, John	Midshipman	INDEFATIGABLE	
	Quarter Master	NYMPHE	Nymphe. 18 June 1793
	Midshipman	INDEFATIGABLE	Indefatigable. 20 April 1796 (Vfd Abd. Not on Roll)
	Master	QUEEN CHARLOTTE	Algiers (See note under NYMPHE)
GROUBE, Thomas	Master's Mate	INDEFATIGABLE	
	Master's Mate	INDEFATIGABLE	Indefatigable. 20 April 1796
HARRY, John	Vol 1st Cl	INDEFATIGABLE	
	Vol 1st Cl	INDEFATIGABLE	Indefatigable. 20 April 1796
HART, Henry	A.B.	INDEFATIGABLE	
	Midshipman	IMPETUEUX	B.S. 29 July 1800
JONES, John	A.B.	INDEFATIGABLE	(Vfd Abd. Not on Roll)
	A B	INDEFATIGABLE	Indefatigable. 20 April 1796
McKERLIE, John	Schoolmaster	INDEFATIGABLE	
	Quarter Gunner	INDEFATIGABLE	Indefatigable. 20 April 1796
	Lieut. R.N.	SPARTIATE	Trafalgar
PATESHALL, Nicholas.L.	Midshipman	INDEFATIGABLE	
	Midshipman	INDEFATIGABLE	Indefatigable. 20 April 1796
	Master's Mate	IMPETUEUX	B.S. 29 July 1800
SIMPSON, Joseph	A.B.	INDEFATIGABLE	(Vfd Abd. Not on Roll)
	Gunner's Crew	NYMPHE	Nymphe. 18 June 1793
	A.B.	INDEFATIGABLE	Indefatigable. 20 April 1796 (Vfd Abd. Not on Roll)
WILLIAMS, Richard.P.	Surgeon's Mate	INDEFATIGABLE	

(6) AMAZON 13 JANY 1797
Destruction of the French "74", DROITS DE L'HOMME, on Penmarch Rocks, Finistere.
(The Muster List for January 1797 has not survived)

BROWN, John	A.B.	AMAZON	(M.L. (1796) as James BROWN)
CROFT, William	Midshipman	AMAZON	
	Midshipman	FOUDROYANT	Egypt
DEVONSHIRE, Richard	Vol 1st Cl	AMAZON	
	Lieut. R.N.	AIGLE	Basque Roads 1809
DIXIE, Alexander	A.B.	AMAZON	
	Lieut. R.N.	PHOEBE	Trafalgar
ELLENDER, John	L.M.	AMAZON	
	Bosun's Mate	NORTHUMBERLAND	St Domingo
REYNOLDS, Barrington	Midshipman	AMAZON	
	Midshipman	IMPETUEUX	B.S. 29 Aug 1800
	Commander	HESPER	Java
	Capt. R.N. C.B.	GANGES	Syria

(348) ST VINCENT (G.M.)
Battle of Cape St Vincent on 14 February 1797. Capture of four Spanish sail of the line.

ABERCROMBIE, James	Ord	GOLIATH	
AINSLIE, Thomas	Ord	BRITANNIA	
	A.B.	GOLIATH	Nile
	Gunner's Mate	CORNELIA	Java
ALLEN, James	2 Borne.A.B. & QM	CAPTAIN	
ANDREW, George	Ord	PRINCE GEORGE	
	A.B.	ORION	Trafalgar (see notes)
APPLEBY, Young	Midshipman	BLENHEIM	
	Bosun's Servant	ALFRED	1 June 1794
ARCHARD, John	L.M.	ORION	(alias ORCHARD)
	Ord	ORION	Nile
ARMSTRONG, James	A.B.	BARFLEUR	
ATWOOD, John	L.M.	BARFLEUR	G.H. 5,202
	Ord	BRITANNIA	Trafalgar
BAIN, Alexander	Midshipman	CULLODEN	
	Quartermaster	CULLODEN	1 June 1794
	Midshipman	CULLODEN	Nile
BAKER, James	Ord	ORION	G.H. 6,363
BARBER, Alexander	A.B.	BARFLEUR	
BARRETT, John	Pte. R.M.	VICTORY	
BATTEN, Richard	A.B.	PRINCE GEORGE	
BEADLE, William	Boy 2nd Cl	GOLIATH	
	Servant	BARFLEUR	1 June 1794
	Boy 2nd Cl	GOLIATH	Nile
BEAVEN, John	A.B.	DIADEM	
BEER, William	Pte. R.M.	CULLODEN	
	Pte. R.M.	CULLODEN	1 June 1794
	Pte. R.M.	CULLODEN	Nile
BELL, John	Ord	BARFLEUR	
BELL, William	A.B.	BLENHEIM	G.H. 7,753
	L.M.	ALFRED	1 June 1794
BELLINCOLE, Thomas	L.M.	NAMUR	
	Ord	ROYAL SOVEREIGN	Trafalgar
BENNETT, William	Carp's Crew	BRITANNIA	
	Carp's Crew	BRITANNIA	14 March 1795
BERRY, Joseph	A.B.	BRITANNIA	
BEST, Thomas	A.B.	CAPTAIN	
BIGGINS, Robert	A.B.	BLENHEIM	
	A.B.	ALFRED	1 June 1794
	A.B.	URANIE	B.S. 21 July 1801
BINNINGTON, Thomas	Boy 2nd Cl	CAPTAIN	(Vfd Abd by G.H. Roll)
	Ord	MARS	Mars. 21 April 1798
			GH.5007. M.L. as BENNINGTON
BLACKMORE, Samuel	A.B.	MINERVE	
	A.B.	MINERVE	Minerve. 19 Decr 1796
	A.B.	MINERVE	B.S. 29 May 1797
BOND, Dyer	Midshipman	BARFLEUR	
BOWDEN, William	L.M.	EXCELLENT	
BOYD, William	L.M.	NAMUR	
BRENHAM, John	A.B.	CULLODEN	
	A.B.	CULLODEN	1 June 1794
	A.B.	CULLODEN	Nile
BRICKNELL, Samuel	A.B.	PRINCE GEORGE	
	Q.M.	GIBRALTAR	Basque Roads. 1809
BRIDGER, Henry	Q.M's Mate	EGMONT	
	A.B.	EGMONT	14 March 1795
BROADHURST, James	L.M.	NAMUR	

BROWN, John	Ord	EGMONT	G.H. 8,796
BROWN, Peter	A.B.	MINERVE	
	A.B.	MINERVE	Minerve. 19 Decr 1796
	A.B.	MINERVE	Egypt
BROWN, Thomas	Ord	PRINCE GEORGE	
BROWN, William	Midshipman	GOLIATH	
BRYDEN, Edward	Q.M's Mate	CULLODEN	
	A.B.	CULLODEN	1 June 1794
	Q.M's Mate	CULLODEN	Nile
BUCKMASTER, Ishmael	A.B.	LIVELY	
	A.B.	LIVELY	Lively. 13 March 1795 (Vfd Abd. Not on Roll)
	A.B.	AUDACIOUS	Nile
BUDD, Francis	A.B.	EGMONT	
	A.B.	SUPERB	St Domingo
	A.B.	SCEPTRE	Guadaloupe
BURBRIDGE, William.C.	Midshipman	BLENHEIM	
	Captain's Servant	ALFRED	1 June 1794
	Midshipman	NASSAU	Nassau. 22 March 1808
BURCH, Peter	Midshipman	BRITANNIA	(Became Gunner)
	Midshipman	GOLIATH	Nile
BURGOYNE, Frederick.W.	Actg Lieut. R.N.	BRITANNIA	
	Midshipman	MONTAGU	1 June 1794
	Master's Mate	NYMPHE	23rd June 1795
BURNETT, William	Surg's 3rd Mate	GOLIATH	
	Surg's 1st Mate	GOLIATH	Nile
	Surgeon	ATHENIENNE	Egypt
	Surgeon	DEFIANCE	Trafalgar. (Kntd 1831)
BURROWS, Henry	L.M.	CULLODEN	
	L.M.	CULLODEN	Nile
CAMERON, John	A.B.	CAPTAIN	
	A.B.	CAPTAIN	14 March 1795
CARTER, Thomas	A.B.	COLOSSUS	
CHADWICK, Samuel	Pte 69th Regt	BRITANNIA	(M.L. as CHADDOCK)
CHAMBERS, James	L.M.	GOLIATH	G.H. 9,443
	L.M.	GOLIATH	Nile
CHAPMAN, John OR George	Pte. R.M.	NAMUR	G.H. 9,465 as JOHN. 2 clasps (Roll as George)
	Pte. R.M.	NEPTUNE	Trafalgar
CHAPMAN, William	A.B.	CAPTAIN	
CHRISTY, William	Schoolmaster	EXCELLENT	
CHRISTIAN, James	Pte. R.M.	NAMUR	G.H. 6,461
CHUBB, John	L.M.	COLOSSUS	
CHUTE, Caled	Capt' 69th Regt	BRITANNIA	
	Capt' 69th Regt	BRITANNIA	14 March 1795
CLARK, Thomas	Pte. R.M.	EXCELLENT	
CLARKE, James	Pte. R.M.	SOUTHAMPTON	
	Pte. R.M.	LATONA	1 June 1794
	Pte. R.M.	SWIFTSURE	Nile
CLARKE, Walter	Pte. R.M.	NIGER	
	Pte. R.M.	NEPTUNE	Martinique
COCKBURN, George	Captain. R.N.	MINERVE	
	Captain. R.N.	MELEAGER	14 March 1795
	Captain. R.N.	MINERVE	Minerve 19 Decr 1796
	Captain. R.N.	MINERVE	Egypt
	Commodore	POMPEE	Martinique
	Rear Admiral	MARLBOROUGH	B.S. Ap & May 1813
COLEMAN, William	Ord	VICTORY	
COLEPACK, John	Vol 1st Cl	BONNE CITOYENNE	
	Capt's Servant	QUEEN CHARLOTTE	1 June 1794
	Boy 3rd Cl	QUEEN CHARLOTTE	23rd June 1795
	Ord	BONNE CITOYENNE	Egypt
CONNOLLY, W.H.	2nd Lt. R.M.	EXCELLENT	
COOK, Thomas Potter	Boy 3rd Cl	RAVEN	(Became famous stage actor)
COOK, William	L.M.	GOLIATH	
	L.M.	GOLIATH	Nile
COOKE, John	A.B.	BARFLEUR	
	A.B.	BARFLEUR	1 June 1794
COOPER, William	A.B.	BARFLEUR	
	Ord	BARFLEUR	1 June 1794
	Ord	BARFLEUR	23rd June 1795
CORAM, James	Boy 3rd Cl	PRINCE GEORGE	
CORBY, Gilbert	L.M.	BARFLEUR	
CORNES, Josiah	Pte. R.M.	EXCELLENT	
COUZENS, Edward	A.B.	NAMUR	(Became Gunner)
COX, Edward	L.M.	VICTORY	
CRABB, John	Pte. R.M.	CAPTAIN	
	Pte. R.M.	THESEUS	Nile
CROMBIE, John	A.B.	CAPTAIN	

ST VINCENT

CULLEN, William	Capt of Top	GOLIATH	GH.5871. Roll may read CULLIN.
	Capt of Top	GOLIATH	Nile
CULLERN, Thomas	L.M.	EXCELLENT	
	L.M.	SEINE	Seine. 20 Augt 1800
CUMMINGS, Nicholas	A.B.	PRINCE GEORGE	
DALLIMORE, James	Pte. R.M.	SOUTHAMPTON	
	Pte. R.M.	SOUTHAMPTON	1 June 1794
	Pte. R.M.	SOUTHAMPTON	Southampton. 9 June 1796
DANE, Gustave	A.B.	BRITANNIA	
	Ord	GOLIATH	Nile
	Ord	ELEPHANT	Copenhagen 1801
DARLINGTON, Joseph	Boy	CULLODEN	
	Servant	CULLODEN	1 June 1794
	Ord	CULLODEN	Nile
DAVIDSON, William	A.B.	BLENHEIM	
DAVIES, John	Ord	SOUTHAMPTON	
	L.M.	SOUTHAMPTON	1 June 1794
	Ord	SOUTHAMPTON	Southampton. 9 June 1796 (Vfd Abd. Not on Roll)
	A.B.	SUPERB	Gut of Gibraltar. 12 July 1801
	A.B.	SUPERB	St Domingo
DAVIS, George or DAVIES	L.M.	PRINCE GEORGE	G.H. 7,030
	A.B.	PHOENIX	Phoenix. 10 Augt 1805
	A.B.	PHOENIX	4 Novr 1805
DAY, Thomas	A.B.	BRITANNIA	
DENCH, Thomas	Midshipman	BRITANNIA	
	Midshipman	GOLIATH	Nile
DE PAGE, John	A.B.	ORION	(M.L. as LE PAGE)
	A.B.	CRESCENT	Crescent. 20 Octr 1793
	A.B.	ORION	23rd June 1795
	A.B.	ORION	Nile
DIAPER, James	Carp's Crew	VICTORY	
DICKEY, Alexander	A.B.	PRINCE GEORGE	
DODDS, Thomas	A.B.	EXCELLENT	
	A.B.	ELING*	Copenhagen 1801 (Ship not in printed List)
DONNELLY, Peter	Ord	CULLODEN	(M.L. as DOUNELL)
	Ord	CULLODEN	Nile
DOWN, Edward.A.	Master's Mate	EXCELLENT	
	Midshipman	BARFLEUR	1 June 1794
	Master's Mate	VINCIEGO	Vinciego. 30 March 1800
DOWNMAN, Hugh	Lieut. R.N.	VICTORY	
	Captain. R.N.	SANTA DOROTEA	Egypt
DUMMER, George	Ord	GOLIATH	
	Vol 1st Cl	GOLIATH	Nile
DWYER, Mathias	L.M.	BRITANNIA	
	L.M.	DEFENCE	1 June 1794
EDDOCK, Thomas	Armourer	NAMUR	
ELLIOT, Hon George	Vol 1st Cl	BRITANNIA	
	Midshipman	GOLIATH	Nile
	Lieut. R.N.	ST GEORGE	Copenhagen 1801
	Captain. R.N.	MODESTE	Java
ELLIS, Francis	A.B.	BLENHEIM	
	A.B.	ALFRED	1 June 1794
ELLIS, John	Lieut. R.N.	GOLIATH	
ELSMERE, Charles	Actg Lt. R.N.	BRITANNIA	
EVANS, Roger	Lieut. R.N.	SOUTHAMPTON	
	Master's Mate	BEDFORD	14 March 1795
FALLICK, William	L.M.	ORION	
	L.M.	ORION	23rd June 1795
	Ord	ORION	Nile
FEA, James	A.B.	PRINCE GEORGE	(M.L. as FEW)
FERGUSON, John	L.M.	GOLIATH	
	L.M.	GOLIATH	Nile
	Ord	ELEPHANT	Copenhagen 1801
FERGUSSON, John	L.M.	CULLODEN	G.H. 9,571
	L.M.	CULLODEN	Nile
FERNANDES, Donald	Lieut. R.N.	BLENHEIM	
	Midshipman	THUNDERER	1 June 1794
	Master's Mate	THUNDERER	23rd June 1795
FERRIS, Abel	Master's Mate	COLOSSUS	
	Master's Mate	IRRESISTIBLE	23rd June 1795
	Lieut. R.N.	PRINCE	Trafalgar
FINDLAY, Gavin	A.B.	PRINCE GEORGE	
FISHENDEN, John	Ord	DIADEM	
	A.B.	DIADEM	Egypt

Name	Rank	Ship	Notes
FLANDRYN, Daniel	Pte. R.M.	GOLIATH	
	Pte. R.M.	GOLIATH	Nile
	Cpl. R.M.	ASTRAEA	Egypt
FORD, Henry	L.M.	BLENHEIM	G.H. 5,731
FORREST, Peter	L.M.	NAMUR	
FRY, Humphrey	A.B.	DIADEM	
	A.B.	DIADEM	14 March 1795
	A.B.	DIADEM	Egypt
GAGE, Nicholas	L.M.	COLOSSUS	G.H. 2,938
	A.B.	AJAX	Egypt
GAGE, William.H.	Lieut. R.N.	MINERVE	
	Midshipman	PCSS ROYAL	14 March 1795
	Lieut. R.N.	MINERVE	Minerve. 19 Decr 1796
	Lieut. R.N.	MINERVE	B.S. 29 May 1797
GAMBRILL, John	A.B.	DIADEM	
GIBSON, William	Midshipman	DIADEM	
	Boy 2nd Cl	LOWESTOFFE	14 March 1795
	Boy 2nd Cl	LOWESTOFFE	Lowestoffe. 24 June 1795
GILES, James	Boy	COLOSSUS	
GILMOUR, Alexander	Lieut. R.N.	ORION	
	Lieut. R.N.	ORION	Nile
GOODALL, Joseph	L.M.	SOUTHAMPTON	(M.L. as alias HIGGINS)
	L.M.	SOUTHAMPTON	Southampton. 9 June 1796
GOODWIN, John	A.B.	BRITANNIA	G.H. 1758
GORDON, James.A.	Midshipman	NAMUR	
	Midshipman	REVOLUTIONNAIRE	23rd June 1795
	Midshipman	GOLIATH	Nile
	Captain. R.N.	MERCURY	Off Rota. 4 April 1808
	Captain. R.N.	ACTIVE	Lissa
	Captain. R.N.	ACTIVE	Pelagosa. 29 Novr 1811
	Captain. R.N.	SEAHORSE	The Potomac. 17 Aug 1814
GRAGGLESTONE, John	Supernumerary	BARFLEUR	G.H. 6,890
GRAHAM, John.H.	Lieut. R.M.	CAPTAIN	
GRANT, John	A.B.	CULLODEN	G.H. 6,459
	A.B.	CULLODEN	Nile
GRAY, Archibald	Caulker's Mate	BARFLEUR	
GREEN, Stephen	Ord	PRINCE GEORGE	
GRIBBLE, John	L.M.	NAMUR	
GRIFFIN, Nicholas	A.B.	VICTORY	
GRIFFITHS, David	Pte. R.M.	SOUTHAMPTON	G.H. 10,127
	Pte. R.M.	SOUTHAMPTON	Southampton. 9 June 1796 (Vfd Abd. Not on Roll)
GROVES, John	A.B.	LIVELY	
	Midshipman	LIVELY	Lively. 13 March 1795
GUNNING, Thomas	Pte. R.M.	EGMONT	
HAINES, Thomas	Ord	SOUTHAMPTON	
	Ord	SOUTHAMPTON	Southampton. 9 June 1796 (Vfd Abd. Not on Roll)
	Coxswain	SUPERB	Gut of Gibraltar. 12 July 1801
	Coxswain	SUPERB	St Domingo
	Gunner	ACASTA	Martinique
	Gunner	POMPEE	Pompee. 17 June 1809 (Vfd Abd. Not on Roll)
	Gunner	POMPEE	Guadaloupe
HALL, Edward	Midshipman	BLENHEIM	
HALL, Joseph	Pte. R.M.	VICTORY	G.H. 8,233
HALL, Thomas	Pte. R.M.	EXCELLENT	
HAMBLY, Edward	Ord	CAPTAIN	
HANCOCK, John	A.B.	BRITANNIA	
HANLIN, Edward	Lieut. R.M.	CAPTAIN	
HARLARTON, Thomas	Pte. R.M.	VICTORY	(M.L. as HARLETON)
	Sgt. R.M.	MUTINE	Nile
HARRIS, William	A.B.	EGMONT	
HASSETT, Nathan	A.B.	EGMONT	
HAYES, George	Lieut. R.N.	LIVELY	
HEDGES, William	Boy	EMERALD	(Not on Ships' List – detached, closely rejoined after action. Medal approved)
HEMMINGS, William	Boy	GOLIATH	G.H. 7,465 May read HEMMING.
	A.B.	HARPY	Copenhagen 1801
HENDERSON, Menzies	A.B.	GOLIATH	
	A.B.	GOLIATH	Nile
	A.B.	RAMILLIES	Copenhagen 1801
HENDERSON, Robert	Ord	GOLIATH	
HERON, John	Ord	NAMUR	
HEWETT, James or HEWITT	A.B.	BLENHEIM	G.H. 283
	Ord	ALFRED	1 June 1794
	Q.M.'s Mate	NAIAD	Trafalgar
HIATT, John	Midshipman	NAMUR	

ST VINCENT

HILL, John	Boy 3rd Cl	GOLIATH	
	Vol 1st Cl	GOLIATH	Nile
	Vol 1st Cl	ELEPHANT	Copenhagen 1801
HILLIER, William.C.	Midshipman	BLENHEIM	
	Midshipman	ALFRED	1 June 1794
	Master's Mate	POMPEE	Gut of Gibraltar. 12 July 1801
	Purser	COMUS	Comus. 15 Augt 1807
HILLMAN, Richard	A.B.	CULLODEN	
	Ord	CULLODEN	1 June 1794
	A.B.	CULLODEN	Nile
HILLS, Thomas	Vol 1st Cl	VICTORY	
	Lieut. R.N.	PHILOMEL	B.S. 1 Nov 1809
HOBBS, Thomas	A.B.	EGMONT	
HODGE, Edward	Quarter Gunner	DIADEM	
	A.B.	DIADEM	14 March 1795
HODGE, William	Boy 3rd Cl	BLENHEIM	
	Capt's Servant	ALFRED	1 June 1794
HODGES, Joseph	Pte. R.M.	EXCELLENT	
	Pte. R.M.	EGGAR (ROLL)	Copenhagen 1801 (EDGAR?)
HOGDEN, Thomas	L.M.	BARFLEUR	
	Ship's Corporal	DIANA	Egypt
HOLDEN, Thomas	L.M.	NAMUR	
HOLLAND, Henry	Pte. R.M.	IRRESISTIBLE	
	Pte. R.M.	LEVIATHAN	Trafalgar
HOLLAND, Thomas	A.B.	LIVELY	
	A.B.	LIVELY	Lively. 13 March 1795 (Vfd Abd. Not on Roll)
	A.B.	ALEXANDER	Nile
HOLLANDS, George	Pte. R.M.	VICTORY	
HOLT, James	Ord	PRINCE GEORGE	
HOSKEN, James	Gunner	IRRESISTIBLE	
	Gunner	IRRESISTIBLE	B.S. 17 Mar 1794
	Gunner	LONDON	23rd June 1795
HOSKINS, William	Pte. R.M.	EGMONT	
HOUGHTON, William	A.B.	EXCELLENT	
	L.M.	DEFENCE	1 June 1794
HOWELS, John	A.B.	NAMUR	
HUDSON, William	Ord	IRRESISTIBLE	G.H. 6,563
HUGHES, George	A.B.	COLOSSUS	
HUNT, W.	A.B.	PRINCE GEORGE	
HUTCHINGS, John	Boy	BONNE CITOYENNE	
HUSTON, Samuel	Pte. 11th Regt	DIADEM	
JACKSON, James	Vol 1st Cl	ORION	
	Vol 1st Cl	ORION	Nile
JACKSON, Thomas	Ord	GOLIATH	
	Ord	GOLIATH	Nile
JEMMIESON, William	A.B.	BRITANNIA	
JOB, William	Pte. R.M.	CULLODEN	
	Pte. R.M.	CULLODEN	1 June 1794
	Pte. R.M.	CULLODEN	Nile
JOHN, Lewis	A.B.	EXCELLENT	
	Actg Master	PODARGUS	Off Mardoe. 6 July 1812
JOHNSON, John	A.B.	BRITANNIA	
	A.B.	BRITANNIA	14 March 1795
	A.B.	GOLIATH	Nile
	A.B.	ELEPHANT	Copenhagen 1801
	Yeoman Sheets	CORNELIA	Java
JOHNSON, Thomas	A.B.	PRINCE GEORGE	
JOHNSTONE, William	Ord	IRRESISTIBLE	(M.L. as JOHNSON)
	A.B.	IRRESISTIBLE	23rd June 1795
JONES, Charles	Pte. R.M.	DIADEM	
JONES, Daniel	Pte. R.M.	PRINCE GEORGE	
	Sgt. R.M.A.	"ANHOLT"	Anholt. 27 March 1811
JONES, Evan	A.B.	EXCELLENT	
JONES, John	Ord	EGMONT	
JONES, Thomas	A.B.	PRINCE GEORGE	
KEAN, Michael	L.M.	ORION	
	A.B.	ORION	Nile
KELLY, William	L.M.	IRRESISTIBLE	
	A.B.	IRRESISTIBLE	23rd June 1795
KENNEDY, Andrew	Vol 1st Cl	VICTORY	
	Midshipman	PENELOPE	Martinique
KESTON, Richard	Ord	EGMONT	
KIER, Robert	L.M.	BRITANNIA	
KING, Henry	Midshipman	NAMUR	
	Lieut. R.N.	SEAHORSE (P)	The Potomac. 17 Aug 1814
KITE, James	A.B.	CULLODEN	
	Ord	CULLODEN	1 June 1794
	A.B.	CULLODEN	Nile

KITT, Joseph	A.B.	ORION	
	A.B.	CRESCENT	Crescent. 20 Octr 1793
	A.B.	ORION	23rd June 1795
	A.B.	ORION	Nile
KNIGHT, John	L.M.	IRRESISTIBLE	
	A.B. or Carp's Crew	IRRESISTIBLE	23rd June 1795
KNIGHT, Thomas	Boy 3rd Cl	CULLODEN	
	Capt's Servant	CULLODEN	1 June 1794
	Boy 3rd Cl	CULLODEN	Nile
KNOTT, William	A.B.	EXCELLENT	
LAKE, John	Purser's Stwd	CULLODEN	
	L.M.	CULLODEN	1 June 1794
	Purser's Stwd	NEPTUNE	Trafalgar
LARKE, William	Midshipman	PRINCE GEORGE	
LAVERTON, William	Pte. R.M.	LIVELY	
	Pte. R.M.	LIVELY	Lively. 13 March 1795 (Vfd Abd. Not on Roll)
LEAR, William	A.B.	PRINCE GEORGE	
LECKEY, Robert	A.B.	CULLODEN	
	Ord	CULLODEN	1 June 1794
	A.B.	CULLODEN	Nile
	A.B.	PIQUE	Egypt
LEITH, William.F.	A.B.	PRINCE GEORGE	(Became Commander. RN)
LENARD, Joseph	Ord	CULLODEN	
	Ord	CULLODEN	1 June 1794
	Ord	CULLODEN	Nile
	Yeoman Sheets	NAIAD	Trafalgar
LIBBY, Edward	Actg Lt. R.N.	BLENHEIM	
	Midshipman	LOWESTOFFE	14 March 1795
	Midshipman	LOWESTOFFE	Lowestoffe. 24 June 1795
	Lieut. R.N.	NAMUR	4 Novr 1805
LLOYD, William	Pte. R.M.	ORION	
	Pte. R.M.	PRINCE	Trafalgar
LOCK, William	Cpl. R.M.	GOLIATH	
LUGG, William	A.B.	EXCELLENT	
LUTWIDGE, Henry.T.	Midshipman	BARFLEUR	
	Midshipman	BARFLEUR	23rd June 1795
MADGE, William	Quarter Gunner	ORION	
	Quarter Gunner	CRESCENT	Crescent. 20 Octr 1793
	M.A.A.	ORION	Nile
MALING, Thomas.J.	Midshipman	VICTORY	
	Actg Lieut. RN	MINERVE	B.S. 29 May 1797
MANSELL, Thomas	Master's Mate	ORION	
	Midshipman	CRESCENT	Crescent. 20 Octr 1793
	Midshipman	ORION	23rd June 1795
	Midshipman	ORION	Nile
MARKHAM, John	Pte. R.M.	BLENHEIM	
MARRETT, Joseph	Midshipman	ORION	
	Midshipman	CRESCENT	Crescent. 20 Octr 1793
	Midshipman	ORION	23rd June 1795 (Vfd Abd. Not on Roll)
	Midshipman	ORION	Nile
	Lieut. R.N.	MARTIAL	Basque Roads. 1809
MARSH, Robert	L.M.	BONNE CITOYENNE	
MARSHALL, Isaac	A.B.	VICTORY	
MARSHALL, John	A.B.	EGMONT	(Became Rtd Commander)
	Ord	EGMONT	14 March 1795
MARSHALL, William	L.M.	VICTORY	
	A.B.	VANGUARD	Nile
MARTIN, John	A.B.	EXCELLENT	
McAUSLAND, Peter	Bosun's Mate	IRRESISTIBLE	
	A.B.	MONTAGU	1 June 1794
	Gunner's Mate	IRRESISTIBLE	23rd June 1795
	Gunner	PETEREL	Egypt
	Gunner	IMPLACABLE	Implacable. 26 Augt 1808
McCARTHY, Dennis	Ord	EGMONT	G.H. 895
McGLADERY, John	Yeoman Sheets	CULLODEN	(May read M'GLADERY)
	Yeoman Sheets	CULLODEN	Nile
	Actg Lt. R.N.	OTTER	Otter. 18 Septr 1810 (Vfd Abd. Not on Roll)
McGORDON, James	L.M.	BARFLEUR	
McKENZIE, Andrew	Pte. R.M.	ORION	
McNAB, George	Boy	IRRESISTIBLE	G.H. 9,883

ST VINCENT

McQUIN, Hugh	A.B.	DIADEM	
	Ord	DIADEM	14 March 1795
	Quarter Gunner	DIADEM	Egypt
MERRYWEATHER, Richard	A.B.	PRINCE GEORGE	
	L.M.	ILLUSTRIOUS	14 March 1795
MILGROVE, John	Pte. 50th Regt	DIADEM	(May read MULGROVE)
MILLS, William	Sgt. R.M.	COLOSSUS	
	Cpl. R.M.	QUEEN	23rd June 1795
	Sgt. R.M.	BELLONA	Copenhagen 1801
MILNE, Benjamin	Ord	COLOSSUS	(M.L. as MILLER)
	Ord	MUTINE	Nile
MITCHELL, James	A.B.	BARFLEUR	
	A.B.	GLORY	1 June 1794
	A.B.	BARFLEUR	23rd June 1795
MITCHELL, Thomas	A.B.	EXCELLENT	
MOBBS, Robert	A.B.	VICTORY	
MOORFIELD, James	Pte. 11th Regt	CAPTAIN	
MORGAN, Thomas	A.B.	CAPTAIN	
	A.B.	CAPTAIN	14 March 1795
MORICE, James	A.B.	BLENHEIM	
MORR, William	L.M.	IRRESISTIBLE	(M.L. as MOORE)
	Boy 2nd Cl	ORION	23rd June 1795
MORRIS, William	A.B.	CAPTAIN	G.H. 4,507
	A.B.	ROYAL GEORGE	1 June 1794
	A.B.	CAPTAIN	14 March 1795
MORSON, Samuel	A.B.	NAMUR	G.H. 7,517
MORTIMORE, Thomas	L.M.	BLENHEIM	
MOULLEN, Nicholas	Ord	ORION	(M.L. as MULLEN)
MUDGE, Thomas	Ord	PRINCE GEORGE	
(MULGROVE, John)	(See MILGROVE)		
MUNDY, George	Lieut. R.N.	BLENHEIM	
	Lieut. R.N.	GOLIATH	Nile
	Captain. R.N.	HYDRA	Hydra. 6 Augt 1807
MURPHY, Thomas	Pte. R.M.	BLENHEIM	G.H. 9,829
MURRAY, Charles	A.B.	EXCELLENT	G.H. 5,836
NEWCOMBE, John	L.M.	BONNE CITOYENNE	
NOBLE, James	Lieut. R.N.	CAPTAIN	
NORMAN, John	A.B.	VICTORY	
OLIVE, John	Midshipman	GOLIATH	
ORMISTON, John	L.M.	IRRESISTIBLE	
	L.M.	IRRESISTIBLE	23rd June 1795
	A.B.	AJAX	Egypt
PARKER, William	Midshipman	BRITANNIA	
	Midshipman	ST GEORGE	14 March 1795
	Midshipman	GOLIATH	Nile
	Lieut. R.N.	DRUID	Egypt (This clasp awarded on a separate NGS Medal)
PARSONS, George.S.	Midshipman	BARFLEUR	
	Actg Lt. R.N.	EL CARMEN	Egypt
PEACOCK, John	A.B.	BARFLEUR	G.H. 6,859
PEARSE, John	Midshipman	CULLODEN	
	Midshipman	CULLODEN	Nile
PEARSON, George	L.M.	ORION	
	Ord	ORION	23rd June 1795
	Ord	ORION	Nile
PEERS, Samuel	A.B.	PRINCE GEORGE	
PERRYMAN, Joseph	Steward's Mate	NAMUR	
PETERS, James	A.B.	EGMONT	
PILE, Thomas	A.B.	CAPTAIN	
	A.B.	CAPTAIN	14 March 1795
PINTO, Thomas	Midshipman	IRRESISTIBLE	
	Master's Mate	NORTHUMBERLAND	Egypt
	Lieut. R.N.	AGAMEMNON	Trafalgar
	Lieut. R.N.	AGAMEMNON	St Domingo
	Commander	ACHATES	B.S. 13 Dec 1809
	Commander	ACHATES	Guadaloupe
POTTER, Joseph	A.B.	BRITANNIA	G.H. 7,631
	A.B.	BRITANNIA	14 March 1795
PREVOST, James	Lieut. R.N.	BARFLEUR	
	Lieut. R.N.	FOUDROYANT	Egypt
REES, John	L.M.	PRINCE GEORGE	(M.L. as REECE)
REYNOLDS, Cornelius	Surgeon	BLENHEIM	
RICHARDSON, William	Midshipman	PRINCE GEORGE	
	Capt's Servant	ALFRED	1 June 1794
RIDER, William.B.	Lieut. R.N.	DIADEM	
	Lieut. R.N.	DIADEM	14 March 1795
RIVERS, William	Vol 1st Cl	VICTORY	
	Midshipman	VICTORY	Trafalgar (Lost left leg)

ROBERTS, William	A.B.	CULLODEN	
	A.B.	TREMENDOUS	1 June 1794
	A.B.	CULLODEN	Nile
ROBINSON, William	A.B.	PRINCE GEORGE	
ROBITSON, James	A.B.	PRINCE GEORGE	
ROGER, Joseph	Carp's Crew	EGMONT	
ROOT, William	Pte. R.M.	VICTORY	
ROPER, James	L.M.	NAMUR	
ROSE, John	Master	CULLODEN	(Became Rtd Cdr 1847)
	Master	CULLODEN	Nile
ROSS, James	L.M.	PRINCE GEORGE	G.H. 7,973
	Cap' After Guard	SEAHORSE	Seahorse Wh Badere Zaffere
ROWE, William	Boy	IRRESISTIBLE	
	Ord	NORTHUMBERLAND	Egypt
ROWSE, John	Boy	NAMUR	
SALTER, John	Pte. R.M.	CULLODEN	
	Pte. R.M.	CULLODEN	1 June 1794
	Pte. R.M.	MUTINE	Nile
SAMWELL, Peter	Master's Mate	CAPTAIN	
	Lieut. R.N.	MUTINE	Nile
SANDBROOK, Thomas	Capt's Servant	EGMONT	A rating. May be SANDBROOKE.
	Boy	EGMONT	14 March 1795
SAUNDERS, Walter	A.B.	CAPTAIN	
	A.B.	CAPTAIN	14 March 1795
SEDEWAY, James	Mid Ship Man	CULLODEN	G.H. 9,099
	Mid Ship Man	CULLODEN	1 June 1794
	Mid Ship Man	CULLODEN	Nile
SELBY, Thomas	A.B.	CULLODEN	(M.L. as SELVIE)
	A.B.	CULLODEN	1 June 1794
	A.B.	CULLODEN	Nile
SHARPE, Joseph	Drummer. R.M.	GOLIATH	
	Drummer. R.M.	GOLIATH	Nile
SHAW, Isaac	Midshipman	BARFLEUR	
	Midshipman	ROMULUS	14 March 1795
			(Vfd Abd. Not on Roll)
	Lieut. R.N.	NEPTUNE	Trafalgar
	Lieut. R.N.	VOLONTAIRE (P)	B.S. 2 May 1813
SHELSON, Henry	Ord	COLOSSUS	
SIMPSON, Benjamin	Vol 1st Cl	LIVELY	
	Vol 1st Cl	LIVELY	Lively. 13 March 1795
SIMPSON, John	L.M.	COLOSSUS	
SIMS, George	A.B.	EGMONT	
	A.B.	NORTHUMBERLAND	Egypt
SKEET, William	Ord	EXCELLENT	
SMITH, Andrew	L.M.	BARFLEUR	
SMITH, James	A.B.	CULLODEN	
	A.B.	CULLODEN	1 June 1794
	A.B.	CULLODEN	Nile
SMITH, John	Pte. 49th Regt	BLENHEIM	
SMITH, John	3 A.Bs Borne	ALFRED	
	3 A.Bs Borne	ALFRED	1 June 1794
SMITH, John	A.B.	BLENHEIM	
SMITH, John	A.B.	PRINCE GEORGE	
SOAMES, John	Bosun's Mate	ORION	
	A.B.	CRESCENT	Crescent. 20 Octr 1793
	Quarter Gunner	ORION	23rd June 1795
	Bosun's Mate	ORION	Nile
SPAWFORTH, Robert	Coxswain	GOLIATH	
SPILL, Samuel	Pte. R.M.	SOUTHAMPTON	(Vfd Abd. Not on Roll)
	Pte. R.M.	SOUTHAMPTON	Southampton. 9 June 1796
SPINKS, James	L.M.	VICTORY	
STANWAY, James	A.B.	COLOSSUS	
STERRICKS, David	Ord	IRRESISTIBLE	
	A.B.	NORTHUMBERLAND	Egypt
STEWART, Peter	L.M.	PRINCE GEORGE	
STRACHAN, James	Yeoman.B.S.Room	SOUTHAMPTON	(B.S. = Boatswain's Store)
	L.M.	SOUTHAMPTON	1 June 1794
	Yeoman.B.S.Room	SOUTHAMPTON	Southampton. 9 June 1796
SWEET, James	Armourer's Mate	CULLODEN	
	Armourer's Mate	CULLODEN	1 June 1794
	Armourer's Mate	CULLODEN	Nile
	Armourer's Mate	TEMERAIRE	Trafalgar
	Armourer	LONDON	London. 13 March 1806
SYMONDS, W.L.	Midshipman	VICTORY	

ST VINCENT

TANCOCK, John	Master's Mate	ORION	
	Master's Mate	CRESCENT	Crescent. 20 Octr 1793
	Master's Mate	ORION	23rd June 1795
	Actg Lieut. RN	ORION	Nile
	Lieut. R.N.	CAESAR	Gut of Gibraltar. 12 July 1801
TAYLOR, George	Pte. R.M.	EGMONT	
TAYLOR, Thomas	Four Borne	BARFLEUR	(3 A.Bs & one R.M.)
THOMAS, Richard	Lieut. R.N.	EXCELLENT	
	Master's Mate	NAUTILUS	B.S. 17 Mar 1794
THOMAS, Thomas	A.B.	CAPTAIN	
THOMPSON, John	A.B.	BRITANNIA	
THOMPSON, Thomas	A.B.	ORION	G.H. 8,953
	A.B.	ORION	1 June 1794
	A.B.	ORION	Nile
THORN, John	Ord	BLENHEIM	G.H. 3,564
	Ord	ALFRED	1 June 1794
TICKNER, Samuel	Ord	CULLODEN	
	Ord	CULLODEN	Nile
TOLHURST, Jeremiah	Ord	ORION	
	Ord	ORION	Nile
TRIGGS, William	Ord	PRINCE GEORGE	
TURNER, John	Pte. R.M.	PRINCE GEORGE	
TURNEY, Samuel	Pte. R.M.	BARFLEUR	
	Pte. R.M.	QUEEN	23rd June 1795
TURPINS, John	L.M.	ORION	
	L.M.	ORION	23rd June 1795
	Ord	ORION	Nile
	Ord	GANGES	Copenhagen 1801
TUTE, Christopher	A.B.	PRINCE GEORGE	
	A.B.	BELLEISLE	Trafalgar
	A.B.	PERLEN	Guadaloupe
TWENDEN, Michael	A.B.	NAMUR	
VAUGHAN, William	A.B.	CAPTAIN	
WAKEHAM, John	A.B.	SOUTHAMPTON	G.H. 5,341
	A.B.	SOUTHAMPTON	Southampton. 9 June 1796 (Vfd Abd. Not on Roll)
WALKER, William or WALLER	A.B.	DIADEM	
	Boy 3rd Cl	DIADEM	14 March 1795
WALLACE, James	Midshipman	VICTORY	
WARD, William	Midshipman	BARFLEUR	
	Midshipman	BARFLEUR	23rd June 1795 (Vfd Abd. Not on Roll)
	Lieut. R.N.	PIQUE	Pique. 26 March 1806
WARD, William	L.M.	BARFLEUR	
WARNER, Samuel	L.M.	BONNE CITOYENNE	G.H. 9,228
WARRAND, Thomas	Master's Mate	VICTORY	
	Lieut Commanding	SEALARK (P)	Sealark. 21 July 1812
WATSON, John	Boy	CAPTAIN	G.H. 9,957
WATTLER, Stephen	Quarter Gunner	BARFLEUR	G.H. 6,710
	A.B.	BARFLEUR	1 June 1794
WATTS, John	A.B.	CAPTAIN	
WEALE, Edward.T.	Vol 1st Cl	ORION	
	Midshipman	ORION	Nile
WEBB, John	A.B.	BARFLEUR	
	Two Ords borne	BARFLEUR	1 June 1794
WEBSTER, William	L.M.	BARFLEUR	
WEEKS, Richard	A.B.	DIADEM	
WELLS, Andrew	Midshipman	COLOSSUS	
	Midshipman	EDGAR	Copenhagen 1801
WHITE, Arthur	A.B.	VICTORY	
WHITSHED, James.H.	Captain R.N.	NAMUR	
WICKS, Richard	A.B.	DIADEM	
WILES, Samuel	A.B.	CULLODEN	
	A.B.	CULLODEN	1 June 1794
	A.B.	CULLODEN	Nile
WILLCOX, Robert	Ord	LIVELY	
	Boy 3rd Cl	LIVELY	Lively. 13 March 1795
	Midshipman	SUPERB	Gut of Gibraltar. 12 July 1801
WILLES, George.W.	Midshipman	PRINCE GEORGE	(Died in command VANGUARD 26 Oct 1846 before issue of advertisement for Naval War Medals.)
WILLIAMS, John	Sailmaker's Mate	BARFLEUR	
WOOD, John	Ord	BLENHEIM	(M.L. as HOOD)
	Ord	ALFRED	1 June 1794
WOOD, Roger	L.M.	NAMUR	
WOODWARD, William	L.M.	BARFLEUR	
WYATT, James	Pte. R.M.	PRINCE GEORGE	
YATES, John	L.M.	NAMUR	

YERBURY, Walter	Pte. R.M.	EXCELLENT	
	Pte. R.M.	BELLONA	Copenhagen 1801
YOUNG, James	Drummer. R.M.	ORION	
	Drummer. R.M.	ORION	Nile

(8) SAN FIORENZO 8 MAR 1797

Capture of the French frigates RESISTANCE and CONSTANCE by H.M. Ships St FIORENZO and NYMPHE, off Brest.

(Real date 9 March 1797)

BROOKMAN, John	Ord	St FIORENZO	G.H. 3,180
COLE, Daniel	Pte. R.M.	St FIORENZO	G.H. 5,129. Incorrectly recorded on NYMPHE roll.
DALLY, William	Boy 3rd Cl	St FIORENZO	(M.L. as DALLY & DALLEY)
EMMERSON, John	Ord	St FIORENZO	G.H. 2,539
	Ord	ACHILLE	(Vfd Abd. Not on Roll) Trafalgar
LEWIS, William	Boy 2nd Cl	St FIORENZO	
MITFORD, Robert	Midshipman	St FIORENZO	
	Commander	ESPOIR	Espoir 25 & 27 June 1809
RENWICK, Thomas	Lieut. R.N.	St FIORENZO	
	Midshipman	BRUNSWICK	1 June 1794
SHEPHERD, Benjamin	Boy 3rd Cl	St FIORENZO	(M.L. as SHEPPARD)

(5) NYMPHE 8 MARCH 1797

Capture of the French frigates RESISTANCE and CONSTANCE by H.M. Ships St FIORENZO and NYMPHE, off Brest.

(Real date 9 March 1797)

BASTIN, Robert	A.B.	NYMPHE	(Vfd Abd. Not on Roll)
	Lieut. R.N.	BELLEISLE	Trafalgar
	Lieut. R.N.	BLANCHE	Blanche 19 July 1806
COOK, John	Pte. R.M.	NYMPHE	
GODBY, John Hardy	Midshipman	NYMPHE	
	Lieut. R.N.	ATHENIENNE	Egypt
MARKLAND, John.D.	Master's Mate	NYMPHE	
	Commander	BUSTARD	B.S. 29 July 1809
OUTRAM, Benjamin.F.	Surgeon	NYMPHE	
	Surgeon	SUPERB	Gut of Gibraltar. 12 July 1801

(3) 29 MAY BOAT SERVICE 1797

Cutting out of the French brig MUTINE by boats of LIVELY and MINERVE, in Bay of Santa Cruz, Teneriffe.

BLACKMORE, Samuel	A.B.	MINERVE	
	A.B.	MINERVE	Minerve 19 Decr 1796
	A.B.	MINERVE	St Vincent
GAGE, William.H.	Lieut. R.N.	MINERVE	
	Midshipman	PRINCESS ROYAL	14 March 1795
	Lieut. R.N.	MINERVE	Minerve 19 Decr 1796
	Lieut. R.N.	MINERVE	St Vincent
MALING, Thomas.J.	Actg Lieut. R.N.	MINERVE	
	Midshipman	VICTORY	St Vincent

(298) **CAMPERDOWN** (G.M.)
Battle of Camperdown on 11 October 1797

ABERNETHY, Charles.K.	Quarter Gunner	BELLIQUEUX	
ADAMSON, Orame	Carp's Crew	POWERFUL	
	Carp's Crew	ACTIVE	Lissa
	Carp's Crew	ACTIVE	Pelagosa. 29 Novr 1811 (Not on Roll. Vfd Abd.)
AITKEN, James	Ord	VENERABLE	
	Ord	KENT	Egypt
	Ord	DEFENCE	Trafalgar
ALLARD, Mark	L.M.	LANCASTER	
ARCHER, Alexander	Pte. R.M.	TRIUMPH	
ASLETT, Thompson	2nd Lt. R.M.	MONTAGU	
ATWELL, Robert	A.B.	RUSSELL	
	A.B.	IRRESISTIBLE	23rd June 1795
	Yeoman of Sheets	RAMILLIES	Copenhagen 1801
	Yeoman of Sheets	PRINCE	Trafalgar
AYLES, John	L.M.	TRIUMPH	
AYRES, John	Midshipman	MONARCH	
BAILEY, Joseph	A.B.	MONMOUTH	
BAKER, John	A.B.	RUSSELL	
	A.B.	RUSSELL	Copenhagen 1801
BALCHIN, William	Boy	VENERABLE	
	Ord	FOUDROYANT	Egypt
BARNES, James	L.M.	MONARCH	(M.L. as BURNS)
	Ord	MONARCH	Copenhagen 1801
BAXTER, John	Ord	MONTAGU	
BENNETT, Thomas	Midshipman	MONARCH	
	Lieut. R.N.	SEAHORSE	Seahorse Wh Badere Zaffere
BICKELL, William	Boy 3rd Cl	BEDFORD	
BINFORD, John	A.B.	ARDENT	
BIRD, Robert	Midshipman	LANCASTER	
	Gunner	St FIORENZO	San Fiorenzo. 8 March 1808
BISHOP, Richard	L.M.	AGINCOURT	
BLIGH, Thomas	Pte. R.M.	BEDFORD	
	Pte. R.M.	EL CARMEN	Egypt
BLOMELY, John	Boy 2nd Cl	BEDFORD	
	Boy 2nd Cl	FOUDROYANT	Egypt
BODAH, Elias	A.B.	VETERAN	
	A.B.	ORION	1 June 1794
	A.B.	VETERAN	Copenhagen 1801
BOWEN, John	A.B.	VETERAN	(Became a Pilot)
BOWMAN, Heine	Pte. R.M.	BELLIQUEUX	
BRADLEY, John	Caulker	ADAMANT	
BRAMLEY, Job	Ord	LANCASTER	G.H. 6,206
BROWN, Evan	A.B.	BEAULIEU	
BROWN, James	Pte. R.M.	ARDENT	
BROWN, Thomas	Ord	RUSSELL	
	Ord	RUSSELL	Copenhagen 1801
BROWN, William	Ord	TRIUMPH	
BULLEN, Charles	Lieut. R.N.	MONMOUTH	(Recd Gold Medal – Trafalgar)
	Lieut. R.N.	RAMILLIES	1 June 1794
BULLY, James	Pte. R.M.	BELLIQUEUX	
BUNCE, Richard	1st Lt. R.M.	MONMOUTH	(M.G.S. Java)
BURGES, William	L.M.	MONARCH	
	Ord	ARDENT	Copenhagen 1801
BURNES, Alexander	L.M.	AGINCOURT	
	Ord	BELLEROPHON	Trafalgar
BURR, Thomas	Boy 3rd Cl	MONTAGU	
BURROWS, Robert	L.M.	MONMOUTH	
	Ord	MONMOUTH	Egypt
	Ord	REVENGE	Trafalgar
BURTON, William	A.B.	RUSSELL	G.H. 4,440
BUSHELL, Richard	Not Given	KING GEORGE	(No M.Ls this period)
BUTLER, John	A.B.	POWERFUL	
BYRNE, James	L.M.	ADAMANT	
CALLOW, John	Midshipman	MONMOUTH	
CAMPBELL, Donald	Lieut. R.N.	RUSSELL	
CANDY, Joseph	Boy	BEDFORD	
CARR, Edward	Vol 1st Cl	RUSSELL	G.H. 9,371
CARTER, George	Ord	MONTAGU	
CATLIN, Benjamin	Ord	AGINCOURT	G.H. 2,373
CAUSEWAY, James	Ord	TRIUMPH	
CHAPMAN, James	Midshipman	RUSSELL	
	Midshipman	RUSSELL	Copenhagen 1801
CHAPMAN, John	A.B.	BEAULIEU	
CHAPMAN, Thomas	Pte. R.M.	POWERFUL	
CHERRIT, Anthony	Boy	VETERAN	
CHURCHILL, Charles	Ord	MONARCH	
	L.M.	IMPREGNABLE	1 June 1794
	Ord	MONARCH	Copenhagen 1801

CLARK, William	Boy 3rd Cl	VENERABLE	
	Boy	KENT	*Egypt*
CLARKE, Ralph	Pte. R.M.	ARDENT	
CLEMENTS, John	Pte. R.M.	BEDFORD	
CLUBB, Alfred	Boy 2nd Cl	DIRECTOR	
	Pte. R.M.	POLYPHEMUS	*Copenhagen 1801*
COLBY, Thomas	Midshipman	BEDFORD	
	Midshipman	FOUDROYANT	*12 Octr 1798*
	Midshipman	CENTURION	*Centurion. 18 Sept 1804*
	Lieut. R.N.	THUNDERER	*Trafalgar*
			(Known 5 Clasp Medal with unlisted "BS. 19 April 1814")
CONDIE, John	Sailmaker's Mate	BEAULIEU	*G.H. 7,143*
COOK, Robert	L.M.	DIRECTOR	
	L.M.	POLYPHEMUS	*Copenhagen 1801*
COOKE, Thomas	Ord	LANCASTER	
COOPER, James	Boy 3rd Cl	BELLIQUEUX	*G.H. 8,270*
CORBET, Daniel	A.B.	MONMOUTH	
	Ord	REVENGE	*Trafalgar*
CORDER, Edward	Ord	MONTAGU	*G.H. 9,136 (M.L. as CORDY)*
	Ord	COLOSSUS	*Trafalgar*
CORNISH, Richard	Midshipman	BEDFORD	
CREAGH, Richard	L.M.	VETERAN	
	L.M.	ORION	*1 June 1794*
	Quarter Gunner	VETERAN	*Copenhagen 1801*
CREMENE, John	A.B.	VETERAN	*(Spelt CREMENI this roll, & CREMMERN & CREMERN others)*
	L.M.	ORION	*1 June 1794*
	A.B.	LEVIATHAN	*23rd June 1795*
	A.B.	VETERAN	*Copenhagen 1801*
CUERDALE, James	L.M.	MONTAGU	
CUNNINGHAM, Robert	Carpenter's Crew	MONTAGU	*G.H. 6,327*
DAVID, Edward	A.B.	MONARCH	
DAVEY, Thomas	Carp's Crew	AGINCOURT	*G.H. 7,381*
DAVIES, David	A.B.	BEDFORD	
	Quarter Gunner	VANGUARD	*Nile*
	A.B.	FOUDROYANT	*Egypt*
DAVIS, Ephraim	Gnr's Mate	VETERAN	
	Qtr Gunner	VETERAN	*Copenhagen 1801*
DAWSON, Richard	Pte. R.M.	CIRCE	
DAWSON, William	A.B.	BEDFORD	
	A.B.	FOUDROYANT	*Egypt*
DE BLAQUIERE, P.B.	Midshipman	DIRECTOR	
DIBBLE, John	L.M.	MONTAGU	
DICKSON, Thomas	A.B.	POWERFUL	*G.H. 8,025*
DONNER, Edward	L.M.	TRIUMPH	
DRUMMOND, Adam	Lieut. R.N.	MONARCH	
EDDY, William	A.B.	BEDFORD	
EDWARDS, Charles	Ord	BEDFORD	
	A.B.	FOUDROYANT	*Egypt*
EDWARDS, Edward	Boy 2nd Cl	AGINCOURT	
	A.B.	AMPHION	*Lissa*
ELLIS, Thomas	Boy	VENERABLE	*G.H. 1,356*
EMMS, William	A.B.	BEAULIEU	*G.H. 2,155*
EVANS, Thomas	Bosun's Mate	TRIUMPH	
	Q.M.	TRIUMPH	*17 June 1795*
EVEREST, John	Schoolmaster	ARDENT	
FALCON, Gordon.T.	Master's Mate	VENERABLE	
FARQUHAR, Alexander	A.B.	BEDFORD	
FIFFE, John	L.M.	VENERABLE	
FIG, William	A.B.	VENERABLE	
	Midshipman	BELLONA	*Copenhagen 1801*
FLEMING, Michael	A.B.	RUSSELL	
FLITT, James	A.B.	BEAULIEU	
	A.B.	CONQUEROR	*Trafalgar*
	A.B.	CONQUEROR	*B.S. 16 July 1806*
FOOTE, W.William	Not Known	DIRECTOR	*Roll incorrect as Lt. RN.*
FORESTER, John	Ord	DIRECTOR	
FROST, Edward	A.B.	VENERABLE	*G.H. 6,853*
GAY, William	Ord	POWERFUL	
GILES, William	A.B.	TRIUMPH	*(ML as William Goblin GILES)*
GILLAM, Thomas	L.M.	ISIS	
	L.M.	ISIS	*Copenhagen 1801*
GOODMAN, James	A.B.	LANCASTER	
GOULD, John	Boatswain	VENERABLE	
	A.B.	KENT	*Egypt (as John Robert GOULD)*
GRAVES, John	Pte. R.M.	ROSE	
GRAY, William	Q.M.	VETERAN	
GREEN, Henry	A.B.	TRIUMPH	
GREIG, James	A.B.	MONARCH	

CAMPERDOWN

Name	Rank	Ship	Notes
GRIFFITHS, Thomas	L.M.	RUSSELL	
	L.M.	RUSSELL	Copenhagen 1801
GUNTER, John	Ord	MONARCH	(Roll may read GUNBER)
HALEY, John	A.B.	BEDFORD	
HALL, John	A.B.	LANCASTER	
HAMILTON, John	Captain ?	ACTIVE	No M.L. A Hired Cutter Applied as Sir John. Unknown.
HAMILTON, Robert	Pte. R.M.	BEDFORD	
	Pte. R.M.	FOUDROYANT	12 Octr 1798
	Pte. R.M.	FOUDROYANT	Egypt
HAMLET, William	Q.M.	TRIUMPH	
	Q.M.	TRIUMPH	17 June 1795
HAMMERSLEY, James/John	Drummer. R.M.	POWERFUL	G.H. 10,033
HARFORD, Thomas	Pte. R.M.	VENERABLE	
	Pte. R.M.	KENT	Egypt
HARVEY, Edward	Midshipman	BEAULIEU	
	Captain. R.N.	IMPLACABLE	Syria
HATTON, John	Ord	VENERABLE	
HAYNES, John	A.B.	MONARCH	
	A.B.	MONARCH	Copenhagen 1801
HENDERSON, Alexander	A.B.	TRIUMPH	
	A.B.	TRIUMPH	17 June 1795
HENWOOD, Peter	Clerk	VETERAN	
	Purser	ACASTA	St Domingo
HEWITT, William	A.B.	TRIUMPH	Medal Roll states "2 clasps to be added". Unknown.
HIGMAN, Henry	Master's Mate	TRIUMPH	(This Roll as HENRY.G.)
	A.B.	CHARON	23rd June 1795
	Lieut. R.N.	ARETHUSA	Arethusa. 23 Augt 1806
	Lieut. R.N.	ARETHUSA	Curacoa
HILL, John	Qtr Gunner	MONMOUTH	G.H. 6,397
HILLIER, George	Midshipman	ARDENT	
	Capt's Servant	ALFRED	1 June 1794
	Lieut. R.N.	ALLIANCE	Acre. 30 May 1799
	Lieut. R.N.	TIGRE	Egypt
HODGES, Samuel	Pte. R.M.	POWERFUL	
HODGES, Thomas	L.M.	MONARCH	
	Ord	MONARCH	Copenhagen. 1801
HOLDMAN, Thomas	L.M.	DIRECTOR	
HORE, Robert	A.B.	MONARCH	
HUISWORTH, Jonas	A.B.	BELLIQUEUX	
HUNT, Thomas	Q.M's Mate	AGINCOURT	
HUNTER, Peter	Yeoman of Sheets	MONARCH	
	A.B. (?)	MONARCH	Copenhagen 1801
HUTCHINS, Charles	L.M.	VENERABLE	
	Ord	KENT	Egypt
IRONMONGER, Joseph	Ord	DIRECTOR	G.H. 6,831
JACKSON, John	Vol 1st Cl	VETERAN	
	Midshipman	VETERAN	Copenhagen 1801
JEFFRIES, John	A.B.	DIRECTOR	G.H. 8,168
JEMISON, Alexander	A.B.	LANCASTER	G.H. 1,384
JENKINS, John	Pte. R.M.	MONMOUTH	
JOHNSTON, James	Ord	POWERFUL	
	Ord	VESTAL	Egypt
JOHNSTON, John	A.B.	TRIUMPH	(This roll only as JOHNSTONE)
	Ord	TRIUMPH	17 June 1795
JOLLEY, John	Ord	POWERFUL	
JONES, James	L.M.	MONTAGU	G.H. 7,049
JONES, Robert.P.	Midshipman	AGINCOURT	
	A.B.	HARPY	Harpy. 5 Feby 1800 (Vfd Abd. Not on Roll)
	Midshipman	HARPY	Copenhagen 1801 (Vfd Abd. Not on Roll)
JUKES, J.B.	A.B.	ARDENT	
KELSALL, Edward	A.B.	AGINCOURT	On Roll as "KELSELL" as 1 Clasp On G.H. Roll as 4 Clasp. Vfd Abd for additional clasps
	Qtr Gunner	POMPEE	Martinique
	Qtr Gunner	POMPEE	Pompee. 17 June 1809
	Q.M's Mate	POMPEE	Guadaloupe GH.7960
KELSON, William	Drummer. R.M.	MONARCH	
KENDRICK, John	Pte. R.M.	DIRECTOR	
KETTLE, Robert	Ord	MONMOUTH	
	A.B.	MONMOUTH	Egypt
KING, Charles	L.M.	BEAULIEU	
KINGDON, Nathaniel	A.B.	TRIUMPH	
KNIGHTON, William	L.M.	LANCASTER	G.H. 6,821

LANGFORD, John	Boy	ISIS	
LANGLEY, Richard	A.B.	KING GEORGE	(Hired Cutter. Allowed)
LEE, George	L.M.	MONARCH	
	Ord	MONARCH	Copenhagen 1801
LESLIE, Alexander	A.B.	MONMOUTH	(Alias JAMES, John)
	A.B.	MONMOUTH	Egypt
LEVERINGTON, Joshua	A.B.	MONTAGU	
LEVERTON, Richard	A.B.	VETERAN	
	A.B.	ORION	1 June 1794
	Gunner's Mate	TEMERAIRE	Trafalgar
	Yeoman Powder Rm	ANSON	Anson. 23 Augt 1806 (Vfd Abd. Not on Roll)
	Yeoman Powder Rm	ANSON	Curacoa
LEWIS, John	Ord	MONMOUTH	
	Ord	MONMOUTH	Egypt
LIGHTON, James	Ord	MONTAGU	
LIPSON, Thomas	Vol 1st Cl	BEDFORD	
	Vol 1st Cl	WINDSOR CASTLE	14 March 1795
	Vol 1st Cl	FOUDROYANT	12 Octr 1798
LITTLE, Simon	Purser	MONTAGU	
	Clerk	AUDACIOUS	1 June 1794
LONGWILL, David	L.M.	LANCASTER	
LOWE, David	A.B.	POWERFUL	G.H. 7,188
LOWRIE, Robert	A.B.	DIRECTOR	
LUMLY, Thomas	Boy	BEDFORD	
LUNDY, Richard	L.M.	MONMOUTH	
MABEY, John	Ord	CIRCE	
MACKENZIE, James	Midshipman	AGINCOURT	G.H. 9224. A Rating.
MAGRATH, George	Actg Surgeon	RUSSELL	(This Roll as MAGARTH)
	Surgeon	KITE	Copenhagen 1801
MALADY, Thomas	Gnr's Mate	POWERFUL	
MANT, Thomas	Surgeon	ADAMANT	
MARCHINE, Irvine	Ord	MONARCH	G.H. 9,330
MARS, Andrew	Pte. R.M.	RUSSELL	
MARSDEN, John	Ord	CIRCE	
MARSHALL, John	L.M.	MONTAGU	
MARTIN, Alexander	Vol 1st Cl	TRIUMPH	
	Midshipman	PRINCE	Trafalgar
MASON, Thomas	L.M.	LANCASTER	
MATTINSON, Thomas	L.M.	BEAULIEU	
	Gunner	CAROLINE	Banda Neira
	Gunner	MUSQUITO	Navarino
MATRAM, George	Midshipman	AGINCOURT	
MAYERS, William	Pte. R.M.	MONTAGU	
McCARTHY, William	A.B.	BEDFORD	G.H. 6,788
McMILLANE, Allan	A.B.	BEDFORD	
	Boy	BEDFORD	14 March 1795
	Midshipman	FOUDROYANT	12 Octr 1798
MERRITT, William	L.M.	VETERAN	
	L.M.	ORION	1 June 1794
MIDMER, Joseph	A.B.	BELLIQUEUX	G.H. 2,123
MITCHELL, Spalding	Midshipman	BEAULIEU	
MONTAGU, William.A.	Midshipman	RUSSELL	
MONTAGUE, Thomas	Pte. R.M.	POWERFUL	G.H. 5,327
MORGAN, James	A.B.	CIRCE	
MORRIS, George	Lieut. R.N.	ARDENT	
	Midshipman	AUDACIOUS	1 June 1794
MORRISH, Nicholas	Drummer. R.M.	VETERAN	
	Drummer. R.M.	ROYAL SOVEREIGN	1 June 1794
	Drummer. R.M.	VETERAN	Copenhagen 1801
MOSS, John	Sailmaker's Mate	MONTAGU	
MOWATT, James	(Not Known)	RUSSELL	(Only on G.H. Roll)
	Quarter Gunner	BRITANNIA	Trafalgar. G.H. 9943.
MURDEN, Edward	Pte. R.M.	TRIUMPH	(M.L. as E. MORTON)
NEAL, William	A.B.	VETERAN	G.H. 6,862
NEALE, John	Midshipman	VENERABLE	(or VETERAN)
	Midshipman	KENT	Egypt
NEILD, Joseph	L.M.	MONARCH	
	L.M.	MONARCH	Copenhagen 1801
NESHAM, Charles.J.W.	Lieut. R.N.	ADAMANT	
	Captain. R.N.	INTREPID	Martinique
NIBLETT, William	Carp's Crew	ARDENT	
OWEN, John	2nd Lt. R.M.	ADAMANT	
	1st Lt. R.M.	BELLEISLE	Trafalgar
OWENS, John	Pte. R.M.	BRACKEL	
	Pte. R.M.	STATELY	Egypt
PAGE, Jonathan	L.M.	MONMOUTH	
PALMER, James	L.M.	BELLIQUEUX	
PARKE, Thomas.A.	1st Lt. R.M.	TRIUMPH	(Later R.M.A. & Col Cmmdt)
PASCALL, Henry	L.M.	ACTIVE	

CAMPERDOWN

PATTERSON, Francis	A.B.	RUSSELL	("Run" removed by Navy Board)
	Ord	PCSS ROYAL	14 March 1795
	A.B.	RUSSELL	Copenhagen 1801
	A.B.	CANOPUS	St Domingo
PATTY, Thomas	L.M.	ISIS	
PAUSNELL, James	A.B.	BEDFORD	
	A.B.	SWIFTSURE	Trafalgar
PEARCE, Richard	L.M.	POWERFUL	
PHILIPS, James.R.	Midshipman	BEAULIEU	
	Lieut. R.N.	CENTURION (P)	Centurion. 18 Sept 1804
PORTEOUS, James	Second Master	MONTAGU	
PRICE, Richard	A.B.	POWERFUL	
	A.B.	VESTAL	Egypt
PRINGLE, John	A.B.	BEDFORD	
	A.B.	FOUDROYANT	12 Octr 1798
PRIVETT, Richard	Boy	POWERFUL	
PRIVETT, Robert	Pte. R.M.	POWERFUL	
RAINS, James	Lieut. R.N.	KING GEORGE	
RICHARDS, John.S.	Purser	VETERAN	
	Purser	VETERAN	Copenhagen 1801
RICHARDSON, Charles	Lieut. R.N.	CIRCE	
	Master's Mate	ROYAL GEORGE	1 June 1794
	Lieut. R.N.	KENT	Egypt
	Captain R.N.	CAESAR	Basque Roads 1809
RIDER, James	L.M.	RUSSELL	
RIGBY, Job	Pte. R.M.	POWERFUL	
ROACH, Garrett	A.B.	MONTAGU	
ROACH, John	Qtr Gunner	BEDFORD	
ROBERTS, James	Ord	MONARCH	
	Ord	MONARCH	Copenhagen 1801
ROBERTS, Samuel	L.M.	MONTAGU	
ROBERTS, William	A.B.	BEDFORD	
	A.B.	WINDSOR CASTLE	14 March 1795
	A.B.	FOUDROYANT	12 Octr 1798
ROBERTSON, Thomas	Not Given	ARDENT	
ROBINSON, Benjamin	A.B.	VENERABLE	
	A.B.	KENT	Egypt
ROBINSON, George	L.M.	RUSSELL	
	L.M.	RUSSELL	Copenhagen 1801
ROBINSON, James	Ord	MONTAGU	
RONDEAU, Edward	Boy 2nd Cl	DIRECTOR	
ROSE, Donald	A.B.	MONARCH	G.H. 7,887
ROSE, John	A.B.	VENERABLE	
ROSS, Adam	L.M.	MONARCH	G.H. 9,175
ROUSE, William	Pte. R.M.	BEDFORD	
	Pte. R.M.	FOUDROYANT	Egypt
	Pte. R.M.	CONQUEROR	Trafalgar
SADD, John	Boy	DIRECTOR	
SALISBURY, Thomas	A.B.	AGINCOURT	
SAMMS, James	L.M.	TRIUMPH	
SAVAGE, William	Midshipman	AGINCOURT	
SCALLON, Robert	Midshipman	CIRCE	
SCOTT, Hugh	Ord	MONMOUTH	
SCOTT, James	Master's Mate	BELLIQUEUX	
SCRUTTON, John	A.B.	POWERFUL	
SHANLEY, John	Pte. R.M.	MONTAGU	
SHANNON, William	Boy	TRIUMPH	
	Coxswain	UNITE	Pelagosa. 29 Novr 1811
SHARP, Thomas.W.	A.B.	POWERFUL	G.H. 5,013
SHILLING, James	L.M.	POWERFUL	G.H. 8,608
SIMPSON, Adam/Thomas	Sgt. R.M.	DIRECTOR	
SIMPSON, Thomas	L.M.	ADAMANT	
	L.M.	Gun-Boat TEAZER	23rd June 1795
SKELTON, William	A.B.	ADAMANT	
SKILLYCOTT, Samuel	Boy	VETERAN	G.H. 8,911
SLAUGHTER, William	Vol 1st Cl	TRIUMPH	
	Vol 1st Cl	TRIUMPH	17 June 1795
	Lieut. R.N.	AMPHION	B.S. 28 Aug 1809
	Lieut. R.N.	AMPHION	B.S. 28 June 1810
SMITH, James	Ord	VENERABLE	
SMITH, John (6th)	L.M.	VENERABLE	("Run Removed" Allowed)
SMITH, John	Midshipman	MARTIN	
	Capt's Servant	IMPREGNABLE	1 June 1794
SNEYD, Clement	Lieut. R.N.	RUSSELL	
SOMERFIELD, James	Pte. R.M.	VETERAN	
	Cpl. R.M.	VETERAN	Copenhagen 1801
SOMERVILLE, William	Master's Mate	ISIS	
	Lieut. R.N.	BABET	Capture of the Desiree

SOUTHCOTT, Henry	A.B.	MONARCH	(M.L. as SOUTHCOTE)
	L.M.	QUEEN CHARLOTTE	1 June 1794
	A.B.	QUEEN CHARLOTTE	23rd June 1795
	Qtr Gunner	VETERAN	Copenhagen 1801
SPALDING, John	L.M.	ISIS	
	L.M.	ISIS	Copenhagen 1801
SPEARS, William	Carp's Crew	BELLIQUEUX	
SPILL, Samuel	Pte. R.M.	POWERFUL	
SPINK, William	L.M.	MONTAGU	
STARLING, Samuel	A.B.	MONARCH	G.H. 4,172
	A.B.	BARFLEUR	1 June 1794
STEVENS, Archibald	A.B.	BEDFORD	
	A.B.	FOUDROYANT	12 Octr 1798
	A.B.	FOUDROYANT	Egypt
STEVENS, Robert	Lt. R.M.	RUSSELL	
	Captain. R.M.	VICTORIOUS	Victorious with Rivoli
STEWART, John	A.B.	CIRCE	
STEWART, John	A.B.	RUSSELL	
	A.B.	RUSSELL	Copenhagen 1801
STILL, Joseph	L.M.	MONMOUTH	
	A.B.	MONMOUTH	Egypt
STUDDART, Thomas	Qtr Gunner	ISIS	
TAYLOR, Leonard	Bosun's Mate	BEDFORD	
	Boatswain	AMETHYST	Amethyst Wh Thetis
TEAR, John	Ord	AGINCOURT	
	Ord	AGINCOURT	Egypt
TERRY, John	Carpenter	LANCASTER	
THOMAS, Rees	Pte. R.M.	POWERFUL	
	Pte. R.M.	VESTAL	Egypt
TOMLINSON, Edward	Pte. R.M.	ARDENT	G.H. 7,670
TOWNSEND, John	L.M.	TRIUMPH	
	L.M.	TRIUMPH	17 June 1795
TRACY, John	Master's Mate	ARDENT	
TRINNAM, John	Ord	VETERAN	(M.L. as TRINNEN)
TROLLOPE, George.B.	Lieut. R.N.	TRIUMPH	
	Master's Mate	TRIUMPH	17 June 1795 (Vfd Abd. Not on Roll)
	Commander	GRIFFON	Griffon. 27 March 1812
TUDMAN, John	Pte. R.M.	MONMOUTH	
	Pte. R.M.	MONMOUTH	Egypt
TURNER, James	Pte. R.M.	BELLIQUEUX	
TURNER, John	A.B.	TRIUMPH	
	A.B.	TRIUMPH	17 June 1795
TYE, Edward	Vol 1st Cl	DIRECTOR	
USHER, Thomas	Surg's 2nd Mate	BRACKEL	(? in RUSSELL)
	Surg's 2nd Mate	RUSSELL	Copenhagen 1801
VANDERSTEEN, William	L.M.	BEAULIEU	
WAGHORN, Daniel	A.B.	ACTIVE	
WAKELING, James	A.B.	MONMOUTH	G.H. 6,050
WALKER, James	Boy	LANCASTER	(M.L. as WALKER, W.J.)
WALKER, Thomas	L.M.	MONARCH	
WALKER, Thomas	Bosun's Mate	DIRECTOR	G.H. 1,253
WALTON, William	L.M.	RUSSELL	
	L.M.	RUSSELL	Copenhagen 1801
WARDAGILL, John	L.M.	BELLIQUEUX	
WARRENER, John	A.B.	LANCASTER	
WATSON, John	L.M.	VETERAN	
WEBB, John	A.B./L.M.	RUSSELL	
	A.B.	RUSSELL	Copenhagen 1801
WEBBER, John	Coxswain	VENERABLE	
WEST, James	A.B.	BEDFORD	
WICKHAM, William	Pte. R.M.	LANCASTER	
	Pte. R.M.	SIR FRANCIS DRAKE	Java
WILKINSON, Henry	Pte. R.M.	BEDFORD	
	Pte. R.M.	TIGRE	Acre. 30 May 1799
	Pte. R.M.	TIGRE	Egypt
WILLIAMS, James	Pte. R.M.	BEDFORD	
WILLIAMS, John	Captain. R.M.	MONTAGU	
YOUNG, George	Pte. R.M.	VETERAN	
	Pte. R.M.	FREIJA	Guadaloupe

PHOEBE 21 DECR 1797
Capture of the French frigate NEREIDE, off the Islands of Scilly.

(5)

ALLEN, Robert	Yeoman of Sheets	PHOEBE	
LAURIE, Stephen	Boy 3rd Cl	PHOEBE	
	Boy 2nd Cl	PHOEBE	*Phoebe. 19 Feby 1801*
	A.B.	PHOEBE	*Trafalgar*
	A.B.	PHOEBE	*Off Tamatave. 20 May 1811*
	A.B.	PHOEBE	*Java*
	Capt Fore Top	PHOEBE	*Phoebe. 28 March 1814*
PECHELL, Samuel.J.B.	Midshipman	PHOEBE	
	Midshipman	PHOEBE	*Phoebe. 19 Feby 1801*
PROWETT, Charles	Midshipman	PHOEBE	
	Master's Mate	PHOEBE	*Phoebe. 19 Feby 1801*
REEDIN, John	Ord	PHOEBE	
	A.B.	PHOEBE	*Phoebe. 19 Feby 1801*
	Quarter Gunner	PHOEBE	*Trafalgar*

MARS 21 APRIL 1798
Capture of the French HERCULE, 74, at Passage du Raz, Brest.

(26)

ADAMS, Richard	A.B.	MARS	(M.L. as ADMANS)
ARTHUR, Robert	Ord	MARS	G.H.6924
	L.M.	MARS	17 June 1795 (Vfd Abd. Not on Roll)
BACCHUS, Robert	Boy 3rd Cl	MARS	G.H.4882
	Boy 3rd Cl	MARS	17 June 1795 (Vfd Abd. Not on Roll)
BADCOCK, Squire	Boy 2nd Cl	MARS	
	Boy 2nd Cl	MARS	17 June 1795
BETTY, Christopher.W.	Midshipman	MARS	
	Midshipman	MAJESTIC	1 June 1794
	Lieut. R.N.	DREADNOUGHT	Trafalgar
BINNINGTON, Thomas	Ord	MARS	G.H.5007 & M.L. as BENNINGTON
	Boy 2nd Cl	CAPTAIN	St Vincent (Vfd Abd.GH Roll)
BOLTON, Francis.L.	Ord	MARS	
	Boy 2nd Cl	MARS	17 June 1795
BOWKER, John	Lieut. R.N.	MARS	
	Lieut. R.N.	MARS	17 June 1795 (Vfd Abd. Not on Roll)
BRADLEY, William	L.M.	MARS	
	Actg Lieut. R.N.	CUMBERLAND	B.S. 1 Nov 1809
BROOM, John	L.M.	MARS	G.H.8083
	L.M.	MARS	17 June 1795 (Vfd Abd. Not on Roll)
CAVANAUGH, Francis	Pte. R.M.	MARS	
DENISON, Edward	Midshipman	MARS	
	A.B.	MARS	17 June 1795
ELLIOTT, John	Vol 1st Cl	MARS	
	Clerk	RUSSELL	Copenhagen 1801
	Purser	ARETHUSA	Arethusa. 23 Augt 1806
	Purser	ARETHUSA	Curacoa (Probably received two Medals. (a) 1 Clasp Copenhagen (b) other 3 clasps)
FOOT, John	Ord	MARS	
GARRETT, James	A.B.	MARS	
	Ord	MARS	17 June 1795
HOWARTH, William	A.B.	MARS	
	Ord	MARS	17 June 1795
MONTGOMERY, John	A.B.	MARS	
	A.B.	MARS	17 June 1795
MORGAN, Thomas. Rev.	Chaplain	MARS	
	Chaplain	ALFRED	1 June 1794
RILEY, Charles	2 Borne Ord & LM	MARS	
SAUNDERS, Thomas	Ord	MARS	
	Ord	MARS	17 June 1795 (Vfd Abd. Not on Roll)
	L.M.	COMUS	Comus. 15 Augt 1807
SAXBY, Francis	A.B.	MARS	
	A.B.	MARS	17 June 1795 (Vfd Abd. Not on Roll)

STEVENS, Richard	Barber	MARS	
	L.M.	MARS	*17 June 1795*
STEWART, Charles	Ord	MARS	*G.H.9346*
	A.B.	VICTORY	*Trafalgar*
TAYLER, Richard	Ord	MARS	*(M.L. as TAYLOR)*
	Boy 2nd Cl	MARS	*17 June 1795*
TUCKER, William	Ord	MARS	*G.H.9101*
	Ord	MARS	*17 June 1795*
WEST, John	Ord	MARS	
	L.M.	MARS	*17 June 1795*
			(Vfd Abd. Not on Roll)

(3) ISLE St MARCOU. 6 MAY 1798

Successful defence of the Islands of St MARCOUF, Le Havre.

(Real date 7 May 1798. Medal Roll has 6 May, Navy Lists have 5 May in text, but 6 May in Index.)

CAMPBELL, John.	Supn Pte. R.M.	BADGER	
ENSOR, James	Supn 2nd Lt R.M.	SANDFLY	
LAWRENCE, Thomas.L.	Supn 2nd Lt R.M.	BADGER	
	Lt. R.M.	PEARL	*Egypt*

(23) LION 15 JULY 1798

Action with four Spanish frigates & capture of one — SANTA DOROTEA, off Cartagena, Spain.

(Date incorrectly shown as 6 July 1798 in Medal Roll)

BOARDY, James	Boy 3rd Cl	LION	*(M.L. as BOORDY)*
BOARDY, William	Ord	LION	*(M.L. as BOORDY)*
BOYES, Henry	Midshipman	LION	
	Lieut. R.N.	CALEDONIA	*Basque Roads. 1809*
	Lieut. R.N.	CALEDONIA	*B.S. 27 Sept 1810*
BULLOCK, William	A.B.	LION	
CROWTHER, Robert	Q.M.	LION	
DECOEURDOUX, George.J.	Midshipman	LION	
	Lieut. R.N.	MARS	*Trafalgar*
DIXON, Manley Hall	Midshipman	LION	
	Lieut. R.N.	HORATIO	*Horatio. 10 Feby 1809*
GODDARD, John	Ord	LION	
GOODING, James.G.	Midshipman	LION	
HOLLINGSHEAD, John	Boy 2nd Cl	LION	
LINKS, James	L.M.	LION	*(M.L. as LYNX)*
MURRY, Robert	Ord	LION	
PARSLOW, Richard	L.M.	LION	
PATEY, Joseph	Midshipman	LION	
RIPP, Robert	Ord	LION	*G.H. 4,293*
STAPLES, William	L.M.	LION	
TAYLOR, Richard	Pte. R.M.	LION	
THOMAS, William	L.M.	LION	
TREMLETT, W.H.B.	Lieut. R.N.	LION	*(see note below)*
	Midshipman	ROYAL SOVEREIGN	*1 June 1794*
	Midshipman	ROYAL SOVEREIGN	*17 June 1795*
TROTTER, Joseph	A.B.	LION	
VICKERY, John	Pte. R.M.	LION	*(M.L. as VICARY/VICARRY)*
	Sgt. R.M.	REDPOLE	*Basque Roads 1809*
WHYBOURN, William	A.B.	LION	*(M.L. as WEYBOURN)*
WRIGHT, Philip	Midshipman	LION	

NOTE. As an example of the accidental mistakes made in the logging and issuing of the clasps to this N.G.S. Medal, the case of TREMLETT's clasps is well documented. His name does not appear on the Medal Roll for the clasps of "LION 15 July 1798" and "17 June 1795". In Admiralty Digest Book for 1849, Section 85a (ADM 12/511) the following statements can be found:—

"Naval Medals. (Undated, but circa February 1849).
  Vice Admiral Tremlett states that his claims for 'Royal Sovereign 17th June 1795' and 'Lion 15th July 1798' have been omitted in the number of clasps to his Medal and requests error to be rectified."

The three clasps mentioned in the Roll above have been sighted on the Medal awarded to W.H.B. TREMLETT.

(326) NILE (G.M.)
Battle of The Nile on 1 August 1798.

ADAIR, Thomas.B.	1st Lt. R.M.	ALEXANDER	
AINSLIE, Thomas	A.B.	GOLIATH	
	Ord	BRITTANIA	*St Vincent*
	Gunner's Mate	CORNELIA	*Java*
ALEXANDER, John	Ord	MINOTAUR	
ANDREWS, John	Ord	ALEXANDER	
ANTRAM, George	Midshipman	VANGUARD	
APPLEBY, Barney	A.B.	ORION	
ARCHARD, John	Ord	ORION	(Alias ORCHARD)
	L.M.	ORION	*St Vincent*
AYLMER, Hon Frederick.W.	Lieut. R.N.	SWIFTSURE	
	Midshipman	SYREN	*B.S. 15 Mar 1793*
	Lieut. R.N.	SWIFTSURE	*Egypt*
	Captain. R.N.	SEVERN	*Algiers*
BABBAGE, Joseph	A.B.	MINOTAUR	
BAIN, Alexander	Midshipman	CULLODEN	
	Quartermaster	CULLODEN	*1 June 1794*
	Midshipman	CULLODEN	*Nile (A Rating ?)*
BAKER, Richard	A.B.	BELLEROPHON	G.H. 6,240
	L.M.	BELLEROPHON	*1 June 1794*
BAKER, William	L.M.	ZEALOUS	G.H. 8,182
BANTON, Leonard	A.B.	VANGUARD	
BARNES, John	Q.M's Mate	MAJESTIC	
	Quarter Gunner	MAJESTIC	*1 June 1794*
BARNS, John	A.B.	MINOTAUR	
BAZING, John.H.	Boy	THESEUS	(Not yet found)
	Boy	THESEUS	*Acre. 30 May 1799 (N' yet F')*
	Ord?	COLOSSUS?	*Trafalgar?*
BEADLE, William	Boy 2nd Cl	GOLIATH	
	Servant	BARFLEUR	*1 June 1794*
	Boy 2nd Cl	GOLIATH	*St Vincent*
BEATTY, George	2nd Lt. R.M.	THESEUS	
	2nd Lt. R.M.	THESEUS	*Acre. 30 May 1799*
BEER, William	Pte. R.M.	CULLODEN	
	Pte. R.M.	CULLODEN	*1 June 1794*
	Pte. R.M.	CULLODEN	*St Vincent*
BELLAMY, George	Surgeon	BELLEROPHON	
	Actg Surgeon	RANGER	*1 June 1794*
BRENHAM, John	A.B.	CULLODEN	
	A.B.	CULLODEN	*1 June 1794*
	A.B.	CULLODEN	*St Vincent*
BRAUND, George	1st Lt. R.M.	ALEXANDER	
BROADERS, Valentine	Ord	MAJESTIC	
BROBIN, Edward	Ord	DEFENCE	(M.L. as BROVIN)
	Ord	DEFENCE	*Copenhagen 1801*
BROADRIB, James	Pte. R.M.	ALEXANDER	
BROMWELL, John	L.M.	DEFENCE	
BROWN, Alexander	A.B.	SWIFTSURE	
	Coxswain	ROYALIST	*Royalist. 29 Decr 1812*
BRYDEN, Edward	Q.M's Mate	CULLODEN	
	A.B.	CULLODEN	*1 June 1794*
	Q.M's Mate	CULLODEN	*St Vincent*
BUCKLAND, Peter	A.B.	ZEALOUS	
BUCKLEY, Benjamin	Pte. R.M.	VANGUARD	
BUCKMASTER, Ishmael	A.B.	AUDACIOUS	
	A.B.	LIVELY	*Lively. 13 March 1795* (Vfd Abd. Not on Roll)
	A.B.	LIVELY	*St Vincent*
BURCH, Peter	Midshipman	GOLIATH	(Became a Gunner)
	Midshipman	BRITANNIA	*St Vincent*
BURGIN, Joseph	Ord	VANGUARD	(M.L. alias COXHEAD) G.H.161.
	Ord	VICTORY	*Trafalgar (GH as BERGWIN)*
BURNETT, William	Surg's 1st Mate	GOLIATH	
	Surg's 3rd Mate	GOLIATH	*St Vincent*
	Surgeon	ATHENIENNE	*Egypt*
	Surgeon	DEFIANCE	*Trafalgar (Kntd 1831)*
BURROUGHS, William	Pte. R.M.	VANGUARD	(M.L. as BURROWS)
BURROWS, Henry	L.M.	CULLODEN	
	L.M.	CULLODEN	*St Vincent*
BURT, John	L.M.	SWIFTSURE	
	L.M.	SWIFTSURE	*Egypt*
BUTLAND, Henry	A.B.	MINOTAUR	
BUTLER, Henry	Pte. R.M.	MINOTAUR	
	Pte. R.M.	MINOTAUR	*Egypt*
	Pte. R.M.	NAIAD	*Trafalgar*
BUTLER, John	A.B.	THESEUS	
	A.B.	THESEUS	*Acre. 30 May 1799* (Vfd Abd. Not on Roll)

BUTLER, Richard	A.B.	SWIFTSURE	
	Ord	SWIFTSURE	Egypt
BYRNE, James	Pte. R.M.	THESEUS	(M.L. as BURNE)
CAMPBELL, John	Q.M's Mate	DEFENCE	
CAMPION, William	Ord	AUDACIOUS	
	Servant	AUDACIOUS	1 June 1794
CAPEL, Thomas Bladen	Lieut. R.N.	VANGUARD	(Member Flag Officer's Cmmtte)
	Midshipman	SANSPAREIL	23rd June 1795
	Captain. R.N.	PHOEBE	Trafalgar
CHALLENOR, Robert	A.B.	DEFENCE	G.H. 7,926 as CHANDLER
	A.B.	DEFENCE	1 June 1794
CHAMBERS, James	L.M.	GOLIATH	G.H. 9,443 (ML as CHALMERS)
	L.M.	GOLIATH	St Vincent
CHAMBERS, Robert	L.M.	MAJESTIC	
	L.M.	MAJESTIC	1 June 1794
CHAPLAN, John	A.B.	MINOTAUR	
CHAPPLE, Joseph	L.M.	MAJESTIC	
CHEALE, Edward	Ord	ZEALOUS	
CLARKE, James	Pte. R.M.	SWIFTSURE	
	Pte. R.M.	LATONA	1 June 1794
	Pte. R.M.	SOUTHAMPTON	St Vincent
CLARKE, Peter	Pte. R.M.	DEFENCE	
COFFIN, C.P.	Chaplain	MINOTAUR	(M.L. alias PYNE, Charles)
COLLIER, Francis.A.	Vol 1st Cl	VANGUARD	
	Commander	CIRCE (P)	Off the Pearl Rock. 13 Dec 1808
	Captain. R.N.	CIRCE	Martinique
CONNOLLY, Richard.L.	A.B.	THESEUS	(Became Rtd Cdr in 1845)
CONSITT, Thomas	Master's Mate	DEFENCE	
	Midshipman	DEFENCE	1 June 1794
COOK, John	Boy	ALEXANDER	
COOK, William	L.M.	GOLIATH	
	L.M.	GOLIATH	St Vincent
COOPER, Andrew	Boy	LEANDER	G.H. 9,386
COOPER, George	L.M.	BELLEROPHON	
CRABB, John	Pte. R.M.	THESEUS	
	Pte. R.M.	CAPTAIN	St Vincent
CRAWFORD, John	Ord	ALEXANDER	
CRAYDON, Richard	A.B.	VANGUARD	
CROSBY, John	L.M.	BELLEROPHON	
CULLIN, William	Captain of Top	GOLIATH	(M.L. as COLLINS) GH.5871
or CULLEN	Captain of Top	GOLIATH	St Vincent
CUMMINGS, James	A.B.	AUDACIOUS	
	A.B.	AUDACIOUS	1 June 1794
CUNNINGHAM, James	L.M.	ALEXANDER	
DANE, Gustave	Ord	GOLIATH	
	A.B.	BRITANNIA	St Vincent
	Ord	ELEPHANT	Copenhagen 1801
DARLINGTON, Joseph	Ord	CULLODEN	
	Servant	CULLODEN	1 June 1794
	Boy	CULLODEN	St Vincent
DASHWOOD, Robert	Boy 2nd Cl	MAJESTIC	G.H. 9,301
DAVENPORT, John	A.B.	SWIFTSURE	
	A.B.	SWIFTSURE	Egypt
DAVEY, Henry	L.M.	MAJESTIC	
DAVIES, David	Qtr Gunner	VANGUARD	
	A.B.	BEDFORD	Camperdown
	A.B.	FOUDROYANT	Egypt
DAVIS, William	Yeoman of Sheets	SWIFTSURE	
DAWES, Daniel.B.	Purser	CULLODEN	
DAY, John	Boy 2nd Cl	ALEXANDER	
DAY, Nathaniel	Ord	DEFENCE	
DEAGON, Edward	Q.M.	MINOTAUR	
	Gunner	PHAETON	B.S. 27 Oct 1800
	Gunner	ATLAS	St Domingo
DENCH, Thomas	Midshipman	GOLIATH	
	Midshipman	BRITANNIA	St Vincent
DENNIS, Philip	Pte. R.M.	BELLEROPHON	G.H. 9,532
	Pte. R.M.	LEVIATHAN	Trafalgar
DE PAGE, John	A.B.	ORION	
	A.B.	CRESCENT	Crescent. 20 Octr 1793
	A.B.	ORION	23rd June 1795
	A.B.	ORION	St Vincent
DONNELL, Peter	Ord	CULLODEN	(M.L. as DOUNELL)
or DONNELLY	Ord	CULLODEN	St Vincent
DOWELL, James	L.M.	MAJESTIC	
DUMMER, George	Vol 1st Cl	GOLIATH	
	Ord	GOLIATH	St Vincent
DUNCANSON, Robert	Master's Mate	AUDACIOUS	
DYKES, John	Pte. R.M.	MAJESTIC	
	Pte. R.M.	LEVIATHAN	Trafalgar
EDWARDS, Henry	A.B.	DEFENCE	
	L.M.	DEFENCE	1 June 1794
EDWARDS, John	A.B.	CULLODEN	

NILE

EGGLISTONE, Francis	Quarter Gunner	BELLEROPHON	
	A.B.	BELLEROPHON	*1 June 1794*
	Sailmaker's Crew	PEGASUS	*Egypt*
ELLIOT, Hon George	Midshipman	GOLIATH	
	Vol 1st Cl	BRITANNIA	*St Vincent*
	Lieut. R.N.	ST GEORGE	*Copenhagen 1801*
	Captain. R.N.	MODESTE	*Java*
ELLIS, James	Pte. R.M.	MINOTAUR	
EVANS, Thomas	Pte. R.M.	ZEALOUS	
EVANS, William (2)	Ord	MINOTAUR	
	Ord	MINOTAUR	*Egypt*
EVANS, William	A.B.	VANGUARD	
EWINS, John	L.M.	LEANDER	
FALLICK, William	Ord	ORION	
	L.M.	ORION	*23rd June 1795*
	L.M.	ORION	*St Vincent*
FEATHER, James	Pte. R.M.	MINOTAUR	
	Pte. R.M.	WEAZLE	*Weazel. 22 Feby 1812*
	Pte. R.M.	WEAZLE	*Weazel. 22 April 1813*
			(Vfd Abd. Not on Roll)
FERGUSON, John	L.M.	GOLIATH	
	L.M.	GOLIATH	*St Vincent*
	Ord	ELEPHANT	*Copenhagen 1801*
FERGUSSON, John	L.M.	CULLODEN	*G.H. 9,571*
	L.M.	CULLODEN	*St Vincent*
FINLAY, John	A.B.	MINOTAUR	
	Midshipman	MINOTAUR	*Egypt*
FLANDRYN, Daniel	Pte. R.M.	GOLIATH	
	Pte. R.M.	GOLIATH	*St Vincent*
	Cpl. R.M.	ASTRAEA	*Egypt*
FORBES, John	Midshipman	MINOTAUR	
	Lieut. R.N.	FLORENTINA	*Egypt*
	Lieut. R.N.	CANOPUS	*St Domingo*
FURY, John	L.M.	SWIFTSURE	*(M.L. as FURSE)*
	Ord	SWIFTSURE	*Egypt*
FURZE, Samuel	A.B.	CULLODEN	
FYNN, John	Ord	ALEXANDER	
GALE, John	A.B.	BELLEROPHON	
	Carp's Crew	BELLEROPHON	*1 June 1794*
	Carp's Crew	BELLEROPHON	*17 June 1795*
	Carp's Mate	SPENCER	*Gut of Gibraltar. 12 July 1801*
	Carpenter	NORTHUMBERLAND	*Northumberland. 22 May 1812*
GALE, John	A.B.	CULLODEN	
	L.M.	CULLODEN	*1 June 1794*
GAMMELL, Robert	L.M.	MAJESTIC	
GARRETT, John	A.B.	DEFENCE	
	Ord	DEFENCE	*1 June 1794*
GHOST, Joseph	L.M.	ZEALOUS	*G.H. 5,073*
GIBSON, William	L.M.	LEANDER	
GILBERT, Michael	A.B.	MINOTAUR	
GILHAM, James	Coxswain	THESEUS	
	Coxswain	THESEUS	*Acre. 30 May 1799*
			(Vfd Abd. Not on Roll)
GILL, James	A.B.	MINOTAUR	
GILMER, James	Ord	ALEXANDER	*(M.L. as GILLMORE)*
GILMOUR, Alexander	Lieut. R.N.	ORION	
	Lieut. R.N.	ORION	*St Vincent*
GODWIN, George	L.M.	ZEALOUS	*(M.L. as GOODING)*
GOODENOUGH, George	Gunner's Mate	DEFENCE	
	Quarter Gunner	DEFENCE	*1 June 1794*
	Q.M's Mate	POLYPHEMUS	*Copenhagen 1801*
GORDON, James.A.	Midshipman	GOLIATH	
	Midshipman	REVOLUTIONNAIRE	*23rd June 1795*
	Midshipman	NAMUR	*St Vincent*
	Captain. R.N.	MERCURY	*Off Rota. 4 April 1808*
	Captain. R.N.	ACTIVE	*Lissa*
	Captain. R.N.	ACTIVE	*Pelagosa. 29 Novr 1811*
	Captain. R.N.	SEAHORSE	*The Potomac. 17 Aug 1814*
GRANT, John	A.B.	CULLODEN	*G.H. 6,459*
	A.B.	CULLODEN	*St Vincent*
GRANT, Joseph	L.M.	BELLEROPHON	
GREEN, James	A.B.	ZEALOUS	
	A.B.	VENERABLE	*Gut of Gibraltar. 12 July 1801*
GREEN, John	A.B.	DEFENCE	
HALL, Robert	L.M.	VANGUARD	
HALL, William	Pte. R.M.	MAJESTIC	
	Pte. R.M.	MONTAGU	*1 June 1794*

HALLON, Lewis	A.B.	DEFENCE	G.H. 4,694
HAMSHIRE, James	Boy	DEFENCE	
	Capt's Servant	DEFENCE	1 June 1794
	Ord	DEFENCE	Copenhagen 1801
HARLARTON, Thomas	Sgt. R.M.	MUTINE	(M.L. as HARLETON)
	Pte. R.M.	VICTORY	St Vincent
HARPER, John	Lieut. R.N.	DEFENCE	
	Lieut. R.N.	EXCELLENT	B.S. 29 July 1809
HARRIS, George	Ord	ALEXANDER	
HART, Richard	Pte. R.M.	VANGUARD	
	Pte. R.M.	IRRESISTIBLE	23rd June 1795
HART, Robert	1st Lt. R.M.	MAJESTIC	(Was present for but not on Roll of "Gut of Gibraltar".)
HARVEY, Charles	Pte. R.M.	MAJESTIC	G.H. 9,093
	Pte. R.M.	MONTAGU	1 June 1794
HASLING, Charles	Boy 3rd Cl	AUDACIOUS	
HATTON, John	Pte. R.M.	BELLEROPHON	
	Pte. R.M.	BELLEROPHON	1 June 1794
	Pte. R.M.	BELLEROPHON	17 June 1795
	Cpl. R.M.	SPENCER	Gut of Gibraltar. 12 July 1801
HAWES, William.J.	Vol 1st Cl	AUDACIOUS	
	Captain's Servant	AUDACIOUS	1 June 1974
	Ord	CONQUEROR	Trafalgar
HAWKER, Thomas	Ord	ALEXANDER	
HAYNE, Thomas	L.M.	SWIFTSURE	
	L.M.	SWIFTSURE	Egypt
HAYWARD, John	L.M.	ZEALOUS	
HENDERSON, Menzies	A.B.	GOLIATH	
	A.B.	GOLIATH	St Vincent
	A.B.	RAMILLIES	Copenhagen 1801
HICKS, William	Boy	MAJESTIC	
	A.B.	CANOPUS	St Domingo
HIGGINS, William	Ord	ALEXANDER	
HILL, George	L.M.	LEANDER	
HILL, John	Vol 1st Cl	GOLIATH	
	Boy 3rd Cl	GOLIATH	St Vincent
	Vol 1st Cl	ELEPHANT	Copenhagen 1801
HILL, John	Lieut. R.N.	MINOTAUR	
	Commander	HEROINE	Egypt
HILLMAN, Richard	A.B.	CULLODEN	
	Ord	CULLODEN	1 June 1794
	A.B.	CULLODEN	St Vincent
HINDMARSH, John	Midshipman	BELLEROPHON	
	Capt's Servant	BELLEROPHON	1 June 1794
	Vol 1st Cl	BELLEROPHON	17 June 1795
	Midshipman	SPENCER	Gut of Gibraltar. 12 July 1801
	Lieut. R.N.	PHOEBE	Trafalgar
	Lieut. R.N.	BEAGLE	Basque Roads 1809
	Lieut. R.N.	NISUS	Java
HOBSON, Thomas	A.B.	DEFENCE	
HOLLAND, Thomas	A.B.	ALEXANDER	G.H. 6,284
	A.B.	LIVELY	Lively. 13 March 1795 (Vfd Abd. Not on Roll)
	A.B.	LIVELY	St Vincent
HOSKIN, George	L.M.	ALEXANDER	
HUGHES, William	A.B.	LEANDER	
HULL, Arthur	2nd Lt. R.M.	THESEUS	
	2nd Lt. R.M.	THESEUS	Acre. 30 May 1799
HUNT, Thomas	L.M.	VANGUARD	
HUNTER, Peter	L.M.	LEANDER	
IRVIN, George	A.B.	LEANDER	
ISAACSON, Sutville	Clerk	VANGUARD	
JACKSON, James	Vol 1st Cl	ORION	
	Vol 1st Cl	ORION	St Vincent
JACKSON, Thomas	Ord	GOLIATH	
	Ord	GOLIATH	St Vincent
JACKSON, William	Ord	VANGUARD	
JAMES, Thomas	Cpl. R.M.	ALEXANDER	
	Pte. R.M.	ORION	1 June 1794
	Sgt. R.M.	MARS	Trafalgar
JARRETT, Thomas	Carpenter	LEANDER	
JENKINS, Daniel	Pte. R.M.	BELLEROPHON	
JOB, William	Pte. R.M.	CULLODEN	
	Pte. R.M.	CULLODEN	1 June 1794
	Pte. R.M.	CULLODEN	St Vincent
JOHNSON, John	A.B.	GOLIATH	
	A.B.	BRITANNIA	14 March 1795
	A.B.	BRITANNIA	St Vincent
	A.B.	ELEPHANT	Copenhagen 1801
	Yeoman of Sheets	CORNELIA	Java

NILE

JOHNSON, William	L.M.	ALEXANDER	
KEAN, Michael	A.B.	ORION	
	L.M.	ORION	St Vincent
KEATS, Robert	A.B.	ALEXANDER	
KILERT, Thomas	A.B.	SWIFTSURE	
KITE, James	A.B.	CULLODEN	
	Ord	CULLODEN	1 June 1794
	A.B.	CULLODEN	St Vincent
KITT, Joseph	A.B.	ORION	
	A.B.	CRESCENT	Crescent. 20 Octr 1793
	A.B.	ORION	23rd June 1795
	A.B.	ORION	St Vincent
KNIGHT, Thomas	Boy 3rd Cl	CULLODEN	
	Capt's Servant	CULLODEN	1 June 1794
	Boy 3rd Cl	CULLODEN	St Vincent
LAURENCE, John	L.M.	THESEUS	
	L.M.	THESEUS	Acre. 30 May 1799
			(Vfd Abd. Not on Roll)
	Ord	EURYALUS	Trafalgar
LAWSON, Gilbert	A.B.	SWIFTSURE	
	A.B.	SWIFTSURE	Egypt
	Quarter Gunner	CAESAR	4 Novr 1805
	Gunner's Mate	CAESAR	Basque Roads 1809
	Gunner	PHOEBE	Phoebe. 28 March 1814
LECKEY, Robert	A.B.	CULLODEN	
	Ord	CULLODEN	1 June 1794
	A.B.	CULLODEN	St Vincent
	A.B.	PIQUE	Egypt
LEE, James	Ord	MINOTAUR	
	A.B.	MINOTAUR	Egypt
LEE, John	Pte. R.M.	DEFENCE	
	Cpl. R.M.	HYDRA	Hydra. 6 Augt 1807
LEE, John	A.B.	AUDACIOUS	(Probably a 2 clasp Medal)
LE MAISTRE, John	Boy	VANGUARD	(M.L. as MASTRASS)
LENARD, Joseph	Ord	CULLODEN	
	Ord	CULLODEN	1 June 1794
	Ord	CULLODEN	St Vincent
	Yeoman of Sheets	NAIAD	Trafalgar
LOWCAY, Henry	Lieut. R.N.	CULLODEN	
LUKE, James	A.B.	MINOTAUR	
	A.B.	MINOTAUR	Egypt
LUKE, Oliver	Cpl. R.M.	ALEXANDER	
LYNCH, Edward	Pte. R.M.	ALEXANDER	
MADGE, William	M.A.A.	ORION	
	Quarter Gunner	CRESCENT	Crescent. 20 Octr 1793
	Quarter Gunner	ORION	St Vincent
MAGIVEREN, Dennis	L.M.	ZEALOUS	
MAHONY, Timothy	Ord	DEFENCE	
	Ord	DEFENCE	Copenhagen 1801
MAINWARING, Rowland	Midshipman	MAJESTIC	
	Midshipman	DEFENCE	Copenhagen 1801
MAITLAND, James	Midshipman	BELLEROPHON	(Never a Lieut. R.N. ? Rating)
	Ord	BELLEROPHON	1 June 1794
MALCOLM, James	A.B.	SWIFTSURE	
MANSELL, Thomas	Midshipman	ORION	
	Midshipman	CRESCENT	Crescent. 20 Octr 1793
	Midshipman	ORION	23rd June 1795
	Master's Mate	ORION	St Vincent
MARRETT, Joseph	Midshipman	ORION	
	Midshipman	CRESENT	Crescent. 20 Octr 1793
	Midshipman	ORION	23rd June 1795
			(Vfd Abd. Not on Roll)
	Midshipman	ORION	St Vincent
	Lieut. R.N.	MARTIAL	Basque Roads 1809
MARSHALL, Henry.M.	A.B.	SWIFTSURE	
	Midshipman	SWIFTSURE	Egypt
MARSHALL, William	A.B.	VANGUARD	
	L.M.	VICTORY	St Vincent
MARTIN, William	A.B.	SWIFTSURE	
	A.B.	GANGES	Copenhagen 1801
MASTERS, John (2)	A.B.	CULLODEN	
McLINTOCK, Robert	A.B.	SWIFTSURE	

McGLADERE, John	Yeoman of Sheets	CULLODEN	(Also as M'GLADERY on Roll)
	Yeoman of Sheets	CULLODEN	St Vincent
	Actg Lieut. R.N.	OTTER	Otter. 18 Septr 1810
			(Vfd Abd. Not on Roll)
McLAUGHLAN, James	A.B.	BELLEROPHON	
	Ord	BELLEROPHON	1 June 1794
	A.B.	THUNDERER	Trafalgar
MICHAEL, Robert	A.B.	CULLODEN	
MIDDLETON, Joseph	Pte. R.M.	VANGUARD	
	Pte. R.M.	VETERAN	Copenhagen 1801
MILLINGTON, Abraham	L.M.	ZEALOUS	G.H. 6,105
MILNE, Benjamin	Ord	MUTINE	(M.L. as MILLER)
	Ord	COLOSSUS	St Vincent
MITCHELL, John	A.B.	SWIFTSURE	
MOODIE, Alexander	Quarter Gunner	CULLODEN	
MORGAN, James	A.B.	SWIFTSURE	
	A.B.	SWIFTSURE	Egypt
MORGAN, Thomas	L.M.	LEANDER	(Alias WARD, Samuel)
MORRIS, Griffiths	Pte. R.M.	AUDACIOUS	G.H. 9,506
	Pte. R.M.	SHANNON	Shannon Wh Chesapeake
MORRISH, Frederick	L.M.	ALEXANDER	
MUNDY, George	Lieut. R.N.	GOLIATH	
	Lieut. R.N.	BLENHEIM	St Vincent
	Captain. R.N.	HYDRA	Hydra. 6 Augt 1807
NAYLOR, Edward	1st Lt R.M.	VANGUARD	
	1st Lt R.M.	ACASTA	St Domingo
NEWTON, Isaac	Carp's Crew	THESEUS	
	Carp's Crew	THESEUS	Acre. 30 May 1799
	Supn (Unrated)	DANGEREUSE	Egypt
NOWLAND, Michael	A.B.	THESEUS	G.H. 5,479 as NEWLAND
or NEWLAND	A.B.	THESEUS	Acre. 30 May 1799
			(Vfd Abd. Not on Roll)
OFFICE, Joshua	Pte. R.M.	VANGUARD	
OFFLEY, Charles	Ord	MAJESTIC	
OSBORNE, Samuel	Ord	VANGUARD	
OSBORNE, William	A.B.	DEFENCE	
OWEN, William	A.B.	THESEUS	(M.L. as OWENS)
	A.B.	THESEUS	Acre. 30 May 1799
	A.B.	THESEUS	Basque Roads 1809
PAGE, William	A.B.	VANGUARD	
PARDY, John	Ord	BELLEROPHON	
	Ord	BELLEROPHON	1 June 1794
PARKER, William	Midshipman	GOLIATH	
	Midshipman	ST GEORGE	14 March 1795
	Midshipman	BRITANNIA	St Vincent
	Lieut. R.N.	DRUID	Egypt. (This clasp issued on a separate Medal)
PARR, Alexander.F.	Midshipman	SWIFTSURE	(Possibly 2 Medals awarded)
	Midshipman	PENELOPE	Egypt
	Midshipman	AGAMEMNON	Trafalgar
	Midshipman	AGAMEMNON	St Domingo (Medal known as single clasp "NILE", agreeing with Navy List – not Roll)
PARR, Thomas	A.B.	AUDACIOUS	
PATRIARCHE, Charles	Master's Mate	DEFENCE	
	Lieut. R.N.	SUPERB	Gut of Gibraltar. 12 July 1801
			(Vfd Abd. Not on Roll)
	Lieut. R.N.	SUPERB	St Domingo
PATTERSON, William	Not Given	ALEXANDER	(M.L. as Walter PATTERSON)
PEALING, Michael	Ord	MUTINE	
	Capt' of Mast	SHANNON	Shannon Wh Chesapeake
PEARCE, John	Ord	ALEXANDER	G.H. 9907
PEARSE, John	Midshipman	CULLODEN	
	Midshipman	CULLODEN	St Vincent
PEARSON, George	Ord	ORION	
	Ord	ORION	23rd June 1795
	L.M.	ORION	St Vincent
PHILIPPS, John.G.	Midshipman	MINOTAUR	
	Midshipman	MINOTAUR	Egypt
PICKTHORN, John	L.M.	ALEXANDER	(Applied as Lieut. R.N.)
POPE, William	Ord	CULLODEN	
	Ord	DREADNOUGHT	Trafalgar
PORTER, John	Boy 3rd Cl	VANGUARD	G.H. 8,672
POUPARD, Abraham	L.M.	SWIFTSURE	
	Ord	SWIFTSURE	Egypt
PRYOR, John	A.B.	MAJESTIC	
	L.M.	MAJESTIC	1 June 1794
RAINSFORTH, Martin	Boy 2nd Cl	ALEXANDER	G.H. 3,192
RANDALL, Daniel.W.	Midshipman	AUDACIOUS	
RANN, John	Carp's Crew	SWIFTSURE	
	Carp's Crew	CHARON	1 June 1794 (M.L. as RAND)
REYNOLDS, James	Pte. R.M.	VANGUARD	G.H. 9305

NILE

RHYMES, George	Ord	ALEXANDER	(M.L. as G. RIMER.)
			Probably a 2 clasp Medal
RICHARDSON, William	L.M.	BELLEROPHON	
RICKERD, Joseph	L.M.	AUDACIOUS	GH.7832 as Philip RICHARDS
RIDETT, William	Quarter Gunner	DEFENCE	
	L.M.	DEFENCE	1 June 1794
	Purser	GLATTON	Copenhagen 1801
ROBERTS, William	A.B.	CULLODEN	
	A.B.	TREMENDOUS	1 June 1794
	A.B.	CULLODEN	Nile
ROSE, John	Master	CULLODEN	(Became Rtd Cdr 1847)
	Master	CULLODEN	St Vincent
ROYER, Charles	A.B.	SWIFTSURE	
	Midshipman	SWIFTSURE	Egypt
	Lieut. R.N.	ASTRAEA	Off Tamatave. 20 May 1811
			(Vfd Abd. Not on Roll)
SALTER, John	Pte. R.M.	MUTINE	
	Pte. R.M.	CULLODEN	1 June 1794
	Pte. R.M.	CULLODEN	St Vincent
SAMBLER, Stephen	A.B.	ZEALOUS	GH.6376 as SUMBLER
	A.B.	NEPTUNE	Martinique
SAMWELL, Peter	Lieut. R.N.	MUTINE	
	Master's Mate	CAPTAIN	St Vincent
SAUNDERS, William	A.B.	DEFENCE	
	A.B.	DEFENCE	Copenhagen 1801
SAVAGE, William	A.B.	ZEALOUS	
	Ord	VENGEANCE	B.S. 17 Mar 1794
SCOBELL, John	2nd Lt. R.M.	ALEXANDER	
SCOTT, Robert	A.B.	BELLEROPHON	
SCOTT, Thomas	Pte. R.M.	ZEALOUS	G.H. 7,398
SCOWN, John	L.M.	SWIFTSURE	
	Ord	SWIFTSURE	Egypt
SEDEWAY, James	Midshipman	CULLODEN	G.H. 9,099 (Thus a Rating)
	Midshipman	CULLODEN	1 June 1794
	Midshipman	CULLODEN	St Vincent
SELBY, Thomas	A.B.	CULLODEN	(M.L. as SELVIE)
	A.B.	CULLODEN	1 June 1794
	A.B.	CULLODEN	St Vincent
SEWARD, Charles	Midshipman	MAJESTIC	
SHARPE, Joseph	Drummer. R.M.	GOLIATH	
	Drummer. R.M.	GOLIATH	St Vincent
SHAW, William	Drummer. R.M.	ALEXANDER	
SHEPHERD, John	Q.M.	AUDACIOUS	
SHIRLEY, George	Q.M's Mate	VANGUARD	
	A.B.	ST GEORGE	14 March 1795
	Q.M's Mate	FOUDROYANT	Egypt
	Gunner	CLEOPATRA	Martinique
SHORTLAND, P.	L.M.	MAJESTIC	
SILOM, James	A.B.	SWIFTSURE	
	A.B.	SWIFTSURE	Egypt
SIMPSON, Robert	A.B.	THESEUS	
	A.B.	THESEUS	Acre. 30 May 1799
			(Vfd Abd. Not on Roll)
SKUCE, William	L.M.	DEFENCE	
	L.M.	DEFENCE	1 June 1794
	L.M.	DEFIANCE	Copenhagen 1801
SMITH, Alexander	A.B.	MINOTAUR	(Applied as "Pilot".)
	A.B.	MINOTAUR	Egypt
SMITH, James	A.B.	CULLODEN	
	A.B.	CULLODEN	1 June 1794
	A.B.	CULLODEN	St Vincent
SMITH, James	A.B.	ALEXANDER	
SMITH, John	Boy	ZEALOUS	
SMITH, William	Drummer. R.M.	ALEXANDER	
SMITH, William.R.	Midshipman	DEFENCE	
	Lieut. R.N.	THESEUS	Basque Roads 1809
SMITH, Zealous.M.	Boy 3rd Cl	ZEALOUS	
SOAMES, John	Bosun's Mate	ORION	
	A.B.	CRESCENT	Crescent. 20 Octr 1793
	Quarter Gunner	ORION	23rd June 1795
	Bosun's Mate	ORION	St Vincent
SOTHEBY, Charles	Midshipman	ALEXANDER	
	Midshipman	FOUDROYANT	Egypt
SPEED, John	A.B.	SWIFTSURE	
STARKEY, John	A.B.	MAJESTIC	(M.L. as SHARKEY)
	L.M.	MAJESTIC	1 June 1794
STEPHENSON, James	L.M.	GOLIATH	
	Ord	ELEPHANT	Copenhagen 1801
	Q.M.	CORNELIA	Java

STEWART, James	L.M.	DEFENCE	
STONE, Robert	Q.M.	ZEALOUS	
	Q.M.	COURAGEUX	B.S. 29 Aug 1800
	Gunner	EXPLOSION	Copenhagen 1801
STONELAKE, William	Ord	MINOTAUR	
	Cook	TONNANT	Trafalgar
STROUD, Henry	Drummer. R.M.	BELLEROPHON	
STURGEON, Roger	Pte. R.M.	VANGUARD	
	Pte. R.M.	AGAMEMNON	Trafalgar
	Corporal R.M.	AGAMEMNON	St Domingo
SULLIVAN, James	A.B.	DEFENCE	
SULLIVAN, John	Boy 3rd Cl	MAJESTIC	G.H. 2,281
	A.B.	NEPTUNE	Martinique
SUMMERS, Edward	A.B.	AUDACIOUS	
	Ord	AUDACIOUS	1 June 1794
SWALLING, William	A.B.	MINOTAUR	
SWEET, James	Armourer's Mate	CULLODEN	
	Armourer's Mate	CULLODEN	1 June 1794
	Armourer's Mate	CULLODEN	St Vincent
	Armourer's Mate	TEMERAIRE	Trafalgar
	Armourer	LONDON	London. 13 March 1806
SYMONDS, John	A.B.	CULLODEN	G.H. 7,966
TANCOCK, John	Act Lieut. R.N.	ORION	
	Master's Mate	CRESCENT	Crescent. 20 Octr 1793
	Master's Mate	ORION	23rd June 1795
	Master's Mate	ORION	St Vincent
	Lieut. R.N.	CAESAR	Gut of Gibraltar. 12 July 1801
TAYLOR, John	A.B.	MINOTAUR	
THOMPSON, James	Quarter Gunner	CULLODEN	
THOMPSON, Thomas	Ord	MUTINE	
THOMPSON, Thomas	A.B.	ORION	as John as G.H. 8,953
	A.B.	ORION	1 June 1794
	A.B.	ORION	St Vincent
TICKNER, Samuel	Ord	CULLODEN	
	Ord	CULLODEN	St Vincent
TOLHURST, Jeremiah	Ord	ORION	
	Ord	ORION	St Vincent
TOMBKIN, John	L.M.	SWIFTSURE	
TOY, Joseph	A.B.	MAJESTIC	
TRACEY, Andrew	A.B.	AUDACIOUS	
	L.M.	AUDACIOUS	1 June 1794
TRIBE, Henry	Ord	THESEUS	
	Ord	THESEUS	Acre. 30 May 1799
TRICK, Richard	A.B.	AUDACIOUS	
TUCKER, Thomas	A.B.	BELLEROPHON	
	Ord	BELLEROPHON	1 June 1794
TURNER, Thomas	A.B.	MINOTAUR	
TURPIN, Edward	A.B.	MINOTAUR	
TURPINS, John	Ord	ORION	(M.L. as TURPIE)
	L.M.	ORION	23rd June 1795
	L.M.	ORION	St Vincent
	Ord	GANGES	Copenhagen 1801
TYRRELL, Thomas	A.B.	ZEALOUS	G.H. 7,265
TYTE, Robert.W.	A.B.	THESEUS	
	Midshipman	THESEUS	Acre 30 May 1799 (Vfd Abd. Not on Roll)
	Lieut. R.N.	DANGEREUSE	Egypt
VENSON, George	Pte. R.M.	MINOTAUR	
	Pte. R.M.	MINOTAUR	Egypt
WADE, Francis	A.B.	MINOTAUR	G.H. 7,903
	A.B.	MINOTAUR	Egypt
WALKER, John	A.B.	THESEUS	
	A.B.	THESEUS	Acre. 30 May 1799
WARD, Stephen	L.M.	ZEALOUS	G.H. 7,820
WATTS, William	A.B.	BELLEROPHON	
	Ord	BELLEROPHON	1 June 1794
WEALE, Edward.T.	Midshipman	ORION	
	Vol 1st Cl	ORION	St Vincent
WEEKS, Thomas	L.M.	ALEXANDER	
WESTERN, Thomas	L.M.	MAJESTIC	
WHIPPLE, John	Lieut. R.N.	ALEXANDER	
	Midshipman	GIBRALTAR	1 June 1794
WHITE, Peter	Ord	DEFENCE	(Aged nine years for 1-6-94)
	Bosun's Servant	LATONA	1 June 1794
	Midshipman	DEFENCE	Copenhagen 1801
	Master's Mate	SULTAN (P)	B.S. 4 Dec. 1811

NILE

WILES, Samuel	A.B.	CULLODEN	
	A.B.	CULLODEN	*1 June 1794*
	A.B.	CULLODEN	*St Vincent*
WILLIAMS, David	L.M.	ALEXANDER	
	A.B.	ALEXANDER	*Egypt*
WILLIAMS, David	L.M.	THESEUS	
	L.M.	THESEUS	*Acre. 30 May 1799*
WILLIAMS, Owen	A.B.	SWIFTSURE	
	A.B.	SWIFTSURE	*Egypt*
WILLIAMS, Richard	A.B.	MINOTAUR	
WILLIAMS, Thomas	Midshipman	MINOTAUR	
	Lieut. R.N.	CANOPUS	*St Domingo*
WILLIAMS, William	A.B.	BELLEROPHON	
	A.B.	BELLEROPHON	*1 June 1794*
WILSON, William	Boy 3rd Cl	MAJESTIC	
WITTS, John	Lieut. R.M.	SWIFTSURE	
WOOD, James	A.B.	BELLEROPHON	
	Midshipman	BELLEROPHON	*1 June 1794 (?Rating)*
WOOD, George	L.M.	MINOTAUR	
WRIGHT, John	2nd Lieut. R.M.	BELLEROPHON	
	1st Lieut. R.M.	RENOWN	*B.S. 29 Aug 1800*
	1st Lieut. R.M.	RENOWN	*Egypt*
	Captain. R.M.	Qn CHARLOTTE	*Algiers*
YATES, Thomas	A.B.	THESEUS	
	A.B.	THESEUS	*Acre. 30 May 1799*
	A.B.	TERROR	*Copenhagen 1801*
YOUNG, James	A.B.	ALEXANDER	
YOUNG, James	Drummer. R.M.	ORION	
	Drummer. R.M.	ORION	*St Vincent*

(1) ESPOIR 7 AUGT 1798

Capture of the Genoese pirate vessel LIGURIA near Gibraltar.
(Real date 6 August 1798)

CHAMBERS, Henry	Ord	ESPOIR	

(78) 12 OCTR 1798

Action with a French Squadron and capture of the HOCHE (74), and three frigates, off North West coast of Ireland. (Warren's Action).

ANDREW, John.W.	A.B.	FOUDROYANT	
	Midshipman	CANOPUS	*St Domingo*
	Commander	WEAZLE	*Weazel. 22 Feby 1812*
ARCHER, James	Pte. R.M.	FOUDROYANT	
	Pte. R.M.	FOUDROYANT	*Egypt*
ARTHURS, Nicholas	L.M.	ROBUST	
	L.M.	BRUNSWICK	*1 June 1794*
	L.M.	ROBUST	*23rd June 1795*
ASH, James	Quarter Gunner	ROBUST	
	A.B.	ROBUST	*23rd June 1795*
BAMFORD, William	Pte. R.M.	ETHALION	
BANKS, John	A.B.	CANADA	
	Lieut. R.N.	NORTHUMBERLAND	(P)*Northumberland 22 May 1812*
BARRETT, William	Purser's Steward	MELAMPUS	
BEBBS, Richard	Ord	FOUDROYANT	
	Ord	FOUDROYANT	*Egypt*
BONNO, Joseph	Boatswain's Mate	ANSON	
	Gunner	ACTIVE	*Egypt*
	Gunner	NAMUR	*4 Novr 1805*
	Gunner	MINOTAUR	*B.S. 25 July 1809*
BOON, John	Ord	CANADA	
	A.B.	ACASTA	*St Domingo*
	A.B.	SCIPION	*Java*
	A.B.	GRANICUS	*Algiers*
BOYES, Edward	A.B.	ETHALION	
BREWER, George	A.B.	ROBUST	
	L.M.	CAESAR	*1 June 1794*
CHUBB, George.J.	Midshipman	ETHALION	
	Capt's Servant	CHARON	*1 June 1794*

CLACK, Thomas	Midshipman	MAGNANIME	
	Sub Lieut. R.N.	EPERVIER	St Domingo
	Lieut. R.N.	GOREE	Martinique
CLARK, John	A.B.	CANADA	
CLARKE, John	2 Borne A.B. & Ord	CANADA	
	Ord	ST GEORGE	14 March 1795
COLBY, Thomas	Midshipman	FOUDROYANT	
	Midshipman	BEDFORD	Camperdown
	Midshipman	CENTURION	Centurion 18 Sept 1804
	Lieut. R.N.	THUNDERER	Trafalgar (B.S. 19 April 1814, unlisted clasp on known 5 bar Medal)
COLE, Thomas.E.	Vol 1st Cl	ROBUST	(Cdr 1821)
COLLINGS, John	Pte. R.M.	FOUDROYANT	
COOK, Richard	Boy 3rd Cl	AMELIA	(COOK this Roll, CROOK = B.S.)
or CROOK	L.M.	AMELIA	B.S. 29 Aug 1800. G.H. 2961
CULLEN, Daniel	Ord	ROBUST	(M.L. as CULLINS)
	L.M.	BRUNSWICK	1 June 1794
	L.M.	ROBUST	23rd June 1795
	L.M.	ROYAL SOVEREIGN	Trafalgar
DASHWOOD, Charles	Lieut. R.N.	MAGNANIME	(Vfd Abd. Not on Roll)
	Lieut. R.N.	IMPREGNABLE	1 June 1794
	Commander	SYLPH (P)	Sylph. 28 Sepr 1801
DRAKE, William	Bosun's Mate	ANSON	
ERSKINE, Francis	L.M.	CANADA	
FERGUSON, William	Boy	CANADA	
	Boatswain	HAZARD	Martinique
	Boatswain	HAZARD	Anse La Barque. 18 Decr 1809
	Boatswain	HAZARD	Guadaloupe
GORNULLY, James	Ord	AMELIA	(M.L. as GORMALLY)
HAMILTON, Robert	Pte. R.M.	FOUDROYANT	
	Pte. R.M.	BEDFORD	Camperdown
	Pte. R.M.	FOUDROYANT	Egypt
HAYCOCK, John	Pte. R.M.	ANSON	(Probably a 2 Clasp Medal)
HEWETT, Thomas	A.B.	ROBUST	
	A.B.	BRUNSWICK	1 June 1794
	Q.M.	CENTAUR	Centaur. 26 Augt 1808
	Q.M.	IMPREGNABLE	Algiers
HODGSON, William	Cpl. R.M.	ETHALION	
	Sgt. R.M.	SENSIBLE	Egypt. (Received two single clasp Medals for Actions)
HOOPER, Benjamin	Midshipman	FOUDROYANT	
	Midshipman	LONDON	London. 13 March 1806
	Lieut. R.N.	CALYPSO	Off Mardoe. 6 July 1812
HOOPER, M or W.	Volunteer	FOUDROYANT	(Roll badly written)
KEMP, Jeremiah	A.B.	MAGNANIME	
LEROUX, Frederick.J.	Midshipman	ETHALION	(Vfd Abd. Not on Roll)
	Capt's Servant	CHARON	1 June 1794 (See Notes)
LIPSON, Thomas	Vol 1st Cl	FOUDROYANT	
	Vol 1st Cl	WINDSOR CASTLE	14 March 1795
	Vol 1st Cl	BEDFORD	Camperdown
LOWRY, James	Surg's Mate	FOUDROYANT	
	Surg's Mate	SWIFTSURE	Egypt
McMILLANE, Allan	Midshipman	FOUDROYANT	(Lieut. R.N. in 1810)
	Boy	BEDFORD	14 March 1795
	A.B.	BEDFORD	Camperdown
MEADE, John	Midshipman	MAGNANIME	
MENDS, William.B.	Midshipman	CANADA	
	Master's Mate	RENOWN	B.S. 29 Aug 1800
MICHOL, Jacob	L.M.	CANADA	(M.L. as MITCHEL)
MILLER, Zaccheus	2nd Lt. R.M.	FOUDROYANT	
	2nd Lt. R.M.	FOUDROYANT	Egypt
MORGAN, James	Ord	ROBUST	
	L.M.	BRUNSWICK	1 June 1794
	Ord	ROBUST	23rd June 1795
	Ord	SPENCER	St Domingo
MORTON, Henderson	Ord	CANADA	
NORTH, James Beach	Quarter Gunner	ETHALION	
NORTH, John	Quarter Gunner	ETHALION	
OGILVIE, Hugh	A.B.	MELAMPUS	
OLIVE, John	Capt's Clerk	ETHALION	
OLIVER, Thomas	Midshipman	CANADA	
PACKMAN, John	Midshipman	ROBUST	
	A.B.	ROBUST	23rd June 1795
PATTE, Joseph	Boy 3rd Cl	ANSON	

12 OCTR 1798

PATTERSON, Alexander	Ord	CANADA	
	Ord	BELLEROPHON	*Trafalgar*
PATTERSON, Theophilus	A.B.	MAGNANIME	
PIGGOTT, Richard	A.B.	CANADA	*(Navy List as PIGOT, Richard. H.H.)*
(PIGOT Egypt Roll)	Midshipman	RENOWN	*Egypt*
POPE, William	Boy	ROBUST	
	Boy	ROBUST	*23rd June 1795*
PRINGLE, John	A.B.	FOUDROYANT	
	A.B.	BEDFORD	*Camperdown*
RABBICH, Henry	A.B.	ROBUST	
	A.B.	BRUNSWICK	*1 June 1794*
	A.B.	ROBUST	*23rd June 1795*
REED, Richard	L.M.	AMELIA	
ROBERTS, Isaac	Boy 3rd Cl	ANSON	
	A.B.	BELLONA	*Basque Roads. 1809*
ROBERTS, Samuel	Boy 2nd Cl	ANSON	
	Lieut. R.N.	UNICORN	*Basque Roads 1809*
	Commander	METEOR	*The Potomac. 17 Aug 1814*
	Commander	METEOR	*B.S. 14 Dec 1814*
ROBERTS, William	A.B.	FOUDROYANT	
	A.B.	WINDSOR CASTLE	*14 March 1795*
	A.B.	BEDFORD	*Camperdown*
SCHAN, Frederick.D.	Master's Mate	CANADA	
SCOTT, Edward.H.	Vol 1st Cl	ANSON	
SHEPHERD, William	Ord	CANADA	
SIDNEY, William	Ord	CANADA	
STEVENS, Archibald	A.B.	FOUDROYANT	
	A.B.	BEDFORD	*Camperdown*
	A.B.	FOUDROYANT	*Egypt*
STREAK, Stephen	Boy	MAGANANIME	
SYMONDS, William.H.	A.B.	CANADA	*(Navy List as SYMONS)*
or SYMONS	Master's Mate	VICTORY	*Trafalgar (Roll = SYMONS)*
TAYLOR, Richard	L.M.	CANADA	
THOMAS, John	Quarter Gunner	MAGNANIME	
THOMAS, William	A.B.	ANSON	*(Probably 2 Clasp Medal)*
TREMLETT, George.N.	Lieut. R.N.	FOUDROYANT	*(Vfd Abd. Not on Roll)*
	Midshipman	QUEEN	*1 June 1794*
	Lieut. R.N.	THALIA	*23rd June 1795*
			(Vfd Abd. Not on Roll)
VAN HEURENHOFF, Derrick	Pte. R.M.	CANADA	
WARD, Richard	Midshipman	ROBUST	
WELCH, Robert	Midshipman	FOUDROYANT	*(Vfd Abd. Not on Roll)*
	Vol 1st Cl	GALATEA	*23rd June 1795*
	Actg Lieut. R.N.	EXPERIMENT	*Egypt*
WHINYATES, Thomas	Master's Mate	ROBUST	
	Capt's Servant	VETERAN	*B.S. 17 Mar 1794*
	Midshipman	ROBUST	*23rd June 1795*
	Commander	FROLIC	*Martinique*
	Commander	FROLIC	*Guadaloupe*
WRIGHT, Peter	A.B.	MELAMPUS	
YOUNG, Andrew	A.B.	FOUDROYANT	
YOUNG, Benjamin	A.B.	ETHALION	*(Probably a two Clasp Medal)*

(9) FISGARD 20 OCTR 1798

Capture of the French frigate IMMORTALITE, off Brest.

BRADY, Charles	Boy 2nd Cl	FISGARD	
BRIGHT, George	L.M.	FISGARD	
CARDEN, John.S.	Lieut. R.N.	FISGARD (P)	
	Master's Mate	MARLBOROUGH	*1 June 1794*
	Commander	SHEERNESS	*Egypt*
COUCH, Daniel.L.	Midshipman	FISGARD	
	Lieut. R.N.	HERO	*4 Novr 1805*
FLEMING, John	Master's Mate	FISGARD	
MARTIN, Thomas.B.	Captain. R.N.	FISGARD	
	Captain. R.N.	SANTA MARGARITA	*Santa Margaritta 8 June 1796 (see Note)*
	Captain. R.N.	IMPLACABLE	*Implacable. 26 Augt 1808*
MAXWORTHY, Richard	Boy 3rd Cl	FISGARD	
PRICE, Thomas	Yeoman of Sheets	FISGARD	
	Q.M's Mate	SANTA MARGARITA	*Santa Margaritta 8 June 1796*
	Boatswain	EUROTAS	*Eurotas. 25 Feby 1814*
TIVER, John	Boy 3rd Cl	FISGARD	
	Vol 1st Cl	RAMILLIES	*Copenhagen 1801*

(12) SYBILLE 28 FEBY 1799

Capture of the French frigate FORTE, in Hooghly River, Bay of Bengal.
(Real date 1 March 1799)

BUTLER, Samuel	A.B.	SYBILLE	
CLOOSTERMAN, Peter	Boy 2nd Cl	SYBILLE	
COOMBE, James	Ord	SYBILLE	
	Ord	CAESAR	*1 June 1794*
HURLEY, Thomas	Ord	SYBILLE	
LONG, James	A.B.	SYBILLE	
LYSAGHT, Arthur	Midshipman	SYBILLE	
	Master's Mate	FORTE	*Egypt*
MANGER, Nicholas	Lieut. R.N.	SYBILLE	
PIERCY, James	Supn (Unrated)	SYBILLE	
RATCLIFFE, Robert	Supn (Unrated)	SYBILLE	
TRIGGS, John	Ord	SYBILLE	*GH.5350 (M.L. as TRIGGE)*
WRIGHT, Joseph	Vol 1st Cl	SYBILLE	
WRIGHT, William.E.	A.B.	SYBILLE	

No Applicants — TELEGRAPH 18 MARCH 1799

Capture of the French corvette HIRONDELLE, off Isle de Bas, Brest.

(51) ACRE 30 MAY 1799

Successful defence of ACRE, and other services during the siege.
(Real date 20/21 May 1799)

ARNOLD, John	Midshipman	TIGRE	
	Midshipman	TIGRE	*Egypt*
BAZING, John.H.	Boy	THESEUS	*(Not yet found)*
	Boy	THESEUS	*Nile. (Not yet found)*
	Ord?	COLOSSUS?	*Trafalgar?*
BEATTY, George	2nd Lt. R.M.	THESEUS	
	2nd Lt. R.M.	THESEUS	*Nile*
BOXER, James	Master's Mate	TIGRE	
	Midshipman	DIAMOND	*Port Spergui. 17 March 1796*
	Lieut. R.N.	TIGRE	*Egypt*
	Commander	SKYLARK	*Skylark. 11 Novr 1811*
BROWN, John	A.B.	TIGRE	
BROWN, Thomas	Pte. R.M.	TIGRE	*G.H. 994*
	Pte. R.M.	TIGRE	*Egypt*
	Pte. R.M.	DREADNOUGHT	*Trafalgar*
BUDD, Hopewell.H.	Midshipman	TIGRE	
	Master's Mate	TIGRE	*Egypt*
BURTON, Charles.F.	2nd Lt. R.M.	TIGRE	
	2nd Lt. R.M.	TIGRE	*Egypt*
	Captain R.M.A.	On CHARLOTTE	*Algiers*
BUSMAN, George.C.	Sgt. R.M.	TIGRE	
	Sgt. R.M.	TIGRE	*Egypt*
BUTLER, John	A.B.	THESEUS	*(Vfd Abd. Not on Roll)*
	A.B.	THESEUS	*Nile*
COLES, James	Pte. R.M.	TIGRE	*(Vfd Abd. Not on Roll)*
	Pte. R.M.	TIGRE	*Egypt*
CONNEY, James	L.M.	TIGRE	
	A.B.	TIGRE	*Egypt*
DEVESE, Peter	Q.M.	ALLIANCE	*(M.L. as DAVIES)*
DIBBIN, John	L.M.	TIGRE	
	L.M.	TIGRE	*Egypt*
DIXON, George	A.B.	TIGRE	*G.H. 6,040. (M.L. as DICKSON)*
DOOLEY, Thomas	L.M.	TIGRE	
DOWDALL, George	Supn. L.M.	TIGRE	
DUDLEY, William	Pte. R.M.	TIGRE	
DUNN, Nicholas.J.C.	Midshipman	TIGRE	
	Midshipman	DANGEREUSE	*Egypt*
	Lieut. R.N.	TOPAZE	*B.S. 1 Nov 1809*
FOLLETT, John	A.B.	TIGRE	
	A.B.	TIGRE	*Egypt*
GILHAM, James	Coxswain	THESEUS	*(Vfd Abd. Not on Roll)*
	Coxswain	THESEUS	*Nile*
GRAMSHAW, Joseph.G.H.	Boy 2nd Cl	TIGRE	
	Midshipman	TIGRE	*Egypt*

ACRE 30 MAY 1799

HILLIER, George	Lieut. R.N.	ALLIANCE	
	Capt's Servant	ALFRED	*1 June 1794*
	Midshipman	ARDENT	*Camperdown*
	Lieut. R.N.	TIGRE	*Egypt*
HULL, Arthur	2nd Lt. R.M.	THESEUS	
	2nd Lt. R.M.	THESEUS	*Nile*
KEMP, John	Ord	TIGRE	*(Vfd Abd. Not on Roll)*
	Ord	TIGRE	*Egypt*
KENT, William.G.C.	Midshipman	THESEUS	
LAURENCE, John	L.M.	THESEUS	*(Vfd Abd. Not on Roll)*
	L.M.	THESEUS	*Nile*
	Ord	EURYALUS	*Trafalgar*
LEO, John	L.M.	TIGRE	
	Ord	TIGRE	*Egypt*
McPHERSON, William	Ord	TIGRE	*(Vfd Abd. Not on Roll)*
	Ord	TIGRE	*Egypt*
MOLLINEUX, Matthew	Ord	TIGRE	
	Ord	TIGRE	*Egypt*
MOURILYAN, Edward	Midshipman	TIGRE	
	Midshipman	TIGRE	*Egypt*
NEWLAND, Michael	A.B.	THESEUS	*G.H.5419. (Vfd Abd. Not on Roll)*
	A.B.	THESEUS	*Nile*
NEWTON, Isaac	Carp's Crew	THESEUS	
	Carp's Crew	THESEUS	*Nile*
	Supn (Unrated)	DANGEREUSE	*Egypt*
OWEN, William	A.B.	THESEUS	*(M.L. as OWENS)*
	A.B.	THESEUS	*Nile*
	A.B.	THESEUS	*Basque Roads 1809*
PLUMMER, Edward	Ord	TIGRE	*(Vfd Abd. Not on Roll)*
	A.B.	TIGRE	*Egypt*
SAMPSON, Adam	Ord	TIGRE	
	Ord	TIGRE	*Egypt*
SIMPSON, Robert	A.B.	THESEUS	*(Vfd Abd. Not on Roll)*
	A.B.	THESEUS	*Nile*
SNELL, John	A.B.	TIGRE	*G.H. 403*
	A.B.	TIGRE	*Egypt*
SWANSON, William	A.B.	ALLIANCE	
TAYLOR, Charles	A.B.	TIGRE	*(Vfd Abd. Not on Roll)*
	A.B.	TIGRE	*Egypt*
THOMPSON, Josiah	Vol 1st Cl	TIGRE	
	Ord	TIGRE	*Egypt*
TOMS, William	A.B.	TIGRE	
	A.B.	TIGRE	*Egypt*
	A.B.	SCORPION	*Scorpion. 31 March 1804*
	Sailmaker	SCORPION	*Scorpion. 12 Jany 1810*
	Sailmaker	SCORPION	*Guadaloupe*
TRIBE, Henry	Ord	THESEUS	
	Ord	THESEUS	*Nile*
TYTE, Robert.W.	Midshipman	THESEUS	*(Vfd Abd. Not on Roll)*
	A.B.	THESEUS	*Nile*
	Lieut. R.N.	DANGEREUSE	*Egypt*
WALKER, John	A.B.	THESEUS	
	A.B.	THESEUS	*Nile*
WILKINSON, Henry	Pte. R.M.	TIGRE	
	Pte. R.M.	BEDFORD	*Camperdown*
	Pte. R.M.	TIGRE	*Egypt*
WILLIAMS, David	L.M.	THESEUS	
	L.M.	THESEUS	*Nile*
WILLIAMS, John	A.B.	TIGRE	
	A.B.	TIGRE	*Egypt*
WILLIS, John	A.B.	TIGRE	
	A.B.	TIGRE	*Egypt*
YARNOLD, John	Pte. R.M.	TIGRE	
	Pte. R.M.	TIGRE	*Egypt*
YATES, Thomas	A.B.	THESEUS	
	A.B.	THESEUS	*Nile*
	A.B.	TERROR	*Copenhagen 1801*

(4) 9 JUNE BOAT SERVICE 1799

Cutting out of the Spanish polacre BELLA AURORA, from La Selva harbour, N.E. coast of Spain.

GREGORY, John	Master's Mate	SUCCESS	
HARDING, George	Ord	SUCCESS	*(M.L. as HARDEN)*
SMITH, Edward	Pte. R.M.	SUCCESS	
STUPART, Gustavus	Lieut. R.N.	SUCCESS	

(9) SCHIERMONNIKOOG 12 AUG 1799

Attack on SCHIERMONNIKOOG (spelt sometimes with one "n"), Holland, and capture of the ex-British gun-boat CRASH. All names entered in Boat Service Action Roll (Adm 171/3).
(Real dates 11 & 13 August 1799)

BESHEECH, John	Gunner	COURIER	(A Hired Armed Vessel M.L. in Adm 41/3)
	Gunner	COURIER	*Courier. 22 Novr 1799*
BRISCOE, William	L.M.	PYLADES	
FEARY, John	Purser's Steward	PYLADES	
KEYS, Richard	A.B.	COURIER	
	A.B.	COURIER	*Courier. 22 Novr 1799*
KILNER, George	L.M.	PYLADES	
SEARLE, Thomas	Lieut. R.N.	COURIER	
	Lieut. R.N.	COURIER	*Courier. 22 Novr 1799*
	Commander	GRASSHOPPER	*Off Rota. 4 April 1808*
	Commander	GRASSHOPPER	*Grasshopper. 24 April 1808*
STROUD, John	L.M.	PYLADES	
TRAVERS, Eaton	Midshipman	JUNO	
WILSON, David	A.B.	ESPEIGLE	

(2) ARROW 13 SEPTR 1799

Capture of the Dutch DRAAK and GIER by ARROW and WOLVERINE, off Cape Caxine, Algeria.

PERKINS, James.M.	Clerk	ARROW	
RICKETTS, George	Boy 2nd Cl	ARROW	(*M.L. as RICKETTS & SMITH*)
	Vol 1st Cl	ARROW	*Copenhagen 1801*

No Applicants WOLVERINE 13 SEPR 1799

Capture of the Dutch DRAAK and GIER by ARROW and WOLVERINE, off Cape Caxine, Algeria.

(7) SURPRISE WITH HERMIONE (G.M.)

Re-capture of the ex-British HERMIONE, previously taken over by her mutinous and murderous crew. The outstanding action by boats of SURPRISE under command of Captain Edward Hamilton earned him a Naval Gold Medal at the time. The HERMIONE was re-taken at PORTO CABALLO, Venezuela, on 25 October 1799.

BARTLETT, Edward	Ship's Corporal	SURPRISE	
HAMILTON, Edward	Captain. R.N.	SURPRISE	
INGRAM, John	Pte. R.M.	SURPRISE	
	Sgt. R.M.	SIRIUS	*Trafalgar*
	Sgt. R.M.	SIRIUS	*Sirius. 17 April 1806*
McGIVERN, Dennis	L.M.	SURPRISE	(*M.L. as McGIVEN*)
ROBARDO, Charles	Boy 3rd Cl	SURPRISE	
TURNER, Thomas	Ord	SURPRISE	
YOUNG, John	Ord	SURPRISE	

(3) SPEEDY 6 NOVR 1799

Action with fifteen Spanish gun-boats, and successful defence of a convoy, off Gibraltar.

LUSCOMBE, John	A.B.	SPEEDY	(*M.L. as LISCOMBE*) (see notes "SPEEDY 6 May 1801")
PEDLAR, George	Master's Mate	SPEEDY	
	Midshipman	FOUDROYANT	*Egypt*
RICKETTS, Charles.S.	Clerk	SPEEDY	
	Midshipman	SPEEDY	*Speedy. 6 May 1801*

COURIER 22 NOVR 1799
(3)

Capture of the French privateer GUERRIER, off Flushing.
(Real date 23 November 1799)

BESHEECH, John	Gunner	COURIER	*(A Hired Armed Vessel M.L. in ADM 41/3)*
	Gunner	COURIER	*Schiermonnikoog 12 Aug 1799*
KEYS, Richard	A.B.	COURIER	
	A.B.	COURIER	*Schiermonnikoog 12 Aug 1799*
SEARLE, Thomas	Lieut. R.N.	COURIER	
	Lieut. R.N.	COURIER	*Schiermonnikoog 12 Aug 1799*
	Commander	GRASSHOPPER	*Off Rota. 4 April 1808*
	Commander	GRASSHOPPER	*Grasshopper. 24 April 1808*

20 DEC BOAT SERVICE 1799
(3)

Re-capture of the Lady Nelson cutter, previously taken by three French privateers in Bay of Gibraltar. (No Muster List survived for Dec 1799)
(Real date 21 December 1799)

FERGUSON, William	2nd Lt R.M.	QUEEN CHARLOTTE	
	2nd Lt R.M.	SANTA DOROTEA	*Egypt*
PEEBLES, Thomas	2nd Lt R.M.	QUEEN CHARLOTTE	
PERKINS, Joseph	A.B.	QUEEN CHARLOTTE	
	Q.M.'s Mate	STATIRA	*Guadaloupe*
	Q.M.'s Mate	STATIRA	*B.S. Ap & May 1813*

VIPER 26 DECR 1799
(2)

Capture of the French privateer FURET, off Dodman Point, Cornwall.

FILE, Charles	A.B.	VIPER	
PADDON, Silas.H.	Midshipman	VIPER	*(Vfd Abd. Not on Roll)*
	Midshipman	VIPER	*B.S. 29 July 1800*

FAIRY 5 FEBY 1800
(4)

Action with the French frigate PALLAS, and her consequent capture by LOIRE, DANAE and RAILLEUR, off Cape Frehel, St Malo.

BEDDRELL, Thomas	L.M.	FAIRY	*(M.L. as BEARD, Thomas?)*
BENJAMEN, John	Purser's Steward	FAIRY	
	Purser's Steward	RENOMMEE	*Egypt*
	Midshipman	PRINCE	*Trafalgar*
CLARK, Abraham	Vol 1st Cl	FAIRY	
HEWITT, Joseph	Clerk	FAIRY	

HARPY 5 FEBY 1800
(4)

Action with the French frigate PALLAS, and her consequent capture by LOIRE, DANAE and RAILLEUR, off Cape Frehel, St Malo.

JONES, Robert.P.	A.B.	HARPY	*(Vfd Abd. Not on Roll)*
	Midshipman	AGINCOURT	*Camperdown*
	Midshipman	HARPY	*Copenhagen 1801 (VA-NOR)*
MATHEWS, Robert.B.	Vol 1st Cl	HARPY	
RIDER, Richard	Boy 2nd Cl	HARPY	**(Joined after this Action)*
	Boy 2nd Cl	HARPY	*Copenhagen 1801*
TALBOT, William	Boy 2nd Cl	HARPY	
	L.M.	HARPY	*Copenhagen 1801*
	Bosun's Mate	WANDERER	*Guadaloupe*

(LOIRE 5 FEBY 1800)

There is circumstantial evidence that this Clasp may have been issued.
PELL, Watkin.O. is verified as a claimant to two clasps;—

Off Rota 4 April 1808.	Lieut. R.N.	H.M.S. MERCURY
Thunder. 9 Octr 1813	Commander	H.M.S. THUNDER

He was aboard LOIRE at the capture of PALLAS as a Midshipman, and applied for a third clasp for this encounter. His application was, . . . "not allowed vide Admiral Sir Byam Martin's Minute on his claim." Nevertheless the Navy List (Allen. 1851) shows him as receiving a three clasp N.G.S. Medal, which if correct would possibly mean that the above clasp may have been allowed at a later stage to the Admiral's decision. Or, his medal may have either the FAIRY or HARPY clasp upon it, also dated 5 Feby 1800.

PETEREL 21 MARCH 1800
(2)

Capture of the French corvette LIGURIENNE, in Bay of Marseilles.

AUSTEN, Francis.W.	Commander	PETEREL (P)	
	Captain R.N.	CANOPUS	St Domingo
HORN, Stephen	Ord	PETEREL	
	Ord	PETEREL	Egypt

PENELOPE 30 MARCH 1800
(11)

Night action with the French "80", GUILLAUME TELL and her consequent capture by LION and FOUDROYANT, in the Mediterranean.

BAYLY, James	Vol 1st Cl	PENELOPE	
	Midshipman	PENELOPE	Egypt
	Midshipman	EURYALUS	Trafalgar
BOROUGH, William	Midshipman	PENELOPE	
BROWN, James	A.B.	PENELOPE	
	Carpenter	THESEUS	Basque Roads 1809
CARTER, John	Vol 1st Cl	PENELOPE	
	Midshipman	PENELOPE	Egypt
	Actg Lt. R.N.	LEVIATHAN	Trafalgar
COLLINS, Darby	Ord	PENELOPE	G.H. 8,878
ELPHICK, James	Master's Mate	PENELOPE	
	Midshipman	PENELOPE	Egypt
MANNING, William	Boy 3rd Cl	PENELOPE	
	Boy 3rd Cl	PENELOPE	Egypt (Vfd Abd. Not on Roll)
OGDEN, Charles	Pte. R.M.	PENELOPE	
PRESCOTT, Henry	Midshipman	PENELOPE	
	Midshipman	PENELOPE	Egypt
	Lieut. R.N.	AEOLUS	4 Novr 1805
	Commander	WEAZLE	Amanthea. 25 July 1810
SMALL, John	L.M.	PENELOPE	
	L.M.	PENELOPE	Egypt (Vfd Abd. Not on Roll)
	L.M.	LOIRE	Guadaloupe
YULE, Robert	Master's Mate	PENELOPE	
	Master's Mate	PENELOPE	Egypt (Vfd Abd. Not on Roll)
	Master's Mate	HERO	4 Novr 1805
	Lieut. R.N.	ILLUSTRIOUS	Java

VINCIEGO 30 MARCH 1800
(2)

As for PENELOPE above. No Muster Lists for VINCIEGO have survived, whose correct spelling is VINCEJO.

DOWN, Edward.A.	Lieut. R.N.	VINCIEGO	
	Midshipman	BARFLEUR	1 June 1794
	Master's Mate	EXCELLENT	St Vincent
OSBORN, John	Master's Mate	VINCIEGO	
	A.B.	IRRESISTIBLE	B.S. 17 Mar 1794
	Master's Mate	VIRAGO	Egypt

(24) CAPTURE OF THE DESIREE

Boarding and capture of the French frigate DESIREE on 8 July 1800, in Dunkirk Roads.

Name	Rank	Ship	Notes
ALCHIN, Henry	Not Given	CAMPERDOWN	*A Hired Cutter. No M. List.*
BLUETT, Richard	Lieut. R.N.	BABET	
CARTHEW, James	Lieut. R.N.	ROSARIO	*(Vfd Abd. Not on Roll)*
	Captain. R.N.	GLOIRE	*Martinique*
CASEY, David.O'B.	Lieut. R.N.	NEMESIS	
	Lieut. R.N.	SENSIBLE	*Egypt*
COLLARD, Stephen	Not given	VIGILANT	*(Unknown alias in 1800)*
DUVAL, Francis	Midshipman	ANDROMEDA	*(Vfd Abd. Not on Roll)*
	Midshipman	DESIREE	*Copenhagen 1801*
FARMAR, Jasper	2nd Lt R.M.	STAG	*(Vfd Abd. Not on Roll)*
	2nd Lt R.M.	STAG	*B.S. 29 Aug 1800*
FIELDING, Charles	L.M.	DART	
	Ord	DART	*Copenhagen 1801*
GOLDSACK, Henry	Not Given	CAMPERDOWN	*(See note above for ALCHIN)*
HOLMES, Joseph	Pte. R.M.	BOXER	
	Pte. R.M.	APOLLO	*B.S. 1 Nov 1809*
HOWARD, Robert	Ship's Corporal	FALCON	
	L.M.	RESOLUTION	*Basque Roads 1809*
JELL, Henry	Not Given	COMET	*M. List for action missing.*
LONGCHAMP, John	Midshipman	ANDROMEDA	
	Midshipman	LEDA	*Egypt*
	Midshipman	DESIREE	*Copenhagen 1801*
MILLER, Samuel	Gunner's Mate	STAG	*G.H. 2953*
	Gunner's Mate	STAG	*B.S. 29 Aug 1800*
MONTGOMERY, Page	A.B.	NEMESIS	
MORRISON, J. H. (Roll)	Supn unrated	ANDROMEDA	*Loaned from ZEALAND. Little doubt he is Midshipman Isaac Hawkins MORRISON. In 1814 became Capt. R.N.*
MOUNT, Stephen	"Hove the Lead" (Entry in Roll)	STAG	*(Neither this name nor duty found on Muster List)*
NASH, John	Not Given	CAMPERDOWN	*(See note above for ALCHIN)*
OWEN, James.W.	Midshipman	DART	
PEAKE, Daniel	Supn Pilot	NEMESIS	
ROBINS, Thomas.L.	Midshipman	TEAZER	*(Also spelt TEASER)*
	Midshipman	TEAZER	*Copenhagen 1801 (Vfd Abd. Not on Roll)*
	Master's Mate	VICTORY	*Trafalgar*
	Lieut. R.N.	PALLAS	*Basque Roads 1809*
SOMERVILLE, William	Lieut. R.N.	BABET	
	Master's Mate	ISIS	*Camperdown*
WATTS, George.E.	A.B.	STAG	
	Lieut. R.N.	COMUS	*Comus 15 Augt 1807*
	Commander	EPHIRA	*B.S. 27 July 1809*
WHYLAND, Nicholas	Not Given	ANDROMEDA	*This name not on M. List*

(4) 29 JULY BOAT SERVICE 1800

Cutting out of the French brig CERBERE, in Port Louis, Lorient.

Name	Rank	Ship	Notes
DUNN, Hugh	L.M.	IMPETUEUX	
	L.M.	IMPETUEUX	*B.S. 29 Aug 1800*
HART, Henry	Midshipman	IMPETUEUX	
	A.B.	INDEFATIGABLE	*Indefatigable. 13 Jany 1797*
PADDON, Silas.H.	Midshipman	VIPER	
	Midshipman	VIPER	*Viper. 26 Decr 1799 (Vfd Abd. Not on Roll)*
PATESHALL, Nicholas.L.	Master's Mate	IMPETUEUX	
	Midshipman	INDEFATIGABLE	*Indefatigable 20 April 1796*
	Midshipman	INDEFATIGABLE	*Indefatigable 13 Jany 1797*

(7) SEINE 20 AUGT 1800

Capture of the French frigate VENGEANCE, off St Domingo, West Indies. (Clasp List gives incorrect date of 2 August 1800)

CHETHAM, Edward	Lieut. R.N.	SEINE	
(STRODE, Edward.C.)	Midshipman	AGAMEMNON	14 March 1795
	Captain. R.N.	LEANDER	Algiers
CROTTY, William	A.B.	SEINE	
CULLERN, Thomas	L.M.	SEINE	
	L.M.	EXCELLENT	St Vincent
DALYELL, William.C.C.	Midshipman	SEINE	
FITZGERALD, James	A.B.	SEINE	
JARRETT, James	Pte. R.M.	SEINE	(M.L. as JERRETT)
OLIVER, Robert	Midshipman	SEINE	

(25) 29 AUG BOAT SERVICE 1800

Cutting out the French privateer GUEPE, in Redondela narrows, Vigo.
(Real date 30 August 1800)

AVERY, David	Drummer. R.M.	RENOWN	
BRIDGEN, James	Drummer. R.M.	BRILLIANT	
CADOGAN, The Hon George	Master's Mate	IMPETUEUX	
	Vol 1st Cl	INDEFATIGABLE	Indefatigable. 29 April 1796
	Vol 1st Cl	INDEFATIGABLE	Indefatigable. 13 Jan 1797
COLLIER, Henry.T.B.	Midshipman	BRILLIANT	
	Lieut. R.N.	LEDA	Java
CROOK, Richard	L.M.	AMELIA	G.H. 2,961
	Boy 3rd Cl	AMELIA	12 Octr 1798
DUNN, Hugh	L.M.	IMPETUEUX	
	L.M.	IMPETUEUX	B.S. 29 July 1800
FAGG, Matthew	Supn. A.B.	RENOWN	(M.L. as FAIG)
	A.B.	ACHILLE	Trafalgar
FARMAR, Jasper	2nd Lt R.M.	STAG	
	2nd Lt R.M.	STAG	Capture of the Desiree (Vfd Abd. Not on Roll)
GLANVILL, George	Lieut. R.N.	CYNTHIA	
	(Lieut. R.N.)	(CYNTHIA)	(Egypt—not on Roll, but present at operations)
HILLS, George	Lieut. R.N.	AMETHYST	
HUGGINS, James.E.	Master's Mate	EURUS	
	Master's Mate	EURUS	Egypt
LAMBERT, Thomas	A.B.	BRILLIANT	
LITCHFIELD, Henry	Midshipman	IMPETUEUX	
LOGIE, William	Pte. R.M.	BRILLIANT	
	Pte. R.M.	COLOSSUS	23rd June 1795
	Pte. R.M.	DONEGAL	St Domingo
MARSHALL, Thomas	2nd Lt. R.M.	AMETHYST	
MENDS, William.B.	Master's Mate	RENOWN	
	Midshipman	CANADA	12 Octr 1798
MILLER, Samuel	Gunner's Mate	STAG	G.H. 2,953
	Gunner's Mate	STAG	Capture of the Desiree
NEVILLE, James	Actg Lieut. R.N.	IPHEGENIA	
	Actg Lieut. R.N.	IPHEGENIA	Egypt
REYNOLDS, Barrington	Midshipman	IMPETUEUX	
	Midshipman	AMAZON	Amazon. 13 Jan 1797
	Commander	HESPER	Java
	Capt. R.N. C.B.	GANGES	Syria
SLANEY, John	Pte. R.M.	RENOWN	
STONE, Robert	Q.M.	COURAGEUX	
	Q.M.	ZEALOUS	Nile
	Gunner	EXPLOSION	Copenhagen 1801
THELWALL, Bevis	Master's Mate	BRILLIANT	
TOMKINS, Charles	Ord	RENOWN	
WILKINSON, William	Pte. R.M.	RENOWN	
WRIGHT, John	1st Lt. R.M.	RENOWN	
	2nd Lt. R.M.	BELLEROPHON	Nile
	1st Lt. R.M.	RENOWN	Egypt
	Captain. R.M.	Qn CHARLOTTE	Algiers

(5) 27 OCT BOAT SERVICE 1800

Cutting out of the Spanish polacre SAN JOSE, in Fuengirola Harbour, near Malaga.
(Real date 28 October 1800)

BEAUFORT, Francis	Lieut. R.N.	PHAETON (P)	
	Master's Mate	AQUILON	1 June 1794
	Master's Mate	PHAETON	17 June 1795
CAMPBELL, Duncan	2nd Lt. R.M.	PHAETON	
DEAGON, Edward	Gunner	PHAETON	
	Q.M.	MINOTAUR	Nile
	Gunner	ATLAS	St Domingo
HAMILTON, A.B.P.P.	Master's Mate	PHAETON	
SHERRARD, John	A.B.	PHAETON	

(6) PHOEBE 19 FEBY 1801

Capture of the French frigate AFRICAINE, off Ceuta, Straits of Gibraltar.

LAURIE, Stephen	Boy 2nd Cl	PHOEBE	
	Boy 3rd Cl	PHOEBE	Phoebe. 21 Decr 1797
	A.B.	PHOEBE	Trafalgar
	A.B.	PHOEBE	Off Tamatave. 20 May 1811
	A.B.	PHOEBE	Java
	Capt Fore Top	PHOEBE	Phoebe. 28 March 1814
MEREDITH, Richard	Vol 1st Cl	PHOEBE	
	A.B.	PHOEBE	Trafalgar
PECHELL, Samuel.J.B.	Midshipman	PHOEBE	
	Midshipman	PHOEBE	Phoebe. 21 Decr 1797
PROWETT, Charles	Master's Mate	PHOEBE	
	Midshipman	PHOEBE	Phoebe. 21 Decr 1797
REEDIN, John	A.B.	PHOEBE	
	Ord	PHOEBE	Phoebe. 21 Decr 1797
	Quarter Gunner	PHOEBE	Trafalgar
WARD, William	Sgt. R.M.	PHOEBE	

(618) EGYPT

For services on land and off the coast of Egypt.
8 March to 2 September 1801.
(This list is an amended copy of the previous privately produced Roll for this Clasp, because the Official Clasp List in a separate book to those for all other N.G.S. Clasps has since been mislaid).

ABRAHAMS, John	Carpenter's Crew	TIGRE	
AIKEN, John	Landsman	RENOWN	
	Landsman	THUNDERER	Trafalgar
AILES, Thomas	L.M.	PIQUE	
AITKEN, James	Ord	KENT	
	Ord	VENERABLE	Camperdown
	Ord	DEFENCE	Trafalgar
ALEXANDER, Nicholas	Vol 1st Cl	HAERLEM	
	Midshipman	DESIREE	Copenhagen 1801
	Lieut. R.N.	DRAGON	B.S. 29 April 1813
ALLEN, Thomas	Pte. R.M.	DIADEM	
	Pte. R.M.	DREADNOUGHT	Trafalgar
ALLEN, Thomas	L.M.	PIQUE	
ALLEYNE, Richard.I.	Midshipman	HAERLEM	
ANDERSON, Donald	A.B.	REGULUS	(May read ADDISON)
ANDERSON, Joseph	Carpenter	GIBRALTAR	
	Carpenter	GIBRALTAR	Basque Roads 1809
ANDERSON, Robert	Pte. R.M.	FOUDROYANT	
ANDREWS, Thomas	Boy	VESTAL	G.H. 3281
	A.B.	STAR	Martinique (As Thomas. J.)
	A.B.	STAR	Guadaloupe ,, ,, ,,
ARABIN, Stephen	Ord	TIGRE	
ARCHER, James	Pte. R.M.	FOUDROYANT	
	Pte. R.M.	FOUDROYANT	12 Octr 1798
ARNOLD, John	Midshipman	TIGRE	
	Midshipman	TIGRE	Acre. 30 May 1799
ARROW, John.J.	Midshipman	KENT	
ASHMAN, Michael	Drummer. R.M.	ROMULUS	G.H. 2152
ASHTON, Benjamin	Boy	CHARON	(May read AISTIN)
ATKINS, Benjamin	Ord	DICTATOR	
ATKINSON, Jacob	Gunner's Mate	PEARL	
AVERY, Henry	Boy	PIQUE	

THE NAVAL GENERAL SERVICE MEDAL ROLL 1793-1840

AYLMER, Hon Frederick.W.	Lieut. R.N.	SWIFTSURE	
	Midshipman	SYREN	B.S. 15 Mar 1793
	Lieut. R.N.	SWIFTSURE	Nile
	Captain. R.N.	SEVERN	Algiers
AYLWARD, John	L.M.	HECTOR	
AYSCOUGH, John	Commander	INCONSTANT	
BAGGERLEY, James	Pte. R.M.	STATELY	
BAGWELL, Joseph	Ord	ACTIVE	
	Ord	FREIJA	Guadaloupe
BAILEY, John	Q.M.	TERMAGENT	
BAILEY, Samuel	Surgeon's Mate	THETIS	
BAILY, Thomas	Boy	CYCLOPS	
BALCHIN, William	Ord	FOUDROYANT	
	Boy	VENERABLE	Camperdown
BARNETT, Edward	A.B.	ALLIGATOR	
BARNETT, John	Ord	RENOMMEE	
BAREENA, Francis	Clerk	PORT MAHON	
BARRYMORE, William	Actg Purser	INFLEXIBLE	
BATTING, John	L.M.	ROEBUCK	
BAYLY, James	Midshipman	PENELOPE	
	Vol 1st Cl	PENELOPE	Penelope. 30 March 1800
	Midshipman	EURYALUS	Trafalgar
BAYNE, George	Midshipman	HAERLEM	
BEBBS, Richard	Ord	FOUDROYANT	
	Ord	FOUDROYANT	12 Octr 1798
BEARDMORE, W.H.	Boy	FURY	G.H. 1622
BEITHIE, George	L.M.	DELFT	
BELL, James	Ord	PORT MAHON	
BENJAMEN, John	Purser's Steward	RENOMMEE	
	Purser's Steward	FAIRY	Fairy. 5 Feby 1800
	Midshipman	PRINCE	Trafalgar
BERRY, John	L.M.	KENT	
BILLINGTON, Thomas	Cpl. R.M.	HEBE	
BINGHAM, John	Midshipman	MINOTAUR	
BIRD, William	Pte. R.M.	BRACKEL	G.H. 2278
BISBEACH, Thomas	Pte. R.M.	STATELY	
BISHOP, Thomas	Ord	MODESTE	
	A.B.	ALBION	G.H. 8058
BISSETT, George	A.B.	KENT	
BLACK, Archibald	Ord	DIANA	(M.L. as CAMERON?)
BLACKMAN, James	Ord	FOUDROYANT	
	Capt Main Top	BELLEISLE	Martinique
BLADES, James	A.B.	STATELY	
BLAKE, George.C.	Midshipman	ROMULUS	
	Lieut. R.N.	SCORPION	Scorpion. 12 Jany 1810
	Lieut. R.N.	SCORPION	Guadaloupe
BLIGH, Thomas	Pte. R.M.	EL CARMEN	
	Pte. R.M.	BEDFORD	Camperdown
BLOMELY, John	Boy 2nd Cl	FOUDROYANT	
	Boy 2nd Cl	BEDFORD	Camperdown
BLYTH, Francis	Ord	KENT	
BONNO, Joseph	Gunner	ACTIVE	
	Bosun's Mate	ANSON	12 Octr 1798
	Gunner	NAMUR	4 Novr 1805
	Gunner	MINOTAUR	B.S. 25 July 1809
BOSS, James	A.B.	DRAGON	
	Capt Main Top	BEAGLE	Basque Roads 1809
BOTHWAY, Joseph	Ord	AGINCOURT	
	Gnr's Mate	POMPEE	Martinique
BOUND, William	A.B.	REGULUS	
	A.B.	ROYAL SOVEREIGN	Trafalgar
	A.B.	NISUS	Java
	A.B.	QUEEN CHARLOTTE	Algiers
BOWDEN, Richard	Ord	PIQUE	
BOXER, James	Lieut. R.N.	TIGRE	
	Midshipman	DIAMOND	Port Spergui. 17 March 1796
	Midshipman	TIGRE	Acre. 30 May 1799
	Commander	SKYLARK	Skylark. 11 Novr 1811
BRADY, Thomas	A.B.	DRAGON	G.H. 2979
BRAY, W.C.	Midshipman	MADRAS	
BRIEN, Edward.H.	Surgeon	PALLAS	
BRIGGS, Thomas	Commander	SALAMINE	
	Midshipman	DIADEM	14 March 1795
BRINE, John	Midshipman	AGINCOURT	
	Lieut. R.N.	GLOIRE	Martinique
	Lieut. R.N.	POMPEE	Guadaloupe
BROAD, William.H.	Q.M.'s Mate	FOUDROYANT	G.H. 3322
BROOKS, George	Midshipman	FLORENTINA	

EGYPT

BROWN, George	Ord	GREYHOUND	
BROWN, John	Boatswain	FLORA	
BROWN, Peter	Ord	WILHELMINA	G.H. 1090
BROWN, Peter	A.B.	MINERVE	
	A.B.	MINERVE	Minerve. 19 Decr 1796
	A.B.	MINERVE	St Vincent
BROWN, Thomas	Lieut. R.N.	FLORA	
BROWN, Thomas	Ord	NIGER	
BROWN, Thomas	Pte. R.M.	TIGRE	G.H. 994
	Pte. R.M.	TIGRE	Acre. 30 May 1799
	Pte. R.M.	DREADNOUGHT	Trafalgar
BUCHANAN, David	A.B.	DRAGON	
BUDD, Hopewell.H.	Master's Mate	TIGRE	
	Midshipman	TIGRE	Acre. 30 May 1799
BURNETT, William	Surgeon	ATHENIENNE	
	Surg's 3rd Mate	GOLIATH	St Vincent
	Surg's 1st Mate	GOLIATH	Nile
	Surgeon	DEFIANCE	Trafalgar (Kntd 1831)
BURNS, Alexander	L.M.	AGINCOURT	
BURROWS, Robert	Ord	MONMOUTH	
	L.M.	MONMOUTH	Camperdown
	Ord	REVENGE	Trafalgar
BURT, John	L.M.	SWIFTSURE	
	L.M.	SWIFTSURE	Nile
BURTON, Charles.F.	2nd Lt. R.M.	TIGRE	
	2nd Lt. R.M.	TIGRE	Acre. 30 May 1799
	Captain. R.M.A.	QUEEN CHARLOTTE	Algiers
BUSMAN, George.C.	Sgt. R.M.	TIGRE	
	Sgt. R.M.	TIGRE	Acre. 30 May 1799
BUTLER, Henry	Pte. R.M.	MINOTAUR	
	Pte. R.M.	MINOTAUR	Nile
	Pte. R.M.	NAIAD	Trafalgar
BUTLER, Richard	Ord	SWIFTSURE	
	A.B.	SWIFTSURE	Nile
BUTLER, William	L.M.	AJAX	
CAHILL, R.S.	Midshipman	TRUSTY	
CARDEN, John.S.	Commander	SHEERNESS	
	Master's Mate	MARLBOROUGH	1 June 1794
	Lieut. R.N.	FISGARD (P)	Fisgard. 20 Octr 1798
CARELESS, Ebenezer	Pte. R.M.	GREYHOUND	
CARSON, John	A.B.	MONDOVI	
CARSTAIRS, John	Not Given	PEGASUS	
CARTER, John	Midshipman	PENELOPE	
	Vol 1st Cl	PENELOPE	Penelope. 30 March 1800
	Actg Lieut. R.N.	LEVIATHAN	Trafalgar
CARTER, Thomas	A.B.	WINCHELSEA	
CARY, Edward	Boy	DELFT	
CASEY, David. O'B.	Lieut. R.N.	SENSIBLE	
	Lieut. R.N.	NEMESIS	Capture of the Desiree
CASNEY, John	A.B.	ROMNEY	
	A.B.	UNICORN	Basque Roads 1809
CASTLEMAN, William	L.M.	LEDA	
CAVENAGH, Edward	Bosun's Mate	HECTOR	
	Yeoman of Sheets	CANOPUS	St Domingo
CAWORTH, William	Boy	EURUS	
CHAMBERLAIN, William.B.	Midshipman	MONMOUTH	
	Lieut. R.N.	AEOLUS	Martinique
CHAMBERS, John	A.B.	MONMOUTH	
CHILCOTT, James	Pte. R.M.	FLORA	
	Pte. R.M.	CLEOPATRA	Martinique
CHRYSTIE, Thomas	Midshipman	AJAX	
	Midshipman	DEFIANCE	Trafalgar
	Midshipman	NEPTUNE	Martinique
CLARK, John	Boy	FOUDROYANT	
	Capt Fore Top	PHAETON	Java
CLARK, William	Boy	KENT	
	Boy 3rd Cl	VENERABLE	Camperdown
CLEMENTS, Charles	Not Given	DOVER	
CLIMO, John	Boy	MINERVE	
COCHRANE, James	Boy	EUROPA	
COCHRANE, Thomas	Midshipman	AJAX	
	Captain R.N.	ETHALION	Martinique
COCKBURN, George	Captain. R.N.	MINERVE	
	Captain. R.N.	MELEAGER	14 March 1795
	Captain. R.N.	MINERVE	Minerve. 19 Decr 1796
	Captain. R.N.	MINERVE	St Vincent
	Commodore	POMPEE	Martinique
	Rear Admiral	MARLBOROUGH	B.S. Ap & May 1813
COGHILL, Josiah.C.	Lieut. R.N.	HAERLEM	

COLE, Francis	Boy	EXPERIMENT	
COLEPACK, John	Ord	BONNE CITOYENNE	
	Capt's Servant	Qn CHARLOTTE	1 June 1794
	Boy 3rd Cl	Qn CHARLOTTE	23rd June 1795
	Vol 1st Cl	BONNE CITOYENNE	St Vincent
COLES, James	Pte. R.M.	TIGRE	
	Pte. R.M.	TIGRE	Acre. 30 May 1799 (Vfd Abd. Not on Roll)
COLLINS, James	Ord	AJAX	
	A.B.	SURVEILLANTE	St Sebastian
COLLINS, Thomas	Pte. R.M.	RENOWN	
CONNEY, James	A.B.	TIGRE	
	L.M.	TIGRE	Acre. 30 May 1799
CONNOR, John	Boy	MADRAS	
COOK, John	Master	NORTHUMBERLAND	
	Master	STATIRA	Guadaloupe
COOK, John	Boy	THETIS	
COOKESLEY, John	Lieut. R.N.	TRUSTY	
	Lieut. R.N.	GIBRALTAR	Basque Roads 1809
COOPER, John	L.M.	HECTOR	
CORBY, William	Pte. R.M.	EUROPA	G.H. 292
COSSACK, Anthony	Ord	ROMNEY	G.H. 1013
COUSINS, Robert	A.B.	NORTHUMBERLAND	
COX, Henry	1st Lt. R.M.	ROMNEY	
	2nd Lt. R.M.	VALIANT	1 June 1794
	Captain. R.M.	DEFENCE	Trafalgar
CRABB, Robert	Ord	BLONDE	
CROFT, William	Midshipman	FOUDROYANT	
	Midshipman	AMAZON	Amazon. 13 Jany 1797
CROKE, Wentworth.P.	Vol 1st Cl	KANGAROO	
CULL, George	2nd Lt. R.M.	HECTOR	
CURRY, Richard	Commander	FURY	
CURRY, Thomas	Boy	MINOTAUR	G.H. 1438
DACRE, George.H.	Midshipman	PHOENIX	
DADD, James	A.B.	MINOTAUR	
DAKINS, Joseph	Boy	WINCHELSEA	
DARSEY, Ernest	Ord	ROEBUCK	
DAVENPORT, John	A.B.	SWIFTSURE	
	A.B.	SWIFTSURE	Nile
DAVENPORT, Thomas	Midshipman	RENOMMEE	
DAVIES, David	A.B.	FOUDROYANT	
	A.B.	BEDFORD	Camperdown
	Qtr Gunner	VANGUARD	Nile
DAVIES, John.G.	Midshipman	HECTOR	
	A.B.	COURAGEUX	4 Novr 1805
DAVIES, Henry.T.	Lieut. R.N.	WINCHELSEA	
	Capt's Servant	GLORY	1 June 1794
	Lieut. R.N.	BLANCHE (P)	Blanche. 19 July 1806
DAVIS, Jonas	Boy	GIBRALTAR	
	L.M.	AJAX	Trafalgar (+China 1842)
DAWSON, William	A.B.	FOUDROYANT	
	A.B.	BEDFORD	Camperdown
DEAKNEY, John	Pte. R.M.	AJAX	
DESPOURRINS, Peter	Lieut. R.N.	MADRAS	
DEMER, George	Pte. R.M.	PEGASUS	G.H. 9740 as DEAMAN
	Pte. R.M.	NEPTUNE	Martinique (as DEEMER)
DIBBIN, John	L.M.	TIGRE	
	L.M.	TIGRE	Acre. 30 May 1799
DICK, John	Commander	CYNTHIA	
	Captain. R.N.	PENELOPE	Martinique
DICKSON, Thomas	Bosun's Mate	INCONSTANT	(May read DIXON)
DONNELLY, James	Pte. R.M.	BRACKEL	GH 1128 or 1178
DORAN, Thomas	Pte. R.M.	HECTOR	
DOUGLAS, John	Not Given	ULYSSES	
DOWNMAN, Hugh	Captain. R.N.	SANTA DOROTEA	
	Lieut. R.N.	VICTORY	St Vincent
DOYLE, John	Carp's Crew	SANTA DOROTEA	
DOYLE, William	Boy	GREYHOUND	
DUFF, Archibald	Lieut. R.N.	MONDOVI	
DUGWELL, Robert	Boy	CYCLOPS	G.H. 5754
DUNDAS, James.W.D.	Midshipman	KENT	
DUNKLEY, Peter	Qtr Gunner	AJAX	
DUNN, Nicholas.J.C.	Midshipman	DANGEREUSE	
	Midshipman	TIGRE	Acre. 30 May 1799
	Lieut. R.N.	TOPAZE	B.S. 1 Nov 1809
DURSTIN, John	Boy 3rd Cl	FOUDROYANT	
EDMUNDS, Gilbert	A.B.	HEROINE	
EDWARDS, Charles	A.B.	FOUDROYANT	
	Ord	BEDFORD	Camperdown
EGGLISTONE, Francis	Sailmaker's Crew	PEGASUS	
	A.B.	BELLEROPHON	1 June 1794
	Qtr Gunner	BELLEROPHON	Nile
ELLIOT, Robert	Commander	GOOD DESIGN	

EGYPT

ELLIS, William	Not Given	FOX	
ELLIS, William	Sailmaker's Crew	NIGER	
ELPHICK, James	Midshipman	PENELOPE	
	Master's Mate	PENELOPE	Penelope. 30 March 1800
ELPHINSTONE, Alexander.F.	Midshipman	FOUDROYANT	
ENSTONE, Benjamin	Pte. R.M.	MADRAS	(May read EUSTONE)
EVANS, William	Pte. R.M.	KENT	
EVANS, William	Ord	MINOTAUR	
	Ord	MINOTAUR	Nile
EYLES, James	Carp's Crew	NORTHUMBERLAND	
FANSHAWE, Henry	Midshipman	KENT	
FAYERMAN, Zaccheus	Lieut. R.M.	PALLAS	
FERGUSON, William	2nd Lt. R.M.	SANTA DOROTEA	
	2nd Lt. R.M.	Qn CHARLOTTE	B.S. 20 Dec 1799
FETLEY, Thomas	Pte. R.M.	MINERVE	
FINCH, John	L.M.	ROMULUS	
FINCH, Thomas	Ord	NORTHUMBERLAND	
FINLAY, John	Midshipman	MINOTAUR	
	A.B.	MINOTAUR	Nile
FINNEY, Thomas	Coxswain	MONMOUTH	
FISHENDEN, John	A.B.	DIADEM	
	Ord	DIADEM	St Vincent
FISHER, John	Midshipman	STATELY	
FISHER, William	Master's Mate	FOUDROYANT	
	Captain. R.N.	ASIA	Syria
FITZROY, William	Lieut. R.N.	PENELOPE	
	Capt's Servant	PHAETON	1 June 1794
	Midshipman	SANS PAREIL	23rd June 1795
			(Vfd Abd. Not on Roll)
	Captain. R.N.	AEOLUS	4 Novr 1805
	Captain. R.N.	AEOLUS	Martinique
FLANDRYN, Daniel	Cpl. R.M.	ASTRAEA	
	Pte. R.M.	GOLIATH	St Vincent
	Pte. R.M.	GOLIATH	Nile
FLETCHER, William	L.M.	ROMNEY	
FLINN, Patrick	Ord	SANTA DOROTEA	
FOLLETT, John	A.B.	TIGRE	
	A.B.	TIGRE	Acre. 30 May 1799
FOOTMAN, John	A.B.	ROEBUCK	
FORBES, John	Lieut. R.N.	FLORENTINA	
	Midshipman	MINOTAUR	Nile
	Lieut. R.N.	CANOPUS	St Domingo
FORD, Christopher	L.M.	STATELY	
FORSTER, Robert	Master's Mate	LEDA	
	Lieut. R.N.	ASIA	B.S. 14 Dec 1814
FOX, George	Lieut. R.N.	MINOTAUR	
FOX, Joseph	Pte. R.M.	AJAX	
FOX, Samuel	Surgeon	MONDOVI	
FRANKS, John	Q.M.	DETERMINEE	
FRASER, J.S.H.	Midshipman	ROEBUCK	
FREATHY, Henry	Carp's Crew	FOUDROYANT	
FREEMAN, William	A.B.	NIGER	
FRIDAY, Israel	A.B.	SWIFTSURE	
	A.B.	ATLAS	St Domingo
FRY, Humphrey	A.B.	DIADEM	
	A.B.	DIADEM	14 March 1795
	A.B.	DIADEM	St Vincent
FURY, John	Ord	SWIFTSURE	(M. L. as FURSE)
	L.M.	SWIFTSURE	Nile
GAGE, Nicholas	A.B.	AJAX	G.H. 2938
	L.M.	COLOSSUS	St Vincent
GAINS, John	Pte. R.M.	RENOMMEE	
GALLAWAY, Alexander	A.B.	RENOWN	
	Midshipman	THUNDERER	Trafalgar
GIBBINS, William	Not Given	ASTRAEA	
GIBBS, John	Surgeon	CHARON	
GILES, Samuel	Purser	ASTRAEA	
	Midshipman	CULLODEN	1 June 1794
	Purser	ULYSSES	Martinique
GILPIN, Thomas	A.B.	DICTATOR	
GODBY, John Hardy	Lieut. R.N.	ATHENIENNE	
	Midshipman	NYMPHE	Nymphe. 8 March 1797
GOOCH, Benjamin	Drummer. R.M.	DELFT	
GOODSON, James	L.M.	MONMOUTH	G.H. 1911
GOULD, John Robert	A.B.	KENT	
	Boatswain	VENERABLE	Camperdown (as John Gould)
GRAMSHAW, Joseph.G.H.	Midshipman	TIGRE	
	Boy 2nd Cl	TIGRE	Acre. 30 May 1799
GRANDY, Samuel	Ord	DIADEM	
GRANT, John	A.B.	PIQUE	

GREEN, Samuel	Pte. R.M.	AJAX	
	Pte. R.M.	VICTORY	*Trafalgar*
GREENWOOD, Thomas	A.B.	TRUSTY	
GREGORY, William	Ord	MINERVE	
GREY, Edward	Boy	DELFT	
GRIEVE, John	Pilot	NIGER	
GRIFFITHS, George	L.M.	MONMOUTH	*G.H. 3750*
	Boy	St GEORGE	*14 March 1795*
GUDGER, James	A.B.	AJAX	
GURNEY, John	Pte. R.M.	NORTHUMBERLAND	
HALBORD, George	Pte. R.M.	FOUDROYANT	*(M.L. as HOLBERT)*
HALL, George	Ord	RESOURCE	
HAMILTON, Robert	Pte. R.M.	FOUDROYANT	
	Pte. R.M.	BEDFORD	*Camperdown*
	Pte. R.M.	FOUDROYANT	*12 Octr 1798*
HAMON, Samuel	L.M.	FOUDROYANT	*(M.L. as HAMMOND)*
HARDING, George	L.M.	RENOWN	
	L.M.	THUNDERER	*Trafalgar*
HARDY, Horace	Boy	THETIS	*G.H. 506*
HARE, Charles	Midshipman	MADRAS	
HARFORD, Thomas	Pte. R.M.	KENT	
	Pte. R.M.	VENERABLE	*Camperdown*
HARMAN, Thomas	Drummer. R.M.	RENOMEE	
HARRIS, Charles	Pte. R.M.	MADRAS	
HARRIS, Joseph	A.B.	NORTHUMBERLAND	*G.H. 796*
HARRISON, Joseph	Midshipman	SPIDER	
HART, William	A.B.	AJAX	
	A.B.	CAESAR	*1 June 1794*
HARVEY, James	Carpenter	GREYHOUND	
HATCH, John	Pte. R.M.	RESOURCE	
HAWTAYNE, Charles.S.J.	Lieut. R.N.	GREYHOUND	
	Midshipman	DEFENCE	*1 June 1794*
HAYNE, Thomas	L.M.	SWIFTSURE	
	L.M.	SWIFTSURE	*Nile*
HAZARD, William	Q.M.	CHARON	
	A.B.	CHARON	*23rd June 1795*
HENDERSON, Matthew	Carpenter	SHEERNESS	
HEPBURN, John	Master	MINOTAUR	
	Master	CANOPUS	*St Domingo*
HICKS, William	Quarter Gunner	HECTOR	
HEGGIE, Archibald	Ord	MADRAS	
	A.B.	BELLEISLE	*Trafalgar*
	A.B.	LONDON	*London. 13 March 1806*
HIGGS, William.H.	Midshipman	FOUDROYANT	
	Lieut. R.N.	ESPOIR	*Espoir. 25 & 27 June 1809*
HILL, Henry	Ord	NORTHUMBERLAND	
HILL, John (a)	Midshipman	EUROPA	
HILL, John	Commander	HEROINE	
	Lieut. R.N.	MINOTAUR	*Nile*
HILL, Joseph	A.B.	DICTATOR	*G.H. 982*
HILLIER, George	Lieut. R.N.	TIGRE	
	Capt's Servant	ALFRED	*1 June 1794*
	Midshipman	ARDENT	*Camperdown*
	Lieut. R.N.	ALLIANCE	*Acre. 30 May 1799*
HILLYAR, William	Midshipman	NIGER	
HILLYAR, Robert.P.	Surgeon	ROEBUCK	
	Surgeon	APOLLO	*B.S. 1 Nov 1809*
	Surgeon	ALBION	*Navarino*
HILTON, Stephen	Midshipman	PEARL	
	Master's Mate	MINOTAUR	*Trafalgar*
	Lieut. R.N.	REVENGE	*Basque Roads 1809 (Vfd Abd. Not on Roll)*
HOARE, Edward.W.	Lieut. R.N.	NORTHUMBERLAND	
	Midshipman	LONDON	*23rd June 1795*
	Captain. R.N.	MINDEN	*Java*
HODGSKIN, Thomas	Ord	ACTIVE	
HODGSON, William	Sgt. R.M.	SENSIBLE	
	Cpl. R.M.	ETHALION	*12 Octr 1798 (Received two single clasp medals)*
HOGDEN, Thomas	Ship's Corporal	DIANA	
	L.M.	BARFLEUR	*St Vincent*
HOLLINWORTH, John	Lieut. R.N.	VICTOR	
HOLMAN, William	Purser	VESTAL	
HOPE, Henry	Midshipman	KENT	
	Captain. R.N.	ENDYMION	*Endymion Wh President*
HORE, James Ryves	2nd Lt. R.M.	DIANA	
	1st Lt. R.M.	IMPERIEUSE	*Basque Roads 1809*
HORN, Stephen	Ord	PETEREL	
	Ord	PETEREL	*Peterel. 21 March 1800*
HORNSBY, William	Boy	EXPERIMENT	
HOSKIN, William	Ord	AJAX	
HUDSON, Joseph	Pte. R.M.	NORTHUMBERLAND	

EGYPT

HUGGINS, James.E.	Master's Mate	EURUS	(In Command of Flat Boat)
	Master's Mate	EURUS	B.S. 29 Aug 1800
HUGHES, George	Boy	MODESTE	
HUSSEY, Thomas	Lieut. R.M.	KENT	
HUTCHINS, Charles	Ord	KENT	
	L.M.	VENERABLE	Camperdown
HUTCHINGS, John	Carpenter's Crew	ROEBUCK	
HUTCHINSON, George	Master's Mate	DIADEM	
	Master's Mate	CAESAR	4 Novr 1805
	Lieut. R.N.	DOLPHIN	B.S. Ap & May 1813
INMAN, John	Surgeon	EXPEDITION	
JACK, Leigh.S.	Midshipman	CYCLOPS	
	Lieut. R.N.	DESIREE	Gluckstadt. 5 Jany 1814
JACKSON, Robert	Commander	BONNE CITOYENNE	
JACOBS, John	Pte. R.M.	CAMELION	
JARMAN, Thomas	A.B.	AJAX	
JAY, Charles.H.	Midshipman	MONMOUTH	
	Midshipman	Gun-Boat No 19	St Sebastian
JEFFRESON, Francis	A.B.	GREYHOUND	
JENNINGS, John	A.B.	REGULUS	
JESSEP. Thomas.F.	Purser	DIANA	
JOB, Charles	Pte. R.M.	FLORENTINA	G.H. 1274
JOHNSON, George.C.	L.M.	NORTHUMBERLAND	
	Lieut. R.N.	AETNA	Basque Roads 1809
JOHNSON, William	A.B.	AJAX	
JOHNSTON, James	Ord	VESTAL	
	Ord	POWERFUL	Camperdown
JONES, Alexander	Lieut. R.N.	MINERVE	
JONES, Edward	A.B.	FLORA	
JONES, James	Ord	NORTHUMBERLAND	
JONES, J.H.	A.B.	PIGMY	G.H. 2409
JONES, Robert	L.M.	MADRAS	
JOREY, John	A.B.	THISBE	(May be JORCY)
JOYCE, George	Boy	THETIS	
JOYCE, Joseph	Bosun's Mate	HEBE	
KEATES, Samuel	L.M.	DIADEM	
KELLY, Benedictus.M.	Master's Mate	GIBRALTAR	
KELLY, William	Lieut. R.N.	MINERVE	
	Lieut. R.N.	PRINCE	Trafalgar
	Lieut. R.N.	CALEDONIA	Basque Roads 1809
	Lieut. R.N.	CALEDONIA	B.S. 27 Sep 1810 (Vfd Abd. Not on Roll)
KEMP, John	Ord	TIGRE	
	Ord	TIGRE	Acre. 30 May 1799 (Vfd Abd. Not on Roll)
KENNEDY, Hugh	A.B.	DRAGON	
KENYON, Thomas	Ord	PEARL	
KERR, Robert	Surgeon	BONNE CITOYENNE	
KETTLE, Robert	A.B.	MONMOUTH	
	Ord	MONMOUTH	Camperdown
KING, James	Boy	ROEBUCK	
KING, James	Boy	THISBE	
KING, John	Ord	ACTIVE	
KIRBY, Thomas	A.B.	AJAX	
KIRBY, Thomas	Quarter Gunner	INCONSTANT	
KIRTON, John	Sgt. R.M.	THETIS	
LACEY, William	Pte. R.M.	PIQUE	G.H. 1686
LAMB, John	Midshipman	NORTHUMBERLAND	
LAMONT, James	Midshipman	HEBE	
LANDY, Richard	Ord	MONMOUTH	(May read LENDY)
LASCELLES, Thomas.A.	Lt. R.M.	DELFT	
LAWRENCE, Daniel	Midshipman	CYNTHIA	
	Lieut. R.N.	HEUREUX	B.S. 28 Nov 1808
	Lieut. R.N.	WANDERER	Guadaloupe
LAWRENCE, Thomas.L.	Lt. R.M.	PEARL	
	Supn 2nd Lt R.M.	BADGER	Isle St Marcou 6 May 1798
LAWSON, Gilbert	A.B.	SWIFTSURE	
	A.B.	SWIFTSURE	Nile
	Quarter Gunner	CAESAR	4 Novr 1805
	Gunner's Mate	CAESAR	Basque Roads 1809
	Gunner	PHOEBE	Phoebe. 28 March 1814
LECKEY, Robert	A.B.	PIQUE	
	Ord	CULLODEN	1 June 1794
	Ord	CULLODEN	St Vincent
	Ord	CULLODEN	Nile
LEE, James	A.B.	MINOTAUR	
	Ord	MINOTAUR	Nile
LEO, John	Ord	TIGRE	
	L.M.	TIGRE	Acre. 30 May 1799

THE NAVAL GENERAL SERVICE MEDAL ROLL 1793-1840

LESLIE, Alexander	A.B.	MONMOUTH	
	A.B.	MONMOUTH	*Camperdown*
LESLIE, Samuel	Lieut. R.N.	HAERLEM	
LETCH, Charles	Midshipman	DRAGON	
LEWIS, James	Ord	EL CARMEN	*G.H. 1471*
LEWIS, John	Ord	MONMOUTH	
	Ord	MONMOUTH	*Camperdown*
LINDSAY, Peter	A.B.	CERES	
LINSTEAD, Michael	L.M.	MONMOUTH	
LIVINGSTONE, Thomas	Captain. R.N.	ATHENIENNE	
LLOYD, Edward	Midshipman	DICTATOR	
	Lieut. R.N.	BOADICEA	*Boadicea. 18 Septr 1810 Rcvd M.G.S. for JAVA*
LLOYD, Samuel	Boy	CYCLOPS	*G.H. 1207*
LOCK, John	Drummer. R.M.	ROMNEY	
LOCK, J.Erskine	Midshipman	MONDOVI	
LOCKHART, James	Midshipman	PIGMY	
LONDON, John	Purser	ROMULUS	
LONGCHAMP, John	Midshipman	LEDA	
	Midshipman	ANDROMEDA	*Capture of the Desiree*
	Midshipman	DESIREE	*Copenhagen 1801*
LOUIS, John	Midshipman	MINOTAUR	
LOVERSUCH, William	Pte. R.M.	AGINCOURT	
	Cpl. R.M.	POLYPHEMUS	*Trafalgar*
LOWE, Richard	A.B.	VESTAL	
LOWRIE, Robert	A.B.	MODESTE	
LOWRY, James	Surg's Mate	SWIFTSURE	
	Surg's Mate	FOUDROYANT	*12 Octr 1798*
LUKE, James	A.B.	MINOTAUR	
	A.B.	MINOTAUR	*Nile*
LYSAGHT, Arthur	Master's Mate	FORTE	
	Midshipman	SYBILLE	*Sybille. 28 Feby 1799*
MACE, Edmund	Boy	INFLEXIBLE	
MACNAMARA, Robert	A.B.	ALLIGATOR	
MACKAY, John	Surg's Mate	MINERVE	
	Surgeon	BELLONA	*Basque Roads 1809*
MACHEM, Andrew	A.B.	CHARON	
MAINWARING, Edward.R.P.	A.B.	ROEBUCK	*(Captain. R.N. 1841)*
MALONE, Henry	Pte. R.M.	CERES	
MANNING, William	Boy 3rd Cl	PENELOPE	*(Vfd Abd. Not on Roll)*
	Boy 3rd Cl	PENELOPE	*Penelope. 30 March 1800*
MANSFIELD, William	A.B.	DOLPHIN	
MARSH, John	Boy	CAMELION	
MARSHALL, Henry.M.	Midshipman	SWIFTSURE	
	A.B.	SWIFTSURE	*Nile*
MARSHALL, John	Lieut. R.N.	RENOMMEE	
MARTIN, William	Pte. R.M.	HECTOR	
	Pte. R.M.	AJAX	*St Sebastian*
MATHEWSON, Daniel	A.B.	STATELY	
	Servant	NIGER	*1 June 1794*
MATRON, Thomas	Pte. R.M.	NORTHUMBERLAND	*(May read MATSON)*
MAUGHAN, Philip	Mid. Bombay E.I.C.	TERNATE	
MAUGHAN, Samuel	Actg Master	DIDO	
MAYHEW, John	Purser	PALLAS	
McAUSLAND, Peter	Gunner	PETEREL	
	A.B.	MONTAGU	*1 June 1794*
	Gunner's Mate	IRRESISTIBLE	*23rd June 1795*
	Bosun's Mate	IRRESISTIBLE	*St Vincent*
	Gunner	IMPLACABLE	*Implacable. 26 Augt 1808*
McCLAY, John	Gunner's Mate	MADRAS	
	Ord	DONEGAL	*St Domingo*
	Q.M.	DONEGAL	*Basque Roads 1809*
McCOLL, Duncan	Surgeon	FOUDROYANT	
McDONOUGH, E.	A.B.	FURY	
McFRANE, Henry	L.M.	KENT	
McGRIGOR, Robert	A.B.	KENT	
McKEY, William	L.M.	ACTIVE	
McKINDY, John	Midshipman	SANTA THERESA	
McPHERSON, William	Ord	TIGRE	
	Ord	TIGRE	*Acre. 30 May 1799 (Vfd Abd. Not on Roll)*
McQUIN, Hugh	Quarter Gunner	DIADEM	
	Ord	DIADEM	*14 March 1795*
	A.B.	DIADEM	*St Vincent*
MILLER, William	A.B.	CYCLOPS	
MILLER, Zaccheus	2nd Lt. R.M.	FOUDROYANT	
	2nd Lt. R.M.	FOUDROYANT	*12 Octr 1798*
MITCHELL, David	Pte. R.M.	THISBE	*(2nd Clasp?)*
MITCHELL, James	Boy	MONMOUTH	*G.H. 1036*
MOLLINEUX, Matthew	Ord	TIGRE	
	Ord	TIGRE	*Acre. 30 May 1799*
MOODIE, James	Pte. R.M.	HEBE	
MOONEY, Stephen	Pte. R.M.	TERMAGANT	

EGYPT

MORGAN, James	A.B.	SWIFTSURE	
	A.B.	SWIFTSURE	Nile
MORGAN, James	Pte. R.M.	RENOWN	G.H. 1749
	Pte. R.M.	TONNANT	Trafalgar
MORTON, Andrew	Pte. R.M.	KENT	
MORTON, James	Not Given	FLORA	
MOULDY, Matthew	Ord	INFLEXIBLE	
MOURILYAN, Edward	Midshipman	TIGRE	
	Midshipman	TIGRE	Acre. 30 May 1799
MULTON, Charles	Boy	EUROPA	
MUNTON, Eusebius	Ord	MADRAS	
MURPHY, James	Boy 3rd Cl	ALLIGATOR	
	Ord	TOPAZE	B.S. 1 Nov 1809
MURRAY, Charles	A.B.	AJAX	
MURRAY, William	A.B.	RESOURCE	
MURRELL, Samuel	A.B.	EUROPA	G.H. 538
MURTON, Henry.J.	2nd Lt R.M.	ROMNEY	
MYSON, James	L.M.	DICTATOR	
NEALE, John	Midshipman	KENT	
	Midshipman	VENERABLE	Camperdown (or VETERAN)
NEALE, Thomas	Pte. R.M.	DETERMINEE	
NEVILLE, Edward	Ord	AGINCOURT	G.H. 1720
NEVILLE, James	Actg Lieut. R.N.	IPHIGENIA	
	Actg Lieut. R.N.	IPHIGENIA	B.S. 29 Aug 1800
NEWTON, Isaac	Supn (Unrated)	DANGEREUSE	
	Carp's Crew	THESEUS	Nile
	Carp's Crew	THESEUS	Acre. 30 May 1799
NICHOLLS, James	A.B.	MINOTAUR	
NICHOLSON, William	Quarter Gunner	EUROPA	
NEILL, John	Surgeon	VICTOR	(Also M.G.S. "Guadaloupe")
NOADS, Thomas	Ord	NORTHUMBERLAND	
NORLEY, William	A.B.	NORTHUMBERLAND	
NORMAN, Masters	Midshipman	DIANA	
NORMAN, Thomas	Carp's Mate	ALLIGATOR	
NUGENT, John	Lieut. R.N.	PHOENIX	
	Capt's Servant	INVINCIBLE	1 June 1794
OAKS, Thomas	L.M.	CYCLOPS	
OGLE, Challoner	Boy	EUROPA	
OGLE, Charles	Captain R.N.	GREYHOUND	
OLIVER, John	Master	SANTA DOROTEA	
OLIVER, Thomas	Midshipman	RENOWN	
OMMANNEY, Henry.M.	Lieut. R.N.	ACTIVE	
ORCHARD, Benjamin	A.B.	NORTHUMBERLAND	
	Carp's Crew	THALIA	23rd June 1795
ORMISTON, John	A.B.	AJAX	
	L.M.	IRRESISTIBLE	23rd June 1795
	L.M.	IRRESISTIBLE	St Vincent
OSBORN, John	Master's Mate	VIRAGO	
	A.B.	IRRESISTIBLE	B.S. 17 Mar 1794
	Master's Mate	VINCIEGO	Vinciego. 30 March 1800
OWENS, John	Pte. R.M.	STATELY	
	Pte. R.M.	BRACKEL	Camperdown
PAGET, John	Master's Mate	MINORCA	
PALMER, Charles	Pte. R.M.	KENT	
	Pte. R.M.	AFRICA	Trafalgar
PARKER, Henry.D.	Actg Lieut. R.N.	PEGASUS	
PARKER, Joseph	Ord	TIGRE	
PARKER, William	Lieut. R.N.	DRUID	(This EGYPT clasp awarded on a separate medal)
	Midshipman	ST GEORGE	14 March 1795
	Midshipman	BRITANNIA	St Vincent
	Midshipman	GOLIATH	Nile
PARNELL, Joseph	Ord	DICTATOR	
PARR, Alexander.F.	Midshipman	PENELOPE	(Possibly 2 medals awarded)
	Midshipman	SWIFTSURE	Nile (Single clasp known)
	Midshipman	AGAMEMNON	Trafalgar
	Midshipman	AGAMEMNON	St Domingo
PARRY, Henry	A.B.	EURUS	
	Master's Mate	PORCUPINE	B.S. 10 July 1808
PARSONS, George.S.	Actg Lieut. R.N.	EL CARMEN	
	Midshipman	BARFLEUR	St Vincent
PATRICK, John	A.B.	AJAX	
PAUL, John.H.	Ord	PIQUE	
PAVEY, John	Boy	PALLAS	
PAYN, Philip	Ord	TERMAGANT	
PEACOCK, Robert	A.B.	MADRAS	
PEACOCK, William	Ord	MADRAS	(M.L. as PEART?)
	Ord	MONTAGU	1 June 1794
PEAKE, Thomas.L.	Midshipman	RENOWN	
	Lieut. R.N.	VICTORIOUS	Victorious With Rivoli

PEARMAN, James	A.B.	RENOMMEE	
PEDLAR, George	Midshipman	FOUDROYANT	
	Master's Mate	SPEEDY	Speedy. 6 Novr 1799
PELLY, Jeremiah	Pte. R.M.	AJAX	
PERFAY, John	Pte. R.M.	AJAX	
PETHERICK, Edward	L.M.	CYNTHIA	
PHILIPPS, John.G.	Midshipman	MINOTAUR	
	Midshipman	MINOTAUR	Nile
PHILLIPS, Charles	L.M.	DELFT	
	A.B.	COLOSSUS	Trafalgar
PHILLIPS, James	A.B.	PEARL	
PIGOT, Richard	Midshipman	RENOWN	
	A.B.	CANADA	12 Octr 1798 (Roll as PIGGOTT. Navy List a PIGOT, Richard.H.H.)
PINTO, Thomas	Master's Mate	NORTHUMBERLAND	
	Midshipman	IRRESISTIBLE	St Vincent
	Lieut. R.N.	AGAMEMNON	Trafalgar
	Lieut. R.N.	AGAMEMNON	St Domingo
	Commander	ACHATES	B.S. 13 Dec 1809
	Commander	ACHATES	Guadaloupe
POCOCK, Robert	L.M.	RENOWN	
PLUMMER, Edward	A.B.	TIGRE	
	Ord	TIGRE	Acre. 30 May 1799 (Vfd Abd. Not on Roll)
PORTLOCK, John	Pte. R.M.	AGINCOURT	
POUPARD, Abraham	Ord	SWIFTSURE	
	L.M.	SWIFTSURE	Nile
POYNTZ, Newdigate	Midshipman	DETERMINEE	
PREEDER, William	Ord	NORTHUMBERLAND	
PRESCOTT, Henry	Midshipman	PENELOPE	
	Midshipman	PENELOPE	Penelope. 30 March 1800
	Lieut. R.N.	AEOLUS	2 Novr 1805
	Commander	WEAZLE	Amanthea. 25 July 1810
PREVOST, James	Lieut. R.N.	FOUDROYANT	
	Lieut. R.N.	BARFLEUR	St Vincent
PRICE, Richard	A.B.	VESTAL	
	A.B.	POWERFUL	Camperdown
PRIDHAM, William	A.B.	CHARON	
PROCTOR, William.B.	Lieut. R.N.	DIANA	
RADLEY, John	Carpenter	CYCLOPS	
RAINS, John	Boy 2nd Cl	PALLAS	
RAMSEY, Edward	Ord	MONMOUTH	
RAMSHAY, George.R.	Master's Mate	NORTHUMBERLAND	
RAVEN, Michael	Ord	MONMOUTH	
REED, Evan	A.B.	FOUDROYANT	
REEDER, John	A.B.	TERMAGANT	
	Actg Gunner	AMPHION	Lissa
REID, Charles.H.	Midshipman	LEDA	
REVANS, Thomas	Master's Mate	DETERMINEE	
	Lieut. R.N.	IMPREGNABLE	Algiers
REYNOLDS, Thomas	Master	DICTATOR	
REYNOLDS, Thomas	Master	FOUDROYANT	
REYNOLDS, Thomas	Pte. R.M.	EXPEDITION	
	Pte. R.M.	DEFENCE	Trafalgar
RICE, John	L.M.	DRAGON	
RICHARDS, Peter	Trumpeter	PEARL	G.H. 2721
RICHARDSON, Charles	Lieut. R.N.	KENT	
	Master's Mate	ROYAL GEORGE	1 June 1794
	Lieut. R.N.	CIRCE	Camperdown
	Captain. R.N.	CAESAR	Basque Roads 1809
RICHARDSON, Charles	L.M.	CAMELION	
ROBERTS, Benjamin	Midshipman	MADRAS	
	Lieut. R.N.	PROCRIS	Java
ROBERTSON, Thomas	Surgeon	LEDA	
	Surgeon	SIRIUS	Trafalgar
	Surgeon	SIRIUS	Sirius. 17 April 1806
ROBINSON, Benjamin	A.B.	KENT	
	A.B.	VENERABLE	Camperdown
ROBINSON, John	A.B.	ACTIVE	G.H. 368
ROBINSON, John	A.B.	STATELY	
ROBLYN, Thomas	Not Given	ULYSSES	
ROCHFORT, R.	A.B.	HAERLEM	
ROSE, Thomas	A.B.	INFLEXIBLE	
ROSS, John	L.M.	TARTARUS	
ROUSE, Joseph	Boy 3rd Cl	RENOMMEE	(M.L. as ROWSE)
	Ord	PHOENIX	Phoenix. 10 Augt 1805
	Ord	PHOENIX	4 Novr 1805

EGYPT

ROUSE, William	Pte. R.M.	FOUDROYANT	
	Pte. R.M.	BEDFORD	*Camperdown*
	Pte. R.M.	CONQUEROR	*Trafalgar*
ROW, Patrick	L.M.	TRUSTY	
ROWE, William	Ord	NORTHUMBERLAND	
	Boy	IRRESISTIBLE	*St Vincent*
ROWLAND, Richard	Pte. R.M.	HECTOR	
ROYER, Charles	Midshipman	SWIFTSURE	
	A.B.	SWIFTSURE	*Nile*
	Lieut. R.N.	ASTRAEA	*Off Tamatave. 20 May 1811 (Vfd Abd. Not on Roll)*
RUBIDGE, Charles	Midshipman	CERES	
	Lieut. R.N.	AETNA	*Basque Roads. 1809*
RYE, George.H.	Midshipman	MODESTE	
SADGROVE, Francis	Pte. R.M.	EXPEDITION	*G.H. 35*
SAMPSON, Adam	Ord	TIGRE	
	Ord	TIGRE	*Acre. 30 May 1799*
SAUNDERS, Edward	Ord	MODESTE	
SCOTT, George	Master's Mate	MINOTAUR	
	Lieut. R.N.	PHOEBE	*Off Tamatave. 20 May 1811*
	Lieut. R.N.	PHOEBE	*Java*
SCOTT, William	Pte. R.M.	HECTOR	
SCOWN, John	Ord	SWIFTSURE	
	L.M.	SWIFTSURE	*Nile*
SEABURN, Robert	A.B.	KENT	
SEARLE, Joseph	Coxswain	AJAX	
SEEDS, Robert	Cook	VESTAL	
	A.B.	BRUNSWICK	*1 June 1794*
SEYMOUR, John	Not Given	NORTHUMBERLAND	
SHAW, John	A.B.	TIGRE	
SHEEN, Alexander	Boy	EUROPA	
SHEEN, John	L.M.	EUROPA	
SHEEN, William	Ord	ROEBUCK	
SHIRLEY, George	Q.M.'s Mate	FOUDROYANT	
	A.B.	ST GEORGE	*14 March 1795*
	Q.M.'s Mate	VANGUARD	*Nile*
	Gunner	CLEOPATRA	*Martinique*
SHORT, William	Pte. R.M.	FOUDROYANT	
	Pte. R.M.	NAMUR	*4 Novr 1805*
SHORTMAN, Samuel	Ord	NORTHUMBERLAND	
SHUTE, Benjamin	Ord	LEDA	*G.H. 3788*
	Ord	NAMUR	*4 Novr 1805*
SILOM, James	A.B.	SWIFTSURE	
	A.B.	SWIFTSURE	*Nile*
SIMMONS, Daniel	L.M.	EUROPA	
SIMMONS, Martin	Boy	MODESTE	
SIMPSON, Benjamin	Ord	PORT MAHON	
SIMS, George	A.B.	NORTHUMBERLAND	
	A.B.	EGMONT	*St Vincent*
SINCLAIR, John	A.B.	STATELY	
SKINNER, Joseph	Q.M.	DRAGON	
SMALL, John	L.M.	PENELOPE	*(Vfd Abd. Not on Roll)*
	L.M.	PENELOPE	*Penelope. 30 March 1800*
	L.M.	LOIRE	*Guadaloupe*
SMALLBRIDGE, William	Coxswain	ROMULUS	
SMITH, Alexander	A.B.	MINOTAUR	
	A.B.	MINOTAUR	*Nile*
SMITH (2), John	Ord	AJAX	
SMITH, John	Ord	EXPEDITION	
SMITHERS, John.J.	L.M.	AGINCOURT	
	Ord	BELLEROPHON	*Trafalgar*
SNELL, John	A.B.	TIGRE	*G.H. 403*
	A.B.	TIGRE	*Acre. 30 May 1799*
SOTHEBY, Charles	Midshipman	FOUDROYANT	
	Midshipman	ALEXANDER	*Nile*
SOUTH, William.W.	Midshipman	FORTE	
SOWERBY, John	Ship's Corporal	MONDOVI	
SPEED, John	Clerk	RENOWN	
SPENCER, Samuel	Midshipman	ACTIVE	
	Master's Mate	VICTORY	*Trafalgar*
SPRINGFIELD, John	L.M.	MONMOUTH	
SPURWAY, John	Ord	MODESTE	
SQUIRES, Thomas	A.B.	PETEREL	
STAPLES, Robert	A.B.	FLORA	
	Q.M's Mate	PENELOPE	*Martinique*
STEEL, James	Pte. R.M.	KENT	
STERRICKS, David	A.B.	NORTHUMBERLAND	
	Ord	IRRESISTIBLE	*St Vincent*
STEVENS, Archibald	A.B.	FOUDROYANT	
	A.B.	BEDFORD	*Camperdown*
	A.B.	FOUDROYANT	*12 Octr 1798*

STILL, Joseph	A.B.	MONMOUTH	
	L.M.	MONMOUTH	*Camperdown*
STOCKWELL, David	A.B.	STATELY	
STODDART, Pringle	Lieut. R.N.	KENT	
	Midshipman	VALIANT	*1 June 1794*
	A.B.	QUEEN CHARLOTTE	*23rd June 1795*
STORY, Anson	Boy 2nd Cl	AJAX	
STRADLING, Thomas	Pte. R.M.	VESTAL	
	Pte. R.M.	HAUGHTY	*Martinique*
	Pte. R.M.	BACCHANTE	*B.S. 6 Jan 1813*
STRINGER, William	Ord	MINERVE	
STUART, James	A.B.	ALLIGATOR	
TAYLOR, Charles	A.B.	TIGRE	
	A.B.	TIGRE	*Acre. 30 May 1799 (Vfd Abd. Not on Roll)*
TAYLOR, John	Midshipman	GIBRALTAR	
	Master's Mate	DONEGAL	*St Domingo*
	Lieut. R.N.	DONEGAL	*Basque Roads 1809*
TAYLOR, William	A.B.	VESTAL	
TEAR, John	Ord	AGINCOURT	
	Ord	AGINCOURT	*Camperdown*
TERRY, Thomas	Carpenter	AJAX	
THOMAS, George	Lieut. R.N.	EUROPA	
THOMAS, John	Boy	BRACKEL	
THOMAS, Rees	Pte. R.M.	VESTAL	
	Pte. R.M.	POWERFUL	*Camperdown*
THOMPSON, Charles	Lieut. R.N.	PHOENIX	
THOMPSON, George	L.M.	MADRAS	
THOMPSON, Jacob	A.B.	EL CARMEN	
THOMPSON, Josiah	Vol 1st Cl	TIGRE	
	Ord	TIGRE	*Acre. 30 May 1799*
THOMSON, David	Quarter Gunner	CAMELION	
	L.M.	TREMENDOUS	*1 June 1794*
THOMSON, William.A.	Midshipman	FLORENTINA	
TILBY, T.M.Ilden	Clerk	HEROINE	
TILLSTONE, Thomas	Ord	INFLEXIBLE	
TINCOMBE, George	Midshipman	DIADEM	*(A of I. AVA. "SLANEY")*
TINDAL, Charles	Vol 1st Cl	LEDA	
TINNEY, George	Boy	AJAX	
TOMS, William	A.B.	TIGRE	
	A.B.	TIGRE	*Acre. 30 May 1799*
	A.B.	SCORPION	*Scorpion. 31 March 1804*
	Sailmaker	SCORPION	*Scorpion. 12 Jany 1810*
	Sailmaker	SCORPION	*Guadaloupe*
TRACHEY, John	Sailmaker's Crew	FLORENTINA	
TRUEMAN, John	Pte. R.M.	PEGASUS	
TUDMAN, John	Pte. R.M.	MONMOUTH	
	Pte. R.M.	MONMOUTH	*Camperdown*
TURNER, John	Pte. R.M.	NIGER	
TURNER, William.J.	Drummer. R.M.	EUROPA	
TYTE, Robert.W.	Lieut. R.N.	DANGEREUSE	
	A.B.	THESEUS	*Nile*
	Midshipman	THESEUS	*Acre. 30 May 1799 (Vfd Abd. Not on Roll)*
UNDERHILL, William	A.B.	CAMELION	
VENN, Benjamin	Capt's Coxswain	DIDO	*G.H. 1595*
VENSON, George	Pte. R.M.	MINOTAUR	
	Pte. R.M.	MINOTAUR	*Nile*
WADE, Francis	A.B.	MINOTAUR	*G.H. 7903*
	A.B.	MINOTAUR	*Nile*
WADGE, George	Boy	MINERVE	
WAKEFIELD, Samuel	A.B.	HECTOR	
WAL(or R)DEN, James	L.M.	LEDA	
WALKER, John	Ord	EL CARMEN	
WALKER, John	A.B.	NIGER	
WALKER, Robert	Q.M's Mate	KENT	
WARD, John	Pte. R.M.	INFLEXIBLE	
WARDELL, John	Midshipman	GREYHOUND	
WATLEY, Thomas	L.M.	ALLIGATOR	
WEAVER, Richard	A.B.	AJAX	
WEBB, Thomas	A.B.	FOUDROYANT	*G.H. 41*
WEBB, William	A.B.	PETEREL	
WEBBER, John	A.B.	BLONDE	
WEBBER, William	Pte. R.M.	HEBE	
	Pte. R.M.	INVINCIBLE	*1 June 1794*
WEDGE, William	Pte. R.M.	AJAX	
WELCH, Robert	Act Lieut. R.N.	EXPERIMENT	
	Vol 1st Cl	GALATEA	*23rd June 1795*
	Midshipman	FOUDROYANT	*12 Octr 1798 (Vfd Abd. Not on Roll)*
WEST, Christopher	Vol 1st Cl	THETIS	
	Midshipman	MINOTAUR	*Trafalgar*
WEST, John	A.B.	DRAGON	

EGYPT

WESTON, Peter	Ord	AGINCOURT	
WHARTON, Francis	Lieut. R.N.	GOOD DESIGN (Armed Ship)	(Navy List John Francis W') ? Not on Roll, received Sultan's Gold Medal
	Midshipman	GIBRALTAR	1 June 1794
WHEATCROFT, Samuel	Pte. R.M.	PEGASUS	
WHITE, Charles.M.	Master	MONMOUTH	
WHITE, Gilbert	A.B.	FOUDROYANT	
	A.B.	LOWESTOFFE	Lowestoffe. 24 June 1795
WHITE, John	Lieut. R.N.	WILHELMINA	
WHITTOCK, John	Pte. R.M.	THETIS	
WIGGAR, Edward	Boy	KENT	
WIGLEY, John.G.	Midshipman	TRUSTY	
WILKINSON, Henry	Pte. R.M.	TIGRE	
	Pte. R.M.	BEDFORD	Camperdown
	Pte. R.M.	TIGRE	Acre. 30 May 1799
WILKINSON, Thomas	A.B.	CHARON	
WILLCOCK, Joseph.F.	Clerk	PEARL	
WILLIAMS, David	A.B.	ALEXANDER	
	L.M.	ALEXANDER	Nile
WILLIAMS, John	A.B.	TIGRE	
	A.B.	TIGRE	Acre. 30 May 1799
WILLIAMS, Owen	A.B.	SWIFTSURE	
	A.B.	SWIFTSURE	Nile
WILLIAMS, Richard.P.	Surgeon	DRUID	
WILLIAMS, William	A.B.	HEBE	
WILLIS, John	A.B.	TIGRE	
	A.B.	TIGRE	Acre. 30 May 1799
WILLIS, William	Ord	CYNTHIA	
WILSON, James	Gunner	MODESTE	
WILSON, James	Midshipman	SANTA THERESA	
WILSON, M.J.	Midshipman	ACTIVE	
WILSON, Robert	Pte. R.M.	THETIS	
WINTERBURN, George	Boy	RENOWN	
	Ord	CAESAR	4 Novr 1805
	Cook	LOIRE	Guadaloupe
WITHERS, Thomas	Ord	CERES	
WITHRILL, Richard	Pte. R.M.	PIQUE	
WOODLEY, James	Ord	EUROPA	
WRIGHT, John	1st Lt R.M.	RENOWN	
	2nd Lt R.M.	BELLEROPHON	Nile
	1st Lt R.M.	RENOWN	B.S. 29 Aug 1800
	Captain R.M.	Qn CHARLOTTE	Algiers
WYCH, Thomas	Pte. R.M.	DICTATOR	
YARNOLD, John	Pte. R.M.	TIGRE	
	Pte. R.M.	TIGRE	Acre. 30 May 1799
YATES, Robert	Sgt. R.M.	VESTAL	
YOULDEN, William	Boy	PIQUE	
YOUNG, John	Ord	ROMNEY	
YULE, Robert	Master's Mate	PENELOPE	(Vfd Abd. Not on Roll)
	Master's Mate	PENELOPE	Penelope. 30 March 1800
	Master's Mate	HERO	4 Novr 1805
	Lieut. R.N.	ILLUSTRIOUS	Java

(555) COPENHAGEN 1801.

The Battle of Copenhagen against the Danes on 2 April 1801.

ABBOTT, Christopher	1st Lt R.M.	GANGES	
	Captain R.M.	INTREPID	Martinique Received M.G.S./Guadaloupe
AITKEN, David	Ord	POLYPHEMUS	
AKROYD, William	Pte. R.M.	WARRIOR	
ALEXANDER, Nicholas	Midshipman	DESIREE	
	Vol 1st Cl	HAERLEM	Egypt
	Lieut. R.N.	DRAGON	B.S. 29 April 1813
ANDREWS, John	Pte. R.M.	POLYPHEMUS	
ANTRAM, Simon.E.	A.B.	ST GEORGE	
	Master's Mate	ILLUSTRIOUS	Basque Roads 1809
APPLETON, John	Ord	MONARCH	
ARBUTHNOTT, Hugh	Capt. 49th Regt	GANGES	
ARMSTRONG, John	Ensign. 49th Regt	ARDENT	
ARNOLD, Enoch	L.M.	DEFIANCE	G.H. 251
ARTHUR, John	A.B.	BELLONA	
ASKEW, Christopher.C.	Midshipman	AMAZON	
ASPERNE, Timothy.P.	Clerk	JAMAICA	
ATKINS, Edward	Pte. R.M.	ST GEORGE	
ATKINS, William	Boy	LONDON	
	Boy	LONDON	23rd June 1795

ATWELL, Robert	Yeoman of Sheets	RAMILLIES	
	A.B.	IRRESISTIBLE	23rd June 1795
	A.B.	RUSSELL	Camperdown
	Yeoman of Sheets	PRINCE	Trafalgar
BADHAM, John	L.M.	DISCOVERY	(Applied as "Engineer")
BAKER, John	A.B.	RUSSELL	
	A.B.	RUSSELL	Camperdown
BAKER, Stephen	L.M.	GLATTON	
BAKER, Thomas	Supernumerary	AMAZON	
BAKER, William	A.B.	MONARCH	G.H. 2923
BALLINGALL, D.J.	Vol 1st Cl	ST GEORGE	
BARLOW, John	Pte. R.M.	ARDENT	
BARNES, James	Ord	MONARCH	(M.L. as BURNS)
	L.M.	MONARCH	Camperdown
BARTER, Thomas	Pte. R.M.	ALCMENE	
BASHAM, James	Vol 1st Cl	RAISONNABLE	
BASHFORD, Thomas	Midshipman	EDGAR	
BATEMAN, Charles	Lieut. R.N.	MONARCH	
BATSON, Joseph	Ord	LONDON	
	Ord	BELLEROPHON	Trafalgar
BATER, Isaac	A.B.	BELLONA	(Entered twice on Roll, also as BAXTER)
BEACH, Samuel	A.B.	DEFIANCE	G.H. 927
BEAL, Richard	Carpenter's Crew	SATURN	
BEALE, Francis	Surgeon	JAMAICA	
BECKETT, Flowers	Master's Mate	LONDON	(Not on Roll. Vfd Aboard)
	Master's Mate	SPARTIATE	Trafalgar
BEECROFT, Henry	Midshipman	OTTER	
BELCHER, Richard	A.B.	DEFIANCE	G.H. 3704
BENSON, Henry	Boy	DESIREE	
BETHELL, John	Pte. R.M.	POLYPHEMUS	
BETTESON, Richard	Ord	WARRIOR	(M.L. as BADDISTON)
BEVIS, Thomas	A.B.	OTTER	
	Lieut. R.N.	GALATEA	Off Tamatave 20 May 1811
BIDDLE, Thomas	L.M.	DEFENCE	
BIGNELL, George	A.B.	LONDON	
	Lieut. R.N.	SPARTIATE	Trafalgar
BIGGS, Abraham	Pte. R.M.	DEFIANCE	
	Pte. R.M.	SUPERB	St Domingo
BIRD, John	L.M.	RUSSELL	G.H. 9964
BISHOP, Thomas.H.	L.M.	RAMILLIES	
BLACK, James	2nd Masters' Mate	VETERAN	
BLACK, Robert	Carpenter	CRUIZER	
BLEAMIRE, William.B.	Capt. 49th Regt	POLYPHEMUS	
BLYTH, John	Ord	ST GEORGE	
BODAH, Elias	A.B.	VETERAN	
	A.B.	ORION	1 June 1794
	A.B.	VETERAN	Camperdown
BOOTH, William	Pte. 49th Regt	DEFIANCE	
BOURCHIER, Henry	Midshipman	VETERAN	
	Commander	HAWKE	Hawke. 18 Augt 1811
BOWEN, Charles	Midshipman	EDGAR	
	Lieut. R.N.	NORTHUMBERLAND	Northumberland. 22 May 1812.
BRADFORD, Thomas	L.M.	BELLONA	
	A.B.	COLOSSUS	Trafalgar
BRASIER, James	Midshipman	DEFENCE	(Vfd Abd. Not on Roll)
	Lieut. R.N.	ALFRED	Guadaloupe
	Lieut. R.N.	REPULSE	B.S. 2 May 1813
BRICE, William	Pte. R.M.	RAMILLIES	
BRITTS, William	Ord	RUSSELL	
BROBIN, Edward	Ord	DEFENCE	(M.L. as BROVIN)
	Ord	DEFENCE	Nile
BROCK, George	Vol. 49th Regt	GANGES	
BROMWELL, John	Ord	DEFENCE	
BROOKS, Benjamin	Quarter Gunner	AGAMEMNON	G.H. 950
BROOM, James	L.M.	SATURN	
BROWELL, James	L.M.	AGAMEMNON	
BROWN, James	Ord	GANGES	
	Ord	DEFIANCE	Trafalgar
BROWN, John	Ord	SATURN	
BROWN, Joseph	A.B.	ALCMENE	
BROWN, Robert	Clerk	EDGAR	
	Purser	ILLUSTRIOUS	Java
BROWN, Robert	Asst Surgeon to 49th Regiment	GLATTON	
BROWN, Thomas	Ord	RUSSELL	
	Ord	RUSSELL	Camperdown
BRUCE, John	Bosun's Mate	AMAZON	
BUCHANAN, John	A.B.	ALCMENE	
BUMPASS, John	Pte. R.M.	DEFENCE	
	Ship's Corporal	GENOA	Navarino
BURBIDGE, John	L.M.	DEFENCE	
BURDWOOD, Thomas	Master's Mate	RAISONNABLE	Received M.G.S./Martinique

COPENHAGEN 1801

BURGES, William	Ord	ARDENT	
	L.M.	MONARCH	*Camperdown*
BURKE, James	Yeoman of Sheets	BELLONA	(ML as SHAW, John. GH 8373)
BURKE, William	L.M.	ISIS	
BURN, Francis	Boy	ALCMENE	
BURN, Peter	Master	RUSSELL	
BUSH, William	Ord	POLYPHEMUS	
BUTCHER, James	Ord	POLYPHEMUS	
BYERLEE, George	Yeoman of Signals	RUSSELL	
	A.B.	RAMILLIES	*1 June 1794*
	Boatswain	CONFIANCE	*Confiance. 14 Jany 1809*
CAFFIN, Samuel	Boy	BELLONA	
CAMPBELL, Patrick	A.B.	POLYPHEMUS	
CANN, John	Pte. R.M.	AGAMEMNON	
CARRE, Robert.R.	Midshipman	VETERAN	(On M.L. as RIDDLE, Robert)
	Commander	BRITOMART	*Algiers*
CARROLL, Francis	L.M.	BLANCHE	
	L.M.	MARS	*Trafalgar*
CARTER, Thomas	L.M.	JAMAICA	
CARTER, Thomas.G.	Midshipman	GANGES	
CARTER, Thomas.W.	Midshipman	WARRIOR	
CARTWRIGHT, John	Pte. R.M.	LONDON	
CASSELLS, William	L.M.	SATURN	
	Ropemaker	GIBRALTAR	*Basque Roads 1809*
CAST, Daniel	A.B.	SHANNON	G.H. 6449
CHAPMAN, James	Midshipman	RUSSELL	
	Midshipman	RUSSELL	*Camperdown*
CHRISTIE, George	Ord	WARRIOR	G.H. 1699
CHURCH, Charles	Boatswain	ALCMENE	
CHURCHILL, Charles	Ord	MONARCH	
	L.M.	IMPREGNABLE	*1 June 1794*
	Ord	MONARCH	*Camperdown*
CLARK, Samuel	Pte. R.M.	GANGES	
CLARKE, John	Pte. R.M.	SATURN	
CLARKE, Samuel	L.M.	AGAMEMNON	
CLARKE, William	L.M.	RUSSELL	
CLEAVELAND, Charles	A.B.	BELLONA	
CLIFT, Samuel	Pte. R.M.	MONARCH	
CLUBB, Alfred	Pte. R.M.	POLYPHEMUS	
	Boy 2nd Cl	DIRECTOR	*Camperdown*
COAD, Barny	Not Given	GLATTON	(M.L. as McCOURT)
COLE, Philip	Ord	EDGAR	
COLLETT, F.J.	Midshipman	DEFIANCE	
COLLIER, William	Cpl. R.M.	ARDENT	
COLLINS, James	Ord	EDGAR	G.H. 3871
COLLINS, Michael	L.M.	CAESAR	(Ship not present)
CONNER, James	L.M.	BELLONA	
CONNOR, Ross	Vol 1st Cl	ARROW	
	Master's Mate	FISGARD	*Curacoa*
CONROY, John	Pte. R.M.	RAMILLIES	
COOK, Robert	L.M.	POLYPHEMUS	
	L.M.	DIRECTOR	*Camperdown*
COOTE, William	Midshipman	EDGAR	(Vfd Abd. Not on Roll)
	Midshipman	ROYAL GEORGE	*23rd June 1795*
	Lieut. R.N.	AGAMEMNON	*Trafalgar*
	Lieut. R.N.	AGAMEMNON	*St Domingo*
	Lieut. R.N.	CERBERUS (P)	*B.S. 2 Jan 1807*
CORAM, James	Ord	AMAZON	
CORNERFORD, Richard	Pte. 49th Regt	RUSSELL	
COTTER, James	Pte. R.M.	MONARCH	
COTTER, James	Pte. R.M.	BELLONA	G.H. 6706
COURT, Henry	L.M.	MONARCH	
COX, Edward	L.M.	BLANCHE	(M.L. as COCK)
CRAIG, John	L.M.	GLATTON	
CRAYDON, Richard	L.M.	JAMAICA	
CREAGH, Richard	Quarter Gunner	VETERAN	
	L.M.	ORION	*1 June 1794*
	L.M.	VETERAN	*Camperdown*
CREMENE, John	A.B.	VETERAN	(May read CREMMERN/ CREMERN)
	L.M.	ORION	*1 June 1794*
	A.B.	LEVIATHAN	*23rd June 1795*
	A.B.	VETERAN	*Camperdown*
CROFT, Richard	Boy	RUSSELL	
CRONCHY, Joseph	Cpl. 49th Regt	DEFIANCE	
CROOM, John	Pte. R.M.	GANGES	
CROSS, Thomas	L.M.	RAMILLIES	G.H. 6088
CROWDY, Charles	Midshipman	GANGES	
CUNNINGHAM, John	Surgeon	VETERAN	

DABINE, Thomas.D.J.	L.M.	RUSSELL	(Lieut. R.N. in 1812)
DANDY, John	Carp's Crew	ARDENT	G.H. 8242
DANE, Gustave	Ord	ELEPHANT	
	A.B.	BRITANNIA	St Vincent
	Ord	GOLIATH	Nile
DASHWOOD, William.B.	Vol 1st Cl	DEFIANCE	
	Lieut. R.N.	ACTIVE	Pelagosa. 29 Novr 1811
	Commander	PROMETHEUS	Algiers
DAVIDGE, William	Q.M.	VOLCANO	
DAVIES, David	A.B.	POLYPHEMUS	
DAVIES, John	A.B.	MONARCH	
DAVIS, Ephraim	Quarter Gunner	VETERAN	
	Gunner's Mate	VETERAN	Camperdown
DAVIS, John	A.B.	DEFIANCE	
DAWSON, John	Pte. R.M.	WARRIOR	
DAY, Henry	Boy	POLYPHEMUS	
DEGEE, George	Boy 2nd Cl	LONDON	
DELAFOSSE, Edward.H.	Vol 1st Cl	CRUIZER	
	Lieut. R.N.	YORK	Martinique
	Lieut. R.N.	HEBRUS	Algiers
DENNIS, James	Lieut. 49th Regt	MONARCH	
DENNISS, Richard	Pte. R.M.	AGAMEMNON	
DESBRISAY, Thomas.H.W.	Lieut. R.M.	EDGAR	
DIAMOND, Henry	A.B.	ARDENT	
DIXON, James	L.M.	ZEBRA	
DOBBINS, James	Gunner	BLANCHE	
DODDS, Thomas	A.B.	ELING	(Ship not on List)
	A.B.	EXCELLENT	St Vincent
DONNELLY, William	Pte. 49th Regt	DEFIANCE	
DOOLEY, Laurence	Pte. 49th Regt	EDGAR	
DOYLE, James	Ord	ST GEORGE/ISIS	(M.L. as CALLAGHAN)
DREDGE, William	Pte. R.M.	ELEPHANT	
DREWETT, James	Pte. R.M.	RUSSELL	
DUVAL, Francis	Midshipman	DESIREE	
	Midshipman	ANDROMEDA	Capture of the Desiree (Vfd Abd. Not on Roll)
ECCLESTON, Samuel	Pte. R.M.	ARDENT	G.H. 10,007
	Pte. R.M.	CAROLINE	Banda Neira
	Cpl. R.M.	CAROLINE	Java
EDMONDS, Thomas	Pte. R.M.	DEFIANCE	
EDWARDS, William	Midshipman	DEFIANCE	
ELLIOT, Hon George	Lieut. R.N.	St GEORGE	
	Vol 1st Cl	BRITANNIA	St Vincent
	Midshipman	GOLIATH	Nile
	Captain. R.N.	MODESTE	Java
ELLIOTT, John	Clerk	RUSSELL	(Known as single Clasp)
	Vol 1st Cl	MARS	Mars. 21 April 1798
	Purser	ARETHUSA	Arethusa. 23 Augt 1806
	Purser	ARETHUSA	Curacoa (Other 3 clasps may be on separate medal)
ELVEN, Robert.O.	Ord	POLYPHEMUS	
ELYARD, William	Surgeon	ZEPHYR	
EWART, James	A.B.	POLYPHEMUS	
FARR, Samuel	Pte. R.M.	DEFENCE	
FARRANT, John	Vol 1st Cl	RUSSELL	
	Midshipman	ROYAL SOVEREIGN	Trafalgar
	Lieut. R.N.	SCOUT	B.S. 14 July 1809
	Lieut. R.N.	SCOUT	B.S. 1 Nov 1809
	Lieut. R.N.	BORER	B.S. 8 April 1814
FATHOM, George	Captain Fore Top	WARRIOR	
FELTON, John	Midshipman	BELLONA	
	Midshipman	VICTORY	Trafalgar
FENNELL, Joseph	Pte. R.M.	RAMILLIES	
	Sgt. R.M.A.	LEANDER	Algiers
FERGUSON, James	Mid Ship Man	WARRIOR	G.H. 6857. A Rating.
FERGUSON, John	Ord	ELEPHANT	
	L.M.	GOLIATH	St Vincent
	L.M.	GOLIATH	Nile
FERRISS, William	Sgt. R.M.	RUSSELL	
FIELDING, Charles	Ord	DART	
	L.M.	DART	Capture of the Desiree
FIG, William	Midshipman	BELLONA	
	A.B.	VENERABLE	Camperdown
FINLAYSON, John	Midshipman	St GEORGE	
FITZGIBBON, James	Pte. RM & Servant	MONARCH	
FITZMAURICE, James	A.B.	ARDENT	
FLYN, James	A.B.	WARRIOR	
FORD, James	L.M.	DEFIANCE	G.H. 9553
	Quarter Gunner	MINDEN	Java

COPENHAGEN 1801

FORD, Simon	L.M.	ARDENT	
FORSITH, John	A.B.	GLATTON	
FORSTER, John	Vol 1st Cl	MONARCH	
	Lieut. R.N.	GALATEA	Off Tamatave. 20 May 1811
FRANKLYN, George	Master's Mate	ELING	(Ship not on printed list)
FRANKLIN, John	Midshipman	POLYPHEMUS	
	Midshipman	BELLEROPHON	Trafalgar
	Lieut. R.N.	BEDFORD	B.S. 14 Dec 1814
FURBER, Thomas	Midshipman	ARDENT	
GALBRAITH, Robert	Ord	MONARCH	G.H. 2472
GALLAGHAN, Thomas	L.M.	ISIS	
GALLAHER, Thomas	L.M.	BELLONA	
GAIN, James	L.M.	RAMILLIES	G.H. 1850 as GREIR
GAINOR, William	Boy 2nd Cl	BELLONA	
GANES, John	Boy	ST GEORGE	(M.L. as GINN)
GARDNER, Richard	L.M.	SATURN	
GAY, William	Lieut. R.N.	MONARCH	
GAZE, William	Drummer. R.M.	RAISONNABLE	G.H. 1038
GEDDES, James	Ord	DEFIANCE	
GIBSON, Thomas	Ord	ZEBRA	
GILBY, Matthew	A.B.	WARRIOR	G.H. 8226
GILES, John	Ord	EDGAR	
GILLAM, Thomas	L.M.	ISIS	
	L.M.	ISIS	Camperdown
GILLMAN, James	Ord	ISIS	
GIMBER, John	Ord	MONARCH	
GLEGG, John.B.	Lieut. R.N.	MONARCH	
GODFREY, Charles	A.B.	JAMAICA	
GOLDSMITH, John	Purser	AMAZON	
	Clerk	THUNDERER	1 June 1794
	Purser	SUPERB	Algiers
GOLDSMITH, Thomas	Ord	DEFIANCE	
GOODENOUGH, George	Q.M's Mate	POLYPHEMUS	
	Quarter Gunner	DEFENCE	1 June 1794
	Gunner's Mate	DEFENCE	Nile
GOOLD, Hugh	Midshipman	ISIS	
GRACE, Percy	Vol 1st Cl	GANGES	
GRATION, George	Pte. R.M.	MONARCH	
GRAY, Thomas	Pte. R.M.	GANGES	
GRAY, William	Q.M.	VETERAN	
GREGSON, William	Carp's Crew	DEFIANCE	
GREEN, Andrew.P.	Lieut. R.N.	GANGES	
	Midshipman	ILLUSTRIOUS	14 March 1795 (Vfd Abd. Not on Roll)
	Lieut. R.N.	NEPTUNE	Trafalgar
	Supn Commander	ELBE gun-boat Flotilla	Gluckstadt. 5 Jany 1814
GREEN, John	2 Borne. AB & LM	DEFIANCE	
GREVES, James.D.	1st Lt R.M.	AMAZON	
GRIFFITHS, Thomas	L.M.	RUSSELL	
	L.M.	RUSSELL	Camperdown
GRIFFITHS, Thomas	Gunner	RAMILLIES	
	Gunner	HARPY	Java
GRINT, William	Midshipman	AMAZON	
	Master's Mate	BRITANNIA	Trafalgar
	Master's Mate	LATONA	Curacoa
GROSCOTT, Joseph	Quarter Gunner	DEFIANCE	
	M.A.A.	CAPTAIN	Martinique
	A.B.	MINDEN	Algiers
HACKETT, John	Midshipman	RAISONNABLE	
HALL, George	Pte. R.M.	WARRIOR	
HALL, Robert	Ord	WARRIOR	
HALLETT, Joseph	Boy	ZEPHYR	
HAMILTON, John	Vol 1st Cl	St GEORGE	
HAMOND, Graham.E.	Captain. R.N.	BLANCHE	
	Midshipman	QUEEN CHARLOTTE	1 June 1794
HAMOND, Philip	L.M.	ELEPHANT	
HAMSHIRE, James	Ord	DEFENCE	
	Capt's Servant	DEFENCE	1 June 1794
	Boy	DEFENCE	Nile
HARRIS, Henry	Gunner	ZEPHYR	
HAWKES, Charles	Drummer. 49th Regt	RAMILLIES	(M.L. as KNOKES)
HAYNES, John	A.B.	MONARCH	
	A.B.	MONARCH	Camperdown
HEATH, Henry	Pte. R.M.	SATURN	
HEMMING, William	A.B.	HARPY	G.H. 7465 May read HEMMINGS
	Boy	GOLIATH	St Vincent
HENDERSON, Menzies	A.B.	RAMILLIES	
	A.B.	GOLIATH	St Vincent
	A.B.	GOLIATH	Nile
HEUGH, Thomas	A.B.	MONARCH	(M.L. as HUGHES)

THE NAVAL GENERAL SERVICE MEDAL ROLL 1793-1840

HEWETT, James	Midshipman	LONDON	
HILL, John	Vol 1st Cl	ELEPHANT	
	Boy 3rd Cl	GOLIATH	St Vincent
	Vol 1st Cl	GOLIATH	Nile
HODGES, Joseph	Pte. R.M.	EGGAR (Roll)	(ADM 171/2/23. EDGAR?)
	Pte. R.M.	EXCELLENT	St Vincent
HODGES, Thomas	Ord	MONARCH	
	L.M.	MONARCH	Camperdown
HOLE, Lewis	Lieut. R.N.	RAMILLIES	
	Lieut. R.N.	REVENGE	Trafalgar
HOLESGROVE, William	L.M.	ST GEORGE	
HOLMAN, Robert	Midshipman	LONDON	
HOLMAN, William	Lieut. R.N.	LONDON	
	Midshipman	ROYAL GEORGE	23rd June 1795
HOSKEN, John	Carpenter	WARRIOR	? An additional clasp
HOUGHTON, Charles.E.	Midshipman	DEFIANCE	
HOWARD, John	A.P.	ST GEORGE	
HUM, John	Ord	ST GEORGE	
HUMPHREYS, John	Lieut. R.M.	DESIREE	
HUMPHRIES, Robert	L.M.	EDGAR	
HUMPHRIES, Robert	L.M.	AMAZON	
HUNTER, Peter	A.B. (?)	MONARCH	
	Yeoman of Sheets	MONARCH	Camperdown
HURCOMBE, Robert	Pte. R.M.	RUSSELL	
	Pte. R.M.	BELLEISLE	Trafalgar
HURST, Charles	Armourer	CRUIZER	
INGRAM, Richard	A.B.	GLATTON	
JACKSON, John	Midshipman	VETERAN	
	Vol 1st Cl	VETERAN	Camperdown
JAMES, D.Grevis	1st Lt R.M.	AMAZON	
JAMES, William	A.B.	RAMILLIES	
	A.B.	RAMILLIES	1 June 1794
JAMESON, Andrew	Pte. 49th Regt	EDGAR	
JEFFERIS, C.	Boy	BELLONA	
JEFFERSON, Robert	Ord	St GEORGE	
JEWELL, John.W.N.	Clerk	DESIREE	
JOHNS, William	Boy	GANGES	
JOHNSON, Edward	Master's Mate	St GEORGE	
	A.B.	BOYNE	B.S. 17 Mar 1794
	Lieut. R.N.	LONDON	London 13 March 1806
JOHNSON, John	A.B.	ELEPHANT	
	A.B.	BRITANNIA	14 March 1795
	A.B.	BRITANNIA	St Vincent
	A.B.	GOLIATH	Nile
	Yeoman of Sheets	CORNELIA	Java
JOHNSON, John	Quarter Gunner	MONARCH	
JOHNSON, William	Sailmaker	LYNX	GH.8503. Ship not Listed.
JOICE, Joseph	Gunner. R.A.	TERROR	
JONES, J.E.	?A.B.	VOLCANO	
JONES, Joseph	Vol 1st Cl	MONARCH	
JONES, Robert.P.	Midshipman	HARPY	(Vfd Abd. Not on Roll)
	Midshipman	AGINCOURT	Camperdown
	A.B.	HARPY	Harpy. 5 Feby 1800 (Vfd Abd. Not on Roll)
JONES, Thomas	L.M.	MONARCH	
JORDON, Thomas	Pte. R.M.	EDGAR	
	Pte. R.M.	PHOENIX	Phoenix. 10 Augt 1805
	Pte. R.M.	PHOENIX	4 Novr 1805 (Vfd Abd. Not on Roll)
JOYCE, Henry	Boy	BELLONA	
JULYAN, Robert	Lieut. R.N.	GLATTON	
KAANA, Nathaniel	M.A.A.	BELLONA	G.H. 8081
KINGSNORTH, Daniel	Boy	WARRIOR	
KINSALA, William	L.M.	BELLONA	
KIRKLAND, Alexander	L.M.	EDGAR	
KITCHEN, William.H.	Lieut. R.N.	LONDON	
	Lieut. R.N.	ASP	Guadaloupe
KNAPP, William	L.M.	EDGAR	
KNIGHT, John	A.B.	TERROR	
KYLE, George	Master's Mate	ELEPHANT	
	Lieut. R.N.	ABOUKIR	B.S. 29 Sep 1812
LAMBERT, Thomas	Yeoman Powder Rm	DISCOVERY	G.H. 8286
LANCASTER, James	Pte. R.M.	WARRIOR	G.H. 9122
LANGLEY, Charles	Pte. R.M.	RAMILLIES	
LANGSTON, George	Pte. R.M.	JAMAICA	
LARKMAN, Robert	L.M.	VETERAN	
LAVERS, William.B.	Midshipman	TERROR	
LEE, George	Ord	MONARCH	
	L.M.	MONARCH	Camperdown
LEE, John	Pte. R.M.	SATURN	(Different man at NILE)
LEE, Robert	Boy	ZEPHYR	
LE FEUVRE, John	Midshipman	DESIREE	
	Actg Lieut. R.N.	FISGARD	Curacoa

COPENHAGEN 1801

LEHEUH, Edward	Boy	DEFIANCE	
LEMPRIERE, George.O.	Midshipman	RUSSELL	
LEONARD, Samuel	Vol 1st Cl	AGAMEMNON	*(May read LENARD)*
LESTER, John	Pte. R.M.	ARDENT	
LE VESCONTE, Henry	Lieut. R.N.	JAMAICA	
	Lieut. R.N.	NAIAD	*Trafalgar*
LE VESCONTE, Philip	Midshipman	MONARCH	
LEVY, Edward	Pte. R.M.	MONARCH	
LIDDERMORE, Samuel	Ord	AMAZON	G.H. 5098
LISTER, James	A.B.	RAMILLIES	
LISTON, Edward	Pte. 49th Regt	GANGES	
LITTLE, James	Surgeon	LONDON	
LOFTIN, George	Midshipman	GANGES	
	Midshipman	NEPTUNE	*Trafalgar*
LONG, John	Quarter Gunner	BLANCHE	
	Quarter Gunner	THALIA	*23rd June 1795*
LONG, John	Pte. 49th Regt	SATURN	
LONGCHAMP, John	Midshipman	DESIREE	*(Vfd Abd. Not on Roll)*
	Midshipman	ANDROMEDA	*Capture of the Desiree*
	Midshipman	LEDA	*Egypt*
LONGDALE, Thomas	A.B.	SULPHUR	
LOUGHLIN, Patrick	Cpl. R.M.	GLATTON	
	Cpl. R.M.	BRITANNIA	*Trafalgar*
LUCKCRAFT, Alfred	Vol 1st Cl	MONARCH	
	Midshipman	MARS	*Trafalgar*
LUMBER, Charles	Ord	St GEORGE	
LYNN, Matthew	L.M.	ELEPHANT	
	L.M.	CORNELIA	*Java*
LYONS, John	Midshipman	St GEORGE	
	Midshipman	VICTORY	*Trafalgar*
MACER, Joseph	L.M.	MONARCH	
MACDONALD, Archibald	Midshipman	ARDENT	
MACDONALD, James	A.B.	ARDENT	
MACKENZIE, Alexander	1st Lt. R.M.	ELEPHANT	
	1st Lt. R.M.	INVINCIBLE	*1 June 1794*
MACKIE, William	Surg's Mate	ALCMENE	
MACKINTOSH, John	2nd Lt. R.M.	POLYPHEMUS	
	1st Lt. R.M.	POLYPHEMUS	*Trafalgar*
	1st Lt. R.M.	POLYPHEMUS	*B.S. 16 July 1806*
MAGRATH, George	Surgeon	RUSSELL	*(M.L. as MacGRATH)*
	Actg Surgeon	RUSSELL	*Camperdown*
MAHONY, Timothy	Ord	DEFENCE	
	Ord	DEFENCE	*Nile*
MAINWARING, Rowland	Midshipman	DEFENCE	
	Midshipman	MAJESTIC	*Nile*
MAJESTIC, Joseph	A.B.	BELLONA	
	A.B.	LEVIATHAN	*1 June 1794*
MALLARD, Samuel	Drummer. R.M.	ARDENT	
MANN, John	Boy 3rd Cl	ARDENT	
	L.M.	NAMUR	*4 Novr 1805*
	Ord	VALIANT	*Basque Roads 1809*
	Ord	VALIANT	*B.S. 27 Sep 1810*
MANSEL, Thomas	Midshipman	ELEPHANT	
MARTELL, Peter	Midshipman	AMAZON	
MARLER, William	L.M.	DEFIANCE	
	Ord	BELLEROPHON	*Trafalgar*
	Ord	INDEFATIGABLE	*Basque Roads 1809*
MARTIN, Richard	Boy	DEFIANCE	
MARTIN, William	A.B.	GANGES	
	A.B.	SWIFTSURE	*Nile*
MAWBEY, John	Midshipman	POLYPHEMUS	
	Midshipman	SPARTIATE	*Trafalgar*
McCANN, John	Pte. R.M.	ARDENT	
	M.A.A.	AGAMEMNON	*Trafalgar*
	M.A.A.	AGAMEMNON	*St Domingo*
McCLEOD, James	Ord	RAISONNABLE	
McGUIRE, Hugh	Ord	ALCMENE	
McKINLEY, George	Commander	OTTER	
	Lieut. R.N.	LIBERTY	*Port Spergui. 17 March 1796*
McNASPY, Daniel	Pte. R.M.	EDGAR	G.H. 2965
McSWEENY, Morgan	Pte. R.M.	WARRIOR	
	Pte. R.M.	ATLAS	*St Domingo*
MEREDITH, Charles	?Lieut.	ALCMENE	
MESSENGER, Edward	Pte. R.M.	LONDON	
	Pte. R.M.	SPENCER	*St Domingo*
MIDDLETON, Joseph	Pte. R.M.	VETERAN	
	Pte. R.M.	VANGUARD	*Nile*
MILLARD, William.S.	Midshipman	MONARCH	
MILLER, James	L.M.	BELLONA	
MILLS, James	Quarter Gunner	BELLONA	
MILLS, Thomas	Gunner. R.A.	TERROR	

MILLS, William	Sgt. R.M.	BELLONA	
	Cpl. R.M.	QUEEN	23rd June 1795
	Sgt. R.M.	COLOSSUS	St Vincent
MILNE, William	Midshipman	ELEPHANT	
	Actg Lieut. R.N. in Command	CARRIER (P)	Carrier. 4 Novr 1807
MITCHENER, James	Pte. R.M.	EDGAR	
	Pte. R.M.	CANOPUS	St Domingo
	Pte. R.M.	ANDROMACHE	St Sebastian
MONTGOMERY, James	Vol 1st Cl	GANGES	
MOORE, William	Ord or A.B.	BELLONA	
MORRIES, Andrew	Midshipman	POLYPHEMUS	
MORRIS, John	Ord	DISCOVERY	
MORRISH, Nicholas	Drummer. R.M.	VETERAN	
	Drummer. R.M.	ROYAL SOVEREIGN	1 June 1794
	Drummer. R.M.	VETERAN	Camperdown
MORTIMER, John	Pte. R.M.	RUSSELL	
MOTT, Joseph	Ord	DEFENCE	
	Capt' Forecastle	RECRUIT	Martinique
	Capt' Forecastle	RECRUIT	Recruit. 17 June 1809 (Vfd Abd. Not on Roll)
MOYCE, Henry	Pte. R.M.	AGAMEMNON	Entered twice. 2nd as Ord.
MULGANNON, John	L.M.	DEFIANCE	
	Ord	CORNELIA	Java
MULLARD, Samuel	Drummer. R.M.	ARDENT	
MUNRO, John	Boy	ARDENT	
NAIRNE, Andrew	Midshipman	POLYPHEMUS	
NAVE, William	Ord	GANGES	
	Ord	DEFIANCE	Trafalgar
	Ord	CORDELIA	Algiers
NIELD, Joseph	L.M.	MONARCH	
	L.M.	MONARCH	Camperdown
NETTLE, Thomas	A.B.	GANGES	(M.L. as NUTTLE)
	A.B.	DEFIANCE	Trafalgar (Roll as NETELL)
NIBLETT, Harry	Clerk	DEFIANCE	
NICHOLSON, James	Boy	EDGAR	
NICKLIN, Benjamin	Pte. R.M.	DEFIANCE	
	Pte. R.M.	IMPREGNABLE	1 June 1794
NORMAN, Thomas	Pte. R.M.	ALCMENE	
	Pte. R.M.	MARS	Trafalgar
O'BRIEN, Andrew	Midshipman	POLYPHEMUS	
O'BRIEN, James	Boy	SATURN	
OLIVER, Harry	Pte. R.M.	AMAZON	
	Pte. R.M.	LEVIATHAN	Trafalgar
ORMOND, Harry Smith	Vol. 49th Regt	GLATTON/DEFENCE	
OSENAM, John	Boy 2nd Cl	RUSSELL	(ML as HUSEMAN)
	Ord	ENDYMION	Endymion Wh President.
PACK, Abraham	Drummer. R.M.	POLYPHEMUS	G.H. 9426
PADOE, Joseph	Boy 2nd Cl	ELEPHANT	(Alias Antonio PASCOA)
	Ord	CORNELIA	Java
PARKER, John	L.M.	MONARCH	G.H. 8050
PARSONS, Elijah	L.M.	RAMILLIES	
PARSONS, William	L.M.	DEFIANCE	
PARSONS, William	Pte. R.M.	BLANCHE	G.H. 7766
	Pte. R.M.	SPARTIATE	Trafalgar
PASLEY, Hugh	Rifleman. 95th Foot	ISIS	
PATTERSON, Christopher	Ord	ST GEORGE	
PATTERSON, Francis	A.B.	RUSSELL	
	Ord	PCSS ROYAL	14 March 1795
	A.B.	RUSSELL	Camperdown
	A.B.	CANOPUS	St Domingo
PEADON, James	Ord	RAMILLIES	(Alias Antonio PEADON)
	Ord	RAMILLIES	1 June 1794
PEARSON, Charles	Boy	St GEORGE	
	Midshipman	SPENCER	St Domingo
	Midshipman	SCIPION	Java
	Lieut. R.N.	PRESIDENT	St Sebastian
PEARSON, Charles	A.B.	ISIS	
	Lieut. R.N.	PHOEBE (P)	Phoebe. 28 March 1814
PEARSON, Hugh	Lieut. R.N.	ELEPHANT	
PEART, Thomas	Pte. R.M.	RAISONNABLE	?Additional Clasp
PEDLER, John	A.B.	AGEMEMNON	
PENNY, John	L.M.	POLYPHEMUS	
PERRY, Edward	Pte. R.M.	ARDENT	
PETERSON, John	A.B.	MONARCH	
	A.B.	QUEEN CHARLOTTE	1 June 1794
PETTIVER, John	L.M.	BELLONA	
PIKE, Thomas	L.M.	EDGAR	
PIM, Silas	Pte. R.M.	LONDON	
PLEASANTS, Benjamin	Drummer. R.M.	MONARCH	

COPENHAGEN 1801

PLENDERLEATH, Charles	Captain 49th Regiment	ARDENT or RAMILLIES	Military Small Gold Medal for Chrysller's Farm
PLUNKETT, Peter	Pte. 49th Regt	DEFIANCE	
POORE, William	Boy	GANGES	
PORTBURY, Henry	Midshipman	ST GEORGE	
PORTELLI, Bernardott	L.M.	ELEPHANT	
PORTER, James	Pte. R.M.	MONARCH	
POTTER, Reuben	Pte. R.M.	LONDON	
POWELL, Thomas	Boy	GANGES	G.H. 10,120
	A.B.	DARTMOUTH	Navarino
PRESTON, John	L.M.	LONDON	
PRICE, David	Vol 1st Cl	ARDENT	
	Midshipman	CENTAUR	Centaur. 26 Augt 1808
	Lieut. R.N.	HAWKE	Hawke. 18 Augt 1811
PRYOR, John	Quarter Gunner	St GEORGE	
PYE, Esau	Boy 2nd Cl	VETERAN	
READ, Thomas	L.M.	ELEPHANT	(Found as Midshipman aboard RAMILLIES)
	Lieut. R.N.	SWIFTSURE	Trafalgar (Vfd Roll & M.L.) (Notes. 3 Clasp medal with 'NILE' known since 1901. Not on "Nile" roll. Allen's Navy List (1849) shows officer at all three of Nelson's Actions, and in receipt of 3 clasp medal)
REDDALL, James	L.M.	GANGES	
	A.B.	DEFIANCE	Trafalgar
REED, William	A.B.	DEFIANCE	
	Ord	BELLEROPHON	Trafalgar
REEVE, John	Midshipman	AGAMEMNON	
	Master's Mate	AGAMEMNON	Trafalgar
	Master's Mate	AGAMEMNON	St Domingo
	Lieut. R.N.	L'AIMABLE	B.S. 27 July 1809
REID, William (1st)	Ord	DEFIANCE	
RENOUF, Servant	A.B.	LONDON	
REPPER, Sydney	L.M.	ARDENT	
RICHARDS, John.S.	Purser	VETERAN	
	Purser	VETERAN	Camperdown
RICHARDS, Joseph	A.B.	JAMAICA	
RICHARDS, Thomas	L.M.	DART	
	Ord	ROYAL SOVEREIGN	Trafalgar
RICHARDSON, William	A.B.	ALCMENE	
RICHFIELD, William	A.B.	GLATTON	G.H. 10,048
RICKETTS, George	Boy	ARROW	
	Boy 2nd Cl	ARROW	Arrow. 13 Septr 1799
RIDETT, William	Purser	GLATTON	(This roll as RIDDETT)
	L.M.	DEFENCE	1 June 1794
	Quarter Gunner	DEFENCE	Nile
RIDEOUT, Samuel	Midshipman	LONDON	
RIDER, Richard	Boy 2nd Cl	HARPY	
	Boy 2nd Cl	HARPY	Harpy. 5 Feby 1800. (On this Roll, but joined vessel after this Action)
RISK, John.E.	Surgeon's Mate	VETERAN	
ROBERTS, James	Ord	MONARCH	
	Ord	MONARCH	Camperdown
ROBERTS, William	Boy	AMAZON	
ROBERTS, William	Boy	RAMILLIES	G.H. 1506
ROBINS, Thomas.L.	Midshipman	TEAZER	(Vfd Abd. Not on Roll)
	Midshipman	TEAZER	Capture of the Desiree
	Master's Mate	VICTORY	Trafalgar
	Lieut. R.N.	PALLAS	Basque Roads 1809
ROBINSON, George	L.M.	RUSSELL	
	L.M.	RUSSELL	Camperdown
ROSS, Robert	Pte. R.M.	EDGAR	(M.L. as Daniel)
ROUSE, Richard	2nd Lt. R.M.	GLATTON	
RUSSELL, Edward	Boy 3rd Cl	St GEORGE	(Alias NORRIS, George)
	Boy 3rd Cl	BRITANNIA	Trafalgar
	A.B.	QUEEN CHARLOTTE	Algiers
	Q.M.	BENBOW	Syria
RYAN, Patrick	L.M.	LONDON	
ST JOHN, James	Midshipman	TIGRESS	(Ship not present)
SARTIN, Joseph	Pte. R.M.	RAMILLIES	
SAUNDERS, William	A.B.	DEFENCE	
	A.B.	DEFENCE	Nile
SEAMAN, John	M.A.A.	POLYPHEMUS	
	M.A.A.	PRINCE	Trafalgar
SELLIS, William	A.B.	ARDENT	G.H. 8137

SENTON, George	Boy	AGAMEMNON	*May read SENTOR*
SERJEANT, Richard	Ord	EDGAR	
SHEAFFE, Roger.H.	Lt Col. 49th Regt	BELLONA	
SHEPHERD, Thomas	A.B.	ISIS	
SHOEBROOKE, John	Not Given	St GEORGE	
SHORT, Jacob	Vol 1st Cl	RAISONNABLE	
SHULDHAM, Molyneux	Lieut. R.N.	EDGAR	
SIMPSON, John	A.B.	RAISSONABLE	
SKUCE, William	L.M.	DEFIANCE	
	L.M.	DEFENCE	*1 June 1794*
	L.M.	DEFENCE	*Nile*
SLAYNES, Dennis	Pte. 49th Regt	EDGAR	
SMALL, Charles	Pte. R.M.	St GEORGE	
SMALL, John	Ord	RUSSELL	*(M.L. as SMALE)*
SMALL, Thomas	Ord	EDGAR	
SMITH, Andrew	Gunner. R.A.	ZEBRA	
SMITH, George.C.	A.B.	AGAMEMNON	
SMITH, John	L.M.	ARROW	*G.H. 3020*
SMITH, John	Ord	DEFENCE	
SMITH, John	L.M.	DEFENCE	
SMITH, John	Ord	GANGES	
SMITH, Robert	Midshipman	BELLONA	
	Captain's Servant	IMPREGNABLE	*1 June 1794*
SMITH, Samuel	Pte. R.M.	EXPLOSION	
SMITH, Samuel	Pte. R.M.	LONDON	
	Pte. R.M.	NEPTUNE	*Trafalgar*
SOMERFIELD, James	Cpl. R.M.	VETERAN	
	Pte. R.M.	VETERAN	*Camperdown*
SOUTHCOTT, Henry	Quarter Gunner	VETERAN	
	L.M.	QUEEN CHARLOTTE	*1 June 1794*
	A.B.	QUEEN CHARLOTTE	*23rd June 1795*
	A.B.	MONARCH	*Camperdown*
SPALDING, John	L.M.	ISIS	
	L.M.	ISIS	*Camperdown*
SPENCER, William	A.B.	HECLA	
SPOONER, James	Pte. R.M.	SATURN	*G.H. 7836*
SPRATT, James	Midshipman	BELLONA	
	Master's Mate	DEFIANCE	*Trafalgar*
STAPLETON, Patrick	L.M.	VICTORIOUS	*(Ship not on printed list)*
STEED, Francis	Ord	EDGAR	
STEPHENSON, James	Ord	ELEPHANT	
	L.M.	GOLIATH	*Nile*
	Q.M.	CORNELIA	*Java*
STEVENS, Thomas	L.M.	EDGAR	*?Additional clasp*
STEWART, Charles	M.A.A.	GLATTON	
STEWART, John	A.B.	RUSSELL	
	A.B.	RUSSELL	*Camperdown*
STIFF, James	Pte. 95th Rifles	ST GEORGE	
STONE, Robert	Gunner	EXPLOSION	
	Q.M.	ZEALOUS	*Nile*
	Q.M.	COURAGEUX	*B.S. 29 Aug 1800*
STRONG, Samuel	Midshipman	ALCMENE	
	Lieut. R.N.	SCORPION	*Scorpion. 12 Jany 1810 (Vfd Abd. Not on Roll)*
	Lieut. R.N.	SCORPION	*Guadaloupe*
SWAIN, Thomas	Master's Mate	RAMILLIES	
TALBOT, William	L.M.	HARPY	
	Boy 2nd Cl	HARPY	*Harpy. 5 Feby 1800*
	Bosun's Mate	WANDERER	*Guadaloupe*
TANCOCK, James	L.M.	BELLONA	
TAYLOR, Nathaniel	Gunner's Mate	AMAZON	
	A.B.	VALIANT	*1 June 1794*
	A.B.	VALIANT	*23rd June 1795*
TAYLOR, Thomas	3 Borne A.Bs(2) and a L.M.	POLYPHEMUS	*G.H. 3838*
TEED, Richard.M.	Vol 1st Cl	MONARCH	
TERRY, George	Boy	DISCOVERY	
THOMPSON, John	A.B.	ARDENT	
THORNE, Thomas	Pte. R.M.	EDGAR	
THRACKSTON, Edwin	Master's Mate	MONARCH	
THRALE, John	Boy 3rd Cl	GLATTON	*(M.L. as FRAILLE, James)*
TIVER, John	Vol 1st Cl	RAMILLIES	
	Boy 3rd Cl	FISGARD	*Fisgard. 20 Octr 1798*
TOMKINS, John	Volunteer	HARPY	
TREADWELL, Frederick	Actg 2nd Master	VETERAN	
TREDGER, Robert	Boy 3rd Cl	EDGAR	
TREEVE, John	Vol 1st Cl	St GEORGE	
	Master's Mate	TONNANT	*Trafalgar*
	Actg Lieut. R.N.	YORK	*Martinique*
TRIST, Stephen	L.M.	RUSSELL	*G.H. 9206 as TWIST*

COPENHAGEN 1801

TRUSS, John	Boy	DESIREE	
	L.M.	PIQUE	*Pique. 26 March 1806*
	Ord	ELIZABETH	*Anse La Barque. 18 Decr 1809*
			(Vfd Abd. Not on Roll)
	Ord	ELIZABETH	*Martinique*
			(Vfd Abd. Not on Roll)
	Captain of Mast	CYANE	*Cyane. 16 Jany 1814*
TUPPER, James	Boy	DEFIANCE	*May read TAPPER*
TURNER, Joseph	A.B.	BELLONA	
TURNER, Richard	Boy	SATURN	
TURPINS, John	Ord	GANGES	
	L.M.	ORION	*23rd June 1795*
	L.M.	ORION	*St Vincent*
	Ord	ORION	*Nile*
UNDERLAND, William	Pte. R.M.	EDGAR	
UNWIN, Thomas	Ord	GLATTON	
	A.B.	PHOENIX	*Phoenix. 10 Augt 1805*
	Bosun's Mate	PHOENIX	*4 Novr 1805*
USHER, Thomas	Surg's 2nd Mate	RUSSELL	
	Surg's 2nd Mate	BRACKEL	*Camperdown (In ? RUSSELL)*
VALLANCE, George	Coxswain	BLANCHE	
VALLANCE, William	Supn Pte. R.M.	ARDENT	
VINCENT, Samuel	Supn Pte. R.M.	EDGAR	
	Pte. R.M.	NAMUR	*4 Novr 1805*
WALLACE, James	Gunner's Mate	POLYPHEMUS	
WALLIS, Samuel	Boy	LONDON	
WALSH, Anthony	Drummer. 49th Regt	BELLONA	
WALTER, Thomas	Pte. R.M.	DESIREE	*G.H. 7125*
WALTON, Robert	A.B.	EDGAR	
WALTON, William	L.M.	RUSSELL	
	L.M.	RUSSELL	*Camperdown*
WARD, John	Pte. R.M.	RAMILLIES	*G.H. 2318*
	Gnr. R.M.A.	CALEDONIA	*Basque Roads 1809*
	Cpl. R.M.A.	AETNA	*The Potomac. 17 Aug 1814*
	Cpl. R.M.A.	BEELZEBUB	*Algiers*
WARDEN, William	Surgeon	ALCMENE	
	Surgeon	PHOENIX	*Phoenix. 10 Augt 1805*
WARNER, Ambrose	P.S. Mate	AGAMEMNON	*(?Purser's Steward's Mate)*
WARREN, James	L.M.	EDGAR	
WATLING, John.W.	Midshipman	VETERAN	
WATSON, Charles	Ord	GLATTON	
WATSON, James	Ord	GANGES	
WATTS, Walter.M.	Midshipman	VOLCANO	
WATTS, William	Boy	ELING	*(Ship not in printed list)*
WEBB, John	A.B.	RUSSELL	
	A.B./L.M.	RUSSELL	*Camperdown*
WEBB, Samuel	Pte. R.M.	EDGAR	*G.H. 9304*
	Pte. R.M.	NISUS	*Java*
WEBSTER, Charles	Pte. R.M.	DEFIANCE	
WELLS, Andrew	Midshipman	EDGAR	
	Midshipman	COLOSSUS	*St Vincent*
WELSH, Anthony	Drummer. R.M.	BELLONA	
WELSH, George	Master's Mate	ELING	*(Ship not in printed list)*
	Lieut. R.N.	BRISEIS	*B.S. 27 July 1809*
	Lieut. R.N.	BRISEIS	*Briseis. 14 Octr 1810*
WEST, Pearson	Sgt. R.M.	POLYPHEMUS	
WESTPHAL, Philip	Master's Mate	BLANCHE	
	Lieut. R.N.	AMAZON	*Amazon. 13 March 1806*
WHEATLY, William	Midshipman	HASTY	
WHIMPER, William	Midshipman	EDGAR	
WHITE, James	Pte. R.M.	ELEPHANT	
WHITE, John	Ord	AGAMEMNON	
WHITE, John	2 Borne.AB & Boy	RUSSELL	
WHITE, Peter	Midshipman	DEFENCE	
	Bosun's Servant	LATONA	*1 June 1794 (Aged Nine)*
	A.B.	DEFENCE	*Nile*
	Master's Mate	SULTAN (P)	*B.S. 4 Dec 1811*
WHITE, Thomas	3 Borne. M.A.A. & A.B. & Ord	St GEORGE	*G.H. 9410*
WHITE, Thomas	L.M.	EDGAR	
WHITELOCK, Robert	L.M.	EXPLOSION	*G.H. 957*
WHITFIELD, Jesse	L.M.	DESIREE	
WHITLEY, John	Ord	EDGAR	*(M.L. as WITHEY)*
WHITMARSH, James	A.B.	BELLONA	
WICKS, John	Pte. R.M.	ISIS	
WILKINSON, Richard	Boy	ISIS	

WILLIAMS, Hugh	L.M.	AMAZON	
WILLIAMS, John	A.B.	HARPY	
WILLIAMS, John	Ord	WARRIOR	
WILLIAMS, Thomas	Boy	VETERAN	
WILLIAMSON, Bartholomew	A.B.	BLANCHE	
	Ord	THALIA	23rd June 1795
WILSON, Thomas	L.M.	AGAMEMNON	
WINGFIELD, William	Quarter Gunner	POLYPHEMUS	
WOODWARD, James	L.M.	AGAMEMNON	
WORTHINGTON, Edward	A.B.	EDGAR	
WRIGHT, James	Ord	EDGAR	
WRIGHT, John	A.B.	ZEPHYR	
YATES, Thomas	A.B.	TERROR	
	A.B.	THESEUS	Acre. 30 May 1799
	A.B.	THESEUS	Nile
YERBURY, Walter	Pte. R.M.	BELLONA	
	Pte. R.M.	EXCELLENT	St Vincent
YOUNG, George	Pte. R.M.	RUSSELL	
YOUNG, Robert	Pte. 49th Regt	BELLONA	

(7) SPEEDY 6 MAY 1801

Capture of the Spanish xebec GAMO, off Barcelona.
(No Muster Lists have survived for this Action)

CAMPBELL, John	A.B.	SPEEDY	(@HUTCHINSON, William)
	A.B.	STORK	Borne as above. Martinique
COCHRANE, Thomas. LORD.	Commander	SPEEDY (P)	Later Earl of Dundonald
	Lieut. R.N.	THETIS	Thetis. 17 May 1795 (Vfd Abd. Not on Roll)
	Captain. R.N.	IMPERIEUSE	Basque Roads. 1809 (Vfd Abd. Not on Roll)
GRAY, David	A.B.	SPEEDY	
LUSCOMBE, John	A.B.	SPEEDY	*Roll states "discharged 5-6-1800, does not appear to re-join. No M.L. for May 1801."
	A.B.	SPEEDY	Speedy. 6 Novr 1799
RICKETTS, Charles	Midshipman	SPEEDY	
	Clerk	SPEEDY	Speedy. 6 Novr 1799
RUST, David	Actg Carpenter	SPEEDY	
THOMPSON, John	Coxswain	SPEEDY	

(144) GUT OF GIBRALTAR 12 JULY 1801

Action with the Franco-Spanish Squadron in the Gut of Gibraltar; destruction of the Spanish REAL CARLOS and SAN HERMENEGILDO (112s), and of the French St ANTOINE (74).

ABERFIELD, Charles	Pte. R.M.	SPENCER	
	Sgt. R.M.	INDEFATIGABLE	Basque Roads 1809
AIRMES, William	Drummer. R.M.	VENERABLE	
AUNEEMS, Joseph	Pte. R.M.	POMPEE	(M.L. as ANNIMS)
BARNETT, William	A.B.	CAESAR	
BEASTALL, Thomas	A.B.	CAESAR	(M.L. as BURSTELL)
BOYD, David	Lieut. R.N.	SPENCER	
BRENTON, John	Master's Mate	CAESAR	(Awd St Vladimir 4th Cl)
	Actg Commander	Squadron of Gun-Boats	B.S. 29 Sep 1812
BUCKLEY, John	L.M.	SUPERB	
BUDD, Henry.H.	Midshipman	THAMES	
BULL, James	Supn Boy 2nd Cl	SPENCER	
BURTON, George.G.	Midshipman	VENERABLE	
	Lieut. R.N.	NEPTUNE	Martinique
	Lieut. R.N.	POMPEE	Guadaloupe
BUTTON, Charles	Boy 3rd Cl	SPENCER	
CAINES, William	Ord	CAESAR	
CARSLAKE, John	A.B.	THAMES	
	Midshipman	VICTORY	Trafalgar
COLE, Edward	Master's Mate	SUPERB	
	Master's Mate	SUPERB	St Domingo
	Lieut. R.N.	STATELY	Stately. 22 March 1808
COLE, Thomas	Ord	THAMES	
COLLIER, John	A.B.	SPENCER	
COLLINS, Michael	A.B.	CAESAR	
	Midshipman	SPARTIATE	Trafalgar
COOK, John	A.B.	POMPEE	

GUT OF GIBRALTAR 12 JULY 1801

COOKE, William.H.	Midshipman	SUPERB	
	Midshipman	SUPERB	*St Domingo*
COOPER, Edward	Pte. R.M.	SUPERB	G.H. 3,979
COOPER, Thomas	Pte. R.M.	AUDACIOUS	
CORBEN, George	Boy 2nd Cl	SUPERB	*(M.L. as CORBIN)*
	Ord	SUPERB	*St Domingo*
CRANE, Poynter	Midshipman	SUPERB	
CROSBY, Thomas	Ord	SPENCER	
	Ord	NORTHUMBERLAND	*St Domingo*
CROSIER, James	A.B.	SUPERB	*(M.L. as CROSSIER)*
	Gunner's Mate	SUPERB	*St Domingo*
	Gunner's Mate	ALFRED	*Guadaloupe*
CURRAN, James	Ord	VENERABLE	G.H. 9,369
CUTTER, Frank	Vol 1st Cl	CAESAR	Navy List as CUTLER.
DAVIES, John	A.B.	SUPERB	
	L.M.	SOUTHAMPTON	*1 June 1794*
	Ord	SOUTHAMPTON	*Southampton. 9 June 1796* (Vfd Abd. Not on Roll)
	Ord	SOUTHAMPTON	*St Vincent*
	A.B.	SUPERB	*St Domingo*
DAVIES, John	Ord	CAESAR	
DAVIS, Samuel	A.B.	CAESAR	
DOUGLAS, Pringle.H.	Actg Lieut. R.N.	AUDACIOUS	
	Lieut. R.N. (P)	Sir THOMAS PASLEY	*Pasley. 28 Octr 1801*
DUNN, Edward	Ord	CAESAR	G.H. 4,728
DYER, William	Two A.Bs borne	SUPERB	
ELLIS, Thomas	Ord	SPENCER	G.H. 10,081
	Captain's Servant	PEGASUS	*1 June 1794* (Rating)
	Boy 3rd Class	AQUILON	*23rd June 1795*
FISHER, James	Ord	SUPERB	G.H. 2,846
	A.B.	SUPERB	*St Domingo*
FLEECROFT, Peter	Ord	SUPERB	Not yet found aboard.
FRAZIER, John	Ord	SUPERB	
	A.B.	SUPERB	*St Domingo*
GALE, John	Carp's Mate	SPENCER	
	Carp's Crew	BELLEROPHON	*1 June 1794*
	Carp's Crew	BELLEROPHON	*17 June 1795*
	A.B.	CULLODEN	*Nile*
	Carpenter	NORTHUMBERLAND	*Northumberland. 22 May 1812*
GALLOW, Martin	Pilot	THAMES	*(M.L. as GALOT)*
	Pilot	FOXHOUND	*Basque Roads 1809*
GIFFARD, James	Chaplain	SPENCER	
GIFFORD, James	Boy 2nd Cl	POMPEE	
GILBERT, William	Ord	CAESAR	
GLEAVE, Thomas	Pte. R.M.	POMPEE	*(M.L. as GLEAVES)*
GODFREY, John	Boy 3rd Cl	THAMES	*(M.L. as John William)*
GORMAN, John	A.B.	AUDACIOUS	
	A.B.	POMPEE	*Martinique*
	A.B.	POMPEE	*Pompee. 17 June 1809*
	A.B.	POMPEE	*Guadaloupe*
	Yeoman Sheets	Qn CHARLOTTE	*Algiers*
GRAPE, Henry	2nd Lt. R.M.	CAESAR	
GREEN, James	A.B.	VENERABLE	
	A.B.	ZEALOUS	*Nile*
GUTTERIDGE, Samuel	Pte. R.M.	SPENCER	G.H. 8,499
HAINES, Thomas	Coxswain	SUPERB	
	Ord	SOUTHAMPTON	*Southampton. 9 June 1796* (Vfd Abd. Not on Roll)
	Ord	SOUTHAMPTON	*St Vincent*
	Coxswain	SUPERB	*St Domingo*
	Gunner	ACASTA	*Martinique*
	Gunner	POMPEE	*Pompee. 17 June 1809* (Vfd Abd. Not on Roll)
	Gunner	POMPEE	*Guadaloupe*
HALE, William	Gunner's Mate	VENERABLE	*(May read HALL on ADM 171/)*
HALES, William	A.B.	VENERABLE	
HALL, Charles	Pte. R.M.	SUPERB	
	Pte. R.M.	SUPERB	*St Domingo*
HALL, William	Midshipman	SUPERB	
HAMMOND, William	Pte. R.M.	SPENCER	
HARRISON, Joseph	A.B.	AUDACIOUS	G.H. 408
(HART, Robert. See "NILE")			

HATTON, John	Cpl. R.M.	SPENCER	
	Pte. R.M.	BELLEROPHON	*1 June 1794*
	Pte. R.M.	BELLEROPHON	*17 June 1795*
	Pte. R.M.	BELLEROPHON	*Nile*
HAYMAN, John	Ord	VENERABLE	
HILL, Edward	Boy 2nd Cl	POMPEE	
HILL, Thomas	Boy 3rd Cl	VENERABLE	
HILLIER, William.C.	Master's Mate	POMPEE	
	Midshipman	ALFRED	*1 June 1794*
	Midshipman	BLENHEIM	*St Vincent*
	Purser	COMUS	*Comus. 15 Augt 1807*
HINDMARSH, John	Midshipman	SPENCER	
	Capt's Servant	BELLEROPHON	*1 June 1794*
	Vol 1st Cl	BELLEROPHON	*17 June 1795*
	Midshipman	BELLEROPHON	*Nile*
	Lieut. R.N.	PHOEBE	*Trafalgar*
	Lieut. R.N.	BEAGLE	*Basque Roads. 1809*
	Lieut. R.N.	NISUS	*Java*
HOLLOWAY, Isaac	L.M.	POMPEE	
HORTON, Amos	Pte. R.M.	AUDACIOUS	
HUGHES, John	L.M.	SPENCER	
	Ord	PRINCE	*Trafalgar*
HYDE, Thomas	A.B.	POMPEE	(M.L. as HIDE)
JACKSON, Thomas	A.B.	SUPERB	
	Midshipman	SUPERB	*St Domingo*
	Actg Lieut. R.N.	NASSAU (P?)	*Nassau. 22 March 1808* (Vfd Abd. Not on Roll)
JAMES, James	Gunner	CALPE	
JEFFERIES, Evan	L.M.	POMPEE	(M.L. as JEFFERY)
JENNINGS, James	Yeoman Powder Rm	THAMES	
JOHNSON, John	2 borne. AB & LM	SUPERB	
	A.B.	SUPERB	*St Domingo*
JONES, Edward	Pte. R.M.	VENERABLE	
	Pte. R.M.	BELLEROPHON	*Trafalgar*
KEARLEY, Benjamin	Ord	THAMES	(M.L. as CARLEY)
	Coxswain	NAMUR	*4 Novr 1805*
	Coxswain	VALIANT	*Basque Roads 1809*
KENNEDY, Alexander	Midshipman	THAMES	
	Commander	PORT d'ESPAGNE	*Martinique*
KENTON, Thomas	Ord	THAMES	
KING, George	Boy 2nd Cl	CALPE	
	L.M.	HYDRA	*Hydra. 6 Augt 1807*
KNOTT, Stephen	Pte. R.M.	SPENCER	(Found as KING on M.L.)
LAMB, Joseph	Ord	CAESAR	
LEWIS, Frederick	Midshipman	POMPEE	
LILLICRAP, James	Lieut. R.N.	VENERABLE	
LLOYD, William	A.B.	SUPERB	
	Midshipman	SUPERB	*St Domingo*
LOVELESS, Bassett.J.	A.B.	AUDACIOUS	
	Actg Lieut. R.N.	FAWN	*Martinique*
	Actg Lieut. R.N.	FAWN	*Guadaloupe*
LOWE, Abraham	Lieut. R.N.	THAMES	
	Lieut. R.N.	TRIUMPH	*17 June 1795*
MANSON, James	Boy 2nd Cl	THAMES	
MELVILLE, William	Drummer. R.M.	SUPERB	G.H. 9,546 (M.L. as MELVIN)
	Pte. R.M.	SUPERB	*St Domingo*
MILLS, Robert	Pte. R.M.	POMPEE	
MOSER, Peter	A.B.	SPENCER	(alias REYNOLDS, Peter)
	A.B.	BRUNSWICK	*17 June 1795*
	A B	VICTORY	*Trafalgar* GH. 1695 (Medal known as REYNOLDS)
MURPHY, John	Ord	SPENCER	G.H. 6,475
NATION, Thomas	Pte. R.M.	POMPEE	
NEEDHAM, Henry	L.M.	POMPEE	
NEWLEY, George	Ord	CAESAR	G.H. 3,392
NICHOLLS, W.	A.B.	VENERABLE	
NICHOLS, Thomas	Boy 3rd Cl	CAESAR	(M.L. as NICHOLLS)
NORGATE, William	Boy	AUDACIOUS	(Not yet found)
OSBORNE, John	Pte. R.M.	CAESAR	
OUTRAM, Benjamin.F.	Surgeon	SUPERB	
	Surgeon	NYMPHE	*Nymphe. 8 March 1797*
PASMORE, Thomas	Pte. R.M.	AUDACIOUS	
PATRIARCHE, Charles	Lieut. R.N.	SUPERB	(Vfd Abd. Not on Roll)
	Master's Mate	DEFENCE	*Nile*
	Lieut. R.N.	SUPERB	*St Domingo*
PHILLIPS, Richard	A.B.	VENERABLE	
PURVIS, John	Ord	SUPERB	
	Ord	SUPERB	*St Domingo*
RATTRAY, James	A.B.	VENERABLE	
	Master's Mate	BRITANNIA	*Trafalgar*
REED, Joseph	Boy 3rd Cl	SPENCER	G.H. 464

GUT OF GIBRALTAR 12 JULY 1801

ROBINSON, James	A.B.	SUPERB	
	Yeoman of Sheets	SUPERB	*St Domingo*
ROCHE, William	L.M.	CAESAR	
ROOK, William	Pte. R.M.	CAESAR	
ROSCOW, Samuel	Midshipman	SPENCER	
RUNDLE, Edward	Vol 1st Cl	VENERABLE	
RUSS, John	Pte. R.M.	CAESAR	*(Ex-deserter as ROSS on ML)*
RYLEY, John	A.B.	SUPERB	
	Q.M.	SUPERB	*St Domingo*
SAYER, William	A.B.	VENERABLE	
SCOTT, Robert	Midshipman	AUDACIOUS	
	Purser	SCIPION (?)	*Java (see this Clasp Roll)*
SIMMONS, William	Pte. R.M.	SPENCER	
SIMPSON, Alexander	L.M.	SPENCER	
SLEATOR, George	A.B.	POMPEE	*(M.L. as SLATER)*
SMITH, Alexander	2nd Lt. R.M.	VENERABLE	
SPEAR, Isaac	L.M.	POMPEE	
STRATH, William	Gunner's Mate	POMPEE	
	Q.M's Mate	IMPREGNABLE	*Algiers*
STRETCH, William	Ord	VENERABLE	*G.H. 143*
SUGG, Edmund	Pte. R.M.	SUPERB	*(ADM 171/- & ML as EDMUND)*
(or Edward)	Sgt. R.M.	SUPERB	*St Domingo*
	Sgt. R.M.	EREBUS	*The Potomac 17 Aug 1814*
SUGGETT, Christopher	Ord	SUPERB	
	Quarter Gunner	SUPERB	*St Domingo*
SYKES, Thomas	Lieut. R.N.	CALPE	
	Lieut. R.N.	SWIFTSURE	*Trafalgar*
TALLERT, William	Pte. R.M.	AUDACIOUS	*(M.L. as TABERT)*
TANCOCK, John	Lieut. R.N.	CAESAR	
	Master's Mate	CRESCENT	*Crescent. 20 Octr 1793*
	Master's Mate	ORION	*23rd June 1795*
	Master's Mate	ORION	*St Vincent*
	Actg Lieut. R.N.	ORION	*Nile*
TATTON, Michael	Ord	VENERABLE	
THOMAS, Richard	A.B.	SPENCER	
TINSLEY, John	Pte. R.M.	SUPERB	
	Pte. R.M.	SUPERB	*St Domingo*
TRISCOTT, Joseph	2nd Lt. R.M.	SPENCER	
	Captain. R.M.	DICTATOR	*Off Mardoe. 6 July 1812*
TURNOUR, Hon Arthur.R.	Midshipman	CAESAR	
UNDERHILL, George	Drummer. R.M.	THAMES	*(Not yet found in M.L.)*
	Drummer. R.M.	TONNANT	*Trafalgar*
WATKINS, James	L.M.	POMPEE	
	L.M.	LONDON	*London. 13 March 1806*
WEBBER, John	Q.M.	VENERABLE	
WELLS, John	Ord	VENERABLE	
WELSH, Joseph	Quarter Gunner	VENERABLE	
WHITE, Hugh.B.	Midshipman	POMPEE	*(Vfd Abd. Not on Roll)*
	Lieut. R.N.	TONNANT	*Trafalgar*
WHITE, James	2 Borne. AB & Ord	POMPEE	
WHITE, John	Midshipman	SUPERB	
	Midshipman	SUPERB	*St Domingo*
	Lieut. R.N.	BARRACOUTA	*Banda Neira*
	Lieut. R.N.	BARRACOUTA	*Java*
WICKHAM, Job	Boy 3rd Cl	AUDACIOUS	
WILLCOX, Robert	A.B.	SUPERB	
	Boy 3rd Cl	LIVELY	*Lively. 13 March 1795*
	Boy 2nd Cl	LIVELY	*St Vincent*
WILLIAMS, William	Cpl. R.M.	VENERABLE	
WILSON, John	2 Borne. AB & LM	SUPERB	
	Ord	SUPERB	*St Domingo*
WOOD, James	Ord	SUPERB	
WOOD, John	L.M.	AUDACIOUS	*(M.L. as WOODS)*
WOODWARD, Henry	A.B.	THAMES	
WRIGHT, Andrew	Q.M.	CAESAR	
	A.B.	BEDFORD	*14 March 1795*

(7) 21 JULY BOAT SERVICE 1801

Cutting out the French corvette CHEVRETTE, in Camaret Bay, near Brest.
(Real date 22 July 1801)

BARRY, John	A.B.	URANIE	
BECK, William	Pte. R.M.	BEAULIEU	
	Pte. R.M.	St FIORENZO	*San Fiorenzo. 14 Feb 1805*
BIGGINS, Robert	A.B.	URANIE	
	A.B.	ALFRED	*1 June 1794*
	A.B.	BLENHEIM	*St Vincent*
BOXER, Edward	Midshipman	DORIS	
	Lieut. R.N.	TIGRE	*B.S. 1 Nov 1809*
	Captain. R.N.	PIQUE	*Syria*
CLEPHAN, James	Master's Mate	DORIS	*(M.L. as CLEPPIN)*
	Lieut. R.N.	SPARTIATE	*Trafalgar*
INCH, John	Sgt. R.M.	DORIS	
	Pte. R.M.	LEVIATHAN	*1 June 1794*
	Pte. R.M.	SANS PAREIL	*23 June 1795*
MORICE, James	Yeoman of Sheets	URANIE	*(M.L. as MORRIS)*

(2) SYLPH 28 SEPR 1801

Action with a French frigate, off Cape Pinas, North coast of Spain.

BURGESS, Samuel	Lieut. R.N.	SYLPH	
	Midshipman	IMPREGNABLE	*1 June 1794*
	Lieut. R.N.	PRINCE	*Trafalgar*
	Lieut. R.N.	PINCHER	*B.S. 27 July 1809*
	Flag Lt. R.N.	QUEEN CHARLOTTE (P)	*Algiers*
DASHWOOD, Charles	Commander	SYLPH (P)	
	Lieut. R.N.	IMPREGNABLE	*1 June 1794*
	Lieut. R.N.	MAGNANIME	*12 Octr 1798*
			(Vfd Abd. Not on Roll)

(4) PASLEY 28 OCTR 1801

Capture of the Spanish polacre VIRGIN del ROSARIO by the hired 16 gun brig Sir THOMAS PASLEY (M.L. Adm 41/14), off Cape de Gata, Southern Spain.

BIGNELL, William	Boatswain	Sir THOMAS PASLEY	
DOUGLAS, Pringle.H.	Lieut. R.N.	Sir THOMAS PASLEY (P)	
	Actg Lieut. R.N.	AUDACIOUS	*Gut of Gibraltar. 12 July 1801*
GLANVILL, Richard	A.B.	Sir THOMAS PASLEY	
HILL, Joshua	A.B.	Sir THOMAS PASLEY	

(5) 27 JUNE BOAT SERVICE 1803

Cutting out of the French brig VENTEUX, off the Isle de Bas.
(Real date 28 June 1803)

BASTIN, Thomas	Clerk	LOIRE	
	Clerk	LOIRE	*B.S. 4 June 1805*
	Purser	GRASSHOPPER	*Off Rota. 4 April 1808*
	Purser	GRASSHOPPER	*Grasshopper. 24 April 1808*
CAMERON, James	A.B.	LOIRE	
	A.B.	LOIRE	*B.S. 4 June 1805*
FERGUSON, George	Midshipman	LOIRE	
TEMPLE, Francis	Lieut. R.N.	LOIRE (P)	
WHITAKER, Richard	A.B.	LOIRE	
	A.B.	LOIRE	*B.S. 4 June 1805*

(1)   4 NOV BOAT SERVICE 1803

Capture of the French schooner VOLTIGEUSE, in Mancenille Bay, St Domingo.

BERKELEY, Maurice.F.F.	Midshipman	BLANCHE	
	Captain. R.N.	THUNDERER	Syria

(The officer nominated for promotion for this Action was court-martialled, and his proposed advancement cancelled. Even so, the creation of this clasp some 45 years later was approved by the Flag Officers' Committee)

(10)   4 FEB BOAT SERVICE 1804

Cutting out of the French brig CURIEUX, at entrance to Fort Royal Harbour, Martinique.

BACKHOUSE, Joseph	Pte. R.M.	CENTAUR	(M.L. as BLACKHOUSE)
CHURCH, Richard	Pte. R.M.	CENTAUR	
COCKBURN, Robert	Pte. R.M.	CENTAUR	G.H. 7,885.
DOBSON, Jeremiah	Ord	CENTAUR	G.H. 540
	Ord	CENTAUR	B.S. 16 July 1806
	Ord	CENTAUR	Centaur 26 Augt 1808
			(Vfd Abd. Not on Roll)
EDWARDS, Joseph	A.B.	CENTAUR	
JAMES, John	Ord	CENTAUR	
	A.B.	CENTAUR	B.S. 16 July 1806
	Capt Main Top	CENTAUR	Centaur 26 Augt 1808
MANNING, Henry	A.B.	CENTAUR	
	Carpenter's Crew	CENTAUR	B.S. 16 July 1806
	Carpenter's Crew	CENTAUR	Centaur 26 Augt 1808
MESSERVEY, John	A.B.	CENTAUR	G.H. 3,506
	Carpenter's Crew	CENTAUR	B.S. 16 July 1806
	Carpenter's Crew	CENTAUR	Centaur 26 Augt 1808
WARNER, George	Ord	CENTAUR	
	Ord	CENTAUR	B.S. 16 July 1806
	Yeoman of Sheets	CENTAUR	Centaur 26 Augt 1808
WINDSOR, Benjamin	Boy 3rd Cl	CENTAUR	
	Boy 3rd Cl	CENTAUR	B.S. 16 July 1806
	Boy 3rd Cl	CENTAUR	Centaur 26 Augt 1808

(4)   SCORPION 31 MARCH 1804

Cutting out of the Dutch corvette ATHALANTE by boats of SCORPION and BEAVER, in Vlie passage to Texel.
(This Ship Action clasp recorded in Boat Service Roll – Adm 171/3/13)

FLAXMAN, Robert	A.B.	SCORPION	(Vfd Abd. Not on Roll)
	Bosun's Mate	SCORPION	Scorpion. 12 Jany 1810
			(Vfd Abd. Not on Roll)
	Bosun's Mate	SCORPION	Guadaloupe
HACKER, Thomas	Supn. L.M.	SCORPION	
	L.M.	SCORPION	Scorpion. 12 Jany 1810
			(Vfd Abd. Not on Roll)
	L.M.	SCORPION	Guadaloupe
SALVEDORE, George	A.B.	SCORPION	(Vfd Abd. Not on Roll)
	A.B.	LOWESTOFFE	14 March 1795
	A.B.	LOWESTOFFE	Lowestoffe. 24 June 1795
TOMS, William	A.B.	SCORPION	(M.L. as THOMS)
	A.B.	TIGRE	Acre. 30 May 1799
	A.B.	TIGRE	Egypt
	Sailmaker	SCORPION	Scorpion. 12 Jany 1810
	Sailmaker	SCORPION	Guadaloupe

No Applicants   BEAVER 31 MARCH 1804

Cutting out of the Dutch corvette ATHALANTE by boats of SCORPION and BEAVER, in Vlie passage to Texel.

(12) CENTURION 18 SEPT 1804

Action with the French MARENGO (80), ATALANTE (40), and SEMILLANTE (36), in Vizagapatam Roads, Madras.

ANDERTON, Thomas	A.B.	CENTURION	*(This Ship was still on a Commission which started on 30 November 1792)*
BOWEN, George	Master's Mate	CENTURION	*(Vfd Abd. Not on Roll)*
	Master's Mate	NAMUR	*4 Novr 1805*
	Lieut. R.N.	CONQUEROR	*B.S. 16 July 1806*
CARROLL, William.F.	Lieut. R.N.	CENTURION	*(& M.G.S. – MAIDA)*
	Vol 1st Cl	DIAMOND	*Port Spergui. 17 March 1796.*
	Lieut. R.N. (P)	GIBRALTAR FLOTILLA	*B.S. 23 Nov 1810.*
COLBY, Thomas	Midshipman	CENTURION	
	Midshipman	BEDFORD	*Camperdown*
	Midshipman	FOUDROYANT	*12 Octr 1798*
	Lieut. R.N.	THUNDERER	*Trafalgar B.S. 19 April 1814, unlisted clasp on known 5 Clasp Medal.*
COLE, James	Ord	CENTURION	
	Ord	REVENGE	*Trafalgar*
	Ord	REVENGE	*Basque Roads 1809*
HAYDON, Nathaniel	Clerk	CENTURION	
	Purser	St FIORENZO	*San Fiorenzo. 8 March 1808*
MEARS, Jacob	Carpenter's Crew	CENTURION	*(Vfd Abd. Not on Roll)*
	Carpenter's Crew	REVENGE	*Trafalgar. GH. 5308*
	Carpenter's Crew	REVENGE	*Basque Roads 1809 (Vfd Abd)*
PHILIPS, James.R.	Lieut. R.N.	CENTURION (P)	
	Midshipman	BEAULIEU	*Camperdown*
SYMES, John	Q.M's Mate	CENTURION	
THOMPSON, John	A.B.	CENTURION	*(Vfd Abd. Not on 17/- Roll On G.H. Roll) GH.6700*
	A.B.	REVENGE	*Trafalgar*
WARD, John	Quarter Gunner	CENTURION	
	Quarter Gunner	REVENGE	*Trafalgar*
	Yeoman Sheets	REVENGE	*Basque Roads 1809 (Vfd Abd)*
WEBB, George	A.B.	CENTURION	*G.H. 8,855. Joined this ship before War, in Dec 1792*

(8) ARROW 3 FEBY 1805

Most gallant and successful protection of 32 sail of British Merchant ships, when attacked by two forty gun French frigates, off Cape Caxine, Algeria.
(H.M. Sloop ARROW finally captured by French. No Muster List survived)
(Real date 4 February 1805)

BROWN, Benjamin	L.M.	ARROW	*G.H. 2,209*
DALY, Cuthbert.F.	Lieut. R.N.	ARROW	*P.O.W. until July 1806.*
	Commander	COMET	*Comet. 11 Augt 1808*
DANE, Richard	Ord	ARROW	
GRAY, Archibald	Carpenter	ARROW	
GREATREX, Robert	Ord (?)	ARROW	*(Not on M.L. at 1 Sept 1804)*
HURLEY, John	Ord	ARROW	*GH.8341. M.L. as HARLEY*
LONGRIDGE, George	A.B.	ARROW	
WHEELER, Thomas	L.M.	ARROW	

(2) ACHERON 3 FEBY 1805

Most gallant and successful protection of 32 sail of British Merchant ships, when attacked by two forty gun French frigates, off Cape Caxine, Algeria.
(H.M. Bomb Vessel ACHERON finally taken by French. No Muster List survived)
(Real date 4 February 1805)

SIMPSON, John	Midshipman	ACHERON	*P.O.W. for 2 months*
	Midshipman	CUTTLE	*Martinique*
WHEELAN, James	Ord	ACHERON	

(13) SAN FIORENZO 14 FEBY 1805

Capture of the French frigate PSYCHE by H.M.S. St FIORENZO,
off Ganjam, Madras.
(Real date 13 Feb 1805)

ACTON, John	L.M.	St FIORENZO	
	L.M.	St FIORENZO	San Fiorenzo. 8 March 1808
BARNEY, George	Ord	St FIORENZO	
	Ord	St FIORENZO	San Fiorenzo. 8 March 1808
BECK, William	Pte. R.M.	St FIORENZO	
	Pte. R.M.	BEAULIEU	B.S. 21 July 1801
COLLIER, Edward	Lieut. R.N.	St FIORENZO	
	Lieut. R.N.	St FIORENZO	San Fiorenzo. 8 March 1808
	Lieut. R.N.	THAMES (P)	Amanthea. 25 July 1810
	Captain. R.N.	CASTOR	Syria
FINN, Samuel	L.M.	St FIORENZO	(Vfd Abd. Not on Roll)
	L.M.	St FIORENZO	San Fiorenzo. 8 March 1808
HOSKINS, Daniel	Pte. R.M.	St FIORENZO	
	Pte. R.M.	St FIORENZO	San Fiorenzo. 8 March 1808
HUGHES, Peter	A.B.	St FIORENZO	
	A.B.	St FIORENZO	San Fiorenzo. 8 March 1808 (Vfd Abd. Not on Roll)
KENNY, Nathaniel	A.B.	St FIORENZO	
	A.B.	St FIORENZO	San Fiorenzo. 8 March 1808
LOVE, George	Ord	St FIORENZO	
	Ord	St FIORENZO	San Fiorenzo. 8 March 1808
MARSINGALL, Samuel	Midshipman	St FIORENZO	
PACEY, John	A.B.	St FIORENZO	
	A.B.	St FIORENZO	San Fiorenzo. 8 March 1808
PIGGOTT, David	A.B.	St FIORENZO	
TROUT, Peter	Ship's Corporal	St FIORENZO	
	Capt Forecastle	St FIORENZO	San Fiorenzo. 8 March 1808

(10) 4 JUNE BOAT SERVICE 1805

Capture of the French corvettes CONFIANCE and BELIER, in Muros Bay,
near Cape Finisterre.

BASTIN, Thomas	Clerk	LOIRE	
	Clerk	LOIRE	B.S. 27 June 1803
	Purser	GRASSHOPPER	Off Rota. 4 April 1808
	Purser	GRASSHOPPER	Grasshopper. 24 April 1808
BERTRAM, Charles	Lieut. R.N.	LOIRE	
	Lieut. R.N.	EMERALD (P)	Emerald. 13 March 1808
CAMERON, James	A.B.	LOIRE	
	A.B.	LOIRE	B.S. 27 June 1803
COLLINS, Richard	A.B.	LOIRE	
CONNOR, Richard	Midshipman	LOIRE	
	Midshipman	EMERALD	Emerald. 13 March 1808
	Midshipman	EMERALD	Basque Roads 1809
DOUGLAS, Joseph	2nd Lt. R.M.	LOIRE	
M'KILLOP, John	Vol 1st Cl	LOIRE	
	Volunteer per Order	EMERALD	Emerald. 13 March 1808
	Master's Mate	ASTRAEA	Off Tamatave. 20 May 1811
SAURIN, Edward	Vol 1st Cl	LOIRE	
	Midshipman	EMERALD	Emerald. 13 March 1808
	Master's Mate	EMERALD	Basque Roads 1809
SOUTHERN, John	Ord	LOIRE	
WHITAKER, Richard	A.B.	LOIRE	
	A.B.	LOIRE	B.S. 27 June 1803

(29) **PHOENIX 10 AUGT 1805**

Capture of the French frigate DIDON, off Cape Finisterre.

ACLAND, Henry	A.B.	PHOENIX	(Vfd Abd. Not on Roll)
	A.B.	PHOENIX	4 Novr 1805. GH.4060
BLANKER, Christopher	Quarter Gunner	PHOENIX	
	Quarter Gunner	PHOENIX	4 Novr 1805
BROWN, Antony	A.B.	PHOENIX	(Anthony on other Roll)
	A.B.	PHOENIX	4 Novr 1805
BROWN, Samuel	Lieut. R.N.	PHOENIX	
	Lieut. R.N.	PHOENIX	4 Novr 1805
BUCKLEY, James	Steward	PHOENIX	
	Steward	PHOENIX	4 Novr 1805
CUMMINGS, James	Q.M's Mate	PHOENIX	(Vfd Abd. Not on Roll)
	Q.M's Mate	PHOENIX	4 Novr 1805. GH.8849
DAVIES, George	A.B.	PHOENIX	G.H. 7,030
or DAVIS	L.M.	PRINCE GEORGE	St Vincent
	A.B.	PHOENIX	4 Novr 1805
EDWARDS, Patrick	L.M.	PHOENIX	
HOBBS, Thomas	L.M.	PHOENIX	
	L.M.	PHOENIX	4 Novr 1805
HORN, John	Pte. R.M.	PHOENIX	(M.L. as HORNE)
	Pte. R.M.	PHOENIX	4 Novr 1805
JOHNSON, Richard	Quarter Gunner	PHOENIX	GH. 9041
	Quarter Gunner	PHOENIX	4 Novr 1805
JORDON, Thomas	Pte. R.M.	PHOENIX	
	Pte. R.M.	EDGAR	Copenhagen. 1801
	Pte. R.M.	PHOENIX	4 Novr 1805
			(Vfd Abd. Not on Roll)
KENNEDY, Bernard	Yeoman of Sheets	PHOENIX	(Vfd Abd. Not on Roll)
	Yeoman of Sheets	PHOENIX	4 Novr 1805
LAWES, Thomas	Ord	PHOENIX	
	Ord	PHOENIX	4 Novr 1805
LESSELS, Thomas	Q.M.	PHOENIX	
	Q.M.	PHOENIX	4 Novr 1805
MACARTY, Bernard	Quarter Gunner	PHOENIX	
PIKE, James	Ord	PHOENIX	
	Ord	PHOENIX	4 Novr 1805
PLIMPTON, Henry	Boy 3rd Cl	PHOENIX	(M.L. as PLYMPTON)
	Boy 3rd Cl	PHOENIX	4 Novr 1805
PYE, Thomas	Sgt. R.M.	PHOENIX	
	Sgt. R.M.	PHOENIX	4 Novr 1805
RAWLINS, Richard	Pte. R.M.	PHOENIX	(M.L. as ROWLAND)
	Pte. R.M.	PHOENIX	4 Novr 1805
ROUSE, Joseph	Ord	PHOENIX	(M.L. as ROWSE)
	Boy 3rd Cl	RENOMMEE	Egypt
	Ord	PHOENIX	4 Novr 1805
SHARRATT, John	Ord	PHOENIX	(M.L. as SHERRARD)
	Ord	PHOENIX	4 Novr 1805
SMITH, Thomas	Midshipman	PHOENIX	
	Midshipman	PHOENIX	4 Novr 1805
	Lieut. R.N.	LYRA	Basque Roads 1809
STEVENS, William	A.B.	PHOENIX	(M.L. as STEPHENS)
	A.B.	PHOENIX	4 Novr 1805. GH.8979
STOGDEN, Richard	A.B.	PHOENIX	4 Novr 1805
			(Vfd Abd. Not on Roll)
TOZER, Aaron	Midshipman	PHOENIX	
	Lieut. R.N.	VICTORIOUS	Victorious with Rivoli
UNWIN, Thomas	A.B.	PHOENIX	
	Ord	GLATTON	Copenhagen 1801
	Bosun's Mate	PHOENIX	4 Novr 1805
WARDEN, William	Surgeon	PHOENIX	
	Surgeon	ALCMENE	Copenhagen 1801
WHYLEY, Thomas	Pte. R.M.	PHOENIX	GH.8973. (M.L. as WHYLY)
	Pte. R.M.	PHOENIX	4 Novr 1805

(1613) **TRAFALGAR** (G.M.)
Battle. 21 October 1805.

ABBOTT, William	Pte. R.M.	LEVIATHAN	G.H. 7976
ABLETT, Thomas	A.B.	PHOEBE	G.H. 7395
	A.B.	AJAX	St Sebastian
ACAMFORD, Ruffiano	Pte. R.M.	ROYAL SOVEREIGN	
ADAM, Samuel	Ord	ACHILLE	G.H. 3343 as ADAMS
ADAMS, Thomas	Landsman	CONQUEROR	
ADAMS, William	Q.M's Mate	VICTORY	G.H. 7529
ADAMSON, John	Master's Mate	BRITANNIA	
ADDISON, Dominic	A.B.	ROYAL SOVEREIGN	
	A.B.	NISUS	Java
AIKEN, John	L.M.	THUNDERER	
	L.M.	RENOWN	Egypt
AIKIN, Matthew	Ord	ROYAL SOVEREIGN	(M.L. as EAKIN)
AITKEN, James	Ord	DEFENCE	
	Ord	VENERABLE	Camperdown
	Ord	KENT	Egypt
AKERS, Thomas	A.B.	PRINCE	(To Commander 1856)
ALDRED, Henry	L.M.	MARS	
ALLEN, Thomas	Pte. R.M.	DREADNOUGHT	
	Pte. R.M.	DIADEM	Egypt
ALLEN, William	Vol 1st Cl	NAIAD	
ALLEN, William	Pte. R.M.	BRITANNIA	
	Pte. R.M.	VICTORIOUS	Victorious With Rivoli
ALLEN, William.E.H.	Midshipman	TEMERAIRE	
	Lieut. R.N.	AKBAR	Java
ALPHEUS, Charles	Pte. R.M.	BRITANNIA	(ML as ALPHERS)
	Pte. R.M.	THESEUS	Basque Roads 1809
	Pte. R.M.	HEBRUS	Algiers
AMBROSE, Prosper	Midshipman	PHOEBE	
ANDERSON, Archibald	L.M.	TEMERAIRE	
ANDERSON, Colin	L.M.	AFRICA	
ANDERSON, John	A.B.	VICTORY	
ANDREWS, Christopher	Pte. R.M.	TONNANT	
ANDREWS, George	A.B.	ORION	(Same man X/978)
			(Roll as ANDREWS)
	Ord	PRINCE GEORGE	St Vincent (Roll as ANDREW)
ANDREWS, Henry	Master	NAIAD	
ANDREWS, Thomas	Pte. R.M.	DEFENCE	
ANDREWS, William	A.B.	MINOTAUR	G.H. 9931
ANDSOR, Thomas	Ord	DEFIANCE	
ANNEEMS, Joseph	Pte. R.M.	MARS	
ANTHORNE, Thomas	A.B.	LEVIATHAN	
ANTHONY, Mark	Midshipman	NAIAD	
APPLEGATE, James	Pte. R.M.	NAIAD	
ARBUTHNOT, Alexander	Midshipman	MARS	
ARMSTRONG, Samuel	Clerk	EURYALUS	
ARTHUR, John	L.M.	AJAX	
ARTHUR, John	L.M.	VICTORY	
ASHCROFT, Thomas	Boy	SWIFTSURE	
ASLETT, Anthony	A.B.	VICTORY	
ASPINALL, Robert	L.M.	CONQUEROR	
ATKINSON, William	A.B.	ACHILLE	
	Ord	PALLAS	17 June 1795
ATWOOD, John	Ord	BRITANNIA	G.H. 5202
	L.M.	BARFLEUR	St Vincent
ATWELL, Robert	Yeoman of Sheets	PRINCE	
	A.B.	IRRESISTIBLE	23rd June 1795
	A.B.	RUSSELL	Camperdown
	Yeoman of Sheets	RAMILLIES	Copenhagen 1801
ATTWELL, Thomas	Pte. R.M.	SPARTIATE	(Roll here as ATWELL)
	Pte. R.M.	AMPHION	Lissa (S/15 both clasps)
AUNGUR, George	Ord	VICTORY	(In Group at R.N. Museum, Portsmouth)
AYMER, Abraham	Drummer. R.M.	NEPTUNE	
BABKIN, Edward	Pte. R.M.	PRINCE	(M.L. as BAMKIN)
BADCOCK, William.S.	Midshipman	NEPTUNE	(Afterwards as LOVELL)
BAGLAY, James	Pte. R.M.	VICTORY	
BAGNELL, Isaac	Pte. R.M.	NEPTUNE	
BAGUE, George	Lieut. R.N.	COLOSSUS	
BAILEY, John.P.	Midshipman	AFRICA	
BAKER, George	A.B.	ROYAL SOVEREIGN	
BAKER, Stephen	Pte. R.M.	MINOTAUR	(M.L. as CABER)
BAKER, William	3 Borne Pte RM(2) and a Boy	BELLEISLE	
BAKER, William	Pte. R.M.	CONQUEROR	
BALL, George	Boy	DEFIANCE	
BALL, Henry	Ord	VICTORY	
BANFIELD, Henry	Pte. R.M.	THUNDERER	
	Pte. R.M.	IMPLACABLE	B.S. 7 July 1809

BANISTER, John	L.M.	BRITANNIA	
BANTOM, Thomas	Boy	DEFIANCE	
BARBER, Stephen	Pte. R.M.	MINOTAUR	
BARCLAY, John	Lieut. R.N.	BRITANNIA	
	Lieut. R.N.	LATONA	Curacoa
	Lieut. R.N.	PRESIDENT	St Sebastian (Vfd Abd. Not on Roll)
BARKER, George	Vol 1st Cl	ORION	
BARNARD, Edward	Actg Lieut. R.N.	ACHILLE	
	Captain. R.N.	CAMBRIDGE	Syria
BARRITT, Joseph	Pte. R.M.	LEVIATHAN	
BARRY, James	A.B.	THUNDERER	
BARWICK, John	A.B.	DREADNOUGHT	
BASTIN, Robert	Lieut. R.N.	BELLEISLE	
	A.B.	NYMPHE	Nymphe. 8 March 1797 (Vfd Abd. Not on Roll)
	Lieut. R.N.	BLANCHE	Blanche. 19 July 1806
BATEMAN, John	A.B.	VICTORY	
BATEMAN, William	A.B.	LEVIATHAN	
BATH, William	Yeoman of Sheets	DEFIANCE	
BATSON, Joseph	Ord	BELLEROPHON	
	Ord	LONDON	Copenhagen 1801
BAXTER, James	Pte. R.M.	DEFENCE	
BAXTON, Francis	Ord	REVENGE	G.H. 10,076
BAYLY, James	Midshipman	EURYALUS	
	Vol 1st Cl	PENELOPE	Penelope. 30 March 1800
	Midshipman	PENELOPE	Egypt
BAZING, John.H.	Ord	COLOSSUS	Only as Henry BAZING
	Boy	THESEUS	Acre. 30 May 1799 (Not yet found aboard ship)
	Boy	THESEUS	Nile
BEATSON, Robert	A.B.	VICTORY	
BECKETT, Flowers	Master's Mate	SPARTIATE	
	Master's Mate	LONDON	Copenhagen 1801 (Vfd Abd. Not on Roll)
BEECH, William	Pte. R.M.	MINOTAUR	(M.L. as BEACH)
BELITHER, James	Boy 3rd Cl	AGAMEMNON	G.H. 7739
	Boy 3rd Cl	AGAMEMNON	St Domingo
BELL, Joseph	A.B.	EURYALUS	
BELL, William	Ord	COLOSSUS	
BELLAIRS, Henry	Midshipman	SPARTIATE	
BELLAMY, John	L.M.	ROYAL SOVEREIGN	
BELLINCOLE, Thomas	Ord	ROYAL SOVEREIGN	
	L.M.	NAMUR	St Vincent
BELLMAN, Walter	L.M.	TONNANT	
BELLMAN, William	Pte. R.M.	AJAX	
BENDELL, James	Pte. R.M.	DEFENCE	
BENGAMIN, Felix	L.M.	REVENGE	
BENJAMEN, John	Midshipman	PRINCE	
	Purser's Steward	FAIRY	Fairy. 5 Feby 1800
	Purser's Steward	RENOMMEE	Egypt
BENNETT, Richard	Pte. R.M.	VICTORY	G.H. 4955
BENTOTE, James	L.M.	VICTORY	
BERRY, George	Drummer. R.M.	SPARTIATE	
BERSLING, Franz	Pte. R.M.	DEFENCE	
BERWICK, Joseph	Ord	ORION	
BEST, William	L.M.	REVENGE	
BETTY, Christopher.W.	Lieut. R.N.	DREADNOUGHT	
	Midshipman	MAJESTIC	1 June 1794
	Midshipman	MARS	Mars. 21 April 1798
BIGNELL, George	Lieut. R.N.	SPARTIATE	
	A.B.	LONDON	Copenhagen. 1801
BINFIELD, Henry	Pte. R.M.	REVENGE	
	Pte. R.M.	REVENGE	Basque Roads 1809
BINFORD, Thomas	Midshipman	PRINCE	
BIRKIN, William	Pte. R.M.	PRINCE	
BISHOP, James	L.M.	PRINCE	
BISHOP, John	Pte. R.M.	ORION	
BLACK, Peter	Boy 2nd Cl	MARS	G.H. 8153
BLADE, John	Ord	BELLEISLE	G.H. 5558
BLAKE, John	A.B.	LEVIATHAN	
BLANDFORD, James	Midshipman	REVENGE	(Roll as BLANFORD)
	Midshipman	REVENGE	Basque Roads 1809
BLENNERHASSETT, J.P.	Midshipman	TONNANT	
BLETHYN, Richard	Ord	TONNANT	
BLIGHT, Emanuel	Midshipman	BRITANNIA	
BLIGHT, William	Lieut. R.N.	BRITANNIA	
BOLT, William	Ord	BELLEROPHON	
BOLTON, Alexander	A.B.	COLOSSUS	
BOLTON, Robert.H.	Asst Surgeon	ORION	Appld from 78th Highlanders
BOND, Henry	Boy	ORION	G.H. 7695
BOND, Robert	Ord	TEMERAIRE	
BONE, George	L.M.	TONNANT	
BONE, Woodhouse	Ord	BELLEROPHON	
BOON, John	Pte. R.M.	CONQUEROR	

TRAFALGAR

BOOTH, John	Pte. R.M.	REVENGE	
BORTHWICK, George	L.M.	VICTORY	
BOULTON, William	Ord	TEMERAIRE	
BOURDA, John	Ord	NEPTUNE	(M.L. as BAUDAIN)
BOUND, William	A.B.	ROYAL SOVEREIGN	
	A.B.	REGULUS	Egypt
	A.B.	NISUS	Java
	A.B.	QUEEN CHARLOTTE	Algiers
BOURKE, Lawrence	A.B.	MARS	GH 6536 as BURKE
BOWDEN, James	Ord	PHOEBE	
	Ord	PHOEBE	Off Tamatave. 20 May 1811 (Vfd Abd. Not on Roll)
	Ord	PHOEBE	Java
	Quarter Gunner	PHOEBE	Phoebe. 28 March 1814 (Vfd Abd. Not on Roll)
BOWDEN, Richard.B.	Midshipman	BRITANNIA	(Roll as BOWDEUX)
BOWEN, Peregrine	Midshipman	PRINCE	
BOWLES, James	Ord	AFRICA	
BOWLES, Thomas	Ord	BRITANNIA	
BOWYER, John	Drummer. R.M.	SWIFTSURE	
BOYCE, William.H.	Lieut. R.N.	MARS	
BRADBURN, John	L.M.	SWIFTSURE	
BRADFORD, Thomas	A.B.	COLOSSUS	
	L.M.	BELLONA	Copenhagen 1801
BRADY, John	Boy 2nd Cl	ORION	
BRAND, William	Carp's Crew	ACHILLE	
BRAND, William.H.	Vol 1st Cl	REVENGE	
	Vol 1st Cl	REDWING	Redwing. 31 May 1808
	Vol 1st Cl	REDWING	Redwing. 7 May 1808
BRANDON, Thomas	L.M.	REVENGE	G.H. 8925
BRANNAN, Patrick	Pte. R.M.	AFRICA	
BRASKETT, John	A.B.	VICTORY	
BRATTLE, Thomas	1st Lt. R.M.	AFRICA	
BRAY, Henry.H.	Sgt. R.M.	SPARTIATE	G.H. 9967
BRAY, James	A.B.	BELLEROPHON	
BRAYLEY, Edward	L.M.	SWIFTSURE	
BRAZIER, James	L.M.	MINOTAUR	
	Ord	MINOTAUR	B.S. 25 July 1809
	Ord	ALBION	Algiers
BREAME, John	Ord	COLOSSUS	
BREMNER, John	Carp's Crew	TONNANT	
	Carpenter	NISUS	Java
BRENAN, Alexander	Midshipman	TEMERAIRE	
BRENNAN, Daniel	Ord	BELLEISLE	
	L.M.	ROYAL GEORGE	1 June 1794
	Boatswain	BARRACOUTA	Banda Neira
	Boatswain	BARRACOUTA	Java
BRICE, William	Midshipman	PRINCE	
BRIDGE, John	L.M.	LEVIATHAN	
BRINN, John	Ord	DREADNOUGHT	
BRISBEN, James	Clerk	CONQUEROR	
BRITTON, James	A.B.	THUNDERER	
BRITTON, Simon.G.	Asst Surgeon	PICKLE	(Vfd Abd. Not on Roll) Allen's Navy List 1854 shows recvd a 1 clasp NGS.
BROOKS, Thomas	Boy	DEFENCE	
BROOKS, William	Pte. R.M.	POLYPHEMUS	
	Pte. R.M.	PRESIDENT	Java
BROWN, Edward	Ord	ORION	
BROWN, George	Lieut. R.N.	VICTORY	
BROWN, Jacob	Pte. R.M.	VICTORY	G.H. 3062
BROWN, James	Ord	DEFIANCE	
	Ord	GANGES	Copenhagen 1801
BROWN, James	A.B.	REVENGE	G.H. 8777
BROWN, James	Pte. R.M.	SWIFTSURE	
BROWN, John	2 Borne. AB & Ord	BELLEISLE	
BROWN, John.C.	A.B.	NEPTUNE	
	A.B.	PERLEN	Guadaloupe
BROWN, John.H.	Midshipman	PRINCE	
BROWN, Joseph	Ord	VICTORY	G.H. 1110
BROWN, Joseph	Boy 3rd Cl	BELLEISLE	
	A.B.	GENOA	Navarino
BROWN, Joshua	Ord	VICTORY	G.H. 7696
BROWN, Thomas	Pte. R.M.	DREADNOUGHT	G.H. 994
	Pte. R.M.	TIGRE	Acre. 30 May 1799
	Pte. R.M.	TIGRE	Egypt
BROWN, William	A.B.	THUNDERER	

BROWNING, William.D.	Pte. R.M.	VICTORY	
BROWNRIGG, John	L.M.	SIRIUS	G.H. 3278
	L.M.	SIRIUS	Sirius 17 April 1806
BRUCE, Henry.W.	Midshipman	EURYALUS	
BRYAN, Jacob	L.M.	DREADNOUGHT	(M.L. as BYRON)
	Ord	CAPTAIN	Martinique
BRYDONE, James.M.	Asst Surgeon	THUNDERER	(On Roll as BRYDON)
BUCHANNAN, William	A.B.	DEFENCE	
	Lieut. R.N.	DICTATOR	Off Mardoe. 6 July 1812
BUCKINGHAM, Henry	Pte. R.M.	MARS	G.H. 6885
	Servant	CULLODEN	1 June 1794.
BUCKLEY, Cornelius	L.M.	VICTORY	G.H. 5225
BUDDLE, William	Pte. R.M.	BELLEISLE	
BUNNING, William	Boy	BELLEISLE	
BURGESS, Samuel	Lieut. R.N.	PRINCE	
	Midshipman	IMPREGNABLE	1 June 1794
	Lieut. R.N.	SYLPH.	Sylph. 28 Sepr 1801
	Lieut. R.N.	PINCHER	B.S. 27 July 1809
	Flag Lt. R.N.	QUEEN CHARLOTTE	
		(P)	Algiers
BURGIN, Joseph	Ord	VICTORY	GH. 161 for 56 Years.
	Ord	VANGUARD	Nile (ML alias COXHEAD)
BURKE, James	L.M.	TEMERAIRE	
	Ord	ANSON	Anson. 23 Augt 1806
	Ord	ANSON	Curacoa
	"Convict"	POMPEE	Martinique (Ex Mutineer)
	Ord	LION	Java (Re-Instated)
BURN, Edward	Ord	MINOTAUR	G.H. 5928
	Ord	MINOTAUR	B.S. 25 July 1809
			(Vfd Abd. Not on Roll)
BURN, James	A.B.	BRITANNIA	G.H. 4994
BURN, James	L.M.	BRITANNIA	
BURNE, Rev Charles	Chaplain	NEPTUNE	
BURNE, Thomas	Quarter Gunner	TONNANT	
BURNES, Alexander	Ord	BELLEROPHON	
	L.M.	AGINCOURT	Camperdown
BURNETT, Thomas	A.B.	TEMERAIRE	
BURNETT, William	Surgeon	DEFIANCE	
	Surg's 3rd Mate	GOLIATH	St Vincent
	Surg's 1st Mate	GOLIATH	Nile
	Surgeon	ATHENIENNE	Egypt
BURNS, James (1)	L.M.	BRITANNIA	(M.L. as BURNE)
BURR, E.T.	Midshipman	DREADNOUGHT	
BURROWS, Robert	Ord	REVENGE	
	L.M.	MONMOUTH	Camperdown
	Ord	MONMOUTH	Egypt
BURTON, Samuel	Pte. R.M.	DEFENCE	
BURTON, William	Boy	AJAX	
BUSH, William	Pte. R.M.	SWIFTSURE	
	Sgt. R.M.	ALBION	Navarino
BUTCHER, Edward	Pte. R.M.	PHOEBE	
	Cpl. R.M.	PHOEBE	Java
BUTLER, Henry	Pte. R.M.	NAIAD	
	Pte. R.M.	MINOTAUR	Nile
	Pte. R.M.	MINOTAUR	Egypt
BUTT, John	L.M.	PRINCE	
BUTTERAL, William	L.M.	TONNANT	
BUTTERS, James	Ord	ACHILLE	
BUTTON, Joseph	L.M.	VICTORY	
BYRN, Simon	Ord	DREADNOUGHT	G.H. 7839 as BYRNE
BYRNE, David	L.M.	MARS	
BYRNE, Morgan	Ord	BRITANNIA	G.H. 5355 as BRYAN
BYRNE, Patrick	Pte. R.M.	NEPTUNE	G.H. 9044
	Pte. R.M.	VICTORIOUS	Victorious with Rivoli
	Pte. R.M.	GRANICUS	Algiers
CAGAN, George	Pte. R.M.	BELLEISLE	(M.L. as GOAHAGAN)
CALDWELL, Thomas	L.M.	BRITANNIA	
CALLAGHAN, Nicholas	L.M.	MARS	G.H. 10,068
CAMP, William	Pte. R.M.	BELLEISLE	G.H. 9738
CAMPBELL, Benjamin	Ord	PRINCE	
CAMPBELL, Colin	Master's Mate	DEFIANCE	
CAMPBELL, Donald	2nd Lt. R.M.	AGAMEMNON	
	2nd Lt. R.M.	AGAMEMNON	St Domingo
	Lieut. R.M.	RESOLUTION	Basque Roads 1809
CAMPBELL, John	Coxswain	DREADNOUGHT	
CAPEL, Thomas Bladen	Captain. R.N.	PHOEBE	
	Midshipman	SANSPAREIL	23rd June 1795
	Lieut. R.N.	VANGUARD	Nile
CAPPEL, Jacob	Pte. R.M.	VICTORY	G.H. 9146

TRAFALGAR

CAREW, John	L.M.	DEFENCE	G.H. 8605
CARKETT, John	Boy	NAIAD	
CARLETON, William	Midshipman	COLOSSUS	
	Midshipman	AMAZON	Amazon. 13 March 1806
CARNEY, Bryan	L.M.	BELLEISLE	
	L.M.	CAPTAIN	Martinique
CARNEY, Hugh	Pte. R.M.	BRITTANIA	
CARNEY, James	A.B.	SPARTIATE	
CARNEY, Patrick	Ord	ACHILLE	
CARNEY, Thomas	Mid Ship Man	PRINCE	G.H. 9945. A Rating.
CARPHY, Thomas	Quarter Gunner	BRITANNIA	
CARRICK, William	L.M.	POLYPHEMUS	
CARROLL, Cornelius	Boy 2nd Cl	VICTORY	
CARROLL, Francis	L.M.	MARS	
	L.M.	BLANCHE	Copenhagen 1801
CARROLL, Patrick	A.B.	BRITANNIA	G.H. 9540
CARROLL, Peter	L.M.	CONQUEROR	
	L.M.	CONQUEROR	B.S. 16 July 1806
CARSLAKE, John	Midshipman	VICTORY	
	A.B.	THAMES	Gut of Gibraltar. 12 July 1801
CARTER, John	Actg Lieut. R.N.	LEVIATHAN	
	Midshipman	PENELOPE	Egypt
	Vol 1st Cl	PENELOPE	Penelope. 30 March 1800
CARTER, Robert	L.M.	REVENGE	G.H. 7567
CARTWRIGHT, Samuel	Pte. R.M.	ORION	
CASKET, Hector	Boy	BELLEISLE	
CASS, William	A.B.	LEVIATHAN	
CASTLE, Henry	Cpl. R.M.	BRITANNIA	
	Cpl. R.M.	HUSSAR	Java
CATHERINE, Joseph	Pte. R.M.	TONNANT	
CHADLEY, John	Pte. R.M.	CONQUEROR	
CHADWICK, William	A.B.	REVENGE	
CHAMBERS, John	Ord	DREADNOUGHT	
	Ord	CAPTAIN	Martinique
CHAMBERS, Thomas	Pte. R.M.	VICTORY	
CHANDLER, James	Ord	SWIFTSURE	(Deserted 5 Sept 1814)
	A.B.	DICTATOR	Off Mardoe. 6 July 1812
	Capt Main Top	SHAMROCK	Gluckstadt. 5 Jany 1814
CHANDLER, William	L.M.	TONNANT	(M.L. as CHARNLY)
CHAPELL, Charles	Midshipman	VICTORY	
CHAPPEL, William	L.M.	MARS	
CHAPPELL, John	Pte. R.M.	AGAMEMNON	
	Pte. R.M.	AGAMEMNON	St Domingo
CHAPMAN, Daniel	L.M.	AFRICA	
CHAPMAN, George	Pte. R.M.	NEPTUNE	G.H. 9465 2 Clasp as JOHN
	Pte. R.M.	NAMUR	St Vincent. (Roll as John)
CHAPMAN, James	L.M.	VICTORY	
CHAPMAN, James	Boy 3rd Cl	ROYAL SOVEREIGN	
	Ord	NISUS	Java
CHAPMAN, Thomas	Pte. R.M.	BELLEROPHON	
CHARD, William	Pte. R.M.	PRINCE	G.H. 8879 as CHARGE
CHARLES, Joseph	L.M.	REVENGE	
CHARLTON, George	A.B.	COLOSSUS	(M.L. as BEALES, Nicholas)
CHESNAYE, John.C.	Midshipman	ORION	
	Actg 2nd Master	SYLVIA	Sylvia. 26 April 1810
CHERRY, Peter	Ord	TEMERAIRE	G.H. 1112
CHIENE, Robert	Coxswain	LEVIATHAN	
	Gunner	HOGUE	B.S. 8 April 1814
CHINNARY, William	Ord	REVENGE	G.H. 8581 as CHINNERY
CHINNOCK, Richard	Pte. R.M.	BRITANNIA	
CHISWICK, Charles	Vol 1st Cl	ROYAL SOVEREIGN	
CHITTLEBOROUGH, James	Ship's Corporal	PHOEBE	
CHRISTEY, John	Pte. R.M.	CONQUEROR	
CHRISTIAN, Francis	A.B.	ROYAL SOVEREIGN	
CHRISTIE, James	Schoolmaster	DEFENCE	
CHRISTOPHER, Samuel	A.B.	SWIFTSURE	
CHRYSTIE, Thomas	Midshipman	DEFIANCE	
	Midshipman	AJAX	Egypt
	Midshipman	NEPTUNE	Martinique
CHURCH, James	L.M.	BELLEISLE	G.H. 1104
CINNAMON, Joseph	2nd Lt. R.M.	AJAX	(Roll as CINNIMOND)
CLACK, James	Boy	ROYAL SOVEREIGN	
CLARK, John	Lieut. R.N.	THUNDERER	
	Midshipman	RUSSELL	23rd June 1795
CLARK, John	Surgeon	DREADNOUGHT	
CLARK, Joseph	A.B.	MINOTAUR	
	Boy 3rd Cl	BLANCHE	Blanche. 4 Jany 1795
	Vol 1st Cl	BLANCHE	Blanche. 19 Decr 1796
CLARK, William	Boy	ROYAL SOVEREIGN	
CLARKE, David	Ord	AJAX	
CLARKE, George	Ord	VICTORY	
CLARKE, William	Ord	BELLEISLE	
CLARKE, William	A.B.	VICTORY	

CLAY, John	Vol 1st Cl	VICTORY	
CLELLAND, James	Ord	BELLEROPHON	
CLEMENTS, Henry	Capt Forecastle	PRINCE	G.H. 3175
CLEMENTS, Michael	Ship's Corporal	VICTORY	G.H. 6392
CLENSEY, Edward	L.M.	COLOSSUS	G.H. 7122
CLERK, Walter	Ord	PRINCE	
CLEPHAN, James	Lieut. R.N.	SPARTIATE	
	Master's Mate	DORIS	B.S. 21 July 1801
CLIFF, John	L.M.	SPARTIATE	G.H. 9039
CLIMO, Thomas	L.M.	NEPTUNE	
	A.B.	SUPERB	Algiers
CLOUDEN, Daniel	A.B.	ROYAL SOVEREIGN	G.H. 9009
CLOW, David	Purser's Steward	COLOSSUS	
COADY, James	L.M.	COLOSSUS	
COAKLEY, Thomas	Lieut. R.N.	TEMERAIRE	
COBBE, Charles	A.B.	REVENGE	
COCK, Robert	Midshipman	THUNDERER	
	Master's Mate	AURORA	Guadaloupe
	Master's Mate	QUEBEC	B.S. 2 Aug 1811
COCKSEDGE, George	Midshipman	POLYPHEMUS	
CODLIN, Robert	A.B.	BELLEISLE	G.H. 8492 as CODLING
CODRINGTON, Edward	Captain. R.N.	ORION	
	Lieut. R.N.	QUEEN CHARLOTTE	1 June 1794
	Commander	BABET	23rd June 1795
	Vice Admiral	ASIA	Navarino (as Sir Edward)
COGGEN, George	Pte. R.M.	AJAX	
COLBURN, John	Pte. R.M.	DEFIANCE	
COLBY, Thomas	Lieut. R.N.	THUNDERER	
	Midshipman	BEDFORD	Camperdown
	Midshipman	FOUDROYANT	12 Octr 1798
	Midshipman	CENTURION	Centurion. 18 Sept 1804 (Known 5 Clasp Medal with unlisted "BS 19 April 1814")
COLE, James	Ord	REVENGE	
	Ord	CENTURION	Centurion. 18 Sept 1804
	Ord	REVENGE	Basque Roads 1809
COLEMAN, Thomas	Vol 1st Cl	BELLEISLE	
COLLIER, Abraham	Pte. R.M.	CONQUEROR	
COLLINS, Joseph	A.B.	LEVIATHAN	
COLLINS, Michael	Midshipman	SPARTIATE	
	A.B.	CAESAR	Gut of Gibraltar. 12 July 1801
COLLINS, Robert	Boy	PHOEBE	
COLLINSON, Robert	Q.M.	BELLEISLE	
	Quarter Gunner	PALLAS	17 June 1795
	Q.M.	LONDON	London. 13 March 1806
COLTHURST, Nicholas	Midshipman	PRINCE	
COMPTON, James	L.M.	TONNANT	
CONDON, Edward	Pte. R.M.	THUNDERER	
	Pte. R.M.	GIBRALTAR	Basque Roads 1809
CONNELL, Joseph	Ord	VICTORY	G.H. 5792 or 5192
CONNOLLY, Patrick	Pte. R.M.	SIRIUS	
	Pte. R.M.	SIRIUS	Sirius. 17 April 1806
CONNOR, James	Pte. R.M.	DREADNOUGHT	
	Pte. R.M.	CAPTAIN	Martinique
CONONRY, Thomas	L.M.	MARS	G.H. 9519 as CONROY
CONWAY, James	L.M.	REVENGE	G.H. 7950
	L.M.	REVENGE	B.S. 16 July 1806 (Vfd Abd. Not on Roll)
	L.M.	REVENGE	Basque Roads 1809 (Vfd Abd. Not on Roll)
COOK, George	Pte. R.M.	BRITANNIA	
	Pte. R.M.	SPARROW	St Sebastian
COOK, James	L.M.	COLOSSUS	G.H. 8193
COOK, Joseph	A.B.	REVENGE	(M.L. as WILLIAMS, Joseph)
	Ord	REVENGE	Basque Roads 1809
COOK, William	R.M. Boy	DEFENCE	
COOK, William	Boy 2nd Cl	DEFIANCE	
COOP, Abraham	L.M.	AGAMEMNON	
	L.M.	AGAMEMNON	St Domingo
	L.M.	PRESIDENT	Java
COOPER, George	Ord	THUNDERER	
COOPER, John	Ord	MARS	
COOPER, John	Sgt. R.M.	SPARTIATE	
COOPER, William	R.M. Boy	BELLEROPHON	
COOPER, William	L.M.	MARS	
COOTE, William	Lieut. R.N.	AGAMEMNON	
	Midshipman	ROYAL GEORGE	23rd June 1795
	Midshipman	EDGAR	Copenhagen 1801 (Vfd Abd. NOR)
	Lieut. R.N.	AGAMEMNON	St Domingo
	Lieut. R.N.	CERBERUS (P)	B.S. 2 Jan 1807

TRAFALGAR

CORBET, Daniel	Ord	REVENGE	
	A.B.	MONMOUTH	Camperdown
CORBETT, Thomas	Pte. R.M.	DEFENCE	
CORDER, Edward	Ord	COLOSSUS	G.H. 9136 as CORDER
	Ord	MONTAGU	Camperdown (both M.Ls as CORDY)
CORDRY, George	Midshipman	POLYPHEMUS	
CORGEARGE, John	A.B.	DEFIANCE	
CORMACK, Thomas	L.M.	CONQUEROR	
CORNELIUS, William	A.B.	PRINCE	
	L.M.	ROYAL GEORGE	1 June 1794
	L.M.	ROYAL GEORGE	23rd June 1795
CORNISH, Robert	Pte. R.M.	TONNANT	
CORP, Henry	Pte. R.M.	MARS	
CORP, Richard	Pte. R.M.	BELLEISLE	
CORYTON, John.R.	2nd Lt. R.M.	SPARTIATE	
COSTELLO, George	A.B.	THUNDERER	
COSTELLO, Thomas	Boy 3rd Cl	TEMERAIRE	
	Boy 2nd Cl	ANSON	Anson. 23 Augt 1806 (Vfd Abd. Not on Roll)
	Boy 2nd Cl	ANSON	Curacoa
COUCH, James	Lieut. R.N.	CONQUEROR	
COUCHER, Christopher	L.M.	COLOSSUS	(This Roll as COURCHER)
	L.M.	ANSON	Anson. 23 Augt 1806
	L.M.	ANSON	Curacoa
	Ord	TONNANT	B.S. 14 Dec 1814
COURT, Henry	Pte. R.M.	MARS	G.H. 9739
COUSINS, John.C.	Midshipman	AGAMEMNON	
	Midshipman	AGAMEMNON	St Domingo
COWAN, James	Pte. R.M.	BELLEISLE	
COWAN, James	Pte. R.M.	BELLEROPHON	
COWLE, John	L.M.	TEMERAIRE	
COX, Henry	Captain. R.M.	DEFENCE	
	2nd Lt. R.M.	VALIANT	1 June 1794
	1st Lt. R.M.	ROMNEY	Egypt
CRABBE, Charles	Yeoman of Sheets	DREADNOUGHT	
CRAIG, James	A.B.	LEVIATHAN	
CRAIG, John	L.M.	CONQUEROR	
CRANE, Robert	Pte. R.M.	TEMERAIRE	
CRAY, Thomas	Pte. R.M.	TONNANT	
CREER, William	A.B.	PRINCE	
CREMER, John	L.M.	SIRIUS	G.H. 5697
	L.M.	SIRIUS	Sirius. 17 April 1806 (Vfd Abd. NOR)
CRETCH, Daniel	Boy 2nd Cl	PHOEBE	(M.L. as CRUTCH)
	Ord	PHOEBE	Off Tamatave. 20 May 1811
	Ord	PHOEBE	Java
	A.B.	PHOEBE	Phoebe. 28 March 1814
CRIBB, Noel	A.B.	DREADNOUGHT	
CROFTON, Morgan.G.	Midshipman	SIRIUS	
	Midshipman	SIRIUS	Sirius. 17 April 1806
CROOKE, Charles.H.	Midshipman	PHOEBE	
	Actg Lieut. R.N.	CIRCE	Off The Pearl Rock. 13 Dec 1808 (Vfd Abd. Not on Roll but M.I.D. L.Gaz.1809.pp 146.)
CROOKSHANKS, Robert	A.B.	DEFENCE	
CROSBY, John	A.B.	THUNDERER	
CROSBY, Robert	L.M.	DEFENCE	
CROSSON, Francis	A.B.	TEMERAIRE	
CROUCH, John	A.B.	ACHILLE	G.H. 2408
CROW, John	Pte. R.M.	ROYAL SOVEREIGN	
CROWLEY, John	L.M.	DEFIANCE	G.H. 8793
	Ord	MINDEN	Algiers
CROWTHER, Jacob	Boy 2nd Cl	NEPTUNE	
CRUMP, William	Boy	MARS	
CRYER, John	Sgt. R.M.	CONQUEROR	
CUDDEFORD, Robert	Carp's Crew	NAIAD	G.H. 7829
CULLEN, Daniel	L.M.	ROYAL SOVEREIGN	
	L.M.	BRUNSWICK	1 June 1794 (as CULLINS)
	L.M.	ROBUST	23rd June 1795
	Ord	ROBUST	12 Octr 1798
CUNNINGHAM, William	Midshipman	PRINCE	
CURLEY, Henry	L.M.	SIRIUS	(Vfd Abd. Not on Roll)
	L.M.	SIRIUS	Sirius 17 April 1806
CURREN, Edward	A.B.	ORION	
DA COSTA, Benjamin	Midshipman	TEMERAIRE	
DALBY, Thomas	Pte. R.M.	DEFENCE	
DALEY, Joseph	L.M.	ROYAL SOVEREIGN	
DALLING, John.W.	Midshipman	DEFENCE	
	Master's Mate	AMPHION	B.S. 28 Aug 1809

DALTON, Charles	Ord	DEFIANCE	
D'MAIRO, Raffaelle	L.M.	BELLEISLE	
DAMON, Christopher	Ord	THUNDERER	
DANIEL, Richard	Seaman	CONQUEROR	Applied as superannuated Gunner
DARWELL, James	A.B.	SWIFTSURE	
DAVIDSON, Edward	L.M.	SWIFTSURE	
DAVIES, Hamilton	Midshipman	CONQUEROR	
DAVIES, William	A.B.	CONQUEROR	
DAVIS, David	Ord	MARS	
DAVIS, Edward	Pte. R.M.	CONQUEROR	
DAVIS, Francis	L.M.	BELLEISLE	
DAVIS, John	A.B.	SIRIUS	
	A.B.	SIRIUS	Sirius 17 April 1806 (Vfd Abd. Not on Roll)
DAVIS, Jonas	L.M.	AJAX	
	Boy	GIBRALTAR	Egypt. (+ China 1842)
DAVIS, Richard	L.M.	BELLEISLE	
DAVIS, Samuel	Boy	ROYAL SOVEREIGN	
DAVIS, Thomas	Sgt. R.M.	ACHILLE	
DAVIS, Thomas	Pte. R.M.	LEVIATHAN	
DAVIS, Thomas	A.B.	BELLOROPHON	
DAWKINS, Henry	Ord	BRITANNIA	
DAY, Edward	Drummer. R.M.	DEFENCE	
	Drummer. R.M.	RESOLUTION	Basque Roads 1809
DAY, Bartholomew.G.S.	Midshipman	REVENGE	
or B.George.S.	Actg Master	SUPERIEURE	Superieure. 10 Feby 1809
	Actg Master	SUPERIEURE	Martinique (Vfd Abd. Not on Roll)
	Actg Master	SUPERIEURE	Guadaloupe
DEAL, George	A.B.	PRINCE	
DEAL, John	A.B.	TEMERAIRE	
DEAN, Stephen	A.B.	PRINCE	(M.L. as DENN)
DE COCK, Baltic	Ord	SWIFTSURE	(M.L. as DE COCK, Batty)
DECOEURDOUX, George.J.	Lieut. R.N.	MARS	
	Midshipman	LION	Lion. 15 July 1798
DENNIS, Philip	Pte. R.M.	LEVIATHAN	G.H. 9532
	Pte. R.M.	BELLEROPHON	Nile
DENNYS, Lardner	Midshipman	ACHILLE	
DENT, Digby	Midshipman	ACHILLE	
	Lieut. R.N.	MINDEN	Algiers
DENT, Robert	Pte. R.M.	DEFENCE	G.H. 10,134
DESBROW, Charles	Pte. R.M.	DEFIANCE	
DEUCHAR, Patrick	Midshipman	SWIFTSURE	
DEVENISH, Henry	Pte. R.M.	ROYAL SOVEREIGN	
DEVINE, Philip	L.M.	SPARTIATE	
DIAMOND, Samuel	Pte. R.M.	TONNANT	
DICK, Daniel	A.B.	ROYAL SOVEREIGN	
	L.M.	TREMENDOUS	1 June 1794
DICKENSON, Thomas	Midshipman	ROYAL SOVEREIGN	
	Lieut. R.N.	ANDROMACHE	St Sebastian
DICKSON, James	A.B.	ORION	
	A.B.	SCEPTRE	Guadaloupe
DIMOCK, Daniel	L.M.	POLYPHEMUS	G.H. 9487
DINEFORD, John	L.M.	NEPTUNE	
DIPPLE, George	Pte. R.M.	BELLEISLE	
DIXIE, Alexander	Lieut. R.N.	PHOEBE	
	A.B.	AMAZON	Amazon 13 Jany 1797
DIXON, John	L.M.	SPARTIATE	
DOBLE, Robert	Carp's Crew	VICTORY	
	Carp's Crew	PERLEN	Guadaloupe
DODD, Robert	Ord	NEPTUNE	
DOLWICK, Frederick	Pte. R.M.	SWIFTSURE	G.H. 3919 as DULWICK
DONOVON, Michael	L.M.	NAIAD	G.H. 2223
DORMAN, William	Quarter Gunner	DEFIANCE	
DOUGHTY, William	A.B.	MINOTAUR	
DOUGLAS, Richard	Midshipman	ACHILLE	
	Midshipman	NEPTUNE	Martinique
DOWLING, Daniel	Boy	DREADNOUGHT	(M.L. as DOLAN)
DOWNEY, John	Ord	DREADNOUGHT	
DOWNEY, Thomas	Boy 2nd Cl	LEVIATHAN	
	A.B.	QUEEN CHARLOTTE	Algiers
	Capt' of Mast	ALBION	Navarino
DOWNIE, John	A.B.	ROYAL SOVEREIGN	
DOYLE, Laurance	L.M.	ORION	
	Ord	SCEPTRE	Guadaloupe
DRAKE, John	Midshipman	DEFIANCE	
	Lieut. R.N.	NORTHUMBERLAND	Northumberland. 22 May 1812
	Lieut. R.N.	ALBION	Navarino
DRAKE, John	L.M.	NEPTUNE	
DRAKE, William	L.M.	ROYAL SOVEREIGN	
DRAPER, Frederick	L.M.	COLOSSUS	
DREW, John	Pte. R.M.	ROYAL SOVEREIGN	
DREW, Thomas	Pte. R.M.	ACHILLE	

TRAFALGAR

DRIBROUGH, Alexander	A.B.	AGAMEMNON	
	A.B.	AGAMEMNON	St Domingo
DRUMMOND, Robert	A.B.	VICTORY	
DUDLEY, James	L.M.	SWIFTSURE	G.H. 8909
DUFF, Norwich	A.B.	MARS	
	Midshipman	ACTIVE	B.S. 28 June 1810
	Midshipman	ACTIVE	Lissa
	Midshipman	ACTIVE	Pelagosa. 29 Novr 1811
DUFF, Thomas	Vol 1st Cl	MARS	(Became "GORDON")
DUGMORE, William	Pte. R.M.	TONNANT	
DUGLASS, James	L.M.	BELLEROPHON	G.H. 8364 as Charles
DUGLASS, James	L.M.	COLOSSUS	G.H. 1764
	Ord	ANSON	Anson 23 Augt 1806 (Vfd Abd. Not on Roll)
	Ord	ANSON	Curacoa
DUMBRECK, William	Midshipman	DEFENCE	
DUNDAS, James	Surgeon	COLOSSUS	
DURMAN, James	Pte. R.M.	SPARTIATE	
DURNELL, Thomas	Pte. R.M.	TEMERAIRE	
	Pte. R.M.	ILLUSTRIOUS	Basque Roads 1809
	Pte. R.M.	ILLUSTRIOUS	Java
DURRANT, George	L.M.	COLOSSUS	G.H.7598 as DURANT
	Ord	ANSON	Curacoa
DYKES, John	Pte. R.M.	LEVIATHAN	
	Pte. R.M.	MAJESTIC	Nile
EAMES, Joseph	Pte. R.M.	ORION	
EARL, James	Ord	LEVIATHAN	
EASMAN, James	L.M.	AFRICA	
EASTICK, Spencer	A.B.	ACHILLE	(M.L. as HAISTICK)
EASTMAN, John	Midshipman	TEMERAIRE	
EATON, Henry	Ord	BELLEROPHON	
EATON, James	Midshipman	TEMERAIRE	
	Lieut. R.N.	LION	Java
EATON, Thomas	L.M.	LEVIATHAN	
EBBS, John	Gunner's Mate	VICTORY	
EDWARDS, George	Ord	ROYAL SOVEREIGN	G.H. 9242
EDWARDS, Henry	Q.M's Mate	NEPTUNE	
EDWARDS, William	A.B.	EURYALUS	
EDDY, William	A.B.	PHOEBE	G.H. 8707 as HEADY/EDEY
ELEVINE, John	Ord	COLOSSUS	G.H. 1096 as ELLIVINE
ELLIOT, Joseph	Pte. R.M.	BRITANNIA	
ELLIOTT, James.B.	Midshipman	PRINCE	
ELLIS, H.	L.M.	ACHILLE	
ELLIS, Samuel.B.	2nd Lt R.M.	AJAX	
	1st Lt. R.M.	STATIRA	Guadaloupe
ELMHIRST, Philip.C.	Midshipman	AFRICA	
EMMERSON, George	Ord	COLOSSUS	
EMMERSON, John	Ord	ACHILLE	G.H. 2539
	Ord	ST FIORENZO	San Fiorenzo. 8 Mar 1797 (Vfd Abd. Not on Roll)
EMERY, George	Ord	THUNDERER	
ENDERB(or L)Y, Samuel	Vol 1st Cl	DEFENCE	To 16th Lancers. A of I Medal.
ENGLISH, John	L.M.	MARS	G.H. 7777
ENTICOTT, William	Pte. R.M.	ACHILLE	
ENTWISTLE, Hugh	A.B.	BELLEROPHON	Became Commander 1839
ERRING, James	Ord	THUNDERER	
ESSEX, Thomas	Pte. R.M.	THUNDERER	
EVANS, Gregory	Boy	TEMERAIRE	
EVANS, William	A.B.	AJAX	
	Boatswain	DISPATCH	St Sebastian
EVERITT, James	Pte. R.M.	POLYPHEMUS	
EWINS, William	Pte. R.M.	SPARTIATE	
EYRE, Thomas	Ord	DEFENCE	
EYRES, William	Pte. R.M.	LEVIATHAN	
EYTON, William.W.	Vol 1st Cl	NEPTUNE	
	Vol 1st Cl	SEAHORSE	Seahorse Wh Badere Zaffere
FAGG, Mathew	A.B.	ACHILLE	
	Supn A.B.	RENOWN	B.S. 29 Aug 1800
FAIRBROTHER, William	Pte. R.M.	BELLEROPHON	
FAIRTLOUGH, H.B.	2nd Lt R.M.	REVENGE	
FARRAN, Joseph	L.M.	NEPTUNE	
FARRANT, Abraham	Carp's Crew	SPARTIATE	
FARRANT, John	Midshipman	ROYAL SOVEREIGN	
	Vol 1st Cl	RUSSELL	Copenhagen 1801
	Lieut. R.N.	SCOUT	B.S. 14 July 1809
	Lieut. R.N.	SCOUT	B.S. 1 Nov 1809
	Lieut. R.N.	BORER	B.S. 8 April 1814
FARRELL, John	L.M.	ACHILLE	
FARRELL, William	L.M.	CONQUEROR	

FEAKES, John	Pte. R.M.	TEMERAIRE	G.H. 6544
FEAR, William	Ord	ROYAL SOVEREIGN	
FEARALL, Daniel	Sgt. R.M.	VICTORY	
FELTON, John	Midshipman	VICTORY	
	Midshipman	BELLONA	Copenhagen 1801
FENNER, John	Ord	POLYPHEMUS	
	Ord	POLYPHEMUS	B.S. 16 July 1806
FERGUSON, Patrick	A.B.	AJAX	G.H.204
FERN, John	Pte. R.M.	TONNANT	
FERRIS, Abel	Lieut. R.N.	PRINCE	
	Master's Mate	IRRESISTIBLE	23rd June 1795
	Master's Mate	COLOSSUS	St Vincent
FESTING, Benjamin.M.	Midshipman	PRINCE	
	Lieut. R.N.	EAGLE	B.S. 17 Sep 1812
FETCH, Joseph	Boy	AGAMEMNON	
FIFE, William	Ord	BELLEISLE	
FINEMORE, John	Vol 1st Cl	MINOTAUR	
FINSLEY, John	Signalman	ROYAL SOVEREIGN	
FISCHER, John.N.	1st Lt. R.M.	CONQUEROR	
	1st Lt. R.M.	"ANHOLT" (P)	Anholt. 27 March 1811
FISHER, Thomas	Quarter Gunner	BELLEROPHON	
FISHER, Thomas	2nd Asst Surgeon	REVENGE	
FITZGERALD, John	Boy 2nd Cl	PHOEBE	
	Ord	PHOEBE	Off Tamatave. 20 May 1811
	Ord	PHOEBE	Java
	A.B.	PHOEBE	Phoebe. 28 March 1814
FITZPATRICK, Thomas	L.M.	DREADNOUGHT	
	L.M.	CAPTAIN	Martinique
FLAHERTY, Thomas	Drummer. R.M.	REVENGE	
FLINT, James	Pte. R.M.	MINOTAUR	
	Pte. R.M.	MINOTAUR	B.S. 25 July 1809
FLITT, James	A.B.	CONQUEROR	
	A.B.	BEAULIEU	Camperdown
	A.B.	CONQUEROR	B.S. 16 July 1806
FLOOK, William	L.M.	DEFIANCE	
FLUKES, John	Pte. R.M.	ORION	
FLUX, Richard	Pte. R.M.	DEFIANCE	
FLYNN, Cornelius	L.M.	AGAMEMNON	G.H. 9705
	L.M.	AGAMEMNON	St Domingo
FLYNN, Peter	Pte. R.M.	AGAMEMNON	
	Pte. R.M.	AGAMEMNON	St Domingo
FOLLEY, James	Boy	DEFENCE	
FOOLEY, Jeremiah	L.M.	NAIAD	G.H. 6647 as FOLEY
FORBES, Henry	A.B.	PHOEBE	
	Lieut. R.N.	DONEGAL	St Domingo
	Lieut. R.N.	DONEGAL	Basque Roads. 1809
FORBES, Phillip	Yeoman of Signals	EURYALUS	
FOSTER, James	Pte. R.M.	PRINCE	
FOWLER, Stephen	Pte. R.M.	ORION	
FOX, George	L.M.	TONNANT	GH.7427 & M.L. as Charles FOX
FOX, Robert	Pte. R.M.	ACHILLE	
FRANPIT, William	Pte. R.M.	THUNDERER	G.H. 9102 as FRANKPIT
FRANKLIN, John	Midshipman	BELLEROPHON	
	Midshipman	POLYPHEMUS	Copenhagen 1801
	Lieut. R.N.	BEDFORD	B.S. 14 Dec 1814
FRAZER, David	Ord	AGAMEMNON	
	Ord	AGAMEMNON	St Domingo
FREEMAN, Charles	Armourer's Mate	ORION	
FRENCH, George	Ord	VICTORY	G.H. 5632
FRENCH, James	Boy	AFRICA	
FRENCH, Robert	Pte. R.M.	REVENGE	
FROST, William	Pte. R.M.	COLOSSUS	
FRY, Edward	L.M.	SPARTIATE	
FULTON, James	A.B.	DREADNOUGHT	
FURZE, Robert	Ord	ORION	
FYNMORE, James	Ord	AFRICA	Died 1887 as Lt Col R.M.
	2nd Lt. R.M.	HEBRUS	Algiers
GAFFEREY, William	L.M.	CONQUEROR	
GALLAWAY, Alexander	Midshipman	THUNDERER	
	A.B.	RENOWN	Egypt
GAPE, Joseph	Vol. 1st Cl	AJAX	
	Midshipman	AMPHION	B.S. 28 Aug 1809
	Midshipman	AMPHION	B.S. 28 June 1810
GARDENER, William	L.M.	COLOSSUS	
GARDNER, William	Pte. R.M.	BELLEROPHON	
	Cpl. R.M.	EURYALUS	The Potomac. 17 Aug 1814
	Sgt. R.M.	MINDEN	Algiers
GARRETT, Edward.W.	Lieut. R.N.	MARS	
	Lieut. R.N.	ONYX	Onyx. 1 Jany 1809
GARRETT, George	Pte. R.M.	TONNANT	
GARRETT, Henry	Midshipman	BELLEISLE	
	Lieut. R.N.	PSYCHE	Java
GARRETT, Richard	A.B.	DEFENCE	

TRAFALGAR

GASKIN, George	L.M.	AFRICA	
GEARY, John	Midshipman	REVENGE	
	Master's Mate	MONARCH	B.S. 16 July 1806
GEE, Thomas	A.B.	ROYAL SOVEREIGN	
GEOGHEGAN, George	Pte. R.M.	BELLEISLE	G.H. 8486 as GOAHAGAN
GERMAN, William	L.M.	SIRIUS	
	L.M.	SIRIUS	Sirius 17 April 1806 (Vfd Abd. Not on Roll)
GIBSON, James	L.M.	ROYAL SOVEREIGN	
	Ord	PENELOPE	Martinique
GILBERT, James	A.B.	MARS	
GILBERT, John	Carp's Crew	ROYAL SOVEREIGN	
GILL, Joseph.C.	Midshipman	ACHILLE	
GILL, William	R.M.Boy	MARS	
GILLETT, William	Ord	SWIFTSURE	G.H. 9570 (or ? BILLETT)
GLASS, Thomas	Pte. R.M.	CONQUEROR	G.H. 8799
GOBLE, Thomas	Master's Mate	VICTORY	
GOODFELLOW, Peter	Pte. R.M.	MARS	(M) Anchor Type LS & GC. 34 Yrs.
GOODLAD, Edward	Midshipman	NEPTUNE	(Vfd Abd. Not on Roll)
	Midshipman	NEPTUNE	Martinique
	Midshipman	POMPEE	Guadaloupe
GOODMAN, Thomas	Ord	PRINCE	
GOODRICK, Thomas	Carp's Mate	COLOSSUS	
	Carpenter	UNITE	Pelagosa. 29 Novr 1811
GOODWIN, James	A.B.	LEVIATHAN	
GORDON, Robert	Ord	COLOSSUS	
GORDON, Robert	Lt. R.M.	SWIFTSURE	
GORMAN, John	L.M.	DREADNOUGHT	G.H. 2830
	Ord	ABERCROMBIE	Guadaloupe
GOUGH, Jonathan	Pte. R.M.	ACHILLE	
GOVIS, Robert	L.M.	ROYAL SOVEREIGN	
	Ord	ROYAL OAK	B.S. 14 Dec 1814
GRAHAM, Thomas	L.M.	VICTORY	
GRANTMAN, Abraham	Sailmaker	SWIFTSURE	G.H. 5937
GRAY, Francis	Midshipman	ORION	
GRAY, Henry	Ord	COLOSSUS	
GREEN, Andrew.P.	Lieut.	NEPTUNE	
	Midshipman	ILLUSTRIOUS	14 March 1795 (Vfd Abd. Not on Roll)
	Lieut. R.N.	GANGES	Copenhagen 1801
	Supn Commander	ELBE gun-boat Flotilla	Gluckstadt. 5 Jany 1814
GREEN, James	Gunner's Mate	NEPTUNE	G.H. 9730
GREEN, John	Ord	BRITANNIA	
GREEN, Samuel	Pte. R.M.	VICTORY	
	Pte. R.M.	AJAX	Egypt
GREEN, Thomas	Pte. R.M.	BRITANNIA	
GREEN, Thomas	Pte. R.M.	TEMERAIRE	
GREENLY, Rev. John	Chaplain	REVENGE	
GREENSLADE, John	L.M.	PRINCE	G.H. 9820
	L.M.	ROYAL GEORGE	1 June 1794
GREENWOOD, John	Pte. R.M.	REVENGE	
GREER, William	L.M.	CONQUEROR	
GREY, John	A.B.	NEPTUNE	G.H. 941
GRIMES, Samuel	Pte. R.M.	SIRIUS	G.H. 9178
GRINT, William	Master's Mate	BRITANNIA	
	Midshipman	AMAZON	Copenhagen 1801
	Master's Mate	LATONA	Curacoa
GROVES, James	A.B.	SPARTIATE	
GULLIVER, Samuel	Boy	ORION	
HAGGETT, William	L.M.	BRITANNIA	(M.L. as HIGATE)
HALE, John	2 L.Ms borne	PRINCE	
HALFPENNY, Christopher	L.M.	TEMERAIRE	
HALL, Charles	Master's Mate	ORION	
HALL, Henry	Ord	ACHILLE	
HALL, John	A.B.	AFRICA	
HALL, William	A.B.	VICTORY	
HAMBLY, Peter.S.	Master's Mate	PRINCE	
HAMILTON, John	L.M.	DEFENCE	
HAMILTON, Thomas	Ord	PRINCE	
HAMMOND, Isaac	A.B.	ACHILLE	G.H. 9653
HANCOCK, John	A.B.	NAIAD	
HAND, Thomas	R.M. Boy	MARS	
HANDLEY, Thomas	A.B.	BELLEROPHON	
HANDS, John	R.M. Boy	ORION	
HANNAM, John	Carp's Crew	AJAX	
HANOVER, William	Ord	PRINCE	
HANSFORD, George	Boy	CONQUEROR	G.H. 8827
HARDEN, George	Ord	EURYALUS	
HARDING, George	L.M.	THUNDERER	
	L.M.	RENOWN	Egypt

HARDING, Henry	Pte. R.M.	VICTORY	G.H. 5893
HARDWICKE, Rev Thomas	Chaplain	DREADNOUGHT	
HARE, William	Ord	ORION	G.H. 7321
HARKER, Michael	Not Given	AGAMEMNON	(alias HAWKER on M.L.)
HARPER, Matthew	L.M.	AFRICA	
HARRIS, Francis	Was Vol 1st Cl	TEMERAIRE	Roll wrong as "Gunner"
	Midshipman	UNITE	Pelagosa. 29 Novr 1811
HARRIS, Henry	Boy	LEVIATHAN	
HARRIS, John	2 Borne. AB & LM	BELLEROPHON	G.H. 1902
HARRIS, Simon	Ord	DEFENCE	
HARRIS, William	Pte. R.M.	MARS	Applied as John HARRIS
HARRISON, John	Pte. R.M.	BELLEISLE	
HARRISON, John	A.B.	EURYALUS	
HARRISON, William	Ord	VICTORY	
HART, William	Cook	COLOSSUS	
HART, William	L.M.	REVENGE	
HARTIGAN, Edward	A.B.	AFRICA	G.H. 7862
HARTNELL, James	Ropemaker	VICTORY	
HARVEY, William	Pte. R.M.	DEFIANCE	
HASSELEREE, Daniel	Ord	NAIAD	G.H. 9240 as HESSELCREE
HASWELL, William.H.	Midshipman	PHOEBE	
	Capt's Servant	LEVIATHAN	1 June 1794. "On the books only, . . . not present" Too young. Lieut. R.N. 1809.
HATTON, George	Pte. R.M.	REVENGE	
HAWES, William.J.	Ord	CONQUEROR	
	Capt's Servant	AUDACIOUS	1 June 1794
	Vol 1st Cl	AUDACIOUS	Nile
HAWKINS, Charles	Midshipman	PICKLE	
	Actg Sub Lt R.N.	PICKLE (P)	Pickle. 3 Jany 1807
HAWKINS, George.D.	2nd Lt. R.M.	SPARTIATE	
HAWSON, William	Boy 3rd Cl	BRITANNIA	
HAY, James	Midshipman	DEFIANCE	
	Lieut. R.N.	AMARANTHE	Martinique
HAY, Matthew	A.B.	ROYAL SOVEREIGN	
HAYES, William	L.M.	CONQUEROR	
HAYNES, Moses	Pte. R.M.	BRITANNIA	G.H. 730
HAYWARD, John	Pte. R.M.	BELLEISLE	
HEAL, John	Ord	PRINCE	
HEALEY, Patrick	L.M.	SPARTIATE	G.H. 9454 as HEELY
	L.M.	HUSSAR	Java
HEATH, John	Carp's Crew	VICTORY	
HEAVEN, Charles	Pte. R.M.	TEMERAIRE	G.H. 9867 as HAVEN
HEGGIE, Archibald	A.B.	BELLEISLE	
	Ord	MADRAS	Egypt
	A.B.	LONDON	London. 13 March 1806
HELM, Thomas	A.B.	DEFENCE	G.H. 6198
HELLARD, William	Pte. R.M.	ACHILLE	
HELPS, Thomas	Pte. R.M.	REVENGE	G.H. 8599
HEMER, Robert	Vol 1st Cl	AJAX	
HENDERSON, John	2 Borne. Ord & Qtr Gunner	BELLEISLE	
HENDERSON, William.W.	Midshipman	BELLEISLE	
	Lieut. R.N.	ACTIVE	B.S. 28 June 1810
	Lieut. R.N.	ACTIVE (P)	Lissa
	Captain. R.N.	EDINBURGH	Syria
HENLEY, Robert	A.B.	TEMERAIRE	
	Quarter Gunner	ANSON	Anson. 23 Augt 1806
	Quarter Gunner	ANSON	Curacoa
HENNAH, John	Pte. R.M.	BELLEROPHON	
HENNESSEY, John	Boy 3rd Cl	SIRIUS	(M.L. as @ SMITH, George)
	Boy 3rd Cl	SIRIUS	Sirius. 17 April 1806
HENNESSEY, Matthew	A.B.	BELLEROPHON	
HENRY, Joseph	A.B.	ACHILLE	
HERBERT, George.F.	Midshipman	NEPTUNE	
HERRICK, Edward	Midshipman	REVENGE	
	Midshipman	REVENGE	Basque Roads 1809
HERRINGHAM, William.A.	Midshipman	COLOSSUS	
	Midshipman	CALEDONIA	B.S. 27 Sep 1810
HERROD, John	Boy 3rd Cl	SPARTIATE	
HEWETT, James or HEWITT	Q.M's Mate	NAIAD	G.H. 283
	Ord	ALFRED	1 June 1794
	A.B.	BLENHEIM	St Vincent
HEWIN, William	Ord	BRITANNIA	
HEWISON, Benjamin	Quarter Gunner	TEMERAIRE	
HEWSON, George	Lieut. R.N.	DREADNOUGHT	
	Midshipman	BRITANNIA	14 March 1795
HIBBERD, James	Ord	AFRICA	
HIBBERT, Richard	Pte. R.M.	DREADNOUGHT	
HICKS, Augustus.T.	Vol 1st Cl	DEFIANCE	
HICKS, John	Pte. R.M.	ACHILLE	
HICKS, Richard	Pte. R.M.	NAIAD	

TRAFALGAR

HICKS, William	Midshipman	CONQUEROR	
	Master's Mate	MILFORD	B.S. 23 Nov 1810
HIGDEN, W.H.	Midshipman	DREADNOUGHT	
HIGGINS, George	A.B.	BELLEROPHON	
HIGHFIELD, Charles	A.B.	ROYAL SOVEREIGN	
HILL, Joseph	A.B.	ACHILLE	
HILLEN, Henry	Pte. R.M.	LEVIATHAN	
HILTON, Robert	Ord	PHOEBE	(M.L. as HITON)
HILTON, Stephen	Master's Mate	MINOTAUR	
	Midshipman	PEARL	Egypt
	Lieut. R.N.	REVENGE	Basque Roads 1809 (Vfd Abd. Not on Roll)
HINDMARSH, John	Lieut. R.N.	PHOEBE	
	Capt's Servant	BELLEROPHON	1 June 1794
	Vol 1st Cl	BELLEROPHON	17 June 1795
	Midshipman	BELLEROPHON	Nile
	Midshipman	SPENCER	Gut of Gibraltar. 12 July 1801
	Lieut. R.N.	BEAGLE	Basque Roads. 1809
	Lieut. R.N.	NISUS	Java
HINDS, James	Ord	SPARTIATE	
HINDS, John	Pte. R.M.	POLYPHEMUS	
	Pte. R.M.	PRESIDENT	Java
HINES, James	A.B.	CONQUEROR	
HIRKWOOD, Alexander	L.M.	ROYAL SOVEREIGN	
HITCHENS, Henry	Pte. R.M.	LEVIATHAN	G.H. 7593
HODGE, William	Boy 3rd Cl	PRINCE	
HODGES, John	Pte. R.M.	SWIFTSURE	G.H. 4651
HOFFMAN, Frederick	Lieut. R.N.	TONNANT	(Later a P.O.W.)
HOGEN, Dennis	L.M.	BRITANNIA	G.H. 8366
HOLBURNE, Thomas.Wm.	Vol 1st Cl	ORION	
HOLE, Lewis	Lieut. R.N.	REVENGE	
	Lieut. R.N.	RAMILLIES	Copenhagen 1801
HOLECOCK, Joseph	Pte. R.M.	BELLEISLE	(May read "HOLICOCK")
HOLLAND, Daniel	Q.M.	SPARTIATE	G.H. 8927 as HOWARD
HOLLAND, Henry	Pte. R.M.	LEVIATHAN	
	Pte. R.M.	IRRESISTIBLE	St Vincent
HOLLIPHANT, James	A.B.	REVENGE	
HOLLIS, Thomas	Pte. R.M.	PRINCE	
HOLLOCK, John	Pte. R.M.	SPARTIATE	G.H. 5447 as James
HOLLOWAY, William	L.M.	DREADNOUGHT	
	Ord	CAPTAIN	Martinique
HOLMAN, William	Purser	AFRICA	
HOLMES, John	R.M. Boy	THUNDERER	
HOLT, John	Pte. R.M.	THUNDERER	G.H. 10,108
HOOD, William.J.T.	Vol 1st Cl	ACHILLE	
	Master's Mate	MALTA	Gaieta. 24 July 1815
HOPE, Robert	Sailmaker's Crew	TEMERAIRE	
HOPKINS, Samuel	R.M. Boy	ACHILLE	
HORWOOD, Joshua	Asst Surgeon	PRINCE	
HOUNSELL, Thomas	L.M.	ROYAL SOVEREIGN	
	Ord	NISUS	Java
HOWE, Alexander.B.	Lieut. R.N.	LEVIATHAN	
HUDSON, John	Midshipman	ORION	
HUGHES, David	L.M.	ACHILLE	
HUGHES, George.W.	Master's Mate	BELLEROPHON	Became G.W.H.D'AETH.
HUGHES, John	Ord	PRINCE	
	L.M.	SPENCER	Gut of Gibraltar.12 July 1801
HUGHES, Morris	A.B.	ROYAL SOVEREIGN	
HUGMAN, William	Ord	POLYPHEMUS	
HUMPHRIES, William	Quarter Gunner	MARS	
HUNTER, John	A.B.	VICTORY	
HUNTER, John	Q.M.	NAIAD	
HURCOMBE, Robert	Pte. R.M.	BELLEISLE	
	Pte. R.M.	RUSSELL	Copenhagen 1801
HURLEY, Timothy	L.M.	DEFIANCE	
HURST, James	Quarter Gunner	TEMERAIRE	
HUTTON, Douglas	A.B.	ROYAL SOVEREIGN	
HYATT, James	L.M.	DEFIANCE	
HYDE, Thomas	L.M.	CONQUEROR	
HYLAND, William	Boy 2nd Cl	TONNANT	
INGHAM, William	Pte. R.M.	AFRICA	
INGLIS, William	A.B.	BRITANNIA	
INGRAM, John	Sgt. R.M.	SIRIUS	
	Pte. R.M.	SURPRISE	Surprise Wh Hermoine
	Sgt. R.M.	SIRIUS	Sirius. 17 April 1806
ISLES, Samuel	Pte. R.M.	NAIAD	Query name as EYLES
JACKSON, George	Ord	LEVIATHAN	
JACKSON, John	A.B.	COLOSSUS	
JAMES, Francis	L.M.	ROYAL SOVEREIGN	
	A.B.	NISUS	Java
JAMES, John	Pte. R.M.	NAIAD	

JAMES, John	L.M.	SPARTIATE	
JAMES, John	A.B.	LEVIATHAN	
JAMES, John	L.M.	TONNANT	
JAMES, Thomas	Sgt. R.M.	MARS	
	Pte. R.M.	ORION	1 June 1794
	Cpl. R.M.	ALEXANDER	Nile
JAMIESON, John	A.B.	AJAX	
JARVIS, George	Pte. R.M.	PRINCE	G.H. 9311
JARVIS, Griffith	A.B.	BELLEROPHON	
JARVIS, John	Boy 3rd Cl	MARS	Signed for as JERVIS
JATER, Mark	Ord	VICTORY	
JAY, Thomas	Ord	ROYAL SOVEREIGN	(M.L. as TRAY & FRAY)
JEFFERIES, William	Pte. R.M.	ROYAL SOVEREIGN	
JEFFERY, William	Trumpeter	DEFENCE	
	Coxswain	ANSON	Anson. 23 Augt 1806
	M.A.A.	ANSON	Curacoa
JERVOIS, Thomas	L.M.	BELLEISLE	
JEWEL, George	Pte. R.M.	BRITANNIA	
JEWELL, William	Midshipman	BELLEROPHON	Wounded.
JOBB, Joseph	Pte. R.M.	BELLEISLE	
JOHNS, Thomas	A.B.	VICTORY	
JOHNSON, James	Q.M.	PRINCE	
JOHNSON, James	Q.M's Mate	VICTORY	
JOHNSON, John	Carp's Crew	COLOSSUS	
JOHNSON, Thomas	A.B.	MINOTAUR	
	A.B.	MINOTAUR	B.S. 25 July 1809
JOHNSTON, Charles.A.	Midshipman	AGAMEMNON	
	Midshipman	AGAMEMNON	St Domingo
JOHNSTON, James.H.	Midshipman	SPARTIATE	
JONES, Charles	L.M.	THUNDERER	
JONES, Edward	Pte. R.M.	BELLEROPHON	
	Pte. R.M.	VENERABLE	Gut of Gibraltar. 12 July 1801
JONES, Griffith	L.M.	LEVIATHAN	
JONES, James	Pte. R.M.	TONNANT	
	Pte. R.M.	BACCHANTE	B.S. 1 & 18 Sep 1812
	Pte. R.M.	BACCHANTE	B.S. 6 Jan 1813
JONES, John	Quarter Gunner	BELLEISLE	
JONES, John	Pte. R.M.	ORION	
JONES, John	L.M.	NEPTUNE	
JONES, John	L.M.	MINOTAUR	
JONES, John	A.B.	SWIFTSURE	
JONES, Joseph	Ord	EURYALUS	G.H. 3166
JONES, Joseph	Pte. R.M.	ROYAL SOVEREIGN	
JONES, Samuel	Pte. R.M.	BELLEISLE	G.H. 598
JONES, Samuel	L.M.	BRITANNIA	G.H. 5987
JONES, Thomas	Quarter Gunner	ORION	G.H. 4144
	Quarter Gunner	SCEPTRE	Guadaloupe
JONES, Thomas	A.B.	LEVIATHAN	
JONES, Thomas (3)	Ord	SPARTIATE	
JONES, William	Pte. R.M.	ACHILLE	G.H. 7907
JONES, William	Pte. R.M.	BRITANNIA	
JONES, William	Pte. R.M.	ORION	
JONES, William	Ord	AGAMEMNON	
	Cooper	AGAMEMNON	St Domingo
JONES, William	Pte. R.M.	EURYALUS	
JOY, Thomas	L.M.	DREADNOUGHT	
JUKES, Ralph	A.B.	REVENGE	G.H. 6479
KAY, Robert	A.B.	THUNDERER	
KAY, William	A.B.	REVENGE	
KEAN, John	Not Given	ROYAL SOVEREIGN	
KEECH, John	A.B.	AJAX	G.H. 5608
KELLEY, Paul	A.B.	ORION	
KELLY, Daniel	L.M.	MARS	G.H.9877
KELLY, Edmund	Ord	AJAX	
KELLY, John	L.M.	ACHILLE	
	2 L.Ms borne	NISUS	Java
KELLY, Matthew	L.M.	NEPTUNE	
KELLY, Patrick	Ord	AJAX	
KELLY, William	L.M.	ACHILLE	
KELLY, William	Lieut. R.N.	PRINCE	
	Lieut. R.N.	MINERVE	Egypt
	Lieut. R.N.	CALEDONIA	Basque Roads. 1809
	Lieut. R.N.	CALEDONIA	B.S. 27 Sep 1810 (Vfd Abd. Not on Roll)
KENDALL, Edward	A.B.	ROYAL SOVEREIGN	G.H. 2113
KENMURE, Viscount A.G.	Vol 1st Cl	AJAX	(M.L. as GORDON, Adam)
	Midshipman	SEAHORSE	Seahorse Wh Badere Zaffere
KENNEDY, John	L.M.	BELLEISLE	
KENNEDY, Thomas	L.M.	BELLEROPHON	G.H. 1011
KENNICOTT, Gilbert	Midshipman	ROYAL SOVEREIGN	
KERBY, Israel	Pte. R.M.	DREADNOUGHT	G.H. 2786 as KIRBY
(or KIRBY)	Pte. R.M.	CAPTAIN	Martinique (Roll as KIRBY)
KETTER, Thomas	Ord	REVENGE	

TRAFALGAR

KINDNESS, Benjamin	Boy 2nd Cl	PHOEBE	
	Ord	PHOEBE	Off Tamatave. 20 May 1811 (Vfd Abd. Not on Roll)
	Ord	PHOEBE	Java
	Ord	PHOEBE	Phoebe. 28 March 1814 (Vfd Abd. Not on Roll)
	Q.M.	ALBION	Navarino
KING, George	Pte. R.M.	POLYPHEMUS	G.H.4556
KING, James	Quarter Gunner	ROYAL SOVEREIGN	
KING, Uriah	R.M. Boy	BELLEISLE	LS & GC. Applied for NGS as Yeoman of Queen's Guard.
KINGDOM, James	Pte. R.M.	MARS	
KINGSTON, Edward	Ord	DREADNOUGHT	
KIRKWOOD, Alexander	L.M.	ROYAL SOVEREIGN	
	Yeoman of Sheets	ALBION	Algiers
	Supn Boatswain	ASIA	Syria
KITCHEN, James	Q.M.	DEFENCE	
KNAPMAN, Edward	Midshipman	SPARTIATE	
	Lieut. R.N.	Gun Boat No 16	St Sebastian
KNAPMAN, John	Midshipman	TEMERAIRE	
KNOWLES, J.	Ord	AFRICA	
LAKE, John	Purser's Steward	NEPTUNE	
	L.M.	CULLODEN	1 June 1794
	Purser's Steward	CULLODEN	St Vincent
LAKE, Mark	A.B.	AGAMEMNON	
LAKING, Charles	Ord	VICTORY	G.H. 1644
LAMB, George	L.M.	COLOSSUS	
LAMBERT, Charles	Vol 1st Cl	ROYAL SOVEREIGN	
LA MOTT, Antonio	Ord	VICTORY	
LANPHIER, Vernon	Midshipman	SPARTIATE	
LANCASTER, Henry	Vol 1st Cl	VICTORY	
	Midshipman	APOLLO	B.S. 1 Nov 1809
LAND, Richard	Drummer. R.M.	ROYAL SOVEREIGN	
LANGDON, William	Pte. R.M.	AJAX	
	Pte. R.M.	SUPERB	Algiers
LASBURY, Thomas	Pte. R.M.	ORION	(M.L. as LASHBURY)
	Pte. R.M.	RACEHORSE	Off Tamatave. 20 May 1811
LATHAN, John	Pte. R.M.	NAIAD	
	Pte. R.M.	AMETHYST*	Amethyst Wh Thetis (Joined after this Action)
	Pte. R.M.	AMETHYST	Amethyst. 5 April 1809
	Pte. R.M.	IMPREGNABLE	Algiers
LATTO, James	Pte. R.M.	REVENGE	
LAURENCE, John	Ord	EURYALUS	
	L.M.	THESEUS	Nile
	L.M.	THESEUS	Acre. 30 May 1799 (Vfd Abd. Not on Roll)
LAURIE, Stephen	A.B.	PHOEBE	
	Boy 3rd Cl	PHOEBE	Phoebe. 21 Decr 1797
	Boy 2nd Cl	PHOEBE	Phoebe. 19 Feby 1801
	A.B.	PHOEBE	Off Tamatave. 20 May 1811
	A.B.	PHOEBE	Java
	Capt Fore Top	PHOEBE	Phoebe. 28 March 1814
LAURIE, Thomas	Ord	VICTORY	
LAUZUM, Francis	Midshipman	BRITANNIA	
LAWFORD, Stephen	L.M.	MINOTAUR	G.H. 6407
LAWLESS, George	L.M.	BRITANNIA	
LAWLESS, Richard	L.M.	ROYAL SOVEREIGN	
LAWRENCE, Elias	Capt. R.M.	COLOSSUS	
LAWRENCE, William	Ord	SWIFTSURE	G.H. 8787
LAYCOCK, Michael	L.M.	COLOSSUS	
LAYKEN, George	A.B.	VICTORY	G.H. 1644
LEADER, James	L.M.	TONNANT	G.H. 7356
LEADOM, Thomas	Pte. R.M.	DEFENCE	
LEAF, Martin	A.B.	TONNANT	
LEAHY, Timothy	L.M.	SPARTIATE	
LEAR, Joseph	L.M.	ROYAL SOVEREIGN	
LEARE, John	Pte. R.M.	THUNDERER	
LEATHES, William	L.M.	MARS	
LECHMERE, John	Midshipman	ORION	
LEE, William	Carp's Crew	LEVIATHAN	
	Carpenter	GLASGOW	Navarino
LEGG, John	L.M.	ACHILLE	? an additional clasp
LEGGE, William	A.B.	DREADNOUGHT	
LEIGHT, John	L.M.	BELLEROPHON	
LEMON, Thomas	1st Lt. R.M.	DREADNOUGHT	

LENARD, Joseph	Yeoman of Sheets	NAIAD	
	Ord	CULLODEN	1 June 1794
	Ord	CULLODEN	St Vincent
	Ord	CULLODEN	Nile
LEONARD, Francis	Boy	ROYAL SOVEREIGN	
	Coxswain	QUEEN CHARLOTTE	Algiers
LEVERICK, Thomas	Ord	VICTORY	
LEVERTON, Richard	Gunner's Mate	TEMERAIRE	G.H. 709 (ML as LIBERTINE)
	A.B.	ORION	1 June 1794
	A.B.	VETERAN	Camperdown
	Yeoman Powder Rm	ANSON	Anson. 23 Augt 1806 (Vfd Abd. Not on Roll)
	Yeoman Powder Rm	ANSON	Curacoa
LE VESCONTE, Henry	Lieut. R.N.	NAIAD	
	Lieut. R.N.	JAMAICA	Copenhagen. 1801
LEWIS, David	2 Borne. AB & Ord	CONQUEROR	
LEWIS, John	A.B.	DREADNOUGHT	
LEWIS, Thomas	Pte. R.M.	CONQUEROR	G.H. 4770
LEWIS, William	Boy 2nd Cl	AGAMEMNON	
	Boy 2nd Cl	AGAMEMNON	St Domingo
LEWIS, William	A.B.	POLYPHEMUS	
	A.B.	POLYPHEMUS	B.S. 16 July 1806
LIDDLE, Roger	A.B.	SWIFTSURE	
LIPSHAP, J.	Ord	ROYAL SOVEREIGN	
LISTER, John	2nd Lt. R.M.	THUNDERER	
LITMAN, Samuel	L.M.	DEFIANCE	
LITTLE, Matthew	Pte. R.M.	AFRICA	
LITTLE, Thomas	Pte. R.M.	POLYPHEMUS	
LIVERSAGE, Samuel	L.M.	TONNANT	G.H. 2643 as LAVERAGE
LLOYD, John	L.M.	DEFIANCE	
LLOYD, John	A.B.	ORION	
LLOYD, William	Pte. R.M.	PRINCE	
	Pte. R.M.	ORION	St Vincent
LLOYDE, Edward	Ord	DEFENCE	G.H. 6002 as LLOYD
LOADER, James	L.M.	TONNANT	
LOCKWOOD, William	Pte. R.M.	BELLEISLE	
LOFTIN, George	Midshipman	NEPTUNE	
	Midshipman	GANGES	Copenhagen 1801
LOMAS, James	A.B.	SWIFTSURE	G.H. 7169
LOMERS, William	L.M.	SWIFTSURE	
LONG, Conroy	L.M.	BRITANNIA	G.H. 4048 as Conrad
LONG, James	Pte. R.M.	ROYAL SOVEREIGN	G.H. 3942
LONGSTRAATH, James	R.M. Boy	BRITANNIA	
	Pte. R.M.	NEREIDE	B.S. 1 May 1810
LORIN, Andrew	A.B.	TEMERAIRE	
LOTTY, Joseph	L.M.	COLOSSUS	(M.L. as LAWTY)
LOUGHLIN, Patrick	Cpl. R.M.	BRITANNIA	
	Cpl. R.M.	GLATTON	Copenhagen. 1801
LOVENEWTON, Samuel	Carpenter	PHOEBE	
	Carpenter	MINDEN	Algiers
LOVERSUCH, William	Cpl. R.M.	POLYPHEMUS	
	Pte. R.M.	AGINCOURT	Egypt
LOWCAY, William	Midshipman	AJAX	
LOWDEN, Thomas	A.B.	SWIFTSURE	G.H. 8982
LUCKCRAFT, Alfred	Midshipman	MARS	
	Vol 1st Cl	MONARCH	Copenhagen 1801
LUDGUTTER, Robert	Pte. R.M.	PRINCE	
LUNN, George	Ord	ROYAL SOVEREIGN	
LYNCH, John	L.M.	NAIAD	
LYON, Primrose	Asst Surgeon	ROYAL SOVEREIGN	
	Surgeon	GLASGOW	Navarino
LYONS, John	Midshipman	VICTORY	
	Midshipman	St GEORGE	Copenhagen 1801
MACAY, Alexander	Ord	BRITANNIA	
MACKENZIE, Alexander	Midshipman	NEPTUNE	
MACKIE, James	A.B.	REVENGE	
MACKINTOSH, John	1st Lt. R.M.	POLYPHEMUS	
	2nd Lt. R.M.	POLYPHEMUS	Copenhagen 1801
	1st Lt. R.M.	POLYPHEMUS	B.S. 16 July 1806
MACLEAN, Rawdon	Midshipman	COLOSSUS	
	Lieut. R.N.	COLOSSUS	B.S. 23 Nov 1810
MADDISON, George	Ord	PRINCE	
MAGIN, William	1st Lt. R.M.	TONNANT	
	1st Lt. R.M.	SIRIUS	Sirius. 17 April 1806
MAHONEY, Joseph	L.M.	LEVIATHAN	(M.L. as James)
MAINLAND, William	A.B.	VICTORY	
	Ord	ASTRAEA	Astraea. 10 April 1795
	Ord	ASTRAEA	23rd June 1795
MAINWARING, B.	A.B.	TEMERAIRE	
MAINWARING, Thomas.F.C.	Lieut. R.N.	NAIAD	
MAJOR, John	L.M.	DREADNOUGHT	
MALCOLM, Andrew	A.B.	BRITANNIA	

TRAFALGAR

MALONE, John	A.B.	DREADNOUGHT	
MANN, Mark	Quarter Gunner	BELLEISLE	
MANNELL, William	Q.M's Mate	VICTORY	
MANNING, George	A.B.	SWIFTSURE	
MANNING, John	Ord	VICTORY	
MANSFIELD, William	L.M.	BRITANNIA	
MANT, James	Pte. R.M.	EURYALUS	(A forgery known. Rim filed)
MANUEL, Joseph	A.B.	BRITANNIA	G.H. 8883
	Captain Fore Top	HARPY	Java
MARAT, Thomas	Supn	VICTORY	
	L.M.	ILLUSTRIOUS	Basque Roads 1809
MARLEY, David	Roll as R.M. only	DREADNOUGHT	? if 2nd Lt David MARLAY
MARLER, William	Ord	BELLEROPHON	
	L.M.	DEFIANCE	Copenhagen 1801
	Ord	INDEFATIGABLE	Basque Roads 1809
MARSH, Henry	Ord	VICTORY	
MARSH, Richard	L.M.	DREADNOUGHT	
MARTIN, Alexander	Midshipman	PRINCE	
	Vol 1st Cl	TRIUMPH	Camperdown
MARTIN, George	A.B.	VICTORY	
MARTIN, James	Bosun's Mate	BRITANNIA	
MARTIN, James	A.B.	NEPTUNE	
MARTIN, John.O.	Surgeon's Mate	BRITANNIA	
	Surgeon	HUSSAR	Java
MARTIN, Thomas	L.M.	REVENGE	
MARTIN, William	Midshipman	MINOTAUR	
MARTIN, William	Ship's Coxswain	NEPTUNE	
MASON, James	A.B.	CONQUEROR	
MASON, Joseph	Midshipman	POLYPHEMUS	Became a Purser in 1808
MASON, William.G.	Clerk	AJAX	
	Purser	PRESIDENT	Java
	Purser	PRINCESS CHARLOTTE	Syria
MATTHEWS, John	A.B.	THUNDERER	
MATTHEWS, Joseph	Ord	ACHILLE	
MAUNDER, George	Pte. R.M.	ROYAL SOVEREIGN	
MAWBEY, John	Midshipman	SPARTIATE	
	Midshipman	POLYPHEMUS	Copenhagen 1801
MAY, Christopher	L.M.	NEPTUNE	
MAY, Isaac	Pte. R.M.	SIRIUS	
	Pte. R.M.	SIRIUS	Sirius 17 April 1806 (Vfd Abd. Not on Roll)
MAY, John	Pte. R.M.	ORION	
McALLISTER, William	L.M.	AGAMEMNON	
	L.M.	AGAMEMNON	St Domingo (Vfd Abd. Not on Roll)
	Ord	BEDFORD	B.S. 14 Dec 1814
McBETH, Alexander	L.M.	VICTORY	
McCANN, John	M.A.A.	AGAMEMNON	
	Pte. R.M.	ARDENT	Copenhagen 1801
	M.A.A.	AGAMEMNON	St Domingo
McCARDLE, Peter	L.M.	BRITANNIA	G.H. 9540 as Patrick
McCARTHY, Charles	Ropemaker	BELLEROPHON	
McCARTHY, James	Pte. R.M.	AJAX	
McCARTHY, James	Ord	DEFENCE	
McCARTHY, Justin	L.M.	TONNANT	
McCARTHY, Owen	L.M.	REVENGE	
McCLEAN, William	Gunner's Mate	MARS	
McCREA, Robert.C.	Midshipman	SWIFTSURE	
McCULLUM, John	1st Lt R.M.	DREADNOUGHT	
McDOWALL, Andrew	Q.M's Mate	VICTORY	
McEVOY, Pierce	L.M.	TEMERAIRE	
McFARLANE, Andrew	Ord	SWIFTSURE	
McFARLANE, James	Purser	BELLEISLE	
	Purser	BELLONA	Basque Roads 1809
McGENNIS, James	Ord	NEPTUNE	
	L.M.	QUEEN CHARLOTTE	1 June 1794
McGILLIVRAY, Alexander	L.M.	TONNANT	
McGILLIVRAY, Thomas	Pte. R.M.	REVENGE	
McGINTY, Daniel	L.M.	DEFIANCE	
McGRATH, William	L.M.	DREADNOUGHT	
McGREHAM, Daniel	L.M.	ROYAL SOVEREIGN	
	Cook	BEELZEBUB	Algiers
McGINN, William @ MAGINN	Ord	POLYPHEMUS	(M.L. as MEQUIN) GH.2585
	Ord	POLYPHEMUS	B.S. 16 July 1806
McGUIRE, Matthew	L.M.	ACHILLE	G.H. 5631
McKAY, B.	L.M.	AJAX	
McKAY, William	A.B.	POLYPHEMUS	
McKERLIE, John	Lieut. R.N.	SPARTIATE	
	Quarter Gunner	INDEFATIGABLE	Indefatigable. 20 April 1796
	Schoolmaster	INDEFATIGABLE	Indefatigable. 13 Jany 1797
McKENNA, Edward	Pte. R.M.	BELLEROPHON	

McLAUGHLAN, James	A.B.	THUNDERER	
	Ord	BELLEROPHON	1 June 1794
	A.B.	BELLEROPHON	Nile
McLAUGHLIN, Archibald	Ord	COLOSSUS	
	Ord	BELLEROPHON	B.S. 7 July 1809
McNAME, John	L.M.	COLOSSUS	(M.L. as McNEILL)
MEAD, William	Pte. R.M.	LEVIATHAN	
	Pte. R.M.	BEAGLE	St Sebastian
MEALEY, Edward	L.M.	SIRIUS	
	L.M.	SIRIUS	Sirius 17 April 1806 (Vfd Abd. Not on Roll)
MEARS, Jacob	Carp's Crew	REVENGE	G.H. 5308
	Carp's Crew	CENTURION	Centurion. 18 Sept 1804 (Vfd Abd. Not on Roll)
	Carp's Crew	REVENGE	Basque Roads. 1809 (Vfd Abd. Not on Roll)
MEECH, Radford.G.	Midshipman	BRITANNIA	
MELLIPHANT, Robert	L.M.	ROYAL SOVEREIGN	G.H. 8203
MELLISH, William	A.B.	REVENGE	
MEREDITH, Richard	A.B.	PHOEBE	
	Vol 1st Cl	PHOEBE	Phoebe. 19 Feby 1801
MIBERRY, George	A.B.	ACHILLE	
MICALLIF, Francis	Pte. R.M.	DEFENCE	G.H. 9783 as McCOLLIFFE. M.L. as MACALLIO
MILES, Henry	Boy	PRINCE	
MILES, William	L.M.	LEVIATHAN	
MILLARD, Michael	Drummer. R.M.	DEFIANCE	
MILLER, Henry	Lieut. R.M	SWIFTSURE	
MILLER, James	A.B.	MINOTAUR	
MILLER, Robert	A.B.	DEFENCE	
MILLER, Samuel	Ord	DEFENCE	
MILLINGTON, James	Pte. R.M.	BRITANNIA	G.H. 9925
MILLS, James	L.M.	DREADNOUGHT	
MILLS, James	A.B.	ROYAL SOVEREIGN	
MITCHELL, James	Ord	DREADNOUGHT	
MITCHELL, William	Pte. R.M.	TONNANT	
MOFFITT, John	Boy	SPARTIATE	
MOLES, Joseph	Pte. R.M.	TONNANT	
MOOR, Edward	Vol 1st Cl	NEPTUNE	
MOORE, Edward	Ord	AGAMEMNON	G.H. 7023
	Ord	AGAMEMNON	St Domingo
	Carp's Crew	BEDFORD	B.S. 14 Dec 1814
MOORE, H.	A.B.	BRITANNIA	Applied as Cmmd Boatman
MOORE, Joseph.H.	Vol 1st Cl	EURYALUS	(? at GLUCKSTADT 1814)
MOORE, Thomas	Pte. R.M.	SPARTIATE	
MOORMAN, William	L.M.	AJAX	
	Ord	QUEEN CHARLOTTE	Algiers
MORGAN, Edward	A.B.	AJAX	G.H. 4813
MORGAN, James	Pte. R.M.	TONNANT	G.H. 1749
	Pte. R.M.	RENOWN	Egypt
MORGAN, John	L.M.	AGAMEMNON	
	L.M.	AGAMEMNON	St Domingo
MORING, John	A.B.	AJAX	G.H. 6847
MORRIS, James	Pte. R.M.	AJAX	
MORRIS, William	Pte. R.M.	BELLEISLE	
	Pte. R.M.	SCIPION	Java
MORRISON, Henry	L.M.	TONNANT	
MORTIMER, John	Surgeon's Asst	AFRICA	
MORTON, Thomas	Pte. R.M.	TEMERAIRE	G.H. 3396 @ MARTIN
MOSELEY, William	A.B.	MINOTAUR	
MOSER, Peter	A.B.	VICTORY	GH.1695 @ REYNOLDS, Peter
	A.B.	BRUNSWICK	17 June 1795
	A.B.	SPENCER	Gut of Gibraltar. 12 July 1801
MOTTERSHEAD, Joseph	Pte. R.M.	DREADNOUGHT	
MOWATT, James	Quarter Gunner	BRITANNIA	G.H. 9943 ? Camperdown
MOUBRAY, George	Lieut. R.N.	POLYPHEMUS	
	Lieut. R.N.	MOSELLE	14 March 1795
MOWBRAY, Robert	Boy	LEVIATHAN	
MUDGE, Thomas	A.B.	POLYPHEMUS	
MUHLEG, William	A.B.	BELLEISLE	(M.L. as MULIG)
	A.B.	LONDON	London. 13 March 1806
MUIR, Andrew	L.M.	ACHILLE	
MULLINS, John	L.M.	PRINCE	
MUNDAY, John	Ord	VICTORY	G.H. 9845
MURCH, John	Sailmaker's Mate	BELLEISLE	
MURLEY, William	Midshipman	BELLEISLE	
MURPHY, John	Ord/LM	NEPTUNE	
MURPHY, Matthew	L.M.	BELLEROPHON	
MURPHY, Michael	L.M.	BRITANNIA	G.H. 9456
MURPHY, Michael	L.M.	NEPTUNE	
NAGLE, Archibald	Vol 1st Cl	ROYAL SOVEREIGN	
NAPIER, James	A.B.	TEMERAIRE	
NASH, William	Boy	BRITANNIA	
NASH, Joseph	Pte. R.M.	EURYALUS	G.H. 5536

TRAFALGAR

NAVE, William	Ord	DEFIANCE	
	Ord	GANGES	Copenhagen 1801
	Ord	CORDELIA	Algiers
NAVEN, Robert	Ord	MARS	
NEALE, Thomas	A.B.	PRINCE	
NESBITT, J.	Caulker	ROYAL SOVEREIGN	
NETTLE, Thomas	A.B.	DEFIANCE	This Roll as NETELL
	A.B.	GANGES	Copenhagen 1801 (ML as NUTTLE)
NEWLAND, John	L.M.	SWIFTSURE	G.H. 8141
NEWTON, Robert	A.B.	NEPTUNE	Became Lieut. R.N. 1815
NEWTON, Samuel	L.M.	REVENGE	
NICHOLLS, Henry	Ord	VICTORY	
NICHOLLS, John	Pte. R.M.	ACHILLE	G.H. 3274
	Pte. R.M.	MINDEN	Algiers
NICHOLSON, William	Sailmaker's Crew	ROYAL SOVEREIGN	
NICOLAS, Paul.H.	1st Lt. R.M.	BELLEISLE	
	1st Lt. R.M.	ARMIDE	B.S. 13 Feb 1810
NIERO, Giovanni	Ord	DEFENCE	
	Coxswain	NASSAU	Nassau. 22 March 1808
NILES, Charles	Boy 2nd Cl	MARS	
NIPPER, James	Q.M.	BRITANNIA	
NIPPER, James	A.B.	VICTORY	
	Capt's Servant	MARLBOROUGH	1 June 1794
	A.B.	AMAZON	Amazon. 13 March 1806 (Vfd Abd. Not on Roll)
NORDING, Frederick	Pte. R.M.	DEFENCE	
NOEL, John	L.M.	TEMERAIRE	
NORMAN, Thomas	Pte. R.M.	MARS	
	Pte. R.M.	ALCMENE	Copenhagen 1801
NORTHGATE, Benjamin	L.M.	TONNANT	G.H. 9590
NORVELL, Robert	Ord	VICTORY	
NUTT, John	A.B.	BRITANNIA	
NUTT, William	Pte. R.M.	DEFIANCE	
O'BRIAN, Peter	A.B.	MINOTAUR	G.H. 9747 as O'BRIEN
O'BRIEN, James	Boy	CONQUEROR	
O'BRYEN, Charles	A.B.	BELLEISLE	
O'HARA, John	L.M.	TEMERAIRE	
ODGERS, William	Pte. R.M.	THUNDERER	
	Sgt. R.M.	HEBRUS	Algiers
OLIVER, Harry	Pte. R.M.	LEVIATHAN	
	Pte. R.M.	AMAZON	Copenhagen 1801
OLIVER, James	A.B.	SWIFTSURE	
	Gunner	ASIA	Syria
OLIVER, Stephen	A.B.	NAIAD	
	Capt After Guard	QUEEN CHARLOTTE	Algiers
ORGAN, Cornelius	Pte. R.M.	SPARTIATE	
OSBORNE, William	Carp's Crew	SWIFTSURE	
OSBORNE, William	Carp's Crew	REVENGE	
	L.M.	IMPREGNABLE	1 June 1794
OSMAND, James	Surgeon's Mate	SWIFTSURE	
	Surgeon	BEELZEBUB	Algiers
OWEN, John	1st Lt. R.M.	BELLEISLE	
	2nd. Lt. R.M.	ADAMANT	Camperdown
OWENS, John	L.M.	BELLEISLE	
OXLEY, William	L.M.	CONQUEROR	
PAFFARD, James	Boy	DEFENCE	(M.L. as PURFORD)
PAGE, Abraham	Boy 2nd Cl	ROYAL SOVEREIGN	
	Ord	TRAAVE	B.S. 14 Dec. 1814
PAGE, Jonathan	Ord	REVENGE	
PALMER, Charles	Pte. R.M.	AFRICA	
	Pte. R.M.	KENT	Egypt
PALMER, Christopher	A.B.	BRITANNIA	
PALMER, James	Pte. R.M.	AFRICA	
	Pte. R.M.	GLASGOW	Algiers
PARISH, Francis	R.M. Boy	MARS	
PARK, Henry	A.B.	BELLEROPHON	
PARKER, Henry	Sgt. R.M.	BRITANNIA	
PARKER, Henry	Midshipman	BELLEISLE	
	Lieut. R.N.	DRAGON	B.S. Ap & May 1813
PARKER, James	Pte. R.M.	VICTORY	
PARKER, John	Pte. R.M.	ACHILLE	
PARKER, John	Pte. R.M.	TEMERAIRE	
PARKER, Joseph	Pte. R.M.	DEFIANCE	
PARKER, Peter	A.B.	DEFENCE	G.H. 7545
PARKIN, John.P.	Midshipman	ACHILLE	
	Commander	CAMBRIDGE	Syria
PARR, Alexander.F.	Midshipman	AGAMEMNON	(Possibly 2 Medals awarded)
	Midshipman	SWIFTSURE	Nile (Known as single clasp)
	Midshipman	PENELOPE	Egypt
	Midshipman	AGAMEMNON	St Domingo

PARRY, Howard	Boy 2nd Cl	TONNANT	(Applied as Commander?)
PARRY, John	Boy	ROYAL SOVEREIGN	G.H. 9749
PARSLEY, James	L.M.	SPARTIATE	
PARSLEY, Michael	L.M.	DREADNOUGHT	G.H. 10,025
	L.M.	CAPTAIN	Martinique
PARSONS, John	Vol 1st Cl	DEFIANCE	
PARSONS, William	Ord	ACHILLE	
PARSONS, William	Pte. R.M.	SPARTIATE	G.H. 7766
	Pte. R.M.	BLANCHE	Copenhagen 1801
PASCOE, John	Flag Lieutenant	VICTORY	Of "confides" to "expects" fame in Nelson's Signal.
PATEY, George.E.	Midshipman	MARS	
PATTERSON, Alexander	Ord	BELLEROPHON	
	Ord	CANADA	12 Octr 1798
PATTON, Hugh	Midshipman	BELLEROPHON	
PATTON, Robert	Midshipman	BELLEROPHON	
PAUSNELL, James	A.B.	SWIFTSURE	
	A.B.	BEDFORD	Camperdown
PEARCE, Nicholas	Caulker's Mate	MARS	
PEARCEY, James	Pte. R.M.	BRITANNIA	
PEARSE, Richard	A.B.	SPARTIATE	
PEARSON, Mathew	A.B.	REVENGE	G.H. 8302
PEEBLES, James	L.M.	ACHILLE	
PELRIN, Pierre	L.M.	MARS	
PENDAR, Shadrack	A.B.	SWIFTSURE	G.H. 6434
PENN, Joseph	Cpl. R.M.	ROYAL SOVEREIGN	
PEPPER, William	Ord	LEVIATHAN	G.H. 6780
PEPPETT, Charles	Boy	VICTORY	G.H. 7669 as PEGLEY
PERCEVAL, Hon George.J.	Vol 1st Cl	ORION	Became Earl of Egmont
	Midshipman	TIGRE	B.S. 1 Nov 1809
	Captain. R.N.	INFERNAL	Algiers
PERRY, Charles	L.M.	NEPTUNE	
PERRY, Hugh	Gunner	SIRIUS	
	Gunner	SIRIUS	Sirius 17 April 1806 (Vfd Abd. Not on Roll)
PERT, Robert	A.B.	AGAMEMNON	
	A.B.	AGAMEMNON	St Domingo
PETERS, William	Ord	DEFENCE	
PETHERICK, Edward	A.B.	TEMERAIRE	
PETTICK, Daniel	Ord	PRINCE	G.H. 9990 as PETTOCK
PETTS, William	L.M.	BRITANNIA	G.H. 9428
PETTY, Richard	Boy 3rd Cl	BELLEROPHON	
PHELPT, Benjamin	Ord	AJAX	Alias PHIPPS
PHEPOE, John	Midshipman	AJAX	(Vfd Abd. Not on Roll)
	Lieut. R.N.	ARMIDE	B.S. 13 Feb 1810
	Lieut. R.N.	ARMIDE	B.S. 27 Sep 1810 (Vfd Abd. Not on Roll)
PHILIPS, John.A.	Midshipman	BELLEISLE	
PHILIPS, John	Carp's Crew	DREADNOUGHT	
PHILLIPS, Benjamin	L.M.	CONQUEROR	
PHILLIPS, Charles	Pte. R.M.	DEFENCE	G.H. 6682
PHILLIPS, Charles	A.B.	COLOSSUS	
	L.M.	DELFT	Egypt
PHILLIPS, Henry	Ord	ACHILLE	G.H. 9285
PHILLIPS, James	Pte. R.M.	NEPTUNE	
PHILLIPS, Richard	L.M.	MARS	
PICKERNELL, John	L.M.	BELLEISLE	G.H. 9095
PICKERNELL, Peter	Lieut. R.N.	REVENGE	
PICKETT, George	L.M.	DEFENCE	G.H. 6413
PICTON, John	L.M.	AFRICA	
PIERCY, James	A.B.	REVENGE	Alias C.BOATWICK
PIERSON, William.H.	Master's Mate	BELLEISLE	
PIGLEY, Charles	Sgt. R.M.	DEFENCE	
PIKE, Walter	Lieut. R.N.	EURYALUS	
PILCH, William	Vol 1st Cl	BELLEROPHON	
	Midshipman	NORTHUMBERLAND	Northumberland. 22 May 1812
PILL, John	A.B.	VICTORY	
PINGRUFF, John	Pte. R.M.	SPARTIATE	
PINKMAN, Richard	Pte. R.M.	SWIFTSURE	G.H. 8527
PINNINGTON, Joseph	L.M.	DREADNOUGHT	
PINTO, Thomas	Lieut. R.N.	AGAMEMNON	
	Midshipman	IRRESISTIBLE	St Vincent
	Master's Mate	NORTHUMBERLAND	Egypt
	Lieut. R.N.	AGAMEMNON	St Domingo
	Commander	ACHATES	B.S. 13 Dec 1809
	Commander	ACHATES	Guadaloupe
PIPER, John	Ord	NEPTUNE	
	A.B.	ASIA	Navarino
PITNEY, Francis	Pte. R.M.	VICTORY	
PITT, George	Ord	VICTORY	
PLUMBLY, Joseph	Cpl. R.M.	PRINCE	
PLUMRIDGE, James.A.	Midshipman	DEFENCE	
PLUNKETT, Luke	L.M.	PRINCE	

TRAFALGAR

POAD, James	Midshipman	VICTORY	
POCKETT, James	Pte. R.M.	BRITANNIA	
POLGAZE, John	A.B.	CONQUEROR	Became a Boatswain
POLLARD, John	L.M.	AFRICA	
POLLARD, John	Midshipman	VICTORY	
POLLARD, John	L.M.	AGAMEMNON	G.H. 7129 (M.L. as Joseph)
	L.M.	AGAMEMNON	St Domingo
POOL, James	L.M.	ROYAL SOVEREIGN	
POOLE, Benjamin	Pte. R.M.	AJAX	
POPE, Peter	A.B.	ACHILLE	
	A.B.	ACHILLE	B.S. 16 July 1806
POPE, William	Ord	DREADNOUGHT	
	Ord	CULLODEN	Nile
POPE, William	Boy	VICTORY	
PORTER, Abraham	Supn	VICTORY	
PORTER, George	Ord	BRITANNIA	
PORTER, Thomas	L.M.	AGAMEMNON	G.H. 10,064
POTTS, Henry	A.B.	DREADNOUGHT	
POWELL, David	Pte. R.M.	VICTORY	
POWELL, John	Ord	CONQUEROR	G.H. 5711
POWELL, Richard	Ord	VICTORY	
POWELL, Thomas (2)	Ord	BELLEROPHON	
POWEES, John	L.M.	PRINCE	
PRICE, Francis.S	Master's Mate	TEMERAIRE	(Roll as F.S.W.PRICE)
PRICE, George	Pte. R.M.	NEPTUNE	
PRICE, James	L.M.	TONNANT	
PRICE, Rees	Pte. R.M.	SPARTIATE	G.H. 10,019
PRICELY, Jonathan	A.B.	SIRIUS	
	A.B.	SIRIUS	Sirius 17 April 1806 (Vfd Abd. Not on Roll)
PRIOR, Thomas.H.	Vol 1st Cl	AJAX	
PRITCHARD, John.W.	Midshipman	BRITANNIA	
PRITCHARD, Richard.D.	Master's Mate	ROYAL SOVEREIGN	
PRITCHARD, William	Ord	LEVIATHAN	
	Ord	CALEDONIA	Basque Roads 1809
	Ord	CALEDONIA	B.S. 27 Sep 1810
PURCELL, John	Sgt. R.M.	NEPTUNE	G.H. 8202 as PURSELL
PURCHES, James.U.	Lieut. R.N.	DEFIANCE	Applicant noted as a "Lunatic"
	Lieut. R.N.	CHALLENGER	St Sebastian
PUGH, John	Ord	ORION	G.H. 4525
PULLING, William	Boy	PRINCE	
PURSELL, Thomas	Carp's Crew	AFRICA	
PURVIS, Henry	Ord	AJAX	G.H. 5225
PYE, William	Midshipman	MINOTAUR	
PYKE, Stephen	L.M.	BRITANNIA	
PYM, Mark	Ord	ROYAL SOVEREIGN	
QUICK, William	Boy	ROYAL SOVEREIGN	
QUINLIN, Patrick	L.M.	ROYAL SOVEREIGN	
QUINTIN, James	Vol 1st Cl	AGAMEMNON	
or ST QUINTIN,	Midshipman	AGAMEMNON	St Domingo
RADFORD, Richard	Pte. R.M.	ROYAL SOVEREIGN	
RAINS, John	A.B.	POLYPHEMUS	
	A.B.	POLYPHEMUS	B.S. 16 July 1806
RAMSAY, Peter	Ord	SPARTIATE	
RANDALL, Charles	Bosun's Mate	COLOSSUS	
RANDEL, Thomas	A.B.	VICTORY	
RATTRAY, James	Master's Mate	BRITANNIA	
	A.B.	VENERABLE	Gut of Gibraltar. 12 July 1801
RAWLINS, Thomas	Vol 1st Cl	MARS	
RAY, B.	A.B.	SWIFTSURE	
READ, Robert	L.M.	DREADNOUGHT	
READ, Thomas	Lieut. R.N.	SWIFTSURE	(Known as 3 clasp with 'Nile')
	L.M.	ELEPHANT	Copenhagen 1801 (See notes)
REDDALL, James	A.B.	DEFIANCE	
	L.M.	GANGES	Copenhagen 1801
REDSTONE, William	Drummer. R.M.	BELLEROPHON	
REED, William	Ord	BELLEROPHON	
	A.B.	DEFIANCE	Copenhagen 1801
REEDIN, John	Quarter Gunner	PHOEBE	(M.L. as REDDING)
	Ord	PHOEBE	Phoebe. 21 Decr 1797
	A.B.	PHOEBE	Phoebe. 19 Feby 1801
REES, James	Pte. R.M.	NEPTUNE	
REES, William	Armourer's Mate	CONQUEROR	
REEVE, John	Master's Mate	AGAMEMNON	
	Midshipman	AGAMEMNON	Copenhagen 1801
	Master's Mate	AGAMEMNON	St Domingo
	Lieut. R.N.	L'AIMABLE	B.S. 27 July 1809
REEVES, Lewis.B.	2nd Lt. R.M.	VICTORY	
REID, Thomas	L.M.	DREADNOUGHT	
REILLY, John	L.M.	MARS	
RENOU, Timothy	Midshipman	COLOSSUS	

RENTALL, J.	Boy	SPARTIATE	
REYNOLDS, John	Pte. R.M.	DEFENCE	
REYNOLDS, Peter	(Alias. See MOSER, Peter.)		
REYNOLDS, Robert	Pte. R.M.	DREADNOUGHT	
REYNOLDS, Thomas	Pte. R.M.	DEFENCE	
	Pte. R.M.	EXPEDITION	Egypt
RICH, Henry	Master	DEFIANCE	Applied as Rtd Cdr.
RICHARDS, Philip	Ord	COLOSSUS	
RICHARDS, Thomas (2)	Ord	ROYAL SOVEREIGN	
	L.M.	DART	Copenhagen 1801
RICHARDSON, Henry	Sgt. R.M.	ORION	G.H. 6783
RICHARDSON, James	A.B.	BRITANNIA	
RICHARDSON, William	A.B.	REVENGE	G.H. 6982
RICKETTS, Thomas	A.B.	DREADNOUGHT	G.H. 5852 as RICKARD
RIELY, James	L.M.	ROYAL SOVEREIGN	G.H. 5010 as RILEY
RILEY, Richard	Boy 3rd Cl	MINOTAUR	
RILEY, Thomas	L.M.	CONQUEROR	(M.L. as RYLEY)
	L.M.	CONQUEROR	B.S. 16 July 1806
RILL, W.B.	Pte. R.M.	POLYPHEMUS	
	Pte. R.M.	PRESIDENT	Java
RITCHINGS, Thomas	Pte. R.M.	ORION	
RIVERS, William	Midshipman	VICTORY	(Lost left leg)
	Vol 1st Cl	VICTORY	St Vincent
ROAF, John	Carpenter	POLYPHEMUS	
ROBERTS, James	Ord	NAIAD	
ROBERTS, John	2 borne.AB & LM	DEFIANCE	
ROBERTS, John	Quarter Gunner	TEMERAIRE	
ROBERTS, Thomas	Yeoman of Sheets	AFRICA	
ROBERTSON, Thomas	Surgeon	SIRIUS	
	Surgeon	LEDA	Egypt
	Surgeon	SIRIUS	Sirius. 17 April 1806
ROBERTSON, William	Midshipman	DEFENCE	
ROBINS, James	Vol 1st Cl	ORION	
ROBINS, Thomas.L.	Master's Mate	VICTORY	
	Midshipman	TEAZER	Capture of the Desiree
	Midshipman	TEAZER	Copenhagen 1801 (Vfd Abd. Not on Roll)
	Lieut. R.N.	PALLAS	Basque Roads 1809
ROBINSON, Charles	Midshipman	SWIFTSURE	
ROBINSON, Edward	A.B.	POLYPHEMUS	
ROBINSON, Hercules	Midshipman	EURYALUS	
ROBINSON, James	A.B.	PHOEBE	
	A.B.	PHOEBE	Off Tamatave. 20 May 1811
	A.B.	PHOEBE	Java
	A.B.	PHOEBE	Phoebe. 28 March 1814
ROBINSON, John	A.B.	COLOSSUS	
ROBINSON, John	Quarter Gunner	POLYPHEMUS	
ROBINSON, Joseph	Ord	AGAMEMNON	
	Ord	AGAMEMNON	St Domingo
ROBINSON, Thomas	A.B.	AGAMEMNON	
	A.B.	AGAMEMNON	St Domingo
	A.B.	ELIZABETH	B.S. 24 May 1814
ROBINSON, Thomas	Boy	BELLEISLE	
ROBINSON, Thomas	A.B.	TEMERAIRE	
ROBINSON, Thomas.P.	Midshipman	ROYAL SOVEREIGN	
	Lieut. R.N.	GENOA	Navarino
ROBINSON, William	Ord	BRITANNIA	
ROBINSON, William	A.B.	AFRICA	
ROCKWELL, John	Midshipman	DREADNOUGHT	
ROOFE, Henry	L.M.	AGAMEMNON	
	L.M.	AGAMEMNON	St Domingo
	Ord	LEANDER	Algiers
ROOKE, Lewis	2nd Lt. R.M.	NEPTUNE	
ROOME, John	L.M.	VICTORY	G.H.9592
ROSS, Henry. P.B.	Vol 1st Cl	AGAMEMNON	
	Vol 1st Cl	AGAMEMNON	St Domingo
ROSS, Robert	A.B.	PRINCE	
ROSS, Robert	L.M.	VICTORY	
ROTELEY, Lewis	2nd Lt. R.M.	VICTORY	
	1st Lt. R.M.	CLEOPATRA	Martinique
ROURKE, Andrew	Pte. R.M.	NEPTUNE	
	Pte. R.M.	SAMARANG	Java
ROUSE, William	Pte. R.M.	CONQUEROR	
	Pte. R.M.	BEDFORD	Camperdown
	Pte. R.M.	FOUDROYANT	Egypt
ROWDEN, James	Bosun's Mate	PICKLE	
	Bosun's Mate	PICKLE	Pickle 3 Jany 1807
ROWE, Henry.N.	Lieut. R.N.	AJAX	
	Commander	ST CHRISTOPHER	Guadaloupe
ROWE, Michael	A.B.	VICTORY	
ROWE, Thomas	Yeoman Powder Rm	NEPTUNE	

TRAFALGAR

ROWE, William	Midshipman	BELLEISLE	
ROWLEY, James	L.M.	ACHILLE	
ROWLEY, Lewis	Pte. R.M.	VICTORY	
ROYAL, Anthony	Bosun's Mate	SPARTIATE	(M.L. as ROYLE)
RUDGE, John	L.M.	SPARTIATE	
RULE, William	Midshipman	POLYPHEMUS	
	Master's Mate	BEDFORD	B.S. 14 Dec 1814
RUNDEL, Henry	Boy	ROYAL SOVEREIGN	
RUSSEL, John	A.B.	DREADNOUGHT	
RUSSELL, Edward	Boy 3rd Cl	BRITANNIA	(Alias NORRIS, George)
	Boy 3rd Cl	ST GEORGE	Copenhagen 1801
	A.B.	QUEEN CHARLOTTE	Algiers
	Q.M.	BENBOW	Syria.
RUST, John	Pte. R.M.	BELLEROPHON	G.H. 7076
RYAN, John	Pte. R.M.	BELLEROPHON	
	Pte. R.M.	MINDEN	Java
SABBEN, James	Midshipman	DREADNOUGHT	
	Midshipman	NEPTUNE	Martinique
	Actg Lt. R.N.	RINGDOVE	Anse La Barque. 18 Decr 1809
	Actg Lt. R.N.	RINGDOVE	Guadaloupe
SADLER, Benjamin	Pte. R.M.	SPARTIATE	
SALTER, John	A.B.	DEFENCE	
SALTER, Thomas	A.B.	ORION	
SAMSBURY, Stephen	Pte. R.M.	SPARTIATE	
SANDERS, John.H.	Master's Mate	SWIFTSURE	
SANDERS, William	A.B.	VICTORY	
SANGER, James	Pte. R.M.	DEFENCE	
SARTORIUS, George	Midshipman	TONNANT	
SAULS, George	A.B.	LEVIATHAN	
SAUNDERS, George	M.A.A.	LEVIATHAN	
SAUNDERS, John	Boy 3rd Cl	VICTORY	
SAUNDERS, Stephen	A.B.	TONNANT	
SAUNDERS, Thomas	Pte. R.M.	BRITANNIA	
SAVAGE, George	Boy 2nd Cl	AFRICA	G.H. 8629
SAWELL, George	A.B.	LEVIATHAN	
SAYE, William	Pte. R.M.	SIRIUS	
SCAMMELL, George	Pte. R.M.	BRITANNIA	Alias SIMMONDS
SCHROONE, Henry	Ord	BRITANNIA	M.L. as SCHOORR
SCOTT, David	Lieut. R.N.	BELLEROPHON	
SCOTT, Patrick	L.M.	MARS	
SCUDDEMORE, Joseph	L.M.	AFRICA	G.H. 8939
SCULLY, Dennis	L.M.	SIRIUS	G.H. 8504
	L.M.	SIRIUS	Sirius 17 April 1806 (Vfd Abd. Not on Roll)
SCUTT, Joseph	Pte. R.M.	BELLEISLE	G.H. 8902 as SCOTT
SEAMAN, John	M.A.A.	PRINCE	
	M.A.A.	POLYPHEMUS	Copenhagen. 1801
SEATON, John	Pte. R.M.	BRITANNIA	
SEDDAN, John	Trumpeter	PRINCE	
	Trumpeter	SURVEILLANTE	St Sebastian
SEDMAN, William	Pte. R.M.	THUNDERER	
SEED, William	L.M.	DEFIANCE	
SEYMOUR, Joseph	Master	CONQUEROR	Applied as Cdr
SHADDOCK, Elias	Quarter Gunner	ROYAL SOVEREIGN	
	Quarter Gunner	BELLEISLE	Martinique
SHARMAN, James	Ord	VICTORY	
SHARP, David	Ord	REVENGE	
	A.B.	REVENGE	Basque Roads 1809
SHARP, John	Ord	THUNDERER	
SHAW, Isaac	Lieut. R.N.	NEPTUNE	
	Midshipman	ROMULUS	14 March 1795 (Vfd Abd. Not on Roll)
	Midshipman	BARFLEUR	St Vincent
	Lieut. R.N.	VOLONTAIRE (P)	B.S. 2 May 1813
SHAW, William	L.M.	ACHILLE	
SHEA, Francis	A.B.	ORION	
SHEARS, James	Ord	ROYAL SOVEREIGN	
SHEARS, John	Ord	BRITANNIA	
SHEEHY, Edmund	L.M.	SIRIUS	(M.L. as SHEEHAN) GH.7024
	L.M.	SIRIUS	Sirius. 17 April 1806 (Vfd Abd. Not on Roll) Both clasps known on Medal since 1874 (Dalton)

SHEPHERD, Benjamin	Midshipman	BRITANNIA	Navy List & O'Byrne as John
	Midshipman	LATONA	Curacoa
	Midshipman	NEPTUNE	Martinique
	Master's Mate	POMPEE	Guadaloupe
	Lieut. R.N.	GRIFFON	Griffon. 27 March 1812
SHEPHERD, William	Vol 1st Cl	TEMERAIRE	
SHEPPARD, William	Pte. R.M.	VICTORY	
SHIELD, William	Pte. R.M.	DEFIANCE	
SHIELDS, William	Boy 3rd Cl	EURYALUS	
SHORT, Charles	Ord	THUNDERER	
SHUTE, John	Pte. R.M.	THUNDERER	
	Pte. R.M.	THETIS	Guadaloupe
SILCOCK, Henry	Ord	AGAMEMNON	(M.L. as SINCOCK)
	Ord	AGAMEMNON	St Domingo
SIMMONDS, Benjamin	Carp's Crew	THUNDERER	
SIMMONDS, George	L.M.	COLOSSUS	G.H. 9433
or SIMONS	Ord	ANSON	Anson. 23 Augt 1806
			(Vfd Abd. Not on Roll)
	Ord	ANSON	Curacoa
SIMMONS, Edward	Midshipman	MINOTAUR	
	Midshipman	ETHALION	Martinique
	Lieut. R.N.	GALATEA	Off Tamatave. 20 May 1811
SIMMONS, Isaac.J.	Pte. R.M.	AJAX	
SIMMONS, John	L.M.	CONQUEROR	
SIMMONS, Thomas	A.B.	MINOTAUR	
SIMMONS, William	L.M.	TEMERAIRE	
SIMMONS, William	Ord	THUNDERER	
SIMMS, Isaac	Pte. R.M.	ORION	
SIMONDS, Richard.S.	Midshipman	DEFENCE	
	Master's Mate	CALEDONIA	B.S. 27 Sep 1810
	Lieut. R.N.	ABOUKIR	B.S. 29 Sep 1812
SINDER, Matthew	Pte. R.M.	POLYPHEMUS	
SINGLETON, David	Pte. R.M.	NEPTUNE	
	Cpl. R.M.	VALIANT	1 June 1794
SKIDDY, Thomas	A.B.	ROYAL SOVEREIGN	
	A.B.	BELLEISLE	Martinique
	A.B.	CHERUB	Cherub. 28 March 1814
SKINNER, John	Pte. R.M.	TONNANT	
SKINNOCK, James	L.M.	NEPTUNE	
SKITT, Thomas	Pte. R.M.	MINOTAUR	(Roll may read SKETT)
SLADE, John	Boy	TONNANT	
	A.B.	MINDEN	Algiers
SLATTERY, John	L.M.	CONQUEROR	
SLEE, William	A.B.	CONQUEROR	
SMALL, Samuel	Carp's Crew	NAIAD	
SMALL, William	L.M.	ORION	
	A.B.	SCEPTRE	Guadaloupe
SMITH, Charles	Pte. R.M.	BRITANNIA	
SMITH, Charles	Pte. R.M.	PRINCE	
SMITH, Charles	Carp's Crew	VICTORY	
SMITH, George	L.M.	SPARTIATE	
SMITH, George	Pte. R.M.	TEMERAIRE	
SMITH, Henry	L.M.	SPARTIATE	
SMITH, Jacob	R.M.Boy	ACHILLE	
SMITH, James or John	Boy	COLOSSUS	G.H. 8289
	Ord	LION	Java (see Notes)
SMITH, James	Pte. R.M.	PRINCE	
SMITH, James	Pte. R.M.	ROYAL SOVEREIGN	
SMITH, John	A.B.	BRITANNIA	
SMITH, John	A.B.	CONQUEROR	G.H. 9998
SMITH, John (3)	A.B.	DEFENCE	
SMITH, John	A.B.	LEVIATHAN	
SMITH, John (1)	L.M.	DEFENCE	
SMITH, John (2)	L.M.	DEFENCE	
SMITH, John	Pte. R.M.	LEVIATHAN	
SMITH, Peter	Ord	SPARTIATE	
	A.B.	VENERABLE	Venerable. 16 Jany 1814
SMITH, Robert	Midshipman	VICTORY	
SMITH, Samuel	Pte. R.M.	NEPTUNE	
	Pte. R.M.	LONDON	Copenhagen 1801
SMITH, Thomas	Pte. R.M.	MINOTAUR	
SMITH, William (1)	Ord	BELLEISLE	(Application "1/22")
	Ord	LONDON	London. 13 March 1806
SMITH, William (2)	Ord	BELLEISLE	(Application "T/349")
	A.B.	LONDON	London. 13 March 1806
SMITH, William	Midshipman	AJAX	
SMITH, William	R.M. Boy	BELLEROPHON	
SMITH, William	R.M. Boy	BRITANNIA	
SMITH, William	A.B.	VICTORY	
SMITHERS, John.J.	Ord	BELLEROPHON	
	L.M.	AGINCOURT	Egypt
SMITHSON, James	A.B.	VICTORY	G.H. 6556

TRAFALGAR

SMYTH, Spencer	Midshipman	DEFIANCE	
	Master's Mate (P)	NORTHUMBERLAND	Northumberland. 22 May 1812
	Lieut. R.N.	VENERABLE	Venerable. 16 Jany 1814
	Lieut. R.N.	DARTMOUTH	Navarino
SNELL, William	Midshipman	BRITANNIA	
SNELLGROVE, Henry	Midshipman	COLOSSUS	
SNOOK, John	Pte. R.M.	ACHILLE	
SNOW, James	Sailmaker's Mate	CONQUEROR	
SOMERS, William	L.M.	SWIFTSURE	
SONNEY, Constance	A.B.	AJAX	
	Ord	GIBRALTAR	1 June 1794
SORTHON, William	Sgt. R.M.	SWIFTSURE	
	Pte. R.M.	PHAETON	1 June 1794
SOUTH, John	Pte. R.M.	VICTORY	
SOUTHWICK, James	L.M.	BELLEISLE	
SPENCER, Samuel	Master's Mate	VICTORY	
	Midshipman	ACTIVE	Egypt
SPENCER, William	Quarter Gunner	TONNANT	
	A.B.	INCONSTANT	14 March 1795
	Gunner's Mate	GLASGOW	Algiers
SPINK, John	A.B.	THUNDERER	
SPOONER, Samuel	A.B.	EURYALUS	
SPRATT, James	Master's Mate	DEFIANCE	
	Midshipman	BELLONA	Copenhagen 1801
SPRATT, John	Pte. R.M.	ROYAL SOVEREIGN	
SPURRIER, Thomas	L.M.	LEVIATHAN	(M.L. as SPERE)
STARR, George	Clerk	ORION	
	Clerk	ALFRED	Guadaloupe
	Purser	ROSARIO	Rosario. 27 March 1812
STARR, William	Pte. R.M.	NEPTUNE	
STARTUP, Henry	Pte. R.M.	REVENGE	
STEVENS, Alexander	Q.M's Mate	MARS	
STEVENS, Samuel	L.M.	VICTORY	
STEVENS, Thomas	L.M.	CONQUEROR	
STEWART, Charles	A.B.	VICTORY	G.H. 9346
	Ord	MARS	Mars. 21 April 1798
STOCKER, John	Ord	BRITANNIA	
STOCKWELL, David	A.B.	POLYPHEMUS	
STODDART, John	Boy 2nd Cl	AGAMEMNON	
	Boy 2nd Cl	AGAMEMNON	St Domingo
	A.B.	ELIZABETH	B.S. 24 May 1814
STONELAKE, William	Ship's Cook	TONNANT	
	Ord	MINOTAUR	Nile
STOREY, George	A.B.	DEFENCE	G.H. 9140
	Q.M's Mate	ENDYMION	Endymion Wh President
STRAHAN, Thomas	L.M.	VICTORY	G.H. 6936 as STRACHAM
ST QUINTON – see QUINTIN			
STRAY, John	A.B.	MARS	
STROPERS, Jacob	Gunner's Mate	ORION	
	Gunner's Mate	QUEEN CHARLOTTE	Algiers
STURGEON, Roger	Pte. R.M.	AGAMEMNON	
	Pte. R.M.	VANGUARD	Nile
	Corporal R.M.	AGAMEMNON	St Domingo
STYLES, Henry	L.M.	VICTORY	G.H. 5376
STYLES, John	L.M.	SPARTIATE	G.H. 9183
SULLIVAN, David	L.M.	MINOTAUR	
SUMMER, John	Pte. R.M.	AJAX	
SUTHER, Peter	Actg Surgeon	SWIFTSURE	
	Surgeon	EURYDICE	Martinique
SUTHERLAND, James	Ord	VICTORY	
SWAN, John	Ord	SPARTIATE	G.H. 1917
SWAN, John	Pte. R.M.	SWIFTSURE	
SWEET, James	Armourer's Mate	TEMERAIRE	(McCARTHY Gallery. R.N. Museum)
	Armourer's Mate	CULLODEN	1 June 1794
	Armourer's Mate	CULLODEN	St Vincent
	Armourer's Mate	CULLODEN	Nile
	Armourer	LONDON	London. 13 March 1806
SWEET, Thomas	Pte. R.M.	BRITANNIA	
SWENY, Mark	Actg Lt. R.N.	COLOSSUS	
SYER, Dey.R.	Midshipman	PRINCE	
	Midshipman	TIGRE	B.S. 1 Nov 1809
	Lieut. R.N.	VOLONTAIRE	B.S. 2 May 1813
SYKES, Thomas	Lieut. R.N.	SWIFTSURE	
	Lieut. R.N.	CALPE	Gut of Gibraltar. 12 July 1801
SYLVIA, Peter	Ropemaker	ROYAL SOVEREIGN	
	Ropemaker	BUCEPHALUS	Java
SYMES, Joseph	Midshipman	TONNANT	
	Lieut. R.N.	BONNE CITOYENNE	Bonne Citoyenne Wh Furieuse

SYMONS, Henry	Boy 2nd Cl	PRINCE	
	A.B.	MALTA	Gaieta. 24 July 1815
	A.B.	IMPREGNABLE	Algiers
SYMONS, William.H.	Master's Mate	VICTORY	
or SYMONDS	A.B.	CANADA	12 Octr 1798
TABOR, John	Cpl. R.M.	CONQUEROR	
TALLENCE, Samuel	A.B.	AGAMEMNON	
	A.B.	AGAMEMNON	St Domingo
	Boatswain	PELORUS	Martinique
	Boatswain	PELORUS	Guadaloupe
	Boatswain	MUTINE	Algiers
TALLON, Thomas	L.M.	MARS	
TANE, Thomas.J.W.	2nd Lt. R.M.	LEVIATHAN	
TARDREW, George	Midshipman	PRINCE	
TARRANT, William	Quarter Gunner	VICTORY	Became Boatswain.
TART, John	Ord	VICTORY	
TAYLOR, Alexander	Pte. R.M.	EURYALUS	
TAYLOR, James	Bosun's Mate	AFRICA	
TAYLOR, James	Boy	TEMERAIRE	G.H. 9,280
TAYLOR, John	Pte. R.M.	ROYAL SOVEREIGN	
	Pte. R.M.	REVENGE	Basque Roads 1809
TAYLOR, John	Pte. R.M.	TEMERAIRE	G.H. 9640
TAYLOR, Moses	Pte. R.M.	SPARTIATE	
TAYLOR, Robert	L.M.	NEPTUNE	
TAYLOR, S.	L.M.	REVENGE	
TAYLOR, William (2)	Pte. R.M.	ORION	
TEMPLE, William	L.M.	BRITANNIA	
THATCHER, William	A.B.	ROYAL SOVEREIGN	G.H. 4897
THISTLEWOOD, Robert	Pte. R.M.	AJAX	
	A.B. (?)	SCIPION	Java
THOMAS, Henry	Pte. R.M.	BELLEROPHON	
	Pte. R.M.	BELLEROPHON	B.S. 7 July 1809
THOMAS, Henry	Pte. R.M.	ORION	G.H. 8498
THOMAS, James	Ord	DREADNOUGHT	
THOMAS, John	Ord	TONNANT	
THOMAS, Joseph	L.M.	CONQUEROR	
THOMAS, S.F.	Actg Lieut. R.N.	SPARTIATE	Probably THOMAS, Frederick.J.
THOMAS, Thomas	R.M. Boy	ACHILLE	
	Pte. R.M.	ACHILLE	B.S. 23 Nov 1810
THOMAS, William	L.M.	SIRIUS	
	L.M.	SIRIUS	Sirius. 17 April 1806
THOMPSON, James	A.B.	LEVIATHAN	
THOMPSON, John	A.B.	REVENGE	G.H. 6700
	A.B.	CENTURION	Centurion. 18 Sept 1804 (Vfd Abd. Not on ADM 171/-Roll, but on G.H. Roll)
THOMPSON, William	A.B.	LEVIATHAN	
THOMPSON, William	Quarter Gunner	TEMERAIRE	G.H. 7827
THOMPSON, William	Ord	VICTORY	
THOMSON, John	A.B.	LEVIATHAN	
	Q.M.	IMPLACABLE	Implacable. 26 Augt 1808
THOMSON, Thomas	Pte. R.M.	COLOSSUS	
THORBURNE, Alexander	A.B.	LEVIATHAN	
THORP, Joseph	Pte. R.M.	BELLEISLE	
THORPE, William	L.M.	MINOTAUR	
THURNELL, John	Boy 2nd Cl	AGAMEMNON	G.H. 9389
	L.M.	AGAMEMNON	St Domingo
TILLEY, Thomas	Pte. R.M.	CONQUEROR	
TIMPSON, Mortimer	Lieut. R.M.	PHOEBE	
TINHAM, James	Boy	PHOEBE	
TINSLEY, John	Ord	ROYAL SOVEREIGN	
TITSALL, John	Pte. R.M.	MINOTAUR	
TODD, John	Pte. R.M.	MINOTAUR	G.H. 8330
TOGWELL, Charles	Ord	PRINCE	G.H. 3444
TOMBLESON, Thomas	Carp's Crew	VICTORY	
TOMS, George	A.B.	MINOTAUR	
TOOTH, James	Cpl. R.M.	AFRICA	
TOWSEY, Henry	Asst Surgeon	ROYAL SOVEREIGN	
TOZER, John	Yeoman Powder Rm	BELLEISLE	
	Quarter Gunner	ROYAL GEORGE	1 June 1794
	Quarter Gunner	ROYAL GEORGE	23rd June 1795
TRAYS, William	A.B.	NAIAD	
TREEVE, John	Master's Mate	TONNANT	
	Vol 1st Cl	ST GEORGE	Copenhagen 1801
	Actg Lt. R.N.	YORK	Martinique
TREGO, Thomas	Ropemaker	PRINCE	
	Ropemaker	ENDYMION	Endymion Wh President
TREVARROW, James	Cpl. R.M.	ACHILLE	
TROTHNAN, William	Pte. R.M.	LEVIATHAN	
TROTMAN, William.H.	Surg's Mate	SPARTIATE	
TROTTER, John.W.	Master	LEVIATHAN	Applied as Retd Cdr

TRAFALGAR

TRUEMAN, Jeremiah	A.B.	LEVIATHAN	
	Q.M.	IMPLACABLE	*Implacable. 26 Augt 1808*
	Q.M.	IMPLACABLE	*B.S. 7 July 1809*
TUCK, John	Pte. R.M.	VICTORY	
TUCKER, William	Pte. R.M.	ROYAL SOVEREIGN	
TURNER, Charles	R.M. Boy	MINOTAUR	
TURNER, Charles	L.M.	NEPTUNE	
TURNER, Richard	L.M.	NEPTUNE	
TURNER, Thomas	Cpl. R.M.	MARS	
TURNER, William	Surg's 1st Mate	CONQUEROR	
	Asst Surgeon	CONQUEROR	*B.S. 16 July 1806*
TUTE, Christopher	A.B.	BELLEISLE	
	A.B.	PRINCE GEORGE	*St Vincent*
	A.B.	PERLEN	*Guadaloupe*
TUTTON, Joseph	Boy 3rd Cl	AFRICA	
TWIGGS, Samuel	L.M.	DREADNOUGHT	*G.H. 8606*
UNDERHILL, George	Drummer. R.M.	TONNANT	
	Drummer. R.M.	THAMES	*Gut of Gibraltar. 12 July 1801*
			(Not yet found on M.L.)
UPCOTT, William	Drummer. R.M.	NAIAD	*G.H. 3420*
VAUGHAN, Peter	Ord	DREADNOUGHT	*G.H. 7258*
VEASEY, George	L.M.	TONNANT	
VEITH, James	Ord	SWIFTSURE	
VERNON, Thomas	Sgt. R.M.	DREADNOUGHT	
VESCONTE, N.	L.M.	NEPTUNE	
VICARY, William	Midshipman	ACHILLE	
VICE, William	Pte. R.M.	NEPTUNE	
WAKEHAM, John	Pte. R.M.	BELLEISLE	
WALFORD, William	Midshipman	BELLEROPHON	
	Lieut. R.N.	SKYLARK	*Skylark. 11 Novr 1811*
WALKER, Henry	Midshipman	BELLEROPHON	
WALKER, Henry	Vol 1st Cl	TEMERAIRE	
	Lieut. R.N.	MOHAWK	*B.S. Ap & May 1813*
WALKER, James.R.	Midshipman	VICTORY	*(Formerly James ROBERTSON)*
	Lieut. R.N.	HAZARD	*Martinique*
	Lieut. R.N.	HAZARD	*Guadaloupe*
WALKER, John	A.B.	TONNANT	
WALL, Edward	Drummer. R.M.	MINOTAUR	*G.H. 9776*
WALLACE, Patrick	A.B.	BELLEISLE	
WALL, James	L.M.	NAIAD	
WALLER, R	A.B.	SWIFTSURE	
WALLIN, James	A.B.	COLOSSUS	
WALLS, Richard	Ord	AGAMEMNON	
	Ord	AGAMEMNON	*St Domingo*
WALPOLE, William	Midshipman	COLOSSUS	
WALTERS, Robert	Not Given	TEMERAIRE	*G.H. 403*
WARD, Edward	Pte. R.M.	VICTORY	
WARD, George	Supn	VICTORY	
WARD, Henry	Pte. R.M.	ORION	
	Pte. R.M.	"ANHOLT"	*Anholt. 27 March 1811*
	Pte. R.M.	HEBRUS	*Hebrus With L'Etoile*
WARD, John	Quarter Gunner	REVENGE	
	Quarter Gunner	CENTURION	*Centurion. 18 Sept 1804*
	Yeoman of Sheets	REVENGE	*Basque Roads. 1809*
			(Vfd Abd. Not on Roll)
WARDALL, Thomas	Captain F.X.	EURYALUS	
WARDELL, Henry	Pte. R.M.	ORION	*G.H. 8744 as WARDLE*
WARDEN, John	Ord	BELLEISLE	*G.H. 8584*
WARMAN, William	Ord	TEMERAIRE	
WARREN, Alexander	Ship's Corporal	NAIAD	
WARREN, Jenkin	A.B.	EURYALUS	
WATERER, William	L.M.	COLOSSUS	
WATERMAN, John	Midshipman	MINOTAUR	
WATERS, James	L.M.	AGAMEMNON	
	L.M.	AGAMEMNON	*St Domingo*
WATERS, John	Pte. R.M.	DEFENCE	
WATSON, George	L.M.	BELLEISLE	
WATSON, John	Ord	PRINCE	*G.H. 8900*
WATSON, Robert	A.B.	REVENGE	*(? 2 separate medals issued)*
	Quarter Gunner	REVENGE	*B.S. 16 July 1806*
	Q.M.	REVENGE	*Basque Roads. 1809*
WEALAND, Peter	Carp's Crew	BRITANNIA	
WEAR, John	A.B.	ROYAL SOVEREIGN	
WEARING, Thomas	Lieut. R.M.	CONQUEROR	
WEAVER, Richard	Ord	BELLEROPHON	*G.H. 9023*
WEAVERS, William	Vol 1st Cl	AGAMEMNON	
	Vol 1st Cl	AGAMEMNON	*St Domingo*
WEBB, John	Pte. R.M.	TONNANT	
WEBB, William	Pte. R.M.	SPARTIATE	
WEBBER, George	R.M. Boy	ACHILLE	
WEBBER, John	A.B.	DEFIANCE	*G.H. 2916. ? Additional Clasp*
WEBSTER, James	Pte. R.M.	REVENGE	
WEEKS, Richard	Bosun's Mate	ROYAL SOVEREIGN	

WELCH, Joseph	A.B.	LEVIATHAN	
WELLS, George	A.B.	LEVIATHAN	
WELLS, Henry	Purser	THUNDERER	
	Clerk	RUSSELL	1 June 1794
	Clerk	RUSSELL	23rd June 1795
WEST, Christopher	Midshipman	MINOTAUR	
	Vol 1st Cl	THETIS	Egypt
WEST, Henry	Master's Mate	AFRICA	
WEST, James	A.B.	BRITANNIA	
WEST, James	L.M.	VICTORY	G.H. 9239
WEST, John	A.B.	BELLEISLE	
WEST, Robert	Ord	DEFENCE	
WEST, William	L.M.	BRITANNIA	
WESTON, Charles	A.B.	THUNDERER	
WESTPHAL, George.A.	Midshipman	VICTORY	
	Lieut. R.N.	BELLEISLE	Martinique
	Lieut. R.N.	MARLBOROUGH	B.S. Ap & May 1813 (Clasp known "29 April")
WHARRIE, George	Ord	COLOSSUS	
WHELAN, John	Carp's Mate	TEMERAIRE	
WHILBY, Christopher	A.B.	COLOSSUS	
WHITE, Frederick	Midshipman	AFRICA	
WHITE, George	Master's Mate	DREADNOUGHT	
	Actg Lieut. R.N.	CAPTAIN	Martinique
WHITE, Hugh.B.	Lieut. R.N.	TONNANT	
	Midshipman	POMPEE	Gut of Gibraltar. 12 July 1801 (Vfd Abd. Not on Roll)
WHITE, James	Q.M's Mate	TONNANT	
WHITE, John	L.M.	AGAMEMNON	
	L.M.	AGAMEMNON	St Domingo
WHITE, John	Q.M.	PRINCE	
WHITE, John	Pte. R.M.	ROYAL SOVEREIGN	G.H. 4826
WHITE, Mark	Midshipman	BELLEROPHON	
WHITE, Robert	Ord	NEPTUNE	
WHITEHEAD, John	Boy 3rd Cl	ACHILLE	
WHITING, John	L.M.	MARS	G.H. 3135
WHITLEY, John	L.M.	TONNANT	G.H. 8828 as WITLEY
WHITLEY, Thomas	Ord	BELLEISLE	
WHITINGTON, Richard	L.M.	LEVIATHAN	
WHITTLE, Thomas	Ord	BELLEISLE	G.H. 9448
WICHELO, R.	Clerk	BRITANNIA	
WICKHAM, John	Ord	CONQUEROR	
WILD, William	Pte. R.M.	TEMERAIRE	
WILKINSON, William	Master	SIRIUS	
WILLCOCKS, Samuel	Clerk	BELLEROPHON	
WILLIAMS, James	Ord	LEVIATHAN	
WILLIAMS, James	Ord	NEPTUNE	(M.L. as Thomas WILLIAMS(4).)
WILLIAMS, John	2 Borne.Ord & LM	BRITANNIA	
WILLIAMS, John	A.B.	DEFIANCE	
WILLIAMS, Richard	2 Bne.AB & Carp's Crew	ORION	
	Quarter Gunner	SCEPTRE	Guadaloupe
WILLIAMS, Stephen	A.B.	REVENGE	
WILLIAMS, Thomas	Ord	DREADNOUGHT	
	Capt' Main Top	CAPTAIN	Martinique
WILLIAMS, William	Ord	BELLEISLE	
	Ord	BELLEISLE	Martinique
WILLIAMS, William	4 Borne	CONQUEROR	(AB & Ords(2) & 1 "Run")
WILLIAMSON, James	L.M.	TEMERAIRE	
WILLIS, James.W.	Midshipman	PHOEBE	
WILLOUGHBY, Thomas	Q.M.	CONQUEROR	
WILLS, James	L.M.	PRINCE	(Medal known with unlisted clasp B.S. 6 May 1814)
WILSON, Charles	Pte. R.M.	AFRICA	
WILSON, David	A.B.	PHOEBE	
	Ord	PHOEBE	Off Tamatave. 20 May 1811 (Vfd Abd. Not on Roll)
	Ord	PHOEBE	Java
WILSON, George	Quarter Gunner	REVENGE	
WILSON, James	A.B.	DREADNOUGHT	G.H. 8462
	A.B.	CAPTAIN	Martinique
	A.B.	HARPY	Java
WILSON, John	Ord	BELLEROPHON	
WILSON, John	Ord	BRITANNIA	G.H. 8096
WILSON, John	L.M.	CONQUEROR	
WILSON, John	2nd Lt. R.M.	DEFENCE	
WILTON, George	Armourer	AGAMEMNON	
	Armourer	AGAMEMNON	St Domingo
WILTSHIRE, Thomas	Armourer's Mate	AGAMEMNON	
	Armourer's Mate	AGAMEMNON	St Domingo
	Armourer	HYACINTH	Malaga. 29 April 1812
WINDWARD, Walter	Pte. R.M.	TEMERAIRE	
WINGROVE, George	Captain. R.M.	LEVIATHAN	
WINN, Rowland	A.B.	ROYAL SOVEREIGN	
WISBY, Thomas	Pte. R.M.	PRINCE	

TRAFALGAR

WISE, Edward	A.B.	VICTORY	
	Boatswain	SPARTAN	*Spartan. 3 May 1810*
WITTS, John	Pte. R.M.	ACHILLE	
WIZEN, George	Pte. R.M.	VICTORY	
WOLRIGE, Charles	Midshipman	MINOTAUR	*(This Roll as WOLRIDGE)*
	Lieut. R.N.	QUEBEC	*B.S. 2 Aug 1811*
WOOD, John	Ord	COLOSSUS	
WOOD, William	A.B.	NEPTUNE	
WOOD, William	A.B.	SWIFTSURE	
WOODCOCK, James	Pte. R.M.	DEFIANCE	
WOODMAN, James	R.M. Boy	REVENGE	*G.H. 9600*
WOODRIFF, Daniel	Master's Mate	BELLEROPHON	
WOODROW, John	Boy 3rd Cl	THUNDERER	
WOODWARD, Joseph	Boy	NEPTUNE	
WOOLETT, Richard	Ord	THUNDERER	*G.H. 1229 as WOOLLETT*
WRIGHT, Thomas	L.M.	AGAMEMNON	*G.H. 8327*
YELLOWLEY, John	L.M.	LEVIATHAN	
YEO, Peter	L.M.	SPARTIATE	
	L.M.	HUSSAR	*Java*
YOUNG, John	Ord	DEFENCE	
YOUNG, John.L.	Boy	NAIAD	

(296)   4 NOVR 1805   (G.M.)

Capture of four French Line-of-Battle Ships, off Cape Finisterre.

ACLAND, Henry	A.B.	PHOENIX	*G.H. 4060*
	A.B.	PHOENIX	*Phoenix. 10 Augt 1805*
			(Vfd Abd. Not on Roll)
ADAMS, Charles	Yeoman Powder Room	PHOENIX	
AGAR, George	A.B.	NAMUR	
APPLECROFT, William	Ord	AEOLUS	*GH.7916. (M.L. as APPLEGOFF)*
ARCHER, Joseph	L.M.	NAMUR	
BARGUS, Thomas	A.B.	REVOLUTIONNAIRE	
	Quarter Master	GENOA	*Navarino*
BARNSLEY, James	Pte. R.M.	HERO	
BARRABLE, William	A.B.	REVOLUTIONNAIRE	
	A.B.	BELLEROPHON	*B.S. 7 July 1809*
BATES, Thomas	L.M.	NAMUR	*G.H. 8262*
BAUR, Conrad	Pte. R.M.	NAMUR	*(M.L. as BORRE)*
	Pte. R.M.	SURVEILLANTE	*St Sebastian*
BEASLEY, Frederick	Vol 1st Cl	NAMUR	
BELL, William	L.M.	REVOLUTIONNAIRE	
	Ord	IMPLACABLE	*Implacable. 26 Augt 1808*
BELLAMY, James	A.B.	NAMUR	*G.H. 6655*
BENTHAM, George	Midshipman	HERO	
	Actg Commander	BRISEIS	*Briseis. 14 Octr 1810*
	Commander	HERON (P)	*Algiers*
BERRY, John	Pte. R.M.	NAMUR	*G.H. 1859*
BLACK, William	Lieut. R.N.	AEOLUS	
BLANKER, Christopher	Quarter Gunner	PHOENIX	
	Quarter Gunner	PHOENIX	*Phoenix. 10 Augt 1805*
BODEY, George	L.M.	REVOLUTIONNAIRE	
	Ord	IMPLACABLE	*Implacable. 26 Augt 1808*
BOLEY, Benjamin	Pte. R.M.	CAESAR	*(Roll as Richard)*
	Pte. R.M.	CAESAR	*Basque Roads. 1809*
			(Vfd Abd. Not on Roll)
BONNO, Joseph	Gunner	NAMUR	
	Boatswain's Mate	ANSON	*12 Octr 1798*
	Gunner	ACTIVE	*Egypt*
	Gunner	MINOTAUR	*B.S. 25 July 1809*
BOWEN, George	Master's Mate	NAMUR	
	Master's Mate	CENTURION	*Centurion. 18 Sept 1804*
			(Vfd Abd. Not on Roll)
	Lieut. R.N.	CONQUEROR	*B.S. 16 July 1806*
BOWYER, William.B.	Midshipman	AEOLUS	
BOYD, John	Boy 3rd Cl	HERO	
BROWN, Anthony	A.B.	PHOENIX	*(ANTONY on PHOENIX ROLL)*
	A.B.	PHOENIX	*Phoenix. 10 Augt 1805*
BROWN, James	Pte. R.M.	NAMUR	
BROWN, John	2 Borne. AB & LM	HERO	
BROWN, Samuel	Lieut. R.N.	PHOENIX	
	Lieut. R.N.	PHOENIX	*Phoenix. 10 Augt 1805*
BROWN, William	2 Ptes R.M. borne	NAMUR	
BUCKLEY, James	Steward	PHOENIX	
	Steward	PHOENIX	*Phoenix. 10 Augt 1805*

BURCH, Isaac	Midshipman	CAESAR	
	Midshipman	CAESAR	Basque Roads. 1809 (Known. One 2 Clasp Medal & another 1 clasp Bsq Rds)
BURDON, Samuel	Ord	HERO	
BURNS, John	A.B.	CAESAR	
CALLEWREN, Jeremiah	Pte. R.M.	CAESAR	(M.L. as CALLANAN)
CAMPBELL, Alexander	2nd Lieut. R.M.	PHOENIX	
CAMPBELL, Hon George	Vol 1st Cl	NAMUR	(Navy List as George.P.)
	Midshipman	SEAHORSE	Seahorse Wh Badere Zaffere
CARTER, John	L.M.	REVOLUTIONNAIRE	
CARTWRIGHT, Richard	A.B.	REVOLUTIONNAIRE	
	A.B.	PRESIDENT	Java
CASE, Archibald	Pte. R.M.	COURAGEUX	
CASTLE, John	L.M.	HERO	
CATER, James	L.M.	HERO	G.H. 8730
CAVE, Samuel	A.B.	HERO	G.H. 7409
CEULL, John	Carpenter's Crew	HERO	
CHADWICK, Charles	L.M.	AEOLUS	G.H. 2141
	L.M.	AEOLUS	Martinique
CHALLIS, Samuel	Ord	NAMUR	(Known 2 Medals issued)
	Steward's Mate	VALIANT	Basque Roads 1809
	Steward's Mate	VALIANT	B.S. 27 Sep 1810 (as CHALLICE)
CHAPMAN, William	A.B.	COURAGEUX	
CHAPMAN, William	L.M.	HERO	G.H. 7969
CLAPP, Samuel	Sgt. R.M.	COURAGEUX	
CLEWES, Phillip	L.M.	CAESAR	
COLLETT, Daniel	R.M. Boy	HERO	
COLLETT, George	Boy 2nd Cl	COURAGEUX	
COLLEY, Thomas	Carpenter's Crew	REVOLUTIONNAIRE	
	Caulker's Mate	IMPLACABLE	Implacable. 26 Augt 1808
COLLERSON, John	Boy	NAMUR	(M.L. as COLLINSON)
COOK, George	L.M.	HERO	
COOPER, Joseph	Pte. R.M.	HERO	
CORKNO, Andrew	Ord	CAESAR	(M.L. as CARGUE)
COUCH, Daniel.L.	Lieut. R.N.	REVOLUTIONNAIRE	
	Midshipman	FISGARD	Fisgard. 20 Octr 1798
COX, James	A.B.	CAESAR	G.H. 9061
COX, John	L.M.	REVOLUTIONNAIRE	
	Ord	DONEGAL	Basque Roads. 1809
CRAIG, Philip	Carpenter's Mate	NAMUR	
	Carpenter's Mate	VALIANT	Basque Roads. 1809
CROXTON, John	Boy	NAMUR	
	L.M.	VALIANT	Basque Roads. 1809
CUMBY, Charles	Lieut. R.N.	CAESAR	
CUMMINGS, James	Q.M's Mate	PHOENIX	G.H. 8849
	Q.M's Mate	PHOENIX	Phoenix. 10 Augt 1805 (Vfd Abd. Not on Roll)
CURSON, John	Pte. R.M.	REVOLUTIONNAIRE	
DANSIE, Jacob	Pte. R.M.	NAMUR	
DANVILL, William	Ord	HERO	
DARBY, William	R.M. Boy	HERO	G.H. 9113
DAVIES, John George	A.B.	COURAGEUX	
	Midshipman	HECTOR	Egypt
DAVIES, George	A.B.	PHOENIX	G.H. 7030
or DAVIS	L.M.	PRINCE GEORGE	St Vincent
	A.B.	PHOENIX	Phoenix 10 Augt 1805
DAVIS, William	Carpenter's Crew	NAMUR	
	Carpenter's Crew	VALIANT	Basque Roads. 1809
DENBY, John	Ship's Corporal	REVOLUTIONNAIRE	
DENFORCE, Charles	2nd Lieut. R.M.	CAESAR	
DENNEY, John.M.	A.B.	SANTA MARGARITA	
DENNIS, James	L.M.	CAESAR	
DICKSON, James	A.B.	HERO	
DILLOW, Thomas	L.M.	HERO	
DODD, James	Ord	NAMUR	
DORCHESTER, John	L.M.	NAMUR	G.H. 8762
DRAFFEN, Frederick	Master's Mate	SANTA MARGARITA	
DRANE, Thomas	L.M.	CAESAR	
	Actg Lieut. R.N.	CAESAR	Basque Roads. 1809
DUNN, Thomas	A.B.	REVOLUTIONNAIRE	
	Captain Forecastle	PRESIDENT	St Sebastian
EDWARDS, John	A.B.	CAESAR	
EDWARDS, Richard	1st Lt. R.M.	COURAGEUX	
ELLIOTT, John	Pte. R.M.	HERO	
ELLIOTT, Richard	Pte. R.M.	REVOLUTIONNAIRE	
ELSTON, Charles	A.B.	HERO	
	Yeoman of Sheets	IMPREGNABLE	Algiers
ELSTONE, John	Pte. R.M.	CAESAR	
EVERSON, William	Boy 2nd Cl	REVOLUTIONNAIRE	
	L.M.	IMPLACABLE	Implacable. 26 Augt 1808
EVERTON, Richard	L.M.	HERO	G.H. 9821

4 NOVR 1805

FARLEY, William	Midshipman	HERO	
	Master's Mate	FAWN	*Martinique*
	Master's Mate	FAWN	*Guadaloupe*
FARQUHARSON, William	Vol 1st Cl	AEOLUS	
	Vol 1st Cl	AEOLUS	*Martinique*
FARRINGTON, James	L.M.	NAMUR	(M.L. as Dennis FLYNN)
FELL, Robert	A.B.	NAMUR	
FERGUSON, William	Boy	NAMUR	G.H. 8042
FERRIS, Thomas	Midshipman	CAESAR	
FITZROY, William	Captain. R.N.	AEOLUS	
	Capt's Servant	PHAETON	*1 June 1794*
	Midshipman	SANS PAREIL	*23rd June 1795*
			(Vfd Abd. Not on Roll)
	Lieut. R.N.	PENELOPE	*Egypt*
	Captain. R.N.	AEOLUS	*Martinique*
FLYNN, Daniel	L.M.	NAMUR	
FOLLETT, Thomas	Ord	CAESAR	
	A.B.	CAESAR	*Basque roads 1809 (Vfd Abd. NOR)*
	Ord	QUEEN CHARLOTTE	*Algiers*
FOREMAN, George	Ord	SANTA MARGARITA	G.H. 8023
FOUNTAIN, Thomas	Ord	NAMUR	
FOWLER, Stephen	Yeoman of Sheets	CAESAR	
	Yeoman of Sheets	CAESAR	*Basque Roads. 1809.*
FRANCIS, Joseph	Boy	BELLONA	
	Boy	BELLONA	*Basque Roads. 1809*
FREESTUN, Humphrey.M.	Midshipman	REVOLUTIONNAIRE	
FRY, Thomas	Pte. R.M.	CAESAR	
FULLER, Thomas	Ord	HERO	
GALE, Stephen	L.M.	COURAGEUX	
GALLICHAN, James	Master's Mate	CAESAR	
GALVIN, Daniel	A.B.	NAMUR	
GARD, Onesephus	Pte. R.M.	NAMUR	
GARDENER, George	L.M.	NAMUR	
GIBBS, John	Ord	CAESAR	
	Ord	CAESAR	*Basque Roads. 1809*
GIBBS, William	Pte. R.M.	COURAGEUX	G.H. 7489
GILBERT, Samuel	A.B.	AEOLUS	
	A.B.	AEOLUS	*Martinique*
GIBBONS, Samuel	Ship's Corporal	HERO	G.H. 7167
GILRAY, Andrew	Boy 2nd Cl	REVOLUTIONNAIRE	
	L.M.	IMPLACABLE	*Implacable. 26 Augt 1808*
GOULLET, Charles	Midshipman	CAESAR	
	Midshipman	CAESAR	*Basque Roads. 1809*
GOULSTON, William	Ord	HERO	G.H. as GOLDSTONE 3195/3105
GRAY, Robert	L.M.	CAESAR	
GRANT, James	L.M.	HERO	
GREENING, Richard	Midshipman	HERO	
GROOM, Peter	Pte. R.M.	SANTA MARGARITA	G.H. 9971
HAMLIN, James	Pte. R.M.	CAESAR	
HAMMOND, Isaac	L.M.	REVOLUTIONNAIRE	
	Ord	IMPLACABLE	*Implacable. 26 Augt 1808*
	A.B.	IMPLACABLE	*B.S. 7 July 1809*
HANDLEY, John.W.H.	Midshipman	NAMUR	
	Midshipman	VALIANT	*Basque Roads. 1809*
HARDY, Thomas	Ord	CAESAR	
HARRISON, William	Ord	HERO	G.H. 4958
HAWKINS, David	A.B.	AEOLUS	G.H. 6918
HEALE, John	Pte. R.M.	CAESAR	
HENDRY, William	Lieut. R.N.	HERO	
	Lieut. R.N.	STATIRA	*Guadaloupe*
HEXT, William	Lieut. R.N.	SANTA MARGARITA	
HILL, Francis	L.M.	HERO	G.H. 8714
HOBBS, Thomas	L.M.	PHOENIX	
	L.M.	PHOENIX	*Phoenix. 10 Augt 1805*
HOGAN, Edward	Boy 3rd Cl	COURAGEUX	
HOLMES, John	Ord	COURAGEUX	
HOOPER, Robert	L.M.	REVOLUTIONNAIRE	
HORN, John	Pte. R.M.	PHOENIX	(M.L. as HORNE)
	Pte. R.M.	PHOENIX	*Phoenix. 10 Augt 1805*
			(Vfd Abd. Not on Roll)
HOWARD, John	Clerk	HERO	
HULL, Christopher.N.	A.B.	CAESAR	G.H. 8853
HUNT, Michael	L.M.	COURAGEUX	
HUNTER, William	Vol 1st Class	HERO	*Rating as G.H. 7645*
HUTCHINSON, George	Master's Mate	CAESAR	
	Master's Mate	DIADEM	*Egypt*
	Lieut. R.N.	DOLPHIN	*B.S. Ap & May 1813*
HYDE, John	Ord	COURAGEUX	
IFGRAVE, Samuel	Carpenter's Crew	AEOLUS	
	Carpenter's Crew	AEOLUS	*Martinique*
JACKSON, Thomas	L.M.	CAESAR	

JAMES, Isaac	Pte. R.M.	CAESAR	G.H. 9144
JEFFERY, Henry	A.B.	REVOLUTIONNAIRE	(As JEFFREY other 2 Rolls)
	A.B.	PRESIDENT	Java
	A.B.	PRESIDENT	St Sebastian
JOHNSON, Richard	Quarter Gunner	PHOENIX	G.H. 9041
	Quarter Gunner	PHOENIX	Phoenix. 10 Augt 1805 (Vfd Abd. Not on Roll)
JONES, Henry	Q.M's Mate	SANTA MARGARITA	
JONES, Richard	Ord	COURAGEUX	
JONES, William	L.M.	CAESAR	
JORDON, Thomas	Pte. R.M.	PHOENIX	(Vfd Abd. Not on Roll)
	Pte. R.M.	EDGAR	Copenhagen 1801
	Pte. R.M.	PHOENIX	Phoenix. 10 Augt 1805
KEARLEY, Benjamin	Coxswain	NAMUR	(M.L. as CARLEY)
	Ord	THAMES	Gut of Gibraltar. 12 July 1801
	Coxswain	VALIANT	Basque Roads. 1809
KENNEDY, Bernard	Yeoman of Sheets	PHOENIX	
	Yeoman of Sheets	PHOENIX	Phoenix. 10 Augt 1805 (Vfd Abd. Not on Roll)
KIDNEY, Patrick	L.M.	COURAGEUX	
LACEY, Thomas	Ord	CAESAR	G.H. 6669
LAMBETH, John.D.	L.M.	NAMUR	(This Roll as LAMBERT)
	Ord	VALIANT	Basque Roads. 1809
	Ord	VALIANT	B.S. 27 Sep 1810
LANGTON, John	L.M.	HERO	G.H. 9112
LAWES, Thomas	Ord	PHOENIX	
	Ord	PHOENIX	Phoenix. 10 Augt 1805
LAWRENCE, Samuel	Corporal. R.M.	REVOLUTIONNAIRE	
	Drummer. R.M.	ROSE	Navarino
LAWSON, Gilbert	Quarter Gunner	CAESAR	
	A.B.	SWIFTSURE	Nile
	A.B.	SWIFTSURE	Egypt
	Gunner's Mate	CAESAR	Basque Roads. 1809
	Gunner	PHOEBE	Phoebe. 28 March 1814
LEA, Edward	Pte. R.M.	NAMUR	
LEE, George	Boy	SANTA MARGARITA	
LESSELS, Thomas	Quarter Master	PHOENIX	
	Quarter Master	PHOENIX	Phoenix. 10 Augt 1805
LEWIS, David	Pte. R.M.	CAESAR	
LOUIS, George	Captain. R.M.	CAESAR	(Applied as Major General George LEWIS. R.M.)
LEWIS, John	Pte. R.M.	CAESAR	
	Pte. R.M.	CAESAR	Basque Roads. 1809
LEWIS, Samuel	Ord	HERO	G.H. 9675
LIBBY, Edward	Lieut. R.N.	NAMUR	
	Midshipman	LOWESTOFFE	14 March 1795
	Midshipman	LOWESTOFFE	Lowestoffe. 24 June 1795
	Actg Lieut. R.N.	BLENHEIM	St Vincent
LIONS, George	Ord	NAMUR	
LLOYD, William	L.M.	HERO	G.H. 8108
LOVE, James	Pte. R.M.	HERO	
LOWER, Henry	R.M. Boy	HERO	
LULLOCK, John	Pte. R.M.	CAESAR	
LUVELL, George	Pte. R.M.	CAESAR	(M.L. as LUVALL)
MANN, John	L.M.	NAMUR	
	Boy 3rd Cl	ARDENT	Copenhagen 1801
	Ord	VALIANT	Basque Roads. 1809
	Ord	VALIANT	B.S. 27 Sep 1810
MANSFIELD, William	Ord	CAESAR	
MARTIN, James	Pte. R.M.	HERO	
MARTIN, John	Pte. R.M.	CAESAR	
MARSHALL, George.E.	Midshipman	PHOENIX	
	Lieut. R.N.	ACASTA	Martinique
McDOUGALL, John	Lieut. R.N.	CAESAR	
MEE, John	Midshipman	SANTA MARGARITA	
MICHLEGAN, Thomas	Ord	CAESAR	
MILES, Joseph	A.B.	NAMUR	
	A.B.	VALIANT	Basque Roads. 1809
MIMMACK, William	A.B.	HERO	(M.L. as MIMMICK)
MORTON, James	L.M.	CAESAR	
MULKAHY, Timothy	L.M.	COURAGEUX	Other Rolls MULCALEY/MULCAHY
	Ord	AETNA	Basque Roads. 1809
	Quarter Gunner	IMPREGNABLE	Algiers
MUNDAY, Thomas	A.B.	REVOLUTIONNAIRE	G.H. 9888
	Sailmaker	PRESIDENT	Java
	Sailmaker	PRESIDENT	St Sebastian
MURIEL, William	Vol 1st Cl	HERO	
MURPHY, Dennis	Boy	PHOENIX	

4 NOVR 1805

NEWMAN, Robert.A.	Vol 1st Cl	COURAGEUX	
O'HARA, John	L.M.	COURAGEUX	
OLAY, Richard	L.M.	HERO	G.H. 2756 as ONEY
	Ord	CALEDONIA	Basque Roads. 1809
OLIVER, Richard	Ord	CAESAR	G.H. 86
	Ship's Corporal	CAESAR	Basque Roads. 1809
O'NEILL, John	L.M.	CAESAR	
or O'NEIL	Carpenter's Crew	CAESAR	Basque Roads. 1809
PAGE, John	L.M.	REVOLUTIONNAIRE	
PARR, John	L.M.	HERO	
PARSIPLE, Thomas	Ord	HERO	
PARSONS, Richard.T.	Lieut. R.M.	REVOLUTIONNAIRE	
PAUL, Richard	2 borne LM & Pte RM	CAESAR	
PENDLETON, John	Ord	CAESAR	
PIKE, James	Ord	PHOENIX	
	Ord	PHOENIX	Phoenix. 10 Augt 1805
PLIMPTON, Henry	Boy 3rd Cl	PHOENIX	(M.L. as PLYMPTON)
	Boy 3rd Cl	PHOENIX	Phoenix. 10 Augt 1805
POLHILL, George	A.B.	REVOLUTIONNAIRE	(Roll may read Charles)
PHILLIPS, Thomas	A.B.	NAMUR	
	A.B.	VALIANT	Basque Roads. 1809
PORTER, William	Ord	NAMUR	
POWELL, John	R.M. Boy	HERO	
PRATT, Samuel	Pte. R.M.	COURAGEUX	
PRESCOTT, Henry	Lieut. R.N.	AEOLUS	
	Midshipman	PENELOPE	Penelope. 30 March 1800
	Midshipman	PENELOPE	Egypt
	Commander	WEAZLE	Amanthea. 25 July 1810
PRICE, William	Boy	NAMUR	
PRIOR, Francis	Master	AEOLUS	
PROBY, Henry.J.P.	Master's Mate	NAMUR	
PUGH, William	Ord	COURAGEUX	
PURCHAS, William.J.	Midshipman	HERO	
	Midshipman	BELLEROPHON	B.S. 7 July 1809
PURCHASE, William	Midshipman	AEOLUS	
	Midshipman	AEOLUS	Martinique
PYE, Thomas	Sergeant. R.M.	PHOENIX	(Vfd Abd. Not on Roll)
	Sergeant. R.M.	PHOENIX	Phoenix. 10 Augt 1805
QUARM, Roger	Pte. R.M.	HERO	
RABY, Edward	A.B.	SANTA MARGARITA	
RAWLINS, Richard	Pte. R.M.	PHOENIX	(Vfd Abd. Not on Roll)
	Pte. R.M.	PHOENIX	Phoenix. 10 Augt 1805
REED, Benjamin	Boy 2nd Cl	NAMUR	
	Ord	VALIANT	B.S. 27 Sep 1805
	A.B.	VALIANT	Basque Roads 1809
REYNOLDS, John	Lieut. R.N.	SANTA MARGARITA	
REYNOLDS, Samuel	Pte. R.M.	HERO	
RICHARDS, Thomas	Pte. R.M.	CAESAR	
RICHARDS, William	Ord	NAMUR	
RICHARDSON, William	Gunner	CAESAR	
RIDING, Joseph	Pte. R.M.	NAMUR	
RILEY, Francis	Pte. R.M.	COURAGEUX	G.H.8999
ROBERTS, Richard	Ord	COURAGEUX	
ROBINSON, Louis.A.	Midshipman	COURAGEUX	
	Master's Mate	LEDA	Java
ROMNEY, Francis.D.	Midshipman	AEOLUS	
	Supn. Lieut. R.N.	No 10 Gun-Boat	Gluckstadt. 5 Jany 1814 (On books of DESIREE)
ROSE, Thomas	A.N.	HERO	G.H. 3752
ROSS, William	Asst Surgeon	NAMUR	
ROSSER, Phillip	Pte. R.M.	CAESAR	
ROUSE, Joseph	Ord	PHOENIX	
	Boy 3rd Cl	RENOMMEE	Egypt
	Ord	PHOENIX	Phoenix. 10 Augt 1805
ROWLAND, Richard	Pte. R.M.	PHOENIX	(On this Roll, see RAWLINS above. Same man?)
ROWLANDSON, Michael	A.B.	CAESAR	
	A.B.	CAESAR	Basque Roads 1809
RYAN, John	Ord	CAESAR	
SAYER, Francis	A.B.	HERO	
SCOTT, Edmund	Midshipman	HERO	
	Master's Mate	BELLEROPHON	B.S. 7 July 1809
SCOTT, George	Ord	CAESAR	
SCOTT, John	Pte. R.M.	NAMUR	
SHAKESHAFT, Edward	L.M.	AEOLUS	
	Ord	AEOLUS	Martinique
SHARRATT, John	Ord	PHOENIX	(M.L. as SHERRARD)
	Ord	PHOENIX	Phoenix. 10 Augt 1805
SHATTERFOOT, Isaac	Pte. R.M.	CAESAR	
	Pte. R.M.	CAESAR	Basque Roads. 1809

SKEKEL, John	Lieut. R.N.	HERO	
	Lieut. R.N.	BELLEROPHON	B.S. 7 July 1809
SHERROCK, Christopher	Pte. R.M.	COURAGEUX	
SHIELS, Clark	A.B.	COURAGEUX	
SHORT, William	Pte. R.M.	NAMUR	
	Pte. R.M.	FOUDROYANT	Egypt
SHUTE, Benjamin	Ord	NAMUR	G.H. 3788
	Ord	LEDA	Egypt
SLAUGHTER, James	Pte. R.M.	REVOLUTIONNAIRE	G.H. 8518
SMERDON, John	Ord	CAESAR	
SMITH, Edward	Ord	BELLONA	G.H. 8363
	L.M.	BELLONA	Basque Roads. 1809
SMITH, Michael	L.M.	CAESAR	G.H. 8493
SMITH, Thomas	Midshipman	PHOENIX	
	Midshipman	PHOENIX	Phoenix. 10 Augt 1805
	Lieut. R.N.	LYRA	Basque Roads. 1809
SPROAT, Thomas	Pte. R.M.	NAMUR	
STEVENS, George	Ord	SANTA MARGARITA	G.H. 5720
STEVENS, William	A.B.	PHOENIX	G.H. 8979. ML as STEPHENS
	A.B.	PHOENIX	Phoenix. 10 Augt 1805 (Vfd Abd. Not on Roll)
STIFF, Peter	Pte. R.M.	NAMUR	
STOGDEN, Richard	A.B.	PHOENIX	(Vfd Abd. Not on Roll)
	A.B.	PHOENIX	Phoenix. 10 Augt 1805
STYLE, William	Master's Mate	REVOLUTIONNAIRE	
SYMONDS, Christopher	Ord	REVOLUTIONNAIRE	ML as SIMMONS/SIMMONDS?
	A.B.	IMPLACABLE	Implacable. 26 Augt 1808
	A.B.	IMPLACABLE	B.S. 7 July 1809
TARRELL, Robert	L.M.	HERO	
TAYSAND, Eleazer	Ord	COURAGEUX	
THOMPSON, William	Ord	CAESAR	
THOMPSON, William	Boy	CAESAR	
	Boy	CAESAR	Basque Roads. 1809
THORNDICK, Robert	A.B.	REVOLUTIONNAIRE	(M.L. as THORNDYKE)
THORNTON, Henry.A.D.	Vol 1st Cl	NAMUR	
TITLEY, George	L.M.	NAMUR	G.H. 2917
TOMKINS, William	A.B.	CAESAR	G.H. 2521
TOSH, David	A.B.	HERO	
TRUSCOTT, George	Lieut. R.N.	COURAGEUX	
TURNER, William	Pte. R.M.	HERO	
UNWIN, Thomas	Bosun's Mate	PHOENIX	
	Ord	GLATTON	Copenhagen 1801
	A.B.	PHOENIX	Phoenix. 10 Augt 1805
VINCENT, Samuel	Pte. R.M.	NAMUR	
WAKEHAM, William	A.B.	NAMUR	
WALTON, James	Sergeant. R.M.	CAESAR	G.H. 8691
WARDEN, William	Surgeon	PHOENIX	(Vfd Abd. Not on Roll)
	Surgeon	PHOENIX	Phoenix. 10 Augt 1805
WARRING, James	L.M.	NAMUR	G.H. 9795 as WARING
WATERS, William	Ord	CAESAR	
WATTS, George	L.M.	CAESAR	
WAYMOUTH, John	R.M. Boy	CAESAR	
WEEKS, William	Boy 2nd Cl	CAESAR	
	Boy 2nd Cl	CAESAR	Basque Roads 1809
WILD, Thomas	L.M.	NAMUR	
WILKINS, Isaac	Pte. R.M.	COURAGEUX	
WILKINS, Samuel	Pte. R.M.	COURAGEUX	
WILLES, James Irwin	2nd Lieut. R.M.	REVOLUTIONNAIRE	
WILLIAMSON, George	Master's Mate	SANTA MARGARITA	
WINTERBURN, George	Ord	CAESAR	
	Boy	RENOWN	Egypt
	Cook	LOIRE	Guadaloupe
WITT or STOKELEY, Stephen	L.M.	AEOLUS	
WOLRIGE, William	Midshipman	CAESAR	
	Lieut. R.N.	VOLAGE (P)	Lissa
WRIFORD, Samuel	Midshipman	CAESAR	
	Lieut. R.N.	CAESAR	Basque Roads. 1809
	Lieut. R.N.	MALTA	Gaieta. 24 July 1815
WRIGHT, Matthew	L.M.	COURAGEUX	
	A.B.	BEAGLE	St Sebastian
WRIGHT, Richard	Ord	PHOENIX	
WRIGHT, Samuel	Ord	SANTA MARGARITA	
WYATT, George	R.M. Boy	BELLONA	
WHYLEY, Thomas	Pte. R.M.	PHOENIX	GH.8973 as WYLIE/WHYLY
	Pte. R.M.	PHOENIX	Phoenix. 10 Augt 1805 (Vfd Abd. Not on Roll)
YARDLEY, John	L.M.	NAMUR	G.H. 6043
YATES, John	Ord	CAESAR	
	Ord	CAESAR	Basque Roads. 1809

4 NOVR 1805

YULE, Robert	Master's Mate	HERO	
	Master's Mate	PENELOPE	Penelope. 30 March 1800
	Master's Mate	PENELOPE	Egypt
			(Vfd Abd. Not on Roll)
	Lieut. R.N.	ILLUSTRIOUS	Java

(396)   **St DOMINGO**   (G.M.)

Battle of Santo Domingo on 6 February 1806. Capture of three and destruction of two French sail of the line.

ADDERLEY, Arden	Lieutenant. R.N.	SUPERB	
AKERS, John	L.M.	DONEGAL	G.H. 7422
ALEXANDER, John	Midshipman	ACASTA	
ALLEN, George	Pte. R.M.	DONEGAL	
ALLEN, Joseph	A.B.	CANOPUS	
ALLEN, Peter	A.B.	ACASTA	G.H. 3290
ALSTON, George	L.M.	SPENCER	
	Ord	VICTORIOUS	Victorious with Rivoli
AMATUCCI, Innocenzo	Pte. R.M.	CANOPUS	G.H. 7400
ANDREW, John.W.	Midshipman	CANOPUS	
	A.B.	FOUDROYANT	12 Octr 1798
	Commander	WEAZLE	Weazel. 22 Feby 1812
ARMSTRONG, William	Ord	SPENCER	
	A.B.	VICTORIOUS	Victorious with Rivoli
ASLETT, William	Ord	SUPERB	G.H. 8362
AUSTEN, Francis.W.	Captain. R.N.	CANOPUS	
	Commander	PETEREL (P)	Peterel. 21 March 1800
BADDELEY, Henry	Clerk	MAGICIENNE	
BAILEY, Walter	L.M.	ACASTA	
	Ord	ACASTA	Martinique
	Ord	SCIPION	Java
BAIN, Henderson	Lieutenant. R.N.	SPENCER	
	Commander	HARPY	Java
BARLOW, Jeffery	Capt' Fore Top	SUPERB	
BARNARD, William	Midshipman	KINGFISHER	
BARNETT, Joseph	L.M.	SPENCER	
BARNETT, Thomas	L.M.	CANOPUS	
BARNSLEY, B.W.	Midshipman	SPENCER	
BARRY, John	A.B.	ACASTA	
BATH, James	Boy 3rd Class	MAGICIENNE	
BAYNTON, William	Landsman	ATLAS	
BELITHER, James	Boy 3rd Class	AGAMEMNON	G.H. 7739
	Boy 3rd Class	AGAMEMNON	Trafalgar
BELL, George	Boy 2nd Class	SUPERB	
BENNING, Daniel	A.B.	NORTHUMBERLAND	
BICKLE, John	Boy 2nd Class	SUPERB	
BIGGS, Abraham	Pte. R.M.	SUPERB	
	Pte. R.M.	DEFIANCE	Copenhagen 1801
BILLETT, William	L.M.	CANOPUS	
BLYTH, John	Drummer. R.M.	ATLAS	
	Sergeant. R.M.	Qn CHARLOTTE	Algiers (ML as BLIGH)
BOND, George	L.M.	CANOPUS	
BOND, William	Ord	CANOPUS	
	Q.M.	GENOA	Navarino
BOON, John	A.B.	ACASTA	
	Ord	CANADA	12 Octr 1798
	A.B.	SCIPION	Java
	A.B.	GRANICUS	Algiers
BOOTH, John	Ord	SPENCER	
BOOTH, William	A.B.	SUPERB	
BOUCHER, William	Pte. R.M.	CANOPUS	
BOYD, John	A.B.	SPENCER	
BROWN, Daniel	A.B.	MAGICIENNE	
BROWN, Lawrence	Pte. R.M.	SUPERB	G.H.8159
BROWN, Robert	A.B.	CANOPUS	
BROWNE, William.E.	Bosun's Mate	ATLAS	
BUCKLE, Robert	A.B.	KINGFISHER	
BUDD, Francis	A.B.	SUPERB	
	A.B.	EGMONT	St Vincent
	A.B.	SCEPTRE	Guadaloupe
BULLION, Thomas	Boy	NORTHUMBERLAND	
BURKE, James	Ord	CANOPUS	
BURNS, Patrick	Boy 2nd Class	SPENCER	
	Ord	VICTORIOUS	Victorious with Rivoli
CAMPBELL, Archibald	A.B.	SPENCER	

CAMPBELL, Donald	2nd Lieut. R.M.	AGAMEMNON	
	2nd Lieut. R.M.	AGAMEMNON	Trafalgar
	Lieut. R.M.	RESOLUTION	Basque Roads 1809
CAMPBELL, James	Lieut. R.M.	ACASTA	
	Lieut. R.M.	ACASTA	Martinique
CAPPOLE, Anthony	L.M.	SUPERB	
CARTHY, Timothy	Ord	NORTHUMBERLAND	
CAVENAGH, Edward	Yeoman of Sheets	CANOPUS	
	Bosun's Mate	HECTOR	Egypt
CHAPMAN, James	Pte. R.M.	KINGFISHER	G.H. 7410
CHAPPELL, Edward	Volunteer 1st Cl	KINGFISHER	
	Midshipman	INTREPID	Martinique
CHAPPELL, John	Pte. R.M.	AGAMEMNON	
	Pte. R.M.	AGAMEMNON	Trafalgar
CHAPPELL, Thomas	Ord	NORTHUMBERLAND	
CHRISTIE, George	Q.M's Mate	MAGICIENNE	
CHRISTIE, Robert	L.M.	SPENCER	
	Gunner's Crew	GENOA	Navarino
CHURCHER, Benjamin	Q.M's Mate	SPENCER	
	Bosun's Mate	VICTORIOUS	Victorious with Rivoli
CLACK, Thomas	Sub Lieut R.N.	EPERVIER	
	Midshipman	MAGNANIME	12 Octr 1798
	Lieutenant. R.N.	GOREE	Martinique
CLEAR, Richard	A.B.	DONEGAL	G.H. 7102
CLIFTON, Richard	Pte. R.M.	CANOPUS	
CLODD, William	Ship's Corporal	SPENCER	G.H. 7653
	Q.M.	VICTORIOUS	Victorious with Rivoli
COLE, Edward	Master's Mate	SUPERB	
	Master's Mate	SUPERB	Gut of Gibraltar. 12 July 1801
	Lieutenant. R.N.	STATELY	Stately. 22 March 1808
COLLINS, James	L.M.	DONEGAL	G.H. 4414
COLTMAN, James	Ord	ACASTA	
CONIFF, John	Ord	CANOPUS	
CONNELL, David	Ord	NORTHUMBERLAND	
	Ord	NEPTUNE	Martinique
CONNOR, James	Boy	NORTHUMBERLAND	
	Ord	NEPTUNE	Martinique
	A.B.	GLASGOW	Navarino
COOKE, William.H.	Midshipman	SUPERB	
	Midshipman	SUPERB	Gut of Gibraltar. 12 July 1801
COOMBS, Joseph	A.B.	CANOPUS	G.H. 4076
COOP, Abraham	L.M.	AGAMEMNON	
	L.M.	AGAMEMNON	Trafalgar
	L.M.	PRESIDENT	Java
COOPER, Thomas	Ord	ATLAS	
COOTE, William	Lieut. R.N.	AGAMEMNON	
	Midshipman	ROYAL GEORGE	23rd June 1795
	Midshipman	EDGAR	Copenhagen 1801 (Vfd Abd. NOR)
	Lieutenant. R.N.	AGAMEMNON	Trafalgar
	Lieutenant. R.N.	CEREBUS (P)	B.S. 2 Jan 1807
CORBEN, George	Ord	SUPERB	
	Boy 2nd Class	SUPERB	Gut of Gibraltar. 12 July 1801
CORFIELD, William	Pte. R.M.	ATLAS	G.H. 9703
COTESWORTH, Charles	Volunteer	ACASTA	
COUSINS, John.C.	Midshipman	AGAMEMNON	
	Midshipman	AGAMEMNON	Trafalgar
COWAN, David	Surgeon	SUPERB	
CREYKE, Richard	Midshipman	ACASTA	
	Lieutenant. R.N.	VALIANT	Basque Roads 1809
CROCKER, Richard	Pte. R.M.	SUPERB	G.H. 7618
	Pte. R.M.	VOLAGE	Lissa
CROSBY, Thomas	Ord	NORTHUMBERLAND	
	Ord	SPENCER	Gut of Gibraltar. 12 July 1801
CROSHALL, Richard	Pte. R.M.	DONEGAL	
CROSIER, James	Gunner's Mate	SUPERB	
	A.B.	SUPERB	Gut of Gibraltar. 12 July 1801
	Gunner's Mate	ALFRED	Guadaloupe
CUPPAGE, Adam	Volunteer 1st Cl	ACASTA	
CURTIS, John	Carp's Crew	SPENCER	
	Carp's Mate	AMETHYST	Amethyst. 5 April 1809
DALRYMPLE, Thomas	A.B.	ACASTA	
DALY, Daniel	L.M.	CANOPUS	
D'ARANDA, William	Midshipman	ATLAS	
DAVIE, James	Pte. R.M.	MAGICIENNE	
DAVIS, John	Ord	NORTHUMBERLAND	
	Capt' Main Top	NEPTUNE	Martinique
DAVIES, John	A.B.	SUPERB	
	Ord	SOUTHAMPTON	Southampton. 9 June 1796 (Vfd Abd. Not on Roll)
	L.M.	SOUTHAMPTON	1 June 1794
	Ord	SOUTHAMPTON	St Vincent
	A.B.	SUPERB	Gut of Gibraltar. 12 July 1801

ST DOMINGO

DAY, John	Actg Lieut. R.N.	CANOPUS	
DEAGON, Edward	Gunner	ATLAS	
	Q.M.	MINOTAUR	*Nile*
	Gunner	PHAETON	*B.S. 27 Oct 1800*
DELAFONS, W.P.	Midshipman	SUPERB	
DENHAM, John	Sergeant. R.M.	DONEGAL	*(M) Anchor Ty LSGC & Ch '42*
	Corporal. R.M.	Qn CHARLOTTE	*Algiers*
DENMEAD, John	Pte. R.M.	NORTHUMBERLAND	
	Pte. R.M.	DRAGON	*B.S. Ap & May 1813*
DICKSON, John	Asst Surgeon	SUPERB	
DISKIE, Frederick	Ord	DONEGAL	*G.H. 7941*
DOWLING, George	Ord	SUPERB	
DRIBROUGH, Alexander	A.B.	AGAMEMNON	*(May read DRIBOROUGH)*
	A.B.	AGAMEMNON	*Trafalgar*
DUNKLEY, George	Ord	NORTHUMBERLAND	
	Ord	NEPTUNE	*Martinique*
	Capt' After Guard	WANDERER	*Guadaloupe*
DUNN, David	Master's Mate	DONEGAL	
	Lieutenant. R.N.	AMPHION (P)	*Lissa*
	Captain. R.N.	VANGUARD	*Syria (Sir David Dunn)*
EAGAN, Thomas	Ord	CANOPUS	
EDGE, Joseph	Secretary's Asst	SUPERB	
EDWARDS, Henry	Lieutenant. R.N.	ATLAS	
ELGAR, John	Ord	SUPERB	
ELLENDER, John	Bosun's Mate	NORTHUMBERLAND	*(M.L. as ELANDER)*
	L.M.	AMAZON	*Amazon. 13 Jany 1797*
ELLIOTT, William	Pte. R.M.	DONEGAL	
EMBLIN, George	Midshipman	CANOPUS	
EVANS, Edward	Ord	DONEGAL	
EVANS, Gustavus	Master's Mate	EPERVIER	
	Lieutenant. R.N.	CHERUB	*Martinique*
	Lieutenant. R.N.	CHERUB	*Guadaloupe*
FAIRHOLME, Adam	Lieutenant R.N.	DONEGAL	
FARRANT, William	Midshipman	CANOPUS	
FEAR, Hugh	A.B.	SUPERB	
	A.B.	SUPERB	*B.S. 11 Aug 1808*
	A.B.	VICTORIOUS	*Victorious with Rivoli*
FERGUSON, John McP.	Lieutenant. R.N.	SUPERB	
	Lieutenant. R.N.	REDWING	*Redwing. 7 May 1808*
	Lieutenant. R.N.	REDWING (P)	*Redwing. 31 May 1808*
FERRIES, John	Boy 2nd Class	DONEGAL	
	Ord	DONEGAL	*Basque Roads 1809*
FIDGE, Richard	L.M.	SPENCER	*G.H. 7715*
	A.B.	VICTORIOUS	*Victorious with Rivoli*
FINN, John	L.M.	CANOPUS	*G.H. 7414*
FISHER, James	A.B.	SUPERB	*G.H. 2846*
	Ord	SUPERB	*Gut of Gibraltar. 12 July 1801*
FISHER, Joseph	A.B.	ATLAS	
FITZGERALD, Thomas	Ord	CANOPUS	
FLYNN, Cornelius	L.M.	AGAMEMNON	*G.H. 9705*
	L.M.	AGAMEMNON	*Trafalgar*
FLYNN, Peter	Pte. R.M.	AGAMEMNON	
	Pte. R.M.	AGAMEMNON	*Trafalgar*
FOOTMAN, John	Ord	ACASTA	
FORBES, Henry	Lieutenant. R.N.	DONEGAL	
	A.B.	PHOEBE	*Trafalgar*
	Lieutenant. R.N.	DONEGAL	*Basque Roads 1809*
FORBES, John	Lieutenant. R.N.	CANOPUS	
	Midshipman	MINOTAUR	*Nile*
	Lieutenant. R.N.	FLORENTINA	*Egypt*
FORD, Joseph	L.M.	SPENCER	
	L.M.	VICTORIOUS	*Victorious with Rivoli*
FOWKES, Joseph	Pte. R.M.	DONEGAL	
FRASER, John	Volunteer 1st Cl	ACASTA	
FRAZER, David	Ord	AGAMEMNON	
	Ord	AGAMEMNON	*Trafalgar*
FRAZIER, John	A.B.	SUPERB	
	Ord	SUPERB	*Gut of Gibraltar. 12 July 1801*
FREER, John	Pte. R.M.	CANOPUS	
FROST, William	Pte. R.M.	NORTHUMBERLAND	
FRIDAY, Israel	A.B.	ATLAS	
	A.B.	SWIFTSURE	*Egypt*
FULLOVE, John	Boy	KINGFISHER	
FURNEAUX, John	Volunteer 1st Cl	ACASTA	
GARDNER, William	L.M.	SPENCER	
GARTH, Ralph	Boy	NORTHUMBERLAND	
GIBBS, William	Ord	ATLAS	
GIBSON, Uriah	Carp's Crew	NORTHUMBERLAND	
GILBERT, Edmund.W.	Midshipman	CANOPUS	
	Lieutenant. R.N.	GLASGOW	*Algiers*
GILBERT, John	L.M.	CANOPUS	
GILL, James	Ord	DONEGAL	*G.H. 308*

GILLESPIE, William	L.M.	NORTHUMBERLAND	
GLOVER, John	Ord	NEPTUNE	Martinique
GLOVER, Walter	Ord	SUPERB	
	Sergeant. R.M.	DONEGAL	
GOFF, Richard	A.B.	ACASTA	
	A.B.	BRUNSWICK	1 June 1794
GOLDSWORTHY, James	Ord	ACASTA	
GOODFELLOW, Thomas	L.M.	ATLAS	
GORDON, William	Midshipman	KINGFISHER	
	Midshipman	IMPERIEUSE	Basque Roads 1809
GOWEN, Elliott	Caulker's Mate	NORTHUMBERLAND	
GRANT, James	Pte. R.M.	NORTHUMBERLAND	
GREEN, Mark	L.M.	CANOPUS	G.H. 10,082
GREEN, Richard	L.M.	ATLAS	G.H. 8307
GRICE, William	Pte. R.M.	CANOPUS	
GRIMMER, William	A.B.	ATLAS	
GRINDRED, John	A.B.	ATLAS	
HAINES, Thomas	Coxswain	SUPERB	
	Ord	SOUTHAMPTON	Southampton. 9 June 1976 (Vfd Abd. Not on Roll)
	Ord	SOUTHAMPTON	St Vincent
	Coxswain	SUPERB	Gut of Gibraltar. 12 July 1801
	Gunner	ACASTA	Martinique
	Gunner	POMPEE	Pompee. 17 June 1809 (Vfd Abd. Not on Roll)
	Gunner	POMPEE	Guadaloupe (Medal displayed.R.N.Museum)
HALL, Charles	Pte. R.M.	SUPERB	
	Pte. R.M.	SUPERB	Gut of Gibraltar 12 July 1801
HARGREAVES, John	Ord	ACASTA	
HARRETT, Robert	Ord	SPENCER	
	A.B.	VICTORIOUS	Victorious with Rivoli
HARRIS, William	Boy	ACASTA	
	Boy	ACASTA	Martinique
	Ord	SCIPION	Java
HARRISON, John	Pte. R.M.	SUPERB	
HASSETT, Nathaniel	A.B.	SUPERB	
HAWES, Richard	L.M.	DONEGAL	
HAWKINS, Joseph	Ord	DONEGAL	
HAWKINS, Joseph	L.M.	NORTHUMBERLAND	
	A.B.	NEPTUNE	Martinique
HAYES, Edward.W.	Midshipman	MAGICIENNE	
HENWOOD, Peter	Purser	ACASTA	
	Clerk	VETERAN	Camperdown
HEPBURN, John	Master	CANOPUS	
	Master	MINOTAUR	Egypt
HERRON, David	Ord	DONEGAL	
HIBBERT, John	Pte. R.M.	CANOPUS	
HICKS, Richard	Ord	CANOPUS	
HICKS, William	A.B.	CANOPUS	
	Boy	MAJESTIC	Nile
HIGGINS, William	Gunner	EPERVIER	
HILL, John	Boy 3rd Class	MAGICIENNE	G.H. 3724
	L.M.	MODESTE	Java
HILL, William	Corporal. R.M.	SPENCER	
HOLMES, John	Ord	SUPERB	
HOOD, William	A.B.	MAGICIENNE	
HORAM, David	L.M.	NORTHUMBERLAND	
HORE, Samuel.B.	Midshipman	SPENCER	
	Lieut. R.N.	CAESAR	Basque Roads 1809
	Flag Lieut. R.N.	SCIPION	Java
HOSKEN, John	Carpenter	CANOPUS	
HUDSON, James	Ord	SUPERB	G.H. 8963
HUGHES, George	Carp's Crew	SUPERB	
HUTCHINSON, John	Ord	DONEGAL	
HUTTON, Lachlan	A.B.	SUPERB	
HYLAND, Patrick	L.M.	CANOPUS	G.H. 8365
IRVINE, Thomas.J.	Volunteer 1st Cl	SUPERB	
ISLES, Samuel	Supn (Unrated)	ACASTA	
JACKSON, Thomas	Midshipman	SUPERB	
	A.B.	SUPERB	Gut of Gibraltar. 12 July 1801
	Actg Lieut. R.N.	NASSAU (P?)	Nassau. 22 March 1808 (Vfd Abd. Not on Roll)
JAMES, William	Pte. R.M.	CANOPUS	
JEFFERY, Samuel	A.B.	ACASTA	
	A.B.	ACASTA	Martinique
	Yeoman of Sheets	SCIPION	Java
JESSEP, Thomas	Purser	NORTHUMBERLAND	
JOHNSON, John	A.B.	SUPERB	
	2 Borne. AB & LM	SUPERB	Gut of Gibraltar. 12 July 1801
JOHNSON, John	Ord	SUPERB	
JOHNSON, Peter	Ord	NORTHUMBERLAND	

ST DOMINGO

JOHNSTON, Charles.A.	Midshipman	AGAMEMNON	
	Midshipman	AGAMEMNON	*Trafalgar*
JONES, John	A.B.	CANOPUS	
JONES, William	Cooper	AGAMEMNON	
	Ord	AGAMEMNON	*Trafalgar*
JONES, William	A.B.	SPENCER	
KEATS, William	Volunteer 1st Cl	SUPERB	
KING, Robert	Ord	SUPERB	
KNIGHT, William	Midshipman	ATLAS	
LANGLEY, James	L.M.	SPENCER	*(M.L. as LONGLEY)*
	Ord	VICTORIOUS	*Victorious with Rivoli*
LAUGHARNE, Thomas.L.P.	Supn Midshipman	NORTHUMBERLAND	
	Lieutenant. R.N.	UNICORN	*Basque Roads 1809*
	Lieutenant. R.N.	NEREIDE	*B.S. 1 May 1810*
	Lieutenant. R.N.	BOADICEA (P)	*Boadicea. 18 Septr 1810*
LAVERIO, Antonie	A.B.	SPENCER	*G.H. 4944 as LOVARIO*
LAWSON, Robert	A.B.	SUPERB	
LEE, Thomas	A.B.	NORTHUMBERLAND	*G.H. 4913*
LEISTER, William	L.M.	KINGFISHER	*G.H. 8147 as LESTER*
Le NOURY, John	L.M.	DONEGAL	
LEWIS, William	Boy 2nd Class	AGAMEMNON	
	Boy 2nd Class	AGAMEMNON	*Trafalgar*
LLOYD, William	Midshipman	SUPERB	
	A.B.	SUPERB	*Gut of Gibraltar. 12 July 1801*
LOGIE, William	Pte. R.M.	DONEGAL	
	Pte. R.M.	COLOSSUS	*23rd June 1795*
	Pte. R.M.	BRILLIANT	*B.S. 29 Aug 1800*
LOVELL, Thomas	Midshipman	SPENCER	
LOWE, Joseph	L.M.	DONEGAL	*G.H. 8097*
LUCAS, Charles	Q.M.	DONEGAL	
	A.B.	TREMENDOUS	*1 June 1794*
MACKEY, John	Boy	CANOPUS	
	Supn Carp's Crew	IMPREGNABLE	*Algiers*
MACKEY, Robert	Boy 3rd Class	CANOPUS	
MANN, Peter	Q.M.	SUPERB	
MANNING, James	Ord	ATLAS	*G.H. 7948*
MANSELL, James	Ord	NORTHUMBERLAND	*G.H. 5668*
	Ord	NEPTUNE	*Martinique*
MARSHALL, John	Pte. R.M.	CANOPUS	
	Pte. R.M.	PHOEBE	*PHOEBE. 28 March 1814 (Ex CHERUB. Roll)*
MARTIN, George	Ord	NORTHUMBERLAND	
MARTIN, John	A.B.	SUPERB	
MATTHEWS, James	Ord	NORTHUMBERLAND	*(Alias MATHER)*
MATTHEWS, Robert	Ord	NORTHUMBERLAND	
MATTHEWS, William	Boy	CANOPUS	
MAXWELL, John	Bosun's Mate	NORTHUMBERLAND	
MAYNING, James	Ord	SPENCER	*(Applied as a Boatswain)*
	A.B.	VICTORIOUS	*Victorious with Rivoli*
McADAM, Alexander	L.M.	NORTHUMBERLAND	
	L.M.	NEPTUNE	*Martinique*
	L.M.	POMPEE	*Guadaloupe*
McALLISTER, William	L.M.	AGAMEMNON	*(Vfd Abd. Not on Roll)*
	L.M.	AGAMEMNON	*Trafalgar*
	Ord	BEDFORD	*B.S. 14 Dec 1814*
McCANN, John	M.A.A.	AGAMEMNON	
	Pte. R.M.	ARDENT	*Copenhagen 1801*
	M.A.A.	AGAMEMNON	*Trafalgar*
McCLAY, John	Ord	DONEGAL	
	Gunner's Mate	MADRAS	*Egypt*
	Q.M.	DONEGAL	*Basque Roads 1809*
McCLUNE, Thomas	L.M.	CANOPUS	
McELROY, John.F.	Ord	SUPERB	
	A.B.	LOIRE	*Guadaloupe*
McKEACHING, Archibald	A.B.	SUPERB	
McLAREN, Thomas	A.B.	NORTHUMBERLAND	*G.H. 5968*
	A.B.	NEPTUNE	*Martinique*
McLAREN, Thomas	L.M.	NORTHUMBERLAND	*G.H. 5641 (M.L. as McLARMAN)*
McLEAN, Alexander	Pte. R.M.	ACASTA	
McSWEENY, Morgan	Pte. R.M.	ATLAS	
	Pte. R.M.	WARRIOR	*Copenhagen 1801*
MESSENGER, Edward	Pte. R.M.	SPENCER	
	Pte. R.M.	LONDON	*Copenhagen 1801*
MELVILLE, William	Pte. R.M.	SUPERB	*G.H. 9546*
	Drummer. R.M.	SUPERB	*Gut of Gibraltar. 12 July 1801*
MILLER, Robert	Drummer. R.M.	NORTHUMBERLAND	*G.H. 9704*
	Drummer. R.M.	STATELY	*Stately. 22 March 1808*
MILLS, Joseph	Qtr Gunner	KINGFISHER	
MILLS, Peter	Armourer's Mate	NORTHUMBERLAND	
MILTON, Edward	Pte. R.M.	ATLAS	

MITCHELL, Henry	A.B.	CANOPUS	(First seaman awarded Anchor Ty LS & GC Medal)
MITCHELL, James	Carp's Crew	AGAMEMNON	
MITCHENER, James	Pte. R.M.	CANOPUS	
	Pte. R.M.	EDGAR	Copenhagen 1801
	Pte. R.M.	ANDROMACHE	St Sebastian
MOLESWORTH, John	Midshipman	CANOPUS	
MONTAGU, Montagu	Actg Flag Lieut. R.N.	SUPERB	
MOORE, Edward	Ord	AGAMEMNON	G.H. 7023
	Ord	AGAMEMNON	Trafalgar
	Carp's Crew	BEDFORD	B.S. 14 Dec 1814
MOORE, John	Gunner	DONEGAL	
MOORE, Thomas	Ord	ATLAS	
MOORMAN, Richard	Master's Mate	DONEGAL	
MORAN, John	Pte. R.M.	NORTHUMBERLAND	G.H. 9461
	Pte. R.M.	NEPTUNE	Martinique
MORGAN, James	Ord	SPENCER	
	L.M.	BRUNSWICK	1 June 1794
	Ord	ROBUST	23rd June 1795
	Ord	ROBUST	12 Octr 1798
MORGAN, John	L.M.	AGAMEMNON	
	L.M.	AGAMEMNON	Trafalgar
MORGAN, Richard	Ord	CANOPUS	
	Supn Midshipman	TONNANT	B.S. 14 Dec 1814
MORGAN, Thomas	Ord	CANOPUS	G.H. 2964
MORRIS, Charles	Midshipman	DONEGAL	
MORRIS, George	Pte. R.M.	CANOPUS	
MURRAY, John	Ord	DONEGAL	
NAYLOR, Edward	1st Lieut. R.M.	ACASTA	
	1st Lieut. R.M.	VANGUARD	Nile
NEAME, William	Midshipman	SPENCER	
NELSON, Charles	Midshipman	SUPERB	
NELSON, William	Supernumerary	NORTHUMBERLAND	
NICHOLLS, William	A.B.	SUPERB	
	Gunner's Mate	BUCEPHALUS	Java
NORTHWOOD, Joseph	A.B.	CANOPUS	
OGILVIE, Henry	Midshipman	DONEGAL	
	Master's Mate	DONEGAL	Basque Roads 1809
	Midshipman	AKBAR	Java
O'MALEY, Edward	Purser	KINGFISHER	
PALMER, Edward.G.	Midshipman	DONEGAL	
PANTON, Paul.G.	Midshipman	CANOPUS	
PARKINSON, James	L.M.	NORTHUMBERLAND	
	Ord	NEPTUNE	Martinique
PARR, Alexander.F.	Midshipman	AGAMEMNON	
	Midshipman	SWIFTSURE	Nile (see notes)
	Midshipman	PENELOPE	Egypt
	Midshipman	AGAMEMNON	Trafalgar
PATIENCE, Hugh	A.B.	NORTHUMBERLAND	
PATRIARCHE, Charles	Lieutenant. R.N.	SUPERB	
	Master's Mate	DEFENCE	Nile
	Lieutenant. R.N.	SUPERB	Gut of Gibraltar. 12 July 1801 (Vfd Abd. Not on Roll)
PATTERSON, Francis	A.B.	CANOPUS	
	Ord	PCSS ROYAL	14 March 1795
	A.B.	RUSSELL	Camperdown
	A.B.	RUSSELL	Copenhagen 1801
PAUL, John.H.	A.B.	CANOPUS	
PEARSON, Charles	Midshipman	SPENCER	
	Boy	St GEORGE	Copenhagen 1801
	Midshipman	SCIPION	Java
	Lieutenant. R.N.	PRESIDENT	St Sebastian
PERT, Robert	A.B.	AGAMEMNON	
	A.B.	AGAMEMNON	Trafalgar
PETERS, James	A.B.	SUPERB	
PHILLIPS, Edward	Pte. R.M.	SUPERB	
PICKARD, James	Lieutenant. R.N.	CANOPUS	
PIDGEON, John	Carp's Crew	ATLAS	
PINTO, Thomas	Lieutenant. R.N.	AGAMEMNON	
	Midshipman	IRRESISTIBLE	St Vincent
	Master's Mate	NORTHUMBERLAND	Egypt
	Lieutenant. R.N.	AGAMEMNON	Trafalgar
	Commander	ACHATES	B.S. 13 Dec 1809
	Commander	ACHATES	Guadaloupe
PITMAN, William	Pte. R.M.	CANOPUS	

ST DOMINGO

POLLARD, John	L.M.	AGAMEMNON	G.H.7129 (ML as Joseph)
	L.M.	AGAMEMNON	Trafalgar
PRITCHARD, Robert	L.M.	MAGICIENNE	
	Ropemaker	MODESTE	Java
PUMMELL, Samuel	Ord	DONEGAL	
	A.B.	RUSSELL	1 June 1794
	A.B.	RUSSELL	23rd June 1795
	Not Given	Not Given	Basque Roads 1809 (See ADM 171/2/69)
PURKIS, James	Boy 2nd Class	MAGICIENNE	
	Boy 1st Class	MODESTE	Java
PURVIS, John	Ord	SUPERB	
	Ord	SUPERB	Gut of Gibraltar. 12 July 1801
PYLE, John	Pte. R.M.	SPENCER	
QUINTON, James	Midshipman	AGAMEMNON	
or St QUINTON	Volunteer 1st Cl	AGAMEMNON	Trafalgar
RAMSAY, Edward	Midshipman	ATLAS	
RANDALL, William	Boy recruit	SUPERB	G.H. 8971
RANT, Job	L.M.	ATLAS	
RASTON, William	Ord	SUPERB	
RAYMOND, William	A.B.	EPERVIER	
REDGRAVE, Simon	A.B.	MAGICIENNE	
REEVE, John	Master's Mate	AGAMEMNON	
	Midshipman	AGAMEMNON	Copenhagen 1801
	Master's Mate	AGAMEMNON	Trafalgar
	Lieutenant. R.N.	L'AIMABLE	B.S. 27 July 1809
RIAN, Edward	L.M.	SPENCER	
RIBISON, William	A.B.	CANOPUS	G.H. 8139 as ROBINSON
ROBBINS, William	Ord	NORTHUMBERLAND	
ROBERTSON, Francis	A.B.	SUPERB	
ROBINSON, James	Yeoman of Sheets	SUPERB	
	A.B.	SUPERB	Gut of Gibraltar. 12 July 1801
ROBINSON, Joseph	Ord	AGAMEMNON	
	Ord	AGAMEMNON	Trafalgar
ROBINSON, Thomas	A.B.	AGAMEMNON	
	A.B.	AGAMEMNON	Trafalgar
	A.B.	ELIZABETH	B.S. 24 May 1814
ROGER, Joseph	Carp's Crew	SUPERB	
ROOD, George	Boy 2nd Class	DONEGAL	
ROOFE, Henry	L.M.	AGAMEMNON	
	L.M.	AGAMEMNON	Trafalgar
	Ord	LEANDER	Algiers
ROOK, Edward	Carp's Crew	DONEGAL	
	Carp's Crew	DONEGAL	Basque Roads 1809
ROPER, John	Q.M.	SPENCER	
ROSS, Henry.P.B.	Volunteer 1st Cl	AGAMEMNON	
	Volunteer 1st Cl	AGAMEMNON	Trafalgar
ROWE, Benjamin	Carp's Crew	ATLAS	G.H. 9598
RUNDLE, James	Ord	ATLAS	
RYLEY, John	Q.M.	SUPERB	
	A.B.	SUPERB	Gut of Gibraltar. 12 July 1801
SALTER, John	Midshipman	SUPERB	
	Master's Mate	NORTHUMBERLAND	Northumberland. 22 May 1812
SAMWAYS, John	Boy	CANOPUS	
SANG, Andrew	Ord	ACASTA	
SARE, Matthew	A.B.	ACASTA	
SEARLE, Thomas	Ord	DONEGAL	
SEYMOUR, George.F.	Lieutenant. R.N.	NORTHUMBERLAND	
	Captain. R.N.	PALLAS	Basque Roads 1809
SHEAD, Peter	L.M.	SPENCER	
	Ord	VICTORIOUS	Victorious with Rivoli
SHELDON, William	Pte. R.M.	ATLAS	G.H. 10,074
SHEPPARD, John	Q.M.	DONEGAL	
SHEPPARD, John	Pte. R.M.	DONEGAL	G.H. 776
SHIVERS, William	L.M.	NORTHUMBERLAND	
SILCOCK, Henry	Ord	AGAMEMNON	(M.L. as SINCOCK)
	Ord	AGAMEMNON	Trafalgar
SMITH, Alexander	2nd Lieut. R.M.	DONEGAL	
SMITH, George	L.M.	SPENCER	
	A.B.	CAPTAIN	Martinique
SMITH, James	Ord	SPENCER	G.H. 8347
	Ord	VICTORIOUS	Victorious with Rivoli
SNETT, William	Sailmaker	DONEGAL	
SPIERS, William	Midshipman	CANOPUS	
STANLAKE, John	A.B.	CANOPUS	
STANLEY, W.P.	Midshipman	NORTHUMBERLAND	
STEVENS, William	A.B.	CANOPUS	

Name	Rank	Ship	Action
STEWART, James.P.	Lieutenant. R.N.	NORTHUMBERLAND	
	Commander	SHELDRAKE	Anholt. 27 March 1811
	Captain. R.N.	DICTATOR	Off Mardoe. 6 July 1812
STEWART, William	Gunner	KINGFISHER	
STODDART, John	Boy 2nd Class	AGAMEMNON	
	Boy 2nd Class	AGAMEMNON	Trafalgar
	A.B.	ELIZABETH	B.S. 24 May 1814
STOPFORD, Robert	Captain. R.N.	SPENCER	
	Captain. R.N.	AQUILON	1 June 1794
	Captain. R.N.	PHAETON	17 June 1795
	Captain R.N.	CAESAR	Basque Roads 1809
	Rear Admiral	SCIPION	Java
	Admiral	PCSS CHARLOTTE	Syria (GCB. GCMG)
STURGEON, Roger	Corporal. R.M.	AGAMEMNON	
	Pte. R.M.	VANGUARD	Nile
	Pte. R.M.	AGAMEMNON	Trafalgar
SUDDRY, John	Pte. R.M.	SUPERB	
SUETT, William	Sailmaker	DONEGAL	
SUGG, Edmund	Sergeant. R.M.	SUPERB	
	Pte. R.M.	SUPERB	Gut of Gibraltar.12 July 1801
	Sergeant. R.M.	EREBUS	The Potomac 17 Aug 1814
SUGGETT, Christopher	Qtr Gunner	SUPERB	
	Ord	SUPERB	Gut of Gibraltar.12 July 1801
SUTHERLAND, Andrew	L.M.	NORTHUMBERLAND	
	A.B.	NEPTUNE	Martinique
	A.B.	ABERCROMBIE	Guadaloupe
SWAMARHEUGE, William	Not Given	CANOPUS	GH.2714 as SWINARCKRUZE
TALLENCE, Samuel	A.B.	AGAMEMNON	
	A.B.	AGAMEMNON	Trafalgar
	Boatswain	PELORUS	Martinique
	Boatswain	PELORUS	Guadaloupe
	Boatswain	MUTINE	Algiers
TAYLOR, Cornelius	L.M.	ATLAS	
TAYLOR, James	Ord	DONEGAL	
TAYLOR, John	Master's Mate	DONEGAL	
	Midshipman	GIBRALTAR	Egypt
	Lieutenant. R.N.	DONEGAL	Basque Roads 1809
TAYLOR, William	2 borne AB & QM	AGAMEMNON	
TEMPLEMAN, John.W.	Midshipman	SPENCER	
THOMAS, William	L.M.	SPENCER	
THOMSON, Thomas	A.B.	ACASTA	
	Qtr Gunner	BELLEISLE	Martinique
THORN, George	Boy 3rd Class	DONEGAL	
	L.M.	DONEGAL	Basque Roads 1809
THORN, John	A.B.	DONEGAL	
THURNELL, John	L.M.	AGAMEMNON	G.H. 9389
	Boy 2nd Class	AGAMEMNON	Trafalgar
TIBBELDS, Thomas	Boy 2nd Class	CANOPUS	G.H. 9324
TINSLEY, John	Pte. R.M.	SUPERB	
	Pte. R.M.	SUPERB	Gut of Gibraltar.12 July 1801
TISDALL, Archibald	Supernumerary	NORTHUMBERLAND	
	Lieutenant. R.N.	SCIPION	Java
TOWNSEND, James	Lieutenant. R.N.	ATLAS	
	Midshipman	SANSPAREIL	23rd June 1795
TREMBLETT, Robert	L.M.	CANOPUS	
TREVERTHERN, Michael	Pte. R.M.	DONEGAL	
TRIGIDJO, William	Ord	NORTHUMBERLAND	
TROMEY/TWOMEY, Patrick	A.B.	CANOPUS	(See note in ALGIERS)
	Capt' After Guard	SUPERB	Algiers
TUCKER, Thomas.T.	Lieutenant. R.N.	NORTHUMBERLAND	
	Commander	CHERUB	Martinique
	Commander	CHERUB	Guadaloupe
	Commander	CHERUB (P)	Cherub 28 March 1814
TURTON, Thomas	Ord	ATLAS	
VINCENT, John	A.B.	SPENCER	
VINICOMBE, James	Pte. R.M.	CANOPUS	
WALKER, George	L.M.	ATLAS	
WALKER, John	3 borne	MAGICIENNE	AB & Ord & LM
WALLS, Richard	Ord	AGAMEMNON	
	Ord	AGAMEMNON	Trafalgar
WATERS, James	L.M.	AGAMEMNON	
	L.M.	AGAMEMNON	Trafalgar
WATERS, John	Ord	ACASTA	
WEAVERS, William	Volunteer 1st Cl	AGAMEMNON	
	Volunteer 1st Cl	AGAMEMNON	Trafalgar
WEBB, Robert	2nd Lieut. R.M.	SUPERB	
WELSTEAD, Frederick	Lieutenant. R.N.	CANOPUS	
WHITALEY, Joseph	Ord	CANOPUS	

ST DOMINGO

WHITE, John	Midshipman	SUPERB	
	Midshipman	SUPERB	*Gut of Gibraltar. 12 July 1801*
	Lieutenant. R.N.	BARRACOUTA	*Banda Neira*
	Lieutenant. R.N.	BARRACOUTA	*Java*
WHITE, John	L.M.	AGAMEMNON	
	L.M.	AGAMEMNON	*Trafalgar*
WHITE, William	A.B.	NORTHUMBERLAND	
	A.B.	NEPTUNE	*Martinique*
WHITE, William	L.M.	SPENCER	
WILCOX, George	Sergeant. R.M.	SPENCER	
WILDS, William	Qtr Gunner	ATLAS	*G.H. 3494*
WILLIAMS, John (4)	A.B.	SUPERB	
WILLIAMS, Thomas	Lieutenant. R.N.	CANOPUS	
	Midshipman	MINOTAUR	*Nile*
WILSON, John	Ord	SUPERB	
	2 borne. AB & LM	SUPERB	*Gut of Gibraltar. 12 July 1801*
WILTON, George	Armourer	AGAMEMNON	
	Armourer	AGAMEMNON	*Trafalgar*
WILTSHIRE, Thomas	Armourer's Mate	AGAMEMNON	
	Armourer's Mate	AGAMEMNON	*Trafalgar*
	Armourer	HYACINTH	*Malaga. 29 April 1812*
WORSLEY, Thomas	Ord	EPERVIER	
WRIGHT, William	Sailmaker's Crew	DONEGAL	
YERBURY, Francis	Corporal. R.M.	CANOPUS	
YOUNG, William	Ord	CANOPUS	

(30) AMAZON 13 MARCH 1806

Capture of the French 80-gun MARENGO and 40-gun BELLE POULE, – the latter by AMAZON, whilst making for Brest.

ACTON, John	A.B.	AMAZON	
BERRY, Thomas	A.B.	AMAZON	
BOWERS, William	Boy 3rd Cl	AMAZON	
CARLETON, William	Midshipman	AMAZON	
	Midshipman	COLOSSUS	*Trafalgar*
COMFORT, Henry	Ord	AMAZON	
COURTENAY, George.W.C.	Vol 1st Cl	AMAZON	
COX, William	A.B.	AMAZON	*G.H. 3,330*
	A.B.	BACCHANTE	*B.S. 6 Jan 1813*
DAWSON, John	L.M.	AMAZON	
DAY, John	Ord	AMAZON	
DEACON, Henry.C.	Midshipman	AMAZON	
	Midshipman	NEREIDE	*B.S. 1 May 1810 (Not on Roll)*
			M.I.D. L.Gaz. 1810. pp1326.
GREEN, William	Sgt. R.M.	AMAZON	
HOSKINS, Samuel	Master's Mate	AMAZON	
HOSKINS, Thomas	Master	AMAZON	
HOWE, John	Ord	AMAZON	*(M.L. as HOW)*
LAVIS, James	Pte. R.M.	AMAZON	*(M.L. as LAVIES)*
LEAN, William	Ord	AMAZON	*(M.L. as LANE)*
MARCUS, John	Q.M.	AMAZON	
MONDAY, John	Boy 3rd Cl	AMAZON	
	Ord	BACCHANTE	*B.S. 1 & 18 Sep 1812*
	Ord	BACCHANTE	*B.S. 6 Jan 1813*
NIPPER, James	A.B.	AMAZON	*(Vfd Abd. Not on Roll)*
	Captain's Servant	MARLBOROUGH	*1 June 1794*
	A.B.	VICTORY	*Trafalgar*
PARKER, William	Captain. R.N.	AMAZON	
	Midshipman	ORION	*1 June 1794*
PAYNE, George	A.B.	AMAZON	
	Yeoman of Sheets	BACCHANTE	*B.S. 1 & 18 Sep 1812*
	Yeoman of Sheets	BACCHANTE	*B.S. 6 Jan 1813*
PAYNE, Joseph	Ord	AMAZON	
	Ord	BACCHANTE	*B.S. 6 Jan 1813*
RUNDLE, William	Carpenter's Crew	AMAZON	
SIMKIN, Thomas.A.	Midshipman	AMAZON	
SINCLAIR, Sir John.G.	Supn Midshipman	AMAZON	
	Commander	REDWING	*B.S. 2 May 1813*
SMITH, James	A.B.	AMAZON	
	Ord	VENGEANCE	*B.S. 17 Mar 1794*
STREATFEILD, Richard	Supn Midshipman	AMAZON	
TURNER, Jacob	A.B.	AMAZON	
WESTPHAL, Philip	Lieut. R.N.	AMAZON	
	Master's Mate	BLANCHE	*Copenhagen 1801*
YEASLEY, Joseph	Pte. R.M.	AMAZON	*(M.L. as YARLEY)*

(27) LONDON 13 MARCH 1806

Capture of the French 80-gun MARENGO and 40-gun BELLE POULE, – the former by LONDON, whilst making for Brest.

BLAKE, John	A.B.	LONDON	
	A.B.	LEVIATHAN	*Trafalgar*
BOOTH, James.R.	Midshipman	LONDON	
BURRARD, Charles	Midshipman	LONDON	
CARDEW, John.T.	2nd Lt. R.M.	LONDON	
COLLINS, Joseph	A.B.	LONDON	
	A.B.	LEVIATHAN	*Trafalgar*
COLLINSON, Robert	Q.M.	LONDON	
	Quarter Gunner	PALLAS	*17 June 1795*
	Q.M.	BELLEISLE	*Trafalgar*
COWLEY, William.K.	Clerk	LONDON	
DARLING, Andrew	Asst Surgeon	LONDON	
DOYLE, Joseph @ James	Boy 2nd Cl	LONDON	*G.H. 1588*
GLEESON, William	Coxswain	LONDON	
HARRIS, Charles	A.B.	LONDON	
HEGGIE, Archibald	A.B.	LONDON	
	Ord	MADRAS	*Egypt*
	A.B.	BELLEISLE	*Trafalgar*
HILL, Edward	A.B.	LONDON	
HOOPER, Benjamin	Midshipman	LONDON	
	Midshipman	FOUDROYANT	*12 Octr 1798*
	Lieut. R.N.	CALYPSO	*Off Mardoe. 6 July 1812*
HOUSE, Terence	L.M.	LONDON	
JOHNSON, Edward	Lieut. R.N.	LONDON	
	A.B.	BOYNE	*B.S. 17 Mar 1794*
	Master's Mate	St GEORGE	*Copenhagen 1801*
JONES, James	Ord	LONDON	
MUHLEG, William	A.B.	LONDON	*(M.L. as MULIG)*
	A.B.	BELLEISLE	*Trafalgar*
MURRAY, Charles	Pte. R.M.	LONDON	
	Pte. R.M.	HUSSAR	*Java*
OSBOURNE, James	Pte. R.M.	LONDON	
SMITH, William (1)	Ord	LONDON	
	Ord	BELLEISLE	*Trafalgar*
SMITH, William (2)	A.B.	LONDON	
	Ord	BELLEISLE	*Trafalgar*
SPARROW, Daniel	Pte. R.M.	LONDON	
SPARROW, James	Pte. R.M.	LONDON	
St CROIX, Alexander	Ord	LONDON	
SWEET, James	Armourer	LONDON	
	Armourer's Mate	CULLODEN	*1 June 1794*
	Armourer's Mate	CULLODEN	*St Vincent*
	Armourer's Mate	CULLODEN	*Nile*
	Armourer's Mate	TEMERAIRE	*Trafalgar*
WATKINS, James	L.M.	LONDON	
	L.M.	POMPEE	*Gut of Gibraltar. 12 July 1801*

(8) PIQUE 26 MARCH 1806

Capture of the French corvettes PHAETON and VOLTIGEUR, off St Domingo, West Indies.

BELL, Christopher	Lieut. R.N.	PIQUE	
BURKE, Benjamin	Boy 3rd Cl	PIQUE	
HUNGATE, William	Ord	PIQUE	
LLOYD, Rickard	Midshipman	PIQUE	
	Lieut. R.N.	SURINAM*	*Martinique (Not yet Abd)*
	Lieut. R.N.	NORGE	*B.S. 14 Decr 1814*
MOULDING, Thomas	Caulker	PIQUE	*G.H. 1183*
TRUSS, John	L.M.	PIQUE	*(M.L. as TRUST)*
	Boy 3rd Cl	DESIREE	*Copenhagen 1801*
	Ord	ELIZABETH	*Anse La Barque. 18 Decr 1809 (Vfd Abd. Not on Roll)*
	Ord	ELIZABETH	*Martinique (Vfd Abd. Not on Roll)*
	Captain of Mast	CYANE	*Cyane. 16 Jany 1814*
WARD, William	Lieut. R.N.	PIQUE	
	Midshipman	BARFLEUR	*23rd June 1795 (Vfd Abd. Not on Roll)*
	Midshipman	BARFLEUR	*St Vincent*
WILLIAMS, John	A.B.	PIQUE	

(20) SIRIUS 17 APRIL 1806

Action with a French flotilla, off CIVITA VECCHIA, and capture of the corvette BERGERE.

BEATSON, Robert	Carpenter	SIRIUS	(M.L. as BETSON)
BROWNRIGG, John	L.M.	SIRIUS	(Vfd Abd. Not on Roll)
	L.M.	SIRIUS	Trafalgar. G.H. 3,278
CONNOLLY, Patrick	Pte. R.M.	SIRIUS	
	Pte. R.M.	SIRIUS	Trafalgar
CREMER, John	L.M.	SIRIUS	(Vfd Abd. Not on Roll)
	L.M.	SIRIUS	Trafalgar. G.H. 5,697 (M.L. as CRAMER)
CROFTON, Morgan.G.	Midshipman	SIRIUS	
	Midshipman	SIRIUS	Trafalgar
CURLEY, Henry	L.M.	SIRIUS	
	L.M.	SIRIUS	Trafalgar. (Vfd Abd. Not on Roll)
DAVIS, John	A.B.	SIRIUS	(Vfd Abd. Not on Roll)
	A.B.	SIRIUS	Trafalgar
GERMAN, William	L.M.	SIRIUS	(Vfd Abd. Not on Roll)
	L.M.	SIRIUS	Trafalgar
HENNESSEY, John	Boy 3rd Cl	SIRIUS	(M.L. as @ SMITH, George)
	Boy 3rd Cl	SIRIUS	Trafalgar
INGRAM, John	Sgt. R.M.	SIRIUS	
	Pte. R.M.	SURPRISE	Surprise Wh Hermione
	Sgt. R.M.	SIRIUS	Trafalgar
MAGIN, William	1st Lt. R.M.	SIRIUS	
	1st Lt. R.M.	TONNANT	Trafalgar
MAY, Isaac	Pte. R.M.	SIRIUS	(Vfd Abd. Not on Roll)
	Pte. R.M.	SIRIUS	Trafalgar
MEALY, Edward	Ord	SIRIUS	(Vfd Abd. Not on Roll)
	L.M.	SIRIUS	Trafalgar
PERRY, Hugh	Gunner	SIRIUS	(Vfd Abd. Not on Roll)
	Gunner	SIRIUS	Trafalgar
PRICELY, Jonathan	A.B.	SIRIUS	(Vfd Abd. Not on Roll)
	A.B.	SIRIUS	Trafalgar
ROBERTSON, Thomas	Surgeon	SIRIUS	
	Surgeon	LEDA	Egypt
	Surgeon	SIRIUS	Trafalgar
SCULLY, Dennis	L.M.	SIRIUS	G.H. 8,504 (Vfd Abd. Not on Roll)
	L.M.	SIRIUS	Trafalgar
SHEEHY, Edward	L.M.	SIRIUS	(Vfd Abd. Not on Roll)
	L.M.	SIRIUS	Trafalgar. G.H. 7,024 (M.L. as SHEEHAN, Edmund)
THOMAS, William	L.M.	SIRIUS	
	L.M.	SIRIUS	Trafalgar
TURNER, John	Supn Midshipman	SIRIUS	

(52) 16 JULY BOAT SERVICE 1806

Cutting out of the French corvette CESAR in the Verdun Roads, off River Gironde.

BAILLIE, William	Pte. R.M.	INDEFATIGABLE	
	Pte. R.M.	INDEFATIGABLE	Basque Roads. 1809
BARNES, John	Pte. R.M.	MONARCH	
BIDDULPH, Edward	Midshipman	INDEFATIGABLE	
	Master's Mate	INDEFATIGABLE	Basque Roads. 1809
BLAKISTON, Thomas	Midshipman	REVENGE	(P.O.W. this Action)
BOWEN, George	Lieut. R.N.	CONQUEROR	
	Master's Mate	CENTURION	Centurion. 18 Sept 1804 (Vfd Abd. Not on Roll)
	Master's Mate	NAMUR	4 Novr 1805
BREHANT, Henry	Gunner	MONARCH	
CARROLL, Peter	L.M.	CONQUEROR	(M.L. as CARROL)
	L.M.	CONQUEROR	Trafalgar
CAVANAGH, Edward	L.M.	IRIS*	(Joined after Action)
CLARK, Alexander	Q.M.'s Mate	MONARCH	G.H. 4,967
CLARK, Daniel	L.M.	CENTAUR	(M.L. as CLARKE) GH. 2886
	L.M.	CENTAUR	Centaur. 26 Augt 1808
CLARKE, William	1st Lieut. R.M.	CENTAUR	
	1st Lieut. R.M.	CENTAUR	Centaur. 26 Augt 1808
CORNMAN, Philip	A.B.	ACHILLE	G.H. 9,296
CONWAY, James	L.M.	REVENGE	(Vfd Abd. Not on Roll)
	L.M.	REVENGE	Trafalgar. G.H. 7,950
	L.M.	REVENGE	Basque Roads. 1809. (Vfd Abd. Not on Roll)
DEARNESS, John	Ord	MONARCH	
	Ord	HOGUE	B.S. 8 April 1814
DOBSON, Jeremiah	Ord	CENTAUR	
	Ord	CENTAUR	B.S. 4 Feb 1804
	Ord	CENTAUR	Centaur. 26 Augt 1808 (Vfd Abd. Not on Roll)

THE NAVAL GENERAL SERVICE MEDAL ROLL 1793–1840

FENNER, John	Ord	POLYPHEMUS	
	Ord	POLYPHEMUS	*Trafalgar*
FISHER, John	Carp's Mate	IRIS	
FLITT, James	A.B.	CONQUEROR	*(M.L. as FLATT)*
	A.B.	BEAULIEU	*Camperdown*
	A.B.	CONQUEROR	*Trafalgar*
GEARY, John	Master's Mate	MONARCH	
	Midshipman	REVENGE	*Trafalgar*
HARRISON, Francis	L.M.	MONARCH	
	Ord	HOGUE	*B.S. 8 April 1814*
HILLIARD, Richard	A.B.	REVENGE	
	A.B.	REVENGE	*Basque Roads. 1809*
HOWSE, Henry	L.M.	MONARCH	*G.H. 3,068*
JAMES, John	A.B.	CENTAUR	
	Ord	CENTAUR	*B.S. 4 Feb 1804*
	Captain Main Top	CENTAUR	*B.S. 26 Augt 1808*
LANE, William	L.M.	MONARCH	
LESLIE, John	A.B.	INDEFATIGABLE	
	A.B.	INDEFATIGABLE	*Basque Roads. 1809*
LEWIS, William	A.B.	POLYPHEMUS	
	A.B.	POLYPHEMUS	*Trafalgar*
MACDONALD, James	L.M.	PRINCE OF WALES	
MACKINTOSH, John	1st Lt R.M.	POLYPHEMUS	
	2nd Lt R.M.	POLYPHEMUS	*Copenhagen 1801*
	1st Lt R.M.	POLYPHEMUS	*Trafalgar*
McGINN, William	Ord	POLYPHEMUS	*(M.L. as MEQUIN)*
@ MAGINN	Ord	POLYPHEMUS	*Trafalgar. GH. 2585*
MANNING, Henry	Carp's Crew	CENTAUR	
	A.B.	CENTAUR	*B.S. 4 Feb 1804*
	Carp's Crew	CENTAUR	*Centaur. 26 Augt 1808*
MESSERVEY, John	Carp's Crew	CENTAUR	*G.H. 3,506*
	A.B.	CENTAUR	*B.S. 4 Feb 1804*
	Carp's Crew	CENTAUR	*Centaur. 26 Augt 1808*
NICHOLAS, John	Vol 1st Cl	ACHILLE	
PARKER, Kenyon.S.	2nd Lt. R.M.	MONARCH	
PLUMMER, William	Pte. R.M.	PRINCE OF WALES	
POPE, Peter	A.B.	ACHILLE	
	A.B.	ACHILLE	*Trafalgar*
RAINS, John	A.B.	POLYPHEMUS	
	A.B.	POLYPHEMUS	*Trafalgar*
RICHARDS, William	L.M.	CENTAUR	
	L.M.	CENTAUR	*Centaur. 26 Augt 1808*
RILEY, Thomas	L.M.	CONQUEROR	*(M.L. as RYLEY)*
	L.M.	CONQUEROR	*Trafalgar*
ROSE, Thomas	Pte. R.M.	CENTAUR	
SHARLAND, John	Ord	MONARCH	
SPARKS, Thomas	R.M. Boy	POLYPHEMUS	
STROVER, Thomas	Vol 1st Cl	CENTAUR	
	Ord	CENTAUR	*Centaur. 26 Augt 1808*
STUBLEY, Edward.J.	L.M.	MONARCH	
	Carp's Crew	HOGUE	*B.S. 8 April 1814*
TRIVIUS, Robert	A.B.	IRIS	*GH. 4383. (M.L. as TREVEIGNS)*
TURNER, William	Asst Surgeon	CONQUEROR	
	Surg's 1st Mate	CONQUEROR	*Trafalgar*
TURTON, James	Ord	PRINCE OF WALES	
WARNER, George	Ord	CENTAUR	
	Ord	CENTAUR	*B.S. 4 Feb 1804*
	Yeoman of Sheets	CENTAUR	*Centaur. 26 Augt 1808*
WATSON, Robert	Quarter Gunner	REVENGE	*(on separate medal)*
	A.B.	REVENGE	*Trafalgar*
	Q.M.	REVENGE	*Basque Roads. 1809*
WIGGINGTON, John	Pte. R.M.	MONARCH	*(M.L. as WIGGINTON)*
WILLIAMS, William	Two L.Ms borne	PRINCE OF WALES	
WILSON, Robert	A.B.	INDEFATIGABLE	
	A.B.	INDEFATIGABLE	*Basque Roads. 1809*
WINDSOR, Benjamin	Boy 3rd Cl	CENTAUR	
	Boy 3rd Cl	CENTAUR	*B.S. 4 Feb 1804*
	Boy 3rd Cl	CENTAUR	*Centaur. 26 Augt 1808.*

(22) BLANCHE 19 JULY 1806

Capture of the French frigate GUERRIERE, off the Faroe Islands.
(On 4 March 1807 BLANCHE was wrecked, off Ushant, many of her crew were made prisoners of war.)

BASTIN, Robert	Lieut. R.N.	BLANCHE	
	A.B.	NYMPHE	Nymphe 8 March 1797
			(Vfd Abd. Not on Roll)
	Lieut. R.N.	BELLEISLE	Trafalgar
CAMPBELL, John	1st Lt R.M.	BLANCHE	P.O.W. Escaped 1810.
COWEN, John	Midshipman (?)	BLANCHE	P.O.W. Attmtd Escape 1811
DAVIES, Henry.T.	Lieut. R.N.	BLANCHE (P)	
	Capt's Servant	GLORY	1 June 1794
	Lieut. R.N.	WINCHELSEA	Egypt
DYER, David	Boy 3rd Cl	BLANCHE	G.H. 6,469
EVANS, David	Ord	BLANCHE	Taken P.O.W. in prize Feb 1807, released March 1807. P.O.W. by Americans June 1813.
HOSKINS, William	Boy 2nd Cl	BLANCHE	P.O.W.
HOY, Robert	Vol 1st Cl	BLANCHE	P.O.W. to end of war.
HUGHES, Thomas	Boy 3rd Cl	BLANCHE	Probably a P.O.W.
IVES, James	Ord	BLANCHE	As EVANS above for 1807.
LONGLEY, William	Ord	BLANCHE	Probably a P.O.W.
MASTERS, Thomas.J.P.	Midshipman	BLANCHE	P.O.W. Escaped in 1808.
NEWELL, John	Ord	BLANCHE	G.H. 9,922 as NOWELL. Probably a P.O.W.
PATTERSON, John	Asst Surgeon	BLANCHE	P.O.W.
RUNDLE, Edward	Midshipman	BLANCHE*	Left ship before Action.
SCOTT, James	Midshipman	BLANCHE	
	Lieut. R.N.	MARLBOROUGH	B.S. Ap & May 1813
			M.G.S. Martinique. China 1842. Samarang/Nemesis
SCOTT, William	Cpl. R.M.	BLANCHE	Probably a P.O.W.
SECRETAN, James.F.	Vol 1st Cl	BLANCHE	P.O.W.
SOBEY, John	Boatswain	BLANCHE	
	Boatswain	SCEPTRE	Guadaloupe
STANTON, Thomas	A.B.	BLANCHE	Probably a P.O.W. GH. 2419
WEBBER, Thomas	Ord	BLANCHE	Probably a P.O.W.
WILLCOCK, Joseph.F.	Purser	BLANCHE	P.O.W. to end of War

(17) ARETHUSA 23 AUGT 1806

Capture of the Spanish frigate POMONA by ARETHUSA and ANSON, off Havana, Cuba.

ALDRIDGE, John.W.	Midshipman	ARETHUSA	
	Midshipman	ARETHUSA	Curacoa
BELLAIRS, John.H.	Midshipman	ARETHUSA	
	Ord	ARETHUSA	Curacoa
CHAPPLE, Michael	Pte. R.M.	ARETHUSA	GH.245 (M.L. as CHAPEL)
			(Vfd Abd. Not on Roll)
	Pte. R.M.	ARETHUSA	Curacoa
CONCANNON, Peter	Ord	ARETHUSA	(Vfd Abd. Not on Roll)
	Ord	ARETHUSA	Curacoa
COWAN, John	L.M.	ARETHUSA	G.H. 9,923 (Vfd Abd. Not on Roll)
	L.M.	ARETHUSA	Curacoa
ELLIOTT, John	Purser	ARETHUSA	
	Vol 1st Cl	MARS	Mars. 21 April 1798
	Clerk	RUSSELL	Copenhagen. 1801
	Purser	ARETHUSA	Curacoa
FIELD, John	Cpl. R.M.	ARETHUSA	(Vfd Abd. Not on Roll)
	Cpl. R.M.	ARETHUSA	Curacoa
FIELDING, Edward	Ord	ARETHUSA	GH. 5935 (M.L. as FLELING)
			(Incorrectly on ANSON Roll)
	Ord	ARETHUSA	Curacoa
FISHINGTON, Charles	A.B.	ARETHUSA	(Vfd Abd. Not on Roll)
	A.B.	ARETHUSA	Curacoa
GREENGRASS, George	Boy 2nd Cl	ARETHUSA	G.H. 6,018 (Vfd Abd. Not on Roll)
	Boy 2nd Cl	ARETHUSA	Curacoa
GRIFFIN, William	Ord	ARETHUSA	(Vfd Abd. Not on Roll)
	Ord	ARETHUSA	Curacoa
HAGLEY, James	L.M.	ARETHUSA	(Vfd Abd. Not on Roll)
	L.M.	ARETHUSA	Curacoa
HIGMAN, Henry	Lieut. R.N.	ARETHUSA	
	A.B.	CHARON	23rd June 1795
	Master's Mate	TRIUMPH	Camperdown
	Lieut. R.N.	ARETHUSA	Curacoa

JOHNSON, John	Ord	ARETHUSA	G.H. 8,836 (Vfd Abd. Not on Roll)
	Ord	ARETHUSA	*Curacoa*
REID, Curtis	Midshipman	ARETHUSA	
	Midshipman	ARETHUSA	*Curacoa*
SHEPHERD, James	A.B.	ARETHUSA	GH. 9917. (Vfd Abd. On G.H. Roll. Not on Adm 171/-)
	A.B.	ARETHUSA	*Curacoa*
SMITH, James	Ord	ARETHUSA	GH.8452. (Vfd Abd. On G.H. Roll. Not on Adm 171/-)
	Ord	ARETHUSA	*Curacoa*

(11) ANSON 23 AUGT 1806

Capture of the Spanish frigate POMONA by ARETHUSA and ANSON, off Havana, Cuba.

BURKE, James	Ord	ANSON	
	L.M.	TEMERAIRE	*Trafalgar*
	Ord	ANSON	*Curacoa*
	"Convict"	POMPEE	*Martinique. (Ex Mutineer)*
	Ord	LION	*Java (Re-instated)*
COSTELLO, Thomas	Boy 2nd Cl	ANSON	*(Vfd Abd. Not on Roll)*
	Boy 3rd Cl	TEMERAIRE	*Trafalgar*
	Boy 2nd Cl	ANSON	*Curacoa*
COUCHER, Christopher	L.M.	ANSON	
	L.M.	COLOSSUS	*Trafalgar*
	L.M.	ANSON	*Curacoa*
	Ord	TONNANT	*B.S. 14 Dec 1814*
COWARD, Stephen	Pte. R.M.	ANSON	G.H. 3,297
	Pte. R.M.	ANSON	*Curacoa*
DUGLASS, James	Ord	ANSON	GH.1764. (M.L. as DOUGLASS) (Vfd Abd. Not on Roll)
	L.M.	COLOSSUS	*Trafalgar*
	Ord	ANSON	*Curacoa*
HENLEY, Robert	Quarter Gunner	ANSON	
	A.B.	TEMERAIRE	*Trafalgar*
	Quarter Gunner	ANSON	*Curacoa*
JEFFERY, William	Coxswain	ANSON	
	Trumpeter	DEFENCE	*Trafalgar*
	M.A.A.	ANSON	*Curacoa*
LEVERTON, Richard	Yeoman Powder Rm	ANSON	GH.709. (M.Ls as LIVERTON & LIBERTINE) Vfd Abd but not on Adm 171/- Roll
	A.B.	ORION	*1 June 1794*
	A.B.	VETERAN	*Camperdown*
	Gunner's Mate	TEMERAIRE	*Trafalgar*
	Yeoman Pdr Room	ANSON	*Curacoa*
SALMON, Charles	Boy 3rd Cl	ANSON	*(Vfd Abd. Not on Roll)*
	Boy 3rd Cl	ANSON	*Curacoa*
SIMONS, George	Ord	ANSON	GH.9433 (M.L. as SIMMONS) (Vfd Abd. Not on Roll)
	L.M.	COLOSSUS	*Trafalgar*
	Ord	ANSON	*Curacoa*
SULLIVAN, Thomas.B.	Lieut. R.N.	ANSON	
	Lieut. R.N.	ANSON	*Curacoa*

(62) CURACOA (G.M.)
Taking of the Island of CURACOA on 1 January 1807.

ALDRIDGE, John.W.	Midshipman	ARETHUSA	
	Midshipman	ARETHUSA	Arethusa 23 Augt 1806
ARCHER, Thomas	Actg Master	MORNE FORTUNEE	
ATKINS, Thomas	Ord	LATONA	G.H. 9,138
BARCLAY, John	Lieut. R.N.	LATONA	
	Lieut. R.N.	BRITANNIA	Trafalgar
	Lieut. R.N.	PRESIDENT	St Sebastian (Vfd Abd. Not on Roll)
BASS, Joseph	L.M.	LATONA	(A "Prest" man shown as "Gangway Volunteer".)
BELLAIRS, John.H.	Ord	ARETHUSA	
	Midshipman	ARETHUSA	Arethusa 23 Augt 1806
BOWDEN, Philip	Midshipman	FISGARD	
BRISTOW, James	L.M.	LATONA	G.H. 7,483
BULLOCK, John	L.M.	LATONA	
BURKE, James	Ord	ANSON	
	L.M.	TEMERAIRE	Trafalgar
	Ord	ANSON	Anson. 23 Augt 1806
	"Convict"	POMPEE	Martinique. (Ex Mutineer)
	Ord	LION	Java (Re-instated)
CHAPPLE, Michael	Pte. R.M.	ARETHUSA	GH.245 (M.L. as CHAPEL)
	Pte. R.M.	ARETHUSA	Arethusa 23 Augt 1806 (Vfd Abd. Not on Roll)
CLARK, Alexander	Ord	MORNE FORTUNEE	(M.L. as Alx CLERK)
	A.B.	MORNE FORTUNEE	Off the Pearl Rock 13 Dec 1808
CONCANNON, Peter	Ord	ARETHUSA	
	Ord	ARETHUSA	Arethusa 23 Augt 1806 (Vfd Abd. Not on Roll)
CONNOR, Ross	Master's Mate	FISGARD	
	Vol 1st Cl	ARROW	Copenhagen. 1801
COOK, Thomas.F.	L.M.	LATONA	
COSTELLO, Thomas	Boy 2nd Cl	ANSON	
	Boy 3rd Cl	TEMERAIRE	Trafalgar
	Boy 2nd Cl	ANSON	Anson. 23 Augt 1806 (Vfd Abd. Not on Roll)
COUCHER, Christopher	L.M.	ANSON	
	L.M.	COLOSSUS	Trafalgar
	L.M.	ANSON	Anson 23 Augt 1806
	Ord	TONNANT	B.S. 14 Dec 1814
COURT, James	L.M.	LATONA	
COWAN, John	L.M.	ARETHUSA	G.H. 9,923
	L.M.	ARETHUSA	Arethusa. 23 Augt 1806 (Vfd Abd. Not on Roll)
COWARD, Stephen	Pte. R.M.	ANSON	G.H. 3,297
	Pte. R.M.	ANSON	Anson. 23 Augt 1806
DALTON, Joseph	Pte. R.M.	FISGARD	
DOWNES, Henry	Midshipman	FISGARD	
DUGLASS, James	Ord	ANSON	GH.1764. (M.L. as DOUGLASS)
	L.M.	COLOSSUS	Trafalgar
	Ord	ANSON	Anson. 23 Augt 1806 (Vfd Abd. Not on Roll)
DURRANT, George	Ord	ANSON	G.H. 7,598 as DURANT
	L.M.	COLOSSUS	Trafalgar
ELLIOTT, John	Purser	ARETHUSA	
	Vol 1st Cl	MARS	Mars. 21 April 1798
	Clerk	RUSSELL	Copenhagen. 1801
	Purser	ARETHUSA	Arethusa. 23 Augt 1806
FIELD, John	Cpl. R.M.	ARETHUSA	
	Cpl. R.M.	ARETHUSA	Arethusa. 23 Augt 1806 (Vfd Abd. Not on Roll)
FIELDING, Edward	Ord	ARETHUSA	GH.5935. (ML as FLELING)
	Ord	ARETHUSA	Arethusa. 23 Augt 1806 (Incorrectly on ANSON Roll)
FISHINGTON, Charles	A.B.	ARETHUSA	
	A.B.	ARETHUSA	Arethusa. 23 Augt 1806 (Vfd Abd. Not on Roll)
FORBESTER, Jacob	Ord	FISGARD	(M.L. as FORGESTER)
GREENGRASS, George	Boy 2nd Cl	ARETHUSA	G.H. 6,018
	Boy 2nd Cl	ARETHUSA	Arethusa. 23 Augt 1806 (Vfd Abd. Not on Roll)
GRIFFIN, William	Ord	ARETHUSA	
	Ord	ARETHUSA	Arethusa. 23 Augt 1806 (Vfd Abd. Not on Roll)
GRINT, William	Master's Mate	LATONA	
	Midshipman	AMAZON	Copenhagen. 1801
	Master's Mate	BRITANNIA	Trafalgar

HAGLEY, James	L.M.	ARETHUSA	
	L.M.	ARETHUSA	Arethusa. 23 Augt 1806 (Vfd Abd. Not on Roll)
HARDY, Thomas	Pte. R.M.	LATONA	
	Pte. R.M.	AJAX	St Sebastian
HARRIS, Charles	Boy 3rd Cl	LATONA	
HAY, John	Lieut. R.M.	LATONA	
HEADINGTON, William	L.M.	LATONA	(M.L. as HADDINGTON)
HENLEY, Robert	Quarter Gunner	ANSON	
	A.B.	TEMERAIRE	Trafalgar
	Quarter Gunner	ANSON	Anson. 23 Augt 1806
HIGMAN, Henry	Lieut. R.N.	ARETHUSA (P)	
	A.B.	CHARON	23rd June 1795
	Master's Mate	TRIUMPH	Camperdown
	Lieut. R.N.	ARETHUSA	Arethusa 23 Augt 1806
JEFFERY, William	M.A.A.	ANSON	
	Trumpeter	DEFENCE	Trafalgar
	Coxswain	ANSON	Anson. 23 Augt 1806
JOHNSON, John	Ord	ARETHUSA	G.H. 8,836
	Ord	ARETHUSA	Arethusa. 23 Augt 1806 (Vfd Abd. Not on Roll)
KENNEDY, James	Boatswain	ARETHUSA	
LEANORD, Jacob.	Ord	ARETHUSA	(M.L. as LENARD)
LEVERTON, Richard	Yeoman Powder Rm	ANSON	GH.709. (M.Ls as LIVERTON and LIBERTINE)
	A.B.	ORION	1 June 1794
	A.B.	VETERAN	Camperdown
	Gunner's Mate	TEMERAIRE	Trafalgar
	Yeoman Pdr Room	ANSON	Anson. 23 Augt 1806 (Vfd Abd. Not on Roll)
Le FEUVRE, John	Actg Lieut. R.N.	FISGARD	
	Midshipman	DESIREE	Copenhagen. 1801
LOWRIE, George	Boy 2nd Cl	FISGARD	
MOORE, Henry	Boy 2nd Cl	LATONA	
	Boy 2nd Cl	BRITANNIA	Trafalgar
QUIN, Kearn	A.B.	FISGARD	
RAND, John	L.M.	LATONA	
	Q.M's Mate	HECLA	Algiers
REID, Curtis	Midshipman	ARETHUSA	
	Midshipman	ARETHUSA	Arethusa. 23 Augt 1806
RENNER, George	Actg Master	FISGARD	
ROBINSON, William	Pte. R.M.	LATONA	
RORIE, John.J.	Lt. R.N. Cmmdg	MORNE FORTUNEE	
	Midshipman	STANDARD	23rd June 1795
	Lt. R.N. Cmmdg	MORNE FORTUNEE	Off the Pearl Rock. 13 Dec 1808 (Vfd Abd. Not on Roll)
SALMON, Charles	Boy 3rd Cl	ANSON	
	Boy 3rd Cl	ANSON	Anson. 23 Augt 1806 (Vfd Abd. Not on Roll)
SEEDS, Robert	Cook	LATONA	
SHEPHERD, Benjamin	Midshipman	LATONA	Benjamin on Medal Roll & ML. "John" in Navy List & O'By.
	Midshipman	BRITANNIA	Trafalgar
	Midshipman	NEPTUNE	Martinique
	Master's Mate	POMPEE	Guadaloupe
	Lieut. R.N.	GRIFFON	Griffon. 27 March 1812
SHEPHERD, James	A.B.	ARETHUSA	G.H. 9,917
	A.B.	ARETHUSA	Arethusa. 23 Augt 1806. (Vfd Abd. Not on 171/- Roll On G.H. applicant Roll)
SIMONS, George	Ord	ANSON	GH.9433 (M.L. as SIMMONS)
	L.M.	COLOSSUS	Trafalgar
	Ord	ANSON	Anson. 23 Augt 1806 (Vfd Abd. Not on Roll)
SMITH, James	Ord	ARETHUSA	G.H. 8,452
	Ord	ARETHUSA	Arethusa. 23 Augt 1806 (Vfd Abd. Not on 171/- Roll. On GH Medal List)
SULLIVAN, Thomas.B.	Lieut. R.N.	ANSON	
	Lieut. R.N.	ANSON	Anson. 23 Augt 1806
WILLIAMS, John	Two men borne A.B. & Pte. R.M.	ANSON	
WORTHINGTON, Benjamin	Midshipman	LATONA	
	Lieut. R.N.	AJAX	St Sebastian

2 JAN BOAT SERVICE 1807

(3)

Cutting out of French sloop, schooner and 'schooner privateer' by boats of CERBERUS, in St Pierre Harbour, Martinique.

COOTE, William	Lieut. R.N.	CERBERUS	(P)
	Midshipman	ROYAL GEORGE	23rd June 1795
	Midshipman	EDGAR	Copenhagen 1801.
			(Vfd Abd. Not on Roll)
	Lieut. R.N.	AGAMEMNON	Trafalgar
	Lieut. R.N.	AGAMEMNON	St Domingo
GILMORE, Thomas	Drummer. R.M.	CERBERUS	
SAYER, George	Midshipman	CERBERUS	

PICKLE 3 JANY 1807

(2)

Capture of the French privateer FAVORITE, off Lizard Head, Cornwall.

HAWKINS, Charles	Actg Sub Lieut. R.N.	PICKLE	(P)
	Midshipman	PICKLE	Trafalgar
ROWDEN, James	Bosun's Mate	PICKLE	
	Bosun's Mate	PICKLE	Trafalgar

21 JAN BOAT SERVICE 1807

(8)

Chase and capture of the French corvette LYNX by boats of GALATEA, off Caracas, Venezuela.

BROWNING, Martin.L.	Pte. R.M.	GALATEA	
BURNETT, Thomas	Caulker	GALATEA	
	Carpenter	GOREE	Martinique
HOWARD, William	L.M.	GALATEA	
	Ord	THUNDER	Basque Roads. 1809
McCARTHY, James	A.B.	GALATEA	(Joined from Diamond Rock)
MILLS, William	A.B.	GALATEA	(Joined from Diamond Rock)
NORRIS, John	A.B.	GALATEA	(Joined from Diamond Rock)
ROUSE, Benjamin	L.M.	GALATEA	
WILLIAMS, James	Pte. R.M.	GALATEA	

19 APRIL BOAT SERVICE 1807

(No applicants)

Cutting out of the Spanish lugger GAILLARD by boats of RICHMOND, in Paderneira Harbour, Portugal.

(Real date of Action 20 April 1807)

(12) HYDRA 6 AUGT 1807

Attack on batteries at BAGUR, Catalonia, and capture of the polacres
PRINCE EUGENE, BELLE CAROLINE and CARMEN del ROSARIO.

(Real date 7 August 1807. Medal applicants on B.S. Roll ADM 171/3)

BENNETT, John	Pte. R.M.	HYDRA	
DREDGE, Thomas	L.M.	HYDRA	
FINLAISON, William	Midshipman	HYDRA	
GODDARD, Robert.H.	Clerk	HYDRA	
	Purser	HECATE	*Java*
HAYES, Robert	1st Lieut. R.M.	HYDRA	
HUNTLEY, James	Capt Fore Top	HYDRA	
KING, George	L.M.	HYDRA	
	Boy 2nd Cl	CALPE	*Gut of Gibraltar 12 July 1801*
LEE, John	Cpl. R.M.	HYDRA	
	Pte. R.M.	DEFENCE	*Nile. (Not at Copenhagen)*
MUNDY, George	Captain. R.N.	HYDRA	
	Lieut. R.N.	BLENHEIM	*St Vincent*
	Lieut. R.N.	GOLIATH	*Nile*
PANTON, Paul.G.	Midshipman	HYDRA	*(Vfd Abd. Not on Roll)*
	Vol 1st Cl	CANOPUS	*St Domingo*
QUADLINE, B.E.	Boy 2nd Cl	HYDRA	*(M.L. as Bartholomew, QUODLINE)*
SMITH, David	Capt Main Top	HYDRA	

(10) COMUS 15 AUGT 1807

Capture of the Danish frigate FREDERIKSCOARN, off Helsingborg, Sweden.

FINLEY, William	A.B.	COMUS	*(M.L. as FINDLEY)*
HILLIER, William.C.	Purser	COMUS	
	Midshipman	ALFRED	*1 June 1794*
	Midshipman	BLENHEIM	*St Vincent*
	Master's Mate	POMPEE	*Gut of Gibraltar 12 July 1801*
MILLER, John	Coxswain	COMUS	
PINNEGAR, David	Pte. R.M.	COMUS	
SAUNDERS, Thomas	L.M.	COMUS	
	Ord	MARS	*17 June 1795 (Vfd Abd. NOR.)*
	Ord	MARS	*Mars. 21 April 1798*
SCAMMEL, William	A.B.	COMUS	*(M.L. as VEALE, William)*
SEALE, Charles.H.	Midshipman	COMUS	
	Midshipman	NEPTUNE	*Martinique*
	Lieut. R.N.	STAR	*Guadaloupe*
	Lieut. R.N.	DESIREE	*Gluckstadt. 5 Jan 1814*
THAIN, James	Purser's Steward	COMUS	
WATTS, George.E.	Lieut. R.N.	COMUS	
	Midshipman	STAG	*Capture of the Desiree*
	Commander	EPHIRA	*B.S. 27 July 1809*
WRAXALL, W.L.	Midshipman	COMUS	

(1) LOUISA 28 OCTR 1807

Action with and repulse of a French privateer, in Irish Sea
(Real date 29 October 1807)

POWELL, Herbert.B.	Supn Lieut. R.N.	LOUISA	*(9 days abd on passage)*
	Lieut. R.N.	VIRGINIE	*Virginie. 19 May 1808*
	Commander	IMPREGNABLE	*Algiers*

(1) CARRIER 4 NOVR 1807

Capture of the French privateer ACTIF, off Dalmatian Coast, Adriatic.
(Real date 14 November 1807)

MILNE, William	Actg Lieut. R.N. in Command	CARRIER (P)	
	Midshipman	ELEPHANT	*Copenhagen. 1801*

(No applicants) ANN 24 NOVR 1807

Capture of the Spanish lugger privateer VINCEJO, and action with ten Spanish gun-boats with surrender of two of them, off Cape Tarifa, Southern Spain.

(2) 13 FEB BOAT SERVICE 1808

Cutting out of the French gun-vessel CANONNIER, off Fort Belem, Tagus River.
(Real date 14 February 1808)

BLACKMAN, John	Yeoman of Sheets	CONFIANCE	
	Yeoman of Sheets	CONFIANCE	*Confiance. 14 Jany 1809*
LEWIS, David	Surgeon	CONFIANCE	

(4) SAPPHO 2 MARCH 1808

Capture of the Danish brig ADMIRAL JAWL, off Scarborough.

BEATTY, Daniel.McN.	Midshipman	SAPPHO	
	Midshipman	SEVERN	*Algiers*
HOWES, William	Pte. R.M.	SAPPHO	*G.H. 6,116*
NICHOLLS, Thomas	Carpenter's Mate	SAPPHO	
PARRY, Charles	L.M.	SAPPHO	*(M.L. as PERRY)*

(18) SAN FIORENZO. 8 MARCH 1808

Capture of the French frigate PIEMONTAISE (Re-named H.M.S. PIEDMONTAISE) by H.M.S. St FIORENZO (Re-named Prize formerly SAN FIORENZO), off Cape Comorin, southern tip of India.

ACTON, John	L.M.	St FIORENZO	
	L.M.	St FIORENZO	*San Fiorenzo. 14 Feby 1805.*
BARNEY, George	Ord	St FIORENZO	
	Ord	St FIORENZO	*San Fiorenzo. 14 Feby 1805.*
BIRD, Robert	Gunner	St FIORENZO	
	Midshipman	LANCASTER	*Camperdown*
CLARK, Matthew	A.B.	St FIORENZO	
COLLIER, Edward	Lieut. R.N.	St FIORENZO	*(Vfd Abd. Not on Roll)*
	Lieut. R.N.	St FIORENZO	*San Fiorenzo. 14 Feby 1805 (Vfd Abd. Not on Roll)*
	Lieut. R.N.	THAMES (P)	*Amanthea. 25 July 1810*
	Captain. R.N.	CASTOR	*Syria*
CROMER, William	Supn A.B.	St FIORENZO	
DIXON, William	A.B.	St FIORENZO	
FINCH, John	Ord	St FIORENZO	
FINN, Samuel	L.M.	St FIORENZO	
	L.M.	St FIORENZO	*San Fiorenzo. 14 Feby 1805 (Vfd Abd. Not on Roll)*
GAUK, Henry	A.B.	St FIORENZO	*G.H. 6,056.*
HAYDON, Nathaniel	Purser	St FIORENZO	
	Clerk	CENTURION	*Centurion. 18 Sept 1804*
HOSKINS, Daniel	Pte. R.M.	St FIORENZO	
	Pte. R.M.	St FIORENZO	*San Fiorenzo. 14 Feby 1805*
HUGHES, Peter	A.B.	St FIORENZO	*(Vfd Abd. Not on Roll)*
	A.B.	St FIORENZO	*San Fiorenzo. 14 Feby 1805*
KENNY, Nathaniel	A.B.	St FIORENZO	
	A.B.	St FIORENZO	*San Fiorenzo. 14 Feby 1805*
LOVE, George	Ord	St FIORENZO	
	Ord	St FIORENZO	*San Fiorenzo. 14 Feby 1805*
PACEY, John	A.B.	St FIORENZO	
	A.B.	St FIORENZO	*San Fiorenzo. 14 Feby 1805*
TROUT, Peter	Capt Forecastle	St FIORENZO	
	Ship's Corporal	St FIORENZO	*San Fiorenzo. 14 Feby 1805*
WYSE, David	Ord	St FIORENZO	*(M.L. as WISE)*

(10) EMERALD. 13 MARCH 1808

Destruction of the French schooner APROPOS and batteries at VIVERO, N.W. Spain.

BAIRD, Daniel	Master's Mate	EMERALD	
	Supn Master's Mate	NORGE	B.S. 14 Dec 1814
BERTRAM, Charles	Lieut. R.N.	EMERALD (P)	
	Lieut. R.N.	LOIRE	B.S. 4 June 1805
CONNOR, Richard	Midshipman	EMERALD	
	Midshipman	LOIRE	B.S. 4 June 1805
	Midshipman	EMERALD*	Basque Roads 1809 (Not at Action. In Prize)
GILLMAN, John	Carpenter's Crew	EMERALD	(M.L. as GILMON)
	Carpenter's Crew	EMERALD	Basque Roads 1809
M'KILLOP, John	Volt per Order	EMERALD	
	Vol 1st Cl	LOIRE	B.S. 4 June 1805
	Master's Mate	ASTRAEA	Off Tamatave. 20 May 1811
NORMAN, John	Pte. R.M.	EMERALD	
	Cpl. R.M.	EMERALD	Basque Roads 1809
POTTS, Thomas	Sailmaker	EMERALD	
	Sailmaker	EMERALD	Basque Roads 1809
SAURIN, Edward	Midshipman	EMERALD	
	Midshipman	LOIRE	B.S. 4 June 1805
	Master's Mate	EMERALD	Basque Roads 1809
THOMPSON, William	A.B.	EMERALD	
	A.B.	EMERALD	Basque Roads 1809
WYLDE, Edward	Boy 2nd Cl	EMERALD	
	Midshipman	EMERALD	Basque Roads 1809

(4) CHILDERS 14 MARCH 1808

Action with the Danish brig LOUGEN, off Midbe, Coast of Norway.

DILLON, William.H.	Commander	CHILDERS	
	Midshipman	DEFENCE	1 June 1794
	Midshipman	PRINCE GEORGE	23rd June 1795
EDMONDS, Thomas	Lieut. R.N.	CHILDERS	
PARKER, Charles (b)	Vol 1st Cl	CHILDERS	(In O'Byrne two men (a) & (b))
	Midshipman	DOTTEREL	Basque Roads 1809
	Master's Mate	Qn CHARLOTTE	Algiers
WILSON, George	Actg Master	CHILDERS	

(31) STATELY 22 MARCH 1808

Destruction of the Danish 74-gun PRINDS CHRISTIAN FREDERIK, at Grenaa, East coast of Jutland.

BAILEY, Joseph	A.B.	STATELY	(M.L. as BAILLEY)
	A.B.	ILLUSTRIOUS	Basque Roads 1809
	A.B.	ILLUSTRIOUS	Java
BARDO, Benjamin	Yeoman Powder Room	STATELY	(M.L. as BARNARD @ BARDO)
BEDDOWS, Joseph	Pte. R.M.	STATELY	
	Pte. R.M.	PRINCESS CAROLINE	B.S. 25 July 1809
BELL, George	A.B.	STATELY	
	Ord	ILLUSTRIOUS	Basque Roads 1809
BRACE, George	L.M.	STATELY	
	L.M.	PCSS CAROLINE	B.S. 25 July 1809
BURGOYNE, John	Boy 3rd Cl	STATELY	(M.L. as BURGOINE)
CARPENTER, Thomas	L.M.	STATELY	
CHAMBERS, John	Quarter Gunner	STATELY	
	Quarter Gunner	ILLUSTRIOUS	Basque Roads 1809
CHAMBERS, Thomas	L.M.	STATELY	G.H. 7,973
CHEVERALL, John	Ord	STATELY	
	Boy 3rd Cl	St GEORGE	14 March 1795
	A.B.	PCSS CAROLINE	B.S. 25 July 1809
COLE, Edward	Lieut. R.N.	STATELY	
	Master's Mate	SUPERB	Gut of Gibraltar. 12 July 1801
	Master's Mate	SUPERB	St Domingo
COOPER, William	L.M.	STATELY	
DAVIS, James	Master's Mate	STATELY	
HALL, Webb	Ord	STATELY	G.H. 6,673
HIBBERT, Onias	Ord	STATELY	
HILL, Samuel	Midshipman	STATELY	
	Actg Lieut. R.N.	ABOUKIR (P)	B.S. 29 Sep 1812. Not on Roll. Verified promoted for services at Action.
JOACHIM, Richard	Midshipman	STATELY	

STATELY 22 MARCH 1808

LEMON, William	A.B.	STATELY	
	A.B.	ILLUSTRIOUS	Basque Roads 1809
	A.B.	ILLUSTRIOUS	Java
LOVE, B.L.	Midshipman	STATELY	
LUNDY, Richard	A.B.	STATELY	(M.L. as LANDY)
MILLER, Robert	Drummer. R.M.	STATELY	G.H. 9,704
	Drummer. R.M.	NORTHUMBERLAND	St Domingo
PARKER, George	Captain. R.N.	STATELY	
	Lieut. R.N.	CRESCENT	Crescent. 20 Octr 1793
PARKES, James	Ord	STATELY	G.H. 2729 (ML as PARKS)
	Ord	PCSS CAROLINE	B.S. 25 July 1809
PASFIELD, Charles	Pte. R.M.	STATELY	G.H. 7,388
	Pte. R.M.	PCSS CAROLINE	B.S. 25 July 1809
SCOTT, James	A.B.	STATELY	
	Ord	PCSS CAROLINE	B.S. 25 July 1809
SHREEVE, George	Ord	STATELY	
	Midshipman	PCSS CAROLINE	B.S. 25 July 1809
STILL, Joseph	A.B.	STATELY	
	Ord	ILLUSTRIOUS	Basque Roads 1809 (Vfd Abd. Not on Roll)
	A.B.	ILLUSTRIOUS	Java
WILSON, Samuel	Pte. R.M.	STATELY	
WILLSON, William	Boy 3rd Cl	STATELY	(M.L. as WILSON)
WITHERICK, John	Ord	STATELY	(M.L. as WITHERHEAD @ WITHERIC)

(31) NASSAU 22 MARCH 1808

Destruction of the Danish 74-gun PRINDS CHRISTIAN FREDERIK, at Grenaa, East coast of Jutland.

AITKIN, Alexander	Midshipman	NASSAU	
BLANCHETT, Thomas	Pte. R.M.	NASSAU	
BURBRIDGE, William.C.	Midshipman	NASSAU	
	Capt's Servant	ALFRED	1 June 1794
	Midshipman	BLENHEIM	St Vincent
CAIN, Edward	L.M.	NASSAU	
CEMMETT, Joseph	A.B.	NASSAU	(M.L. as CEMMITT)
	A.B.	EAGLE	B.S. 17 Sep 1812
CHAPMAN, James	Midshipman	NASSAU	
CLARK, James	Carpenter's Crew	NASSAU	G.H.1508
	Caulker's Mate	EAGLE	B.S. 17 Sep 1812
COLLINS, Christopher	A.B.	NASSAU	
COLLINS, James	2 Borne.AB & Ord	NASSAU	
DEVERELL, Thomas	Boy 3rd Cl	NASSAU	
DEXTER, George	Pte. R.M.	NASSAU	
ELLIS, William	2 Ptes RM borne	NASSAU	
HACKFORD, Thomas	Sailmaker's Mate	NASSAU	GH. 209
HARDY, James	Boy 3rd Cl	NASSAU	
HENSLEY, Charles	Midshipman	NASSAU	
HOLLOWAY, Thomas	Ord	NASSAU	G.H. 6,526
	Ord	ALBION	Algiers
HUSSEY, Charles	L.M.	NASSAU	
	Ord	EAGLE	B.S. 17 Sep 1812
JACKSON, Thomas	Actg Lieut. R.N.	NASSAU (P?)	(Vfd Abd. Not on Roll)
	A.B.	SUPERB	Gut of Gibraltar.12 July 1801
	Midshipman	SUPERB	St Domingo
JOHNSON, Edward.J.	Vol 1st Cl	NASSAU	
LAYTON, Buxton	Midshipman	NASSAU	
LOCK, James	Ord	NASSAU	
MOULLEN, James	A.B.	NASSAU	(M.L. as MOULLAN)
NIERO, Giovanni	Coxswain	NASSAU	
	Ord	DEFENCE	Trafalgar
RICHARDS, John	A.B.	NASSAU	
SCHULTZ, George.A.	Lieut. R.N.	NASSAU	
SEYMOUR, Samuel	Ord	NASSAU	
	A.B.	EAGLE	B.S. 17 Sep 1812
SMAIL, William.A.	Midshipman	NASSAU	
SMITH, John	Pte. R.M.	NASSAU	
TOOTH, James	L.M.	NASSAU	
WALKER, John	L.M.	NASSAU	
WELSH, George	Ord	NASSAU	

(19) OFF ROTA 4 APRIL 1808

Action with Spanish gun-boats and convoy, resulting in destruction of several vessels, near Cadiz

BASTIN, Thomas	Purser	GRASSHOPPER	*(No Muster Lists survived)*
	Clerk	LOIRE	*B.S. 27 June 1803*
	Clerk	LOIRE	*B.S. 4 June 1805*
	Purser	GRASSHOPPER	*Grasshopper. 24 April 1808*
BROOM, George	Vol 1st Cl	MERCURY	
	Midshipman	ABERCROMBIE	*Guadaloupe*
CROUCH, Joseph	Boy 3rd Cl	MERCURY	
DISNEY, William	L.M.	ALCESTE	
Du CANE, Charles	Master's Mate	MERCURY	
FRENCH, James	L.M.	MERCURY	*G.H. 965*
GAIN, Jonathan	Clerk	GRASSHOPPER	
	Clerk	GRASSHOPPER	*Grasshopper. 24 April 1808*
	Purser	REDPOLE	*Basque Roads. 1809*
GORDON, James.A.	Captain. R.N.	MERCURY	
	Midshipman	REVOLUTIONNAIRE	*23rd June 1795*
	Midshipman	NAMUR	*St Vincent*
	Midshipman	GOLIATH	*Nile*
	Captain. R.N.	ACTIVE	*Lissa*
	Captain. R.N.	ACTIVE	*Pelagosa. 29 Novr 1811*
	Captain. R.N.	SEAHORSE	*The Potomac. 17 Aug 1814.*
HODGE, Stephen	Midshipman	GRASSHOPPER	
	Midshipman	GRASSHOPPER	*Grasshopper. 24 April 1808*
NASH, Smith	Ord	ALCESTE	
	Ord	ALCESTE	*Pelagosa. 29 Novr 1811*
PARKER, William	Midshipman	MERCURY	
PELL, Watkin.O.	Lieut. R.N.	MERCURY	*(Lost left leg Feby 1800)*
	Commander	THUNDER	*Thunder 9 Octr 1813*
			(See ("LOIRE 5 Feby 1800") for probable 3rd clasp)
PHILLIPS, Joseph	Carp's Crew	MERCURY	*G.H. 2,526*
RAGAN, John	Ord	MERCURY	*(M.L. as REGIN)*
RICHARDSON, John	A.B.	MERCURY	
SEARLE, Thomas	Commander	GRASSHOPPER	
	Lieut. R.N.	COURIER	*Schiermonnikoog. 12 Aug 1799*
	Lieut. R.N.	COURIER	*Courier. 27 Novr 1799*
	Commander	GRASSHOPPER	*Grasshopper. 24 April 1808*
SIMPSON, James	(Not yet joined)	ALCESTE*	
	Pte. R.M.	ALCESTE	*Pelagosa 29 Novr 1811*
WATSON, Samuel	Ord	MERCURY	
WHYLOCK, James	1st Lieut. R.M.	MERCURY	
	Captain. R.M.	PIQUE/STROMBOLI	*Syria (Acre medal in gold)*

(7) GRASSHOPPER 24 APRIL 1808

Capture of two Spanish merchant vessels, off Faro; action with the escorting gun-boats, two being captured and the other two destroyed, off Faro, Southern Portugal.

No Muster Lists for this period from GRASSHOPPER have survived.

BASTIN, Thomas	Purser	GRASSHOPPER	
	Clerk	LOIRE	*B.S. 27 June 1803*
	Clerk	LOIRE	*B.S. 4 June 1805*
	Purser	GRASSHOPPER	*Off Rota. 4 April 1808*
GAIN, Jonathan	Clerk	GRASSHOPPER	
	Clerk	GRASSHOPPER	*Off Rota. 4 April 1808*
	Purser	REDPOLE	*Basque Roads 1809*
HODGE, Stephen	Midshipman	GRASSHOPPER	
	Midshipman	GRASSHOPPER	*Off Rota. 4 April 1808*
HOLDEWAY, James	Pte. R.M.	GRASSHOPPER	
LEGGE, James	L.M.	GRASSHOPPER	
POTTINGER, Samuel.J.	L.M.	GRASSHOPPER	
SEARLE, Thomas	Commander	GRASSHOPPER	
	Lieut. R.N.	COURIER	*Schiermonnikoog. 12 Aug 1799*
	Lieut. R.N.	COURIER	*Courier. 27 Novr 1799*
	Commander	GRASSHOPPER	*Off Rota. 4 April 1808*

(1) RAPID 24 APRIL 1808
Same Action as for GRASSHOPPER above.

BAUGH, Henry	Lieut. R.N.	RAPID (P)	*(No Muster List)*

(7) REDWING 7 MAY 1808
Action with seven armed vessels and a convoy of twelve sail; capture or destruction of six of the escort and eleven of the convoy, off Cape Trafalgar, Spain.

BRAND, William.H.	Vol 1st Cl	REDWING	
	Vol 1st Cl	REVENGE	*Trafalgar*
	Vol 1st Cl	REDWING	*Redwing. 31 May 1808*
DAVIS, John	Actg Master	REDWING	
	Actg Master	REDWING	*Redwing. 31 May 1808*
			(Vfd Abd. Not on Roll)
FERGUSON, John.McP.	Lieut. R.N.	REDWING	
	Lieut. R.N.	SUPERB	*St Domingo*
	Lieut. R.N.	REDWING (P)	*Redwing. 31 May 1808*
HALLAHAN, Thomas	Midshipman	REDWING	
	Midshipman	REDWING	*Redwing. 31 May 1808*
	Midshipman	UNDAUNTED	*B.S. 2 May 1813*
HORNIMAN, Robert.L.	Purser	REDWING	
	Purser	REDWING	*Redwing. 31 May 1808*
			(Vfd Abd. Not on Roll)
MARTIN, William	Boatswain	REDWING	
	Boatswain	REDWING	*Redwing. 31 May 1808*
USSHER, Thomas	Commander	REDWING (P)	
	Midshipman	INVINCIBLE	*1 June 1794*
	Captain. R.N.	REDWING	*Redwing. 31 May 1808*
	Captain. R.N.	HYACINTH	*Malaga. 29 April 1812*
	Captain. R.N.	UNDAUNTED	*B.S. 2 May 1813*

(21) VIRGINIE 19 May 1808
Capture of the Dutch frigate GELDERLAND by VIRGINIE in the Western Approaches.

BAILEY, John	A.B.	VIRGINIE	*alias TREGARDON*
BLANCHARD, William	L.M.	VIRGINIE	
BOLD, Edward	Midshipman	VIRGINIE	
BRACE, Francis	Midshipman	VIRGINIE	
DAVIS, Thomas.E.	Capt Main Top	VIRGINIE	
	A.B.	BERWICK	*Gaieta. 24 July 1815*
FATHOM, George	Capt Fore Top	VIRGINIE	
FOSBERY, Godfrey	Vol 1st Cl	VIRGINIE	
FREDERICK, John	Sailmaker	VIRGINIE	
GOUGH, James	A.B.	VIRGINIE	*Entered incorrectly on Roll under "COMET 11 Augt 1808"*
HOLBROOK, Thomas	Pte. R.M.	VIRGINIE	
McALLISTER, John	Ord	VIRGINIE	*(M.L. as McALISTER)*
McINTYRE, Peter	2nd Lt R.M.	VIRGINIE	
O'CONNOR, George	Boy 3rd Cl	VIRGINIE	
PHILLIPS, John	Ship's Cook	VIRGINIE	
POWELL, Herbert Brace	Lieut. R.N.	VIRGINIE	
	Lieut. R.N.	LOUISA	*Louisa. 28 Octr 1807*
	Commander	IMPREGNABLE	*Algiers*
SULLIVAN, Daniel	L.M.	VIRGINIE	
WARREN, Charles	Ord	VIRGINIE	
WATSON, William	Boy 3rd Class	VIRGINIE	*(A Lieut's Servant)*
WILLIAMS, John	Q.M.	VIRGINIE	
WILSON, John	L.M.	VIRGINIE	
WITHEY, Frederick	Pte. R.M.	VIRGINIE	*G.H.8245 as WITHY*

(CURTIS, James entered on Roll as "Not Found". A John Curtis joined VIRGINIE as L.M. after the Action, who deserted Jan 1811 from CAESAR.)

(CAMPBELL, John. Lt R.M. was aboard for action but Not on Roll. A different Lt John CAMPBELL R.M. was awarded clasp "BLANCHE 19 July 1806")

(7) REDWING 31 MAY 1808

Capture of two Spanish vessels and destruction of a third and a battery at BOLONIA, off Bolonia.
(Real date 1 June 1808)

BRAND, William.H.	Vol·1st Cl	REDWING	
	Vol 1st Cl	REVENGE	*Trafalgar*
	Vol 1st Cl	REDWING	*Redwing. 7 May 1808*
DAVIS, John	Actg Master	REDWING	*(Vfd Abd. Not on Roll)*
	Actg Master	REDWING	*Redwing. 7 May 1808*
FERGUSON, John.McP.	Lieut. R.N.	REDWING (P)	
	Lieut. R.N.	SUPERB	*St Domingo*
	Lieut. R.N.	REDWING	*Redwing. 7 May 1808*
HALLAHAN, Thomas	Midshipman	REDWING	
	Midshipman	REDWING	*Redwing. 7 May 1808*
	Midshipman	UNDAUNTED	*B.S. 2 May 1813*
HORNIMAN, Robert.L.	Purser	REDWING	*(Vfd Abd. Not on Roll)*
	Purser	REDWING	
MARTIN, William	Boatswain	REDWING	
	Boatswain	REDWING	*Redwing. 7 May 1808*
USSHER, Thomas	Captain. R.N.	REDWING	
	Midshipman	INVINCIBL	*1 June 1794*
	Commander	REDWING (P)	*Redwing. 7 May 1808*
	Captain. R.N.	HYACINTH	*Malaga. 29 April 1812*
	Captain. R.N.	UNDAUNTED	*B.S. 2 May 1813*

(32) SEAHORSE Wh BADERE ZAFFERE (G.M.)

Action with and capture of the Turkish frigate BADERE ZAFFER on 5 & 6 July 1808, off Khiliodromia in Greek Archipelago.

ATKINSON, William	A.B.	SEAHORSE	
BENNETT, Thomas	Lieut. R.N.	SEAHORSE	
	Midshipman	MONARCH	*Camperdown*
BOLT, James	L.M.	SEAHORSE	
BROWN, Richard	Ord	SEAHORSE	*(M.L. as BROWNE)*
CADMAN, Joseph	Ord	SEAHORSE	*G.H. 7,476*
CAMPBELL, Hon George.P.	Midshipman	SEAHORSE	
	Vol 1st Cl	NAMUR	*4 Novr 1805*
CURTIS, Thomas	Master	SEAHORSE	
DICKENS, George	Boy 3rd Cl	SEAHORSE	
EYTON, William.W.	Vol 1st Cl	SEAHORSE	
	Vol 1st Cl	NEPTUNE	*Trafalgar*
FARR, David	Ord	SEAHORSE	
GREEN, William	Q.M's Mate	SEAHORSE	*G.H. 4,122*
HAY, Lord John	Midshipman	SEAHORSE	
HEMSLEY, Richard	A.B.	SEAHORSE	*(M.L. as HELMSLEY)*
JENDERS, Edward	Pte. R.M.	SEAHORSE	
JENKINS, Thomas	Boy 2nd Cl	SEAHORSE	*G.H. 7,879*
KENMURE, Viscount A.G.	Midshipman	SEAHORSE	*(M.L. as GORDON, Adam)*
	Vol 1st Cl	AJAX	*Trafalgar*
LESTER, William	Master's Mate	SEAHORSE	
MAWBEY, C.E.	Boy 3rd Cl	SEAHORSE	
MELON, John	A.B.	SEAHORSE	
MONTEITH, John	Q.M.	SEAHORSE	
OASTLER, William	Surgeon	SEAHORSE	
PALMER, Thomas	Ord	SEAHORSE	
PARSONS, Samuel	Ord	SEAHORSE	*G.H. 4,776*
PHILLIPS, Henry.C.M.	Boy 2nd Cl	SEAHORSE	
RICH, Edwin.L.	Midshipman	SEAHORSE	
ROSS, James	Capt After Guard	SEAHORSE	*G.H. 7,973*
	L.M.	PRINCE GEORGE	*St Vincent*
SEED, Thomas	Pte. R.M.	SEAHORSE	
SMITH, Richard	Q.M.'s Mate	SEAHORSE	*G.H. 9,182*
STEVENS, James.A.	Midshipman	SEAHORSE	
THOMAS, William	A.B.	SEAHORSE	*G.H. 8,607*
VALLACK, Richard.G.	Lieut. R.N.	SEAHORSE	
	Lieut. R.N.	AETNA	*The Potomac. 17 Aug 1814*
VALLANCE, Thomas	A.B.	SEAHORSE	*(M.L. as VALENCE)*

(8) 10 JULY BOAT SERVICE 1808

Cutting out of the Spanish polacra N.S. del ROSARIO, off Port d'Anzio, south of Rome.

ADAMS, Charles.J.	Vol 1st Cl	PORCUPINE	
ANDERSON, George	Clerk	PORCUPINE	
	Purser	FANTOME	BS. Ap & May 1813
CAMPBELL, John	Q.M's Mate	PORCUPINE	
JOHNS, Francis	Boy 3rd Cl	PORCUPINE	
LANE, George.D.	L.M.	PORCUPINE	
PARRY, Henry	Master's Mate	PORCUPINE	
	A.B.	EURUS	Egypt
SMARTLEY, Henry	Master	PORCUPINE	
TOWNSEND, Thomas	Pte. R.M.	PORCUPINE	
	Pte. R.M.	UNDAUNTED	

(4) COMET 11 AUGT 1808

Action with two French brigs and capture of one, – the SYLPHE, in the Bay of Biscay.
(Real date 9 August 1808)

DALY, Cuthbert.F.	Commander	COMET	
	Lieut. R.N.	ARROW	Arrow. 3 Feby 1805
DEW, George	Vol 1st Cl	COMET	
	Midshipman	PHOEBE	Phoebe. 28 March 1814
CAFFREY, Daniel	Boy 2nd Cl	COMET	(M.L. as CAFFERY)
			(Vfd Abd. Not on Roll)
	Ord	HUSSAR	Java
VANSTON, Edward	Pte. R.M.	COMET	

(17) 11 AUG BOAT SERVICE 1808

Capture of the Danish corvettes FAMA and SALORMAN by boats from Rear Admiral Richard.G.Keat's squadron, in Nyborg Harbour, Funen Island, Denmark.
(Real date 9 August 1808)

COLLINS, E.J.	L.M.	BRUNSWICK	(M.L. as Edward COLLINS)
CROOME, Samuel	Pte. R.M.	SUPERB	
DAVIES, William.R.	Midshipman	SUPERB	
DODD, Henry.W.	Midshipman	EDGAR	
FEAR, Hugh	A.B.	SUPERB	
	A.B.	SUPERB	St Domingo
	A.B.	VICTORIOUS	Victorious with Rivoli
JACKSON, Caleb	Master's Mate	EDGAR	
LOFT, David	Ord	EDGAR	
MARSHAM, Henry.S.	Boy. 2nd Cl	SUPERB	
	Midshipman	NORTHUMBERLAND	Northumberland 22 May 1812
McGUIRE, Hugh	Gunner's Mate	EDGAR	
RADDON, William	A.B.	EDGAR	(M.L. as READING @ RADDON)
RAYMOND, George	Midshipman	EDGAR	(Vfd Abd. Not on Roll)
	Midshipman	SHANNON	Shannon Wh Chesapeake
	A.B.	ROYAL OAK	B.S. 14 Dec 1814
SMITH, James	2 Ptes R.M. borne	EDGAR	G.H. 1,110
SMITHSON, William	Ord	EDGAR	
TAYLOR, John	Purser	BRUNSWICK	
TEMPLE, Henry Edward	Midshipman	EDGAR	(Vfd Abd. Not on Roll)
	Midshipman	EUROTAS	Eurotas. 25 Feby 1814
WARREN, John.T.	Midshipman	SUPERB	
WILLIAMS, Thomas	Ord	EDGAR	

(42) CENTAUR 26 AUGT 1808

Chase of the Russian fleet and capture of the SEVOLOD (74), off Hango Point, Finland.

BERRY, James	L.M.	CENTAUR	(On Roll IMPLACABLE. Wrong)
BIDGOOD, Samuel	Trumpeter	CENTAUR	
BUDGEN, John	Midshipman	CENTAUR	
BUDGEN, Richard	Ord	CENTAUR	
CANE, John	A.B.	CENTAUR	
CASE, William	Lieut. R.N.	CENTAUR	
CLARK, Daniel	L.M.	CENTAUR	G.H. 2886
			(M.L. as CLARKE)
	L.M.	CENTAUR	B.S. 16 July 1806
CLARKE, William	1st Lieut. R.M.	CENTAUR	
	1st Lieut. R.M.	CENTAUR	B.S. 16 July 1806
CLAYTON, Robert	A.B.	CENTAUR	
DAVIES, Wm. St George	Asst Surgeon	CENTAUR	
	Surgeon	DOTTEREL	Basque Roads. 1809.
DENYER, James.R.	Ord	CENTAUR	
DOBSON, Jeremiah	Ord	CENTAUR	(Vfd Abd. Not on Roll)
	Ord	CENTAUR	B.S. 4 Feb 1804
	Ord	CENTAUR	B.S. 16 July 1806
DODSON, Nathaniel	Pte. R.M.	CENTAUR	
GISBOLD, Samuel	R.M. Boy	CENTAUR	
GOSLIN, James	L.M.	CENTAUR	
GRACE, Dennis	L.M.	CENTAUR	G.H. 6289
GRANGER, Daniel	Pte. R.M.	CENTAUR	(M.L. as GRANGE)
HENN, Richard	Boy 2nd Cl	CENTAUR	
HEWETT, Thomas	Q.M.	CENTAUR	
	A.B.	BRUNSWICK	1 June 1794
	A.B.	ROBUST	12 Octr 1798
	Q.M.	IMPREGNABLE	Algiers
ILLINGWORTH, Abraham	Asst Surgeon	CENTAUR	
JAMES, John	Capt Main Top	CENTAUR	
	Ord	CENTAUR	B.S. 4 Feb 1804
	A.B.	CENTAUR	B.S. 16 July 1806
LAWRENCE, Thomas	L.M.	CENTAUR	
LESLIE, Thomas	Midshipman	CENTAUR	
MANNING, Henry	Carpenter's Crew	CENTAUR	
	A.B.	CENTAUR	B.S. 4 Feb 1804
	Carpenter's Crew	CENTAUR	B.S. 16 July 1806
MESSERVEY, Henry	Carpenter's Crew	CENTAUR	G.H. 3506
	A.B.	CENTAUR	B.S. 4 Feb 1804
	Carpenter's Crew	CENTAUR	B.S. 16 July 1806
NICHOLLS, William	Ord	CENTAUR	
POLLETT, Nicholas	R.M. Boy	CENTAUR	
PRICE, David	Midshipman	CENTAUR	
	Vol 1st Cl	ARDENT	Copenhagen 1801
	Lieut. R.N.	HAWKE	Hawke. 18 Augt 1811
RICHARDS, John	Boy 2nd Cl	CENTAUR	
RICHARDS, William	L.M.	CENTAUR	
	L.M.	CENTAUR	B.S. 16 July 1806
ROBERTS, Nicholas	A.B.	CENTAUR	
SCOTT, Robert	A.B.	CENTAUR	
SEYMOUR, Francis.E.	Actg Lieut. R.N.	CENTAUR	
SIMMONDS, John	A.B.	CENTAUR	
STROVER, Thomas	Ord	CENTAUR	
	Vol 1st Cl	CENTAUR	B.S. 16 July 1806
TEED, Richard.M.	Midshipman	CENTAUR	
TREFUSIS, Hon G.R.W.	Vol 1st Cl	CENTAUR	
	Midshipman	THAMES	Amanthea. 25 July 1810
WALCOTT, John.E.	Master's Mate	CENTAUR	
WARD, John	Ord	CENTAUR	G.H. 10,152
WARNER, George	Yeoman of Sheets	CENTAUR	
	Ord	CENTAUR	B.S. 4 Feb 1804
	Ord	CENTAUR	B.S. 16 July 1806
WARREN, Charles	Admiral's Domestic	CENTAUR	
WINDSOR, Benjamin	Boy 3rd Cl	CENTAUR	
	Boy 3rd Cl	CENTAUR	B.S. 4 Feb 1804
	Boy 3rd Cl	CENTAUR	B.S. 16 July 1806

(44) IMPLACABLE 26 AUGT 1808
Chase of the Russian fleet and capture of the SEVOLOD (74), off Hango Point, Finland.

ABRAHAMS, Joseph	A.B.	IMPLACABLE	
BALDWIN, Augustus	Lieut. R.N.	IMPLACABLE	
BELL, William	Ord	IMPLACABLE	
	L.M.	REVOLUTIONNAIRE	4 Novr 1805
BERE, William	Pte. R.M.	IMPLACABLE	(M.L. as BEER)
BOBBETT, Thomas	Pte. R.M.	IMPLACABLE	
BODEY, George	Ord	IMPLACABLE	
	L.M.	REVOLUTIONNAIRE	4 Novr 1805
BURD, John	L.M.	IMPLACABLE	(Vfd Abd. Not on Roll)
	L.M.	IMPLACABLE	B.S. 7 July 1809
CARR, William	L.M.	IMPLACABLE	(Vfd Abd. Not on Roll)
	L.M.	IMPLACABLE	B.S. 7 July 1809
CAUGHLAN, William	L.M.	IMPLACABLE	(M.L. as COGLAN & COGHLAN)
COLLEY, Thomas	Caulker's Mate	IMPLACABLE	
	Carpenter's Crew	REVOLUTIONNAIRE	4 Novr 1805
COX, Henry	Midshipman	IMPLACABLE	
	Midshipman	PELICAN	Pelican. 14 Augt 1813
CRACKNELL, James.T.	Actg 1st Lieut. R.M.	IMPLACABLE	
	Actg 1st Lieut. R.M.	IMPLACABLE	B.S. 7 July 1809
			(Vfd Abd. Not on Roll)
CRAWLEY, John	L.M.	IMPLACABLE	
	L.M.	IMPLACABLE	B.S. 7 July 1809
DAVIS, Thomas	Pte. R.M.	IMPLACABLE	
DOUGHT, William	Pte. R.M.	IMPLACABLE	(M.L. as DOUBT)
EVERSON, William	L.M.	IMPLACABLE	
	Boy 2nd Cl	REVOLUTIONNAIRE	4 Novr 1805
FANSHAWE, Arthur	Midshipman	IMPLACABLE	
	Midshipman	SCIPION	Java
	Lieut. R.N.	ENDYMION	B.S. 8 April 1814
	Lieut. R.N.	ENDYMION	Endymion Wh President
	Captain. R.N.	PRINCESS CHARLOTTE	Syria
FITZGERALD, John (1)	L.M. (two borne)	IMPLACABLE	(Both applied this clasp)
FITZGERALD, John (2)	L.M. (two borne)	IMPLACABLE	(1 of 2 appld B.S. clasp)
	L.M.	IMPLACABLE	B.S. 7 July 1809
FRY, Robert	Pte. R.M.	IMPLACABLE	(M.L. as PRY @ FRY)
	Pte. R.M.	(HMS ANHOLT)	Anholt. 27 March 1811
GARBY, John	Midshipman	IMPLACABLE	
GILRAY, Andrew	L.M.	IMPLACABLE	(M.L. as GUILREAY)
	Boy 2nd Cl	REVOLUTIONNAIRE	4 Novr 1805
GREEN, Samuel	Sailmaker's Mate	IMPLACABLE	
	Sailmaker's Mate	IMPLACABLE	B.S. 7 July 1809
HAMMOND, Isaac	Ord	IMPLACABLE	
	L.M.	REVOLUTIONNAIRE	4 Novr 1805
	A.B.	IMPLACABLE	B.S. 7 July 1809
HARRIS, John	2 Ptes R.M. Borne	IMPLACABLE	(Both at Action)
	2 Ptes R.M. left ship (Neither aboard at action)	IMPLACABLE*	B.S. 7 July 1809 (one Pte claimed) G.H. 10,053
HYMERS, James	L.M.	IMPLACABLE	
JEFFERY, John	Ord	IMPLACABLE	(M.L. & @ RABY/RABEY,John)
LESLY, John	A.B.	IMPLACABLE	(M.L. as LESLIE)
	A.B.	IMPLACABLE	B.S. 7 July 1809
LUSCOMBE, Edward	Midshipman	IMPLACABLE	
MALLETT, William	Pte. R.M.	IMPLACABLE	
MARTIN, Thomas Byam	Captain. R.N.	IMPLACABLE	
	Captain. R.N.	SANTA MARGARITA	Santa Margaritta 8 June 1796 (see note)
	Captain. R.N.	FISGARD	Fisgard. 20 Octr 1798
McAUSLAND, Peter	Gunner	IMPLACABLE	
	A.B.	MONTAGU	1 June 1794
	Gunner's Mate	IRRESISTIBLE	23rd June 1795
	Bosun's Mate	IRRESISTIBLE	St Vincent
	Gunner	PETEREL	Egypt
MEAR, William	Pte. R.M.	IMPLACABLE	(M.L. as MEARD)
	Pte. R.M.	(HMS ANHOLT)	Anholt. 27 March 1811
ORMOND, Francis	Midshipman	IMPLACABLE	
	Master's Mate	IMPLACABLE	B.S. 7 July 1809
	Actg Flag Lieut. R.N.	ABOUKIR	B.S. 29 Sep 1812
	Lieut. R.N.	ENDYMION	Endymion Wh President
	Lieut. R.N.	IMPREGNABLE	Algiers
PETERS, William	L.M.	IMPLACABLE	(M.L. as James PETERS)
SERVANTE, Frederick	Midshipman	IMPLACABLE	

STANBURY, James	L.M.	IMPLACABLE	
SYMONDS, Christopher	A.B.	IMPLACABLE	(M.L. as SIMMONS, & in other ships as SIMMONDS, SYMMONDS)
	Ord	REVOLUTIONNAIRE	4 Novr 1805
	A.B.	IMPLACABLE	B.S. 7 July 1809
THOMSON, John	Q.M.	IMPLACABLE	
	A.B.	LEVIATHAN	Trafalgar
TRUEMAN, Jeremiah	Q.M.	IMPLACABLE	
	A.B.	LEVIATHAN	Trafalgar
	Q.M.	IMPLACABLE	B.S. 7 July 1809
WARE, Charles.B.	Vol 1st Cl	IMPLACABLE	
	Midshipman	LEANDER	Algiers
WATERS, William	Pte. R.M.	IMPLACABLE	G.H. 10,306
WHITE, John	Ord	IMPLACABLE	(Vfd Abd. Not on Roll) G.H. 9,787
	A.B.	IMPLACABLE	B.S. 7 July 1809
WILLIAMS, O.G. Rev.	Chaplain	IMPLACABLE	

(4) CRUIZER 1 NOVR 1808

Action with a Danish flotilla of twenty sail, and capture of the schuyt privateer RINALDO, off Gothenburgh, Sweden.

ALLEN, John	Lieut. R.N.	CRUIZER	
ELLIS, Francis.W.	Midshipman	CRUIZER	
FORREST, James.R.	Vol 1st Cl	CRUIZER	
WALKER, W.J.	Ord	CRUIZER	(Only a James WALKER fnd)

(31) AMETHYST Wh THETIS (G.M.)

Capture of the French frigate THETIS on 10 November 1808, off Isle de Groix, Lorient.

ANDERSON, Thomas	A.B.	AMETHYST	
BOULTON, Samuel	Gunner	AMETHYST	
	Gunner	AMETHYST	Amethyst 5 April 1809
BOWEN, John	Surgeon	AMETHYST	
	Surgeon	AMETHYST	Amethyst 5 April 1809
BUTLER, Daniel	Ord	AMETHYST	
	Ord	AMETHYST	Amethyst 5 April 1809
CHAPPLE, Richard	Ord	AMETHYST	
COCKER, Francis	Ord	AMETHYST	G.H. 8,924
	Ord	AMETHYST	Amethyst 5 April 1809
COOPER, William	Armourer	AMETHYST	
	Armourer	AMETHYST	Amethyst 5 April 1809
CUMMINGS, Thomas	Ord	AMETHYST	
	Ord	AMETHYST	Amethyst 5 April 1809
CUSSACK, John	L.M.	AMETHYST	(M.L. as CUSACK)
	L.M.	AMETHYST	Amethyst 5 April 1809
DODGIN, Gideon	Q.M's Mate	AMETHYST	(M.L. as DODGEON)
	Q.M's Mate	AMETHYST	Amethyst 5 April 1809
DUNTHORNE, John	Asst Surgeon	AMETHYST	
GOULD, James	A.B.	AMETHYST	
	Midshipman	AMETHYST	Amethyst 5 April 1809
GRAY, Andrew	Capt Fore Top	AMETHYST	(M.L. as GREY)
	Yeoman of Sheets	AMETHYST	Amethyst 5 April 1809
HOLLANDS, Thomas	A.B.	AMETHYST	
	A.B	AMETHYST	Amethyst 5 April 1809
JENKINS, James	Pte. R.M.	AMETHYST	
LATHAN, John	Pte. R.M.	AMETHYST*	(Joined after this Action)
	Pte. R.M.	NAIAD	Trafalgar
	Pte. R.M.	AMETHYST	Amethyst 5 April 1809
	Pte. R.M.	IMPREGNABLE	Algiers
LAUTENBURGH, Christian	Carpenter's Crew	AMETHYST	
	L.M.	AMETHYST	Amethyst 5 April 1809
MACDONALD, John	Capt Main Top	AMETHYST	
	Capt Main Top	AMETHYST	Amethyst 5 April 1809
MARLAND, John	Pte. R.M.	AMETHYST	(M.L. MAITLAND @ MARLAND)
MILES, Lawford	Midshipman	AMETHYST	
	Master's Mate	AMETHYST	Amethyst 5 April 1809
	Master's Mate	QUEEN CHARLOTTE	Algiers
PEARCE, John	Boy 2nd Cl	AMETHYST	
	Boy 2nd Cl	AMETHYST	Amethyst 5 April 1809 (Vfd Abd. Not on Roll)
REARDON, Patrick	L.M.	AMETHYST	
	L.M.	AMETHYST	Amethyst 5 April 1809
	L.M.	ASTRAEA	Off Tamatave. 20 May 1811

AMETHYST Wh THETIS

RUTTER, John	Sgt. R.M.	AMETHYST	
	Sgt. R.M.	AMETHYST	*Amethyst 5 April 1809*
SEYMOUR, John C.	Midshipman	AMETHYST	
	Midshipman	AMETHYST	*Amethyst 5 April 1809*
SEYMOUR, Matthew C.	Vol 1st Cl	AMETHYST	
SIMS, Robert	Pte. R.M.	AMETHYST	*(Not found on Muster List ADM 37/709)*
SMITH, Isaac	Pte. R.M.	AMETHYST	
STEVENS, Vivian	Master's Mate	AMETHYST	
TAYLOR, Leonard	Boatswain	AMETHYST	
	Bosun's Mate	BEDFORD	*Camperdown*
WALKER, George	Ord	AMETHYST	
	Ord	AMETHYST	*Amethyst 5 April 1809*
WHATLEY, John	Pte. R.M.	AMETHYST	

(2) 28 NOV BOAT SERVICE 1808

Attack on the batteries in MAHAULT BAY, GUADALOUPE, and capture of two vessels.
(Real date 29 November 1808)

LAWRENCE, Daniel	Lieut. R.N.	HEUREUX	
	Midshipman	CYNTHIA	*Egypt*
	Lieut. R.N.	WANDERER	*Guadaloupe*
MILNE, James	Carpenter	HEUREUX	

(16) OFF THE PEARL ROCK 13 DEC 1808

Action with batteries at MARTINIQUE; – and the destruction of the French corvette CYGNE and two schooners. Mainly a boat service type of Action.
(Real dates 12 & 13 December 1808)

CLARK, Alexander	A.B.	MORNE FORTUNEE	
	Ord	MORNE FORTUNEE	*Curacoa*
COLLIER, Francis.A.	Commander	CIRCE	*(P)*
	Vol 1st Cl	VANGUARD	*Nile*
	Captain. R.N.	CIRCE	*Martinique*
CROOKE, Charles.H.	Act Lieut. R.N.	CIRCE	*(V/d Abd. Not on Roll but M.I.D. L.Gaz. 1809.p146.)*
	Midshipman	PHOEBE	*Trafalgar*
FRY, Richard	Pte. R.M.	STORK	
	Pte. R.M.	STORK	*Martinique*
GARRICK, James	Ord	AMARANTHE	
	Ord	AMARANTHE	*Martinique*
	A.B.	AMARANTHE	*Guadaloupe*
HARDING, George	A.B.	STORK	
	A.B.	STORK	*Martinique*
HARRISON, Joseph	Lieut. R.N.	EPERVIER	
JAGO, John	A.B.	CIRCE	*(M.L. as JAGOE)*
	A.B.	CIRCE	*Martinique*
Le GEYT, George	Commander	STORK	
	Commander	STORK	*Martinique*
RIGMAIDEN, James	Midshipman	AMARANTHE	
	Midshipman	AMARANTHE	*Martinique*
ROBERTS, Alexander	Yeoman of Sheets	CIRCE	
	Yeoman of Sheets	CIRCE	*Martinique*
RORIE, John.J.	Lt. R.N. Cmmdg	MORNE FORTUNEE	*(V/d Abd. Not on Roll)*
	Midshipman	STANDARD	*23rd June 1795*
	Lt. R.N. Cmmdg	MORNE FORTUNEE	*Curacoa*
RUSSELL, Peter	(Not Found)	MORNE FORTUNEE*	
	Supn. Un-Rated	NEPTUNE	*Martinique*
UNDERWOOD, George	Ord	CIRCE	
	Ord	CIRCE	*Martinique*
WEATHERHEAD, William	A.B.	AMARANTHE	*G.H. 7,039*
WILLANS, Joseph	Vol 1st Cl	AMARANTHE	
	Vol 1st Cl	AMARANTHE	*Martinique*

(NOTE. This Action was a combination of bombardment from sea and fierce fighting by boat's crews sent inshore. It would appear that a number of men from AMARANTHE, CIRCE and STORK who were awarded Martinique & Guadaloupe clasps, – and who were entitled to this clasp, – did not claim for it. Perhaps such men thought that this was a "Boat Service Action", and since they had not served in the boats at the time, did not consider that their claim for this clasp would receive approval.)

ONYX 1 JANY 1809

(5)

Capture of the Dutch brig MANLY, in the North Sea.

BARNES, John	Ord	ONYX	
DUTCHMAN, Hewson	Clerk	ONYX	(M.L. as HEUSEN)
EDWARDS, Henry	Quarter Gunner	ONYX	G.H. 5,197
GARRETT, Edward.Wm	Lieut. R.N.	ONYX	
	Lieut. R.N.	MARS	Trafalgar
WHITE, William	Master's Mate	ONYX	

CONFIANCE 14 JANY 1809

(8)

Taking of CAYENNE, French Guiana.

BLACKMAN, John	Yeoman of Sheets	CONFIANCE	
	Yeoman of Sheets	CONFIANCE	B.S. 13 Feb 1808
BRYANT, Edward	Midshipman	CONFIANCE	
BYERLEE, George	Boatswain	CONFIANCE	(M.L. also as BYERLEIGH)
	A.B.	RAMILLIES	1 June 1794
	Yeoman of Signals	RUSSELL	Copenhagen. 1801
HINNICK, Thomas	Ord	CONFIANCE	
HOSAN, Christopher	L.M.	CONFIANCE	(M.L. as HOUSEN)
MOORE, William	Midshipman	CONFIANCE	
O'CALLOGHAN, Henry.J.	Vol 1st Cl	CONFIANCE	
WARD, Thomas	Cpl R.M.	CONFIANCE	

MARTINIQUE

(486)

Capture of Martinique on 24 February 1809, for which a medal was bestowed upon the Army.

ABBOTT, Christopher	Captain. R.M.	INTREPID	
	1st Lieut. R.M.	GANGES	Copenhagen 1801. Also received M.G.S./Guadaloupe.
ABBOTT, Thomas	L.M.	CAPTAIN	
ADAMSON, John	A.B.	NEPTUNE	
ALLEN, John	Carp's Crew	CIRCE	G.H. 7705
ALLEN, William	Pte. R.M.	POMPEE	
	Pte. R.M.	POMPEE	Pompee. 17 June 1809 (Vfd Abd. Not on Roll)
	Pte. R.M.	POMPEE	Guadaloupe
ANDREWS, Thomas.J.	A.B.	STAR	G.H. 3281
	Boy	VESTAL	Egypt (Roll as Thomas)
	A.B.	STAR	Guadaloupe
ANGIER, Ezekiel	Coxswain	BELLEISLE	
	Coxswain	POMPEE	Pompee. 17 June 1809
	Coxswain	ABERCROMBIE	Guadaloupe
ANLEY, William	Midshipman	NEPTUNE	
	Midshipman	POMPEE	Guadaloupe
ARCHER, Thomas	Clerk	BELLEISLE	
	Clerk	POMPEE	Pompee. 17 June 1809
	Clerk	ABERCROMBIE	Guadaloupe
ATKINS, James (a)	Lieut. R.N.	MOZAMBIQUE	
BAILEY, Walter	Ord	ACASTA	
	L.M.	ACASTA	St Domingo
	Ord	SCIPION	Java
BAKER, William.H.	Master	CAPTAIN	
BALDWIN, Benjamin	Ord	STORK	
(BALHETCHET, William)	(2nd Lieut. R.M.)	(NEPTUNE)	Awarded M.G.S. medal & clasps for Martinique & Guadaloupe. Became Purser
BALL, James	Not given	POMPEE	
BALLINGALL, James	Master	PELORUS	
	Master	PELORUS	Guadaloupe
BARKER, Francis	Boy	ETHALION	
BARLOW, John	Ord	STORK	
BARKLEY, Charles	Vol 1st Cl	BELLEISLE	
BARTHOLOMEW, John	A.B.	INTREPID	G.H. 3146
	A.B.	POMPEE	Guadaloupe
BATT, William	Midshipman	EXPRESS	
BAYLIS, William	L.M.	POMPEE	
	L.M.	POMPEE	Pompee. 17 June 1809 (Vfd Abd. Not on Roll)
	L.M.	POMPEE	Guadaloupe
BEARD, Hugh	A.B.	NEPTUNE	
BECK, John	L.M.	ETHALION	
BEDFORD, Joseph	A.B.	POMPEE	
	A.B.	POMPEE	Pompee. 17 June 1809
	A.B.	POMPEE	Guadaloupe

MARTINIQUE

Name	Rank	Ship	Notes
BEER, Christopher	Master's Mate	SURINAM	
BENNY, Thomas	A.B.	INTREPID	
(BIGLAND, Wilson B.)	(Lieut. R.N.)	(POMPEE)	Awarded M.G.S. Medal
(BIRDWOOD, Thomas)	(Lieut. R.N.)	(BELLEISLE)	Awarded M.G.S. Medal
BIRTH, Thomas	Pte. R.M.	ACASTA	
BISHOP, John	Armourer's Mate	EURYDICE	G.H. 8812
	Armourer's Mate	BACCHANTE	B.S. 1 & 18 Sep 1812
	Armourer	BACCHANTE	B.S. 6 Jan 1813
BISHOP, Thomas	Surgeon	BELLETTE	
BLACKMAN, James	Capt' Main Top	BELLEISLE	
	Ord	FOUDROYANT	Egypt
BLAKE, Edward J.	Midshipman	POMPEE	
BONE, William	Drummer. R.M.	POMPEE	(M.L. as Will BONES)
	Drummer. R.M.	POMPEE	Pompee. 17 June 1809
	Drummer. R.M.	POMPEE	Guadaloupe
BORNSTEAD, George	Ord	HAZARD	
BOTHWAY, Joseph	Gunner's Mate	POMPEE	
	Ord	AGINCOURT	Egypt
BOURCHIER, Thomas	Actg Lieut. R.N.	FORESTER	
BOWEN, Thomas	A.B.	GLOIRE	
	A.B.	GLOIRE	Guadaloupe
BOWERMAN, Thomas	Pte. R.M.	NEPTUNE	
	Pte. R.M.	BLONDE	Guadaloupe
BRICE, Rev. Edward	Chaplain	YORK	
BRIGGS, John	L.M.	POMPEE	(M.L. as BIGGS)
	L.M.	POMPEE	Pompee. 17 June 1809 (Vfd Abd. Not on Roll)
BRINE, John	Lieut. R.N.	GLOIRE	
	Midshipman	AGINCOURT	Egypt
	Lieut. R.N.	POMPEE	Guadaloupe
BRITTON, William	A.B.	NEPTUNE	
BROCK, Edward	Pte. R.M.	AMARANTHE	
	Pte. R.M.	AMARANTHE	Guadaloupe (Vfd Abd. Not on Roll)
BROCKFIELD, John	L.M.	FORESTER	
	L.M.	FORESTER	Guadaloupe
BRODERICK, Luke	Pte. R.M.	YORK	
BROOKMAN, William	Qtr Gunner	ETHALION	G.H. 8136
BROOKS, John	Sailmaker	INTREPID	
BROWN, John	Master	PORT d'ESPAGNE	
	Master	St PIERRE	Guadaloupe
BRYAN, Dennis	L.M.	STORK	
BRYAN, Jacob	Ord	CAPTAIN	(M.L. as BYRON)
	L.M.	DREADNOUGHT	Trafalgar
BRYAN, John	Purser	EURYDICE	
	Purser	ALCMENE	Guadaloupe
	Purser	EUROTAS	Eurotas. 25 Feby 1814
BUCKLAND, Benjamin	Pte. R.M.	NEPTUNE	
BUCKLER, William	Pte. R.M.	NEPTUNE	
	Pte. R.M.	BLONDE	Guadaloupe
BUCKLEY, John	Ord	ETHALION	
BULFORD, John	Actg Lieut. R.N.	INTREPID	
BURCHELL, T.	Pte. R.M.	EURYDICE	
BURKE, James	"Convict"	POMPEE	Courtmartialled Mutineer
	L.M.	TEMERAIRE	Trafalgar
	Ord	ANSON	Anson. 23 Augt 1806
	Ord	ANSON	Curacoa
	Ord	LION	Java. (re-instated Ord)
BURNETT, Thomas	Carpenter	GOREE	
	Caulker	GALATEA	B.S. 21 Jan 1807
BURTON, George.G.	Lieut. R.N.	NEPTUNE	
	Midshipman	VENERABLE	Gut of Gibraltar. 12 July 1801
	Lieut. R.N.	POMPEE	Guadaloupe
BUTTER, Henry	Pte. R.M.	POMPEE	
	Pte. R.M.	POMPEE	Pompee. 17 June 1809 (Vfd Abd. Not on Roll)
	Pte. R.M.	GUADALOUPE	Guadaloupe. (Vfd Abd. Brig GUADALOUPE. Not on Roll)
BUTTON, Henry	Pte. R.M.	NEPTUNE	
CAMPBELL, Archibald	Gunner's Mate	CAPTAIN	
CAMPBELL, James	Lieut. R.M.	ACASTA	
	Lieut. R.M.	ACASTA	St Domingo
CAMPBELL, John	A.B.	STORK	(M.L. as HUTCHINSON, Wm)
	A.B.	SPEEDY	Speedy. 6 May 1801
CAMPBELL, William	Master's Mate	GLOIRE	
	Lieut. R.N.	ROSAMUND	Guadaloupe
CARNEY, Bryan	L.M.	CAPTAIN	(M.L. as Barney)
	L.M.	BELLEISLE	Trafalgar
CARNEY, James	L.M.	ETHALION	
CARTER, Samuel.J.	Actg Lieut. R.N.	INTREPID	
	Lieut. R.N.	ROSAMUND	Guadaloupe

CARTER, Thomas	A.B.	PENELOPE	G.H. 3335
CARTHEW, James	Captain. R.N.	GLOIRE	
	Lieut. R.N.	ROSARIO	Capture of the Desiree (Vfd Abd. Not on Roll)
CASHMORE, John	Pte. R.M.	NEPTUNE	
CHADWICK, Charles	L.M.	AEOLUS	G.H. 2141
	L.M.	AEOLUS	4 Novr 1805
CHAMBERLAIN, William.B.	Lieut. R.N.	AEOLUS	
	Midshipman	MONMOUTH	Egypt
CHAMBERS, John	Ord	CAPTAIN	
	Ord	DREADNOUGHT	Trafalgar
CHAPPELL, Edward	Midshipman	INTREPID	
	Vol 1st Cl	KINGFISHER	St Domingo
CHATFIELD, Charles	A.B.	PENELOPE	
CHESTON, John	A.B.	YORK	G.H. 6925
CHILCOTT, James	Pte. R.M.	CLEOPATRA	
	Pte. R.M.	FLORA	Egypt
CHILD, Charles	A.B.	STORK	
CHRISTIE, Thomas	Midshipman	WOLVERINE	
CHRYSTIE, Thomas	Midshipman	NEPTUNE	
	Midshipman	AJAX	Egypt
	Midshipman	DEFIANCE	Trafalgar
CLACK, Thomas	Lieut. R.N.	GOREE	
	Midshipman	MAGNANIME	12 Octr 1798
	Sub Lieut. R.N.	EPERVIER	St Domingo
CLARE, James	A.B.	EURYDICE	(M.L. as CLEAR)
CLARK, Edward	Ord	POMPEE	
	Ord	POMPEE	Pompee. 17 June 1809
	Ord	POMPEE	Guadaloupe
CLARK, John	Purser's Steward	PELORUS	
	Purser's Steward	PELORUS	Guadaloupe
CLARK, William	Q.M.	NEPTUNE	
CLARKE, George	Ord	NEPTUNE	
CLARKE, Walter	Pte. R.M.	NEPTUNE	
	Pte. R.M.	NIGER	St Vincent
CLARKE, William	Yeoman of Sheets	YORK	
COATES, Richard	Lieut. R.N.	SURINAM	
COCHRANE, Thomas	Captain. R.N.	ETHALION	
	Midshipman	AJAX	Egypt
COCK, George	Pte. R.M.	NEPTUNE	G.H. 7105
COCKBURN, George	Commodore	POMPEE	
	Captain. R.N.	MELEAGER	14 March 1795
	Captain. R.N.	MINERVE	Minerve. 19 Decr 1796
	Captain. R.N.	MINERVE	St Vincent
	Captain. R.N.	MINERVE	Egypt
	Rear Admiral	MARLBOROUGH	B.S. Ap & May 1813
COLLIER, Edward	Midshipman	BELLEISLE	
	Master's Mate	EURYALUS	The Potomac. 17 Aug 1814
COLLIER, Francis.A.	Captain. R.N.	CIRCE	
	Vol 1st Cl	VANGUARD	Nile
	Commander	CIRCE (P)	Off the Pearl Rock. 13 Dec 1808
CONNELL, David	Ord	NEPTUNE	
	Ord	NORTHAMPTON	St Domingo
CONNOLLEY, George	Purser	SNAP	(Alias Wm POWERS)
	Purser	SNAP	Guadaloupe
CONNOR, Daniel	Boy 3rd Class	WOLVERINE	
CONNOR, James	Pte. R.M.	CAPTAIN	
	Pte. R.M.	DREADNOUGHT	Trafalgar
CONNOR, James	Ord	NEPTUNE	
	Boy	NORTHUMBERLAND	St Domingo
	A.B.	GLASGOW	Navarino
COOPER, James	R.M. Boy	POMPEE	
	R.M. Boy	POMPEE	Pompee. 17 June 1809
	R.M. Boy	POMPEE	Guadaloupe
COOPER, Jonathan	Pte. R.M.	NEPTUNE	
	Pte. R.M.	BLONDE	Guadaloupe
COX, Douglas	Lieut. R.N.	SNAP	
	Lieut. R.N.	SNAP	Guadaloupe
CRAIG, Robert	Ord	ACASTA	
CRAWFORD, George	A.B.	CAPTAIN	
CRAWLEY, Bryan	Boy	PENELOPE	
CROFTON, Hon G.A.	Commander	FAWN	
	Commander	FAWN	Guadaloupe
CROMBIE, William	Boy	CHERUB	
	Supn. L.M.	CHERUB	Cherub. 28 March 1814
CULLERN, William	Pte. R.M.	BELLEISLE	
DALEY, Michael	Pte. R.M.	NEPTUNE	
	Pte. R.M.	BLONDE	Guadaloupe

MARTINIQUE

DANIEL, John	A.B.	POMPEE	
	A.B.	POMPEE	Pompee. 17 June 1809 (Vfd Abd. Not on Roll)
	A.B.	POMPEE	Guadaloupe
	A.B.	ASTRAEA	Of Tamatave. 20 May 1811
DAVID, William	Carp's Crew	INTREPID	
	A.B.	POMPEE	Guadaloupe
DAVIES, Richard	Ord	NEPTUNE	
DAVIS, John	Capt' Main Top	NEPTUNE	
	Ord	NORTHUMBERLAND	St Domingo
DAVIS, John	Boy 3rd Class	RECRUIT	
	Boy 3rd Class	RECRUIT	Recruit. 17 June 1809
DAVISON, Kilgour	Midshipman	NEPTUNE	
	Actg Lieut. R.N.	VIMIERA	Guadaloupe
DAWSON, Dixon	Yeoman of Sheets	INTREPID	
DAY, Bartholomew.G.S.	Actg Master	SUPERIEURE	(Vfd Abd. Not on Roll)
	Midshipman	REVENGE	Trafalgar
	Actg Master	SUPERIEURE	Superieure. 10 Feby 1809
	Actg Master	SUPERIEURE	Guadaloupe
DELAFOSSE, Edward.H.	Lieut. R.N.	YORK	
	Vol 1st Cl	CRUIZER	Copenhagen 1801
	Lieut. R.N.	HEBRUS	Algiers
DEEMER, George	Pte. R.M.	NEPTUNE	G.H. 9740 as DEAMAN
	Pte. R.M.	PEGASUS	Egypt (Roll as DEMER)
DICK, John	Captain. R.N.	PENELOPE	
	Commander	CYNTHIA	Egypt
DICKIE, John	A.B.	NEPTUNE	
	Secretary's Clerk	NEPTUNE	Guadaloupe
DICKSON, Daniel.J.H.	Physician	NEPTUNE	
DIGMAN, Andrew	A.B.	BELLETTE	(or DIGNAM)
	A.B.	BELLETTE	Guadaloupe
DOUGLAS, James.S.	Midshipman	ACASTA	
	Midshipman	NISUS	Java
DOUGLAS, Richard	Midshipman	NEPTUNE	
	Midshipman	ACHILLE	Trafalgar
DUNKLEY, George	Ord	NEPTUNE	
	Ord	NORTHUMBERLAND	St Domingo
	Capt' After Guard	WANDERER	Guadaloupe
DUNNING, William	Pte. R.M.	BELLEISLE	
DUNSTAN, Octavius	Master's Mate	ETHALION	
	Master's Mate	HOGUE	B.S. 8 April 1814
EAGLES, Joseph	Pte. R.M.	FAWN	G.H. 5556
	Pte. R.M.	FAWN	Guadaloupe
ELLIOTT, George.Edwd.	Midshipman	FORESTER	(O'Byrne as Edward George)
	Midshipman	FORESTER	Guadaloupe
EPPS, John	L.M.	POMPEE	G.H. 5997
	L.M.	POMPEE	Pompee. 17 June 1809 (Vfd Abd. Not on Roll)
	L.M.	POMPEE	Guadaloupe
EVANS, Gustavus	Lieut. R.N.	CHERUB	
	Master's Mate	EPERVIER	St Domingo
	Lieut. R.N.	CHERUB	Guadaloupe
EVANS, John	Ord	INTREPID	
EVANS, Thomas	Ord	POMPEE	
	Ord	POMPEE	Pompee. 17 June 1809 (Vfd Abd. Not on Roll)
	Ord	POMPEE	Guadaloupe
EVANS, Thomas	Bosun's Mate	ULYSSES	
FAIRHEAD, James	A.B.	ELIZABETH	
FARLEY, William	Master's Mate	FAWN	
	Midshipman	HERO	4 Novr 1805
	Master's Mate	FAWN	Guadaloupe
FARQUHARSON, William	Vol 1st Cl	AEOLUS	
	Vol 1st Cl	AEOLUS	4 Novr 1805
FELLOWS, Richard	Pte. R.M.	YORK	G.H. 9515
	Pte. R.M.	CYDNUS	B.S. 14 Dec 1814
FELT, Hans Christian	Ord	POMPEE	G.H. 8855 as O'FELL
	Ord	POMPEE	Pompee. 17 June 1809 (Vfd Abd. Not on Roll)
	Ord	POMPEE	Guadaloupe
FERGUSON, William	Boatswain	HAZARD	
	Boy	CANADA	12 Octr 1798
	Boatswain	HAZARD	Anse La Barque. 18 Decr 1809
	Boatswain	HAZARD	Guadaloupe
FERRIS, James	Pte. R.M.	CLEOPATRA	
FISHER, Edward	A.B.	EXPRESS	

FITZGERALD, Thomas	Ord	POMPEE	
	Ord	POMPEE	Pompee. 17 June 1809
	Ord	POMPEE	Guadaloupe
FITZPATRICK, Thomas	L.M.	CAPTAIN	
	L.M.	DREADNOUGHT	Trafalgar
FITZROY, Lord William	Captain. R.N.	AEOLUS	
	Captain's Servant	PHAETON	1 June 1794
	Midshipman	SANS PAREIL	23rd June 1795 (Vfd Abd. Not on Roll)
	Lieut. R.N.	PENELOPE	Egypt
	Captain. R.N.	AEOLUS	4 Novr 1805
FLEMING, Peter	A.B.	NEPTUNE	G.H. 8549
FLEMING, Richard.H.	Actg Lieut. R.N.	YORK	
	Lieut. R.N.	Qn CHARLOTTE	Algiers
FORD, Ambrose	Bosun's Mate	HAZARD	
	Bosun's Mate	HAZARD	Guadaloupe
FORSTER, Joseph	A.B.	POMPEE	(Vfd Abd. Not on Roll)
	A.B.	POMPEE	Pompee. 17 June 1809 (Vfd Abd. Not on Roll)
	A.B.	POMPEE	Guadaloupe
FRANCILLON, John.G.	Midshipman	POMPEE	
	Midshipman	MARLBOROUGH	B.S. Ap & May 1813
FRANCILLON, Thomas	Midshipman	POMPEE	
	Midshipman	MARLBOROUGH	B.S. Ap & May 1813
	Supn Lieut. R.N.	RAMILLIES	B.S. 14 Dec 1814
FRANCIS, Robert	Ord	BELLEISLE	
FREEMAN, Henry	Capt' Forecastle	NEPTUNE	
FROST, William	Ord	YORK	G.H. 7663
FRY, Richard	Pte. R.M.	STORK	
	Pte. R.M.	STORK	Off the Pearl Rock. 13 Dec 1808
FRYATT, John	Ord	RINGDOVE	
FURNEAUX, Theophilus	Capt' Main Top	EURYDICE	
	A.B.	BACCHANTE	B.S. 1 & 18 Sep 1812
	A.B.	BACCHANTE	B.S. 6 Jan 1813
FUSHAW, Joseph	L.M.	YORK	
GARRICK, James	Ord	ARAMANTHE	
	Ord	ARAMANTHE	Off the Pearl Rock. 13 Dec 1808
	A.B.	ARAMANTHE	Guadaloupe
GEORGE, William	A.B.	NEPTUNE	
GIBSON, James	Ord	PENELOPE	
	L.M.	ROYAL SOVEREIGN	Trafalgar
GIFFARD, Henry	Boy	NEPTUNE	
	Boy	POMPEE	Guadaloupe
GILBERT, Samuel	A.B.	AEOLUS	
	A.B.	AEOLUS	4 Novr 1805
GILES, Samuel	Purser	ULYSSES	
	Midshipman	CULLODEN	1 June 1794
	Purser	ASTRAEA	Egypt
GILLESPIE, William	Ord	NEPTUNE	
	L.M.	NORTHUMBERLAND	St Domingo
GOODLAD, Edward	Midshipman	NEPTUNE	
	Midshipman	NEPTUNE	Trafalgar (Vfd Abd. Not on Roll)
	Midshipman	POMPEE	Guadaloupe
GORE, Martin	A.B.	WOLVERINE	G.H. 8489 or 5489
GORMAN, John	A.B.	POMPEE	
	A.B.	AUDACIOUS	Gut of Gibraltar. 12 July 1801
	A.B.	POMPEE	Pompee. 17 June 1809
	A.B.	POMPEE	Guadaloupe
	Yeoman of Sheets	Qn CHARLOTTE	Algiers
GOULD, William	Midshipman	NEPTUNE	
GOWLAND, Thomas	A.B.	POMPEE	
	A.B.	POMPEE	Pompee. 17 June 1809 (Vfd Abd. Not on Roll)
	Capt' Main Top	ABERCROMBIE	Guadaloupe
GRANT, James	Pte. R.M.	ETHALION	
GRAVES, James	Q.M.	POMPEE	
	Q.M.	POMPEE	Pompee. 17 June 1809 (Vfd Abd. Not on Roll)
	Q.M.	POMPEE	Guadaloupe
GREY, James	L.M.	POMPEE	(M.L. as GRAY)
	L.M.	POMPEE	Pompee. 17 June 1809
	L.M.	POMPEE	Guadaloupe
GRIFFITHS, Lewellyn	Pte. R.M.	ACASTA	
GROSCOTT, Joshua or Joseph	M.A.A.	CAPTAIN	(Roll also as HMS YORK)
	Qtr Gunner	DEFIANCE	Copenhagen 1801
	A.B.	MINDEN	Algiers
GROVES, John	Corporal R.M.	NEPTUNE	
GUILD, George	L.M.	PENELOPE	
GWYNNE, Samuel	Capt' Forecastle	HAUGHTY	G.H. 278
HADLEY, William	Pte. R.M.	NEPTUNE	

MARTINIQUE

HAINES, Edward	Ord	NEPTUNE	
HAINES, Thomas	Gunner	ACASTA	
	Ord	SOUTHAMPTON	Southampton. 9 June 1796 (Vfd Abd. Not on Roll)
	Ord	SOUTHAMPTON	St Vincent
	Coxswain	SUPERB	Gut of Gibraltar. 12 July 1801
	Coxswain	SUPERB	St Domingo
	Gunner	POMPEE	Pompee. 17 June 1809 (Vfd Abd. Not on Roll)
	Gunner	POMPEE	Guadaloupe
HALKETT, David	Yeoman Powder Rm	RINGDOVE	
	Yeoman Powder Rm	RINGDOVE	Anse La Barque. 18 Decr 1809
	Bosun's Mate	RINGDOVE	Guadaloupe
HALL, Charles.J.	A.B.	ULYSSES	
HALLILAY, Richard	Purser	ETHALION	
	Purser	ABERCROMBIE	Guadaloupe
HARDING, George	A.B.	STORK	
	A.B.	STORK	Off The Pearl Rock. 13 Dec 1808
HARGER, James	Drummer. R.M.	CAPTAIN	(M.L. as MAYER)
HARRINGTON, Henry	Lieut. R.M.	PENELOPE	
HARRIS, William	Boy	ACASTA	
	Boy	ACASTA	St Domingo
	Ord	SCIPION	Java
HARRIS, William	Pte. R.M.	ETHALION	
HARRIS, William.B.	Carp's Crew	CLEOPATRA	G.H. 3962
HARVEY, William	Pte. R.M.	FORESTER	
	Pte. R.M.	FORESTER	Guadaloupe
HARWOOD, John.L	Pte. R.M.	PENELOPE	
HARWOOD, Richard	Q.M's Mate	WOLVERINE	
HAWK, Thomas	L.M.	ULYSSES	
HAWKES, John	Capt' Main Top	HAZARD	
	Yeoman Powder Rm	HAZARD	Anse La Barque. 18 Decr 1809
	Yeoman Powder Rm	HAZARD	Guadaloupe
HAWKINS, George	A.B.	CAPTAIN	
HAWKINS, George	L.M.	PENELOPE	G.H. 6227
HAWKINS, Joseph	A.B.	NEPTUNE	
	L.M.	NORTHUMBERLAND	St Domingo
HAWKSFORD, John	Pte. R.M.	NEPTUNE	
HAY, James	Lieut. R.N.	AMARANTHE	
	Midshipman	DEFIANCE	Trafalgar
HAYDON, Charles	Master's Mate	CHERUB	
	Master's Mate	POMPEE	Guadaloupe
HAYDON, William.P.	Master's Mate	NEPTUNE	
	Lieut. R.N.	GUADALOUPE	Guadaloupe
HAZELDINE, John	Pte. R.M.	YORK/DOLPHIN (?)	
	Pte. R.M.	ALCMENE	Guadaloupe
HENDERSON, James	Surgeon	STAR	
HENRY (Roll), Alphonso	Midshipman	GLOIRE	O'Byrne as HENRI
HENRY, William	Midshipman	NEPTUNE	
	Midshipman	POMPEE	Guadaloupe
HEWLETT, William	Midshipman	ULYSSES	
HILL, William	L.M.	YORK	
HITCHCOCK, Thomas	A.B.	POMPEE	2 medals issued. P–M & G
	A.B.	POMPEE	Pompee. 17 June 1809
	Capt' After Guard	POMPEE	Guadaloupe
HOLE, William	Midshipman	WOLVERINE	
	Midshipman	BACCHUS	B.S. 13 Dec 1809
	Midshipman	BACCHUS	Guadaloupe
	Master's Mate	TRAAVE	B.S. 14 Dec 1814
HOLLOWAY, William	Ord	CAPTAIN	
	L.M.	DREADNOUGHT	Trafalgar
(HOOKEY, George)	(2nd Lieut. R.M.)	(ACASTA)	Awarded M.G.S. Medal
HOOPER, Benjamin	Pte. R.M.	POMPEE	G.H. 2231
	Pte. R.M.	POMPEE	Pompee. 17 June 1809 (Vfd Abd. Not on Roll)
	Pte. R.M.	POMPEE	Guadaloupe
HORNE, Benjamin	Pte. R.M.	INTREPID	
HOWELL, John.S.	Purser's Steward	YORK	
HOWES, William	Pte. R.M.	POMPEE	
	Pte. R.M.	POMPEE	Pompee. 17 June 1809 (Vfd Abd. Not on Roll)
	Pte. R.M.	POMPEE	Guadaloupe
HULKS, John	Ord	YORK	
HUNTER, Hugh	Midshipman	HAZARD	
	Midshipman	HAZARD	Anse La Barque. 18 Decr 1809
	Midshipman	HAZARD	Guadaloupe
HURD, Thomas	A.B.	AMARANTHE	
	Capt' Fore Top	AMARANTHE	Guadaloupe

HUTCHINGS, George	L.M.	POMPEE	
	L.M.	POMPEE	Pompee. 17 June 1809 (Vfd Abd. Not on Roll)
	L.M.	POMPEE	Guadaloupe
HUTCHINS, William	Capt' Forecastle	NEPTUNE	
IFGRAVE, Samuel	Carp's Crew	AEOLUS	
	Carp's Crew	AEOLUS	4 Novr 1805
(JACKSON, Charles.S.)	(Vol 1st Cl)	(CAPTAIN)	Awarded M.G.S. Medal
JACKSON, Henry	Midshipman	FROLIC	
JAGO, John	A.B.	CIRCE	(M.L. as JAGOE)
	A.B.	CIRCE	Off the Pearl Rock. 13 Dec 1808
JAMES, Horatio	Master's Mate	ETHALION	
JEFFERY, Samuel	A.B.	ACASTA	
	A.B.	ACASTA	St Domingo
	Yeoman of Sheets	SCIPION	Java
JOHNSON, John	Q.M.	YORK	
JOHNSON, Joseph	A.B.	YORK	G.H. 6574
JONES, John	Carp's Crew	ACASTA	
	Carp's Crew	SCIPION	Java
JONES, William	Vol 1st Cl	CAPTAIN	
	Midshipman	CONSTANT	St Sebastian
JONES, William	Carp's Crew	CAPTAIN	
KARLEY, Alexander	Master's Mate	CLEOPATRA	
KELSALL, Edward	Qtr Gunner	POMPEE	G.H. 7960
	A.B.	AGINCOURT	Camperdown (See notes)
	Qtr Gunner	POMPEE	Pompee. 17 June 1809
	Q.M's Mate	POMPEE	Guadaloupe
KENNEDY, Alexander	Commander	PORT d'ESPAGNE	
	Midshipman	THAMES	Gut of Gibraltar. 12 July 1801
KENNEDY, Andrew	Midshipman	PENELOPE	
	Vol 1st Cl	VICTORY	St Vincent
KERBY, Israel	Pte. R.M.	CAPTAIN	G.H. 2786
	Pte. R.M.	DREADNOUGHT	Trafalgar
KERRISON, James	Pte. R.M.	SUPERIEURE	
	A.B. (? Roll)	SUPERIEURE	Guadaloupe
KILLOCK, Robert	Pte. R.M.	BELLEISLE	
	Pte. R.M.	ALFRED	Guadaloupe
	Pte. R.M.	SURVEILLANTE	St Sebastian
KING, Samuel	Pte. R.M.	NEPTUNE	
	Pte. R.M.	FROLIC	Guadaloupe
KIRBY, John	A.B.	BELLEISLE	
KIRBY, Walter	Midshipman	ETHALION	
KITE, James	Ord	FORESTER	
KNOWLES, Joseph	Pte. R.M.	ETHALION	
LACK, Stephen	Pte. R.M.	POMPEE	
	Pte. R.M.	POMPEE	Pompee. 17 June 1809 (Vfd Abd. Not on Roll)
	Pte. R.M.	POMPEE	Guadaloupe
LAKE, William	Armourer's Mate	ACASTA	
LAKE, William	Boy	PENELOPE	
LANE, William	Midshipman	PELORUS	
	Midshipman	ALCMENE	Guadaloupe
LANGDON, John	A.B.	ETHALION	
LAURENCE, Thomas	L.M.	PENELOPE	
LAY, James	Ord	POMPEE	
	Ord	POMPEE	Pompee. 17 June 1809
	Ord	POMPEE	Guadaloupe
LEAR, Daniel	L.M.	CIRCE	G.H. 9343
	L.M.	ABERCROMBIE	Guadaloupe
LEATHERBY, John	A.B.	NEPTUNE	
LEECH, Robert	Master	PULTUSK	
	Midshipman	POMPEE	Guadaloupe
LEECH, Robert	A.B.	POMPEE	
	A.B.	POMPEE	Guadaloupe
Le GEYT, George	Commander	STORK	
	Commander	STORK	Off the Pearl Rock. 13 Dec 1808
LEITCH, James	Surgeon	AMARANTHE	
	Surgeon	AMARANTHE	Guadaloupe
LETHBRIDGE, Thomas	Carp's Crew	FAWN	
LEWIS, William	Ord	POMPEE	G.H. 7160
	Ord	POMPEE	Pompee. 17 June 1809
	Ord	POMPEE	Guadaloupe
LINDSAY, John	Coxswain	GOREE	
LINES, Thomas	Boy	NEPTUNE	
LITHERLAND, William	Pte. R.M.	PENELOPE	
LLOYD, Rickard	(Actg?) Lieut. R.N.	SURINAM	(Not yet aboard?)
	Midshipman	PIQUE	Pique 26 March 1806
	Lieut. R.N.	NORGE	B.S. 14 Dec 1814
LOCK, James	Pte. R.M.	PENELOPE	
LOCK, Robert	Pte. R.M.	NEPTUNE	
	Pte. R.M.	ABERCROMBIE	Guadaloupe

MARTINIQUE

LOVELESS, Bassett.J.	Actg Lieut. R.N.	FAWN	
	A.B.	AUDACIOUS	Gut of Gibraltar. 12 July 1801
	Actg Lieut. R.N.	FAWN	Guadaloupe
LOWE, Thomas	Pte. R.M.	POMPEE	
	Pte. R.M.	POMPEE	Pompee. 17 June 1809
	Pte. R.M.	POMPEE	Guadaloupe
LUCKSINGER, Nelson	Ord	HAUGHTY	
LYNCH, Richard	A.B.	ETHALION	
MACLEOD, John	Purser	YORK	
(MACNEVIN – see McNEVIN)			
MAILES, George	Pte. R.M.	BELLEISLE	
	Pte. R.M.	ALFRED	Guadaloupe
MALCOLM, John	Master's Mate	FAWN	(May read MALCOLME)
MALLARD, Charles	Midshipman	ETHALION	
MANNAH, William	Boy	BELLETTE	
MANSELL, James	Ord	NEPTUNE	G.H. 5668
	Ord	NORTHUMBERLAND	St Domingo
MARSHALL, George E.	Lieut. R.N.	ACASTA	
	Midshipman	PHOENIX	4 Novr 1805
MARTIN, Thomas	Lieut. R.N.	PENELOPE	
MASON, James	A.B.	POMPEE	
	A.B.	POMPEE	Pompee. 17 June 1809 (Vfd Abd. Not on Roll)
	A.B.	POMPEE	Guadaloupe
MATTHEWS, John	Ord	STAR	
	Ord	STAR	Guadaloupe
	A.B.	MALTA	Gaieta. 24 July 1815
	A.B.	IMPREGNABLE	Algiers
MAXWELL, John	A.B.	BELLEISLE	
MAY, Henry	A.B.	LIBERTY	(Alias HODGMAN)
MAYNARD, James	Gunner	STAR	
	Gunner	STAR	Guadaloupe
McADAM, Alexander	L.M.	NEPTUNE	
	L.M.	NORTHUMBERLAND	St Domingo
	L.M.	POMPEE	Guadaloupe
McADAM, Daniel	A.B.	NEPTUNE	
McLAREN, David	Pte. R.M.	STAR	
	Pte. R.M.	STAR	Guadaloupe
McLAREN, Thomas	A.B.	NEPTUNE	G.H. 5968
	A.B.	NORTHUMBERLAND	St Domingo
McLEOD, Alexander	Ord	STAR	
	Ord	STAR	Guadaloupe
	A.B.	MALTA	Gaieta. 24 July 1815
McMULLEN, Laughlan	Carp's Crew	CIRCE	
McNAMARA, Patrick	Ord	BELLEISLE	
McNEVIN, John	Lieut. R.N.	SUPERIEURE	
	Lieut. R.N.	SUPERIEURE	Guadaloupe
MERCER, John D.	Master's Mate	BELLEISLE	
	Master's Mate	POMPEE	Pompee. 17 June 1809
	Lieut. R.N.	PULTUSK	B.S. 13 Dec 1809
	Lieut. R.N.	PULTUSK	Guadaloupe
MEYER, Anthony	Carp's Crew	ETHALION	
MILLER, Canute	Pte. R.M.	EURYDICE	G.H. 2125
MILLER, James	Ord	POMPEE	
	Ord	POMPEE	Pompee. 17 June 1809
	Ord	POMPEE	Guadaloupe
MILLS, Benjamin	A.B.	BELLEISLE	
MILLS, James	Boy	PELORUS	
	Ord	ALFRED	Guadaloupe
MILWARD, Clement	Lieut. R.N.	POMPEE	
	Midshipman	ALARM	B.S. 17 March 1794
MITCHELL, John	Ord	PULTUSK	
	Ord	PULTUSK	Guadaloupe
MITCHELL, Joseph	Boy	SURINAM	
	Boy	SURINAM	Guadaloupe
MITCHELL, Thomas	L.M.	POMPEE	G.H. 3120
	L.M.	POMPEE	Pompee. 17 June 1809
	L.M.	POMPEE	Guadaloupe (Vfd Abd. Not on Roll)
MOORE, Henry	Ord	CAPTAIN	
MOORE, Thomas	A.B.	ULYSSES	
MORAN, John	Pte. R.M.	NEPTUNE	G.H. 9461
	Pte. R.M.	NORTHUMBERLAND	St Domingo
MORAN, Peter	Drummer. R.M.	NEPTUNE	
MORGAN, Joseph	L.M.	POMPEE	
	L.M.	POMPEE	Pompee. 17 June 1809
	L.M.	POMPEE	Guadaloupe

MOTT, Joseph	Capt' Forecastle	RECRUIT	
	Ord	DEFENCE	Copenhagen 1801
	Capt' Forecastle	RECRUIT	Recruit. 17 June 1809 (Vfd Abd. Not on Roll)
MULLIGAN, Thomas	L.M.	YORK	
MURPHY, Daniel	Capt' After Guard	GOREE	
MURRAY, James	Lieut. R.N.	INTREPID	
MUSTART or MUSTARD, Robert	Carpenter	RECRUIT	(Vfd Abd. Not on Roll)
	Carpenter	RECRUIT	Recruit. 17 June 1809
NAPIER, Charles	Commander	RECRUIT	(Vfd Abd all clasps)
	Commander	RECRUIT (P)	Recruit. 17 June 1809
	Captain. R.N.	EURYALUS	The Potomac. 17 Aug 1814
	Commodore	POWERFUL	Syria
NASH, Samuel	Ord	SURINAM	
	A.B.	SURINAM	Guadaloupe
NEIL, John	Ord	STAR	
	Ord	STAR	Guadaloupe
	A.B.	MALTA	Gaieta. 24 July 1815
	Capt' Forecastle	IMPREGNABLE	Algiers
NEILL/NIELL, Christopher	Ord	AMARANTHE	
	A.B.	AMARANTHIE	Guadaloupe
NESHAM, Charles.J.W.	Captain. R.N.	INTREPID	
	Lieut. R.N.	ADAMANT	Camperdown
NEVIN, James	Ord	SURINAM	
	Q.M.	SURINAM	Guadaloupe
NEWTON, George	A.B.	NEPTUNE	
NICHOLLS, John	L.M.	ETHALION	
NOLBOROUGH, Joseph	Capt' of Mast	ETHALION	G.H. 8239
NOTT, John.T.	Lieut. R.N.	PORT d'ESPAGNE	
ODLAM, William.E.	Surgeon	INTREPID	
	Surgeon	ABERCROMBIE	Guadaloupe
OKEY, Benjamin	Boy 3rd Class	YORK	
ORR, Robert	L.M.	ACASTA	
	L.M.	SCIPION	Java
OSBORN, William (2)	A.B.	POMPEE	
	A.B.	POMPEE	Pompee. 17 June 1809 (Vfd Abd. Not on Roll)
	A.B.	POMPEE	Guadaloupe
OTWAY, Robert	Master's Mate	BELLEISLE	
OXFORD, John	Midshipman	BELLEISLE	
PARKER, Francis	Boy	ETHALION	
PARKER, Peter	Master	RINGDOVE	
	Master	ABERCROMBIE	Guadaloupe
PARKINSON, James	Ord	NEPTUNE	
	L.M.	NORTHUMBERLAND	St Domingo
PARRY, Thomas	A.B.	NEPTUNE	
PARSLEY, Michael	L.M.	CAPTAIN	G.H. 10,025
	L.M.	DREADNOUGHT	Trafalgar
PAXMAN, John	A.B.	ETHALION	
PATTINSON, Robert	L.M.	RECRUIT	
	L.M.	RECRUIT	Recruit. 17 June 1809
PEARCE, William	A.B.	CIRCE	
PEARSON, John	Q.M.	RECRUIT	(Vfd Abd. Not on Roll)
	Q.M.	RECRUIT	Recruit. 17 June 1809
PETRIE, Peter	Midshipman	CAPTAIN	
	Supn Midshipman	TONNANT	B.S. 14 Dec 1814
PHILLIPS, Robert	Ord	FORESTER	G.H. 8308
PICKERING, John	Pte. R.M.	BELLEISLE	
PINNEGAR, James	Pte. R.M.	DEMERARA	
PLUMB, Richard	Capt' Forecastle	BELLEISLE	
PLUMPTON, William	L.M.	YORK	
PRICE, Edward	Pte. R.M.	POMPEE	
	Pte. R.M.	POMPEE	Pompee. 17 June 1809 (Vfd Abd. Not on Roll)
PRICE, Hugh	Midshipman	FORESTER	
	Midshipman	FORESTER	Guadaloupe
PRICE, William	Corporal. R.M.	CLEOPATRA	
PRYKE, Edward	Pte. R.M.	STAR	
	Pte. R.M.	ASP	Guadaloupe
	Pte. R.M.	SEVERN	Algiers
PURCHASE, William	Midshipman	AEOLUS	
	Midshipman	AEOLUS	4 Novr 1805
QUINTON, James	Caulker	AEOLUS	
RAFFIN, Richard	Boatswain	PENELOPE	
RATCLIFFE, Edward	Ord	POMPEE	G.H. 2940
	Ord	POMPEE	Pompee. 17 June 1809
	Ord	POMPEE	Guadaloupe
RENNY, Thomas	A.B.	CAPTAIN	
(RICHARDS, Edwin)	(Master's Mate)	(POMPEE)	Awarded M.G.S. Medal

MARTINIQUE

RICHARDS, William	Qtr Gunner	ULYSSES	
RICHES, John.H.	Midshipman	DOMINICA	
	Midshipman	ALCMENE	*Guadaloupe*
RICKERBY, David	L.M.	PENELOPE	
RICKFORD, Thomas	Purser	BELLEISLE	
RIDLEY, John	Pte. R.M.	POMPEE	
	Pte. R.M.	POMPEE	*Pompee. 17 June 1809 (Vfd Abd. Not on Roll)*
	Pte. R.M.	POMPEE	*Guadaloupe*
RIDSDALE, Thomas	Supn Boy	ACASTA	
RIGMAIDEN, James	Midshipman	ARAMANTHE	
	Midshipman	ARAMANTHE	*Off the Pearl Rock. 13 Dec 1808*
ROBERTS, Alexander	Yeoman of Sheets	CIRCE	
	Yeoman of Sheets	CIRCE	*Off the Pearl Rock. 13 Dec 1808*
ROBERTS, William	Ord	NEPTUNE	
ROBINSON, James	Boy	YORK	*G.H. 3287*
ROBINSON, Joseph	Boy 3rd Class	INTREPID	
ROBINSON, Peter	L.M.	BELLEISLE	*(Additional clasp ?)*
ROBINSON, Thomas	L.M.	BELLEISLE	
ROBINSON, Thomas	Ord	CAPTAIN	
(ROBYNS, John)	(Captain. R.M.)	(NEPTUNE)	*Awarded M.G.S. Medal*
ROGERS, John	Pte. R.M.	NEPTUNE	
ROGERS, John	Supn Boy	POMPEE	
	Boy	ALCMENE	*Guadaloupe*
ROLLS, William	A.B.	RINGDOVE	
	A.B.	RINGDOVE	*Guadaloupe*
ROSE, Edward	A.B.	RINGDOVE	
	Qtr Gunner	RINGDOVE	*Anse la Barque. 18 Decr 1809*
	A.B.	RINGDOVE	*Guadaloupe*
ROSS, James	Master	DEMERARA	*G.H. 4626*
ROTELEY, Lewis	1st Lieut. R.M.	CLEOPATRA	
	2nd Lieut. R.M.	VICTORY	*Trafalgar*
RUSSELL, Peter	Supn Unrated	NEPTUNE	
	On Roll but not found	MORNE FORTUNEE	*Off the Pearl Rock. 13 Dec 1808*
RYLAND, John	Pte. R.M.	BELLEISLE	
	Pte. R.M.	SCEPTRE	*Guadaloupe*
SABBEN, James	Midshipman	NEPTUNE	
	Midshipman	DREADNOUGHT	*Trafalgar*
	Actg Lieut. R.N.	RINGDOVE	*Anse La Barque. 18 Decr 1809*
	Actg Lieut. R.N.	RINGDOVE	*Guadaloupe*
SALTER, William	L.M.	CHERUB	*G.H. 9794*
	L.M.	CHERUB	*Guadaloupe*
	Ord	CHERUB	*Cherub. 28 March 1814*
SALTER, William	Boy 3rd Class	FAWN	
	L.M.	FAWN	*Guadaloupe*
SAMBLER, Stephen	A.B.	NEPTUNE	*G.H. 6376 as SUMBLER*
	A.B.	ZEALOUS	*Nile*
SANGER, James	Ord	POMPEE	
	Ord	POMPEE	*Pompee. 17 June 1809 (Vfd Abd. Not on Roll)*
	Ord	ABERCROMBIE	*Guadaloupe*
SAUL, John	L.M.	BELLEISLE	
	A.B.	SUPERB	*Algiers*
SAVILLE, John	L.M.	GLOIRE	
	L.M.	GLOIRE	*Guadaloupe*
(SCOTT, James)	(Master's Mate)	(POMPEE)	*Awarded M.G.S. Medal (Also received N.G.S. clasps) Blanche. 19 Jan 1806 B.S. Ap & May 1813*
SCOTT, George	Ord	HAUGHTY	
SEALE, Charles.H.	Midshipman	NEPTUNE	
	Midshipman	COMUS	*Comus. 15 Augt 1807*
	Lieut. R.N.	STAR	*Guadaloupe*
	Lieut. R.N.	DESIREE	*Gluckstadt. 5 Jan 1814*
SEAR, George	Ord	POMPEE	
	Ord	POMPEE	*Pompee. 17 June 1809*
	Ord	ABERCROMBIE	*Guadaloupe*
SHADDOCK, Elias	Qtr Gunner	BELLEISLE	
	Qtr Gunner	ROYAL SOVEREIGN	*Trafalgar*
SHAKESHAFT, Edward	Ord	AEOLUS	
	L.M.	AEOLUS	*4 Novr 1805*
SHANKS, Thomas	Corporal. R.M.	BELLEISLE	
SHASONY, Edward	L.M.	INTREPID	
SHAW, James	L.M.	NEPTUNE	
SHEPHERD, Benjamin	Midshipman	NEPTUNE	*Navy List & O'Byrne as John*
	Midshipman	BRITANNIA	*Trafalgar*
	Midshipman	LATONA	*Curacoa*
	Master's Mate	POMPEE	*Guadaloupe*
	Lieut. R.N.	GRIFFON	*Griffon. 27 March 1812*

SHIPTON, James	Master's Mate	PENELOPE	
SHIRLEY, George	Gunner	CLEOPATRA	
	A.B.	St GEORGE	14 March 1795
	Q.M's Mate	VANGUARD	Nile
	Q.M's Mate	FOUDROYANT	Egypt
SHORTLAND, Pierce	Pte. R.M.	AEOLUS	
SHREEVE, William	A.B.	POMPEE	G.H. 8532
	A.B.	POMPEE	Pompee. 17 June 1809 (Vfd Abd. Not on Roll)
	Caulker's Mate	POMPEE	Guadaloupe
SHUTTLEWORTH, George	L.M.	ACASTA	
	L.M.	SCIPION	Java
SHUTTLEWORTH, George	Pte. R.M.	PENELOPE	
SILVERS, Robert	Bosun's Mate	CLEOPATRA	
SIMMONS, Edward	Midshipman	ETHALION	
	Midshipman	MINOTAUR	Trafalgar
	Lieut. R.N.	GALATEA	Off Tamatave. 20 May 1811
SIMPSON, James	Ord	ULYSSES	
SIMPSON, John	Midshipman	CUTTLE	
	Midshipman	ACHERON	Acheron. 3 Feby 1805
SIMPSON, John	Commander	WOLVERINE	
SIMS, Andrew	Midshipman	ACASTA	
	Master's Mate	NISUS	Java
SKIDDY, Thomas	A.B.	BELLEISLE	
	A.B.	ROYAL SOVEREIGN	Trafalgar
	A.B.	CHERUB	Cherub. 28 March 1814
SLINGSBY, Robert	Capt' Main Top	AMARANTHE	
	Sailmaker	AMARANTHE	Guadaloupe
SMITH, George	A.B.	CAPTAIN	
	L.M.	SPENCER	St Domingo
SMITH, George	L.M.	STORK	G.H. 8633
SMITH, William.H.	Midshipman	NEPTUNE	
	Lieut. R.N.	SNAP	Guadaloupe
SOMERVILLE, George.F.	Lieut. R.N.	ULYSSES	
SPECK, William	Lieut. R.N.	BELLEISLE	
STAPLES, Robert	Q.M's Mate	PENELOPE	
	A.B.	FLORA	Egypt
STEEL, David	Midshipman	POMPEE	
	Midshipman	POMPEE	Pompee. 17 June 1809
STEPHENSON, Henry	Capt' After Guard	ACASTA	
	Not Given	HESPER	Java
STEWART, James	Carp's Crew	RECRUIT	
	Carp's Crew	RECRUIT	Recruit. 17 June 1809 (Vfd Abd. Not on Roll)
STOCKLEY, William	L.M.	INTREPID	
STOKES, George	Ord	BELLEISLE	
STONEFORD, Richard	Carp's Crew	YORK	G.H. 5521
STRADLING, Thomas	Pte. R.M.	HAUGHTY	
	Pte. R.M.	VESTAL	Egypt
	Pte. R.M.	BACCHANTE	B.S. 6 Jan 1813
STRONGITHARM, Joseph.L.	L.M.	CAPTAIN	
STRUGNELL, William.B.	Midshipman	AEOLUS	
STYLES, Edward	Ord	YORK	
SULLIVAN, John	A.B.	NEPTUNE	G.H. 2281
	Boy 3rd Class	MAJESTIC	Nile
SUTHER, Peter	Surgeon	EURYDICE	
	Actg Surgeon	SWIFTSURE	Trafalgar
SUTHERLAND, Andrew	A.B.	NEPTUNE	
	L.M.	NORTHUMBERLAND	St Domingo
	A.B.	ABERCROMBIE	Guadaloupe
SUTHERLAND, George	Ord	ULYSSES	
SWANE, Hans	Boy	NEPTUNE	
	Boy	POMPEE	Guadaloupe
TALLANCE, Samuel	Boatswain	PELORUS	
	A.B.	AGAMEMNON	Trafalgar
	A.B.	AGAMEMNON	St Domingo
	Boatswain	PELORUS	Guadaloupe
	Boatswain	MUTINE	Algiers
TAYLOR, John	Gunner	BELLEISLE	
TAYLOR, Robert	A.B.	ETHALION	
TELLION, J. Benjamin	Ord	YORK	(Alias SELLIEN)
TELLOGRAM, William	Pte. R.M.	HAZARD	
	Pte. R.M.	HAZARD	Guadaloupe
TENNANT, John	A.B.	NEPTUNE	
	Master's Mate	ABERCROMBIE	Guadaloupe
THOMAS, William	L.M.	CAPTAIN	
THOMPSON, Charles	L.M.	FORESTER	
THOMSON, Thomas	Qtr Gunner	BELLEISLE	
	A.B.	ACASTA	St Domingo
TOLEMAN, James	Pte. R.M.	NEPTUNE	
TOWN, Henry	Master's Mate	WOLVERINE	

MARTINIQUE

TREEVE, John	Actg Lieut. R.N.	YORK	
	Vol 1st Cl	St GEORGE	*Copenhagen 1801*
	Master's Mate	TONNANT	*Trafalgar*
TRUMBLE, William	Ord	POMPEE	
	Ord	POMPEE	*Pompee. 17 June 1809*
	Ord	ABERCROMBIE	*Guadaloupe*
TRUSS, John	Ord	ELIZABETH	*(Vfd Abd. Not on Roll)*
	Boy	DESIREE	*Copenhagen 1801*
	L.M.	PIQUE	*Pique. 26 March 1806*
	Ord	ELIZABETH	*Anse La Barque. 18 Decr 1809*
			(Vfd Abd. Not on Roll)
	Capt' of Mast	CYANE	*Cyane. 16 Jany 1814*
TUCKER, Thomas.T.	Commander	CHERUB	
	Lieut. R.N.	NORTHUMBERLAND	*St Domingo*
	Commander	CHERUB	*Guadaloupe*
	Commander	CHERUB (P)	*Cherub. 28 March 1814*
TURNLEY, James	Ord	BELLEISLE	*(May read TRIMLEY)*
UNDERWOOD, George	Ord	CIRCE	
	Ord	CIRCE	*Off the Pearl Rock. 13 Dec 1808*
VEAL, Richard	L.M.	ACASTA	
	L.M.	SCIPION	*Java*
WAKEN, Nicholas	Boy	YORK	
WALKER, George	Carp's Mate	INTREPID	
	Carpenter	FROLIC	*Guadaloupe*
WALKER, James.R.	Lieut. R.N.	HAZARD	*(Formerly James ROBERTSON)*
	Midshipman	VICTORY	*Trafalgar*
	Lieut. R.N.	HAZARD	*Guadaloupe*
WALKER, William	Purser	SNAP	
	Purser	SNAP	*Guadaloupe*
	Purser	EREBUS	*The Potomac. 17 Aug 1814*
WALL, Allen	Master's Mate	DEMERARA	
WALLACE, John	Ord	NEPTUNE	
WALLER, George	Secretary's Clerk	NEPTUNE	
WALLS, Jeremiah	Pte. R.M.	ETHALION	*G.H. 10,008 as WALL*
WALSH, Frederic	Midshipman	INTREPID	
WALSH, John	A.B.	GOREE	*(May read WALCH)*
WALSH, Patrick	Surgeon	WOLVERINE	
WARDLE, John	Midshipman	POMPEE	
	Midshipman	POMPEE	*Pompee. 17 June 1809*
			(Vfd Abd. Not on Roll)
	Actg Lieut. R.N.	PULTUSK	*Guadaloupe*
WATSON, John	A.B.	ETHALION	
WAY, John	L.M.	CLEOPATRA	
WEAVER, William	Pte. R.M.	AMARANTHE	
	Sgt. R.M.	AMARANTHE	*Guadaloupe*
(WELLS, William)	(A.B.)	(AMARANTHE)	*Awarded M.G.S. Medal*
WESTON, Peter	A.B.	NEPTUNE	*G.H. 10,029 as WESTERN*
WESTPHAL, George.A.	Lieut. R.N.	BELLEISLE	
	Midshipman	VICTORY	*Trafalgar*
	Lieut. R.N.	MARLBOROUGH	*B.S. Ap & May 1813*
			(Clasp known "29 April")
WEYLIE, Thomas	L.M.	ACASTA	
WHEATLEY, William	Ord	YORK	*G.H. 9915*
WHINYATES, Thomas	Commander	FROLIC	
	Capt's Servant	VETERAN	*B.S. 17 Mar 1794*
	Midshipman	ROBUST	*23rd June 1795*
	Master's Mate	ROBUST	*12 Octr 1798*
	Commander	FROLIC	*Guadaloupe*
WHITE, George	Actg Lieut. R.N.	CAPTAIN	
	Master's Mate	DREADNOUGHT	*Trafalgar*
WHITE, William	A.B.	NEPTUNE	
	A.B.	NORTHUMBERLAND	*St Domingo*
WILKINS, Thomas	Ord	BELLEISLE	*G.H. 4768*
WILKINSON, Samuel	L.M.	POMPEE	
	L.M.	POMPEE	*Pompee. 17 June 1809*
	L.M.	POMPEE	*Guadaloupe*
WILKINSON, Stephen	Midshipman	YORK	
	Midshipman	DISPATCH	*St Sebastian*
WILLANS, Joseph	Vol 1st Cl	AMARANTHE	
	Vol 1st Cl	AMARANTHE	*Off the Pearl Rock. 13 Dec 1808*
WILLIAMS, John	Clerk	GLOIRE	
	Supernumerary	FROLIC	*Guadaloupe*
WILLIAMS, Richard.P.	Surgeon	ACASTA	
WILLIAMS, Thomas	Capt' Main Top	CAPTAIN	
	Ord	DREADNOUGHT	*Trafalgar*
WILLIAMS, Walter	Carp's Crew	INTREPID	
WILLIAMS, William	Ord	BELLEISLE	
	Ord	BELLEISLE	*Trafalgar*

WILLIAMS, William.C.	L.M.	YORK	
WILLIAMSON, Robert	L.M.	CIRCE	G.H. 10,005 Roll states "Not aboard. In hospital"
WILSON, James	A.B.	CAPTAIN	G.H. 8462
	A.B.	DREADNOUGHT	Trafalgar
	A.B.	HARPY	Java
WILSON, William	Pte. R.M.	ETHALION	
WINNETT, William	Boy 2nd Class	CLEOPATRA	
WISE, Charles	Corporal. R.M.	NEPTUNE	
	Corporal. R.M.	GUADALOUPE	Guadaloupe
WITT, Stephen	Midshipman (Roll)	AEOLUS	Applied as Lt?
	L.M.	AEOLUS	4 Novr 1805 (as STOKELEY)
WOOD, James	Ord	CLEOPATRA	(Alias John Pine)
WOOD, James	Q.M.	HAUGHTY	
	Q.M.	ABERCROMBIE	Guadaloupe
WOOD, John	Pte. R.M.	NEPTUNE	
WORSLEY, William	Drummer. R.M.	YORK	Applied as "Late C/Sgt RM"
WYATT, James	Carpenter	INTREPID	
YARNALL, William	Pte. R.M.	ULYSSES	
YEOMAN, James	Pte. R.M.	SURINAM	
YOULL, Alexander	A.B.	BELLEISLE	

(13) HORATIO 10 FEBY 1809

Capture of the French frigate JUNON, off Virgin Islands, West Indies.

ALLEN, Joseph	Ord	HORATIO	
BESWICK, Samuel	Boy 3rd Cl	HORATIO	
BLAKENEY, Richard	1st Lieut. R.M.	HORATIO	
CRAWFORD, Joseph	Pte. R.M.	HORATIO	G.H. 8,726
DISNEY, Garret. R.T.	Boy 2nd Cl	HORATIO	
DIXON, Manley Hall	Lieut. R.N.	HORATIO	
	Midshipman	LION	Lion. 15 July 1798
HURLEY, Morris	L.M.	HORATIO	(M.L. as Maurice HURLEY) G.H. 8,487
LANE, John	Capt Fore Top	HORATIO	
PLUMB, Richard	A.B.	HORATIO	
VINCENT, George	Sgt. R.M.	HORATIO	
WARDEN, John	Purser	HORATIO	
WEBB, Nicholas	Midshipman	HORATIO	
YOUNG, Thomas	Drummer. R.M.	HORATIO	G.H. 9,500

(1) SUPERIEURE 10 FEBY 1809

Capture of the French frigate JUNON, off Virgin Islands, West Indies.

DAY, Bartholomew. G.S.	Actg Master	SUPERIEURE	Trafalgar
or B. George. S.	Midshipman	REVENGE	Martinique
	Actg Master	SUPERIEURE	(Vfd Abd. Not on Roll)
	Actg Master	SUPERIEURE	Guadaloupe

(27) AMETHYST 5 APRIL 1809

Capture of the French frigate NIEMEN in the Bay of Biscay.

BOULTON, Samuel	Gunner	AMETHYST	
	Gunner	AMETHYST	Amethyst Wh Thetis (10 Nov 1808)
BOWEN, John	Surgeon	AMETHYST	
	Surgeon	AMETHYST	Amethyst Wh Thetis
BUTLER, Daniel	Ord	AMETHYST	
	Ord	AMETHYST	Amethyst Wh Thetis
COCKER, Francis	Ord	AMETHYST	G.H. 8,924
	Ord	AMETHYST	Amethyst Wh Thetis
COOPER, William	Armourer	AMETHYST	
	Armourer	AMETHYST	Amethyst Wh Thetis
CUMMINGS, Thomas	Ord	AMETHYST	
	Ord	AMETHYST	Amethyst Wh Thetis
CURTIS, John	Carpenter's Mate	AMETHYST	
	Carpenter's Crew	SPENCER	St Domingo
CUSSACK, John	L.M.	AMETHYST	(M.L. as CUSACK)
	L.M.	AMETHYST	Amethyst Wh Thetis
DODGIN, Gideon	Q.M.'s Mate	AMETHYST	(M.L. as DODGEON)
	Q.M.'s Mate	AMETHYST	Amethyst Wh Thetis
DOWN, John	Pte. R.M.	AMETHYST	
EDWARDS, Adams	Midshipman	AMETHYST	

AMETHYST 5 APRIL 1809

GOULD, James	Midshipman	AMETHYST	
	A.B.	AMETHYST	Amethyst Wh Thetis
GRAY, Andrew	Yeoman of Sheets	AMETHYST	(M.L. as GREY)
	Capt Fore Top	AMETHYST	Amethyst Wh Thetis
HAWKEY, Nicholas	L.M.	AMETHYST	
HOLLANDS, Thomas	A.B.	AMETHYST	
	A.B.	AMETHYST	Amethyst Wh Thetis
ISAAC, John	Pte. R.M.	AMETHYST	
LAMB, James.T.	Vol 1st CL	AMETHYST	
LATHAN, John	Pte. R.M.	AMETHYST	
	Pte. R.M.	NAIAD	Trafalgar
	Pte. R.M.	AMETHYST*	Amethyst Wh Thetis (Joined after this Action)
	Pte. R.M.	IMPREGNABLE	Algiers
LAUTENBURGH, Christian	L.M.	AMETHYST	
	Carpenter's Crew	AMETHYST	Amethyst Wh Thetis
MACDONALD, John	Capt Main Top	AMETHYST	
	Capt Main Top	AMETHYST	Amethyst Wh Thetis
MILES, Lawford	Master's Mate	AMETHYST	
	Midshipman	AMETHYST	Amethyst Wh Thetis
	Master's Mate	QUEEN CHARLOTTE	Algiers
PEARCE, John	Boy 2nd Cl	AMETHYST	(Vfd Abd. Not on Roll)
	Boy 2nd Cl	AMETHYST	Amethyst Wh Thetis
PURCHASE, William	Boy 2nd Cl	AMETHYST	
	Ord	WESER	B.S. 14 Dec 1814 (Later received Vic Wide LSGC Medal with 43 Yrs)
REARDON, Patrick	L.M.	AMETHYST	
	L.M.	AMETHYST	Amethyst Wh Thetis
	L.M.	ASTRAEA	Off Tamatave. 20 May 1811
RUTTER, John	Sgt. R.M.	AMETHYST	
	Sgt. R.M.	AMETHYST	Amethyst Wh Thetis
SEYMOUR, John.C.	Midshipman	AMETHYST	
	Midshipman	AMETHYST	Amethyst Wh Thetis
WALKER, George	Ord	AMETHYST	
	Ord	AMETHYST	Amethyst Wh Thetis

(529) BASQUE ROADS 1809

Destruction of French ships in Basque Roads 11 & 12 April 1809.

ABERFIELD, Charles	Sgt. R.M.	INDEFATIGABLE	
	Pte. R.M.	SPENCER	Gut of Gibraltar. 12 July 1801
ADDINGTON, William.S.	Lieut. R.N.	REVENGE	
ALLAN, John	Asst Surgeon	EMERALD	
ALDRIDGE, John	Ord	RESOLUTION	G.H. 9248
ALPHEUS, Charles	Pte. R.M.	THESEUS	
	Pte. R.M.	BRITANNIA	Trafalgar
	Pte. R.M.	HEBRUS	Algiers
ANDERSON, Joseph	Carpenter	GIBRALTAR	
	Carpenter	GIBRALTAR	Egypt
ANDREWS, Walter	Boy	AIGLE	
ANDREWS, William	Two L.Ms borne	GIBRALTAR	G.H. 9581
ANTRAM, Simon.E.	Master's Mate	ILLUSTRIOUS	
	A.B.	St GEORGE	Copenhagen 1801
ATKINSON, Henry.E.	Midshipman	HERO	
BABBIDGE, John	A.B.	ILLUSTRIOUS	
	A.B.	ILLUSTRIOUS	Java
BAGSHAW, Joseph	Pte. R.M.	LYRA	
BAILEY, Joseph	A.B.	ILLUSTRIOUS	
	A.B.	STATELY	Stately. 22 March 1808
	A.B.	ILLUSTRIOUS	Java
BAILEY, Samuel	Not Given	INDEFATIGABLE	
BAILLIE, William	Pte. R.M.	INDEFATIGABLE	
	Pte. R.M.	INDEFATIGABLE	B.S. 16 July 1806
BAKER, Samuel	Midshipman	VALIANT	
	Midshipman	VALIANT	B.S. 27 Sep 1810
BAKER, William	Pte. R.M.	ILLUSTRIOUS	(May read BABER)
BAPTISTE, John or BABTISTE	French Pilot	DOTTEREL	
	A.B.	VOLAGE	Lissa
BARBER, James	Pte. R.M.	VALIANT	
BARKER, Philip	Ord	THESEUS	G.H. 7340
BARNES, Peter	Midshipman	EMERALD	
BARTLETT, Arthur	Pte. R.M.	CALEDONIA	G.H. 483
BAYFIELD, Henry.W.	Vol 1st Cl	BEAGLE	
BAYFORD, John	Pte. R.M.	THESEUS	G.H. 8741
BEARD, Charles	L.M.	AIGLE	

THE NAVAL GENERAL SERVICE MEDAL ROLL 1793-1840

Name	Rank	Ship	Notes
BEER, Daniel	Qtr Gunner	CALEDONIA	G.H. 2716
	Qtr Gunner	CALEDONIA	B.S. 27 Sep 1810
BELL, Frederick	Ord	MARTIAL	
BELL, George	Ord	ILLUSTRIOUS	
	A.B.	STATELY	Stately. 22 March 1808
BENNET, Martin	Midshipman	ILLUSTRIOUS	
	Actg Lieut. R.N.	SCEPTRE	Anse La Barque. 18 Decr 1809
	Actg Lieut. R.N.	SCEPTRE	Guadaloupe
BENSON, Thomas	Ord	REVENGE	
BERNARD, Andrew	Ord	INDEFATIGABLE	(Additional clasp ?)
BEST, Thomas.F.	Vol 1st Cl	CALEDONIA	
BEZANT, John	1st Lieut. R.M.A.	THUNDER	
	1st Lieut. R.M.A.	"ANHOLT"	Anholt. 27 March 1811
BIDDULPH, Edward	Master's Mate	INDEFATIGABLE	
	Midshipman	INDEFATIGABLE	B.S. 16 July 1806
BIGGS, John	Not Given	GIBRALTAR	
BINFIELD, Henry	Pte. R.M.	REVENGE	
	Pte. R.M.	REVENGE	Trafalgar
BIRCH, William	L.M.	GIBRALTAR	G.H. 1442
BIRMINGHAM, Henry	Bosun's Mate	FERVENT	
BISHOP, William	Ord	PALLAS	G.H. 7580
BLAND, George	Midshipman	PALLAS	
BLANFORD, James or BLANDFORD	Midshipman	REVENGE	Roll & M.L. as BLANFORD
	Midshipman	REVENGE	Trafalgar. O'By = BLANDFORD
BLYTH, Charles	A.B.	INDEFATIGABLE	
	Midshipman	SCIPION	Java
	Midshipman	PRESIDENT	St Sebastian
BOES, James	Pte. R.M.	GIBRALTAR	
BOLEY, Benjamin	Pte. R.M.	CAESAR	(Vfd Abd. Not on Roll)
	Pte. R.M.	CAESAR	4 Novr 1805. (ML = Richard)
BOLTON, Peter	Boy	RESOLUTION	
BOSS, James	Capt' Main Top	BEAGLE	
	A.B.	DRAGON	Egypt
BOUKESS, Matthew or BOUKAS	Pte. R.M.	ILLUSTRIOUS	
	Pte. R.M.	ILLUSTRIOUS	Java
BOULTON, Robert	Corporal R.M.	IMPERIEUSE	
BOYES, Henry	Lieut. R.N.	CALEDONIA	
	Midshipman	LION	Lion. 15 July 1798
	Lieut. R.N.	CALEDONIA	B.S. 27 Sep 1810
BOYNS, George	Ord	INDEFATIGABLE	
BREWER, James	Pte. R.M.	UNICORN	
BRICKELL, Elias	Qtr Gunner	THUNDER	
BRICKNELL, Samuel	Q.M.	GIBRALTAR	
	A.B.	PRINCE GEORGE	St Vincent
BROAD, Thomas	A.B.	CALEDONIA	
BROTHERS, John	Boy	INSOLENT	
BROWN, James	Carpenter	THESEUS	
	A.B.	PENELOPE	Penelope. 30 March 1800
BROWN, Zachariah	A.B.	IMPERIEUSE	G.H. 6830
BRUCE, John	Ord	INDEFATIGABLE	
BRYDGES, Thomas	Vol 1st Cl	AETNA	
BUCKHOLTZ, Frederick	Pte. R.M.	THESEUS	
BUNN, Thomas	Midshipman	RESOLUTION	
BURCH, Isaac	Midshipman	CAESAR	(2 medals. see 4 Nov '05)
	Midshipman	CAESAR	4 Novr 1805
BURNISTON, Hugh.S.	Midshipman	CAESAR	
	Master's Mate	Qn CHARLOTTE	Algiers
BURROWS, John	Trumpeter	GIBRALTAR	
BURTON, Robert	A.B.	CALEDONIA	(Vfd Abd. Not on Roll)
	A.B.	CALEDONIA	B.S. 27 Sep 1810
BUTLER, Charles.G.	Vol 1st Cl	CALEDONIA	
	Midshipman	CALEDONIA	B.S. 27 Sep 1810
BUTLER, Patrick	Pte. R.M.	GIBRALTAR	
	Pte. R.M.	Qn CHARLOTTE	Algiers
CAMPBELL, Donald	Lieut. R.M.	RESOLUTION	
	2nd Lieut. R.M.	AGAMEMNON	Trafalgar
	2nd Lieut. R.M.	AGAMEMNON	St Domingo
CAMPBELL, Ebenezer	A.B.	THESEUS	
CAREY, William	Ord	DONEGAL	
CARR, George	Ord	RESOLUTION	G.H. 10,009
CASNEY, John	A.B.	UNICORN	
	A.B.	ROMNEY	Egypt
CASSELLS, William	Ropemaker	GIBRALTAR	
	L.M.	SATURN	Copenhagen 1801
CASTLE, Samuel	Ord	THESEUS	
CHALLIS, Samuel	Steward's Mate	VALIANT	(Known. 2 Medals issued)
	Ord	NAMUR	4 Novr 1805
	Steward's Mate	VALIANT	B.S. 27 Sep 1810
CHALMERS, James	A.B.	UNICORN	
CHAMBERS, John	Qtr Gunner	ILLUSTRIOUS	
	Qtr Gunner	STATELY	Stately. 22 March 1808
CHARLESSON, Richard.W.	Midshipman	AETNA	
CHEGWYN, Joseph	Master's Mate	REVENGE	
CHINN, Thomas	Pte. R.M.	INDEFATIGABLE	
CHURCHILL, John	A.B.	PALLAS	

BASQUE ROADS 1809

CLARK, John	L.M.	DREADNOUGHT (Not present)	G.H. 1047 states DREADNOUGHT
CLARKE, Patrick	Boy	THESEUS	
	Ord	HEBRUS	Hebrus with L'Etoile
CLARKE, William	Gunner. R.M.A.	AETNA	
CLAYDON, Thomas	Sgt. R.M.	THESEUS	
CLAYTON, William	Surgeon	LYRA	(Vfd Abd. Not on Roll)
	Surgeon	LYRA	St Sebastian
CLEEV, Edward	A.B.	IMPERIEUSE	G.H. 2377 as CLEAVE
CLEMENTS, James	Gunner. R.M.A.	WHITING	(This Roll CLEMMENTS)
	Gunner. R.M.A.	AETNA	The Potomac. 17 Aug 1814
CLARK, Maurice	Clerk	AETNA	
COATES, Joseph	Sgt. R.M.	BELLONA	
COCHRANE, Thomas. Lord.	Captain. R.N.	IMPERIEUSE	(Vfd Abd. Not on Roll)
	Lieut. R.N.	THETIS	Thetis 17 May 1795 (Vfd Abd. Not on Roll)
	Commander	SPEEDY (P)	Speedy 6 May 1801
COLE, James	Ord	REVENGE	
	Ord	CENTURION	Centurion. 18 Sept 1809
	Ord	REVENGE	Trafalgar
COLLINS, John	Boy	EMERALD	
COLQUHON, Humphrey	Vol 1st Cl	FOXHOUND	
CONDE, George	Boy	CAESAR	
CONDE, John	Boy	HERO	
CONDON, Edward	Pte. R.M.	GIBRALTAR	
	Pte. R.M.	THUNDERER	Trafalgar
CONEYBEAR, William	Ord	INDEFATIGABLE	
CONNOR, Richard	Midshipman	EMERALD	(Not present. In Prize)
	Midshipman	LOIRE	B.S. 4 June 1805
	Midshipman	EMERALD	Emerald. 13 March 1808
CONNER, William.H.	Volunteer	EMERALD	
CONWAY, James	L.M.	REVENGE	(Vfd Abd. Not on Roll)
	L.M.	REVENGE	Trafalgar. G.H. 7950
	L.M.	REVENGE	B.S. 16 July 1806 (Vfd Abd. Not on Roll)
COOK, Joseph	Ord	REVENGE	(Alias WILLIAMS)
	A.B.	REVENGE	Trafalgar
COOKE, Thomas	Volunteer	AIGLE	
COOKESLEY, John	Lieut. R.N.	GIBRALTAR	
	Lieut. R.N.	TRUSTY	Egypt
COOKNEY, James.T.	Midshipman	DONEGAL	
COOPER, James	Carpenter	UNICORN	
COOPER, Samuel	Not Given	RESOLUTION	
COPELAND, Richard	Midshipman	REVENGE	
CORNISH, William	A.B.	UNICORN	
CORNUTT, Ralph	A.B.	LYRA	
CORTON, William	(Not on Bsq Rds Roll)		See B.S. 27 Sep 1810
CORYNDON, Joseph	Pte. R.M.	GIBRALTAR	
COUCH, John	1st Lieut. R.M.	CALEDONIA	(Vfd Abd. Not on Roll)
	1st Lieut. R.M.	CALEDONIA	B.S. 27 Sep 1810
COX, John	Ord	DONEGAL	
	L.M.	REVOLUTIONNAIRE	4 Novr 1805
COX, Jonathan	Boy	REVENGE	
CRAIG, Philip	Carp's Mate	VALIANT	
	Carp's Mate	NAMUR	4 Novr 1805
CRANK, James	L.M.	THESEUS	
CREYKE, Richard	Lieut. R.N.	VALIANT	
	Midshipman	ACASTA	St Domingo
CROKER, James	A.B.	THESEUS	
CROXTON, John	L.M.	VALIANT	
	Boy	NAMUR	4 Novr 1805
CUMMINS, Edward	L.M.	IMPERIEUSE	
DAN, Thomas	Pte. R.M.	IMPERIEUSE	
DANE, Richard	Ord	BELLONA	G.H. 10,134
DARTNETT, Michael	L.M.	RESOLUTION	
DAVIES, William St.G.	Surgeon	DOTTEREL	
	Asst Surgeon	CENTAUR	Centaur 26 Augt 1808
DAVIS, David	A.B.	LYRA	G.H. 9882 as DAVIES
	A.B.	LYRA	St Sebastian
DAVIS, John	Midshipman	RESOLUTION	
DAVIS, William	Carp's Crew	VALIANT	
	Carp's Crew	NAMUR	4 Novr 1805
DAVIS, William	Two borne (Armourer)	VALIANT	Armourer & Carp's Crew (see name above)
DAY, Edward	Drummer.R.M.	RESOLUTION	
	Drummer.R.M.	DEFENCE	Trafalgar
DEANE, Daniel	L.M.	RESOLUTION	
DELANEY, Mark	Ord	GIBRALTAR	
DELANY, Jeremiah	Pte. R.M.	PALLAS	
DEVONSHIRE, Richard	Lieut. R.N.	AIGLE	
	Vol 1st Cl	AMAZON	Amazon 13 Jany 1797
DEWAR, John	Master's Mate	CALEDONIA	
DINGLE, John	A.B.	CALEDONIA	

DONELLAN, Malachi	Lieut. R.N.	REVENGE	
DOWLIN, John	Pte. R.M.	HERO	
DRAKE, Francis	Qtr Gunner	CALEDONIA	G.H. 9934
DRAKE, James.R.	Midshipman	THESEUS	
DRANE, Thomas	Actg Lieut. R.N.	CAESAR	
	L.M.	CAESAR	4 Novr 1805
DRUMMOND, James	L.M.	ILLUSTRIOUS	
DRY, Robert	Ord	UNICORN	G.H. 8635
DUFFETT, Solomon	Pte. R.M.	GIBRALTAR	G.H. 5370 or 3701
DUNCAN, George	A.B.	MEDIATOR	G.H. 9455
	Q.M.	BERWICK	Gaieta. 24 July 1815
DUNN, John	A.B.	CALEDONIA	G.H. 3232
	A.B.	ASIA	Navarino
DUNTHORN, John	Asst Surgeon	GIBRALTAR	
DURNELL, Thomas	Pte. R.M.	ILLUSTRIOUS	
	Pte. R.M.	TEMERAIRE	Trafalgar
	Pte. R.M.	ILLUSTRIOUS	Java
EDMONDS, Henry	Pte. R.M.	PALLAS	G.H. 9863
EDMUNDS, George	Pte. R.M.	THESEUS	G.H. 2448 as EDMONDS
EDWARDS, Richard	Ord	UNICORN	G.H. 6161
EGAN, Thomas	L.M.	GIBRALTAR	
ELMORE, John	Ord	THUNDER	
	Ord	THUNDER	Thunder. 9 Octr 1813 (Vfd Abd. Not on Roll)
ENGLISH, William	Ord	BELLONA	G.H. 6570
EVANSON, Alleyn	Volunteer	DONEGAL	
FALKNER, Charles.L.	Midshipman	DONEGAL	
	Lieut. R.N.	SHANNON	Shannon Wh Chesapeake
FARRELL, Robert	Not Given	CALEDONIA	
FELKINS, Thomas	Boy 3rd Class	THESEUS	
FENTON, William	A.B.	RESOLUTION	G.H. 6389
FERRIES, John	Ord	DONEGAL	
	Boy 2nd Class	DONEGAL	St Domingo
FINN, David	A.B.	THUNDER	
	Q.M.	THUNDER	Thunder. 9 Octr 1813
FINNIE, James	Q.M.	CAESAR	
FISHER, Richard	Boy	INDEFATIGABLE	G.H. 2730
FLETCHER, Charles	Ord	AETNA	
FLEXMAN, James	2nd Lieut. R.M.	ILLUSTRIOUS	
FLYNN, Josiah	Actg Boatswain	INDEFATIGABLE	
FOLLARD, Hugh	Ord	BELLONA	G.H. 9899 as FALLARD
FOLLETT, Thomas	A.B.	CAESAR	(Vfd Abd. Not on Roll)
	Ord	CAESAR	4 Novr 1805
	Ord	Qn CHARLOTTE	Algiers
FORBES, Alexander.W.	Vol 1st Cl	IMPERIEUSE	
	Midshipman	ARMIDE	B.S. 14 Dec 1814
FORBES, Henry	Lieut. R.N.	DONEGAL	
	A.B.	PHOEBE	Trafalgar
	Lieut. R.N.	DONEGAL	St Domingo
FORSTER, James	A.B.	CAESAR	
FOWLER, John	Pte. R.M.	DONEGAL	
FOWLER, Stephen	Yeoman of Sheets	CAESAR	
	Yeoman of Sheets	CAESAR	4 Novr 1805
FOY, John	Capt' Main Top	ENCOUNTER	G.H. 1215
FRANCIS, Joseph	Boy	BELLONA	
	Boy	BELLONA	4 Novr 1805
FRY, James	R.M. Boy	CAESAR	
FRY, James	Pte. R.M.	EMERALD	
FRY, John	A.B.	BEAGLE	
FURZE, Robert	Midshipman	CAESAR	
GAIN, Jonathan	Purser	REDPOLE	
	Clerk	GRASSHOPPER	Off Rota. 4 April 1808
	Clerk	GRASSHOPPER	Grasshopper. 24 April 1808
GAINOR, Benjamin	Carp's Crew	RESOLUTION	G.H. 5201
GALLOW, Martin	Pilot	FOXHOUND	
	Pilot	THAMES	Gut of Gibraltar. 12 July 1801
GAWD, Matthew	L.M.	IMPERIEUSE	
GIBBS, John	Ord	CAESAR	
	Ord	CAESAR	4 Novr 1805
GILBERT, George	Asst Surgeon	IMPERIEUSE	
GILBERT, James	Ord	THESEUS	
GILLMAN, John	Carp's Crew	EMERALD	(M.L. as GILMON)
	Carp's Crew	EMERALD	Emerald. 13 March 1808
GLOVER, Henry	Pte. R.M.	INDEFATIGABLE	G.H. 2920
GOLIFER, Joseph	Ord	AIGLE	
GOLLAN, Timothy	L.M.	THESEUS	(May read GALLAN)
GOMS, John	A.B.	DONEGAL	
	A.B.	BELLE POULE	B.S. 14 Dec 1814
GORDON, James.G.	Midshipman	ILLUSTRIOUS	
	Actg Lieut. R.N.	FREIJA	Anse la Barque. 18 Decr 1809
	Actg Lieut. R.N.	FREIJA	Guadaloupe
GORDON, John	Ord	IMPERIEUSE	G.H. 7971
GORDON, William	Midshipman	IMPERIEUSE	
	Midshipman	KINGFISHER	St Domingo

BASQUE ROADS 1809

GORE, Ralph	Vol 1st Cl	THESEUS	
GOSTLING, Philip	Vol 1st Cl	UNICORN	
	Midshipman	ARMIDE	B.S. 27 Sep 1810
	Lieut. R.N.	SEVERN	Algiers
GOULLET, Charles	Midshipman	CAESAR	
	Midshipman	CAESAR	4 Novr 1805
GOWAN, Samuel	R.M. Boy	REVENGE	
GRANT, Edward	Midshipman	GIBRALTAR	
	Midshipman	ANDROMACHE	St Sebastian
	Actg Lieut. R.N.	CYANE	Cyane. 16 Jany 1814
GRANT, James	Boy 2nd Class	AETNA	
	L.M.	HARDY	B.S. 23 Nov 1810
GREEN, John	Pte. R.M.	DONEGAL	G.H. 2839
GREGORY, William	Pte. R.M.	CAESAR	
GRIFFITHS, William	A.B.	CAESAR	
HAGGIS, James	Ord	BELLONA	G.H. 9961
HAIG, Richard	Secretary's Clerk	CALEDONIA	
HALL, William	Two Ptes RM borne	GIBRALTAR	G.H. 9771
HALPIN, John	Pte. R.M.	DONEGAL	
HAM, John	Capt' Main Top	THUNDER	G.H. 221
	A.B.	THUNDER	Thunder. 9 Octr 1813 (Vfd Abd. Not on Roll)
HAMOND, Philip	L.M.	RESOLUTION	
HANDLEY, John.W.H.	Midshipman	VALIANT	
	Midshipman	NAMUR	4 Novr 1805
HARDING, George	Carp's Crew	INDEFATIGABLE	
HARRIS, Charles	Ord	ILLUSTRIOUS	(M.G.S. medal for Java)
HARRIS, James	Midshipman	THESEUS	
HARRISON, John	Master's Mate	VALIANT	Joined after action
	Master's Mate	VALIANT	B.S. 27 Sep 1810
HARTHORN, Joseph	A.B.	THESEUS	
HARVEY, Charles	Ord	IMPERIEUSE	
HARVEY, Joseph	Sailmaker's Mate	RESOLUTION	
HAWKINS, Josh	Pte. R.M.	DONEGAL	
HAYDON, John	Bosun's Mate	AIGLE	
HEDGCOCK, Thomas	Master	REDPOLE	
HERRICK, Edward	Midshipman	REVENGE	
	Midshipman	REVENGE	Trafalgar
HEWITT, Samuel	Pte. R.M.	CAESAR	
HIGGINS, Thomas	Midshipman	CAESAR	
HILL, James	Boy 3rd Class	AETNA	
	Boy 3rd Class	AETNA	The Potomac. 17 Aug 1814
HILLIARD, Richard	A.B.	REVENGE	
	A.B.	REVENGE	B.S. 16 July 1806
HILTON, Stephen	Lieut. R.N.	REVENGE	(Vfd Abd. Not on Roll)
	Midshipman	PEARL	Egypt
	Master's Mate	MINOTAUR	Trafalgar
HINDMARSH, John	Lieut. R.N.	BEAGLE	
	Capt's Servant	BELLEROPHON	1 June 1794
	Vol 1st Cl	BELLEROPHON	17 June 1795
	Midshipman	BELLEROPHON	Nile
	Midshipman	SPENCER	Gut of Gibraltar. 12 July 1801
	Lieut. R.N.	PHOEBE	Trafalgar
	Lieut. R.N.	NISUS	Java
HOCKINGS, Robert	Lieut. R.N.	CALEDONIA	
	Master's Mate	PALLAS	17 June 1795
HODGSON, Thomas	A.B.	RESOLUTION	G.H. 3792
HOLLAND, Thomas	A.B.	VALIANT	
HOLLMAN, John	L.M.	MEDIATOR	G.H. 10,011
HORE, Henry.C.	Midshipman	CAESAR	
HORE, James.R.	1st Lieut. R.M.	IMPERIEUSE	
	2nd Lieut. R.M.	DIANA	Egypt
HORE, Samuel.B.	Lieut. R.N.	CAESAR	
	Midshipman	SPENCER	St Domingo
	Flag Lieut. R.N.	SCIPION	Java
HOWARD, Robert	L.M.	RESOLUTION	
	Ship's Corporal	FALCON	Capture of the Desiree
HOWARD, William	Ord	THUNDER	
	L.M.	GALATEA	B.S. 21 Jan 1807
HUGHES, Edward	Pte. R.M.	CALEDONIA	
HUGHES, James	Actg Carpenter	CAESAR	
HUMPHRIES, James	Pte. R.M.	BEAGLE	G.H. 9658
HUNTER, Robert	Midshipman	UNICORN	
	Master's Mate	ARMIDE	B.S. 13 Feb 1810
	Master's Mate	ARMIDE	B.S. 27 Sep 1810
HUTCHINS, William	Ord	UNICORN	
HUTCHINSON, Charles	Lieut. R.N.	VALIANT	
HYDE, John	Pte. R.M.	GIBRALTAR	
ISUM, Edward	A.B.	IMPERIEUSE	
JACKSON, John	Pte. R.M.	BELLONA	
JACKSON, John	L.M.	ILLUSTRIOUS	
	A.B.	ILLUSTRIOUS	Java

JAGO, John.S.	Midshipman	INDEFATIGABLE	
JAMES, John	A.B.	RESOLUTION	
JEFFREYS, Richard	1st Lieut. R.M.	AETNA	
JEFFRIES, Edward	Pte. R.M.	IMPERIEUSE	G.H. 6633
JENKINS, Arthur	A.B.	CALEDONIA	
JENNINGS, Edward	Midshipman	VALIANT	
	Midshipman	VALIANT	B.S. 27 Sep 1810
JENNINGS, Thomas	Pte. R.M.	CALEDONIA	
JERAM, William	Cooper	BEAGLE	
	Cooper	BEAGLE	St Sebastian
JEWERS, Richard.F.	Master's Mate	THESEUS (P)	
JOHNSON, George	Carpenter	REDPOLE	
JOHNSON, George.C.	Lieut. R.N.	AETNA	
	L.M.	NORTHUMBERLAND	Egypt
JOINT, Thomas	Pte. R.M.	ENCOUNTER	
	Pte. R.M.	DRAGON	B.S. Ap & May 1813
JOLLIFFE, William	Lieut. R.M.	THESEUS	
	Captain. R.M.	EDINBURGH	Syria
JONES, Abraham	Ropemaker	RESOLUTION	G.H. 9337
JONES, Henry.P.	Midshipman	REVENGE	
	Midshipman	REVENGE	B.S. 23 Nov 1810
JONES, James	Lieut. R.M.	HERO	
JORDAN, Joseph	Pte. R.M.	REDPOLE	
JORNEAS, Jacob	Qtr Gunner	CALEDONIA	
KEARLEY, Benjamin	Coxswain	VALIANT	
	Ord	THAMES	Gut of Gibraltar. 12 July 1801
	Coxswain	NAMUR	4 Novr 1805
KEARNS, Patrick	L.M.	IMPERIEUSE	
KEATS, William	Armourer	GIBRALTAR	
KELLY, William	Lieut. R.N.	CALEDONIA	
	Lieut. R.N.	MINERVE	Egypt
	Lieut. R.N.	PRINCE	Trafalgar
	Lieut. R.N.	CALEDONIA	B.S. 27 Sep 1810 (Vfd Abd. Not on Roll)
KING, William	Pte. R.M.	BELLONA	
KINGCOME, John	Vol 2nd Cl	EMERALD	(M) A of I(AVA) & Ch 1842.
KINRADE, Michael	Ord	GIBRALTAR	(M.L. as KINDRID)
	A.B.	BEDFORD	B.S. 14 Dec 1814 (See note)
LAING, Robert	A.B.	REVENGE	G.H. 9634
LAKE, William	Ord	CALEDONIA	
LAMB, George	L.M.	VALIANT	
LAMBETH, John.D.	Ord	VALIANT	(M.L. as John LAMBETH)
	L.M.	NAMUR	4 Novr 1805
	Ord	VALIANT	B.S. 27 Sep 1810
LANGLEY, Robert	Boy 1st Class	RESOLUTION	G.H. 9634
LAUGHARNE, Thomas.L.P.	Lieut. R.N.	UNICORN	
	Supn Midshipman	NORTHUMBERLAND	St Domingo
	Lieut. R.N.	NEREIDE	B.S. 1 May 1810
	Lieut. R.N.	BOADICEA (P)	Boadicea. 18 Septr 1810
LAWRENCE, John	Gunner. R.M.A.	AETNA	
	Gunner. R.M.A.	AETNA	B.S. 23 Nov 1810
LAWSON, Gilbert	Gunner's Mate	CAESAR	
	A.B.	SWIFTSURE	Nile
	A.B.	SWIFTSURE	Egypt
	Qtr Gunner	CAESAR	4 Novr 1805
	Gunner	PHOEBE	Phoebe. 28 March 1814
LEAN, James.S.	Master's Mate	ZEPHYR	(Borne in REDPOLE)
LEE, William	Pte. R.M.	BELLONA	
LEITH, Nicholas	Qtr Gunner	ILLUSTRIOUS	
LEMON, William	A.B.	ILLUSTRIOUS	
	A.B.	STATELY	Stately. 22 March 1808
	A.B.	ILLUSTRIOUS	Java
LESLIE, John	A.B.	INDEFATIGABLE	
	A.B.	INDEFATIGABLE	B.S. 16 July 1806
LEWIS, George	Ord	INSOLENT	
LEWIS, John	Pte. R.M.	CAESAR	
	Pte. R.M.	CAESAR	4 Novr 1805
LEY, Nicholas	A.B.	RESOLUTION	
LIFTON, James	A.B.	RESOLUTION	
LILLY, William	Carpenter	LYRA	
LLOYD, John.J.	A.B.	AETNA	
	Midshipman	ABERCROMBIE	Guadaloupe
LLOYD, William.H.	Midshipman	CAESAR	
LODWICK, John	Ord	CALEDONIA	
LODWICK, William	Carpenter	IMPERIEUSE	
	Carpenter	VICTORIOUS	Victorious With Rivoli
LONEY, Robery	Midshipman	AIGLE	
	2nd Master	SCIPION	Java
	Lieut. R.N.	REINDEER	St Sebastian ('disallowed'?)

BASQUE ROADS 1809

LORING, Oliver	A.B.	BELLONA	
	A.B.	ALFRED	*Guadaloupe*
LORY, William	Vol 1st Cl	UNICORN	
	Vol 1st Cl	ARMIDE	*B.S. 13 Feb 1810*
	Midshipman	ARMIDE	*B.S. 27 Sep 1810*
MACKAY, John	Surgeon	BELLONA	
	Surgeon's Mate	MINERVE	*Egypt*
MANN, John	Ord	VALIANT	
	Boy 3rd Class	ARDENT	*Copenhagen 1801*
	L.M.	NAMUR	*4 Novr 1805*
	Ord	VALIANT	*B.S. 27 Sep 1810*
MANNING, John	Ord	CALEDONIA	
MARAT, Thomas	L.M.	ILLUSTRIOUS	
	Supernumerary	VICTORY	*Trafalgar*
MARLER, William	Ord	INDEFATIGABLE	
	L.M.	DEFIANCE	*Copenhagen 1801*
	Ord	BELLEROPHON	*Trafalgar*
MARRETT, Joseph	Lieut. R.N. Cmdg	MARTIAL	
	Midshipman	CRESCENT	*Crescent. 20 Octr 1793*
	Midshipman	ORION	*23rd June 1795*
			(Vfd Abd. Not on Roll)
	Midshipman	ORION	*St Vincent*
	Midshipman	ORION	*Nile*
MARRIOTT, John	Ord	INSOLENT	
MARRYAT, Frederick	Midshipman	IMPERIEUSE	*Author.*
MARTIN, Antonio	Ord	ILLUSTRIOUS	
	Ord	ILLUSTRIOUS	*Java*
MARTIN, Francis	Carp's Crew	RESOLUTION	
MARTIN, William	L.M.	IMPERIEUSE	
MASTERS, James	Lieut. R.N.	BELLONA	
MATTHEWS, John	L.M.	UNICORN	
MAWSON, Thomas	A.B.	GIBRALTAR	
McADAM, David	Lieut. R.M.	AIGLE	
	Lieut. R.M.	THAMES	*Amanthea. 25 July 1810*
McCARTHY, John	Two Borne	CALEDONIA	*Carp's Crew & Ord*
McCLAY, John	Q.M.	DONEGAL	
	Gunner's Mate	MADRAS	*Egypt*
	Ord	DONEGAL	*St Domingo*
McFARLANE, James	Purser	BELLONA	
	Purser	BELLEISLE	*Trafalgar*
McLEAN, Charles.C.	Vol 1st Cl	GIBRALTAR	
McMURTY, John	Pte. R.M.	BELLONA	
MEARS, Jacob	Carp's Crew	REVENGE	*(Vfd. Abd. Not on Roll)*
	Carp's Crew	CENTURION	*Centurion. 18 Sept 1804*
			(Vfd Abd. Not on Roll)
	Carp's Crew	REVENGE	*Trafalgar. G.H.5308*
MILES, Joseph	A.B.	VALIANT	
	A.B.	NAMUR	*4 Novr 1805*
MILLER, William	L.M.	INDEFATIGABLE	
MILTON, Samuel	Coxswain	IMPERIEUSE	*G.H. 6538*
MORGAN, Francis	Not given	THESEUS	*Lieut crossed out. 171/2/170*
MOORE, John	Pte. R.M.	REVENGE	*(Additional clasp?)*
MOOR, Philip	Midshipman	UNICORN	
	Midshipman	ARMIDE	*B.S. 13 Feb 1810*
MORLEY, John	Pte. R.M.	THESEUS	*G.H. 9951*
	Sgt. R.M.	ALBION	*Algiers*
MORTON, Thomas.C.P.	Midshipman	ILLUSTRIOUS	
	Midshipman	ILLUSTRIOUS	*Java*
MULCAHY, Timothy	Ord	AETNA	
or MULCALEY or	L.M.	COURAGEUX	*4 Novr 1805*
MULKAHY	Qtr Gunner	IMPREGNABLE	*Algiers*
MURPHY, James	Sgt. R.M.	VALIANT	*Known paired Anchor Ty LSGC*
MURPHY, Michael	Ord	CALEDONIA	*G.H. 9456*
MURTHA or MURTA, Owen	L.M.	CALEDONIA	*G.H. 2051 as MURTO*
MUSTON, Thomas.G.	Lieut. R.N.	CALEDONIA	
NORMAN, John	Corporal R.M.	EMERALD	
	Pte. R.M.	EMERALD	*Emerald. 13 March 1808*
NORTON, John	Ord	CALEDONIA	
O'CONNOR, John	Ord	WHITING	
OGILVIE, Henry	Master's Mate	DONEGAL	
	Midshipman	DONEGAL	*St Domingo*
	Midshipman	AKBAR	*Java*
OLAY, Richard	Ord	CALEDONIA	*G.H. 2756 as ONEY*
	L.M.	HERO	*4 Novr 1805*
OLDMIXON, George	Vol 1st Cl	BELLONA	
OLDREY, William	Midshipman	DOTTEREL	
	Lieut. R.N.	UNDAUNTED	*B.S. 2 May 1813*
OLIVER, John	Master	DONEGAL	
OLIVER, Richard	Ship's Corporal	CAESAR	*G.H. 86*
	Ord	CAESAR	*4 Novr 1805*

O'NEIL, John or O'NEILL	Carp's Crew L.M.	CAESAR CAESAR	4 Novr 1805
ORAM, William	Pte. R.M.	GIBRALTAR	
OTTY, Allen	Master's Mate	CALEDONIA	
OWEN, William	A.B.	THESEUS	(M.L. as OWENS)
	A.B.	THESEUS	Nile
	A.B.	THESEUS	Acre. 30 May 1799
PARKE, John	Yeoman of Sheets	THESEUS	
PARKER, Charles (B)	Midshipman	DOTTEREL	
	Vol 1st Cl	CHILDERS	Childers. 14 March 1808
	Master's Mate	Qn CHARLOTTE	Algiers (Explosion vessel)
PARKER, Peter	Ord	AIGLE	
PARNELL, Robert	A.B.	CALEDONIA	
PARR, John	Pte. R.M.	CALEDONIA	
PASCOE, John.E.	Midshipman	INDEFATIGABLE	
PASTON, Charles	Pte. R.M.	RESOLUTION	
PATTE, Joseph	Lieut. R.N.	GIBRALTAR	
PATTERSON, John	Sgt. R.M.	CALEDONIA	
PAYNTER, Charles	Midshipman	INDEFATIGABLE	
PAYNTER, John.P.	Midshipman	INDEFATIGABLE	
	Lieut. R.N.	EURYALUS	The Potomac. 17 Aug 1814
PEAT, John	Boy 2nd Class	ILLUSTRIOUS	
	Boy 2nd Class	ILLUSTRIOUS	Java
PERFERRY, John	Gunner. R.M.A.	AETNA	
	Gunner. R.M.A.	"ANHOLT"	Anholt. 27 March 1811
PETERS, John	Pte. R.M.	INDEFATIGABLE	
PHILLIPS, Frederick	Midshipman	BELLONA	
PHILLIPS, George	Ord	AIGLE	
PHILLIPS, Thomas	A.B.	VALIANT	
	A.B.	NAMUR	4 Novr 1805
PHIPPS, William	Midshipman	INDEFATIGABLE	
PLUMMER, William	Ord	BEAGLE	
POCOCK, George	L.M.	THESEUS	G.H. 5485
POPE, Edmund	Midshipman	VALIANT	
	Midshipman	VALIANT	B.S. 27 Sep 1810 (Vfd Abd. Not on Roll)
POPE, John	Midshipman	REDPOLE	
POPPLE, William	Ord	ILLUSTRIOUS	
POTTS, Thomas	Sailmaker	EMERALD	
	Sailmaker	EMERALD	Emerald. 13 March 1808
PRESTON, James	Pte. R.M.	GIBRALTAR	
PRICE, James.H.	Lieut. R.N.	BEAGLE	
PRICE, Samuel	Midshipman	THESEUS	
PRICE, Thomas	Pte. R.M.	BEAGLE	
PRINCE, John	Lieut. R.N.	RESOLUTION	
PRITCHARD, William	Ord	CALEDONIA	
	Ord	LEVIATHAN	Trafalgar
	Ord	CALEDONIA	B.S. 27 Sep 1810
PUMMELL, Samuel	Not Given	Not Given	(see ADM 171/2/69)
	A.B.	RUSSELL	1 June 1794
	A.B.	RUSSELL	23rd June 1795
	Ord	DONEGAL	St Domingo
RANDALL, Henry	Midshipman	PALLAS	
RANDY, Johannes	L.M.	RESOLUTION	G.H. 9441
RANDOLPH, Charles.G.	Midshipman	DONEGAL	
	Lieut. R.N.	EUROTAS	Eurotas. 25 Feby 1814
READ, George	Midshipman	VALIANT	
	Midshipman	VALIANT	B.S. 27 Sep 1810
READ, George	Ord	BEAGLE	
READ, Henry	Boatswain	VALIANT	
READ, Robert.M.	Clerk	AIGLE	
READ, Thomas	2nd Master	CAESAR	
REDMAN, John	A.B.	RESOLUTION	(Might read NEDMAN)
REED, Benjamin	A.B.	VALIANT	(M.L. as REID)
	Boy 2nd Class	NAMUR	4 Novr 1805
	Ord	VALIANT	B.S. 27 Sep 1810
REES, Frederick	Pte. R.M.	CAESAR	
REYNOLDS, George	Pte. R.M.	REVENGE	G.H. 9758
REYNOLDS, Joseph	A.B.	RESOLUTION	
RICE, Thomas	Pte. R.M.	PALLAS	G.H. 10,064
RICH, Charles	Master's Mate	DOTTEREL	
RICHARDSON, Charles	Captain. R.N.	CAESAR	
	Master's Mate	ROYAL GEORGE	1 June 1794
	Lieut. R.N.	CIRCE	Camperdown
	Lieut. R.N.	KENT	Egypt
ROBERTS, Daniel	Master's Mate	ILLUSTRIOUS	
	Lieut. R.N.	ILLUSTRIOUS	Java
ROBERTS, Isaac	A.B.	BELLONA	
	Boy 3rd Class	ANSON	12 Octr 1798
ROBERTS, Lazarus	Midshipman	REVENGE	
ROBERTS, Obadiah	Midshipman	CAESAR	

BASQUE ROADS 1809

ROBERTS, Samuel	Lieut. R.N.	UNICORN	
	Boy 2nd Class	ANSON	*12 Octr 1798*
	Commander	METEOR	*The Potomac. 17 Aug 1814*
	Commander	METEOR	*B.S. 14 Dec 1814*
ROBERTSON, Archibald	Asst Surgeon	CALEDONIA	
	Surgeon	CYDNUS	*B.S. 14 Dec 1814*
ROBINS, Thomas.L.	Lieut. R.N.	PALLAS	
	Midshipman	TEAZER	*Capture of the Desiree*
	Midshipman	TEAZER	*Copenhagen 1801*
			(Vfd Abd. Not on Roll)
	Master's Mate	VICTORY	*Trafalgar*
ROBINS, William	Gunner's Mate	THESEUS	
	Gunner's Mate	TONNANT	*B.S. 14 Dec 1814*
ROBINSON, Charles	2nd Lieut. R.M.	VALIANT	
	Captain. R.M.	HASTINGS	*Syria*
ROBINSON, Edward	Midshipman	Not Given	
ROBINSON, William	Two Borne	GIBRALTAR	*GH.3180. A.B. & L.M.*
RONEY, James	Sailmaker	BEAGLE	
ROOK, Edward	Carp's Crew	DONEGAL	
	Carp's Crew	DONEGAL	*St Domingo*
ROSE, Thomas	Ord	RESOLUTION	
ROWE, Richard	Coxswain	LYRA	*G.H. 7000*
	Coxswain	LYRA	*St Sebastian*
ROWLANDSON, Michael	A.B.	CAESAR	*(M.L. as RAWLINSON)*
	A.B.	CAESAR	*4 Novr 1805*
RUBIDGE, Charles	Lieut. R.N.	AETNA	
	Midshipman	CERES	*Egypt*
SALTER, Samuel	A.B.	THESEUS	
SALTER, William	Pte. R.M.	RESOLUTION	
SAUNDERS, James	Pte. R.M.	REVENGE	
SAURIN, Edward	Master's Mate	EMERALD	
	Midshipman	LOIRE	*B.S. 4 June 1805*
	Midshipman	EMERALD	*Emerald. 13 March 1808*
SAVAGE, James	Pte. R.M.	AIGLE	*G.H. 1517*
SAXBY, Robert	1st Lieut. R.M.	GIBRALTAR	
SCHULTE, Wilheim	Pte. R.M.	RESOLUTION	
SCOTT, John	A.B.	INDEFATIGABLE	*G.H. 8135*
SEAGROVE, John	Not Given	HERO	
SEARLE, William	A.B.	REVENGE	
SEYMOUR, George.F.	Captain R.N.	PALLAS	
	Lieut. R.N.	NORTHUMBERLAND	*St Domingo*
SEYMOUR, Matthew.C.	Midshipman	GIBRALTAR	*(?AMETHYST clasps 1809)*
SHADS, William	Ord	AIGLE	
SHARP, David	A.B.	REVENGE	
	Ord	REVENGE	*Trafalgar*
SHATTERFOOT, Isaac	Pte. R.M.	CAESAR	
	Pte. R.M.	CAESAR	*4 Novr 1805*
SHEPPARD, John	Capt' Forecastle	RESOLUTION	
SHERMAN, Thomas	Captain. R.M.	CALEDONIA	*(Vfd Abd. Not on Roll)*
	2nd Lieut. R.M.	DRYAD	*Dryad. 13 June 1796*
	Captain. R.M.	CALEDONIA	*B.S. 27 Sep 1810*
SHORE, Josiah	R.M. Boy	PALLAS	
SHOWAN, Elijah	Gunner's Mate	CALEDONIA	
	Capt's Servant	QUEEN	*A domestic. M.L. as SHOWEN*
	Boy 2nd Class	QUEEN	*23rd June 1795*
SHUTER, Thomas	Pte. R.M.	CALEDONIA	
SIMMONS, Absalom	Corporal. R.M.	INDEFATIGABLE	
SIMMONS, Robert	Volunteer	HERO	
SIMPLE, Walter	Ord	INDEFATIGABLE	
SIMPSON, Thomas	Qtr Gunner	INDEFATIGABLE	
SKINLEY, John	Midshipman	THESEUS	
SLOAMON, John	Ord	IMPERIEUSE	*(M.L. as SOLOMON)*
SMITH, Charles	Midshipman	CAESAR	
SMITH, Edward	L.M.	BELLONA	*G.H. 8363*
	Ord	BELLONA	*4 Novr 1805*
SMITH, James	Ord	REVENGE	
	M.A.A.	SUPERB	*Algiers*
	M.A.A.	ALBION	*Navarino*
			(M) Known Anchor Type LSGC
SMITH, John	Pte. R.M.	CALEDONIA	
SMITH, John	Capt' After Guard	IMPERIEUSE	*G.H. 6994*
	Gunner's Mate	GRANICUS	*Algiers*
SMITH, Thomas	Lieut. R.N.	LYRA	
	Midshipman	PHOENIX	*4 Novr 1805*
	Midshipman	PHOENIX	*Phoenix. 10 Augt 1805*
SMITH, William.R.	Lieut. R.N.	THESEUS	
	Midshipman	DEFENCE	*Nile*
SNELLERS, Edward	Q.M.	AIGLE	
SNEROING, Francis	L.M.	RESOLUTION	*G.H. 2780 as SNEVERE*
SNOOK, Walter	Boy	VALIANT	

SOUTH, John	A.B.	UNICORN	G.H. 6816
SPARSHOTT, Samuel	Master's Mate	CALEDONIA	
SPENCER, Thomas	Pte. R.M.	BELLONA	
STOCKPOLE, Philip	Pte. R.M.	REVENGE	G.H. 2726
STANBURY, William	Midshipman	CALEDONIA	
	Midshipman	CALEDONIA	B.S. 27 Sep 1810
STEPHENS, John	A.B.	THESEUS	G.H. 1423 as STEVENS?
STEVENS, Edward	Pte. R.M.	IMPERIEUSE	G.H. 8246
STEVENS, Vivian	Master's Mate	VALIANT	
STEVENS, William	Boy	ILLUSTRIOUS	
STEWART, John	Asst Surgeon	GIBRALTAR	
	Asst Surgeon	PIEDMONTAISE	Banda Neira
	Actg Surgeon	CAROLINE	Java
STILL, Joseph	Ord	ILLUSTRIOUS	(Vfd Abd. Not on Roll)
	A.B.	STATELY	Stately. 22 March 1808
	A.B.	ILLUSTRIOUS	Java
STILL, William	Master's Mate	LYRA	
STIVEY, John	L.M.	INDEFATIGABLE	
STOCKWELL, William	Pte. R.M.	UNICORN	
STONES, Thomas	Pte. R.M.	REVENGE	
STOPFORD, Robert	Captain. R.N.	CAESAR	
	Captain. R.N.	AQUILON	1 June 1794
	Captain. R.N.	PHAETON	17 June 1795
	Captain. R.N.	SPENCER	St Domingo
	Rear Admiral	SCIPION	Java
	Admiral	Pcss CHARLOTTE	Syria
STRICKLAND, Joseph	Carp's Crew	AIGLE	G.H. 2105
	Carp's Crew	INFERNAL	Algiers
SUTTON, Robert	Pte. R.M.	UNICORN	
SWIFF, Joseph	Ord	BELLONA	G.H. 9597
TABART, Francis.G.	Purser	DOTTEREL	
TANCOCK, O. F or J.	Midshipman	MARTIAL	
TAPLEY, John.T.	Master	NIMROD	
TAYLOR, James	Ord	INSOLENT	
TAYLOR, John	Lieut. R.N.	DONEGAL	
	Midshipman	GIBRALTAR	Egypt
	Master's Mate	DONEGAL	St Domingo
TAYLOR, John	Pte. R.M.	REVENGE	
	Pte. R.M.	ROYAL SOVEREIGN	Trafalgar
TAYLOR, John	Pte. R.M.	VALIANT	
	Pte. R.M.	VALIANT	B.S. 27 Sep 1810
TAYLOR, William	Yeoman of Sheets	CALEDONIA	
TEIGHE, Charles	Volunteer	REVENGE	
THACKER, Henry or THACHER	Ord	CALEDONIA	
THOMAS, George	Ord	CAESAR	G.H. 9005
THOMAS, John	Qtr Gunner	INDEFATIGABLE	G.H. 10,114
THOMAS, John	A.B.	PALLAS	
THOMPSON, Thomas	A.B.	THUNDER	
	Q.M's Mate	THUNDER	Thunder. 9 Octr 1813
THOMPSON, William	A.B.	EMERALD	
	A.B.	EMERALD	Emerald. 13 March 1808
THOMPSON, William	Boy	CAESAR	
	Boy	CAESAR	4 Novr 1805
THORN, George	L.M.	DONEGAL	
	Boy 3rd Class	DONEGAL	St Domingo
THORN, Thomas	A.B.	RESOLUTION	
TINK, Henry	Ord	CALEDONIA	
TOBIN, John	Asst Surgeon	HERO	
TOMBLESON, William	Boy	DOTTEREL	
TOMKIN, William	Ord	CALEDONIA	
TOMLIN, James	Actg Master	GOLDFISH	Ship not in list. Medal signed for by TOMLIN
TOMLINSON, Robert.C.	Master's Mate	AETNA	
TOOLE, Michael	Ord	CALEDONIA	
	Ord	CALEDONIA	B.S. 27 Sep 1810
TREASURE, James or Josh	Pte. R.M.	GIBRALTAR	
TRESIZE, Thomas	Gunner	REVENGE	
TRUSTI, Daniel	Ord	CALEDONIA	
TUCKER, James	Pte. R.M.	CAESAR	
TUCKER, Robert	Midshipman	GIBRALTAR	
UPCOTT, Joseph	Pte. R.M.	IMPERIEUSE	
VICKERY, John	Sgt. R.M.	REDPOLE	
	Pte. R.M.	LION	Lion. 15 July 1798
VINNIE, James	Q.M.	CAESAR	
WALKER, William	Lieut. R.N.	MARTIAL	
WALLIS, William	Clerk	VALIANT	
WALSTER, William	L.M.	AETNA	
	Barber	ROYAL OAK	B.S. 14 Dec 1814
WALLS, James	Carp's Crew	CALEDONIA	(May read WATTS)
WALPOLE, John	Clerk	THESEUS	

BASQUE ROADS 1809

WARD, John	Yeoman of Sheets	REVENGE	(Vfd Abd. Not on Roll)
	Qtr Gunner	CENTURION	Centurion. 18 Sept 1804
	Qtr Gunner	REVENGE	Trafalgar
WARD, John	Gunner. R.M.A.	CALEDONIA	G.H. 2318
	Pte. R.M.	RAMILLIES	Copenhagen 1801
	Corporal. R.M.A.	AETNA	The Potomac. 17 Aug 1814
	Corporal. R.M.A.	BEELZEBUB	Algiers
WATNOUGH, James	Gunner. R.M.A.	CALEDONIA	
WATSON, Robert	Q.M.	REVENGE	
	A.B.	REVENGE	Trafalgar } on one medal
	Qtr Gunner	REVENGE	B.S. 16 July 1806 on separate medal
WEBB, James	Coxswain	THUNDER	
	Gunner's Mate	THUNDER	Thunder. 9 Octr 1813
WEEKS, William	Boy 2nd Class	CAESAR	
	Boy 2nd Class	CAESAR	4 Novr 1805
WHEELER, Benjamin	Pte. R.M.	IMPERIEUSE	G.H.8497
WHEELER, Nicholas	Pte. R.M.	INDEFATIGABLE	
WHITE, Robert	Gunner. R.M.A.	WHITING (Schooner)	G.H. 2957
WHITE, Thomas	Boy	REVENGE	
WHITE, Thomas	Pte. R.M.	RESOLUTION	G.H.3055
WILLIAMS, William	Purser's Steward	THESEUS	
WILLIAMS, William	Ord	CALEDONIA	
WILLOUGHBY, Richard	Capt' Main Top	CALEDONIA	
WILLSON, George	Capt' Forecastle	REVENGE	
WILSON, David	A.B.	CALEDONIA	G.H. 8217
WILSON, Robert	A.B.	INDEFATIGABLE	
	A.B.	INDEFATIGABLE	B.S. 16 July 1806
WITHAM, Charles	Midshipman	GIBRALTAR	
WOOD, John	Cook	UNICORN	
WOOLCOMBE, George	Vol 1st Cl	CALEDONIA	
WOOLRIDGE, John	Pte. R.M.	AIGLE	
WRIFORD, Samuel	Lieut. R.N.	CAESAR	
	Midshipman	CAESAR	4 Novr 1805
	Lieut. R.N.	MALTA	Gaieta. 24 July 1815
WYATT, Henry.B.	Master's Mate	UNICORN	
WYLDE, Edward	Midshipman	EMERALD	
	Boy 2nd Class	EMERALD	Emerald. 13 March 1808
WYTHAM, Francis	Midshipman	GIBRALTAR	
YATES, John	Ord	CAESAR	
	Ord	CAESAR	4 Novr 1805
YOUNG, John	Pte. R.M.	REVOLUTIONNAIRE	
YOUNG, Archibald.H.	Pte. R.M.	RESOLUTION	

(47) POMPEE 17 JUNE 1809

Chase and capture of the French "74" D'HAUTPOUL, off Lower Sainte, Guadaloupe.

(Real date 17 April 1809)

ALLEN, William	Pte. R.M.	POMPEE	(Vfd Abd. Not on Roll)
	Pte. R.M.	POMPEE	Martinique
	Pte. R.M.	POMPEE	Guadaloupe
ANGIER, Ezekiel	Coxswain	POMPEE	
	Coxswain	BELLEISLE	Martinique
	Coxswain	ABERCROMBIE	Guadaloupe
ARCHER, Thomas	Clerk	POMPEE	
	Clerk	BELLEISLE	Martinique
	Clerk	ABERCROMBIE	Guadaloupe
BAYLIS, William	L.M.	POMPEE	(Vfd Abd. Not on Roll)
	L.M.	POMPEE	Martinique
	L.M.	POMPEE	Guadaloupe
BEDFORD, Joseph	A.B.	POMPEE	
	A.B.	POMPEE	Martinique
	A.B.	POMPEE	Guadaloupe
BONE, William	Drummer. R.M.	POMPEE	(Vfd Abd. Not on Roll) (M.L. as Will BONES)
	Drummer. R.M.	POMPEE	Martinique
	Drummer. R.M.	POMPEE	Guadaloupe
BRIGGS, John	L.M.	POMPEE	(Vfd Abd. Not on Roll) (M.L. as BIGGS)
	L.M.	POMPEE	Martinique
	Admiral's Domestic	POMPEE	Guadaloupe
BUTTER, Henry	Pte. R.M.	POMPEE	(Vfd Abd. Not on Roll)
	Pte. R.M.	POMPEE	Martinique
	Pte. R.M.	GUADALOUPE	Guadaloupe Vfd Abd Brig GUADALOUPE.NOR.

CLARK, Edward	Ord	POMPEE	
	Ord	POMPEE	*Martinique*
	Ord	POMPEE	*Guadaloupe*
COOPER, James	R.M. Boy	POMPEE	
	R.M. Boy	POMPEE	*Martinique*
	R.M. Boy	POMPEE	*Guadaloupe*
COSBY, W.	Lieut 63rd Regt	POMPEE	"Doing duty as a Marine"
DANIEL, John	A.B.	POMPEE	*(Vfd Abd. Not on Roll)*
	A.B.	POMPEE	*Martinique*
	A.B.	POMPEE	*Guadaloupe*
	A.B.	ASTRAEA	*Off Tamatave. 20 May 1811.*
EPPS, John	L.M.	POMPEE	*(Vfd Abd. Not on Roll)*
	L.M.	POMPEE	*Martinique G.H. 5997*
	L.M.	POMPEE	*Guadaloupe*
EVANS, Thomas	Ord	POMPEE	*(Vfd Abd. Not on Roll)*
	Ord	POMPEE	*Martinique*
	Ord	POMPEE	*Guadaloupe*
FELT, Hans Christian	Ord	POMPEE	*(Vfd Abd. Not on Roll)*
	Ord	POMPEE	*Martinique G.H. 8855*
	Ord	POMPEE	*Guadaloupe*
FITZGERALD, Thomas	Ord	POMPEE	
	Ord	POMPEE	*Martinique*
	Ord	POMPEE	*Guadaloupe*
FORSTER, Joseph	A.B.	POMPEE	*(Vfd Abd. Not on Roll)*
	A.B.	POMPEE	*Martinique*
			(Vfd Abd. Not on Roll)
	A.B.	POMPEE	*Guadaloupe*
GORMAN, John	A.B.	POMPEE	
	A.B.	AUDACIOUS	*Gut of Gibraltar. 12 July 1801*
	A.B.	POMPEE	*Martinique*
	A.B.	POMPEE	*Guadaloupe*
	Yeoman Sheets	Qn CHARLOTTE	*Algiers*
GOWLAND, Thomas	A.B.	POMPEE	*(Vfd Abd. Not on Roll)*
	A.B.	POMPEE	*Martinique*
	Capt Main Top	ABERCROMBIE	*Guadaloupe*
GRAVES, James	Q.M.	POMPEE	*(Vfd Abd. Not on Roll)*
	Q.M.	POMPEE	*Martinique*
	Q.M.	POMPEE	*Guadaloupe*
GREY, James	L.M.	POMPEE	*(M.L. as GRAY)*
	L.M.	POMPEE	*Martinique*
	L.M.	POMPEE	*Guadaloupe*
HAINES, Thomas	Gunner	POMPEE	*(Vfd Abd. Not on Roll)*
	Ord	SOUTHAMPTON	*Southampton. 9 June 1796*
			(Vfd Abd. Not on Roll)
	Ord	SOUTHAMPTON	*St Vincent*
	Coxswain	SUPERB	*Gut of Gibraltar 12 July 1801*
	Coxswain	SUPERB	*St Domingo*
	Gunner	ACASTA	*Martinique*
	Gunner	POMPEE	*Guadaloupe*
HITCHCOCK, Thomas	A.B.	POMPEE	*2 Medals issued. P & M+G*
	A.B.	POMPEE	*Martinique*
	Capt After Guard	POMPEE	*Guadaloupe*
HOOPER, Benjamin	Pte. R.M.	POMPEE	*(Vfd Abd. Not on Roll)*
	Pte. R.M.	POMPEE	*Martinique*
	Pte. R.M.	POMPEE	*Guadaloupe G.H.2231*
HOWES, William	Pte. R.M.	POMPEE	*(Vfd Abd. Not on Roll)*
	Pte. R.M.	POMPEE	*Martinique*
	Pte. R.M.	POMPEE	*Guadaloupe*
HUTCHINGS, George	L.M.	POMPEE	*(Vfd Abd. Not on Roll)*
	L.M.	POMPEE	*Martinique*
	L.M.	POMPEE	*Guadaloupe*
KELSALL, Edward	Quarter Gunner	POMPEE	*(Vfd Abd. Not on Roll)*
			On G.H. Roll as 4 Clasp.
	A.B.	AGINCOURT	*Camperdown (On 171/- Roll)*
	Quarter Gunner	POMPEE	*Martinique*
			(Vfd Abd. Not on Roll)
	Q.M's Mate	POMPEE	*Guadaloupe GH.7960*
			(Vfd Abd. Not on Roll)
LACK, Stephen	Pte. R.M.	POMPEE	*(Vfd Abd. Not on Roll)*
	Pte. R.M.	POMPEE	*Martinique*
	Pte. R.M.	POMPEE	*Guadaloupe*
LAY, James	Ord	POMPEE	
	Ord	POMPEE	*Martinique*
	Ord	POMPEE	*Guadaloupe*
LEWIS, William	Ord	POMPEE	*G.H. 7,160*
	Ord	POMPEE	*Martinique*
	Ord	POMPEE	*Guadaloupe*

POMPEE 17 JUNE 1809

LOWE, Thomas	Pte. R.M.	POMPEE	
	Pte. R.M.	POMPEE	*Martinique*
	Pte. R.M.	POMPEE	*Guadaloupe*
MASON, James	A.B.	POMPEE	*(Vfd Abd. Not on Roll)*
	A.B.	POMPEE	*Martinique*
	A.B.	POMPEE	*Guadaloupe*
MERCER, John.D.	Master's Mate	POMPEE	
	Master's Mate	BELLEISLE	*Martinique*
	Lieut. R.N.	PULTUSK	*B.S. 13 Dec 1809*
	Lieut. R.N.	PULTUSK	*Guadaloupe*
MILLER, James	Ord	POMPEE	
	Ord	POMPEE	*Martinique*
	Ord	POMPEE	*Guadaloupe*
MITCHELL, Thomas	L.M.	POMPEE	*G.H.3,120*
	L.M.	POMPEE	*Martinique*
	L.M.	POMPEE	*Guadaloupe*
			(Vfd Abd. Not on Roll)
MORGAN, Joseph	L.M.	POMPEE	
	L.M.	POMPEE	*Martinique*
	L.M.	POMPEE	*Guadaloupe*
OSBORN, William	A.B.	POMPEE	*(Vfd Abd. Not on Roll)*
	A.B.	POMPEE	*Martinique*
	A.B.	POMPEE	*Guadaloupe*
PRICE, Edward	Pte. R.M.	POMPEE	*(Vfd Abd. Not on Roll)*
	Pte. R.M.	POMPEE	*Martinique*
RATCLIFFE, Edward	Ord	POMPEE	*G.H.2,940*
	Ord	POMPEE	*Martinique*
	Ord	POMPEE	*Guadaloupe*
RIDLEY, John	Pte. R.M.	POMPEE	*(Vfd Abd. Not on Roll)*
	Pte. R.M.	POMPEE	*Martinique*
	Pte. R.M.	POMPEE	*Guadaloupe*
SANGER, James	Ord	POMPEE	*(Vfd Abd. Not on Roll)*
	Ord	POMPEE	*Martinique*
	Ord	ABERCROMBIE	*Guadaloupe*
SEAR, George	Ord	POMPEE	
	Ord	POMPEE	*Martinique*
	Ord	ABERCROMBIE	*Guadaloupe*
SHREEVE, William	A.B.	POMPEE	*(Vfd Abd. Not on Roll)*
	A.B.	POMPEE	*Martinique. G.H.8532*
	Caulker's Mate	POMPEE	*Guadaloupe*
STEEL, David	Midshipman	POMPEE	*(Vfd Abd. Not on Roll)*
	Midshipman	POMPEE	*Martinique*
TRUMBLE, William	Ord	POMPEE	
	Ord	POMPEE	*Martinique*
	Ord	ABERCROMBIE	*Guadaloupe*
WARDLE, John	Midshipman	POMPEE	*(Vfd Abd. Not on Roll)*
	Midshipman	POMPEE	*Martinique*
	Actg Lieut. R.N.	PULTUSK	*Guadaloupe*
WILKINSON, Samuel	L.M.	POMPEE	
	L.M.	POMPEE	*Martinique*
	L.M.	POMPEE	*Guadaloupe*

(13) CASTOR 17 JUNE 1809

Chase and capture of the French "74" D'HAUTPOUL, off Lower Sainte, Guadaloupe.
(Real date 17 April 1809)

ANDREWS, William	Boy 2nd Cl	CASTOR	
	Boy 2nd Cl	CASTOR	*Anse La Barque. 18 Decr 1809*
			(Vfd Abd. Not on Roll)
	L.M.	CASTOR	*Guadaloupe*
DIXON, James.T.T.	Midshipman	CASTOR	
	Master's Mate	CASTOR	*Anse La Barque. 18 Decr 1809*
	Master's Mate	CASTOR	*Guadaloupe*
	Midshipman	MAGICIENNE	*St Sebastian*
FORBES, John	Surgeon	CASTOR	*(Incorrectly on "POMPEE"*
			ADM 171/– Roll)
	Surgeon	NETLEY	*Guadaloupe*
	Surgeon	DESIREE	*Gluckstadt. 5 July 1814*
			Probably discharged before this action
HUSON, Joseph	Pte. R.M.	CASTOR	*(Vfd Abd. Not on Roll)*
	Pte. R.M.	CASTOR	*Anse La Barque. 18 Decr 1809*
			(Vfd Abd. Not on Roll)
	Pte. R.M.	CASTOR	*Guadaloupe*
McCAROGHER, Joseph	Surgeon	CASTOR	

McLAUGHLAN, James	A.B.	CASTOR	(Vfd Abd. Not on Roll)
	A.B.	CASTOR	Anse La Barque. 18 Decr 1809
			(Vfd Abd. Not on Roll)
	A.B.	CASTOR	Guadaloupe
MILLS, Samuel	Pte. R.M.	CASTOR	(Vfd Abd. Not on Roll)
	Pte. R.M.	CASTOR	Anse La Barque. 18 Decr 1809
			(Vfd Abd. Not on Roll)
	Pte. R.M.	CASTOR	Guadaloupe
NESBITT, Alexander	A.B.	CASTOR	(Vfd Abd. Not on Roll)
	Ord	CASTOR	Anse La Barque. 18 Decr 1809
			(Vfd Abd. Not on Roll)
	Ord	CASTOR	Guadaloupe. GH.3909
PACKE, George	Pte. R.M.	CASTOR	(Vfd Abd. Not on Roll)
	Pte. R.M.	CASTOR	Anse La Barque. 18 Decr 1809
			(Vfd Abd. Not on Roll)
	Pte. R.M.	CASTOR	Guadaloupe
PEVERINY, Anthony	Cook	CASTOR	(Vfd Abd. Not on Roll)
	Cook	CASTOR	Anse La Barque. 18 Decr 1809
			(Vfd Abd. Not on Roll)
	Cook	CASTOR	Guadaloupe
RAVEN, Michael	Lieut. R.N.	CASTOR	(Vfd Abd. Not on Roll)
	Lieut. R.N.	CASTOR	Anse La Barque. 18 Decr 1809
			(Vfd Abd. Not on Roll)
	Lieut. R.N.	CASTOR	Guadaloupe
ROSS, John	Pte. R.M.	CASTOR	G.H. 1,894
SELLON, W.B. (Roll)			
W.R.B. (Navy List)	Lieut. R.N.	CASTOR	(M.L. as SMITH, William)

(7) RECRUIT 17 JUNE 1809

Chase and capture of the French "74" D'HAUTPOUL, off Lower Sainte, Guadaloupe.

(Real date 17 April 1809)

DAVIS, John	Boy 3rd Cl	RECRUIT	
	Boy 3rd Cl	RECRUIT	Martinique
MOTT, Joseph	Capt Forecastle	RECRUIT	(Vfd Abd. Not on Roll)
	Ord	DEFENCE	Copenhagen 1801
	Capt Forecastle	RECRUIT	Martinique
MUSTART or			
MUSTARD, Robert	Carpenter	RECRUIT	
	Carpenter	RECRUIT	Martinique
			(Vfd Abd. Not on Roll)
NAPIER, Charles	Commander	RECRUIT (P)	(Vfd Abd. for all clasps)
	Commander	RECRUIT	Martinique
	Captain. R.N.	EURYALUS	The Potomac. 17 Aug 1814
	Commodore	POWERFUL	Syria.
			(Known to have received 4 clasp
			Medal. Not on Rolls)
PATTINSON, Robert	L.M.	RECRUIT	
	L.M.	RECRUIT	Martinique
PEARSON, John	Q.M.	RECRUIT	
	Q.M.	RECRUIT	Martinique
			(Vfd Abd. Not on Roll)
STEWART, James	Carp's Crew	RECRUIT	(Vfd Abd. Not on Roll)
	Carp's Crew	RECRUIT	Martinique

(5) CYANE 25 & 27 JUNE 1809

Action with the Franco-Neapolitan frigate CERES, and capture of eighteen gun-boats and destruction of four, off Naples.

(Real dates 26 & 27 June 1809)

ALLNUTT, Joseph	Midshipman	CYANE
CROGAN, John	Boy 3rd Cl	CYANE
STUART, William	1st Lt. R.M.	CYANE
TAPSON, John	Purser	CYANE
TAYLOR, John	Midshipman	CYANE

(5) ESPOIR 25 & 27 JUNE 1809

Action with the Franco-Neapolitan frigate CERES, and capture of eighteen gun-boats and destruction of four, off Naples.

(Real dates 26 & 27 June 1809)

BOYCE, Edward	Ord	ESPOIR	
HIGGS, William.H.	Lieut. R.N.	ESPOIR	
	Midshipman	FOUDROYANT	*Egypt*
MITFORD, Robert	Commander	ESPOIR	
	Midshipman	St FIORENZO	*San Fiorenzo. 8 Mar 1797*
OLIVER, Robert	Actg Lt. R.N.	ESPOIR	
TAYLOR, John	L.M.	ESPOIR	*G.H. 3,188*

(12) BONNE CITOYENNE Wh FURIEUSE (G.M.)

Capture of the French frigate FURIEUSE on 6 July 1809 in mid Atlantic.

ATWATERS, Thomas	Carpenter	BONNE CITOYENNE	
BUTTONSHAW, Edward	Ord	BONNE CITOYENNE	
CHAPMAN, Richard	Pte. R.M.	BONNE CITOYENNE	
CROSDALE, John	Supn Boy 2nd Cl	BONNE CITOYENNE	
JOLLEY, James	Pte. R.M.	BONNE CITOYENNE	*(M.L. as JOLLY)*
ROBERTS, Richard	Capt Fore Top	BONNE CITOYENNE	
ROUTH, Nathaniel	Midshipman	BONNE CITOYENNE	*G.H. 7,625*
SANDOM, William	Lieut. R.N.	BONNE CITOYENNE	
SMITH, Joseph	Pte. R.M.	BONNE CITOYENNE	
SYMES, Joseph	Lieut. R.N.	BONNE CITOYENNE	
	Midshipman	TONNANT	*Trafalgar*
TAYSAND, Eliazer	Capt Fore Top	BONNE CITOYENNE	*(M.L. as TYSUM/TYSAM)*
WHITE, William	Ord	BONNE CITOYENNE	*(Claim not refused, yet he "Ran" Oct 1810)*

(35) 7 JULY BOAT SERVICE 1809

Capture and destruction of seven gun-boats and twelve merchantmen at PERCOLA POINT, Baro Sound, Finland.

ALLEN, Charles	Lieut. R.N.	BELLEROPHON	
ALLEN, Robert	Boatswain	BELLEROPHON	
BANFIELD, Henry	Pte. R.M.	IMPLACABLE	
	Pte. R.M.	THUNDERER	*Trafalgar*
BARRABLE, William	A.B.	BELLEROPHON	
	A.B.	REVOLUTIONNAIRE	*4 Novr 1805*
BROOKS, Henry	Pte. R.M.	BELLEROPHON	
BURD, John	L.M.	IMPLACABLE	
	L.M.	IMPLACABLE	*Implacable 26 Augt 1808 (Vfd Abd. Not on Roll)*
CARR, William	L.M.	IMPLACABLE	
	L.M.	IMPLACABLE	*Implacable 26 Augt 1808 (Vfd Abd. Not on Roll)*
CRACKNELL, James. T.	Actg 1st Lieut.RM.	IMPLACABLE	*(Vfd Abd. Not on Roll)*
	Actg 1st Lieut.RM.	IMPLACABLE	*Implacable 26 Augt 1808*
CRAWLEY, John	L.M.	IMPLACABLE	
	L.M.	IMPLACABLE	*Implacable 26 Augt 1808*
CREAGH, James	Vol 1st Cl	MELPOMENE	
	Master's Mate	HEBRUS	*Algiers*
DIGNUM, Philip	Ord	MELPOMENE	*(M.L. as DIGMON)*
FITZGERALD, John (2)	L.M. (two borne)	IMPLACABLE	*(1 of 2 applied B.S. clasp)*
	L.M.	IMPLACABLE	*Implacable 26 Augt 1808*
GREEN, Samuel	Sailmaker's Mate	IMPLACABLE	
	Sailmaker's Mate	IMPLACABLE	*Implacable 26 Augt 1808*
HAMMOND, Isaac	A.B.	IMPLACABLE	
	L.M.	REVOLUTIONNAIRE	*4 Novr 1805*
	Ord	IMPLACABLE	*Implacable 26 Augt 1808*
HARCOURT, Frederick.E.V.	Lieut. R.N.	IMPLACABLE	*Formerly & on M.L. as VERNON, Frederick.E.*
HARRIS, John	2 Ptes R.M. borne	IMPLACABLE	**(Both left before Action)*
	2 Ptes R.M. borne	IMPLACABLE	*Implacable 26 Augt 1808 (1 of 2 appld both clasps)*
HARVEY, William	Pte. R.M.	IMPLACABLE	
KING, George	Pte. R.M.	MELPOMENE	
LAKEMAN, William	Sgt. R.M.	BELLEROPHON	
LESLY, John	A.B.	IMPLACABLE	*(M.L. as LESLIE)*
	A.B.	IMPLACABLE	*Implacable 26 Augt 1808*
LOCK, Samuel	Pte. R.M.	MELPOMENE	

MATSON, George.W.	Midshipman	BELLEROPHON	
McCALLUM, John	Master's Mate	PRESIDENT	*Java*
McLAUGHLIN, Archibald	Bosun's Mate	BELLEROPHON	(M.L. as McCALLEM)
	Ord	BELLEROPHON	(M.L. as McLACHLIN)
	Ord	COLOSSUS	*Trafalgar*
McKINNON, Malcolm	Cook	PROMETHEUS	(Joined by Warrant 14-I-1808)
or MACKINNON	Cook	PROMETHEUS	B.S. 25 July 1809
	Cook	PROMETHEUS	Algiers (M.L. as McKENNION)
ORMOND, Francis	Master's Mate	IMPLACABLE	
	Midshipman	IMPLACABLE	*Implacable 26 Augt 1808*
	Actg Flag Lieut. R.N.	ABOUKIR	B.S. 29 Sep 1812
	Lieut. R.N.	ENDYMION	*Endymion Wh President*
	Lieut. R.N.	IMPREGNABLE	*Algiers*
PURCHAS, William.J.	Midshipman	BELLEROPHON	
	Midshipman	HERO	*4 Novr 1805*
SCOTT, Edmund	Master's Mate	BELLEROPHON	
	Midshipman	HERO	*4 Novr 1805*
SKEKEL, John	Lieut. R.N.	BELLEROPHON	
	Lieut. R.N.	HERO	*4 Novr 1805*
SHERIDAN, John	Lieut. R.N.	BELLEROPHON	
SYMONDS, Christopher	A.B.	IMPLACABLE	(M.L. as SIMMONS & other ships as SIMMONDS, SYMMONDS)
	Ord	REVOLUTIONNAIRE	*4 Novr 1805*
	A.B.	IMPLACABLE	*Implacable 26 Augt 1808*
THOMAS, Henry	Pte. R.M.	BELLEROPHON	
	Pte. R.M.	BELLEROPHON	*Trafalgar*
TRUEMAN, Jeremiah	Q.M.	IMPLACABLE	
	A.B.	LEVIATHAN	*Trafalgar*
	Q.M.	IMPLACABLE	*Implacable 26 Augt 1808*
WHITE, John	A.B.	IMPLACABLE	
	Ord	IMPLACABLE	*Implacable 26 Augt 1808*
WILSON, John	Ord	MELPOMENE	

(7) 14 JULY BOAT SERVICE 1809

Storming a battery near CARRY, on River Rhone, by boats of SCOUT.
(Real date 16 July 1809)

ADAMS, John	Midshipman	SCOUT	G.H. 7,577 (Rating)
	Midshipman	SCOUT	B.S. 1 Nov 1809
ATKINS, Thomas	A.B.	SCOUT	
BLACKMORE, Robert	Carpenter	SCOUT	
BROWN, Philip	A.B.	SCOUT	
FARRANT, John	Lieut. R.N.	SCOUT	
	Vol 1st Cl	RUSSELL	*Copenhagen. 1801*
	Midshipman	ROYAL SOVEREIGN	*Trafalgar*
	Lieut. R.N.	SCOUT	B.S. 1 Nov 1809
	Lieut. R.N.	BORER	B.S. 8 April 1814
HOULDER, James	Pte. R.M.	SCOUT	
	Pte. R.M.	SCOUT	B.S. 1 Nov 1809
HOWARD, Thomas	Capt Fore Top	SCOUT	G.H. 8,472
	Capt Fore Top	SCOUT	B.S. 1 Nov 1809

No Applicants. 25 JULY BOAT SERVICE 1809 (a)

Cutting out and capture of a French cutter and a schooner in St Marie Bay, Guadaloupe by boats from H.M.S. FAWN on 26 July 1809 — real date.

(36) 25 JULY BOAT SERVICE 1809 (b)

Cutting out of a Russian brig and three gun-boats at FREDERIKSHAMN, in Gulf of Finland.

ARROWSMITH, William	Pte. R.M.	MINOTAUR	
BEDDOWS, Joseph	Pte. R.M.	PRINCESS CAROLINE	
	Pte. R.M.	STATELY	*Stately. 22 March 1808*
BONNO, Joseph	Gunner	MINOTAUR	*(M.L. as BONUO)*
	Bosun's Mate	ANSON	*12 Octr 1798*
	Gunner	ACTIVE	*Egypt*
	Gunner	NAMUR	*4 Novr 1805*
BRACE, George	L.M.	PCSS CAROLINE	
	L.M.	STATELY	*Stately. 22 March 1808*
BRAZIER, James	Ord	MINOTAUR	
	L.M.	MINOTAUR	*Trafalgar*
	Ord	ALBION	*Algiers*
BURDEN, John	Pte. R.M.	PCSS CAROLINE	*(He deserted before this Action, on 1st Dec 1808 at Yarmouth)*
BURN, Edward	Ord	MINOTAUR	*GH.5928. M.L. as BURNES. (Vfd Abd. Not on Roll)*
	Ord	MINOTAUR	*Trafalgar*
CANE, Robert	Master's Mate	PROMETHEUS	
CHAMBERS, Charles	Surgeon	PROMETHEUS	
CHEVERALL, John	A.B.	PCSS CAROLINE	
	Boy 3rd Cl	ST GEORGE	*14 March 1795*
	Ord	STATELY	*Stately. 22 March 1808*
COX, Joseph	Pte. R.M.	PCSS CAROLINE	
ELVY, George	Midshipman	MINOTAUR	
FLINT, James	Pte. R.M.	MINOTAUR	
	Pte. R.M.	MINOTAUR	*Trafalgar*
HART, Benjamin	Midshipman	MINOTAUR	
HAYES, John	Ord	MINOTAUR	
HODGES, Richard	Pte. R.M.	MINOTAUR	
HUME, David	A.B.	PCSS CAROLINE	
JOHNSON, Thomas	Master	PCSS CAROLINE	
JOHNSON, Thomas	A.B.	MINOTAUR	
	A.B.	MINOTAUR	*Trafalgar*
M'CHRYSTAL, John	Asst Surgeon	MINOTAUR	
McKINNON, Malcolm	Cook	PROMETHEUS	*(M.L. as McKENNION)*
	Cook	PROMETHEUS	*B.S. 7 July 1809*
	Cook	PROMETHEUS	*Algiers*
PARK, John.S.	Midshipman	PCSS CAROLINE	
PARKER, William	Ord	PCSS CAROLINE	*G.H. 2,511*
PARKES, James	Ord	PCSS CAROLINE	*GH. 2729 M.L. as PARKS*
	Ord	STATELY	*Stately. 22 March 1808*
PASFIELD, Charles	Pte. R.M.	PCSS CAROLINE	
	Pte. R.M.	STATELY	*Stately. 22 March 1808*
REED, John	Two L.Ms borne	PCSS CAROLINE	*Applicant G.H. 10,073*
SCOTT, James	Ord	PCSS CAROLINE	
	A.B.	STATELY	*Stately. 22 March 1808*
SHERWOOD, William	Vol 1st Cl	CERBERUS	
	Midshipman	CERBERUS	*B.S. 28 June 1810*
	Midshipman	CERBERUS	*Lissa*
SHREEVE, George	Midshipman	PCSS CAROLINE	*(M.L. as SHRIEVE)*
	Ord	STATELY	*Stately. 22 March 1808*
SINCLAIR, David	Ord	PCSS CAROLINE	*G.H. 103*
SMITH, William	Quarter Gunner	PCSS CAROLINE	*G.H. 8,261*
STEVENS, Thomas	1st Lt. R.M.	CERBERUS	
STRATTON, Samuel	Pte. R.M.	PROMETHEUS	
TAYLOR, Robert	Midshipman	CERBERUS	
TILLETT, James	Ord	PCSS CAROLINE	
	A.B.	GLASGOW	*Algiers*
VERNON, Henry	Supn Boy 3rd Cl	MINOTAUR	

(10) 27 JULY BOAT SERVICE 1809

Taking and destroying the battery at GESSENDORF (Wesermunde).

BANKS, William.H.	Surgeon	BRISEIS	
BIRD, William	Pte. R.M.	MUSQUITO	
BURGESS, Samuel	Lt Cmmdg R.N.	PINCHER	
	Midshipman	IMPREGNABLE	*1 June 1794*
	Lieut. R.N.	SYLPH	*Sylph. 28 Sepr 1801*
	Lieut. R.N.	PRINCE	*Trafalgar*
	Flag Lt. R.N.	QUEEN CHARLOTTE	*Algiers (P)*
COTGRAVE, Rowland.B.	Midshipman	PINCHER	
FROST, Edward	A.B.	MUSQUITO	
HAWKINS, Abraham.M.	Lieut. R.N.	L'AIMABLE	
REEVE, John	Lieut. R.N.	L'AIMABLE	
	Midshipman	AGAMEMNON	*Copenhagen 1801*
	Master's Mate	AGEMEMNON	*Trafalgar*
	Master's Mate	AGEMEMNON	*St Domingo*
THOMPSON, Denzil.J.	Not Given	Not Given	**Not yet found on M.L. of any ship at this Action.*
WATTS, George.E.	Commander	EPHIRA	
	Midshipman	STAG	*Capture of the Desiree*
	Lieut. R.N.	COMUS	*Comus. 15 Augt 1807*
WELSH, George	Lieut. R.N.	BRISEIS	
	Master's Mate	ELING	*Copenhagen 1801*
	Lieut. R.N.	BRISEIS	*Briseis. 14 Octr 1810*

(11) 29 JULY BOAT SERVICE 1809

Cutting out of six Italian gun-boats and ten laden trabaccolos at DUINO, near Trieste.

FOORD, James.J.	Midshipman	EXCELLENT	
HARPER, John	Lieut. R.N.	EXCELLENT	
	Lieut. R.N.	DEFENCE	*Nile*
HILTON, John	Lieut. R.N.	BUSTARD	
HOW, Thomas	2nd Lt. R.M.	EXCELLENT	
LASTON, Samuel.H.	Master's Mate	BUSTARD	*(Navy List shows recd two clasp Medal. ? +Algiers)*
MARKLAND, John.D.	Commander	BUSTARD	
	Master's Mate	NYMPHE	*Nymphe. 8 March 1797*
PROWSE, William	Midshipman	EXCELLENT	
RICHARDS, William	Ord	BUSTARD	*G.H. 7,890*
SAINSBURY, Thomas	Pte. R.M.	BUSTARD	*G.H. 9,106*
WISE, James	Purser	BUSTARD	
WOLFE, William	Ord	BUSTARD	*(M.L. as WOOLFE)*

(15) 28 AUG BOAT SERVICE 1809

Destroying a battery and capturing six gun-boats and seven trabaccolas at CORTELLAZZO, in the Adriatic.
(Real date 27 August 1809)

ANGAS, Jonathan	Surgeon's Asst	AMPHION	
	Surgeon	ACTIVE	*Lissa (13 March 1811)*
BAILEY, John	Ord	AMPHION	*(M.L. as BAYLEY)*
	Ord	AMPHION	*B.S. 28 June 1810*
	Ord	AMPHION	*Lissa*
BLYTH, Francis	Capt Forecastle	AMPHION	*(M.L. as BLYTHE)*
	Capt Forecastle	AMPHION	*B.S. 28 June 1810*
	Q.M.	AMPHION	*Lissa*
BOARDMAN, Thomas	Master's Mate	AMPHION	
BRUCE, Charles	Midshipman	AMPHION	
	Midshipman	AMPHION	*B.S. 28 June 1810*
	(Not Yet Joined)	BACCHANTE	*B.S. 1 & 18 Sep 1812 (On Roll)*
	Mid Ordinary	BACCHANTE	*B.S. 6 Jan 1813*
BUCHANAN, David	Yeoman of Sheets	AMPHION	
	Yeoman of Sheets	AMPHION	*B.S. 28 June 1810*
	Yeoman of Sheets	AMPHION	*Lissa*
DALLING, John.W.	Master's Mate	AMPHION	
	Midshipman	DEFENCE	*Trafalgar*

28 AUG BOAT SERVICE 1809

GAPE, Joseph	Midshipman	AMPHION	
	Vol 1st Cl	AJAX	*Trafalgar*
	Midshipman	AMPHION	*B.S. 28 June 1810*
KEMPTHORN, Charles.H.	Midshipman	AMPHION	
	Midshipman	AMPHION	*Lissa*
MOORE, Thomas	1st Lieut. R.M.	AMPHION	
	1st Lieut. R.M.	AMPHION	*B.S. 28 June 1810*
	1st Lieut. R.M.	AMPHION	*Lissa*
PHILLOTT, C.G.R.	Lieut. R.N.	AMPHION	
ROSS, Charles.H.	Midshipman	AMPHION	
	Master's Mate	AMPHION	*B.S. 28 June 1810*
	Actg Lieut. R.N.	AMPHION	*Lissa*
SLAUGHTER, William	Lieut. R.N.	AMPHION	
	Vol 1st Cl	TRIUMPH	*17 June 1795*
	Vol 1st Cl	TRIUMPH	*Camperdown*
	Lieut. R.N.	AMPHION	*B.S. 28 June 1810*
WESTON, George	Pte. R.M.	AMPHION	
	Pte. R.M.	AMPHION	*B.S. 28 June 1810*
	Pte. R.M.	AMPHION	*Lissa*
WHISKER, William	L.M.	AMPHION	
	L.M.	AMPHION	*B.S. 28 June 1810*
	L.M.	AMPHION	*Lissa*
	A.B.	BACCHANTE	*B.S. 1 & 18 Sep 1812*

(8) DIANA 11 SEPTR 1809

Capture of the Dutch corvette ZEFIER, off Fort Monado, Island of Celebes, East Indies.

BRITTAL, Noah	Pte. R.M.	DIANA	(M.L. as BRITTLE)
	Pte. R.M.	DIANA	B.S. 24 Dec 1810
	Pte. R.M.	ENDYMION	*Endymion Wh President*
BROWN, Ambrose	Pte. R.M.	DIANA	G.H.3627
	Pte. R.M.	DIANA	B.S. 24 Dec 1810
BURKE, James	Supn Boy 2nd Cl	DIANA	
KNOCKER, John.B.	Midshipman	DIANA	(Vfd Abd. Not on Roll)
(Henry on Roll)	Master's Mate	DIANA	B.S. 24 Dec 1810
NEWELL, Julius.J.F.	Ord	DIANA	(Vfd Abd. Not on Roll)
	Midshipman	DIANA	B.S. 24 Dec 1810
ROWELL, Richard	Ord	DIANA	
WHITE, George	Ship's Corporal	DIANA	(Vfd Abd. Not on Roll)
	Ship's Corporal	DIANA	B.S. 24 Dec 1810
WILSON, George	A.B.	DIANA	

(110) 1 NOV BOAT SERVICE 1809

Capture and destruction of four armed vessels and seven of a convoy at ROSAS, N.E. coast of Spain.

ADAMS, John	Midshipman	SCOUT	G.H. 7,577
	Midshipman	SCOUT	B.S. 14 July 1809
ARCHER, Charles	L.M.	VOLONTAIRE	
	Ord	VOLONTAIRE	B.S. 2 May 1813
ARTHUR, William	Boy 2nd Cl	CUMBERLAND	
	Ord	TONNANT	B.S. 14 Dec 1814
ATHILL, James	Midshipman	TIGRE	
ATKINSON, Christopher	A.B.	APOLLO	
BALGONIE, Viscount	Lieut. R.N.	TOPAZE	(Became Lord Leven)
BANNATYNE, John	Master's Mate	VOLONTAIRE	
	Master's Mate	VOLONTAIRE	B.S. 2 May 1813
BARRETT, William	Clerk	PHILOMEL	
BARTLETT, John	Boy 3rd Cl	APOLLO	
BEDWORTH, Thomas	Boy 3rd Cl	TOPAZE	
BELL, William (1)	Ord	CUMBERLAND	
BOXER, Edward	Lieut. R.N.	TIGRE	
	Midshipman	DORIS	B.S. 21 July 1801
	Captain R.N.	PIQUE	*Syria*
BOYTER, Alexander	Master's Mate	TOPAZE	
	Master's Mate	ENDYMION	*Endymion Wh President*
BRADLEY, William	Actg Lt. R.N.	CUMBERLAND	
	L.M.	MARS	*Mars. 21 April 1798*
BRADY, William.H.	Midshipman	CUMBERLAND	
BREWING, Daniel	Ord	TOPAZE	(M.L. as BREWER) GH.7556.
BRIDGES, George.F.	Midshipman	TIGRE	

BRICKWITH, Thomas	Ord	CUMBERLAND	(M.L. as BRICKWORTH)
BRUTTON, John	2nd Lt. R.M.	TIGRE	
BULL, Benjamin	Pte. R.M.	TIGRE	
BUTT, John	Ord	VOLONTAIRE	
CALLAN, Matthew	Pte. R.M.	TUSCAN	
CLIFFORD, Augustus.W.J.	Lieut. R.N.	TIGRE	
COCK, Henry	Master	PHILOMEL	
COMMANDER, Samuel	Pte. R.M.	TOPAZE	G.H. 8,306
COOK, Thomas	Pte. R.M.	TOPAZE	(M.L. as COOKE)
CRAFERS, Robert	Pte. R.M.	TOPAZE	(Not yet found in TOPAZE)
CROW, Patrick	A.B.	CUMBERLAND	G.H. 9,665
DAVIS, Simon	Cpl. R.M.	CUMBERLAND	
	Pte. R.M.	VOLONTAIRE	B.S. 2 May 1813
DICKSON, William	Quarter Gunner	TOPAZE	Recd Medal aged 84.
DODSON, Francis	Pte. R.M.	TIGRE	
DONOVAN, Timothy	Pte. R.M.	TIGRE	
DOVE, Francis	Yeoman of Sheets	APOLLO	
DUNCAN, James	Capt's Coxswain	VOLONTAIRE	
DUNN, Nicholas.J.C.	Lieut. R.N.	TOPAZE	
	Midshipman	TIGRE	Acre. 30 May 1799
	Midshipman	DANGEREUSE	Egypt
ETHERINGTON, William	Pte. R.M.	CUMBERLAND	"Not Found aboard"
EVANS, Thomas	Capt Afterguard	TIGRE	
FARRANT, John	Lieut. R.N.	SCOUT	
	Vol 1st Cl	RUSSELL	Copenhagen 1801
	Midshipman	ROYAL SOVEREIGN	Trafalgar
	Lieut. R.N.	SCOUT	B.S. 14 July 1809
	Lieut. R.N.	BORER	B.S. 8 April 1814
FAWCETT, Henry.A.	Midshipman	TIGRE	
FINNEY, Benjamin	Pte. R.M.	TIGRE	(M.L. as FINEY)
FORSTER, John	Lieut. R.N.	APOLLO	
FREEMAN, Andrew	Carpenter's Crew	TIGRE	G.H. 8,952
FRENCH, John.O.	Clerk	APOLLO	
FROST, Thomas	A.B.	CUMBERLAND	G.H. 534
GILLMAN, James	Gunner	PHILOMEL	
	Gunner	HEBRUS	Hebrus with L'Etoile
GRAHAM, Robert	L.M.	TIGRE	
HAMMOND, Charles	Lieut. R.N.	TOPAZE	
HARCOURT, Octavius.V.	Midshipman	TIGRE	Formerly and on M.L. as Octavius VERNON.
HARNESS, Richard.S.	Midshipman	VOLONTAIRE	
HARRIS, John	Pte. R.M.	TOPAZE	
HAY, George.J.	Vol 1st Cl	APOLLO	To Midshipman 2nd Nov 1809.
HEW, Robert	Sgt. R.M.	TOPAZE	(M.L. as KEW)
HILLS, Thomas	Lieut. R.N.	PHILOMEL	
	Vol 1st Cl	VICTORY	St Vincent
HILLYAR, Robert.P.	Surgeon	APOLLO	
	Surgeon	ROEBUCK	Egypt
	Surgeon	ALBION	Navarino
HOLMES, Joseph	Pte. R.M.	APOLLO	
	Pte. R.M.	BOXER	Capture of the Desiree
HOULDER, James	Pte. R.M.	SCOUT	
	Pte. R.M.	SCOUT	B.S. 14 July 1809
HOWARD, Thomas	Capt Fore Top	SCOUT	G.H. 8,472
	Capt Fore Top	SCOUT	B.S. 14 July 1809
HUME, Joseph	Midshipman	TOPAZE	
HYNSON, Joseph	Master's Mate	TIGRE	
JONES, William	Ord	SCOUT	G.H. 9,903
LANCASTER, Henry	Midshipman	APOLLO	
	Vol 1st Cl	VICTORY	Trafalgar
LAWRENCE, William	Ord	CUMBERLAND	
Le BUFF, Francis	Ord	APOLLO	(M.L. as Le BEEF)
LEEKE, Henry.J.	Supn Midshipman	VOLONTAIRE	
LEER, Thomas	Ord	CUMBERLAND	
MARKS, John	Ord	TIGRE	G.H. 2,039 (M.L. as MACKS)
M'DOUGALL, John	Midshipman (P)	Loaned to Boats ex UNITE via VILLE DE PARIS	
	Lieut. R.N.	UNITE	Pelagosa. 29 Novr 1811
	Lieut. R.N.	SUPERB	Algiers
McLAUGHLIN, Peter	A.B.	TIGRE	G.H. 7,352
McNAMARA, Robert	Capt Fore Top	TOPAZE	
MILLER, Hugh	L.M.	TIGRE	G.H. 7,064
MONTAGU, James	Midshipman	TIGRE	
	Lieut. R.N.	ALCESTE	Pelagosa. 29 Novr 1811
MOULD, Thomas	Pte. R.M.	VOLONTAIRE	
	Cpl. R.M.	VOLONTAIRE	B.S. 2 May 1813
MURPHY, James	Ord	TOPAZE	
	Boy 3rd Cl	ALLIGATOR	Egypt
MURRAY, Robert	L.M.	VOLONTAIRE	(M.L. as MOREY)
NASH, Philip	Ord	CUMBERLAND	G.H. 2,765
OAKS, Samuel	L.M.	TIGRE	G.H. 2,839
PERCEVAL, Hon George.J.	Midshipman	TIGRE	Became Earl of Egmont
	Vol 1st Cl	ORION	Trafalgar
	Captain. R.N.	INFERNAL	Algiers

1 NOV BOAT SERVICE 1809

PRIEST, Joseph	Pte. R.M.	APOLLO	
RAMSDEN, Frank	Vol 1st Cl	TIGRE	
REYNOLDS, John	Pte. R.M.	TIGRE	
ROONEY, James	Ord	TOPAZE	
RUBY, Thomas	Pte. R.M.	TOPAZE	G.H. 2,997
SEAMORE, Thomas	Pte. R.M.	TOPAZE	
	Sgt. R.M.	SUPERB	Algiers
SIMPLE, Robert	Asst Surgeon	TIGRE	(M.L. as SEMPLE)
SISON, Samuel	Lieut. R.N.	VOLONTAIRE	
SLADE, Henry	Lieut. R.N.	PHILOMEL	
STANWAY, John	Cpl. R.M.	TIGRE	
STANYERS, Joseph	Pte. R.M.	CUMBERLAND	
STEDDY, John	Midshipman	TUSCAN	
STEWART, James	Capt Main Top	TOPAZE	
STUART, Richard	Lieut. R.N.	CUMBERLAND	
SULLIVAN, Dennis	L.M.	TOPAZE	
SUMMERS, Joseph	Ropemaker	TIGRE	
SYER, Dey.R.	Midshipman	TIGRE	
	Midshipman	PRINCE	Trafalgar
	Lieut. R.N.	VOLONTAIRE	B.S. 2 May 1813
TRAPPESS, Thomas	Pte. R.M.	APOLLO	
TURTON, James	Ord	CUMBERLAND	
VINCENT, William	Pte. R.M.	TIGRE	
WADSWORTH, David	Pte. R.M.	CUMBERLAND	
WALDEGRAVE, William	Lieut. R.N.	Loaned for boats from VILLE DE PARIS	
			Became Earl WALDEGRAVE.
	Captain. R.N.	REVENGE	Syria
WALKER, Daniel	L.M.	TUSCAN	
WEBSTER, Gunderland (?)	Ord	TIGRE	
WEST, George	Cpl. R.M.	TOPAZE	
WHITE, John	A.B.	CUMBERLAND	
WILKINSON, William	L.M.	VOLONTAIRE	
WILLIAMS, William	Three Borne	CUMBERLAND	
WILSON, Robert	Sgt. R.M.	TUSCAN	
WILSON, Thomas	Boy 2nd Cl	VOLONTAIRE	
	L.M.	VOLONTAIRE	B.S. 2 May 1813
WRIGHT, Samuel	Drummer. R.M.	TIGRE	
YOUNG, James	Armourer	VOLONTAIRE	
	Armourer	VOLONTAIRE	B.S. 2 May 1813
YOUNG, John	M.A.A.	APOLLO	

(9) 13 DEC BOAT SERVICE 1809

Cutting out of the French corvette NISUS and destruction of a battery, in Hayes Harbour, N.W. Guadaloupe.
(Real date 12 December 1809)

COOKE, Jervis	2nd Lt. R.M.	THETIS	
	2nd Lt. R.M.	THETIS	Anse la Barque. 18 Decr 1809
			(Vfd Abd. Not on Roll)
	2nd Lt. R.M.	THETIS	Guadaloupe
HOLE, William	Midshipman	BACCHUS	
	Midshipman	WOLVERENE	Martinique
	Midshipman	BACCHUS	Guadaloupe
	Master's Mate	TRAAVE	B.S. 14 Dec 1814
MERCER, John.D.	Lieut. R.N.	PULTUSK	
	Master's Mate	BELLEISLE	Martinique
	Master's Mate	POMPEE	Pompee 17 June 1809
	Lieut. R.N.	PULTUSK	Guadaloupe
MURRAY, Daniel	Boatswain	THETIS	
	Boatswain	THETIS	Anse la Barque. 18 Decr 1809
	Boatswain	THETIS	Guadaloupe
PINTO, Thomas	Commander	ACHATES	
	Midshipman	IRRESISTIBLE	St Vincent
	Master's Mate	NORTHUMBERLAND	Egypt
	Lieut. R.N.	AGAMEMNON	Trafalgar
	Lieut. R.N.	AGAMEMNON	St Domingo
	Commander	ACHATES	Guadaloupe
ROSS, John	A.B.	ATTENTIVE	
	A.B.	ATTENTIVE	Guadaloupe
RUEL, John.G.	1st Lt. R.M.	THETIS	(Vfd Abd. Not on Roll)
	1st Lt. R.M.	THETIS	Anse la Barque. 18 Decr 1809
			(Vfd Abd. Not on Roll)
	1st Lt. R.M.	THETIS	Guadaloupe

SODEN, Benjamin	Purser	THETIS	
	Purser	THETIS	*Anse la Barque. 18 Decr 1809*
	Purser	THETIS	*Guadaloupe*
UNDERHILL, Alexander	Ord	ATTENTIVE	
	Ord	ATTENTIVE	*Guadaloupe*

(52) ANSE LA BARQUE 18 DECR 1809

Storming batteries at Barque Bay, Guadaloupe, and capture of the French frigates LOIRE and SEINE.

ANDREWS, William	Boy 2nd Cl	CASTOR	*(Vfd Abd. Not on Roll)*
	Boy 2nd Cl	CASTOR	*Castor. 17 June 1809*
	L.M.	CASTOR	*Guadaloupe*
BAKER, William.H.	Midshipman	CASTOR	
	Midshipman	CASTOR	*Guadaloupe*
BATTERSBY, John.P.	Vol 1st Cl	FREIJA	
	Vol 1st Cl	FREIJA	*St Sebastian*
BELL, James	Ord	SCEPTRE	
	Ord	SCEPTRE	*Guadaloupe*
BENNET, Martin	Actg Lt. R.N.	SCEPTRE	
	Midshipman	ILLUSTRIOUS	*Basque Roads 1809*
	Actg Lt. R.N.	SCEPTRE	*Guadaloupe*
BLAKE, Thomas	Boy (?)	Not Given	
	Boy (?)	CASTOR	*Guadaloupe (Not yet found)*
BULL, Benjamin	A.B.	THETIS	
	A.B.	THETIS	*Guadaloupe*
CARTER, James	Midshipman	SCEPTRE	
	Midshipman	SCEPTRE	*Guadaloupe*
CARTER, William.F.	Surgeon	BLONDE	
	Surgeon	BLONDE	*Guadaloupe*
	Surgeon	ROYALIST	*Royalist. 29 Decr 1812*
CLEMENTS, John	L.M.	ELIZABETH	*(Vfd Abd. Not on Roll)*
COLWELL, John	Vol 1st Cl	SCEPTRE	*(Vfd Abd. Not on Roll)*
	Vol 1st Cl	SCEPTRE	*Guadaloupe*
	Paymaster	PHOENIX	*Syria (+Crimea Medals)*
COOKE, Jervis	2nd Lt. R.M.	THETIS	*(Vfd Abd. Not on Roll)*
	2nd Lt. R.M.	THETIS	*B.S. 13 Dec 1809*
	2nd Lt. R.M.	THETIS	*Guadaloupe*
COVE, William	Trumpeter	THETIS	
	Trumpeter	THETIS	*Guadaloupe*
DIXON, James.T.T.	Master's Mate	CASTOR	
	Midshipman	CASTOR	*Castor. 17 June 1809*
	Master's Mate	CASTOR	*Guadaloupe*
	Midshipman	MAGICIENNE	*St Sebastian*
FERGUSON, William	Boatswain	HAZARD	
	Boy	CANADA	*12 Octr 1798*
	Boatswain	HAZARD	*Martinique*
	Boatswain	HAZARD	*Guadaloupe*
FRANCIS, John	Drummer. R.M.	BLONDE	
	Drummer. R.M.	BLONDE	*Guadaloupe*
GORDON, James.G.	Actg Lt. R.N.	FREIJA	
	Midshipman	ILLUSTRIOUS	*Basque Roads 1809*
	Actg Lt. R.N.	FREIJA	*Guadaloupe*
HALKETT, David	Yeoman Pdr Rm	RINGDOVE	
	Yeoman Pdr Rm	RINGDOVE	*Martinique*
	Bosun's Mate	RINGDOVE	*Guadaloupe*
HAMLING, John	A.B.	SCEPTRE	
	A.B.	SCEPTRE	*Guadaloupe*
HARDEN, James	Midshipman	SCEPTRE	
	Midshipman	SCEPTRE	*Guadaloupe*
HAWKES, John	Yeo Powder Rm	HAZARD	
	Capt Main Top	HAZARD	*Martinique*
	Yeo Powder Rm	HAZARD	*Guadaloupe*
HUNTER, Hugh	Midshipman	HAZARD	
	Midshipman	HAZARD	*Martinique*
	Midshipman	HAZARD	*Guadaloupe*
HUSON, Joseph	Pte. R.M.	CASTOR	*(Vfd Abd. Not on Roll)*
	Pte. R.M.	CASTOR	*Castor. 17 June 1809 (Vfd Abd. Not on Roll)*
	Pte. R.M.	CASTOR	*Guadaloupe*
KNEVITT, Thomas.L.	Master's Mate	SCEPTRE	
	Master's Mate	SCEPTRE	*Guadaloupe*
	Master's Mate	VENERABLE	*Venerable. 16 Jany 1814*
McLAUGHLAN, James	A.B.	CASTOR	*(Vfd Abd. Not on Roll)*
	A.B.	CASTOR	*Castor. 17 June 1809 (Vfd Abd. Not on Roll)*
	A.B.	CASTOR	*Guadaloupe*

ANSE LA BARQUE 18 DECR 1809

MILLS, Samuel	Pte. R.M.	CASTOR	(Vfd Abd. Not on Roll)
	Pte. R.M.	CASTOR	Castor. 17 June 1809
			(Vfd Abd. Not on Roll)
	Pte. R.M.	CASTOR	Guadaloupe
MOLESWORTH, Bourchier	Lieut. R.N.	SCEPTRE	
	Lieut. R.N.	SCEPTRE	Guadaloupe
MONTGOMERIE, Alexander	Midshipman	SCEPTRE	
	Actg Lieut. R.N.	FREIJA	Guadaloupe
MURRAY, Daniel	Boatswain	THETIS	
	Boatswain	THETIS	B.S. 13 Dec 1809
	Boatswain	THETIS	Guadaloupe
NESBITT, Alexander	Ord	CASTOR	(Vfd Abd. Not on Roll)
	A.B.	CASTOR	Castor. 17 June 1809
			(Vfd Abd. Not on Roll)
	Ord	CASTOR	Guadaloupe
PACKE, George	Pte. R.M.	CASTOR	(Vfd Abd. Not on Roll)
	Pte. R.M.	CASTOR	Castor. 17 June 1809
			(Vfd Abd. Not on Roll)
	Pte. R.M.	CASTOR	Guadaloupe
PETERSON, Andrew	L.M.	BLONDE	
	L.M.	BLONDE	Guadaloupe
PEVERINY, Anthony	Cook	CASTOR	(Vfd Abd. Not on Roll)
	Cook	CASTOR	Castor. 17 June 1809
			(Vfd Abd. Not on Roll)
	Cook	CASTOR	Guadaloupe
PITT, Edward.W.	Lieut. R.N.	SCEPTRE	
	(Lieut. R.N.)	(SCEPTRE)	Awarded M.G.S. Guadaloupe
RAVEN, Michael	Lieut. R.N.	CASTOR	(Vfd Abd. Not on Roll)
	Lieut. R.N.	CASTOR	Castor. 17 June 1809
			(Vfd Abd. Not on Roll)
	Lieut. R.N.	CASTOR	Guadaloupe
RILEY, James	Pte. R.M.	CYGNET	G.H. 3,288
	Pte. R.M.	CYGNET	Guadaloupe
ROSE, Edward	Quarter Gunner	RINGDOVE	
	A.B.	RINGDOVE	Martinique
	A.B.	RINGDOVE	Guadaloupe
RUEL, John.G.	1st Lt. R.M.	THETIS	(Vfd Abd. Not on Roll)
	1st Lt. R.M.	THETIS	Guadaloupe
	1st Lt. R.M.	THETIS	B.S. 13 Dec 1809
			(Vfd Abd. Not on Roll)
SABBEN, James	Actg Lt. R.N.	RINGDOVE	
	Midshipman	DREADNOUGHT	Trafalgar
	Midshipman	NEPTUNE	Martinique
	Actg Lt. R.N.	RINGDOVE	Guadaloupe
SHARLAND, John	Capt Fore Top	SCEPTRE	
	Capt Fore Top	SCEPTRE	Guadaloupe
SHARP, John	Carp's Mate	BLONDE	
	Carp's Mate	BLONDE	Guadaloupe
SODEN, Benjamin	Purser	THETIS	
	Purser	THETIS	B.S. 13 Dec 1809
	Purser	THETIS	Guadaloupe
STEEL, James	L.M.	THETIS	(M.L. as STEELE, Patrick)
	L.M.	THETIS	Guadaloupe
TRIBE, Thomas	Midshipman	SCEPTRE	
	Midshipman	SCEPTRE	Guadaloupe
TRUSS, John	Ord	ELIZABETH	(Vfd Abd. Not on Roll)
	Boy 3rd Cl	DESIREE	Copenhagen 1801
	L.M.	PIQUE	Pique 26 March 1806
	Ord	ELIZABETH	Martinique
			(Vfd Abd. Not on Roll)
	Capt of Mast	CYANE	Cyane 16 Jany 1814
WALLIS, Provo.W.P.	Lieut. R.N.	GLOIRE	Anse La Barque 18 Decr 1809
		(Ship not on List)	
	Lieut. R.N.	GLOIRE	Guadaloupe
	Lieut. R.N.	SHANNON	Shannon Wh Chesapeake
WEBB, Christopher	L.M.	BLONDE	G.H. 2,919
	L.M.	BLONDE	Guadaloupe
			(Vfd Abd. Not on Roll)
WEBER, Ludwig	Pte. R.M.	FREIJA	
	Pte. R.M.	FREIJA	Guadaloupe
WEST, Thomas	Pte. R.M.	FREIJA	
	Pte. R.M.	FREIJA	Guadaloupe
WILSON, Robert	2nd Lt. R.M.	BLONDE	
	2nd Lt. R.M.	BLONDE	Guadaloupe
WRIGHT, Alexander	L.M.	SCEPTRE	
	L.M.	SCEPTRE	Guadaloupe
YOUNG, William	Pte. R.M.	SCEPTRE	
	Pte. R.M.	SCEPTRE	Guadaloupe

(4) CHEROKEE 10 JANY 1810

Capture of the French privateer AIMABLE NELLY, in Dieppe Harbour.

(Real date 11 January 1810)

ARGUILE, George	Ord	CHEROKEE	(M.L. as ARGYLE)
BARBER, Henry	Supn Pilot	CHEROKEE	
PILCHER, Henry	Supn Pilot	CHEROKEE	
WEBB, Joseph.R.R.	Lieut. R.N.	CHEROKEE	

(8) SCORPION 12 JANY 1810

Capture of the French corvette ORESTE, in Basse Terre Bay, Guadaloupe.

BENSON, John.R.	Midshipman	SCORPION	
	Midshipman	SCORPION	*Guadaloupe*
BLAKE, George.C.	Lieut. R.N.	SCORPION	
	Midshipman	ROMULUS	*Egypt*
	Lieut. R.N.	SCORPION	*Guadaloupe*
FLAXMAN, Robert	Bosun's Mate	SCORPION	*(Vfd Abd. Not on Roll)*
	A.B.	SCORPION	*Scorpion. 31 March 1804 (Vfd Abd. Not on Roll)*
	Bosun's Mate	SCORPION	*Guadaloupe*
HACKER, Thomas	L.M.	SCORPION	*(Vfd Abd. Not on Roll)*
	Supn L.M.	SCORPION	*Scorpion. 31 March 1804*
	L.M.	SCORPION	*Guadaloupe. GH.10,014*
PETERS, Adam	A.B.	SCORPION	GH.6746. *(Vfd Abd. Not on 171/- Roll. On G.H. Roll)*
	A.B.	SCORPION	*Guadaloupe*
SCOTT, John	Lieut. R.N.	(BLONDE)	*On B.S. Roll ADM 171/3/28 for "BLONDE 10 Jany 1810", capture of L'ORESTE. B.S. Clasp ?*
	Lieut. R.N.	BLONDE	*Guadaloupe*
(SMITH, James)	—	—	*(See Guadaloupe Roll)*
STRONG, Samuel	Lieut. R.N.	SCORPION	*(Vfd Abd. Not on Roll)*
	Midshipman	ALCMENE	*Copenhagen 1801*
	Lieut. R.N.	SCORPION	*Guadaloupe*
TOMS, William	Sailmaker	SCORPION	
	A.B.	TIGRE	*Acre. 30 May 1799*
	A.B.	TIGRE	*Egypt*
	A.B.	SCORPION	*Scorpion. 31 March 1804*
	Sailmaker	SCORPION	*Guadaloupe*

(483) GUADALOUPE

Capture of Guadaloupe on 5 February 1810, for which a medal was bestowed upon the Army.

(ABBOTT, Christopher)	(Captain. R.M.)	(POMPEE)	*Awarded M.G.S. Medal also awarded N.G.S. medal Copenhagen 1801 Martinique clasps*
ALLEN, James	R.M. Boy	ALFRED	
ALLEN, Paul	L.M.	ABERCROMBIE	
ALLEN, William	Pte. R.M.	POMPEE	
	Pte. R.M.	POMPEE	*Martinique*
	Pte. R.M.	POMPEE	*Pompee. 17 June 1809 (Vfd Abd. Not on Roll)*
AYMOT, Richard.G.	Lieut. R.N.	LOIRE	
ANDREWS, Benjamin	Midshipman	SAVAGE	
	Midshipman	HEBRUS	*Hebrus with L'Etoile*
ANDREWS, James	Vol 1st Cl	VIMIERA	
ANDREWS, Thomas.J.	A.B.	STAR	G.H. 3281
	Boy	VESTAL	*Egypt*
	A.B.	STAR	*Martinique*
ANDREWS, William	L.M.	CASTOR	
	Boy 2nd Class	CASTOR	*Castor. 17 June 1809*
	Boy 2nd Class	CASTOR	*Anse La Barque. 18 Decr 1809*
ANGIER, Ezekiel	Coxswain	ABERCROMBIE	
	Coxswain	BELLEISLE	*Martinique*
	Coxswain	POMPEE	*Pompee. 17 June 1809*
ANLEY, William	Midshipman	POMPEE	
	Midshipman	NEPTUNE	*Martinique*
APPLEBY, Abraham	Gunner	HAZARD	
ARCHER, Thomas	Clerk	ABERCROMBIE	
	Clerk	BELLEISLE	*Martinique*
	Clerk	POMPEE	*Pompee. 17 June 1809*

GUADALOUPE

ARCHLEY, John	Boy	ROSAMUND	G.H. 3555 as ASCHLEY
ARMSTRONG, Francis	Ord	SCEPTRE	
BAGWELL, Joseph	Ord	FREIJA	
	Ord	ACTIVE	Egypt
BAILEY, George	Ord	LOIRE	
BAKER, James	Pte. R.M.	SCEPTRE	(Additional clasp ?)
BAKER, William.H.	Midshipman	CASTOR	
	Midshipman	CASTOR	Anse La Barque. 18 Decr 1809
BALDWIN, Thomas	Sgt. R.M.	BLONDE	
(BALHETCHET, William)	(2nd Lieut. R.M.)	(POMPEE)	Awarded M.G.S. Medal & clasps for Martinique & Guadaloupe. Became a Purser.
BALLANTYNE, Richard	Boy 3rd Class	ROSAMUND	
BALLINGALL, James	Master	PELORUS	
	Master	PELORUS	Martinique
BANNISTER, William	Ord	LOIRE	G.H. 7752
BARTHOLOMEW, John	A.B.	POMPEE	G.H. 3146
	A.B.	INTREPID	Martinique
BARTON, John	Ord	ALCMENE	
BASTARD, Richard	Lieut. R.N.	PERLEN	
	Lieut. R.N.	FREIJA	St Sebastian (Vfd Abd. Not on Roll)
BATEY, John	Carpenter	ASP	
BAYLIS, William	L.M.	POMPEE	
	L.M.	POMPEE	Martinique
	L.M.	POMPEE	Pompee. 17 June 1809 (Vfd Abd. Not on Roll)
BECK, John	Gunner	FAWN	
	Gunner	FAWN	Martinique
BECK, Michael	Ord	ROSAMUND	
BEDFORD, Joseph	A.B.	POMPEE	
	A.B.	POMPEE	Martinique
	A.B.	POMPEE	Pompee. 17 June 1809
BEDWELL, Edward.P.	Master's Mate	SNAP	
	Midshipman	HOGUE	B.S. 8 April 1814
BELL, James	Ord	SCEPTRE	
	Ord	SCEPTRE	Anse La Barque. 18 Decr 1809
BENNET, Martin	Actg Lieut. R.N.	SCEPTRE	
	Midshipman	ILLUSTRIOUS	Basque Roads 1809
	Actg Lieut. R.N.	SCEPTRE	Anse La Barque. 18 Decr 1809
BENNETT, Henry	Boy	ALFRED	
BENSON, John.R.	Midshipman	SCORPION	
	Midshipman	SCORPION	Scorpion. 12 Jany 1810
BLAKE, George.C.	Lieut. R.N.	SCORPION	
	Midshipman	ROMULUS	Egypt
	Lieut. R.N.	SCORPION	Scorpion. 12 Jany 1810
BLAKE, Thomas	Boy (?)	CASTOR	Not found on M.L.
	Boy (?)	Not Given	Anse La Barque. 18 Decr 1809
BLOOMFIELD, William	L.M.	ORPHEUS	G.H. 2776
BOND, Richard	Corporal	FREIJA	
BONE, William	Drummer. R.M.	POMPEE	(M.L. as Will BONES)
	Drummer. R.M.	POMPEE	Martinique
	Drummer. R.M.	POMPEE	Pompee. 17 June 1809 (Vfd Abd. Not on Roll)
BOOTH, William	Ord	ALFRED	
BOTTLE, Thomas	Boy 2nd Class	LOIRE	
BOWEN, Thomas	A.B.	GLOIRE	
	A.B.	GLOIRE	Martinique
BOWERMAN, Thomas	Pte. R.M.	BLONDE	
	Pte. R.M.	NEPTUNE	Martinique
BRADEN, William	Boy	ALFRED	
BRASIER, James	Lieut. R.N.	ALFRED	
	Midshipman	DEFENCE	Copenhagen 1801 (Vfd Abd. Not on Roll)
	Lieut. R.N.	REPULSE	B.S. 2 May 1813
BREETZ, Daniel	Capt' Fore Top	BLONDE	(M.L. as BRADY)
BRIGGS, John	Admiral's Domestic	POMPEE	(M.L. as BIGGS)
	L.M.	POMPEE	Martinique
	L.M.	POMPEE	Pompee. 17 June 1809 (Vfd Abd. Not on Roll)
BRIGGS, Stephen	Lieut. R.N.	GRANADA	
BRINE, John	Lieut. R.N.	POMPEE	
	Midshipman	AGINCOURT	Egypt
	Lieut. R.N.	GLOIRE	Martinique
BROCK, Edward	Pte. R.M.	AMARANTHE	(Vfd Abd. Not on Roll)
	Pte. R.M.	AMARANTHE	Martinique
BROCKFIELD, John	L.M.	FORESTER	
	L.M.	FORESTER	Martinique
BROOM, George	Midshipman	ABERCROMBIE	
	Vo 1st Cl	MERCURY	Off Rota. 4 April 1808
BROUGHTON, John	Ord	OBSERVATEUR	
BROWN, Charles	Midshipman	LAURA	
BROWN, John	Master	St PIERRE	
	Master	PORT d'ESPAGNE	Martinique

BROWN, John.C.	A.B.	PERLEN	
	A.B.	NEPTUNE	Trafalgar
BROWN, William	Drummer. R.M.	ORPHEUS	
BRYAN, John	Purser	ALCMENE	
	Purser	EURYDICE	Martinique
	Purser	EUROTAS	Eurotas. 25 Feby 1814
BUCKLER, William	Pte. R.M.	BLONDE	
	Pte. R.M.	NEPTUNE	Martinique
BUDD, Francis	A.B.	SCEPTRE	
	A.B.	EGMONT	St Vincent
	A.B.	SUPERB	St Domingo
BULL, Benjamin	A.B.	THETIS	
	A.B.	THETIS	Anse La Barque. 18 Decr 1809
BURNEY, George	Gunner	AURORA	
BURTON, George.G.	Lieut. R.N.	POMPEE	
	Midshipman	VENERABLE	Gut of Gibraltar. 12 July 1801
	Lieut. R.N.	NEPTUNE	Martinique
BUTLER, George	Midshipman	LOIRE	
BUTTER, Henry	Pte. R.M.	GUADALOUPE	(Vfd Abd Brig GUADALOUPE. NOR)
	Pte. R.M.	POMPEE	Martinique
	Pte. R.M.	POMPEE	Pompee. 17 June 1809 (Vfd Abd. Not on Roll)
BYRNE, Michael	Pte. R.M.	MELAMPUS	(Application No. B/25)
	A.B.	MINDEN	Algiers (Application No. B/25)
CAIN, Roger	Pte. R.M.	LOIRE	
CAMPBELL, William	Lieut. R.N.	ROASMUND	
	Master's Mate	GLOIRE	Martinique
CANDLER, John	Ord	ALFRED	
CARTER, James	Midshipman	SCEPTRE	
	Midshipman	SCEPTRE	Anse La Barque. 18 Decr 1809
CARTER, Samuel.J.	Lieut. R.N.	CASTOR	
	Actg Lieut. R.N.	INTREPID	Martinique
CARTER, William.F.	Surgeon	BLONDE	
	Surgeon	BLONDE	Anse La Barque. 18 Decr 1809
	Surgeon	ROYALIST	Royalist. 29 Decr 1812 (Vfd Abd. Not on Roll)
CHADWELL, Joseph	Pte. R.M.	SCEPTRE	(Found M.L. as Thomas)
CHAMBERS, John	Q.M.	ALFRED	
CHARLES, Hugh	Surgeon	STAR	
CHERRY, Henry	Q.M.'s Mate	STATIRA	
CHURCH, Thomas	Pte. R.M.	SCEPTRE	
CLACK, Robert	Ord	LOIRE	
CLARK, Edward	Ord	POMPEE	
	Ord	POMPEE	Martinique
	Ord	POMPEE	Pompee. 17 June 1809
(CLARK, James)	(2nd Lieut. R.M.)	(POMPEE)	Awarded M.G.S. Medal. Also received N.G.S. medal clasp Algiers
CLARK, John	Purser's Steward	PELORUS	
	Purser's Steward	PELORUS	Martinique
CLARKE, James	Ord	PERLEN	
CLEMENT, Samuel	Pte. R.M.	SCEPTRE	G.H. 3426
COCK, Robert	Master's Mate	AURORA	
	Midshipman	THUNDERER	Trafalgar
	Master's Mate	QUEBEC	B.S. 2 Aug 1811
COHEN, John	Ord	LOIRE	G.H. 5904
COLE, John	Pte. R.M.	FREIJA	
COLLINS, Daniel	Ord	ABERCROMBIE	
COLLINS, John	L.M.	ALCMENE	
COLLINS, Joseph	Capt' Fore Top	PERLEN	
COLWELL, John	Vol 1st Cl	SCEPTRE	
	Vol 1st Cl	SCEPTRE	Anse La Barque. 18 Decr 1809 (Vfd Abd. Not on Roll)
	Paymaster	PHOENIX	Syria (& Crimea medals)
COMPTON, Richard	Master's Mate	STATIRA	
CONNOLLEY, George	Purser	SNAP	(Alias William POWERS)
	Purser	SNAP	Martinique
CONWAY, George	Ord	ORPHEUS	
COOK, John	Master	STATIRA	
	Master	NORTHUMBERLAND	Egypt
COOK, John	Pte. R.M.	ALFRED	
COOKE, Jervis	2nd Lieut. R.M.	THETIS	
	2nd Lieut. R.M.	THETIS	B.S. 13 Dec 1809
	2nd Lieut. R.M.	THETIS	Anse La Barque. 18 Decr 1809 (Vfd Abd. Not on Roll)
COOPER, James	R.M. Boy	POMPEE	
	R.M. Boy	POMPEE	Martinique
	R.M. Boy	POMPEE	Pompee. 17 June 1809
COOPER, Jonathan	Pte. R.M.	BLONDE	
	Pte. R.M.	NEPTUNE	Martinique
COPEMAN, John	A.B.	BLONDE	
COPPIN, Frederic	Midshipman	STATIRA	
CORNISH, William	Boy	OBSERVATEUR	
COTGRAVE, Edward.S.	Lieut. R.N.	ACHATES	

GUADALOUPE

COVE, William	Trumpeter	THETIS	
	Trumpeter	THETIS	Anse La Barque. 18 Decr 1809
COX, Douglas	Lieut. R.N.	SNAP	
	Lieut. R.N.	SNAP	Martinique
COX, John	Pte. R.M.	ALCMENE	
COX, John	Pte. R.M.	PERLEN	
CRESER, Thomas	Vol 1st Cl	FREIJA	
	Vol 1st Cl	GALATEA	Off Tamatave. 20 May 1811
CROFTON, Hon George.A.	Commander	FAWN	
	Commander	FAWN	Martinique
CROSIER, James	Gunner's Mate	ALFRED	(M.L. as CROSSIER)
	A.B.	SUPERB	Gut of Gibraltar. 12 July 1801
	Gunner's Mate	SUPERB	St Domingo
CUMMINGS, Thomas	Pte. R.M.	VIMIERA	
CURRAN, Charles	A.B.	MELAMPUS	
CURRAN, Peter	Pte. R.M.	ABERCROMBIE	G.H. 9077
DALEY, Michael	Pte. R.M.	BLONDE	
	Pte. R.M.	NEPTUNE	Martinique
DALL, Patrick	Actg Master	PERLEN	
DALY, James	Pte. R.M.	FREIJA	
	M.A.A.	GANGES	Syria
DANIEL, John	A.B.	POMPEE	
	A.B.	POMPEE	Martinique
	A.B.	POMPEE	Pompee. 17 June 1809 (Vfd Abd. Not on Roll)
	A.B.	ASTRAEA	Off Tamatave. 20 May 1811
DANIELS, Samuel	L.M.	SCEPTRE	
	Ord	MINDEN	Algiers
DAVID, William	A.B.	POMPEE	
	Carp's Crew	INTREPID	Martinique
DAVIDSON, John	L.M.	LOIRE	
DAVIES, John	Master's Mate	LOIRE	
DAVISON, Kilgour	Actg Lieut. R.N.	VIMIERA	
	Midshipman	INTREPID	Martinique
DAY, Bartholomew.G.	Actg Master	SUPERIEURE	
	Midshipman	REVENGE	Trafalgar
	Actg Master	SUPERIEURE	Superieure. 10 Feby 1809
	Actg Master	SUPERIEURE	Martinique (Vfd Abd. Not on Roll)
DENSTEN, Thomas	Master's Mate	POMPEE	
	Lieut. R.N.	SPARROW	St Sebastian
DICKENSON, John	Ord	MELAMPUS	
DICKIE, John	Secretary's Clerk	POMPEE	
	A.B.	NEPTUNE	Martinique
DICKSON, James	A.B.	SCEPTRE	
	A.B.	ORION	Trafalgar
DIGNAM or DIGMAN, Andrew	A.B.	BELLETTE	
	A.B.	BELLETTE	Martinique
DILLON, Thomas	Ord	ALFRED	
	Ord	MUTINE	Algiers
DIXON, James.T.T.	Master's Mate	POMPEE	
	Master's Mate	CASTOR	Anse La Barque. 18 Decr 1809
	Midshipman	CASTOR	Castor. 17 June 1809
	Midshipman	MAGICIENNE	St Sebastian
DOBLE, Robert	Carp's Crew	PERLEN	
	Carp's Crew	VICTORY	Trafalgar
DONAHOE, Michael	L.M.	ALFRED	
DONOVAN, James	Pte. R.M.	AURORA	also Jeremiah pencil Roll (Alias DENMAN)
DONOVON, Timothy	Carp's Crew	SCEPTRE	
DOWKER, Richard	A.B.	PERLEN	
DOYLE, Lawrance	Ord	SCEPTRE	
	L.M.	ORION	Trafalgar
DRAPER, John	Pte. R.M.	ORPHEUS	
DREW, James	Ord	LOIRE	
DRIVER, Thomas	Master	FREIJA	
DRIVER, William	Ord	MELAMPUS	
DUNCAN, David	Gunner	LOIRE	
DUNKLEY, George	Capt' After Guard	WANDERER	
	Ord	NORTHUMBERLAND	St Domingo
	Ord	NEPTUNE	Martinique
DUPE, William	Pte. R.M.	ALCMENE	
DURNFORD, Thomas	Ord	CYGNET	
	A.B.	SEALARK	Sealark. 21 July 1812
DUSON, Benjamin	L.M.	ATTENTIVE	
DWARRIS, William.H.	Midshipman	LOIRE	
DYAS, William	Pte. R.M.	STATIRA	

EAGLES, Joseph	Pte. R.M.	FAWN	G.H. 5556
	Pte. R.M.	FAWN	Martinique
EASTO, Richmond	Midshipman	STATIRA	
	Master	CAMBRIAN	Navarino
ELLIOTT, George Edwd	Midshipman	FORESTER	(O'Byrne as Edward George)
	Midshipman	FORESTER	Martinique
ELLIS, Samuel.B.	1st Lieut. R,M.	STATIRA	
	2nd Lieut. R.M.	AJAX	Trafalgar
ELLIS, William	Bosun's Mate	ASP	
ELRINGTON, George	Lieut. R.N.	THETIS	
EPPS, John	L.M.	POMPEE	G.H.5997
	L.M.	POMPEE	Martinique
	L.M.	POMPEE	Pompee. 17 June 1809 (Vfd Abd. Not on Roll)
ETHERINGTON, William	Boy	PERLEN	
EVANS, Gustavus	Lieut. R.N.	CHERUB	
	Master's Mate	EPERVIER	St Domingo
	Lieut. R.N.	CHERUB	Martinique
EVANS, Thomas	Ord	POMPEE	
	Ord	POMPEE	Martinique
	Ord	POMPEE	Pompee. 17 June 1809 (Vfd Abd. Not on Roll)
EVELYN, George.J.	Lieut. R.N.	ECLAIR	
FARRELL, Robert	Sgt. R.M.	STATIRA	
FARLEY, William	Master's Mate	FAWN	
	Midshipman	HERO	4 Novr 1805
	Master's Mate	FAWN	Martinique
FELT, Hans Christian	Ord	POMPEE	G.H. 8855 as O'FELL
	Ord	POMPEE	Martinique
	Ord	POMPEE	Pompee. 17 June 1809 (Vfd Abd. Not on Roll)
FERGUSON, William	Boatswain	HAZARD	
	Boy	CANADA	12 Octr 1798
	Boatswain	HAZARD	Martinique
	Boatswain	HAZARD	Anse La Barque. 18 Decr 1809
FERTH, Daniel	Pte. R.M.	ORPHEUS	
FINLAYSON, John	Lieut. R.N.	ALCMENE	
FITZGERALD, Thomas	Ord	POMPEE	
	Ord	POMPEE	Martinique
	Ord	POMPEE	Pompee. 17 June 1809
FLAXMAN, Robert	Bosun's Mate	SCORPION	G.H.7802
	A.B.	SCORPION	Scorpion 31 March 1804 (Vfd Abd. NOR)
	Bosun's Mate	SCORPION	Scorpion 12 Jany 1810 (Vfd Abd. NOR)
FLOWER, John	Corporal. R.M.	GLOIRE	
FORBES, John	Surgeon	NETLEY	
	Surgeon	CASTOR	Castor. 17 June 1809
	Surgeon	DESIREE	Gluckstadt. 5 Jany 1814. Probably discharged before this action.
FORD, Ambrose	Bosun's Mate	HAZARD	
	Bosun's Mate	HAZARD	Martinique
FOREMAN, Richard	Pte. R.M.	PERLEN	
FORSTER, Joseph	A.B.	POMPEE	
	A.B.	POMPEE	Martinique (Vfd Abd. Not on Roll)
	A.B.	POMPEE	Pompee. 17 June 1809 (Vfd Abd. Not on Roll)
FRANCIS, John	Drummer	BLONDE	
	Drummer	BLONDE	Anse La Barque. 18 Decr 1809
GALLOWAY, John	Ord	SCEPTRE	
	Ord	MINDEN	Algiers
GARRICK, James	A.B.	AMARANTHE	
	Ord	AMARANTHE	Off the Pearl Rock. 13 Dec 1808
	Ord	AMARANTHE	Martinique
GIFFARD, Henry	Boy	POMPEE	
	Boy	NEPTUNE	Martinique
GILES, John	Clerk	PERLEN	
GILES, William	Master's Mate	ALFRED	
GOODLAD, Edward	Midshipman	POMPEE	
	Midshipman	NEPTUNE	Trafalgar (Vfd Abd. Not on Roll)
	Midshipman	NEPTUNE	Martinique
GORDON, James.G.	Actg Lieut. R.N.	FREIJA	
	Midshipman	ILLUSTRIOUS	Basque Roads 1809
	Actg Lieut. R.N.	FREIJA	Anse La Barque. 18 Decr 1809
GORMAN, John	A.B.	POMPEE	
	A.B.	AUDACIOUS	Gut of Gibraltar. 12 July 1801
	A.B.	POMPEE	Martinique
	A.B.	POMPEE	Pompee. 17 June 1809
	Yeoman of Sheets	Qn CHARLOTTE	Algiers

GUADALOUPE

GORMAN, John	Ord	ABERCROMBIE	G.H. 2830
	L.M.	DREADNOUGHT	Trafalgar
GOWLAND, Thomas	Capt' Main Top	ABERCROMBIE	
	A.B.	POMPEE	Martinique
	A.B.	POMPEE	Pompee. 17 June 1809 (Vfd Abd. Not on Roll)
GRANT, George	Boy	PERLEN	
GRANT, Lewis	Pte. R.M.	ORPHEUS	
GRAVES, James	Q.M.	POMPEE	
	Q.M.	POMPEE	Martinique
	Q.M.	POMPEE	Pompee. 17 June 1809 (Vfd Abd. Not on Roll)
GREY, James	L.M.	POMPEE	(M.L. as GRAY)
	L.M.	POMPEE	Martinique
	L.M.	POMPEE	Pompee. 17 June 1809
GRIFFIN, Robert	Sgt. R.M.	ALCMENE	
HACKER, Thomas	L.M.	SCORPION	G.H. 10,014
	Supn L.M.	SCORPION	Scorpion. 31 March 1804
	L.M.	SCORPION	Scorpion. 12 Jany 1810 (Vfd Abd. Not on Roll)
HADDON, David	Boatswain	ORPHEUS	
HAINES, Thomas	Gunner	POMPEE	
	Ord	SOUTHAMPTON	Southampton. 9 June 1796 (Vfd Abd. Not on Roll)
	Ord	SOUTHAMPTON	St Vincent
	Coxswain	SUPERB	Gut of Gibraltar. 12 July 1801
	Coxswain	SUPERB	St Domingo
	Gunner	ACASTA	Martinique
	Gunner	POMPEE	Pompee. 17 June 1809 (Vfd Abd. Not on Roll)
HALKETT, David	Bosun's Mate	RINGDOVE	
	Yeoman Powder Rm	RINGDOVE	Martinique
	Yeoman Powder Rm	RINGDOVE	Anse La Barque. 18 Decr 1809
HALLILAY, Richard	Purser	ABERCROMBIE	
	Purser	ETHALION	Martinique
HALLION, John.W.	Asst Surgeon	ALFRED	
HAMILTON, James	Actg Surgeon	CHERUB	
HAMLING, John	A.B.	SCEPTRE	
	A.B.	SCEPTRE	Anse La Barque. 18 Decr 1809
HARDEN, James	Midshipman	SCEPTRE	
	Midshipman	SCEPTRE	Anse La Barque. 18 Decr 1809
HARDY, John	Pte. R.M.	SCEPTRE	
HARVEY, William	Pte. R.M.	FORESTER	
	Pte. R.M.	FORESTER	Martinique
HANSCHMANN, Johann.G.	Not Given	ABERCROMBIE	
HAVERS, Benjamin	Pte. R.M.	ASP	
HAWKER, Edward	Captain. R.N.	MELAMPUS	
HAWKES, John	Yeoman Powder Rm	HAZARD	
	Capt' Main Top	HAZARD	Martinique
	Yeoman Powder Rm	HAZARD	Anse La Barque. 18 Decr 1809
HAYDON, Charles	Master's Mate	POMPEE	
	Master's Mate	CHERUB	Martinique
HAYDON, William.P.	Lieut. R.N.	GUADALOUPE	
	Master's Mate	NEPTUNE	Martinique
HAZELDINE, John	Pte. R.M.	ALCMEME	
	Pte. R.M.	YORK/DOLPHIN (?)	Martinique
HENDRY, William	Lieut. R.N.	STATIRA	
	Lieut. R.N.	HERO	4 Novr 1805
HENRY, William	Midshipman	POMPEE	
	Midshipman	NEPTUNE	Martinique
HERBERT, Thomas	Master's Mate	BLONDE	(Rcd China 1842 Medal)
	Lieut. R.N.	EURYALUS (P)	The Potomac. 17 Aug 1814
HIGGINS, John	Boy 3rd Class	STATIRA	
HITCHCOCK, James	Sgt. R.M.	GUADALOUPE	
HITCHCOCK, Thomas	Ord	POMPEE	2 medals issued. P. – M & G
	A.B.	POMPEE	Martinique
	A.B.	POMPEE	Pompee. 17 June 1809
HOBDAY, Thomas	Pte. R.M.	FREIJA	
HOLE, William	Midshipman	BACCHUS	
	Midshipman	WOLVERINE	Martinique
	Midshipman	BACCHUS	B.S. 13 Dec 1809
	Master's Mate	TRAAVE	B.S. 14 Dec 1814
HOOPER, Benjamin	Pte. R.M.	POMPEE	G.H. 2231
	Pte. R.M.	POMPEE	Martinique
	Pte. R.M.	POMPEE	Pompee. 17 June 1809 (Vfd Abd. Not on Roll)
HOPKINS, Edward.J.	Volunteer	STATIRA	
HOPKINS, John	Pte. R.M.	STATIRA	G.H. 3079
HORTON, Frederick	Purser	SAVAGE	

HOWES, William	Pte. R.M.	POMPEE	
	Pte. R.M.	POMPEE	*Martinique*
	Pte. R.M.	POMPEE	*Pompee. 17 June 1809*
			(Vfd Abd. Not on Roll)
HUBBARD, John	L.M.	LOIRE	G.H. 6997
HUNTER, Hugh	Midshipman	HAZARD	
	Midshipman	HAZARD	*Martinique*
	Midshipman	HAZARD	*Anse La Barque. 18 Decr 1809*
HURD, Thomas	Capt' Fore Top	AMARANTHE	
	A.B.	AMARANTHE	*Martinique*
HUSON, Joseph	Pte. R.M.	CASTOR	
	Pte. R.M.	CASTOR	*Castor. 17 June 1809*
			(Vfd Abd. Not on Roll)
	Pte. R.M.	CASTOR	*Anse La Barque. 18 Decr 1809*
			(Vfd Abd. Not on Roll)
HUTCHINGS, George	L.M.	POMPEE	
	L.M.	POMPEE	*Martinique*
	L.M.	POMPEE	*Pompee. 17 June 1809*
			(Vfd Abd. Not on Roll)
HUTCHINS, Charles	A.B.	MELAMPUS	
JACOBS, John	Ord	PLUMPER	
JACOBS, William	Midshipman	POMPEE	
JACKSON, John	L.M.	MORNE FORTUNEE	
JAMES, Hugh	Midshipman	ASP	
JARRATT, Thomas	Pte. R.M.	PERLEN	G.H. 8808
JANUS, Charles	Lieut. R.N.	L'ECLAIR	
JEFFRIES, John	L.M.	SCEPTRE	
JENNINGS, Thomas	Purser	MELAMPUS	
JERVOIS, Sampson	Lieut. R.N.	ASP	
JOHNS, William	Not Given	MORNE FORTUNEE	*(Probably Master)*
JOHNSON, James	Bosun's Mate	PERLEN	
JOHNSON, Peter	Actg Master	SURINAM	
JONES, James	Not Given	ASP	*(also shown as Sgt R.M.)*
JONES, John	A.B.	STATIRA	
	Ord	STATIRA	B.S. Ap & May 1813
JONES, Thomas	Qtr Gunner	SCEPTRE	G.H. 4144
	Qtr Gunner	ORION	*Trafalgar*
KEEN, James	Pte. R.M.	ALFRED	
KELLY, John	Ord	PERLEN	
KELSALL, Edward	Q.M.'s Mate	POMPEE	*(Vfd Abd. Not on Roll)*
	A.B.	AGINCOURT	*Camperdown. (On Roll)*
			(On Roll as KELSELL)
			On G.H. list – 4 clasps, all verified by M.L.
	Qtr Gunner	POMPEE	*Martinique*
	Qtr Gunner	POMPEE	*Pompee. 17 June 1809*
			G.H. 7960
KERRISON, James	A.B.	SUPERIEURE	
	Pte. R.M. (Roll ?)	SUPERIEURE	*Martinique*
KILLOCK, Robert	Pte. R.M.	ALFRED	
	Pte. R.M.	BELLEISLE	*Martinique*
	Pte. R.M.	SURVEILLANTE	*St Sebastian*
KING, John	Ord	PERLEN	
KING, Samuel	Pte. R.M.	FROLIC	
	Pte. R.M.	NEPTUNE	*Martinique*
KING, William	L.M.	ORPHEUS	G.H. 2623
KITCHEN, William.H.	Lieut. R.N.	ASP	
	Lieut. R.N.	LONDON	*Copenhagen 1801*
KNEVITT, Thomas.L.	Master's Mate	SCEPTRE	
	Master's Mate	SCEPTRE	*Anse La Barque. 18 Decr 1809*
	Master's Mate	VENERABLE	*Venerable. 16 Jany 1814*
LACK, Stephen	Pte. R.M.	POMPEE	
	Pte. R.M.	POMPEE	*Martinique*
	Pte. R.M.	POMPEE	*Pompee. 17 June 1809*
			(Vfd Abd. Not on Roll)
LANE, William	Midshipman	ALCMENE	
	Midshipman	PELORUS	*Martinique*
LATHAM, John.W.	Surgeon	OBSERVATEUR	
LAWLER, John	Yeoman Powder Rm	THETIS	
LAWLESS, Henry	Midshipman	PERLEN	
LAWRENCE, Daniel	Lieut. R.N.	WANDERER	
	Midshipman	CYNTHIA	*Egypt*
	Lieut. R.N.	HEREUX	B.S. 28 Nov 1808
LAY, James	Ord	POMPEE	
	Ord	POMPEE	*Martinique*
	Ord	POMPEE	*Pompee. 17 June 1809*
LEAPER, William	Actg Carpenter	VIMIERA	
	Carpenter	GOSHAWK	*Malaga. 29 April 1812*
LEAR, Daniel	L.M.	ABERCROMBIE	G.H. 9343
	L.M.	CIRCE	*Martinique*
LEECH, Robert	Midshipman	POMPEE	
	Master	PULTUSK	*Martinique*
LEECH, Robert	A.B.	POMPEE	
	A.B.	POMPEE	*Martinique*

GUADALOUPE

LEITCH, James	Surgeon	AMARANTHE	
	Surgeon	AMARANTHE	*Martinique*
LEMPRIERE, George.O.	Lieut. R.N.	LOIRE	
LEWIS, John	Cook's Mate	ORPHEUS	
LEWIS, William	Ord	POMPEE	*G.H. 7160*
	Ord	POMPEE	*Martinique*
	Ord	POMPEE	*Pompee. 17 June 1809*
LIMINGTON, Joseph	Ord	MELAMPUS	
LLOYD, Benjamin	Ord	PERLEN	*G.H. 7044*
LLOYD, John.J.	Midshipman	ABERCROMBIE	
	A.B.	AETNA	*Basque Roads 1809*
LOCK, Robert	Pte. R.M.	ABERCROMBIE	
	Pte. R.M.	NEPTUNE	*Martinique*
LONGE, William	L.M.	SCEPTRE	
LORING, Oliver	A.B.	ALFRED	
	A.B.	BELLONA	*Basque Roads 1809*
LOVELESS, Bassett.J.	Actg Lieut. R.N.	FAWN	
	A.B.	AUDACIOUS	*Gut of Gibraltar. 12 July 1801*
	Actg Lieut. R.N.	FAWN	*Martinique*
LOVIE, Alexander	Midshipman	ROSAMUND	
LOWE, Thomas	Pte. R.M.	POMPEE	
	Pte. R.M.	POMPEE	*Martinique*
	Pte. R.M.	POMPEE	*Pompee. 17 June 1809*
LOWRIE, Richard	Gunner	ACHATES	
MACNEVIN or McNEVIN, John	Lieut. R.N.	SUPERIEURE	
	Lieut. R.N.	SUPERIEURE	*Martinique*
MAEN, George	Yeoman of Sheets	ALCMENE	
MAILES, George	Pte. R.M.	ALFRED	
	Pte. R.M.	BELLEISLE	*Martinique*
MARTIN, John	Capt' Forecastle	ALFRED	
MARTIN, William	Pte. R.M.	LOIRE	
MARTIN, William.H.	Midshipman	PULTUSK	
MASON, George	Vol 1st Cl	FREIJA	
MASON, James	A.B.	POMPEE	
	A.B.	POMPEE	*Martinique*
	A.B.	POMPEE	*Pompee. 17 June 1809 (Vfd Abd. Not on Roll)*
MATTHEWS, John	Ord	STAR	
	Ord	STAR	*Martinique*
	A.B.	MALTA	*Gaieta. 24 July 1815*
	A.B.	IMPREGNABLE	*Algiers*
MAYNARD, James	Gunner	STAR	
	Gunner	STAR	*Martinique*
McADAM, Alexander	L.M.	POMPEE	
	L.M.	NOTHUMBERLAND	*St Domingo*
	L.M.	NEPTUNE	*Martinique*
McELROY, John.F.	A.B.	LOIRE	
	Ord	SUPERB	*St Domingo*
McELVOY, John	Pte. R.M.	SCEPTRE	
McKEY, William	Ord	PELORUS	
McLAREN, David	Pte. R.M.	STAR	
	Pte. R.M.	STAR	*Martinique*
McLAUGHLAN, James	A.B.	CASTOR	
	A.B.	CASTOR	*Castor. 17 June 1809 (Vfd Abd. Not on Roll)*
	A.B.	CASTOR	*Anse La Barque. 18 Decr 1809 (Vfd Abd. Not on Roll)*
McLEOD, Alexander	Ord	STAR	
	Ord	STAR	*Martinique*
	A.B.	MALTA	*Gaieta. 24 July 1815*
McNICOL, Duncan	Lieut. R.M.	ABERCROMBIE	
	Lieut. R.M.	GLASGOW	*Algiers*
MERCER, John.D.	Lieut. R.N.	PULTUSK	
	Master's Mate	BELLEISLE	*Martinique*
	Master's Mate	POMPEE	*Pompee. 17 June 1809*
	Lieut. R.N.	PULTUSK	*B.S. 13 Dec 1809*
METCALF, Rawson	A.B.	SCEPTRE	*G.H. 8625 as MEDCALF*
MILLER, James	Ord	POMPEE	
	Ord	POMPEE	*Martinique*
	Ord	POMPEE	*Pompee. 17 June 1809*
MILLS, James	Ord	ALFRED	
	Boy	PELORUS	*Martinique*
MILLS, Samuel	Pte. R.M.	CASTOR	*(Vfd Abd as McLAUGHLAN above)*
MILLS, William	A.B.	ROSAMUND	
MITCHELL, John	Ord	PULTUSK	
	Ord	PULTUSK	*Martinique*
MITCHELL, Joseph	Boy	SURINAM	
	Boy	SURINAM	*Martinique*
MITCHELL, Thomas	Boatswain	ORPHEUS	

MITCHELL, Thomas	L.M.	POMPEE	*(Vfd Abd. Not on Roll)*
	L.M.	POMPEE	*Martinique. GH.3120*
	L.M.	POMPEE	*Pompee. 17 June 1809*
MOLESWORTH, Bourchier	Lieut. R.N.	SCEPTRE	
	Lieut. R.N.	SCEPTRE	*Anse La Barque. 18 Decr 1809*
MONAGHAM, Edward	Boy 3rd Class	LOIRE	
MONTGOMERIE, Alexander	Actg Lieut. R.N.	FREIJA	
	Midshipman	SCEPTRE	*Anse La Barque. 18 Decr 1809*
MOODY, James	A.B.	ALFRED	
	A.B.	ALFRED	*B.S. 23 Nov 1810*
MOORE, John	Midshipman	ORPHEUS	
	Midshipman	SEAHORSE (P)	*The Potomac. 17 Aug 1814*
MORGAN, Joseph	L.M.	POMPEE	
	L.M.	POMPEE	*Martinique*
	L.M.	POMPEE	*Pompee. 17 June 1809*
MORGAN, Robert	Master's Mate	ALFRED	
MONK, Stephen	Q.M's Mate	PERLEN	*(Alias John WARD)*
MURRAY, Daniel	Boatswain	THETIS	
	Boatswain	THETIS	*B.S. 13 Dec 1809*
	Boatswain	THETIS	*Anse La Barque. 18 Decr 1809*
MUSTART, James	Boy 2nd Class	VIMIERA	
	A.B.	BEDFORD	*B.S. 14 Dec 1814*
NASH, Samuel	A.B.	SURINAM	
	Ord	SURINAM	*Martinique*
NEIGHBOUR, Edward	L.M.	BLONDE	
NEIL, John	Ord	STAR	
	Ord	STAR	*Martinique*
	A.B.	MALTA	*Gaieta. 24 July 1815*
	Capt' Forecastle	IMPREGNABLE	*Algiers*
NESBITT, Alexander	Ord	CASTOR	*G.H. 3909. (Vfd Abd as for McLAUGHLAN above)*
NEVIN, James	Q.M.	SURINAM	
	Q.M.	SURINAM	*Martinique*
NIELL/NEILL, Christopher	A.B.	AMARANTHE	
	Ord	AMARANTHE	*Martinique*
(NIELL, John)	(Surgeon)	(SCEPTRE)	*Awarded M.G.S. Medal*
NICHOLSON, Thomas	A.B.	ORPHEUS	
NORIE, James	Master	MELAMPUS	
NORRIS, John	2nd Lieut. R.M.	MELAMPUS	
	1st Lieut. R.M.	REVOLUTIONNAIRE	*St Sebastian*
	1st Lieut. R.M.	SUPERB	*Algiers*
	1st Lieut. R.M.	GLASGOW	*Navarino*
NUTT, John	Dummer. R.M.	FREIJA	
ODLAM, William.E.	Surgeon	ABERCROMBIE	
	Surgeon	INTREPID	*Martinique*
OGILVIE, James	Carpenter	ALCMENE	
OSBORN, William (2)	A.B.	POMPEE	
	A.B.	POMPEE	*Martinique*
	A.B.	POMPEE	*Pompee. 17 June 1809* *(Vfd Abd. Not on Roll)*
OSBORNE, Alick	Asst Surgeon	ALFRED	
PACE, Edmund.H.	Vol 1st Cl	FREIJA	
	Supn Adm Mid	GLASGOW	*Algiers. (Known medal with Martinique Clasp) (M) A of I. AVA Clasp.*
PACKE, George	Pte. R.M.	CASTOR	*(and as for McLAUGHLAN previously)*
PAGE, Nathaniel	Pte. R.M.	PERLEN	
PARKER, Joseph	Capt' Fore Top	ORPHEUS	
PARKER, Peter	Master	ABERCROMBIE	
	Master	RINGDOVE	*Martinique*
PARKINSON, Benjamin	A.B.	ORPHEUS	
PAYNE, James	Boy	ALCMENE	
PEARSON, William	L.M.	FREIJA	
PEAVER, Thomas	Sgt. R.M.	SURINAM	
PEDDIGREE, Joseph	Ord	MELAMPUS	*G.H. 1632*
PEMITER, William	L.M.	STATIRA	*(M.L. as PAINTER)*
	Ord	STATIRA	*B.S. Ap & May 1813*
PENNYFATHER, William	Ord	SCEPTRE	
PERKINS, Joseph	Q.M's Mate	STATIRA	
	A.B.	Qn CHARLOTTE	*B.S. 20 Dec 1799*
	Q.M's Mate	STATIRA	*B.S. Ap & May 1813*
PETERS, Adam	A.B.	SCORPION	
	A.B.	SCORPION	*Scorpion. 12 Jany 1810 (Vfd Abd. Not on ADM 171/- but on G.H.Roll. 6746.)*
PETERS, Peter	A.B.	FREIJA	*G.H. 4142*
PETERSON, Andrew	L.M.	BLONDE	
	L.M.	BLONDE	*Anse La Barque. 18 Decr 1809*
PEVERINY, Anthony	Cook	CASTOR	*(and as for McLAUGHLAN previously)*

GUADALOUPE

PINTO, Thomas	Commander	ACHATES	
	Midshipman	IRRESISTIBLE	*St Vincent*
	Master's Mate	NORTHUMBERLAND	*Egypt*
	Lieut. R.N.	AGAMEMNON	*Trafalgar*
	Lieut. R.N.	AGAMEMNON	*St Domingo*
	Commander	ACHATES	*B.S. 13 Dec 1809*
PITMAN, Stephen	Pte. R.M.	FREIJA	
(PITT, Edward.W.)	(Lieut. R.N.)	(SCEPTRE)	*Awarded M.G.S. Medal also awarded N.G.S. Medal clasp Anse La Barque. 18 Decr 1809*
PORTER, William	Pte. R.M.	SCEPTRE	
PRESTON, Charles	A.B.	ORPHEUS	
PRICE, Hugh	Midshipman	FORESTER	
	Midshipman	FORESTER	*Martinique*
PRIDHAM, William.D.	Master's Mate	AURORA	*(M.L. as William PRIDHAM)*
	Lieut. R.N.	PROMETHEUS	*Algiers*
PRIO, James	A.B.	GLOIRE	*(Alias PRIOR)*
PRYKE, Edward	Pte. R.M.	ASP	
	Pte. R.M.	STAR	*Martinique*
	Pte. R.M.	SEVERN	*Algiers*
QUAMMAM, Samuel	Pte. R.M.	AURORA	
QUIN, John	Boy	ASP	
RADFORD, John	Pte. R.M.	ALFRED	
RANDS, John	Vol 1st Cl	ALCMENE	*(May read RAND)*
RATCLIFFE, Edward	Ord	POMPEE	*G.H. 2940*
	Ord	POMPEE	*Martinique*
	Ord	POMPEE	*Pompee. 17 June 1809*
RAVEN, John	Corporal. R.M.	PULTUSK	
RAVEN, Michael	Lieut. R.N.	CASTOR	*(Vfd as for McLAUGHLAN previously)*
REDMOND, Thomas	Carp's Crew	GLOIRE	
REED, James	Sgt. R.M.	CASTOR	
REGAN, Patrick	L.M.	POMPEE	
RICHES, John.H.	Midshipman	ALCMENE	
	Midshipman	DOMINICA	*Martinique*
RIDLEY, John	Pte. R.M.	POMPEE	
	Pte. R.M.	POMPEE	*Martinique*
	Pte. R.M.	POMPEE	*Pompee. 17 June 1809 (Vfd Abd. Not on Roll)*
RILEY, James	Pte. R.M.	CYGNET	*G.H. 3288*
	Pte. R.M.	CYGNET	*Anse La Barque. 18 Decr 1809*
RIXSON, Peter	L.M.	BACCHUS	
ROBERTS, Henry	Boy	LAURA	
ROBINSON, James	Yeoman of Sheets	ALFRED	
ROGERS, John	Boy	ALCMENE	
	Supn Boy	POMPEE	*Martinique*
ROLLS, William	A.B.	RINGDOVE	
	A.B.	RINGDOVE	*Martinique*
ROSE, Edward	A.B.	RINGDOVE	
	A.B.	RINGDOVE	*Martinique*
	Qtr Gunner	RINGDOVE	*Anse La Barque. 18 Decr 1809*
ROSS, John	A.B.	ATTENTIVE	
	A.B.	ATTENTIVE	*B.S. 13 Dec 1809*
ROWE, Henry.N.	Commander	St CHRISTOPHER	
	Lieut. R.N.	AJAX	*Trafalgar*
ROWSE, Joseph	A.B.	ALCMENE	*(Additional clasp ?)*
RUEL, John.G.	1st Lieut. R.M.	THETIS	
	1st Lieut. R.M.	THETIS	*B.S. 13 Dec 1809 (Vfd Abd. Not on Roll)*
	1st Lieut. R.M.	THETIS	*Anse La Barque. 18 Decr 1809 (Vfd Abd. Not on Roll)*
RUGARD, Jacob	L.M.	AURORA	
RYLAND, John	Pte. R.M.	SCEPTRE	
	Pte. R.M.	BELLEISLE	*Martinique*
SABBEN, James	Actg Lieut. R.N.	RINGDOVE	
	Midshipman	DREADNOUGHT	*Trafalgar*
	Midshipman	NEPTUNE	*Martinique*
	Actg Lieut. R.N.	RINGDOVE	*Anse La Barque. 18 Decr 1809*
SALTER, William	L.M.	CHERUB	*G.H. 9794*
	L.M.	CHERUB	*Martinique*
	Ord	CHERUB	*Cherub. 28 March 1814*
SALTER, William	L.M.	FAWN	
	Boy 3rd Class	FAWN	*Martinique*
SANGER, JAMES	Ord	ABERCROMBIE	
	Ord	POMPEE	*Martinique*
	Ord	POMPEE	*Pompee. 17 June 1809 (Vfd Abd. Not on Roll)*
SARGEANT, John	Boy	SCEPTRE	
SAVE, William	Pte. R.M.	ALCMENE	*G.H. 7056*

SAVILLE, John	L.M.	GLOIRE	
	L.M.	GLOIRE	*Martinique*
SCHOMBERG, Alexander.W.	Captain. R.N.	LOIRE	
SCOTT, James	Ord	OBSERVATEUR	
SCOTT, John	Lieut. R.N.	BLONDE	
	Lieut. R.N.	(BLONDE)	*B.S. type of action. Scorpion, 12 Jany 1810. See notes SCORPION*
SCRIVEN, William	Cooper	STATIRA	
SEALE, Charles.H.	Lieut. R.N.	STAR	
	Midshipman	COMUS	*Comus. 15 Augt 1807*
	Midshipman	NEPTUNE	*Martinique*
	Lieut. R.N.	DESIREE	*Gluckstadt. 5 Jan 1814*
SEAR, George	Ord	ABERCROMBIE	
	Ord	POMPEE	*Martinique*
	Ord	POMPEE	*Pompee. 17 June 1809*
SHARLAND, John	Capt' Fore Top	SCEPTRE	
	Capt' Fore Top	SCEPTRE	*Anse La Barque. 18 Decr 1809*
SHARP, John	Carp's Mate	BLONDE	
	Carp's Mate	BLONDE	*Anse La Barque. 18 Decr 1809*
SHEPHERD, Benjamin	Master's Mate	POMPEE	*Navy List & O'Byrne as John*
	Midshipman	BRITANNIA	*Trafalgar*
	Midshipman	LATONA	*Curacoa*
	Midshipman	NEPTUNE	*Martinique*
	Lieut. R.N.	GRIFFON	*Griffon. 27 March 1812*
SHREEVE, William	Caulker's Mate	POMPEE	*G.H.8532*
	A.B.	POMPEE	*Martinique*
	A.B.	POMPEE	*Pompee. 17 June 1809 (Vfd Abd. Not on Roll)*
SHUTE, John	Pte. R.M.	THETIS	
	Pte. R.M.	THUNDERER	*Trafalgar*
SLINGSBY, Robert	Sailmaker	AMARANTHE	
	Capt' Main Top	AMARANTHE	*Martinique*
SMALL, John	L.M.	LOIRE	
	L.M.	PENELOPE	*Penelope. 30 March 1800*
	L.M.	PENELOPE	*Egypt (Vfd Abd. Not on Roll)*
SMALL, William	A.B.	SCEPTRE	
	L.M.	ORION	*Trafalgar*
SMITH, James	Two Borne	SCORPION	*Ord & L.M. Both aboard for Scorpion 12 Jany 1810. Not on that Roll*
SMITH, John	A.B.	LOIRE	
SMITH, Samuel	Pte. R.M.	ALFRED	
SMITH, Thomas	Master's Mate	OBSERVATEUR	
SMITH, Thomas	A.B.	BLONDE	
SMITH, William.H.	Lieut. R.N.	SNAP	
	Midshipman	NEPTUNE	*Martinique*
SMURTHWAIT, William	Carps' Crew	ROSAMUND	
SOBEY, John	Boatswain	SCEPTRE	
	Boatswain	BLANCHE	*Blanche. 19 July 1806*
SODEN, Benjamin	Purser	THETIS	
	Purser	THETIS	*B.S. 13 Dec 1809*
	Purser	THETIS	*Anse La Barque. 18 Decr 1809*
SPIERS, John	Carpenter	THETIS	
SPODE, J.	Midshipman	ALFRED	
STARR, George	Capt's Clerk	ALFRED	
	Clerk	ORION	*Trafalgar*
	Purser	ROSARIO	*Rosario. 27 March 1812*
STEEL, James	L.M.	THETIS	*(M.L. as STEELE, Patrick)*
	L.M.	THETIS	*Anse La Barque. 18 Decr 1809*
STRONG, Samuel	Lieut. R.N.	SCORPION	
	Midshipman	ALCMENE	*Copenhagen 1801*
	Lieut. R.N.	SCORPION	*Scorpion. 12 Jany 1810 (Vfd Abd. Not on Roll)*
STRONG, William	Ord	BLONDE	
SUTHERLAND, Andrew	A.B.	ABERCROMBIE	
	L.M.	NORTHUMBERLAND	*St Domingo*
	A.B.	NEPTUNE	*Martinique*
SWANE, Hans	Boy	POMPEE	
	Boy	NEPTUNE	*Martinique*
TALBOT, William	Bosun's Mate	WANDERER	
	Boy 2nd Class	HARPY	*Harpy. 5 Feby 1800*
	L.M.	HARPY	*Copenhagen 1801*
TALLENCE, Samuel	Boatswain	PELORUS	
	A.B.	AGAMEMNON	*Trafalgar*
	A.B.	AGAMEMNON	*St Domingo*
	Boatswain	PELORUS	*Martinique*
	Boatswain	MUTINE	*Algiers*
TELLOGRAM, William	Pte. R.M.	HAZARD	
	Pte. R.M.	HAZARD	*Martinique*

GUADALOUPE

TENNANT, John	Master's Mate	ABERCROMBIE	
THOMPSON, John.L.	A.B.	NEPTUNE	*Martinique*
THOMPSON, Richard	Actg Master	BLONDE	
THOMPSON, Robert	A.B.	ROSAMUND	
THOMPSON, William	Ord	LOIRE	
THORNE, Samuel	L.M.	WANDERER	
TILLICK, William	Ord	MELAMPUS	*G.H. 8542*
TOMLINSON, William	A.B.	MELAMPUS	*G.H. 4441*
	Carp's Crew	SCEPTRE	
TOMS, William	Sailmaker	SCORPION	
	A.B.	TIGRE	*Acre. 30 May 1799*
	A.B.	TIGRE	*Egypt*
	A.B.	SCORPION	*Scorpion. 31 March 1804*
	Sailmaker	SCORPION	*Scorpion. 12 Jany 1810*
TOUGH, Alexander	L.M.	VIMIERA	*(Alias SANDY)*
TOWNE, John	Master's Mate	POMPEE	
TRIBE, Thomas	Midshipman	SCEPTRE	
	Midshipman	SCEPTRE	*Anse La Barque. 18 Decr 1809*
TRUMBLE, William	Ord	ABERCROMBIE	
	Ord	POMPEE	*Martinique*
	Ord	POMPEE	*Pompee. 17 June 1809*
TUCKER, John.T.	2nd Lieut. R.M.	ALFRED	
TUCKER, Thomas.T.	Commander	CHERUB	
	Lieut. R.N.	NORTHUMBERLAND	*St Domingo*
	Commander	CHERUB	*Martinique*
	Commander	CHERUB (P)	*Cherub. 28 March 1814*
TULL, John	Armourer	ORPHEUS	*G.H. 4840*
TUTE, Christopher	A.B.	PERLEN	
	A.B.	PRINCE GEORGE	*St Vincent*
TYSON, John	A.B.	AURORA	
UNDERHILL, Alexander	Ord	ATTENTIVE	
	Ord	ATTENTIVE	*B.S. 13 Dec 1809*
VEASEY, George	Ord	ALFRED	
VICK, Richard	L.M.	ALFRED	
VINALL, John	A.B.	GLOIRE	*G.H. 6749 (M.L. as VINON)*
WALKER, David	Pte. R.M.	ABERCROMBIE	
WALKER, George	Carpenter	FROLIC	
	Carp's Mate	INTREPID	*Martinique*
WALKER, James.R.	Lieut. R.N.	HAZARD	*(M.L. as James ROBERTSON)*
	Midshipman	VICTORY	*Trafalgar*
	Lieut. R.N.	HAZARD	*Martinique*
WALKER, Richard	L.M.	ALFRED	
WALKER, William	Purser	SNAP	
	Purser	SNAP	*Martinique*
	Purser	EREBUS	*The Potomac. 17 Aug 1814*
WALLIS, Provo.W.P.	Lieut. R.N.	GLOIRE	
	Lieut. R.N.	GLOIRE	*Anse La Barque. 18 Decr 1809*
		(Ship not on list)	*Vfd on Roll.*
	Lieut. R.N.	SHANNON	*Shannon Wh Chesapeake*
WARDLE, John	Actg Lieut. R.N.	PULTUSK	
	Midshipman	POMPEE	*Martinique*
	Midshipman	POMPEE	*Pompee. 17 June 1809 (Vfd Abd. Not on Roll)*
WARNE, Dennis	Pte. R.M.	ABERCROMBIE	
WARREN, William	Vol 1st Cl	LOIRE	*(M) China 1842 Medal*
WATERS, Dominick.C.	Midshipman	PELORUS	
WATSON, Joseph	Ord	ASP	
WATTS, James	Pte. R.M.	ROSAMUND	
WEAVER, William	Sgt. R.M.	AMARANTHE	
	Pte. R.M.	AMARANTHE	*Martinique*
WEBB, Christopher	L.M.	BLONDE	*(Vfd Abd. Not on Roll)*
	L.M.	BLONDE	*Anse La Barque. 18 Decr 1809 G.H. 2919*
WEBER, Ludwig	Pte. R.M.	FREIJA	
	Pte. R.M.	FREIJA	*Anse La Barque. 18 Decr 1809*
(WESLEY, Samuel.R.)	(2nd Lieut. R.M.)	(ABERCROMBIE)	*Awarded M.G.S. Medal*
WEST, Thomas	Pte. R.M.	FREIJA	
	Pte. R.M.	FREIJA	*Anse La Barque. 18 Decr 1809*
WETHERALL, Frederick.A.	Lieut. R.N.	OBSERVATEUR	
WHIFFEN, Thomas	Drummer. R.M.	SCEPTRE	
WHITE, George	A.B.	VIMIERA	
WHITE, William	2nd Lieut. R.M.	ALCMENE	
WHINYATES, Thomas	Commander	FROLIC	
	Capt's Servant	VETERAN	*B.S. 17 Mar 1794*
	Midshipman	ROBUST	*23rd June 1795*
	Master's Mate	ROBUST	*12 Octr 1798*
	Commander	FROLIC	*Martinique*

WILDING, Alexander	Midshipman	AURORA	
WILKINSON, Samuel	L.M.	POMPEE	
	L.M.	POMPEE	Martinique
	L.M.	POMPEE	Pompee. 17 June 1809
WILLIAMS, Edward	Pte. R.M.	ALFRED	
WILLIAMS, John	Boatswain (?)	ACHATES	
WILLIAMS, John	Two borne	ABERCROMBIE	A.B. and Ord
WILLIAMS, John	Supernumerary	FROLIC	
	Clerk	GLOIRE	Martinique
WILLIAMS, John	Surgeon	PERLEN	
WILLIAMS, Joseph	Pte. R.M.	MELAMPUS	
WILLIAMS, Richard	Qtr Gunner	SCEPTRE	
	A.B. or Carp's Crew	ORION	Trafalgar
WILSON, Harry	Midshipman	ALFRED	
	Midshipman	ALFRED	B.S. 23 Nov 1810 (Vfd Abd. Not on Roll)
	Lieut. R.N.	BERWICK	Gaieta. 24 July 1815 (Vfd Abd. Not on Roll)
WILSON, John	L.M.	SNAP	
WILSON, Robert	2nd Lieut. R.M.	BLONDE	
	2nd Lieut. R.M.	BLONDE	Anse La Barque. 18 Decr 1809
WINALL, George	L.M.	PERLEN	
WINGFIELD, William	Q.M.	CYGNET	
WINNISTER, John.F.	Capt' Fore Top	ALCMENE	(Vfd Abd. Not on Roll)
	Ship's Corporal	SHANNON	Shannon Wh Chesapeake
WINTERBURN, George	Cook	LOIRE	
	Boy	RENOWN	Egypt
	Ord	CAESAR	4 Novr 1805
WISE, Charles	Corporal. R.M.	GUADALOUPE	
	Corporal. R.M.	NEPTUNE	Martinique
WOOD, James	Q.M.	ABERCROMBIE	
	Q.M.	HAUGHTY	Martinique
WRIGHT, Alexander	L.M.	SCEPTRE	
	L.M.	SCEPTRE	Anse La Barque. 18 Decr 1809
WRIGHT, Cuthbert	A.B.	STATIRA	
WYLIE, William	A.B.	ALFRED	
YEOMAN, James	Pte. R.M.	SURINAM	
	Pte. R.M.	SURINAM	Martinique
YOUNG, George	Pte. R.M.	FREIJA	
	Pte. R.M.	VETERAN	Camperdown
YOUNG, William	Pte. R.M.	SCEPTRE	
	Pte. R.M.	SCEPTRE	Anse La Barque. 18 Decr 1809

No applicants.

THISTLE 10 FEBY 1810

Capture of the Dutch corvette HAVIK, off Bermuda.

(20) 13 FEB BOAT SERVICE 1810

Attack on nine French gun-boats in Basque Roads, and capture of one of them.

BECKERLY, Richard	A.B.	CHRISTIAN VII	(M.L. as BICKERLEGS) (R) Entered on Adm 171/- Roll under "Basque Roads 1809"
CAMBRIDGE, Samuel	Sgt. R.M.	CHRISTIAN VII	(R) see above. G.H. 4758
COLE, William. J.	Midshipman	CHRISTIAN VII	
DAVIES, John	L.M.	ARMIDE	(M.L. as DAVIS)
	L.M.	ARMIDE	B.S. 27 Sep 1810
HARPER, John	Pte. R.M.	CHRISTIAN VII	
HENNING, Alexander	Midshipman	CHRISTIAN VII	
	Midshipman	GALATEA	Off Tamatave. 20 May 1811
HOWELL, William	Pte. R.M.	CHRISTIAN VII	(R) see above
HUNTER, Robert	Master's Mate	ARMIDE	
	Midshipman	UNICORN	Basque Roads 1809
	Master's Mate	ARMIDE	B.S. 27 Sep 1810
JONES, John	Two Ptes R.M. borne	CHRISTIAN VII	
LANGDON, William	A.B.	CHRISTIAN VII	
LORY, William	Vol 1st Cl	ARMIDE	
	Vol 1st Cl	UNICORN	Basque Roads 1809
	Midshipman	ARMIDE	B.S. 27 Sep 1810
MATTHEWS, John	Pte. R.M.	CHRISTIAN VII	(R) see above
McARTHUR, John	2nd Lt. R.M.	ARMIDE	
MOOR, Philip	Midshipman	ARMIDE	
	Midshipman	UNICORN	Basque Roads 1809
NICOLAS, Paul.H.	1st Lt. R.M.	ARMIDE	
	1st Lt. R.M.	BELLEISLE	Trafalgar

13 FEB BOAT SERVICE 1810

PHEPOE, John	Lieut. R.N.	ARMIDE	
	Midshipman	AJAX	*Trafalgar (Vfd Abd. N.O.R.)*
	Lieut. R.N.	ARMIDE	*B.S. 27 Sep 1810*
			(Vfd Abd. Not on Roll)
ROBERTS, Robert	L.M.	ARMIDE	
	L.M.	ARMIDE	*B.S. 27 Sep 1810*
SCOTT, Edward.F.	Lieut. R.N.	CHRISTIAN VII	
SPRATT, John	Pte. R.M.	CHRISTIAN VII	
STEELE, Henry.P.	Midshipman	CHRISTIAN VII	

(1) SURLY 24 APRIL 1810

Capture of the French privateer ALCIDE by SURLY & FIRM (this Action recorded in Boat Service Actions Roll ADM 171/3), in Granville Bay, Grenada, West Indies.
(Real date 20 April 1810)

NORSTER, Abraham	Clerk	SURLY	

(1) FIRM 24 APRIL 1810

Capture of the French privateer ALCIDE by SURLY & FIRM (this Action recorded in Boat Service Actions Roll ADM 171/3), in Granville Bay, Grenada, West Indies.
(Real date 20 April 1810)

WIGLEY, Henry	Pte. R.M.	FIRM	

(1) SYLVIA 26 APRIL 1810

Capture of the Dutch brig ECHO, off Edam Island, Java.

CHESNAYE, John.C.	Actg 2nd Master	SYLVIA	
	Midshipman	ORION	*Trafalgar*

(15) 1 MAY BOAT SERVICE 1810

Capture of the French schooner ESTAFETTE and a fort at JACOTET, Isle de France (Muster Lists of NEREIDE for year 1810 have not survived).

CHERRIT, Anthony	L.M.	NEREIDE	
COSTERTON, Samuel	Midshipman	NEREIDE	
DEACON, Henry.C.	Lieut. R.N.	NEREIDE	*(Not on Roll. L. Gaz. 1810)*
	Midshipman	AMAZON	*Amazon. 13 March 1806*
EDWARDS, William	Capt Forecastle	NEREIDE	
GRIFFEN, Thomas	A.B.	NEREIDE	
LAUGHARNE, Thomas.L.P.	Lieut. R.N.	NEREIDE	
	Supn Midshipman	NORTHUMBERLAND	*St Domingo*
	Lieut. R.N.	UNICORN	*Basque Roads 1809*
	Lieut. R.N.	BOADICEA (P)	*Boadicea 18 Septr 1810*
LONGSTRAATH, James	Pte. R.M.	NEREIDE	
	R.M. Boy	BRITANNIA	*Trafalgar*
LYNCH, Richard	Ord	NEREIDE	
MANNING, Thomas	Gunner	NEREIDE	
PATTON, Thomas	Midshipman	NEREIDE	
REID, Charles	L.M.	NEREIDE	
SANDERSON, John.W.	Gunner's Mate	NEREIDE	
SANDERSON, William	Not Given	NEREIDE	
SUTHERLAND, James	Ord	NEREIDE	
WILLOUGHBY, Nesbit.J.	Actg Captain. RN.	NEREIDE (P)	

(30) SPARTAN 3 MAY 1810

Action with the Franco-Neapolitan frigate CERES and consorts, and capture of the brig SPARVIERE in the Bay of Naples.

ANDROS, Charles	Midshipman	SPARTAN	
	Midshipman	DICTATOR	*Off Mardoe. 6 July 1812*
BASDEN, Charles	Midshipman	SPARTAN	
BAYNES, Simcoe	Vol 1st Cl	SPARTAN	
BOURNE, Henry	Lieut. R.N.	SPARTAN	
BURR, Thomas	Clerk	SPARTAN	
COWAN, James	Pte. R.M.	SPARTAN	
DOWNS, Richard	Ord	SPARTAN	*G.H. 1,008*
DUNN, James	Purser	SPARTAN	
EBORALL, Samuel	Midshipman	SPARTAN	
FARRELL, Timothy	Pte. R.M.	SPARTAN	
FEGEN, Charles	Lieut. R.M.	SPARTAN	
	Captain. R.M.	GORGON	*Syria*
FERRALL, Patrick	Pte. R.M.	SPARTAN	*(M.L. as FARRELL)*
GALLICK, James	R.M. Boy	SPARTAN	*(M.L. as GOLLICK)*
JOB, Thomas	Gunner's Mate	SPARTAN	
JONES, Robert	L.M.	SPARTAN	*G.H. 8089*
LOVICK, John	Ord	SPARTAN	*G.H. 6525*
MORRISON, Richard.J.	Midshipman Ord	SPARTAN	
PINCOMBE, John	Ord	SPARTAN	*G.H. 6290 (M.L. as PINCOMB)*
ROBERTSON, John	Vol 1st Cl	SPARTAN	
ROBINSON, John	Capt Main Top	SPARTAN	
ROGINSON, Joseph	A.B.	SPARTAN	
SAUMAREZ, Richard	Midshipman	SPARTAN	
SEARLE, John	Gunner	SPARTAN	
SOUTHERN, John	A.B.	SPARTAN	
SWIFT, John	Boy 3rd Cl	SPARTAN	
WALKER, Francis	Pte. R.M.	SPARTAN	
WESTON, James	L.M.	SPARTAN	
WILLIAMS, John	A.B.	SPARTAN	
WILLIAMS, Richard	Capt Forecastle	SPARTAN	
WISE, Edward	Boatswain	SPARTAN	
	A.B.	VICTORY	*Trafalgar*

(3) ROYALIST MAY & JUNE 1810

Action with and capture of six armed vessels on different dates whilst on English Channel service.

(Real dates. Nov 1809 to Feb 1810)

BOWLES, Anthony	Supn Pilot	ROYALIST	*(Joined after Actions)
SELBY, George	Boy 3rd Cl	ROYALIST	
THORNTON, Henry.A.D.	Midshipman	ROYALIST	

(26) 28 JUNE BOAT SERVICE 1810

Capture of twenty and destruction of eleven vessels at PORTO GRADO, N.E. of Venice.

(Real date 29 June 1810)

BAILEY, John	Ord	AMPHION	*(M.L. as BAYLEY)*
	Ord	AMPHION	*B.S. 28 Aug 1809*
	Ord	AMPHION	*Lissa*
BASSETT, Samuel	L.M.	CERBERUS	
	L.M.	CERBERUS	*Lissa*
BLYTH, Francis	Capt Forecastle	AMPHION	*(M.L. as BLYTHE)*
	Capt Forecastle	AMPHION	*B.S. 28 Aug 1809*
	Q.M.	AMPHION	*Lissa*
BOWEN, Richard	Midshipman	ACTIVE	
	Midshipman	ACTIVE	*Lissa*
	Midshipman	ACTIVE	*Pelagosa. 29 Novr 1811.*
BRUCE, Charles	Midshipman	AMPHION	
	Midshipman	AMPHION	*B.S. 28 Aug 1809*
	(Not yet joined)	BACCHANTE	*B.S. 1 & 18 Sep 1812 (On Roll)*
	Mid Ordinary	BACCHANTE	*B.S. 6 Jan 1813*
BUCHANAN, David	Yeoman of Sheets	AMPHION	
	Yeoman of Sheets	AMPHION	*B.S. 28 Aug 1809*
	Yeoman of Sheets	AMPHION	*Lissa*

28 JUNE BOAT SERVICE 1810

CAMMILLERI, Joseph	(Not yet aboard)	ACTIVE	(On Roll)
	A.B.	ACTIVE	Lissa
	Midshipman	ACTIVE	Pelagosa. 29 Novr 1811
	Master's Mate	SEAHORSE	The Potomac. 17 Aug 1814
	Master's Mate	SEAHORSE	B.S. 14 Dec 1814
CHRISTIE, George	L.M.	AMPHION	G.H. 8658 (Vfd Abd. Not on Roll) (M.L. as CHRISTIAN)
	L.M.	AMPHION	Lissa
DAVIES, Evan	Capt After Guard	ACTIVE	G.H. 6262 (Vfd Abd. Not on 171/- Roll. On GH Roll) M.L. as DAVIS
	Capt After Guard	ACTIVE	Lissa
	Capt After Guard	ACTIVE	Pelagosa. 29 Novr 1811
DUFF, Norwich	Midshipman	ACTIVE	
	A.B.	MARS	Trafalgar
	Midshipman	ACTIVE	Lissa
	Midshipman	ACTIVE	Pelagosa. 29 Novr 1811
FRIEND, Charles	Midshipman	ACTIVE	
	Master's Mate	ACTIVE	Lissa
	Master's Mate	ACTIVE	Pelagosa. 29 Novr 1811
GAPE, Joseph	Midshipman	AMPHION	
	Vol 1st Cl	AJAX	Trafalgar
	Midshipman	AMPHION	B.S. 28 Aug 1809
HAWKES, John	Pte. R.M.	ACTIVE	(M.L. as HAWKE)
	Pte. R.M.	ACTIVE	Lissa
	Pte. R.M.	ACTIVE	Pelagosa. 29 Novr 1811
HENDERSON, William.W.	Lieut. R.N.	ACTIVE	
	Midshipman	BELLEISLE	Trafalgar
	Lieut. R.N.	ACTIVE (P)	Lissa
	Captain. R.N.	EDINBURGH	Syria
HEWETT, John.H.	Pte. R.M.	ACTIVE	(M.L. as HEWITT, Henry.J.)
	Pte. R.M.	ACTIVE	Lissa
	Pte. R.M.	ACTIVE	Pelagosa. 29 Novr 1811
LAMMING, John	Ord	CERBERUS	
	Ord	CERBERUS	Lissa
MEARES, John	2nd Lieut. R.M.	ACTIVE	
	2nd Lieut. R.M.	ACTIVE	Lissa
	2nd Lieut. R.M.	ACTIVE	Pelagosa. 29 Novr 1811
MOORE, Thomas	1st Lieut. R.M.	AMPHION	
	1st Lieut. R.M.	AMPHION	B.S. 28 Aug 1809
	1st Lieut. R.M.	AMPHION	Lissa
O'BRIEN, Donat.H.	Lieut. R.N.	AMPHION	
	Lieut. R.N.	AMPHION	Lissa
	Lieut. R.N.	BACCHANTE (P)	B.S. 1 & 18 Sep 1812
	Lieut. R.N.	BACCHANTE	B.S. 6 Jan 1813
ROSS, Charles.H.	Master's Mate	AMPHION	
	Midshipman	AMPHION	B.S. 28 Aug 1809
	Actg Lieut. R.N.	AMPHION	Lissa
SHERWOOD, William	Midshipman	CERBERUS	
	Vol 1st Cl	CERBERUS	B.S. 25 July 1809
	Midshipman	CERBERUS	Lissa
SLAUGHTER, William	Lieut. R.N.	AMPHION	
	Vol 1st Cl	TRIUMPH	17 June 1795
	Vol 1st Cl	TRIUMPH	Camperdown
	Lieut. R.N.	AMPHION	B.S. 28 Aug 1809
SPARKES, John	Pte. R.M.	ACTIVE	
	Pte. R.M.	ACTIVE	Lissa
	Pte. R.M.	ACTIVE	Pelagosa. 29 Novr 1811
STAMER, Lovelace	L.M.	CERBERUS	N.O.R. but on Java list "Medal issued with addl clasp for Grae".
	L.M.	CERBERUS	Java ("Run" 25-11-1811)
STOKES, Joseph	Cpl. R.M.	ACTIVE	
	Cpl. R.M.	ACTIVE	Lissa
	Cpl. R.M.	ACTIVE	Pelagosa. 29 Novr 1811 (Vfd Abd. Not on Roll)
WESTON, George	Pte. R.M.	AMPHION	
	Pte. R.M.	AMPHION	B.S. 28 Aug 1809
	Pte. R.M.	AMPHION	Lissa
WHISKER, William	L.M.	AMPHION	
	L.M.	AMPHION	B.S. 28 Aug 1809
	L.M.	AMPHION	Lissa
	A.B.	BACCHANTE	B.S. 1 & 18 Sep 1812

(23) AMANTHEA 25 JULY 1810

Action with gun-boats, and capture and destruction of a number of transports, at AMANTEA, Italy.

BURGESS, James	Pte. R.M.	PILOT	
COLLIER, Edward	Lieut. R.N.	THAMES (P)	
	Lieut. R.N.	St FIORENZO	San Fiorenzo. 14 Feby 1805 (Vfd Abd. Not on Roll)
	Lieut. R.N.	St FIORENZO	San Fiorenzo. 8 March 1808 (Vfd Abd. Not on Roll)
	Captain. R.N.	CASTOR	Syria
COPPIN, Charles.P.	Lieut. R.N.	WEAZLE	
CORNWALL, John	Midshipman	THAMES	
	Midshipman	VOLONTAIRE	B.S. 2 May 1813
GOSLIN, William.H.	Midshipman	WEAZLE	
LIDDON, Matthew	Master's Mate	THAMES	
	Lieut. R.N.	MAIDSTONE	B.S. Ap & May 1813
	Lieut. R.N.	MAIDSTONE	B.S. 8 April 1814
McADAM, David	Lieut. R.M.	THAMES	
	Lieut. R.M.	AIGLE	Basque Roads. 1809
MOODY, William	Boy 2nd Cl	THAMES	G.H. 9,912
MULLINS, William	Boatswain	THAMES	
NICOLAS, John.T.	Commander	PILOT	(Named changed to NICHOLAS in 1818)
PENRUDDOCK, George	Lieut. R.N.	PILOT	
PRESCOTT, Henry	Commander	WEAZLE	
	Midshipman	PENELOPE	Penelope. 30 March 1800
	Midshipman	PENELOPE	Egypt
	Lieut. R.N.	AEOLUS	4 Novr 1805
RICKETTS, William	Boy 2nd Cl	THAMES	
ROBBINS, Richard	Supn Boy 3rd Cl	PILOT	
SAXTON, John	Ord	WEAZLE	
	Ord	WEAZLE	Weazel. 22 Feby 1812
	Ord	WEAZLE	B.S. 6 Jan 1813
	Ord	WEAZLE	Weazel. 22 April 1813
TREFUSIS, Hon George.R.W.	Midshipman	THAMES	
	Vol 1st Cl	CENTAUR	Centaur. 26 Augt 1808
VEAR, Joseph	Coxswain	WEAZLE	
WALDEGRAVE, Hon G.G.	Captain. R.N.	THAMES	(Afterwards Lord RASSTOCK)
WARING, John	Boy 3rd Cl	THAMES	
WHITEWAY, Samuel	Lieut. R.N.	THAMES	
WILKINSON, James	Midshipman	THAMES	
	Master's Mate	EURYALUS	The Potomac. 17 Aug 1814 (Revd A of India/AVA)
WRIGLEY, James	Quarter Gunner	PILOT	
WYVILL, Christopher	Midshipman	THAMES	
	Midshipman	VOLONTAIRE	B.S. 2 May 1813

(68) BANDA NEIRA (G.M.)

Capture of BANDA NEIRA (NEIRA Island in the BANDA group of the MOLUCCAS), on 9 August 1810.

ALLEN, Charles	Yeoman of Pdr Rm	CAROLINE	
ALLEN, Thomas	Boy 3rd Cl	BARRACOUTA	
	Boy 2nd Cl	BARRACOUTA	Java (July/Sept 1811)
ANTHONY, John	L.M.	CAROLINE	
APPLEGATE, William	Ship's Corporal	CAROLINE	
	Ship's Corporal	CAROLINE	Java
AUSTIN, William	Ord	CAROLINE	
	Ord	CAROLINE	Java
BARKER, Robert	Lieut. R.N.	PIEDMONTAISE	
BARNETT, John	Ord	PIEDMONTAISE	
BEST, John	L.M.	CAROLINE	
BRENNAN, Daniel	Boatswain	BARRACOUTA	
	L.M.	ROYAL GEORGE	1 June 1794
	Ord	BELLEISLE	Trafalgar
	Boatswain	BARRACOUTA	Java
BROWN, William	A.B.	BARRACOUTA	
CARR, Arthur	Pte. R.M.	CAROLINE	(Not yet found)
CAWLEY, James	Coxswain's Mate	CAROLINE	(M.L. as CONLEY)
	Coxswain's Mate	CAROLINE	Java
CHEESEMAN, Robert	Sailmaker's Mate	CAROLINE	G.H. 7,338

BANDA NEIRA

COLE, William	Ord	CAROLINE	G.H. 8,214
COTTON, John	Ship's Corporal	BARRACOUTA	
	Ship's Corporal	BARRACOUTA	Java
CROSSWELL, Thomas	A.B.	CAROLINE	
	Captain Forecastle	CAROLINE	Java
	Q.M.	Qn CHARLOTTE	Algiers
CUNNINGHAM, George	Pte. R.M.	PIEDMONTAISE	
DAVENPORT, Thomas	Master's Mate	CAROLINE	
DAVIS, John	Yeoman of Sheets	CAROLINE	
	Yeoman of Sheets	CAROLINE	Java
DICKER, John	L.M.	CAROLINE	
	L.M.	CAROLINE	Java
ECCLESTON, Samuel	Pte. R.M.	CAROLINE	G.H. 10,007
	Pte. R.M.	ARDENT	Copenhagen 1801
	Cpl. R.M.	CAROLINE	Java
FRANCIS, William	Ord	CAROLINE	
FRANKLIN, Henry	Two Ptes RM borne.	PIEDMONTAISE	
FRENCH, John	Supn. Unrated.	PIEDMONTAISE	A re-taken deserter.
GOODWIN, Nathaniel	Master's Mate	CAROLINE	
	Master's Mate	CAROLINE	Java
GRIPTON, Richard	Ord	PIEDMONTAISE	
HARDY, Robert.W.H.	Midshipman	CAROLINE	
HENDERSON, Henry	A.B.	PIEDMONTAISE	
HIGGINS, Henry	Ord	PIEDMONTAISE	
HULL, William	Ord	CAROLINE	
	Ord	CAROLINE	Java
INNES, Thomas	A.B.	BARRACOUTA	
	A.B.	BARRACOUTA	Java
JACOBS, Joseph	Purser	PIEDMONTAISE	
JONES, Benjamin	A.B.	BARRACOUTA	G.H. 2,744
	A.B.	BARRACOUTA	Java
JONES, Edward	Ord	CAROLINE	
	Ord	CAROLINE	Java
	A.B.	TONNANT	B.S. 14 Dec 1814
JONES, John (2)	Ord	CAROLINE	
	Ord	CAROLINE	Java
LYONS, Edmund	Lieut. R.N.	BARRACOUTA	
	Lieut. R.N.	MINDEN	B.S. 30 July 1811
	Lieut. R.N.	MINDEN	Java
MANNING, George	L.M.	CAROLINE	
	L.M.	CAROLINE	Java
MATHEWS, Peter	L.M.	PIEDMONTAISE	(M.L. as MATTHEWS)
MATTINSON, Thomas	Gunner	CAROLINE	
	L.M.	BEAULIEU	Camperdown
	Gunner	MUSQUITO	Navarino
MILTON, Thomas	Pte. R.M.	CAROLINE	
	Pte. R.M.	CAROLINE	Java
MYLINS, Charles.A.S.	Midshipman	PIEDMONTAISE	
NOTLEY, Henry	Q.M's Mate	CAROLINE	
PAGE, Robert	L.M.	BARRACOUTA	G.H. 10,181
	L.M.	BARRACOUTA	Java
PARKER, Robert	A.B.	CAROLINE	
	Sailmaker's Mate	CAROLINE	Java
PARROTT, William	Carp's Crew	BARRACOUTA	G.H. 2,695
	Carp's Crew	CAROLINE	Java
PHILLIPS, Paul	A.B.	BARRACOUTA	
	A.B.	BARRACOUTA	Java
PRESTOPINO, Antonio	Capt Main Top	PIEDMONTAISE	(M.L. as PRESIPINO)
PULFER, Charles	Carp's Crew	CAROLINE	
	Carp's Crew	CAROLINE	Java
RACE, John	L.M.	CAROLINE	G.H. 9,784
	L.M.	CAROLINE	Java
RENTON, William	Master's Mate	PIEDMONTAISE	
ROSSER, William	A.B.	PIEDMONTAISE	
SCOLLARD, Michael	Ord	CAROLINE	(Not yet found)
SMITH, Abraham	Supn. Un-rated.	PIEDMONTAISE	
SMITH, George	Ord	PIEDMONTAISE	
STEWART, John	Asst Surgeon	PIEDMONTAISE	
	Asst Surgeon	GIBRALTAR	Basque Roads. 1809
	Actg Surgeon	CAROLINE	Java
STEWART, Peter	Q.M's Mate	CAROLINE	
	Capt Forecastle	CAROLINE	Java
SUBBINS, James	Yeoman of Sheets	PIEDMONTAISE	M.L. as STUBBINS.
SWAINE, Matthew	Actg Armourer	CAROLINE	
	Actg Armourer	CAROLINE	Java
SWANSON, Andrew	Ord	CAROLINE	
	Ord	CAROLINE	Java
THORPE, Edward	Supn. Un-Rated.	PIEDMONTAISE	G.H. 6,995
WADDELL, Henry	Ord	CAROLINE	
	Ord	CAROLINE	Java
WATSON, George	Ord	BARRACOUTA	
	Carp's Crew	BARRACOUTA	Java
WEST, Joseph	Midshipman	PIEDMONTAISE	

WHITE, Henry	Ord	BARRACOUTA	
	Ord	BARRACOUTA	*Java*
WHITE, John	Lieut. R.N.	BARRACOUTA	
	Midshipman	SUPERB	*Gut of Gibraltar. 12 July 1801*
	Midshipman	SUPERB	*St Domingo*
	Lieut. R.N.	BARRACOUTA	*Java*
WHITE, William	Ord	CAROLINE	
	Ord	CAROLINE	*Java*
WOOD, John	Actg Ropemaker	CAROLINE	
YEATS, John.S.	Midshipman	CAROLINE	

(15) BOADICEA 18 SEPTR 1810

Capture of the French frigate VENUS and re-capture of the CEYLON, off Isle of Reunion.

BORROWS, John	Pte. R.M.	BOADICEA	(M.L. as BURROWS)
CAREY, William	Ord	BOADICEA	
CHAMBERLAYNE, John	Midshipman	BOADICEA	
CLIFFORD, Herbert.J.	Actg Lieut. R.N.	BOADICEA	
GRIFFITHS, Richard	Pte. R.M.	BOADICEA	
	Pte. R.M.	ALBION	*Algiers*
LAMB, Philip	L.M.	BOADICEA	
LAUGHARNE, Thomas.L.P.	Lieut. R.N.	BOADICEA (P)	
	Supn. Midshipman	NORTHUMBERLAND	*St Domingo*
	Lieut. R.N.	UNICORN	*Basque Roads. 1809*
	Lieut. R.N.	NEREIDE	*B.S. 1 May 1810*
LLOYD, Edward	Lieut. R.N.	BOADICEA	
	Midshipman	DICTATOR	*Egypt*
			Revd M.G.S. for JAVA
PAGE, William	A.B.	BOADICEA	
RAMSEY, Samuel	Midshipman	BOADICEA	
ROBERTS, Thomas	Cpl. R.M.	BOADICEA	
STOCKER, Stewart	Boy 3rd Cl	BOADICEA	
SWIGG, James	Pte. R.M.	BOADICEA	
TAYLOR, William	Ord	BOADICEA	
WILSON, James	Two Boys 3rd Cl borne	BOADICEA	

(8) OTTER 18 SEPTR 1810

Capture of the French frigate VENUS and re-capture of the CEYLON, off Isle of Reunion.

GRASSUM, John	Pte. R.M.	OTTER	
HEARN, Owen	Boy 2nd Cl	OTTER	
JEFFERY, John	A.B.	OTTER	
MANNING, Thomas	Quarter Gunner	OTTER	(Had left ship before action)
McGLADERY, John or M'GLADERY	Actg Lieut. R.N.	OTTER	(Vfd Abd. Not on Roll)
	Yeoman of Sheets	CULLODEN	*St Vincent*
	Yeoman of Sheets	CULLODEN	*Nile*
PRATT, Benjamin	Pte. 69th Regt	OTTER	
SUTHERLAND, James	Ord	OTTER	(Taken P.O.W. before action)
TAYLOR, Francis	Actg Purser	OTTER	

(2) STAUNCH 18 SEPR 1810

Capture of the French frigate VENUS and re-capture of the CEYLON, off Isle of Reunion.

EDWARDS, John	Ord	STAUNCH	
	Carpenter's Crew	HYACINTH	*Malaga. 29 April 1812*
			(Vfd Abd. Not on Roll)
SAINTHILL, Richard.T.	Actg Sub Lt. R.N.	STAUNCH	

(36) 27 SEP BOAT SERVICE 1810

Storming a battery at CHE POINT, Basque Roads and capture of two French brigs and destruction of a third brig.

(Real date 28 September 1810)

AYERS, James	Boy (?)	VALIANT (?)	Roll as VALIANT, Not found.
BAKER, Samuel	Midshipman	VALIANT	
	Midshipman	VALIANT	Basque Roads 1809
BEER, Daniel	Quarter Gunner	CALEDONIA	G.H. 2716
	Quarter Gunner	CALEDONIA	Basque Roads 1809
BOYES, Henry	Flag Lieut. R.N.	CALEDONIA*	*Had left ship Feb 1810
	Midshipman	LION	Lion. 15 July 1798
	Flag Lieut. R.N.	CALEDONIA	Basque Roads 1809
BURTON, Robert	A.B.	CALEDONIA	
	A.B.	CALEDONIA	Basque Roads 1809 (Vfd Abd. Not on Roll)
BUTLER, Charles.G.	Midshipman	CALEDONIA	
	Vol 1st Cl	CALEDONIA	Basque Roads 1809
CHALLIS, Samuel	Steward's Mate	VALIANT	(M.L. as CHALLICE)
	Ord	NAMUR	4 Novr 1805 (see note)
	Steward's Mate	VALIANT	Basque Roads 1809
CORTON, William	Pte. R.M.	CALEDONIA	Probably noted incorrectly on Medal Roll under B.S. List at ADM 171/3/29.
COUCHE, John	1st Lt. R.M.	CALEDONIA	
	1st Lt. R.M.	CALEDONIA	Basque Roads 1809 (Vfd Abd. Not on Roll)
DAVIES, John	L.M.	ARMIDE	(M.L. as DAVIS)
	L.M.	ARMIDE	B.S. 13 Feb 1810
FOOTE, John	Lieut. R.N.	CALEDONIA	
GOSTLING, Philip	Midshipman	ARMIDE	
	Vol 1st Cl	UNICORN	Basque Roads 1809
	Lieut. R.N.	SEVERN	Algiers
HAMILTON, Arthur.P.	Lieut. R.N.	CALEDONIA (P)	
HARRISON, John	Master's Mate	VALIANT	
	Master's Mate	VALIANT	Basque Roads
HERRINGHAM, William.A.	Midshipman	CALEDONIA	
	Midshipman	COLOSSUS	Trafalgar
HUNTER, Robert	Master's Mate	ARMIDE	
	Midshipman	UNICORN	Basque Roads 1809
	Master's Mate	ARMIDE	B.S. 13 Feb 1810
JENNINGS, Edward	Midshipman	VALIANT	
	Midshipman	VALIANT	Basque Roads 1809
KELLY, William	Lieut. R.N.	CALEDONIA	(Vfd Abd. Not on Roll)
	Lieut. R.N.	MINERVE	Egypt
	Lieut. R.N.	PRINCE	Trafalgar
	Lieut. R.N.	CALEDONIA	Basque Roads 1809
KINGSTON, George	C in C's Domestic	CALEDONIA*	Vfd on Roll. Had left ship Feb 1810
LAMBETH, John.D.	Ord	VALIANT	(M.L. as John LAMBETH)
	L.M.	NAMUR	4 Novr 1805
	Ord	VALIANT	Basque Roads 1809
LITTLE, Robert.J.	1st Lt. R.M.A.	CALEDONIA	
LORY, William	Midshipman	ARMIDE	
	Vol 1st Cl	UNICORN	Basque Roads 1809
	Vol 1st Cl	ARMIDE	B.S. 13 Feb 1810
MANN, John	Ord	VALIANT	
	Boy 3rd Cl	ARDENT	Copenhagen 1801
	L.M.	NAMUR	4 Novr 1805
	Ord	VALIANT	Basque Roads 1809
NUCKEN, Peter	Pte. R.M.	CALEDONIA	(M.L. as NINKEN)
PHEPOE, John	Lieut. R.N.	ARMIDE	(Vfd Abd. Not on Roll)
	Midshipman	AJAX	Trafalgar (Vfd Abd. Not on Roll)
	Lieut. R.N.	ARMIDE	B.S. 13 Feb 1810
POPE, Edmund	Midshipman	VALIANT	(Vfd Abd. Not on Roll)
	Midshipman	VALIANT	Basque Roads 1809
PRITCHARD, William	Ord	CALEDONIA	
	Ord	LEVIATHAN	Trafalgar
	Ord	CALEDONIA	Basque Roads 1809
READ, George	Midshipman	VALIANT	
	Midshipman	VALIANT	Basque Roads 1809
REED, Benjamin	Ord	VALIANT	(M.L. as REID)
	Boy 2nd Cl	NAMUR	4 Novr 1805
	Ord	VALIANT	Basque Roads 1809
ROBERTS, Robert	L.M.	ARMIDE	
	L.M.	ARMIDE	B.S. 13 Feb 1810

SHERMAN, Thomas	Captain. R.M.	CALEDONIA		
	2nd Lt. R.M.	DRYAD	Dryad. 13 June 1796	
	Captain. R.M.	CALEDONIA	Basque Roads 1809	
			(Vfd Abd. Not on Roll)	
SIMONDS, Richard.S.	Master's Mate	CALEDONIA		
	Midshipman	DEFENCE	Trafalgar	
	Lieut. R.N.	ABOUKIR	B.S. 29 Sep 1812	
SMITH, Edward	Master's Mate	CALEDONIA		
STANBURY, William	Midshipman	CALEDONIA		
	Midshipman	CALEDONIA	Basque Roads 1809	
TAYLOR, John	Pte. R.M.	VALIANT		
	Pte. R.M.	VALIANT	Basque Roads 1809	
TOOLE, Michael	Ord	CALEDONIA		
	Ord	CALEDONIA	Basque Roads 1809	

(2) BRISEIS 14 OCTR 1810

Capture of the French privateer SANS SOUCI in the North Sea.

BENTHAM, George	Actg Commander	BRISEIS		
	Midshipman	HERO	4 Novr 1805	
	Commander	HERON (P)	Algiers	
WELSH, George	Lieut. R.N.	BRISEIS		
	Master's Mate	ELING	Copenhagen 1801	
	Lieut. R.N.	BRISEIS	B.S. 27 July 1809	

(1) 4 NOV BOAT SERVICE 1810

Capture of the French privateer CESAR, off Cape Sicie, S.W. Toulon.

BARRINGTON, James	Ord	BLOSSOM	

(42) 23 NOV BOAT SERVICE 1810

Attack and destruction of shipping at PUERTO de SANTA MARIA by bomb and mortar vessels, and boats of fleet operating off CADIZ.

ANDERSON, Matthew	Asst Surgeon	MILFORD	
BALDOCK, Thomas	Supn Midshipman	NORGE	
BATT, David	Carpenter	MILFORD	
BOWYER, William.B.	Lieut. R.N.	NORGE	
BROOKER, Henry	2nd Master & Pilot	HARDY	
BROWNING, George	Clerk	THUNDER	
CARROLL, William.F.	Lieut. R.N. (P)	GIBRALTAR FLOTILLA	
		DIAMOND	Port Spergui. 17 March 1796
		CENTURION	Centurion. 18 Sept 1804
			(& M.G.S. Maida)
CHAPMAN, James	Ord	MILFORD	
CORK, Charles	?	?	(Not found as on Roll)
DICKEN, Henry.P.	Midshipman	MILFORD	
DONLEVY, George.M.	Vol 1st Cl	NORGE	
	Midshipman	NORGE	B.S. 14 Dec 1814
DRINKWATER, Thomas	2nd Lieut. R.M.	MILFORD	
DYER, Robert	Ord	ATLAS	
FELLOWES, Thomas	Commander	CADIZ FLOTILLA of GUNBOATS	(P)
	Captain. R.N.	DARTMOUTH	Navarino (Kt for services)
GRANT, James	L.M.	HARDY	
	Boy 2nd Cl	AETNA	Basque Roads. 1809
HICKS, William	Master's Mate	MILFORD	
	Midshipman	CONQUEROR	Trafalgar
HILL, George	A.B.	MILFORD	(M.L. as MEADOR, Charles)
JACKSON, James	Pte. R.M.	ATLAS	
JERRARD, Michael	Master's Mate	REVENGE*	(Joined after Action)
JONES, Henry.P.	Midshipman	REVENGE	
	Midshipman	REVENGE	Basque Roads. 1809
KITCHEN, James	A.B.	ATLAS	
LANDMANN, George	Captain. R.E.	MILFORD *?	(Not found this Muster List)
LAWRENCE, John	Gnr. R.M.A.	AETNA	
	Gnr. R.M.A.	AETNA	Basque Roads. 1809
LECOUNT, Peter	Midshipman	THUNDER	
	Midshipman	INFERNAL	Algiers
MACLEAN, Rawdon	Lieut. R.N.	COLOSSUS	
	Midshipman	COLOSSUS	Trafalgar
MASCALL, John.R.	2nd Lieut. R.M.	NORGE	
McDONALD, William	A.B.	HOUND	

23 NOV BOAT SERVICE 1810

MOODY, James	A.B.	ALFRED	
	A.B.	ALFRED	Guadaloupe
MORROGH, David	L.M.	MILFORD	(M.L. as MURROGH)
NAYLOR, Joseph	A.B.	HOUND	(M.L. as NAILOR)
OKES, Charles	Lieut. R.N.	In Cmd GUN-BOAT of CADIZ FLOTILLA	
PRESTON, Henry	L.M.	ALFRED	
ROOKE, Frederick.W.	Lieut. R.N.	GIBRALTAR FLOTILLA of GUN-BOATS.	
SHACKLOCK, Edward	Master's Mate	AETNA	
SMITHERS, George	Master's Mate	AETNA*	(Left ship before Action)
SMYTH, William.H.	Midshipman	GUN-BOAT MORS AUT GLORIA	
SOADY, Joseph	Lieut. R.N.	COLOSSUS	
	Lieut. R.N.	SUPERB	Algiers
THOMAS, Thomas	Pte. R.M.	ACHILLE	
	R.M. Boy	ACHILLE	Trafalgar
WALKER, John	Midshipman	NORGE	
	Master's Mate	NORGE	B.S. 14 Dec 1814
WEEDON, John	A.B.	NORGE	
WOOD, John	Pte. R.M.	NORGE	
WILSON, Harry	Midshipman	ALFRED	(Vfd Abd. Not on Roll)
	Midshipman	ALFRED	Guadaloupe
	Lieut. R.N.	BERWICK	Gaieta. 24 July 1815 (Vfd Abd. Not on Roll)

(6) 24 DEC BOAT SERVICE 1810

Destruction of the French frigate ELISA, at La Hogue, East Cotentin peninsular.

BRITTAL, Noah	Pte. R.M.	DIANA	(M.L. as BRITTLE)
	Pte. R.M.	DIANA	Diana. 11 Septr 1809
	Pte. R.M.	ENDYMION	Endymion Wh President
BROWN, Ambrose	Pte. R.M.	DIANA	G.H.3627
	Pte. R.M.	DIANA	Diana. 11 Septr 1809
KNOCKER, John.B.	Master's Mate	DIANA	(171/- Roll as Henry.)
	Midshipman	DIANA	Diana. 11 Septr 1809 (Vfd Abd. Not on Roll)
MAXWELL, William	Vol 1st Cl	DIANA	
	Midshipman	VENERABLE	Venerable. 16 Jan 1814
NEWELL, Julius.J.F.	Midshipman	DIANA	
	Ord	DIANA	Diana. 11 Septr 1809 (Vfd Abd. Not on Roll)
WHITE, George	Ship's Corporal	DIANA	
	Ship's Corporal	DIANA	Diana. 11 Septr 1809 (Vfd Abd. Not on Roll)

(124) LISSA (G.M.)

Action with a Franco-Venetian squadron; capture of the BELLONA and CORONA, and destruction of the FAVORITE, on 13 March 1811, in the Adriatic.

ADAMSON, Orame	Carpenter's Crew	ACTIVE	
	Carpenter's Crew	POWERFUL	Camperdown
	Carpenter's Crew	ACTIVE	Pelagosa. 29 Novr 1811 (Vfd Abd. Not on Roll)
ALBERRY, Samuel	L.M.	CERBERUS	
ALLINGTON, Samuel	Pte. R.M.	ACTIVE	
	Pte. R.M.	ACTIVE	Pelagosa. 29 Novr 1811 (Vfd Abd. Not on Roll)
ANGAS, Jonathan	Surgeon	ACTIVE	
	Surgeon's Asst	AMPHION	B.S. 28 Aug 1809
ATKINSON, Thomas	Carp's Crew	AMPHION	
ATTWELL, Thomas	Pte. R.M.	AMPHION	
	Pte. R.M.	SPARTIATE	Trafalgar
BADSEY, Thomas	Master's Mate	ACTIVE	
	Master's Mate	ACTIVE	Pelagosa. 29 Novr 1811
BAILEY, John	Ord	AMPHION	(M.L. as BAYLEY)
	Ord	AMPHION	B.S. 28 Aug 1809
	Ord	AMPHION	B.S. 28 June 1810
BAKER, John	Carpenter's Crew	AMPHION	
BANKS, Kennett	Master	CERBERUS	
BABTISTE, John or BAPTISTE	A.B.	VOLAGE	(M.L. as BATESTIE)
	French Pilot	DOTTEREL	Basque Roads 1809
BARTLE, Henry	Qtr Gunner	CERBERUS	(M.L. as BARTLETT)

BASSETT, Samuel	L.M.	CERBERUS	
	L.M.	CERBERUS	B.S. 28 June 1810
BLYTH, Francis	Q.M.	AMPHION	
	Capt Forecastle	AMPHION	B.S. 28 Aug 1809
	Capt Forecastle	AMPHION	B.S. 28 June 1810
BOWEN, Richard	Midshipman	ACTIVE	
	Midshipman	ACTIVE	B.S. 28 June 1810
	Midshipman	ACTIVE	Pelagosa. 29 Novr 1811
BRENT, William	Purser	VOLAGE	
BRYANT, John	R.M.Boy	VOLAGE	G.H. 6,248
BUCHANAN, David	Yeoman of Sheets	AMPHION	
	Yeoman of Sheets	AMPHION	B.S. 28 Aug 1809
	Yeoman of Sheets	AMPHION	B.S. 28 June 1810
BURNS, Charles	L.M.	CERBERUS	
BURNS, John	Ord	VOLAGE	(M.L. as BURNE)
BUSHELL, John	L.M.	CERBERUS	
CAMMILLERI, Joseph	A.B.	ACTIVE	
	(Not yet Aboard)	ACTIVE	B.S. 28 June 1810 (On Roll)
	Midshipman	ACTIVE	Pelagosa. 29 Novr 1811
	Master's Mate	SEAHORSE	The Potomac. 17 Aug 1814
	Master's Mate	SEAHORSE	B.S. 14 Dec 1814
CHRISTIE, George	L.M.	AMPHION	GH.8658. (ML. as CHRISTIAN)
	L.M.	AMPHION	B.S. 28 June 1810
			(Vfd Abd. Not on Roll)
CLEMENTS, Richard	A.B.	CERBERUS	
CLIFF, Thomas	Ord	CERBERUS	(M.L. as CLIFT)
COLEMAN, John	Sgt. R.M.	VOLAGE	
COLLINS, John	L.M.	ACTIVE	
	L.M.	ACTIVE	Pelagosa. 29 Novr 1811
CORBET, John	A.B.	ACTIVE	(Roll also as CORBETT)
	A.B.	ACTIVE	Pelagosa. 29 Novr 1811
			(Vfd Abd. Not on Roll)
			G.H. 4,258
CORNELIUS, Robert	Quarter Gunner	AMPHION	
CRILLY, William	A.B.	VOLAGE	(M.L. as CRILLEY)
CROCKER, Richard	Pte. R.M.	VOLAGE	G.H. 7,618
	Pte. R.M.	SUPERB	St Domingo
DAVIES, Evan	Capt After Guard	ACTIVE	G.H.6262 (M.L. as DAVIS)
	Capt After Guard	ACTIVE	B.S. 28 June 1810
			(Vfd Abd. Not on 171/- Roll. On G.H. Roll)
	Capt After Guard	ACTIVE	Pelagosa. 29 Novr 1811
DAVIS, James	Ord	CERBERUS	
DAWSON, John	Quarter Gunner	ACTIVE	
	Quarter Gunner	ACTIVE	Pelagosa. 29 Novr 1811
DAWSON, John	Midshipman Ord	ACTIVE	
DUFF, Norwich	Midshipman	ACTIVE	
	A.B.	MARS	Trafalgar
	Midshipman	ACTIVE	B.S. 28 June 1810
	Midshipman	ACTIVE	Pelagosa. 29 Novr 1811
DUNN, David	Lieut. R.N.	AMPHION (P)	
	Master's Mate	DONEGAL	St Domingo
	Captain R.N.	VANGUARD	Syria
EDWARDS, Edward	A.B.	AMPHION	
	Boy 2nd Cl	AGINCOURT	Camperdown
ELVIN, William	L.M.	ACTIVE	
	L.M.	ACTIVE	Pelagosa. 29 Novr 1811
EVERARD, George	Capt Main Top	ACTIVE	
	Capt Main Top	ACTIVE	Pelagosa. 29 Novr 1811
FIELDING, Thomas	Pte. R.M.	AMPHION	
FITZMAURICE, Edmund.H.	Master's Mate	VOLAGE	
FRIEND, Charles	Master's Mate	ACTIVE	
	Midshipman	ACTIVE	B.S. 28 June 1810
	Master's Mate	ACTIVE	Pelagosa. 29 Novr 1811
GLEESON, William	Gunner	VOLAGE	
GOLDING, Edward	Q.M's Mate	AMPHION	
GOODE, Sephas	Midshipman	CERBERUS	
GORDON, Abraham	Pte. R.M.	CERBERUS	GH.5223 (M.L. as GARDNER)
GORDON, James.A.	Captain. R.N.	ACTIVE	
	Midshipman	REVOLUTIONNAIRE	23rd June 1795
	Midshipman	NAMUR	St Vincent
	Midshipman	GOLIATH	Nile
	Captain. R.N.	MERCURY	Off Rota. 4 April 1808
	Captain. R.N.	ACTIVE	Pelagosa. 29 Novr 1811
	Captain. R.N.	SEAHORSE	The Potomac. 17 Aug 1814
GREVILLE, Henry.F.	Midshipman	VOLAGE	
HALL, John (2)	Q.M.	CERBERUS	

LISSA

HAWKES, John	Pte. R.M.	ACTIVE	
	Pte. R.M.	ACTIVE	B.S. 28 June 1810
	Pte. R.M.	ACTIVE	Pelagosa. 29 Novr 1811
HAYE, George	Lieut. R.N.	ACTIVE	
	Lieut. R.N.	ACTIVE	Pelagosa. 29 Novr 1811
HAYS, William	Carpenter	AMPHION	
HENDERSON, William.W.	Lieut. R.N.	ACTIVE (P)	
	Midshipman	BELLEISLE	*Trafalgar*
	Lieut. R.N.	ACTIVE	*B.S. 28 June 1810*
	Captain. R.N.	EDINBURGH	*Syria*
HEWITT, John Henry	Pte. R.M.	ACTIVE	*(M.L. as HEWITT, Henry.J.)*
	Pte. R.M.	ACTIVE	*B.S. 28 June 1810*
	Pte. R.M.	ACTIVE	*Pelagosa. 29 Novr 1811*
HICKEY, Cornelius	Ord	CERBERUS	
HILL, John	Two borne. Ord & Qtr Gunner	ACTIVE	
	" " " "	ACTIVE	*Pelagosa. 29 Novr 1811 (Vfd Abd. Not on Roll)*
HILL, Samuel	Boy 3rd Cl	ACTIVE	
	Boy 3rd Cl	ACTIVE	*Pelagosa. 29 Novr 1811 (Vfd Abd. Not on Roll)*
HORNBY, Phipps.	Captain. R.N.	VOLAGE	
HORROCK, David	Pte. R.M.	AMPHION	*(M.L. as ARROCK)*
HUGHES, Thomas	A.B.	ACTIVE	
	A.B.	ACTIVE	*Pelagosa. 29 Novr 1811*
JOHNSON, Thomas	Coxswain	ACTIVE	*(M.L. as JOHNSTON)*
	Coxswain	ACTIVE	*Pelagosa. 29 Novr 1811 (Vfd Abd. Not on Roll)*
JONES, William	Boy 2nd Cl	ACTIVE	
	Boy 2nd Cl	ACTIVE	*Pelagosa. 29 Novr 1811*
JUSTICE, Thomas	A.B.	ACTIVE	*G.H.7005.*
	A.B.	ACTIVE	*Pelagosa. 29 Novr 1811 (Vfd Abd. Not on Roll)*
KAY, James	Asst Surgeon	ACTIVE	
	Asst Surgeon	ACTIVE	*Pelagosa. 29 Novr 1811*
KEMPTHORN, Charles.H.	Midshipman	AMPHION	
	Midshipman	AMPHION	*B.S. 28 Aug 1809*
KENNY, Nathaniel	Q.M.	CERBERUS	
KINGSTONE, Robert	Midshipman	ACTIVE	
KNAPMAN, William.S.	1st Lieut. R.M.	VOLAGE	
LAMMING, John	Ord	CERBERUS	
	Ord	CERBERUS	*B.S. 28 June 1810*
LANGTON, Thomas.W.	Midshipman	AMPHION	
	Midshipman	BACCHANTE	*B.S. 1 & 18 Sep 1812*
LEAR, William	Gunner's Mate	AMPHION	
LONG, Charles	A.B.	ACTIVE	*G.H. 7,057*
	A.B.	ACTIVE	*Pelagosa. 29 Novr 1811 (Vfd Abd. Not on Roll)*
MACKENZIE, Nathaniel	L.M.	ACTIVE	
	L.M.	ACTIVE	*Pelagosa. 29 Novr 1811 (Vfd Abd. Not on Roll)*
MACKLIN, Joseph	A.B.	ACTIVE	
	Capt Fore Top	ACTIVE	*Pelagosa. 29 Novr 1811 (Vfd Abd. Not on Roll)*
MARSH, Samuel	Capt Forecastle	VOLAGE	
MARSHALL, Edward.O or C.	Boy	AMPHION	*(Not yet found)*
MARTIN, John	Purser	AMPHION	
MASON, William	Ord	AMPHION	
McCULLOCH, Allan	Ord	AMPHION	
McDONALD, John	A.B.	AMPHION	
McINTYRE, James	Carp's Crew	VOLAGE	
MEARES, John	2nd Lt. R.M.	ACTIVE	
	2nd Lt. R.M.	ACTIVE	*B.S. 28 June 1810*
	2nd Lt. R.M.	ACTIVE	*Pelagosa. 29 Novr 1811*
MELHUISH, G.	Pte. R.M.	VOLAGE	*(M.L. as John.)*
MILFORD, William	Boy 3rd Cl	ACTIVE	
	Boy 3rd Cl	ACTIVE	*Pelagosa. 29 Novr 1811*
MILFORD, William	L.M.	CERBERUS	
	L.M.	IMPREGNABLE	*Algiers*
MILLER, Samuel	Ord	AMPHION	
MILLS, Robert	Ord	ACTIVE	
	Ord	ACTIVE	*Pelagosa. 29 Novr 1811*
MOFFATT, John	Actg Lieut. R.N.	CERBERUS (P)	
MOORE, Thomas	1st Lt. R.M.	AMPHION	
	1st Lt. R.M.	AMPHION	*B.S. 28 Aug 1809*
	1st Lt. R.M.	AMPHION	*B.S. 28 June 1810*
NUTTER, Ellis	Pte. R.M.	CERBERUS	

O'BRIEN, Donat.H.	Lieut. R.N.	AMPHION	
	Lieut. R.N.	AMPHION	B.S. 28 June 1810
	Lieut. R.N.	BACCHANTE (P)	B.S. 1 & 18 Sep 1812
	Lieut. R.N.	BACCHANTE	B.S. 6 Jan 1813
PARKER, John	Two Borne. Q.M.& Carp's Crew	ACTIVE	
PARRATT, Samuel	Ord	ACTIVE	G.H. 2,567
	Ord	ACTIVE	Pelagosa. 29 Novr 1811
PENGELLY, Robert.L.	Vol 1st Cl	VOLAGE	
PENTON, James	Capt Forecastle	CERBERUS	
PETERS, William	Boy 2nd Cl	AMPHION	
PHILMORE, Richard	Boy 2nd Cl	VOLAGE	
READ, Robert	Ord	AMPHION	
REEDER, John	Actg Gunner	AMPHION	
	A.B.	TERMAGENT	Egypt
RENNIE, James	Master's Mate	CERBERUS	
RISHEN, William	L.M.	CERBERUS	
	A.B.	CAMBRIAN	Navarino
ROLLIER, Louis	Midshipman Ord	CERBERUS	
ROSS, Charles.H.	Actg Lieut. R.N.	AMPHION	
	Midshipman	AMPHION	B.S. 28 Aug 1809
	Master's Mate	AMPHION	B.S. 28 June 1810
SANDEMAN, Charles	Pte. R.M.	AMPHION	
SANTULLO, Francis	Pte. R.M.	AMPHION	G.H. 7,734
SCANNELL, David	Cooper	AMPHION	
SEARLES, William.G.	Gunner	ACTIVE	
	Gunner	ACTIVE	Pelagosa. 29 Novr 1811
SHERWOOD, William	Midshipman	CERBERUS	
	Vol 1st Cl	CERBERUS	B.S. 25 July 1809
	Midshipman	CERBERUS	B.S. 28 June 1810
SPARKES. John	Pte. R.M.	ACTIVE	(M.L. as SPARKS)
	Pte. R.M.	ACTIVE	B.S. 28 June 1810
	Pte. R.M.	ACTIVE	Pelagosa. 29 Novr 1811
STAMER, Lovelace	L.M.	CERBERUS	"Run 25-11-1811". Later removed.
	L.M.	CERBERUS	B.S. 28 June 1810. (See note)
STOKES, Joseph	Cpl. R.M.	ACTIVE	
	Cpl. R.M.	ACTIVE	B.S. 28 June 1810
	Cpl. R.M.	ACTIVE	Pelagosa. 29 Novr 1811
			(Vfd Abd. Not on Roll)
SULLIVAN, Dennis	Pte. R.M.	ACTIVE	
	Pte. R.M.	ACTIVE	Pelagosa. 29 Novr 1811
SWAYNE, Stephen.J.	Surgeon	VOLAGE	
	Surgeon	ACTIVE	Pelagosa. 29 Novr 1811
	Surgeon	SEAHORSE	The Potomac. 17 Aug 1814
			(Vfd Abd. Not on Roll)
	Surgeon	SEAHORSE	B.S. 14 Dec 1814
TAYLOR, James	L.M.	ACTIVE	
	L.M.	ACTIVE	Pelagosa. 29 Novr 1811
TUCKEY, William	L.M.	ACTIVE	
	L.M.	ACTIVE	Pelagosa. 29 Novr 1811
	Blacksmith	BELLEROPHON	Syria
VALENTINE, David	Pte. R.M.	CERBERUS	
WATERHOUSE, William	L.M.	ACTIVE	
	L.M.	ACTIVE	Pelagosa. 29 Novr 1811
WESTON, George	Pte. R.M.	AMPHION	
	Pte. R.M.	AMPHION	B.S. 28 Aug 1809
	Pte. R.M.	AMPHION	B.S. 28 June 1810
WHISKER, William	L.M.	AMPHION	
	L.M.	AMPHION	B.S. 28 Aug 1809
	L.M.	AMPHION	B.S. 28 June 1810
	A.B.	BACCHANTE	B.S. 1 & 18 Sep 1812
WILSON, Thomas	Drummer. R.M.	CERBERUS	
WOLRIGE, William	Lieut. R.N.	VOLAGE (P)	
	Midshipman	CAESAR	4 Novr 1805
WOODS, Thomas	Vol 1st Cl	ACTIVE	
	Midshipman	ACTIVE	Pelagosa. 29 Novr 1811
	Midshipman	SEAHORSE	The Potomac. 17 Aug 1814
	Midshipman	SEAHORSE	B.S. 14 Dec 1814
	Supn Master's Mate	IMPREGNABLE	Algiers
WORSLEY, Marcus	Midshipman	VOLAGE	

(40) ## ANHOLT 27 MARCH 1811

Repulse of the Danish attack on the Island of ANHOLT.
(The Island was commissioned as one of H.M.Ships. See Adm 37/3513. The only clasp known which stems partially from the promotion of Royal Marine Officers.)

Name	Rank	Ship	Notes
ANDREWS, Charles	Pte. R.M.	"ANHOLT"	
BAKER, Henry.L.	Lieut. R.N.	"ANHOLT" (P)	Second in Command of Island.
BAYLEY, James	Pte. R.M.	"ANHOLT"	G.H. 2,991
BEZANT, John	1st Lt. R.M.A.	"ANHOLT"	
	1st Lt. R.M.A.	THUNDER	Basque Roads 1809
BROOKS, James	Pte. R.M.	"ANHOLT"	
BROWN, Thomas	Pte. R.M.	"ANHOLT"	G.H. 3,349
CLEAL, James	Pte. R.M.	"ANHOLT"	G.H. 7,562
DAVIES, Richard	A.B.	"ANHOLT"	G.H. 10,132
DONOVAN, Thomas	Pte. R.M.	"ANHOLT"	
FISCHER, John.N.	1st Lt. R.M.	"ANHOLT" (P)	
	1st Lt. R.M.	CONQUEROR	Trafalgar
FORD, William	1st Lt. R.M.	"ANHOLT"	(Vfd Abd. Not on Roll)
FRY, Robert	Pte. R.M.	"ANHOLT"	(M.L. as PRY @ FRY)
	Pte. R.M.	IMPLACABLE	Implacable. 26 Augt 1808
GRAY, Thomas	Actg Surgeon	"ANHOLT"	
GREAVES, Edward	Pte. R.M.	"ANHOLT"	
GROVER, George	Pte. R.M.	"ANHOLT"	
HALL, Stephen	Pte. R.M.	"ANHOLT"	
HARDY, John	Pte. R.M.	"ANHOLT"	(Not yet found on M.L.)
HAYMER, James	Pte. R.M.	"ANHOLT"	(M.L. as HAMER)
JELLICOE, Richard	1st Lt. R.M.	"ANHOLT"	
JOHNS, John	Pte. R.M.	"ANHOLT"	
JONES, Daniel	Sgt. R.M.A.	"ANHOLT"	
	Pte. R.M.	PRINCE GEORGE	St Vincent
KING, Thomas	Pte. R.M.	"ANHOLT"	G.H. 2,366
LUCKCRAFT, William	Lieut. R.N.	SHELDRAKE	
	Commander	BELLEROPHON	Syria
MAURICE, James.W.	Captain. R.N.	"ANHOLT"	C.O. and Governor of Island. (Previously as a Lt. R.N. he commanded another Island, – H.M.S. DIAMOND ROCK)
MOSS, Charles	Midshipman	SHELDRAKE	
MEAR, William	Pte. R.M.	"ANHOLT"	(M.L. as MEARS)
	Pte. R.M.	IMPLACABLE	Implacable. 26 Augt 1808
PERFERRY, John	Gnr. R.M.A.	"ANHOLT"	(M.L. as PERRY)
	Gnr. R.M.A.	AETNA	Basque Roads 1809
PRICE, Edward	Pte. R.M.	"ANHOLT"	
RIDDEFORD, Arthur	Pte. R.M.	"ANHOLT"	
	Pte. R.M.	MINDEN	Algiers
SANDERS, Charles	Pte. R.M.	"ANHOLT"	(M.L. as SAUNDERS)
SEXSMITH, Thomas	Pte. R.M.	"ANHOLT"	
SHORE, Thomas	Pte. R.M.	"ANHOLT"	
STEWART, Edward.H.	1st Lt. R.M.	"ANHOLT"	
STEWART, James.R.	Commander	SHELDRAKE	
	Lieut. R.N.	NORTHUMBERLAND	St Domingo
	Captain. R.N.	DICTATOR	Off Mardoe. 6 July 1812
SULLIVAN, Florence	Pte. R.M.	"ANHOLT"	G.H. 9,372
TORRENS, Robert	Captain. R.M.	"ANHOLT" (P)	
TUBBY, Benjamin	Pte. R.M.	"ANHOLT"	(Vfd Abd. Only G.H. Roll)
	Pte. R.M.	RAMILLIES	B.S. 14 Dec 1814. GH. 3157
WEEKES, Sampson	Cpl. R.M.A.	"ANHOLT"	
WITHERSBY, William	Pte. R.M.	"ANHOLT"	(M.L. as WEATHERSBY) G.H. 3750
WARD, Henry	Pte. R.M.	"ANHOLT"	
	Pte. R.M.	ORION	Trafalgar
	Pte. R.M.	HEBRUS	Hebrus with L'Etoile

No applicants. ## ARROW 6 APRIL 1811

Action with batteries and capture of FREDERICK and PAIX DESIREE — chasse-marees, off the coast of France.
(Real date 30 March 1811)

(10) 4 MAY BOAT SERVICE 1811

Destruction of a French brig of war at PORTO di PARENZO, off Istria, Adriatic.

(Real date 5 May 1811)

BEILLY, George	A.B.	BELLE POULE	G.H. 3070 (M.L. as BAILEY)
BOARDMAN, Robert.B.	Lieut. R.N.	BELLE POULE	
BOWDEN, James	2 Ptes R.M. borne	BELLE POULE	
CHAPMAN, Charles.M.	Midshipman	BELLE POULE	
CROKER, Charles	Midshipman	ALCESTE	
	Midshipman	ALCESTE	Pelagosa. 29 Novr 1811
GROSE, Arthur	A.B.	BELLE POULE	
KING, John	Midshipman	ALCESTE	
	Midshipman	ALCESTE	Pelagosa. 29 Novr 1811
ROWCLIFFE, George	Ord	BELLE POULE	
STANBURY, Peter	L.M.	ALCESTE	
	L.M.	ALCESTE	Pelagosa. 29 Novr 1811
WOODWARD, Robert	Pte. R.M.	BELLE POULE	
	Pte. R.M.	BERWICK	Gaieta. 24 July 1815

(87) OFF TAMATAVE 20 MAY 1811

Action with three French frigates, capture of RENOMMEE and surrender of NEREIDE, off East coast of Madagascar.

ALLEN, Daniel	Ord	RACEHORSE	
ANDREWS, James	Carpenter	PHOEBE	
	Carpenter	PHOEBE	Java
BAILEY, Samuel	Surgeon	ASTRAEA	
BAKER, William	Cpl. R.M.	ASTRAEA	
BARTON, Richard	Ord	PHOEBE	
	Ord	PHOEBE	Java
	Ord	PHOEBE	Phoebe. 28 March 1814
BEECHEY, Frederick.W.	Midshipman	ASTRAEA	
BEECHIN, Michael	Ord	PHOEBE	(Vfd Abd. Not on Roll)
	Ord	PHOEBE	Java
	Ord	PHOEBE	Phoebe. 28 March 1814
BEVIS, Thomas	Lieut. R.N.	GALATEA	
	A.B.	OTTER	Copenhagen 1801
BILL or BULL, Charles	Sgt. R.M.	ASTRAEA	
BOWDEN, James	Ord	PHOEBE	(Vfd Abd. Not on Roll)
	Ord	PHOEBE	Trafalgar
	Ord	PHOEBE	Java
	Ord	PHOEBE	Phoebe. 28 March 1814
			(Vfd Abd. Not on Roll)
CALDER, John	Ord	RACEHORSE	
CAMPBELL, John.N.	Lieut. R.N.	ASTRAEA	
	Commander	ALBION	Navarino (see notes)
CLIFFORD, William	Surgeon	RACEHORSE	
COCKBURN, John	Ord	PHOEBE	
	Ord	PHOEBE	Java
CONDON, Patrick	Boy 3rd Cl	PHOEBE	(Vfd Abd. Not on Roll)
	Boy 3rd Cl	PHOEBE	Java
	Boy 3rd Cl	PHOEBE	Phoebe. 28 March 1814
COOK, William	L.M.	PHOEBE	(Vfd Abd. Not on Roll)
	L.M.	PHOEBE	Java
	Ord	PHOEBE	Phoebe. 28 March 1814
COX, John	Pte. R.M.	PHOEBE	
	Pte. R.M.	PHOEBE	Java
CRESER, Thomas	Vol 1st Cl	GALATEA	
	Vol 1st Cl	FREIJA	Guadaloupe
CRETCH, Daniel	Ord	PHOEBE	(M.L. as CRUTCH)
	Boy 2nd Cl	PHOEBE	Trafalgar
	Ord	PHOEBE	Java
	A.B.	PHOEBE	Phoebe. 28 March 1814
DANIEL, John	A.B.	ASTRAEA	
	A.B.	POMPEE	Martinique
	A.B.	POMPEE	Pompee. 17 June 1809
			(Vfd Abd. Not on Roll)
	A.B.	POMPEE	Guadaloupe
DOUGLAS, Henry	Midshipman	ASTRAEA	
DUCKHAM, George	L.M.	PHOEBE	(Vfd Abd. Not on Roll)
	A.B.	PHOEBE	Java
	Ord	PHOEBE	Phoebe. 28 March 1814
			(Vfd Abd. Not on Roll)
DUNN, Michael	Pte. R.M.	ASTRAEA	(M.L. as DUNNE)
EDWARDS, John.Thomas.	A.B.	ASTRAEA	(M.L. as EDWARDS, Thomas)

OFF TAMATAVE 20 MAY 1811

FIELDHOUSE, George	Pte. R.M.	PHOEBE	
	Pte. R.M.	PHOEBE	*Java*
	Pte. R.M.	PHOEBE	*Phoebe. 28 March 1814*
			(Vfd Abd. Not on Roll)
FITZGERALD, John	Ord	PHOEBE	
	Boy 2nd Cl	PHOEBE	*Trafalgar*
	Ord	PHOEBE	*Java*
	A.B.	PHOEBE	*Phoebe. 28 March 1814*
FOLCUS, Thomas	Supn. L.M.	ASTRAEA	
FORSTER, John	Lieut. R.N.	GALATEA	
	Vol 1st Cl	MONARCH	*Copenhagen 1801*
GEDDES, John	Vol 1st Cl	ASTRAEA	
GORDON, Robert	Vol 1st Cl	PHOEBE	
	Midshipman	PHOEBE	*Java*
	Actg Lt. R.N.	Qn CHARLOTTE	*Algiers*
GRAHAM, George	Pte. R.M.	RACEHORSE	
GRAY, James	A.B.	ASTRAEA	
GREEN, William	Ord	GALATEA	
HALE, William	Boatswain	GALATEA	
HASWELL, John.S.	1st Lt. R.M.	PHOEBE	
	1st Lt. R.M.	PHOEBE	*Java*
HENNING, Alexander	Midshipman	GALATEA	
	Midshipman	CHRISTIAN VII	*B.S. 13 Feb 1810*
HEWITT, Thomas	L.M.	PHOEBE	
HOPE, Andrew.J.	Boy 3rd Cl	PHOEBE	
	Boy 3rd Cl	PHOEBE	*Java*
	L.M.	PHOEBE	*Phoebe. 28 March 1814*
JENKINS, Thomas	Ord	GALATEA	
JEYES, John	Vol 1st Cl	GALATEA	*(M.L. as JAYES)*
KELLY, Edward	Vol 1st Cl	GALATEA	
KINDNESS, Benjamin	Ord	PHOEBE	*(Vfd Abd. Not on Roll)*
	Boy 2nd Cl	PHOEBE	*Trafalgar*
	Ord	PHOEBE	*Java*
	Ord	PHOEBE	*Phoebe. 28 March 1814*
			(Vfd Abd. Not on Roll)
	Q.M.	ALBION	*Navarino*
KNIGHT, Charles	Midshipman	ASTRAEA	
KNIGHT, Christopher	Midshipman	ASTRAEA	
	Lieut. R.N.	IMPREGNABLE	
KNIGHT, John	A.B.	GALATEA	
LAKE, William	Armourer	ASTRAEA	
LASBURY, Thomas	Pte. R.M.	RACEHORSE	*(M.L. as LASHBURY)*
	Pte. R.M.	ORION	*Trafalgar*
LAURIE, Stephen	A.B.	PHOEBE	
	Boy 3rd Cl	PHOEBE	*Phoebe. 21 Decr 1797*
	Boy 2nd Cl	PHOEBE	*Phoebe. 19 Feby 1801*
	A.B.	PHOEBE	*Trafalgar*
	A.B.	PHOEBE	*Java*
	Capt Fore Top	PHOEBE	*Phoebe. 28 March 1814*
LEWIS, Henry	2nd Lt. R.M.	ASTRAEA	
LOVELESS, Robert	L.M.	GALATEA	
MANNING, Joseph	L.M.	PHOEBE	
	L.M.	PHOEBE	*Java*
	Ord	PHOEBE	*Phoebe. 28 March 1814*
MAYBEE, Henry	A.B.	RACEHORSE	*(M.L. as MABEY)*
McGEE, Christopher	L.M.	RACEHORSE	*(M.L. as MAGEE)*
MACGILLEN, Hugh	L.M.	RACEHORSE	*(M.L. as McGILLAN)*
M'KILLOP, John	Master's Mate	ASTRAEA	
	Vol 1st Cl	LOIRE	*B.S. 4 June 1805*
	Volt per Order	EMERALD	*Emerald. 13 March 1808*
MEARS, George	Q.M.	RACEHORSE	
MILLERY, Thomas	Actg Sailmaker	PHOEBE	
	Actg Sailmaker	PHOEBE	*Java*
	Sailmaker	PHOEBE	*Phoebe. 28 March 1814*
MORGAN, William	Pte. R.M.	PHOEBE	*G.H. 9,765*
	Cpl. R.M.	PHOEBE	*Phoebe. 28 March 1814*
	(Pte. R.M.)	(PHOEBE)	*(M.G.S. with JAVA Clasp)*
NICHOLS, Thomas.G.	Actg Lt. R.N.	RACEHORSE	
PARKIN, Thomas	Pte. R.M.	ASTRAEA	
PASCOE, Richard.W.	2nd Lt. R.M.	PHOEBE	
	Captain. R.M.	IMPLACABLE	*Syria*
	(2nd Lt. R.M.)	(PHOEBE)	*(M.G.S. with JAVA Clasp)*
PITTS, Edward	Midshipman	GALATEA	
RABETT, George.W.	Boy 3rd Cl	GALATEA	
	Midshipman	CYDNUS	*B.S. 14 Dec 1814*
	Lieut. R.N.	MUSQUITO	*Navarino*

REARDON, Patrick	L.M.	ASTRAEA	
	L.M.	AMETHYST	*Amethyst Wh Thetis*
	L.M.	AMETHYST	*Amethyst. 5 April 1809*
REED, Nehemiah.J.	Midshipman	ASTRAEA	
RICE, Henry	Lieut. R.N.	PHOEBE	
	Lieut. R.N.	PHOEBE	*Java*
RICHARDSON, George	Supn Boy	ASTRAEA	
ROBERTS, John	Boy 2nd Cl	PHOEBE	
	Boy 2nd Cl	PHOEBE	*Java*
ROBINSON, James	A.B.	PHOEBE	
	A.B.	PHOEBE	*Trafalgar*
	A.B.	PHOEBE	*Java*
	A.B.	PHOEBE	*Phoebe. 28 March 1814*
ROSS, Robert	A.B.	GALATEA	
ROYER, Charles	Lieut. R.N.	ASTRAEA	*(Vfd Abd. Not on Roll)*
	A.B.	SWIFTSURE	*Nile*
	Midshipman	SWIFTSURE	*Egypt*
SCOTT, George	Lieut. R.N.	PHOEBE	
	Master's Mate	MINOTAUR	*Egypt*
	Lieut. R.N.	PHOEBE	*Java*
SIMMONS, Edward	Lieut. R.N.	GALATEA	
	Midshipman	MINOTAUR	*Trafalgar*
	Midshipman	ETHALION	*Martinique*
SLYMAN, Daniel	Midshipman	GALATEA	*(On Roll in error on ADM 171/2/44)*
SMITH, James	Boy 3rd Cl	ASTRAEA	
SNOOKE, George	Caulker	ASTRAEA	
SOMERVILLE, Lord Kenelm	Lieut. R.N.	PHOEBE	
	Lieut. R.N.	PHOEBE	*Java*
SPARKS, John	L.M.	PHOEBE	
	L.M.	PHOEBE	*Java*
	L.M.	PHOEBE	*Phoebe. 28 March 1814*
			(Vfd Abd. Not on Roll)
TATTNALL, James.B.	Lieut. R.N.	RACEHORSE	*(Vfd Abd. Not on Roll)*
	Lieut. R.N.	PRESIDENT	*St Sebastian*
	Lieut. R.N.	TONNANT	*B.S. 14 Dec 1814*
TAYLOR, George.R.	Midshipman	ASTRAEA	*(Roll as TAYLER – wrong)*
THOMPSON, Thomas.S.	Boy 2nd Cl	GALATEA	
VINCENT, Thomas	Sgt. R.M.	RACEHORSE	
WADSWORTH, Elijah	Pte. R.M.	GALATEA	
WHITE, James	Pte. R.M.	ASTRAEA	
WILLIAMS, Henry	Midshipman	GALATEA	
WILSON, David	Ord	PHOEBE	*(Vfd Abd. Not on Roll)*
	A.B.	PHOEBE	*Trafalgar*
	Ord	PHOEBE	*Java*
YATES, George	Boy 2nd Cl	PHOEBE	*(M.L. as YEATES)*
	L.M.	PHOEBE	*Java*
	Ord	PHOEBE	*Phoebe 28 March 1814*

(4) 30 JULY BOAT SERVICE 1811
Capture of Fort Marrack, JAVA.

ELLMORE, William	Quarter Gunner	MINDEN	
	Quarter Gunner	MINDEN	*Java*
			(Vfd Abd. Not on Roll)
LYONS, Edmund	Lieut. R.N.	MINDEN	
	Lieut. R.N.	BARRACOUTA	*Banda Neira*
	Lieut. R.N.	MINDEN	*Java*
ROBERTS, Stephen	A.B.	MINDEN	
	A.B.	MINDEN	*Java*
SCOTT, William	A.B.	MINDEN	
	A.B.	MINDEN	*Java*

(9) 2 AUG BOAT SERVICE 1811

Capture of four French gun-boats at NORDENEY, North Germany.
(Real date 3 August 1811)

CLARK, William	Carpenter's Crew	RAVEN	
COCK, Robert	Master's Mate	QUEBEC	
	Midshipman	THUNDERER	*Trafalgar*
	Master's Mate	AURORA	*Guadaloupe*
HARE, Thomas	Sub Lieut. R.N.	EXERTION	
HAWKINS, Benjamin	L.M.	QUEBEC	
RUSSELL, William	A.B.	PRINCESS AUGUSTA	(Not found on Muster list ADM 37/2962)
SMITH, John	Pte. R.M.	ALERT	
TATE, John	Pte. R.M.	QUEBEC	(M.L. as TAIT)
WOLRIGE, Charles	Lieut. R.N.	QUEBEC	
	Midshipman	MINOTAUR	*Trafalgar*
WRIGHT, Edmund @ E. RICHMOND (Roll)	A.B.	PRINCESS AUGUSTA	(Not found on Muster list ADM 37/2962)

(6) HAWKE 18 AUGT 1811

Capture of the French corvette HERON and three vessels of a convoy, off Barfleur, Cherbourg.

BOURCHIER, Henry	Commander	HAWKE	
	Midshipman	VETERAN	*Copenhagen 1801*
KEADY, John	Ord	HAWKE	
LANGWORTHY, John	Midshipman	HAWKE	
MONTIETH, John	Carpenter's Crew	HAWKE	
PERKIS, William	Ord	HAWKE	
PRICE, David	Lieut. R.N.	HAWKE	
	Vol 1st Cl	ARDENT	*Copenhagen 1801*
	Midshipman	CENTAUR	*Centaur 26 Augt 1808*

(665) JAVA

Capture of JAVA, for which a medal was bestowed on the Army, for Action from July until surrender on 18 September 1811.

(Captain George SAYER R.N. was awarded the (Military) Field Officer's Gold Medal — the only naval officer who received it at any time. Captain Richard BUNCE R.M. also received the Field Officer's Gold Medal, being the only Royal Marine Officer so distinguished.)

ABLE, James	A.B.	SCIPION	G.H. 3144 as ABEL
ADAMS, Peter	Quarter Gunner	MINDEN	
ADDIS, Edward.B.	Lieutenant. R.N.	Sir FRANCIS DRAKE	
ADDISON, Dominic	A.B.	NISUS	
	A.B.	ROYAL SOVEREIGN	*Trafalgar*
AINSLIE, Thomas	Gunner's Mate	CORNELIA	
	Ord	BRITANNIA	*St Vincent*
	A.B.	GOLIATH	*Nile*
AKEN, James	A.B.	PHAETON	
ALCOCK, John	A.B.	ILLUSTRIOUS	
ALFORD, Robert	Corporal. R.M.	MODESTE	
	Sergeant. R.M.	GLASGOW	*Navarino*
ALLEN, John	Landsman	PROCRIS	
ALLEN, Thomas	Boy 2nd Class	BARRACOUTA	
	Boy 3rd Class	BARRACOUTA	*Banda Neira (9 Augt 1810)*
ALLEN, William	Lieut. R.M.	LEDA	
ALLEN, William.E.H.	Lieutenant. R.N.	AKBAR	
	Midshipman	TEMERAIRE	*Trafalgar*
ANDERSON, John	Carp's Crew	PHAETON	
ANDOE, James.H.	Master's Mate	MINDEN	
ANDREWS, Charles	Ord	PHAETON	G.H. 7983
ANDREWS, James	Carpenter	PHAETON	
ANDREWS, James	Carpenter	PHOEBE	
	Carpenter	PHOEBE	*Off Tamatave. 20 May 1811*
ANDREWS, John	Capt' Fore Top	MODESTE	
APPLEBY, John	Ord	MODESTE	
APPLEGATE, William	Ship's Corporal	CAROLINE	
	Ship's Corporal	CAROLINE	*Banda Neira*
ARCHER, Alexander	Capt's Cook	HUSSAR	G.H. 7850
ARLE, James	A.B.	AKBAR	G.H. 9577
ARNOTT, James	Ord	BUCEPHALUS	
ASPINALL, James	A.B.	CORNELIA	
ATALETT, William	A.B.	NISUS	
AUSTIN, William	Ord	CAROLINE	
	Ord	CAROLINE	*Banda Neira*
AVERY, John	Pte. R.M.	SCIPION	

BABBIDGE, John	A.B.	ILLUSTRIOUS	
	A.B.	ILLUSTRIOUS	Basque Roads 1809
BAILEY, John	Actg Boatswain	AKBAR	
BAILEY, John	Sailmaker	SAMARANG	
BAILEY, Joseph	A.B.	ILLUSTRIOUS	
	A.B.	STATELY	Stately. 22 March 1808
	A.B.	ILLUSTRIOUS	Basque Roads. 1809
BAILEY, Walter	Ord	SCIPION	
	Landsman	ACASTA	St Domingo
	Ord	ACASTA	Martinique
BAILEY, William	Master's Mate	LION	
BAIN, Henderson	Commander	HARPY	
	Lieutenant. R.N.	SPENCER	St Domingo
BAKER, George	A.B.	MINDEN	
BALL, Thomas	Qtr Gunner	PSYCHE	
BALLINGER, Thomas	Pte. R.M.	MINDEN	
(BANISTER, Henry)	(A.B.)	(ILLUSTRIOUS)	Received M.G.S. Medal
BARKER, Joseph	Landsman	LEDA	
BARNES, John	Ord	PSYCHE	
BARRINGTON, Mark	Landsman	AKBAR	
BARTLETT, Benjamin	Qtr Gunner	Sir FRANCIS DRAKE	G.H. 2907
BARTON, Richard	Ord	PHOEBE	
	Ord	PHOEBE	Off Tamatave. 20 May 1811
	Ord	PHOEBE	Phoebe. 28 March 1814
BARTON, Amos	Pte. R.M.	HUSSAR	
BAXTER, William	Ord	PROCRIS	
BEAL, John	Clerk	HECATE	
BEALES, Robert	Pte. R.M.	HUSSAR	(BEALS on known medal)
BEAN, William	Bosun's Mate	HARPY	
BEASLEY, Thomas	Ord	CORNELIA	
BEAZLEY, John	Landsman	PROCRIS	
BEECHIN, Michael	Ord	PHOEBE	
	Ord	PHOEBE	Off Tamatave. 20 May 1811 (Vfd Abd. Not on Roll) Phoebe. 28 MARCH 1814
	Ord	PHOEBE	
BENNETT, Thomas	Landsman	ILLUSTRIOUS	
BIGGINS, James	Pte. R.M.	NISUS	
BILLINGER, Edward	Ord	MINDEN	
(BIRTLES, Thomas)	(Landsman)	(SCIPION)	Received M.G.S. Medal
BISHOP, Joseph	A.B.	LEDA	
BISHOP, William	Ord	SCIPION	G.H. 10,103
BLADES, James	Ship's Corporal	PHAETON	
BLAND, Richard	A.B.	ILLUSTRIOUS	G.H. 9111 (alias GRIFFITHS)
BLATCHLEY, Edward	Drummer. R.M.	SCIPION	
BLYTH, Charles	Midshipman	SCIPION	
	A.B.	INDEFATIGABLE	Basque Roads. 1809
	Midshipman	PRESIDENT	St Sebastian
BOND, Philip	Master's Mate	Sir FRANCIS DRAKE	
BONNER, Thomas	Ord	PSYCHE	
BOON, John	A.B.	SCIPION	
	Ord	CANADA	12 Octr 1798
	A.B.	ACASTA	St Domingo
	A.B.	GRANICUS	Algiers
BOSTON, William	A.B.	ILLUSTRIOUS	
BOUKESS, Matthew	Pte. R.M.	ILLUSTRIOUS	
	Pte. R.M.	ILLUSTRIOUS	Basque Roads. 1809 (BOUKAS)
BOUND, William	A.B.	NISUS	
	A.B.	REGULUS	Egypt
	A.B.	ROYAL SOVEREIGN	Trafalgar
	A.B.	Qn CHARLOTTE	Algiers
BOWDEN, James	Ord	PHOEBE	
	Ord	PHOEBE	Trafalgar
	Ord	PHOEBE	Off Tamatave. 20 May 1811 (Vfd Abd. Not on Roll)
	Quarter Gunner	PHOEBE	Phoebe. 28 March 1814 (Vfd Abd. Not on Roll)
BOWLING, John	A.B.	PHAETON	
BOWMAN, John	Caulker	PSYCHE	
BRADLEY, Richard	Pte. R.M.	NISUS	
BRAWLEY, James	Landsman	PRESIDENT	
	Landsman	PRESIDENT	St Sebastian
BRAY, William	Boy 3rd Class	ILLUSTRIOUS	
	Ord	ALBION	Algiers
	Capt' Main Top	ASIA	Navarino
BREMNER, John	Carpenter	NISUS	
	Carp's Crew	TONNANT	Trafalgar

JAVA

BRENNAN, Daniel	Boatswain	BARRACOUTA	
	Landsman	ROYAL GEORGE	*1 June 1794*
	Ord	BELLEISLE	*Trafalgar*
	Boatswain	BARRACOUTA	*Banda Neira*
BRETT, Henry	Lieutenant. R.N.	DORIS	
BRISCOE, John	Pte. R.M.	MINDEN	*G.H. 10,013*
BRISTOW, James	Landsman	MODESTE	*(M.L. as BRISTER)*
BRISTOW, John	Ord	CORNELIA	
BRITTON, John	Pte. R.M.	SCIPION	
BRODIE, John	Landsman	SCIPION	*(Roll also as BRAWDIE)*
BROMLEY, Enoch	A.B.	PHAETON	
BROOKS, William	Pte. R.M.	PRESIDENT	
	Pte. R.M.	POLYPHEMUS	*Trafalgar*
BROWN, James	Ord	PHAETON	
BROWN, James	Ropemaker	LION	
BROWN, John	Not Given	PHAETON	
BROWN, Robert	Purser	ILLUSTRIOUS	
	Clerk	EDGAR	*Copenhagen. 1801*
BROWN, William	4 seaman borne	LION	
BUCHANAN, Alexander	Midshipman	HUSSAR	
BUNCE, John	A.B.	SCIPION	
BURKE, James	Ord	LION	*(re-instated ex-convict)*
	Landsman	TEMERAIRE	*Trafalgar*
	Ord	ANSON	*Anson. 23 Augt 1806*
	Ord	ANSON	*Curacoa*
	"Convict"	POMPEE	*Martinique (ex mutineer)*
BURKETT, Henry	Capt' Main Top	HARPY	
BUTCHART, Daniel	Capt's Cook	AKBAR	
BUTCHER, Edward	Corporal. R.M.	PHOEBE	
	Pte. R.M.	PHOEBE	*Trafalgar*
BUTTLER, George	Lieutenant. R.N.	DORIS	
BUTTON, Ephraim	Ord	SCIPION	*G.H. 3657*
BYRNE, Gerald	Pte. R.M.	ILLUSTRIOUS	
(CABBURN, John.E.)	(Master's Mate)	(CORNELIA)	*Received M.G.S. Medal*
CAFFREY, Daniel	Ord	HUSSAR	
	Boy 2nd Class	COMET	*Comet. 11 Augt 1808* *(Vfd Abd. Not on Roll)*
(CALAMY, James)	(2nd Lieut. R.M.)	NISUS	*Received M.G.S. Medal*
CALLAGHAN, William	Boy	MODESTE	
CARTER, John	Ord	SCIPION	
CARTER, Thomas	Capt' of Mast	SCIPION	
CARTER, William	Landsman	PSYCHE	
CARTWRIGHT, Richard	A.B.	PRESIDENT	
	A.B.	REVOLUTIONNAIRE	*4 Novr 1805*
CASTLE, Daniel	Ord	PRESIDENT	
	Ord	PRESIDENT	*St Sebastian*
CASTLE, Henry	Corporal. R.M.	HUSSAR	
	Corporal. R.M.	BRITANNIA	*Trafalgar*
CAWLEY, James	Coxswain's Mate	CAROLINE	
	Coxswain's Mate	CAROLINE	*Banda Neira*
CHAPMAN, James	Ord	NISUS	
	Boy 3rd Class	ROYAL SOVEREIGN	*Trafalgar*
CHAPMAN, John	Pte. R.M.	HUSSAR	
CHARLESTON, Charles	A.B.	CAROLINE	
CHISHOLM, William	A.B.	PROCRIS	
CHOWN, Charles	Master	PRESIDENT	
CHURCH, John	Midshipman	PRESIDENT	
CLARK, John	Capt' Fore Top	PHAETON	
	Boy	FOUDROYANT	*Egypt*
CLARK, Samuel	Qtr Gunner	MINDEN	
CLOSEN, Frederick	Capt' Main Top	PRESIDENT	
COCK, James	Ord	PSYCHE	
(COCKS see COX)			
COCKBURN, George	Ord	PHOEBE	
	Ord	PHOEBE	*Off Tamatave. 20 May 1811*
COCKERILL, R.M.	Surgeon	HESPER	
COGGLE, Donald	Qtr Gunner	MINDEN	
COLLIER, Henry. T.B.	Lieutenant. R.N.	LEDA	
	Midshipman	BRILLIANT	*B.S. 29 Aug 1800*
COLLIER, James	Q.M.	PSYCHE	
COLLIS, James	A.B.	NISUS	
COLLINS, John	Landsman	LEDA	
COLMAN, George	Master's Mate	AKBAR	
CONDON, Patrick	Boy 3rd Class	PHOEBE	
	Boy 3rd Class	PHOEBE	*Off Tamatave. 20 May 1811* *(Vfd Abd. Not on Roll)*
	Boy 3rd Class	PHOEBE	*Phoebe. 28 March 1814*
CONNELL, W.G.	Midshipman	MODESTE	
COOK, James	Ord	PSYCHE	

COOK, William	Landsman	PHOEBE	
	Landsman	PHOEBE	Off Tamatave. 20 May 1811 (Vfd Abd. Not on Roll)
	Ord	PHOEBE	Phoebe. 28 March 1814
COOKE, James	Landsman	SAMARANG	
	Carp's Crew	ENDYMION	Endymion Wh President
COOKE, William	Pte. R.M.	SCIPION	
COOP, Abraham	Landsman	PRESIDENT	
	Landsman	AGAMEMNON	Trafalgar
	Landsman	AGAMEMNON	St Domingo
COOPER, Richard	Ord	Sir FRANCIS DRAKE	
COSTELLO, Thomas	Landsman	PRESIDENT	
COSTOR, William	Capt' Fore Top	HESPER	G.H. 8122
COTTON, John	Ship's Corporal	BARRACOUTA	
	Ship's Corporal	BARRACOUTA	Banda Neira
COX, John	Pte. R.M.	PHOEBE	
	Pte. R.M.	PHOEBE	Off Tamatave. 20 May 1811
COX, Robert	Ord	PRESIDENT	(Known medal with COCKS)
	Ord	PRESIDENT	St Sebastian
CRAIG, John	Cook	Sir FRANCIS DRAKE	
CRAIG, Robert	Mid. H.E.I.C.S.	Not Given	
CRAISE, James	Landsman	AKBAR	
CREASE, Henry	Lieutenant. R.N.	PHAETON	
CREIGHTON, William	Capt' After Guard	LION	
(CRESSY, John)	(Sergeant. R.M.)	(PRESIDENT)	Received M.G.S. Medal
CROSSWELL, Thomas	Capt' Forecastle	CAROLINE	
	A.B.	CAROLINE	Banda Neira
	Q.M.	Qn CHARLOTTE	Algiers
CRUNKTHORN, Thomas	Landsman	HESPER	
CRETCH, Daniel	Ord	PHOEBE	
	Boy 2nd Class	PHOEBE	Trafalgar
	Ord	PHOEBE	Off Tamatave. 20 May 1811
	A.B.	PHOEBE	Phoebe. 28 March 1814
CURTIS, Thomas	Landsman	SAMARANG	
DALEY, John	Qtr Gunner	MINDEN	(M.L. as DAILEY)
DAVIS, Alexander	Yeoman of Sheets	SCIPION	
DAVIS, John	Yeoman of Sheets	CAROLINE	
	Yeoman of Sheets	CAROLINE	Banda Neira
DAVISON, Robert	A.B.	MINDEN	
DEAVIN, James	Carp's Mate	LION	
(DENNEHY, Lawrence)	(Master's Mate)	(ILLUSTRIOUS)	Received M.G.S. Medal
DERRETT, William	Pte. R.M.	PRESIDENT	
	Pte. R.M.	PRESIDENT	St Sebastian
DICKER, John	Landsman	CAROLINE	
	Landsman	CAROLINE	Banda Neira
DODDS, Thomas	Landsman	PROCRIS	"additional claim"
DODGE, Francis	Ord	PHAETON	
DOHERTY, John	Landsman	HESPER	
DONOVAN, Morley	Un-Rated aboard	ILLUSTRIOUS	
DOUGLAS, James.S.	Midshipman	NISUS	
	Midshipman	ACASTA	Martinique
DOWELL, George	Actg Purser	PROCRIS	
DOWLAND, William	Cooper	PSYCHE	G.H. 601
DOWLIN, John	Landsman	SCIPION	
DOWN, James	A.B.	Sir FRANCIS DRAKE	G.H. 7915
DOYLE, James	Boy 3rd Class	NISUS	G.H. 5739
DREW, George	Lieutenant. R.N.	CAROLINE	
DRUDGE, James	Qtr Gunner	HUSSAR	
DUNCAN, Edward	Ord	HUSSAR	
DUCKHAM, George	A.B.	PHOEBE	
	Landsman	PHOEBE	Off Tamatave. 20 May 1811 (Vfd Abd. Not on Roll)
	Ord	PHOEBE	Phoebe. 28 March 1814 (Vfd Abd. Not on Roll)
DUNN, John	Yeoman of Sheets	PHAETON	
DURNELL, Thomas	Pte. R.M.	ILLUSTRIOUS	
	Pte. R.M.	TEMERAIRE	Trafalgar
	Pte. R.M.	ILLUSTRIOUS	Basque Roads. 1809
DYER, Samuel	Landsman	PRESIDENT	
EARP, Richard	Pte. R.M.	SCIPION	
EASTER, Charles	Cooper	MODESTE	
EASTES, William	Landsman	PRESIDENT	(may read EASTER)
EATON, James	Lieutenant. R.N.	LION	
	Midshipman	TEMERAIRE	Trafalgar
EATON, James	Pte. R.M.	Sir FRANCIS DRAKE	
ECCLESTON, Samuel	Corporal. R.M.	CAROLINE	G.H. 10,007
	Pte. R.M.	ARDENT	Copenhagen 1801
	Pte. R.M.	CAROLINE	Banda Neira
EDMONDS, Thomas	A.B.	PHAETON	
EDWARDS, John	Ord	CORNELIA	
ELLIOT, Henry	1st Lieut. R.M.	PRESIDENT	
ELLIOT, John.F.	2nd Lieut. R.M.	SCIPION	

JAVA

ELLIOT, Hon George	Captain. R.N.	MODESTE	
	Volunteer 1st Cl	BRITANNIA	St Vincent
	Midshipman	GOLIATH	Nile
	Lieutenant. R.N.	St GEORGE	Copenhagen 1801
ELLIS, Charles	Pte. R.M.	PROCRIS	
EMERY, James	Pte. R.M.	SCIPION	
EVANS, James	Pte. R.M.	LION	G.H. 6292
EVANS, John	Landsman	PROCRIS	
EVANS, William	Surgeon	PRESIDENT	
	Surgeon	PRESIDENT	St Sebastian
EVERITT, John	Pte. R.M.	CORNELIA	
	Supn Gnr. R.M.A.	BEELZEBUB	Algiers
EVERSON, Robert	Boy	SCIPION	
EVERY, William	Q.M's Mate	NISUS	
	Q.M's Mate	TRAAVE	B.S. 14 Dec 1814
FANSHAWE, Arthur	Midshipman	SCIPION	
	Midshipman	IMPLACABLE	Implacable 26 Augt 1808
	Lieutenant. R.N.	ENDYMION	B.S. 8 April 1814
	Lieutenant. R.N.	ENDYMION	Endymion Wh President
	Captain. R.N.	PCSS CHARLOTTE	Syria
FARNES, Barney	A.B.	MODESTE	
FARWOOD, John	A.B.	SCIPION	
(FESTING, Robert.W.G.)	(Actg Captain R.N.)	(ILLUSTRIOUS)	Received M.G.S. Medal
(FIELD, Francis)	(Pte. R.M.)	(PRESIDENT)	Received M.G.S. Medal
FIELD, John.S.	2nd Lieut. R.M.	HUSSAR	
FIELDHOUSE, George	Pte. R.M.	PHOEBE	
	Pte. R.M.	PHOEBE	Off Tamatave. 20 May 1811
	Pte. R.M.	PHOEBE	Phoebe. 28 March 1814
			(Vfd Abd. Not on Roll)
FIELDING, Alexander	A.B.	AKBAR	
FINNEY, George	Boy	PRESIDENT	
FITZGERALD, John	Ord	PHOEBE	
	Boy 2nd Class	PHOEBE	Trafalgar
	Ord	PHOEBE	Off Tamatave. 20 May 1811
	A.B.	PHOEBE	Phoebe. 28 March 1814
FLACKFIELD, John	Landsman	LION	
FONT, John	Master	DORIS	
FORD, James	Qtr Gunner	MINDEN	G.H. 9553
	Landsman	DEFIANCE	Copenhagen 1801
FORSTER, Richard	Ship's Corporal	PRESIDENT	
(FOX, Dennis)	(Private R.M.)	(SCIPION)	Received M.G.S. Medal
FRANKS, Francis	Boy	ILLUSTRIOUS	
FRENCH, James	Carpenter	SCIPION	
FRENCH, John	Private R.M.	HUSSAR	
FRESHWATER, James	Ord	SCIPION	
FREWIN, James	Qtr Gunner	AKBAR	
FURLONG, Joseph	Landsman	ILLUSTRIOUS	
GADSO, James	Landsman	LION	
GALE, Jonathan	Private R.M.	MINDEN	
(GARNISTON, Samuel)	(1st Lieut. R.M.)	(BUCEPHALUS)	Received M.G.S. Medal
GARRETT, Henry	Lieutenant. R.N.	PSYCHE	
	Midshipman	BELLEISLE	Trafalgar
GATES, Charles	Landsman	CORNELIA	
GAYNOR, James	Ord	PHAETON	
GEARING, William	Landsman	LION	
GEORGE, James	Actg Lieut. R.N.	ILLUSTRIOUS	
GHERKIN, Jacob	Q.M.	SCIPION	(M) A of I. AVA
GIBBESON, John	Landsman	LION	
GILBERT, John	Landsman	MINDEN	
(GILL, George)	(2nd Lieut. R.M.)	(SCIPION)	Received M.G.S. Medal
GLADING, George	Ord	CORNELIA	
GLENISTER, Sibley	Ord	Sir FRANCIS DRAKE	
GLOVER, Thomas	Landsman	DASHER	
GODDARD, Robert.H.	Purser	HECATE	
	Clerk	HYDRA	Hydra. 6 Augt 1807
GOLDIE, William	Carpenter	Sir FRANCIS DRAKE	
GOODRICHE, Thomas	Landsman	LEDA	(M.L. as GOODRICK)
GOODWIN, Francis	Carpenter	SAMARANG	
GOODWIN, Nathaniel	Master's Mate	CAROLINE	
	Master's Mate	CAROLINE	Banda Neira
GORDON, Charles	Boy	HUSSAR	
GORDON, Robert	Midshipman	PHOEBE	
	Volunteer 1st Cl	PHOEBE	Off Tamatave. 20 May 1811
	Actg Lieut. R.N.	Qn CHARLOTTE	Algiers
GOTT, John	A.B.	ILLUSTRIOUS	G.H. 9103
GOWDY, Thomas	Actg Master	HESPER	
GRANT, Richard	Lieutenant. R.N.	PRESIDENT	
GREAVES, George	Master's Mate	Sir FRANCIS DRAKE	

GREEN, Edward	Ord	LION	
GREENHARD, William	Ord	PSYCHE	
GREENHILL, Mark	Sergeant. R.M.	MINDEN	
GRIFFITH, Richard	Surgeon	Sir FRANCIS DRAKE	
GRIFFITHS, Thomas	Gunner	HARPY	
	Gunner	RAMILLIES	Copenhagen 1801
GUE, Thomas	Pte. R.M.	LION	G.H. 2756 (M.L. as GUEX)
GULLEY, John	A.B.	NISUS	
GUY, James.W.	Mid. H.E.I.C.S.	AURORA	(M) A of I. AVA
HAGAN, Edward	Ord	MINDEN	
HAINES, Robert	Pte. R.M.	SCIPION	
HALL, John	1st Lieut. HEICS	VESTAL	
HALL, Samuel	Qtr Gunner	CORNELIA	
HALL, Thomas	Sergeant. R.M.	SCIPION	
	Sergeant. R.M.	REVOLUTIONNAIRE	St Sebastian
HAMILTON, Hugh	Landsman	LION	
HARDELL, W.H.	Volunteer 1st Cl	CORNELIA	
(HARRIS, Charles)	(Ord)	(ILLUSTRIOUS)	Received M.G.S. Medal
	Ord	ILLUSTRIOUS	Basque Roads 1809 (N.G.S.)
HARRIS, Thomas	Carpenter	PRESIDENT	
HARRIS, Thomas	A.B.	PHAETON	G.H. 6151
HARRIS, William	Ord	SCIPION	
	Boy	ACASTA	St Domingo
	Boy	ACASTA	Martinique
HARRISON, James	Landsman	ILLUSTRIOUS	
HART, Timothy	Ord	MINDEN	G.H. 8628
HARTWELL, James	Landsman	SCIPION	
HARVEY, John	Ord	MODESTE	
HASWELL, John.S.	1st Lieut. R.M.	PHOEBE	
	1st Lieut. R.M.	PHOEBE	Off Tamatave. 20 May 1811
HAWKINS, George	Landsman	HARPY	
HAWKINS, George	Pte. R.M.	PHAETON	
HAWKINS, William	Ord	DASHER	
HAWKESWORTH, William	Pte. R.M.	NISUS	G.H. 8213
HEALEY, Patrick	Landsman	HUSSAR	G.H. 9454 as HEELEY
	Landsman	SPARTIATE	Trafalgar
HEATH, Francis	Landsman	MODESTE	G.H. 9451
HEATHCOTE, Henry	Captain. R.N.	LION	
	Midshipman	PCSS ROYAL	14 March 1795
HENRY, Charles	A.B.	MINDEN	
HENRY, Francis	Ord	LEDA	
HIGGINS, John	Ord	SCIPION	
HIGGINSON, Joseph	Sergeant. R.M.	PRESIDENT	
HILL, Benjamin	Boy	LEDA	
HILL, John	Landsman	MODESTE	G.H.3724
	Boy 3rd Cl	MAGICIENNE	St Domingo
HILL, John	A.B.	NISUS	
HINDMARSH, John	Lieutenant. R.N.	NISUS	
	Captain's Servant	BELLEROPHON	1 June 1794
	Volunteer 1st Cl	BELLEROPHON	17 June 1795
	Midshipman	BELLEROPHON	Nile
	Midshipman	SPENCER	Gut of Gibraltar.12 July 1801
	Lieutenant. R.N.	PHOEBE	Trafalgar
	Lieutenant. R.N.	BEAGLE	Basque Roads 1809
HINDS, John	Pte. R.M.	PRESIDENT	
	Pte. R.M.	POLYPHEMUS	Trafalgar
HOARE, Edward.W.	Captain. R.N.	MINDEN	
	Midshipman	LONDON	23rd June 1795
	Lieutenant. R.N.	NORTHUMBERLAND	Egypt
HOARE, Thomas	Landsman	DORIS	(alias WOOD)
HOLBECH, George	Midshipman	SCIPION	
HOLBERTON, John	Volunteer 1st Cl	SCIPION	
	Midshipman	AJAX	St Sebastian
	Master's Mate	IMPREGNABLE	Algiers
HOLLISTER, William	Landsman	ILLUSTRIOUS	
HOOD, Richard	Ord	MINDEN	G.H. 9819
HOPE, Andrew.J.	Boy 3rd Class	PHOEBE	
	Boy 3rd Class	PHOEBE	Off Tamatave. 20 May 1811
	Landsman	PHOEBE	Phoebe. 28 March 1814
HOPKINS, E.	Pte. R.M.	SCIPION	
HORCASTLE, William	A.B.	Sir FRANCIS DRAKE	
HORE, Henry.C.	Lieutenant. R.N.	HARPY	
HORE, Samuel.B.	Flag. Lieut. R.N.	SCIPION	
	Midshipman	SPENCER	St Domingo
	Lieutenant. R.N.	CAESAR	Basque Roads 1809
HORLEY, Joseph	Not Given	PHAETON	(may read HARLEY)
HOWARD, George	Boy	MODESTE	
HOWARD, James	A.B.	Sir FRANCIS DRAKE	G.H. 8074
HOUNSELL, Thomas	Ord	NISUS	
	Landsman	ROYAL SOVEREIGN	Trafalgar
HUBBARD, John	Two borne	SCIPION	(Ord & A.B.)
HUBBARD, William	Volunteer 1st Cl	ILLUSTRIOUS	

JAVA

HULL, William	Ord	CAROLINE	
	Ord	CAROLINE	Banda Neira
HURT, Abraham	Corporal. R.M.	SAMARANG	(May read HUNT)
HUSTWAYTE, George	Pte. R.M.	MODESTE	
IBBETSON, John	Ord	MINDEN	
INNES, Robert.W.	Midshipman	CORNELIA	
	Lieutenant. R.N.	GLASGOW	Algiers
INNES, Thomas	A.B.	BARRACOUTA	
	A.B.	BARRACOUTA	Banda Neira
IRVIN, Henry	Landsman	CAROLINE	
JACKSON, John	A.B.	ILLUSTRIOUS	
	Landsman	ILLUSTRIOUS	Basque Roads 1809
JACOB, Robert	Lieutenant. R.N.	SCIPION	
JAMES, Francis	A.B.	NISUS	
	Landsman	ROYAL SOVEREIGN	Trafalgar
JAMES, William.T.	Purser	NISUS	
JEFFREY, Henry	A.B.	PRESIDENT	
(or JEFFERY)	A.B.	REVOLUTIONNAIRE	4 Novr 1805
	A.B.	PRESIDENT	St Sebastian
JEFFERY, Samuel	Yeoman of Sheets	SCIPION	
	A.B.	ACASTA	St Domingo
	A.B.	ACASTA	Martinique
JOHNSON, Harry	A.B.	MODESTE	G.H. 5254
JOHNSON, Henry	A.B.	LEDA	
JOHNSON, John	Yeoman of Sheets	CORNELIA	
	A.B.	BRITANNIA	14 March 1795
	A.B.	BRITANNIA	St Vincent
	A.B.	GOLIATH	Nile
	A.B.	ELEPHANT	Copenhagen 1801
JOHNSON, John	Ord	PRESIDENT	G.H. 8220
	Ord	PRESIDENT	St Sebastian
JOHNSON, John	A.B.	SCIPION	(May read JOHNSTON)
JOHNSTON, John	A.B.	HUSSAR	
JOHNSTONE, James	Ord	DORIS	
JOICE, Robert	Ord	Sir FRANCIS DRAKE	
JOLLEY, John	Landsman	HUSSAR	G.H. 291 as JOLLY
JONES, Benjamin	A.B.	BARRACOUTA	G.H. 2744
	A.B.	BARRACOUTA	Banda Neira
JONES, Edward	Ord	CAROLINE	
	Ord	CAROLINE	Banda Neira
	A.B.	TONNANT	B.S. 14 Dec 1814
JONES, Evan	Pte. R.M.	HARPY	
JONES, George	Landsman	PHAETON	
JONES, Hugh	A.B.	SCIPION	
JONES, John (2)	Ord	CAROLINE	
	Ord	CAROLINE	Banda Neira
JONES, John	Pte. R.M.	HUSSAR	
JONES, John	Carp's Crew	PHAETON	
	Carp's Crew	PHOEBE	Phoebe. 28 March 1814
JONES, John	Carp's Crew	SCIPION	
	Carp's Crew	ACASTA	Martinique
JONES, Thomas	Landsman	PRESIDENT	
JONES, William	A.B.	CAROLINE	
JONES, William	Pte. R.M.	PHAETON	G.H. 9818
KAINE, John	A.B.	PHAETON	
KANE, John	Ord	PHAETON	G.H. 9839
	Ord	SEAHORSE	The Potomac. 17 Aug 1814
KELLY, John	2 borne as L.M.	NISUS	
	Landsman	ACHILLE	Trafalgar
KEMP, John	Ord	PRESIDENT	G.H. 2720
KEMPTON, James	A.B.	AKBAR	G.H. 1238
	A.B.	PHAETON	1 June 1794
KENNEDY, Patrick	Landsman	NISUS	
KEWN, Edward	Ord	PRESIDENT	
KILIAN, Gottfried	Pte. R.M.	LION	(M.L. as KILGANE)
KIMBER, John	Ord	BUCHEPHALUS	
KINDNESS, Benjamin	Ord	PHOEBE	
	Boy 2nd Class	PHOEBE	Trafalgar
	Ord	PHOEBE	Off Tamatave. 20 May 1811 (Vfd Abd. Not on Roll)
	Ord	PHOEBE	Phoebe. 28 March 1814 (Vfd Abd. Not on Roll)
	Q.M.	ALBION	Navarino
KING, Richard	Ord	ILLUSTRIOUS	G.H. 6844
KING, William	A.B.	LION	
KINGSLAND, Thomas	Ord	HUSSAR	
KNIGHT, George	Landsman	LION	G.H. 9808
LAHIFF, James	Ord	PRESIDENT	
LANE, John	Purser	MINDEN	

LATA, Alexander	Pte. R.M.	SAMARANG	(M.L. as LATTY)
LAURIE, Stephen	A.B.	PHOEBE	
	Boy 3rd Class	PHOEBE	Phoebe. 21 Decr 1797
	Boy 2nd Class	PHOEBE	Phoebe. 19 Feby 1801
	A.B.	PHOEBE	Trafalgar
	A.B.	PHOEBE	Off Tamatave. 20 May 1811
	Capt' Fore Top	PHOEBE	Phoebe. 28 March 1814
LEARY, Timothy	A.B.	LION	
LEE, John	Ord	Sir FRANCIS DRAKE	
LEIGHTON, William	Pte. R.M.	NISUS	
LEITH, Andrew	A.B.	AKBAR	
	A.B.	GLASGOW	Navarino
LEMON, William	A.B.	ILLUSTRIOUS	
	A.B.	STATELY	Stately. 22 March 1808
	A.B.	ILLUSTRIOUS	Basque Roads. 1809
LEONARD, William	Boy	BUCHEPHALUS	(M.L. as LENNARD)
	Capt's Coxswain	CAMBRIAN	Navarino
			(M) Anchor Type LS & GC
LEPPERT, Richard	Carp's Crew	ILLUSTRIOUS	
Le SAGE, James	Ord	ILLUSTRIOUS	G.H. 9249
LEWIS, John	A.B.	ILLUSTRIOUS	
LINES, Peter	Ord	PRESIDENT	
LINGARD, John	A.B.	MINDEN	
LLOYD, William	Ord	SCIPION	
LOFTUS, Arthur	Supn A.B.	SCIPION	
LONEY, Robert	2nd Master	SCIPION	
	Midshipman	AIGLE	Basque Roads 1809
	Lieut. R.N.	REINDEER	St Sebastian. ("disallowed"?)
LUFF, James	Ord	LION	
LUTTICK, John.C.	Pte. R.M.	PRESIDENT	(M.L. as LUTTECK)
LYNCH, Richard	Ord	NISUS	
LYNN, Matthew	Landsman	CORNELIA	
	Landsman	ELEPHANT	Copenhagen 1801
LYONS, Edmund	Lieutenant. R.N.	MINDEN	(C in C at Crimea)
	Lieutenant. R.N.	BARRACOUTA	Banda Neira
	Lieutenant. R.N.	MINDEN	B.S. 30 July 1811
MACDONOUGH, John	Landsman	MINDEN	
MAGIN, Joseph	Lieutenant, R.N.	SCIPION	
MALCOLM, Robert	Carp's Mate	PRESIDENT	
MALDEN, Charles.R.	Midshipman	NISUS	
MALLETT, William	A.B.	NISUS	
MALLINSON, Michael	Pte. R.M.	LEDA	
MANLEY, William.P.	A.B.	NISUS	
MANNING, George	Landsman	CAROLINE	
	Landsman	CAROLINE	Banda Neira
MANNING, Joseph	Landsman	PHOEBE	
	Landsman	PHOEBE	Off Tamatave. 20 May 1811
	Ord	PHOEBE	Phoebe. 28 March 1811
MANUEL, Joseph	Capt' Fore Top	HARPY	G.H. 8883
	A.B.	BRITANNIA	Trafalgar
MARGERSON, Lawrence	Landsman	PRESIDENT	
MARTIN, Antonio	Ord	ILLUSTRIOUS	
	Ord	ILLUSTRIOUS	Basque Roads 1809
MARTIN, John.O.	Surgeon	HUSSAR	
	Surgeon's Mate	BRITANNIA	Trafalgar
MARTING, George	Ord	PHAETON	(alias McDONALD)
MASON, William.G.	Purser	PRESIDENT	
	Clerk	AJAX	Trafalgar
	Purser	PCSS CHARLOTTE	Syria
MATTHEWS, Michael	Lieutenant. R.N.	MINDEN	
MATSON, George.W.	Master's Mate	PRESIDENT	
	Midshipman	BELLEROPHON	B.S. 7 July 1809
MAYNARD, John	Pte. R.M.	PRESIDENT	
McCARTHY, Daniel	A.B.	CORNELIA	
McDERMOTT, James	Carp's Crew	HESPER	
McDONALD, D.	1st Lieut. HEICS	ARIEL	
McDONALD, John	Ord	SCIPION	
McDONALL, Thomas	Ord	AKBAR	
McMULLEN, Michael	Landsman	NISUS	
MEADOWS, William	Lieutenant. R.N.	BUCEPHALUS	
MILLARD, George	Master	Sir FRANCIS DRAKE	
MILLERY, Thomas	Actg Sailmaker	PHOEBE	
	Actg Sailmaker	PHOEBE	Off Tamatave. 20 May 1811
	Sailmaker	PHOEBE	Phoebe. 28 March 1814
MILTON, Thomas	Pte. R.M.	CAROLINE	
	Pte. R.M.	CAROLINE	Banda Neira
MITCHELL, James	Armourer's Mate	LION	
MITSCHER, Michael	Pte. R.M.	LION	
MOGGS, William	A.B.	ILLUSTRIOUS	G.H. 8734
MOLESWORTH, Arthur	1st Lieut. R.M.	HUSSAR	
MOORE, Benjamin	Pte. R.M.	LION	
MOORE, Charles	Pte. R.M.	BUCEPHALUS	
MOORE, William	Midshipman	LION	

JAVA

MORGAN, William	Ord	ILLUSTRIOUS	G.H. 2324
(MORGAN, William)	(Pte. R.M.)	(PHOEBE)	Received (Java) M.G.S. Medal
	Pte. R.M.	PHOEBE	Off Tamatave. 20 May 1811
	Corporal R.M.	PHOEBE	Phoebe. 28 March 1814
			(Rcd 2 clasp N.G.S.)
			G.H. 9765
MORRIS, John	Carp's Crew	LEDA	
MORRIS, William	Pte. R.M.	SCIPION	
	Pte. R.M.	BELLEISLE	Trafalgar
MORRISON, James	A.B.	PSYCHE	
MORTON, T.C.P.	Midshipman	ILLUSTRIOUS	
	Midshipman	ILLUSTRIOUS	Basque Roads 1809
MOSLEY, Samuel	Ord	ILLUSTRIOUS	
MOSS, Thomas	Ord	SCIPION	
MULGANNON, John	Ord	CORNELIA	
	Landsman	DEFIANCE	Copenhagen 1801
MUMFORD, William	Boy 3rd Class	MODESTE	G.H. 8905
	A.B.	EDINBURGH	Syria
MUNDAY, Edward	Pte. R.M.	LION	
MUNDAY, Thomas	Sailmaker	PRESIDENT	G.H. 9888
	A.B.	REVOLUTIONNAIRE	4 Novr 1805
	Sailmaker	PRESIDENT	St Sebastian
MURPHY, Francis	Landsman	SCIPION	(M.L. as MONAGHAN)
MURPHY, John	Pte. R.M.	SCIPION	
MURRAY, Charles	Pte. R.M.	HUSSAR	
	Pte. R.M.	LONDON	London. 13 March 1806
MURRAY, Michael	Ord	ILLUSTRIOUS	G.H. 5840
MYERS, Joseph	Ord	HECATE	
NAZER, Kelly	Lieutenant. R.N.	LEDA	
NEALE, Thomas	Pte. R.M.	ILLUSTRIOUS	
NECHAN, Lewis	Landsman	LION	
	A.B.	PROMETHEUS	Algiers
NELENCE, Thomas	A.B.	AKBAR	G.H. 3006
NELSON, Alexander	A.B.	DORIS	G.H. 6729
NEWENHAM, William.P.	Lieutenant. R.N.	HARPY	
NEWMAN, John	Boy	LION	
NICHOLLS, William	Gunner's Mate	BUCEPHALUS	
	A.B.	SUPERB	St Domingo
NIXON, James	Actg Lieut. R.N.	HESPER	
NOAKES, James	Boy 3rd Class	LION	
NORCOT, Edmund	Midshipman	MINDEN	
	Lieutenant. R.N.	ALBION	Navarino
(NORRIS, John)	(Coxswain)	(LEDA)	Awarded M.G.S. Medal
NORTH, Joseph	Corporal. R.M.	CORNELIA	
NOULTON, James.G.	Landsman	BUCEPHALUS	
NOULAN, John	Landsman	PROCRIS	
OGDEN, William	Ord	MINDEN	
OGILVIE, Henry	Midshipman	AKBAR	
	Midshipman	DONEGAL	St Domingo
	Master's Mate	DONEGAL	Basque Roads 1809
O'GRADY, Waller	Volunteer	HARPY	
OLDHALL, John	Master's Mate	LION	
OLDHAM, George	Landsman	LEDA	
OLDMIXON, John.W.	Master's Mate	PHAETON	
O'READ, John	Landsman	MINDEN	
ORR, James	Lieut. R.M.	PHAETON	
ORR, Robert	Landsman	SCIPION	
	Landsman	ACASTA	Martinique
OSBORN, John	Armourer	BUCHEPHALUS	
OSBORNE, Robert	Pte. R.M.	PROCRIS	G.H. 3279
OWEN, William.F.	Commander	BARRACOUTA	
	Midshipman	CULLODEN	1 June 1794
OXBOROUGH, William	Clerk	MODESTE	
PADOE, Joseph	Ord	CORNELIA	(Alias Antonio PASCOA)
or PODOA	Boy 3rd Class	ELEPHANT	Copenhagen 1801
PAGE, Edward	Landsman	LION	
PAGE, Robert	Landsman	BARRACOUTA	G.H. 10,181
	Landsman	BARRACOUTA	Banda Neira
PALIAN, John	Pte. R.M.	MINDEN	
PARKER, Robert	Sailmaker's Mate	CAROLINE	
	A.B.	CAROLINE	Banda Neira
PARROTT, William	Carp's Crew	CAROLINE	G.H. 2695
	Carp's Crew	BARRACOUTA	Banda Neira
(PASCOE, Richard.W.)	(Lieut. R.M.)	(PHOEBE)	Awarded M.G.S. Medal
PATRICK, James	Carp's Crew	NISUS	G.H. 9642
PAYNE, Benjamin	Pte. R.M.	PRESIDENT	
PEARSON, Charles	Midshipman	SCIPION	
	Boy	St GEORGE	Copenhagen 1801
	Midshipman	SPENCER	St Domingo
	Lieutenant. R.N.	PRESIDENT	St Sebastian

PEAT, John	Boy 2nd Class	ILLUSTRIOUS	
	Boy 2nd Class	ILLUSTRIOUS	Basque Roads 1809
PELLEW, Fleetwood	Captain. R.N.	PHAETON	
PEMKIN, George	Landsman	PROCRIS	
PENPRASE, Alexander	Purser	CAROLINE	
PETERS, John	Q.M's Mate	LION	
PETTITT, John	Pte. R.M.	CORNELIA	
PHELPS, Joseph	Pte. R.M.	HUSSAR	
PHILLIPS, John	A.B.	PHAETON	
PHILLIPS, Joseph	Ord	HECATE	
PHILLIPS, Paul	A.B.	BARRACOUTA	
	A.B.	BARRACOUTA	Banda Neira
PHIPPS, William	Landsman	MODESTE	G.H. 2934
PIKE, Peter	Carp's Mate	HECATE	
	Caulker's Mate	ALBION	Navarino
PIKE, William	Pte. R.M.	HARPY	
PINHEY, William.T.	Lieut. R.M.	LION	
PITT, William (2)	Midshipman	PHAETON	
PLATT, James	Pte. R.M.	SCIPION	
POINDESTER, James	Ord	PRESIDENT	
POWERS, William	Boy 3rd Class	NISUS	
PRIOR, James	Surgeon	NISUS	
PRITCHARD, Robert	Ropemaker	MODESTE	
	Landsman	MAGICIENNE	St Domingo
PUCKFORD, James	Midshipman	NISUS	
PULFER, Charles	Carp's Crew	CAROLINE	
	Carp's Crew	CAROLINE	Banda Neira
PUNCHARD, James	Caulker	ILLUSTRIOUS	
PURKIS, James	Boy 1st Class	MODESTE	
	Boy 2nd class	MAGICIENNE	St Domingo
QUARRIER, David	Carp's Crew	CORNELIA	G.H. 7018
QUIN, John	Boy	ILLUSTRIOUS	
RACE, John	Landsman	CAROLINE	G.H. 9784
	Landsman	CAROLINE	Banda Neira
RAMSAY, Charles	Landsman	HARPY	
RAWLINGS, Richard	Ord	PSYCHE	G.H. 3101
REDDICK, John	Ord	BARRACOUTA	
REES, Mansel	Purser's Steward	SCIPION	
REID, Thomas	A.B.	MODESTE	
REINHARD, J.	Volunteer 1st Cl	ILLUSTRIOUS	
REYNOLDS, Barrington	Commander	HESPER	
	Midshipman	AMAZON	Amazon. 13 Jany 1797
	Midshipman	IMPETUEUX	B.S. 29 Aug 1800
	Captain.R.N. C.B.	GANGES	Syria
(REYNOLDS, Jeremiah)	(Ord)	(MINDEN)	Awarded M.G.S. Medal
REYNOLDS, John	Qtr Gunner	LION	(alias OUTRAM)
RICE, Henry	Lieutenant. R.N.	PHOEBE	
	Lieutenant. R.N.	PHOEBE	Off Tamatave. 20 May 1811
RICHARDS, William	Pte. R.M.	HUSSAR	G.H. 8551
RICHARDSON, Thomas	Yeoman Powder Rm	PSYCHE	
RICHARDSON, William	A.B.	MINDEN	G.H. 8084
RICHES, Watson.T.	Midshipman	ILLUSTRIOUS	
	Master's Mate	Gun Boat	Gluckstadt. 5 Jany 1814
			(Vfd in Gn Bt. Not on Roll)
RIDER, Francis	Corporal. R.M.	LEDA	
RILL, W.B.	Pte. R.M.	PRESIDENT	
	Pte. R.M.	POLYPHEMUS	Trafalgar
RISCON, George	Landsman	LEDA	
RITSON, George	Ord	MINDEN	G.H. 7944
ROBBINS, Thomas	Boy	SAMARANG	
ROBERTS, Benjamin	Lieutenant. R.N.	PROCRIS	
	Midshipman	MADRAS	Egypt
ROBERTS, Daniel	Lieutenant. R.N.	ILLUSTRIOUS	
	Master's Mate	ILLUSTRIOUS	Basque Roads 1809
ROBERTS, George	Asst Surgeon	NISUS	
ROBERTS, John	Boy 2nd Class	PHOEBE	
	Boy 2nd Class	PHOEBE	Off Tamatave. 20 May 1811
ROBERTS, Stephen	A.B.	MINDEN	
	A.B.	MINDEN	B.S. 30 July 1811
ROBINSON, C.F.	Midshipman	SCIPION	
ROBINSON, George	A.B.	SCIPION	G.H. 1287
ROBINSON, James	A.B.	DORIS	
ROBINSON, James	A.B.	PHOEBE	
	A.B.	PHOEBE	Trafalgar
	A.B.	PHOEBE	Off Tamatave. 20 May 1811
	A.B.	PHOEBE	Phoebe. 28 March 1814
ROBINSON, Louis.A.	Master's Mate	LEDA	
	Midshipman	COURAGEUX	4 Novr 1805
ROGERS, John	Ord	HUSSAR	
ROONEY, Thomas	Ord	HUSSAR	G.H. 8833
ROPER, Thomas	Ord	MINDEN	

JAVA

ROURKE, Andrew	Pte. R.M.	SAMARANG	
	Pte. R.M.	NEPTUNE	*Trafalgar*
RUNDLE, Edward	A.B.	LION	
RUSSELL, James	A.B.	MINDEN	
	A.B.	BEAGLE	*St Sebastian*
RUTHERFORD, G.S.	Asst Surgeon	LION	
RYAN, John	Pte. R.M.	MINDEN	
	Pte. R.M.	BELLEROPHON	*Trafalgar*
SALMON, John	Pte. R.M.	HUSSAR	
SALMON, Thomas	Pte. R.M.	NISUS	
SALTER, George	Landsman	LION	
SAYER, Robert.R.	Midshipman	CAROLINE	
SCHULTZ, John	A.B.	AKBAR	
SCOTT, George	Lieutenant.R.N.	PHOEBE	
	Master's Mate	MINOTAUR	*Egypt*
	Lieutenant. R.N.	PHOEBE	*Off Tamatave. 20 May 1811*
SCOTT, John	Q.M's Mate	CAROLINE	
SCOTT, Robert	Purser (Roll)	SCIPION/AKBAR	*Was in CORNWALLIS?*
	Midshipman	AUDACIOUS	*Gut of Gibraltar. 12 July 1801*
SCOTT, William	A.B.	MINDEN	
	A.B.	MINDEN	*B.S. 30 July 1811*
SEAL, James	Pte. R.M.	SCIPION	*G.H. 7723*
SERGEANT, William	Pte. R.M.	LION	
SHAIRP, Alexander	Midshipman	HUSSAR	
	Midshipman	BERWICK	*Gaieta. 24 July 1815*
SHEARMAN, Benjamin	Boy	HUSSAR	
SHEERING, Henry	Landsman	LION	
SHELLSHEAR, Hugh	Gunner	SCIPION	
	A.B.	PHAETON	*1 June 1974*
	A.B.	PHAETON	*17 June 1795*
SHEPHARD, Samuel	A.B.	PROCRIS	
SHORE, William	Pte. R.M.	SCIPION	
SHUTE, George	Ord	MODESTE	
SHUTTLEWORTH, George	Landsman	SCIPION	
	Landsman	ACASTA	*Martinique*
(SIMMONS,W.C.)	(Midshipman)	(ILLUSTRIOUS)	*Awarded M.G.S. Medal*
SIMS, Andrew	Master's Mate	NISUS	
	Midshipman	ACASTA	*Martinique*
SISK, Mathias	Master	SCIPION	
SLADE, John	Ord	HESPER	
SLATER, William	Capt' Fore Top	ILLUSTRIOUS	
SLAUGHTER, Thomas	Ord	PHAETON	
SLOBY, James	Midshipman	ILLUSTRIOUS	
SMITH, George	Pte. R.M.	HUSSAR	
SMITH, John or James	Ord	LION (Roll)	*G.H. 8289 as in Scipion? (alias Charles)*
	Boy	COLOSSUS	*Trafalgar*
SMITH, John	Pte. R.M.	NISUS (Roll)	*G.H. 9031 as in Lion? (See B.S. 2 Aug 1811 ?)*
SMITH, Richard	Q.M.	DASHER	*G.H. 9564*
SMITH, Samuel	Boy	HARPY	
SMITH, Thomas	Ord	CORNELIA	
SMITH, Thomas	Landsman	MODESTE	
SMITH, William	A.B.	ILLUSTRIOUS	*G.H. 9973*
	Capt' Forecastle	MINDEN	*Algiers*
SMITH, William	Ord	PHAETON	
SMITHSON, John	Ord	DORIS	
SMOUT, Thomas	Pte. R.M.	SCIPION	
SNELL, Thomas	Pte. R.M.	ILLUSTRIOUS	
SOMERVILLE, Lord Kenelm	Lieutenant. R.N.	PHOEBE	
	Lieutenant. R.N.	PHOEBE	*Off Tamatave. 20 May 1811*
SOUTH, William	Domestic	PSYCHE	
	Admiral's Domestic	Qn CHARLOTTE	*Algiers*
SPARKES, George	A.B.	AKBAR	
SPARKS, John	Landsman	PHOEBE	
	Landsman	PHOEBE	*Off Tamatave. 20 May 1811*
	Landsman	PHOEBE	*Phoebe. 28 March 1814 (Vfd Abd. Not on Roll)*
SPEAKMAN, Thomas	Pte. R.M.	SCIPION	
(SPEAR, William)	(Pte. R.M.)	(SCIPION)	*Awarded M.G.S. Medal*
SPEARE, Michael	Landsman	HESPER	
SPEARMAN, Boddy	Carp's Crew	LEDA	
SPONG, George	Volunteer 1st Cl	PRESIDENT	
STACKPOOLE, James	Pte. R.M.	NISUS	
STAFFORD, Richard	Pte. R.M.	CAROLINE	*G.H.8401*
STANLEY, John	Landsman	PRESIDENT	
STAPP, Charles	Boy	ILLUSTRIOUS	
STARKEY, Thomas	A.B.	PHAETON	*G.H. 4074*
(STEEL, F.)	(2nd Lieut. R.M.)	(ILLUSTRIOUS)	*Awarded M.G.S. Medal*
STEPHENSON, Henry	Not Given	HESPER	
	Capt' After Guard	ACASTA	*Martinique*

STEPHENSON, James	Q.M.	CORNELIA	
	Landsman	GOLIATH	*Nile*
	Ord	ELEPHANT	*Copenhagen 1801*
STEVENS, William	Boy	ILLUSTRIOUS	
STEWARD, James	A.B.	LEDA	*G.H.8923*
STEWART, Frederick.A.	Midshipman	DORIS	*(O'Byrne as F.A.B. STEWART)*
STEWART, James	Midshipman	ILLUSTRIOUS	
STEWART, John	Actg Surgeon	CAROLINE	
	Asst Surgeon	GIBRALTAR	*Basque Roads 1809*
	Asst Surgeon	PIEDMONTAISE	*Banda Neira*
STEWART, Peter	Capt Forecastle	CAROLINE	
	Q.M's Mate	CAROLINE	*Banda Neira*
STILL, Joseph	A.B.	ILLUSTRIOUS	
	A.B.	STATELY.	*Stately. 22 March 1808*
	Ord	ILLUSTRIOUS	*Basque Roads 1809*
			(Vfd Abd. Not on Roll)
STOCKDALE, Charles.B.	Master's Mate	ILLUSTRIOUS	
STOCKER, James	A.B.	HUSSAR	*A of I/AVA. Boatswain?*
STOCKER, Stephen	Master's Mate	BUCEPHALUS	
STOPFORD, Montagu	Volunteer 1st Cl	SCIPION	
STOPFORD, Robert	Rear Admiral	SCIPION	
	Captain. R.N.	AQUILON	*1 June 1794 (see this Roll)*
	Captain. R.N.	PHAETON	*17 June 1795*
	Captain. R.N.	SPENCER	*St Domingo*
	Captain. R.N.	CAESAR	*Basque Roads 1809*
	Admiral	Pcss CHARLOTTE	*Syria*
STOVE, John.L.	Boatswain	HUSSAR	
	A.B.	ASSURANCE	*B.S. 17 Mar 1794*
			(alias John LISK. ML as LESK)
STUART, Alexander	Q.M's Mate	HECATE	
SULLIVAN, Owen	Ord	Sir FRANCIS DRAKE	
SULLIVAN, Timothy	A.B.	CAROLINE	
SULLIVAN, Timothy	A.B.	ILLUSTRIOUS	
SWAINE, Matthew	Actg Armourer	CAROLINE	
	Actg Armourer	CAROLINE	*Banda Neira*
SWANSON, Andrew	Ord	CAROLINE	
	Ord	CAROLINE	*Banda Neira*
SWEENY, Edward	A.B.	ILLUSTRIOUS	
SWINTON, James	A.B.	ILLUSTRIOUS	
SYLVESTER, George	Asst Surgeon	LION	
SYLVIA, Peter	Ropemaker	BUCEPHALUS	
	Ropemaker	ROYAL SOVEREIGN	*Trafalgar*
TABART, C.M.	Midshipman	LION	
	Midshipman	ANDROMACHE	*St Sebastian*
TAIT, Robert	Midshipman	SCIPION	
TANNER, Thomas	A.B. HEICoy	Not Given	*Applied as a Commander*
TAYLOR, George	A.B.	SCIPION	
TAYLOR, John	A.B.	ILLUSTRIOUS	*G.H. 9015*
TAYLOR, John	Ord	AKBAR	
TAYLOR, Joseph	A.B.	ILLUSTRIOUS	
THISTLEWOOD, Robert	A.B.	SCIPION	
	Pte. R.M. (?)	AJAX	*Trafalgar*
THOMAS, John	A.B.	LEDA	*(Alias William)*
THOMAS, Owen	Ord	MODESTE	
THOMAS, William.G.	Midshipman	SCIPION	
	Lieutenant. R.N.	AETNA	*The Potomac. 17 Aug 1814*
THOMPSON, George	Sergeant. R.M.	HUSSAR	
THOMPSON, James	A.B.	MODESTE	
THOMPSON, Joseph	Ord	AKBAR	
THORNE, Benjamin	Pte. R.M.	LION	
THORN, John	Clerk	HUSSAR	
	Purser	HECLA	*Algiers*
THORNTON, Abraham	Landsman	ILLUSTRIOUS	
THRUSTON, Charles.T.	Lieutenant. R.N.	SCIPION	
TIMMS, Joseph	Ord	LION	
TISDALL, Archibald	Lieutenant. R.N.	SCIPION	
	Supernumerary	NORTHUMBERLAND	*St Domingo*
TONSHAW, Timothy	Landsman	DORIS	
TOOL, James	Bosun's Mate	HUSSAR	
TOOMEY, Jeremiah	Landsman	DORIS	
TOWNLEY, John	A.B.	HECATE	
TRAYNIER, J.B.	A.B.	HUSSAR	
TRUELOVE, James	Ord	Sir FRANCIS DRAKE	*G.H. 3861*
	Qtr Gunner	GLASGOW	*Algiers*
TULLOH, John	Lieutenant. R.N.	ILLUSTRIOUS	
	Supn' Lieut. R.N.	No 4 Gun Boat	*Gluckstadt. 5 Jany 1814*
TWYSDEN, Henry D.	Midshipman	HUSSAR	
TYRRELL, George	Midshipman	ILLUSTRIOUS	
VEAL, Richard	Landsman	SCIPION	
	Landsman	ACASTA	*Martinique*
VINER, John	Ord	HUSSAR	
WADDELL, Henry	Ord	CAROLINE	
	Ord	CAROLINE	*Banda Neira*

JAVA

WALDERS, James	A.B.	MINDEN	G.H. 5742
WALKER, Thomas	Landsman	LEDA	
WALTON, George	Sailmaker	Sir FRANCIS DRAKE	
WARD, Charles	Qtr Gunner	Sir FRANCIS DRAKE	
WARD, William	Boy	ILLUSTRIOUS	
WARE, John	Pte. R.M.	NISUS	
WARNER, William	Capt' Fore Top	HUSSAR	G.H. 935
WASHPEAR, James	A.B.	SCIPION	
WATERS, Thomas	Armourer	HUSSAR	
WATERS, William	Ord	MINDEN	(M.L. as BOWEN)
WATERWORTH, Thomas	Ord	CORNELIA	
WATSON, George	Carp's Crew	BARRACOUTA	
	Ord	BARRACOUTA	Banda Neira
WEAVER, William	Midshipman	PRESIDENT	
	Supn Admty Mid'	FURY	Algiers
WEBB, James	Coxswain	PRESIDENT	
WEBB, Samuel	Pte. R.M.	NISUS	G.H. 9304
	Pte. R.M.	EDGAR	Copenhagen 1801
WHATLEY, Richard	Drummer. R.M.	PHAETON	
WHEELER, William	Ord	Sir FRANCIS DRAKE	
WHITE, Charles	Ord	PRESIDENT	
	Ord	PRESIDENT	St Sebastian
WHITE, Henry	Ord	BARRACOUTA	
	Ord	BARRACOUTA	Banda Neira
WHITE, John	Lieutenant. R.N.	BARRACOUTA	
	Midshipman	SUPERB	Gut of Gibraltar.12 July 1801
	Midshipman	SUPERB	St Domingo
	Lieutenant. R.N.	BARRACOUTA	Banda Neira
WHITE, William	Ord	CAROLINE	
	Ord	CAROLINE	Banda Neira
WICKHAM, William	Pte. R.M.	Sir FRANCIS DRAKE	
	Pte. R.M.	LANCASTER	Camperdown
WILKINSON, John	A.B.	MINDEN	
WILLIAMS, James	Pte. R.M.	MINDEN	
WILLIAMS, John	Landsman	SAMARANG	
WILLIAMS, Joseph	Pte. R.M.	PHAETON	
WILLIAMS, Robert	A.B.	SCIPION	
WILLIAMS, William	Landsman	ILLUSTRIOUS	
WILLIAMS, William	Landsman	SCIPION	
WILMSHURST, George	Landsman	CORNELIA	
WILSON, David	Ord	PHOEBE	
	A.B.	PHOEBE	Trafalgar
	Ord	PHOEBE	Off Tamatave. 20 May 1811 (Vfd Abd. Not on Roll)
WILSON, James	A.B.	HARPY	G.H. 8462
	A.B.	DREADNOUGHT	Trafalgar
	A.B.	CAPTAIN	Martinique
WILSON, Martin	Sailmaker's Mate	PSYCHE	
WILSON, Peter	Qtr Gunner	AKBAR	G.H. 2138 as WESTRAM?
WINDSOR, Thomas	Boy	BUCHEPHALUS	
WINDWARD, Walter	Pte. R.M.	NISUS	
WINGET, John	Landsman	SCIPION	
WISE, Robert	Actg Master	PROCRIS	
WOOD, Henry	Landsman	ILLUSTRIOUS	
WORBOYS, James	A.B.	DORIS	
WORLD, Thomas	Ord	HECATE	
WORTHAM, James	Midshipman	LION	
WORTHINGTON, George	A.B.	SCIPION	G.H. 9497
WRIGHT, Charles	Ord	Sir FRANCIS DRAKE	
WRIGHT, Samuel	Ord	PRESIDENT	
	Capt' Fore Top	PRESIDENT	St Sebastian
WRIGHT, Thomas	Landsman	LEDA	
WRIGHT, William	A.B.	SCIPION	
WYNN, William	Surgeon (? Roll)	DORIS	G.H. 1015 as WYNNE
YATES, George	Landsman	PHOEBE	(M.L. as YEATES)
	Boy 2nd Class	PHOEBE	Off Tamatave. 20 May 1811
	Ord	PHOEBE	Phoebe. 28 March 1814
YEO, Peter	Landsman	HUSSAR	
	Landsman	SPARTIATE	Trafalgar
YOUNG, George	Lieutenant. R.N.	LION	
YULE, Robert	Lieutenant. R.N.	ILLUSTRIOUS	
	Master's Mate	PENELOPE	Penelope. 30 March 1800
	Master's Mate	PENELOPE	Egypt (Vfd Abd. Not on Roll)
	Master's Mate	HERO	4 Novr 1805

(6) 20 SEP BOAT SERVICE 1811

Capture of two Danish privateers in WINGO SOUND (VINGA SAND), Baltic.
(Real date 21 September 1811)

BASON, John	Pte. R.M.	VICTORY
LAND, Gabriel	Quarter Gunner	VICTORY
MOUNTFORD, Charles	Pte. R.M.	VICTORY
PURCELL, Edward	Midshipman	VICTORY (P)
ROSTON, Joseph	A.B.	VICTORY
St CLAIR, David.L.	Lieut. R.N.	VICTORY (P)

(4) SKYLARK 11 NOVR 1811

Action with the Boulogne invasion flotilla and capture of the gun-brig Number 26.
(Real date 10 November 1811)

BIRD, William	Boy 2nd Cl	SKYLARK	
BOXER, James	Commander	SKYLARK	
	Midshipman	DIAMOND	*Port Spergui. 17 March 1796*
	Midshipman	TIGRE	*Acre 30 May 1799*
	Lieut. R.N.	TIGRE	*Egypt*
DYER, Richard	(Unknown)	SKYLARK	*(At first "Not Found" by Cmmtte, then "Found" under unknown alias at Action)*
WALFORD, William	Lieut. R.N.	SKYLARK	
	Midshipman	BELLEROPHON	*Trafalgar*

(2) LOCUST 11 NOVR 1811

Action with the Boulogne invasion flotilla and capture of the gun-brig Number 26.
(Real date 10 November 1811)

BACHELL, Samuel	Ord	LOCUST
GEDGE, John	Lieut. R.N.	LOCUST (P)

(74) PELAGOSA 29 NOVR 1811

Action with three French frigates, capture of POMONE and PERSANNE, in the Adriatic.

ADAMSON, Orame	Carp's Crew	ACTIVE	*(Vfd Abd. Not on Roll)*
	Carp's Crew	POWERFUL	*Camperdown*
	Carp's Crew	ACTIVE	*Lissa*
ALLINGTON, Samuel	Pte. R.M.	ACTIVE	*(Vfd Abd. Not on Roll)*
	Pte. R.M.	ACTIVE	*Lissa*
BADSEY, Thomas	Master's Mate	ACTIVE	
	Master's Mate	ACTIVE	*Lissa*
BARNETT, James	Boy 3rd Cl	UNITE	*G.H. 2,905*
BARROW, James	Actg Master	UNITE	
	Master	PRESIDENT	*St Sebastian*
BARWELL, Nathaniel	Midshipman	ACTIVE	*(Joined ACTIVE 10-5-1811. This Action also known as "2nd action off Lissa")*
BEECHING, George	Supn Pte. R.M.	ALCESTE	*(M.L. as BEACHAM)*
BIDDULPH, John	Cpl. R.M.	UNITE	
BOWEN, Richard	Midshipman	ACTIVE	
	Midshipman	ACTIVE	*B.S. 28 June 1810*
	Midshipman	ACTIVE	*Lissa*
CAMMILLIERI, Joseph	Midshipman	ACTIVE	
	(Not yet aboard)	ACTIVE	*B.S. 28 June 1810 (On Roll)*
	A.B.	ACTIVE	*Lissa*
	Master's Mate	SEAHORSE	*The Potomac. 17 Aug 1814*
	Master's Mate	SEAHORSE	*B.S. 14 Dec 1814*
COLLINS, John	L.M.	ACTIVE	
	L.M.	ACTIVE	*Lissa*
CORBET, John	A.B.	ACTIVE	*(Vfd Abd. Not on Roll)*
	A.B.	ACTIVE	*Lissa. GH.4258*
CRABB, Joseph.W.	Lieut. R.N.	UNITE	
CROKER, Charles	Midshipman	ALCESTE	
	Midshipman	ALCESTE	*B.S. 4 May 1811*

PELAGOSA 29 NOVR 1811

CULLERN, William	Pte. R.M.	ALCESTE	(Name may be CUTTERIN)
DASHWOOD, William.B.	Lieut. R.N.	ACTIVE	
	Vol 1st Cl	DEFIANCE	Copenhagen 1801
	Commander	PROMETHEUS	Algiers
DAVIES, Evan	Capt After Guard	ACTIVE	(M.L. as DAVIS)
	Capt After Guard	ACTIVE	B.S. 28 June 1810. (Vfd Abd. Not on 171/- Roll. On G.H. Roll) GH.6262
	Capt After Guard	ACTIVE	Lissa
DAWSON, John	Quarter Gunner	ACTIVE	
	Quarter Gunner	ACTIVE	Lissa
DUCK, Thomas	Sailmaker	UNITE	
DUFF, Norwich	Midshipman	ACTIVE	
	A.B.	MARS	Trafalgar
	Midshipman	ACTIVE	B.S. 28 June 1810
	Midshipman	ACTIVE	Lissa
ELVIN, William	L.M.	ACTIVE	
	L.M.	ACTIVE	Lissa
EVERARD, George	Capt Main Top	ACTIVE	
	Capt Main Top	ACTIVE	Lissa
FLANAGAN, Lawrence	Ord	UNITE	G.H. 6,902
FRIEND, Charles	Master's Mate	ACTIVE	
	Midshipman	ACTIVE	B.S. 28 June 1810
	Master's Mate	ACTIVE	Lissa
FRY, John	Pte. R.M.	UNITE	
GASO, Antonio	L.M.	UNITE	
GODFREY, Charles	A.B.	ALCESTE	
GOODRICK, Thomas	Carpenter	UNITE	
	Carp's Mate	COLOSSUS	Trafalgar
GOODRIDGE, Richard	Midshipman	UNITE	
GORDON, James.A.	Captain. R.N.	ACTIVE	
	Midshipman	REVOLUTIONNAIRE	23rd June 1795
	Midshipman	NAMUR	St Vincent
	Midshipman	GOLIATH	Nile
	Captain. R.N.	MERCURY	Off Rota. 4 April 1808
	Captain. R.N.	ACTIVE	Lissa
	Captain. R.N.	SEAHORSE	The Potomac. 17 Aug 1814
HARRIS, Francis	Midshipman	UNITE	(Died in 1883 aged 87)
	Vol 1st Cl	TEMERAIRE	Trafalgar
HAWKES, John	Pte. R.M.	ACTIVE	(M.L. as HAWKE)
	Pte. R.M.	ACTIVE	B.S. 28 June 1810
	Pte. R.M.	ACTIVE	Lissa
HAYE, George	Lieut. R.N.	ACTIVE	
	Lieut. R.N.	ACTIVE	Lissa
HEWETT, John.H.	Pte. R.M.	ACTIVE	(M.L. as HEWITT, Henry.J.)
	Pte. R.M.	ACTIVE	B.S. 28 June 1810
	Pte. R.M.	ACTIVE	Lissa
HILL, John	Two borne. Ord & Qtr Gunner	ACTIVE	(Vfd Abd. Not on Roll)
	Two borne. ,, ,,	ACTIVE	Lissa
HILL, Samuel	Boy 3rd Cl	ACTIVE	(Vfd Abd. Not on Roll)
	Boy 3rd Cl	ACTIVE	Lissa
HOTHAM, William	Actg Lieut. R.N.	UNITE	
HUGHES, Thomas	A.B.	ACTIVE	
	A.B.	ACTIVE	Lissa
JEFFERSON, Robert	Quarter Gunner	UNITE	
JOHNSON, Thomas	Coxswain	ACTIVE	(Vfd Abd. Not on Roll)
	Coxswain	ACTIVE	Lissa
JOHNSTON, John	Ord	ACTIVE	
JONES, William	Boy 2nd Cl	ACTIVE	
	Boy 2nd Cl	ACTIVE	Lissa
JUSTICE, Thomas	A.B.	ACTIVE	(Vfd Abd. Only on G.H.Roll)
	A.B.	ACTIVE	Lissa GH.7005.
KAY, James	Asst Surgeon	ACTIVE	
	Asst Surgeon	ACTIVE	Lissa
KENNEDY, Thomas	Ord	UNITE	
KING, John	Midshipman	ALCESTE	
	Midshipman	ALCESTE	B.S. 4 May 1811
Le MESURIER, Edward	Midshipman	UNITE	
LEAKEY, Robert	Bosun's Mate	UNITE	
LONG, Charles	A.B.	ACTIVE	(Vfd Abd. Not on Roll)
	A.B.	ACTIVE	Lissa G.H. 7,057
LUGG, William	Pte. R.M.	ALCESTE	
MACKENZIE, Nathaniel	L.M.	ACTIVE	(Vfd Abd. Not on Roll)
	L.M.	ACTIVE	Lissa
MACKLIN, Joseph	Capt Fore Top	ACTIVE	(Vfd Abd. Not on Roll)
	A.B.	ACTIVE	Lissa
M'DOUGALL, John	Lieut. R.N.	UNITE	
	Midshipman	Boats ex UNITE	B.S. 1 Nov 1809
	Lieut. R.N.	SUPERB	Algiers

MEARES, John	2nd Lt. R.M.	ACTIVE	
	2nd Lt. R.M.	ACTIVE	*B.S. 28 June 1810*
	2nd Lt. R.M.	ACTIVE	*Lissa*
MILFORD, William	Boy 3rd Cl	ACTIVE	
	Boy 3rd Cl	ACTIVE	*Lissa*
MILLS, Robert	Ord	ACTIVE	
	Ord	ACTIVE	*Lissa*
MONTAGU, James	Lieut. R.N.	ALCESTE	
	Midshipman	TIGRE	*B.S. 1 Nov 1809*
MORIATY, Redmond	Actg Lt. R.N.	ACTIVE	
NASH, Smith	Ord	ALCESTE	
	Ord	ALCESTE	*Off Rota. 4 April 1808*
PARRATT, Samuel	Ord	ACTIVE	*G.H. 2,567*
	Ord	ACTIVE	*Lissa*
SEARLES, William.G.	Gunner	ACTIVE	
	Gunner	ACTIVE	*Lissa*
SHANNON, William	Coxswain	UNITE	
	Boy	TRIUMPH	*Camperdown*
SIMPSON, James	Pte. R.M.	ALCESTE	
	(Not yet joined)	ALCESTE*	*Off Rota. 4 April 1808*
SPARKES, John	Pte. R.M.	ACTIVE	*(M.L. as SPARKS)*
	Pte. R.M.	ACTIVE	*B.S. 28 June 1810*
	Pte. R.M.	ACTIVE	*Lissa*
STANBURY, Peter	L.M.	ALCESTE	
	L.M.	ALCESTE	*B.S. 4 May 1811*
STOKES, Joseph	Cpl. R.M.	ACTIVE	*(Vfd Abd. Not on Roll)*
	Cpl. R.M.	ACTIVE	*B.S. 28 June 1810*
	Cpl. R.M.	ACTIVE	*Lissa*
SULLIVAN, Dennis	Pte. R.M.	ACTIVE	
	Pte. R.M.	ACTIVE	*Lissa*
SWAYNE, Stephen.J.	Surgeon	ACTIVE	
	Surgeon	VOLAGE	*Lissa*
	Surgeon	SEAHORSE	*The Potomac. 17 Aug 1814*
			(Vfd Abd. Not on Roll)
	Surgeon	SEAHORSE	*B.S. 14 Dec 1814*
TAYLOR, James	L.M.	ACTIVE	
	L.M.	ACTIVE	*Lissa*
TUCKEY, William	L.M.	ACTIVE	
	L.M.	ACTIVE	*Lissa*
	Blacksmith	BELLEROPHON	*Syria*
VICTOR, George	2nd Lt. R.M.	UNITE	
WATERHOUSE, William	L.M.	ACTIVE	
	L.M.	ACTIVE	*Lissa*
WILLIAMS, John	Ord	ALCESTE	
	A.B.	Qn CHARLOTTE	*Algiers (? same man)*
WOODS, Thomas	Midshipman	ACTIVE	
	Vol 1st Cl	ACTIVE	*Lissa*
	Midshipman	SEAHORSE	*The Potomac. 17 Aug 1814*
	Midshipman	SEAHORSE	*B.S. 14 Dec. 1814*
	Supn Master's Mate	IMPREGNABLE	*Algiers*

(19) 4 DEC BOAT SERVICE 1811

Capture of the French settee LANGUEDOC and brig CASTOR, off Bastia, Corsica.

BROOKS, Joseph	A.B.	SULTAN	*G.H. 2,380*
CHITTLE, Thomas	A.B.	SULTAN	*G.H. 9,888*
CROSLAND, Joseph	Pte. R.M.	SULTAN	*M.L. as CROSSLAND*
FARRELL, John	Ord	SULTAN	*GH.3382. M.L. as FERRALL*
GREEN, William	Ord	SULTAN	
GREGORY, Richard.B.	2nd Master	SULTAN	*Roll. @ THOMPSON, Charles.*
HANNABEL, Daniel	Q.M.	SULTAN	*(M.L. as HANABLE.)*
KIRKEE, Robert	A.B.	SULTAN	*(M.L. as KIRKIE)*
MANT, Joseph	Pte. R.M.	SULTAN	*GH.1882. G.H. Roll as MONK*
			(Entered incorrectly on 171/- Roll
			for B.S. 4 April 1812)
QUIN, Michael	Master's Mate	SULTAN (P)	
	Lieut. R.N.	WEAZLE	*Weazel. 22 April 1813.*
SIMONS, Simon	A.B.	SULTAN	
	Gunner's Servant	ROYAL SOVEREIGN	*1 June 1794*
SLOANE, Barnard	Ord	SULTAN	*G.H. 5,824*
THOMSON, Thomas	Pte. R.M.	SULTAN	
TWIGG, Robert	Ord	SULTAN	
WELCH, Thomas	Ord	SULTAN	*GH.4521. M.L. as WELSH.*
WHEELER, John	Ord	SULTAN	

4 DEC BOAT SERVICE 1811

WHITE, Peter	Master's Mate	SULTAN (P)	
	Bosun's Servant	LATONA	(Born 1 Aug 1785. Aged 9) 1 June 1794
	A.B.	DEFENCE	Nile
	Midshipman	DEFENCE	Copenhagen. 1801.
WILSON, Richard	Sgt. R.M.	SULTAN	G.H. 9,752
WOOD, John	Pte. R.M.	SULTAN	

(67) VICTORIOUS WITH RIVOLI (G.M.)

Capture of the French "74" RIVOLI, and the destruction of the corvette MERCURE, on 22 February 1812, off Venice.

AISTIN, Benjamin	A.B.	VICTORIOUS	(M.L. as ASHTON)
ALEXANDER, William	Pte. R.M.	VICTORIOUS	
ALLEN, William	Pte. R.M.	VICTORIOUS	
	Pte. R.M.	BRITANNIA	Trafalgar
ALSTON, George	Ord	VICTORIOUS	
	L.M.	SPENCER	St Domingo
ARMSTRONG, William	A.B.	VICTORIOUS	
	Ord	SPENCER	St Domingo
ARNOLD, Charles	Pte. R.M.	VICTORIOUS	
AYTON, George.H.	Master's Mate	VICTORIOUS	
BAILEY, Stephen	Pte. R.M.	VICTORIOUS	
BOLTON, Henry	Midshipman	VICTORIOUS	
BRIGGS, Richard	Two Borne A.B. & Ord	VICTORIOUS	
BROMFIELD, William	Pte. R.M.	VICTORIOUS	
BRUCE, George	Carpenter's Crew	VICTORIOUS	
BURNS, Patrick	Ord	VICTORIOUS	(M.L. as BYRNE)
	Boy 2nd Class	SPENCER	St Domingo
BUSH, William	Pte. R.M.	VICTORIOUS	
BYRNE, Patrick	Pte. R.M.	VICTORIOUS	G.H.9044
	Pte. R.M.	NEPTUNE	Trafalgar
	Pte. R.M.	GRANICUS	Algiers
CAWETT, Andrew	A.B.	VICTORIOUS	(M.L. as COWET)
CHERRY, Richard	L.M.	VICTORIOUS	
CHURCHER, Benjamin	Bosun's Mate	VICTORIOUS	
	Q.M's Mate	SPENCER	St Domingo
CLODD, William	Q.M.	VICTORIOUS	G.H. 7,653
	Ship's Corporal	SPENCER	St Domingo
COFFIN, John.T.	Lieut. R.N.	VICTORIOUS	
CRAWFORD, James.R.	Midshipman	VICTORIOUS	
CUTLER, William	Pte. R.M.	VICTORIOUS	
DANKS, John	Pte. R.M.	VICTORIOUS	
DAVIS, John	Two borne. Armr & Ord	VICTORIOUS	
DIGHTON, Joseph	A.B.	VICTORIOUS	
DIXON, John	L.M.	VICTORIOUS	
FEAR, Hugh	A.B.	VICTORIOUS	
	A.B.	SUPERB	St Domingo
	A.B.	SUPERB	B.S. 11 Aug 1808
FIDGE, Richard	A.B.	VICTORIOUS	(M.L. as FEDGE) GH.7715
	L.M.	SPENCER	St Domingo
FORD, Joseph	L.M.	VICTORIOUS	(M.L. as McFORD)
	L.M.	SPENCER	St Domingo
FURSMAN, Joseph	A.B.	VICTORIOUS	
GOULD, William	Ord	VICTORIOUS	
GURLEY, John	Midshipman	VICTORIOUS	
	A.B.	VICTORIOUS	
HARRETT, Robert	Ord	SPENCER	St Domingo
HARRIES, William.A.	Clerk	VICTORIOUS	
HONSLOW, William	Drummer. R.M.	VICTORIOUS	(M.L. as ONSLOW)
HOWELL, William	Pte. R.M.	VICTORIOUS	
JEFFRIES, William	Sgt. R.M.	VICTORIOUS	
JENKINS, John	A.B.	VICTORIOUS	G.H. 8,092
KEELING, John.J.	Master's Mate	VICTORIOUS	
LANGLEY, James	Ord	VICTORIOUS	
	L.M.	SPENCER	St Domingo
LODWICK, William	Carpenter	VICTORIOUS	
	Carpenter	IMPERIEUSE	Basque Roads 1809
MAYNING, James	A.B.	VICTORIOUS	
	Ord	SPENCER	St Domingo
MILES, William	Boy 3rd Cl	VICTORIOUS	
MULLINS, William	Boatswain	VICTORIOUS	
PEAKE, Thomas.L.	Lieut. R.N.	VICTORIOUS	
	Midshipman	RENOWN	Egypt
PHILLIPS, John	Pte. R.M.	VICTORIOUS	
RADNALL, Richard	Pte. R.M.	VICTORIOUS	
RAY, Joseph	Midshipman	VICTORIOUS	
READ, William	Pte. R.M.	VICTORIOUS	

REYNOLDS, Paul	Cpl. R.M.	VICTORIOUS	
RICH, Francis	Carp's Crew	VICTORIOUS	
ROBERTS, John	Yeoman of Powder Rm	VICTORIOUS	
RUSH, William	Pte. R.M.	VICTORIOUS	
SAVAGE, John	A.B.	VICTORIOUS	
SHAW, John	A.B.	VICTORIOUS	
	Ship's Cook	BELLEROPHON	Syria
SHEAD, Peter	Ord	VICTORIOUS	(M.L. as SHADE)
	L.M.	SPENCER	St Domingo
SILVERTHORN, Joseph	Pte. R.M.	VICTORIOUS	
SMITH, George	Pte. R.M.	VICTORIOUS	
SMITH, James	Ord	VICTORIOUS	G.H. 8,347
	Ord	SPENCER	St Domingo
SMITH, John	Two A.Bs borne	VICTORIOUS	
SPARROW, Benjamin.H.	A.B.	VICTORIOUS	
STEVENS, Robert	Captain. R.M.	VICTORIOUS	
	Lt. R.M.	RUSSELL	Camperdown
TALBOT, John	Captain. R.N.	VICTORIOUS	also Small Naval Gold Medal.
	Lieut. R.N.	ASTRAEA (P)	Astraea. 10 April 1795
THOMAS, Philip	A.B.	VICTORIOUS	
TOZER, Aaron	Lieut. R.N.	VICTORIOUS	
	Midshipman	PHOENIX	Phoenix 10 Augt 1805
TUCKER, William	Pte. R.M.	VICTORIOUS	G.H. 3,842
WHITE, Jacob	Pte. R.M.	VICTORIOUS	

(6) WEAZEL 22 FEBY 1812

Capture of the French 74-gun RIVOLI, and destruction of the corvette MERCURE by VICTORIOUS and WEAZLE, off Venice.

ANDREW, John.W.	Commander	WEAZLE	
	A.B.	FOUDROYANT	12 Octr 1798
	Midshipman	CANOPUS	St Domingo
FEATHER, James	Pte. R.M.	WEAZLE	(M.L. as FEATHERS)
	Pte. R.M.	MINOTAUR	Nile
	Pte. R.M.	WEAZLE	Weazel. 22 April 1813 (Vfd Abd. Not on Roll)
KIERNAN, Francis	Asst Surgeon	WEAZLE	
	Asst Surgeon	WEAZLE	Weazel. 22 April 1813
MILLY, John	Ord	WEAZLE	(M.L. as MELLY)
	A.B.	WEAZLE	Weazel. 22 April 1813 (Vfd Abd. Not on Roll)
SAXTON, John	Ord	WEAZLE	
	Ord	WEAZLE	Amanthea. 25 July 1810
	Ord	WEAZLE	B.S. 6 Jan 1813
	Ord	WEAZLE	Weazel. 22 April 1813
YOUNG, William	Pte. R.M.	WEAZLE	
	Pte. R.M.	WEAZLE	Weazel. 22 April 1813 (Vfd Abd. Not on Roll)

(7) ROSARIO. 27 MARCH 1812

Capture of three French brigs-of-war by ROSARIO and GRIFFON, off Dieppe.

BROWN, John	Actg Master	ROSARIO	
GILLMAN, James	Supn Pilot	ROSARIO	
NORRIS, George	Pte. R.M.	ROSARIO	
ROTHERY, James	Midshipman	ROSARIO	
STARR, George	Purser	ROSARIO	
	Clerk	ORION	Trafalgar
	Clerk	ALFRED	Guadaloupe
WATSON, William	Surgeon	ROSARIO	
WEBBER, John	Gunner	ROSARIO	

(3) GRIFFON 27 MARCH 1812

Capture of three French brigs-of-war by ROSARIO and GRIFFON, off Dieppe.

PRICE, Carteret	Master's Mate	GRIFFON	
SHEPHERD, Benjamin	Lieut. R.N.	GRIFFON	*(In Navy List & O'By as JOHN)*
	Midshipman	BRITANNIA	*Trafalgar*
	Midshipman	LATONA	*Curacoa*
	Midshipman	NEPTUNE	*Martinique*
	Master's Mate	POMPEE	*Guadaloupe*
TROLLOPE, George.B.	Commander	GRIFFON	
	Master's Mate	TRIUMPH	*17 June 1795*
			(Vfd Abd. Not on Roll)
	Lieut. R.N.	TRIUMPH	*Camperdown*

(4) 4 APRIL BOAT SERVICE 1812

Capture of the French xebec MARTINET, off Cape de Gatt, S.E.Spain.

CASWELL, William	Master's Mate	MAIDSTONE	
	Lieut. R.N.	SUPERB	*Algiers*
LIGHTBODY, George	Ord	MAIDSTONE	
REA, Andrew.C.	1st Lt. R.M.	MAIDSTONE	
SMITH, William	Pte. R.M.	MAIDSTONE	
	Pte. R.M.	MAIDSTONE	*B.S. Ap & May 1813*

(19) MALAGA 29 APRIL 1812

At MALAGA; capture of French privateers BRAVE & NAPOLEON.
(Printed list date of 29 May was incorrect)

ANDREWS, John	Ord	HYACINTH	
BELL, Joseph	Actg Boatswain	HYACINTH	
BARBER, John	Pte. R.M.	HYACINTH	
	Pte. R.M.	MALTA	*Gaieta. 24 July 1815*
	Pte. R.M.	GLASGOW	*Algiers*
BIRD, Richard	Pte. R.M.	RESOLUTE	
BLATCHLEY, Charles	Clerk	HYACINTH	
CULL, Thomas	Lieut. R.N. I/Cmd.	Gun Boat No 16.	*(Vfd Abd. Not on Roll)*
	Lieut. R.N.	LYRA	*St Sebastian*
EDWARDS, John	Carpenter's Crew	HYACINTH	*(Vfd Abd. Not on Roll)*
	Ord	STAUNCH	*Staunch. 18 Sepr 1810.*
FILE, Charles	Yeoman Powder Room	GOSHAWK	
HASTINGS, Thomas	Lieut. R.N.	HYACINTH	
HEAVISIDE, Marshal	Pte. R.M.	GOSHAWK	*(M.L. as HEAVISIDES)*
HOFFMEISTER, John.M.	Clerk	GOSHAWK	
LEAPER, William	Carpenter	GOSHAWK	
	Actg Carpenter	VIMIERA	*Guadaloupe*
OTTY, Allen	Lieut. R.N.	GOSHAWK	
PARROTT, George.L.	Master	GOSHAWK	
SHACKLE, Charles	A.B.	GOSHAWK	
USSHER, Thomas	Captain. R.N.	HYACINTH	
	Midshipman	INVINCIBLE	*1 June 1794*
	Commander	REDWING	*Redwing. 7 May 1808*
	Captain. R.N.	REDWING	*Redwing. 31 May 1808*
	Captain. R.N.	UNDAUNTED	*B.S. 2 May 1813*
VAZZEY, John	Pte. R.M.	RESOLUTE	
WEEKS, George	Capt Fore Top	HYACINTH	*GH.7501. M.L. @ BATT,G.*
WILTSHIRE, Thomas	Armourer	HYACINTH	
	Armourer's Mate	AGAMEMNON	*Trafalgar*
	Armourer's Mate	AGAMEMNON	*St Domingo*

(63) NORTHUMBERLAND 22 MAY 1812
Destruction of the French frigates ARIANE and ANDROMAQUE and the brig MAMELUK, off Isle de Groix, Lorient.

ASHBURNE, John	L.M.	NORTHUMBERLAND	
ALLEN, Jacob	Pte. R.M.	NORTHUMBERLAND	
BAKER, George	Midshipman	NORTHUMBERLAND	
BANKS, John	Lieut. R.N.	NORTHUMBERLAND (P)	
	A.B.	CANADA	12 Octr 1798
BEASLEY, Thomas	Two borne. Qtr Gnr & Ord	NORTHUMBERLAND	
BELLAMY, John	Boy 2nd Cl	NORTHUMBERLAND	G.H. 2,016
BOWEN, Charles	Lieut. R.N.	NORTHUMBERLAND	
	Midshipman	EDGAR	Copenhagen 1801
BRADY, Daniel	L.M.	NORTHUMBERLAND	
CARON, James	Ord	NORTHUMBERLAND	(M.L. as CARRON.GH. 5064)
CARTER, John	Trumpeter	NORTHUMBERLAND	
CROSS, George	Quarter Gunner	NORTHUMBERLAND	
DILLON, Robert	L.M.	NORTHUMBERLAND	
DRAKE, John	Lieut. R.N.	NORTHUMBERLAND	
	Midshipman	DEFENCE	Trafalgar
	Lieut. R.N.	ALBION	Navarino
DOYLE, Patrick	A.B.	NORTHUMBERLAND	
FERRY, John	Pte. R.M.	NORTHUMBERLAND	
FOURACRES, Nicholas	A.B.	NORTHUMBERLAND	
GALE, John	Carpenter	NORTHUMBERLAND	
	Carp's Crew	BELLEROPHON	1 June 1794
	Carp's Crew	BELLEROPHON	17 June 1795
	A.B.	CULLODEN	Nile
	Carp's Mate	SPENCER	Gut of Gibraltar.12 July 1801
GOLDSMITH, Samuel	Boy 3rd Cl	NORTHUMBERLAND	G.H. 8,831
HARDING, Francis	Boy 2nd Cl	NORTHUMBERLAND	
HARP, George	Pte. R.M.	NORTHUMBERLAND	
HATHERLEY, Edward	A.B.	NORTHUMBERLAND	G.H. 6,893
HAWKINS, James	Pte. R.M.	NORTHUMBERLAND	
HILL, Henry	A.B.	NORTHUMBERLAND	
HOTHAM, George.F.	Vol 1st Cl	NORTHUMBERLAND	
	Vol 1st Cl	MINDEN	Algiers
IRVING, John	Clerk	NORTHUMBERLAND	
LARDNER, Philip	Midshipman	NORTHUMBERLAND	
LEWIS, Joseph	Pte. R.M.	NORTHUMBERLAND	
LOW, John	Yeoman Powder Rm	NORTHUMBERLAND	
LUMBY, William	Boy 3rd Cl	NORTHUMBERLAND	
MAHONY, Thomas	A.B.	NORTHUMBERLAND	
MARSHAM, Henry.S.	Midshipman	NORTHUMBERLAND	
	Boy 2nd Cl	SUPERB	B.S. 11 Aug 1808
MAY, Francis	Midshipman	NORTHUMBERLAND	
McFERNAN, James	Asst Surgeon	NORTHUMBERLAND	
MOGDRIDGE, Abraham	Boy 2nd Cl	NORTHUMBERLAND	(M.L. as MOGRIDGE)
MOUNTFORD, Joseph	2nd Lt. R.M.	NORTHUMBERLAND	
NEIL, Thomas	Ord	NORTHUMBERLAND	
OWEN, Price	A.B.	NORTHUMBERLAND	
PAIN, Edward	Pte. R.M.	NORTHUMBERLAND	
PEARSE, Joseph	Midshipman	NORTHUMBERLAND	
PEARSON, John	Vol 1st Cl	NORTHUMBERLAND	
PILCH, William	Midshipman	NORTHUMBERLAND	
	Vol 1st Cl	BELLEROPHON	Trafalgar
PILE, Benjamin	Pte. R.M.	NORTHUMBERLAND	
PIPER, Edward.J.	Midshipman	NORTHUMBERLAND	
PLUMMER, William	Pte. R.M.	NORTHUMBERLAND	
PRICE, John	L.M.	NORTHUMBERLAND	
ROACH, William	A.B.	NORTHUMBERLAND	
ROWE, James	Midshipman	NORTHUMBERLAND	
ROWE, Robert	A.B.	NORTHUMBERLAND	
SALTER, John	Master's Mate	NORTHUMBERLAND	
	Midshipman	SUPERB	St Domingo
SAUNDERS, George	L.M.	NORTHUMBERLAND	
SAUNDERS, John	Yeoman of Sheets	NORTHUMBERLAND	
SHEPPARD, Joseph	Pte. R.M.	NORTHUMBERLAND	
	Pte. R.M.	Qn CHARLOTTE	Algiers
SIMMONDS, Edward	Pte. R.M.	NORTHUMBERLAND	GH.7721 (ML as SIMMONS)
SMITH, Abraham	Armourer	NORTHUMBERLAND	(Recd Medal aged 82)
SMITHWICK, Robert	2nd Lt. R.M.	NORTHUMBERLAND	
SMYTH, Spencer	Master's Mate	NORTHUMBERLAND (P)	
	Midshipman	DEFIANCE	Trafalgar
	Lieut. R.N.	VENERABLE	Venerable. 16 Jany 1814
	Lieut. R.N.	DARTMOUTH	Navarino
SPURWAY, John	Midshipman	NORTHUMBERLAND	
STEAD, William	R.M.Boy	NORTHUMBERLAND	(M.L. as STEED)
STEPHENS, William.L.	Midshipman	NORTHUMBERLAND	

NORTHUMBERLAND 22 MAY 1812

STYLE, Sir Thomas.C.Bart	Vol 1st Cl	NORTHUMBERLAND	
TRUSSLER, John	A.B.	NORTHUMBERLAND	*(M.L. as TRUSLER)*
WELCH, George	A.B.	NORTHUMBERLAND	*(M.L. as WELSH)*
WOLLEY, Godfrey.L.	Boy 2nd Cl.	NORTHUMBERLAND	

(1) GROWLER 22 MAY 1812

Destruction of the French frigates ARIANE and ANDROMAQUE and the brig MAMELUK, off Isle de Groix, Lorient.

EDWARDS, Henry	Midshipman	GROWLER	

(The following names on the GROWLER clasp roll served in NORTHUMBERLAND, and have been included in the former clasp list. DILLON, Robert. ROWE, Robert & STEPHENS, William.L.)

(47) OFF MARDOE 6 JULY 1812

Destruction of the Danish frigate NAYADEN and action with three corvettes, off Norwegian Coast.

ANDROS, Charles	Midshipman	DICTATOR	
	Midshipman	SPARTAN	*Spartan. 3 May 1810*
BAUGH, Edward	Vol 1st Cl	PODARGUS	
BEALE, William	Pte. R.M.	DICTATOR	*(Not yet found)*
BISHOP, William	L.M.	DICTATOR	
BROWN, Samuel	Bosun's Mate	PODARGUS	G.H. 5,986
BUCHANNAN, William	Lieut. R.N.	DICTATOR	
	A.B.	DEFENCE	*Trafalgar*
BURR, William	Armourer's Mate	DICTATOR	G.H. 2,228
CHANDLER, James	A.B.	DICTATOR	*(Deserted 5 Sept 1814)*
	Ord	SWIFTSURE	*Trafalgar*
	Capt Main Top	SHAMROCK	*Gluckstadt. 5 Jany 1814*
CROOKE, Thomas.L.	Midshipman	DICTATOR	
DIXON, John	Ord	DICTATOR	
DUTTON, Benjamin	Lieut. R.N.	DICTATOR	
EDWARDS, Richard	Lieut. R.N.	DICTATOR	
EDWARDS, William	A.B.	DICTATOR	
FOWLES, James	A.B.	DICTATOR	G.H. 9,756
GOODYER, John	A.B.	DICTATOR	
GRANGER, William	Pte. R.M.	DICTATOR	G.H. 3,599
GURNEY, John	Ord	CALYPSO	
HOOPER, Benjamin	Lieut. R.N.	CALYPSO	
	Midshipman	FOUDROYANT	*12 Octr 1798*
	Midshipman	LONDON	*London. 13 March 1806*
JOHN, Lewis	Actg Master	PODARGUS	
	A.B.	EXCELLENT	*St Vincent*
JONES, Samuel	Ord	DICTATOR	
LANE, William	Ord	DICTATOR	
LEDAN, John	Quarter Gunner	PODARGUS	
LEWIS, George	A.B.	DICTATOR	G.H. 6,438
LOVELL, James.E.	Midshipman	DICTATOR	
MANNER, George	Capt Main Top	CALYPSO	GH.7867. *(ML as MANNERS)*
MATTHEWS, Henry	Ord	DICTATOR	
MacNAMARA, F.F.	2nd Lt. R.M.	DICTATOR	*(M.L. as F.M.J.F.McN')*
MILLER, John	Ord	DICTATOR	
MORIN or MORAN, Barnabas	Ord	DICTATOR	
NISBETT, John	Pte. R.M.	DICTATOR	*(M.L. as NESBIT)*
POWELL, John	Midshipman	FLAMER	
PRICE, Edward	A.B.	CALYPSO	
ROBILLIARD, Thomas	Vol 1st Cl	PODARGUS	
SANDERSON, Henry	Asst Surgeon	DICTATOR	
SMITH, James	A.B.	DICTATOR	G.H. 8,829
SMITH, John	Surgeon	CALYPSO	
STEPHENS, Michael.C.	Purser	CALYPSO	
STEWART, James.P.	Captain.R.N.	DICTATOR	
	Lieut. R.N.	NORTHUMBERLAND	*St Domingo*
	Commander	SHELDRAKE	*Anholt. 27 March 1811*
STITCHBURY, William	Pte. R.M.	DICTATOR	G.H. 9,194
TAUNTON, James	A.B.	DICTATOR	*(M.L. as TANTON)* GH.1271
TAYLOR, Richard	A.B.	DICTATOR	G.H. 2,588
THOMAS, John	Armourer's Mate	CALYPSO	
THOMPSON, Joseph.F.	Midshipman	DICTATOR	
TRISCOTT, Joseph	Captain. R.M.	DICTATOR	
	2nd Lt. R.M.	SPENCER	*Gut of Gibraltar. 12 July 1801*
WARREN, Thomas	Ord	DICTATOR	G.H. 6,895
WHITEHEAD, Abraham	Midshipman	DICTATOR	
WISE, William	Pte. R.M.	DICTATOR	GH.2910 *(M.L. as WIRE)*

(4) SEALARK 21 JULY 1812

Capture of the French privateer VILLE DE CAEN, off Start Point, Devon.

CUMMINGS, James	Gunner's Mate	SEALARK	
DURNFORD, Thomas	A.B.	SEALARK	
	Ord.	CYGNET	*Guadaloupe*
WAKEHAM, John	Cpl. R.M.	SEALARK	
WARRAND, Thomas	Lieut Commanding	SEALARK (P)	
	Master's Mate	VICTORY	*St Vincent*

(21) 1 & 18 SEP BOAT SERVICE 1812

Action with and capture of two French gun-boats, the xebec TISIPHONE and seven vessels of a convoy by boats of BACCHANTE in Port Lemo, Istria, Adriatic.

(The real and only date of this Action was 1 September 1812. The Medal Committee became muddled on the date, and altered it four times in the Medal Roll. Similar bother occurred with BACCHANTE's other Boat Action on 6 January 1813. The issue of these two clasps may well have become confused.)

ALDERSON, George	Ord	BACCHANTE	G.H. 1,877
	Ord	BACCHANTE	B.S. 6 Jan 1813
ARNOLL, James	Ord	BACCHANTE	(M.L. as ARNELL)
	Ord	BACCHANTE	B.S. 6 Jan 1813
BISHOP, John	Armourer's Mate	BACCHANTE	G.H. 8,812
	Armourer's Mate	EURYDICE	*Martinique*
	Armourer	BACCHANTE	B.S. 6 Jan 1813
BRUCE, Charles	(Not yet joined)	BACCHANTE	(Not aboard. On Roll)
	Midshipman	AMPHION	B.S. 28 Aug 1809
	Midshipman	AMPHION	B.S. 28 June 1810
	Midshipman Ord	BACCHANTE	B.S. 6 Jan 1813
(BRYAN, John)	(See B.S. 7 Jan 1813 Roll)		
CLARE, James	A.B.	BACCHANTE	(M.L. as CLEAR)
	Coxswain	BACCHANTE	B.S. 6 Jan 1813
FARROW, Alexander	Pte. R.M.	BACCHANTE	
	Pte. R.M.	BACCHANTE	B.S. 6 Jan 1813
FURNEAUX, Theophilus	A.B.	BACCHANTE	
	Capt Main Top	EURYDICE	*Martinique*
	A.B.	BACCHANTE	B.S. 6 Jan 1813
HAIG, William	1st Lt. R.M.	BACCHANTE	
	1st Lt. R.M.	BACCHANTE	B.S. 6 Jan 1813
HOOD, Silas.T.	Lieut. R.N.	BACCHANTE	
	Lieut. R.N.	CONFLICT	*Basque Roads. 1809*
	Lieut. R.N.	BACCHANTE	B.S. 6 Jan 1813
JONES, James	Pte. R.M.	BACCHANTE	
	Pte. R.M.	TONNANT	*Trafalgar*
	Pte. R.M.	BACCHANTE	B.S. 6 Jan 1813
LANGTON, Thomas.W.	Midshipman	BACCHANTE	
	Midshipman	AMPHION	*Lissa*
LLOYD, John	L.M.	BACCHANTE	
	L.M.	BACCHANTE	B.S. 6 Jan 1813
MELVILL, Thomas	Capt Forecastle	BACCHANTE	(M.L. as MELVIN)
	Capt Forecastle	BACCHANTE	B.S. 6 Jan 1813
MONDAY, John	Ord	BACCHANTE	
	Boy 3rd Cl	AMAZON	*Amazon. 13 March 1806*
	Ord	BACCHANTE	B.S. 6 Jan 1813
O'BRIEN, Donat.H.	Lieut. R.N.	BACCHANTE (P)	
	Lieut. R.N.	AMPHION	B.S. 28 June 1810
	Lieut. R.N.	AMPHION	*Lissa*
	Lieut. R.N.	BACCHANTE	B.S. 6 Jan 1813
PAYNE, George	Yeoman of Sheets	BACCHANTE	
	A.B.	AMAZON	*Amazon. 13 March 1806*
	Yeoman of Sheets	BACCHANTE	B.S. 6 Jan 1813
POWELL, George.E.	Master's Mate	BACCHANTE	
	Master's Mate	BACCHANTE	B.S. 6 Jan 1813 (? awarded)
	Lieut. R.N.	CORDELIA	*Algiers*
ROUS, Henry.J.	Midshipman	BACCHANTE	
	Midshipman	BACCHANTE	B.S. 6 Jan 1813
SPENCER, James	Ord	BACCHANTE	
	Ord	BACCHANTE	B.S. 6 Jan 1813
TURNER, William	Two Borne A.B. & Pte. R.M.	BACCHANTE	G.H. 2,690
	(as above)	BACCHANTE	B.S. 6 Jan 1813
WHISKER, William	A.B.	BACCHANTE	
	L.M.	AMPHION	B.S. 28 Aug 1809
	L.M.	AMPHION	B.S. 28 June 1810
	L.M.	AMPHION	*Lissa*

(11) 17 SEP BOAT SERVICE 1812

Action with and capture of two gun-boats and twenty-one of a convoy, off Goro, near Ancona, Adriatic.

BINES, Robert	L.M.	EAGLE	(Clasp altered from "17 Dec" to "17 Sep")
CEMMETT, Joseph	A.B.	EAGLE	(M.L. as CEMMITT)
	A.B.	NASSAU	Nassau 22 March 1808
CLARK, James	Caulker's Mate	EAGLE	(M.L. as CLARKE)
	Carpenter's Crew	NASSAU	Nassau 22 March 1808 G.H. 1508
FESTING, Benjamin.M.	Lieut. R.N.	EAGLE	
	Midshipman	PRINCE	Trafalgar
GOOD, John	Pte. R.M.	EAGLE	(M.L. as GOODE)
HEINE, Richard	Pte. R.M.	EAGLE	(M.L. as HEARNE)
HUSSEY, Charles	Ord	EAGLE	
	L.M.	NASSAU	Nassau. 22 March 1808
LLOYD, Samuel	2nd Lt R.M.	EAGLE	
MOORE, Charles	Master's Mate	EAGLE (P)	
NICHOLSON, James	Q.M.	EAGLE	
SEYMOUR, Samuel	A.B.	EAGLE	
	Ord	NASSAU	Nassau. 22 March 1808

(25) 29 SEP BOAT SERVICE 1812

Attack and occupation of MITTAU (JELGAVA), Gulf of Riga, Estonia.

BEAMSON, Robert	Caulker	ABOUKIR	
BELLAMY, John	Ord	ABOUKIR	
BRENTON, John	Actg Cdr of Squadron of gun-boats	(ABOUKIR) (P)	Supernumerary abd ABOUKIR Awd St Vladimir 4th Cl.
	Master's Mate	CAESAR	Gut of Gibraltar. 12 July 1801 (At R.N. Museum)
COLBIE, William	L.M.	ABOUKIR	
D'ALTON, Edward.N.	Midshipman	ABOUKIR	
DRAMGOD, Patrick	A.B.	ABOUKIR	GH.3176. ML as DRUMGOLD
ELVIN, Thomas	Drummer. R.M.	ABOUKIR	G.H. 3211
FORDE, William	A.B.	ABOUKIR	M.L. as FORD
GENT, Thomas	Pte. R.M.	ABOUKIR	
HAYMES, Philip.G.	Supn Actg Lt.RN.	ABOUKIR	
HILL, Samuel	Supn Actg Lt.RN.	ABOUKIR (P)	Not on Roll. Late Applictn. Pmtd for services at Action.
	Midshipman	STATELY	STATELY. 22 March 1808. (Verified on Roll)
HORTH, John	Pte. R.M.	ABOUKIR	
HOWARD, John	Sailmaker	ABOUKIR	
KYLE, George	Lieut. R.N.	ABOUKIR	
	Master's Mate	ELEPHANT	Copenhagen 1801
MARSHALL, John	L.M.	ABOUKIR	G.H. 3000
MATTHEWS, John	Quarter Gunner	ABOUKIR	
ORMOND, Francis	Actg Flag Lieut	ABOUKIR	(At Action. Supn Lt.RN)
	Midshipman	IMPLACABLE	Implacable. 26 Augt 1808
	Master's Mate	IMPLACABLE	B.S. 7 July 1809
	Lieut. R.N.	ENDYMION	Endymion Wh President
	Lieut. R.N.	IMPREGNABLE	Algiers
OWEN, George	Cpl. R.M.	ABOUKIR	G.H. 752
PIKE, James	A.B.	ABOUKIR	G.H. 9995
ROBERTS, Andrew	A.B.	ABOUKIR	G.H. 10,117
ROBINSON, Joseph	Vol 1st Cl.	ABOUKIR	(12 years old)
SALTMARSH, John	Ord	ABOUKIR	
SIMONDS, Richard.S.	Supn Lieut. RN.	ABOUKIR	
	Midshipman	DEFENCE	Trafalgar
	Master's Mate	CALEDONIA	B.S. 27 Sep 1810
USHER, Charles	A.B.	ABOUKIR	
WARNER, William	Ord	ABOUKIR	G.H. 1512. (Original medal stolen in Admiralty. Duplicate issued.)

ROYALIST 29 DECR 1812
(4)

Capture of the French privateer RUSE, off Hythe, Kent.
(Recorded in Boat Service Roll, — ADM 171/3/148.)

BROWN, Alexander	Coxswain	ROYALIST	
	A.B.	SWIFTSURE	Nile
CARTER, William.F.	Surgeon	ROYALIST	(Vfd Abd. Not on Roll)
	Surgeon	BLONDE	Anse La Barque. 18 Decr 1809
	Surgeon	BLONDE	Guadaloupe
HACKMAN, Henry	A.B.	ROYALIST	
REES, Lewis	Midshipman	ROYALIST	

6 JAN BOAT SERVICE 1813
(25)

Capture of five French gun-boats off OTRANTO, Italy, by boats of BACCHANTE and WEAZLE.

(The date of this Action caused the Medal Committee a lot of bother. As did the date for the action by the boats of BACCHANTE on 1 September 1812. The issue of these two clasps may well have become confused.)

ALDERSON, George	Ord	BACCHANTE	G.H.1,877
	Ord	BACCHANTE	B.S. 1 & 18 Sep 1812
ARNOLL, James	Ord	BACCHANTE	(M.L. as ARNELL)
	Ord	BACCHANTE	B.S. 1 & 18 Sep 1812
BISHOP, John	Armourer	BACCHANTE	G.H. 8,812
	Armourer's Mate	EURYDICE	Martinique
	Armourer's Mate	BACCHANTE	B.S. 1 & 18 Sep 1812
BRUCE, Charles	Midshipman Ord	BACCHANTE	
	Midshipman	AMPHION	B.S. 28 Aug 1809
	Midshipman	AMPHION	B.S. 28 June 1810
	(Not yet joined)	BACCHANTE	B.S. 1 & 18 Sep 1812 (On 171/3/38 Roll)
BRYAN, John	Ord	WEAZLE	(Medal known with B.S. clasp dated 1 Sep 1812. See heading on "confusion".)
	Ord	WEAZLE	Weazel. 22 April 1813.
CLARE, James	Coxswain	BACCHANTE	(M.L. as CLEAR)
	A.B.	BACCHANTE	B.S. 1 & 18 Sep 1812
COX, William	A.B.	BACCHANTE	G.H. 3,330
	A.B.	AMAZON	Amazon. 13 March 1806
FARROW, Alexander	Pte. R.M.	BACCHANTE	
	Pte. R.M.	BACCHANTE	B.S. 1 & 18 Sep 1812
FURNEAUX, Theophilus	A.B.	BACCHANTE	
	Capt Main Top	EURYDICE	Martinique
	A.B.	BACCHANTE	B.S. 1 & 18 Sep 1812
HAIG, William	1st Lt. R.M.	BACCHANTE	
	1st Lt. R.M.	BACCHANTE	B.S. 1 & 18 Sep 1812
HOOD, Silas.T.	Lieut. R.N.	BACCHANTE	
	Lieut. R.N.	CONFLICT	Basque Roads. 1809
	Lieut. R.N.	BACCHANTE	B.S. 1 & 18 Sep 1812
JONES, James	Pte. R.M.	BACCHANTE	
	Pte. R.M.	TONNANT	Trafalgar
	Pte. R.M.	BACCHANTE	B.S. 1 & 18 Sep 1812
LLOYD, John	L.M.	BACCHANTE	
	L.M.	BACCHANTE	B.S. 1 & 18 Sep 1812
MELVILL, Thomas	Capt Forecastle	BACCHANTE	(M.L. as MELVIN)
	Capt Forecastle	BACCHANTE	B.S. 1 & 18 Sep 1812
MONDAY, John	Ord	BACCHANTE	
	Boy 3rd Cl	AMAZON	Amazon. 13 March 1806
	Ord	BACCHANTE	B.S. 1 & 18 Sep 1812
O'BRIEN, Donat.H.	Lieut. R.N.	BACCHANTE	
	Lieut. R.N.	AMPHION	B.S. 28 June 1810
	Lieut. R.N.	AMPHION	Lissa
	Lieut. R.N.	BACCHANTE (P)	B.S. 1 & 18 Sep 1812
PAYNE, George	Yeoman of Sheets	BACCHANTE	
	A.B.	AMAZON	Amazon. 13 March 1806
	Yeoman of Sheets	BACCHANTE	B.S. 1 & 18 Sep 1812
PAYNE, Joseph	Ord	BACCHANTE	
	L.M.	AMAZON	Amazon. 13 March 1806
POWELL, George.E.	Master's Mate	BACCHANTE	(Query if clasp awarded)
	Master's Mate	BACCHANTE	B.S. 1 & 18 Sep 1812
	Lieut. R.N.	CORDELIA	Algiers
RICHARDSON, Samuel	Vol 1st Cl	BACCHANTE	
ROUS, Henry.J.	Midshipman	BACCHANTE	
	Midshipman	BACCHANTE	B.S. 1 & 18 Sep 1812

6 JAN BOAT SERVICE 1813

SAXTON, John	Ord	WEAZLE	
	Ord	WEAZLE	Amanthea. 25 July 1810
	Ord	WEAZLE	Weazel. 22 Feby 1812
	Ord	WEAZLE	Weazel. 22 April 1813
SPENCER, James	Ord	BACCHANTE	
	Ord	BACCHANTE	B.S. 1 & 18 Sep 1812
STRADLING, Thomas	Pte. R.M.	BACCHANTE	
	Pte. R.M.	HAUGHTY	Martinique
	Pte. R.M.	VESTAL	Egypt
TURNER, William	Two Borne A.B. & Pte. RM.	BACCHANTE	G.H. 2,690
	(as above)	BACCHANTE	B.S. 1 & 18 Sep 1812

(3) 21 MARCH BOAT SERVICE 1813

Capture of the Danish gun-boats JONGE TROUTMAN and LIEBE, in River Elbe, Germany.

DAVIES, Thomas	Asst Surgeon	BREVDAGEREN	
DEVON, Frederick	Midshipman	BREVDAGEREN (P)	
WHITEMAN, James	Pte. R.M.	BLAZER	
	Pte. R.M.	BLAZER	Gluckstadt. 5 Jany 1814 (Vfd Abd. Not on Roll)

(8) WEAZEL 22 APRIL 1813

Destruction of six French gun-boats in BOSCALINE, off Venice.

BRYAN, John	Ord	WEAZLE	
	Ord	WEAZLE	B.S. 6 Jan 1813 (See Note)
FEATHER, James	Pte. R.M.	WEAZLE	(Vfd Abd. Not on Roll) M.L. as FEATHERS
	Pte. R.M.	MINOTAUR	Nile
	Pte. R.M.	WEAZLE	Weazel. 22 Feby 1812
KIERNAN, Francis	Asst Surgeon	WEAZLE	
	Asst Surgeon	WEAZLE	Weazel. 22 Feby 1812
MILLY, John	A.B.	WEAZLE	(Vfd Abd. Not on Roll)
	Ord	WEAZLE	Weazel. 22 Feby 1812
QUIN, Michael	Lieut. R.N.	WEAZLE	
	Master's Mate	SULTAN (P)	B.S. 4 Dec 1811
SAXTON, John	Ord	WEAZLE	
	Ord	WEAZLE	Amanthea. 25 July 1810
	Ord	WEAZLE	Weazel. 22 Feby 1812
	Ord	WEAZLE	B.S. 6 Jan 1813
WATSON, William	Ord	WEAZLE	
YOUNG, William	Pte. R.M.	WEAZLE	(Vfd Abd. Not on Roll)
	Pte. R.M.	WEAZLE	Weazel. 22 Feby 1812

(2) 29 APRIL BOAT SERVICE 1813 (a)

Destruction of the American letter of marque WAMPOE, off North American Coast.

(Real date 28 April 1813)

DANCE, William.F.	Actg Lieut. R.N.	ORPHEUS (P)
MacDONALD, Gordon.G.	Midshipman	ORPHEUS

(57) ## AP & MAY BOAT SERVICE 1813
also as
29 APRIL BOAT SERVICE 1813 (b)

(Real dates 29 April and 3 May 1813)

Destruction of battery, stores and vessels at Frenchtown, and cannon foundry and battery at Havre de Grace, up Elk River, Chesapeake Bay.

(The Medal Roll shows the original entry of "29 April" crossed out, with correction of "April & May", – no doubt to avoid confusion with previous clasp. Clasps are known with both engraved dates, with a distinct probability that the "29 April" variety appeared on the clasps issued to early applicants.)

ALEXANDER, Nicholas	Lieut. R.N.	DRAGON	
	Vol 1st Cl	HAERLEM	Egypt
	Midshipman	DESIREE	Copenhagen 1801
ANDERSON, George	Purser	FANTOME	
	Clerk	PORCUPINE	B.S. 10 July 1808
BARTLETT, John	Ord	MARLBOROUGH	
BISCON, Peter	L.M.	DRAGON	(Not yet found)
BISHOP, George	Lieut. R.N.	STATIRA	(Known "29 April")
BLANDFORD, George	L.M.	MARLBOROUGH	
BRIDSON, Robert	L.M.	DRAGON	
BUCK, Robert	L.M.	MARLBOROUGH	
COCKBURN, George	Rear Admiral	MARLBOROUGH	(Known "29 April")
	Captain. R.N.	MELEAGER	14 March 1795
	Captain. R.N.	MINERVE	Minerve. 19 Decr 1796
	Captain. R.N.	MINERVE	St Vincent
	Captain. R.N.	MINERVE	Egypt
	Commodore	POMPEE	Martinique
CRANE, John	A.B.	FANTOME	Maybe Ishmael CRANE.
DENMEAD, John	Pte. R.M.	DRAGON	
	Pte. R.M.	NORTHUMBERLAND	St Domingo
DOWELL, Thomas	Pte. R.M.	DRAGON	
EDMONDS, Evan	A.B.	STATIRA	
FITZPATRICK, James	L.M.	HIGHFLYER	(M.L. missing)
FRANCILLON, John.G.	Midshipman	MARLBOROUGH	
	Midshipman	POMPEE	Martinique
FRANCILLON, Thomas	Midshipman	MARLBOROUGH	
	Midshipman	POMPEE	Martinique
	Supn Lieut. R.N.	RAMILLIES	B.S. 14 Dec 1814
GOSLING, William	Capt Forecastle	MARLBOROUGH	G.H. 5,743
GREENBERRY, David	Ord	MARLBOROUGH	(Known "Ap & May")
GROWSE, John	L.M.	MARLBOROUGH	
HANDOLL, Samuel	Pte. R.M.	MARLBOROUGH	(Known "Ap & May") (M.L. as HANDELL)
HAWKINS, George. D.	1st Lt. R.M.	DRAGON	
HORNSBY, William	Boy 3rd Cl	MARLBOROUGH	
HOY, John	Pte. R.M.	DRAGON	(Known "Ap & May")
HUTCHINSON, George	Lieut. R.N.	DOLPHIN	
	Master's Mate	DIADEM	Egypt
	Master's Mate	CAESAR	4 Novr 1805
HUTCHINSON, William	Lieut. R.N.	MOHAWK	
JOINT, Thomas	Pte. R.M.	DRAGON	
	Pte. R.M.	ENCOUNTER	Basque Roads 1809
JONES, John	Ord	STATIRA	
	A.B.	STATIRA	Guadaloupe
KENT, Henry	Lieut. R.N.	FANTOME	
KILNER, Richard	Pte. R.M.	MARLBOROUGH	
LAMB, Joseph	Boy 2nd Cl	DRAGON	
LAWRENCE, John	Commander	FANTOME	
	Midshipman	WINDSOR CASTLE	14 March 1795
	Captain. R.N.	HASTINGS	Syria
LEARY, John	Ord	FANTOME	
L'ESTRANGE, Frederick	Vol 1st Cl	MAIDSTONE	
	Midshipman	MAIDSTONE	B.S. 8 April 1814
LIDDON, Matthew	Lieut. R.N.	MAIDSTONE	(Known "April & May")
	Master's Mate	THAMES	Amanthea. 25 July 1810
	Lieut. R.N.	MAIDSTONE	B.S. 8 April 1814
LYON, Francis	Master's Mate	STATIRA	(Known "Ap & May")
LYONS, Thomas	Boy 3rd Cl	MARLBOROUGH	
MACNAMARA, Burton	Midshipman	STATIRA	
MILLS, Charles	Pte. R.M.	MARLBOROUGH	
MOODY, Samuel	Pte. R.M.	DRAGON	
PARKER, Henry	Lieut. R.N.	DRAGON	
	Midshipman	BELLEISLE	Trafalgar
PEMITER, William	Ord	STATIRA	
	L.M.	STATIRA	Guadaloupe

AP & MAY BOAT SERVICE 1813 also as 29 APRIL BOAT SERVICE 1813

PERKINS, Joseph	Q.M's Mate	STATIRA	(Known "Ap & May")
	A.B.	QUEEN CHARLOTTE	B.S. 20 Dec 1799
	Q.M's Mate	STATIRA	Guadaloupe
PILGRIM, John	Ord	MAIDSTONE	(Known "Ap & May")
RAMMAGE, John	Coxswain	DRAGON	(Known "29 April")
			(M.L. as RUMMAGE)
RENDLE, William	Ord	DRAGON	
RICHARDSON, Michael	L.M.	MARLBOROUGH	
ROBERTSON, Frederick	Lieut. R.A.	MARLBOROUGH	(Known "Ap & May")
SCOTT, James	Lieut. R.N.	MARLBOROUGH	
	Midshipman	BLANCHE	Blanche. 19 July 1806
			M.G.S. Martinique.
			China 1842. Samarang/Nemesis
SMITH, William	A.B.	MARLBOROUGH	
SMITH, William	Pte. R.M.	MAIDSTONE	
	Pte. R.M.	MAIDSTONE	B.S. 4 April 1812
SNOWDELL, James	L.M.	MARLBOROUGH	(Known "Ap & May")
SWAINSON, William	Midshipman	DRAGON	(Known "29 April")
TAYLOR, Timothy	Ord	MARLBOROUGH	G.H. 9,341
WALKER, Henry	Lieut. R.N.	MOHAWK	
	Vol 1st Cl	TEMERAIRE	Trafalgar
WEST, Richard	L.M.	MARLBOROUGH	
WESTPHAL, George.A.	Lieut. R.N.	MARLBOROUGH (P)	(Known "29 April")
	Midshipman	VICTORY	Trafalgar
	Lieut. R.N.	BELLEISLE	Martinique
WOODROW, Charles	Ord	HIGHFLYER	

(48) 2 MAY BOAT SERVICE 1813

Destruction of batteries and capture of six merchant vessels at MORGIOU, near Toulon.

ARCHER, Charles	Ord	VOLONTAIRE	
	L.M.	VOLONTAIRE	B.S. 1 Nov 1809
BANNATYNE, John	Master's Mate	VOLONTAIRE	
	Master's Mate	VOLONTAIRE	B.S. 1 Nov 1809
BARRATTE, Augustus.G.	Midshipman	UNDAUNTED	
BOWLINE, James	Boy 3rd Cl	UNDAUNTED	
BRASIER, James	Lieut. R.N.	REPULSE	
	Midshipman	DEFENCE	Copenhagen 1801 (Vfd Abd)
	Lieut. R.N.	ALFRED	Guadaloupe
CLARE, James	Ord	REPULSE	G.H. 1,635 (M.L. as CLEAR)
CLARKE, William.N.	Lieut. R.N.	REDWING	
COOPER, Edward.W.	A.B.	REPULSE	G.H. 1,935
CORNWALL, John	Midshipman	VOLONTAIRE	
	Midshipman	THAMES	Amanthea. 25 July 1810
DAVIS, Simon	Pte. R.M.	VOLONTAIRE	(M.L. as DAVIES)
	Cpl. R.M.	CUMBERLAND	B.S. 1 Nov 1809
DOW, William	Midshipman	UNDAUNTED	
DOWNS, Daniel	Ord	REPULSE	(M.L. as DOWNES)
DRUMMER, William	Cpl. R.M.	REPULSE	
FISHER, Charles	Pte. R.M.	REPULSE	
FULCHER, William	A.B.	VOLONTAIRE	
GIRVIN, John	A.B.	UNDAUNTED	
GORDON, William.F.	L.M.	UNDAUNTED	G.H. 9,892
GUY, Thomas	Ord	REPULSE	
HALEY, James	Ord	REPULSE	
HALLAHAN, Thomas	Midshipman Ord	UNDAUNTED	
	Midshipman	REDWING	Redwing. 7 May 1808
	Midshipman	REDWING	Redwing. 31 May 1808
HARPER, James	Master's Mate	REPULSE	(Roll as HARPUR)
HOSEY, John	A.B.	VOLONTAIRE	
KELLY, John	L.M.	UNDAUNTED	
KEWSON, William	Ord	UNDAUNTED	(M.L. as KUESON)
LIARDET, William	Midshipman	REDWING	
LEITH, James	M.A.A.	REPULSE	
MIDGELEY, John	Pte. R.M.	REPULSE	
MORGAN, Richard	L.M.	REPULSE	
MOULD, Thomas	Cpl. R.M.	VOLONTAIRE	
	Pte. R.M.	VOLONTAIRE	B.S. 1 Nov 1809
O'CONNOR, John	A.B.	UNDAUNTED	
OLDREY, William	Lieut. R.N.	UNDAUNTED	
	Midshipman	DOTTEREL	Basque Roads 1809
PETERSON, John	A.B.	REPULSE	G.H. 1,281
ROBINSON, John	A.B.	REPULSE	
SALKELD, Thomas	Master's Mate	UNDAUNTED	

SHAW, Isaac	Lieut. R.N.	VOLONTAIRE (P)	
	Midshipman	ROMULUS	14 March 1795 (Vfd Abd)
	Midshipman	BARFLEUR	St Vincent
	Lieut. R.N.	NEPTUNE	Trafalgar
SINCLAIR, Sir John.G.	Commander	REDWING	
	Supn Midshipman	AMAZON	Amazon. 13 March 1806
STEPHENSON, James	A.B.	VOLONTAIRE	
SYER, Dey Richard	Lieut. R.N.	VOLONTAIRE	
	Midshipman	PRINCE	Trafalgar
	Midshipman	TIGRE	B.S. 1 Nov 1809
TARPLETT, George	A.B.	REPULSE	
TOD, John	Midshipman	REPULSE	
	Midshipman	TONNANT	B.S. 14 Dec 1814
TOWNSEND, Thomas	Pte. R.M.	UNDAUNTED	
	Pte. R.M.	PORCUPINE	B.S. 10 July 1808
USSHER, Thomas	Captain. R.N.	UNDAUNTED	
	Midshipman	INVINCIBLE	1 June 1794
	Commander	REDWING (P)	Redwing. 7 May 1808
	Captain. R.N.	REDWING	Redwing. 31 May 1808
	Captain. R.N.	HYACINTH	Malaga. 29 April 1812.
WELLS, George	Ord	REDWING	
WHITE, William	A.B.	UNDAUNTED	
WILSON, Thomas	L.M.	VOLONTAIRE	
	Boy 2nd Cl	VOLONTAIRE	B.S. 1 Nov 1809
WYVILL, Christopher	Midshipman	VOLONTAIRE	
	Midshipman	THAMES	Amanthea. 25 July 1810
YOUNG, James	Armourer	VOLONTAIRE	
	Armourer	VOLONTAIRE	B.S. 1 Nov 1809
YOUNG, James.L.	Actg Lieut. R.N.	UNDAUNTED	

(42) SHANNON WH CHESAPEAKE (G.M.)

Capture of the American frigate CHESAPEAKE on 1 June 1813, off Boston Harbour.

ALEXANDER, John	Pte. R.M.	SHANNON	
BEACH, Samuel	Pte. R.M.	SHANNON	
BOYD, Robert	Cooper	SHANNON	
CADET, John.P.	Ord	SHANNON	G.H. 3,497
	Supn Ord	HECLA	Algiers
CENTER, Joseph	Capt After Guard	SHANNON	G.H. 3,363
	A.B.	VENUS	1 June 1794
			(M.L. as KINTER, CANTER & CENTRE.)
COLLIER, John	Gunner's Mate	SHANNON	
CONNOLLY, James	Boy 2nd Cl	SHANNON	
	Ord	GENOA	Navarino
	A.B.	IMPLACABLE	Syria
COOPER, Isaac	Pte. R.M.	SHANNON	
DIAMOND, William	Ord	SHANNON	
DOWNHAM, William	Ord	SHANNON	
DOUGHERTY, John	A.B.	SHANNON	G.H. 1508
			(Not found on M.L. by this name. ? Alias.)
ELDER, Thomas	A.B.	SHANNON	
ETOUGH, Henry.G.	Actg Master	SHANNON	
	Lieut. R.N.	BEDFORD	B.S. 14 Dec 1814
FALKNER, Charles.L.	Lieut. R.N.	SHANNON	
	Midshipman	DONEGAL	Basque Roads 1809
FILER, John	Pte. R.M.	SHANNON	
FRENCH, James	Ord	SHANNON	G.H. 7,335
GIFFORD, John	Ord	SHANNON	(M.L. GIFFARD)
HARDY, James	Sailmaker	SHANNON	
	Sailmaker	SEAHORSE	The Potomac. 17 Aug 1814
	Sailmaker	SEAHORSE	B.S. 14 Dec 1814
HOILER, Daniel	Pte. R.M.	SHANNON	
JOHNSTON, Joseph	A.B.	SHANNON	(M.L. as JOHNSON)
LAW, John	2nd Lt. R.M.	SHANNON	
MATTHEWS, Robert	Caulker	SHANNON	
McCLENNON, Alexander	Pte. R.M.	SHANNON	
MENDHAM, William	A.B.	SHANNON	
MOLLYNEAUX, Richard	Sgt. R.M.	SHANNON	
MORRIS, Griffiths	Pte. R.M.	SHANNON	G.H. 9,506
	Pte. R.M.	AUDACIOUS	Nile
PARREY, Edward.Iggulden.	Midshipman	SHANNON	(Roll may read PARRY) (A released P.O.W.)
PEALING, Michael	Capt of Mast	SHANNON	
	Ord	MUTINE	Nile
PURCELL, Thomas	Ord	SHANNON	(M.L. as PERSALL)

SHANNON WH CHESAPEAKE

RAYMOND, George	Midshipman	SHANNON	
	Midshipman	EDGAR	B.S. 11 Aug 1808
			(Vfd Abd. Not on Roll)
REED, Adam	A.B.	ROYAL OAK	B.S. 14 Dec 1814
	Supn Seaman	SHANNON	(A released P.O.W.)
			(M.L. as REID)
ROBERTS, Richard	Ord	SHANNON	
ROBINSON, John	Vol 1st Cl	SHANNON	
ROBINSON, Laurence	Ord	SHANNON	
SAMWELL, John	Midshipman	SHANNON	"Discharged Dead (D.D.) Halifax Hospital of wounds"

(Note by Adm Byam Martin in Roll. "Wounded in Action, and died 19 June 1813. Mother claimed (circa 1847), this claim may be allowed if the Admiralty approve of our recommendation, provided there is no widow or son living. The Mother must produce a certificate of marriage")

SMITH, William	Master's Mate	SHANNON	(M) A of I / AVA.
SMITH, William	Ord	SHANNON	
STACK, William	Coxswain	SHANNON	(M.L. as STARK)
TAYLOR, Richard	A.B.	SHANNON	G.H. 982
VAN LOO, Peter	L.M.	SHANNON	(M.L. as VAN LEWIS, Peter)
WALLIS, Provo.W.P.	Lieut. R.N.	SHANNON	Died aged 100 as Admiral of Fleet on 13 Feb 1892.
	Lieut. R.N.	GLOIRE	Anse La Barque 18 Decr 1809 (Ship not on List)
	Lieut. R.N.	GLOIRE	Guadaloupe
WINNISTER, John.F.	Ship's Corporal	SHANNON	
	Capt' Fore Top	ALCMENE	Guadaloupe (Vfd Abd. Not on Roll)

(4) PELICAN 14 AUGT 1813

Capture of the American brig ARGUS, off St David's Head, South Wales.

BAKER, William	A.B.	PELICAN	
COX, Henry	Midshipman	PELICAN	
	Midshipman	IMPLACABLE	Implacable. 26 Augt 1808 (+Gold (1835) and Silver (1840) Life Saving Medals). R.N. Museum.
FOX, Francis	Cook	PELICAN	
MAIDES, William	Pte. R.M.	PELICAN	

(293) St SEBASTIAN

Capture of St Sebastian on 8 September 1813, for which a medal was bestowed on the Army.

ABLETT, Thomas	A.B.	AJAX	G.H. 7395
	A.B.	PHOEBE	Trafalgar
AITKEN, John	L.M.	SURVEILLANTE	
ALLEN, Joseph	Pte. R.M.	MAGICIENNE	
ALLEN, Thomas	Ord	AJAX	
ALLFREE, John	A.B.	DISPATCH	(Alias John THOMPSON)
AMMANETT, John	Q.M.	MAGICIENNE	
ANDERSON, John	A.B.	SURVEILLANTE	
ANGEL, William	Armourer's Mate	AJAX	
ANNING, Owen	Carp's Crew	REVOLUTIONNAIRE	
APLIN, John.George.	Lieut RN Cmmdg	ARROW	Roll incorrect as ALPIN
BAILEY, John	Pte. R.M.	REVOLUTIONNAIRE	
	Pte. R.M.	SEVERN	Algiers
BAKE, John.W.	Midshipman	RACER	
BAKER, George	Yeoman of Sheets	BEAGLE	
BANKS, Joseph	Pte. R.M.	FREIJA	
BARCLAY, John	Lieutenant.R.N.	PRESIDENT	(Vfd Abd. Not on Roll)
	Lieutenant. R.N.	BRITANNIA	Trafalgar
	Lieutenant. R.N.	LATONA	Curacoa
BARNARD, David	Gunner	SPARROW	
BARNES, John	Capt' Fore Top	SURVEILLANTE	
BARROW, James	Master	PRESIDENT	
	Actg Master	UNITE	Pelagosa. 29 Novr 1811
BASTARD, Richard	Lieut. R.N.	FREIJA	(Vfd Abd. Not on Roll)
	Lieut. R.N.	PERLEN	Martinique
BATTERSBY, John	Pte. R.M.	AJAX	
BATTERSBY, John.P.	Vol 1st Cl	FREIJA	
	Vol 1st Cl	FREIJA	Anse La Barque.18 Decr 1809
BAUR, Conrad	Pte. R.M.	SURVEILLANTE	(M.L. as BORRE)
	Pte. R.M.	NAMUR	4 Novr 1805
BAXTER, Isaac	A.B.	SURVEILLANTE	

BEECH, John	Pte. R.M.	ANDROMACHE	
BELL, Frederick	A.B.	FREIJA	
BENDALL, Joseph	Pte. R.M.	IRIS	
BLACKNEY, John	A.B.	MAGICIENNE	(M.L. as BLACKMAN)
BLOYE, Robert	Commander	LYRA (P)	
	Midshipman	MARLBOROUGH	1 June 1794
BLYTH, Charles	Midshipman	PRESIDENT	
	A.B.	INDEFATIGABLE	Basque Roads 1809
	Midshipman	SCIPION	Java
BRACKNALL, William	Ord	AJAX	
BRADLEY, Henry	Ord	ARROW	
BRAWLEY, James	L.M.	PRESIDENT	
	L.M.	PRESIDENT	Java
BREWIN, Samuel	Ord	AJAX	G.H. 9777
BROOKE, Samuel	Corporal. R.M.	JUNIPER	
BROWN, Joseph.W.	Midshipman	MAGICIENNE	
BURNES, George	Q.M.	MAGICIENNE	Additional clasp ?
BUTTON, Simon.G.	Surgeon	MAGICIENNE	
CALLAGHAN, Patrick	Pte. R.M.	ANDROMACHE	
CALLIFORD, John	Ord	AJAX	
CAMPBELL, John	Actg Commander	SPARROW	
CAMPBELL, John	Bosun's Mate	AJAX	(Alias CAMMELL)
	Boatswain	ASIA	Syria
CARSON, Joshua	Capt' Forecastle	REINDEER	(Ship not on List)
CARTHEW, William	Carp's Crew	REVOLUTIONNAIRE	
CASTLE, Daniel	Ord	PRESIDENT	
	Ord	PRESIDENT	Java
CHAMBERS, John	Master's Mate	Gun Boat No 14	
CHAPMAN, James	A.B.	AJAX	
CHILDS, William	Ord	ANDROMACHE	
CLARKE, Joseph	Pte. R.M.	ANDROMACHE	
CLAYTON, William	Surgeon	LYRA	
	Surgeon	LYRA	Basque Roads 1809 (VA-NOR)
CLEVELAND, William	Master's Mate	AJAX	
COCHRANE, William	Gunner. R.M.A.	FREIJA	
COLLINS, Charles	Pte. R.M.	REVOLUTIONNAIRE	
COLLINS, James	A.B.	SURVEILLANTE	
	Ord	AJAX	Egypt
COLLIS, William	1st Lieut. R.M.	AJAX	
(COLVILLE, Thomas)	(Ord)	(SURVEILLANTE)	Received M.G.S. Medal
COMMINGS, Robert	Pte. R.M.	REVOLUTIONNAIRE	
CONNEEN, Peter	Ord	Gunboat No 16	
	Ord	IMPREGNABLE	Algiers
COOK, George	Pte. R.M.	SPARROW	
	Pte. R.M.	BRITANNIA	Trafalgar
COX, Matthew	Boy 3rd Class	REVOLUTIONNAIRE	
COX, Robert	Ord	PRESIDENT	
	Ord	PRESIDENT	Java
COX, Thomas	Pte. R.M.	REVOLUTIONNAIRE	
CRABB, William	Q.M.	REVOLUTIONNAIRE	
CRAIG, John	Capt Forecastle	SPARROW	
CROWE, William	L.M.	AJAX	G.H. 2887
CULL, Thomas	Lieutenant. R.N.	LYRA	
	Lieut. R.N. I/Cmd	Gun Board No 16	Malaga. 29 April 1812 (Vfd Abd. Not on Roll)
DALL, William	Sailmaker's Mate	SURVEILLANTE	
DAVIES, George	Vol 1st Cl	AJAX	
	Midshipman	Qn CHARLOTTE	Algiers
DAVIS, David	A.B.	LYRA	G.H. 9882 as DAVIES
	A.B.	LYRA	Basque Roads 1809
DENSTEN, Thomas	Lieut. R.N.	SPARROW	
	Master's Mate	POMPEE	Guadaloupe
DERRETT, William	Pte. R.M.	PRESIDENT	
	Pte. R.M.	PRESIDENT	Java
DEVONPORT, Ellis	Pte. R.M.	AJAX	
DEW, Andrew	Corporal. R.M.	REVOLUTIONNAIRE	
	Pte. R.M.	TREMENDOUS	1 June 1794
DICKENSON, Thomas	Lieut. R.N.	ANDROMACHE	
	Midshipman	ROYAL SOVEREIGN	Trafalgar
DIGMAN, Daniel	Pte. R.M.	LYRA	
DIXON, James.T.T.	Midshipman	MAGICIENNE	
	Midshipman	CASTOR	Castor. 17 June 1809
	Master's Mate	CASTOR	Anse La Barque.18 Decr 1809
	Master's Mate	CASTOR	Guadaloupe
DOBBS, John	Pte. R.M.	BEAGLE	
DUFFIN, Thomas	Pte. R.M.	CONSTANT	
DUNN, Thomas	Capt' Forecastle	PRESIDENT	
	A.B.	REVOLUTIONNAIRE	4 Novr 1805
DOWAL, Thomas	L.M.	REVOLUTIONNAIRE	
DWYER, Michael	Lieut. R.N.	REVOLUTIONNAIRE	
ELLIOTT, James	Pte. R.M.	ANDROMACHE	
ELLIS, James	Pte. R.M.	AJAX	
EVANS, Thomas	Master's Mate	EPERVIER	

ST SEBASTIAN

EVANS, William	Boatswain	DISPATCH	
	A.B.	AJAX	Trafalgar
EVANS, William	Surgeon	PRESIDENT	
	Surgeon	PRESIDENT	Java
FADDY, Peter	Captain. R.A.	FREIJA	
FARR, William	Surgeon	GOLDFINCH	
FOOKS, Robert	Gunner	IRIS	
FORD, William	L.M.	Gun Boat No 20	
FORDYCE, George	A.B.	SURVEILLANTE	
FOSTER, Henry.D.	Vol 1st Cl	AJAX	
FOWLER, Stephen	Qtr Gunner	SURVEILLANTE	
FREDERICK, John	A.B.	Gun Boat No 19	
FROST, George	A.B.	AJAX	G.H. 6200
FULLER, William	Vol 1st Cl	DISPATCH	
GARLAND, Travers	Ord	MAGICIENNE	
GEAR, James	M.A.A.	AJAX	
GILBERT, John	A.B.	AJAX	
GOFF, George	L.M.	MAGICIENNE	
GORDON, Hon William	Midshipman	MAGICIENNE	
GOUGH, William	Ord	AJAX	
GRANT, Duncan.B.G.	Vol 1st Cl	ANDROMACHE	
	Mate	GENOA (P)	Navarino
GRANT, Edward	Midshipman	ANDROMACHE	
	Midshipman	GIBRALTAR	Basque Roads 1809
	Actg Lieut. R.N.	CYANE	Cyane. 16 Jany 1814
GREER, James	A.B.	MAGICIENNE	(M.L. as GREEN)
GRIFFIN, John	Ord	SURVEILLANTE	
GRIFFITHS, Thomas	Pte. R.M.	ANDROMACHE	
HACKMAN, Henry	Clerk	DISPATCH	
HAGAN, Robert	Master's Mate	SURVEILLANTE	
HALL, Alexander	Gunner's Mate	FREIJA	
HALL, Thomas	Sgt. R.M.	REVOLUTIONNAIRE	
	Sgt. R.M.	SCIPION	Java
HANNON, John	Ord	REVOLUTIONNAIRE	
HARDING, William	L.M.	MAGICIENNE	
HARDY, Thomas	Pte. R.M.	AJAX	
	Pte. R.M.	LATONA	Curacoa
HARRIOTT, William	Volunteer	REVOLUTIONNAIRE	
HAYDEN, Bartholomew	Midshipman	SPARROW	
HICKS, William	Qtr Gunner	CHALLENGER	
HILL, John	Ord	ANDROMACHE	
HILL, William	Ord	PRESIDENT	
HOGAN, Patrick	Boy 3rd Class	STORK	
HOLBERTON, John	Midshipman	AJAX	
	Vol 1st Cl	SCIPION	Java
	Master's Mate	IMPREGNABLE	Algiers
HOLLAND, William	Boy	SPARROW	
HOOPER, William	Midshipman	PRESIDENT	
HOPKINS, William	L.M.	ANDROMACHE	
HORTON, Frederick	Purser	REVOLUTIONNAIRE	
HOWARD, John	L.M.	Gunboat No 19	G.H. 7060 in G.Bt. No 22
HOWARD, Michael	Carpenter	BEAGLE	
HUBBARD, William	Ship's Corporal	CHALLENGER	
HUGOE, Samuel	2nd Lieut. R.M.	ANDROMACHE	
HUNSELL, Joseph	Not Given	REVOLUTIONNAIRE	(May read HERNSELL)
JAY, Charles.H.	Midshipman	Gun Boat No 19	
	Midshipman	MONMOUTH	Egypt
JEFFREY, Henry	A.B.	PRESIDENT	
(or JEFFERY)	A.B.	REVOLUTIONNAIRE	4 Novr 1805
	A.B.	PRESIDENT	Java
JENNER, George	Midshipman	AJAX	
JERAM, William	Cooper	BEAGLE	
	Cooper	BEAGLE	Basque Roads 1809
JOHNS, Richard	Actg Master	REINDEER	(Ship not on List)
JOHNSON, John	Ord	PRESIDENT	G.H. 8220
	Ord	PRESIDENT	Java
JONES, John	Pte. R.M.	JUNIPER & AJAX	
JONES, William	Midshipman	CONSTANT	
	Vol 1st Cl	CAPTAIN	Martinique
JONES, William	Ord	PRESIDENT	
JONES, William	Lieut. R.N.	STORK	
KIDDELL, Joseph	L.M.	AJAX	
KILLOCK, Robert	Pte. R.M.	SURVEILLANTE	
	Pte. R.M.	BELLEISLE	Martinique
	Pte. R.M.	ALFRED	Guadaloupe
KING, William	A.B.	Gun Boat No 19	G.H. 8064 as G.Bt No 22
KNAPMAN, Edward	Lieut. R.N.	Gun Boat No 16	
	Midshipman	SPARTIATE	Trafalgar
KNIGHT, John	Boy	BEAGLE	
KNIGHT, John.E.	Midshipman	BEAGLE	
KNOLLES, Henry	Midshipman	REVOLUTIONNAIRE	(M) Group includes King John, Portugal jewel.
LAING, Andrew	Ship's Corporal	ANDROMACHE	

LANGLEY, William	Master's Mate	MAGICIENNE	
LAVIS, John	L.M.	REVOLUTIONNAIRE	
LEQUISTE, Richard	Pte. R.M.	PRESIDENT	
LETHBRIDGE, John	Midshipman	ANDROMACHE	
LEWIS, John	A.B.	CONSTANT	G.H. 3360
LITTLE, Henry	L.M.	MAGICIENNE	
LIVESAY, Robert	Pte. R.M.	SURVEILLANTE	
LLOYD, Samuel	Coxswain	BEAGLE	
LLOYD, Vaughan	Midshipman	AJAX	
LONDON, John	A.B.	DISPATCH	
LONEY, Robert	Lieut. R.N.	REINDEER	(Ship not on List)
	Midshipman	AIGLE	Basque Roads 1809
	2nd Master	SCIPION	Java
LUCAS, William	Boy 3rd Class	AJAX	
LYNCH, John	Qtr Gunner	ANDROMACHE	
MACINTOSH, Angus	Midshipman	AJAX	
MALLOCK, Thomas	Volunteer	AJAX	
MARA, Edward	Ord	CONSTANT	
MARSH, Digby	Master's Mate	SURVEILLANTE	
MARTIN, Joseph	Pte. R.M.	SURVEILLANTE	
MARTIN, William	Pte. R.M.	AJAX	
	Pte. R.M.	HECTOR	Egypt
MASON, Francis	Captain. R.N.	PRESIDENT	
	Midshipman	RUSSELL	1 June 1794
	Midshipman	RUSSELL	23rd June 1795
MASTERTON, William	Ord	AJAX	
McCARTHY, James	A.B.	CONSTANT	
McCLINTOCK, William.B.	Vol 1st Cl	AJAX	(In 1846 became BUNBURY)
	Midshipman	SEVERN	Algiers
McDONALD, Edward	Boy	SURVEILLANTE	
McLEOD, William	A.B.	ANDROMACHE	G.H. 3703
MEAD, William	Pte. R.M.	BEAGLE	
	Pte. R.M.	LEVIATHAN	Trafalgar
MEARS, John.D.	Pte. R.M.	REVOLUTIONNAIRE	
MERRY, Francis	Midshipman	STORK	
MIDGLEY, John	Ord	FREIJA	
	Ord	LEANDER	Algiers
MILLS, James	Capt' Main Top	REVOLUTIONNAIRE	
MITCHELL, Thomas	Lieut. R.N.	AJAX	
MITCHENER, James	Pte. R.M.	ANDROMACHE	
	Pte. R.M.	EDGAR	Copenhagen 1801
	Pte. R.M.	CANOPUS	St Domingo
MORGAN, Thomas	A.B.	REVOLUTIONNAIRE	
MUNDAY, Thomas	Sailmaker	PRESIDENT	G.H. 9888
	A.B.	REVOLUTIONNAIRE	4 Novr 1805
	Sailmaker	PRESIDENT	Java
NICHOLS, Thomas	Boy 3rd Class	SURVEILLANTE	
NORRIS, John	1st Lieut. R.M.	REVOLUTIONNAIRE	
	2nd Lieut. R.M.	MELAMPUS	Guadaloupe
	1st Lieut. R.M.	SUPERB	Algiers
	1st Lieut. R.M.	GLASGOW	Navarino
NOXON, Richard	Corporal R.M.	SURVEILLANTE	
NUDD, Charles	Pte. R.M.	DISPATCH	
OLDMIXON, William.H.	Schoolmaster	REVOLUTIONNAIRE	(Lieut. R.N. in 1815)
ORMES, John	Ord	Gun Boat No 22	
OWSTON, William	Actg Master	ANDROMACHE	
PAGE, Robert	A.B.	DISPATCH	
PAKENHAM, John	Lieut. R.N.	MAGICIENNE	
PEARCE, Samuel	Pte. R.M.	JUNIPER/AJAX	G.H. 2427 as Nathaniel, late application.
PEARCY, David	Swabber	ANDROMACHE	
PEARSON, Charles	Lieut. R.N.	PRESIDENT	
	Boy	St GEORGE	Copenhagen 1801
	Midshipman	SPENCER	St Domingo
	Midshipman	SCIPION	Java
PEARSON, William	Ord	AJAX	G.H. 10,700 May have received additional clasp.
PEDDER, William	L.M.	AJAX	
PEERS, Martin	Q.M.	CONSTANT	
PELLOWE, John	Boy	SPARROW	
PERRY, James	Pte. R.M.	AJAX	
PHILIPS, John	Pte. R.M.	DISPATCH	
PINEO, Obidiah	Surgeon	REVOLUTIONNAIRE	
PIPPETT, Thomas	Boy	SURVEILLANTE	G.H. 1022
	A.B.	GLASGOW	Navarino
POLGLAZE, Henry	A.B.	SURVEILLANTE	
POOL, Thomas	Boy	SURVEILLANTE	
PORTER, James	Q.M.	AJAX	G.H.7385
POUTHAM, John	Capt' Forecastle	BEAGLE	G.H. 1480 as POULSHAM
POWELL, David	A.B.	PRESIDENT	
PRESTON, Thomas	Midshipman	AJAX	

ST SEBASTIAN

PURCHES, James.U.	Lieut. R.N.	CHALLENGER	*Application marked 'Lunatic'*
	Lieut. R.N.	DEFIANCE	*Trafalgar*
RAYE, Henry.R.	2nd Lieut. R.M.	AJAX	
REDDING, Owen	L.M.	MAGICIENNE	*(M) Anchor Type LS & GC*
REEVES, Samuel	Pte. R.M.	BEAGLE	
REMINGTON, John	L.M.	MAGICIENNE	
REYNOLDS, Joseph	Pte. R.M.	PRESIDENT	
RICHMOND, Henry	Midshipman	SURVEILLANTE	
ROBERTS, John	Ord	CHALLENGER	
ROBERTSON, William	Carp's Mate	SURVEILLANTE	
ROSE, James	Pte. R.M.	JUNIPER/AJAX	
ROSKY, Johann	L.M.	AJAX	
ROWE, Richard	Coxswain	LYRA	*G.H. 7000*
	Coxswain	LYRA	*Basque Roads 1809*
RUBIDGE, Robert.H.	Lieut. R.N.	SPARROW	
RUMP, John	Boy	FREIJA	
RUSSELL, James	A.B.	BEAGLE	
	A.B.	MINDEN	*Java*
SAUNDERS, Richard	Q.M.	CHALLENGER	
SAVAGE, George	Pte. R.M.	PRESIDENT	
SCAPING, Joseph	Carp's Crew	AJAX	
SCOTT, John	Carpenter	PRESIDENT	
SCOTT, William.I.	Captain. R.N.	FREIJA	
SEDDAN, John	Trumpeter	SURVEILLANTE	
	Trumpeter	PRINCE	*Trafalgar*
SELLWOOD, John	A.B.	AJAX	
SHAPCOTT, Thomas	Q.M's Mate	REVOLUTIONNAIRE	
SHEILL, John	L.M.	SURVEILLANTE	*(Roll "or CHAIN")*
SIMMONDS, G.W.	Clerk	AJAX	
SIMMS, John	Capt' Forecastle	SURVEILLANTE	
SKILLY, Evan	Armourer's Mate	DISPATCH	
SMITH, James	A.B.	SURVEILLANTE	
SMITH, James	A.B.	Gun Boat No 14	
SMITH, William	Ord	SURVEILLANTE	
SNELL, John	Not Given	PRESIDENT	*(M.L. as John LOVE)*
	A.B.	GANGES	*Syria. Ex-Smuggler. Impressed 5 yrs. LSGC later refused.*
SNELL, Thomas	Boy	AJAX	
SPENCE, John	Clerk	SURVEILLANTE	
SPROWLES, Stephen	Pte. R.M.	PRESIDENT	
STAGG, Leonard	Vol 1st Cl	MAGICIENNE	
STANBURY, James	Ord	REVOLUTIONNAIRE	
STANNARD, Charles	A.B.	CONSTANT	*G.H. 8571*
STAPLES, Thomas	Midshipman	AJAX	
STENT, John.B.	Actg Master	ROVER	
STEPTOE, William	A.B.	SURVEILLANTE	
STOCKIE, Edward	Boy	REVOLUTIONNAIRE	
STOKES, William	Pte. R.M.	MAGICIENNE	
STOWELL, George	Supn Boy 3rd Cl	ANDROMACHE	
STRINGER, Daniel	Ord	SURVEILLANTE	
SUTHERLAND, James	Ord	ANDROMACHE	*G.H. 3333*
SWINFILD, John	Pte. R.M.	SURVEILLANTE	
TABART, C.M.	Midshipman	ANDROMACHE	
	Midshipman	LION	*Java*
TARN, John	Asst Surgeon	PRESIDENT	
TATTNALL, James.B.	Lieut. R.N.	PRESIDENT	
	Lieut. R.N.	RACEHORSE	*Off Tamatave. 20 May 1811 (Vfd Abd. Not on Roll)*
	Lieut. R.N.	TONNANT	*B.S. 14 Dec 1814*
TAWS, George	L.M.	SURVEILLANTE	
	Yeoman of Signals	GLASGOW	*Navarino*
TAYLER, Joseph.N.	Commander	SPARROW	
TIDBURY, James	Pte. R.M.	MAGICIENNE	
	Pte. R.M.	LEANDER	*Algiers*
TISBURY, Peter	Q.M.	SURVEILLANTE	
TRILL, William	Pte. R.M.	AJAX	
TROUNSELL, George.P.	Midshipman	DISPATCH	
TRUEMAN, John	Bosun's Mate	SURVEILLANTE	
TURNER, John	Ord	ANDROMACHE	
TYNDALE, Edward	Vol 1st Cl	AJAX	
	Mate	TALBOT (P)	*Navarino*
VINE, John	Carpenter	SPARROW	
WADDY, William	A.B.	SURVEILLANTE	*G.H. 9743*
WAINWRIGHT, John	Pte. R.M.	ANDROMACHE	*(Alias William)*
WALLACE, James	Ord	REINDEER	*(Ship not on List)*
WALLSWORTH, John	Boy	REVOLUTIONNAIRE	
WALSH, Jonathan.W.	Midshipman	SURVEILLANTE	
WARD, Samuel	Pte. R.M.	SURVEILLANTE	
WEBSTER, Thomas	Pte. R.M.	ANDROMACHE	*G.H. 3843*
WELSH, William	Volunteer	REVOLUTIONNAIRE	
WHITAKER, Richard	A.B.	FREIJA	

WHITE, Charles	Ord	PRESIDENT	
	Ord	PRESIDENT	*Java*
WHITE, John	A.B.	REVOLUTIONNAIRE	
WICKET, George	Yeoman Powder Rm	MAGICIENNE	
WILKINSON, Stephen	Midshipman	DISPATCH	
	Midshipman	YORK	*Martinique*
WILLIAMS, George	Ord	AJAX	
WILLIAMS, Joseph	Pte. R.M.	REVOLUTIONNAIRE	
WILLS, John	Midshipman	LYRA	
WILLSON, John	Q.M.	AJAX	
WILSON, James	A.B.	AJAX	G.H. 9776
WILSON, James.H.R.	Vol 1st Cl	CHALLENGER	
WITHERS, William	Pte. R.M.	PRESIDENT	
WITHROW, Andrew	L.M.	JUNIPER/AJAX	
WOODWARD, Joseph	Sailmaker	BEAGLE	
WORTHINGTON, Benjamin	Lieut. R.N.	AJAX	
	Midshipman	LATONA	*Curacoa*
WORTHINGTON, George	Pte. R.M.	DISPATCH	
WRIGHT, James	L.M.	ANDROMACHE	
WRIGHT, Matthew	A.B.	BEAGLE	
	L.M.	COURAGEUX	4 Novr 1805
WRIGHT, Samuel	Capt' Fore Top	PRESIDENT	
	Ord	PRESIDENT	*Java*
WYNN, Daniel	L.M.	AJAX	

(9) THUNDER 9 OCTR 1813

Capture of the French privateer NEPTUNE, off the Owers Light, English Channel.

COTTEREL, Charles.E.	Purser	THUNDER	
ELMORE, John	Ord	THUNDER	*(Vfd Abd. Not on Roll)*
	Ord	THUNDER	*Basque Roads 1809*
FINN, David	Q.M.	THUNDER	
	A.B.	THUNDER	*Basque Roads 1809*
HAM, John	A.B.	THUNDER	*(Vfd Abd. Not on Roll)*
	Capt Main Top	THUNDER	*Basque Roads 1809*
MACKENZIE, Thomas.H.	Lieut. R.N.	THUNDER	
PELL, Watkin.O.	Commander	THUNDER (P)	*Lost left leg Feby 1800*
	Lieut. R.N.	MERCURY	*Off Rota. 4 April 1808. (See "Fairy 5 Feby 1800" for probable 3rd Clasp)*
THOMPSON, Thomas	Q.M's Mate	THUNDER	
	A.B.	THUNDER	*Basque Roads 1809*
WEBB, James	Gunner's Mate	THUNDER	
	Coxswain	THUNDER	*Basque Roads 1809*
WHITTMEE, William.S.	Midshipman	THUNDER	

(44) GLUCKSTADT 5 JANY 1814

Fortress of GLUCKSTADT captured by H.M.Ships, and ELBE flotilla of gun-boats.

ARCHER, Thomas	Lieut. R.N.	DESIREE	
ASHBURY, Henry	Pte. R.M.	HEARTY	
BATTAWS, John	Capt Main Top	HEARTY	*(M.L. as BATTERS)*
BRITT, Joseph	A.B.	DESIREE	
BROUNCKER, John.P.	Midshipman	DESIREE	
BULL, George.S.	Midshipman	DESIREE	
CHANDLER, James	Capt Main Top	SHAMROCK	*Deserted 5 Sept 1814*
	Ord	SWIFTSURE	*Trafalgar*
	A.B.	DICTATOR	*Off Mardoe. 6 July 1812*
CLERY, James	Purser	BLAZER	
CONNOR, James	A.B.	DESIREE	*(M.L. as CONNER)*
DOIG, David	Sgt. R.M.	REDBREAST	
FORBES, John	Surgeon	DESIREE	*Probably discharged before this action.*
	Surgeon	CASTOR	*Castor. 17 June 1809*
	Surgeon	NETLEY	*Guadaloupe*
FORDYCE, Alexander.D.	Vol 1st Cl	DESIREE	
	Midshipman	ALBION	*Algiers*
GREATREX, Charles.B.	1st Lt. R.M.	DESIREE	
GREEN, Andrew.P.	Supn Cdr	ELBE gun-boat Flotilla	*(On books of DESIREE)*
	Midshipman	ILLUSTRIOUS	*14 March 1795 (Vfd Abd. Not on Roll)*
	Lieut. R.N.	GANGES	*Copenhagen 1801*
	Lieut. R.N.	NEPTUNE	*Trafalgar*
HALL, David	L.M.	DESIREE	
HALLOWES, John	Supn Midshipman	No 5 Gun-Boat	*(On books of DESIREE)*

GLUCKSTADT 5 JANY 1814

HARRISON, John	Cpl. R.M.	DESIREE	
HERRICK, John	Supn. A.B.	ELBE gun-boat Flotilla	G.H. 4,449
			(On books of DESIREE)
JACK, Leigh.S.	Lieut. R.N.	DESIREE	
	Midshipman	CYCLOPS	Egypt
KITCHEN, James	Supn A.B.	No 5 Gun-Boat	(On books of SHAMROCK)
MARSHALL, John	Commander	SHAMROCK (P)	
	Lieut. R.N.	ABOUKIR	B.S. 29 Sept 1812
PASLEY, James	Ord	DESIREE	(M.L. as PARSLEY)
PHIPPS, William	Supn Lieut. R.N.	DESIREE	
RAINIER, John	Midshipman	DESIREE	
RAYBOULD, Benjamin	Pte. R.M.	HEARTY	
RICHES, Watson.T.	Master's Mate	Gun Boat	(Not on Roll. Vfd in Gun Boat)
	Midshipman	ILLUSTRIOUS	Java
RIDDLE, James	Pte. R.M.	DESIREE	GH. 1245 M.L. as REDDALL
ROCHFORD, William	Ord	REDBREAST	
ROMNEY, Francis.D.	Supn. Lieut. RN.	No 10 Gun-Boat	(On books of DESIREE)
	Midshipman	AEOLUS	4 Novr 1805
SAXTON, Thomas	Sgt. R.M.	DESIREE	(M.L. as SEXTON)
	C/Sgt. R.M.	Qn CHARLOTTE	Algiers
SCOTT, Thomas	Carpenter's Crew	DESIREE	
SCRIVEN, Thomas.S.	Midshipman	PIERCER	
SEALE, Charles.H.	Supn Lieut. RN.	No 3 Gun-Boat	(On books of DESIREE)
	Midshipman	COMUS	Comus. 15 Augt 1807
	Midshipman	NEPTUNE	Martinique
	Lieut. R.N.	STAR	Guadaloupe
SLOWLY, George	Ord	PIERCER	
SPARKS, William	Ord	DESIREE	(M.L. as SPARKES)
STONNELL, Thomas	L.M.	DESIREE	
SWEENY, Owen	Pte. R.M.	DESIREE	(M.L. as Dennis SWEENY)
THOMPSON, James	A.B.	DESIREE	
TULLOH, John	Supn. Lieut. RN.	No 4 Gun-Boat	(On books of DESIREE)
	Lieut. R.N.	ILLUSTRIOUS	Java
WELLS, James	Supn. A.B.	DESIREE	(M.L. as WALLS)
WHALEY, Joseph	Ord	SHAMROCK	(M.L. as WILEY)
WHEELER, Josh	Pte. R.M.	DESIREE	
WITCHER, Benjamin	Ord	DESIREE	(M.L. as WHITCHER)
WHITEMAN, James	Pte. R.M.	BLAZER	(Vfd Abd. Not on Roll)
	Pte. R.M.	BLAZER	B.S. 21 March 1813

(42) VENERABLE 16 JANY 1814

Capture of the French frigates ALCMENE and IPHIGENIE, off the Canary Islands.

(Real dates 16 & 20 Jan 1814)

ALDER, Peter	Ord	VENERABLE	
BARNHOUSE, William	Not Given	?	Not on M.L. or in CYANE
BEARDWELL, John	Pte. R.M.	VENERABLE	
BOUGH, James	Not Given	?	Not on M.L. or in CYANE
BRIGGS, David	Master's Mate	VENERABLE	
BROOKMAN, William	Pte. R.M.	VENERABLE	
CARPENTER, Augustus	A.B.	VENERABLE	
CHRISTIE, William	Midshipman	VENERABLE	
FIGGINS, William	L.M.	VENERABLE	(M.L. as FIGGIS)
FOWLER, William	Supn Boy 3rd Cl	VENERABLE	
GILLETT, William	A.B.	VENERABLE	G.H.2166 & on G.H.Roll
			Not entered on Adm 171/-.
HACKLEY, John	Ord	VENERABLE	(M.L. as HICKLEY)
HALL, George	Sgt. R.M.	VENERABLE	
HARE, Richard	Midshipman	VENERABLE	
HARRIS, Elijah	Pte. R.M.	VENERABLE	
HUBBARD, James	Captain's Cook	VENERABLE	
KNEVITT, Thomas.L.	Master's Mate	VENERABLE	
	Master's Mate	SCEPTRE	Anse La Barque. 18 Decr 1809
	Master's Mate	SCEPTRE	Guadaloupe
KING, Thomas	Captain Main Top	VENERABLE	
LEDNER, Thomas	Ord	VENERABLE	(see "ALGIERS" as LARDNER)
LUDDETT, Charles	A.B.	VENERABLE	G.H. 8094
MAXWELL, William	Midshipman	VENERABLE	
	Vol 1st Cl	DIANA	B.S. 24 Dec 1810
MOLE, Alexander	Ord	VENERABLE	G.H. 5578
MORRISON, Adam	Q.M.	VENERABLE	
MORTIMER, George	Lieut. R.N.	VENERABLE	
	Lieut. R.N.	MALTA	Gaieta. 24 July 1815
MORTIMER, John	Passenger	VENERABLE	Not known if civil or naval
PLATT, Thomas	L.M.	VENERABLE	G.H. 9895
PORTER, William	Cpl. R.M.	VENERABLE	
RISK, Henry	L.M.	VENERABLE	

ROBINSON, John	Pte. R.M.	VENERABLE	
RODD, Thomas	Ord	VENERABLE	
SIMKIN, William	Ord	VENERABLE	G.H. 4619 as SIMKINS (M.L. as SIMPKINS)
SKINNER, Arthur McGregor	Midshipman	VENERABLE	
	Midshipman	GLASGOW	Algiers (+A of I/AVA)
SMITH, Peter	A.B.	VENERABLE	
	Ord	SPARTIATE	Trafalgar
SMYTH, Spencer	Lieut. R.N.	VENERABLE	
	Midshipman	DEFIANCE	Trafalgar
	Master's Mate	NORTHUMBERLAND	Northumberland. 22 May 1812
	Lieut. R.N.	DARTMOUTH	Navarino
STEWART, James	A.B.	VENERABLE	
WALKER, B.J.	Master's Mate	VENERABLE	
WATSON, Alexander	Capt Fore Top	VENERABLE	
WATSON, James	A.B.	VENERABLE	
	Carpenter	ASIA	Syria
WHITE, John	Q.M.	VENERABLE	
WILLIAMS, George	Ord	VENERABLE	
WILSON, Thomas	Pte. R.M.	VENERABLE	
WORTH, Henry.John.	Midshipman	VENERABLE	
	Commander	HASTINGS	Syria. (M) A of I/AVA

(7) CYANE 16 JANY 1814

Capture of the French frigates ALCMENE and IPHIGENIE, off the Canary Islands.

(Real dates 16 & 20 Jan 1814)

AITON, William	Surgeon	CYANE	
GRANT, Edward	Actg Lieut. R.N.	CYANE	
	Midshipman	GIBRALTAR	Basque Roads 1809
	Midshipman	ANDROMACHE	St Sebastian
HURWOOD, John	Supn Boy 2nd Cl	CYANE	(M.L. as HARWOOD)
SCULL, William	Supn Boy 2nd Cl	CYANE	(M.L. as SKULL)
THOMPSON, James	Master's Mate	CYANE	
TRUSS, John	Capt of Mast	CYANE	(M.L. as TRUST)
	Boy 3rd Cl	DESIREE	Copenhagen 1801
	L.M.	PIQUE	Pique. 26 March 1806
	Ord	ELIZABETH	Anse La Barque 18 Decr 1809 (Vfd Abd. Not on Roll)
	Ord	ELIZABETH	Martinique (Vfd Abd. Not on Roll)
YOUNG, Daniel	Midshipman	CYANE	

(32) EUROTAS 25 FEBY 1814

Action with the French frigate CLORINDE, leading to its subsequent surrender to other ships the next day.

BATES, Samuel	Pte. R.M.	EUROTAS	
BRIGSTOCKE, Thomas.R.	Midshipman	EUROTAS	
BRYAN, John	Purser	EUROTAS	
	Purser	EURYDICE	Martinique
	Purser	ALCMENE	Guadaloupe
CRESE, Thomas	Yeoman of Sheets	EUROTAS	(M.L. as CREESE)
DREW, Andrew	Master's Mate	EUROTAS	(Actg Lt RN at Action)
DRUMMOND, James	Vol 1st Cl	EUROTAS	
EGAN, John	Ord	EUROTAS	
GALLYER, Thomas	Ord	EUROTAS	(M.L. as GALLYAN)
HAMPTON, John	Supn Boy 2nd Cl	EUROTAS	
HARRISON, James	Pte. R.M.	EUROTAS	
HAY, Thomas.P.	Boy 3rd Cl	EUROTAS	
HIGGINSON, Francis	Boy 3rd Cl	EUROTAS	
HORROX, Richard	Pte. R.M.	EUROTAS	(M.L. as HORROCKS)
JAMES, William	L.M.	EUROTAS	
JONES, Thomas.C.	Surgeon	EUROTAS	
KING, John	Yeoman of Sheets	EUROTAS	
LAMBERT, William	Pte. R.M.	EUROTAS	
MEES, John	L.M.	EUROTAS	
PRICE, Thomas	Boatswain	EUROTAS	
	Q.M's Mate	SANTA MARGARITA	Santa Margaritta 8 June 1796
	Yeoman of Sheets	FISGARD	Fisgard. 20 Octr 1798
RANDOLPH, Charles.G.	Lieut. R.N.	EUROTAS	
	Midshipman	DONEGAL	Basque Roads 1809
ROSSER, Philip	Pte. R.M.	EUROTAS	(M.L. as PROSSER, Wm)

EUROTAS 25 FEBY 1814

SIZMUR, John	L.M.	EUROTAS	*(M.L. as SIZMURE)*
SHAKESPEARE, John	Pte. R.M.	EUROTAS	
STANHOPE, William	L.M.	EUROTAS	
SMITH, John	Pte. R.M.	EUROTAS	
SMITH, Robert	Lieut. R.N.	EUROTAS (P)	
TEMPLE, Henry Edw	Midshipman	EUROTAS	
	Midshipman	EDGAR	*B.S. 11 Aug 1808*
			(Vfd Abd. Not on Roll)
TEMPLE, Robert	L.M.	EUROTAS	
TOVEY, William	L.M.	EUROTAS	
WARBUTON, James	Pte. R.M.	EUROTAS	*(M.L. as WARBUTTON)*
WEBBER, William.C.	Midshipman	EUROTAS	
WILMSHURST, George	A.B.	EUROTAS	*(M.L. as WILMHURST)*

(40) HEBRUS WITH L'ETOILE (G.M.)

Capture of the French frigate ETOILE on 27 March 1814, off the Island of Alderney.

ANDREWS, Benjamin	Midshipman	HEBRUS	
	Midshipman	SAVAGE	*Guadaloupe*
ARKWRIGHT, John	Boy 2nd Cl	HEBRUS	
BANNISTER, Edward	Ord	HEBRUS	*(M.L. as BENNISTER)*
BARRETT, Robert.J.	Midshipman	HEBRUS	
	Actg 2nd Master	HEBRUS	*Algiers*
BOYTER, David	Surgeon	HEBRUS	
BURTON, Joseph	L.M.	HEBRUS	*(M.L. as BURDON)*
CASTLE, Samuel	A.B.	HEBRUS	
CHRISTIAN, Francis	A.B.	HEBRUS	
CHURCH, Frederick	Vol 1st Cl	HEBRUS	
CLARK, John	Pte. R.M.	HEBRUS	*(M.L. as CLARKE)*
CLARKE, Patrick	Ord	HEBRUS	
	Boy	THESEUS	*Basque Roads 1809*
CRAWFORD, Christopher	Carpenter	HEBRUS	
	Carpenter	HEBRUS	*Algiers*
DARBY, Joseph	Ord	HEBRUS	
DRAY, James	Clerk	HEBRUS	
ELLIOTT, Stephen	Ord	HEBRUS	*(M.L. as ELLIOT)*
GALLOWAY, Daniel	Ord	HEBRUS	
GAZEY, John	Supn Boy 3rd Cl	HEBRUS	
GILLMAN, James	Gunner	HEBRUS	
	Gunner	PHILOMEL	*B.S. 1 Nov 1809*
GILLMAN, William	Armourer's Mate	HEBRUS	
GOODWIN, Charles	Supn Boy 2nd Cl	HEBRUS	
GOSTON, Richard	A.B.	HEBRUS	
HIGHTON, Gerrard	Cpl. R.M.	HEBRUS	
JAMES, James	A.B.	HEBRUS	
JONES, John	Ord	HEBRUS	
	A.B.	HEBRUS	*Algiers*
MABLE, Francis	Pte. R.M.	HEBRUS	*(Not yet found)*
MADDOCK, John	Purser	HEBRUS	
MASON, George	Trumpeter	HEBRUS	
McLAUCHLAN, John	2nd Lt. R.M.	HEBRUS	
ORMES, Samuel	Supn Boy 2nd Cl	HEBRUS	
ROBERTS, William	Caulker	HEBRUS	
SALTER, Samuel	A.B.	HEBRUS	
SCARESBRICK, Joseph	Pte. R.M.	HEBRUS	*(M.L. as SCARISBRICK)*
SHOTTEN, James	Pte. R.M.	HEBRUS	
SMITH, William (1)	Yeo Powder Rm	HEBRUS	
SMITH, William (2)	A.B.	HEBRUS	
STANFORD, William	Cooper	HEBRUS	*G.H. 6,149*
STONE, John	L.M.	HEBRUS	
TURNER, Michael	Midshipman	HEBRUS	
	Midshipman	HEBRUS	*Algiers*
WARD, Henry	Pte. R.M.	HEBRUS	
	Pte. R.M.	ORION	*Trafalgar*
	Pte. R.M.	"ANHOLT"	*Anholt. 27 March 1811*
WILLIAMSON, Joseph	Pte. R.M.	HEBRUS	

(36) PHOEBE 28 MARCH 1814

Capture of the American frigate ESSEX and her tender ESSEX JUNIOR, off Valparaiso, Chile.

BARTON, Richard	Ord	PHOEBE	
	Ord	PHOEBE	*Off Tamatave. 20 May 1811*
	Ord	PHOEBE	*Java*
BEECHIN, Michael	Ord	PHOEBE	
	Ord	PHOEBE	*Off Tamatave. 20 May 1811*
			(Vfd Abd. Not on Roll)
	Ord	PHOEBE	*Java*
BOWDEN, James	Quarter Gunner	PHOEBE	*(Vfd Abd. Not on Roll)*
	Ord	PHOEBE	*Trafalgar*
	Ord	PHOEBE	*Off Tamatave. 20 May 1811*
			(Vfd Abd. Not on Roll)
	Ord	PHOEBE	*Java*
CLARK, John	Capt Afterguard	PHOEBE	*G.H. 9,517*
CONDON, Patrick	Boy 3rd Cl	PHOEBE	
	Boy 3rd Cl	PHOEBE	*Off Tamatave. 20 May 1811*
			(Vfd Abd. Not on Roll)
	Boy 3rd Cl	PHOEBE	*Java*
COOK, William	Ord	PHOEBE	
	L.M.	PHOEBE	*Off Tamatave. 20 May 1811*
			(Vfd Abd. Not on Roll)
	L.M.	PHOEBE	*Java*
CRETCH, Daniel	A.B.	PHOEBE	*(M.L. as CRUTCH)*
	Boy 2nd Cl	PHOEBE	*Trafalgar*
	Ord	PHOEBE	*Off Tamatave. 20 May 1811*
	Ord	PHOEBE	*Java*
DAY, Thomas	Pte. R.M.	PHOEBE	*(Ex "CHERUB..." Roll)*
DEW, George	Midshipman	PHOEBE	
	Vol 1st Cl	COMET	*Comet. 11 Augt 1808*
DUCKHAM, George	Ord	PHOEBE	*(Vfd Abd. Not on Roll)*
	L.M.	PHOEBE	*Off Tamatave. 20 May 1811*
			(Vfd Abd. Not on Roll)
	A.B.	PHOEBE	*Java*
FEAR, George	Pte. R.M.	PHOEBE	
FIELDHOUSE, George	Pte. R.M.	PHOEBE	*(Vfd Abd. Not on Roll)*
	Pte. R.M.	PHOEBE	*Off Tamatave. 20 May 1811*
	Pte. R.M.	PHOEBE	*Java*
FITZGERALD, John	A.B.	PHOEBE	
	Boy 2nd Cl	PHOEBE	*Trafalgar*
	Ord	PHOEBE	*Off Tamatave. 20 May 1811*
	Ord	PHOEBE	*Java*
HAMILTON, John	Supn Boy 3rd Cl	PHOEBE	
HOPE, Andrew.J.	L.M.	PHOEBE	
	Boy 3rd Cl	PHOEBE	*Off Tamatave. 20 May 1811*
	Boy 3rd Cl	PHOEBE	*Java*
JONES, John	Carp's Crew	PHOEBE	
	Carp's Crew	PHAETON	*Java*
KINDNESS, Benjamin	Ord	PHOEBE	*(Vfd Abd. Not on Roll)*
	Boy 2nd Cl	PHOEBE	*Trafalgar*
	Ord	PHOEBE	*Off Tamatave. 20 May 1811*
			(Vfd Abd. Not on Roll)
	Ord	PHOEBE	*Java*
	Q.M.	ALBION	*Navarino*
LARK, Thomas	Pte. R.M.	PHOEBE	
LAURIE, Stephen	Capt Fore Top	PHOEBE	
	Boy 3rd Cl	PHOEBE	*Phoebe. 21 Decr 1797*
	Boy 2nd Cl	PHOEBE	*Phoebe. 19 Feby 1801*
	A.B.	PHOEBE	*Trafalgar*
	A.B.	PHOEBE	*Off Tamatave. 20 May 1811*
	A.B.	PHOEBE	*Java*
LAWSON, Gilbert	Gunner	PHOEBE	
	A.B.	SWIFTSURE	*Nile*
	A.B.	SWIFTSURE	*Egypt*
	Quarter Gunner	CAESAR	*4 Novr 1805*
	Gunner's Mate	CAESAR	*Basque Roads 1809*
LUNN, John	Midshipman	PHOEBE	
MANNING, Joseph	Ord	PHOEBE	
	L.M.	PHOEBE	*Off Tamatave. 20 May 1811*
	L.M.	PHOEBE	*Java*

PHOEBE 28 MARCH 1814

MARSHALL, John	Pte. R.M.	PHOEBE	(Ex "CHERUB..." Roll)
	Pte. R.M.	CANOPUS	*St Domingo*
MILLER, John	Actg Master	PHOEBE	
	Master	MINDEN	*Algiers*
MILLERY, Thomas	Sailmaker	PHOEBE	
	Actg Sailmaker	PHOEBE	*Off Tamatave. 20 May 1811*
	Actg Sailmaker	PHOEBE	*Java*
MORGAN, William	Cpl. R.M.	PHOEBE	
	Pte. R.M.	PHOEBE	*Off Tamatave. 20 May 1811*
	(Pte. R.M.)	(PHOEBE)	*(M.G.S. with JAVA clasp)*
PEARSON, Charles	Lieut. R.N.	PHOEBE (P)	
	A.B.	ISIS	*Copenhagen 1801*
RANDALL, Robert	Pte. R.M.	PHOEBE	
RAWDON, Charles.W.	Boy 3rd Cl	PHOEBE	
	Midshipman	MINDEN	*Algiers*
ROBINSON, James	A.B.	PHOEBE	
	A.B.	PHOEBE	*Trafalgar*
	A.B.	PHOEBE	*Off Tamatave. 20 May 1811*
	A.B.	PHOEBE	*Java*
SIMPSON, Adam	Asst Surgeon	PHOEBE	(Ex "CHERUB..." Roll)
SMART, George	A.B.	PHOEBE	
SPARKS, John	L.M.	PHOEBE	*(Vfd Abd. Not on Roll)*
	L.M.	PHOEBE	*Off Tamatave. 20 May 1811*
	L.M.	PHOEBE	*Java*
THORNTON, Samuel	Midshipman	PHOEBE	
WILLIAMS, Lawrence.B.	Midshipman Ord	PHOEBE	
YATES, George	Ord	PHOEBE	*(M.L. as YEATES)*
	Boy 2nd Cl	PHOEBE	*Off Tamatave. 20 May 1811*
	L.M.	PHOEBE	*Java*

CHERUB 28 MARCH 1814

(7)

Capture of the American frigate ESSEX and her tender ESSEX JUNIOR, off Valparaiso, Chile.

CROMBIE, William	Supn L.M.	CHERUB	
	Boy 3rd Cl	CHERUB	*Martinique*
GRIFFIN, Jonathan	Boy 2nd Cl	CHERUB	
RAMSAY, Peter	Surgeon	CHERUB	
RANDALL, John	Vol 1st Cl	CHERUB	*(M.L. as RANDOLL)*
SALTER, William	Ord	CHERUB	*G.H. 9,794*
	L.M.	CHERUB	*Martinique*
	L.M.	CHERUB	*Guadaloupe*
SKIDDY, Thomas	A.B.	CHERUB	*(M.L. as SCIDDY)*
	A.B.	ROYAL SOVEREIGN	*Trafalgar*
	A.B.	BELLEISLE	*Martinique*
TUCKER, Thomas.T.	Commander	CHERUB (P)	
	Lieut. R.N.	NORTHUMBERLAND	*St Domingo*
	Commander	CHERUB	*Martinique*
	Commander	CHERUB	*Guadaloupe*

(24) 8 APRIL BOAT SERVICE 1814
Destruction of twenty-seven vessels in the CONNECTICUT River.

BEDWELL, Edward.P.	Midshipman	HOGUE	
	Master's Mate	SNAP	*Guadaloupe*
CHIENE, Robert	Gunner	HOGUE	
	Coxswain	LEVIATHAN	*Trafalgar*
CHITTLEBOROUGH, James	Q.M.	HOGUE	
DEARNESS, John	Ord	HOGUE	(M.L. as DEERNESS)
	Ord	MONARCH	B.S. 16 July 1806
DICKSON, William	A.B.	HOGUE	
DUNSTAN, Octavius	Master's Mate	HOGUE	
	Master's Mate	ETHALION	*Martinique*
ELLIOTT, Isaac	Pte. R.M.	MAIDSTONE	
FANSHAWE, Arthur	Lieut. R.N.	ENDYMION	
	Midshipman	IMPLACABLE	*Implacable.* 26 Augt 1808
	Midshipman	SCIPION	*Java*
	Lieut. R.N.	ENDYMION	*Endymion* Wh *President*
	Captain. R.N.	PRINCESS CHARLOTTE	*Syria*
FARRANT, John	Lieut. R.N.	BORER	
	Vol 1st Cl	RUSSELL	*Copenhagen.* 1801
	Midshipman	ROYAL SOVEREIGN	*Trafalgar*
	Lieut. R.N.	SCOUT	B.S. 14 July 1809
	Lieut. R.N.	SCOUT	B.S. 1 Nov 1809
FOWLER, John	Yeoman of Sheets	HOGUE	G.H. 4,993
HARRISON, Francis	Ord	HOGUE	
	L.M.	MONARCH	B.S. 16 July 1806
HEYLAND, James	Midshipman	ENDYMION	
JAMESON, John	Ord	BORER	(Joined ship after Action)
JONES, Evan	Pte. R.M.	HOGUE	
Le NEVE, Anselm.P.	Master's Mate	MAIDSTONE	
L'ESTRANGE, Frederick	Midshipman	MAIDSTONE	
	Vol 1st Cl	MAIDSTONE	B.S. Ap & May 1813
LIDDON, Matthew	Lieut. R.N.	MAIDSTONE	
	Master's Mate	THAMES	*Amanthea.* 25 July 1810
	Lieut. R.N.	MAIDSTONE	B.S. Ap & May 1813
MASTERMAN, Joseph	Quarter Gunner	HOGUE	G.H. 1,876
PARRY, William.Edw.	Lieut. R.N.	HOGUE	(Arctic Explorer)
ROUSE (ROWSE), Joseph	A.B.	HOGUE	
SKINLEY, John	Master's Mate	MAIDSTONE	
	Midshipman	THESEUS	*Basque Roads.* 1809
SMITH, John	Midshipman	HOGUE	
SMITH, William	A.B.	HOGUE	(Deserted before Action)
STUBLEY, Edward.J.	Carpenter's Crew	HOGUE	
	L.M.	MONARCH	B.S. 16 July 1806

(12) 24 MAY BOAT SERVICE 1814
Capture of the French xebec AIGLE, off Vide, Corfu.
(Real date 25 May 1814)

AARON, William	L.M.	ELIZABETH	
COLLIER, John	Pte. R.M.	ELIZABETH	
EVANS, John	Ord	ELIZABETH	
KEAYS, Richard	Master's Mate	ELIZABETH	
LIPSCOMB, Edwin	Midshipman	ELIZABETH	
McADAMS, Daniel	Carpenter's Crew	ELIZABETH	
ROBERTS, Mitchell	Lieut. R.N.	ELIZABETH	
ROBINSON, Thomas	A.B.	ELIZABETH	
	A.B.	AGAMEMNON	*Trafalgar*
	A.B.	AGAMEMNON	*St Domingo*
SAVORY, John	L.M.	ELIZABETH	G.H. 8,328
STODDART, John	A.B.	ELIZABETH	
	Boy 2nd Cl	AGAMEMNON	*Trafalgar*
	Boy 2nd Cl	AGAMEMNON	*St Domingo*
TAYLOR, Henry	Ord	ELIZABETH	G.H. 4,779
TOWNING, Henry	L.M.	ELIZABETH	(Not found on Muster List. ADM 37/5061)

(108) THE POTOMAC 17 AUG 1814

Capitulation of ALEXANDRIA (U.S.A.) and capture of shipping in the Potomac River.

(Real dates 17 to 29 August 1814)

AGNEW, Thomas	Pte. R.M.	EURYALUS	
ALEXANDER, Thomas	A.B.	SEAHORSE	
	A.B.	SEAHORSE	B.S. 14 Dec 1814
BAGNALL, John	Pte. R.M.	REGULUS	Ship not present, – nor below.
	Pte. R.M.	REGULUS	B.S. 14 Dec 1814 (M.L. as BAGNELL)
BAKER, Henry.L.	Commander	FAIRY	
	Lieut. R.N.	"ANHOLT" (P)	Anholt. 27 March 1811
BALL, John	Drummer. R.M.	EURYALUS	
BARRON, John	A.B.	FAIRY	G.H. 7,721
BERRYMAN, George	Pte. R.M.	SEAHORSE	(M.L. as BARRYMAN)
	Pte. R.M.	SEAHORSE	B.S. 14 Dec 1814
BROWN, James	A.B.	SEAHORSE	
BUCKLAND, Robert	Capt Main Top	SEAHORSE	
	Capt Main Top	SEAHORSE	B.S. 14 Dec 1814
BURROWS, William	Pte. R.M.	EURYALUS	
BURTON, Thomas	L.M.	METEOR	
CAMMILLIERI, Joseph	Master's Mate	SEAHORSE	
	Not yet Aboard	ACTIVE	B.S. 28 June 1810
	A.B.	ACTIVE	Lissa
	Midshipman	ACTIVE	Pelagosa. 29 Novr 1811
	Master's Mate	SEAHORSE	B.S. 14 Dec 1814
CLEMENTS, James	Gnr. R.M.A.	AETNA	
	Gnr. R.M.A.	WHITING	Basque Roads 1809
COLLIER, Edward	Master's Mate	EURYALUS	
	Midshipman	BELLEISLE	Martinique
COX, Thomas	A.B.	SEAHORSE	
	A.B.	SEAHORSE	B.S. 14 Dec 1814
CRUWYS, Thomas	Carp's Crew	EURYALUS	
CUMMINGS, John	Pte. R.M.	EREBUS	(M.L. as CUMMINS)
DAVIS, John	Master	EURYALUS	
DAWSON, John	Capt of Mast	SEAHORSE	
	Capt of Mast	SEAHORSE	B.S. 14 Dec 1814
DICKINSON, Thomas	L.M.	SEAHORSE	(Vfd Abd. Not on Roll)
	L.M.	SEAHORSE	B.S. 14 Dec 1814 (M.L. as DUKESON)
DIXON, William.H.	Lieut. R.N.	DEVASTATION	
DOBIE, Robert	Supn Asst Surg	SEAHORSE	
DORAN, William	Ord	DEVASTATION	
DOYLE, James @ Joseph	A.B.	EURYALUS	
DUFTON, William	Pte. R.M.	SEAHORSE	
FAWCONER, Samuel	Midshipman	DEVASTATION	
FORSYTH, Alexander	Cpl. R.M.	EURYALUS	
GARDNER, William	Cpl. R.M.	EURYALUS	
	Pte. R.M.	BELLEROPHON	Trafalgar
	Sgt. R.M.	MINDEN	Algiers
GAYNOR, Richard	L.M.	EURYALUS	(M.L. as GANER)
GOGGIN, Edward	Ord	SEAHORSE	GH.7699. M.L. as GOGAN
	Ord	SEAHORSE	B.S. 14 Dec 1814
GORDON, Charles	Midshipman	EREBUS	
GORDON, James.A.	Captain. R.N.	SEAHORSE	
	Midshipman	REVOLUTIONNAIRE	23rd June 1795
	Midshipman	NAMUR	St Vincent
	Midshipman	GOLIATH	Nile
	Captain. R.N.	MERCURY	Off Rota. 4 April 1808
	Captain. R.N.	ACTIVE	Lissa
	Captain. R.N.	ACTIVE	Pelagosa. 29 Novr 1811
GORDON, John	Lieut. R.N.	SEAHORSE	
GRAY, Robert	A.B.	SEAHORSE	
	A.B.	SEAHORSE	B.S. 14 Dec 1814
GREEN, Daniel	A.B.	DEVASTATION	G.H. 9,989
GREW, John	Sgt. R.M.	SEAHORSE	
HARDY, James	Sailmaker	SEAHORSE	
	Sailmaker	SHANNON	Shannon Wh Chesapeake
	Sailmaker	SEAHORSE	B.S. 14 Dec 1814
HARRIOTT, Thomas	Midshipman	EREBUS	
HERBERT, Thomas	Lieut. R.N.	EURYALUS (P)	(Recd China 1842 Medal)
	Master's Mate	BLONDE	Guadaloupe
HILL, Edward	A.B.	EURYALUS	
HILL, James	Boy 3rd Cl	AETNA	
	Boy 3rd Cl	AETNA	Basque Roads 1809
HOLLAND, Rupert.C.	1st Lt. R.M.	EURYALUS	
	1st Lt. R.M.	QN CHARLOTTE	Algiers
HYDE, John	Boatswain	DEVASTATION	

JAMES, Henry	Pte. R.M.	REGULUS	*Ship not present, – nor below*
	Pte. R.M.	REGULUS	*B.S. 14 Dec 1814*
JENNINGS, Thomas	Purser	SEAHORSE	
JEWELL, John.N.	Purser	EURYALUS	
JONES, Henry	Boy 3rd Cl	EREBUS	
JONES, James	Ship's Corporal	EURYALUS	
JONES, John	Coxswain	DEVASTATION	*(M.L. as JAMES, Jones)*
JONES, John	Two A.Bs borne	EURYALUS	
KAINS, Thomas	Purser	DEVASTATION	
KANE, John	Ord	SEAHORSE	*G.H.9839. M.L. as KAIN*
	Ord	PHAETON	*Java*
KING, Henry	Lieut. R.N.	SEAHORSE (P)	
	Midshipman	NAMUR	*St Vincent*
LAPPING, Benjamin	Supn Boy 2nd Cl	EREBUS	
LEARY, Daniel	Carp's Crew	SEAHORSE	
	Carp's Crew	SEAHORSE	*B.S. 14 Dec 1814*
Le MARKQUAND, James	Yeo Powder Room	EREBUS	
LEYSON, William	Asst Surgeon	EURYALUS	
LIVINGSTONE, Archibald	A.B.	EURYALUS	
LLOYD, David	Supn Boy 2nd Cl	SEAHORSE	
LUCAS, Edward	Pte. R.M.	EREBUS	
LUCY, John	Supn Boy 3rd Cl	SEAHORSE	*(M.L. as LACY)*
MACKLIN, Joseph	Ship's Corporal	SEAHORSE	*(Vfd Abd. Not on Roll)*
	Ship's Corporal	SEAHORSE	*B.S. 14 Dec 1814*
MATTHEWS, William	Pte. R.M.	EURYALUS	*G.H. 9,260*
MAY, Christopher	Midshipman	FAIRY	
MAYNARD, James	Gunner	METEOR	
McLAUGHLAN, William	Carp's Crew	SEAHORSE	
McMANUS, David	Asst Surg	SEAHORSE	*(Vfd Abd. Not on Roll)*
	Asst Surg	SEAHORSE	*B.S. 14 Dec 1814*
	Surgeon	PROMETHEUS	*Algiers (Vfd Abd. N. on R.)*
MOFFITT, George	A.B.	SEAHORSE	
	A.B.	SEAHORSE	*B.S. 14 Dec 1814*
MOORE, John	Midshipman	SEAHORSE (P)	
	Midshipman	ORPHEUS	*Guadaloupe*
MORRIS, John	Ord	SEAHORSE	
MURPHY, Richard	Ord	EURYALUS	*G.H. 3,853*
NAPIER, Charles	Captain. R.N.	EURYALUS	
	Commander	RECRUIT	*Martinique*
	Commander	RECRUIT (P)	*Recruit. 17 June 1809*
	Commodore	POWERFUL	*Syria*
			(Known to have recd 4 clasp Medal. Not on any Roll)
NICHOLS, Christopher	Ord	SEAHORSE	*GH.9230. M.L. as NICHOLLS*
PAYNTER, John.P.	Lieut. R.N.	EURYALUS	
	Midshipman	INDEFATIGABLE	*Basque Roads 1809*
PETCH, Charles. A.	Midshipman	EURYALUS	
PIKEWOOD, Stephen	A.B.	FAIRY	*G.H. 2,528*
POWELL, John	Ord	EREBUS	
PRICE, Owen	Pte. R.M.	SEAHORSE	
	Pte. R.M.	SEAHORSE	*B.S. 14 Dec 1814*
REA, Alexander	Surgeon	EURYALUS	
ROBERTS, Samuel	Commander	METEOR	
	Boy 2nd Cl	ANSON	*12 Octr 1798*
	Lieut. R.N.	UNICORN	*Basque Roads 1809*
	Commander	METEOR	*B.S. 14 Dec 1814*
SEBBORNE, James	Not Given	EREBUS	*(Not found on M.L.)*
SHAW, John	A.B.	EURYALUS	
SHIPLEY, James	Boy 2nd Cl	DEVASTATION	
SIMMONS, James	Ord	SEAHORSE	*(M.L. as SIMMONDS)*
SMITH, John	Supn Boy 2nd Cl	EREBUS	
SMITH, Joseph	Boy 2nd Cl	SEAHORSE	
SMITH, William	Capt Fore Top	EURYALUS	
SONNERAT, Thomas	Clerk	DEVASTATION	
SUGG, Edward	Sgt. R.M.	EREBUS	
	Pte. R.M.	SUPERB	*Gut of Gibraltar. 12 July 1801*
	Sgt. R.M.	SUPERB	*St Domingo*
SWAYNE, Stephen.J.	Surgeon	SEAHORSE	*(Vfd Abd. Not on Roll)*
	Surgeon	VOLAGE	*Lissa*
	Surgeon	ACTIVE	*Pelagosa. 29 Novr 1811*
	Surgeon	SEAHORSE	*B.S. 14 Dec 1814*
TAYLOR, Charles	L.M.	SEAHORSE	
	L.M.	SEAHORSE	*B.S. 14 Dec 1814*
THOMAS, George	Lieut. R.N.	EREBUS	
THOMAS, John	A.B.	EURYALUS	
THOMAS, William.G.	Lieut. R.N.	AETNA	
	Midshipman	SCIPION	*Java*
THOMPSON, George	Ord	SEAHORSE	
THORN @ THOM, Jonathan	L.M.	SEAHORSE	

THE POTOMAC 17 AUG 1814

THORPE, Charles	Boy 3rd Cl	SEAHORSE	
	Boy 3rd Cl	SEAHORSE	B.S. 14 Dec 1814
URWIN, George	Carpenter	SEAHORSE	
VALLACK, Richard.G.	Lieut. R.N.	AETNA	
	Lieut. R.N.	SEAHORSE	Seahorse Wh Badere Zaffere
WALKER, William	Purser	EREBUS	
	Purser	SNAP	Martinique
	Purser	SNAP	Guadaloupe
WARD, John	Cpl. R.M.A.	AETNA	G.H. 2,318
	Pte. R.M.	RAMILLIES	Copenhagen 1801
	Gnr. R.M.A.	CALEDONIA	Basque Roads 1809
	Cpl. R.M.A.	BEELZEBUB	Algiers
WARING, John	Clerk	EURYALUS	
WARREN @ WARRAM, Joseph	Pte. R.M.	EURYALUS	
WATERS, Adam	A.B.	SEAHORSE	
	A.B.	SEAHORSE	B.S. 14 Dec 1814
WHEATLEY, William	Ord	METEOR	
WILKINSON, James	Master's Mate	EURYALUS	(M) A of I/AVA
	Midshipman	THAMES	Amanthea. 25 July 1810
WOODS, Thomas	Midshipman	SEAHORSE	
	Vol 1st Cl	ACTIVE	Lissa
	Midshipman	ACTIVE	Pelagosa. 29 Novr 1811
	Midshipman	SEAHORSE	B.S. 14 Dec 1814
	Supn Master's Mate	IMPREGNABLE	Algiers
WRIGHT, Robert	2nd Lt. R.M.A.	AETNA	

(1) 3 & 6 SEP BOAT SERVICE 1814

Capture of the American schooners TIGRESS and SCORPION by boats in the Detour Passage, Lake Huron.

BULGER (or BULGEN), Andrew	Lieutenant	Royal Newfoundland Fencible Infantry	(Disbanded 24 June 1816)

(205) 14 DEC BOAT SERVICE 1814

Capture of five American gun vessels and a sloop on Lake Borgne, New Orleans.

ALEXANDER, Thomas	A.B.	SEAHORSE	
	A.B.	SEAHORSE	The Potomac. 17 Aug 1814
ALLEN, James Henry	Supn Boy 2nd Cl	DIOMEDE	
ALLEN, William	Pte. R.M.	SOPHIE	
ARTHUR, William	Ord	TONNANT	
	Boy 2nd Cl	CUMBERLAND	B.S. 1 Nov 1809
AUSTIN, Horatio.T.	Midshipman	RAMILLIES	
	Captain. R.N.	CYCLOPS	Syria
BACKWELL, Henry	Yeo Powder Rm	RAMILLIES	(M.L. as BAKEWELL)
BAGNALL, John	Pte. R.M.	REGULUS	(M.L. as Thomas BAGNELL)
	Pte. R.M.	REGULUS	The Potomac. 17 Aug 1814
BAIRD, Daniel	Supn Master's Mate	NORGE	
	Midshipman	EMERALD	Emerald. 13 March 1808
BARKLEY, Charles	A.B.	ROYAL OAK	
BARNES, Richard.K.	Lieut. R.M.	BEDFORD	
BATTISON, Thomas	Pte. R.M.	ROYAL OAK	
BELL, William	Asst Surgeon	BELLE POULE	(Vfd Abd. Not on Roll)
	Surgeon	IMPLACABLE	Syria
BERRYMAN, George	Pte. R.M.	SEAHORSE	(M.L. as BARRYMEN)
	Pte. R.M.	SEAHORSE	The Potomac. 17 Aug 1814
BEWS, James	A.B.	ALCESTE	
BLACKWOOD, Thomas	A.B.	RAMILLIES	G.H.4295
BOWKER, Henry	Ord	NORGE	(M.L. as BOUKER)
BOYCE, Edward	Ord	WESER	(M.L. as BOYS)
BRAGG, David	A.B.	BEDFORD	G.H.2063
BROOKS, John.H.	Purser's Steward	CYDNUS	
BROWN, William	2 Borne	ROYAL OAK	
BUCKLAND, Robert	Capt Main Top	SEAHORSE	
	Capt Main Top	SEAHORSE	The Potomac. 17 Aug 1814
BYWATER, Thomas	Pte. R.M.	NORGE	

CAMMILLERI, Joseph	Master's Mate	SEAHORSE	
	(Not Abd. On Roll)	ACTIVE	B.S. 28 June 1810
	A.B.	ACTIVE	Lissa
	Midshipman	ACTIVE	Pelagosa. 29 Novr 1811
	Master's Mate	SEAHORSE	The Potomac. 17 Aug 1814
CAMPBELL, James	1st Lieut. R.M.	TONNANT	(Roll RAMILLIES. Wrong)
CARR, Henry John	Master's Mate	ROYAL OAK	
CARTER, Lot	L.M.	RAMILLIES	
CASTLES, Thomas	L.M.	DIOMEDE	
CAVANAGH, Cain or Ryan or Kyer	Ord	ROYAL OAK	
CHIGNELL, James	A.B.	TONNANT	(M.L. as CHEGNILL)
CHOPPIN, William	L.M.	ROYAL OAK	
CLARK, James	Ord	CYDNUS	(M.L. as CLARKE)
CLERK, Lawrence	Supn A.B.	METEOR	(M.L. as Laurence CLARKE)
COLE, George.W.	Master's Mate	TONNANT	
CONNOLLY, Thomas	Ord	TONNANT	
	Ord	ALBION	Algiers
CONNOR, John	Ord	TONNANT	
COOPER, Benjamin	Pte. R.M.	ASIA	
CORLEY, George	Ord	ROYAL OAK	
CORRIGAN, John	Pte. R.M.	TONNANT	G.H. 9509
	Pte. R.M.	MINDEN	Algiers
COUCHER, Christopher	Ord	TONNANT	
	L.M.	COLOSSUS	Trafalgar
	L.M.	ANSON	Anson. 23 Aug 1806
	L.M.	ANSON	Curacoa
COX, Thomas	A.B.	SEAHORSE	
	A.B.	SEAHORSE	The Potomac. 17 Aug 1814
CREAK, William	Midshipman	TONNANT	
	Lieut. R.N.	MUTINE	Algiers
CULLEN, Anthony	Ord	TONNANT	
DANGERFIELD, William	Pte. R.M.	NORGE	G.H. 9904
	Pte. R.M.	MINDEN	Algiers
DAVIES, John	Qtr Gnr	ARMIDE	
DAVIS, Thomas	Ord	ALCESTE	
DAWSON, John	Capt Mast	SEAHORSE	
	Capt Mast	SEAHORSE	The Potomac. 17 Aug 1814
DICKINSON, Thomas	L.M.	SEAHORSE	(M.L. as DUKESON)
	L.M. (Not on Roll)	SEAHORSE	The Potomac. 17 Aug 1814 (Vfd Abd. Not on Roll)
DILLOW, Thomas	Ord	ROYAL OAK	
DOBSON, Francis	Pte. R.M.	RAMILLIES	(M.L. as DODSON)
DONLEVY, George.M.	Midshipman	NORGE	
	Vol 1st Cl	NORGE	B.S. 23 Nov 1810
DORMAN, George	Ord	RAMILLIES	
DORNFORD, Francis	Midshipman	ROYAL OAK	
DRAPPER, George	Ropemaker	ROYAL OAK	
EDWARDS, Thomas	Ord	NORGE	
ETOUGH, Henry.G.	Lieut. R.N.	BEDFORD	
	Actg Master	SHANNON	Shannon Wh Chesapeake
EVANS, De Lacy	Lt 3rd Dragoons	METEOR	(Not abd this Action. Discharged 5 Nov 1814)
EVANS, William	2 Borne	TONNANT	
EVERY, William	Q.M's Mate	TRAAVE	
	Q.M's Mate	NISUS	Java
FELLOWS, Richard	Pte. R.M.	CYDNUS	
	Pte. R.M.	YORK	Martinique. G.H.9515
FORBES, Alexander.W.	Midshipman	ARMIDE	
	Vol 1st Cl	IMPERIEUSE	Basque Roads 1809
FORSTER, Robert	Lieut. R.N.	ASIA	
	Master's Mate	LEDA	Egypt
FRANCILLON, Thomas	Supn Lieut. R.N.	RAMILLIES	
	Midshipman	POMPEE	Martinique
	Midshipman	MARLBOROUGH	B.S. Ap & May 1813
FRANKLIN, John	Lieut. R.N.	BEDFORD	
	Midshipman	POLYPHEMUS	Copenhagen 1801
	Midshipman	BELLEROPHON	Trafalgar
FRANKS, William	Ord	ALCESTE	
FREMANTLE, Charles.H.	Midshipman	RAMILLIES	
FRUIN, William	L.M.	DIOMEDE	
FURLOUGH, Patrick	A.B.	RAMILLIES	
GAYNOR, James	A.B.	RAMILLIES	
GILLESPIE, William	A.B.	CARRON	
GILMORE, John	Midshipman	TONNANT	
GOGGIN, Edward	Ord	SEAHORSE	(M.L. as GOGAN. G.H.7699)
	Ord	SEAHORSE	The Potomac. 17 Aug 1814
GOMS, John	A.B.	BELLE POULE	(M.L. as GUMS)
	A.B.	DONEGAL	Basque Roads 1809
GOVIS, Robert	Ord	ROYAL OAK	
	L.M.	ROYAL SOVEREIGN	Trafalgar
GRAY, Matthew	Lieut. R.N.	TONNANT	(ex "Potomac - -" Roll)

14 DEC BOAT SERVICE 1814

Name	Rank	Ship	Notes
GRAY, Robert	A.B.	SEAHORSE	
	A.B.	SEAHORSE	The Potomac. 17 Aug 1814
GREEN, John	Vol 1st Cl	SOPHIE	
GREY, John	L.M.	RAMILLIES	(M.L. as GRAY. G.H. 5090)
HAMILTON, James	Qtr Gnr	ROYAL OAK	alias Samuel HAMMERTON
HAMPTON, Samuel.R.	Pte. R.M.	TONNANT	
HARDY, James	Sailmaker	SEAHORSE	
	Sailmaker	SHANNON	Shannon Wh Chesapeake
	Sailmaker	SEAHORSE	The Potomac. 17 Aug 1814
HARRIS, George	A.B.	NORGE	
HARTLEY, Michael	Armourer's Mate	ROYAL OAK	
HAWKESFORD, Samuel	Pte. R.M.	RAMILLIES	(M.L. as HOXFORD)
HAY, Patrick.D.H.	Lieut. R.N.	RAMILLIES	
HAYWOOD, Richard	Pte. R.M.	?	Roll TONNANT. Not Found.
HENNESSEE, Matthew	A.B.	BEDFORD	(M.L. as HENNESSY)
HENRY, Thomas John	L.M.	DIOMEDE	
HERRING, William	A.B.	BEDFORD	
HOCKING, William	Pte. R.M.	TONNANT	
HOLDER, James	Ord	ALCESTE	(M.L. as HOULDER)
HOLE, William	Master's Mate	TRAAVE	
	Midshipman	WOLVERENE	Martinique
	Midshipman	BACCHUS	B.S. 13 Dec 1809
	Midshipman	BACCHUS	Guadaloupe
HOLLAND, Jacob	Pte. R.M.	NORGE	
HOUNSELL, Thomas	A.B.	TRAAVE	
HOUSE, Terence	L.M.	ROYAL OAK	
HUGHES, William	Pte. R.M.	ARMIDE	
HUNTER, James	Master's Mate	BEDFORD	
HUNTER, Peter	Qtr Gnr	SOPHIE	
HUSSEY, Richard	Master's Mate	DIOMEDE	
	Master's Mate	GLASGOW	Algiers
INCHES, Charles	Asst Surgeon	ROYAL OAK	
	Surgeon	CAMBRIAN	Navarino
JACKSON, Thomas	Ord	HYDRA	
JAMES, Henry	Pte. R.M.	REGULUS	(Ship not present)
	Pte. R.M.	REGULUS	The Potomac. 17 Aug 1814
JAMES, Mark	Pte. R.M.	BEDFORD	
JONES, Edward	A.B.	TONNANT	
	Ord	CAROLINE	Banda Neira
	Ord	CAROLINE	Java
JONES, John	Capt After Guard	RAMILLIES	
JONES, John	Ord	RAMILLIES	
JOSEPHSON, Henry	Gunner (W.O.)	SOPHIE	
KEITH, John	Sgt. R.M.	ALCESTE	G.H.4769
KINRADE, Michael	A.B.	BEDFORD	Roll SEAHORSE. Wrong.
	Ord	GIBRALTAR	Basque Roads 1809
LAMB, George	Ord	TONNANT	
LAWS, John.M.	Midshipman	RAMILLIES	
LAYTON, Henry	Midshipman	RAMILLIES	
LEACH, James	Supn Pte. R.M.	TONNANT	(M.L. as David LEACH)
LEARY, Daniel	Carp's Crew	SEAHORSE	
	Carp's Crew	SEAHORSE	The Potomac. 17 Aug 1814
LEVEQUE, William.O.	Actg Master	SOPHIE	
LEWIN, William	Ord	TONNANT	G.H.7858
LEY, Nicholas	Q.M.	SOPHIE	
LITTLEMORE, Matthew	L.M.	NORGE	
LLOYD, Rickard	Lieut. R.N.	NORGE	
	Midshipman	PIQUE	Pique. 26 March 1806
	Lieut. R.N.	SURINAM	Martinique (Not yet Abd)
LONSDALE, John	Pte. R.M.	CYDNUS	
LONTON, Benjamin	L.M.	SOPHIE	(M.L. as LUNTON)
LUFF, Thomas	Ord	RAMILLIES	
LYNN, David	Q.M.	ALCESTE	
MACKLIN, Joseph	Ship's Corporal	SEAHORSE	
	Ship's Corporal	SEAHORSE	The Potomac. 17 Aug 1814 (Vfd Abd. Not on Roll)
MAGENNIS, John	Cpl. R.M.	SOPHIE	
	Pte. R.M.	Qn CHARLOTTE	Algiers
MAGNIES, John	A.B.	SOPHIE	
MALLETT, William	A.B.	TRAAVE	
MANN, John	Ord	CYDNUS	(M.L. as Joseph MANN)
MANNING, Michael	Ord	TONNANT	
	Ord	SUPERB	Algiers
MATSELL, Robert	Pte. R.M.	RAMILLIES	(May be John @ Robert)
MATHEWS, Peter	2 A.Bs Borne	NORGE	
McALLISTER, William	Ord	BEDFORD	
	L.M.	AGAMEMNON	Trafalgar
	L.M. (Not on Roll)	AGAMEMNON	St Domingo (Vfd Abd)
McCARTHY, Daniel	Ord	CYDNUS	
McCOY, James	A.B.	SOPHIE	G.H.6753
McCROSKEY, Henry	Ord	TONNANT	(M.L. as McCLOSKY)

Name	Rank/Rating	Ship	Notes
McDONALD, John	Capt Main Top	RAMILLIES	G.H.1193
McMANUS, David	Asst Surgeon	SEAHORSE	
	A/Surg (not on Roll)	SEAHORSE	The Potomac 1814 (Vfd Abd)
	Surg (not on Roll)	PROMETHEUS	Algiers (Vfd Abd)
MILLER, James	A.B.	ASIA	
MILLS, William	Pte. R.M.	GORGON	
MITCHEL, Peter	A.B.	SOPHIE	
MOFFITT, George	A.B.	SEAHORSE	
	A.B.	SEAHORSE	The Potomac. 17 Aug 1814
MOODY, Thomas	Pte. R.M.	TONNANT	G.H.7544
MOORE, Edward	Carp's Crew	BEDFORD	G.H.7023
	Ord	AGAMEMNON	Trafalgar
	Ord	AGAMEMNON	St Domingo
MORGAN, Charles	Lieut. R.M.	ARMIDE	
MORGAN, Richard	Supn Midshipman	TONNANT	
	Ord	CANOPUS	St Domingo
MORRIS, Evan	Pte. R.M.	NORGE	G.H.3846
MORRIS, Peter	Master's Mate	ALCESTE	
MOTT, Richard	Pte. R.M.	TONNANT	
MULCAHY, Timothy	A.B.	ROYAL OAK	
	L.M.	COURAGEUX	4 Nov 1805
	Ord	AETNA	Basque Roads 1809
	Qtr Gnr	IMPREGNABLE	Algiers
MUSTART, James	A.B.	BEDFORD	
	Boy 2nd Cl	VIMIERA	Guadaloupe
O'HEA, Matthew	Master's Mate	BEDFORD	
O'REILLY, John	Midshipman	TONNANT	
OSBORNE, Robert	Cpl. R.M.	ARMIDE	(Medal known dated 5 Dec 1814)
PAGE, Abraham	Ord	TRAAVE	
	Boy 2nd Cl	ROYAL SOVEREIGN	Trafalgar
PAGETT, Matthew	Ord	NORGE	
PARK, John	A.B.	NORGE	
PETRIE, Peter	Supn Midshipman	TONNANT	
	Midshipman	CAPTAIN	Martinique
POLLARD, Joseph	Ord	BEDFORD	
PRICE, Owen	Pte. R.M.	SEAHORSE	
	Pte. R.M.	SEAHORSE	The Potomac. 17 Aug 1814
PURCHASE, William	Ord	WESER	
	Boy 2nd Cl	AMETHYST	Amethyst 5 April 1809
RABETT, George.W.	Midshipman	CYDNUS	
	Boy 3rd Cl	GALATEA	Off Tamatave. 20 May 1811
	Lieut. R.N.	MUSQUITO	Navarino
RAYMOND, George	A.B.	ROYAL OAK	
	Midshipman	EDGAR	B.S. 11 Aug 1808 (Vfd Abd. Not on Roll)
	Midshipman	SHANNON	Shannon Wh Chesapeake
REDDING, Thomas	Pte. R.M.	BEDFORD	
REYNOLDS, Thomas	Supn. Gnr. R.M.A.	TONNANT	
RITSON, George	Armourer	SEAHORSE	On G.H.Roll. Not on 171/Roll
	Ord	MINDEN	Java. G.H.7944
ROBERTS, Robert	A.B.	ARMIDE	
ROBERTS, Samuel	Commander. R.N.	METEOR	
	Boy 2nd Cl	ANSON	12 Oct 1798
	Lieut. R.N.	UNICORN	Basque Roads 1809
	Commander. R.N.	METEOR	The Potomac. 17 Aug 1814
ROBERTSON, Archibald	Surgeon	CYDNUS	
	Asst Surgeon	CALEDONIA	Basque Roads 1809
ROBINS, William	Gunner's Mate	TONNANT	
	Gunner's Mate	THESEUS	Basque Roads 1809
ROBINSON, Joseph	A.B.	BEDFORD	
RULE, William	Master's Mate	BEDFORD	
	Midshipman	POLYPHEMUS	Trafalgar
SCOTT, John	Pte. R.M.	ROYAL OAK	
SHILLINGFORD, Alexander	Actg Lieut. R.N.	CYDNUS	
SMALLWOOD, James	L.M.	BEDFORD	G.H.8041
SMITH, Thomas	L.M.	ROYAL OAK	
SPENCER, John	2 Borne	NORGE	
STEPHENS, Christopher	Pte. R.M.	RAMILLIES	
SWAYNE, Stephen.J.	Surgeon	SEAHORSE	
	Surgeon	VOLAGE	Lissa
	Surgeon	ACTIVE	Pelagosa. 29 Novr 1811
	Surgeon	SEAHORSE	The Potomac. 17 Aug 1814 (Vfd Abd. Not on Roll)
SWEET, James	Pte. R.M.	TONNANT	
TAILOR, James	2 Borne	TONNANT	
TATNEY, John	Cook	ALCESTE	

14 DEC BOAT SERVICE 1814

TATTNALL, James.B.	Lieut. R.N.	TONNANT	
	Lieut. R.N.	RACEHORSE	Off Tamatave. 20 May 1811 (Vfd Abd. Not on Roll)
	Lieut. R.N.	PRESIDENT	St Sebastian
TAYLOR, Charles	L.M.	SEAHORSE	
	L.M.	SEAHORSE	The Potomac. 17 Aug 1814
THOMAS, Benjamin	Q.M's Mate	TONNANT	G.H.5048
THOMAS, Robert	Actg Lieut. R.N.	ROYAL OAK	
THORPE, Charles	Boy 3rd Cl	SEAHORSE	
	Boy 3rd Cl	SEAHORSE	The Potomac. 17 Aug 1814
TOD, John	Midshipman	TONNANT	
	Midshipman	REPULSE	B.S. 2 May 1813
TODD, John	Pte. R.M.	ASIA	
TRILL, James	L.M.	TRAAVE	(M.L. as John TRILL)
TRIPP, John.U.	Lieut. R.N.	RAMILLIES	
TUBBY, Benjamin	Pte. R.M.	RAMILLIES	G.H.3157
	Pte. R.M.	HMS ANHOLT	On G.H.Roll. Not on 171/Roll Anholt. 27 March 1811
TUCKER, William	Capt of Mast	TONNANT	
WALKER, John	Master's Mate	NORGE	
	Midshipman	NORGE	B.S. 23 Nov 1810
WALSTER, William	Barber	ROYAL OAK	(M.L. as Wm WALLITIE)
	L.M.	AETNA	Basque Roads 1809
WATERS, Adam	A.B.	SEAHORSE	
	A.B.	SEAHORSE	The Potomac. 17 Aug 1814
WATTS, Thomas	A.B.	ASIA	G.H.3103
WEDDERKOFF, Johann.C.	Ord	ROYAL OAK	
WELLS, James	Ord	NORGE	
WESTCOTT, John	Ord	?	Roll SEAHORSE. Not found
WILKINSON, John James	Master's Mate	RAMILLIES	
WILLIAMS, John	2 Borne	TONNANT	
WILLIAMS, Thomas.M.	Supn Midshipman	TONNANT	
WILLS, John	Capt of Fore Top	METEOR	
WOODS, Thomas	Midshipman	SEAHORSE	
	Vol 1st Cl	ACTIVE	Lissa
	Midshipman	ACTIVE	Pelagosa. 29 Novr 1811
	Midshipman	SEAHORSE	The Potomac. 17 Aug 1814
	Supn Master's Mate	IMPREGNABLE	Algiers
WROOT, Michael.M.	Lieut. R.N.	ROYAL OAK	

(58) ENDYMION WH PRESIDENT (G.M.)

Action by ENDYMION with the American frigate PRESIDENT on 15 January 1815, which surrendered to other ships of British squadron, off Sandy Hook, New Jersey.

ATHERTON, John	Supn L.M.	ENDYMION	
BAKER, John	2nd Lieut. R.M.	ENDYMION	
BARNETT, John	Supn Pte. R.M.	ENDYMION	
BEAN, William	Actg Carpenter	ENDYMION	
	Carpenter	IMPLACABLE	Syria
BEAUMONT, Richard	Midshipman	ENDYMION	
BENNETT, James.C.	Vol 1st Cl	ENDYMION	
BOYTER, Alexander	Master's Mate	ENDYMION	
	Master's Mate	TOPAZE	B.S. 1 Nov 1809
BRIGHT, John.R.	Supn Pte. R.M.	ENDYMION	
BRITTAL, Noah	Supn Pte. R.M.	ENDYMION	(M.L. as BRITTLE)
	Pte. R.M.	DIANA	Diana. 11 Sept 1809
	Pte. R.M.	DIANA	B.S. 24 Dec 1810
COLE, Robert	L.M.	ENDYMION	
COOKE, James	Carp's Crew	ENDYMION	(M.L. as COOK)
	L.M.	SAMARANG	Java
DART, John	L.M.	ENDYMION	
DILLON, Edward	Purser's Steward	ENDYMION	
DISTON, John	Ord	ENDYMION	
EMSLEY, James	Carpenter's Mate	ENDYMION	(M.L. as ENSLEY)
EVANS, John	2 Borne	ENDYMION	
FANSHAWE, Arthur	Lieut. R.N.	ENDYMION	
	Midshipman	IMPLACABLE	Implacable. 26 Aug 1808
	Midshipman	SCIPION	Java
	Lieut. R.N.	ENDYMION	B.S. 8 April 1814
	Captain. R.N.	PRINCESS CHARLOTTE	Syria
FARMILO, John	Supn Boy 2nd Cl	ENDYMION	
FIELD, Francis	Sgt. R.M.	ENDYMION	
FORD, Dominic	A.B.	ENDYMION	
GIBSON, John	A.B.	ENDYMION	

GOODALL, Joseph	Supn. A.B.	ENDYMION	
GREEN, John	Vol 1st Cl	ENDYMION	
GREENHALGH, William	Supn Pte. R.M.	ENDYMION	
GUEST, Joseph	Ord	ENDYMION	
HAGLEY, James	Q.M's Mate	ENDYMION	
HEXTER, Samuel	Supn Ord	ENDYMION	*(M.L. as EXETER)*
HICKEY, Owen	Pte. R.M.	ENDYMION	
HILL, William	Ord	ENDYMION	
HITCHMAN, Henry	Ord	ENDYMION	
HOPE, Henry	Captain. R.N.	ENDYMION	
	Midshipman	KENT	*Egypt*
JELLETT, Cornelius	Pte. R.M.	ENDYMION	
JOB, Thomas	Ord	ENDYMION	
JONES, Thomas	Supn Pte. R.M.	ENDYMION	
JONES, William	Capt of Mast	ENDYMION	G.H.7305
KENNEDY, Thomas	Supn Boy 3rd Cl	ENDYMION	
KITCHEN, James	Capt of Fore Top	ENDYMION	
LINGARD, John	Supn A.B.	ENDYMION	
MACKIE, William	Capt of Fore Top	ENDYMION	
NIGHTINGALE, William	Supn A.B.	ENDYMION	
ORMOND, Francis	Lieut. R.N.	ENDYMION	
	Midshipman	IMPLACABLE	*Implacable. 26 Aug 1808*
	Master's Mate	IMPLACABLE	*B.S. 7 July 1809*
	Actg Flag Lieut. RN.	ABOUKIR	*B.S. 29 Sep 1812*
	Lieut. R.N.	IMPREGNABLE	*Algiers*
OSENAM, John	Ord	ENDYMION	*(M.L. as OXMAN)*
	Boy 2nd Cl	RUSSELL	*Copenhagen. 1801*
OUGHTON, George.V.	Purser	ENDYMION	*(M.L. as OUTON)*
PRATT, William	L.M.	ENDYMION	
RICHARDSON, James	A.B.	ENDYMION	
ROBERTS, William	Pte. R.M.	ENDYMION	
ROWLANDS, Thomas	Supn Boy 3rd Cl	ENDYMION	*(M.L. as ROWLAND)*
SADLER, Benjamin.P.	Supn Midshipman	ENDYMION	
SPARSHOTT, William	Armourer	ENDYMION	G.H.8265
STOREY, George	Q.M's Mate	ENDYMION	G.H.9140
	A.B.	DEFENCE	*Trafalgar*
TREGO, Thomas	Ropemaker	ENDYMION	
	Ropemaker	PRINCE	*Trafalgar*
TREHEARNE, David	Supn Pte. R.M.	ENDYMION	
WAGLIN, Christopher @ LLOYD, Charles	A.B.	ENDYMION	*(M.L. as WAGLING)*
WEBB, Joseph	Sailmaker's Crew	ENDYMION	
WILLIAMS, Henry	Midshipman	ENDYMION	
WITTLE, James	L.M.	ENDYMION	*(M.L. as WHITTLE)*
WOODS, Robert	Ord	ENDYMION	
YULE, James	Vol 1st Cl	ENDYMION	

(89) GAIETA 24 July 1815

For attack and reduction of GAETA, Italy.
(Real Date – The fortress did not surrender until 8 Aug 1814)

BARBER, John	Pte. R.M.	MALTA	
	Pte. R.M.	HYACINTH	*Malaga. 29 April 1812*
	Pte. R.M.	GLASGOW	*Algiers*
BARCLAY, Charles	L.M.	BERWICK	
BARNES, William	Pte. R.M.	BERWICK	
BARNETT, Edward	Midshipman	MALTA	
	Midshipman	SUPERB	*Algiers*
BARTON, Samuel	Ship's Corporal	BERWICK	
BECK, Michael	A.B.	BERWICK	*(M.L. as BACK)*
BELCHER, Edward	Midshipman	MALTA	
	Midshipman	SUPERB	
BERRY, James	Pte. R.M.	MALTA	
	Pte. R.M.	IMPREGNABLE	
BEST, Thomas	L.M.	MALTA	
BIGNALL, George	Ord	BERWICK	G.H.9530
BIRD, John	Ord	BERWICK	
BLENKARNE, William	Midshipman	BERWICK	
	Master's Mate	IMPREGNABLE	*Algiers*
BLOIS, John Ralph	Midshipman	BERWICK	
BRACE, Edward	Vol 1st Cl	BERWICK	
BULFORD, Robert	Yeoman of Sheets	BERWICK	G.H.7994
CLARKE, George	Boy 2nd Cl	BERWICK	
	L.M.	IMPREGNABLE	*Algiers*
COCKSHOT, George	Capt of Fore Top	BERWICK	
COOK, Thomas	Pte. R.M.	BERWICK	
CRODEN, William	Pte. R.M.	MALTA	*(M.L. as CRAYDEN)*
CRUTCHLEY, James	Master's Mate	BERWICK	
	Master's Mate	IMPREGNABLE	*Algiers*

GAIETA 24 JULY 1815

DALMAHOY, William	Ord	BERWICK	
DAVIS, John	Pte. R.M.	BERWICK	
DAVIS, Thomas.E.	A.B.	BERWICK	
	Capt Main Top	VIRGINIE	*Virginie. 19 May 1808*
DENHAM, William	Capt Forecastle	MALTA	
DUNCAN, George	Q.M.	BERWICK	*G.H. 9455*
	A.B.	MEDIATOR	*Basque Roads 1809*
EVANS, William.B.	Ord	BERWICK	
FITCHETT, Isaac	Pte. R.M.	BERWICK	
FOX, William	Ord	BERWICK	
GILSON, Thomas Andrew	Midshipman	MALTA	
HANDCOCK, James	A.B.	BERWICK	
HOOD, William.J.T.	Master's Mate	MALTA	
	Vol 1st Cl	ACHILLE	*Trafalgar*
HOOPER, Edward	Pte. R.M.	WOODLARK	*G.H.2536. Ship not present.*
HOSKIN, Thomas	A.B.	MALTA	
HUDSMITH, John	Q.M.	MALTA	*(M.L. as HERTSMITH)*
JAMESON, William	A.B.	MALTA	*(M.L. as JAMIESON)*
JELBARD, Richard	Midshipman	MALTA	
JONES, Edward	Vol 1st Cl	MALTA	
KEAN, Michael	Vol 1st Cl	MALTA	
KNIGHT, Nathaniel	Pte. R.M.	BERWICK	
LARCOMBE, Robert	Ord	MALTA	
LUTMAN, Charles	Lieut. R.N.	BERWICK	
	Lieut. R.N.	IMPREGNABLE	*Algiers*
			(Vfd Abd. Not on Roll)
MACKAY, John	Surgeon	MALTA	
	Surgeon	MUTINE	*Algiers*
MARSHALL, Robert	Ord	BERWICK	
MATTHEWS, John	A.B.	MALTA	
	Ord	STAR	*Martinique*
	Ord	STAR	*Guadaloupe*
	A.B.	IMPREGNABLE	*Algiers*
McLEOD, Alexander	A.B.	MALTA	
	Ord	STAR	*Martinique*
	Ord	STAR	*Guadaloupe*
MITCHELL, Thomas	Midshipman	BERWICK	
	Midshipman	IMPREGNABLE	*Algiers*
MONK, John	Lieut. R.N.	BERWICK	
	Lieut. R.N.	IMPREGNABLE	*Algiers*
MORTIMER, George	Lieut. R.N.	MALTA	
	Lieut. R.N.	VENERABLE	*Venerable. 16 Jany 1814*
NEIL, John	A.B.	MALTA	
	Ord	STAR	*Martinique*
	Ord	STAR	*Guadaloupe*
	Capt Forecastle	IMPREGNABLE	*Algiers*
NEWMAN, Thomas	Quarter Gunner	BERWICK	*G.H.592*
NIXON, Adam	Midshipman	BERWICK	
O'BRIEN, Joseph	Lieut. R.N.	BERWICK	
	Lieut. R.N.	IMPREGNABLE	*Algiers*
PARKER, Edward.A.	2nd Lt R.M.	MALTA	
POLETTI, Stephen	Boy 3rd Cl	BERWICK	
PRIGG, Thomas	Pte. R.M.	BERWICK	
REDMOND, Timothy	Capt Fore Top	BERWICK	
REYNOLDS, James	Pte. R.M.	BERWICK	
RICHMOND, Edward	A.B.	PRINCESS AUGUSTA	*alias WRIGHT, Edward Ship not present*
	A.B.	PNCSS AUGUSTA	*B.S. 2 Augt 1811*
	A.B.	PNCSS AUGUSTA	*Gluckstadt. 5 Jan 1814*
RILEY, Charles.W.	Master's Mate	MALTA	
ROBILLIARD, John	Vol 1st Cl	MALTA	
SAMUEL, Joseph	Carpenter's Crew	BERWICK	
SANGESTER, George	A.B.	BERWICK	
SHAIRP, Alexander	Midshipman	BERWICK	
	Midshipman	HUSSAR	*Java*
SHAW, Elisha	Ord	MALTA	
SHAW, John	Carpenter's Crew	MALTA	
SILK, John	L.M.	MALTA	
SYMONS, Henry	A.B.	MALTA	
	Boy 2nd Cl	PRINCE	*Trafalgar*
	A.B.	IMPREGNABLE	*Algiers*
SIMS, James	Boy 2nd Cl	BERWICK	*(M.L. as SIME & SIMMS)*
SMITH, John	A.B.	MALTA	
SMITH, Thomas	Pte. R.M.	MALTA	
SMITH, Thomas	2 Borne Ord & Drummer.R.M.	MALTA	
SPOONER, W.	Pte. R.M.	WOODLARK	*G.H.2045. Ship not present.*

STANHOPE, William.S.	Lieut. R.N.	BERWICK	Appld as RODDAM, William
	Lieut. R.N.	IMPREGNABLE	Algiers
THIRKELL, Thomas	A.B.	BERWICK	(M.L. as THURKIN & THURKELLS & THURKILLS)
THOMPSON, John	Midshipman	MALTA	
TIERNEY, Thomas	L.M.	BERWICK	
TRACE, John	Ord	BERWICK	G.H.9671
TURNER, John	2 Pte R.Ms borne	MALTA	
VAUGHAN, John	Boy 3rd Cl	MALTA	
	Boatswain	VANGUARD	Syria
VERNON, Thomas	Quarter Gunner	BERWICK	
WALKER, George	L.M.	MALTA	
WELSH, John	Ord	BERWICK	G.H.2296
WILKINSON, Frederick.A.	College Volunteer	BERWICK	
	Midshipman	SUPERB	Algiers
WILLIAMS, John	Ord	MALTA	
WILSON, Harry	Lieut. R.N.	BERWICK	(Vfd Abd. Not on Roll)
	Midshipman	ALFRED	Guadaloupe
	Midshipman	ALFRED	B.S. 23 Nov 1810 (Vfd Abd. Not on Roll)
WILSON, John	Pte. R.M.	BERWICK	
WRIFORD, Samuel	Lieut. R.N.	MALTA	
	Midshipman	CAESAR	4 Nov 1805
	Lieut. R.N.	CAESAR	Basque Roads 1809
WOODS, Richard	Pte. R.M.	BERWICK	G.H.9107
WOODWARD, Robert	Pte. R.M.	BERWICK	
	Pte. R.M.	BELLE POULE	B.S. 4 May 1811

(1328) ALGIERS

Lord Exmouth's bombardment of ALGIERS on 27 August 1816.

ABBOTT, William	Steward's Mate	LEANDER	
ACKLAND, Richard	Pte. R.M.	MINDEN	
ADAMS, Robert	Ord	GRANICUS	
ADAMSON, John	Surgeon	SUPERB	
ADDCOCK, Thomas	Armourer	FURY	(ML as ADCOCK)
ADDINGTON, Thomas	Boatswain	PROMETHEUS	
	Boatswain	ALBION	Navarino
ADKINS, Joshua	Pte. R.M.	IMPREGNABLE	
ADLAM, James	Gnr. R.M.A.	IMPREGNABLE	(May read ALLAM on roll)
AFFORD, James	Pte. R.M.	ALBION	
AITCHISON, Edward	Master's Mate	LEANDER	
AITCHISON, Robert	Lieutenant. R.N.	LEANDER	Commanded the forecastle & gangway guns.
AKER/AHER, Morris	Carp's Crew	IMPREGNABLE	(not yet found aboard)
ALEXANDER, John	Bosun's Mate	GLASGOW	alias & ML as THOMPSON, John.
ALEXANDER, Samuel	L.M.	LEANDER	(not yet found aboard)
ALLEN, James	Pte. R.M.	IMPREGNABLE	
ALLEN, Joseph	Supn Gnr. R.H.A.	GRANICUS	Rocket Corps
ALLEN, Thomas	Pte. R.M.	LEANDER	
ALLESLEY, Dennis	A.B.	PROMETHEUS	
ALMOND, George	Pte. R.M.	ALBION	
ALPHEUS, Charles	Supn Pte. R.M.	HEBRUS	
	Pte. R.M.	BRITANNIA	Trafalgar
	Pte. R.M.	THESEUS	Basque Roads 1809
ALSBURY, James	Supn Pte. R.M.	HEBRUS	(ML as AYLESBURY)
ALVEY, Isaac	Pte. R.M.	PROMETHEUS	
ANDERSON, James	Ord	IMPREGNABLE	
ANDERSON, Thomas	Ord	Qn CHARLOTTE	
ANDREWS, Thomas	Boy 3rd Cl	IMPREGNABLE	
ANGELL, William	Pte. R.M.	GLASGOW	
ARCHER, William	Ord	LEANDER	
ARMSTRONG, Benjamin	A.B.	ALBION	
ARMSTRONG, Henry	Ord	Qn CHARLOTTE	
ARMSTRONG, James Wm	A.B.	FALMOUTH Lighter	Promoted "Master" 1825
ARMSTRONG, Matthew	Pte. R.M.	MINDEN	
ARMSTRONG, Robert	Asst Surgeon	ALBION	
ARMSTRONG, Thomas	Master	FALMOUTH Lighter	
	A.B.	WINDSOR CASTLE	14 March 1795
ARQUIMBAU, Joseph	Supn Midshipman	SEVERN	
ARROWSMITH, William	Ord	Qn CHARLOTTE	
ASH, Isaac	Supn Boy 3rd Cl	BRITOMART	
AVERY, William	L.M.	SUPERB	(ML as EVERY)
AXFORD, William	Pte. R.M.	SEVERN	
AYLMER, Hon. F.W.	Captain	SEVERN	
	Midshipman	SYREN	B.S. 15 Mar 1793 (Earliest NGS clasp issued)
	Lieut. R.N.	SWIFTSURE	Nile
	Lieut. R.N.	SWIFTSURE	Egypt

ALGIERS

BAILEY, Bartholomew	Pte. R.M.	Qn CHARLOTTE	
BAILEY, John	Pte. R.M.	SEVERN	
	Pte. R.M.	REVOLUTIONNAIRE	St Sebastian
BAKER, Charles	Boy 3rd Cl	LEANDER	
BAKER, Charles.H.	Midshipman	ALBION	
BAKER, James	Supn Yeo of Sheets	Qn CHARLOTTE	
BAKER, James	Supn Boy 2nd Cl	INFERNAL	
BAKER, William	A.B.	GLASGOW	
BALL, James	Bosun's Mate	SUPERB	
BALL, John.A.	Midshipman	IMPREGNABLE	
BALL, Thomas	Pte. R.M.	Qn CHARLOTTE	
BAMBRIDGE, William	Pte. R.M.	GLASGOW	
BAMFIELD, Thomas	Q.M.	HERON	
BARBER, John	Pte. R.M.	GLASGOW	
	Pte. R.M.	HYACINTH	Malaga 29 April 1812
	Pte. R.M.	MALTA	Gaieta. 24 July 1815
BARCLAY, James	Supn Mate	FALMOUTH Lighter.	GH 9524.
BARKER, James	Pte. R.M.	IMPREGNABLE	
BARKHAM, John	Qtr Gunner	LEANDER	
BARLOW, Charles.A.	Midshipman	Qn CHARLOTTE	
BARNARD, Charles.J.	Midshipman	MINDEN	
BARNES, John	Qtr Gunner	MINDEN	
BARNES, Thomas	Ord	MINDEN	
BARNETT, Edward	Midshipman	SUPERB	
	Midshipman	MALTA	Gaieta 24 July 1815
BARON, Jonathan	1st Lieut. R.M.	ALBION	
BARRETT, Robert John	Actg 2nd Master	HEBRUS	
	Midshipman	HEBRUS	Hebrus with L'Etoile (27-3-1814)
BARTON, George	L.M.	IMPREGNABLE	
	Ward Room Cook	EDINBURGH	Syria
BATEMAN, John	Pte. R.M.	Qn CHARLOTTE	(ML as BAKEMAN)
BAYLIS, Jeremiah	Boy 2nd Cl	ALBION	(ML as BAILEY)
	A.B.	HASTINGS	Syria
BEACHE, George	Pte. R.M.	SUPERB	(ML as BEACH)
BEAN, James	Boy 2nd Cl	SEVERN	(ML as BAIN)
BEARD, William	Pte. R.M.	IMPREGNABLE	
BEATON, James. Luke.	Boy 3rd Cl	Qn CHARLOTTE	(ML as BETON)
BEATTY, Daniel. McN.	Midshipman	SEVERN	Gun Boat Yawl No 9. Sly Wnd.
	Midshipman	SAPPHO	Sappho 2 March 1808
BEATTY, Rev Edward	Chaplain	SUPERB	
BEAUCHANT, T.S.	1st Lieut R.M.A.	IMPREGNABLE	Mortar Boat Launch No 2
BEAUMONT, Charles	Pte. R.M.	ALBION	(M) Anchor Ty LS & GC
BEAVER, John.N.	Volunteer 1st Cl	GLASGOW	
BEDWELL, James	Boy 3rd Cl	HEBRUS	
BELCHER, Edward	Midshipman	SUPERB	(Applied as "Sir Edward")
	Midshipman	MALTA	Gaieta 24 July 1815
BELL, Francis	Ord	LEANDER	
BELL, John	Supn L.M.	GRANICUS	
BELL, John	Midshipman	HECLA	
BELL, Joseph	Ord	IMPREGNABLE	
BELL, Joseph	A.B.	MINDEN	(Only found as BALL Pte. RM)
BELL, William	Purser	CORDELIA	
BELLAIRS, W.T.	Supn Adm Mid	LEANDER	
BELLAMY, Charles.P.	Supn Midshipman	ALBION	
BELLMAN, Walter	Supn Ord	IMPREGNABLE	
BENHAM, John	L.M.	LEANDER	
BENNETT, John	Ord	LEANDER	GH.4827
BENNETT, John	L.M.	LEANDER	
BENNETT, Richard	Pte. R.M.	Qn CHARLOTTE	
BENNETT, Samuel	Boy 2nd Cl	MINDEN	
BENNETT, Thomas	Cooper	MUTINE	
BENNETT, William	Supn Boy 2nd Cl	Qn CHARLOTTE	
BENTHAM, George	Commander	HERON (P)	
	Midshipman	HERO	4 Novr 1805
	Actg Commander	BRISEIS	Briseis 14 Octr 1810
BENWOOD, William	Carp's Crew	GLASGOW	(Roll may read BERWOOD)
BERRY, James	Pte. R.M.	IMPREGNABLE	
	Pte. R.M.	MALTA	Gaieta 24 July 1815
BERRIDGE, Josh	Ord	MINDEN	
BETTY, Robert	L.M.	SUPERB	
BEVAN, John.Wm.	Pte. R.M.	ALBION	(ML as BEVENS)
BIAS, John	Boatswain.	SEVERN	
BIDD, John	Pte. R.M.	Qn CHARLOTTE	
BIGGS, Stephen	Pte. R.M.	SUPERB	
BILLINGTON, Edward	Pte. R.M.	Qn CHARLOTTE	
BINGHAM, Parker.D.	Midshipman	ALBION	Mortar Boat Launch No 5
BINSTEAD, Stephen	Supn Ropemaker	IMPREGNABLE	
BIRD, Edward.J.	Midshipman	ALBION	
BISHOP, Thomas	A.B.	ALBION	GH 8058
	Ord	MODESTE	Egypt
BLAIR, Peter	Carpenter	IMPREGNABLE	

BLEACH, Thomas	Ord	Qn CHARLOTTE	
	Captain Main Top	TALBOT	Navarino
	Gunner's Mate	VANGUARD	Syria
			(This medal displayed with Anchor Type LS & GC at R.N.Museum)
BLENKARNE, William	Master's Mate	IMPREGNABLE	
	Midshipman	BERWICK	Gaieta 24 July 1815
BLOWER, William	Pte. R.M.	IMPREGNABLE	
BLURTON, George	Lieut. R.N.	MUTINE	
BLYTH, John	Sgt. R.M.	Qn CHARLOTTE	(ML as BLIGH)
	Drummer. R.M.	ATLAS	St Domingo
BOBBETT, Thomas	Cpl. R.M.	GRANICUS	
BOLTON, James	Supn Midshipman	SEVERN	Gun Boat Barge No 12
BOND, James	Sapper & Miner	Qn CHARLOTTE	
BOND, Thomas.B.	Midshipman	GLASGOW	
BONETT, John	L.M.	ALBION	(ML as BORRETT)
BOON, John	A.B.	GRANICUS	
	Ord	CANADA	12 Octr 1798
	A.B.	ACASTA	St Domingo
	A.B.	SCIPION	Java
			(Awarded when 80 years old)
BOSTICK, Richard	Carp's Crew	IMPREGNABLE	(ML as BOSTOCK)
BOTHAM, John	Master	FURY	
BOUND, William	A.B.	Qn CHARLOTTE	(Awarded when 78 years old)
	A.B.	REGULUS	Egypt
	A.B.	ROYAL SOVEREIGN	Trafalgar
	A.B.	NISUS	Java
BOWING, Jeremiah	Supn A.B.	SUPERB	
BOWYER, Joseph	Pte. R.M.	LEANDER	
BRACKENBURY, Edwin	Volunteer 1st Cl	BRITOMART	
BRADEN, William	Ord	Qn CHARLOTTE	
BRADLEY, James	Pte. R.M.	SEVERN	
BRADLEY, John	Ord	ALBION	
	Gunner's Crew	ASIA	Navarino
	A.B.	PIQUE	Syria
			(M) Anchor Type LS & GC
BRANSFIELD, Edward	Master	SEVERN	
BRAY, Dennis	Ord	MUTINE	
BRAY, William	Ord	ALBION	
	Boy 3rd Cl	ILLUSTRIOUS	Java
	Captain Main Top	ASIA	Navarino
BRAZIER, James	Ord	ALBION	
	L.M.	MINOTAUR	Trafalgar
	Ord	MINOTAUR	B.S. 25 July 1809
BRENTON, Henry	Actg Purser	BEELZEBUB	
	Purser	DAPHNE	Syria
BRENTON, William	A.B.	IMPREGNABLE	(An impressed convicted smuggler)
BREWER, James	Pte. R.M.	SUPERB	
BRICE, Robert	Pte. R.M.	SUPERB	
BRIMER, John	Ord	IMPREGNABLE	
BRISTOW, Benjamin	A.B.	SUPERB	
BROOKS, John.H.	Purser's Steward	LEANDER	
BROWN, George	A.B.	Qn CHARLOTTE	
BROWN, George	Ord	MINDEN	GH.8975
BROWN, James	Ord	MINDEN	
BROWN, John	2 Ords borne	ALBION	
BROWN, John	A.B.	FURY	
BROWN, Nicholas	A.B.	SUPERB	GH.9599
BROWN, Samuel	Pte. R.M.	Qn CHARLOTTE	
BROWN, Thomas	2 borne	HEBRUS	SB.106 Ord & 219 Gnr's Mate
BROWN, Thomas	Pte. R.M.	GRANICUS	
BROWN, Thomas	Ord	LEANDER	"wounded in action"
BROWNE, John	Ord	MUTINE	(ML as BROWN)
BROWNE, William.C.	Volunteer 1st Cl	MINDEN	
BROWNING, Colin.A.	Asst Surgeon	HEBRUS	
BROWNING, Samuel	Pte. R.M.	SUPERB	
BRUNKER, John	L.M.	GLASGOW	GH.2701
BUCHANAN, William	L.M.	SUPERB	(ML as BUCHANNON)
BUCKLEY, Thomas	Ord	IMPREGNABLE	
	Gunner's Crew	GENOA	Navarino
BUNBURY, George.B.	Midshipman	MINDEN	(On ML as G.B.B.ISSAC, by 1846 changed to G.B.BUNBURY.)
BURGE, John	Boy 2nd Cl	Qn CHARLOTTE	
BURGESS, Samuel	Flag Lt R.N.	Qn CHARLOTTE (P)	
	Midshipman	IMPREGNABLE	1 June 1794
	Lieut. R.N.	SYLPH	Sylph 28 Sepr 1801
	Lieut. R.N.	PRINCE	Trafalgar
	Lieut. R.N.	PINCHER	B.S. 27 July 1809

ALGIERS

Name	Rank	Ship	Notes
BURKHILL, William	Supn Pte. R.M.	HEBRUS	(ML as BROCKALL)
BURNISTON, Hugh.S.	Master's Mate	Qn CHARLOTTE	
	Midshipman	CAESAR	Basque Roads 1809
BURNS, Daniel	Ord	Qn CHARLOTTE	(Only found a James & Edward)
BURNS, Patrick	Ord	IMPREGNABLE	
BURR, Charles	Pte. R.M.	ALBION	
BURRELLS, Joseph	L.M.	HEBRUS	(ML as BURLS)
BURT, William	Midshipman	SUPERB	
BURTON, Charles.F.	Captain. R.M.A.	Qn CHARLOTTE	
	2nd Lieut. R.M.	TIGRE	Acre 30 May 1799
	2nd Lieut. R.M.	TIGRE	Egypt
BURTON, James.R.	Lieut. R.N.	ALBION	I/Cmd No 19 Gun Boat
BURTON, Thomas	Ord	Qn CHARLOTTE	(ML as BORTON)
BUSH, Matthew.C.	Pte. R.M.	Qn CHARLOTTE	
	Ship's Corporal	POWERFUL	Syria
BUTCHER, Thomas	Ord	LEANDER	
BUTLER, Patrick	Pte. R.M.	Qn CHARLOTTE	
	Pte. R.M.	GIBRALTAR	Basque Roads 1809
BUTTON, Joseph	L.M.	MINDEN	
BYRNE, Patrick	Pte. R.M.	GRANICUS	GH.9044
	Pte. R.M.	NEPTUNE	Trafalgar
	Pte. R.M.	VICTORIOUS	Victorious with Rivoli
BYRNE, Michael	A.B.	MINDEN	(Application No B/25)
	Pte. R.M.	MELAMPUS	Guadaloupe ,, ,,
BYRON, William	Pte. R.M.	Qn CHARLOTTE	
CABLE, Thomas	A.B.	LEANDER	
CADDY, John	Ord	SEVERN	
CADET, John.P.	Supn Ord	HECLA	GH.3497 as Peter
	Ord	SHANNON	Shannon Wh Chesapeake
CADLOCK, William	L.M.	GRANICUS	
CALDWELL, Edward	Surgeon	CORDELIA	
	Surgeon	CAMBRIDGE	Syria
CALEY, Charles	Supn Midshipman	SEVERN	
CALLAGHAN, Thomas	L.M.	HEBRUS	
CALLAWAY, William	Boy 2nd Cl	MINDEN	
CAMILLOR, Joseph	A.B.	Qn CHARLOTTE	
CAMM, John	Pte. R.M.	GLASGOW	
CAMP, Daniel	L.M.	SEVERN	
CAMPBELL, H.F.	Midshipman	Qn CHARLOTTE	
CAMPBELL, John	Pte. R.M.	MINDEN	
CAMPBELL, William	Pte. R.M.	LEANDER	
CARNAC, John Rivett	Midshipman	Qn CHARLOTTE	By 1846 was John RIVETT-CARNAC Gun Boat Barge No 1
CARR, Edward	Supn Boy 3rd Cl	Qn CHARLOTTE	
CARR, Thomas	A.B.	Qn CHARLOTTE	
CARR, William	M.A.A.	HEBRUS	
CARRE, Robert Riddle	Commander	BRITOMART	Surname & ML RIDDLE to 1817
	Midshipman	VETERAN	Copenhagen 1801
CARRINGTON, Charles	Pte. R.M.	LEANDER	
CARTER, John	Pte. R.M.	Qn CHARLOTTE	
CARTWRIGHT, Thomas	Midshipman	Qn CHARLOTTE	
CASH, Edward	Carpenter	HERON	(ML as COSH)
CASTLE, William	Ord	GRANICUS	
CASWELL, William	Lieut. R.N.	SUPERB	
	Master's Mate	MAIDSTONE	B.S. 4 April 1812
CATOR, Thomas	Q.M's Mate	Qn CHARLOTTE	
	Ship's Corporal	ASIA	Navarino
CAUGHLAN, William	Ord	MINDEN	(ML as COCKLAND)
CHADWICK, Thomas	Pte. R.M.	SUPERB	
CHAMBERLAIN, Edward	Pte. R.M.	SUPERB	(ML as CHAMBERLAINE)
CHAMBERS, William	Pte. R.M.	Qn CHARLOTTE	
	Pte. R.M.	ALBION	Navarino
CHAPLIN, Edward	Ord	IMPREGNABLE	
CHAPMAN, Daniel	Pte. R.M.	Qn CHARLOTTE	
CHAPMAN, George	Pte. R.M.	LEANDER	
CHAPPELL, William	L.M.	IMPREGNABLE	(ML as CHAPPEL)
CHARDS, James	L.M.	GRANICUS	
CHARLESTON, Charles	Capt' Forecastle	MINDEN	
CHEAL, Thomas	Ord	LEANDER	(ML as CHIELL)
CHEAL, Wm.M or Wm.T	Ord	LEANDER	(ML as CHIELL)
CHETHAM, Edward	Captain. R.N.	LEANDER	Since 1845 became Sir Edward Chetham STRODE, KCB, KCH.
	Midshipman	AGAMEMNON	14 March 1795
	Lieut. R.N.	SEINE	Seine 20 Augt 1800
CHEYNE, George	Lieut. R.N.	ALBION	
CHISHOLM, William	Ord	MINDEN	
CHORLEY, James	Pte. R.M.	SUBERB	
CHORLEY, William	Pte. R.M.	IMPREGNABLE	
CHRISTIAN, Peter	A.B.	LEANDER	
CHRISTIE, Gabriel	Lieut. R.N.	GRANICUS	
CHURM, John	Drummer. R.M.	GRANICUS	
CLARK, Joseph	Supn Adm Mid	LEANDER	(ML as CLARKE)

THE NAVAL GENERAL SERVICE MEDAL ROLL 1793-1840 279

CLARK, Thomas	Ord	MINDEN	*(ML as CLARKE)*
CLARKE, George	L.M.	IMPREGNABLE	
	Boy 2nd Cl	BERWICK	*Gaieta. 24 July 1815*
CLARKE, James	2nd Lieut. R.M.	SUPERB	*& M.G.S. Clasp "Guadaloupe"*
CLARKE, James	A.B.	HERON	
CLARKE, James	A.B.	GRANICUS	
CLARKE, Joseph	Pte. R.M.	SUPERB	
CLARKE, William	Gunner. R.M.A.	LEANDER	
CLAYTON, John	Pte. R.M.	SUPERB	
CLAYTON, John.L.	Midshipman	Qn CHARLOTTE	
CLEMENTS, George	Cpl. R.M.	Qn CHARLOTTE	
CLIFFORD, Patrick	Pte. R.M.	SUPERB	
CLIMO, Thomas	A.B.	SUPERB	
	L.M.	NEPTUNE	*Trafalgar*
CLOUGH, Samuel	Pte. R.M.	GRANICUS	
COGHLAN, Francis.R.	Lieut. R.N.	MINDEN	*I/Cmd No 23 Gun Boat*
COHAN, James	L.M.	LEANDER	*GH.8383*
COLDTHREAD, Francis	A.B.	LEANDER	
COLE, George	Ord	GRANICUS	
COLE, Robert	A.B.	ALBION	*(ML as CALE)*
COLE, Samuel	Ord	PROMETHEUS	
COLE, William	Supn Adm Mid	LEANDER	
COLES, Edward	Pte. R.M.	ALBION	*GH.9174. (ML as COLE)*
COLES, William	Flag Officer's Domestic	Qn CHARLOTTE	
COLLEY, George.F.	Midshipman	ALBION	*Formerly & ML as POMEROY.G.F.*
COLLINS, Samuel	Pte. R.M.	ALBION	
COLLINS, William	Ord	ALBION	
COMBEN, Jonathan	L.M.	MINDEN	
COMIN, William.A.C.	Ord	GLASGOW	*(ML as Charles COMIN)*
CONN, James	Pte. R.M.	GLASGOW	
CONNEEN, Peter	Ord	IMPREGNABLE	
	Ord	Gun Boat No 16.	*St Sebastian*
CONNELLY, Michael	A.B.	LEANDER	
CONNELLY, Patrick	Supn L.M.	SUPERB	
CONNOLLY, Barney	Pte. R.M.	ALBION	
CONNOLLY, Thomas	Ord	ALBION	
	Ord	TONNANT	*B.S. 14 Dec 1814*
CONNOR, Daniel	Ord	HEBRUS	
CONNOR, Thomas (1)	L.M.	GLASGOW	
COODE, John	Captain. R.N.	ALBION	
COOMBS, Thomas	L.M.	SUPERB	
COOPER, William	Pte. R.M.	IMPREGNABLE	
CORBEN, George	Bosun's Mate	Qn CHARLOTTE	
CORCHRAN, John	Ord	MINDEN	*Roll also as CORCHORAN. (ML as COCKRAN)*
CORRIGAN, John	Pte. R.M.	MINDEN	*GH.9509*
	Pte. R.M.	TONNANT	*B.S. 14 Dec 1814*
COSFORD, William	Pte. R.M.	LEANDER	
COSTELLO, Charles	Ord	GRANICUS	
COSTON, James	Captain of Hold	IMPREGNABLE	*(Adm 171/1/376 as "Syria")*
COTGRAVE, Thomas.E.	Midshipman	SUPERB	
COTTLE, William	Pte. R.M.	LEANDER	
COUCH, William	L.M.	IMPREGNABLE	
COULT, James	Gunner. R.M.A.	INFERNAL	
COURTNEY, Abraham	Asst Surgeon	MUTINE	
COUSINS, William	Ord	Qn CHARLOTTE	
COVELL, Daniel	Carp's Crew	SUPERB	
COX, George	Pte. R.M.	ALBION	
COX, John	Pte. R.M.	Qn CHARLOTTE	
COX, Richard	Pte. R.M.	SUPERB	
CRAIG, Richard	Ord	SUPERB	*(ML as CREIG)*
CRAWFORD, Christopher	Carpenter	HEBRUS	
	Carpenter	HEBRUS	*Hebrus with L'Etoile*
CRAWLEY, John	Supn Ord	Qn CHARLOTTE	
CREAGH, James	Master's Mate	HEBRUS	*Gun Boat Yawl No 15*
	Volunteer 1st Cl	MELPOMENE	*B.S. 7 July 1809*
CREAK, William	Lieut. R.N.	MUTINE	
	Midshipman	TONNANT	*B.S. 14 Dec 1814*
CREMER, John	Ord	IMPREGNABLE	
CRISPIN, William	Purser's Steward	HERON	*(ML as CRISPEN)*
	Purser's Steward	GENOA	*Navarino*
CRONIN, Matthew	Armourer	HERON	
CROOK, John	Supn Q.M.	HECLA	
CROSSON, Francis	Supn A.B.	Qn CHARLOTTE	*(ML as CRAWSON)*
CROSSWELL, Thomas	Q.M.	Qn CHARLOTTE	
	A.B.	CAROLINE	*Banda Neira*
	Capt' Forecastle	CAROLINE	*Java*
CROWLEY, John	Ord	MINDEN	*GH. 8793*
	L.M.	DEFIANCE	*Trafalgar*
CRUIZE, John	A.B.	IMPREGNABLE	*(ML as CRUISE)*
	Gunner's Crew	ROSE	*Navarino*
CRUTCHLEY, James	Master's Mate	IMPREGNABLE	
	Master's Mate	BERWICK	*Gaieta 24 July 1815*
CRYER, William	Pte. R.M.	IMPREGNABLE	
CUMMINGS, James	Capt' Afterguard	GRANICUS	*GH.8849 (ML as CUMMINS)*

ALGIERS

CURTIS, Hart	Pte. R.M.	MINDEN	
CUTBEARD, William	L.M.	ALBION	(ML as CUTBAIRD)
CUTLER, Richard	Ord	GLASGOW	
DALE, John	Ord	HERON	
DALEY, Bryan	A.B.	SUPERB	
DALEY, John	Ord	Qn CHARLOTTE	(ML as DEALLY)
	Ord	ALBION	Navarino
DALY, Edward	Ord	LEANDER	GH.9801 & ML as DALEY
DANBY, Henry	L.M.	ALBION	
DANGERFIELD, William	Pte. R.M.	MINDEN	GH.9904
	Pte. R.M.	NORGE	B.S. 14 Dec 1814
DANIELS, Samuel	Ord	MINDEN	
	L.M.	SCEPTRE	Guadaloupe
DANIELS, William	L.M.	LEANDER	(ML as DANIEL)
DARE, Samuel	L.M.	MINDEN	(An impressed convicted smuggler)
DASHWOOD, William.B.	Commander	PROMETHEUS	
	Volunteer 1st Cl	DEFIANCE	Copenhagen 1801
	Lieut. R.N.	ACTIVE	Pelagosa 29 Novr 1811
DAVEY, James	A.B.	GLASGOW	
DAVIDSON, John	A.B.	Qn CHARLOTTE	
DAVIES, George	Midshipman	Qn CHARLOTTE	
	Volunteer 1st CL	AJAX	St Sebastian
DAVIS, James	Capt' Afterguard	ALBION	
DAVIS, James	Q.M.	GLASGOW	
DAVIS, John	Pte. R.M.	IMPREGNABLE	
DAVIS, John	Pte. R.M.	MINDEN	
DAVIS, William	A.B.	ALBION	GH.7977
DAWSON, Thomas	A.B.	LEANDER	GH. 9133 or 10,133
DAWTRY, William	Ship's Corporal	MINDEN	GH. 627
DAY, Robert	Supn Ord	Qn CHARLOTTE	
DAY, William	Capt' Forecastle	HERON	
DAYMAN, William	Pte. R.M.	Qn CHARLOTTE	
DEANE, Samuel	Pte. R.M.	Qn CHARLOTTE	
DEELY or DEALLY or DAELEY, William	L.M.	GRANICUS	(ML as DAELY)
DELAFOSSE, Edward.H.	Lieut. R.N.	HEBRUS	
	Volunteer 1st Cl	CRUIZER	Copenhagen 1801
	Lieut. R.N.	YORK	Martinique
DELME, George	Lieut. R.N.	SEVERN	
DENHAM, John	Cpl. R.M.	Qn CHARLOTTE	(M) Anchor Ty LSGC & Ch '42
	Sgt. R.M.	DONEGAL	St Domingo
DENNIS, George	Boy 3rd Cl	HECLA	
DENT, Charles.C.	Master's Mate	MINDEN	Gun Boat Yawl No. 6. Slightly wounded
DENT, Digby	Lieut. R.N.	MINDEN	
	Midshipman	ACHILLE	Trafalgar
DENT, William	Pte. R.M.	GLASGOW	
DICKENSON, John	Artificer, Royal Laboratory, Woolwich	Qn CHARLOTTE	
DICKER, John	A.B.	MINDEN	(ML as DECKER)
DICKSON, David.J.	Lieut. R.N.	BRITOMART	
DICKSON, James	L.M.	Qn CHARLOTTE	
DICKSON, William	Adm Midshipman	MINDEN	
DILLON, Thomas	Ord	MUTINE	
	Ord	ALFRED	Guadaloupe
DIVINE, John	Purser's Steward	MUTINE	
DIX, Christopher.C.	Supn Boy 2nd Cl	Qn CHARLOTTE	(ML Christopher DICKS)
DIXON, John	Ord	MINDEN	
DIXON, John	A.B.	PROMETHEUS	
DIXON, John.S.	Lieut. R.N.	LEANDER	
DOBBS, Conway.R.	Midshipman	SUPERB	
DONNELLY, Maurice	L.M.	GLASGOW	(ML as DUNLEARY)
DOUTY, William	Supn Boy 2nd Cl	Qn CHARLOTTE	(ML as DOUGHTY)
DOUGHTY, James	Supn Ord	LEANDER	
DOUGLASS, Edward.R.	A.B.	SUPERB	(ML as DOUGLAS)
	Boatswain	STROMBOLI	Syria
DOUGLAS, John	Midshipman	BRITOMART	
DOWNEY, John	A.B.	MUTINE	
	A.B.	ASIA	Navarino
DOWNEY, Thomas	A.B.	Qn CHARLOTTE	
	Boy 2nd Cl	LEVIATHAN	Trafalgar
	Capt' of Mast	ALBION	Navarino
DOWNING, John	A.B.	Qn CHARLOTTE	
DRAKE, William	Boy 3rd Cl	Qn CHARLOTTE	
DREW, John	A.B.	Qn CHARLOTTE	
DUCK, Isaac	Gnr. R.M.A.	Qn CHARLOTTE	
DUFFELL, Jacob	Pte. R.M.	BRITOMART	
DUFFELL, John	Carp's Crew	MINDEN	(ML as John.D.DUFFELL). (M) Army of India "AVA". (M) Anchor Ty LSGC as DUFFILL.
DUFFILL, John	Midshipman	GLASGOW	(M) A of I."AVA". Larne.
DUKE, John	Pte. R.M.	IMPREGNABLE	GH.8703
DUMMER, George	Q.M's Mate	LEANDER	

DUNBAVEN, William	Pte. R.M.	LEANDER	
DUNBRILL, Edward	Supn Boy 2nd Cl	MUTINE	(ML & 171/1 Roll as DUNBRILL. ADM 171/4/35 Roll. DUMBRILL)
DUNLOP, Robert	Supn Ord	Qn CHARLOTTE	
DUNN, James	Ord	GRANICUS	GH. 9383
DUNN, William	Supn A.B.	IMPREGNABLE	Impressed as convicted smuggler.
DUXBURY, George	Pte. R.M.	LEANDER	(ML as DUXBERRY)
DYER, John	Ord	LEANDER	
DYSON, Edward	Pte. R.M.	ALBION	
EARL, Charles	A.B.	GLASGOW	(ML as EARLE)
EATON, John	Supn Pte. R.M.	HEBRUS	
EBURNE, Daniel	Pte. R.M.	IMPREGNABLE	(ML as EBOURNE)
EDMONDS, Thomas	Boy 2nd Cl	INFERNAL	(ML as EDMOND)
EDWARDS, John	Ord	SEVERN	
EKINS, Charles	Captain R.N.	SUPERB	
ELLICE, Alexander	Lieut. R.N.	MINDEN	
ELLIS, John	Supn A.B.	IMPREGNABLE	
ELLIOT, Charles	Supn Midshipman	MINDEN	
ELLIOT, Robert.J.	Midshipman	MINDEN	
ELLIOT, William	L.M.	IMPREGNABLE	(ML as ELLIOTT)
ELLISON, Samuel	A.B.	ALBION	
ELLMERS, Richard	A.B.	GLASGOW	(ML as HELMAS)
ELSTON, Charles	Yeoman of Sheets	IMPREGNABLE	
	A.B.	HERO	4 Novr 1805
ELSWORTHY, Thomas	Pte. R.M.	Qn CHARLOTTE	
EMMING, Robert	Pte. R.M.	Qn CHARLOTTE	(ML as EMMINGS)
EVANS, David	Pte. R.M.	HERON	
EVANS, John	2 borne. LM & AB	SUPERB	
EVANS, Richard	Pte. R.M.	HEBRUS	
EVANS, William	Carp's Crew	SUPERB	
EVERS or IVIES, Richard	Supn Ord	Qn CHARLOTTE	
EVERIDGE, John	Boy 2nd Cl	SUPERB	
EVERITT, John	Supn Gnr R.M.A.	BEELZEBUB	
	Pte. R.M.	CORNELIA	Java
EVINSON, John.C.	Midshipman	ALBION	No 19 Gun Boat
FAIRBAIRN, Peter	Asst Surgeon	SUPERB	
FAIRFIELD, William	Pte. R.M.	PROMETHEUS	
FARMER, Thomas	Sapper & Miner.RE.	Qn CHARLOTTE	
FARMER, William	Supn Gnr R.M.A.	BEELZEBUB	
FARMILO, Daniel	Pte. R.M.	SUPERB	(ML as FARMILLO)
FARROW, Alexander	Pte. R.M.	MUTINE	
FEATHERSTONE, Craven.J.	Midshipman	FURY	
FENNELL, Joseph	Supn Sgt R.M.A.	LEANDER	
	Pte. R.M.	RAMILLIES	Copenhagen 1801
FENTON, Joseph	Pte. R.M.	GRANICUS	
FERRALL, John	L.M.	LEANDER	GH.8708 as FARRELL (ML as FARROLL)
FERRAR, William.A.	Midshipman	SEVERN	
FIFE, William	A.B.	IMPREGNABLE	
FILE, Charles	Q.M.	SUPERB	
FINLAYSON, William	Midshipman	IMPREGNABLE	
	Admiral's Clerk	ASIA	Navarino
FISHER, John	Ord	SUPERB	
FISHER, Thomas	Yeoman of Sheets	Qn CHARLOTTE	
FISHER, William	Ord	ALBION	
FITZGERALD, Charles	Supn Adm Mid	HECLA	
FITZGERALD, David	L.M.	GLASGOW	
FITZGERALD, Thomas	Supn Ship's Cpl	BEELZEBUB	
FITZPATRICK, James	Supn Ord	Qn CHARLOTTE	GH.2849
FITZROY, Francis.C.	Midshipman	DARTMOUTH	
FLAHERTY, John	L.M.	LEANDER	(ML as FLAHARTY)
FLEMING, Richard.H.	Lieut. R.N.	Qn CHARLOTTE	I/Cmd No 5 Gun Boat & then Explosion Vessel
	Actg Lieut. R.N.	YORK	Martinique
FLEMING, Robert	Pte. R.M.	SEVERN	
FLINN, Charles	Supn A.B.	IMPREGNABLE	(ML as FLYNN)
FLUTTER, Henry	Pte. R.M.	MINDEN	
FLUX, George	Boy 3rd Cl	INFERNAL	
FOLLETT, Thomas	Ord	Qn CHARLOTTE	
	Ord	CAESAR	4 Novr 1805
	A.B.	CAESAR	Basque Roads 1809. (Verified aboard. Not on Roll)
FOOT, John	Pte. R.M.	SUPERB	
FORD, Daniel	Pte. R.M.	Qn CHARLOTTE	
FORDYCE, Alexander.D.	Midshipman	ALBION	Gun Boat Yawl No 7
	Volunteer 1st Cl	DESIREE	Gluckstadt 5 Jany 1814
FORSTER, James	Q.M's Mate	IMPREGNABLE	
FORSTER, John	A.B.	LEANDER	(ML as FOSTER)
FORTESCUE, Henry	Volunteer 1st Cl	MINDEN	
FOWKE, Thomas.T.	Volunteer 1st Cl	SEVERN	
FOWLER, William	A.B.	IMPREGNABLE	
FOX, Thomas	Boy 3rd Cl	BRITOMART	
	A.B.	ZEBRA	Syria
FRANCE, William.F.	Pte. R.M.	CORDELIA	(Displayed with Anchor Ty LSGC in RM Museum, Eastney)

ALGIERS

FRAMPTON, Thomas.R.	Midshipman	MINDEN	
FRASER, James	Pte. R.M.	LEANDER	
FRASER, Thomas	Supn Adm Mid	LEANDER	(M) Army of India/"AVA".
FREEMAN, Thomas	Pte. R.M.	Qn CHARLOTTE	
FREEMAN, William.L.	Supn Clerk	GLASGOW	
FRENCH, John	A.B.	GLASGOW	
FRENCH, Samuel	Boy 2nd Cl	Qn CHARLOTTE	
FROWD, Rev. John.B.	Chaplain	Qn CHARLOTTE	
FRY, Charles	Pte. R.M.	SUPERB	
FUGE, John	L.M.	SUPERB	
FULLER, John Thomas	Lieut Rocket Bde. R.H.A.	MINDEN	I/Cmd Division Rocket Boats
FULTON, Robert	Master	GLASGOW	Wounded.
	Ord	HUSSAR	Java. (Vfd Abd. Not on Roll) (M). China 1842 & life saving Medals.
FURNESS, James	L.M.	HEBRUS	
FYNMORE, James	2nd Lieut R.M.	HEBRUS	(Died 1887 as Lt Col R.M.)
	Ord	AFRICA	Trafalgar
GADD, Thomas	A.B.	LEANDER	
GALE, John	Yeoman Powder Rm	HECLA	
GALLAHER, Jeremiah	L.M.	GLASGOW	
GALLOWAY, John	Ord	MINDEN	
	Ord	SCEPTRE	Guadaloupe
GANDY, John	Capt's Cook	GLASGOW	(Not yet found aboard)
GANNON, John	Asst Surgeon	HECLA	
GARDENER, John	Pte. R.M.	Qn CHARLOTTE	(ML as GARDNER)
GARDINER, John	Volunteer 1st Cl	GLASGOW	
GARDNER, Joseph	Ord	GRANICUS	
GARDNER, Richard	Q.M.	Qn CHARLOTTE	
GARDNER, William	Sgt. R.M.	MINDEN	
	Pte. R.M.	BELLEROPHON	Trafalgar
	Cpl. R.M.	EURYALUS	The Potomac. 17 Aug 1814
GARLICK, Henry	Pte. R.M.	MINDEN	
GARMSTON, Samuel	1st Lieut. R.M.	SEVERN	(M.G.S. Clasp "Java")
GARNER, Josh	Pte. R.M.	PROMETHEUS	
GARRETT, John	Midshipman	GRANICUS	Gun Boat Yawl No 10
GARRETT, William	Pte. R.M.	GLASGOW	(Torn page Roll. ? GARRATT)
	Sgt. R.M.	BRISK	Navarino
GARRETT, William	Supn L.M.	LEANDER	
	L.M.	ALBION	Navarino
GATES, William	Carp's Crew	Qn CHARLOTTE	
GAY, John	Boy 2nd Cl	SUPERB	
	Ship's Cpl	RODNEY	Syria
GAZE, John	Additional Master	Qn CHARLOTTE	
	Quarter Master	NYMPHE	Nymphe 18 June 1793
	Midshipman	INDEFATIGABLE	Indefatigable. 20 April 1796 (Vfd Abd. Not on Roll)
	Midshipman	INDEFATIGABLE	Indefatigable. 13 Jany 1797

(It appears probable that the claimant received four single clasp medals for these four Actions, and that one was changed to (known) unofficial clasp of "ARETHUSA 23 Aug 1806", – possibly to match an incorrect private Medal Roll. He was never aboard ARETHUSA in 1806, nor on that Roll.)

GEAR, Henry	Carp's Crew	GLASGOW	(ML as Henry Wm GEAR)
GEORGE, Henry	Gnr. R.M.A.	INFERNAL	
GEORGE, William (2)	A.B.	LEANDER	
	A.B.	PHILOMEL	Navarino
GIBBONS, John	A.B.	GLASGOW	
GIBBS, George	A.B.	ALBION	
GILBERT, Edmund.W.	Lieut. R.N.	GLASGOW	
	Midshipman	CANOPUS	St Domingo
GILBERT, John	2 Ptes RM borne	MINDEN	
GILBERT, Thomas	Qtr Gnr	SEVERN	
GILBERTSON, Henry	Ord	MINDEN	(Should never have been awarded. He deserted from Prometheus 29 Augt 1816)
GILES, Benjamin	Supn Q.M's Mate	SUPERB	
GILHAM, Thomas	Sgt. R.M.	IMPREGNABLE	
GILL, William.Y.	Master's Mate	ALBION	Gun Boat Barge No 10
GILLARD, Charles	Supn Capt' F.Top	IMPREGNABLE	
	Boatswain	IMPLACABLE	Syria
GILLARD, Richard	Qtr Gnr	SUPERB	(Not yet found aboard)
GILLARD, William	Pte. R.M.	IMPREGNABLE	
GILLETT, Thomas	L.M.	MINDEN	Impressed as a convicted "Poacher"
GIMBER, Josh	Pte. R.M.	GLASGOW	
GINN, William	Pte. R.M.	GLASGOW	
GLASSON, Richard	L.M.	HEBRUS	
GODBY, William	Pte. R.M.	IMPREGNABLE	
GODDEN, John	Pte. R.M.	SEVERN	

GOLDSMITH, John	Purser	SUPERB	
	Clerk	THUNDERER	1 June 1794
	Purser	AMAZON	Copenhagen 1801
GOODE, Robert	Pte. R.M.	CORDELIA	
GOODMAN, John	L.M.	GLASGOW	
GOODMAN, John	Supn A.B.	SUPERB	
GOODMAN, Samuel	Boy 3rd Cl	GLASGOW	(Found only as Thomas)
GOODWIN, David	Pte. R.M.	IMPREGNABLE	
GOOGE, Stephen	Boy 2nd Cl	MINDEN	(ML as GOUGE)
GORDON, Anthony John	Pte. R.M.	Qn CHARLOTTE	(Only man found is John GORDON, Royal Rocket Corps, ex Severn)
GORDON, John	Pte. R.M.	MINDEN	
GORDON, Robert	Actg Lieut. R.N.	Qn CHARLOTTE	
	Volunteer 1st Cl	PHOEBE	Off Tamatave 20 May 1811
	Midshipman	PHOEBE	Java
GORE, Hon Edward	Master's Mate	FURY	
GORE, John	Boy 3rd Cl	SEVERN	
GORE, Ralph	Supn Midshipman	SEVERN	
GORMAN, John	Supn Yeoman Sheets	Qn CHARLOTTE	
	A.B.	AUDACIOUS	Gut of Gibraltar.12 July 1801
	A.B.	POMPEE	Martinique
	A.B.	POMPEE	Pompee 17 June 1809
	A.B.	POMPEE	Guadaloupe
GOSBY, Jeshra	A.B.	MINDEN	(ML as Guthero.W. GOSBY) Impressed & convicted smuggler.
GOSLING, Robert	Pte. R.M.	SEVERN	
GOSMAN, David	Master	MUTINE	Often also spelt GOSSMAN. (M) King John VI of Portugal Jewel. Lively. 1824.
GOSNOLD, George	A.B.	BRITOMART	
GOSTLING, Philip	Lieut. R.N.	SEVERN	
	Volunteer 1st Cl	UNICORN	Basque Roads 1809
	Midshipman	ARMIDE	B.S. 27 Sep 1810
GOWER, Samuel	L.M.	HERON	
GRANT, Edward	Ropemaker	PROMETHEUS	
GRASSUM, John	Gnr. R.M.A.	Qn CHARLOTTE	(ML as GROSSUM)
GRAY, James	A.B.	GLASGOW	
GRAY, Joseph	Supn A.B.	IMPREGNABLE	
GREEN, Edward	Pte. R.M.	Qn CHARLOTTE	
GREEN, George	Supn Boy 3rd Cl	Qn CHARLOTTE	
GREEN, James	Drummer.R.M.	IMPREGNABLE	
GREEN, James	2 Ptes RM borne	MINDEN	
GREEN, William	Supn L.M.	SUPERB	
	Gunner's Crew	ALBION	Navarino
GREENBANK, Robert	Pte. R.M.	LEANDER	
GREENING, William	Pte. R.M.	IMPREGNABLE	
GREY, Thomas	Pte. R.M.	Qn CHARLOTTE	
GRIFFIN, William	Midshipman	MINDEN	
	Commander	GANGES	Syria
GRIFFITHS, Howell	Pte. R.M.	IMPREGNABLE	GH.8779
GRIFFITHS, John	Pte. R.M.	ALBION	
GRIFFITHS, Richard	Pte. R.M.	ALBION	
	Pte. R.M.	BOADICEA	Boadicea 18 Septr 1810
GRIFFITHS, William	Captain Fore Top	SEVERN	GH.9763
GRIMES, Cornelius	Ord	Qn CHARLOTTE	
GRIMMER, William	Carp's Mate	Qn CHARLOTTE	(Not yet found aboard)
GROSCOTT, Joseph	A.B.	MINDEN	
	Qtr Gunner	DEFIANCE	Copenhagen 1801
	M.A.A.	CAPTAIN	Martinique
GROVE, Francis	Midshipman	LEANDER	
GROVES, Richard	Supn Ord	Qn CHARLOTTE	GH.9264
GUNN, William	L.M.	Qn CHARLOTTE	GH.9548
HALL, Alexander	Supn Q.M's Mate	Qn CHARLOTTE	
HALL, Henry	A.D.	Qn CHARLOTTE	
HALL, James	Surgeon	HECLA	Roll states "Duplicate issued to Acct Gen 24 Feb 1911."
HALL, John	Pte. R.M.	ALBION	
HALL, John	Pte. R.M.	LEANDER	
HALL, Roger	Lieut. R.N.	IMPREGNABLE	
HALL, Stephen	Pte. R.M.	IMPREGNABLE	
HAMILTON, John	Master	ALBION	
HAMILTON, William	Schoolmaster	GRANICUS	(ex Midshipman)
HAMMETT, John	Ord	SUPERB	
	Ord	GENOA	Navarino
HAMMONT, William	Pte. R.M.	HEBRUS	
HANCOCK, Josh	Ord	SUPERB	
HANGER, William	L.M.	SUPERB	
HANKS, Thomas	Pte. R.M.	Qn CHARLOTTE	(Known paired with Anchor Ty LSGC. Engraved "Late Private Royal Marine" 1833.)
HANKS, Thomas	Pte. R.M.	SUPERB	(Ply Div. 43 Coy)
HANLON, Michael	A.B.	Qn CHARLOTTE	(ML as HANLOW)
HANSLER, Thomas	Pte. R.M.	Qn CHARLOTTE	(ML as HENSLOR)

ALGIERS

Name	Rank	Ship	Notes
HARFORD, John	Cpl. R.M.	GLASGOW	(ML as HARTFORD)
HARPER, George	L.M.	MINDEN	Impressed & convicted Smuggler
HARPER, William	Pte. R.M.	Qn CHARLOTTE	
HARRIS, Daniel	Bmbdr. R.M.A.	IMPREGNABLE	
HARRIS, William	Pte. R.M.	ALBION	
HARRISON, George	Supn Midshipman	MINDEN	(May have Vol 1st Cl)
HARRISON, G.B.	Purser	MINDEN	
HARSENT, John	Carp's Crew	GLASGOW	(ML as HARSANT)
HARTE, Thomas	Supn A.B.	IMPREGNABLE	(ML as HART)
HARTLEY, John	Boy 2nd Cl	GRANICUS	
	Captain of Mast	CAMBRIDGE	Syria
HARVEY, James	Gnr. R.M.A.	FURY	
HARVEY, John	Ord	GLASGOW	
HATT, John	Ord	GRANICUS	
HAWES, Edward	Master's Mate	BRITOMART	
HAWKINS, William	Yeoman of Sheets	Qn CHARLOTTE	GH.5822
HAWKSHAW, Hugh	Midshipman	SEVERN	
HAWTHORN, Robert	Supn Gnr. R.M.A.	LEANDER	(ML as HAWTHORNE)
HAY, James.B.L.	Midshipman	Qn CHARLOTTE	
HAYDON, Samuel	Purser	SEVERN	
HAYES, John	Ord	MINDEN	GH.9542
HAYES, Richard	Pte. R.M.	LEANDER	
HAYTER, Benjamin	Midshipman	IMPREGNABLE	Gun Boat Barge No 4
HAYWARD, John	Pte. R.M.	MUTINE	
HAYWARD, Richard	Pte. R.M.	IMPREGNABLE	
	Pte. R.M.	TONNANT	B.S. 14 Dec 1814. (On Roll, but not yet found aboard)
HEALD, Samuel	Pte. R.M.	LEANDER	
HEALE, John	Pte. R.M.	GRANICUS	
HEANEY, John	Pte. R.M.	IMPREGNABLE	(ML as HEANY)
HEATHCOTE, George.H.	Supn Adm Mid	GLASGOW	
HEDDY, Sampson	Supn L.M.	ALBION	
HEGINBOTTOM, James	Pte. R.M.	SUPERB	
HELBY, John.H.	Midshipman	Qn CHARLOTTE	
HEMMINGS, John	Ord	GLASGOW	
HEMMS, Thomas	A.B.	CORDELIA	(ML as HEMS)
HENDERSON, Andrew	Asst Surgeon	Qn CHARLOTTE	
HENDERSON, Henry	Supn Capt'.Mn Top	IMPREGNABLE	
HENRY, George	Supn Ord	HECLA	
HENRY, Robert	2nd Lieut. R.M.A.	BEELZEBUB	
HERRING, John	Cpl. R.M.	LEANDER	First man recommended to receive Anchor Type LSGC Medal. November 1830.
HERRING, Thomas	Pte. R.M.	GRANICUS	
HESLIP, John	Ord	ALBION	
HETHRIDGE, William	Pte. R.M.	SUPERB	(ML as HETHERIDGE)
HEWITT, Thomas	Q.M.	IMPREGNABLE	
HICKS, Hugh	L.M.	MINDEN	Impressed & convicted smuggler
HICKS, John	Supn Ord	BEELZEBUB	
HICKSON, Richard	Supn Pte. R.M.	HEBRUS	
HIGGINS, James	Boy 3rd Class	GLASGOW	(Not yet found aboard)
HIGINSON, Charles	Ord	ALBION	(ML as HIGGINSON)
HIGMAN, John	L.M.	MINDEN	
HILL, Henry.Wm.	Supn Adm Mid	HEBRUS	
HILL, John	Pte. R.M.	Qn CHARLOTTE	
HILL, Robert	Supn Pte. R.M.	HEBRUS	(Only found as Richard)
HINTON, Samuel	Boatswain	GLASGOW	
HIPWELL, Samuel	Boatswain	GLASGOW	
HIPWELL, William	Supn Gnr R.M.A.	MINDEN	"for Rocket Boat"
HISCOCK, William	Pte. R.M.	Qn CHARLOTTE	
HOGAN, Charles	L.M.	Qn CHARLOTTE	
HOGAN, Matthew	A.B.	SEVERN	
HOLBERT, Samuel	Pte. R.M.	IMPREGNABLE	
HOLBERTON, John	Master's Mate	IMPREGNABLE	Mortar Boat Launch No 2
	Volunteer 1st Cl	SCIPION	Java
	Midshipman	AJAX	St Sebastian
HOLDEN, William	Pte. R.M.	LEANDER	
HOLDING, Arthur	Q.M's Mate	Qn CHARLOTTE	
HOLL, Benjamin	L.M.	GRANICUS	
HOLLAND, Daniel	L.M.	SEVERN	
HOLLAND, Edward	Midshipman	ALBION	
HOLLAND, Rupert.C.	1st Lieut. R.M.	Qn CHARLOTTE	
	1st Lieut. R.M.	EURYALUS	The Potomac 17 Aug 1814
HOLLAND, Thomas	Ord	Qn CHARLOTTE	
HOLLAND, William	Supn Ord	Qn CHARLOTTE	
HOLLIDAY, William	Caulker's Mate	LEANDER	
	Caulker's Mate	HASTINGS	Syria
HOLLOWAY, Thomas	Supn Ord	ALBION	GH.6526
	Ord	NASSAU	Nassau 22 March 1808
HOLMES, William	Boy 2nd Cl	HERON	
HOLTON, Daniel	Pte. R.M.	LEANDER	(ML as HALTON)
	Pte. R.M.	GLASGOW	Navarino
HOOPER, James	Pte. R.M.	Qn CHARLOTTE	

HOOPER, Joseph	L.M.	MINDEN	
HOOPER, Thomas	Supn Q.M.	IMPREGNABLE	
HOPE, George	Volunteer per Order	GRANICUS	(Rank of young trainee officer after completing 2 years at the R.N.College)
HOPKINS, Thomas	Pte. R.M.	ALBION	
HORNBY, William	Midshipman	MINDEN	Gun Boat Barge No 7
HOTHAM, George	Lieut. R.E.	MINDEN (?)	(Roll at ADM 171/4/32)
HOTHAM, George.F.	Volunteer 1st Cl	MINDEN	
	Volunteer 1st Cl	NORTHUMBERLAND	Northumberland 22 May 1812
HOWE, Edward	Sgt Rocket Bde. R.H.A.	MINDEN	
HOWELL, Charles	Drummer. R.M.	MINDEN	
HOWELL, Joseph.B.	Lieut. R.N.	MINDEN	
HOWELL, William	Pte. R.M.	MINDEN	
HOWLETT, Robert	Pte. R.M.	GLASGOW	
HUBBARD, William	Ord	HEBRUS	
HUBBARD, William	Midshipman	HERON	
HUDSON, William	Carp's Crew	SEVERN	
HUGH, Philip	Ord	GLASGOW	(ML as HUGHES)
HUGHES, David	Carpenter	MUTINE	
HUGHES, Thomas	Pte. R.M.	Qn CHARLOTTE	
HULME, Robert	Pte. R.M.	IMPREGNABLE	
HULTON, William	Pte. R.M.	LEANDER	
HUMBY, John	Lieut. R.M.	SEVERN	
HUMPHRIES, Francis	Pte. R.M.	GLASGOW	
HUMPHRIES, Stephen	Pte. R.M.	IMPREGNABLE	
HUNTER, Robert	Ord	Qn CHARLOTTE	
HURLEY, Michael	Cpl. R.M.	INFERNAL	
HUSSEY, Richard	Master's Mate	GLASGOW	
	Master's Mate	DIOMEDE	B.S. 14 Dec 1814
HUTCHESON, Francis.D.	Midshipman	IMPREGNABLE	
HUXLEY, Thomas	Pte. R.M.	SUPERB	
HUXTABLE, James	Gnr. R.M.A.	Qn CHARLOTTE	
HYATT, John	Pte. R.M.	IMPREGNABLE	
HYATT, William	Pte. R.M.	SUPERB	
IRWIN, David	Q.M.	SUPERB	(ML as IRVIN)
INNES, Robert.W.	Lieut. R.N.	GLASGOW	
	Midshipman	CORNELIA	Java
ISLES, Samuel	Ord	SUPERB	(ML as AYLES)
(IVIES see EVERS)			
JACKSON, George.V.	Lieut. R.N.	HECLA	
(JACKSON.H.P. see PLANTAGENT, Henry)			
JAGO, John.S.	Actg Lieut. R.N.	Qn CHARLOTTE	Slightly wounded
JAMES, Henry	2nd Lieut. R.M.A.	HECLA	
JAMES, Thomas	Supn Boy 3rd Cl	SEVERN	
JEFFERIES, James	Supn L.M.	HEBRUS	
JENKINS, Thomas	L.M.	ALBION	
JENNINGS, John	Pte. R.M.	IMPREGNABLE	
JENNINGS, Thomas	Pte. R.M.	LEANDER	
JESSE, Henry	Clerk	GLASGOW	
JESSE, Robert	Cooper	GLASGOW	
JOHNS, William	2 Ords borne	HEBRUS	
JOHNSON, James	Capt' Main Top	HERON	
JOHNSON, John	L.M.	IMPREGNABLE	
	Armourer's Mate	CAMBRIAN	Navarino
JOHNSON, John	Captain of Mast	SUPERB	
JOHNSON, John.S.W.	Lieut. R.N.	Qn CHARLOTTE	
JOHNSON, Matthew	Pte. R.M.	LEANDER	
JOHNSON, William	Supn Ord	IMPREGNABLE	SLVO 1116
JOHNSON, William	Supn Ord	IMPREGNABLE	SLVO 1129
JOHNSTON, Henry	Adm Midshipman	LEANDER	
JOHNSTON, Robert	Asst Surgeon	GRANICUS	
JOHNSTONE, Robert.B.	Supt Lieut. R.N.	SUPERB	I/Cmd No 24 Gun Boat
JONES, Edmund	Pte. R.M.	HEBRUS	
JONES, Essex	Ord	ALBION	
JONES, Henry	Pte. R.M.	Qn CHARLOTTE	
JONES, James	Pte. R.M.	GRANICUS	
JONES, James	Pte. R.M.	MINDEN	
JONES, John	Ord	ALBION	
JONES, John	Supn A.B.	HEBRUS	
	Ord	HEBRUS	Hebrus with L'Etoile
JONES, John	A.B.	IMPREGNABLE	
JONES, John (1)	Ord	PROMETHEUS	
JONES, Lewis.T.	Midshipman	GRANICUS	(In Group at R.N.Museum)
	Actg Commander	Pcss CHARLOTTE	Syria
JONES, Patrick	Supn. L.M.	ALBION	
JONES, William	Drummer. R.M.	ALBION	
JOREY/JURY, Thomas	Sapper & Miner	IMPREGNABLE	
JUSTICE, Robert	Adm Midshipman	MINDEN	
KEEFE, James	Ord	IMPREGNABLE	
KELLY, Cornelius	Pte. R.M.	SEVERN	
KEMPSTER, Thomas	Ord	IMPREGNABLE	
KENNAR, William	Ord	MINDEN	(ML as KENNER)
KENNIGHT, Richard	L.M.	SEVERN	

ALGIERS

KENNY, Peter	Ord	ALBION	
	Gunner's Mate	PHILOMEL	Navarino
KENT, William	Volunteer 1st Cl	LEANDER	
KEOGH, John	Supn Ord	Qn CHARLOTTE	GH.9751
KERKEN, George	No Rate	IMPREGNABLE	Impressed & convicted smuggler. alias KIRKINS.
KERR, John James	Midshipman	IMPREGNABLE	
KEYSER, John	Boy 2nd Cl	SEVERN	
KEYSER, Joseph	M.A.A.	SEVERN	
KIDSTONE, Robert	Pte. R.M.	ALBION	(ML as KIDSTON)
KILLER, James	Pte. R.M.	ALBION	GH.8706
KING, George.M.	Lieut. R.N.	Qn CHARLOTTE	
KINGABY, Richard	Boy 3rd Cl	HEBRUS	
KINGDOM, Arthur	A.B.	IMPREGNABLE	
KIRBY, John	L.M.	SEVERN	
KIRK, George	Gnr. R.M.A.	HECLA	
KIRKWOOD, Alexander	Yeoman of Sheets	ALBION	
	L.M.	ROYAL SOVEREIGN	Trafalgar
	Supn Boatswain	ASIA	Syria
KNIGHT, Christopher	Lieut. R.N.	IMPREGNABLE	
	Midshipman	ASTRAEA	Off Tamatave. 20 May 1811
KNIGHT, Richard	Pte. R.M.	Qn CHARLOTTE	
KNIGHT, William	A.B.	Qn CHARLOTTE	
KNOCKER, William	Lieut. R.N.	HERON	
KNOWLSON, John	Ord	GLASGOW	
LACK, John	Pte. R.M.	ALBION	
LANGDON, William	Pte. R.M.	SUPERB	
	Pte. R.M.	AJAX	Trafalgar
LANGLEY, Isaac	Pte. R.M.	GRANICUS	
LANGTON, Charles	Volunteer 1st Cl	SEVERN	
LANGWITH, Henry	A.B.	HEBRUS	
LANYON, William	Supn Boy 2nd Cl	IMPREGNABLE	
LAPTHORN, James	L.M.	IMPREGNABLE	
LARDNER, Thomas	L.M.	Qn CHARLOTTE	(Roll may suggest he is also Thomas LEDNER, entitled to "Venerable 16 Jany 1814")
LATHAN, John	Pte. R.M.	IMPREGNABLE	
	Pte. R.M.	NAIAD	Trafalgar
	Pte. R.M.	AMETHYST	Amethyst Wh Thetis. (On Roll. but joined after Action)
	Pte. R.M.	AMETHYST	Amethyst 5 April 1809
LAWLER, Thomas	Ord	SUPERB	(Only found a John LAWLER)
LAWRENCE, John	Cpl. R.M.A.	HECLA	(May read LAURENCE)
LAWS, John	Supn Boy 3rd Cl	MINDEN	
LAWSON, Richard	Pte. R.M.	GRANICUS	
LEAHY, Timothy	Supn Ord	SUPERB	
LEARY, John	Supn Ord	Qn CHARLOTTE	
LECOUNT, Peter	Supn Adm Mid	INFERNAL	
	Midshipman	THUNDER	B.S. 23 Nov 1810
LEE, George	Pte. R.M.	SUPERB	
LEE, James	A.B.	LEANDER	
LEE, John	Supn Ord	HECLA	
LEECH, James	Supn Ord	Qn CHARLOTTE	
LEEDS, Alexander	Gunner	LEANDER	
LEGG, James	Boatswain	BEELZEBUB	(ML as LEGGE)
LEGGATT, George	A.B.	FALMOUTH	(Lighter)
Le MESURIER, Frederick.H.	Supn Adm Mid	FURY	
LEONARD, Francis	Coxswain	Qn CHARLOTTE	
	Boy	ROYAL SOVEREIGN	Trafalgar
LESLIE, Andrew	Surgeon	SEVERN	
LEVENS, Michael	A.B.	Qn CHARLOTTE	(ML as LEVEN)
LEWER, Joseph.R.	L.M.	MINDEN	
LEWIS, James	Pte. R.M. 3rd Cl	IMPREGNABLE	
LEWIS, John	Capt' Fore Top	Qn CHARLOTTE	
LEWIS, Michael	Boy	IMPREGNABLE	
	A.B.	RODNEY	Syria
LIDDELL, James	Midshipman	ALBION	Rocket Flat boat No 4
LIDDLE, James	Pte. R.M.	Qn CHARLOTTE	
LIDDON, John	Pte. R.M.	SUPERB	
LINDSEY, William	Pte. R.M.	SEVERN	
LINFIELD, Joseph	Supn A.B.	SEVERN	GH.5386
LITTLEJOHN, Joseph	Boy 2nd Cl	Qn CHARLOTTE	
LIVERTON, James	L.M.	IMPREGNABLE	
LLOYD, James	Supn Ord	SUPERB	
LLOYD, John.H.	Volunteer 1st Cl	HERON	
LOAD, William	Ord	CORDELIA	
LOBB, Richard	Ord	IMPREGNABLE	
LOCK, James	Artificer, Royal Laboratory, Woolwich	Transport "FRIENDS"	On Roll 171/3/81 as "Carpenter" Medal known with "Carpenter" on edge.

Name	Rank/Role	Ship	Notes
LOCK, James	Ord	MINDEN	Aged 32. Born Isle of Wight.
	Captain's Servant	Qn CHARLOTTE	1 June 1794.
			A domestic aged 10 years.
LOCK, James	Sgt. R.M.	Qn CHARLOTTE	
LOCKYER, Abraham	Pte. R.M.	SUPERB	
LOCKYER, John	Ord	MINDEN	
LONDON, Joseph	Boy 2nd Cl	Qn CHARLOTTE	
LONG, William	Boy 2nd Cl	MUTINE	
	Q.M.	BELLEROPHON	Syria. (M) Anchor Ty LS&GC
LONGMAN, David	Ord	HERON	
LOVE, Daniel	Gunner's Mate	IMPREGNABLE	
LOVE, William	Pte. R.M.	IMPREGNABLE	
LOVENEWTON, Samuel	Carpenter	MINDEN	
	Carpenter	PHOEBE	Trafalgar
LOVERN, John	Pte. R.M.	SUPERB	(ML as LOUVERNE)
LOVESAY, Thomas	Pte. R.M.	SEVERN	
LOVETT, John	Pte. R.M.	SEVERN	
LOW, John	Pte. R.M.	GLASGOW	
LOXTON, Hugh	Supn Pte. R.M.	HEBRUS	
LOXTON, James	Pte. R.M.	MINDEN	(ML as LUXTON)
LUCAS, Daniel	Supn L.M.	Qn CHARLOTTE	
LUMSDALE, Alexander	Master	Qn CHARLOTTE	(For Ship not Squadron duties)
LUTMAN, Charles	Lieut. R.N.	IMPREGNABLE	(Vfd Aboard. Not on Roll)
	Lieut. R.N.	BERWICK	Gaieta 24 July 1815 (On Roll)
LYNCH, Thomas	Supn A.B.	Qn CHARLOTTE	
LYNCH, Thomas	Ord	GLASGOW	
LYS, Matthew	Mate (Roll)	MINDEN	(ML as Admiralty Midshipman)
MACKAY, John	Surgeon	MUTINE	
	Surgeon	MALTA	Gaieta 24 July 1815
MACKEY, John	Supn Carp's Crew	IMPREGNABLE	
	Boy	CANOPUS	St Domingo
MacKENNY, John	Ord	SUPERB	(ML as McKENNY)
MACKINNON or			
McKINNON, Malcolm	Cook	PROMETHEUS	(Joined ship by Warrant dated 14 Jan 1808)
	Cook	PROMETHEUS	B.S. 7 July 1809
	Cook	PROMETHEUS	B.S. 25 July 1809
MADDEN, James.M.	Supn Asst Surgeon	IMPREGNABLE	(On Medal Roll, but not at Action. Joined ex Ister 2 Sept 1816)
MAGENNIS, John	Pte. R.M.	Qn CHARLOTTE	
	Cpl. R.M.	SOPHIE	B.S. 14 Dec 1814
MAHER, Thomas	Pte. R.M.	GLASGOW	(ML as MAHAR)
MAITLAND, Hon Anthony	Captain R.N.	GLASGOW	
MAKIN, John	Pte. R.M.	LEANDER	
MALCOLM, James	Pte. R.M.	MINDEN	
MANLEY, John	L.M.	HERON	
MANNELL, John	Pte. R.M.	ALBION	(?ML as James MUNNELL)
MANNERS, Russell.H.	Volunteer per Order	MINDEN	(Ex R.N. College 6 March 1816)
MANNING, James	Pte. R.M.	SUPERB	
MANNING, Michael	Ord	SUPERB	
	Ord	TONNANT	B.S. 14 Dec 1814 (M) (Group known includes Anchor LSGC & China 1842 medals)
MANSEL, George	Actg Lieut. R.N.	MINDEN	
	Commander	WASP	Syria
MAPLE, Thomas	L.M.	SUPERB	
MARCH, Charles	Supn Adm Mid	SUPERB	
MARSH, John	Ord	LEANDER	
MARSHALL, John (2)	A.B.	ALBION	
MARSHALL, William	Pte. R.M.	GRANICUS	
MARTIN, Henry	Ord	LEANDER	
MARTIN, John (1)	L.M.	Qn CHARLOTTE	
MARTIN, Peter	Supn Qtr Gunner	Qn CHARLOTTE	
MASON, Edward	Pte. R.M.	GRANICUS	
MATCHETT, William	Pte. R.M.	Qn CHARLOTTE	(ML as MATCHELL)
MATTHEWS, John	Supn A.B.	IMPREGNABLE	
	Ord	STAR	Martinique
	Ord	STAR	Guadaloupe
	A.B.	MALTA	Gaieta 24 July 1815
MATTHEWSON, Walter	Capt' Forecastle	Qn CHARLOTTE	(Not yet found aboard)
MAY, Francis	Supn Passed Clerk	SEVERN	
MAYCOCK, Josh	Pte. R.M.	GLASGOW	
	Pte. R.M.	GANGES	Syria
MAYNE, Dawson	Midshipman	LEANDER	
McCADE, Terence	Pte. R.M.	IMPREGNABLE	
McCALL, Charles	Supn L.M.	IMPREGNABLE	
McCANN, Neil	Pte. R.M.	Qn CHARLOTTE	
	Pte. R.M.	CAMBRIAN	Navarino
McCARTHY, William	Supn Ord	Qn CHARLOTTE	
McCLINTOCK, Wm.Bunbury	Midshipman	SEVERN	
	Volunteer 1st Cl	AJAX	St Sebastian. (In 1846 took name of Wm. Bunbury McLintock BUNBURY.)

ALGIERS

Name	Rank/Rating	Ship	Notes
McCONNELL, Alexander	A.B.	IMPREGNABLE	
McDERMOTT, James	Pte. R.M.	ALBION	
McDONALD, Angus	M.A.A.	LEANDER	GH.9944
McDONALD, Donald	Pte. R.M.	ALBION	
McDONALD, John	A.B.	ALBION	
McDONALD, John (1)	L.M.	Qn CHARLOTTE	
McDONALD, John (2)	A.B.	Qn CHARLOTTE	
McDONALD, William	Carp's Mate	MUTINE	
McDONNELL, Thomas	L.M.	IMPREGNABLE	(ML as McDANIEL)
McDONOUGH, Edward	Ord	SUPERB	GH.2721
McDOUGALL, John	Lieut. R.N.	SUPERB	
	Midshipman	UNITE	B.S. 1 Nov 1809
	Lieut. R.N.	UNITE	Pelagosa 29 Novr 1811
McGREGOR, George	Ord	SUPERB	
McGREHAM, Daniel	Cook	BEELZEBUB	
	L.M.	ROYAL SOVEREIGN	Trafalgar
McKENSIE, John	Ord	GLASGOW	(ML as McKENSEY)
McKENSIE, Robert	Capt Fore Top	ALBION	(ML as McKENZIE)
McKENZIE, Alexander	Sapper & Miner	Qn CHARLOTTE	
McLEAN, Alexander	L.M.	Qn CHARLOTTE	
McLEOD, Daniel	Supn Gnr Rocket Brigade. R.H.A.	GLASGOW	
McMANUS, David	Surgeon	PROMETHEUS	(Vfd Aboard. Not on Roll)
	Asst Surgeon	SEAHORSE	The Potomac 17 Aug 1814 (Vfd Abd. Not on Roll)
	Asst Surgeon	SEAHORSE	BS. 14 Dec 1814. (On Roll)
McNICOL, Duncan	Lieut. R.M.	GLASGOW	
	Lieut. R.M.	ABERCROMBIE	Guadaloupe
MELVILLE, Ninian	Sgt. Sappers & Miners	Qn CHARLOTTE	
MICHELL, Frederick.T.	Lieut. R.N.	Qn CHARLOTTE	I/Cmd the Flotilla of Gun & Mortar Boats
	Captain. R.N.	MAGICIENNE	Syria
MIDGLEY, John	Ord	LEANDER	(ML as MIDGELEY)
	Ord	FREIJA	St Sebastian
MILBOURNE, Francis	Supn Capt' Mn Top	Qn CHARLOTTE	
	Captain Main Top	GANGES	Syria
MILES, Lawford	Master's Mate	Qn CHARLOTTE	
	Midshipman	AMETHYST	Amethyst Wh Thetis
	Master's Mate	AMETHYST	Amethyst 5 April 1809
MILFORD, William	Supn L.M.	IMPREGNABLE	
	L.M.	CERBERUS	Lissa
MILHAM, John	Gnr. R.M.A.	HECLA	
MILLER, Christopher	L.M.	SUPERB	
MILLER, John	Boy 3rd Cl	BRITOMART	
MILLER, John	Clerk of Ordnance Stores	Transport "FRIENDS"	(ML as Deputy Asst Commy)
MILLER, John	Master	MINDEN	
	Actg Master	PHOEBE	Phoebe 28 March 1814
MILLER, Morris	Pte. R.M.	IMPREGNABLE	
MILLS, George	Ord	ALBION	
MILLS, John	Pte. R.M.	LEANDER	
MILTON, Edward	Sgt. R.M.	Qn CHARLOTTE	
MILTON, William	Carp's Crew	MINDEN	
MINGAR, James	Boy 3rd Cl	SUPERB	
MINGO, Samuel	Pte. R.M.	MINDEN	
MITCHELL, Abraham	A.B.	BRITOMART	
	Ward Room Steward	Pcss CHARLOTTE	Syria
MITCHELL, James	Ship's Cpl	GRANICUS	
MITCHELL, Joseph	Clerk	LEANDER	(Not yet found aboard)
MITCHELL, Lewis.D.	Midshipman	GRANICUS	
MITCHELL, Thomas	Midshipman	IMPREGNABLE	
	Midshipman	BERWICK	Gaieta 24 July 1815
MOGGS, Thomas	L.M.	Qn CHARLOTTE	(ML as MOGG) GH.9050
MONK, George.M.	Extra Lieut. R.N.	LEANDER	
MONK, John	Lieut. R.N.	IMPREGNABLE	
	Lieut. R.N.	BERWICK	Gaieta 24 July 1815
MOORE, Francis	Pte. R.M.	Qn CHARLOTTE	(Not yet found aboard)
MOORE, James	Supn Ord	Qn CHARLOTTE	
MOORE, John	Pte. R.M.	IMPREGNABLE	GH.8804
MOORE, John	Ord	ALBION	
MOORE, Thomas	Supn Ord	MINDEN	
MOORE, William	Pte. R.M.	SUPERB	
MOORE, William	Pte. R.M.	Qn CHARLOTTE	
	Pte. R.M.	TALBOT	Navarino
MOORMAN, William	Ord	Qn CHARLOTTE	
	L.M.	AJAX	Trafalgar
MOORSOM, Constantine.R.	Captain R.N.	FURY	
MORAN, John Owen	L.M.	Qn CHARLOTTE	(ML as John MORAN)
MORGAN, James	Ord	SUPERB	
	Capt' Fore Top	DARTMOUTH	Navarino
MORGAN, John	Pte. R.M.	LEANDER	
MORGAN, Thomas	Supn Bosun's Mte	Qn CHARLOTTE	
MORGAN, William	Gnr. R.M.A.	INFERNAL	
MORGAN, William	L.M.	MINDEN	

MORLEY, John	Sgt. R.M.	ALBION	GH.9951
	Pte. R.M.	THESEUS	Basque Roads 1809
MORRES, Elliot	Supn Adm Mid	GLASGOW	Gun Boat Yawl No 14
MORRIS, Charles	Supn Boy 2nd Cl	ALBION	
MORRIS, Thomas	L.M.	Qn CHARLOTTE	
MORRISON, Robert	Ord	LEANDER	
MORRISS, Edward.J.	Lieut. R.N.	BEELZEBUB	
MORTIMER, John (2)	Supn Sailmaker	IMPREGNABLE	
	Sailmaker	TALBOT	Navarino
MORTIMER, Robert	Boy 3rd Cl	GRANICUS	
MUGFORD, Hugh	L.M.	IMPREGNABLE	
MULKAHY, Timothy	Supn Qtr Gunner	IMPREGNABLE	
	L.M.	COURAGEUX	4 Novr 1805
	Ord	AETNA	Basque Roads 1809
MULLHOLLAND, William	Ord	IMPREGNABLE	(ML as HOLLAND)
MULLICE, William	Boatswain	HERON	
MULLINS, William	Boatswain	MINDEN	
MUNRO, Matthew	Lieut. R.N.	IMPREGNABLE	I/Cmd No 1 Gun Boat
MURFORD, John	Ord	LEANDER	
MURPHY, Dennis	Ord	ALBION	
MURPHY, William	Gunner's Tailor	HEBRUS	
MURRAY, Hugh	Pte. R.M.	SUPERB	
NASH, Richard	A.B.	HEBRUS	(ML alias Joseph PHALIN)
NASON, Samuel	Pte. R.M.	Qn CHARLOTTE	
NAVE, William	Ord	CORDELIA	(ML as KNAVE)
	Ord	GANGES	Copenhagen 1801
	Ord	DEFIANCE	Trafalgar
NECHAN, Lewis	A.B.	PROMETHEUS	(ML as NECAN)
	L.M.	LION	Java
NEIL, James	Ord	GRANICUS	(ML as NEAL)
NEIL, John	Supn Capt' Fcsle	IMPREGNABLE	
	Ord	STAR	Martinique
	Ord	STAR	Guadaloupe
	A.B.	MALTA	Gaieta 24 July 1815
NEILL, John	Supn Carp's Crew	SEVERN	(ML as NEALE)
NELSON, John	Ord	ALBION	
NEWBURY, Joseph	Pte. R.M.	BRITOMART	(ML as NEWBERRY)
NEWLAND, Abraham	Pte. R.M.	IMPREGNABLE	
NEWMAN, Richard	Ord	Qn CHARLOTTE	
NEWSTEAD, Robert	Ord	GLASGOW	
NEWTON, Charles	Boy 2nd Cl	MINDEN	
NICHOLS, Thomas	Pte. R.M.	MUTINE	
NICHOLS, William	A.B.	ALBION	
NICHOLLS, John	Pte. R.M.	MINDEN	GH.3274
	Pte. R.M.	ACHILLE	Trafalgar
NICKELS, George	Carpenter	SUPERB	
NOBLE, Michael	Pte. R.M.	SUPERB	
NOOKS, Joseph	Pte. R.M.	IMPREGNABLE	(ML as NOOKES)
NORMAN, Abraham	Ord	SUPERB	
NORRIS, John	1st Lieut. R.M.	SUPERB	
	2nd Lieut. R.M.	MELAMPUS	Guadaloupe
	1st Lieut. R.M.	REVOLUTIONNAIRE	St Sebastian
	1st Lieut. R.M.	GLASGOW	Navarino
NORTH, Charles	Supn Armr's Mate	Qn CHARLOTTE	
NORTHCOTT, Robert	L.M.	SUPERB	
NOTT, John	Boy 3rd Cl	SUPERB	
NOWELL, Charles	L.N.	MINDEN	(ML as Charles.S.NOEL)
O'BRIEN, Joseph	Lieut. R.N.	IMPREGNABLE	
	Lieut. R.N.	BERWICK	Gaieta 24 July 1815
O'BRIEN, Patrick (2)	Ord	IMPREGNABLE	
OCCLESTON, John	Pte. R.M.	IMPREGNABLE	(M) Anchor Ty LSGC as M.A.A.
O'CONNOR, John	Ord	SEVERN	
O'CONNOR, Patrick	L.M.	SEVERN	GH.9565
ODGERS, William	Sgt. R.M.	HEBRUS	
	Pte. R.M.	THUNDERER	Trafalgar
OGILVIE, Simon.T.	Supn Adm Mid	HEBRUS	
OLIVER, Stephen	Supn Capt' Aft Gd	Qn CHARLOTTE	
	A.B.	NAIAD	Trafalgar
OLVER, John	L.M.	SUPERB	
O'NEIL, Henry	Pte. R.M.	MINDEN	
O'NEILL, John	Carp's Crew	IMPREGNABLE	
	Carp's Crew	GENOA	Navarino
ORMOND, Francis	Lieut. R.N.	IMPREGNABLE	
	Midshipman	IMPLACABLE	Implacable 26 Augt 1808
	Master's Mate	IMPLACABLE	B.S. 7 July 1809
	Actg Flag Lieut.	ABOUKIR	B.S. 29 Sep 1812
	Lieut. R.N.	ENDYMION	Endymion Wh President
OSMAND, James	Surgeon	BEELZEBUB	
	Surgeon's Mate	SWIFTSURE	Trafalgar

ALGIERS

Name	Rank	Ship	Notes
OWEN, James	Pte. R.M.	MINDEN	
PACE, Edmund.H.	Supn Adm Mid	GLASGOW	Mortar Boat Launch No 9
	Volunteer 1st Cl	FREIJA	Guadaloupe (Known but issued with Martinique clasp) (M) A of I/AVA.
PAINE, William	Purser	FURY	
PALMER, James	Pte. R.M.	GLASGOW	
	Pte. R.M.	AFRICA	Trafalgar
PALMER, James	Pte. R.M.	IMPREGNABLE	
PALMER, John	Purser	GLASGOW	
PARKER, Benjamin	Pte. R.M.	MINDEN	
PARKER, Charles (B)	Master's Mate	Qn CHARLOTTE	Explosion Vessel
	Volunteer 1st Cl	CHILDERS	Childers 14 March 1808
	Midshipman	DOTTEREL	Basque Roads 1809
PARKER, John	2 Ptes RM borne	LEANDER	
PARKER, William	Lieut. R.N.	HECLA	
PARKIN, James.L.	Master's Mate	MINDEN	
PARLBY, James	Midshipman	SUPERB	
PARPATH, John	Pte. R.M.	Qn CHARLOTTE	(ML as PARPETH)
PARRY, Richard	Sapper & Miner	IMPREGNABLE	
PARSON, John	Lieut. R.N.	GRANICUS	
PARSONS, Henry	Pte. R.M.	GLASGOW	
PARSONS, James	A.B.	ALBION	
PAWLEY, Robert	Sgt. R.M.	ALBION	
PEACOCK, Samuel	Supn Boy 2nd Cl	HEBRUS	
PEARCE, Christopher	Supn L.M.	IMPREGNABLE	
PEARCE, Thomas	L.M.	MINDEN	
PEARN, Henry	Supn Boy 2nd Cl	BEELZEBUB	(ML as PEARNE)
PEARSON, John	Pte. R.M.	BRITOMART	
PECK, William	Ord	LEANDER	GH.9250
PEED, James	Supn A.B.	SUPERB	
	A.B.	MUSQUITO	Navarino
PERCEVAL, George.J.	Captain. R.N.	INFERNAL	
Earl of Egmont	Volunteer 1st Cl	ORION	Trafalgar
	Midshipman	TIGRE	B.S. 1 Nov 1809
PERCY, William	Cpl. R.M.	MINDEN	
PERFECT, Joseph	Pte. R.M.	HEBRUS	
PERKINS, Henry.A.	Lieut. R.N.	GRANICUS	
PERRIN, William (2)	Armourer	GRANICUS	(ML as PERRING)
PETERS, John	Cpl. R.M.	IMPREGNABLE	
PEW, George	Master's Mate	BEELZEBUB	
PHILIPS, John	Caulker	Qn CHARLOTTE	(ML as PHILLIPS)
PHILLIPS, George	Supn Boy 3rd Cl	Qn CHARLOTTE	
PHILLIPS, Henry	Boy 3rd Cl	GRANICUS	
PICKFORD, James	Pte. R.M.	IMPREGNABLE	
PIERCE, George	Lieut. R.N.	BEELZEBUB	
PILE, Benjamin	Pte. R.M.	Qn CHARLOTTE	
PITFIELD, Joseph.E.C.	Lieut. R.N.	SUPERB	
PLANT, Francis	L.M.	GLASGOW	
PLANTAGENET, Henry	Boy 3rd Cl	SUPERB	
PLAYER, George	Pte. R.M.	SUPERB	(ML as PLYER)
PLEDGER, John	Gnr. R.M.A.	ALBION	
PLOMER, Matthew.H.	Pte. R.M.	Qn CHARLOTTE	
PLUMMER, William	Carp's Crew	ALBION	
POLDEN, Samuel	Pte. R.M.	ALBION	
PONTIN, Humphry	Pte. R.M.	IMPREGNABLE	
PONTON, William	Ord	IMPREGNABLE	(ML as PARTON)
POOLE, John	Ord	IMPREGNABLE	(ML as POOL)
POPE, William	Ord	MINDEN	
POPHAM, William	Captain. R.N.	HECLA	
PORTER, Thomas	Supn Ord	SUPERB	
POTTER, Thomas	L.M.	GLASGOW	
POWELL, Herbert.B.	Supn Commander	IMPREGNABLE	"Volunteer" for Expedition
	Supn Lieut. R.N.	LOUISA	Louisa 28 Octr 1807 (The only recipient)
	Lieut. R.N.	VIRGINIE	Virginie 19 May 1808
POWELL, George.E.	Lieut. R.N.	CORDELIA	
	Master's Mate	BACCHANTE	B.S. 1 & 18 Sep 1812
	Master's Mate	BACCHANTE	B.S. 6 Jan 1813 (? awarded)
POWELL, William	Cpl. R.M.	MINDEN	
POWER, John	A.B.	ALBION	
PRATT, James	Admiralty Mid	BRITOMART	
PRIANE, Andrew	Ord	GRANICUS	
PRIDHAM, William.D.	Lieut. R.N.	PROMETHEUS	(ML as Wm PRIDHAM)
	Master's Mate	AURORA	Guadaloupe
PRIEST, Bartholomew	Midshipman	MINDEN	
PRIEST, Charles	Pte. R.M.	MINDEN	
PRIEST, Joshua	Pte. R.M.	PROMETHEUS	
PRIEST, William	L.M.	ALBION	
PRYKE, Edward	Pte. R.M.	SEVERN	(ML as PYKE)
	Pte. R.M.	STAR	Martinique
	Pte. R.M.	ASP	Guadaloupe
PROBERT, William	Cook	HECLA	

PURCELL, Robert	Caulker's Mate	SUPERB	
QUIN, Henry	Midshipman	IMPREGNABLE	
QUINTON, John	Capt' of Mast	GLASGOW	
RADCLIFF, John	Supn Adm Mid	ALBION	Gun Boat Barge No 9
RADCLIFFE, William	Supn Adm Mid	GLASGOW	Gun Boat Barge No 15
RADDON, Samuel	Ord	MINDEN	Impressed & convicted Smuggler
RAND, John	Supn Q.M's Mate	HECLA	(ML as Jonathan)
	L.M.	LATONA	Curacoa
RANDALL, William	Supn L.M.	Qn CHARLOTTE	
RANT, Edward	Ropemaker	PROMETHEUS	(ML as Charles RAWDEN)
RAW, Joseph	Pte. R.M.	Qn CHARLOTTE	
RAWDON, Charles.W.	Midshipman	MINDEN	
	Boy 3rd Cl	PHOEBE	Phoebe 28 March 1814
RAYMOND, James.G.	Supn Midshipman	SUPERB	Rocket Flat Boat No 3
REAY, Walter	Pte. R.M.	ALBION	GH.9670
REDFORD, William	Boy 3rd Cl	GRANICUS	
REDMAN, John	Pte. R.M.	SUPERB	
REEVES, George	Boy 3rd Cl	HEBRUS	
REID, William	Captain. R.E.	Qn CHARLOTTE	(ML as REED)
REVANS, Thomas	Flag Lieutenant R.N.	IMPREGNABLE	I/Cmd Gun Boat Division
	Master's Mate	DETERMINEE	Egypt
REYNOLDS, Edward	Supn A.B.	BEELZEBUB	
REYNOLDS, John	Pte. R.M.	SUPERB	
REYNOLDS, Joseph	Pte. R.M.	ALBION	
RHODES, John	A.B.	ALBION	(ML as ROWANS alias RHODES)
RICHARDS, Henry	Boy 3rd Cl	SUPERB	
RICHARDS, John	Pte. R.M.	SEVERN	GH.9983
RICHARDS, Peter	Lieut. R.N.	Qn CHARLOTTE	
RICHARDSON, Edward	Ord	GRANICUS	
RICHARDSON, E.T.	Midshipman	Qn CHARLOTTE	
RICHARDSON, Henry	Ord	ALBION	
RIDDEFORD, Arthur	Pte. R.M.	MINDEN	
	Pte. R.M.	"ANHOLT"	Anholt 27 March 1811
RIDDING, Owen	A.B.	Qn CHARLOTTE	
	Capt' of Mast	ASIA	Navarino
RILEY, George	Carp's Crew	SEVERN	
RILEY, John (1)	Carp's Crew	Qn CHARLOTTE	
ROBB, John	Master's Mate	CORDELIA	
	Lieut I/Cmd	HIND (Tender)	Navarino (to Asia)
ROBBINS, George	Pte. R.M.	HEBRUS	(ML as ROBINS)
ROBERTS, Edward	Ord	LEANDER	
ROBERTS, James	Pte. R.M.	ALBION	
ROBERTS, John	Admiralty Mid	MINDEN	(Is incorrectly stated as "Charles" on ADM 171/4/33)
ROBERTS, Peter	L.M.	SUPERB	
ROBERTSON, James	Pte. R.M.	GRANICUS	(Only found as ROBINSON)
ROBERTSON, John	Carp's Mate	IMPREGNABLE	
ROBERTSON, Patrick	1st Lieut. R.M.	Qn CHARLOTTE	
ROBINSON, James	2 borne AB & Ord	ALBION	GH.740
ROBINSON, John	L.M.	ALBION	
ROBINSON, Richard	L.M.	ALBION	
RODBURN, Charles	L.M.	SUPERB	
ROGERS, Charles	Pte. R.M.	MINDEN	
ROGERS, Francis	Sapper & Miner	Qn CHARLOTTE	
ROGERS, Frederick	Lieut. R.N.	Qn CHARLOTTE	
ROOFE, Henry	Ord	LEANDER	
	L.M.	AGAMEMNON	Trafalgar
	L.M.	AGAMEMNON	St Domingo
ROOK, Richard	Supn Gnr R.M.A.	BEELZEBUB	(ML as ROOKE)
ROSS, Hamilton	A.B.	GRANICUS	GH.9919
ROSSER, Philip	Pte. R.M.	IMPREGNABLE	
ROUSE, John	Pte. R.M.	Qn CHARLOTTE	
(ROW see RAW, Joseph)			(Roll either. ML as RAW)
ROW, William	Armourer	IMPREGNABLE	(ML as ROWE)
ROWDEN, John	L.M.	SUPERB	GH.9296
ROWE, John	Ord	MUTINE	
	A.B.	TALBOT	Navarino
ROWE, William	Capt' After Guard	SEVERN	(ML as ROW)
ROWLEY, Joshua	L.M.	IMPREGNABLE	
ROWLEY, William	Pte. R.M.	MUTINE	
RUCKHAM, John	Pte. R.M.	LEANDER	
RUMKER, Charles	Schoolmaster	ALBION	
RUNCIMAN, John	Asst Surgeon	ALBION	
	Surgeon	POWERFUL	Syria
RUSH, George	Ord	Qn CHARLOTTE	
RUSSELL, Edward	A.B.	Qn CHARLOTTE	(ML as George NORRIS)
	Boy 3rd Cl	St GEORGE	Copenhagen 1801
	Boy 3rd Cl	BRITANNIA	Trafalgar
	Q.M.	BENBOW	Syria. (M) Anchor Type LS&GC
RYDER, Nathaniel	Pte. R.M.	SUPERB	
RYDER, William	Master's Mate	SEVERN	Mortar Boat Launch No 6
SAFFRON, James	Supn Qtr Gunner	IMPREGNABLE	

ALGIERS

Name	Rank/Rating	Ship	Notes
SAINTHILL, Alfred	Supn Adm Mid	Qn CHARLOTTE	Gun Boat Yawl No 2
SALE, James	Ord	SUPERB	GH.2777
SALMON, Henry	Pte. R.M.	SUPERB	
SALMON, Thomas	Sgt. R.M.	SUPERB	
SALMONS, William	Pte. R.M.	Qn CHARLOTTE	
SALTER, Barney	Pte. R.M.	SEVERN	
SALTER, John	Gnr. R.M.A.	ALBION	
SAMWELL, William	Midshipman	IMPREGNABLE	(ML incorrectly as SAMUELS)
SANDERS, Thomas	Lieut. R.N.	LEANDER	
SANDERSON, John	Master's Mate	HEBRUS	Mortar Boat Launch No 10
SARDI, Thomas	Boy 2nd Cl	CORDELIA	
SARGENT, Edward	Conductor of Stores	Qn CHARLOTTE	
SAUL, John	A.B.	SUPERB	
	L.M.	BELLEISLE	Martinique
SAUNDERS, Francis	Pte. R.M.	Qn CHARLOTTE	
SAUNDERS, John	L.M.	IMPREGNABLE	
SAUNDERS, Richard	Supn Gnr. R.M.A.	SUPERB	
SAUNDERS, Thomas	Pte. R.M.	IMPREGNABLE	GH.10,102
SAVAGE, George	Ord	ALBION	GH.8629
SAWYER, William	L.M.	MINDEN	
SAXTON, Thomas	C/Sgt. R.M.	Qn CHARLOTTE	
	Sgt. R.M.	DESIREE	Gluckstadt. 5 Jany 1814
SCALLAN, James	Actg Gunner	HECLA	
SCOTCHMAN, Mark	Gnr. R.M.A.	GRANICUS	
SCOTT, John	Ord	ALBION	
SCOTT, John	Boy 3rd Cl	SUPERB	
SCREEN, John	Pte. R.M.	IMPREGNABLE	
SEABRIDGE, Thomas	Pte. R.M.	Qn CHARLOTTE	
SEAMORE, Thomas	Sgt. R.M.	SUPERB	(ML as SEYMOUR)
	Pte. R.M.	TOPAZE	B.S. 1 Nov 1809
SEAVER, Charles	Volunteer 1st Cl	PROMETHEUS	
SELBY, George	Ord	HEBRUS	
SEYMOUR, Edward.W.	Lieut. R.N.	GLASGOW	
SHAW, William	Pte. R.M.	MINDEN	
SHEA, John	Purser	GLASGOW	
SHEARS, Henry	A.B.	Qn CHARLOTTE	
SHEPPARD, Joseph	Pte. R.M.	Qn CHARLOTTE	
	Pte. R.M.	NORTHUMBERLAND	Northumberland 22 May 1812
SHEPPARD, William	Supn Ord	SUPERB	
SHERGOLD, Samuel	Pte. R.M.	Qn CHARLOTTE	GH. March 1850
SHERRY, Michael	Ord	SUPERB	
SHERWOOD, Stephen	A.B.	GRANICUS	
SHEWBRIDGE, William	Pte. R.M.	ALBION	GH.8663 (ML as SHOCBRIDGE)
SHIPLEY, William	Pte. R.M.	BRITOMART	
SHORT, Charles	Supn Ord	HEBRUS	GH.2200
SHORTRIDGE, John	A.B.	HERON	
SHUTE, John	Pte. R.M.	SUPERB	
SHUTTLEWORTH, George	Pte. R.M.	SUPERB	
SIBLY, John	Midshipman	MINDEN	No 23 Gun Boat
SIMMS, James	2 borne. AB & Ord	IMPREGNABLE	
SINCLAIR, James.S.	Midshipman	GLASGOW	
(SINGER, Richard see WALKER, Richard S.)			
SKELTON, William	Boy 2nd Cl	SEVERN	
SKINNER, Arthur.McG.	Midshipman	GLASGOW	
	Midshipman	VENERABLE	Venerable 16 Jany 1814 (M) A of I/AVA. Liffey
SLADE, John	A.B.	MINDEN	
	Boy	TONNANT	Trafalgar
SLAUGHTER, George	Supn L.M.	FURY	
SLOACOMBE, Joseph	Pte. R.M.	SUPERB	(ML as SLOCOMBE)
SMART, Robert	Midshipman	GLASGOW	
	Lieut. R.N.	CAMBRIAN	Navarino
SMITH, Alexander	Drummer. R.E.Corps.	Qn CHARLOTTE	
SMITH, Charles	Ord	MINDEN	
SMITH, Henry	2 Ords borne	Qn CHARLOTTE	
SMITH, James (3)	Capt' Forecastle	GLASGOW	
SMITH, James	A.B.	Qn CHARLOTTE	
SMITH, James	M.A.A.	SUPERB	
	Ord	REVENGE	Basque Roads 1809
	M.A.A.	ALBION	Navarino (M) Anchor Type LSGC
SMITH, John	Gunner's Mate	GRANICUS	GH.6994
	Capt Aft Guard	IMPERIEUSE	Basque Roads 1809
SMITH, John	Midshipman	HECLA	
SMITH, John.E.	A.B. & Ord borne	ALBION	GH.3823. Both as John SMITH.
SMITH, Peter	Pte. R.M.	HEBRUS	
SMITH, Thomas	Ord	IMPREGNABLE	
SMITH, William	Capt' Forecastle	MINDEN	GH.9973
	A.B.	ILLUSTRIOUS	Java
SMITH, William Sidney	Midshipman	HERON	
SMITHSON, Joseph	A.B.	SUPERB	
SOADY, Joseph	Lieut. R.N.	SUPERB	
	Lieut. R.N.	COLOSSUS	B.S. 23 Nov 1810

SODEN, James.B.E.	Clerk	GRANICUS	*(Purser 1827)*
SOUTH, William	Admiral's Domestic	Qn CHARLOTTE	*(ADM 171/1/464)*
	Domestic	PSYCHE	*Java*
SOUTHWORTH, John	Supn Gnr R.M.A.	GLASGOW	
SPARSHOTT, James	Purser	PROMETHEUS	
SPEECHLY, Samuel	Bmbdr. R.M.A.	Qn CHARLOTTE	
SPENCER, James	Pte. R.M.	Qn CHARLOTTE	
	Pte. R.M.	CAMBRIAN	*Navarino*
SPENCER, William	Gunner's Mate	GLASGOW	
	A.B.	INCONSTANT	*14 March 1795*
	Quarter Gunner	TONNANT	*Trafalgar*
SPROULE, Oliver	Asst Surgeon	LEANDER	
SQUIRES, Henry	Pte. R.M.	MINDEN	
STANBURY, Peter	Ord	IMPREGNABLE	
STANFORD, David	L.M.	SUPERB	
STANHOPE, William.S.	Lieut. R.N.	IMPREGNABLE	*(Changed name to Wm RODDAM)*
	Lieut. R.N.	BERWICK	*Gaieta 24 July 1815*
STANLEY, Edward	Midshipman	Qn CHARLOTTE	
STEARS, Harry.G.	Volunteer 1st Cl	Qn CHARLOTTE	
STEPHENS, John	Pte. R.M.	MINDEN	
STEPHENS, Robert.L.	Volunteer 1st Cl	SUPERB	
STEPHENS, William	L.M.	SEVERN	
STEVENS, George	L.M.	SUPERB	
STEVENS, Henry	Pte. R.M.	Qn CHARLOTTE	*GH.7717*
STEVENS, John.Harry	1st Lieut. R.M.A.	Qn Ch & INFERNAL	*1/Cmd Div of Rocket Boats*
STEVENSON, George	L.M.	Qn CHARLOTTE	
STEVENSON, John	L.M.	GLASGOW	
STEWART, Alexander	Asst Surgeon	GLASGOW	
STILES, William	L.M.	GRANICUS	
STOCKER, Walter.B.	Supn Adm Mid	PROMETHEUS	
STONE, William	L.M.	SUPERB	
STOREY, James	Admiral's Domestic	IMPREGNABLE	
STRAHAN, Alexander	Boy 3rd Cl	LEANDER	*(ML as STRACHAN)*
STRATH, William	Q.M's Mate	IMPREGNABLE	
	Gunner's Mate	POMPEE	*Gut of Gibraltar 12 July 1801*
STRICKLAND, Charles	Supn Carp's Crew	INFERNAL	
STRICKLAND, Joseph	Carp's Crew	INFERNAL	*GH. 2105*
	Carp's Crew	AIGLE	*Basque Roads 1809*
STRONG, Henry	Pte. R.M.	MINDEN	
STRONG, Joseph.T.	Midshipman	Qn CHARLOTTE	
STRONG, William	Supn Capt' After Gd	IMPREGNABLE	
STROPERS, Jacob	Supn Gnr's Mate	Qn CHARLOTTE	
	Gunner's Mate	ORION	*Trafalgar*
STROUD, George	Ord	HEBRUS	*(ML as G.F. STROUD)*
STUART, William	Sapper & Miner	Qn CHARLOTTE	*(ML as STEWART)*
STURT, Henry.R.	Midshipman	LEANDER	
	Lieut. R.N.	GENOA	*Navarino*
SWAN, Matthew	Supn Ord	IMPREGNABLE	
SWANEY, Jacob	Boatswain	HECLA	*(ML as SWANCEA)*
SWEETING, William	Supn Adm Mid	SUPERB	
SWINDLER, Thomas	Pte. R.M.	Qn CHARLOTTE	
SYMES, Aaron.S.	Supn Adm Mid	HEBRUS	*Rocket Flat Boat No 8*
SYMONS, Henry	A.B.	IMPREGNABLE	*(Various spellings of name)*
	Boy 2nd Cl	PRINCE	*Trafalgar*
	A.B.	MALTA	*Gaieta 24 July 1815*
TALBOT, James	Ship's Cpl	PROMETHEUS	*(Not yet found aboard)*
TALLENCE, Samuel	Boatswain	MUTINE	
	A.B.	AGAMEMNON	*Trafalgar*
	A.B.	AGAMEMNON	*St Domingo*
	Boatswain	PELORUS	*Martinique*
	Boatswain	PELORUS	*Guadaloupe*
TAMPLIN, Robert	Pte. R.M.	SEVERN	
TAYLER, John	A.B.	GLASGOW	*(ML as TAYLOR)*
TAYLOR, Edward	Gnr. R.M.A.	HECLA	
TAYLOR, Israel	Pte. R.M.	IMPREGNABLE	*(Only found as Samuel)*
TAYLOR, James	L.M.	SEVERN	
TAYLOR, John	Ord	ALBION	
	Ord	GANGES	*Syria*
TAYLOR, John	Carp's Crew	HECLA	
TAYLOR, John	Ord	IMPREGNABLE	*GH.10,049*
TAYLOR, Samuel	L.M.	IMPREGNABLE	
TAYLOR, Simon	Pte. R.M.	LEANDER	
TAYLOR, Thomas	Pte. R.M.	IMPREGNABLE	
TAYLOR, Thomas	Pte. R.M.	MINDEN	
TAYLOR, William	Gunner. R.M.A.	FURY	
TAYLOR, William	A.B.	LEANDER	
TAYLOR, William	Ord	IMPREGNABLE	
TELLOGRAM, William	Ord	IMPREGNABLE	
TENNANT, John	A.B.	LEANDER	
THERRY, Bryan.K.	Master's Mate	HERON	
THOMAS, George	Pte. R.M.	IMPREGNABLE	
THOMAS, James	Pte. R.M.	SEVERN	
THOMAS, James	Qtr Gunner	SUPERB	

ALGIERS

Name	Rank	Ship	Notes
THOMAS, Richard	Pte. R.M.	GRANICUS	
THOMAS, William	L.M.	IMPREGNABLE	
THOMAS, William	Pte. R.M.	MINDEN	
THOMPSON, George	Drummer. R.M.	Qn CHARLOTTE	
(THOMPSON, John see ALEXANDER, John)			
THOMPSON, William	Pte. R.M.	Qn CHARLOTTE	
THORPE, John	Pte. R.M.	SEVERN	(ML as THORP)
THORN, John	Purser	HECLA	
	Clerk	HUSSAR	Java
THORNTON, Richard	Pte. R.M.	GLASGOW	
TIDBURY, James	Pte. R.M.	LEANDER	
	Pte. R.M.	MAGICIENNE	St Sebastian
TILLETT, James	A.B.	GLASGOW	
	Ord	Pcss CAROLINE	B.S. 25 July 1809
TILLS, William	Midshipman	GRANICUS	
	Mate	ASIA	Navarino
TILMOUTH, Robert.C.	Master	CORDELIA	
TINLING, Edward.B.	Midshipman	Qn CHARLOTTE	
TIPPINGS, Thomas	Supn Ord	SUPERB	
TOM, John	Volunteer 1st Cl	ALBION	
TOMKINS, Henry.W.	Supn Adm Mid	CORDELIA	
TOMLIN, James	Pte. R.M.	Qn CHARLOTTE	
TOMLINSON, Thomas	Pte. R.M.	Qn CHARLOTTE	
TORSELL, Joseph	Ord	SEVERN	
TRACEY, Benjamin.W.	Volunteer 1st Cl	ALBION	
TREADWELL, Samuel	Supn Boy.	GRANICUS	
TREBEY, James	A.B.	MINDEN	(ML as TRABEY)
TREGASKING, John	Sailmaker	MUTINE	
	Sailmaker	ASIA	Navarino
	Sailmaker	REVENGE	Syria (M) Anchor Type LSGC.
TREGENNA, Thomas	L.M.	SUPERB	
TRISCOTT, Richard.S.	Midshipman	Qn CHARLOTTE	
TRUELOVE, James	Qtr Gunner	GLASGOW	GH.3861
	Ord	Sir FRANCIS DRAKE	Java
TUCKER, Benjamin	Pte. R.M.	SUPERB	
TUCKER, James	Pte. R.M.	HERON	
TURNER, John	Ord	SUPERB	
TURNER, Michael	Midshipman	HEBRUS	Gun Boat Barge No 16
	Midshipman	HEBRUS	Hebrus with L'Etoile
TWOMEY/TROMEY, Patrick	Capt' Aft Guard	SUPERB	(ML as TWOMEY)
	A.B.	CANOPUS	St Domingo (ADM 171/4/42. "Gone to Mint as St Domingo. TROMEY")
UNDERDOWN, Thomas	Supn Boy 2nd Cl	GLASGOW	
UNDERWOOD, James	Ord	Qn CHARLOTTE	
UPTON, William	Pte. R.M.	ALBION	
UREN, Andrew	L.M.	IMPREGNABLE	(ML as URAN)
VERDINE, Joseph	Cook	SUPERB	
VOWELL, William	L.M.	SUPERB	
WAKEFIELD, John.W.	Volunteer 1st Cl	HEBRUS	
WALCOTT, Charles	Midshipman	HEBRUS	
WALKER, Richard.S.	A.B.	Qn CHARLOTTE	
WALKER, William	Master	BEELZEBUB	
WALKER, William	Cpl. R.M.	MUTINE	
WALKER, William (2)	L.M.	MINDEN	Convicted & impressed Poacher
WALL, John	Pte. R.M.	ALBION	
WALL, Joseph	Ord	SUPERB	GH.1122
WALLIS, William.R.	Pte. R.M.	ALBION	
WALSH/WELSH, James	Supn Ord	Qn CHARLOTTE	(Roll read either. ML=WALSH)
WALSH, Jonathan.W.	Midshipman	SUPERB	
WALSH, John	Ord	SUPERB	
WALSH, Patrick	Carp's Mate	HERON	
WARD, Benjamin	Pte. R.M.	IMPREGNABLE	
WARD, John	Supn Cpl R.M.A.	BEELZEBUB	GH.2318
	Pte. R.M.	RAMILLIES	Copenhagen 1801
	Gnr. R.M.A.	CALEDONIA	Basque Roads 1809
	Cpl. R.M.A.	AETNA	The Potomac. 17 Aug 1814
(WARD, Samuel see MORGAN, Thomas)			
WARD, William	Supn Ord	IMPREGNABLE	
WARD, William	Supn Boy 2nd Cl	LEANDER	
WARE, Charles.B.	Midshipman	LEANDER	Gun Boat Yawl No 12
	Volunteer 1st Cl	IMPLACABLE	Implacable 26 Augt 1808
WARNER, William	Capt' Forecastle	SUPERB	
WARREN, Benjamin	L.M.	ALBION	
WARREN, John	Pte. R.M.	GLASGOW	
WATERMAN, John	Supn L.M.	IMPREGNABLE	
WATERMAN, Oliver	L.M.	IMPREGNABLE	
WATKINS, Thomas	Pte. R.M.	MINDEN	
WATSON, Henry	A.B.	ALBION	

Name	Rate/Rank	Ship	Notes
WATSON, Henry	Ord	ALBION	
	A.B.	EDINBURGH	Syria
WEAVER, William	Supn Adm Mid	FURY	
	Midshipman	PRESIDENT	Java
WEBB, Charles	Midshipman	SUPERB	GH. 10,078.
WEBBER, George.W.	Midshipman	HEBRUS	Gun Boat Yawl No 15
WEBSTER, Thomas	Ord	SEVERN	GH.3117
WEIRS, Josh	Ord	Qn CHARLOTTE	
WELCH, John	Gunner's Mate	SUPERB	
WELCHMAN, George.T.	1st Lieut. R.M.	MINDEN	
WELHAM, George	Boy 2nd Cl	Qn CHARLOTTE	(ML as WELLHAM)
WELLER, John.H.	Midshipman	ALBION	
WELLS, Thomas.B.	Midshipman	GRANICUS	Gun Boat Barge No 13
WELSH, John	2 borne	SUPERB	Qtr Gnr & Ord
WELSH, John	Pte. R.M.	IMPREGNABLE	(ML as WELCH)
WENTWORTH, William.F.	Lieut. R.N.	HEBRUS	
WEST, George	L.M.	SUPERB	
WEST, John	Boy 3rd Cl	HEBRUS	
WESTLAKE, William	Pte. R.M.	IMPREGNABLE	
	Pte. R.M.	GENOA	Navarino
WHEATLEY, William	Ord	GRANICUS	
WHEELER, Samuel	Pte. R.M.	Qn CHARLOTTE	
WHEELER, William	Supn Bosun's Mate	Qn CHARLOTTE	
WHEELER, William	Ord	SUPERB	
	Capt' Fore Top	TALBOT	Navarino
WHINYATES, Frederick.W.	Lieut. R.E.	IMPREGNABLE	
WHISH, William.G.H.	Master's Mate	MUTINE	No 5 Gun Boat
WHITE, Robert	Ord	CORDELIA	
WHITE, Thomas	2 Landsmen borne	MINDEN	SB.565.alias STONE a convicted & impressed smuggler SB.571. Convtd/Impds poacher
WHITE, William	2nd Lieut. R.M.	IMPREGNABLE	
WHITEHEAD, William	L.M.	SUPERB	
WHITMARSH, Thomas	Supn Boy 2nd Cl	MINDEN	
WIGHT, Andrew	Midshipman	LEANDER	
WILBY, John	Pte. R.M.	GLASGOW	(ML as WELBY)
WILCOX, John	Ord	MINDEN	
WILD, Richard	Pte. R.M.	Qn CHARLOTTE	
WILKINS, Joseph	Supn Pte. R.M.	HEBRUS	
WILKINSON, Frederick.A.	Supn Adm Mid	SUPERB	Mortar Boat Launch No 3
	College Volunteer	BERWICK	Gaieta 24 July 1815
WILLCOX, John	Pte. R.M.	SEVERN	(ML as WILCOX)
WILLIAMS, John	A.B.	Qn CHARLOTTE	
WILLIAMS, John	"Several borne"	Qn CHARLOTTE	Roll does not show Rate (Note. 4 similar names for "Pelagosa 29 Novr 1811", Martinique & Guadaloupe Rolls.)
WILLIAMS, John	Pte. R.M.	BRITOMART	
WILLIAMS, Poulton	Midshipman	SUPERB	
WILLIAMS, Thomas	Pte. R.M.	Qn CHARLOTTE	
WILLIAMS, Thomas	Pte. R.M.	MINDEN	(Not yet found aboard)
WILLIS, James	Pte. R.M.	IMPREGNABLE	
WILMORE, George/John	A.B.	FURY	(ML as John)
	Capt's Coxswain	ZEBRA	Syria (Two Rolls differ. WILLMORE/ WILMORE & George/John)
WILSEY, Martin	Supn Slmkr' Mte	BEELZEBUB	
WILSON, Charles	Supn A.B.	IMPREGNABLE	(? additional clasp)
WILSON, David	Pte. R.M.	Qn CHARLOTTE	(Not yet found aboard)
WILSON, James	"2 borne"	Qn CHARLOTTE	Slmaker's Mate and Ord
WILSON, John (2)	A.B.	LEANDER	
	A.B.	CAMBRIAN	Navarino
WILSON, John (1)	Ord	LEANDER	
WILSON, Josh	Ord	MINDEN	(Alias John HAYES on ML) (M) Anchor Ty LSGC. Was at Syria/Asia. Not on Roll.
WINGROVE, Henry.E.	Midshipman	PROMETHEUS	
WINNETT, Clement	A.B.	ALBION	
WINSOR, George	Midshipman	FURY	
WINTER, George	Boy 2nd Cl	MUTINE	(Only found as Supn, James)
WOLRIDGE, Ambrose.A.R.	Lieut. R.M.A.	Qn CHARLOTTE	Mortar Boat Launch No 1
WOOD, James	Master	GRANICUS	
WOOD, James	Armourer	CORDELIA	
WOOD, John	Pte. R.M.	SUPERB	
WOOD, Joseph	L.M.	GRANICUS	
WOOD, Thomas	L.M.	HECLA	
	A.B.	Pcss CHARLOTTE	Syria
WOODNUTT, George	Carp's Crew	Qn CHARLOTTE	
WOODRUFF, Henry	Midshipman	Qn CHARLOTTE	

ALGIERS

WOODS, Thomas	Master's Mate	IMPREGNABLE	Gun Boat Yawl No 4
	Volunteer 1st Cl	ACTIVE	Lissa
	Midshipman	ACTIVE	Pelagosa 29 Novr 1811
	Midshipman	SEAHORSE	The Potomac. 17 Aug 1814
	Midshipman	SEAHORSE	B.S. 14 Dec 1814
WRIGHT, Charles	Carp's Crew	GLASGOW	
WRIGHT, James	Pte. R.M.	ALBION	
WRIGHT, John	Captain. R.M.	Qn CHARLOTTE	
	2nd Lieut. R.M.	BELLEROPHON	Nile
	1st Lieut. R.M.	RENOWN	B.S. 29 Aug 1800
	1st Lieut. R.M.	RENOWN	Egypt
WRIGHT, William	Boy 2nd Cl	GRANICUS	
WYATT, Thomas.H.G.	Midshipman	MINDEN	
YARRINGTON, William	Pte. R.M.	MINDEN	GH.3126
	Pte. R.M.	BRISK	Navarino
YORK, Thomas	Carp's Crew	GLASGOW	
YORK, Hon Charles.P.	Supn Adm Mid	Qn CHARLOTTE	No 5 Gun Boat
YOUNG, John	2 Ords borne	LEANDER	
YOUNG, William	Armourer's Mate	LEANDER	
YULE, Robert	Gunner	HERON	

(1142) NAVARINO

Defeat of the Turko-Egyptian Fleet by the English, French and Russian Squadrons on 20 October 1827. The Last Fleet Action of the sailing Navy.

AARON, John	A.B.	ASIA	
ABBOTT, James	Pte. R.M.	ALBION	
ABERCROMBIE, James	Gunner's Crew	ALBION	
ABERLEY, James	Pte. R.M.	ALBION	
ADAMS, John (1)	Ord	ASIA	
ADDINGTON, Thomas	Boatswain	ALBION	Severely wounded. L.Gaz 1827.p.2324.
	Boatswain	PROMETHEUS	Algiers
ADDOMS, John	Ord	ASIA	
AFFLICK, William	A.B.	TALBOT	
ALDRED, William	A.B.	GENOA	
ALEXANDER, George	Ord	DARTMOUTH	
	A.B.	PIQUE	Syria
ALFORD, Robert	Sergeant. R.M.	GLASGOW	
	Corporal. R.M.	MODESTE	Java
ALLCOCK, James	Pte. R.M.	ASIA	
ALLEN, Alexander.S.	Asst Surgeon	ASIA	
ALLEN, Charles	L.M.	ASIA	
ALLEN, James	Pte. R.M.	DARTMOUTH	
ALLEN, John	Pte. R.M.	ASIA	
ALLEN, Thomas	A.B.	ASIA	
ANDERSON, Alexander	Lieut. R.M.	ALBION	
	Lieut. R.M.	THUNDERER	Syria
ANDERSON, John	Capt' Forecastle	ASIA	
ANDREWS, Charles.E.	Purser	GENOA	
ANGLIN, William	A.B.	CAMBRIAN	
ANSON, Samuel	Q.M.	TALBOT	
ARAM, Charles	A.B.	ALBION	(Despatched 7/1849 to ARHAM)
ARMITAGE, Edward	Pte. R.M.	BRISK	
ARTHUR, James	Ord	GENOA	
ASHDOWN, John	Cooper	GENOA	
ASHFORD, William	Boy	GLASGOW	(M). China 1842/Samarang. Baltic. Cr/Seb. Tu/Cr.
ASHTON, James	Pte. R.M.	GENOA	
ATKINSON, Robert.L.	Vol 1st Cl	ASIA	
AYLES, J.G.A.	Supny Clerk	ASIA	
BAGOT, Henry	Midshipman	TALBOT	
BAILEY, Henry	Ord	GLASGOW	
BAILLIE, Thomas	Vol 1st Cl	DARTMOUTH	
BAKER, George	A.B.	GENOA	
BAKER, John	Ord	ALBION	
BAKER, William	Cooper	ALBION	
BALL, Samuel	L.M.	DARTMOUTH	
BALLANTYNE, John	Ord	ASIA	
BALWIN, George	Pte. R.M.	DARTMOUTH	
BAMBER, John	Ord	TALBOT	
BAMFIELD, David	Pte. R.M.	GENOA	
BANCROFT, Thomas	Pte. R.M.	ALBION	
BANE, Robert	Ord	ROSE	(M.L. as BAIN)
	A.B.	BELLEROPHON	Syria

BANKS, George	A.B.	CAMBRIAN	
	Gunner's Crew	WASP	Syria
BANKS, William	Bosun's Yeoman	DARTMOUTH	
BARGENT, William	Boy 1st Cl	DARTMOUTH	
BARGUS, Thomas	Q.M.	GENOA	
	A.B.	REVOLUTIONNAIRE	4 Novr 1805
BARKER, John	Boy 1st Cl	ALBION	
BARNACOTT, Richard	Carp's Crew	GENOA	
BARNETT, Patrick	A.B.	GENOA	
BARNETT, Thomas	Pte. R.M.	ROSE	
BARRY, John	Ord	DARTMOUTH	
BARTER, Abraham	A.B.	TALBOT	(alias FORREST, James.)
BARTLETT, William	Capt' Forecastle	DARTMOUTH	
BARTON, Richard	Gunner's Crew	TALBOT	
BASS, Josh	Boy	GLASGOW	
BATE, William	L.M.	GENOA	
BATEMAN, F.W.	Senior Master's Assistant	GENOA	(Died Dec 1892 as Cdr RN)
	Acting Master	CARYSFORT	Syria
BATTERSON, Thomas	Ord	GENOA	
BAXTER, George	A.B.	BRISK	
BAYNES, Robert.L.	Commander. R.N.	ASIA	
BAZELEY, John	Boy	CAMBRIAN	
	A.B.	RODNEY	Syria
BEATTIE, William	Pte. R.M.	ASIA	
BEAUMONT, Josh	Pte. R.M.	CAMBRIAN	
	Pte. R.M.	REVENGE	Syria
BEAVER, James	Boy 1st Class	ASIA	
BECK, William	Sailmaker	MUSQUITO	
BECKETT, James	A.B.	PHILOMEL	Impressed ex-Smuggler
BEEMAN, Robert	Boy 2nd Class	BRISK	
BEERES, Robert	A.B.	CAMBRIAN	(M.L. as BELFOOT)
BELL, John	Ord	GENOA	
BENNETT, James	Carp's Crew	ALBION	
BENNETT, William	Pte. R.M.	ASIA	
BERRITTS, Matthew	Pte. R.M.	ASIA	
BERRY, John	A.B.	ALBION	
	A.B.	RODNEY	Syria
BETHELL, William	Pte. R.M.	DARTMOUTH	
	Pte. R.M.	THUNDERER	Syria
BIRCH, Edward	A.B.	TALBOT	
BIRD, John	Pte. R.M.	ASIA	
BIRT, James	A.B.	ASIA	Impressed ex-Smuggler
BISHOP, Charles	Pte. R.M.	ALBION	
BISS, James	Pte. R.M.	ALBION	
BLACK, John	A.B.	GENOA	
BLACKBURN, James	Pte. R.M.	GENOA	
BLACKNEY, John	Boy 1st Class	TALBOT	
BLAIR, Horatio	Lieutenant. R.N.	ASIA	
BLAND, David	A.B.	ALBION	
BLEACH, Thomas	Capt' Main Top	TALBOT	(M) Anchor Type LS & GC
	Ord	Qn CHARLOTTE	Algiers
	Gunner's Mate	VANGUARD	Syria
			(Displayed at R.N. Museum)
BLIGHT, John	A.B.	CAMBRIAN	
BLUNDELL, Thomas	Boy	ALBION	
BOAK, Richard	Ord	ASIA	
	A.B.	CARYSFORT	Syria
BOAKES, Thomas	Corporal. R.M.	BRISK	
	Sergeant R.M.	STROMBOLI	Syria
BODMAN, Benjamin	Pte. R.M.	ROSE	
BOGHURST, J.H.	Clerk	DARTMOUTH	
BOLLIN, John	Pte. R.M.	ALBION	
BOND, George	Boy	GENOA	
BOND, Samuel	A.B.	ALBION	
BOND, William	Q.M.	GENOA	
	Ord	CANOPUS	St Domingo
BOND, William.H.	Purser	ROSE	
BONETT, John	L.M.	ALBION	
BOSSENCE, John	A.B.	GLASGOW	
BOTELER, John.H.	Lieutenant. R.N.	ALBION	Author "Recollections of my sea life. 1808-1830"
BOWLEY, John	A.B.	TALBOT	
BOYS, William	Midshipman	ALBION	
BRADBURY, Thomas	Ord	ALBION	
BRADLEY, Alexander	L.M.	ALBION	
BRADLEY, John	Gunner's Crew	ASIA	(M) Anchor Type LS & GC
	Ord	ALBION	Algiers
	A.B.	PIQUE	Syria
BRADLEY, John	Ord	GLASGOW	
BRAY, John	Ord	GENOA	
BRAY, William	Capt' Main Top	ASIA	
	Boy 3rd Class	ILLUSTRIOUS	Java
	Ord	ALBION	Algiers
BREND, William	Carp's Mate	TALBOT	
BRETT, John	Carp's Crew	ALBION	

NAVARINO

BRIGGS, Joseph	Gunner	ASIA	
	Gunner	Pcss CHARLOTTE	Syria
BRIMMER, James	Pte. R.M.	ASIA	
	Pte. R.M.	BENBOW	Syria
BRISSINGTON, William	Pte. R.M.	GENOA	
	Pte. R.M.	THUNDERER	Syria
BROKE, George.N.	Midshipman	GENOA	
	Lieutenant. R.N.	WASP	Syria
BROKE, Philip	Lieutenant. R.N.	GENOA	(Acceded to baronetcy 1/1841)
BROOKS, Henry	A.B.	ALBION	
BROOKS, Thomas	Ord	DARTMOUTH	
BROOKS, William	Pte. R.M.	GENOA	
BROWN, James	Ropemaker	ALBION	(M) Anchor Type LS & GC.
BROWN, John	A.B.	ALBION	
	A.B.	CAMBRIDGE	Syria
BROWN, John.F.	Capt's Coxswain	TALBOT	(M) China 1842
BROWN, Joseph	A.B.	GENOA	
	Boy 3rd Class	BELLEISLE	Trafalgar
BROWN, William	A.B.	GLASGOW	
BROWN, William	Pte. R.M.	GLASGOW	
	Pte. R.M.	EDINBURGH	Syria
BROWN, William	A.B.	CAMBRIAN	
BROWN, William.D.	Master's Asst	ASIA	
BROWN, William.H.	Purser	MUSQUITO	
BROWNING, Benjamin	Asst Surgeon	ASIA	
BRYAN, Jacob	Gunner's Crew	ALBION	(M.L. as BRYON)
BRYAN, Michael	Bosun's Mate	ALBION	
BUCKLEY, Thomas	Gunner's Crew	GENOA	
	Ord	IMPREGNABLE	Algiers
BUMPASS, John	Ship's Corporal	GENOA	
	Pte. R.M.	DEFENCE	Copenhagen 1801
BUNBURY, Richard.H.	Volunteer 1st Cl	ASIA	Severely wnd. Gaz 1827/2324 (M) Ry Humane Scty
BUNNEY, William	Pte. R.M.	DARTMOUTH	
BURCH, Edward	Ord	GLASGOW	
BURLA, James	Pte. R.M.	GENOA	
BURNETT, Joseph	A.B.	GLASGOW	May be named Richard
BURROUGH, John	Mate	ASIA	(Promoted)
BUSH, William	Sergeant. R.M.	ALBION	
	Pte. R.M.	SWIFTSURE	Trafalgar
BUTLER, Edward	Pte. R.M.	ALBION	
	A.B.(?)	CASTOR	Syria
BUTT, James	Carp's Crew	GLASGOW	
BUTT, William	Pte. R.M.	PHILOMEL	
BUTTER, James	A.B.	CAMBRIAN	
BUTTERWORTH, John	Pte. R.M.	GLASGOW	
CAFFIN, James.C.	Midshipman	CAMBRIAN	(M) Civil CB. Baltic
CALDWELL, James.T.	Midshipman	CAMBRIAN	
CALLAGHAN, John	A.B.	GENOA	GH. 3758
CALLAGHAN, Peter	Ord	GENOA	
CAMPBELL, Charles.J.F.	Midshipman	ROSE	
CAMPBELL, James	Gunner's Crew	MUSQUITO	
CAMPBELL, John.N.	Commander	ALBION	(P). Slty Wnd Gaz 1827/2324
	Lieutenant. R.N.	ASTRAEA	Off Tamatave. 20 May 1811 (M) 11/1837 CB. 1834 Rdmr of Greece.
CANNON, David	Caulker	ASIA	
CARDEW, John	L.M.	GENOA	(May read JAMES)
CARLISLE, Edward.J.	A.B.	DARTMOUTH	
CARR, George	Capt' Forecastle	PHILOMEL	(M) Anchor Type LS & GC
CARR, Hugh	Ord	CAMBRIAN	
CARRINGTON, George	Capt' Main Top	CAMBRIAN	(or KENNINGTON)
CARTLIDGE, Joseph	Pte. R.M.	ASIA	(M) Anchor LSGC as CARTLEDGE.
CASEY, Daniel	Pte. R.M.	ASIA	
CASSALL, Michael	Capt's Cook	PHILOMEL	
CASTLES, William	Pte. R.M.	ALBION	
CATER, Samuel	Pte. R.M.	TALBOT	
CATOR, Thomas	Ship's Corporal	ASIA	
	Q.M's Mate	Qn CHARLOTTE	Algiers
CATTARALL, James	Pte. R.M.	MUSQUITO	
CAVELL, John	Pte. R.M.	ASIA	
CAWLEY, John	Midshipman	GENOA	Died 7-2-1896. Aged 96.
CEENEY, Henry	Armourer	GLASGOW	
CEENEY, John	Armr's Mate	GLASGOW	
CHADWICK, John.F.	Mate	ALBION	
CHAMBERS, James	Volunteer 2nd Cl.	GENOA	Slty Wnd. Gaz 1827/2325
CHAMBERS, William	Pte. R.M.	ALBION	
	Pte. R.M.	Qn CHARLOTTE	Algiers
CHEETHAM, Thomas	Carp's Crew	GENOA	
CHESTERMAN, William	A.B.	GLASGOW	
CHILDS, William	Carp's Mate	DARTMOUTH	
CHIPP, James	Sailmaker's Mate	ALBION	

CHORLTON, William	Pte. R.M.	MUSQUITO	
	Pte. R.M.	Pcss CHARLOTTE	Syria
CHOWLER, Charles	Boy 1st Class	TALBOT	
CHRISTIAN, Henry	Boy	ALBION	
CHRISTIE, Peter	Lieutenant. R.N.	CAMBRIAN	(Promoted)
CHRISTIE, Robert	Gunner's Crew	GENOA	
	Landsman	SPENCER	St Domingo
CHRISTIE, Thomas	A.B.	DARTMOUTH	
	Bosun's Mate	HAZARD	Syria
CLAIZE, Benjamin	Pte. R.M.	ASIA	
CLARK, Andrew	Q.M.	ALBION	
CLARK, John	A.B.	ALBION	
CLARK, John	Ord	ASIA	
CLARK, John	Pte. R.M.	ASIA	
CLARK, John	A.B.	CAMBRIAN	
CLARK, Charles	Pte. R.M.	ASIA	
CLARKE, Edwin	Carp's Crew	TALBOT	
CLARKE, John	Pte. R.M.	ASIA	
CLARKE, John	Ord	GENOA	
CLARKE, Josh	Ord	CAMBRIAN	
CLEMENTS, Henry	Boy	DARTMOUTH	
	A.B.	CAMBRIDGE	Syria
CLEWER, William	Pte. R.M.	PHILOMEL	
CLINTON, Henry	A.B.	PHILOMEL	
COBBY, Richard	A.B.	ASIA	Impressed ex-smuggler
COCK, John	Ord	TALBOT	
CODRINGTON, Sir Edward	Vice Admiral	ASIA	
	Lieutenant. R.N.	Qn CHARLOTTE	1 June 1794
	Captain	BABET	23rd June 1795
	Captain	ORION	Trafalgar
	(See L.Gaz. 1827. pages 2320-4. (M) GCB for services at Navarino, also Grand Cross of St Louis, Order of St George of Russia, & Gold Cross of Redeemer of Greece)		
CODRINGTON, Henry.J.	Midshipman	ASIA	(Son of Sir Edward)
	Captain	TALBOT	Syria
			Severely wounded at Navarino.
COE, Abraham	Pte. R.M.	ASIA	
COFFEY, James	A.B.	DARTMOUTH	
COFFIN, William.C.	Midshipman	CAMBRIAN	
COGHLAN, Michael	Ord	GENOA	
COKER, James	A.B.	PHILOMEL	
	A.B.	PIQUE	Syria
COLE, James	Adm Codrington's servant	ASIA	
COLE, John	Pte. R.M.	ASIA	
COLE, John (1)	A.B.	GENOA	
COLE, John (2)	Ord	GENOA	
COLLERO, Vincent	Ord	ALBION	
	Gun Rm Steward	HAZARD	Syria
COLLIER, James	Q.M.	GENOA	(aged 38 years)
	Ord	PSYCHE	Java
COLLINS, John	L.M.	ALBION	
COLLINS, John	Q.M.	ASIA	
	Q.M.	HASTINGS	Syria
COLLINS, Richard	Ord	ROSE	
	Bosun's Mate	HECATE	Syria
COLLINS, Samuel	Pte. R.M.	ALBION	
COLLINS, William	Ord	ALBION	
COLLISTER, John	Ord	ASIA	
COMELATI, William	Clerk	ASIA	
COMERFORD, John	A.B.	ASIA	
CONNOLLY, James	Ord	GENOA	
	Boy 2nd Class	SHANNON	Shannon Wh Chesapeake
	A.B.	IMPLACABLE	Syria
CONNOR, James	A.B.	GLASGOW	
	Boy	NORTHUMBERLAND	St Domingo
	Ord	NEPTUNE	Martinique
CONSTABLE, John	A.B.	ALBION	
	A.B.	EDINBURGH	Syria
CONSTANT, Edward	Pte. R.M.	GENOA	
COOCH, Richard	Landsman	GENOA	
COOK, George	A.B.	ASIA	
	Gunner's Mate	DAPHNE	Syria
COOK, Joseph	Pte. R.M.	ASIA	
	Pte. R.M.	BENBOW	Syria
COOKE, John.M.	Volunteer 1st Cl	ASIA	
COOPER, William	Pte. R.M.	ALBION	
COPPLESTONE, Thomas	Carp's Crew	GENOA	
CORKING, William	A.B.	ASIA	
COTTON, Alexander	College Midshipman	TALBOT	Slty wounded. Gaz.1827/2325
COTTON, Thomas	Boy	CAMBRIAN	
COTTON, William	Boy	CAMBRIAN	
COUZENS, Edward.S.	Volunteer 2nd Cl	GENOA	(M.L. as COZENS)
COUZENS, John	Ord	TALBOT	
	Gunner	MEDEA	Syria

NAVARINO

COWD, William	L.M.	DARTMOUTH	
COX, Charles	Ord	GLASGOW	
COX, Edward	Carp's Crew	GENOA	
CRABB, Samuel	Pte. R.M.	GENOA	
CRADOCK, H.	Lieut Colonel	ASIA	Slty Wounded. Gaz.1827/2324 Became Lord Howden
CRAGIE, William	Carp's Crew	MUSQUITO	
CRANE, Edward	A.B.	ALBION	
CRANG, John.H.	Volunteer 1st Cl	ALBION	(M) China 1842
CRAWLEY, Joseph	Pte. R.M.	ASIA	
CRAY, Paul	Pte. R.M.	ASIA	
CRISPIN, William	Purser's Steward	GENOA	
	Purser's Steward	HERON	Algiers
CROFTS, Richard	Pte. R.M.	ALBION	
CROSS, William	Pte. R.M.	CAMBRIAN	
CROSSE, T.H.B.	Asst Surgeon	MUSQUITO	
CRUIZE, John	Gunner's Crew	ROSE	
	A.B.	IMPREGNABLE	Algiers
CULLIVER, Thomas	Gunner's Crew	GENOA	G.H. 7159
CULLUM, Thomas.F.	Carp's Crew	GENOA	
CULVERHOUSE, James	A.B.	ROSE	(M) Anchor Type LS & GC.
	A.B.	PIQUE	Syria
CUNNINGHAM, Andrew	Ord	GENOA	
CURRANT, Samuel	Pte. R.M.	ASIA	
CURRIN, William	Ord	ASIA	
	A.B.	BENBOW	Syria
CURRY, Douglas	Midshipman	ROSE	Svyl Wounded. Gaz.1827/2325
	Midshipman	PIQUE	Syria
CURTIS, James	Bosun's Mate	GENOA	(M) Anchor Type LS & GC
CURZON, Edward	Flag Captain (to Adm Codrington)	ASIA	L.Gaz.1827/2322 & 2331. CB 1827. St Louis of France, St Vladimir of Russia & Redeemer of Greece
DAFT, Henry	Pte. R.M.	DARTMOUTH	
DALEY, Bryant	A.B.	GENOA	
DALEY, John	Ord	ALBION	(ML as DEALY)
	Ord	Qn CHARLOTTE	Algiers (ML as DAYLY)
DALLIMORE, Henry	Ord	TALBOT	
DAMON, Henry	A.B.	CAMBRIAN	
DANCE, James	Ord	ALBION	(or John.D.)
DANIELL, George	Lieutenant. R.N.	MUSQUITO	
DANIELS, Alexander.L.	Not Given	ASIA	(Not found in Asia)
DARSEY, John	Corporal. R.M.	ALBION	
DAVEY, Joseph	Boy 1st Class	GENOA	
DAVIS, Charles	A.B.	ASIA	
DAVIS, John	Three borne	ASIA	2 A.Bs & Pte RM. Alias WILLIAMS, Thomas.
DAVIS, William	Pte. R.M.	DARTMOUTH	
DAVIS, William	Pte. R.M.	ASIA	
DAWSON, Thomas	Pte. R.M.	ASIA	
	Pte. R.M.	HECATE	Syria
DEACON, John	Pte. R.M.	ALBION	
	Pte. R.M.	MAGICIENNE	Syria
DEAKIN, Richard	Pte. R.M.	ROSE	
DELLAMORE, John	Actg Schoolmaster	TALBOT	Svly Wounded. Gaz.1827/2325
DENNIS, James	Caulker's Mate	GENOA	
DEVAN, Thomas	Capt' Fore Top	ALBION	
DIBBEN, George	Pte. R.M.	ALBION	
DIBBS, William	Ord	ASIA	
DICKIN, John	Armourer	GENOA	
DILKE, Thomas	Flag Lieutenant	ASIA	Promoted to Command Rose.
DIMOND, John	Ord	GLASGOW	(M.L. as DIAMOND)
DOBREE, Thomas.P.	Lieutenant. R.N.	BRISK	
DOLE, Joseph	Pte. R.M.	ALBION	
DOLL, Peter	Gunner's Crew	ALBION	
DONOVAN, James	Pte. R.M.	GENOA	
DONOVAN, James	Ord	ASIA	
DOOLEY, Lawrence	Ord	GENOA	
DORAN, William	Boy	GENOA	
DOREHILL, Arthur.L.	Midshipman	ASIA	
DORIZAC, John	A.B.	GLASGOW	
DOVE, James	Pte. R.M.	CAMBRIAN	
DOWNES, James	Ord	TALBOT	
DOWNEY, John	A.B.	ASIA	
	A.B.	MUTINE	Algiers
DOWNEY, Thomas	Capt' of Mast	ALBION	
	Boy 2nd Class	LEVIATHAN	Trafalgar
	A.B.	Qn CHARLOTTE	Algiers
DOWNS, Thomas	Bosun's Mate	GENOA	
DRAKE, John	Lieutenant. R.N.	ALBION	
	Midshipman	DEFIANCE	Trafalgar
	Lieutenant. R.N.	NORTHUMBERLAND	Northumberland 22 May 1812

DREDGE, James	Pte. R.M.	ALBION	
	Pte. R.M.	BENBOW	Syria
DRISCOLL, James	Landsman	ASIA	(or Jeremiah)
DRURY, Thomas	A.B.	TALBOT	
	A.B.	ZEBRA	Syria
DUKES, James	Boy	MUSQUITO	
	Capt's Coxswain	REVENGE	Syria
DUNN, John	Boy 1st Class	TALBOT	(M) LSGC. Vic.Wide.Dtd 1848.
DUNN, John	A.B.	ASIA	G.H. 3232
	A.B.	CALEDONIA	Basque Roads. 1809
DUNNETT, William	Pte. R.M.	ASIA	
DUNSTONE, Henry	A.B.	DARTMOUTH	
	A.B.	ASIA	Syria
DYE, Martin	A.B.	DARTMOUTH	
DYER, Henry.S.	Admiral's Secy	ASIA	Slty Wounded. Gaz 1827/2324
EAGLE, James	Pte. R.M.	DARTMOUTH	
EARL, John	A.B.	ROSE	
EASTO, Richmond	Master	CAMBRIAN	
	Midshipman	STATIRA	Guadaloupe
EASTON, Nathaniel	Ord	GENOA	
EATON, Joseph	Pte. R.M.	GLASGOW	
EATON, William	Boy 1st Class	CAMBRIAN	
EDGCOMBE, James	Pte. R.M.	ALBION	
EDWARDS, Isaac	Bosun's Mate	CAMBRIAN	
EDWARDS, James	A.B.	BRISK	
EDWARDS, Thomas	Pte. R.M.	ASIA	
ELLIOTT, Robert	Sergeant. R.M.	DARTMOUTH	
ELLIOTT, Thomas	Actg Boatswain	PHILOMEL	Confirmed after Action.
ELLIS, Robert	Midshipman	GLASGOW	
ELLIS, Thomas	Pte. R.M.	ALBION	
ELLIS, Thomas	Boy	GENOA	
	Bosun's Mate	PHOENIX	Syria
ELLISON, Samuel	A.B.	ALBION	
EMANEY, William	Pte. R.M.	GENOA	
EMPTISH, Charles	Capt' After Guard	CAMBRIAN	
ETWELL, Thomas	Pte. R.M.	ASIA	
EVANS, Thomas	A.B.	GENOA	
EVELEIGH, Rev James	Chaplain	GLASGOW	
FELIX, Edward	Gunner's Crew	GENOA	
FELLOWES, Sir Thomas	Captain. R.N.	DARTMOUTH	
	Commander	Gun Boats	B.S. 23 Nov 1810. (P) Knighthood for conspicuous gallantry at Navarino. Knight of Spanish Order of Charles III, L of H, St Anne of Russia & Redeemer of Greece.
FELLOWES, Thomas.A.	Boy 1st Class	DARTMOUTH	
FELLOWES, William.A.	Volunteer 1st Cl	DARTMOUTH	(Son of Sir Thomas)
FELLOWS, Edward	Pte. R.M.	GENOA	
FENLER, John	A.B.	ALBION	
FEWSTER, Francis	Pte. R.M.	ASIA	
FIGG, James	Pte. R.M.	ASIA	G.H. 269
FINLAYSON, William	Adm's Clerk	ASIA	
	Midshipman	IMPREGNABLE	Algiers
FINNEY, George	Capt' Main Top	GENOA	
FITZPATRICK, James	L.M.	ASIA	
FITZROY, F.Charles.	Midshipman	DARTMOUTH	
FLEMING, Samuel	A.B.	TALBOT	
FLETCHER, Samuel	Pte. R.M.	ALBION	
FLINN, Michael	Gunner's Crew	CAMBRIAN	G.H. 8206 as FLYNN(?)
FLINN, Thomas	Capt' Forecastle	ROSE	
FLOWERS, John	A.B.	ASIA	
FLYNN, John	Ship's Corporal	GENOA	
FLYNN, Josiah	Actg Boatswain	TALBOT	
FORBES, Thomas	Yeoman of Signals	CAMBRIAN	
FORBES, Thomas.G.	Midshipman	DARTMOUTH	
	Lieutenant. R.N.	Pcss CHARLOTTE	Syria
FORD, Henry	Ord	ALBION	
FORD, Thomas	Capt's Coxswain	MUSQUITO	
FOSS, Henry	Capt' Fore Top	GLASGOW	
	Bosun's Mate	CYCLOPS	Syria
FOSTER, Rev Thomas	Chaplain	GENOA	
FOWLER, Samuel	Pte. R.M.	GLASGOW	
FRANCE, Joseph	Boy	GLASGOW	
FREELAND, John.O.	Volunteer 1st Cl	ALBION	
	Lieutenant. R.N.	STROMBOLI	Syria
FRENCH, Thomas	Boy 2nd Class	ALBION	
	Capt' Main Top	POWERFUL	Syria
FREW, James	Ord	CAMBRIAN	
FRIEND, Robert	A.B.	CAMBRIAN	(Alias FITTALL)
FRISTRY, John	Pte. R.M.	TALBOT	
	Pte. R.M.	BENBOW	Syria
FURNACE, Robert	A.B.	GENOA	(M) Anchor Ty LSGC. China 1842.
FYNMORE, Thomas	Lieut. R.M.	ASIA	
GALBREATH, John	Coxswain Launch	GENOA	
GAMBIER, Robert.F.	Lieutenant. R.N.	ASIA	

NAVARINO

GANDY, John	Capt's Cook	TALBOT	
GANE, Francis	Corporal. R.M.	ASIA	
GARRATT, William	Sergeant. R.M.	BRISK	
	Sergeant. R.M.	GLASGOW	Algiers
GARRETT, William	A.B.	ALBION	
	Landsman	LEANDER	Algiers
GASKIN, John	Pte. R.M.	ASIA	
GATT, Vincent	Ord	ASIA	
GEE, John	Pte. R.M.	GENOA	
GENNYS, John.H.	Midshipman	CAMBRIAN	
GEORGE, William	A.B.	PHILOMEL	
	A.B.	LEANDER	Algiers
GERRARD, William	Pte. R.M.	GENOA	
GIBBON, George.J.	Volunteer	ASIA	
GIFFARD, Henry.W.	Midshipman	ASIA	(M) Ch 1842.
GILES, Henry.J.	Midshipman	GENOA	
GILLIES, James	Volunteer 2nd Cl	ASIA	
	Schoolmaster	EDINBURGH	Syria
GILLOTT, Charles	Pte. R.M.	ASIA	
GLADDING, William	Pte. R.M.	GENOA	
GODFREY, Richard	Pte. R.M.	GENOA	
GOLDNEY, Harry	Asst Surgeon	GLASGOW	
GOODE, Thomas	Cooper	TALBOT	
GOODMAN, Edward	Pte. R.M.	PHILOMEL	
	Pte. R.M.	BENBOW	Syria
GORE, James	Boy	DARTMOUTH	(M) Ch 1842. Baltic. Arctic.
GOUGH, I.	Capt's Steward	TALBOT	
GOULD, Thomas	Landsman	GENOA	
GRAHAM, Francis	Pte. R.M.	ASIA	
GRANT, George	Pte. R.M.	ALBION	
GRANT, Duncan.B.G.	Mate	GENOA	(P)
	Volunteer 1st Cl	ANDROMACHE	St Sebastian
GRASSIE, Alexander	A.B.	GLASGOW	
GRAVES, Thomas	Pte. R.M.	GENOA	
GRAY, Frederick	Midshipman	ALBION	Svly Wounded. Gaz.1827/2325
GRAY, Henry	Capt's Coxswain	ALBION	
GRAY, Herbert.B.	Midshipman	GENOA	Svly Wounded. Gaz.1827/2325
GRAY, Thomas	A.B.	ASIA	
GRAY, Thomas.B.	Lieut. R.M.	ASIA	
GREEN, Benjamin	Pte. R.M.	GENOA	(Additional clasp?)
GREEN, Thomas	Pte. R.M.	ASIA	
GREEN, William	Gunner's Crew	ALBION	
	Landsman	SUPERB	Algiers
GREET, John	Pte. R.M.	DARTMOUTH	
GREGORY, Thomas	Ord	ALBION	
	A.B.	IMPLACABLE	Syria
GREGORY, William	Pte. R.M.	ALBION	
GREY, Hon George	Midshipman	TALBOT	
GRILLS, James	Ord	GENOA	
GROUBE, William	A.B.	GENOA	
GROWSMITH, George	Carpenter's Crew	BRISK	(M.L. as Henry)
GUARD, William,	A.B.	CAMBRIAN	
GUTTRIDGE, William	Pte. R.M.	CAMBRIAN	
GWILLIM, David	Pte. R.M.	GENOA	
HADLEY, Samuel	A.B.	GLASGOW	
HADLEY, Thomas	Pte. R.M.	GENOA	
HAGGARTY, Timothy	A.B.	GENOA	
HAINES, Thomas	Pte. R.M.	GENOA	
	Pte. R.M.	POWERFUL	Syria
HAINES, William	A.B.	GENOA	
HALLIWELL, Joseph	Pte. R.M.	ROSE	
	Pte. R.M.	PHOENIX	Syria
HAM, Walter	Ord	TALBOT	
HAMBLY, Edward	Gunner's Crew	GENOA	
HAMILTON, John	Ord	CAMBRIAN	
HAMILTON, John	Lieutenant. R.N.	BRISK	(P)
HAMILTON, Peter.W.	Volunteer 1st Cl	BRISK	(M) China 1842
HAMMETT, John	A.B.	GENOA	
	Ord	SUPERB	Algiers
HAMOND, Andrew.S.	Midshipman	TALBOT	
HANAM, George	Ord	CAMBRIAN	(M.L. as HANNAM)
HANCOCK, John	A.B.	GENOA	
	A.B.	POWERFUL	Syria
HARDIMAN, James	Boy	ASIA	
HARDING, James	Pte. R.M.	ASIA	
HARDING, James	Boy	PHILOMEL	
HARDING, William	Pte. R.M.	ALBION	
	Pte. R.M.	REVENGE	Syria
HARKER, Thomas	Pte. R.M.	GLASGOW	
HARMAN, William	Pte. R.M.	GLASGOW	
HARRIGAN, John	Ord	DARTMOUTH	(or HARROGAN)
HARRIS, Job	Pte. R.M.	GENOA	
HARRIS, Robert	Midshipman	CAMBRIAN	(M) China 1842

HARRIS, Robert	Pte. R.M.	GENOA	
HARRIS, Thomas	Capt's Coxswain	DARTMOUTH	(M) Anchor Type LS & GC
	Admiral's Coxswain	Pcss CHARLOTTE	Syria
HARRIS, William	Pte. R.M.	CAMBRIAN	
	Pte. R.M.	REVENGE	Syria
HARRIS, William	A.B.	GENOA	
HARRISS, William	Gunner's Crew	ASIA	
HARRISON, Charles	Ord	ALBION	
HARRISON, John	Sergeant. R.M.	CAMBRIAN	
HARVEY, Benjamin	Pte. R.M.	ALBION	
HARVEY, Henry	Midshipman	ASIA	
HARVEY, John	A.B.	GENOA	
HARVEY, Richard	Landsman	ALBION	
HARVEY, Robert.B.	Volunteer 1st Cl	ASIA	
HARVEY, William	A.B.	ALBION	(Alias as HARDY)
HASTINGS, Charles	Boy	GLASGOW	
	Yeoman Signals	MAGICIENNE	Syria
HAWKES, Robert	Ord	ASIA	
HAWKINS, Daniel	Landsman	GENOA	
HAWKINS, Richard	A.B.	CAMBRIAN	
HAWKINS, William	Ord	DARTMOUTH	(M) China 1842
HAY, Robert.S.	Lieutenant. R.N.	TALBOT	Slty Wounded. Gaz.1827/2325
HAYES, John (1)	Ord	TALBOT	
	A.B.	TALBOT	Syria
HAYES, John (2)	Ord	TALBOT	(M) LSGC. Vic Wide. Dtd 1848.
HAYES, Patrick	Ord	GENOA	
	Capt' After Guard	THUNDERER	Syria
HAYTER, Stephen	Pte. R.M.	ASIA	
HAYWARD, James	Boy	ROSE	
	A.B.	Pcss CHARLOTTE	Syria
HEAD, William	Corporal. R.M.	ASIA	
HEATHMAN, John.C.	Clerk	GLASGOW	
HEDGE, Mathew.B.	Pte. R.M.	ALBION	
HEGAN, Edward	A.B.	ALBION	
HEMING, Francis	Capt's Cook	GLASGOW	
HEMSLEY, William	Master	BRISK	
HENDERSON, Jonathan	Boy	GENOA	Died 6 Feb 1906.
HENDERSON, George	Pte. R.M.	ASIA	
	Pte. R.M.	BENBOW	Syria
HENRY, George.A.	Midshipman	TALBOT	
HENSHAW, John	Pte. R.M.	ALBION	
HERRY, Thomas	Pte. R.M.	GENOA	
HEYWOOD, Josh	Pte. R.M.	ASIA	
HILDRETH, Joseph	Pte. R.M.	GENOA	
HILL, Joshua	Actg 2nd Master	GENOA	
HILL, Walter	Ord	GENOA	
HILL, William	Boy	ASIA	
HILL, William	Boy	GENOA	
HILLIER, Henry	A.B.	PHILOMEL	
HILLS, Samuel	A.B.	ASIA	
HILLYAR, Robert.P.	Surgeon	ALBION	
	Surgeon	ROEBUCK	Egypt
	Surgeon	APOLLO	B.S. 1 Nov 1809 (M) 1824. Knight Tower & Sword, King John jewel – Windsor Castle.
HINES, Francis	Boy	ASIA	
	A.B.	Pcss CHARLOTTE	Syria
HOARE, Gerrard.N.	Volunteer	GLASGOW	
HOBBS, Edward	Pte. R.M.	PHILOMEL	
HOBBS, John	A.B.	ASIA	
HODGSKIN, James.A.	A.B.	ALBION	
HODGSKINS, George	Purser	ALBION	
	Clerk	SCORPION	Scorpion 31 March 1804
HOLBERTON, Henry	Pte. R.M.	GENOA	
HOLBORN, Thomas	Pte. R.M.	GENOA	(or OBURN, John)
HOLINWOOD, David	Pte. R.M.	GLASGOW	
HOLLAND, Robert	Pte. R.M.	GENOA	
HOLLOWAY, Pryse.A.	Midshipman	BRISK	
HOLMES, Henry	A.B.	GLASGOW	
HOLMWOOD, David	Pte. R.M.	GLASGOW	G.H. 8321
	Pte. R.M.	ZEBRA	Syria
HOLTON, Daniel	Pte. R.M.	GLASGOW	
	Pte. R.M.	GLASGOW	Algiers
HOLYOAK, Edward	Pte. R.M.	PHILOMEL	
	Pte. R.M.	STROMBOLI	Syria
HOPE, Hon George	Volunteer 1st Cl	CAMBRIAN	
HOPE, Thomas	Midshipman	GLASGOW	
HOPKINSON, Samuel	Carp's Crew	DARTMOUTH	
HORN, Alexander	Master	DARTMOUTH	
HORNBROOK, William	Boy	ASIA	
HORTH, James	Ord	GENOA	
HOUGHTON, Edward	A.B.	DARTMOUTH	
HOWES, John	A.B.	ASIA	(May read HOWS)
HOWLETT, John	Ord	GLASGOW	

NAVARINO

Name	Rank	Ship	Notes
HUGGINS, John	Boy	TALBOT	
	A.B.	WASP	Syria
HUGHES, Henry	A.B.	CAMBRIAN	
	Capt' Fore Top	BENBOW	Syria
HUGHES, Henry	Pte. R.M.	TALBOT	
HUGHES, John	A.B.	TALBOT	
	A.B.	CASTOR	Syria
HUGHES, Stephen	A.B.	ALBION	
HUGHES, Thomas	A.B.	GLASGOW	
HUGHES, Thomas	Pte. R.M.	GENOA	
HUMBY, James	Boy	DARTMOUTH	
HUNT, Henry	Pte. R.M.	ALBION	
HUNT, John	Ord	GLASGOW	
HUNT, Moses	Ord	CAMBRIAN	
HUNT, Samuel	Pte. R.M.	DARTMOUTH	
HUNT, William	Ord	GENOA	
HUNTLEY, Charles	Pte. R.M.	ALBION	
HURDLE, Thomas	2nd Lieut. R.M.	ALBION	Died 7-6-1889 a General
HURLOCK, Richard	Ord	ALBION	
HUSON, Thomas	Ord	GENOA	
HUSSEY, Bartholomew	Pte. R.M.	MUSQUITO	G.H. 8708
HUTCHINSON, William	Capt' Forecastle	TALBOT	(M) Anchor Type LS & GC
	Q.M.	BENBOW	Syria
HYDE, James	Pte. R.M.	TALBOT	
HYNE, William.E.	Volunteer 1st Cl	ALBION	(M) China 1842
INCHES, Charles	Surgeon	CAMBRIAN	
	Asst Surgeon	ROYAL OAK	B.S. 14 Dec 1814
INSKIP, Peter.P.	Midshipman	GENOA	(M) Royal Humane Society.
IRVINE, Samuel	Surgeon	DARTMOUTH	(M) A of I. Gilbert Blane.
IRVING, Samuel	Capt' Fore Top	CAMBRIAN	(or William)
IZZO, Giovanni	A.B.	ALBION	
JACKSON, John	Sergeant. R.M.	GENOA	(M) China 1842
JACKSON, Thomas	A.B.	ALBION	
	A.B.	VANGUARD	Syria
JACOBS, George	Carp's Crew	ASIA	
JACOBS, Richard	A.B.	ASIA	
	Coxswain Pinnace	POWERFUL	Syria
JAMIESON, James	A.B.	GLASGOW	
JARVIS, Thomas	Ord	BRISK	
JEFFREY, Robert.M.	Clerk	PHILOMEL	(May read JEFFERY)
JEFFRIES, James	Landsman	ALBION	
JEFFRIES, Richard	Pte. R.M.	GENOA	
JENKINS, William	A.B.	DARTMOUTH	(M) Anchor Type LS & GC
JENNETT, John	Ord	ALBION	
JOHNS, Samuel	A.B.	GENOA	(M) LSGC. Vic Wide. Dtd 1848
JOHNSON, Francis.H.	Pte. R.M.	ASIA	
JOHNSON, John (1)	Armourer's Mate	CAMBRIAN	(or JOHNSTONE)
	Landsman	IMPREGNABLE	Algiers
JOHNSON, John (2)	A.B.	CAMBRIAN	
	A.B.	EDINBURGH	Syria
JOHNSON, John	Ord	GLASGOW	
	Ord	ASIA	Syria
JOHNSTON, James.C.	Mate	ASIA	(P)
JOHNSTON, Thomas	Pte. R.M.	ALBION	
JONES, Edward	Pte. R.M.	ASIA	
JONES, James	Pte. R.M.	CAMBRIAN	
JONES, John	Ord	CAMBRIAN	
JONES, Stephen	A.B.	ASIA	
	Carp's Crew	MEDEA	Syria
JONES, Thomas	Pte. R.M.	ASIA	
JONES, Thomas	Cook's Mate	TALBOT	
JONES, William	Carp's Crew	ASIA	
JORDAN, John	Capt's Steward	MUSQUITO	
JORDAN, William	Pte. R.M.	GENOA	
JORDON, Michael	Pte. R.M.	DARTMOUTH	
KEEMER, George	A.B.	ROSE	
	Capt' Forecastle	PHOENIX	Syria
KEFFER, William	A.B.	GENOA	
KELL, William	Boy	DARTMOUTH	
KELLOCK, John	Volunteer 2nd Cl	DARTMOUTH	
KELLY, James	Corporal R.M.	TALBOT	
KELLY, Nicholas	Cook	ASIA	
KELNER, Charles	A.B.	GLASGOW	
KEMP, George	Caulker's Mate	ASIA	
KEMP, James	Boy	GLASGOW	
KEMP, John	Drummer. R.M.	ALBION	
KEMP, John	Pte. R.M.	ROSE	
KEMP, John	Pte. R.M.	ASIA	G.H. 2726
KEMPSTER, Robert	Ord	CAMBRIAN	
	A.B.	CAMBRIDGE	Syria
KENNEDY, John	A.B.	ASIA	
KENNELL, John	Ord	ASIA	
	A.B.	REVENGE	Syria

KENNY, Peter	Gunner's Mate	PHILOMEL	
	Ord	ALBION	Algiers
KENT, Frederick	A.B.	ASIA	(Duplicate issued 12-12-1850)
KERSLEY, William	Ord	ALBION	
KEYS, Charles	A.B.	PHILOMEL	
	Gunner	STROMBOLI	Syria
KINDNESS, Benjamin	Q.M.	ALBION	
	Boy	PHOEBE	Trafalgar
	Ord	PHOEBE	Java
			(Also entitled but not on Roll for 'Off Tamatave 20 May 1814' & 'Phoebe 28 March 1814')
KING, Abraham	Pte. R.M.	GENOA	
KING, John	Boy	ASIA	
KING, Joseph.N.	Actg 2nd Master	ALBION	
KING, Samuel	Drummer. R.M.	ASIA	
KING, Thomas	Landsman	ASIA	
KINGDOM, William	Carp's Crew	ASIA	
KNIGHT, George	A.B.	GENOA	
KNIGHT, Robert	Boy	GLASGOW	
KNOWLES, James	Boy	MUSQUITO	(M.L. as John)
	Sailmaker's Crew	STROMBOLI	Syria
KNOX, Thomas	A.B.	CAMBRIAN	
	A.B.	POWERFUL	Syria
LAKE, William	A.B.	GENOA	
LAMB, George	A.B.	ASIA	
LANDER, Thomas	A.B.	GLASGOW	
LANE, John	Coxswain	ALBION	
LANE, Thomas	A.B.	ASIA	
LANGAN, Michael	Pte. R.M.	ASIA	
LANGFORD, John	A.B.	GLASGOW	
	A.B.	CASTOR	Syria
LANGTRY, Joseph.M.	Mate	ALBION	(P)
LANGTRY, William.H.	Volunteer 1st Cl	DARTMOUTH	O'By.631. Died in 1846. Medal should not have been approved.
LANIN, John	Ord	ASIA	(May read LANNON)
LASKEY, George	Landsman	ALBION	
LASSERA, Henry	A.B.	CAMBRIAN	(or LASSARE, Honore)
LATIMER, George	Yeoman Signals	ASIA	
LAURENCE, James	Ord	GENOA	
LAVITON, William	Pte. R.M.	CAMBRIAN	
LAWRENCE, Samuel	Corporal. R.M.	ROSE	
	Corporal. R.M.	REVOLUTIONNAIRE	4 Nov 1805
LAYTON, Francis	Ord	ASIA	(or LATINE)
LEAH, Edward	Asst Surgeon	ALBION	
LEAT, Charles	A.B.	ASIA	
LECQUIRE, Henry	Boy	GLASGOW	
LEE, William	Carpenter	GLASGOW	
	Carp's Crew	LEVIATHAN	Trafalgar
LEE, William.V.	Mate	ASIA	(P) Svly Wnd. Gaz.1827/2324
LEGARD, James.A.	Mate	MUSQUITO	(M) Kt Tower & Sword
LEITH, Andrew	A.B.	GLASGOW	
	A.B.	AKBAR	Java
LEONARD, William	Capt's Coxswain	CAMBRIAN	(Alias LENNARD)
	Boy	BUCEPHALUS	Java
			(M) Anchor Type LS & GC
LEVERT, John	Q.M.	DARTMOUTH	
LEVETT, James	Pte. R.M.	GLASGOW	
	Pte. R.M.	CAMBRIDGE	Syria
LEWIS, David	Boy	ASIA	
LIDDELL, John	Surgeon	ASIA	
LINDSAY, William	Asst Surgeon	GENOA	
LLOYD, William	A.B.	ASIA	G.H. 7311
LONG, John	A.B.	GLASGOW	G.H. 9851
LOVE, Henry	Capt' Main Top	ASIA	
LOVE, Robert	A.B.	ROSE	
LOVELL, William	Gunner's Mate	GENOA	
LOWE, Robert	Ord	ASIA	
LUCAS, Thomas	Ord	GENOA	G.H. 9024
LUMSDEN, William	Landsman	GENOA	
LUSHINGTON, Stephen	Lieutenant. R.N.	CAMBRIAN	(M) St Louis of France, Redeemer of Greece
LYHANE, Daniel	Ord	DARTMOUTH	
LYON, Primrose	Surgeon	GLASGOW	
	Asst Surgeon	ROYAL SOVEREIGN	Trafalgar
MACKENZIE, James.G.	Midshipman	PHILOMEL	
MACKEY, Alexander	Drummer. R.M.	GENOA	
MACKLIN, George	A.B.	ASIA	
MADREN, John	Capt' Fore Top	GENOA	(or MADDRIN)
MALLARD, Edward	Schoolmaster	ALBION	
MALONE, Michael	M.A.A.	CAMBRIAN	
MAN, George	Ord	ALBION	
MANN, William	Pte. R.M.	TALBOT	
MARLEY, William	Landsman	ALBION	
MARSDEN, John	Pte. R.M.	GLASGOW	

NAVARINO

MARSH, Samuel	Q.M.	GENOA	
MARTIN, Abraham	A.B.	GLASGOW	
MARTIN, George.B.	Commander	MUSQUITO	I/Cmd. Rcd C.B., K.S.L., K.S.A. & K.R.G. for services.
MARTIN, Thomas	Ord	GENOA	
MARTIN, William	Ord	DARTMOUTH	
MASON, James	A.B.	PHILOMEL	
MASON, Joseph	Pte. R.M.	ALBION	
	Bombdr. R.M.A.	HECATE	Syria
MASON, Thomas	Pte. R.M.	GENOA	
MASON, William	Pte. R.M.	MUSQUITO	
MASSIE, Thomas.L.	Mate	ASIA	(P) Lt in death vacancy.
	Lieutenant. R.N.	THUNDERER	Syria (P) to Captain. Died 20-7-1898 aged 95 yrs as an Admiral.
MATLESS, John	Pte. R.M.	GLASGOW	
MATTHEWS, George	A.B.	ASIA	
	A.B.	EDINBURGH	Syria
MATTHEWS, Samuel	Ord	CAMBRIAN	
MATTINSON, Thomas	Gunner	MUSQUITO	
	Landsman	BEAULIEU	Camperdown
	Gunner	CAROLINE	Banda Neira
MATTOCKS, James	Pte. R.M.	GENOA	
	Pte. R.M.	STROMBOLI	Syria
MAUNDER, William	Pte. R.M.	GENOA	
MAY, John	Boy 1st Class	GENOA	
MAYBEER, Nicholas	Carp's Crew	GENOA	
MAYER, George.H.	Drummer. R.M.	GLASGOW	
McBRIDE, Peter	Pte. R.M.	GLASGOW	
McCANN, Neil	Pte. R.M.	CAMBRIAN	
	Pte. R.M.	Qn CHARLOTTE	Algiers
McCARTHY, Daniel	Boy	ASIA	
McCLEVERTY, James.J.	Midshipman	ASIA	(M) China 1842
McCUGH, Pugh	Pte. R.M.	ALBION	
	Pte. R.M.	BENBOW	Syria
McGAREY, Michael	Pte. R.M.	ROSE	
McILWAINE, Samuel	Ord	CAMBRIAN	
McINDOE, Patrick	Boy	ASIA	
McKAY, Hugh	Pte. R.M.	BRISK	
	Pte. R.M.	HASTINGS	Syria
McLEOD, Joseph	L.M.	DARTMOUTH	
McMAHON, Thomas	A.B.	GENOA	
MEALING, Henry	Pte. R.M.	DARTMOUTH	
MELLING, John	Pte. R.M.	GENOA	
MELLISH, James	A.B.	GENOA	
MENEAR, John	A.B.	CAMBRIAN	
MERRELLS, Joseph	Pte. R.M.	TALBOT	
METCALFE, William.C.	College Volunteer	ASIA	(M) China 1842
MILBANK, James	Pte. R.M.	TALBOT	
MILLER, James	Pte. R.M.	ALBION	
MILLER, John	2nd Lieut. R.M.	GENOA	
	Captain. R.M.	POWERFUL	Syria
MILLER, William	Master	GENOA	
MILLCOCK, John	Pte. R.M.	GENOA	
MILLS, John	Q.M.	DARTMOUTH	Impressed ex-smuggler.
MILLS, William	Q.M.	TALBOT	
MINIFEE, Robert	Pte. R.M.	GENOA	G.H. 8733
MITCHELL, John	Q.M.	GENOA	
MITCHELL, John	Corporal. R.M.	GENOA	
MOARHEAD, Fergus	Landsman	DARTMOUTH	
MOGFORD, John	Landsman	DARTMOUTH	
MOGG, George	Purser's Steward	PHILOMEL	
MONCK, William	Pte. R.M.	TALBOT	(or as MOUNK)
MONDAY, John	Lieutenant. R.N.	GLASGOW	
MONFALCAN, John	Ship's Corporal	GLASGOW	
MOON, Thomas	Pte. R.M.	ASIA	
MOOR, William	Cook	CAMBRIAN	
MOORE, James	Pte. R.M.	GENOA	
MOORE, Thomas	A.B.	GLASGOW	
	Sailmaker's Mate	EDINBURGH	Syria
MOORE, William	Pte. R.M.	CAMBRIAN	
MOORE, William	Pte. R.M.	TALBOT	
	Pte. R.M.	Qn CHARLOTTE	Algiers
MOREY, William	Pte. R.M.	CAMBRIAN	
	Corporal. R.M.	STROMBOLI	Syria
MORGAN, James	Capt' Fore Top	DARTMOUTH	
	Ord	SUPERB	Algiers
MORGAN, John	Ord	ASIA	
MORGAN, Thomas	Admiral's Retinue	ASIA	(Additional clasp?)
MORGAN, Thomas	Pte. R.M.	GENOA	
MORLEY, James	Landsman	ALBION	
MORRIS, Evan	Pte. R.M.	CAMBRIAN	
MORRIS, Henry.G.	College Midshipman	GLASGOW	

MORRIS, John	Boy	TALBOT	
MORRIS, William	Lieutenant. R.N.	GENOA	
MORTIMER, John	Sailmaker	TALBOT	(M) Anchor Type LS & GC
	Sailmaker	IMPREGNABLE	Algiers
MORTON, Rev David	Chaplain	ASIA	
MOTLEY, Francis	A.B.	PHILOMEL	
MOULTON, John	A.B.	TALBOT	
MURPHY, John	A.B.	ASIA	G.H. 9548
MURRAY, Alexander	Midshipman	PHILOMEL	(M) A of I/AVA
MURRAY, Alexander	Landsman	DARTMOUTH	
MURRAY, Thomas	Boy 1st Class	TALBOT	G.H. 6911
MURTON, Henry.F.	2nd Lieut. R.M.	ASIA	
MUSGROVE, Peter	Gunner's Crew	MUSQUITO	
NANCARRON, William	Pte. R.M.	GLASGOW	
NAPLETON, John	Ord	TALBOT	
NEAL, John	Pte. R.M.	ASIA	
	Corporal. R.M.	VANGUARD	Syria
NEALE, William.J.	Volunteer 2nd Cl	TALBOT	Died March 1893. Aged 80 Yrs.
NELDER, Peter	Carp's Crew	ALBION	(M) Anchor Type LS & GC
NEW, Joseph	Boy	ALBION	
	Ord	Pcss CHARLOTTE	Syria
NEWBERRY, William	Pte. R.M.	DARTMOUTH	
NEWBURY, George	Gunner's Crew	PHILOMEL	(Or NEWBERRY. From Liffey)
	Boatswain	RODNEY	Syria
			(M) A of I. AVA. as NEWBERRY.
NEWBY, Thomas	Pte. R.M.	ALBION	
NEWMAN, Robert	Pte. R.M.	ASIA	
NEWPORT, William	Pte. R.M.	ASIA	
	Sergeant. R.M.	CAMBRIDGE	Syria
NIAS, Joseph	Lieutenant. R.N.	ASIA	(M) China 1842 & Arctic
NICHOLL, William	A.B.	ASIA	(& as NICOLL)
NICHOLLS, James	Ord	TALBOT	
NICHOLSON, Francis	Landsman	ALBION	
NORCOT, Edmund	Lieutenant. R.N.	ALBION	
	Midshipman	MINDEN	Java
NORRIS, John	1st Lieut. R.M.	GLASGOW	
	2nd Lieut. R.M.	MELAMPUS	Guadaloupe
	1st Lieut. R.M.	REVOLUTIONNAIRE	St Sebastian
	1st Lieut. R.M.	SUPERB	Algiers
NORRIS, Joseph	Pte. R.M.	ROSE	
NOSTER, Richard	Boy	DARTMOUTH	
NOWLAN, John	Pte. R.M.	ASIA	
OAKES, John	Ord	ALBION	
OATRIDGE, William	A.B.	GENOA	
(OBORN see HOLBORN)			
OLIVER, Richard.A.	Midshipman	GLASGOW	
	Lieutenant. R.N.	ASIA	Syria
O'MALEY, James	Gunner's Crew	TALBOT	
OMMANNEY, Erasmus	Volunteer 1st Cl	ALBION	
OMMANNEY, John.A.	Captain. R.N.	ALBION	(M). C.B. for Navarino
			& K.S.L., K.S.V., K.R.G.
	Lieutenant. R.N.	Qn CHARLOTTE	23rd June 1795.
			Died 21-12-1904. 90 as Adm.
O'NEILL, John	Carp's Crew	GENOA	
	Carp's Crew	IMPREGNABLE	Algiers
ORGAN, William	Carp's Yeoman	GENOA	
ORMOND, Thomas	Pte. R.M.	TALBOT	
OSBORNE, John	A.B.	GENOA	
OSMOND, Elisha	Pte. R.M.	CAMBRIAN	
	Pte. R.M.	POWERFUL	Syria
OTTER, Henry.C.	Midshipman	CAMBRIAN	
OVENS, Charles	Pte. R.M.	GENOA	
OWENS, Owen	A.B.	ASIA	
PACK, John	Boy	GLASGOW	
PAGE, Nicholas	A.B.	ASIA	
PAGET, Lord Clarence.E.	Midshipman	TALBOT	Died aged 83 as Adm 3-1895.
PARK, John	A.B.	GLASGOW	
PARKER, John	A.B.	ASIA	
PARKER, Johnathan	A.B.	ALBION	
PARKER, Stephen	A.B.	CAMBRIAN	
	A.B.	RODNEY	Syria
PARKINS, John	A.B.	ASIA	
PARKINSON, John	A.B.	CAMBRIAN	
PARNELL, H.W.	Midshipman	GLASGOW	Died as Lord Congleton aged 87 years
			10-10-1896.
PARR, James	A.B.	CAMBRIAN	
PARSONS, George	Pte. R.M.	CAMBRIAN	
PARTRIDGE, Richard	Pte. R.M.	GENOA	
PASMORE, Henry	Boy	GLASGOW	
PATTERSON, Thomas	Capt' Main Top	DARTMOUTH	
PAYNTER, James.A.D.	Midshipman	GENOA	
PEARN, George	A.B.	GENOA	

NAVARINO

PEARSON, Andrew	A.B.	ALBION	(M) Anchor Type LS & GC
	Capt' Forecastle	EDINBURGH	Syria
PEARSON, John	Boy	GENOA	
PEED, James	A.B.	MUSQUITO	(M.L. as PEID)
	A.B.	SUPERB	Algiers
PELHAM, Hon. D.W.A.	Volunteer 1st Cl	DARTMOUTH	
PENDLEBURY, Gerard	Pte. R.M.	GLASGOW	
PENFOUND, James	Carp's Crew	DARTMOUTH	
PEPERDAY, Benjamin	Pte. R.M.	ASIA	
PETTY, Edward	Pte. R.M.	GENOA	
PHILIPS, Griffith.G.	Midshipman	DARTMOUTH	
PHILIPS, William	Q.M.	MUSQUITO	(M.L. as PHILLIPS)
PHILLIPS, Alexander	Capt's Coxswain	ASIA	
	Capt's Coxswain	HASTINGS	Syria
PHILLIPS, James	Ord	ALBION	
PHILP, Henry	Ord	GENOA	
	Ord	TALBOT	Syria
PHYSICK, Joseph	Caulker	DARTMOUTH	
PICKWICK, John	Corporal. R.M.	CAMBRIAN	
PIKE, Peter	Caulker's Mate	ALBION	
	Carpenter's Mate	HECATE	Java
PIPER, John	A.B.	ASIA	
	Ord	NEPTUNE	Trafalgar
PIPPETT, Thomas	A.B.	GLASGOW	G.H. 1022
	Boy	SURVEILLANTE	St Sebastian
PITMAN, John.C.	Volunteer 1st Cl	ROSE	Died Capt' aged 84 yrs 7-1898
POLACCA, Lewis	Supn Boy	GENOA	
POLLARD, Thomas	Pte. R.M.	DARTMOUTH	
POOLE, Samuel	A.B.	PHILOMEL	(From Liffey. Not A of I Roll)
	Cook	PIQUE	Syria
POPE, James	A.B.	DARTMOUTH	
POPHAM, Thomas	Ship's Corporal	ALBION	
PORTEOUS, Francis.P.	Volunteer 1st Cl	GENOA	
PORTMAN, Wyndham.B.	Lieutenant. R.N.	TALBOT	
POTTS, John	Boy	ROSE	
POUNDS, Thomas	Q.M.	MUSQUITO	
POWELL, James	A.B.	DARTMOUTH	
POWELL, John	Pte. R.M.	ALBION	
POWELL, John	A.B.	TALBOT	
POWELL, Thomas	Carpenter's Crew	GLASGOW	
POWELL, Thomas	A.B.	DARTMOUTH	G.H. 10,120
	Boy	GANGES	Copenhagen 1801
POWER, John	A.B.	GLASGOW	
POWERS, Martin	Capt' Fore Top	GLASGOW	G.H. 9004
POWERS, Thomas	Ord	DARTMOUTH	
PRAED, James	Ord	ALBION	
PRENDERGAST, John	A.B.	ALBION	
PRIDEAUX, John	A.B.	TALBOT	(M) China 1842. Anchor Ty & Vic Wide LSGC medals. Group 4 known 1881, all separated by 1905.
PRITCHARD, Samuel	Pte. R.M.	GLASGOW	
PRYNN, John	A.B.	ALBION	
	A.B.	RODNEY	Syria
PURVES, Archibald	Pte. R.M.	ASIA	
PYNE, James	Pte. R.M.	TALBOT	
QUAYLE, Thomas	A.B.	ALBION	
	A.B.	STROMBOLI	Syria
QUINTON, George	A.B.	CAMBRIAN	
QUINTON, John	Capt' of Mast	GLASGOW	
RABETT, George.W.	Lieutenant. R.N.	MUSQUITO	
	Boy 3rd Class	GALATEA	Off Tamatave. 20 May 1811
	Midshipman	CYDNUS	B.S. 14 Dec 1814
RACKETT, Edward	Ord	ASIA	
RADFORD, William	Landsman	DARTMOUTH	(M) Vic Wide LSGC dated 1848.
RAMPLY, Thomas	Capt's Steward	DARTMOUTH	
RAMSAY, William	Lieutenant. R.N.	ALBION	
RANCE, James	Pte. R.M.	ALBION	
RAVELLING, John	Gunner's Crew	GLASGOW	
RAWKINS, James	Pte. R.M.	ASIA	
RAY, Joshua	Landsman	ASIA	
RAY, William	Ord	GLASGOW	
	A.B.	CAMBRIDGE	Syria
REARDON, Simon	Boy	ALBION	
REDMAN, John	Pte. R.M.	ALBION	
	Pte. R.M.	THUNDERER	Syria
REEVES, Jeremiah	Ord	ROSE	
REMINGTON, George	Not Given	PHILOMEL	(Not found in Philomel)
RENNY, William	Boy	ROSE	
RESHEN, William	A.B.	CAMBRIAN	
RETSON, John	Landsman	ALBION	
REVINGTON, Patrick	A.B.	GENOA	
RHODES, Thomas	Pte. R.M.	ALBION	
RHODES, Thomas	Pte. R.M.	GENOA	

RIALL, William.H.	Mate	CAMBRIAN	(P)
RICHARDS, James	Ord	GLASGOW	
RICHARDS, John	Ord	CAMBRIAN	
RICHARDS, William	Ord	ASIA	
	A.B.	RODNEY	Syria
RICHARDS, William	A.B.	CAMBRIAN	
RICHARDSON, Henry	Ord	ALBION	
RIDDING, Owen	Capt' of Mast	ASIA	
	A.B.	Qn CHARLOTTE	Algiers
RILEY, Thomas	Ord	GENOA	
RIND, David	A.B.	ASIA	
RIORDAN, Daniel	Ord	DARTMOUTH	(M.L. as REARDON)
RIPPON, John	A.B.	GENOA	G.H. 7013
	A.B.	ASIA	Syria
RISHEN, William	A.B.	CAMBRIAN	(Found as RESHEN)
	Landsman	CERBERUS	Lissa
ROBB, John	Lieutenant. R.N.	HIND	(Tender to Asia)
	Master's Mate	CORDELIA	Algiers
ROBERTS, George	Boy	DARTMOUTH	
ROBERTSON, Andrew	A.B.	GLASGOW	
ROBINSON, Daniel	Ord	ASIA	
ROBINSON, George	Gunner's Yeoman	GENOA	
ROBINSON, John	A.B.	MUSQUITO	
ROBINSON, Reuben	Pte. R.M.	ASIA	
ROBINSON, Richard	Landsman	ALBION	
ROBINSON, Thomas.P.	Lieutenant. R.N.	GENOA	
	Midshipman	ROYAL SOVEREIGN	Trafalgar
ROBINSON, William	A.B.	CAMBRIAN	(M) Anchor Type LS & GC
	Q.M.	BENBOW	Syria
ROBINSON, William	Purser's Steward	GENOA	
ROGERS, George	Landsman	ALBION	
ROGERS, John	Ord	GLASGOW	
ROLLINS, James	Pte. R.M.	CAMBRIAN	
	Pte. R.M.	HASTINGS	Syria
ROPER, John	Boy	ALBION	
ROSE, John	Boy	DARTMOUTH	
	Gunner's Mate	POWERFUL	Syria
ROSE, Thomas	A.B.	ROSE	
ROSS, David	Carp's Crew	GENOA	
ROSS, Thomas	Pte. R.M.	BRISK	
ROSSO, Mathio	A.B.	ASIA	
ROTHERAM, Thomas	Landsman	ALBION	
ROWE, John	A.B.	TALBOT	
	Ord	MUTINE	Algiers
ROWLAND, John	Ord	GLASGOW	
RUDD, William	Pte. R.M.	GENOA	
RUNDLE, John	Ord	GENOA	
RUSH, Edward	Pte. R.M.	ASIA	
RUSSELL, Lord Edward	Lieutenant. R.N.	PHILOMEL	
RUSSELL, Godfrey	Midshipman	ALBION	
RUSSELL, John	Boy	ASIA	
RUSSELL, Josh	Pte. R.M.	MUSQUITO	
RUSSELL, William	A.B.	ASIA	
RYDER, Michael	Ord	ASIA	
	A.B.	THUNDERER	Syria
SACKREE, Thomas	A.B.	PHILOMEL	Impressed ex-smuggler
SAFFIN, William	Pte. R.M.	GENOA	
SANDERS, Richard	Pte. R.M.	ALBION	
SANDFORD, James	Ord	DARTMOUTH	
SANDY, Stephen	Pte. R.M.	ALBION	
SANKEY, Francis	Surgeon	MUSQUITO	
SANKEY, Frederic	Landsman	MUSQUITO	
SARRIDGE, John	Pte. R.M.	TALBOT	
SAUNDERS, John	Cooper's Crew	ALBION	
SAUNDERS, Samuel	A.B.	ALBION	
	A.B.	HYDRA	Syria
SAVAGE, Henry	Ord	GLASGOW	
SAVAGE, John	Pte. R.M.	ASIA	
SAVAGE, William	Ord	ALBION	
SAVORY, Richard.F.	Acting Clerk	ASIA	
SCANDLING, John.H.	Gunner's Mate	MUSQUITO	
SCHOMBERG, Henry.C.	Lieutenant. R.N.	GLASGOW	
SCOATES, William	Q.M.	CAMBRIAN	(M) Anchor Type LS & GC
SCOTT, Charles	Lieut. R.M.	DARTMOUTH	
SCOTT, Henry	A.B.	CAMBRIAN	
SCOTT, Thomas	Lieut. R.M.	DARTMOUTH	
SCOTT, William.J.	Cooper	ASIA	
SCREECH, Josh	Bosun's Mate	GENOA	
SEAGROVE, Charles	Boy	ASIA	
	Capt' After Guard	POWERFUL	Syria
SERGEANT, John	A.B.	DARTMOUTH	
SHACKLES, William	Pte. R.M.	GENOA	(M) Anchor Type LS & GC
SHALL, James	Color Sgt. R.M.	TALBOT	
SHANNON, James	Pte. R.M.	GENOA	
	Pte. R.M.	CAMBRIDGE	Syria

NAVARINO

SHEATH, James	Pte. R.M.	ALBION	
SHEPHERD, John	Pte. R.M.	ASIA	(also as SHEPPEAR)
SHERGOLD, Isaac	Armourer's Mate	ASIA	
SHERWELL, Thomas	Boy	DARTMOUTH	
	Bosun's Mate	MAGICIENNE	Syria
SHIELDS, Edward	A.B.	ROSE	
	Gunner	HYDRA	Syria
SHORT, William	Ord	CAMBRIAN	
SHOTTER, William	Boy	GENOA	
	A.B.	RODNEY	Syria
SILLY, William	Carpenter	GENOA	
	Carpenter	LYRA	Basque Roads. 1809
SIM (or SYM), Thomas	Pte. R.M.	GLASGOW	
SIMMONDS, Jacob	Pte. R.M.	ALBION	
SIMMONDS, John	Not given	ASIA	"additional claim"
SIMMONS, William	Carp's Crew	ASIA	
SITTON, James	Landsman	ASIA	
SKEATES, William	Pte. R.M.	ALBION	
SLATER, John	Pte. R.M.	DARTMOUTH	
SMALE, John	Pte. R.M.	GENOA	(also as SMALL)
SMART, Robert	Lieutenant. R.N.	CAMBRIAN	
	Midshipman	GLASGOW	Algiers
SMITH, Andrew	Asst Surgeon	DARTMOUTH	
SMITH, Charles	A.B.	GENOA	
SMITH, Henry	Carp's Mate	ASIA	G.H. 5260
SMITH, Henry	A.B.	ASIA	
SMITH, James	Boy 1st Class	ALBION	
	Purser's Steward	ASIA	Syria
SMITH, James	M.A.A.	ALBION	
	Ord	REVENGE	Basque Roads. 1809
	M.A.A.	SUPERB	Algiers
			(M) Anchor Type LS & GC
SMITH, John	Pte. R.M.	ASIA	3 entries. 3 medals?
SMITH, John	Not Given	ASIA	Borne. 6 Seamen & 5 R.Ms.
SMITH, John	Gunner. R.M.A.	ALBION	
SMITH, John	Pte. R.M.	ROSE	
SMITH, Joseph	Boy 2nd Class	ALBION	
SMITH, Joseph	Ord	DARTMOUTH	
SMITH, Robert	Pte. R.M.	ALBION	
SMITH, Samuel	Armourer's Mate	GENOA	
SMITH, William	Not Given	ALBION	(Ord or Purser's Steward)
SMITH, William	Pte. R.M.	ASIA	
SMITH, William	Carp's Crew	ASIA	
SMITHWICK, Thomas	Cooper's Crew	ALBION	
SMYTH, Spencer	Lieutenant. R.N.	DARTMOUTH	(P) Slty Wnd. Gaz.1827/2325
	Midshipman	DEFIANCE	Trafalgar
	Mate	NORTHUMBERLAND	Northumberland. 22 May 1812
	Lieutenant. R.N.	VENERABLE	Venerable. 16 Jan 1814
SNOWDEN, Henry	Boy	ASIA	
SOFFIN, William	Pte. R.M.	GENOA	
SOWTER, Robert	Landsman	ALBION	
SPARKMAN, James	Boy	CAMBRIAN	
	A.B.	GANGES	Syria
SPEAR, William	Ord	GENOA	
SPENCE, John	Capt's Steward	GLASGOW	
SPENCER, Earl, Rt Hon Frederick	Captain. R.N.	TALBOT	(M) For Navarino. C.B., K.S.L., K.S.A. & K.R.G.
SPENCER, James	Pte. R.M.	CAMBRIAN	
	Pte. R.M.	Qn CHARLOTTE	Algiers
SPICER, Joseph	Pte. R.M.	ALBION	
SPILLER, John	A.B.	CAMBRIAN	
SPRATT, William	Pte. R.M.	ALBION	
STAINER, John	Landsman	TALBOT	He was the last survivor. Died at Binstead, Ryde I.O.W. aged 99 yrs on 3 March 1907.
STANDFIELD, James	Carp's Mate	CAMBRIAN	
STANWAY, George	Pte. R.M.	GLASGOW	
STEELE, Thomas	Pte. R.M.	DARTMOUTH	
STENT, John	Pte. R.M.	DARTMOUTH	
STEPHENS, Joseph	A.B.	GENOA	
STEVENS, George	Landsman	ALBION	
	Capt's Coxswain	WASP	Syria
STEWART, Hon Keith	Volunteer 1st Cl	ASIA	
STILLMAN, William	Pte. R.M.	CAMBRIAN	
STOKES, Samuel	Bosun's Mate	ROSE	
STONE, James	Pte. R.M.	ASIA	
STONE, James	Pte. R.M.	ROSE	
STOODLEY, William	Cooper	GLASGOW	
STOREY, Richard	Boy	PHILOMEL	
STRANGE, Lot	Actg Armourer	TALBOT	(M) Anchor Type LS & GC

STRANSHAM, Anthony.B.	Lieut. R.M.	CAMBRIAN	(M) China 1842 & Baltic. Died Oct 1900 aged 94 years as a General.
STRETTELL, John	Midshipman	CAMBRIAN	(M) China 1842
STROUD, Henry	Boy	DARTMOUTH	(M) Baltic & Vic Wide LSGC.
STUBBINGTON, James	Bosun's Mate	GENOA	
STUDWELL, Robert	Volunteer	ASIA	
STURT, Henry.R.	Lieutenant. R.N.	GENOA	Slty Wounded. Gaz.1827/2325
	Midshipman	LEANDER	Algiers
SULLIVAN, Cornelius	Ord	GENOA	
SULLIVAN, Simon	Ord	ALBION	
SUMMERS, William	Master	ROSE	
SURRIDGE, John	Pte. R.M.	TALBOT	
SUTER, William.E.	Purser's Steward	DARTMOUTH	
SWAIN, William or SWAINE	Landsman	DARTMOUTH	
	Bosun's Mate	VANGUARD	Syria
SWATHRIDGE, James	Purser's Steward	MUSQUITO	(also at SWATHERIDGE)
SWATTON, John	Ord	DARTMOUTH	
SWEEPER, Ralph	Corporal R.M.	GLASGOW	
SWEET, Thomas	A.B.	ASIA	G.H. 8684
TABNER, John	A.B.	CAMBRIAN	
TALBOT, John.T.	Lieutenant. R.N.	ROSE	
TASKAR, Richard	Ord	DARTMOUTH	
TAVERNAR, James	Pte. R.M.	ASIA	G.H. 8685
TAWS, George	Yeoman Signals	GLASGOW	
	Landsman	SURVEILLANTE	St Sebastian
TAYLOR, Frederick.F.F.	Master's Asst	GLASGOW	
	2nd Master	MAGICIENNE	Syria
TAYLOR, John.S.	Master's Asst	GLASGOW	
TAYLOR, Henry	Pte. R.M.	ROSE	
TAYLOR, Robert	Ord	CAMBRIAN	
TAYLOR, Thomas	Sergeant. R.M.	GLASGOW	
TAYLOR, Thomas	Gunner's Crew	GLASGOW	
TAYLOR, William	Pte. R.M.	ASIA	
TELFER, James	A.B.	ALBION	
TERRELL, Edward	Ord	GENOA	
THOMAS, Richard	Capt' After Guard	GENOA	
THOMPSON, James	A.B.	ALBION	
THOMPSON, John	A.B.	TALBOT	
THOMPSON, Joseph	A.B.	GENOA	
THOMPSON, Samuel	A.B.	CAMBRIAN	
THOMPSON, Thomas	Gunner's Crew	GENOA	
TILDESLEY, Thomas.E.	Volunteer	DARTMOUTH	
TILLS, William	Mate	ASIA	
	Midshipman	GRANICUS	Algiers
TOUZEAU, James.C.M.	Midshipman	GENOA	(M) China 1842
TRATHEN, Walter	Sailmaker	CAMBRIAN	
TREGASKING, John	Sailmaker	ASIA	(M) Anchor Type LS & GC
	Sailmaker	MUTINE	Algiers
	Sailmaker	REVENGE	Syria
TREWAVES, James	A.B.	GENOA	
TROHEAR, John	A.B.	ALBION	
TROUNCE, John	Ord	ASIA	
TRYON, Robert	Midshipman	CAMBRIAN	
TUCKER, William	Ord	GLASGOW	
TUCKEY, Davys	Midshipman	GLASGOW	
TURNBULL, James	Boy	DARTMOUTH	
	A.B.	EDINBURGH	Syria
TURNBULL, William.C.	Capt' Fore Top	TALBOT	
TURNER, Charles	A.B.	GLASGOW	
TURNER, Thomas	Pte. R.M.	ALBION	
TYLER, Samuel	Boy	ASIA	
	A.B.	GANGES	Syria
TYNDALE, Edward	Mate	TALBOT	(P)
	Volunteer 1st Cl	AJAX	St Sebastian
UNDERHILL, John	Gunner	TALBOT	
VASS, George.C.	Boy	ALBION	
VEAL, James	Ord	DARTMOUTH	
VEARY, George	A.B.	GLASGOW	
VENN, William	Pte. R.M.	GENOA	
VICKS, Joseph	A.B.	ASIA	(or VICK)
VINES, Mark	Pte. R.M.	ALBION	
VINTON, Charles.T.	Ord	ALBION	
WAGLIN, Christopher	Sailmaker's Crew	GENOA	(alias LLOYD, Charles)
WALDRIDGE, George	Pte. R.M.	ASIA	
WALKER, Francis.M.	Pte. R.M.	DARTMOUTH	
WALKER, James	A.B.	ASIA	(M) IGS/PEGU & S.A. 1853.
WALKER, Thomas	Pte. R.M.	CAMBRIAN	
WALKER, William	Boy	DARTMOUTH	
WALKER, William	Boy	GENOA	discharged before battle.
WALL, John	Ord	GENOA	
WALLELL, James	Ord	ALBION	
WALLIS, John	Pte. R.M.	CAMBRIAN	
	Pte. R.M.	BENBOW	Syria
WALSH, William	Ord	DARTMOUTH	

NAVARINO

Name	Rank	Ship	Notes
WALTER, Samuel	Landsman	GENOA	
WALWIN, Edward	Pte. R.M.	ASIA	
WARD, Charles	Boy	ASIA	
WARD, William	Pte. R.M.	ASIA	
WARDEN, Thomas	Capt' of Mast	TALBOT	
WARN, John	A.B.	GENOA	
WARN, William	Q.M.	GENOA	
WARNER, Henry	Landsman	ALBION	
	Gunner's Mate	GORGON	Syria
WARREN, Charles.B.	Midshipman	ALBION	
	Lieutenant. R.N.	MAGICIENNE	Syria
WARREN, John	Caulker	GENOA	
	Caulker	Pcss CHARLOTTE	Syria
WARREN, Thomas	Not Given	DARTMOUTH	
WARREN, Thomas	Boy	GENOA	
WATTINS, William	Gunner's Crew	GLASGOW	(also as WATKINS)
WATTS, James	A.B.	CAMBRIAN	
WEBB, John	Ord	GENOA	
WEBB, John	Landsman	GENOA	
WEBB, Richard	A.B.	GENOA	Impressed ex-smuggler (Displayed at R.N.Museum)
WEBB, Stephen	Pte. R.M.	CAMBRIAN	
WEBB, Thomas	Pte. R.M.	DARTMOUTH	
WEEKS, William	Q.M.	PHILOMEL	
WELLS, Edward	Ship's Corporal	DARTMOUTH	
	A.B.	EDINBURGH	Syria
WELLS, John	Pte. R.M.	GLASGOW	
WELLS, William	Pte. R.M.	ASIA	
WELSH, William	Ord	DARTMOUTH	
WESBURY, William	Ord	ALBION	(or as WESTBURY)
WEST, Thomas	Pte. R.M.	ALBION	
WEST, Thomas	Ord	GENOA	
WESTLAKE, William	Pte. R.M.	GENOA	
	Pte. R.M.	IMPREGNABLE	Algiers
WHARTON, Richard.H.	Volunteer 1st Cl	GENOA	
WHEELER, William	Capt' Fore Top	TALBOT	
	A.B.	SUPERB	Algiers
WHIGTON, John	Pte. R.M.	GLASGOW	(also as WIGHTON)
WHITCOMBE, Thomas	A.B.	ALBION	
WHITE, Jacob	Boy	DARTMOUTH	
WHITE, James	Pte. R.M.	DARTMOUTH	(M) N.Z. 1845-46
WHITE, John	Capt' Fore Top	DARTMOUTH	
WHITE, Joseph	Boy	ALBION	
	A.B.	HYDRA	Syria
WHITE, William	Master	ALBION	
WHITE, William	Ord	GLASGOW	
WHITEHEAD, James	Pte. R.M.	CAMBRIAN	
WHITEHOUSE, James	Corporal R.M.	DARTMOUTH	
	Corporal R.M.	Pcss CHARLOTTE	Syria
WIGLEY, Robert	Ord	GENOA	
WILKES, William	Pte. R.M.	GENOA	
WILKS, John	A.B.	ASIA	
WILLCOX, Thomas	A.B.	GENOA	Impressed ex-smuggler
WILLIAMS, Charles	Color Sgt. R.M.	DARTMOUTH	
WILLIAMS, Daniel	Gunner's Crew	CAMBRIAN	
WILLIAMS, Elias	Landsman	ASIA	
WILLIAMS, George.B.	Midshipman	GLASGOW	1824 rcd Order Tower & Sword, King John's jewel. HMS Windsor Castle
WILLIAMS, Henry	Ord	ASIA	
WILLIAMS, John	Ord	ALBION	
WILLIAMS, John	Boy	MUSQUITO	
WILLIAMS, John	A.B.	CAMBRIAN	
	A.B.	GANGES	Syria
WILLIAMS, John	A.B.	GLASGOW	G.H. 3013
	Q.M.	BELLEROPHON	Syria
WILLIAMS, John	Ord	TALBOT	
WILLIAMS, Joseph	Ord	TALBOT	
WILLIAMS, Richard	Boy	GLASGOW	
WILLIAMS, Thomas	Not Given	ALBION	Three borne.
WILLIAMS, William	Pte. R.M.	GENOA	two R.M.s borne
WILLIAMS, William	Not given	GENOA	Ship's Ck & 2 A.Bs.
	Not given	RODNEY	Syria
WILLIAMS, Woodford.J.	College Midshipman	ROSE	Slty Wounded. Gaz.1827/2325
	Commander	STROMBOLI	Syria
WILLIAMSON, John	Boy	DARTMOUTH	
	Capt's Coxswain	CARYSFORT	Syria
WILLIAMSON, William	Gunner's Crew	ASIA	
	Gunner's Crew	GANGES	Syria
WILLIS, William	Ord	GENOA	(Also as WILLIS, Wm.J.)
WILLISON, John	Ord	DARTMOUTH	
WILLSON, Samuel	Pte. R.M.	ALBION	

WILSON, George	Master's Asst	ALBION	
	Master	MEDEA	Syria
WILSON, George.K.	Lieutenant. R.N.	TALBOT	Father of a future First Sea Lord. V.C.
WILSON, James	A.B.	TALBOT	
WILSON, John (2)	A.B.	CAMBRIAN	
	A.B.	LEANDER	Algiers
WILSON, John	Ord	ASIA	
WILSON, John	A.B.	ASIA	G.H. 3267
WILSON, William	Q.M.	PHILOMEL	
WILTSHIRE, James	Pte. R.M.	ALBION	
WINDADD, Jeremiah	A.B.	GENOA	(also as WINDATT)
WINDSOR, George	Gunner's Crew	GLASGOW	
	A.B.	GANGES	Syria
WINKS, George	A.B.	ALBION	
WINLEY, Matthew	A.B.	DARTMOUTH	
WINSLOW, George	Pte. R.M.	ALBION	G.H. 6235
WINSLOW, William	A.B.	GLASGOW	
WINTER, Henry	Ord	CAMBRIAN	
WINTER, John	Ord	ASIA	Impressed ex-smuggler
WISE, Robert	A.B.	ASIA	
WITTS, Robert	Boy	GLASGOW	
WODEHOUSE, George	Midshipman	ASIA	Died 15 Feb 1900 aged 89 years as Vice Admiral
WOOD, John	Capt' Fore Top	ALBION	(M) Anchor Type LS & GC
WOOD, John	Ord	DARTMOUTH	
WOOD, Robert	A.B.	ALBION	
WOODMAN, James	Carp's Mate	ALBION	
WOODMAN, John	Ord	ASIA	
WOODMAN, Joseph	Boy	ASIA	
WOODMASON, John	A.B.	TALBOT	
WOODS, Thomas	Ord	GLASGOW	
WOOLLEY, Joseph	Pte. R.M.	GENOA	
	Pte. R.M.	REVENGE	Syria
WRIGHT, Henry	Midshipman	ASIA	
WRIGHT, John	Ord	GLASGOW	
WRIGHT, Thomas	Pte. R.M.	TALBOT	
WYBURN, John	A.B.	ASIA	
YARRINGTON, William	Pte. R.M.	BRISK	G.H. 3126
	Pte. R.M.	MINDEN	Algiers
YOULTON, George	Pte. R.M.	CAMBRIAN	
YOUNG, Alfred	Volunteer 1st Cl	MUSQUITO	
YOUNG, David	A.B.	PHILOMEL	
YOUNG, Jacob	Pte. R.M.	ALBION	
	Pte. R.M.	BELLEROPHON	Syria
YOUNG, Thomas	Pte. R.M.	CAMBRIAN	
ZAMITT, Antonio	Gun Rm Cook	ROSE	(M.L. as ZAMID)
	Gun Rm Cook	RODNEY	Syria

(6,978) SYRIA

Operations on the coast of SYRIA from 10 September 1840 until surrender of ACRE on 4 November 1840, and blockade of Egyptian ports Sept/Dec 1840.

ABBOTT, John	A.B.	Pcss CHARLOTTE
ABBOTT, John	Pte. R.M.	VANGUARD
ABELLO, Antonio	A.B.	ASIA
ABELLO, Lorenzo	A.B.	ASIA
ABELTSHAUSER, Charles	A.B.	BENBOW
ABLE, Daniel	Carp's Crew	BELLEROPHON
ABLE, Michael.W.	Caulker	HAZARD
ABLETT, John	Pte. R.M.	CAMBRIDGE
ABLETT, Silas	A.B.	Pcss CHARLOTTE
ABRAHAMS, James	Pte. R.M.	Pcss CHARLOTTE
ABRAM, Frank	Boy	PIQUE
ABRAMS, James	Ord	BELLEROPHON
ABRAMS, John	Ord	EDINBURGH
ABRAMS, S.	A.B.	GANGES
ABSALOM, George	A.B.	BELLEROPHON
ABUTT, Charles	Stoker	HYDRA
ACHESON, J.H.	Surgeon	EDINBURGH
ACKFORD, Samuel	Capt' Fore Top	CAMBRIDGE
ACKLAND, William	Pte. R.M.	Pcss CHARLOTTE
ACTON, John	Asst Surgeon	HECATE
ACTON, William	Ord	DIDO
ADAIR, Charles.W.	Lieut. R.M.	HASTINGS
ADAMS, Adam	Pte. R.M.	WASP
ADAMS, Francis.W.	Ord	Pcss CHARLOTTE
ADAMS, George	Ord	MEDEA
ADAMS, George.C.	Lieut. R.N.	MAGICIENNE
ADAMS, Jabes	A.B.	Pcss CHARLOTTE
ADAMS, James	A.B.	BELLEROPHON

SYRIA

ADAMS, James	Ord	EDINBURGH	
ADAMS, John	Pte. R.M.	EDINBURGH	
ADAMS, John	Pte. R.M.	PIQUE	
ADAMS, Joseph	Pte. R.M.	THUNDERER	
ADAMS, Joseph	Pte. R.M.	STROMBOLI	
ADAMS, Robert	Fifer	RODNEY	
ADAMS, Thomas	Ord	BENBOW	
ADAMS, Thomas	Fifer	IMPLACABLE	
ADAMS, Thomas	A.B.	RODNEY	
ADAMS, William	Pte. R.M.	IMPLACABLE	
ADAMSON, J.McL	Pte. R.M.	CASTOR	
ADAMSON, Thomas	Carp's Mate	POWERFUL	
ADCOCK, William	Pte. R.M.	BENBOW	
ADDISON, Richard	Boy	HASTINGS	
ADLAM, John	Pte. R.M.	Pcss CHARLOTTE	
ADLAM, Richard	Pte. R.M.	BENBOW	
ADMONDS, Henry	Carp's Crew	RODNEY	
ADYE, Samuel	Pte. R.M.	STROMBOLI	
AFFLICK, Richard	Gunner R.A.	PIQUE & others	
AGAR, John	Boy	REVENGE	
AGNEW, J.W.	A.B.	ASIA	
AGUIS, Angelo	A.B.	ASIA	
AGUIS, Christopher	Ord	VANGUARD	
AGUIS, Frank	A.B.	ASIA	
AGUIS, Pepin	A.B.	CAMBRIDGE	
AGUIS, Vincenzo	A.B.	ASIA	
AHEARN, John	Ord	THUNDERER	
AHEARN, Timothy	A.B.	POWERFUL	
AHERN, Simon	A.B.	EDINBURGH	
AHERN, William	Carp's Crew	REVENGE	
AIKMAN, William	Ord	BENBOW	
AINSWORTH, William	A.B.	BELLEROPHON	
ALCHISS, George	A.B.	Pcss CHARLOTTE	
ALDERSLADE, Thomas	A.B.	GANGES	
ALDERSLADE, William	Ord	VANGUARD	
ALDERSON, R.C.	Lieut Colonel.R.E.	HECATE	
ALDRED, William.F.J.	Boy	VANGUARD	
ALDRICH, Edward	Asst Mil Sec (R.E.)	Pcss CHARLOTTE	
ALDRIDGE, Francis	Ord	HAZARD	
ALEXANDER, George	A.B.	PIQUE	
	Ord	DARTMOUTH	*Navarino*
ALEXANDER, George.J.	Gun Room Steward	Pcss CHARLOTTE	
ALEXANDER, John	Pte. R.M.	STROMBOLI/ HASTINGS	
ALEXANDER, John	Pte. R.M.	STROMBOLI/ CASTOR	
ALEXANDER, Richard	Pte. R.M.	STROMBOLI	
ALEXANDER, Robert	Pte. R.M.	BENBOW	
ALFORD, Thomas	Capt' of Mast	THUNDERER	
ALLARD, James	Pte. R.M.	BELLEROPHON	
ALLBERRY, James	Pte. R.M.	EDINBURGH	
ALLBURY, Thomas	Pte. R.M.	PIQUE	
ALLCOCK, Henry	A.B.	Pcss CHARLOTTE	
ALLCOCK, William	Ord	PIQUE	
ALLEN, Charles	Stoker	MEDEA	
ALLEN, David	A.B.	BENBOW	
ALLEN, George	Drummer. R.M.	HECATE	
ALLEN, George	Boy	Pcss CHARLOTTE	
ALLEN, James	A.B.	RODNEY	
ALLEN, John	Stoker	CYCLOPS	
ALLEN, John	Ord	VANGUARD	
ALLEN, Thomas	Pte. R.M.	REVENGE	
ALLEN, Thomas	Pte. R.M.	CARYSFORT	
ALLEN, Thomas	Barber	BELLEROPHON	
ALLEN, Thomas	A.B.	EDINBURGH	
ALLEN, Thomas	Captain's Steward	MAGICIENNE	
ALLEN, William	Ord	BELLEROPHON	
ALLINGHAM, Thomas	Pte. R.M.	STROMBOLI	
ALLISON, Michael	Pte. R.M.	REVENGE	
ALLPORT, Edward	Pte. R.M.	POWERFUL	
ALOSSA, John	Pte. R.M.	IMPLACABLE	
ALRIDGE, Thomas	Capt' After Guard	RODNEY	
ALVES, George	A.B.	REVENGE	
AMOS, Luke	A.B.	ASIA	
ANDERSON, Alexander	Lieut. R.M.	THUNDERER	
	Lieut. R.M.	ALBION	*Navarino*
ANDERSON, Edward	Pte. R.M.	ASIA	
ANDERSON, John	A.B.	Pcss CHARLOTTE	
ANDERSON, John	Boy	RODNEY	
ANDERSON, Robert	Ord	CARYSFORT	
ANDERSON, Robert	Asst Surgeon	Pcss CHARLOTTE	
ANDERSON, William	Q.M.	HYDRA	
ANDERSON, William	Ord	BENBOW	

ANDERTON, James	Pte. R.M.	HAZARD	
ANDREWS, Henry	Pte. R.M.	BELLEROPHON	
ANDREWS, James (1)	Pte. R.M.	BELLEROPHON	
ANDREWS, James (2)	Pte. R.M.	BELLEROPHON	
ANDREWS, James.R.	Clerk	MAGICIENNE	
ANDREWS, John	A.B.	Pcss CHARLOTTE	
ANDREWS, John	Boy	MAGICIENNE	
ANDREWS, Richard	A.B.	CAMBRIDGE	
ANDREWS, Robert	Supn. Pte. R.M.	BELLEROPHON	
ANDREWS, Robert	Pte. R.M.	EDINBURGH	
ANDREWS, Samuel	Pte. R.M.	VANGUARD	
ANDREWS, William	Gunner	GORGON	
ANDREWS, William	Boy	GANGES	
ANDREWS, William	A.B.	HASTINGS	
ANGEL, George	Ord	BENBOW	
ANGUS, John	Q.M.	EDINBURGH	
ANNABONA, George	A.B.	RODNEY	
ANNETT, William	A.B.	DAPHNE	
ANNO, Edward	A.B.	IMPLACABLE	(May read ARNO)
ANSCOMBE, Thomas	Pte. R.M.	BELLEROPHON	
ANSTEY, Charles	Ord	CARYSFORT	
ANTHONY, William	Ord	REVENGE	
ANTRAM, John	Ord	PIQUE	
APPLEBY, John	A.B.	POWERFUL	
APPLEDORE, Samuel	Ord	THUNDERER	
APPLETON, Edward	Lieut. R.M.	BELLEROPHON	
APPS, Reuben	Gunner. R.M.A.	STROMBOLI	
ARAM, Thomas	Gunner's Mate	BELLEROPHON	
ARBELA, Joseph	A.B.	IMPLACABLE	
ARBELA, Luigi	A.B.	IMPLACABLE	
ARBERY, John	Pte. R.M.	THUNDERER	
ARCHER, George	Ord	GORGON	
ARCHIBALD, William	Capt' of Mast	RODNEY	
ARCHIBOLD, Edward	Ord	CASTOR	
ARMOUR, Richard	Boy	CARYSFORT	
ARMSTRONG, James	A.B.	VANGUARD	
ARMSTRONG, John	Painter	Pcss CHARLOTTE	
ARNETT, William	A.B.	DAPHNE	(M.L. as HARNETT)
ARNEY, John	Ord	BELLEROPHON	
ARNOALT, William	Carp's Mate	ASIA	
ARNOLD, Edwin	Pte. R.M.	CAMBRIDGE	
ARNOLD, George.P.	Seaman's Schoolmaster	CAMBRIDGE	
ARNOLD, Richard	Pte. R.M.	EDINBURGH	
ARNOLD, Samuel	A.B.	VANGUARD	
ARNOLD, Thomas	Pte. R.M.	EDINBURGH	
ARTERTON, John	L.M.	THUNDERER	
ARY, William	Ord	IMPLACABLE	
ASH, Alexander	Pte. R.M.	RODNEY	
ASH, John	Pte. R.M.	VANGUARD	
ASH, Oliver.J.	Sailmaker	PHOENIX	
ASH, R.W.	Ord	BENBOW	
ASH, William	Gunner. R.M.A.	VESUVIUS	
ASHBY, George	Pte. R.M.	CAMBRIDGE	
ASHBY, William	Boy	WASP	
ASHCROFT, Charles	A.B.	IMPLACABLE	
ASHCROFT, William	Boy	ASIA	
ASHE, Edward.D.	Gunner's Mate	DAPHNE	
ASHFORD, John	Pte. R.M.	RODNEY	
ASHFORD, Robert	Ord	EDINBURGH	
ASHFORD, William	Capt' of Mast	RODNEY	
ASHMORE, Edward	Gunner. R.A.	PIQUE & other vessels	
ASHTON, James	Pte. R.M.	ASIA	
ASHWORTH, James	Pte. R.M.	POWERFUL	
ASLETT, John.T.	2nd Lieut. R.M.	STROMBOLI & WASP	
ASPINALL, William.T.	Ord	HASTINGS	
ASPLIN, William	Gunner. R.M.A.	PIQUE	
ASPLIN, William	Pte. R.M.	PIQUE	
ATHERTON, Charles	Yeoman Store Room	BENBOW	
ATHERTON, William	Supn Pte. R.M.	STROMBOLI	
ATHILL, James	Pte. R.M.	VANGUARD	(M.L. as ATTRILL)
ATHURSON, James	Cooper	CASTOR	
ATKEY, George	Pte. R.M.	STROMBOLI & HASTINGS	
ATKEY, John	A.B.	Pcss CHARLOTTE	
ATKIN, William	A.B.	BELLEROPHON	
ATKINS, Robert	Pte. R.M.	VANGUARD	
ATKINS, Thomas	Ord	Pcss CHARLOTTE	
ATKINS, William	Sergeant. R.M.	Pcss CHARLOTTE	
ATRILL, William	Gunner's Mate	CAMBRIDGE	
ATTARD, Antonio	Not Given	EDINBURGH	(M.L. as Albert)
ATTARD, Joseph	A.B.	HYDRA	
ATTRIDGE, Richard	A.B.	Pcss CHARLOTTE	
ATTRILL, George	Ord	Pcss CHARLOTTE	
ATTRILL, Henry	L.M.	Pcss CHARLOTTE	
ATTRILL, Henry	Pte. R.M.	BELLEROPHON	

SYRIA

ATTWELL, Thomas	A.B.	POWERFUL	
ATWILL, Richard.A.W.	Purser's Steward	IMPLACABLE	(? an additional clasp)
AUGUSTIN, A.	Ord	CAMBRIDGE	
AUSTEN, Algernon.S.	Mate	BENBOW	
AUSTEN, Charles.J.	Mate	BELLEROPHON	
AUSTEN, Charles.J.	Captain. R.N.	BELLEROPHON	
	Midshipman	UNICORN	Unicorn. 8 June 1796
AUSTEN, Herbert.G.	Mate	MEDEA	
AUSTIN, Horatio.T.	Captain. R.N.	CYCLOPS	
	Midshipman	RAMILLIES	B.S. 14 Dec 1814
AVALLI, Phillipp	A.B.	GANGES	
AVERY, Morris	Ord	CASTOR	
AVERY, William	Pte. R.M.	POWERFUL	
AYERS, J.William.	Pte. R.M.	VANGUARD	
AYLEN, John.R.	Actg Master	WASP	
AYLEN, Jonathan	Master	HASTINGS	
AYLETT, William	Pte. R.M.	CAMBRIDGE	
AYLEY, Thomas	Q.M.	PHOENIX	(M) Anchor Type LS & GC
AYLING, Richard	Pte. R.M.	PIQUE	
AYLING, Robert	L.M.	REVENGE	
AYLING, Thomas	Ord	BENBOW	
AYLWARD, George	A.B.	HASTINGS	
AYRES, George	Pte. R.M.	THUNDERER	
AZZOPARDI, Frank	Ord	EDINBURGH	
AZZOPARDI, Rosario	Capt's Cook	BENBOW	
AZZOPARDI, Salro	A.B.	IMPLACABLE	
BAARING, Henry	Stoker	MEDEA	
BACON, Henry	Mate	CAMBRIDGE	
BACON, Joseph	Boy	BENBOW	
BAGG, George	Pte. R.M.	STROMBOLI	
BAGGETT, William	A.B.	ASIA	
BAGSHAW, Edward	Pte. R.M.	PIQUE	
BAID, William	Boy	VANGUARD	
BAILEY, Benjamin	Stoker	PHOENIX	
BAILEY, Charles	Stoker	HYDRA	
BAILEY, Edward	A.B.	EDINBURGH	
BAILEY, George	Boy	THUNDERER	
BAILEY, Henry	Ord	VANGUARD	
BAILEY, Henry	Gunner. R.A.	HECATE	
BAILEY, James	Q.M.	BENBOW	
BAILEY, James	Coxswain Pinnace	VANGUARD	
BAILEY, Job	Pte. R.M.	BELLEROPHON	
BAILEY, John	Pte. R.M.	ASIA	
BAILEY, Robert.L.	A.B.	RODNEY	
BAILEY, Thomas	Ord	RODNEY	
BAILEY, Thomas	Pte. R.M.	STROMBOLI	
BAILEY, William	Pte. R.M.	ASIA	
BAILEY, William	Pte. R.M.	THUNDERER	
BAILEY, William	Pte. R.M.	CASTOR	
BAILEY, William	Ord	REVENGE	
BAILEY, William	Boy	DAPHNE	
BAINES, John	A.B.	ASIA	
BAINES, William	A.B.	GANGES	
BAIRD, Charles	A.B.	EDINBURGH	
BAIRD, John	Pte. R.M.	CARYSFORT	
BAIRD, Robert	Carp's Mate	EDINBURGH	
BAKER, Benjamin	A.B.	RODNEY	
BAKER, Charles	Stoker	GORGON	
BAKER, Charles.H(?).	A.B.	EDINBURGH	
BAKER, George	Pte. R.M.	STROMBOLI	
BAKER, George	Pte. R.M.	THUNDERER	
BAKER, George	Ord	ASIA	
BAKER, Henry	A.B.	CAMBRIDGE	
BAKER, Henry	Asst Surgeon	REVENGE	
BAKER, Henry	A.B.	ASIA	
BAKER, James	Sick Berth Attdt	BENBOW	
BAKER, James	Q.M.	HASTINGS	
BAKER, James.E.	A.B.	CARYSFORT	
BAKER, John.G.	Boy	PHOENIX	
BAKER, John.R.	Lieutenant. R.N.	RODNEY	
BAKER, Matthias	A.B.	GORGON	
BAKER, Robert	Carp's Crew	BENBOW	
BAKER, Samuel	A.B.	CASTOR	
BAKER, Thomas	Seaman's Schoolmaster	POWERFUL	
BAKER, Thomas	Capt' Forecastle	MAGICIENNE	
BAKER, William	Ship's Corporal	VANGUARD	
BAKER, William	Pte. R.M.	GANGES	
BAKER, William	Pte. R.M.	REVENGE	
BAKER, William	A.B.	POWERFUL	
BAKER, William	Ord	IMPLACABLE	
BAKER, William	A.B.	IMPLACABLE	
BAKER, William	Pte. R.M.	EDINBURGH	
BALDACHINO, Salvo	Ord	HAZARD	

BALDWIN, George	Boy	ZEBRA	
BALDWIN, John	A.B.	CASTOR	
BALFE, Thomas	Ord	BELLEROPHON	
BALL, Charles	A.B.	EDINBURGH	
BALL, John	Pte. R.M.	HASTINGS	
BALL, Richard	Actg Cook	CARYSFORT	(M) Anchor Type LS & GC
BALL, William	A.B.	CASTOR	
BALL, William	Pte. R.M.	Pcss CHARLOTTE	
BALLANCHER, Joseph	Boy	DIDO	
BALLARD, James	Pte. R.M.	VANGUARD	
BALLARD, John	Pte. R.M.	BELLEROPHON	
BALLISTON, John	Boy	ZEBRA	(M.L. as BAPTISTA)
BALLS, William	A.B.	ASIA	
BALMAN, Edward	Pte. R.M.	REVENGE	
BALSON, Thomas	Actg Carpenter	ZEBRA	
BALZON, Joseph	Pte. R.M.	Pcss CHARLOTTE	
BAMBER, Henry.K.	Paymaster & Purser	CARYSFORT	
BANBROOK, John	Pte. R.M.	GANGES	
BAND, Charles	Boy 2nd Class	HYDRA	
BAND, Robert	Carp's Mate	EDINBURGH	
BANE, Robert	A.B.	BELLEROPHON	
	A.B.	ROSE	Navarino
BANGHURST, John	Pte. R.M.	Pcss CHARLOTTE	
BANGHURST, Thomas	Pte. R.M.	BELLEROPHON	
BANKS, George	Gunner's Crew	WASP	
	A.B.	CAMBRIAN	Navarino
BANKS, Henry	L.M.	REVENGE	
BANNISTER, W.G.	Ord	Pcss CHARLOTTE	
BANNISTER, William	Pte. R.M.	CAMBRIDGE	
BANTICK, Thomas	Pte. R.M.	CAMBRIDGE	
BARBER, James	A.B.	BELLEROPHON	
BARBER, John	Engineer's Boy 3rd Class	VESUVIUS	
BARBER, John	Ord	BELLEROPHON	
BARBER, John	Fifer	ASIA	
BARBER, Joseph	Ord	CASTOR	
BARBER, William	Stoker	GORGON	
BARBER, William	A.B.	Pcss CHARLOTTE	
BARCLAY, Alexander	Carpenter	THUNDERER	
BARDEN, Thomas	Pte. R.M.	Pcss CHARLOTTE	
BARDIN, John	A.B.	EDINBURGH	
BARDIN, William	A.B.	GANGES	
BARFOOT, John	Ord	HYDRA	
BARFORD, John	Pte. R.M.	CAMBRIDGE	
BARKER, George	Pte. R.M.	TALBOT	
BARKER, George	Pte. R.M.	POWERFUL	
BARKER, James	A.B.	REVENGE	
BARKER, Joseph	Ord	CAMBRIDGE	
BARKER, Thomas	Pte. R.M.	POWERFUL	
BARKER, William	Pte. R.M.	WASP	
BARKER, William	Pte. R.M.	REVENGE	
BARKER, William	Pte. R.M.	CAMBRIDGE	
BARLOW, John.C.	Master	PIQUE	
BARLING, William	Pte. R.M.	CAMBRIDGE	
BARNARD, Charles.L.	Clerk's Asst	CAMBRIDGE	
BARNARD, Edward	Captain. R.N.	CAMBRIDGE	
	Actg Lieut. R.N.	ACHILLE	Trafalgar
BARNARD, Thomas	Corporal. R.M.	EDINBURGH	
BARNARD, William	Boy	HASTINGS	
BARNES, Charles	A.B.	BELLEROPHON	
BARNES, Edgar.B.	Naval Instructor	TALBOT	
BARNES, George	Boy	Pcss CHARLOTTE	
BARNES, John	Pte. R.M.	CASTOR	
BARNES, John	Carpenter	GORGON	
BARNES, John	Ropemaker	BENBOW	
BARNES, Richard	Pte. R.M.	MAGICIENNE	
BARNES, Thomas	Capt's Steward	CAMBRIDGE	
BARNES, William	Pte. R.M.	PIQUE	
BARNES, William.H.	Carp's Mate	REVENGE	
BARNET, Robert	Boy	EDINBURGH	
BARNETT, T.W.	Pte. R.M.	POWERFUL	
BARNHAM, Richard	Boy	RODNEY	(May read BURNCAM)
BARNHAM, Thomas	Pte. R.M.	GANGES	
BARNS, James	A.B.	HASTINGS	
BARRATT, Edward	Pte. R.M.	STROMBOLI	
BARRATT, William	A.B.	CASTOR	
BARRAY, James	A.B.	RODNEY	
BARRELL, William	Boy	BENBOW	
BARRETT, Abel	Pte. R.M.	PIQUE	
BARRETT, Abraham	Pte. R.M.	GANGES	
BARRETT, George	A.B.	CARYSFORT	
BARRETT, Henry	Bosun's Mate	MEDEA	
BARRETT, John	Boy	HASTINGS	
BARRETT, John	Boy	STROMBOLI	
BARRETT, Richard	Sergeant. R.M.	HASTINGS	

SYRIA

BARRETT, Robert	Q.M.	ZEBRA	
BARRETT, Thomas	A.B.	VANGUARD	
BARRETT, William	A.B.	DIDO	
BARRETT, William	Ord	BELLEROPHON	
BARROW, Arthur	Mate	RODNEY	
BARRY, George	Pte. R.M.	REVENGE	
BARRY, James	Bosun's Mate	BELLEROPHON	
BARRY, James	Ord	POWERFUL	
BARRY, James.G.	Bosun's Mate	BELLEROPHON	
BARRY, Michael	Q.M.	TALBOT	
BARRY, Michael	Carp's Crew	Pcss CHARLOTTE	
BARRY, William	Cooper	VANGUARD	(M) Anchor Type LS & GC
BARSBY, William	Sergeant. R.M.	BELLEROPHON	
BARTER, William	Boy	HAZARD	
BARTHOLOMEW, John	A.B.	THUNDERER	
BARTHOLOMEW, William	Stoker	GORGON	
BARTHOLOMEW, William	Pte. R.M.	BENBOW	
BARTLETT, Arthur	Ship's Corporal	IMPLACABLE	
BARTLETT, George	Gunner. R.M.A.	VESUVIUS	
BARTLETT, George	Carp's Crew	VANGUARD	
BARTLETT, Henry	A.B.	RODNEY	
BARTLETT, James	Boy	POWERFUL	
BARTLETT, John.A.	Pte. R.M.	VESUVIUS & HYDRA	
BARTLETT, J.A.	Pte. R.M.	Pcss CHARLOTTE	
BARTLETT, Thomas	A.B.	EDINBURGH	
BARTLETT, William	L.M.	HAZARD	
BARTLETT, William	A.B.	PIQUE	
BARTON, George	Pte. R.M.	BELLEROPHON	
BARTON, George	Ward Room Cook	EDINBURGH	
	L.M.	IMPREGNABLE	Algiers
BARTON, James	Ord	BELLEROPHON	
BARTON, Miles	Pte. R.M.	HASTINGS	
BARTON, William	A.B.	BELLEROPHON	
BARYER, George	A.B.	EDINBURGH	(May read BANGER)
BASDEN, John	A.B.	ASIA	
BASE, Thomas	Carp's Crew	Pcss CHARLOTTE	
BASKERVILLE, Charles	Mate	IMPLACABLE	
BASKERVILLE, William	A.B.	IMPLACABLE	
BASS, William	Bombadier. R.A.	THUNDERER	
BASS, William	Gunner. R.M.A.	PIQUE	
BASSENT, William	Cooper	IMPLACABLE	
BASSETT, Thomas	A.B.	THUNDERER	
BASTARD, James	Carp's Crew	THUNDERER	
BASTION, Thomas	A.B.	RODNEY	
BATCHELOR, George	A.B.	VANGUARD	
BATCHELOR, Henry	Boy	DIDO	
BATCHELOR, John	A.B.	HAZARD	
BATCHELOR, Richard	Clerk's Asst	REVENGE	
BATEMAN, Edwin	Carp's Crew	PHOENIX	
BATEMAN, F.W.	Actg Master	CARYSFORT	
	Sen Master's Asst	GENOA	Navarino
BATEMAN, William	Asst Surgeon	GANGES	
BATEMAN, William	Pte. R.M.	CAMBRIDGE	
BATES, John	Ord	POWERFUL	
BATEY, James.N.	A.B.	CAMBRIDGE	
BATH, John	Blacksmith	CARYSFORT	
BATH, Robert	Ord	RODNEY	
BATRIDGE, James	L.M.	EDINBURGH	
BATTEN, Richard	Capt' Fore Top	VANGUARD	
BATTERBURY, Christopher	Pte. R.M.	Pcss CHARLOTTE	
BATTY, Charles	Bosun's Mate	BENBOW	
BAXENDINE, Thomas	A.B.	BENBOW	
BAXTER, George	A.B.	BENBOW	
BAXTER, James	Ord	PHOENIX	
BAYLEY, Thomas	A.B.	CAMBRIDGE	
BAYLEY, William	A.B.	IMPLACABLE	
BAYLEY, William	Capt' After Guard	CASTOR	
BAYLEY, William	A.B.	RODNEY	
BAYLEY, William	Two borne	THUNDERER	
BAYLIS, Jeremiah	A.B.	HASTINGS	
	Boy	ALBION	Algiers
BAYNE, James	A.B.	CASTOR	
BAYNES, William	Pte. R.M.	GANGES	
BAYNTON, William	Pte. R.M.	STROMBOLI	
BAZELEY, John	A.B.	RODNEY	
	Boy	CAMBRIAN	Navarino
BEACH, William	A.B.	Pcss CHARLOTTE	
BEACHEY, Stephen	Ord	POWERFUL	
BEAL, James	Gunner. R.M.A.	PIQUE	
BEAL, James	Pte. R.M.	PIQUE	
BEAL, James	Boy 1st Class	BENBOW	
BEAL, Thomas	Pte. R.M.	Pcss CHARLOTTE	
BEAL, William	Pte. R.M.	POWERFUL	

BEALE, Joseph.T.	Ord	HASTINGS	
BEALE, Nathaniel	A.B.	REVENGE	
BEALE, Robert.B.	Midshipman	ZEBRA	
BEALES, John	Pte. R.M.	CAMBRIDGE	
BEALEY, George	Pte. R.M.	THUNDERER	
BEAN, William	Carpenter	IMPLACABLE	
	Actg Carpenter	ENDYMION	*Endymion Wh President*
BEAN, William	Bosun's Mate	IMPLACABLE	*(M) Anchor Type LS & GC*
BEANLEY, Christopher	Ord	RODNEY	
BEAR, Charles	A.B.	EDINBURGH	
BEARD, Benjamin	A.B.	GANGES	
BEARD, Edward	Pte. R.M.	CAMBRIDGE	
BEARD, William	Caulker's Mate	MEDEA	
BEATON, John	Bosun's Mate	RODNEY	
BEATTIE, John	Boy	BENBOW	
BEAVER, Samuel	A.B.	REVENGE	
BEAUCHAMP, James	Pte. R.M.	CYCLOPS	
BEAUMONT, Jesse	A.B.	EDINBURGH	
BEAUMONT, Joseph	Pte. R.M.	REVENGE	
	Pte. R.M.	CAMBRIAN	*Navarino*
BEAUVAIS, Frederick.J.	A.B.	POWERFUL	
BEAZLEY, Thomas	Pte. R.M.	GANGES	
BEBELL, Edward	A.B.	REVENGE	
BECK, George	Sailmaker	GANGES	
BECKLEY, Edward	Ord	PIQUE	
BEDELLA, Thomas	A.B.	CAMBRIDGE	
BEDFORD, Robert.T.	Mate	HASTINGS	
BEDFORD, Thomas	Ord	VANGUARD	
BEDFORD, William	Stoker	MEDEA	
BEDWELL, George	Boy	GANGES	
BEDWELL, Henry	Ord	MAGICIENNE	
BEDWELL, John	Ord	Pcss CHARLOTTE	
BEE, George	Fifer	CYCLOPS	
BEEBY, John	Gunner. R.A.	PIQUE & other vessels	
BEECH, Samuel	Pte. R.M.	STROMBOLI	
BEER, Charles	Sapper & Miner	Pcss CHARLOTTE & other vessels	
BEER, Thomas	A.B.	PHOENIX	
BEEVIS, M.Henry.	Ord	HAZARD	
BELGRAVE, Thomas	Mate	RODNEY	
BELL, Alexander	Pte. R.M.	CAMBRIDGE	
BELL, Charles	A.B.	EDINBURGH	
BELL, David	Pte. R.M.	Pcss CHARLOTTE	
BELL, John	A.B.	GANGES	
BELL, John	Corporal. R.M.	CASTOR	
BELL, Thomas	Pte. R.M.	THUNDERER	
BELL, Thomas	Boy 1st Class	POWERFUL	
BELL, Thomas	A.B.	BELLEROPHON	
BELL, William	Asst Surgeon	IMPLACABLE	
	Asst Surgeon	BELLE POULE	*B.S. 14 Dec 1814* (Vfd Abd. Not on Roll)
BELLINGTON, John	Pte. R.M.	ASIA	*(May read BILLINGTON)*
BELLUTI, Giovanni	Capt's Steward	ASIA	*(May read BELLULI)*
BELSEY, John	Ord	HASTINGS	
BENDALL, John	Boy	PHOENIX	
BENFIELD, Thomas	Ord	BENBOW	
BENHAM, Arthur	Ord	Pcss CHARLOTTE	
BENHAM, William	A.B.	Pcss CHARLOTTE	
BENN, Josiah	Stoker	STROMBOLI	
BENNELL, George	Pte. R.M.	BENBOW	
BENNELL, George	Supn Corporal. RM.	BENBOW	
BENNESS, William	Boy	VESUVIUS	
BENNETT, Benjamin	Carp's Crew	BENBOW	
BENNETT, David	Boy	DAPHNE	
BENNETT, Edmund	Ord	POWERFUL	
BENNETT, Edward	Pte. R.M.	BELLEROPHON	
BENNETT, John	Coxswain of Launch	PIQUE	
BENNETT, John	Boy	CASTOR	
BENNETT, Samuel	Q.M.	POWERFUL	
BENNETT, William	Mate	GANGES	
BENNY, John	Stoker	HYDRA	
BENNY, Joseph	A.B.	VANGUARD	
BENNY, Richard	Capt' of Hold	TALBOT	
BENOY, John	A.B.	RODNEY	
BENSON, William	Capt' Fore Top	GANGES	
BENSON, William	A.B.	THUNDERER	
BENTLEY, Robert	Fifer. R.M.	GORGON	
BENTON, John	Pte. R.M.	TALBOT	
BENWELL, Henry	Capt' Fore Top	HASTINGS	
BENZEY, Henry	A.B.	HASTINGS	
BERESFORD, Henry	Not Given	TALBOT	
BERESFORD, Henry.B.	Mate	VANGUARD	*(Roll as J.B. BERESFORD)*
BERKELEY, Maurice.F.F.	Captain. R.N.	THUNDERER	
	Midshipman	BLANCHE	*B.S. 4 Nov 1803*
BERNARD, John	A.B.	RODNEY	

SYRIA

BERREY, James	A.B.	RODNEY	
BERRINGTON, E.J.	Pte. R.M.	BENBOW	
BERRY, Bartholomew	Ord	THUNDERER	
BERRY, John	A.B.	RODNEY	
	A.B.	ALBION	*Navarino*
BERRY, John	Ord	THUNDERER	
BERRY, Patrick	Ord	POWERFUL	
BERRY, Samuel	A.B.	MAGICIENNE	
BERRY, William	Boy	TALBOT	
BERRY, William	Pte. R.M.	GANGES	
BERTOLLE, James	Clr Sgt. R.M.	ZEBRA	
BESANT, Christopher	Ord	BELLEROPHON	
BEST, Joseph	Pte. R.M.	HASTINGS	
BETHELL, William	Pte. R.M.	THUNDERER	
	Pte. R.M.	DARTMOUTH	*Navarino*
BETO, Samuel	Pte. R.M.	VESUVIUS	*(May read BELO)*
BETTS, Frederick	Sailmaker	WASP	
BETTS, Samuel	A.B.	Pcss CHARLOTTE	
BETTSWORTH, James	Ord	HASTINGS	
BEVANS, Thomas	Pte. R.M.	GANGES	
BEVEN, John	Boy	CYCLOPS	
BEVERIDGE, Charles	Boy	REVENGE	
BEVERIDGE, David	Bosun's Mate	VANGUARD	
BEVERIDGE, H.T.S.	Asst Surgeon	HASTINGS	
BEW, William	Q.M.	CAMBRIDGE	
BICKELL, William	Caulker's Mate	THUNDERER	
BICKFORD, J.G.	Master	GANGES	
BIDDECOMB, John	Ord	TALBOT	
BIDDLECOMBE, William	Ord	EDINBURGH	
BIDDLESCOMBE, George	Master	TALBOT	
BIGGINS, Charles	Stoker	CYCLOPS	
BILLATT, Thomas	Pte. R.M.	GANGES	
BILLING, Edwin	Ord	THUNDERER	
BILLING, William	A.B.	RODNEY	
BINGHAM, Henry.H.	Lieutenant. R.N.	Pcss CHARLOTTE	
BINGHAM, Jonathan	Pte. R.M.	POWERFUL	
BINMORE, Thomas	A.B.	IMPLACABLE	
BIRCH, John.N.	Pte. R.M.	ASIA	
BIRCH, Thomas	A.B.	CASTOR	
BIRCH, William	Pte. R.M.	Pcss CHARLOTTE	
BIRD, Andrew	Pte. R.M.	THUNDERER	
BIRD, James	Boy	VANGUARD	
BIRD, J.	A.B.	RODNEY	
BIRD, William	Pte. R.M.	GANGES	
BIRD, William	Gunner. R.A.	HECATE	
BIRDS, Joseph	Ord	BENBOW	
BIRKETT, Henry	A.B.	VANGUARD	
BIRNIE, Alexander	Engineer	VESUVIUS	
BISHOP, George	Pte. R.M.	ASIA	
BISHOP, John	Caulker	VANGUARD	
BISHOP, Joseph	Pte. R.M.	STROMBOLI	
BISHOP, Thomas	Pte. R.M.	IMPLACABLE	
BISHOP, William	Boy	ASIA	*(Alias James)*
BISHOP, William	A.B.	CARYSFORT	
BISHOP, William	Pte. R.M.	EDINBURGH or THUNDERER	
BISHOP, William	Boy 1st Class	EDINBURGH	
BISSETT, John	Pte. R.M.	IMPLACABLE	
BISSHOPP, Edward.C.	Clerk's Asst	VESUVIUS	
BITLER, Joseph	Ord	REVENGE	
BITTON, Joseph	Ord	ASIA	
BLACK, James	Carp's Crew	BENBOW	
BLACK, William	A.B.	RODNEY	
BLACK, William	Sgt. Sapper & Miner	Pcss CHARLOTTE	
BLACK, W.T.	A.B.	RODNEY	
BLACKETT, Edward.A.	Midshipman	IMPLACABLE	
BLACKIER, James	Pte. R.M.	Pcss CHARLOTTE	*(M.L. as BLACKER)*
BLACKMAN, George	L.M.	BENBOW	
BLACKMAN, William	Capt's Steward	BENBOW	*(M) Anchor Type LS & GC*
BLACKMAN, William	Ord	IMPLACABLE	
BLACKMORE, George	Ord	POWERFUL	
BLACKMORE, James	Pte. R.M.	STROMBOLI	
BLACKMORE, John	Mate	EDINBURGH	
BLACKMORE, Robert	Bosun's Mate	HASTINGS	
BLACKMORE, William	Ship's Cook	VANGUARD	*(M) Anchor Type LS & GC*
BLADES, James	A.B.	DAPHNE	
BLADES, James.P.	A.B.	VANGUARD	
BLAGRAVE, James	Pte. R.M.	BENBOW	
BLAKE, Edward	Ord	REVENGE	
BLAKE, Edward	Boy	MAGICIENNE	
BLAKE, George	Boy 2nd Class	CAMBRIDGE	
BLAKE, John	Ord	REVENGE	
BLAKE, Richard	Pte. R.M.	RODNEY	

BLAKE, Robert	Pte. R.M.	RODNEY	
BLAKE, William	Carp's Crew	MAGICIENNE	
BLAKIE, Jasper	Ord	CAMBRIDGE	
BLAMEY, John	Boy	IMPLACABLE	(May read BLAMCY)
BLAMPIN, Jonah	Ord	BENBOW	
BLANCHARD, William	Pte. R.M.	POWERFUL	
BLANCHARD, William	Supn Gnr R.M.A.	PIQUE	
BLAND, Richard	Ord	DIDO	
BLAND, William	Ord	BELLEROPHON	
BLANE, George	Lieutenant. R.N.	BENBOW	
BLANHAM, Thomas	Ord	THUNDERER	
BLANN, Thomas	Sergeant. R.M.	STROMBOLI	
BLASS, John	A.B.	GANGES	(Alias GLASS)
BLEACH, Thomas	Gunner's Mate	VANGUARD	
	Ord	QUEEN CHARLOTTE	Algiers
	Capt' Main Top	TALBOT	Navarino
BLEASDALE, John	Qtr Gunner	ASIA	
BLELLOCK, John	Painter	VANGUARD	
BLENHEIM, William	A.B.	HASTINGS	
BLIGHT, John	Pte. R.M.	STROMBOLI	
BLIGHT, John	Pte. R.M.	VESUVIUS	
BLIGHT, Samuel	Boy	RODNEY	
BLISSENDEN, William	Ord	IMPLACABLE	
BLIZARD, Thomas	Ord	Pcss CHARLOTTE	
BLOCK, William	Gunner's Crew	TALBOT	
BLOMFIELD, Henry.J.	Volunteer. 1st Cl	THUNDERER	
BLOUNT, John	Pte. R.M.	BELLEROPHON	
BLUETT, Frederick.B.	2nd Lieut. R.M.	CAMBRIDGE & GANGES	
BLUNDEN, Joseph	M.A.A.	BENBOW	
BLUTCHFORD, Henry	Ropemaker	TALBOT	(May read BLATCHFORD)
BLY, William.H.B.	Ord	HASTINGS	(M.L. as Wm BLY)
BLYGH, James	A.B.	GANGES	
BLYGHT, James	A.B.	THUNDERER	
BLYTH, David	Lieut. R.M.	CAMBRIDGE	
BOAK, Richard	A.B.	CARYSFORT	
	Ord	ASIA	Navarino
BOAKES, Thomas	Sergeant. R.M.	STROMBOLI	
	Corporal	BRISK	Navarino
BOARD, Henry	Pte. R.M.	RODNEY	
BOARDLEY, Henry	A.B.	DAPHNE	
BODDY, George	Gunner's Mate	PIQUE	
BODEN, Thomas	Corporal R.M.	BELLEROPHON	(M.L. as BOWDEN)
BOGGELN, John	M.A.A.	WASP	
BOGGINS, William	Pte. R.M.	POWERFUL	
BOGGISS, Robert	Pte. R.M.	GANGES	
BOKELL, Thomas	A.B.	RODNEY	
BOLESLAND, Archibald	A.B.	EDINBURGH	
BOLEY, James.R.	A.B.	CAMBRIDGE	
BOLING, Michael	Ord	VANGUARD	
BOLITHO, William	Ord	THUNDERER	
BOLT, Robert	Pte. R.M.	RODNEY	
BOLTON, James	Boy	Pcss CHARLOTTE	
BOLTON, James	Pte. R.M.	STROMBOLI	
BOLTON, Thomas	A.B.	RODNEY	
BOND, Henry	Pte. R.M.	GANGES	
BOND, Thomas	Pte. R.M.	DIDO	
BOND, William	Pte. R.M.	IMPLACABLE	
BONDS, John	Young Gentleman's Steward	HASTINGS	
BONE, James	A.B.	HAZARD	
BONEFACE, George	Pte. R.M.	BENBOW	
BONNER, James	Ord	ASIA	
BONNER, Richard	A.B.	CASTOR	
BONNEY, Alfred	Ord	BELLEROPHON	
BONNEY, William.C.	Pte. R.M.	RODNEY	
BONNICE, John	A.B.	POWERFUL	
BOOKER, George	Ord	Pcss CHARLOTTE	
BOOKER, George	Ord	BENBOW	
BOOTH, Augustus.St.C.	Lieutenant. R.N.	THUNDERER	
BOOTH, Thomas	Ord	POWERFUL	
BOOTH, William	Ord	CAMBRIDGE	
BORE, George	M.A.A.	MAGICIENNE	
BORLER, George	A.B.	CARYSFORT	
BORLEY, Jeremiah	Pte. R.M.	CASTOR	
BORNEAR, William	Ord	RODNEY	
BOSWARD, George	Boy	BENBOW	
BOSWELL, John	Engineer	HYDRA	
BOULTER, Samuel	Pte. R.M.	BELLEROPHON	
BOULTON, William	A.B.	CARYSFORT	
BOULTON, W.H.	Boy	HASTINGS	
BOUCHER, Richard	A.B.	HASTINGS	
BOUNDEN, Robert	A.B.	STROMBOLI	
BOUNSALL, James	A.B.	TALBOT	
BOURCHIER, MacDonald	Mate	GANGES	

SYRIA

BOURKE, James	A.B.	VANGUARD	
BOURKE, Michael	Steward	CAMBRIDGE	
BOURKE, William	Steward	CAMBRIDGE	(M) Anchor Type LS & GC
BOURNE, Thomas	Pte. R.M.	ASIA	
BOURNE, Thomas	Pte. R.M.	POWERFUL	
BOW, Elias	Pte. R.M.	BELLEROPHON	
BOWDEN, James	Ord	CAMBRIDGE	
BOWDEN, John	Carp's Crew	CAMBRIDGE	
BOWDEN, Joseph	Pte. R.M.	EDINBURGH	
BOWDEN, Richard	Pte. R.M.	RODNEY	
BOWDEN, Thomas	A.B.	CAMBRIDGE	
BOWDEN, William	Volunteer	STROMBOLI	
BOWEN, George	Stoker	STROMBOLI	
BOWEN, James	Q.M.	HYDRA	
BOWEN, James	Gun Room Steward	HYDRA	
BOWEN, John	Ord	POWERFUL	
BOWEN, Thomas	Pte. R.M.	IMPLACABLE	
BOWEN, William	Pte. R.M.	PIQUE & other vessels	
BOWER, John	Asst Surgeon	CASTOR	
BOWERS, William	A.B.	RODNEY	
BOWES, John	L.M.	REVENGE	
BOWIE, John	Pte. R.M.	CASTOR	
BOWMAN, F.William	Capt' Mizzen Top	CARYSFORT	
BOWMAN, Phillip	A.B.	PIQUE	
BOWYER, James	Pte. R.M.	Pcss CHARLOTTE	
BOXER, Edward	Captain. R.N.	PIQUE	
	Midshipman	DORIS	B.S. 21 July 1801
	Lieut. R.N.	TIGRE	B.S. 1 Nov 1809
BOXER, John	Mate	VESUVIUS	
BOXER, James.M.	Mate	PIQUE	
BOXER, William	Ord	TALBOT	
BOYD, Henry	Boy	ZEBRA	
BOYD, John	Ord	IMPLACABLE	
BOYD, John.A.H.	Mate	CASTOR	
BOYD, Robert	Pte. R.M.	Pcss CHARLOTTE	
BOYD, William	Carp's Crew	RODNEY	
BOYD, Wilson	Ord	PIQUE	
BOYDELL, Samuel	Carpenter	WASP	
BOYETT, Henry	A.B.	GANGES	
BOYLE, Charles	A.B.	POWERFUL & CARYSFORT	
BOYLE, John	Pte. R.M.	BENBOW	
BOYNES, Charles	A.B.	IMPLACABLE	
BOYNES, William	Not Given	HASTINGS	
BOYS, Henry	Midshipman	EDINBURGH	
BOYSE, Frederick.W.	Mate	BELLEROPHON	
BOYTON, James	Pte. R.M.	CAMBRIDGE	
BRADBURY, Richard	Ord	ASIA	
BRADFORD, Abraham.R.	Surgeon	HAZARD	
BRADLEY, John	A.B.	PIQUE	(M) Anchor Type LS & GC
	Ord	ALBION	Algiers
	Gunner's Crew	ASIA	Navarino
BRADLY, Stephen	Lieutenant R.N.	POWERFUL	A.D.C. to Commodore Napier
BRADSHAW, Benjamin	Ord	EDINBURGH	
BRADSHAW, Robert.A.	Lieutenant. R.N.	ASIA	
BRADY, Robert	Ship's Corporal	VANGUARD	(M) Anchor Type LS & GC
BRAGG, James	Sergeant. R.M.	HYDRA	
BRAKE, Thomas	A.B.	HYDRA	
BRAKSPEAIR, Francis	Sailmaker	DAPHNE	
BRAMPTON, Henry	Pte. R.M.	VESUVIUS	
BRAND, John	Pte. R.M.	BELLEROPHON	
BRANFORD, G(?).	Pte. R.M.	GANGES	
BRANGEN, William	Boy	CYCLOPS	
BRANNON, Thomas	L.M.	ASIA	
BRASIER, Thomas	Bosun's Mate	CAMBRIDGE	
BRASIER, William	Boy	BENBOW	
BRAXTON, Henry	Ord	REVENGE	
BRAXTON, Robert	A.B.	HASTINGS	
BRAY, John	Capt's Coxswain	TALBOT	
BRAY, Thomas	Ord	IMPLACABLE	
BRAYLEY, William	Boy	PIQUE	
BRAZIER, George	Pte. R.M.	GANGES	
BRAZIER, James	Ord	ASIA	
BREADSTREY, William	A.B.	DAPHNE	
BREAKER, John	Pte. R.M.	HASTINGS	
BREMER, George	Ord	CAMBRIDGE	
BRENCHLEY, Richard	Q.M.	MEDEA	
BRENNEN, Thomas	A.B.	RODNEY	
BRENTNALL, Alfred	Ord	IMPLACABLE	
BRENTON, Henry	Purser	DAPHNE	
	Clerk	BEELZEBUB	Algiers
BRESNEHAN, M.	A.B.	WASP	
BRETT, George	A.B.	POWERFUL	

BRETT, William	A.B.	CAMBRIDGE	
BRETTELL, Joseph.C.	Mining Engineer	BENBOW	(British refugee)
BREWER, George	Ord	CAMBRIDGE	
BREWER, Richard	Capt' Main Top	TALBOT	
BREWER, Richard	Not Given	CAMBRIDGE	
BREWER, Stephen	Ord	HASTINGS	
BREWER, William	A.B.	CYCLOPS	
BRICKWELL, Samuel.J.	Mate	ASIA	
BRIDAL, Robert	Pte. R.M.	POWERFUL	
BRIDE, H.M.	A.B.	Pcss CHARLOTTE	
BRIDGE, Ethelred.W.	Midshipman	PIQUE	
BRIDGES, James.H.	Lieutenant. R.N.	THUNDERER	
BRIDGES, Peter	Ord	BENBOW	
BRIDGES, William	Ord	BENBOW	
BRIDGMAN, Arthur.A.	Naval Instructor	THUNDERER	
BRIDGMAN, Henry	A.B.	THUNDERER	
BRIDLE, Francis	A.B.	MAGICIENNE	
BRIGGS, Joseph	Gunner	Pcss CHARLOTTE	
	Gunner	ASIA	Navarino
BRIGGS, Reuben	Pte. R.M.	HASTINGS	
BRIGGS, William	Caulker's Mate	REVENGE	
BRIMBLEY, Samuel	Pte. R.M.	CAMBRIDGE	
BRIMMER, James	Pte. R.M.	BENBOW	
	Pte. R.M.	ASIA	Navarino
BRINNAN, Joseph	Pte. R.M.	PHOENIX	
BRINSON, Joseph	Boy	MEDEA	
BRISCOLL, Henry	Pte. R.M.	Pcss CHARLOTTE	
BRISON, G.H.	Boy	REVENGE	
BRISSINGTON, William	Pte. R.M.	THUNDERER	
	Pte. R.M.	GENOA	Navarino
BRITTANCY, Benjamin	A.B.	BELLEROPHON	
BRITTLE, Robert	Pte. R.M.	RODNEY	
BRITTON, Isaac	Pte. R.M.	CAMBRIDGE	
BRITTON, William	Yeoman Store Rms	CASTOR	
BROAD, John	Ord	MEDEA	
BROAD, Thomas	A.B.	CAMBRIDGE	
BROADBENT, Thomas	Pte. R.M.	Pcss CHARLOTTE	(in Stromboli?)
BROADBRIDGE, Augustus	Pte. R.M.	BELLEROPHON	
BROCKHURST, John	Pte. R.M.	Pcss CHARLOTTE	
BROCKLESS, Richard	Gunner. R.A.	PIQUE & HYDRA	
BROCKWELL, John	Stoker	CYCLOPS	
BRODERICK, Denis	Ord	THUNDERER	
BRODERICK, William	L.M.	CAMBRIDGE	
BRODING, George	Gunner	VANGUARD	
BROKE, George.N.	Lieutenant. R.N.	WASP	
	Midshipman	GLASGOW	Navarino
BROMFIELD, George	A.B.	CYCLOPS	
BROMLEY, Charles	Midshipman	Pcss CHARLOTTE	
BROOK, Benjamin	Pte. R.M.	Pcss CHARLOTTE	
BROOKER, Henry.W.	Lieut. R.M.	REVENGE	
BROOKER, John	A.B.	HASTINGS	
BROOKING, John (2)	A.B.	THUNDERER	
BROOKS, Alfred	Boy	CASTOR	
BROOKS, Frederick.R.	Pte. R.M.	GANGES	
BROOKS, Henry	Pte. R.M.	RODNEY	
BROOKS, Henry	A.B.	PIQUE	
BROOKS, John	Pte. R.M.	GANGES	
BROOKS, John	Pte. R.M.	IMPLACABLE	
BROOKS, William	Pte. R.M.	CASTOR	
BROOKS, William	A.B.	RODNEY	
BROOM, James	Pte. R.M.	EDINBURGH	
BROOM, William	Gunner	THUNDERER	
BROOME, James	Pte. R.M.	BENBOW	
BROOMFIELD, Thomas	Q.M.	EDINBURGH	(Or ? Thunderer)
BROPHEY, Philip	Q.M.	VESUVIUS	
BROUNSDEN, James	Pte. R.M.	CASTOR	
BROWN, Alexander	Gunner	CASTOR	
BROWN, Alfred	Ord	Pcss CHARLOTTE	
BROWN, Benjamin	A.B.	GANGES	
BROWN, Charles	A.B.	GANGES	
BROWN, David	A.B.	EDINBURGH	
BROWN, David	Gunner's Crew	BELLEROPHON	
BROWN, Edward	Ord	Pcss CHARLOTTE	
BROWN, Edward	Carp's Crew	THUNDERER	
BROWN, Francis	Ord	REVENGE	
BROWN, Francis.T.	Lieutenant. R.N.	GORGON	
BROWN, Frederick	A.B.	Pcss CHARLOTTE	
BROWN, G.A.	Boy 1st Class	ASIA	
BROWN, George	Pte. R.M.	HASTINGS	
BROWN, Henry	Pte. R.M.	RODNEY	
BROWN, Henry	Corporal. Sapper & Miner	PIQUE & POWERFUL	
BROWN, Henry.F.	Volunteer 1st Cl	POWERFUL	
BROWN, Henry.J.	Ord	BELLEROPHON	
BROWN, Jacob	Pte. R.M.	CAMBRIDGE & BELLEROPHON	

SYRIA

BROWN, James	Caulker	DAPHNE	
BROWN, James	A.B.	RODNEY	
BROWN, James	Pte. R.M.	Pcss CHARLOTTE	
BROWN, James	Pte. R.M.	GANGES	
BROWN, James	Pte. R.M.	HECATE	
BROWN, James	Pte. R.M.	ASIA	
BROWN, James	Pte. R.M.	CAMBRIDGE	
BROWN, James	Capt' After Guard	EDINBURGH	
BROWN, John	A.B.	PIQUE	
BROWN, John	2 Ptes RM borne	MAGICIENNE	
BROWN, John	A.B.	CAMBRIDGE	
	A.B.	ALBION	Navarino
BROWN, John	Sailmaker	MAGICIENNE	
BROWN, John	Coxswain of Pinnace	MAGICIENNE	
BROWN, John	Pte. R.M.	ASIA	
BROWN, John	Ord	RODNEY	
BROWN, John	A.B. or M.A.A.	VANGUARD	(Two borne)
BROWN, John.J.	Ord	GANGES	
BROWN, John.T.	Lieut. R.M.	VESUVIUS	
BROWN, John.V.	Sergeant. R.M.	EDINBURGH	
BROWN, Joseph	Pte. R.M.	STROMBOLI	(May read J.B. Brown)
BROWN, Joseph	Pte. R.M.	POWERFUL	
BROWN, Joseph	Pte. R.M.	THUNDERER	
BROWN, Pasco	Pte. R.M.	Pcss CHARLOTTE	
BROWN, Richard	Capt' After Guard	BELLEROPHON	
BROWN, Richard	Boy	THUNDERER	
BROWN, Robert	Pte. R.M.	EDINBURGH	
BROWN, Robert	A.B.	REVENGE	
BROWN, Robert	A.B.	VANGUARD	
BROWN, Samuel	Pte. R.M.	REVENGE	
BROWN, Samuel.V.	A.B.	ASIA	
BROWN, Thomas	Pte. R.M.	Pcss CHARLOTTE	
BROWN, Thomas	A.B.	BELLEROPHON	
BROWN, Thomas	A.B.	GANGES	
BROWN, Thomas	A.B.	RODNEY	
BROWN, Thomas	Boy 1st Class	THUNDERER	
BROWN, Thomas	Ord	RODNEY	
BROWN, Thomas	Stoker	CYCLOPS	
BROWN, William	Gunner	THUNDERER	
BROWN, William	Capt' of Mast	GORGON	
BROWN, William	Pte. R.M.	EDINBURGH	
	Pte. R.M.	GLASGOW	Navarino
BROWN, William	L.M.	IMPLACABLE	
BROWN, W.O.	A.B. or Ord	Pcss CHARLOTTE	(Two J. BROWNs borne only)
BROWNE, William	A.B.	EDINBURGH	
BROWNE, William	Capt' Forecastle	GANGES	
BROWNING, James	A.B.	BELLEROPHON	
BROWNING, William	Boy	BENBOW	
BROWNING, William	A.B.	EDINBURGH	
BROWNSELL, William	A.B.	HASTINGS	
BRUCE, Thomas.C.	Midshipman	BELLEROPHON	
BRUCE, William	Surgeon	HASTINGS	
BRUNDRITT, Isaac	Sergeant. R.M.	HASTINGS	
BRYAN, Edward	A.B.	CARYSFORT	
BRYAN, Thomas	A.B.	RODNEY	
BRYANT, Daniel	Capt' Fore Top	PIQUE	
BRYANT, James	Gunner's Mate	HYDRA	
BRYANT, John	Pte. R.M.	Pcss CHARLOTTE	(Alias BRYHUNT)
BRYANT, Richard	Boy	Pcss CHARLOTTE	
BRYANT, Thomas	A.B.	IMPLACABLE	
BRYCE, Philip	Pte. R.M.	ASIA	
BRYDONE, William	Purser	HYDRA	
BRYHURST, John	Pte. R.M.	Pcss CHARLOTTE	
BUCHANAN, Colin	A.B.	Pcss CHARLOTTE	
BUCHANAN, James	Lieut. R.M.	PIQUE	
BUCHANAN, James.G.	Asst Surgeon	VANGUARD	(O'Byrne. 1861. p.138) Roll as "Asst Engineer". (M) Baltic
BUCK, James	Sergeant. R.M.	GORGON	
BUCKETT, John	Boy	REVENGE	
BUCKINGHAM, William	Yeoman of Signals	PIQUE	
BUCKLEY, Daniel	Boy	THUNDERER	
BUCKLEY, George	Boy	THUNDERER	
BUCKLEY, James	A.B.	Pcss CHARLOTTE	
BUCKLY, George	Pte. R.M.	ASIA	
BUDD, James	Pte. R.M.	ASIA	
BUDDELL, John	Ord	EDINBURGH	
BUDDEN, G.H.	Pte. R.M.	Pcss CHARLOTTE	
BUDDEN, William	Boy	THUNDERER	
BUDGE, Thomas	A.B.	CAMBRIDGE	
BULL, Charles	Boy	VANGUARD	
BULL, Edward	Pte. R.M.	VANGUARD	
BULL, George	Ord	BENBOW	
BULL, James	Mate	VANGUARD	

BULL, John	Boy	MAGICIENNE	
BULL, Richard	Cook	CARYSFORT	
BULL, William	Ord	PIQUE	
BULLEN, Charles	Mate	EDINBURGH	
BULLEY, William	Ord	RODNEY	
BULLIONS, Thomas	Engineer	HECATE	
BULLMORE, Richard	Boatswain 3rd Cl	CARYSFORT	
BUNDAY, John	Pte. R.M.	CAMBRIDGE & HASTINGS	
BUNKER, John	Ord	CAMBRIDGE	
BUNN, John	Corporal R.M.	CAMBRIDGE	
BUNN, William	Pte. R.M.	STROMBOLI	
BUNNING, Robert	Pte. R.M.	BELLEROPHON	
BUNSKILL, Abraham	A.B.	REVENGE	
BUNTER, Luke	Pte. R.M.	BELLEROPHON	
BUNTING, James	Pte. R.M.	GANGES	
BURBRIDGE, Samuel	A.B.	HASTINGS	
BURCH, James	Ord	IMPLACABLE	
BURCH, James	Capt's Cook	DAPHNE	
BURCHALL, Edward	Carp's Crew	HECATE	
BURDEN, George	A.B.	Pcss CHARLOTTE	
BURDETT, Isiah	Ord	Pcss CHARLOTTE	
BURGESS, David	Boy	CARYSFORT	
BURGESS, Henry	A.B.	POWERFUL	
BURGESS, John.W.	A.B.	POWERFUL	
BURGESS, Thomas	Pte. R.M.	PIQUE	
BURGESS, William	Stoker	CYCLOPS	
BURGHOPE, James	Pte. R.M.	HASTINGS	
BURGONIE, Samuel	A.B.	IMPLACABLE	
BURKSAND, William	Bosun's Mate	HAZARD	
BURLING, William	Pte. R.M.	CAMBRIDGE	
BURMILE, William	Pte. R.M.	THUNDERER	
BURN, Edwin	Pte. R.M.	IMPLACABLE	
BURN, Joseph	Ord	VANGUARD	
BURNARD, Richard.L.	Q.M.	IMPLACABLE	
BURNELL, William	Pte. R.M.	THUNDERER	
BURNETT, Charles	Carp's Crew	VANGUARD	
BURNETT, George	Carp's Crew	THUNDERER	
BURNETT, James	Pte. R.M.	BENBOW	
BURNETT, Thomas	Not Given	THUNDERER	
BURNETT, William	Pte. R.M.	REVENGE	(M) Anchor Type LS & GC
BURNETT, William	A.B.	GANGES	
BURNETT, William	Lieutenant. R.N.	VESUVIUS	
BURNS, Edward	Pte. R.M.	Pcss CHARLOTTE	
BURNS, George	Ord	THUNDERER	
BURNS, John.J.D.	Asst Surgeon	CARYSFORT	
BURNS, Joseph	A.B.	RODNEY	(May read JAMES)
BURNS, William	A.B.	RODNEY	
BURRIN, Christopher	Pte. R.M.	GANGES	
BURROOUGHS, Frederick	A.B.	Pcss CHARLOTTE	('Run' removed in 1845)
BURROUGH, William	Mid's Steward	EDINBURGH	
BURROWS, James	Boy	VANGUARD	
BURROWS, Montagu	Midshipman	EDINBURGH	
BURROWS, William	A.B.	VANGUARD	
BURSTAL, Edward	Midshipman	CAMBRIDGE	
BURT, George.M.	3rd Engineer	HECATE	
BURT, John	Q.M.	THUNDERER	
BURT, Thomas	Clerk's Asst	MAGICIENNE	
BURTON, David	A.B.	REVENGE	
BURTON, David	Pte. R.M.	REVENGE	
BURTON, Thomas	A.B.	POWERFUL	
BURY, Thomas	A.B.	EDINBURGH	
BUSH, Matthew.C.	Ship's Corporal	POWERFUL	
	Pte. R.M.	QUEEN CHARLOTTE	Algiers
BUSH, Thomas	Pte. R.M.	CARYSFORT	
BUSH, William J	Ord	CYCLOPS	
BUSMAN, George	Boatswain 3rd Cl	HAZARD	
BUSSELL, Henry	Pte. R.M.	GANGES	
BUSVINE, Edward	Pte. R.M.	POWERFUL	
BUTCHER, Edward	Corporal R.M.	POWERFUL	
BUTLER, Daniel	Pte. R.M.	ASIA	
BUTLER, Edward	A.B.	CASTOR	(? if R.M. A.B. on Roll)
	Pte. R.M.	ALBION	Navarino
BUTLER, James	Ord	ASIA	
BUTLER, John	A.B.	VANGUARD	
BUTLER, John	A.B.	HASTINGS	
BUTLER, John	Drummer. R.M.	VANGUARD	
BUTLER, Thomas	Pte. R.M.	Pcss CHARLOTTE	
BUTLER, Thomas	Pte. R.M.	BENBOW	
BUTLER, Thomas	Pte. R.M.	HASTINGS	
BUTLER, Thomas	A.B.	GANGES	
BUTLER, William	Boatswain	VESUVIUS	
BUTT, George	Ord	BENBOW	
BUTT, Richard	Gunner. R.M.A.	CYCLOPS	
BUTTERS, Benjamin	Ord	CAMBRIDGE	

SYRIA

BUTTLE, Jacob	Pte. R.M.	THUNDERER	
BUTTON, Charles	Ord	REVENGE	
BUTTON, William	Capt' Forecastle	DAPHNE	(M) Anchor Type LS & GC
BYERS, Richard	Gunner. R.A.	PIQUE & other vessels	
BYFORD, Thomas	Capt' Mizzen Top	VANGUARD	
BYFORD, Thomas	Drummer. R.M.	CAMBRIDGE	
BYLES, John	Boy	STROMBOLI	
BYNG, J.R.M.	Midshipman	Pcss CHARLOTTE	
BYRCH, Edward	Pte. R.M.	STROMBOLI	
BYRNE, Edward	A.B.	IMPLACABLE	
CABLE, William	Ord	GANGES	
CADOGAN, Cornelius	Ship's Corporal	CAMBRIDGE	
CAFFALL, Richard	Pte. R.M.	CAMBRIDGE	
CAGER, James	Pte. R.M.	BENBOW	
CAIN, Daniel	Boy	BELLEROPHON	
CAIN, John	Boy 1st Class	THUNDERER	
CAINS, Christopher	Ord	BELLEROPHON	
CAINS, George	Ropemaker	VANGUARD	
CALAMY, William	Captain. R.M.	REVENGE	Received MGS Medal 'Java'
CALARGUE, Peter	Pilot	EDINBURGH	
CALDWELL, E.	Surgeon	CAMBRIDGE	
	Surgeon	CORDELIA	Algiers
CALIS, Francis	A.B.	CAMBRIDGE	
CALLAGHAN, Cornelius	Boy	THUNDERER	
CALLAGHAN, James	A.B.	VANGUARD	
CALLAGHAN, William	A.B.	THUNDERER	
CALLAGHAN, John	Boy	THUNDERER	
CALLAM, James	A.B.	THUNDERER	
CALLAWAY, Charles	Painter	HASTINGS	
CALLAWAY, Edward	Boy	CASTOR	
CALLICOTT, William	A.B.	IMPLACABLE	
CALLOW, Dennis	Not Given	HYDRA	
CAMILEN, Frank	Ord	EDINBURGH	
CAMMILLERI, Antonio	Ord	PHOENIX	
CAMPBELL, Allen	A.B.	REVENGE	
CAMPBELL, James (b)	Lieutenant. R.N.	BELLEROPHON	
CAMPBELL, John	A.B.	EDINBURGH	
CAMPBELL, John	Boatswain	ASIA	(Alias CAMMELL)
	Bosun's Mate	AJAX	St Sebastian
CAMPBELL, John	Cooper's Crew	IMPLACABLE	
CAMPBELL, John	Boy	RODNEY	
CAMPBELL, R.	A.B.	CASTOR	
CAMPBELL, Robert	A.B.	Pcss CHARLOTTE	
CAMPBELL, Robert	Boy	RODNEY	
CAMPBELL, Thomas	Boatswain	EDINBURGH	
CAMPLIN, Henry	Sailmaker's Crew	CAMBRIDGE	
CANDISH, Samuel	A.B.	RODNEY	
CANDY, George	A.B.	CAMBRIDGE	
CANE, Richard	Carp's Crew	BENBOW	
CANE, Samuel	Ord	MAGICIENNE	
CANHAM, William	A.B.	GANGES	
CANN, Henry	Not Given	VESUVIUS	
CANNON, J.	Corporal R.M.	CAMBRIDGE	
CANNON, William	Pte. R.M.	STROMBOLI	
CANONICO, George	Cooper	CARYSFORT	
CANTLE, George	A.B.	BELLEROPHON	
CAPPER, Joseph	A.B.	STROMBOLI	
CARBINE, James	Pte. R.M.	RODNEY	
CAREY, Michael (a)	Ord	POWERFUL	(Two borne. Both Applied)
CAREY, Michael (b)	Ord	POWERFUL	
CAREY, Richard	Boy 1st Class	POWERFUL	
CARKETT, George	Boy	THUNDERER	
CARMAN, Walter	Ord	BELLEROPHON	
CARMICHAEL, J.J.O'F.	Midshipman	POWERFUL	
CARNALL, James	A.B.	BELLEROPHON	
CARNEY, George	Yeoman of Signals	CARYSFORT	
CARNEY, John	Ord	POWERFUL	
CARPENTER, Edward	Ord	POWERFUL	
CARR, George	Q.M.	HYDRA	
CARR, George	Boy	ASIA	
CARR, Richard	Ord	THUNDERER	
CARR, Samuel	Blacksmith	MEDEA	
CARROLL, Michael	Ord	PIQUE	
CARSTAIRS, David	Boy	BENBOW	
CARSWELL, Henry	Pte. R.M.	THUNDERER	
CART, Henry	A.B.	POWERFUL	
CARTER, Charles	Pte. R.M.	CASTOR	
CARTER, Charles	Mate	GANGES	
CARTER, Harry	Pte. R.M.	STROMBOLI	
CARTER, Henry	Carp's Crew	Pcss CHARLOTTE	
CARTER, Henry	Pte. R.M.	Pcss CHARLOTTE	
CARTER, James	Pte. R.M.	CARYSFORT	
CARTER, John	Pte. R.M.	TALBOT	
CARTER, John	Pte. R.M.	HASTINGS	

CARTER, Joseph	Sergeant. R.M.	HASTINGS	
CARTER, Robert	Carp's Crew	EDINBURGH	
CARTER, Robert	Ord	EDINBURGH	
CARTER, Thomas	Supn A.B.	GANGES	
CARTER, Thomas	Pte. R.M.	RODNEY	
CARTER, William	Pte. R.M.	HAZARD	
CARTER, William	Pte. R.M.	CAMBRIDGE	
CARTHY, L.	Ord	CASTOR	
CARTWRIGHT, John	Mate	POWERFUL	
CARVER, George	Pte. R.M.	STROMBOLI	
CASELDINE, William	A.B.	EDINBURGH	
CASEY, Daniel	Sergeant. R.M.	ASIA	
CASHION, Thomas	A.B.	Pcss CHARLOTTE	
CASHMAN, James	Sailmaker's Mate	VESUVIUS	
CASHMAN, Michael	Ord	IMPLACABLE	
CASHMAN, William	Mate	EDINBURGH	
CASLEY, Thomas	Boy	IMPLACABLE	
CASLEY, William	Pte. R.M.	Pcss CHARLOTTE	
CASLICK, John	Blacksmith	EDINBURGH	
CASON, Richard	Ord	Pcss CHARLOTTE	
CASSAR, Paolo	Gun Room Cook	MAGICIENNE	
CASSFORD, W.B.	Pte. R.M.	EDINBURGH	
CASTLES, William	Boy	GANGES	(Alias W.Brown)
CATER, J.H.	Not Given	CAMBRIDGE	
CATER, Richard	Pte. R.M.	RODNEY	
CATHERINE, John	Pte. R.M.	CAMBRIDGE	
CATLING, Thomas	A.B.	IMPLACABLE	
CAUHIE, John	Not Given	HASTINGS	(M.L. as COWICK)
CAUSE, Samuel	Pte. R.M.	TALBOT	
CAUSLEY, William	Pte. R.M.	THUNDERER	
CAVANAGH, Edward	Ord	MAGICIENNE	
CAVANNAGH, Daniel	Yeoman of Signals	GANGES	
CAVELL, John	Ord	ASIA	
CAVENDISH, John	M.A.A.	EDINBURGH	
CAWKELL, Edward	A.B.	CAMBRIDGE	
CEILEY, John	Ord	TALBOT	
CHACKLE, John	Pte. R.M.	GANGES	
CHAFFEY, Henry	Ord	BENBOW	
CHALK, William.M.	A.B.	Pcss CHARLOTTE	
CHALLEN, William	A.B.	EDINBURGH	
CHAMBERLAIN, Charles	Gunner	EDINBURGH	
CHAMBERLAIN, William.C.	Mate	STROMBOLI	
CHAMBERS, Joseph	A.B.	MAGICIENNE	
CHAMBERS, William	Pte. R.M.	POWERFUL	
CHAMPION, Samuel	Pte. R.M.	RODNEY	
CHANDLER, James	A.B.	WASP	
CHANGARO, Antonio	A.B.	ASIA	
CHANNINGS, Nicholas	Engineer's Boy	MEDEA	
CHANNON, John	A.B.	RODNEY	
CHAPEL, James	Pte. R.M.	BENBOW	
CHAPLIN, Thomas	Boy	ZEBRA	
CHAPMAN, A.B.	Gunner	CYCLOPS	
CHAPMAN, Henry	Stoker	BELLEROPHON	
CHAPMAN, James	Corporal. R.M.	BELLEROPHON	
CHAPMAN, John	Pte. R.M.	Pcss CHARLOTTE	
CHAPMAN, John.R.	Pte. R.M.	THUNDERER	
CHAPMAN, Samuel	A.B.	CARYSFORT	
CHAPMAN, William	Yeoman of Signals	VANGUARD	
CHAPMAN, William	Ord	BELLEROPHON	
CHAPMAN, William	A.B.	PIQUE	
CHAPMAN, W.P.	Mate	GANGES	
CHAPPELL, James	Pte. R.M.	EDINBURGH	
CHAPPELL, John	Gunner. R.M.A.	CYCLOPS	
CHAPPELL, John	A.B.	DAPHNE	
CHAPPELL, John	Pte. R.M.	STROMBOLI	
CHARDE, Samuel	Boy	WASP	
CHARLES, George.F.	Second Master	THUNDERER	
CHARLES, William	A.B.	BELLEROPHON	
CHARLETON, Henry	Mate	THUNDERER	
CHARLEWOOD, Edward.P.	Lieutenant. R.N.	BENBOW	
CHARLO, George	Ord	HASTINGS	
CHARLWOOD, William	A.B.	IMPLACABLE	
CHARNOCK, Henry	A.B.	ASIA	
CHARTERS, Alexander.G.	Carp's Crew	THUNDERER	
CHASE, Edward	Pte. R.M.	BENBOW	
CHASE, George	Pte. R.M.	RODNEY	
CHASE, Parkhurst	Volunteer 1st Cl	VANGUARD	
CHASE, William	Pte. R.M.	DAPHNE	
CHATFIELD, John	Pte. R.M.	EDINBURGH	
CHATFIELD, Richard	Pte. R.M.	EDINBURGH	
CHEELS, Edward	Capt' of Mast	VANGUARD	
CHEERE, John	Lieutenant. R.N.	BELLEROPHON	
CHEERY, William	Pte. R.M.	STROMBOLI	
CHEESMAN, James	Pte. R.M.	CAMBRIDGE	
CHEESMAN, Robert.G.	Asst Clerk	PIQUE	

SYRIA

CHERRY, William	Ord	POWERFUL	
CHERTES, John	Ord	THUNDERER	
CHESHAM, George	Pte. R.M.	GANGES	
CHESNEY, Samuel	Gnr(?) R.A.	HECATE	
CHESNUT, Thomas	L.M.	REVENGE	
CHEVERTON, Thomas	A.B.	STROMBOLI	
CHIBERS, James	Pte. R.M.	RODNEY	
CHIDDICK, Stephen	Pte. R.M.	DIDO	
CHIFFINCE, George	Pte. R.M.	BENBOW	
CHILD, John	A.B.	BELLEROPHON	
CHILDS, George	A.B.	TALBOT	
CHILDS, Joseph	A.B.	VANGUARD	
CHILDS, Joseph	Captain. R.M.	REVENGE	
CHILDS, Philip	Pte. R.M.	CAMBRIDGE	
CHILDS, Richard	Pte. R.M.	STROMBOLI	
CHILDS, Thomas	Capt' Main Top	BELLEROPHON	
CHILLINGFORD, Richard	A.B.	BELLEROPHON	
CHILMAN, John	Pte. R.M.	GANGES	
CHINERY, John	Pte. R.M.	GORGON	
CHINNERY, John	Pte. R.M.	GORGON	(same man as above?)
CHIPP, Abraham	A.B.	EDINBURGH	
CHIPP, William	Gunner's Crew	DIDO	
CHISLETT, John	Pte. R.M.	THUNDERER	
CHITTENDEN, Edward	A.B.	WASP	
CHITTENDEN, William	Ord	MAGICIENNE	
CHIVERS, Thomas	Clr Sgt. R.M.	Pcss CHARLOTTE	(M) Anchor Type LS & GC
CHIVERTON, Richard	A.B.	PIQUE	
CHIVERTON, Thomas	A.B.	STROMBOLI	
CHORLTON, William	Pte. R.M.	Pcss CHARLOTTE	
	Pte. R.M.	MUSQUITO	Navarino
CHRISTIAN, Thomas.H.	Lieut. R.N.	Pcss CHARLOTTE	
CHRISTIE, Thomas	Bosun's Mate	HAZARD	
	A.B.	DARTMOUTH	Navarino
CHUBB, George	Carp's Crew	CAMBRIDGE	
CHUBB, George	Ord	BELLEROPHON	
CHUBB, Henry	Carp's Crew	RODNEY	
CHUBB, Isaac	Pte. R.M.	THUNDERER	
CHUMPRESS, Richard	A.B.	CAMBRIDGE	(May read CHAMPNESS)
CHURCH, Daniel	A.B.	CAMBRIDGE	
CHURCH, Joseph	Ord	POWERFUL	
CHURCH, Matthew	Pte. R.M.	VESUVIUS	
CHURCH, William	Ord	BENBOW	
CHURCHER, Joseph	A.B.	Pcss CHARLOTTE	
CHURCHMAN, Henry	Pte. R.M.	Pcss CHARLOTTE	
CHURCHWARD, John	A.B.	MEDEA	
CLACK, James	Pte. R.M.	VANGUARD	
CLAIG, Benjamin	Pte. R.M.	Pcss CHARLOTTE	
CLANCEY, William	Bosun's Mate	BENBOW	
CLARE, Francis	Pte. R.M.	HASTINGS	
CLARE, Joseph	Carp's Crew	EDINBURGH	
CLARINGBOULD, Charles.G.	Boy	GANGES	
CLARINGBOULD, William	L.M.	GANGES	
CLARK, David	Boy 1st Class	WASP	
CLARK, Frederick	A.B.	BELLEROPHON	
CLARK, George	Boy	EDINBURGH	
CLARK, James	Pte. R.M.	VANGUARD	
CLARK, James (or CLARKE)	Sailmaker's Crew	IMPLACABLE	
CLARK, Robert	Pte. R.M.	BELLEROPHON	
CLARK, Thomas	Pte. R.M.	HASTINGS	
CLARK, Thomas	Ord	BENBOW	
CLARK, Thomas	Ord	VANGUARD	
CLARK, William	Lieutenant. R.N.	EDINBURGH	
CLARK, William	A.B.	EDINBURGH	
CLARKE, Edward.F.	Mate	BELLEROPHON	
CLARKE, Edwin	Carp's Crew	TALBOT	
CLARKE, George	Purser	VESUVIUS	
CLARKE, George.H.	Mate	HYDRA	
CLARKE, John	Boy 2nd Class	VANGUARD	
CLARKE, Latimore	A.B.	PIQUE	
CLARKE, Philip	Pte. R.M.	THUNDERER	
CLARKE, Richard	Boy	THUNDERER	
CLARKE, Richard	Not Given	PIQUE	
CLARKE, William	A.B.	HAZARD	
CLARKE, William	Carp's Crew	BENBOW	
CLARKE, William	Ord	BENBOW	
CLAVELL, Richard.K.	2nd Lieut. R.M.	GANGES	
CLAVERING, H.A.	Midshipman	IMPLACABLE	
CLAY, Christopher	Fifer. R.M.	VESUVIUS	
CLAY, John	Pte. R.M.	BELLEROPHON	
CLAY, Thomas	Pte. R.M.	EDINBURGH	(Additional clasp?)
CLAYTON, George	A.B.	DIDO	
CLEAR, Thomas	A.B.	GANGES	

CLEAVELAND, George	Mate	Pcss CHARLOTTE	
CLEGG, Charles	Boy 1st Class	VESUVIUS	
CLEMENSON, James	A.B.	ASIA	
CLEMENTS, Charles	A.B.	DAPHNE	
CLEMENTS, George	3rd Engineer	STROMBOLI	
CLEMENTS, Henry	A.B.	CAMBRIDGE	
	Boy	DARTMOUTH	*Navarino*
CLEMENTS, James	Pte. R.M.	GANGES	
CLEMENTS, William	A.B.	Pcss CHARLOTTE	
CLEMENTS, William	Ord	THUNDERER	
CLENCY, William	Bosun's Mate	BELLEROPHON	
CLEVELAND, Robert	Ord	ZEBRA	
CLEVERLY, James	Ship's Corporal	BELLEROPHON	(M) Anchor Type LS & GC
CLEVERTY, Richard	Carp's Mate	CAMBRIDGE	
CLEWS, John	A.B.	HASTINGS	
CLIFFORD, James	Boy	EDINBURGH	
CLIFT, Daniel	Ord	HASTINGS	
CLIFT, Robert	Ord	BENBOW	
CLIFTON, George	Volunteer 1st Cl	BELLEROPHON	
CLINCH, Timothy	Clerk	STROMBOLI	
CLISSOLD, Daniel	Sergeant. R.M.	IMPLACABLE	
CLIVE, James	Pte. R.M.	CASTOR	
CLOAKE, Henry	Ord	BENBOW	
CLOKE, Charles	Pte. R.M.	CASTOR	
CLOSE, William	Ord	RODNEY	
COAKLEY, D.J.	A.B.	BELLEROPHON	
COATES, Daniel	A.B.	EDINBURGH	
COBB, George	Capt's Coxswain	EDINBURGH	
COBDEN, Joseph	Gunner's Mate	Pcss CHARLOTTE	
COBHAM, John	Pte. R.M.	CAMBRIDGE	
COCHRAN, Thomas	Mate	ASIA	
COCHRANE, Arthur.A.	Volunteer 1st Cl	BENBOW	
COCHRANE, John	A.B.	BELLEROPHON	
COCK, Aaron	Sergeant. R.M.	THUNDERER	
COCKBURN, David	Cooper's Mate	HASTINGS	
COCKBURN, J.H.	Mate	CASTOR	
COCKING, Nicholas	Pte. R.M.	PHOENIX	
COCKING, William	Ord	RODNEY	
CODD, Edward	Lieutenant. R.N.	TALBOT	
CODRINGTON, H.J.	Captain R.N.	TALBOT	
	Midshipman	ASIA	*Navarino*
COE, John	A.B.	CAMBRIDGE	
COE, Philip	A.B.	ASIA	
COFFIN, James	L.M.	STROMBOLI	
COFFIN, Richard	Pte. R.M.	THUNDERER	
COGHLAN, John	A.B.	CYCLOPS	
COGHLAN, Thomas	Caulker	POWERFUL	*(May read COGLAN)*
COHEN, William	A.B.	MAGICIENNE	
COHNBURN, Daniel	Gunner's Mate	ZEBRA	
COKER, Charles	Boy	REVENGE	
COKER, James	A.B.	PIQUE	
	A.B.	PHILOMEL	*Navarino*
COLBERT, Bartholomew	Ord	POWERFUL	
COLE, Alfred	Ord	CARYSFORT	
COLE, Charles.A.	Second Master	CASTOR	
COLE, Daniel	A.B.	THUNDERER	
COLE, Edward	Pte. R.M.	POWERFUL	
COLE, Edwin	Pte. R.M.	REVENGE	
COLE, Edwin	Pte. R.M.	POWERFUL	
COLE, James	Pte. R.M.	STROMBOLI	
COLE, James	Pte. R.M.	EDINBURGH	
CALE, James	Ord	RODNEY	
COLE, Matthew	A.B.	VANGUARD	
COLE, Nathaniel	Bosun's Mate	GANGES	
COLE, Philip	Pte. R.M.	RODNEY	
COLE, Theophilus	Stoker	PHOENIX	
COLE, William	Pte. R.M.	POWERFUL	
COLEMAN, Frederick	Pte. R.M.	BENBOW	
COLEMAN, John	Armourer	ASIA	
COLEMAN, John	A.B.	REVENGE	
COLEMAN, J.M.	Ord	CASTOR	
COLES, Cowper.P.	Mate	GANGES	
COLES, Richard	A.B.	PHOENIX	
COLES, Thomas	Engineer's Boy	VESUVIUS	
COLES, William	Gunner's Mate	BENBOW	
COLLERO, Vincent	Ord	HAZARD	
	Ord	ASIA	*Navarino*
COLLERY, Michael	Ord	VANGUARD	
COLLETT, Joseph	Pte. R.M.	STROMBOLI	
COLLEY, William	Ord	DIDO	
COLLEY, William	A.B.	CAMBRIDGE	
COLLEYS, Henry	Q.M.	ZEBRA	

SYRIA

COLLIER, Edward	Captain. R.N.	CASTOR	
	Lieutenant. R.N.	St FIORENZO	San Fiorenzo. 14 Feby 1805
	Lieutenant. R.N.	St FIORENZO	San Fiorenzo. 8 March 1808
	Lieutenant. R.N.	THAMES (P)	Amanthea. 25 July 1810
COLLIER, Joseph	Boy 2nd Class	Pcss CHARLOTTE	
COLLIN, Henry	A.B.	REVENGE	(Alias COLLIER)
COLLINGS, Bartholomew	Ord	CASTOR	
COLLINGS, James.S.	Sergeant. R.M.	IMPLACABLE	
COLLINGS, John	A.B.	BELLEROPHON	
COLLINGS, Joseph	Ord	VANGUARD	
COLLINGS, Richard.G.	Capt' After Guard	IMPLACABLE	
COLLINGS, William	A.B.	PHOENIX	
COLLINGTON, John	Pte. R.M.	EDINBURGH	
COLLINS, Bartholomew	Ord	THUNDERER	
COLLINS, Dennis	Ord	RODNEY	
COLLINS, George	Gunner's Crew	BELLEROPHON	
COLLINS, George	Capt's Coxswain	IMPLACABLE	
COLLINS, Henry	Bosun's Mate	Pcss CHARLOTTE	
COLLINS, Henry	Two Borne Ord & AB	GANGES	
COLLINS, James	Capt's Steward	CARYSFORT	
COLLINS, Jeremiah	Ord	IMPLACABLE	
COLLINS, John	Q.M.	HASTINGS	
	Q.M.	ASIA	Navarino
COLLINS, John	Ord	CYCLOPS	
COLLINS, Michael	Ord	THUNDERER	
COLLINS, Michael	L.M.	RODNEY	
COLLINS, Richard	Bosun's Mate	HECATE	
	Ord	ROSE	Navarino
COLLINS, Richard	Carp's Crew	THUNDERER	
COLLINS, Richard	Pte. R.M.	RODNEY	(Additional clasp?)
COLLINS, Robert	A.B.	RODNEY	
COLLINS, Robert	A.B.	CAMBRIDGE	
COLLINS, Thomas	Pte. R.M.	IMPLACABLE	
COLLINS, Thomas	Ord	HYDRA	
COLLINS, William	Two Borne	GANGES	Capt FX and A.B.
COLLIS, Frederick	Pte. R.M.	VESUVIUS	(M.L. as COLLINS)
COLLIS, George	Pte. R.M.	BENBOW	
COLLIS, James	A.B.	VANGUARD	
COLLISTER, John	Q.M.	RODNEY	
COLMAN, Charles.E.	Clerk	VESUVIUS	
COLMAN, George	Capt' Main Top	DAPHNE	
COLQUHON, F.H.	Lieut Colonel R.A.	HECATE	
COLSON, George	Ord	TALBOT	
COLSON, Samuel	Q.M.	STROMBOLI	
COLSON, Samuel	Q.M.	REVENGE	
COLVILE, George.T.	Volunteer 1st Cl	TALBOT	
COLWELL, John	Paymaster & Purser	PHOENIX	
	Vol 1st Cl	SCEPTRE	Anse La Barque 18 Decr 1809 (Vfd Abd. Not on Roll)
	Vol 1st Cl	SCEPTRE	Guadaloupe
COMBER, Thomas	Pte. R.M.	EDINBURGH	
COMBS, Moses	A.B.	EDINBURGH	
COMEFORD, Garrit	A.B.	VANGUARD	
COMEN, W.A.C.	Ord	GLASGOW	
COMETY, John	A.B.	HECATE	
COMPTON, Henry	A.B.	MAGICIENNE	
COMPTON, William	Boy 1st Class	Pcss CHARLOTTE	
COMUS, John	Pilot	CASTOR	(or CORNUS)
CONEY, Daniel.S.	M.A.A.	BELLEROPHON	
CONGRAM, Henry	Boy	THUNDERER	
CONNELL, Bernard	Pte. R.M.	BELLEROPHON	
CONNELL, James	Pte. R.M.	Pcss CHARLOTTE	
CONNOLLY, James	A.B.	IMPLACABLE	(Spelt CONNELLY also Roll)
	Boy 2nd Class	SHANNON	Shannon Wh Chesapeake
	Ord	GENOA	Navarino
CONNOLLY, Matthew	Mate	CASTOR	
CONNOR, Daniel	Ord	POWERFUL	
CONNOR, Edward	Ord	POWERFUL	(Alias O'CONNELL)
CONNOR, John	A.B.	EDINBURGH	
CONNOR, John	Ord	HECATE	
CONNOR, Michael	A.B.	ASIA	
CONNOR, Patrick	A.B.	REVENGE	
CONSTABLE, John	A.B.	EDINBURGH	
	A.B.	ALBION	Navarino
CONSTANT, James	Boy	CAMBRIDGE	
CONSTANT, Jesse	Pte. R.M.	GANGES	
CONSTINE, Joseph	A.B.	Pcss CHARLOTTE	
CONTSTONAY, William	Ord	POWERFUL	
CONWAY, James	A.B.	IMPLACABLE	
COOK, Charles	Pte. R.M.	CAMBRIDGE	
COOK, George	Gunner's Mate	DAPHNE	
	A.B.	ASIA	Navarino

COOK, George	L.M.	REVENGE	
COOK, George	Boy	CASTOR	
COOK, Henry	Pte. R.M.	Pcss CHARLOTTE	
COOK, Henry	Ord	RODNEY	
COOK, James	A.B.	IMPLACABLE	
COOK, James	Boy	CARYSFORT	
COOK, John	Pte. R.M.	HYDRA	
COOK, John	Capt' Main Top	Pcss CHARLOTTE	
COOK, John	Two borne	POWERFUL	Blacksmith or A.B.
COOK, John	Ord	THUNDERER	
COOK, John (2)	A.B.	POWERFUL	
COOK, Joseph	Pte. R.M.	BENBOW	
	Pte. R.M.	ASIA	Navarino
COOK, Matthew	Bosun's Mate	IMPLACABLE	
COOK, Peter	A.B.	BELLEROPHON	
COOK, Richard	A.B.	Pcss CHARLOTTE	
COOK, Robert	Pte. R.M.	REVENGE	
COOK, Thomas	Pte. R.M.	HASTINGS	
COOKE, Henry	Two borne	RODNEY	Ord or Boy
COOKE, Samuel	Pte. R.M.	CASTOR	
COOKE, William	Carpenter	RODNEY	
COOMBE, H.	Boy	IMPLACABLE	
COOMBE, Stephen	Bosun's Mate	CAMBRIDGE	
COOMBES, George	Pte. R.M.	VANGUARD	
COOMBES, John	Pte. R.M.	THUNDERER	
COOMBES, John	Stoker	GORGON	
COOMBS, Charles	Pte. R.M.	REVENGE	
COOMBS, Roger	Q.M.	GORGON	
COONEY, James	L.M.	REVENGE	
COONEY, John	A.B.	RODNEY	
COOPER, George	Ord	BENBOW	
COOPER, Henry	A.B.	GORGON	
COOPER, James	Ord	PIQUE	
COOPER, John	Capt' Main Top	GANGES	
COOPER, Richard	Pte. R.M.	BELLEROPHON	
COOPER, Thomas	Clr Sgt. R.M.	PHOENIX	
COOPER, Thomas	Bombdr. R.M.A.	STROMBOLI	
COOPER, William	A.B.	EDINBURGH	
COOPER, William	Boy	PIQUE	
COOPER, William	Capt' of Mast	Pcss CHARLOTTE	
COOTE, John	Boy	CARYSFORT	
COOTE, Robert	Mate	DAPHNE	
COOTE, William	A.B.	VANGUARD	
COOTER, William	Boy 2nd Class	VESUVIUS	
COOTES, James	A.B.	EDINBURGH	
COPPLESTONE, Joseph	A.B.	GANGES	
CORBETT, John	Midshipman	CARYSFORT	
CORCORAN, William	Not Given	POWERFUL	(M.L. as CORKLIN)
CORK, John	Pte. R.M.	Pcss CHARLOTTE	
CORK, John	Pte. R.M.	THUNDERER	
CORKEREY, John	A.B.	HASTINGS	
CORNELIUS, Henry	Ropemaker	IMPLACABLE	(M) Anchor Type LS & GC
CORNELL, Timothy	A.B.	CASTOR	
CORNEY, William	A.B.	Pcss CHARLOTTE	
CORNISH, Anthony	Ord	RODNEY	
CORNISH, Frederick	Boy	PIQUE	
CORNISH, M.	Carp's Crew	THUNDERER	(M.L. as John)
CORP, William	Pte. R.M.	POWERFUL	
CORPS, William	Ord	EDINBURGH	
CORSAR, Frederick	Pte. R.M.	Pcss CHARLOTTE	
CORYTON, George.H.	Captain. R.M.	ASIA	
COSSAR, Walter	1st Lieut. R.M.	RODNEY	
COSSEY, Robert	Ship's Corporal	POWERFUL	
COSTER, John	Pte. R.M.	REVENGE	
COTGROVE, Henry	A.B.	CAMBRIDGE	
COTTER, Patrick	Ord	THUNDERER	
COTTON, Frederick.L.	Midshipman	BELLEROPHON	
COTTON, James	Pte. R.M.	REVENGE	
COUCH, Thomas	Carp's Crew	POWERFUL	
COULSON, Richard	A.B.	ASIA	
COUNTRY, Jeremiah	Ord	THUNDERER	
COUPER, James	Carp's Crew	CYCLOPS	
COURME, Frank	Ord	EDINBURGH	
COURT, William	Yeoman of Signals	CAMBRIDGE	
COURTENAY, Richard.W.	Mate	EDINBURGH	
COURTNALL, Joseph	A.B.	POWERFUL	
COURTNELL, Henry	Caulker	EDINBURGH	
COURTS, John	Capt' Main Top	CARYSFORT	
COUSER, James	Capt' Forecastle	CARYSFORT	
COUSINS, Matthew	Pte. R.M.	HASTINGS	
COUSINS, Thomas	Gunner's Crew	Pcss CHARLOTTE	(May read COUSENS)
COUZENS, James	Ord	BENBOW	
COUZENS, John	Gunner	MEDEA	
	Ord	TALBOT	Navarino
COUZINS, William	Boy	EDINBURGH	

SYRIA

COVENTRY, James	Pte. R.M.	BELLEROPHON	
COVEY, William.H.	Boy	PHOENIX	
COWARD, Charles	L.M.	REVENGE	
COWLEY, James	A.B.	ASIA	
COWLING, Stephen	Yeoman of Signals	HASTINGS	
COWLING, William	A.B.	IMPLACABLE	
COX, Charles	Capt' of Mast	BELLEROPHON	
COX, Francis	Pte. R.M.	Pcss CHARLOTTE	
COX, Henry	Pte. R.M.	ASIA	
COX, James	A.B.	RODNEY	
COX, John	Pte. R.M.	ASIA	
COX, John	Ord	THUNDERER	
COX, Josiah	Capt' Fore Top	BELLEROPHON	
COX, Matthew	Sailmaker	ASIA	
COX, Thomas	A.B.	EDINBURGH	
COX, Thomas.C.	Boy	PIQUE	
COX, William	Boy	ASIA	
COXELL, Joseph	A.B.	HYDRA	
COXHEAD, William	Pte. R.M.	VANGUARD	
COZENS, Charles	Ord	EDINBURGH	
COZENS, Thomas	A.B.	HYDRA	
CRACKLAND, William	Pte. R.M.	CAMBRIDGE	
CRADDOCK, James	Boy	ZEBRA	
CRAGO, John	Boy	THUNDERER	
CRAIG, George	A.B.	REVENGE	
CRANCH, William	Fifer. R.M.	IMPLACABLE	
CRANE, George	Sergeant. R.M.	STROMBOLI	
CRANE, John	Q.M.	TALBOT	
CRANN, Thomas	A.B.	CAMBRIDGE	(M) Anchor Type LS & GC
CRANTON, George	Pte. R.M.	IMPLACABLE	
CRAUFURD, F.A.B.	Midshipman	BENBOW	
CRAUFURD, H.W.	Commander	POWERFUL	
CRAWFORD, William	Mate	RODNEY	
CRAWLE, George	Capt' of Mast	IMPLACABLE	
CRAWLEY, Charles	A.B.	RODNEY	
CRAWLEY, William	Ord	POWERFUL	
CREBER, William	Ord	CAMBRIDGE	
CREED, William	A.B.	HASTINGS	
CREEK, William	Pte. R.M.	ASIA	
CREMOR, William	Bosun's Mate	TALBOT	
CRESSY, William	A.B.	MAGICIENNE	
CREW, Charles	Pte. R.M.	Pcss CHARLOTTE	
CREW, Robert	Pte. R.M.	Pcss CHARLOTTE	
CREWS, William	Gunner's Mate	GANGES	
CREWS, William	Capt' Main Top	RODNEY	
CREYKE, Richard.B.	Mate	BELLEROPHON	
CRIDDLE, Thomas	Pte. R.M.	STROMBOLI	
CRIPPS, Joseph	Ord	MAGICIENNE	
CRISP, William	Blacksmith	DIDO	
CRISPIN, Thomas	Boy	TALBOT	
CROAD, William.M.	Carp's Mate	BELLEROPHON	
CROCKER, George	Boy	TALBOT	
CROFT, Edward	Pte. R.M.	RODNEY	
CROFT, Emmerson	Pte. R.M.	ASIA	
CROKER, Henry	Ord	IMPLACABLE	
CROOKS, Samuel	Boy	POWERFUL	
CROSBY, John.G.	A.B.	VANGUARD	(M.L. as John CROSBY)
CROSS, Charles	Pte. R.M.	HASTINGS	
CROSS, Edward	A.B.	CAMBRIDGE	
CROSS, James	Ord	EDINBURGH	
CROSS, Thomas	Pte. R.M.	EDINBURGH	
CROSS, William	Pte. R.M.	REVENGE	
CROSSCOMBE, George	A.B.	RODNEY	
CROSTON, William	A.B.	REVENGE	
CROUCH, Frederick	Boy	REVENGE	
CROUCH, George	Ord	BENBOW	
CROUCHER, James.H.	A.B.	BELLEROPHON	
CROW, John	A.B.	BELLEROPHON	
CROW, Josiah	Boy	BENBOW	
CROW, Lewis	Ord	ASIA	
CROWDY, Thomas	Pte. R.M.	STROMBOLI	
CROWHURST, John	Pte. R.M.	PIQUE & CARYSFORT	
CROWLEY, George	Boy	BENBOW	
CROWLEY, Patrick	Ship's Cook	MEDEA	
CROWSON, Thomas	Clr Sgt. R.M.	HAZARD	(M) Waterloo Medal Anchor Type LS & GC
CROZIER, William.P.	Lieutenant. R.N.	WASP	
CRUMPLIN, John	Ord	BENBOW	
CRUNDEN, Edward	Pte. R.M.	Pcss CHARLOTTE	
CRUYS, William	Sergeant. R.M.	STROMBOLI	
CRUYS, William.H.	Boy	STROMBOLI	
CUDLIP, Matthew	A.B.	CAMBRIDGE	
CUDLIPP, Benjamin	A.B.	Pcss CHARLOTTE	

CUDLIPP, George	Ord	Pcss CHARLOTTE	
CUDLIPP, Nicholas	Ord	THUNDERER	
CULBUSH, William	Pte. R.M.	HASTINGS	
CULLAMORE, John	A.B.	EDINBURGH	
CULLUM, William	Boy 2nd Class	GORGON	
CULLINGS, Edward	Pte. R.M.	HASTINGS	
CULLIS, Henry	Capt' Main Top	MAGICIENNE	
CULVER, James	Pte. R.M.	CASTOR	
CULVERHOUSE, James	A.B.	PIQUE	(M) Anchor Type LS & GC
	A.B.	ROSE	Navarino
CUMBER, Henry	Boy	CYCLOPS	
CUMMING, Arthur	Mate	CYCLOPS	
CUMMINGS, Andrew	A.B.	IMPLACABLE	
CUMMINGS, James.J.	A.B.	BELLEROPHON	
CUMMINGS, John	A.B.	EDINBURGH	
CUMMINGS, Robert	A.B.	VANGUARD	
CUMMINS, Joseph	Boy	HASTINGS	
CUNDY, George	A.B.	CAMBRIDGE	
CUNLIFFE, Jonathan	Sergeant. R.M.	WASP	
CUNNINGHAM, Michael	A.B.	REVENGE	
CURETON, Phillip	Pte. R.M.	THUNDERER	
CURME, David	Pte. R.M.	ASIA	
CURRAN, William	Boy	IMPLACABLE	
CURRIN, William	A.B.	BENBOW	
	Ord	ASIA	Navarino
CURRY, Douglas	Lieutenant. R.N.	PIQUE	(Incorrect "Mid" on Roll)
	Midshipman	ROSE	Navarino
CURRY, Robert.M.	1st Lieut. R.M.	THUNDERER	
CURRY, William	Ord	THUNDERER	
CURTIS, Henry	A.B.	BELLEROPHON	
CURTIS, James	Ord	PHOENIX	
CURTIS, John	Pte. R.M.	HASTINGS	
CURTIS, Samuel	A.B.	REVENGE	
CURTIS, William	Pte. R.M.	GORGON	
CUSWORTH, Richard	Gunner. R.M.A.	GORGON	
CUTFIELD, Alfred.B.	Asst Surgeon	EDINBURGH	
CUTLER, Joseph	Ord	BENBOW	
CUTLER, Thomas	Bosun's Mate	BELLEROPHON	
CUZRUNGTON, Joseph	Pte. R.M.	ASIA	
CYCLUNA, Frank	A.B.	BENBOW	
DADD, John	Boy	EDINBURGH	
D'AETH, Edward.H.H.	Midshipman	BELLEROPHON	
DAGWELL, John	Ord	BENBOW	
DAINES, John	Ord	DIDO	
DALE, William	Pte. R.M.	REVENGE	
DALEY, William	A.B.	TALBOT	
DALGLISH, David	Pte. R.M.	STROMBOLI	
DALL, Henry	Boy	CYCLOPS	
DALLY, Philip	Pte. R.M.	STROMBOLI	
DALTON, James	Pte. R.M.	IMPLACABLE	
DALTON, Silvanus	Sailmaker	Pcss CHARLOTTE	
DALY, James	M.A.A.	GANGES	(M) Anchor Type LS & GC
	Pte. R.M.	FREIJA	Guadaloupe
DALY, John	L.M.	VESUVIUS	
DAN, Richard	Boy	TALBOT	
DAN, William	Ord	IMPLACABLE	
DANIELS, John	Armourer	Pcss CHARLOTTE	
DANIELLS, W.B.	Capt' of Hold	CYCLOPS	
DANN, John	Pte. R.M.	VANGUARD	
DANN, William	Ord	CAMBRIDGE	
DARCH, Jesse	Gunner. R.A.	HECATE	(DOUCH?)
DAREL, James.S.	Midshipman	PIQUE	
DARK, Henry	A.B.	RODNEY	
DARK, John	Pte. R.M.	EDINBURGH	
DARK, Joseph	Capt' Fore Top	CASTOR	
DARNELL, Philip.W.	Midshipman	HAZARD	
DARRAGH, John	Ord	RODNEY	
DASH, John	Ord	BENBOW	
DAVENPORT, Thomas	Pte. R.M.	THUNDERER	
DAVERS, Cornelius	Ord	THUNDERER	
DAVEY, John	Boy	RODNEY	
DAVEY, George	Sailmaker's Crew	Pcss CHARLOTTE	
DAVEY, Samuel	Boy	RODNEY	
DAVIDGE, George	Pte. R.M.	THUNDERER	
DAVIDGE, John	M.A.A.	REVENGE	(M) Anchor Type LS & GC
DAVIDGE, John	Boy	REVENGE	
DAVIDSON, Edwin.C.	Clerk	ASIA	
DAVIDSON, Hugh	A.B.	GORGON	
DAVIDSON, James	Asst Surgeon	DAPHNE	
DAVIDSON, Robert	A.B.	GANGES	
DAVIDSON, William	Q.M.	CAMBRIDGE	
DAVIES, Benjamin	Pte. R.M.	MEDEA	
DAVIES, Daniel	A.B.	BELLEROPHON	
DAVIES, David	Color Sgt. R.M.	THUNDERER	
DAVIES, David	A.B.	TALBOT	

SYRIA

DAVIES, Jacob	Pte. R.M.	Pcss CHARLOTTE	
DAVIES, James	Pte. R.M.	DIDO	
DAVIES, James	Ord	ASIA	
DAVIES, John	Pte. R.M.	BELLEROPHON	
DAVIES, John	Pte. R.M.	IMPLACABLE	
DAVIES, John	Pte. R.M.	POWERFUL	
DAVIES, John	Master	EDINBURGH	
DAVIES, Thomas (b)	Mate	GANGES	
DAVIES, William	Pte. R.M.	POWERFUL	
DAVIS, Charles	Pte. R.M.	Pcss CHARLOTTE	
DAVIS, Edward	Pte. R.M.	THUNDERER	
DAVIS, George	A.B.	BELLEROPHON	
DAVIS, George	A.B.	CAMBRIDGE	
DAVIS, George	Ord	Pcss CHARLOTTE	
DAVIS, Henry	Capt' Main Top	POWERFUL	
DAVIS, Henry	Pte. R.M.	Pcss CHARLOTTE	
DAVIS, H.B.	Lieutenant. R.N.	REVENGE	
DAVIS, John	Pte. R.M.	BELLEROPHON	
DAVIS, John	Gunner	VESUVIUS	
DAVIS, John	A.B.	MAGICIENNE	
DAVIS, John	A.B.	BELLEROPHON	
DAVIS, John	Ord	CAMBRIDGE	(M.L. as DAVIES)
DAVIS, Owen	Ord	VANGUARD	
DAVIS, Richard	Gunner's Crew	DIDO	
DAVIS, Richard	Capt' Fore Top	DIDO	
DAVIS, Richard	A.B.	THUNDERER	
DAVIS, Robert	Ship's Cook	PHOENIX	
DAVIS, Thomas	Capt' Fore Top	THUNDERER	
DAVIS, Thomas	Pte. R.M.	Pcss CHARLOTTE	
DAVIS, Thomas	Pte. R.M.	BELLEROPHON	
DAVIS, William	Pte. R.M.	CAMBRIDGE	
DAVISON, James.S.	Mate	HASTINGS	
DAVISON, John	Capt's Coxswain	PIQUE	
DAVY, Henry	Master	THUNDERER	
DAVY, Joseph	Capt' Fore Top	WASP	
DAVY, Samuel	Engineer's Apprentice	GORGON	
DAW, Edmund	Pte. R.M.	GANGES	
DAW, Henry	Gunner. R.M.A.	STROMBOLI	
DAW, Joseph	Ord	REVENGE	
DAWE, George	Boy	Pcss CHARLOTTE	
DAWE, Henry	Ord	REVENGE	
DAWE, James	Boy	RODNEY	
DAWE, William	A.B.	RODNEY	
DAWKES, James	Pte. R.M.	REVENGE	
DAWKINGS, George	A.B.	ASIA	
DAWKINS, Charles	Pte. R.M.	EDINBURGH	
DAWKINS, William	Boy	HASTINGS	
DAWSON, Henry	Boy	CASTOR	
DAWSON, H.W.	Volunteer	VANGUARD	
DAWSON, John	Ord	REVENGE	
DAWSON, Thomas	Pte. R.M.	HECATE	
	Pte. R.M.	ASIA	Navarino
DAWSON, William	Pte. R.M.	PHOENIX	
DAY, Charles	Ord	THUNDERER	
DAY, George	Pte. R.M.	ASIA	
DAY, George.F.	Mate	BENBOW	
DAY, Jabez	Sailmaker	GORGON	
DAY, J.A.	Clerk's Asst	VANGUARD	
DAY, Joseph	Pte. R.M.	VANGUARD	
DAY, William	Ord	POWERFUL	
DEACON, John	Pte. R.M.	MAGICIENNE	
	Pte. R.M.	ALBION	Navarino
DEACON, Jonathan	Pte. R.M.	PIQUE	
DEACTON, Charles.B.	A.B.	BELLEROPHON	
DEAN, James	Pte. R.M.	ASIA	
DEAR, George	Boy	BELLEROPHON	
DEAS, David	Surgeon	HYDRA	
DEATHERS, Thomas	Sailmaker's Crew	PHOENIX	
DEBOUS, Lawrence	Capt's Cook	MAGICIENNE	(or DEBOUR)
DEDAMEES, George	Q.M.	DAPHNE	
DEE, John	Pte. R.M.	STROMBOLI	
DEE, Patrick	A.B.	EDINBURGH	
De GORGIO, Pascalli	Gun Rm Steward	DAPHNE	
De HORSEY, Algernon.F.R.	Not Given	VANGUARD	
DEIGHTON, George.R.	Clerk	CASTOR	
DEMARE, James	Capt's Cook	VANGUARD	
DEMPSTER, Robert	Pte. R.M.	CARYSFORT	
DENAHAY, M.	Ord	POWERFUL	
DENHAM, Matthew	Boy	Pcss CHARLOTTE	
DENMAN, James	A.B.	ASIA	
DENMAN, John	Pte. R.M.	VESUVIUS	
DENNIS, James.S.A.	Lieutenant. R.N.	PHOENIX	
DENNIS, Joseph	Pte. R.M.	THUNDERER	

DENNIS, Robert	Pte. R.M.	HASTINGS	
DENT, Christopher	Pte. R.M.	GANGES	
DENTY, Elias	Pte. R.M.	WASP	
DENYER, Henry	Capt's Coxswain	STROMBOLI	
DERRETT, William	Pte. R.M.	ASIA	
DESMOND, Richard	Ord	CAMBRIDGE	
DEVELIN, William	Ord	REVENGE	
DEVENPORT, Joseph	Pte. R.M.	RODNEY	
DEVEREUX, Thomas.M.	Boy	CASTOR	
DEVONPORT, William	Q.M.	VANGUARD	
DEVONSHIRE, John	Gunner's Mate	PIQUE	
DEVONSHIRE, William	Bosun's Mate	POWERFUL	
DEW, Alfred	Boy	MAGICIENNE	
DEW, Roderick	Midshipman	HYDRA	
DEYKIN, Samuel	Boy	PIQUE	
DICK, William	Ord	HASTINGS	
DICKENSON, George	Pte. R.M.	EDINBURGH	
DICKINSON, Edward	Pte. R.M.	CAMBRIDGE	
DICKINSON, James	A.B.	Pcss CHARLOTTE	
DICKSON, Charles	Midshipman	EDINBURGH	
DICKSON, Patrick	Ord	CASTOR	(Alias DIXON)
DICKSON, Walter	Ord	Pcss CHARLOTTE	
DIDHAM, Charles.J.	Volunteer	POWERFUL	
DIDHAM, Richard.G.	Purser	POWERFUL	
DIGNAM, Daniel	Pte. R.M.	VESUVIUS	
DILLON, William	Ord	IMPLACABLE	
DIMICK, Simon	Boy	BELLEROPHON	
DIMMOCK, George	A.B.	Pcss CHARLOTTE	
DIMOCK, Joseph	A.B.	ASIA	
DINEN, James	Ord	THUNDERER	
DINGLE, William	Pte. R.M.	THUNDERER	
DINHAM, Thomas	Ord	STROMBOLI	(M.L. as DINHIM)
DITON, Thomas	Ord	GANGES	
DITTMAN, Gustavus	Naval Instructor	RODNEY	
DIX, Charles	Ord	BELLEROPHON	
DIXON, Herbert	A.B.	BELLEROPHON	
DIXON, Robert	Ord	BELLEROPHON	
DIXON, William	A.B.	GANGES	
DIXON, William	A.B.	DAPHNE	
DOBBIE, William.H.	Lieutenant. R.N.	GANGES	
DOCKINGS, John.R.	Ord	BELLEROPHON	
DODGE, Charles	A.B.	IMPLACABLE	
DOIGE, David	A.B.	GANGES	
DOIGE, Peter	Boy	GANGES	
DOIGE, Richard	Boy	RODNEY	
DOLBEAR, John	Pte. R.M.	THUNDERER	
DOLBY, John	Gunner. R.A.	HECATE	
DOMINEY, Thomas	Carp's Crew	BELLEROPHON	
DOMINICK, Benjamin	A.B.	VANGUARD	
DOMVILLE, Henry.J.	Asst Surgeon	REVENGE	
DONAGHUE, Michael	Gunner R.A.	PIQUE & other vessels	
DONALD, Jeremiah	A.B.	PIQUE	
DONAVAN, Daniel	A.B.	CASTOR	
DONKIN, Andrew	Pte. R.M.	REVENGE	
DONNELL, James	Pte. R.M.	STROMBOLI	
DONNELLY, Samuel	Asst Surgeon	TALBOT	
DONNET, James.J.L.	Asst Surgeon	VESUVIUS	
DONNOHUE, Michael	Stoker	CYCLOPS	
DONOGAN, Morris	A.B.	THUNDERER	
DONOGHUE, John	A.B.	Pcss CHARLOTTE	
DONOGUE, Dennis	A.B.	THUNDERER	(M) Anchor Type LS&GC. Baltic
DONOVAN, Dennis	Boy	THUNDERER	
DONOVAN, Dennis	Bosun's Mate	GORGON	
DONOVAN, James	Pte. R.M.	CASTOR	
DONOVAN, John	Ord	POWERFUL	
DONOVAN, John	L.M.	THUNDERER	
DONOVAN, John	Seaman	GORGON	
DORAN, James	Ord	CARYSFORT	(M) C.G.M. Group of 6
DORE, James	A.B.	HYDRA & EDINBURGH	(Additional clasp?)
DORE, Michael	Pte. R.M.	ASIA	
DORE, William	A.B.	GANGES	
DOREY, George	Pte. R.M.	Pcss CHARLOTTE	
DOREY, Joseph	A.B.	RODNEY	(Alias DORIE)
DORGAN, David	Ord	POWERFUL	
DORMER, John	Gunner's Mate	CAMBRIDGE	
DORNEY, Luke	Ord	POWERFUL	
DORVILLE, John.W.	Mate	BELLEROPHON	
DOTTLE, G.W.	Pte. R.M.	RODNEY	(May read DOBBLE)
DOUBT, William	Pte. R.M.	IMPLACABLE	(May raed DOUGH)
DOUDENAY, John	A.B.	EDINBURGH	
DOUGLAS, Hon G.H.	Midshipman	CARYSFORT	
DOUGLAS, Henry. J.	Lieutenant. R.N.	HASTINGS	
DOUGLAS, M.C.	Ship's Corporal	BENBOW	
DOUGLAS, Peter	Bosun's Mate	POWERFUL	(M) Anchor Type LS & GC

SYRIA

DOUGLAS, S.J.	Midshipman	THUNDERER	
DOUGLASS, Edward.R.	Boatswain	STROMBOLI	
	A.B.	SUPERB	Algiers
DOUST, John	Ord	POWERFUL	
DOVE, James	Ord	Pcss CHARLOTTE	
DOVE, Richard	Stoker	GORGON	
DOVE, William	Boy 2nd Cl	GORGON	
DOVER, Joseph	Carp's Mate	GANGES	
DOWLING, John	Pte. R.M.	CAMBRIDGE	
DOWMAN, James	Captain. R.M.	VESUVIUS	
DOWN, Thomas	Pte. R.M.	THUNDERER	
DOWN, William	A.B.	RODNEY	
DOWNER, Jacob	Pte. R.M.	Pcss CHARLOTTE	
DOWNER, William	Capt' After Guard	Pcss CHARLOTTE	
DOWNES, Thomas.H.	Lieutenant. R.N.	ZEBRA	A of I/AVA & Baltic
DOWNEY, James	Carp's Crew	CAMBRIDGE	
DOWNEY, John	Ord	CAMBRIDGE	(May read DOWING)
DOWNEY, William	L.M.	REVENGE	
DOWNS, Ebenezer	Ord	GANGES	
DOWNS, James	A.B. & Gn Rm Cook	TALBOT	
DOWS, Thomas	A.B.	HYDRA	
DOYLE, John	A.B.	ASIA	
DOYLE, William	A.B.	RODNEY	
DRAGO, Francis	Pte. R.M.	CAMBRIDGE	
DRAGSON, Daniel	Ord	EDINBURGH	
DRAKE, George	Carp's Yeoman	IMPLACABLE	
DRAKE, James	Boy	DIDO	
DRANER, James	Q.M.	Pcss CHARLOTTE	
DREDGE, James	Pte. R.M.	BENBOW	
	Pte. R.M.	ALBION	Navarino
DREW, James	A.B.	REVENGE	
DREW, John	Pte. R.M.	RODNEY	
DREWITT, Daniel	A.B.	BELLEROPHON	
DRINKWATER, William	Not Given	CASTOR	
DRISCOLL, Dennis	Ord	GANGES	
DROVER, John	Ord	GANGES	
DRUDGE, James	Q.M.	EDINBURGH	(M) Anchor Type LS & GC
DRUITT, Nathaniel	Boy 1st Class	VANGUARD	
DRUMGOOLE, Charles	Capt's Steward	GANGES	
DRUMMOND, Edgar.A.	Volunteer 1st Cl	TALBOT	
DRUMMOND, John	A.B.	BELLEROPHON	
DRURY, Thomas	A.B.	ZEBRA	
	A.B.	TALBOT	Navarino
DRURY, William	Passed Clerk	CARYSFORT	
DUBBER, William	Ord	STROMBOLI	
DUCKHAM, John	Ord	THUNDERER	
DUDDRIDGE, William	Pte. R.M.	BELLEROPHON	
DUDFIELD, Thomas	Pte. R.M.	DAPHNE	
DUDLEY, John	A.B.	BELLEROPHON	
DUFF, John	A.B.	Pcss CHARLOTTE	
DUFFY, George	Carp's Crew	IMPLACABLE	
DUGAN, Thomas	A.B.	HASTINGS	
DUGDELL, George	Purser's Steward	Pcss CHARLOTTE	
DUGGAN, Cornelius	Ord	POWERFUL	
DUGGINS, William	Carp's Mate	HYDRA	
DUKES, James	Capt's Coxswain	REVENGE	
	Boy	MUSQUITO	Navarino
DUKES, Thomas	A.B.	EDINBURGH	
DUKES, William	A.B.	BELLEROPHON	
DULUG, Jeremiah	Pte. R.M.	THUNDERER	(May read DUHIG)
DUNBAR, David	Ship's Cook	THUNDERER	
DUNCAN, James	Stoker	VESUVIUS	
DUNCAN, Robert	Lieutenant. R.N.	POWERFUL	
DUNCAN, Thomas	Corporal. R.M.	PIQUE	
DUNCOM, John	Boy 1st Class	CAMBRIDGE	
DUNDAS, Thomas	A.B.	CAMBRIDGE	(M) Anchor Type LS & GC
DUNFORD, George	Pte. R.M.	WASP	
DUNHAM, John	A.B.	BELLEROPHON	
DUNKERLEY, John	Pte. R.M.	POWERFUL	
DUNLOP, George.G.	Boy	HASTINGS	(Alias GARVIN, George)
DUNN, Allen	Pte. R.M.	EDINBURGH	
DUNN, Daniel	Pte. R.M.	THUNDERER	
DUNN, Sir David	Captain R.N.	VANGUARD	
	Master's Mate	DONEGAL	St Domingo
	Lieutenant. R.N.	AMPHION (P)	Lissa
DUNN, Edward	Pte. R.M.	POWERFUL	
DUNN, George	A.B.	RODNEY	
DUNN, Thomas	Stoker	STROMBOLI	
DUNN, William	Ord	ASIA	
DUNNING, James	Ord	CASTOR	
DUNSTER, Edward	Ord	CASTOR	
DUNSTERVILLE, Edward	Master	CAMBRIDGE	
DUNSTERVILLE, John	Mate	ASIA	

DUNSTONE, Henry	A.B.	ASIA		
	A.B.	DARTMOUTH	Navarino	
DUNST..., Henry	A.B.	CAMBRIDGE	(Torn edge to Roll)	
DURANT, Samuel	Blacksmith	Pcss CHARLOTTE		
DURHAM, Thomas	A.B.	POWERFUL		
DURNDELL, George	Boy	REVENGE		
DUTTON, George	Cook	GANGES		
DYALL, John	Sailmaker	PIQUE		
DYCE, Thomas	Boy 1st Class	RODNEY		
DYER, Benjamin	Purser	TALBOT		
DYER, H.C.P.	2nd Lieut. R.M.	RODNEY		
DYER, James	Pte. R.M.	POWERFUL		
DYER, Richard	Pte. R.M.	VANGUARD		
DYER, Thomas	Boy	RODNEY		
DYER, William	Boy	HASTINGS		
DYKE, Charles	Mate	HECATE		
DYKE, Thomas.W.	A.B.	GANGES		
DYKES, J.	Ord	DAPHNE		
DYNAN, John	A.B.	THUNDERER		
EAGERS, George	Boy	CAMBRIDGE		
EAGLE, John	Pte. R.M.	BENBOW		
EALES, George	A.B.	REVENGE		
EALES, George.B.	Clerk's Asst	POWERFUL		
EALES, William	Purser	BENBOW		
EARL, Frederick.J.	Ord	REVENGE		
EARL, George	Gun Room Cook	RODNEY		
EARL, James	Ord	REVENGE		
EARL, Richard	Carpenter	PHOENIX		
EARL, Thomas	Carpenter	CARYSFORT		
EARL, William	Pte. R.M.	REVENGE		
EARL, William	Pte. R.M.	BENBOW		
EARLY, Henry.W.	Fifer. R.M.	EDINBURGH		
EARP, William	Pte. R.M.	DAPHNE		
EARSWELL, Charles	Carp's Crew	BELLEROPHON		
EASON, Richard	Boy	Pcss CHARLOTTE		
EASTCOTT, George	Capt' Main Top	PIQUE		
EASTER, John.J.	Gun Room Steward	MEDEA		
EASTERBROOKE, George	Boatswain	MAGICIENNE		
EASTHER, Henry	Gun Room Steward	GANGES		
EASTHOOF, Frederick	Boy	VANGUARD		
EASTMAN, Joseph	Pte. R.M.	Pcss CHARLOTTE		
EASTMAN, Thomas	Schoolmaster	ASIA		
EASTMEAD, John	Pte. R.M.	CALCUTTA	On Roll. Ship not present	
EASTON, Robert.T.	Asst Surgeon	Pcss CHARLOTTE		
EASTON, William	Ord	IMPLACABLE		
EBURNE, Daniel	Boy	STROMBOLI		
ECCLES, William	Cooper's Crew	EDINBURGH		
ECCLESTONE, James	Ord	HASTINGS		
EDDICKER, Joseph	A.B.	EDINBURGH		
EDDRINGTON, Thomas	Sapper & Miner	PIQUE & other vessels		
EDDRINGTON, Thomas	Pte. R.M.	PIQUE		
EDEN, Sir William	Not Given	CARYSFORT		
EDES, William	A.B.	BENBOW		
EDESS, Daniel	Pte. R.M.	POWERFUL		
EDEY, Edward	Gunner. R.M.A.	VESUVIUS		
EDGAR, John	Midshipman's Stwd	HAZARD		
EDGAR, William	Gunner's Mate	RODNEY		
EDGCOME, William	Ord	IMPLACABLE		
EDGECOMBE, John	A.B.	PHOENIX		
EDGECOMBE, Joseph	Ord	THUNDERER		
EDINGTON, F.	Sapper & Miner	GORGON		
EDMINSTON, William	Pte. R.M.	HASTINGS		
EDMONDS, Joseph	Pte. R.M.	Pcss CHARLOTTE		
EDMONDS, Thomas	Drummer. R.M.	BELLEROPHON		
EDMONDS, Thomas	Ord	VESUVIUS		
EDMONDSON, John	Pte. R.M.	POWERFUL		
EDMUNDS, Ephraim	Pte. R.M.	IMPLACABLE		
EDSELL, Henry	Pte. R.M.	EDINBURGH		
EDWARDS, Alexander	Carp's Crew	GORGON		
EDWARDS, Alfred.E.	Stoker	PHOENIX		
EDWARDS, Andrew	Pte. R.M.	BELLEROPHON		
EDWARDS, Andrew	A.B.	RODNEY		
EDWARDS, Charles	Ord	WASP		
EDWARDS, David	Lieut. R.N.	POWERFUL		
EDWARDS, Horatio	Boy	Pcss CHARLOTTE		
EDWARDS, John	Pte. R.M.	STROMBOLI		
EDWARDS, Nicholas	Pte. R.M.	GORGON		
EDWARDS, Richard	Pte. R.M.	RODNEY		
EDWARDS, Watkin	Pte. R.M.	RODNEY		
EDWARDS, William	Not Given	HASTINGS		
EDY, John	Pte. R.M.	CAMBRIDGE		
EGAN, Edmund	Pte. R.M.	Pcss CHARLOTTE		
EGAN, John	A.B.	BELLEROPHON		
EGERTON, Francis	Volunteer 1st Cl	Pcss CHARLOTTE		
EKENS, Allen.J.	Ord	CAMBRIDGE		

SYRIA

ELBROW, John	Pte. R.M.	Pcss CHARLOTTE	
ELDRIDGE, Thomas	Boy	GANGES	
ELLAM, Edward	Pte. R.M.	REVENGE	
ELLERY, John	A.B.	EDINBURGH	
ELLICOMBE, Hugh.M.	Lieut. R.N.	RODNEY	
ELLINGTON, Robert	Ship's Cook	ASIA	
ELLIOT, Hon Charles.G.J.B.	Commander	HAZARD	
ELLIOT, John.H.	Ord	IMPLACABLE	
ELLIOT, Robert.H.	Lieut. R.N.	POWERFUL	
ELLIOTT, Charles	Gunner. R.M.A.	STROMBOLI	
ELLIOTT, David	A.B.	BENBOW	
ELLIOTT, Edward	Ord	VANGUARD	
ELLIOTT, Edwin	Cooper	BELLEROPHON	
ELLIOTT, Hugh	Ord	BELLEROPHON	
ELLIOTT, James	Capt' of Hold	PIQUE	
ELLIOTT, John	A.B.	REVENGE	
ELLIOTT, John.W.	Surgeon	ZEBRA	
ELLIOTT, William	Pte. R.M.	CAMBRIDGE	
ELLIOTT, William	Pte. R.M.	STROMBOLI	
ELLIOTT, William.C.P.	2nd Lieut. R.M.	IMPLACABLE	
ELLIS, Charles	Pte. R.M.	VANGUARD	
ELLIS, Charles	Boy	POWERFUL	
ELLIS, Christopher	Pte. R.M.	IMPLACABLE	
ELLIS, John	A.B.	GANGES	
ELLIS, John	Boy	CASTOR	
ELLIS, John	Pte. R.M.	CAMBRIDGE	
ELLIS, John	M.A.A.	CARYSFORT	*(M) Anchor Type LS & GC*
ELLIS, Richard	Capt's Coxswain	VANGUARD	
ELLIS, Richard	Ord	RODNEY	
ELLIS, Solomon	Pte. R.M.	RODNEY	
ELLIS, Thomas	Bosun's Mate	PHOENIX	
	Boy	GENOA	*Navarino*
ELLIS, Thomas	Pte. R.M.	ASIA	
ELLIS, William	A.B.	BENBOW	
ELLISON, James.H.	Pte. R.M.	IMPLACABLE	
ELLISS, Richard	Pte. R.M.	Pcss CHARLOTTE	
ELLUL, Angelo	Boy	BENBOW	
ELMORE, Charles	Boy	DIDO	
ELMS, Joseph	Pte. R.M.	REVENGE	
ELRIDGE, John	Ship's Cook	MEDEA	
ELSON, Thomas	Actg Master	Pcss CHARLOTTE	
ELSTON, John	Pte. R.M.	MEDEA	
ELY, John	Pte. R.M.	CASTOR	
ELY, John	A.B.	GANGES	
EMBLETON, Thomas	Coxswain Pinnace	GANGES	
EMBRY, William	Pte. R.M.	POWERFUL	
EMMERSON, George	Boy	BENBOW	
EMERY, James	Boy	EDINBURGH	
EMES, William.H.	Master	MAGICIENNE	
ENDACOTT, John	Pte. R.M.	THUNDERER	
ENGLAND, Charles	Carp's Crew	TALBOT	
ENNIS, James	A.B.	BELLEROPHON	
ENNIS, Neal	Ship's Cook	Pcss CHARLOTTE	
ENOS, George	Ord	CASTOR	
EPPS, William	Boy 2nd Class	VANGUARD	
ERRIDGE, William	Ord	ASIA	
ERRINGTON, James	Boy	REVENGE	
ESSAM, Sindall	A.B.	HASTINGS	
ETHERINGTON, James	A.B.	BELLEROPHON	
EUSTACE, Thomas	Pte. R.M.	STROMBOLI	
EVANS, James	A.B.	Pcss CHARLOTTE	*(Alias NEWDOM)*
EVANS, John	Ord	CAMBRIDGE	
EVANS, Joseph	Ord	PIQUE	
EVANS, Joseph	Not Given	THUNDERER	
EVANS, Robert	Boy	GANGES	
EVANS, Samuel	Pte. R.M.	RODNEY	
EVANS, Samuel	Ord	RODNEY	
EVANS, Samuel	Pte. R.M.	POWERFUL	
EVANS, Thomas	A.B.	EDINBURGH	
EVANS, Thomas	A.B.	CASTOR	
EVANS, Thomas	Pte. R.M.	BENBOW	
EVANS, William	Pte. R.M.	RODNEY	
EVANS, William	Ord	POWERFUL	
EVANS, William	Boy 2nd Class	THUNDERER	
EVEREST, Henry.B.	Mate	VANGUARD	
EVERHURST, William	Pte. R.M.	GANGES	
EVERIDGE, John	Boy	SUPERB	
EVES, Samuel	A.B.	VANGUARD	
EVES, William	Boy	VESUVIUS	
EVINS, John	Gunner's Crew	IMPLACABLE	
EWANS, John	Boy	PIQUE	
EYERS, William	Engineer's Boy	HYDRA	
EYLEY, Jeremiah	A.B.	EDINBURGH	

EYLEY, Jeremiah	Q.M.	EDINBURGH	
EYLEY, Robert	Pte. R.M.	EDINBURGH	
EYNON, William	A.B.	HASTINGS	
EYRE, John.J.	Pte. R.M.	HASTINGS	
EYRES, William	A.B.	DAPHNE	
FABIAN, Benjamin	Carp's Crew	HYDRA	
FACEY, George	Ord	Pcss CHARLOTTE	
FACEY, Solomon	Sgt. R.M.	BELLEROPHON	
FANSHAWE, Arthur	Captain. R.N.	Pcss CHARLOTTE	
	Midshipman	IMPLACABLE	*Implacable. 26 Augt 1808*
	Midshipman	SCIPION	*Java*
	Lieut. R.N.	ENDYMION	*B.S. 8 April 1814*
	Lieut. R.N.	ENDYMION	*Endymion Wh President*
FANSHAWE, Edward.G.	Lieut. R.N.	DAPHNE	
FARDY, William	Ord	REVENGE	*(May read FORDY)*
FARENDEN, William	M.A.A.	HECATE	
FAREWELL, Emanuel	Capt' of Hold	GORGON	
FARNDELL, Thomas	A.B.	BELLEROPHON	
FARO, John	A.B.	THUNDERER	
FARQUHAR, Arthur	Mate	Pcss CHARLOTTE	
FARR, William.J.	Pte. R.M.	PIQUE	
FARRALL, John	L.M.	PIQUE	
FARRANDS, George	Pte. R.M.	POWERFUL	
FARRANT, Augustus.D.L.	Lieut. R.M.	POWERFUL	
FARRELL, Cornelius	A.B.	Pcss CHARLOTTE	
FARRELL, James	Boy 2nd Class	BELLEROPHON	
FARRER, Joseph	A.B.	WASP	
FARROWE, John	Ord	PHOENIX	
FARRUGIA, Lorenzo	Capt's Cook	ZEBRA	
FARTHING, Henry	Fifer. R.M.	GANGES	
FAULKENER, Thomas	Carp's Crew	WASP	
FAULKNER, Joseph	Coxswain	HECATE	
FAULKNER, Thomas	Ord	RODNEY	
FAULKNER, William	Pte. R.M.	HASTINGS	
FAW, Edward	Ord	THUNDERER	*(May read FAIR)*
FAWKES, Richard	Ord	POWERFUL	
FAYERS, George	Pte. R.M.	BELLEROPHON	
FEARINGSIDE, Thomas	Pte. R.M.	GORGON & EDINBURGH	
FEARYES, David	Pte. R.M.	BELLEROPHON	
FEARNOUGHT, John	A.B.	BELLEROPHON	
FEAST, Charles	Pte. R.M.	BELLEROPHON	
FEATHERSTONE, John	Pte. R.M.	PIQUE	
FEATHERSTONE, William	Caulker's Mate	ASIA	
FEENEY, James	Ord	IMPLACABLE	
FEGEN, Charles	Captain R.M.	GANGES	
	Lieut. R.M.	SPARTAN	*Spartan. 3 May 1810*
FELICE, Vincenzo	Capt's Cook	WASP	
FELLINGHAM, William	Boy	BENBOW	
FELSTEAD, Richard	Pte. R.M.	HASTINGS	
FELTON, William	Pte. R.M.	REVENGE	
FENNELL, Alfred	Boy	POWERFUL	
FENNELL, Robert	Pte. R.M.	ZEBRA	
FERGUSON, Alexander	Cooper	VANGUARD	
FERGUSON, Thomas	Boy	CASTOR	
FERNANDEZ, Richard	Q.M.	RODNEY	*(M.L. as John PETERSON)* *(M) Anchor Type LS & GC*
FERNIE, Joseph	A.B.	BENBOW	
FERRELL, Reuben	A.B.	BENBOW	*(May read FERRETT)*
FERRELL, Richard.C.	Bosun's Mate	CAMBRIDGE	*(May read FERRETT)*
FERRETT, William	Gunner's Mate	THUNDERER	
FERRIS, Charles	Sgt. R.M.	Pcss CHARLOTTE	
FERRIS, John	Boy	EDINBURGH	
FERRIS, William	Armourer	BELLEROPHON	
FERRUDGE, Nicholas	A.B.	PHOENIX	
FERRY, Robert	A.B.	VANGUARD	
FEWKES, William	Pte. R.M.	CASTOR	*(May read FAWKES)*
FIBIAN, Daniel	A.B.	BELLEROPHON	
FIBIAN, John	A.B.	HYDRA	
FICKERS, John	A.B.	ASIA	*(or FICKUS/FICKINS)*
FIELD, John	Ord	IMPLACABLE	
FIELDER, James	Pte. R.M.	BENBOW	
FIELDER, William	Boy	MEDEA	
FIELDER, William	Boy	VANGUARD	
FIELDER, William	A.B.	CAMBRIDGE	
FIELDING, Thomas	A.B.	IMPLACABLE	
FIGGING, Thomas	A.B.	VANGUARD	
FIGGINS, John	Carp's Crew	BELLEROPHON	
FILMER, George	Actg Master	CASTOR	
FINDLEY, James	Ord	VANGUARD	
FINLAY, George	Ord	VANGUARD	
FINNAMORE, Richard	A.B.	CAMBRIDGE	
FISHER, Francis	L.M.	REVENGE	

SYRIA

FISHER, Isaac	Pte. R.M.	IMPLACABLE	
FISHER, Stephen	Clerk	DAPHNE	
FISHER, Thomas	Pte. R.M.	BELLEROPHON	
FISHER, Thomas	Pte. R.M.	CASTOR	
FISHER, William	Captain. R.N.	ASIA	
	Master's Mate	FOUDROYANT	Egypt
FISHER, William.E.	Mate	GANGES	
FITSMORRIS, Edward	A.B.	Pcss CHARLOTTE	
FITZE, Thomas	Stoker	VESUVIUS	
FITZGERALD, Richard	Pte. R.M.	POWERFUL	
FITZJAMES, James	Lieut. R.N.	GANGES	
FITZPATRICK, James	A.B.	EDINBURGH	
FIZZARD, William	L.M.	HYDRA	
FLACK, William	A.B.	EDINBURGH	
FLEETWOOD, Thomas	Ship's Corporal	EDINBURGH	(M) Anchor Type LS & GC
FLEMING, Charles	A.B.	BELLEROPHON	
FLEMING, James	Ord	THUNDERER	
FLEMING, James	Carp's Mate	WASP	
FLEMING, John	Pte. R.M.	PIQUE	
FLEMING, John	Gunner's Yeoman	GANGES	
FLEMING, Joseph	Ord	CASTOR	
FLEMING, Richard	Ord	CASTOR	
FLEMING, William	Ord	RODNEY	
FLEMMING, John	Boy	HAZARD	
FLETCHER, Archibald.D.W.	Midshipman	GANGES	
FLETCHER, Charles	Gun Room Cook	PIQUE	
FLETCHER, David	Ord	BENBOW	
FLETCHER, Edward	Painter	PIQUE	
FLETCHER, George	Pte. R.M.	POWERFUL	
FLETCHER, John	Pte. R.M.	CAMBRIDGE	
FLETCHER, Joseph	Carp's Mate	BELLEROPHON	
FLETCHER, Joseph	A.B.	ASIA	
FLINN, Daniel	Pte. R.M.	GANGES	(May read David)
FLINN, Thomas	Ord	BENBOW (?)	
FLOOD, Peter	Sgt. R.M.	POWERFUL	
FLOOD, William	Pte. R.M.	PIQUE	
FLOOKS, Job.G.	Boy	POWERFUL	
FLORENCE, Richard	Caulker's Mate	BENBOW	(or Carp's Mate)
FLOUD, Ross.M.	Mate	HAZARD	
FLOWERDEW, Edward	Pte. R.M.	ASIA	
FLOWERS, Francis	Boy	BENBOW	
FLOWERS, George	Pte. R.M.	BENBOW	
FLY, John	Fifer. R.M.	THUNDERER	
FLYNN, Charles	Boy	IMPLACABLE	
FLYNN, Dennis	Capt' Fore Top	THUNDERER	
FLYNN John	Capt' Forecastle	VANGUARD	(M) Anchor Type LS & GC
FLYNN, John	Ord	Pcss CHARLOTTE	
FOGDEN, George	A.B.	GANGES	
FOGDEN, Henry	Capt' of Hold	THUNDERER	
FOGG, Francis	A.B.	CYCLOPS	
FOLDS, William	Surgeon	PIQUE	
FOLEY, Augustus.J.	Midshipman	CASTOR	
FOLEY, William	Ord	REVENGE	
FOOT, Charles	Pte. R.M.	PIQUE	
FOOT, George	Ord	HASTINGS	
FOOT, John	Pte. R.M.	THUNDERER	
FOOT, Robert	Pte. R.M.	THUNDERER	
FOOT, William	Ord	HASTINGS	
FOOTE, Henry.R.	Mate	GORGON	
FOOTE, John	Pte. R.M.	STROMBOLI	
FOOTE, John	Cook	GORGON	
FORBES, James	Q.M.	ASIA	
FORBES, James	Not Given	ASIA	(Additional clasp?)
FORBES, Thomas.G.	Lieut. R.N.	Pcss CHARLOTTE	
	Midshipman	DARTMOUTH	Navarino
FORD, Alfred	Ord	HASTINGS	
FORD, Henry	Ord	BELLEROPHON	
FORD, John	A.B.	VANGUARD	
FORD, Nicholas	Not Given	DIDO	
FORD, Nathaniel	Pte. R.M.	BELLEROPHON	
FORD, Richard	A.B.	CAMBRIDGE	
FORD, S.G. or L.G.	A.B.	TALBOT	
FORD, William	Capt' Fore Top	ASIA	
FORD, William	Ord	REVENGE	
FORDYCE, George	Capt' Forecastle	GANGES	
FOREMAN, John	Ropemaker	ASIA	
FOROLU, Henry	Pte. R.M.	CYCLOPS	(May read FOROLEE)
FORMOSA, Michael	Carp's Crew	ASIA	
FORREST, John	A.B.	Pcss CHARLOTTE	(May read FORIEST) M.L. as FORRESTER
FORREST, Joseph	Ord	BELLEROPHON	
FORREST, Robert	Pte. R.M.	CAMBRIDGE	
FORSYTH, James	Pte. R.M.	REVENGE	

FORTESCUE, Thomas.D.A.	Midshipman	VANGUARD	
FORTESCUE, Thomas.K.	Mate	CAMBRIDGE	
FORWARD, James	Sgt. R.M.	MAGICIENNE	
FORWARD, Thomas	Ward Rm Cook	IMPLACABLE	
FOSS, Henry	Bosun's Mate	CYCLOPS	
	Capt' Fore Top	GLASGOW	*Navarino*
FOSTER, Edward	A.B.	CAMBRIDGE	
FOSTER, James	Pte. R.M.	RODNEY	
FOSTER, John	A.B.	IMPLACABLE	
FOSTER, Joseph	Pte. R.M.	DAPHNE	
FOSTER, William	A.B.	IMPLACABLE	
FOUK, Anthony	A.B.	POWERFUL	
FOULHAM, William	Capt' Mizzen Top	CASTOR	*(May read FORDHAM)*
FOWELL, Benjamin	A.B.	CAMBRIDGE	
FOWELL, John	Capt' of Mast	Pcss CHARLOTTE	*(M) Anchor Type LS & GC*
FOWELL, Samuel	Mate	CARYSFORT	
FOWELLS, George	A.B.	VANGUARD	
FOWLER, Henry	Pte. R.M.	CYCLOPS	
FOWLER, James	Fifer. R.M.	STROMBOLI	
FOWLER, James	Drummer. R.M.	BENBOW	
FOWLER, Richard	Ord	POWERFUL	
FOWLER, William	Pte. R.M.	THUNDERER	
FOWLES, Richard	A.B.	BENBOW	
FOX, Edward.W.	Boy 1st Class	BENBOW	
FOX, Thomas	A.B.	ZEBRA	
	Boy 3rd Class	BRITOMART	*Algiers*
FOY, James	Ord	VANGUARD	
FOY, William	Boy	VANGUARD	*(May read FRY)*
FOYLE, William	A.B.	GANGES	
FRAMPTON, Ambrose	A.B.	RODNEY	
FRAMPTON, George	Carp's Crew	THUNDERER	
FRANCES, Joseph	Pte. R.M.	DAPHNE	
FRANCIS, James	Pte. R.M.	CAMBRIDGE	
FRANCIS, John	Ord	IMPLACABLE	
FRANCIS, Lot	Pte. R.M.	VANGUARD	
FRANCIS, Osborne	Capt's Cook	POWERFUL	
FRANCIS, Thomas	Pte. R.M.	GANGES	
FRANKHAM, Isaac	Pte. R.M.	VANGUARD	
FRANKLIN, John	L.M.	Pcss CHARLOTTE	
FRANKLIN, William	Ord	HASTINGS	
FRAPPELL, William	Pte. R.M.	STROMBOLI	
FRASER, Nathaniel	A.B.	EDINBURGH	
FRASER, Simon	Lieut. R.M.	Pcss CHARLOTTE	
FRASER, Thomas	Lieut. R.N.	VANGUARD	
FRAZER, John	Coxswain Pinnace	EDINBURGH	
FRAZER, William	Ord	THUNDERER	
FRAZER, William	A.B.	CYCLOPS	*(Additional clasp?)*
FREE, James	Pte. R.M.	CAMBRIDGE	
FREELAND, John.O	Lieut. R.N.	STROMBOLI	
	Volunteer 1st Cl	ALBION	*Navarino*
FREEMAN, Henry	Bosun's Mate	MAGICIENNE	
FREEMAN, James	Pte. R.M.	EDINBURGH	
FREEMAN, John	Capt' Main Top	REVENGE	
FREEMAN, John	Pte. R.M.	BELLEROPHON	
FREEMAN, Josiah	Gunner. R.M.A.	PIQUE	
FREEMAN, Pearce	Gunner	CAMBRIDGE	
FREEMANTLE, William	Pte. R.M.	POWERFUL	
FRENCH, Benjamin	Pte. R.M.	THUNDERER	
FRENCH, George	Ord	CARYSFORT	
FRENCH, Thomas	Capt' Main Top	POWERFUL	
	Boy 2nd Class	ALBION	*Navarino*
FRETHAM, Thomas	Ord	ASIA	*(M.L. as FELTHAM)*
FRERE, John.J.B.E.	Lieut. R.N.	Pcss CHARLOTTE	
FREW, Thomas	A.B.	IMPLACABLE	
FRICKER, Henry	Pte. R.M.	Pcss CHARLOTTE	
FRIEND, Thomas	Ord	PIQUE	
FRISTRY, John	Pte. R.M.	BENBOW	
	Pte. R.M.	TALBOT	*Navarino*
FROST, H.	Sgt. R.M.	STROMBOLI	
FROST, John	Carp's Crew	Pcss CHARLOTTE	
FROST, Sampson	A.B.	MEDEA	
FROST, Thomas	Carp's Mate	RODNEY	
FROWELL, Richard	L.M.	THUNDERER	
FRUDD, William	Gunner. R.A.	PIQUE & other vessels	
FRUIN, James	A.B.	MEDEA	
FRY, George	Carp's Crew	RODNEY	
FRY, John	Ord	HASTINGS	
FRY, Joseph	Boy	IMPLACABLE	
FRYER, John	Ord	HAZARD	
FRYER, Robert	Boy	DAPHNE	
FRYER, William	Ord	ASIA	
FUGE, John	A.B.	REVENGE	*(Alias BALL)*
FULFORD, John	Lieut. R.N.	TALBOT	*(M) A of I/AVA. Tamar*
FULLER, John	Ord	BENBOW	
FULLER, Robert	Ord	CASTOR	

SYRIA

Name	Rank	Ship	Notes
FULLERTON, James	A.B.	Pcss CHARLOTTE	
FULLERTON, James	Ord	VANGUARD	
FULLERTON, William	Ord	VANGUARD	
FULLICK, William	Ord	BELLEROPHON	
FUNT, William	Boy (?)	REVENGE	
FURGUSON, Edward	Pte. R.M.	THUNDERER	(or Edmund)
FURGUSON, James	Pte. R.M.	BELLEROPHON	
FURNACE, William	A.B.	MAGICIENNE	
FURZE, James	Pte. R.M.	Pcss CHARLOTTE	
FURZE, Samuel	Boy	ZEBRA	
FURZEY, Robert	Pte. R.M.	RODNEY	
FUSSELL, William	Pte. R.M.	POWERFUL	
GABRIEL, Thomas	Ord	REVENGE	
GABRIEL, William	Fifer. R.M.	CARYSFORT	
GAFFORD, Patrick	Pte. R.M.	POWERFUL	
GAGE, John	A.B.	ASIA	
GALAVAN, Jeremiah	Boy	CASTOR	
GALAVIN, John	Ord	RODNEY	
GALE, Barnet	Pte. R.M.	RODNEY	
GALE, George	Carpenter	PIQUE	
GALE, James	Pte. R.M.	MAGICIENNE	
GALLEHAWK, John	Boy	CYCLOPS	Duplicate issued in 1894
GALLEY, Charles	Bosun's Mate	REVENGE	
GALLIES, John	Ord	REVENGE	
GALLOP, George.H.	Pte. R.M.	REVENGE	
GALLWEY, Henry.J.W.S.P.	Lieut. R.N.	PIQUE	
GAMBIER, Henry	Ord	CAMBRIDGE	
GAMBLE, John	Pte. R.M.	VANGUARD	
GAMBLIN, Francis	Q.M.	POWERFUL	
GAMBLING, George	Boy	WASP	
GAMBRELL, Benjamin	Capt's Steward	EDINBURGH	
GAMMON, Lawrence	Ship's Cook	MAGICIENNE	(Alias GANNIMORE) (M) Anchor Type LS & GC
GANE, Henry	Pte. R.M.	BELLEROPHON	
GAPE, William	Pte. R.M.	VANGUARD	
GARD, George	Boy	BELLEROPHON	
GARDINER, Daniel	Pte. R.M.	Pcss CHARLOTTE	
GARDINER, James	Ord	PIQUE	
GARDINER, Richard	Ship's Cook	CAMBRIDGE	
GARDNER, Allen.M.	Mate	DIDO	
GARDNER, George	Boy	HECATE	
GARDNER, James	Pte. R.M.	ASIA	
GARDNER, John	Pte. R.M.	PIQUE	
GARLAND, Peter	Boy	EDINBURGH	
GARLAND, William	A.B.	GANGES	
GARNER, John	2nd Master	DIDO	
GARNETT, Thomas	Capt' Main Top	HASTINGS	
GARROD, James	Gnr Royal Arty	HECATE	
GARTHWAITE, Edward	L.M.	REVENGE	
GARVIN, George	Boy	VANGUARD	(Alias DUNLOP, G.G.)
GARVIN, John	Ord	IMPLACABLE	
GARVIS, Thomas	Pte. R.M.	STROMBOLI	
GASKELL, John	Pte. R.M.	POWERFUL	
GASKIN, James	Corporal. R.M.	REVENGE	
GASTON, Gideon	Pte. R.M.	EDINBURGH	
GATCOMB, John	A.B.	STROMBOLI	
GATEHOUSE, William	Ord	CASTOR	
GATER, William	Ropemaker	CARYSFORT	
GATES, W.J.	Pte. R.M.	CAMBRIDGE	
GATT, Emanuel	Sailmaker	ZEBRA	
GAUCHI, Antonio	Not Given	CYCLOPS	
GAUDIN, Albert	Pte. R.M.	PIQUE	
GAUL, Joseph	Ropemaker	GANGES	
GAUNT, James	A.B.	VANGUARD	
GAUNTLETT, Charles	Gunner's Mate	PHOENIX	
GAUNTLETT, John	Capt' Main Top	CASTOR	
GAUSSEN, Thomas.L.	Mate	ASIA	
GAY, George	Pte. R.M.	REVENGE	
GAY, George	Pte. R.M.	THUNDERER	
GAY, John	Ship's Corporal	RODNEY	
	Boy	SUPERB	Algiers
GAY, John	Ord	IMPLACABLE	
GAYTE, Peter	Gnr Royal Arty	HECATE	
GEACH, John	Carp's Mate	IMPLACABLE	
GEARD, George	A.B.	REVENGE	
GEARD, John	Pte. R.M.	TALBOT	
GEARING, John.F.	Capt's Coxswain	ASIA	(May read John J.)
GEARY, James	A.B.	THUNDERER	
GEARY, James	A.B.	Pcss CHARLOTTE	
GEARY, William	Pte. R.M.	VANGUARD	
GEER, Richard	Ord	THUNDERER	
GENNYS, William.H.	Mate	CARYSFORT	
GENSHLEA, Michael	Pte. R.M.	POWERFUL	

GEORGE, Matthew	L.M.	REVENGE	
GEORGE, Thomas	Bombdr Royal Arty	PIQUE & other vessels	
GERMAIN, Arthur	A.B.	GANGES	
GERMAN, Lawrence	Pte. R.M.	GANGES	
GERRARD, James	Pte. R.M.	ASIA	
GERRARD, Thomas	Pte. R.M.	REVENGE	
GIBBING, John	Pte. R.M.	Pcss CHARLOTTE	
GIBBONS, Edward	Pte. R.M.	VANGUARD	
GIBBONS, George	Gunner's Mate	REVENGE	
GIBBONS, George	Pte. R.M.	BELLEROPHON	
GIBBONS, William	Pte. R.M.	Pcss CHARLOTTE	
GIBBS, Hair or Hais	Pte. R.M.	THUNDERER	
GIBBS, John	Ord	VANGUARD	
GIBBS, Soloman	Pte. R.M.	GANGES	
GIBBS, William	Pte. R.M.	VANGUARD	
GIBSON, Benjamin	Pte. R.M.	POWERFUL	
GIBSON, Charles	Boy	THUNDERER	
GIBSON, George	Ord	BELLEROPHON	
GIBSON, John	Ord	CARYSFORT	
GIBSON, John	A.B.	Pcss CHARLOTTE	
GIBSON, Thomas	Boy	REVENGE	
GIBSON, William	A.B.	THUNDERER	
GIDDENS, George	A.B.	GANGES	
GIFFARD, George	Lieut. R.N.	CYCLOPS	
GILBERT, Edward	Bosun's Mate	THUNDERER	
GILBERT, James	A.B.	RODNEY	
GILBERT, William	Boy	EDINBURGH	
GILCHRIST, Archibald	Surgeon	VESUVIUS	
GILES, George	Boy 1st Class	THUNDERER	
GILES, George	Pte. R.M.	WASP	
GILES, Henry	Pte. R.M.	RODNEY	
GILES, William	A.B.	IMPLACABLE	
GILL, Charles	Pte. R.M.	HASTINGS	
GILL, John	Ord	VANGUARD	
GILL, Richard	A.B.	IMPLACABLE	
GILL, Samuel	Ord	CARYSFORT	
GILL, Thomas	Pte. R.M.	Pcss CHARLOTTE	
GILLARD, Charles	Boatswain	IMPLACABLE	
	Capt' Fore Top	IMPREGNABLE	Algiers
GILLARD, James	Pte. R.M.	RODNEY	
GILLATLEY, P.	Carp's Crew	BENBOW	
GILLETT, Edward	Ord	DAPHNE	
GILLETT, William	Pte. R.M.	HASTINGS	
GILLIES, James	Schoolmaster	EDINBURGH	
	Volunteer 2nd Cl	ASIA	Navarino
GILLILAND, John	A.B.	EDINBURGH	
GILLIS, William	A.B.	BENBOW	
GILLOTT, Charles	Pte. R.M.	Pcss CHARLOTTE	
GILLOTT, William	A.B.	EDINBURGH	
GINGELL, Stephen	Pte. R.M.	IMPLACABLE	
GLANVILL, Francis	Ord	IMPLACABLE	
GLANVILLE, Robert	A.B.	IMPLACABLE	
GLANVILLE, Samuel	Ord	CAMBRIDGE	
GLANVILLE, William.F.	Flag Lieut. R.N.	Pcss CHARLOTTE	
GLANVIN, John	A.B.	CARYSFORT	
GLASCOTT, Charles	Yeoman of Signals	THUNDERER	
GLASS, James	Ord	PIQUE	
GLASS, James	Pte. R.M.	CASTOR	
GLINN, Constantine.G.	Mate	CYCLOPS	
GLINN, Charles.J.P.	Mate	GORGON	
GLOVER, John	Stoker	HYDRA	
GLOVER, William	A.B.	ASIA	
GLUE, Thomas	Pte. R.M.	MAGICIENNE	
GOBLE, George	L.M.	BELLEROPHON	
GODDARD, David	A.B.	EDINBURGH	
GODDARD, Henry	Pte. R.M.	GANGES	
GODDARD, James	Pte. R.M.	GANGES	
GODDARD, Robert	Boy	CAMBRIDGE	
GODFREY, Peter.McK.	Mate	POWERFUL	
GODFREY, Samuel	Coxswain of Launch	Pcss CHARLOTTE	
GODHEARD, Thomas	Pte. R.M.	CAMBRIDGE	
GODWIN, Thomas	Pte. R.M.	GORGON & REVENGE	
GODWIN, Thomas	Pte. R.M.	REVENGE	
GOFF, James	Ord	CAMBRIDGE	
GOFF, Joseph	Pte. R.M.	GANGES	
GOFF, Thomas	Q.M.	POWERFUL	
GOLDFINCH, George	Lieut. R.N.	GANGES	(M) A of I/AVA. Sophie
GOLDING, John	Pte. R.M.	BELLEROPHON	(M.L. as William)
GOLDING, Richard	Ord	Pcss CHARLOTTE	
GOLDSACK, Isaac	A.B.	IMPLACABLE	
GOLDSMITH, John	A.B.	GANGES	
GOLDSMITH, Thomas	A.B.	Pcss CHARLOTTE	
GOLIGHTLY, George	Boy	THUNDERER	
GOLSTON, Jonathan	Gun Room Cook	CYCLOPS	
GOOCH, James	Pte. R.M.	DIDO	

SYRIA

GOODALL, Charles	Pte. R.M.	Pcss CHARLOTTE	
GOODCHILD, Edward	Pte. R.M.	REVENGE	
GOODENOUGH, Thomas	Pte. R.M.	CAMBRIDGE	
GOODEY, Edward	Pte. R.M.	CAMBRIDGE	
GOODFELLOW, John	Pte. R.M.	THUNDERER	
GOODING, George	Stoker	GORGON	
GOODMAN, Edward	Pte. R.M.	BENBOW	
	Pte. R.M.	PHILOMEL	*Navarino*
GOODYER, Richard	Ord	BENBOW	
GOOGE, George	Ord	GANGES	
GORDON, David.M.	Mate	THUNDERER	
GORDON, William	Ord	VANGUARD	
GOSNELL, William	Carp's Crew	ASIA	
GOSS, Samuel	A.B.	BENBOW	
GOSSAGE, George	Ord	BENBOW	
GOTT, William	Capt' Mizzen Top	EDINBURGH	
GOUGH, Daniel	Pte. R.M.	THUNDERER	
GOUGH, Edward	A.B.	GANGES	
GOUGH, James	Pte. R.M.	POWERFUL	
GOUGH, Joseph	Corporal. R.M.	POWERFUL	
GOULD, George	Pte. R.M.	VESUVIUS	
GOULD, James	Pte. R.M.	RODNEY	
GOULD, James	Pte. R.M.	THUNDERER	
GOULD, Thomas	A.B.	EDINBURGH	
GOULDSWORTHY, John	Bosun's Mate	CYCLOPS	
GOURD, Charles.D.	Clerk	HECATE	
GOVER, James	Pte. R.M.	EDINBURGH	
GOWANS, John	Naval Instructor	HASTINGS	
GOWER, John	Pte. R.M.	EDINBURGH	
GOWING, George	Bosun's Mate	WASP	*(M) Anchor Type LS & GC*
GOWLAND, Ferguson	Capt' Fore Top	BELLEROPHON	
GRACE, James	Ord	RODNEY	
GRAHAM, Robert.B.	Actg Master	HAZARD	
GRAHAM, William	Pte. R.M.	CAMBRIDGE	
GRAIG, Mitchell	Ord	GANGES	
GRANGER, William	Pte. R.M.	RODNEY	
GRANT, Charles	Bosun's Mate	EDINBURGH	
GRANT, Charles	Ord	GANGES	
GRANT, Edward	Pte. R.M.	Pcss CHARLOTTE	
GRANT, George	Master	STROMBOLI	
GRANT, George	Gunner	CARYSFORT	
GRANT, George	Admiral's Stwd	Pcss CHARLOTTE	
GRANT, Henry	A.B.	REVENGE	
GRANT, Henry.J.	Midshipman	VANGUARD	
GRANT, James	Capt's Coxswain	POWERFUL	*(M) Anchor Type LS & GC*
GRANT, James	Boy	POWERFUL	
GRANT, James	Ord	BELLEROPHON	
GRANT, John	Ord	BELLEROPHON	
GRANT, Richard	Carp's Crew	REVENGE	
GRANT, Robert	Sapper & Miner	HECATE	
GRANT, Thomas	Boy	CASTOR	
GRANT, William	Pte. R.M.	GORGON	
GRANT, William	Pte. R.M.	STROMBOLI	
GRANT, William	Carpenter	GANGES	
GRANT, William	Capt's Steward	GORGON	
GRANT, William	Bosun's Mate	RODNEY	
GRANT, William.C.P.	Clerk	CYCLOPS	
GRANVILLE, Frederick	Boy	WASP	
GRANVILLE, Henry	A.B.	THUNDERER	
GRANVILLE, James	Ord	VANGUARD	
GRARD, George	Pte. R.M.	REVENGE	
GRATTON, William	Pte. R.M.	CARYSFORT	
GRAVENER, Edward	Ord	HASTINGS	
GRAVENER, William	Pte. R.M.	GANGES	
GRAY, Archilans	Pte. R.M.	BELLEROPHON	
GRAY, Henry	Ord	HASTINGS	
GRAY, John	Q.M.	THUNDERER	
GRAY, John	A.B.	IMPLACABLE	
GRAY, Robert	Coxswain of Pinnace	EDINBURGH	
GRAY, William	Ord	REVENGE	
GRAY, William	A.B.	Pcss CHARLOTTE	
GREADY, James	Boy	GANGES	
GREANES, Joseph	Gunner. R.M.A.	PIQUE	
GREAVES, James	A.B.	RODNEY	
GREAVES, John.H.	Paymaster & Purser	HAZARD	
GREEN, Alexander	A.B.	GANGES	
GREEN, Daniel	Capt' of Mast	HASTINGS	
GREEN, George	Ord	CAMBRIDGE	
GREEN, James	A.B.	HASTINGS	
GREEN, James	Ord	CAMBRIDGE	
GREEN, James	Gunner. R.M.A.	MEDEA	
GREEN, John	Pte. R.M.	HAZARD	
GREEN, John	Pte. R.M.	VANGUARD	

GREEN, John	Pte. R.M.	ASIA	
GREEN, John	Boy	DAPHNE	
GREEN, John	Boy	RODNEY	
GREEN, John.G.	Gun Room Stwd	CAMBRIDGE	
GREEN, Peter	A.B.	POWERFUL	
GREEN, Robert	Pte. R.M.	ZEBRA	
GREEN, Stephen	Ord	DIDO	
GREEN, Thomas	A.B.	EDINBURGH	
GREEN, Thomas	Pte. R.M.	VANGUARD	
GREEN, Thomas	Pte. R.M.	BENBOW	
GREEN, William	A.B.	IMPLACABLE	
GREEN, William	Q.M.	VANGUARD	
GREEN, William	Pte. R.M.	STROMBOLI	
GREENACRE, Robert	Ord	BENBOW	
GREENAWAY, James	Pte. R.M.	REVENGE	
GREENFIELD, Henry	A.B.	HASTINGS	
GREENHALL, Middleton	Pte. R.M.	Pcss CHARLOTTE	
GREENLAND, Albion	Pte. R.M.	VANGUARD	
GREENSLADE, John	Pte. R.M.	THUNDERER	
GREENSTREET, John	Boy	PIQUE	
GREEVES, Henry	Pte. R.M.	POWERFUL	
GREGG, Henry	Ord	BELLEROPHON	
GREGORY, Edward	A.B.	DAPHNE	
GREGORY, Henry	Ord	HASTINGS	
GREGORY, James	Pte. R.M.	IMPLACABLE	
GREGORY, John	Pte. R.M.	STROMBOLI	
GREGORY, John	Q.M.	GANGES	
GREGORY, Joseph	Pte. R.M.	Pcss CHARLOTTE	
GREGORY, Thomas	A.B.	IMPLACABLE	
	Ord	ALBION	*Navarino*
GREGSON, John	Pte. R.M.	POWERFUL	
GRENFELL, Sidney	Lieut. R.N.	CYCLOPS	
GRENTER, Henry	Pte. R.M.	THUNDERER	
GREY, David.H.	L.M.	GANGES	
GRIFFEN, Edward	Pte. R.M.	PIQUE	
GRIFFIN, George	Captain. R.M.	CAMBRIDGE	
GRIFFIN, Joseph	Pte. R.M.	MEDEA	
GRIFFIN, William	Commander.	GANGES	
	Midshipman	MINDEN	*Algiers*
GRIFFITHS, Albert	Boy	STROMBOLI	
GRIFFITHS, George	Gunner's Mate	WASP	
GRIFFITHS, Henry	Fifer. R.M.	HASTINGS	
GRIFFITHS, John	A.B.	GANGES	
GRIFFITHS, John	Carpenter	VESUVIUS	
GRIFFITHS, John	A.B.	DIDO	
GRIFFITHS, William	Pte. R.M.	BELLEROPHON	
GRIFFITHS, William	Pte. R.M.	POWERFUL	
GRIFFITHS, William	2 borne	EDINBURGH	
GRIGG, Thomas	Capt' Main Top	IMPLACABLE	
GRIGG, William	Ord	ZEBRA	
GRILLS, Francis	Pte. R.M.	TALBOT	
GRIMA, Vincent	Boy	IMPLACABLE	
GRISBROOK, John	A.B.	Pcss CHARLOTTE	
GROOM, Richard	Ord	BENBOW	
GROOM, Samuel	A.B.	BENBOW	
GROONES, Henry	Boy	WASP	
GROSVENOR, Thomas	Ord	BENBOW	
GROVE, James	Pte. R.M.	IMPLACABLE	
GROVES, Charles	Pte. R.M.	VANGUARD	
GROVES, Edward	Asst Surgeon	CAMBRIDGE	
GROVES, George	Pte. R.M.	Pcss CHARLOTTE	
GROVES, George	Pte. R.M.	MAGICIENNE	
GROVES, James	Ord	BENBOW	
GROVES, John	Pte. R.M.	IMPLACABLE	
GROVES, Thomas	Ord	HASTINGS	*(May read GROVER)*
GROVES, William	Ord	BENBOW	
GROVES, William	Q.M.	GORGON	
GROVES, W.T.	Capt' Fore Top	VANGUARD	
GRUBB, Henry	Capt' of Mast	HASTINGS	
GRUBB, Stephen	Pte. R.M.	BENBOW	
GRUETT, William	Ord	THUNDERER	
GRUZELIER, Frederick.J.	2nd Master	BENBOW	
GUARD, John	Ord	POWERFUL	
GUBBY, William	A.B.	GANGES	*(May read GUBBEY)*
GUEST, William	Sailmaker's Crew	BELLEROPHON	
GUILAND, Peter	A.B.	EDINBURGH	*(May read GARLAND)*
GULAND, William	Surgeon	BELLEROPHON	
GULLIFORD, John	Carp's Crew	Pcss CHARLOTTE	
GULLIVER, Charles	Pte. R.M.	STROMBOLI	
GULLIVER, Henry	Pte. R.M.	THUNDERER	
GULLY, Joseph	Ord	RODNEY	
GUMB, George	Ord	HAZARD	
GUMBLE, James	Capt' Fore Top	HASTINGS	
GUMMER, John	Pte. R.M.	CAMBRIDGE	
GUMMETT, John	Pte. R.M.	ASIA	

SYRIA

GUNTUR, George	Ord	VANGUARD	*(Very badly written – Roll)*
GUNDRY, James	A.B.	THUNDERER	
GURMAN, William	A.B.	POWERFUL	
GURNEY, William	Stoker	STROMBOLI	
GUTTERIDGE, George	A.B.	BELLEROPHON	
GUY, James	Boy 1st Class	EDINBURGH	
GUY, John	Pte. R.M.	THUNDERER	
GUY, Thomas	Pte. R.M.	BELLEROPHON	*(M.L. as GREY)*
GUYON, John.F.	Lieut. R.N.	CYCLOPS	
GWINNELL, Henry	Pte. R.M.	BENBOW	
GWYNE, John	Midshipman	BENBOW	
HAASE, Samuel	Pte. R.M.	CAMBRIDGE	
HABDALLAH, Joseph	Not Given	EDINBURGH	
HACKETT, Thomas	Pte. R.M.	BENBOW	
HACKEE(?), George	A.B.	IMPLACABLE	*Surname indecipherable*
HADLEY, Charles	Pte. R.M.	IMPLACABLE	
HADRILL, James	Pte. R.M.	Pcss CHARLOTTE	
HAIGH, James	Pte. R.M.	CYCLOPS	
HAIN, Joseph	Pte. R.M.	Pcss CHARLOTTE	
HAINES, James	Pte. R.M.	EDINBURGH	
HAINES, Thomas	Pte. R.M.	POWERFUL	
	Pte. R.M.	GENOA	*Navarino*
HAKE, John	Ropemaker	Pcss CHARLOTTE	*(M) Anchor Type LS & GC*
HALE, Henry	Pte. R.M.	STROMBOLI	
HALE, John	Pte. R.M.	PIQUE	
HALE, Thomas	Pte. R.M.	ASIA	
HALE, William	Pte. R.M.	BELLEROPHON	
HALES, John	Ord	EDINBURGH	
HALES, R.M.	Stoker	CYCLOPS	
HALES, Thomas	Carp's Crew	EDINBURGH	
HALES, William	Pte. R.M.	BENBOW	
HALEY, John	Ord	REVENGE	
HALEY, John	Capt' Fore Top	CARYSFORT	
HALEY, Michael	Ord	Pcss CHARLOTTE	
HALFYEAR, Job	Pte. R.M.	RODNEY	
HALISSY, Cornelius	Pte. R.M.	VESUVIUS	
HALL, Charles.E.P.	Clerk	RODNEY	
HALL, James	A.B.	RODNEY	
HALL, James	Boy	BELLEROPHON	
HALL, Job	Pte. R.M.	ASIA	
HALL, Joseph	Cooper's Crew	Pcss CHARLOTTE	
HALL, Richard	A.B.	VANGUARD	
HALL, Thomas	Ord	STROMBOLI	
HALL, William	A.B.	POWERFUL	
HALL, William.H.	Lieut. R.N.	THUNDERER	*(M) A of I/AVA. Alligator*
HALL, William.K.	Mate	BENBOW	
HALL, William.R.	Addtl Clerk	RODNEY	
HALLATT, Richard	Ord	ZEBRA	
HALLETT, Hughes	Lieut. R.N.	BELLEROPHON	
HALLING, Edward	Blacksmith	REVENGE	
HALLIWELL, Joseph	Pte. R.M.	PHOENIX	
	Pte. R.M.	ROSE	*Navarino*
HALLS, Edwin	A.B.	GANGES	
HALLOWES, Ramsey.H.	Volunteer 1st Cl	POWERFUL	
HALSEY, Edward	Ord	POWERFUL	
HALSEY, Thomas	A.B.	EDINBURGH	
HALTON, William	Drummer. R.M.	DIDO	
HAMBLEY, James	Q.M.	CASTOR	
HAMBLIN, James	Ord	CARYSFORT	
HAMBLYN, William	A.B.	CAMBRIDGE	
HAMBROOK, John	Ord	CASTOR	
HAMILTON, Alexander	Mate	POWERFUL	
HAMILTON, George	Ord	BENBOW	
HAMILTON, John	A.B.	Pcss CHARLOTTE	
HAMILTON, Joseph	A.B.	DAPHNE	*(May read James)*
HAMILTON, Thomas	A.B.	THUNDERER	
HAMILTON, William	Pte. R.M.	GANGES	
HAMILTON, William	A.B.	VANGUARD	
HAMILTON, William	Boy	REVENGE	
HAMLEY, Charles.O.	1st Lieut. R.M.	PIQUE	
HAMLEY, Wymond	Lieut. R.N.	EDINBURGH	
HAMLIN, Henry	Pte. R.M.	MAGICIENNE	
HAMLIN, Isaac	Sgt. R.M.	RODNEY	
HAMMETT, Lacon.U.	Mate	BELLEROPHON	
HAMMING, John	Pte. R.M.	BELLEROPHON	
HAMMOND, James	Gun Room Cook	GORGON	
HAMMOND, Thomas	Ord	PIQUE	
HAMMOND, William	Ord	POWERFUL	
HAMPTON, Robert	Boy 1st Class	POWERFUL	
HANCE, Alfred	Pte. R.M.	REVENGE	
HANCOCK, Ely	Pte. R.M.	PIQUE	
HANCOCK, Henry	A.B.	RODNEY	

HANCOCK, John	A.B.	POWERFUL	
	A.B.	GENOA	*Navarino*
HANCOCK, John	A.B.	RODNEY	
HANCOCK, Richard	Ord	THUNDERER	
HANCOCK, Richard	Pte. R.M.	PIQUE	
HANCOX, John	2 borne	RODNEY	
HANDLEY, William	Pte. R.M.	PHOENIX	
HANDS, Joseph	Pte. R.M.	BELLEROPHON	
HANES, G.S.R.	Pte. R.M.	VANGUARD	*(May read G.T.N.)*
HANHAM, Thomas.B.	Volunteer 1st Cl	HASTINGS	
HANLEY, George	Pte. R.M.	POWERFUL	
HANLON, Michael.J.	Ord	BENBOW	
HANN, Alfred	Pte. R.M.	PIQUE	
HANN, Edward	Pte. R.M.	EDINBURGH	
HANN, Thomas	Pte. R.M.	Pcss CHARLOTTE	
HANNELL, William	Pte. R.M.	STROMBOLI	
HANNER, John	A.B.	PIQUE	
HANRAHAN, Maurice	Pte. R.M.	HASTINGS	
HANSARD, Alfred.O.	Mate	IMPLACABLE	
HANSFORD, Samuel	A.B.	CASTOR	
HAPLEY, William	Pte. R.M.	VANGUARD	
HARBIN, Stephen	Pte. R.M.	VANGUARD	
HARBOR, John	Pte. R.M.	VANGUARD	
HARBOUR, Robert	Pte. R.M.	EDINBURGH	
HARBOUR, William	Pte. R.M.	Pcss CHARLOTTE	
HARBOWE, William.E.	Engineer	HECATE	
HARBUTT, Peter	Pte. R.M.	Pcss CHARLOTTE	
HARDING, Henry	Ord	VANGUARD	
HARDING, John	Ord	THUNDERER	
HARDING, Thomas	Q.M.	HASTINGS	
HARDING, William	Pte. R.M.	REVENGE	
	Pte. R.M.	ALBION	*Navarino*
HARDING, William	Pte. R.M.	HASTINGS	
HARDING, William	Stoker	CYCLOPS	
HARDIWAY, William	Ord	GANGES	
HARDY, Charles	Sailmaker	HAZARD	
HARDY, John	Ord	POWERFUL	
HARDY, Thomas	A.B.	CASTOR	
HARE, William	A.B.	DAPHNE	
HARE, William	Purser's Steward	DAPHNE	
HARFLEET, Thomas	Pte. R.M.	HASTINGS	
HARGEAR, Henry	Boy	GANGES	
HARHEN, William	Cooper	DAPHNE	*(May read HARBEN)*
HARLAND, Charles	Boy	HASTINGS	
HARLOW, Henry	Boy	IMPLACABLE	
HARLOW, John.P.	Carp's Crew	GORGON	
HARMAN, James	Pte. R.M.	BENBOW	
HARMAN, Thomas	Not Given	GANGES	
HARMOND, John	A.B.	GANGES	
HARNDEN, Edward	Painter	CASTOR	
HARPER, Alfred	Boy 2nd Class	RODNEY	
HARPER, George	A.B.	IMPLACABLE	
HARPER, George	A.B.	HAZARD	
HARPER, Henry	Capt's Coxswain	HAZARD	
HARPER, H.	Ord	VANGUARD	
HARPER, James	Pte. R.M.	PIQUE	
HARPER, John	2 A.Bs borne	RODNEY	
HARPER, Richard	A.B.	VANGUARD	
HARPING, John	A.B.	CAMBRIDGE	
HARPUR, George	A.B.	IMPLACABLE	
HARPUR, James	A.B.	RODNEY	
HARRIGAN, James	Ord	Pcss CHARLOTTE	
HARRINGTON, David	Carp's Crew	CAMBRIDGE	
HARRINGTON, Dennis	Ord	CAMBRIDGE	
HARRINGTON, Dennis	Ord	ASIA	
HARRINGTON, Frederick	Pte. R.M.	WASP	
HARRINGTON, James	A.B.	ASIA	
HARRINGTON, James	A.B.	Pcss CHARLOTTE	
HARRINGTON, John	Ord	VANGUARD	
HARRINGTON, William	Pte. R.M.	POWERFUL	
HARRIS, Abraham	Ord	REVENGE	
HARRIS, Alfred	Ord	VANGUARD	
HARRIS, Charles	A.B.	EDINBURGH	
HARRIS, E.T.	Pte. R.M.	CAMBRIDGE	
HARRIS, George	Boatswain	REVENGE	
HARRIS, George	Ord	REVENGE	
HARRIS, Henry	A.B.	RODNEY	
HARRIS, Henry	Pte. R.M.	BELLEROPHON	
HARRIS, Isaac	A.B.	PIQUE	
HARRIS, Jacob	Pte. R.M.	RODNEY	
HARRIS, James	Fifer. R.M.	STROMBOLI	
HARRIS, James	Gunner. R.M.A.	VESUVIUS	
HARRIS, James	Pte. R.M.	HASTINGS	
HARRIS, James	Pte. R.M.	BELLEROPHON	
HARRIS, John	Pte. R.M.	Pcss CHARLOTTE	

SYRIA

HARRIS, John	Pte. R.M.	PHOENIX	
HARRIS, John	Ord	REVENGE	
HARRIS, John	Pte. R.M.	STROMBOLI	
HARRIS, John	Fifer. R.M.	VESUVIUS	
HARRIS, John	A.B.	IMPLACABLE	
HARRIS, John	Boy	THUNDERER	
HARRIS, Joseph	A.B.	TALBOT	
HARRIS, N.H.	Addtl Clerk	CAMBRIDGE	
HARRIS, Robert	Gunner	VANGUARD	
HARRIS, Samuel	Pte. R.M.	VANGUARD	
HARRIS, Samuel	A.B.	RODNEY	
HARRIS, Samuel	Ord	MAGICIENNE	
HARRIS, Stephen	Boy	THUNDERER	
HARRIS, Thomas	Admiral's Coxswain	Pcss CHARLOTTE	(M) Anchor Type LS & GC
	Capt's Coxswain	DARTMOUTH	Navarino
HARRIS, William	Pte. R.M.	IMPLACABLE	
HARRIS, William	A.B.	THUNDERER	
HARRIS, William	Pte. R.M.	THUNDERER	
HARRIS, William	Pte. R.M.	HYDRA	
HARRIS, William	Pte. R.M.	REVENGE	
	Pte. R.M.	CAMBRIAN	Navarino
HARRISON, Charles	Boy	DIDO	
HARRISON, Edward	Pte. R.M.	BELLEROPHON	
HARRISON, James	Q.M.	MAGICIENNE	(M) Anchor Type LS & GC
HARRISON, Job	Pte. R.M.	TALBOT	
HARRISON, John	Caulker's Mate	POWERFUL	
HARRISON, John	Bosun's Mate	BELLEROPHON	
HARRISON, John	Pte. R.M.	VANGUARD	
HARRISON, Joseph	Boy	Pcss CHARLOTTE	
HARRISON, Octavius.S.	Chaplain	POWERFUL	
HARRISON, Robert.S.	Lieut. R.M.	BENBOW	
HART, Daniel	Q.M.	BENBOW	
HART, David	Q.M.	Pcss CHARLOTTE	
HART, George	Pte. R.M.	Pcss CHARLOTTE	
HART, Henry	Pte. R.M.	BENBOW	
HART, James	A.B.	BELLEROPHON	
HART, James	A.B.	PIQUE	
HART, Joseph	Pte. R.M.	BENBOW	
HART, William	A.B.	POWERFUL	
HARTLEY, John	A.B.	CAMBRIDGE	
	Boy 2nd Class	GRANICUS	Algiers
HARTLEY, John	A.B.	HASTINGS	
HARVEY, Edward	Captain. R.N.	IMPLACABLE	
	Midshipman	BEAULIEU	Camperdown
HARVEY, Edward	Captain R.M. (? unknown)	HECATE	Probably an Army Officer
HARVEY, Edward	Pte. R.M.	TALBOT	
HARVEY, Edwin	Corporal. R.M.	REVENGE	
HARVEY, George	A.B.	GANGES	
HARVEY, George	Pte. R.M.	RODNEY	
HARVEY, Gillmore	Lieut. R.N.	MEDEA	
HARVEY, Henry	Midshipman	IMPLACABLE	
HARVEY, James	Capt' After Guard	HAZARD	
HARVEY, James	Boy	CARYSFORT	
HARVEY, John	Bosun's Mate	Pcss CHARLOTTE	
HARVEY, Robert	Not Given	RODNEY	
HARVEY, Thomas	Pte. R.M.	ASIA	
HARVEY, William	Carp's Crew	HAZARD	
HARVEY, William	Bosun's Mate	VESUVIUS	
HARWARD, John.R.	Midshipman	PIQUE	
HARWOOD, Richard	Pte. R.M.	BENBOW	
HARWOOD, Robert	Pte. R.M.	PIQUE	
HASTED, Samuel	Boy 1st Class	VANGUARD	
HASTINGS, Charles	Yeoman of Signals	MAGICIENNE	
	Boy	GLASGOW	Navarino
HASTINGS, Francis.D.	Commander	EDINBURGH	
HASTINGS, John	Ord	Pcss CHARLOTTE	
HASTINGS, Richard	Boy 2nd Class	REVENGE	
HASWELL, William.H.	Mate	TALBOT	
HATCH, James	Boy	IMPLACABLE	
HATCH, John	Pte. R.M.	THUNDERER	
HATCH, John	L.M.	RODNEY	
HATCHARD, Daniel	Stoker	STROMBOLI	
HATCHARD, George	Carp's Crew	POWERFUL	
HATCHER, Henry	A.B.	HASTINGS	
HATFIELD, George	Pte. R.M.	WASP	
HATHORN, George	Commander	BENBOW	
HAUNT(?), Richard	A.B.	Pcss CHARLOTTE	(Very badly written. HAM(?))
HAVES, William	Carp's Crew	Pcss CHARLOTTE	
HAWKER, George	Blacksmith	HAZARD	
HAWKER, Henry	Lieut. R.N.	EDINBURGH	
HAWKER, Joseph	Boy	HASTINGS	
HAWKER, William	Ord	HASTINGS	
HAWKEY, Charles	Mate	STROMBOLI	

HAWKINS, Charles	A.B.	IMPLACABLE	
HAWKINS, Charles	A.B.	BENBOW	
HAWKINS, Charles	Coxswain of Pinnace	DAPHNE	
HAWKINS, Frank.K.	Midshipman	PIQUE	
HAWKINS, George	Capt's Cook	EDINBURGH	
HAWKINS, Henry	A.B.	REVENGE	
HAWKINS, James	A.B.	EDINBURGH	
HAWKINS, John	Ord	THUNDERER	
HAWKINS, Thomas	A.B.	IMPLACABLE	
HAWKINS, Thomas	A.B.	BENBOW	
HAWTON, William	Ord	IMPLACABLE	
HAY, Edward	Pte. R.M.	BENBOW	
HAY, John	Sgt. R.M.	CASTOR	
HAY, John.C.D.	Midshipman	BENBOW	
HAYES, George	Lieut. R.M.	ASIA	
HAYES, James	Ord	REVENGE	
HAYES, James	A.B.	BENBOW	
HAYES, John	Ord	THUNDERER	
HAYES, John	A.B.	TALBOT	
	Ord	TALBOT	Navarino
HAYES, John	Boy	REVENGE	
HAYES, Patrick	Capt' After Guard	THUNDERER	
	Ord	GENOA	Navarino
HAYES, Thomas	A.B.	EDINBURGH	
HAYLES, Benjamin	Capt's Steward	VANGUARD	
HAYNES, Benjamin	Boy	THUNDERER	
HAYNES, Charles	Not Given	MEDEA	
HAYNES, John.C.	A.B.	VANGUARD	
HAYNES, Rowling	Purser's Steward	HAZARD	
HAYNES, William	Boy	THUNDERER	
HAYNES, William	Ord	VANGUARD	
HAYNES, William	A.B.	PIQUE	
HAYTER, Thomas	Pte. R.M.	REVENGE	
HAYWARD, George	Gunner's Mate	IMPLACABLE	
HAYWARD, James	A.B.	Pcss CHARLOTTE	
	Boy	ROSE	Navarino
HAYWARD, John	Ord	BELLEROPHON	
HAYWARD, William	Pte. R.M.	HASTINGS	
HAYWOOD, Thomas	Pte. R.M.	THUNDERER	(May read HEYWOOD)
HAZLEWOOD, James	Ord	CASTOR	
HEAD, John	A.B.	Pcss CHARLOTTE	
HEAD, Richard	Carp's Crew	CYCLOPS	
HEAD, William	Corporal. R.M.	ASIA	
HEADE, Thomas	A.B.	POWERFUL	alias HEAD
HEADEN, Charles	Capt' Forecastle	DAPHNE	
HEADLAND, William	Boy	VANGUARD	
HEAL, William	Ord	BELLEROPHON	
HEALY, William	Gunner. R.M.A.	STROMBOLI	(M) M.S.M. Gallantry 1857
HEARD, Thomas	Mate	POWERFUL	
HEARLE, Edmund	Captain. R.M.	RODNEY	
HEARLE, Nicholas	Pte. R.M.	RODNEY	
HEARN, Beverley	Ord	THUNDERER	
HEARN, Charles.J.	A.B.	BELLEROPHON	
HEARN, Thomas.C.	Q.M.	POWERFUL	
HEARN, William	Pte. R.M.	BENBOW	
HEARN, William	Ord	POWERFUL	
HEASBY, George	Pte. R.M.	HASTINGS	(May read HENSBY)
HEATH, Edward	Ord	CARYSFORT	
HEATH, Henry	Ord	GANGES	
HEATH, John	Pte. R.M.	EDINBURGH	
HEATH, Thomas	Pte. R.M.	HASTINGS	
HEATH, William.A.J.	College Mate	PIQUE	
HEATHCOTE, Henry	A.B.	Pcss CHARLOTTE	
HEATHCOTE, Richard	A.B.	STROMBOLI	
HEATHCOTE, Thomas	Boy	PIQUE	
HEATHCOTE, William	Sapper & Miner	HECATE	
HEATHER, Thomas	Ord	EDINBURGH	
HEATHER, William	Pte. R.M.	Pcss CHARLOTTE	
HEATHORN, Charles	Pte. R.M.	VESUVIUS & STROMBOLI	
HEBLEY, John	Ord	HASTINGS	
HEDGECOCK, George	Boy	HASTINGS	
HEDINGTON, William	A.B.	HASTINGS	
HEGARTY, Patrick	L.M.	REVENGE	
HEIGHWAY, Edward	Pte. R.M.	EDINBURGH	
HELBORN, William	Carp's Crew	EDINBURGH	
HEMMETT, Richard	A.B.	IMPLACABLE	
HEMMINGS, William	A.B.	HASTINGS	
HEMPSTEAD, William	Pte. R.M.	GORGON	
HENDERSON, David	Pte. R.M.	REVENGE	
HENDERSON, George	Pte. R.M.	BENBOW	
	Pte. R.M.	ASIA	Navarino
HENDERSON, James	Caulker's Mate	BENBOW	
HENDERSON, John	A.B.	IMPLACABLE	
HENDERSON, Samuel.H.	Midshipman	EDINBURGH	

SYRIA

HENDERSON, Thomas	Commander	VESUVIUS	
HENDERSON, William.H.	Captain. R.N.	GORGON	
HENDERSON, William.W.	Captain. R.N.	EDINBURGH	
	Midshipman	BELLEISLE	*Trafalgar*
	Lieut. R.N.	ACTIVE	*B.S. 28 June 1810*
	Lieut. R.N.	ACTIVE	*(P) Lissa*
HENDY, Joseph	A.B.	POWERFUL	
HENLEY, Charles	Pte. R.M.	HAZARD	
HENLEY, Thomas	A.B.	GANGES	
HENRY, John	Royal Artillery	HECATE	*Collarmaker (?). HENERY (?)*
HENSON, William	Ord	REVENGE	
HENTY, John	2nd Engineer	PHOENIX	
HENWOOD, Thomas	Pte. R.M.	BELLEROPHON	
HERBERT, Douglas	Midshipman	EDINBURGH	
HERBERT, John	Ord	GANGES	
HERD, Robert	A.B.	POWERFUL	
HERN, Lewis	Pte. R.M.	EDINBURGH	
HERRING, Richard	Gunner's Mate	Pcss CHARLOTTE	
HESTER, James	Gunner's Mate	VANGUARD	
HETHERIDGE, Joseph	A.B.	GANGES	
HEWETT, Isaac	Boy 2nd Class	HECATE	
HEWITSON, James	Gun Room Cook	HAZARD	
HEWITT, John	A.B.	EDINBURGH	
HEWITT, William	A.B.	MAGICIENNE	
HEWLETT, Richard.S.	Lieut. R.N.	ASIA	
HIAMS, John	Pte. R.M.	STROMBOLI	
HIBBARD, Charles	Pte. R.M.	VANGUARD	
HIBBERD, Richard	Ord	ASIA	
HICKER, Owen	Gunner's Mate	HECATE	
HICKEY, William	Ord	VANGUARD	
HICKINGBOTTOM, John	Pte. R.M.	Pcss CHARLOTTE	
HICKMAN, Henry	A.B.	STROMBOLI	
HICKMAN, James	Coxswain of Launch	BENBOW	
HICKMAN, John	Gunner	PHOENIX	
HICKOX, John	A.B.	GANGES	
HICKS, George	A.B.	Pcss CHARLOTTE	
HICKS, George	A.B.	PIQUE	
HICKS, George	Sgt. R.M.	BENBOW	
HICKS, Henry	Sailmaker's Crew	GORGON	
HICKS, William	A.B.	HASTINGS	
HICKSON, Richard	Pte. R.M.	CASTOR	
HIERTA, C.J.	Steward's Mate	EDINBURGH	
HIGGINS, Elias	Pte. R.M.	STROMBOLI	
HIGGINS, T.Gordon	Major Ryl Arty	THUNDERER	
HIGGINS, William	A.B.	THUNDERER	
HILL, Charles	Ord	HASTINGS	
HILL, Charles	A.B.	REVENGE	
HILL, Charles	Pte. R.M.	RODNEY	
HILL, David	Pte. R.M.	REVENGE	
HILL, Edward	Pte. R.M.	STROMBOLI	
HILL, George	A.B.	EDINBURGH	
HILL, George	2 borne	EDINBURGH	
HILL, Henry	A.B.	MEDEA	
HILL, Henry	Boy	Pcss CHARLOTTE	
HILL, Henry	Boy	CARYSFORT	
HILL, Henry.W.	Pte. R.M.	EDINBURGH	
HILL, Hickford	A.B.	POWERFUL	
HILL, James	Ord	HASTINGS	
HILL, John	Carp's Crew	THUNDERER	
HILL, John	Ord	GANGES	
HILL, John	A.B.	HASTINGS	
HILL, John	Carpenter	MAGICIENNE	
HILL, John	Boy	PIQUE	
HILL, Joseph	Pte. R.M.	THUNDERER	
HILL, Pascoe.G.	Chaplain	ASIA	
HILL, Richard	Boy	TALBOT	
HILL, Richard	Pte. R.M.	RODNEY	
HILL, Samuel	Bosun's Mate	POWERFUL	
HILL, Theophilus	A.B.	IMPLACABLE	
HILL, Thomas	Ship's Corporal	Pcss CHARLOTTE	
HILL, Thomas	Ship's Corporal	CAMBRIDGE	
HILL, Thomas	Royal Artillery	HECATE	
HILL, Thomas	Boy	RODNEY	
HILL, William	Pte. R.M.	EDINBURGH	
HILL, William	Pte. R.M.	THUNDERER	
HILL, William	2 borne	IMPLACABLE	
HILL, William.H.	Ord	POWERFUL	
HILL, W.H.(?)	Bosun's Mate	HYDRA	*Initials indistinct*
HILLIARD, John	Pte. R.M.	BELLEROPHON	
HILLIMAN, John	Pte. R.M.	VESUVIUS	
HILLMAN, Uriah	Pte. R.M.	PIQUE	

HILLYAR, Henry.S.	Midshipman	ASIA	
HILLS, William	Pte. R.M.	REVENGE	
HILMAN, Arthur	Pte. R.M.	REVENGE	
HILMAN, Peter	Gun Room Steward	RODNEY	
HINDE, Edward.G.	Ward Room Steward	THUNDERER	
HINE, Henry	Pte. R.M.	BENBOW	
HINES, Daniel	Capt' Main Top	BENBOW	(Additional clasp?)
HINES, Francis	A.B.	Pcss CHARLOTTE	
	Boy	ASIA	Navarino
HINGSTON, A.	Caulker	GANGES	
HINGSTON, Bevil (?)	Carp's Mate	RODNEY	
HINKINS, Henry	Capt' Main Top	ZEBRA	
HINKS, George	A.B.	EDINBURGH	
HISCOCK, Thomas	Sailmaker's Crew	CAMBRIDGE	
HISCOX, Richard	Sailmaker's Crew	CAMBRIDGE	(Same man as above (?))
HITCHCOCK, James	Pte. R.M.	DAPHNE	
HITCHCOCK, William	Pte. R.M.	STROMBOLI	
HITCHENS, Joseph	Ord	HASTINGS	
HITCHINS, John	A.B.	POWERFUL	
HITCHOX, Thomas	Pte. R.M.	BELLEROPHON	
HOAR, Henry	Ord	STROMBOLI	
HOAR, John	Pte. R.M.	IMPLACABLE	
HOARE, William	A.B.	ASIA	
HOBBS, George	Gun Room Steward	BENBOW	
HOBBS, George	Boy	CARYSFORT	
HOBBS, George	Pte. R.M.	VANGUARD	
HOBBS, George.W.	A.B.	EDINBURGH	
HOBBS, Henry	Pte. R.M.	THUNDERER	
HOBBS, James	A.B.	Pcss CHARLOTTE	
HOBBS, James	Ord	BENBOW	
HOBBS, Samuel	Boy	RODNEY	
HOBBS, Thomas	Pte. R.M.	RODNEY	
HOBBS, William	A.B.	BELLEROPHON	
HOBBS, William	Ord	IMPLACABLE	
HOBDAY, George	A.B.	HYDRA	
HOBLEDAY, John	A.B.	RODNEY	
HOBLIN, John	A.B.	RODNEY	
HOBSON, James	Pte. R.M.	REVENGE	
HOBSON, John	Pte. R.M.	Pcss CHARLOTTE	
HOCKEN, William	Carp's Crew	THUNDERER	
HOCKER, Edward	1st Lieut. R.M.	STROMBOLI & VESUVIUS	
HOCKHAM, Thomas	Stoker	PHOENIX	
HOCKIN, Andrew	Ord	RODNEY	
HOCKIN, Charles.L.	Lieut. R.N.	DIDO	
HOCKING, James	Pte. R.M.	CAMBRIDGE	
HOCKING, Richard	A.B.	CAMBRIDGE	
HOCKING, Thomas	Boy	RODNEY	
HOCKLEY, Richard	Carp's Mate	CASTOR	
HODD, Frederick.H.	Engineer's Boy	STROMBOLI	
HODDER, Job	L.M.	REVENGE	
HODGE, Edward	A.B.	RODNEY	
HODGE, John	A.B.	REVENGE	
HODGE, John	Pte. R.M.	RODNEY	
HODGES, Samuel	Cooper's Crew	VANGUARD	
HODGES, Thomas	Boy 1st Class	GANGES	
HODGES, William	Pte. R.M.	BELLEROPHON	
HODGES, William	Pte. R.M.	GANGES	
HODGKINS, James	A.B.	HYDRA	
HODGKINSON, Thomas	Mate	GANGES	
HODGKISS, Samuel	A.B.	CAMBRIDGE	(M) Anchor Type LS & GC
HODGKISS, William	2 borne	CAMBRIDGE	A.B. & Boy
HODGSON, Joseph.L.	Naval Instructor	VANGUARD	
HOFF, William	Capt' Main Top	Pcss CHARLOTTE	
HOGG, William	Pte. R.M.	HASTINGS	
HOGGETT, Charles	A.B.	EDINBURGH	
HOILE, Daniel	Boy 1st Class	EDINBURGH	
HOLBROOK, Edward	A.B.	RODNEY	
HOLBROOK, Joseph	Ord	BENBOW	
HOLDEN, James	Pte. R.M.	CAMBRIDGE	
HOLDER, George	Sailmaker	HASTINGS	
HOLDER, George	Pte. R.M.	STROMBOLI	
HOLDER, John	Pte. R.M.	BELLEROPHON	
HOLDER, William	Pte. R.M.	GANGES	
HOLDHAM, Joseph	Gunner's Mate	HASTINGS	
HOLEYARD, Samuel	Pte. R.M.	RODNEY	
HOLLAND, James	A.B.	BENBOW	
HOLLANDALE, John	Ord	EDINBURGH	(Alias ALLANDALE)
HOLLAY, Richard	Pte. R.M.	RODNEY	
HOLLEY, John	Pte. R.M.	HASTINGS	
HOLLIDAY, David	A.B.	RODNEY	
HOLLIDAY, William	Caulker's Mate	HASTINGS	
	Caulker's Mate	LEANDER	Algiers
HOLLINWORTH, Henry	Mate	THUNDERER	
HOLLINWORTH, Horatio.W.	Clerk	IMPLACABLE	

SYRIA

HOLLOWAY, Robert	Pte. R.M.	POWERFUL	
HOLLOWAY, Thomas	A.B.	CARYSFORT	
HOLMARD, James	A.B.	ASIA	
HOLMES, David	Boy	VANGUARD	
HOLMES, James	Capt' After Guard	VANGUARD	
HOLMES, John	A.B.	CARYSFORT	
HOLMES, William	A.B.	IMPLACABLE	(M) Anchor Type LS & GC
HOLMES, William	Pte. R.M.	BELLEROPHON	
HOLMES, William	Ord	ASIA	
HOLMES, William	Boy	THUNDERER	
HOLMES, William	A.B.	GANGES	
HOLMES, William	Royal Artillery	HECATE	
HOLMWOOD, David	Pte. R.M.	ZEBRA	G.H. 8321
	Pte. R.M.	GLASGOW	Navarino
HOLROYD, Richard	Pte. R.M.	REVENGE	
HOLT, Edward	Pte. R.M.	POWERFUL	
HOLYOAK, Edward	Pte. R.M.	STROMBOLI	
	Pte. R.M.	PHILOMEL	Navarino
HONEY, William	Pte. R.M.	RODNEY	
HONEYBURN, James	Ord	BENBOW	
HOOD, Arthur.W.A.	Midshipman	VANGUARD	
HOOK, William	Pte. R.M.	VESUVIUS	
HOOK, William	Bosun's Mate	Pcss CHARLOTTE	
HOOKER, William	Pte. R.M.	POWERFUL	
HOOKS, William	Pte. R.M.	CAMBRIDGE	
HOOPER, Henry	Sailmaker's Crew	DIDO	
HOOPER, James	Pte. R.M.	IMPLACABLE	
HOOPER, Robert	A.B.	IMPLACABLE	
HOOPER, Tom	Carp's Crew	Pcss CHARLOTTE	
HOOPER, William	A.B.	BENBOW	
HOOPS, Richard	Mate	GANGES	
HOPE, Sackett	Commander	REVENGE	
HOPKINS, Charles	Pte. R.M.	Pcss CHARLOTTE	
HOPKINS, Charles	Ord	MAGICIENNE	
HOPKINS, George	Pte. R.M.	STROMBOLI	
HOPKINS, Thomas	Pte. R.M.	STROMBOLI	
HOPKINS, William.B.	A.B.	REVENGE	
HOPPER, John	A.B.	Pcss CHARLOTTE	
HOPPING, William	Boy	ASIA	
HOPSON, Christopher	Pte. R.M.	Pcss CHARLOTTE	
HORDEN, John	L.M.	RODNEY	
HORE, Christopher.T.	Clerk's Asst	BELLEROPHON	
HORE, Edward.G.	Midshipman	CASTOR	
HORE, Jonah	Ord	RODNEY	
HORGAN, David	Carp's Mate	PIQUE	(May read HOGAN)
HORN, George	A.B.	BENBOW	
HORN, James	A.B.	BELLEROPHON	
HORN, Robert	Capt' Mizzen Top	VANGUARD	
HORN, Thomas	Ord	GORGON	
HORN, Thomas	Capt' Main Top	TALBOT	
HORN, William	Ord	BENBOW	
HORN, William	Boy	REVENGE	
HORN, William	A.B.	VANGUARD	
HORNBROOK, Richard	Ord	RODNEY	
HORNBY, Geoffry.T.B.	Midshipman	Pcss CHARLOTTE	
HORNSBY, Joseph	Pte. R.M.	BELLEROPHON	
HORRELL, William	A.B.	THUNDERER	
HORTON, Henry	Pte. R.M.	VANGUARD	
HORTON, William	College Mate	TALBOT	
HORTON, William	Pte. R.M.	STROMBOLI	
HOSEASON, John.C.	Lieut. R.N.	CAMBRIDGE	
HOSKINS, Henry	Sailmaker's Mate	THUNDERER	
HOSKINS, James	A.B.	IMPLACABLE	
HOSKINS, John	Capt' Fore Top	Pcss CHARLOTTE	
HOSKINS, William	Ord	REVENGE	
HOSSACK, James	A.B.	CAMBRIDGE	
HOUGHTON, William	Asst Surgeon	STROMBOLI	
HOUSE, Samuel	Pte. R.M.	ASIA	
HOW, Thomas	Gunner. R.M.A.	PIQUE	
HOWARD, Henry	Volunteer 1st Cl	RODNEY	
HOWARD, James	Capt' Main Top	CAMBRIDGE	
HOWARD, Robert	Gunner. R.M.A.	GORGON	
HOWARD, Robert.StD.	Pte. R.M.	ASIA	
HOWARD, Thomas	Ord	POWERFUL	
HOWARD, William	A.B.	HASTINGS	
HOWE, James	Fifer. R.M.	HASTINGS	
HOWE, John	Pte. R.M.	BENBOW	
HOWE, John	Pte. R.M.	VESUVIUS	
HOWE, John	Pte. R.M.	GANGES	
HOWE, Thomas	Domestic	Pcss CHARLOTTE	
HOWE, William	Not Given	WASP	
HOWELL, George	Pte. R.M.	POWERFUL	
HOWES, John	Q.M.	VANGUARD	

HOWSON, John	Pte. R.M.	STROMBOLI	
HOYE, Edmond	Boy	BELLEROPHON	
HOYLE, Frederick	Capt' of Mast	REVENGE	
HOYTON, George	Boy	VANGUARD	
HUCKER, Charles	Pte. R.M.	THUNDERER	
HUDD, Joseph	Pte. R.M.	CAMBRIDGE	
HUDD, Joseph	Pte. R.M.	EDINBURGH	
HUDSON, Henry	Ord	BENBOW	
HUDSON, James	Pte. R.M.	RODNEY	
HUDSON, Robert	Gunner. R.M.A.	CYCLOPS	
HUDSON, William	Ord	VANGUARD	
HUGGINS, John	A.B.	WASP	
	Boy	TALBOT	*Navarino*
HUGGINS, Richard	Pte. R.M.	CAMBRIDGE	
HUGHES, George	Ord	BENBOW	
HUGHES, George	A.B.	Pcss CHARLOTTE	
(HUGHES, Hallett see HALLETT)			
HUGHES, Henry	Capt' Fore Top	BENBOW	
	A.B.	CAMBRIAN	*Navarino*
HUGHES, John	Pte. R.M.	BELLEROPHON	
HUGHES, John	A.B.	CASTOR	
	A.B.	TALBOT	*Navarino*
HUGHES, John	A.B.	CAMBRIDGE	
HUGHES, John	Armourer's Mate	ASIA	
HUGHES, John	A.B.	VANGUARD	
HUGHES, Joseph	Boy	CAMBRIDGE	
HUGHES, Robert	A.B.	BENBOW	
HUGHES, Thomas	Corporal. R.M.	POWERFUL	
HULBERT, Thomas	Pte. R.M.	VANGUARD	
HULL, William	Pte. R.M.	CAMBRIDGE	
HULLOTT, Frederick	Bosun's Mate	GORGON	
HUMBER, Thomas	A.B.	VANGUARD	
HUME (?), John	Pte. R.M.	CAMBRIDGE	*Could read HINNE*
HUMPHRIES, David	Ord	HASTINGS	
HUMPHRIES, Frederick	Pte. R.M.	BENBOW	
HUMPHRIES, Henry	Boy	CASTOR	
HUMPHRIES, Joseph	Pte. R.M.	POWERFUL	
HUMPHREY, William	Pte. R.M.	HASTINGS	
HUMPHREYS, Edward	Gunner's Mate	CASTOR	
HUNNEYMAN, Robert	Ord	THUNDERER	
HUNSON, Samuel	Ord	BELLEROPHON	
HUNT, George.E.	1st Lieut. R.M.	MAGICIENNE	
HUNT, Gideon	Corporal R.M.	BENBOW	
HUNT, James	Mate	STROMBOLI	
HUNT, John	A.B.	EDINBURGH	
HUNT, John	Pte. R.M.	POWERFUL	
HUNT, Thomas	Sailmaker's Mate	PIQUE	
HUNT, Thomas	A.B.	HASTINGS	
HUNT, Thomas	Boy	VANGUARD	
HUNT, William	Pte. R.M.	VANGUARD	
HUNT, William	Ord	BELLEROPHON	
HUNTER, Edward	A.B.	THUNDERER	
HUNTER, James	Ord	ASIA	
HUNTER, Richard	A.B.	IMPLACABLE	
HUNTER, William	Pte. R.M.	REVENGE	
HUNTER, William	Pte. R.M.	VANGUARD	
HUNTINGDON, Joseph	Ord	BENBOW	
HUNTINGDON, James	Capt's Steward	HYDRA	
HUNTLEY, Levey	Gunner. R.M.A.	PIQUE	
HURCOMB, James	Pte. R.M.	Pcss CHARLOTTE	
HURD, John	Pte. R.M.	STROMBOLI	
HURD, Joseph	Pte. R.M.	REVENGE	*(May read HARD)*
HURLEY, John	Ord	POWERFUL	*(M.L. as HORLEY)*
HURLEY, Michael	Ord	VANGUARD	
HURLEY, Timothy	Capt' of Mast	CASTOR	*(M) A of I/AVA and Anchor Type LS & GC*
HURRELL, James	Color Sgt. R.M.	DIDO	
HURROLL, William	Pte. R.M.	ASIA	
HURST, Elijah	Pte. R.M.	BENBOW	
HURST, Henry	Boy 1st Class	HAZARD	
HUSKISSON, John	2nd Lieut. R.M.	CAMBRIDGE	
HUTCHINGS, George	A.B.	POWERFUL	
HUTCHINGS, Henry	Master's Asst	HECATE	
HUTCHINGS, James	A.B.	DAPHNE	
HUTCHINGS, Robert	Pte. R.M.	BELLEROPHON	
HUTCHINGS, Samuel	Ord	BELLEROPHON	
HUTCHINS, John	Gun Room Cook	WASP	
HUTCHINSON, David	A.B.	CARYSFORT	
HUTCHINSON, Joshua	Lieut. R.N.	BELLEROPHON	
HUTCHINSON, John	A.B.	CAMBRIDGE	
HUTCHINSON, William	Q.M.	BENBOW	*(M) Anchor type LS & GC*
	Capt' Forecastle	TALBOT	*Navarino*
HUTTON, Frederick	Commander	VANGUARD	*(M) A of I/AVA. Tees*
HUTTON, James	Pte. R.M.	GANGES	
HUTTON, Joseph	Ord	RODNEY	

SYRIA

HUTTON, Matthew	A.B.	CAMBRIDGE	
HUXLEY, Robert	A.B.	GANGES	
HYAM, George	Pte. R.M.	THUNDERER	
HYDE, Henry	Ord	RODNEY	
HYDE, Henry	Bombdr. R.M.A.	PIQUE	
HYDE, Hugh	A.B.	THUNDERER	
HYDE, James	Ord	POWERFUL	
HYMEN, Elijah	Pte. R.M.	REVENGE	
HYNES, Thomas	Pte. R.M.	CAMBRIDGE	
ICKS, Joseph	Ord	EDINBURGH	
IDESON, Charles	A.B.	RODNEY	
ILLMAN, Thomas	Sick Berth Attdt	THUNDERER	
INGLEFIELD, Edward.A.	Mate	THUNDERER	
INGLEFIELD, Valentine.O.	Midshipman	Pcss CHARLOTTE	
INGLIS, James	Carp's Crew	BENBOW	
INGLIS, James	Lieut. R.N.	EDINBURGH	
INGRAM, Herbert.F.W.	Mate	TALBOT	
INGRAM, John	Ord	EDINBURGH	
INGRAM, William (?)	Boy	POWERFUL	*(Roll indecipherable)*
INGRAM, William	Pte. R.M.	PIQUE	
INKPEN, James	Ord	Pcss CHARLOTTE	
INSLEY, Thomas	Pte. R.M.	GANGES	
IRELAND, James	Sapper & Miner	HECATE	
IRISH, Alfred	A.B.	REVENGE	
IRVING, Edward.G.	Asst Surgeon	BELLEROPHON	
IRVING, John	Ord	Pcss CHARLOTTE	
IRVING, John	Pte. R.M.	POWERFUL	
IRWING, George	Q.M.	Pcss CHARLOTTE	
ISAAC, John	A.B.	IMPLACABLE	
ISAAC, William	L.M.	REVENGE	
ISAACS, George	Capt' Main Top	VANGUARD	
ISBESTER, Samuel	Gunner's Crew	BELLEROPHON	*(May read ISHESTER)*
ISHUS, William	Ord	IMPLACABLE	
ISSLES, Thomas.P.	Ord	REVENGE	*(Or ISLES)*
ISTED, Henry	Ord	GANGES	
ISUM, John	A.B.	VANGUARD	
ISUM, William	A.B.	Pcss CHARLOTTE	
IVERS, James	A.B.	EDINBURGH	
IVORY, George	Pte. R.M.	GANGES	
IZAAC, James	Sgt. R.M.	REVENGE	
IZZO, Vincent	Capt's Steward	ZEBRA	
JACKETT, Richard	Ord	CAMBRIDGE	
JACKSON, Charles.K.	College Mate	ASIA	
JACKSON, Edward	A.B.	RODNEY	
JACKSON, George	Ord	GANGES	
JACKSON, H.G.	2nd Master	CARYSFORT	
JACKSON, James	Cook	HASTINGS	
JACKSON, John	A.B.	VANGUARD	
JACKSON, Joseph	Ord	VANGUARD	
JACKSON, Mark	A.B.	RODNEY	*(M) Anchor Type LS & GC*
JACKSON, Thomas	A.B.	VANGUARD	
	A.B.	ALBION	*Navarino*
JACKSON, William	Ord	HAZARD	
JACKSON, William	A.B.	ASIA	
JACKSON, William	A.B.	RODNEY	
JACMAN, Thomas	Q.M.	PIQUE	
JACOBS, James	Pte. R.M.	CASTOR	
JACOBS, John	A.B.	Pcss CHARLOTTE	
JACOBS, Richard	Coxswain of Pinnace	POWERFUL	
	A.B.	ASIA	*Navarino*
JAGO, James	Boy	TALBOT	
JAGO, Joseph	Ord	CAMBRIDGE	
JAGO, Samuel	Ropemaker	GORGON	
JAGO, Thomas	Sailmaker's Mate	STROMBOLI	
JAMES, Charles	Not Given	ASIA	
JAMES, George	A.B.	Pcss CHARLOTTE	
JAMES, George	A.B.	RODNEY	
JAMES, James	Q.M.	HAZARD	
JAMES, John	Ord	THUNDERER	
JAMES, John	Pte. R.M.	ASIA	
JAMES, Thomas	Ord	IMPLACABLE	
JAMES, William	Boy	BELLEROPHON	
JAMES, William	Boy	DAPHNE	
JAMES, William	Purser's Steward	REVENGE	
JAMES, William	M.A.A.	CYCLOPS	
JAMESON, George	A.B.	RODNEY	
JAMESON, Hugh	Surgeon	CASTOR	
JAMESON, John	A.B.	ASIA	
JAMESON, Scott	Ord	CASTOR	
JAMESON, William	A.B.	POWERFUL	
JAMIESON, John	Gunner. R.M.A.	PIQUE	
JAMIESON, William	A.B.	POWERFUL	
JARDINE, David	Capt's Clerk	GORGON	

JARRETT, James	Pte. R.M.	HASTINGS	
JARRETT, Richard	Boy	CAMBRIDGE	
JARRETT, Thomas	A.B.	BENBOW	
JARVIS, James	Ord	RODNEY	
JARVIS, Richard	Pte. R.M.	RODNEY	
JARVIS, Robert	Pte. R.M.	CAMBRIDGE	
JARVIS, Samuel	Ord	RODNEY	
JASPER, Thomas	Bosun's Mate	THUNDERER	
JEANS, George	Pte. R.M.	VANGUARD	
JEANS, William	Not Given	BELLEROPHON	
JEFFERIES, William	Pte. R.M.	DIDO	
JEFFERSON, Henry	Boy	IMPLACABLE	
JEFFERY, Isaac	Pte. R.M.	HASTINGS	
JEFFERY, John	Ship's Cook	IMPLACABLE	
JEFFERY, John.W.	Boy	Pcss CHARLOTTE	
JEFFREY, John	A.B.	VANGUARD	
JEFFREY, John	A.B.	BELLEROPHON	
JEFFREY, Phillip	A.B.	RODNEY	
JEFFREYS, Henry.C.	Mate	Pcss CHARLOTTE	
JEFFRIES, Thomas	Boy	POWERFUL	
JEFFRIES, Thomas	Pte. R.M.	REVENGE	
JEFFRIES, William	A.B.	Pcss CHARLOTTE	
JEFFRIES, William	A.B.	CAMBRIDGE	
JENKINS, Charles	Boy	RODNEY	
JENKINS, Charles.A.	Clerk	HAZARD	
JENKINS, George	Boy	BELLEROPHON	
JENKINS, James	A.B.	GANGES	
JENKINS, James	2 A.Bs borne	Pcss CHARLOTTE	
JENKINS, John	Carp's Mate	POWERFUL	
JENKINS, John	A.B.	HASTINGS	
JENKINS, Rev John	Chaplain	BENBOW	
JENKINS, Joseph	Boy 1st Class	RODNEY	
JENKINS, Robert	Midshipman	HASTINGS	
JENKS, John	Pte. R.M.	Pcss CHARLOTTE	
JENMAN, Henry	Ord	BELLEROPHON	
JENNER, Robert	Mate	EDINBURGH	
JENNER, Robert	Pte. R.M.	GORGON	
JENNER, William	Pte. R.M.	EDINBURGH	
JENNINGS, Benjamin	Purser	REVENGE	
JENNINGS, James	Ord	IMPLACABLE	
JENNINGS, William.H.	Pte. R.M.	Pcss CHARLOTTE	
JENNISON, Henry.G.	Pte. R.M.	CAMBRIDGE	
JEROME, James	Ord	BELLEROPHON	
JEROME, S.H.	Ord	Pcss CHARLOTTE	
JERRAM, George	Boy	DAPHNE	
JERRARD, Benjamin	Capt's Cook	BELLEROPHON	
JESSUP, W.S.	Stoker	HECATE	
JEWELS, William	Pte. R.M.	THUNDERER	
JOB, John	Boy	EDINBURGH	
JOHN, William.H.	Carp's Crew	CAMBRIDGE	
JOHNS, Charles	Pte. R.M.	GANGES	
JOHNS, Henry	Boy	RODNEY	
JOHNS, James	Pte. R.M.	EDINBURGH	
JOHNS, John	Carp's Mate	STROMBOLI	
JOHNS, John	A.B.	BELLEROPHON	
JOHNS, John	2 borne	RODNEY	(A.B. & Ord)
JOHNS, Richard	Boy	THUNDERER	
JOHNS, Samuel	Ord	THUNDERER	
JOHNS, Simon	Carp's Crew	HASTINGS	(M) Anchor Type LS & GC
JOHNS, Thomas	A.B.	IMPLACABLE	
JOHNS, William	Ord	CAMBRIDGE	
JOHNS, William	A.B.	RODNEY	
JOHNSON, Abraham	Capt' of Mast	CAMBRIDGE	(M) Anchor Type LS & GC
JOHNSON, Andrew	Ord	CAMBRIDGE	
JOHNSON, Benjamin	A.B.	GANGES	
JOHNSON, Charles	A.B.	ASIA	
JOHNSON, Charles.R.	Lieut. R.N.	Pcss CHARLOTTE	
JOHNSON, Edward	Boy	BENBOW	
JOHNSON, George.C.J.	Midshipman	IMPLACABLE	
JOHNSON, Henry	Pte. R.M.	BELLEROPHON	
JOHNSON, James	A.B.	CARYSFORT	
JOHNSON, John	A.B.	RODNEY	
JOHNSON, John	A.B.	EDINBURGH	
	A.B.	CAMBRIAN	Navarino
JOHNSON, John	Ord	ASIA	
	Ord	GLASGOW	Navarino
JOHNSON, John	A.B.	Pcss CHARLOTTE	
JOHNSON, Jonah	Pte. R.M.	Pcss CHARLOTTE	
JOHNSON, Mathias	Stoker	THUNDERER	
JOHNSON, Peter	Carpenter	REVENGE	
JOHNSON, Richard	Pte. R.M.	GANGES	
JOHNSON, Robert	Ord	THUNDERER	
JOHNSON, Thomas	Ropemaker	BELLEROPHON	
JOHNSON, Thomas	A.B.	CASTOR	
JOHNSON, Thomas	A.B.	HASTINGS	

SYRIA

JOHNSON, William	Ord	CASTOR	
JOHNSON, William (1)	A.B.	HASTINGS	
JOHNSON, William (2)	A.B.	HASTINGS	
JOHNSON, William	Ord	Pcss CHARLOTTE	
JOHNSON, William	Pte. R.M.	EDINBURGH	
JOHNSON, William	Boatswain	PHOENIX	
JOHNSTON, James	Pte. R.M.	REVENGE	
JOHNSTON, Moses	Royal Artillery	HECATE	
JOHNSTONE, George	A.B.	ZEBRA	
JOHNSTONE, Thomas	A.B.	PIQUE	
JOHNSTONE, William	Boy	REVENGE	
JOHNSTONE, William	Lieut. R.N.	GANGES	
JOINT, William	Pte. R.M.	IMPLACABLE	
JOLLIFFE, William	Captain. R.M.	EDINBURGH	
	Lieut. R.M.	THESEUS	Basque Roads 1809
JOLLIFFE, William	2nd Lieut. R.M.	POWERFUL	
JOLLY, George	Ldg Stoker	MEDEA	
JONES, Charles	Ord	HASTINGS	
JONES, Evan	Pte. R.M.	PIQUE	
JONES, Griffith	Stoker	HECATE	
JONES, Henry	A.B.	Pcss CHARLOTTE	
JONES, Henry	A.B.	CARYSFORT	
JONES, Horatio.N.	Boy 2nd Class	CAMBRIDGE	
JONES, Hugh	A.B.	Pcss CHARLOTTE	
JONES, James	Pte. R.M.	Pcss CHARLOTTE	
JONES, James	Pte. R.M.	PIQUE	
JONES, James.A.	Caulker	GORGON	
JONES, James.E.	Drummer. R.M.	STROMBOLI & POWERFUL	
JONES, John	Ord	BELLEROPHON	
JONES, John	Pte. R.M.	TALBOT	
JONES, John	A.B.	PIQUE	
JONES, John	L.M.	GANGES	
JONES, John	A.B.	BENBOW	
JONES, John	A.B.	RODNEY	
JONES, John	Boy 1st Class	MEDEA	
JONES, John	Clerk	THUNDERER	
JONES, John	A.B.	REVENGE	
JONES, John	3rd Engineer	HYDRA	
JONES, John	Ord	RODNEY	
JONES, John	Ord	BENBOW	
JONES, Joseph	A.B.	PIQUE	
JONES, Joseph	Pte. R.M.	PIQUE	
JONES, Joshua	L.M.	GANGES	
JONES, J.	Gunner's Mate	HASTINGS	
JONES, Lewis.T.	Actg Commander	Pcss CHARLOTTE	
	Midshipman	GRANICUS	Algiers
JONES, Peter	Capt's Cook	ASIA	
JONES, Richard	Bosun's Mate	PIQUE	
JONES, Stephen	Carp's Crew	MEDEA	
	A.B.	ASIA	Navarino
JONES, Thomas	Carp's Crew	Pcss CHARLOTTE	
JONES, Thomas	Painter	BENBOW	
JONES, William	A.B.	EDINBURGH	
JONES, William	Carp's Crew	Pcss CHARLOTTE	
JONES, William	Pte. R.M.	Pcss CHARLOTTE	
JONES, William	A.B.	ASIA	
JONES, William	A.B.	HASTINGS	
JONES, William	Pte. R.M.	PIQUE	
JONES, William	A.B.	DIDO	
JONES, William	Sailmaker	TALBOT	
JONES, William	A.B.	GANGES	
JONES, William	Boy	BELLEROPHON	
JORDAN, Francis	A.B.	EDINBURGH	
JORDAN, George	Pte. R.M.	Pcss CHARLOTTE	
JORDAN, William	A.B.	POWERFUL	
JORDAN, William.A.	A.B.	ZEBRA	
JOREY, Thomas	Sapper & Miner	IMPLACABLE	(M.L. as JURY)
JOSEPH, John	A.B.	GORGON	
JOYCE, Richard	Capt' Forecastle	RODNEY	
JOYCE, Thomas	Gunner. R.M.A.	STROMBOLI	
JUDD, Archibald	A.B.	Pcss CHARLOTTE	
JUDD, Henry	Ord	EDINBURGH	
JUFFS, Richard	Capt' of Hold	CASTOR	
JUFFS, Thomas	Ord	CASTOR	
JUKES, Thomas	Pte. R.M.	CYCLOPS	
JULIAN, Thomas	Boy 1st Class	CAMBRIDGE	
JUPP, Benjamin	Pte. R.M.	EDINBURGH	
JUPP, George	Pte. R.M.	EDINBURGH	
JUPP, John	Pte. R.M.	VANGUARD	
JUSLEY, Thomas	Pte. R.M.	GANGES	
KAIN, John	L.M.	POWERFUL	
KAMMELL, John	Painter	CYCLOPS	

KANWAY, Thomas	Capt' After Guard	HASTINGS	
KARSLEY, Thomas	Pte. R.M.	BENBOW	
KATON, James.E.	Lieut. R.N.	CAMBRIDGE	
KAY, John	Surgeon	Pcss CHARLOTTE	
KEANE, George.D.	Mate	PHOENIX	
KEARSLEY, John	Boy	RODNEY	
KEAST, James	Ord	DIDO	
KEAST, John	Ord	IMPLACABLE	
KEATING, John	Ord	POWERFUL	
KEATING, Joseph	Pte. R.M.	POWERFUL	
KEATS, David	Pte. R.M.	PIQUE	
KEEMER, George	Capt' Forecastle	PHOENIX	
	A.B.	ROSE	Navarino
KEENE, Henry	Pte. R.M.	BELLEROPHON	
KEENAN, James	Gnr. Ryl Arty.	PIQUE & other vessels	
KEEP, Charles	Ord	POWERFUL	
KEER, Bernard	A.B.	Pcss CHARLOTTE	
KELLY, John	A.B.	HASTINGS	(M) Anchor Type LS & GC
KELLY, John.W.	Ship's Corporal	IMPLACABLE	
KELLY, Michael	Cooper's Crew	THUNDERER	
KEMMISH, Henry	Ord	MAGICIENNE	
KEMP..., George	Pte. R.M.	POWERFUL	(Roll torn)
KEMP, Henry	A.B.	Pcss CHARLOTTE	
KEMP, John	Stoker	GORGON	
KEMP, John	Ord	IMPLACABLE	
KEMP, Samuel	A.B.	HASTINGS	
KEMP, Samuel	Capt' Fore Top	Pcss CHARLOTTE	
KEMPSTER, John	Boy 1st Class	Pcss CHARLOTTE	
KEMPSTER, Robert	A.B.	CAMBRIDGE	
	Ord	CAMBRIAN	Navarino
KENFELL, William	A.B.	CASTOR	
KENNEDY, Charles.D.B.	Midshipman	HASTINGS	
KENNEDY, David	Pte. R.M.	POWERFUL	
KENNEDY, Hugh	Pte. R.M.	ASIA	
KENNEDY, James	L.M.	WASP	
KENNEDY, John	A.B.	IMPLACABLE	
KENNEDY, John	Blacksmith	CASTOR	
KENNELL, John	A.B.	REVENGE	
	Ord	ASIA	Navarino
KENT, Barney	Ord	REVENGE	
KENT, James	Pte. R.M.	GANGES	
KENT, John	Gunner. R.M.A.	MEDEA	
KEOHANE, Michael	Boy 1st Class	RODNEY	
KEON, Henry	A.B.	REVENGE	
KEOWN, Thomas.H.	Asst Surgeon	POWERFUL	
KEPRIES, Demts.	Pilot	GORGON	
KERBY, Damiel	Boy 2nd Class	Pcss CHARLOTTE	
KERMER, John	Pte. R.M.	PIQUE	
KERNECK, William	Pte. R.M.	IMPLACABLE	(or KERNICK)
KERR, Henry.A.	Midshipman	Pcss CHARLOTTE	
KERR, Lord Frederick.H.	Lieut. R.N.	GORGON	
KERR, William	Naval Instructor	POWERFUL	
KERR, William.D.	Surgeon	DIDO	
KERSHAW, J.T.	Fifer. R.M.	Pcss CHARLOTTE	
KESSON, David	A.B.	GANGES	
KEST, George.C.	Mate	HASTINGS	
KETTLE, James	Sgt. R.M.	CASTOR	
KEVERN, F.J.	A.B.	RODNEY	
KEYFORD, Thomas	A.B.	CAMBRIDGE	
KEYS, Charles	Gunner	STROMBOLI	
	A.B.	PHILOMEL	Navarino
KIBLER, John	Pte. R.M.	BELLEROPHON	
KIDD, John	Pte. R.M.	DIDO	
KIDHAM, William	A.B.	Pcss CHARLOTTE	
KIDNEY, John	A.B.	EDINBURGH	
KILBEY, Thomas	A.B.	POWERFUL	
KILLICK, Thomas.H.	Boy 1st Class	POWERFUL	
KIMBER, Edward	Not Given	CAMBRIDGE	(Duplicate issued)
KIMBER, Thomas.B.	Carp's Crew	Pcss CHARLOTTE	
KING, Charles	Pte. R.M.	THUNDERER	
KING, Edward	Stoker	VESUVIUS	
KING, George	Pte. R.M.	GANGES	
KING, George	Ord	BELLEROPHON	
KING, George	2 others borne	BELLEROPHON	(Q.M. & A.B.)
KING, Henry.B.	Midshipman	DAPHNE	
KING, James	Engineer's Boy	HECATE	
KING, John	M.A.A.	PIQUE	
KING, John	Not Given	CAMBRIDGE	
KING, John	Pte. R.M.	CAMBRIDGE	
KING, Joseph	Capt' of Mast	BENBOW	
KING, Peter	Pte. R.M.	RODNEY	
KING, Richard	A.B.	Pcss CHARLOTTE	
KING, Robert	Pte. R.M.	RODNEY	
KING, Thomas	Domestic	Pcss CHARLOTTE	
KING, Thomas	Ord	CARYSFORT	

SYRIA

KING, William	Purser's Steward	VESUVIUS	
KING, William	Pte. R.M.	Pcss CHARLOTTE	
KING, William	Pte. R.M.	GANGES	
KING, William	A.B.	ASIA	
KING, William.K.	Clerk's Asst	GANGES	
KINGMAN, James	Pte. R.M.	Pcss CHARLOTTE	
KINGS, Thomas	Pte. R.M.	HASTINGS	
KINGSFORD, William	Q.M.	ASIA	
KINGSNORTH, John	A.B.	CAMBRIDGE	
KINGSTON, Bevil	Not Given	RODNEY	(M.L. as HINGSTON)
KINGSTON, John	Ord	REVENGE	
KINSEY, Joseph	Pte. R.M.	POWERFUL	
KINSIE, Thomas	Pte. R.M.	EDINBURGH	
KINSMAN, Richard	Boy	DIDO	
KINSON, Walter	Corporal. R.M.	Pcss CHARLOTTE	
KIRBY, Henry	Pte. R.M.	BELLEROPHON	
KIRBY, James	Ord	Pcss CHARLOTTE	
KIRK, Edward	Gunner	BELLEROPHON	
KIRK, William	Boy	GANGES	
KIRKWOOD, Alexander	Supn Boatswain	ASIA	
	L.M.	ROYAL SOVEREIGN	Trafalgar
	Yeoman of Sheets	ALBION	Algiers
KIRVILL, Edward	A.B.	POWERFUL	
KISBY, Thomas	Boy 2nd Class	CYCLOPS	
KITSON, Edward	Chaplain	Pcss CHARLOTTE	
KNAPP, William	Pte. R.M.	RODNEY	
KNEEBONE, Peter	A.B.	Pcss CHARLOTTE	
KNIGHT, Charles	Pte. R.M.	IMPLACABLE	
KNIGHT, Charles	A.B.	EDINBURGH	
KNIGHT, Daniel	Ord	REVENGE	
KNIGHT, H.W.	Not Given	VANGUARD	
KNIGHT, John	Pte. R.M.	PIQUE	
KNIGHT, John	Boy	MAGICIENNE	
KNIGHT, John	Ord	PIQUE	
KNIGHT, Matthew	Pte. R.M.	IMPLACABLE	
KNIGHT, Richard	Gunner's Crew	Pcss CHARLOTTE	
KNIGHT, Richard	Pte. R.M.	CARYSFORT	
KNIGHT, Samuel	Ord	Pcss CHARLOTTE	
KNIGHT, William	Pte. R.M.	EDINBURGH	
KNIGHT, William	Mid's Steward	STROMBOLI	
KNIGHT, William.H.	Pte. R.M.	THUNDERER	
KNOLSON, William	Pte. R.M.	REVENGE	
KNOTT, James	A.B.	BENBOW	
KNOTT, John	A.B.	IMPLACABLE	
KNOWLES, James	Sailmaker's Crew	STROMBOLI	
	Boy	MUSQUITO	Navarino
KNOWLES, John	A.B.	EDINBURGH	
KNOWLES, John	Boy	BENBOW	
KNOWLES, William	A.B.	EDINBURGH	
KNOX, Robert	Q.M.	EDINBURGH	
KNOX, Thomas	A.B.	POWERFUL	
	A.B.	CAMBRIAN	Navarino
KYNASTON, Augustus.F.	Mate	VANGUARD	
LACEY, Charles	A.B.	BENBOW	
LACEY, Francis	Boy	HECATE	
LACEY, James	A.B.	VANGUARD	
LACEY, Richard	A.B.	BELLEROPHON	
LACEY, William	Pte. R.M.	HASTINGS	
LACK, John	A.B.	RODNEY	
LACY, John	Ord	IMPLACABLE	
LACY, Robert	Ord	HASTINGS	
LACY, William	Pte. R.M.	GANGES	
LADD, Thomas	Carpenter	STROMBOLI	
LAIGHT, Brandon	Pte. R.M.	REVENGE	
LAING, William	Ord	THUNDERER	
LAIRS, William	Pte. R.M.	EDINBURGH	(May read as LAVIS)
LAKE, Willoughby.J.	Mate	Pcss CHARLOTTE	
LAKEMAN, Samuel	A.B.	GANGES	
LAKEMAN, William	A.B.	THUNDERER	
LAMB, John	Pte. R.M.	VANGUARD	
LAMB, Richard	A.B.	PIQUE	
LAMB, William	Stoker	STROMBOLI	
LAMB, William	A.B.	CARYSFORT	
LAMB, William	Pte. R.M.	POWERFUL	
LAMBARD, William	Volunteer 1st Cl	REVENGE	
LAMBART, Frank.H.	Volunteer 1st Cl	RODNEY	
LAMBERT, Alfred	Ord	RODNEY	
LAMBERT, George	Pte. R.M.	STROMBOLI	
LAMBERT, Henry	Pte. R.M.	DIDO	
LAMBERT, Thomas	Pte. R.M.	REVENGE	
LAMBERT, William	Pte. R.M.	CAMBRIDGE	
LAMKIN, William	Pte. R.M.	EDINBURGH	
LAMPALE, William	A.B.	CAMBRIDGE	(Alias LAMPARD)

LAMPEN, Samuel	Ord	MAGICIENNE	
LANCASTER, William.F.	A.B.	RODNEY	
LAND, John	Lieut. R.M.	EDINBURGH	
LANDER, James	Boy 2nd Class	HASTINGS	
LANE, George	A.B.	POWERFUL	
LANE, John	A.B.	IMPLACABLE	
LANE, John	Pte. R.M.	GANGES	
LANE, John	Pte. R.M.	THUNDERER	
LANE, Thomas	Pte. R.M.	BELLEROPHON	
LANE, William	Pte. R.M.	TALBOT	
LANER, John	Boy	HAZARD	
LANG, Nicholas	Pte. R.M.	THUNDERER	
LANG, William	Capt' Mizzen Top	TALBOT	
LANGDON, George	Ord	HASTINGS	
LANGFORD, George	Boy 1st Class	BELLEROPHON	
LANGFORD, James	Boy	BELLEROPHON	
LANGFORD, John	A.B.	CASTOR	
	A.B.	GLASGOW	Navarino
LANGFORD, John	Bosun's Mate	VANGUARD	
LANGFORD, William	Boy	GANGES	
LANGHORN, James	Carp's Crew	REVENGE	
LANGLEY, John	Ord	REVENGE	
LANGLEY, Philip	A.B.	THUNDERER	
LANGLEY, Richard	Ord	HAZARD	
LANGMAID, R.T.	Boy	GANGES	
LANGMEED, William	Ord	BELLEROPHON	
LANGRIDGE, William	Pte. R.M.	BENBOW	
LANSDOWN, George	Pte. R.M.	PIQUE & CARYSFORT	
LANSDOWN, John	Pte. R.M.	HAZARD	
LANSDOWN, John	Pte. R.M.	REVENGE	
LAPPAGE, Edward	Pte. R.M.	CASTOR	
LARCOM, John	A.B.	POWERFUL	
LARCOMBE, Edward	Ord	IMPLACABLE	
LARK, John	Gunner. R.M.A.	THUNDERER	
LARK, John	Gnr. Ryl Artly.	PIQUE & other vessels	
LARK, John	A.B.	GANGES	
LARK, William	Gnr. Ryl Artly	PIQUE & other vessels	
LARKINS, Joseph	Pte. R.M.	DIDO	
LARRAD, George	Boy	MAGICIENNE	
LASHAM, Jonathan	Gunner's Mate	CYCLOPS	
LASHBROOK, Thomas	A.B.	ASIA	
LATH, William.B.	Not Given	Pcss CHARLOTTE	
LATHAM, Thomas.W.	Armourer	POWERFUL	
La TOUCHE, Ashley	Mate	REVENGE	
LATTIMER, George	Q.M.	STROMBOLI	
LATTO, James	Gunner	PIQUE	
LAURENCE, David	Carp's Mate	DAPHNE	
LAURENCE, John	Capt' Fore Top	POWERFUL	
LAURENCE, Richard	Pte-R.M.	THUNDERER	
LAVENDER, George	Ord	Pcss CHARLOTTE	
LAVENDER, Joseph	Ord	EDINBURGH	
LAVIE, George	Lieut. R.N.	REVENGE	
LAVIS, Alexander	A.B.	PIQUE	
LAWES, James	Ord	BENBOW	
LAWES, James	Pte. R.M.	VANGUARD	
LAWFORD, John	Q.M.	BELLEROPHON	
LAWLER, Edward	A.B.	VANGUARD	(Could read LAINLER) (M) Anchor Type LS & GC
LAWLER, John	Gunner's Mate	VESUVIUS	
LAWRENCE, Benjamin	Pte. R.M.	GORGON	
LAWRENCE, Cornelius	Ord	CAMBRIDGE	
LAWRENCE, Edward	Ord	REVENGE	
LAWRENCE, John	Captain. R.N.	HASTINGS	
	Midshipman	WINDSOR CASTLE	14 March 1795
	Commander	FANTOME	B.S. Ap & May 1813
LAWRENCE, Richard	Pte R.M.	EDINBURGH	
LAWRENCE, Thomas	Ord	VANGUARD	
LAWRENSON, James	A.B.	IMPLACABLE	(May read LAURENSON)
LAWS, William	Ord	POWERFUL	
LAWSON, Robert	A.B.	GANGES	
LAYTON, Thomas	A.B.	ASIA	(M.L. LATINE)
LAYTON, William	Boy	MAGICIENNE	
LEACH, Charles	A.B.	VESUVIUS	
LEACH, Henry.W.	Pte. R.M.	HASTINGS	
LEACH, Thomas	A.B.	Pcss CHARLOTTE	
LEAMAN, George	Carp's Crew	VANGUARD	
LEAN, William	Pte. R.M.	TALBOT	
LEARY, James	A.B.	EDINBURGH	
LEARY, John	Bosun's Mate	Pcss CHARLOTTE	
LEAT, William	Pte. R.M.	STROMBOLI	
LECORNEY, William	A.B.	HASTINGS	
LEE, Francis	Pte. R.M.	HASTINGS	
LEE, George	Ord	POWERFUL	
LEE, Henry	Carp's Crew	IMPLACABLE	
LEE (or LEY), Henry	Mate	VANGUARD	

SYRIA

LEE, James	Ord	VANGUARD	
LEE, John	Pte. R.M.	HYDRA	
LEE, John	Bosun's Mate	REVENGE	
LEE, Nicholas	A.B.	RODNEY	
LEE, Richard	A.B.	REVENGE	
LEE, Thomas	A.B.	Pcss CHARLOTTE	
LEE, Thomas	Sailmaker	CYCLOPS	
LEE, Thomas	Ord	IMPLACABLE	
LEE, Timothy	A.B.	BENBOW	
LEE, William	Ord	THUNDERER	
LEE, William	Q.M.	CAMBRIDGE	
LEE, William	Pte. R.M.	RODNEY	
LEE, William.J.	A.B.	ASIA	
LEESON, Charles	Pte. R.M.	PIQUE	
LEGG, Edward	Ord	THUNDERER	
LEGG, Jacob	Pte. R.M.	EDINBURGH	
LEGG, James	Pte. R.M.	EDINBURGH	
LEGG, William	Ord	VANGUARD	
LEGGITT, William	Admiral's Domestic	Pcss CHARLOTTE	
LEGGOE, Frederick	A.B.	THUNDERER	
Le GRAND, Frederick.W.	Surgeon	CYCLOPS	
LEIGH, Frederick.G.	Mate	CASTOR & MEDEA	
LEMMON, George	Ord	Pcss CHARLOTTE	
LEMMON, Sidney	A.B.	BELLEROPHON	
LENNOX, Hugh	A.B.	BENBOW	
LENNOX, Walter.W.	Asst Surgeon	CAMBRIDGE	
LENOY, Richard	Corporal	POWERFUL	
LEONARD, John	Boy	VANGUARD	
LEONARD, Robert	Captain. R.M.	VESUVIUS & STROMBOLI	
LESLIE, John	Boy	CASTOR	
LETCH, Samuel	Pte. R.M.	HASTINGS	
LETTON, Thomas	Pte. R.M.	IMPLACABLE	
LETTY, William	Boy	VANGUARD	
LEVELL, William	Pte. R.M.	GANGES	
LEVERICK, Thomas	Capt' of Mast	ASIA	
LEVETT, James	Pte. R.M.	CAMBRIDGE	
	Pte. R.M.	GLASGOW	Navarino
LEVETT, Nicholas	Painter	BELLEROPHON	
LEWARN, John	Ord	RODNEY	
LEWIN, George.R.	Chaplain	GANGES	
LEWIN, William	Pte. R.M.	THUNDERER	
LEWIS, Benjamin	Boy	PIQUE	
LEWIS, David	Pte. R.M.	THUNDERER	
LEWIS, Edward	Ord	TALBOT	
LEWIS, J.	Boy	PIQUE	
LEWIS, James	A.B.	VANGUARD	
LEWIS, James	Pte. R.M.	VANGUARD	
LEWIS, John	Bosun's Mate	STROMBOLI	
LEWIS, John	Ord	CAMBRIDGE	
LEWIS, John	A.B.	RODNEY	
LEWIS, Michael	A.B.	RODNEY	
	Boy	IMPREGNABLE	Algiers
LEWIS, Robert	Pte. R.M.	HAZARD	
LEWIS, William	A.B.	REVENGE	
LEWIS, William.F.	Carpenter	HASTINGS	(or F. William)
LEY, Francis.E.	Pte. R.M.	PHOENIX	
LEY, William	3 borne	IMPLACABLE	Bo Mte & A.B. & Ord
LEYCESTER, Edmund.M.	Mate	VANGUARD	
LIARDET, Francis	Commander	POWERFUL	
LIAS, William	Pte. R.M.	RODNEY	
LIDDEARD, Robert.T.	Fifer. R.M.	PIQUE & other vessels	
LIDDELL, Henry	Asst Surgeon	IMPLACABLE	
LIDDICOAT, William	Pte. R.M.	THUNDERER	
LIDDLE, William	A.B.	EDINBURGH	
LIDDON, William	Pte. R.M.	THUNDERER	
LIDE, Henry	Pte. R.M.	Pcss CHARLOTTE	
LIGHT, George	A.B.	VANGUARD	
LIGHT, William	A.B.	RODNEY	
LIGHTFOOT, William	Pte. R.M.	POWERFUL	
LILLEY, Jonas	Pte. R.M.	ASIA	
LILLEY, Samuel	Boy	GANGES	
LILLEY, William	L.M.	BELLEROPHON	
LILLICRAP, Robert.G.A.W.	Clerk	Pcss CHARLOTTE	
LILLICRAP, Walter.W.	Lieut. R.M.	GANGES	
LILLIWHITE, Thomas	Blacksmith	MAGICIENNE	
LILLYWHITE, George	A.B.	EDINBURGH	
LILLYWHITE, Joseph	A.B.	VANGUARD	
LINDSAY, John	Boy	CAMBRIDGE	
LINDSAY, John	Pte. R.M.	REVENGE	
LINDUP, William	Ord	CASTOR	(M.L. as LENTUP)
LINHAM, Richard	Supn Corporal. R.M.	PIQUE	
LINNINGTON, Henry	A.B.	Pcss CHARLOTTE	

LINWAY, James	Corporal. R.M.	TALBOT	
LIPPLE, George	A.B.	GANGES	
LIPSHAIN, John	L.M.	GANGES	
LISCOMBE, John	A.B.	THUNDERER	
LISCOMBE, William	Pte. R.M.	REVENGE	
LISK, James	Capt's Coxswain	PHOENIX	
LISTER, P.	A.B.	Pcss CHARLOTTE	
LISTON, Andrew	A.B.	CARYSFORT	
LITLEY, Robert	Pte. R.M.	IMPLACABLE	
LITTLE, Alexander	Lieut. R.N.	THUNDERER	
LITTLE, David	Stoker	CYCLOPS	
LITTLE, Richard	Pte. R.M.	DAPHNE	
LITTLEJOHNS, Richard	A.B.	IMPLACABLE	
LITTON, Thomas	A.B.	BELLEROPHON	
LIVESAY, Salter	Asst Surgeon	ASIA	
LLOYD, Edward.A.T.	Midshipman	RODNEY	
LLOYD, George	A.B.	THUNDERER	(M.L. as James)
LLOYD, John	Pte. R.M.	IMPLACABLE	
LLOYD, Thomas	Pte. R.M.	REVENGE	
LLOYD, Thomas	A.B.	CAMBRIDGE	
LLOYD, William	A.B.	BELLEROPHON	
LLOYD, William	Pte. R.M.	DIDO	
LOBB, Charles	A.B.	REVENGE	
LOCK, Charles	Bosun's Mate	THUNDERER	
LOCK, Charles	Pte. R.M.	VANGUARD	
LOCK, George	Boy	DAPHNE	
LOCK, Henry	A.B.	POWERFUL	
LOCK, John.T.	Boy	POWERFUL	
LOCK, William	Sgt. R.M.	PIQUE	
LOCK, William	Pte. R.M.	IMPLACABLE	
LOCKE, George	Boy	RODNEY	
LOCKETT, Joseph	Boy 2nd Class	GORGON	
LODDER, Charles.A.	Midshipman	POWERFUL	
LODGE, George	Boy	GANGES	
LODGE, John	Pte. R.M.	PIQUE	
LOFFT, George	Stoker	VESUVIUS	(Also on Roll as LOFT)
LOFTS, Edward	Pte. R.M.	GANGES	
LOGAN, James	Q.M.	REVENGE	
LOMAS, Thomas	Boy	Pcss CHARLOTTE	
LONEY, Jonathan	Sgt. R.M.	Pcss CHARLOTTE	
LONEY, Peter	Master	Pcss CHARLOTTE	
LONG, FitzJames	Sgt. R.M.	CAMBRIDGE	
LONG, Job	Pte. R.M.	EDINBURGH	
LONG, John	A.B.	THUNDERER	
LONG, John	A.B.	BELLEROPHON	
LONG, John	A.B.	Pcss CHARLOTTE	
LONG, Patrick	Ord	Pcss CHARLOTTE	
LONG, Richard	A.B.	ASIA	
LONG, Samuel	Bosun's Mate	HASTINGS	
LONG, William	A.B.	CAMBRIDGE	
LONG, William	Ord	ASIA	
LONG, William	Q.M.	BELLEROPHON	(M) Anchor Type LS & GC
	Boy 2nd Class	MUTINE	Algiers
LONGBOTTOM, William.H.	A.B.	GANGES	
LONGLEY, Joseph	Bosun's Mate	BENBOW	
LONGOBARDO, Benjamin	A.B.	CAMBRIDGE	
LOOKER, William	A.B.	CAMBRIDGE	
LORD, R.W.	Pte. R.M.	PIQUE	
LORD, William	Corporal. R.M.	GANGES	
LORING, William	Lieut. R.N.	CARYSFORT	
LOTT, George	Boy	HECATE	
LOTT, William	Ord	CAMBRIDGE	
LOUDON, John	Secretary	Pcss CHARLOTTE	(Purser since 1799)
LOUIS, Charles	2nd Lieut. R.M.	Pcss CHARLOTTE	
LOURY, Francis	A.B.	VANGUARD	
LOVATT, William	Pte. R.M.	REVENGE	
LOVE, Henry	Not Given	HASTINGS	
LOVEDAY, Edwin	Pte. R.M.	EDINBURGH	
LOVELESS, John	Gunner's Mate	MAGICIENNE	
LOVELL, Samuel	Ord	CARYSFORT	
LOVELL, William	A.B.	CARYSFORT	
LOVELOCK, George	A.B.	HASTINGS	
LOVERING, William	Capt' Main Top	BELLEROPHON	
LOVETT, Jonathan	Pte. R.M.	ASIA	
LOWE, Arthur	Lieut. R.N.	HASTINGS	
LOWE, Charles	Ord	EDINBURGH	(M.L. as LOW)
LOWE, Gower	Lieut. R.N.	REVENGE	
LOWE, Thomas	Ord	MAGICIENNE	
LOWRIN, Stephen	Not Given	MEDEA	(May read LOWRIA)
LOWRY, John	Bosun's Mate	PIQUE	
LOWRY, Simpson	A.B.	CAMBRIDGE	
LOWDER, Benjamin	Pte. R.M.	HASTINGS	
LOWTHER, Marcus	Mate	HASTINGS	
LUCAS, John	A.B.	VANGUARD	
LUCAS, Richard	Pte. R.M.	THUNDERER	

SYRIA

LUCAS, William	Boy	THUNDERER	
LUCAS, William	Pte. R.M.	EDINBURGH	
LUCAS, William	Ship's Cook	HECATE	
LUCE, John	Volunteer 1st Cl	THUNDERER	
LUCIA, Thomas	A.B.	EDINBURGH	
LUCIA, William	Carp's Crew	GORGON	
LUCK, Emanuel	Pte. R.M.	GANGES	
LUCKCRAFT, Charles.M.	Mate	CAMBRIDGE	
LUCKCRAFT, William	Commander	BELLEROPHON	
	Lieut. R.N.	SHELDRAKE	Anholt. 27 March 1811
LUCRAFT, Edward	Boy	THUNDERER	
LUDLOW, Benjamin	A.B.	CAMBRIDGE	
LUMBER, John	Sgt. R.M.	STROMBOLI	
LUMBY, Bartholomew	Ord	THUNDERER	
LUMLEY, John	A.B.	THUNDERER	
LUMSDEN, Robert	Ord	ASIA	
LUNDAY, George	A.B.	EDINBURGH	(May read LONDAY)
LUNT, Luke	Pte. R.M.	THUNDERER	(and as a Supn)
LURWAY, James	Corporal. R.M.	TALBOT	
LUPARDI, Andrew	Young Gentleman's Steward	GORGON	(Alias AZZOPARDI)
LUSCOMBE, Henry	Ord	Pcss CHARLOTTE	
LUSH, Isaac	A.B.	HASTINGS	
LUSH, Silas	Pte. R.M.	POWERFUL	
LYE, William	Barber	IMPLACABLE	(M.L. as LEY)
LYNCH, Peter	A.B.	VANGUARD	
LYNCH, William	A.B.	REVENGE	
LYNE, Charles	Clerk	TALBOT	
LYNE, George	A.B.	VANGUARD	
LYNE, Richard	A.B.	CAMBRIDGE	
LYON, John	Boy	CARYSFORT	
LYONS, Edward	Pte. R.M.	REVENGE	
LYONS, Henry	A.B.	CARYSFORT	
LYONS, James	L.M.	POWERFUL	
LYONS, William	Yeoman of Signals	THUNDERER	
LYSTER, Henry	Lieut. R.N.	VANGUARD	
MacARTHUR, John	Purser	CAMBRIDGE	
MACEY, John	Capt's Steward	IMPLACABLE	
MACFARLANE, Henry	Asst Surgeon	HAZARD	
MACKEENE, Daniel	A.B.	IMPLACABLE	
MACKENSIE, John	A.B.	MAGICIENNE	
MACKETT, William	Yeoman of Signals	HASTINGS	
MACKEY, Alexander.M.P.	Actg Master	GANGES	
MACKIE, Thomas	A.B.	ASIA	
MACKINNON, Lauchlan.B.	Mate	VANGUARD	
MACKLIN, James	Ord	POWERFUL	
MACKLY, David	A.B.	EDINBURGH	
MACLAREN, George.D.	Surgeon	MAGICIENNE	
MACLEOD, Robert.B.A.	Mate	THUNDERER	(Roll wrong as B.B.A.)
MacMICHAEL, John.F.	Naval Instructor	PIQUE	
MACNAMARA, Dennis	A.B.	GANGES	
MADDEN, Peter	Coxswain Pinnace	BELLEROPHON	
MADGE, John	A.B. (Roll)	PIQUE	Found M.L. as Pte R.M.
MAGRATH, Joseph	A.B.	CAMBRIDGE	
MAGUIRE, Rochfort	Mate	WASP	
MAGUIRE, Terence	Pte. R.M.	THUNDERER	
MAHONEY, Charles	Pte. R.M.	HASTINGS	
MAHONEY, David	A.B.	Pcss CHARLOTTE	
MAHONEY, John	Boy 1st Class	Pcss CHARLOTTE	
MAHONEY, Lawrence	A.B.	CASTOR	
MAHONEY, Michael	A.B.	HASTINGS	
MAINE, Edward	Pte. R.M.	CAMBRIDGE	
MAINPRIZE, William.T.	2nd Master	TALBOT	
MAJOR, Joseph	A.B.	Pcss CHARLOTTE	
MALE, Arthur	Ord	HASTINGS	
MALLACHIP, James	Pte. R.M.	Pcss CHARLOTTE	
MALLIN, John	Not Given	DIDO	
MALLIN, John	Gun Room Steward	POWERFUL	
MALOKIN, William	Sailmaker's Crew	PIQUE	(May read MALCKIN)
MALPAS, Edward	A.B.	VANGUARD	
MANCHESTER, Isaac	Capt' Mizzen Top	POWERFUL	
MANLEY, James	Boy	POWERFUL	
MANN, James.S.	Midshipman	CAMBRIDGE	
MANNAN, Michael	A.B.	THUNDERER	
MANNING, George	Q.M.	BELLEROPHON	(additional clasp?)
MANNING, James	Capt' of Mast	HAZARD	
MANNING, James	Pte. R.M.	PHOENIX	
MANNING, John	Ord	THUNDERER	
MANNING, Thomas	Ord	POWERFUL	
MANNINGS, Joseph	A.B.	Pcss CHARLOTTE	
MANNLEM, Emanuel	Gun Room Steward	PHOENIX	
MANSEL, George	Commander	WASP	
	Actg Lieut. R.N.	MINDEN	Algiers

MANSEL, Robert	Cook	WASP	
MANSFIELD, Richard	Ord	CYCLOPS	
MANSFIELD, Walter.G.	Mate	VANGUARD	
MANSER, William	Pte. R.M.	POWERFUL	
MANT, William	A.B.	GANGES	
MANUEL, John	A.B.	POWERFUL	
MAPLE, Albert	Boy 1st Class	EDINBURGH	
MARCER, William	Barber	GANGES	
MARCH, John	L.M.	REVENGE	
MARCHANT, Esau	Pte. R.M.	GORGON	
MARCHANT, George	Pte. R.M.	GANGES & Pcss CHARLOTTE	
MARDOE, Henry	Cooper	HASTINGS	
MARKS, Thomas	Pte. R.M.	THUNDERER	
MARKS, William	Ropemaker	CASTOR	
MARKS, William	Sailmaker's Crew	EDINBURGH	
MARRIOTT, Richard	Pte. R.M.	ASIA	
MARRYAT, Frank	Volunteer	VANGUARD	
MARSH, Charles	Capt' Forecastle	DIDO	
MARSH, Daniel	Ord	MAGICIENNE	
MARSH, George	Gunner. R.M.A.	CYCLOPS	
MARSH, John	Pte. R.M.	Pcss CHARLOTTE	
MARSH, N.H.	Carp's Crew	IMPLACABLE	
MARSH, William	A.B.	CAMBRIDGE	
MARSH, William	Supn Sgt. R.M.	PIQUE	
MARSHAL, Edward	A.B.	Pcss CHARLOTTE	
MARSHALL, Abraham	A.B.	EDINBURGH	
MARSHALL, Charles	Pte. R.M.	REVENGE	
MARSHALL, Henry	A.B.	CAMBRIDGE	
MARSHALL, John	Sailmaker	CARYSFORT	
MARSHALL, John	Ord	RODNEY	
MARSHALL, John	A.B.	REVENGE	
MARSHALL, John	Chaplain	PIQUE	
MARSHALL, John.H.	Engineer 1st Cl	PHOENIX	
MARSHALL, Joseph	Chaplain	CASTOR	
MARSHALL, Matthew	A.B.	VANGUARD	
MARSHALL, William	A.B.	CARYSFORT	
MARSHMAN, Samuel	Pte. R.M.	ASIA	
MARSLEM, James	Boy	BELLEROPHON	
MARTEN, Francis	Mate	PHOENIX	
MARTIAL, Edward	A.B.	Pcss CHARLOTTE	
MARTIN, George	Capt's Coxswain	CYCLOPS	
MARTIN, George	Sick Berth Attdt	POWERFUL	
MARTIN, G.T.M.	Asst Surgeon	HASTINGS	
MARTIN, Henry	Ord	REVENGE	
MARTIN, Henry Byam	Captain. R.N.	CARYSFORT	
MARTIN, Jacob	Pte. R.M.	THUNDERER	
MARTIN, James	Ord	THUNDERER	
MARTIN, James	Pte. R.M.	EDINBURGH	
MARTIN, James	Ord	STROMBOLI	
MARTIN, James	A.B.	Pcss CHARLOTTE	
MARTIN, John	Pte. R.M.	GANGES	
MARTIN, John	Pte. R.M.	THUNDERER	
MARTIN, John	A.B.	RODNEY	
MARTIN, John	Boy	Pcss CHARLOTTE	
MARTIN, Richard	Q.M.	THUNDERER	
MARTIN, Robert	Pte. R.M.	GANGES	
MARTIN, Samuel	Gunner's Steward	CASTOR	
MARTIN, Thomas	Boy 1st Class	VESUVIUS	
MARTIN, Thomas	Capt' Main Top	Pcss CHARLOTTE	
MARTIN, William	Carp's Crew	BELLEROPHON	
MARTIN, William	Ord	GANGES	
MARTIN, William	A.B.	Pcss CHARLOTTE	
MARTIN, William	A.B.	EDINBURGH	
MARTIN, William	Pte. R.M.	WASP	
MASON, Abraham	Boy	ASIA	
MASON, Edward	Boy	CAMBRIDGE	
MASON, George	A.B.	BENBOW	
MASON, George	Ord	BELLEROPHON	
MASON, George	Carp's Crew	TALBOT	
MASON, Joseph	Pte. R.M.	IMPLACABLE	
MASON, Joseph	Bombdr. R.M.A.	HECATE	
	Pte. R.M.	ALBION	Navarino
MASON, William.G.	Purser	Pcss CHARLOTTE	
	Clerk	AJAX	Trafalgar
	Purser	PRESIDENT	Java
MASSEY, John	Ord	Pcss CHARLOTTE	
MASSEY, Joseph	Pte. R.M.	POWERFUL	
MASSEY, William	Pte. R.M.	MAGICIENNE	
MASSIE, John.B.	Lieut. R.N.	DAPHNE	
MASSIE, Thomas.L.	Lieut. R.N.	THUNDERER	
	Mate	ASIA	Navarino (see notes)
MASTERS, Charles	Pte. R.M.	VANGUARD	
MASTERS, John.S.	A.B.	RODNEY	
MATHER, James	Pte. R.M.	POWERFUL	

SYRIA

MATHEWS, Robert	A.B.	BENBOW	
MATSON, W.C.	Boy	CYCLOPS	
MATTHEWS, Alfred	Boy	PIQUE	
MATTHEWS, Benjamin	Not Given	IMPLACABLE	
MATTHEWS, Charles	Pte. R.M.	BELLEROPHON	
MATTHEWS, George	A.B.	EDINBURGH	
	A.B.	ASIA	*Navarino*
MATTHEWS, George	Boy 2nd Class	BENBOW	
MATTHEWS, Jacob	A.B.	HAZARD	
MATTHEWS, James	2 borne	POWERFUL	*(Cox Launch & A.B.)*
MATTHEWS, John	Ord	BELLEROPHON	
MATTHEWS, John.W.	Ord	BELLEROPHON	*(M.L. as John)*
MATTHEWS, Nicholas	Ord	POWERFUL	
MATTHEWS, Thomas	Q.M.	WASP	
MATTHEWS, Thomas	Pte. R.M.	HASTINGS	
MATTHEWS, Thomas	Pte. R.M.	EDINBURGH	
MATTHEWS, William	Ord	VANGUARD	
MATTHIAS, James	Capt' Forecastle	BELLEROPHON	
MATTHISON, John	Q.M.	HASTINGS	
MATTOCKS, James	Pte. R.M.	STROMBOLI	
MAUNDER, William	Carp's Crew	HYDRA	
MAUNSELL, Robert	2 borne	RODNEY	*(A.B. & Ord)*
MAW, Cornelius	Pte. R.M.	PIQUE	
MAXWELL, Robert	Surgeon	TALBOT	
MAY, John	Boy 1st Class	THUNDERER	
MAY, John	Capt' Forecastle	ASIA	
MAY, John	A.B.	BELLEROPHON	
MAY, John	A.B.	VANGUARD	
MAY, John	A.B.	VESUVIUS	
MAYCOCK, Joseph	Pte. R.M.	GANGES	
	Pte. R.M.	GLASGOW	*Algiers*
MAYNARD, Frank	Pte. R.M.	CAMBRIDGE	
MAYNE, John	Pte. R.M.	RODNEY	
MAYO, John	A.B.	BENBOW	*(M) Anchor Type LS & GC*
MAZZE, Laurence	A.B.	IMPLACABLE	
McARTHUR, Charles	A.B.	VANGUARD	
McBEAN, Graham	A.B.	ZEBRA	
McBRIDE, Henry	A.B.	Pcss CHARLOTTE	
McBRIDE, John	Pte. R.M.	IMPLACABLE	
McCALLEY, Hugh	A.B.	POWERFUL	
McCALLUM, Henry.A.	Lieut. R.M.	GORGON	
McCAN, John	A.B.	GANGES	
McCANN, Charles	A.B.	HASTINGS	
McCARTHY, Austin	Ord	HECATE	
McCARTHY, Eugene	A.B.	ASIA	
McCARTHY, Henry.H.	2nd Lieut. R.M.	IMPLACABLE	
McCARTHY, James	A.B.	EDINBURGH	
McCARTHY, James	A.B.	GORGON	
McCARTHY, Jeremiah	Pte. R.M.	POWERFUL	
McCARTHY, John	Ord	THUNDERER	
McCARTHY, John	A.B.	GORGON	
McCARTHY, Patrick	Ord	THUNDERER	
McCARTHY, Thomas	A.B.	EDINBURGH	
McCARTHY, William	A.B.	HASTINGS	
McCATHIE, William	A.B.	BENBOW	
McCAULEY, James	Pte. R.M.	POWERFUL	
McCLEAN, John	Coxswain Launch	THUNDERER	
McCLUNE, Thomas	Ord	HASTINGS	
McCOLE, Robert	Not Given	GANGES	
McCORMACK, Patrick	Capt' Main Top	BENBOW	
McCOY, John	A.B.	MAGICIENNE	
McCOY, Niel	A.B.	CAMBRIDGE	
McCREA, John	Corporal. R.M.	GANGES	
McCREE, Philip	Sailmaker's Crew	REVENGE	
McCUE, Thomas	Corporal. R.M.A.	PIQUE	
McCUGH, Pugh	Pte. R.M.	BENBOW	
	Pte. R.M.	ALBION	*Navarino*
McCULLAGH, Robert	Ord	RODNEY	
McCULLUM, John	Capt's Steward	REVENGE	
McDAID, Michael	L.M.	RODNEY	
McDERMOTT, James	L.M.	REVENGE	
McDONALD, Alexander	Q.M.	REVENGE	
McDONALD, Archibald	Pte. R.M.	ASIA	
McDONALD, Hugh	Pte. R.M.	VANGUARD	
McDONALD, James	Pte. R.M.	EDINBURGH	
McDONALD, Jeremiah	Ord	VANGUARD	
McDONALD, John	Boy 1st Class	POWERFUL	*(M.L. as McDONNELL)*
McDONALD, Malcolm	A.B.	EDINBURGH	
McDONALD, Thomas	Ord	Pcss CHARLOTTE	
McDOUGAL, David	Pte. R.M.	RODNEY	*(Alias Robert)*
McDOUGAL, Hugh	Bosun's Mate	CAMBRIDGE	
McDOUGALL, John	Lieut. R.N.	PIQUE	
McFARLANE, William	Pte. R.M.	BENBOW	

McFAGDEN, John	A.B.	ASIA	
McFEE, Frederick	Pte. R.M.	HASTINGS	
M'GRATH, John	A.B.	POWERFUL	
McGRATH, Michael	Ord	Pcss CHARLOTTE	
McGRATH, Philip	A.B.	CAMBRIDGE	
McGREGOR, Andrew	3rd Engineer	VESUVIUS	
McGREGOR, Fitzjames.S.	Lieut. R.N.	BELLEROPHON	
McGREGOR, William	Ord	CARYSFORT	
McGUGIN, Hugh	Cooper's Crew	REVENGE	
McGUIRE, John	Stoker	CYCLOPS	
McGURK, John	Ord	HECATE	
McINTYRE, William	A.B.	VANGUARD	
McJANES, Thomas	Boy 1st Class	EDINBURGH	(M.L. as McJAMES)
McKAY, Hugh	Pte. R.M.	HASTINGS	
	Pte. R.M.	BRISK	Navarino
McKAY, James	Bosun's Yeoman	BELLEROPHON	
McKENDRY, James	Ord	POWERFUL	
McKENNA, Dennis	A.B.	RODNEY	
McKENNY, Ralph	Gunner. R.M.A.	PIQUE	
McKENZIE, John.F.C.	Midshipman	ZEBRA	
McKIE, George	Pte. R.M.	POWERFUL	
McKIE, James	Corporal. R.M.	HASTINGS	
McKINNA, John	Ord	THUNDERER	
McKOWAN, William	A.B.	BENBOW	
McLANE, Tate	Carp's Crew	Pcss CHARLOTTE	
McLAUGHLAN, John	Q.M.	GANGES	
McLAUGLAN, Thomas	A.B.	BELLEROPHON	
McLEAN, Augustus.B.	Master	REVENGE	
McLEAN, John	A.B.	BELLEROPHON	
McLENNON, Murdoch	Not Given	ASIA	
McLEOD, Alexander	Boy	THUNDERER	
McMAHON, James	A.B.	CAMBRIDGE	
McMANNING, George	Gnr. Ryl Arty	PIQUE & other vessels	
McMULLIN, Daniel	A.B.	HASTINGS	
McNAMARA, John	Gunner's Crew	ASIA	
McNEAL, James	A.B.	PIQUE	
McNEIL, George	Pte. R.M.	CAMBRIDGE	
McNEIL, James	Cooper	GANGES	
McNEIL, Neil	Pte. R.M.	CASTOR	
McNULTY, James	Pte. R.M.	GORGON	
McPHAIL, John	A.B.	BENBOW	
McPHAIL, Robert	Carp's Crew	GANGES	
McPHERSON, William	Pte. R.M.	HASTINGS	
McQUICK, David	Ord	Pcss CHARLOTTE	
MEAD, Thomas	Stoker	GORGON	
MEADBOWLES, Charles	A.B.	IMPLACABLE	
MEADER, Charles	Boatswain	DIDO	
MEADON, William	Pte. R.M.	EDINBURGH	
MEADOWS, Thomas	A.B.	ASIA	
MEADOWS, William	Pte. R.M.	HASTINGS	
MEARS, Joseph	Carpenter	ASIA	
MEATHERELL, William	Bosun's Mate	REVENGE	
MEDES, William	Ord	CAMBRIDGE	
MEDLAND, James	Ord	IMPLACABLE	
MEEHAN, John	A.B.	RODNEY	
MEEK, John	A.B.	EDINBURGH	
MEEKINS, John	Pte. R.M.	BENBOW	
MEHEGAN, James	Ord	THUNDERER	
MEHEUX, Thomas.C.	Lieut. R.N.	CARYSFORT	
MELBOURNE, Benjamin	Gunner	CASTOR	
MELDREN, Joseph	Ord	RODNEY	
MELERICK, William	L.M.	REVENGE	
MELLERSH, Arthur	Lieut. R.N.	HYDRA	
MELLIN, John	A.B.	BENBOW	
MELLON, Frederick	Boy	THUNDERER	
MELVILLE, William	Carp's Mate	REVENGE	
MENEAR, William	A.B.	THUNDERER	(Could read MINCAR)
MENDS, George.C.	Lieut. R.N.	CAMBRIDGE	
MENDS, Martin	A.B.	CAMBRIDGE	
MERCER, Thomas	Carp's Crew	GANGES	
MERCHANT, Henry	Pte. R.M.	CAMBRIDGE	
MERCHANT, William	Q.M.	BELLEROPHON	(M) Anchor Type LS & GC
MERRETT, Peter	Ship's Corporal	CAMBRIDGE	
MERRITT, Charles	A.B.	HASTINGS	
MERRITT, Thomas	Blacksmith	PIQUE	
MERRITT, William	Not Given	VANGUARD	
MERRY, William	Pte. R.M.	REVENGE	
MESSENGER, Henry	Boy	DIDO	
MESSUM, Joseph	Ord	POWERFUL	(M.L. as MASSUM)
MEYER, George	Pte. R.M.	CAMBRIDGE	
MIALL, Henry	Boy	BENBOW	(Alias MILES)
MICH, Thomas	Ord	HASTINGS	(May read MEEK)
MICHEL, Solomon	Pilot	BELLEROPHON	
MICHELL, Frederick.T.	Captain. R.N.	MAGICIENNE	
	Lieut. R.N.	Qn CHARLOTTE	Algiers

SYRIA

MICHELSON, William	Carpenter	BELLEROPHON	
MIDDLETON, Thomas	Pte. R.M.	BENBOW	
MIDLAND, James	Ord	IMPLACABLE	
MIDLANE, John	Gun Room Steward	MAGICIENNE	
MIHELL, William	Drummer. R.M.	BELLEROPHON	
MILBOURNE, Francis	Capt' Main Top	GANGES	
	Supn Capt' M.T.	Qn CHARLOTTE	Algiers
MILDMAY, Hervey.G.St.J.	Mate	TALBOT	
MILDON, Thomas	Ord	RODNEY	
MILES, James	Pte. R.M.	POWERFUL	
MILLAR, Andrew	Surgeon	CARYSFORT	
MILLAR, Moses	Gunner. R.M.A.	GORGON	
MILLARD, Henry	A.B.	HAZARD	
MILLER, David	Lieut. R.N.	RODNEY	
MILLER, Frederick	A.B.	BENBOW	(M) Anchor Type LS & GC
MILLER, Henry	Boy	RODNEY	
MILLER, James	A.B.	DAPHNE	
MILLER, James	Pte. R.M.	Pcss CHARLOTTE	
MILLER, James	Boy	MEDEA	
MILLER, John	A.B.	GANGES	
MILLER, John	Gunner's Crew	IMPLACABLE	
MILLER, John	Captain. R.M.	POWERFUL	
	2nd Lieut. R.M.	GENOA	Navarino
MILLER, John	Pte. R.M.	GORGON	
MILLER, Jonathan	Pte. R.M.	REVENGE	
MILLER, Lewis	Sgt. R.M.	VANGUARD	
MILLER, William	Pte. R.M.	EDINBURGH	
MILLER, William	Pte. R.M.	Pcss CHARLOTTE	
MILLETT, James	A.B.	THUNDERER	
MILLS, George	Pte. R.M.	CASTOR	
MILLS, George	Drummer. R.M.	WASP	
MILLS, George	Ord	BENBOW	
MILLS, Henry	A.B.	Pcss CHARLOTTE	
MILLS, John	Pte. R.M.	BENBOW	
MILLS, Thomas	Pte. R.M.	DIDO	
MILLS, Thomas	Ord	Pcss CHARLOTTE	
MILLS, William	Capt' Main Top	CAMBRIDGE	
MILLS, William	Pte. R.M.	CAMBRIDGE	
MILLS, William	Carpenter	CASTOR	
MILROY, Andrew	Ord	GANGES	
MILTON, Edward	Ord	VANGUARD	
MILTON, Edward	Boy	PIQUE	
MINCHIN, David	Pte. R.M.	BELLEROPHON	
MINELL, William	Pte. R.M.	BENBOW	
MINNS, Martin	A.B.	CAMBRIDGE	
MINTER, Henry	Ord	EDINBURGH	
MINTER, John	Asst Surgeon	IMPLACABLE	
MIRCHANT, William	Q.M.	BELLEROPHON	
MISK, John	Dragoman	POWERFUL	
MISKIN, John	Boy 2nd Class	GORGON	(May read MISKEN)
MIST, Charles	Pte. R.M.	STROMBOLI	
MITCHAM, Charles	A.B.	BENBOW	
MITCHEAR, John	Capt' of Mast	CYCLOPS	
MITCHELL, Abraham	Ward Rm Steward	Pcss CHARLOTTE	
	A.B.	BRITOMART	Algiers
MITCHELL, Charles	Trumpeter	HASTINGS	
MITCHELL, George	L.M.	PIQUE	
MITCHELL, George	A.B.	CARYSFORT	
MITCHELL, Henry	Capt' Mizzen Top	ASIA	
MITCHELL, H.V.	Pte. R.M.	POWERFUL	
MITCHELL, James	Pte. R.M.	THUNDERER	
MITCHELL, James	A.B.	HASTINGS	
MITCHELL, James	A.B.	GANGES	
MITCHELL, John	Sgt. R.M.	Pcss CHARLOTTE	
MITCHELL, John	A.B.	GANGES	
MITCHELL, Thomas	Ord	CARYSFORT	
MITCHELL, Thomas	Pte. R.M.	VANGUARD	
MITCHELL, Thomas	A.B.	EDINBURGH	
MITCHELL, William	Not Given	THUNDERER	
MITCHELLMORE, William	Pte. R.M.	IMPLACABLE	
MITCHEN, Peter	Bosun's Mate	IMPLACABLE	
MITFORD, Henry.G.	1st Lieut. R.M.	CARYSFORT	
MIZEN, Edward	Pte. R.M.	STROMBOLI	
MIZEN, John	Pte. R.M.	WASP	
MOALA, Luigi	Boy	CARYSFORT	
MOCKETT, Alexander	Pte. R.M.	BENBOW	
MODINO, Destino	Pilot	POWERFUL	
MOFFETT, Benjamin	Carp's Crew	RODNEY	
MOFFETT, John	Ord	CASTOR	
MOFFITT, Edward	Ord	EDINBURGH	
MOGG, William	L.M.	IMPLACABLE	
MOLISON, Robert	A.B.	Pcss CHARLOTTE	
MOLTON, George	A.B.	HASTINGS	

MONAGHAN, Stephen	Pte. R.M.	VANGUARD	
MONHAGAN, Thomas	A.B.	RODNEY	
MONRO, Charles	A.B.	DIDO	
MONTAGUE, John	Pte. R.M.	BELLEROPHON	
MOODY, James	A.B.	THUNDERER	
MOODY, Mark	Pte. R.M.	BELLEROPHON	
MOODY, William	Pte. R.M.	GANGES	
MOON, Thomas	Pte. R.M.	BENBOW	
MOON, William	Midshipman's Stwd	PIQUE	
MOONEY, Henry	Ord	Pcss CHARLOTTE	
MOONEY, Joseph	Pte. R.M.	HAZARD	
MOOR, Edmund	A.B.	ASIA	
MOORE, Edwin	Boy	RODNEY	
MOORE, Egbert	Ord	VANGUARD	
MOORE, George	Boy	DIDO	
MOORE, James	Pte. R.M.	CAMBRIDGE	
MOORE, James	Pte. R.M.	REVENGE	
MOORE, James	Pte. R.M.	DAPHNE	
MOORE, John	Sapper & Miner	PIQUE & STROMBOLI	
MOORE, John	Pte. R.M.	POWERFUL	
MOORE, Joseph	L.M.	REVENGE	
MOORE, Lewis	Boatswain 1st Cl	HASTINGS	
MOORE, Michael	Ord	POWERFUL	
MOORE, N.	H.B.M's Consul	—	
MOORE, Peter	Carp's Crew	EDINBURGH	
MOORE, Pierce	Pte. R.M.	Pcss CHARLOTTE	
MOORE, Richard	Pte. R.M.	BENBOW	
MOORE, Richard	A.B.	ASIA	
MOORE, Richard	Pte. R.M.	THUNDERER	
MOORE, Robert.S.	Mate	HASTINGS	
MOORE, Thomas	Sailmaker's Mate	EDINBURGH	
	A.B.	GLASGOW	*Navarino*
MOORE, Thomas	Pte. R.M.	REVENGE	
MOORE, William	A.B.	HASTINGS	
MOORE, William	L.M.	GANGES	
MOORES, William	Pte. R.M.	Pcss CHARLOTTE	
MOOREY, Henry	Ord	Pcss CHARLOTTE	
MOOREY, William	Ord	IMPLACABLE	
MORAN, Martin	Ord	RODNEY	
MORECOMB, G.J.	Pte. R.M.	CAMBRIDGE	
MORESBY, Fairfax	Volunteer 1st Cl	PIQUE	
MORETON, Hon Herbert.A.	Vol 1st Class	THUNDERER	
MOREY, William	Corporal. R.M.	STROMBOLI	
	Pte. R.M.	CAMBRIAN	*Navarino*
MOREY, William	Ord	BELLEROPHON	
MOREY, William	A.B.	MAGICIENNE	
MORGAN, Alexander	Boy	CAMBRIDGE	
MORGAN, G.J.	Fifer. R.M.	STROMBOLI	
MORGAN, George	Drummer. R.M.	WASP	
MORGAN, Henry	Pte. R.M.	PIQUE	
MORGAN, James	Ord	EDINBURGH	
MORGAN, John	Capt' Forecastle	Pcss CHARLOTTE	
MORGAN, John	Boy 1st Class	VANGUARD	
MORGAN, John	Pte. R.M.	RODNEY	
MORGAN, Samuel	Pte. R.M.	VANGUARD	
MORGAN, Samuel	Boy	RODNEY	
MORGAN, Thomas	Pte. R.M.	IMPLACABLE	
MORIATY, Henry.A.	2nd Master	GANGES	
MORIATY, Joseph	A.B.	HYDRA	
MORLEY, William	Boy	REVENGE	
MORRIS, Frederick	Mate	PIQUE	
MORRIS, Henry	Q.M.	CYCLOPS	
MORRIS, James	Boatswain	MEDEA	
MORRIS, John	Pte. R.M.	POWERFUL	
MORRIS, Joseph	A.B.	HASTINGS	*(M) Anchor Type LS & GC*
MORRIS, Peter	A.B.	PIQUE	
MORRISS, James	Pte. R.M.	PIQUE	
MORRISON, Arthur	Captain. R.M.	Pcss CHARLOTTE	
MORRISON, James	Fifer. R.M.	ZEBRA	
MORRISON, James	Capt' After Guard	REVENGE	
MORRISON, John	Sgt. R.M.	VESUVIUS	
MORRISON, R.F.E.	Seaman's Schoolmaster	RODNEY	
MORRISON, William	Bosun's Mate	ASIA	
MORSHEAD, John	Lieut. R.N.	HASTINGS	
MORSSON, John	A.B.	HASTINGS	
MORTIMER, William	A.B.	BENBOW	
MORTIMORE, John	Pte. R.M.	HASTINGS	
MORTIMORE, William	Pte. R.M.	Pcss CHARLOTTE	
MORTLOCK, Thomas	Pte. R.M.	ASIA	
MOSES, Charles	A.B.	BELLEROPHON	
MOSES, John	Pte. R.M.	ASIA	
MOSTON, Joseph	Sgt. R.M.	EDINBURGH	
MOTTLEY, James.C.	Clerk	HASTINGS	
MOTTLEY, Joseph.M.	Lieut. R.N.	REVENGE	
MOUBRAY, William.H.	Midshipman	HASTINGS	

SYRIA

MOULAND, Joseph	Boy	BELLEROPHON	
MOULD, Frederick	Pte. R.M.	STROMBOLI & POWERFUL	
MOULD, John.A.	Surgeon	PHOENIX	
MOUNTSTEVEN, James.S.	Purser	MEDEA	
MOWBRAY, Richard.Y.S.	Lieut. R.M.	CASTOR	*MOUBRAY in Navy List*
MOWER, J.	Pte. R.M.	CAMBRIDGE	
MOWLES, Isaac	Gunner Ryl Arty	HECATE	
MUGFORD, John	Mid's Cook	Pcss CHARLOTTE	
MUGFORD, William	Ord	VANGUARD	
MUGRIDGE, Edward	Ord	GANGES	
MUIR, George	Capt's Steward	Pcss CHARLOTTE	
MUIR, John	Ord	BELLEROPHON	
MULCAHY, David	A.B.	POWERFUL	
MULHOLLAND, Neal	Pte. R.M.	EDINBURGH	
MULLETT, George	Purser's Steward	STROMBOLI	
MULLETT, James	Ord	EDINBURGH	
MULLINS, John	Boy	POWERFUL	
MULLINGER, John	A.B.	POWERFUL	
MULLINGS, John	Pte. R.M.	Pcss CHARLOTTE	
MULLINS, James	A.B.	EDINBURGH	
MULLINS, Joseph	Pte. R.M.	RODNEY	
MUMFORD, William	A.B.	EDINBURGH	G.H.8905
	Boy 3rd Class	MODESTE	*Java*
MUMMERY, Charles	Ord	EDINBURGH	
MUNCY, William	Pte. R.M.	GANGES	
MUNROE, John	A.B.	VANGUARD	
MUNSEY, Thomas	Pte. R.M.	ASIA	
MUNSON, Richard	A.B.	THUNDERER	
MURKS, Charles	Barber	POWERFUL	
MURPHY, James	A.B.	ASIA	
MURPHY, John	A.B.	Pcss CHARLOTTE	
MURPHY, John	A.B.	VANGUARD	
MURPHY, John	Ord	RODNEY	
MURPHY, Laurence	Ord	RODNEY	
MURPHY, Michael	Ord	Pcss CHARLOTTE	
MURPHY, Patrick	Ord	REVENGE	
MURPHY, Patrick	L.M.	REVENGE	
MURPHY, William	A.B.	HASTINGS	
MURRAY, Alexander	Lieut. R.N.	Pcss CHARLOTTE (P)	(M) A of I/AVA
MURRAY, Alexander	L.M.	MEDEA	
MURRAY, Augustus.G.E.	Midshipman	ASIA	
MURRAY, James	A.B.	ASIA	
MURRAY, James	A.B.	CAMBRIDGE	
MURRAY, James	Pte. R.M.	Pcss CHARLOTTE	
MURRAY, John	Capt's Coxswain	DIDO	
MURRAY, Robert	Pte. R.M.	POWERFUL	
MURRAY, William	Corporal. R.M.A.	GORGON	
MUSKET, Henry	Pte. R.M.	ASIA	
MUSTARD, James.M.	Asst Surgeon	POWERFUL	
MUSTY, William	Pte. R.M.	THUNDERER	
MUTLO, John	Gunner. Ryl Arty	HECATE	
MUTLOW, John	Pte. R.M.	EDINBURGH	
MUTTON, James	Pte. R.M.	ASIA	
MYERS, Edward	A.B.	BELLEROPHON	
MYERS, Joseph	Not Given	CAMBRIDGE	
NADIELD, John	Boy 2nd Class	CARYSFORT	
NADRUM, George	A.B.	CAMBRIDGE	
NAGHORN, Charles	Ord	RODNEY	
NAISH, Henry.E.	Boy	REVENGE	
NAISH, Thomas	Ord	GANGES	
NANCARROW, Henry	Boy	DIDO	
NANT, Peter	A.B.	BELLEROPHON	
NAPIER, Charles	Ord	WASP	
NAPIER, E.	Lieut Colonel	HYDRA & HECATE	"duplicate worked up"
NASH, Charles	Boy 1st Class	DIDO	
NASH, Charles	Pte. R.M.	EDINBURGH	
NASH, John	Pte. R.M.	PIQUE	
NASH, John.W.	Carp's Crew	POWERFUL	
NASH, Richard	Armourer	CASTOR	
NASH, Samuel	A.B.	GANGES	
NASH, Thomas	Pte. R.M.	BENBOW	
NASH, William	Boy	MEDEA	
NAVIN, Michael	Pte. R.M.	EDINBURGH	
NAYLOR, A.	A.B.	RODNEY	
NAYLOR, Charles	Ord	RODNEY	
NEAL, John	Corporal. R.M.	VANGUARD	
	Pte. R.M.	ASIA	*Navarino*
NEALE, Charles	A.B.	DIDO	
NEALE, William	Capt' Main Top	BELLEROPHON	
NEARY, Michael	A.B.	EDINBURGH	
NEBITT, Henry	Pte. R.M.	ASIA	
NEELS, William	Corporal. R.M.	Pcss CHARLOTTE	

NEIL, Robert	Fifer. R.M.	Pcss CHARLOTTE	
NEILL, William	Ropemaker	POWERFUL	
NEILSON, Matthew	Gunner. Ryl Arty	PIQUE & other vessels	
NEGAL, Michael	Coxswain Pinnace	CAMBRIDGE	
NELLER, George	Pte. R.M.	STROMBOLI	
NELSON, Horatio	Midshipman	IMPLACABLE	
NERTON, J.F.	Pte. R.M.	HASTINGS	
NESS, Alexander	A.B.	CASTOR	
NETHERCOT, James	Carp's Crew	REVENGE	
NETHERTON, Samuel	A.B.	THUNDERER	
NETTLE, William	Pte. R.M.	IMPLACABLE	
NETTLETON, Peter.G.	Mate	CAMBRIDGE	
NEVILLE, Thomas	A.B.	GANGES	
NEVILLE, William	Q.M.	CASTOR	
NEVIN, James	Q.M.	GANGES	
NEW, Joseph	Ord	Pcss CHARLOTTE	
	Boy	ALBION	Navarino
NEW, Matthew	A.B.	CARYSFORT	
NEW, Moses	A.B.	WASP	
NEW, Thomas	A.B.	WASP	
NEWBERY, William	Pte. R.M.	Pcss CHARLOTTE	
NEWBURY, George	Boatswain	RODNEY	(M) A of I/AVA as NEWBERRY
	Gunner's Crew	PHILOMEL	Navarino
NEWBY, Matthew	A.B.	BELLEROPHON	
NEWDICK, Thomas	Boy	CASTOR	
NEWELL, James	A.B.	EDINBURGH	
NEWELL, John	Pte. R.M.	BELLEROPHON	
NEWHAM, William	A.B.	RODNEY	
NEWICK, Samuel	Pte. R.M.	PIQUE	
NEWINGTON, Abel	Pte. R.M.	STROMBOLI	
NEWINGTON, Henry	Pte. R.M.	REVENGE	
NEWLAN, Thomas	A.B.	BELLEROPHON	
NEWMAN, Jacob	Pte. R.M.	THUNDERER	
NEWMAN, Jeremiah	Pte. R.M.	BELLEROPHON	
NEWMAN, John	Carp's Crew	BENBOW	
NEWMAN, John	Boy	GANGES	
NEWMAN, Joseph	A.B.	GANGES	
NEWMAN, Joseph	A.B.	EDINBURGH	
NEWMAN, Richard	A.B.	CARYSFORT	
NEWMAN, Richard	Ord	TALBOT	
NEWMAN, Robert	Capt' Forecastle	TALBOT	(M) Anchor Type LS & GC
NEWMAN, Robert	A.B.	REVENGE	
NEWMAN, Robert	Bosun's Yeoman	IMPLACABLE	
NEWMAN, William	A.B.	BENBOW	
NEWMAN, William	Boy	DAPHNE	
NEWNHAM, Barnabus	Ord	Pcss CHARLOTTE	
NEWNHAM, Edward	Ord	VANGUARD	
NEWNHAM, George	Boy	ASIA	
NEWNHAM, John	Carp's Yeoman	BELLEROPHON	
NEWNHAM, Thomas	A.B.	BENBOW	
NEWNHAM, Thomas	Pte. R.M.	VANGUARD	
NEWPORT, William	Sgt. R.M.	CAMBRIDGE	
	Pte. R.M.	ASIA	Navarino
NEWTON, Abraham	Stoker	GORGON	
NEWTON, Henry	Ord	Pcss CHARLOTTE	
NEWTON, Joseph	Boy 1st Class	CASTOR	
NEWTON, Joseph	A.B.	HASTINGS	
NEWTON, William	Pte. R.M.	BENBOW	
NIBLETT, Robert	Ord	ASIA	
NICHOLLS, Thomas	A.B.	RODNEY	
NICHOLLS, William	Ord	ASIA	
NICHOLSON, David	Cooper	ASIA	
NICHOLSON, Frederick.F.	Midshipman	DIDO	
NICHOLSON, James	Q.M.	MAGICIENNE	
NICHOLSON, Joseph	Capt' of Mast	Pcss CHARLOTTE	
NICHOLSON, Josiah	Ord	BELLEROPHON	(M.L. as Joseph)
NICHOLSON, Samuel	Trumpeter	PIQUE	
NICKLIN, William	Sgt. R.M.	VANGUARD	
NICOL, Robert	Boatswain	CASTOR	
NIDDRIE, Peter	Asst Surgeon	Pcss CHARLOTTE	
NIMMO, James	Q.M.	PIQUE	
NIX, Joseph	Capt' Forecastle	HYDRA	
NOAKE, Francis	Boy	VANGUARD	
NOBLE, William	Sgt. R.M.	POWERFUL	
NODIN, William	Pte. R.M.	POWERFUL	
NOLL, William.G.	Boy	Pcss CHARLOTTE	
NORGATE, Robert	A.B.	RODNEY	
NORMAN, Benjamin	Pte. R.M.	IMPLACABLE	
NORMAN, Charles	A.B.	GANGES	
NORMAN, Charles.S.	Mate	EDINBURGH	
NORMAN, Henry	L.M.	REVENGE	
NORRIS, John	A.B.	EDINBURGH	
NORRIS, Thomas	Supn Pte. R.M.	STROMBOLI	
NORRISS, James	Pte. R.M.	STROMBOLI	
NORSWORTHY, James	Boy	THUNDERER	

SYRIA

NORTH, Francis	Ord	POWERFUL	
NORTHCOTE, John	A.B.	DAPHNE	
NORTHCOTT, Richard.H.	Boy	GANGES	
NORTHMORE, Joseph	Sgt. R.M.	MEDEA	
NORTON, John	Fifer. R.M.	REVENGE	
NORTON, Joseph	Pte. R.M.	Pcss CHARLOTTE	
NORTON, Peter	Ord	VANGUARD	
NORTON, Thomas	Pte. R.M.	Pcss CHARLOTTE	
NORWAY, Nevill	Lieut. R.N.	PHOENIX	
NOWLAN, John	Ord	Pcss CHARLOTTE	
NUNN, Robert	Carp's Crew	CASTOR	
NURSALL, George	Pte. R.M.	CAMBRIDGE	
NURSSALL, James	Pte. R.M.	ASIA	
NUTCHER, Frederic	Ord	POWERFUL	
NUTCHER, William	Carpenter	CYCLOPS	
NUTE, John	A.B.	BENBOW	
NUTT, Richard.C.	Surgeon	GORGON	
NYE, Thomas	Boy 1st Class	HECATE	
OADES, Edward	A.B.	CAMBRIDGE	
OADES, Thomas	Carp's Crew	PIQUE	
OAKLEY, Charles	Pte. R.M.	VANGUARD	
OATES, William	Corporal. R.M.	THUNDERER	
OBOURNE, Jacob	Pte. R.M.	RODNEY	
O'BRIEN, Harry	Boy	HECATE	
O'BRIEN, Henry	A.B.	CAMBRIDGE	
O'BRIEN, Samuel	A.B.	CAMBRIDGE	
O'BRIEN, William	Boy	GANGES	
O'CONNOR, George	Capt' After Guard	GANGES	
O'CONNOR, Patrick	Purser	ZEBRA	
ODGERS, Matthew	A.B.	IMPLACABLE	
O'DONNELL, Anthony	Ord	RODNEY	
O'DONNELL, William	Pte. R.M.	GANGES	
OGLE, Graham	Lieut. R.N.	EDINBURGH	
OGLESBY, Matthew	Pte. R.M.	POWERFUL	
O'GUYLE, William	A.B.	EDINBURGH	
O'HAGAN, Hugh	Asst Surgeon	GORGON	
OKE, Walter	Pte. R.M.	RODNEY	
OKINS, George	Pte. R.M.	ASIA	
OLCON, William	Pte. R.M.	CAMBRIDGE	
OLDEN, Michael	A.B.	DAPHNE	
OLDHAM, Henry.J.	Sgt. R.M.	CYCLOPS	
OLDING, Michael	Capt' Forecastle	HASTINGS	
OLDSON, Stephen	A.B.	WASP	
O'LEARY, John	Ord	BELLEROPHON	
O'LEARY, William	Ord	Pcss CHARLOTTE	
OLIVE, James	Pte. R.M.	CASTOR	
OLIVER, James	Gunner	ASIA	
	A.B.	SWIFTSURE	*Trafalgar*
OLIVER, James	A.B.	HAZARD	
OLIVER, John	Coxswain Pinnace	THUNDERER	
OLIVER, Richard.A.	Lieut. R.N.	ASIA	
	Midshipman	GLASGOW	*Navarino*
OLIVER, William	Pte. R.M.	Pcss CHARLOTTE	
OLIVER, William	Boy 2nd Class	Pcss CHARLOTTE	
OLIVER, Wilson	Caulker	DIDO	*(May read Wilsa)*
OMAN, Robert	A.B.	VANGUARD	
ONSLOW, Pitcairn	Lieut. R.M.	STROMBOLI	
ORAM, Edward	A.B.	ASIA	
ORAM, John	Pte. R.M.	BELLEROPHON	
ORCHARD, William	A.B.	IMPLACABLE	
ORGAN, Joseph	Boy	RODNEY	
ORME, Oswald	Sgt. R.M.	POWERFUL	
ORMES, Edward	Gunner's Crew	IMPLACABLE	
ORSMOND, Robert	A.B.	BENBOW	
OSBORN, William	A.B.	IMPLACABLE	
OSBORNE, Henry	Boy	DIDO	
OSBORNE, John	A.B.	BELLEROPHON	
OSBORNE, John	Capt' Main Top	CAMBRIDGE	
OSMOND, Edward	Supn Pte. R.M.	BELLEROPHON	
OSMOND, Elisha	Pte. R.M.	POWERFUL	
	Pte. R.M.	CAMBRIAN	*Navarino*
OTTEN, Henry	Pte. R.M.	THUNDERER	
OUGH, Charles	Boy	HASTINGS	
OUTEN, Thomas	A.B.	MAGICIENNE	
OUTFIN, Henry	Boy	TALBOT	
OVERING, Richard	Ord	STROMBOLI	
OWEN, John	A.B.	RODNEY	
OWEN, William	Boy	POWERFUL	
OWENS, Francis	Pte. R.M.	VANGUARD	
OWENS, Henry	Boy	DIDO	
OWENS, Richard	A.B.	STROMBOLI	
OXENHAM, Richard	A.B.	CAMBRIDGE	
OXENHAM, William	A.B.	CAMBRIDGE	

OXLAND, Thomas	Caulker's Mate	IMPLACABLE	
OZZARD, James.W.	Clerk	WASP	
PACE, Gaetano	Sailmaker's Mate	BELLEROPHON	
PACHE, Michael	Sailmaker's Mate	ASIA	
PACKMAN, John	Capt's Steward	PHOENIX	
PADWICK, Joseph	A.B.	GANGES	
PADWICK, Thomas	A.B.	EDINBURGH	
PAFFARD, Peter	Ord	VANGUARD	
PAGE, Henry	Ord	REVENGE	
PAGE, James	Carp's Mate	ZEBRA	
PAGE, Joseph	Ord	CAMBRIDGE	
PAGE, Richard	Pte. R.M.	CAMBRIDGE	
PAGE, William	Ord	BELLEROPHON	
PAGE, William	Pte. R.M.	GANGES	
PAGE, William	Pte. R.M.	CAMBRIDGE	
PAIN, James	Pte. R.M.	GANGES	
PAIN, William	Ord	ASIA	
PAINE, Robert	Stoker	MEDEA	
PAINTER, Michael	Boy	IMPLACABLE	
PAISLEY, Robert	Bombdr Ryl Arty	HECATE	
PALMER, Edward	Sgt. R.M.	THUNDERER	(M) Anchor Type LS & GC
PALMER, George	Pte. R.M.	STROMBOLI	
PALMER, George	A.B.	CAMBRIDGE	
PALMER, George	Pte. R.M.	REVENGE	
PALMER, Henry	Boy	VANGUARD	(Alias Hy ROBERTS)
PALMER, Henry	Pte. R.M.	IMPLACABLE	
PALMER, James	Pte. R.M.	PIQUE	
PALMER, James	Boy	VANGUARD	
PALMER, Jeremiah	Pte. R.M.	BELLEROPHON	
PALMER, John	Caulker	STROMBOLI	
PALMER, John	Boy	VANGUARD	
PALMER, John	Q.M.	GANGES	
PALMER, John	Coal Trimmer	HYDRA	
PALMER, Joseph	Ord	DIDO	
PALMER, Reuben	Pte. R.M.	Pcss CHARLOTTE	
PALMER, Reuben	Pte. R.M.	CAMBRIDGE & REVENGE	
PALMER, Robert	Pte. R.M.	RODNEY	
PALMER, Thomas	A.B.	RODNEY	
PALMER, William	Purser's Steward	DIDO	
PALMER, William	Purser's Steward	EDINBURGH	
PALMER, William	Pte. R.M.	RODNEY	
PALMERS, Thomas	Pte. R.M.	THUNDERER	
PAMPHILON, Frederick	Pte. R.M.	GANGES	
PANALIGAN, John	Ord	CAMBRIDGE	
PANKHURST, David	Pte. R.M.	STROMBOLI & HAZARD	
PAPAREL, Robert	Ord	THUNDERER	
PAPPALARDO, Charles	Supn Pilot	BENBOW	
PARADISE, Thomas	Pte. R.M.	ZEBRA	
PARFITT, George	Pte. R.M.	POWERFUL	
PARIER, William	Midshipman	GORGON	
PARK, Edward	Pte. R.M.	THUNDERER	
PARKE, Hamnett	1st Lieut. R.M.	PIQUE	(Hammett incorrectly roll)
PARKER, David	Boy	POWERFUL	
PARKER, Frederick	Pte. R.M.	VANGUARD	
PARKER, George	A.B.	GANGES	
PARKER, John	Boy	BELLEROPHON	
PARKER, Richard	A.B.	BENBOW	
PARKER, Robert	Pte. R.M.	HAZARD	
PARKER, Stephen	A.B.	RODNEY	
	A.B.	CAMBRIAN	Navarino
PARKER, Thomas	Bosun's Mate	POWERFUL	
PARKER, Thomas	Boy 1st Class	EDINBURGH	
PARKER, William	Ord	VANGUARD	
PARKIN, George.H.	Volunteer 1st Cl	CAMBRIDGE	
PARKIN, John.P.	Commander	CAMBRIDGE	
	Midshipman	ACHILLE	Trafalgar
PARKINSON, Thomas	Pte. R.M.	PIQUE	
PARKS, Henry	A.B.	HASTINGS	
PARKS, Thomas	A.B.	HASTINGS	
PARMETER, William.G.	Clerk	ZEBRA	
PARMINTER, William.W.	Clerk	PHOENIX	(Roll as Watson.W.)
PARR, Joseph	Boy	CAMBRIDGE	
PARR, Thomas	Corporal Ryl Arty	PIQUE & other vessels	
PARR, Thomas	Blacksmith	CAMBRIDGE	
PARRICK, Joseph	Boy	Pcss CHARLOTTE	
PARRY, James	A.B.	BENBOW	
PARSONS, Henry	A.B.	RODNEY	(Initials may be H.Y.)
PARSONS, William	Ord	CAMBRIDGE	
PARSONS, William	Gunner's Mate	CASTOR	
PARTRIDGE, Frederick.J.	Vol 1st Class	PIQUE	
PARTRIDGE, John	Drummer. R.M.	EDINBURGH	
PARTRIDGE, John	Ord	RODNEY	(M.L. as John.W.)
PARTRIDGE, William	A.B.	VANGUARD	

SYRIA

Name	Rank/Rating	Ship	Notes
PARTRIDGE, William.L.	Mate	DIDO	
PASCO, G.M. & G.L.M.	Clerk's Asst	THUNDERER	Two applications for medal
PASCOE, Bennet	A.B.	CAMBRIDGE	
PASCOE, Richard.W.	Captain. R.M.	IMPLACABLE	
	2nd Lieut. R.M.	PHOEBE	Off Tamatave. 20 May 1811
	(2nd Lieut. R.M.)	(PHOEBE)	(M.G.S. JAVA clasp)
PASCOE, Walter	A.B.	RODNEY	
PASCOE, William	Ship's Corporal	BENBOW	(M) Anchor Type LS & GC
PASFIELD, William	Pte. R.M.	GANGES	
PASHEN, Robert	Pte. R.M.	IMPLACABLE	
PASSMORE, William	Pte. R.M.	Pcss CHARLOTTE	
PATEMAN, Joseph	Pte. R.M.	ASIA	
PATERSON, David	Caulker's Mate	GANGES	
PATEY, Charles.G.E.	Lieut. R.N.	CASTOR	"Planted flag on ramparts"
PATEY, George.E.	Mate	CARYSFORT	
PATEY, John	Ord	Pcss CHARLOTTE	
PATEY, Richard	A.B.	CAMBRIDGE	
PATRICK, Charles	A.B.	THUNDERER	
PATTENDEN, Joseph	Boy 1st Class	VANGUARD	
PATTER, John	Pte. R.M.	EDINBURGH	
PATTERN, John.J.	Pte. R.M.	STROMBOLI	
PATTERSON, George	A.B.	EDINBURGH	
PATTERSON, John	Pte. R.M.	VANGUARD	
PATTERSON, John	Q.M.	HECATE	
PATTISON, James	Boy	HAZARD	
PATTISON, Joseph	Ord	VANGUARD	
PAUL, James	Ord	THUNDERER	(Alias HILL)
PAUL, James	Ord	REVENGE	
PAUL, John	Pte. R.M.	IMPLACABLE	
PAUL, John	Coxswain Launch	RODNEY	(M) Vic Wide dated 1848 LS&GC
PAUL, Joseph	M.A.A.	HASTINGS	
PAUL, William	Ord	MAGICIENNE	
PAVETT, Samuel	Ord	ASIA	
PAVEY, William	Pte. R.M.	THUNDERER	
PAXTON, James	A.B.	POWERFUL	
PAY, Richard	Pte. R.M.	DIDO	
PAYNE, Benjamin	Carp's Crew	GANGES	
PAYNE, Charles	Ord	GANGES	
PAYNE, George	A.B.	CARYSFORT	
PAYNE, John	A.B.	EDINBURGH	
PAYNE, John	A.B.	STROMBOLI	
PAYNE, Phillip	Pte. R.M.	VANGUARD	
PAYNE, Samuel	Coxswain Pinnace	Pcss CHARLOTTE	(M) Anchor Type LS & GC
PAYNE, William	A.B.	BELLEROPHON	
PAYNE, William.H.	Mate	GORGON	
PAYTON, John	Pte. R.M.	ASIA	
PEACH, William	Pte. R.M.	IMPLACABLE	
PEACHELL, Thomas	A.B.	Pcss CHARLOTTE	
PEACOCK, William	Ord	POWERFUL	
PEARCE, Edward	Ord	VANGUARD	
PEARCE, Edward.S.	Lieut. R.N.	Pcss CHARLOTTE	
PEARCE, George	A.B.	CAMBRIDGE	
PEARCE, James	Pte. R.M.	IMPLACABLE	
PEARCE, James	Ord	RODNEY	
PEARCE, John	Pte. R.M.	MEDEA	
PEARCE, John	Ord	REVENGE	
PEARCE, John	Pte. R.M.	VESUVIUS	
PEARCE, John	A.B.	BENBOW	
PEARCE, Joseph	Pte. R.M.	VANGUARD	
PEARCE, Thomas	Pte. R.M.	CAMBRIDGE	
PEARCE, Thomas	Ord	Pcss CHARLOTTE	
PEARCE, Thomas.W.	Boy	Pcss CHARLOTTE	
PEARCE, William	Pte. R.M.	DAPHNE	
PEARCE, William	Ord	IMPLACABLE	
PEARCE, William.B.	Asst Clerk	BENBOW	
PEARMAN, James	Ord	BELLEROPHON	
PEARN, Edward.J.P.	Master	POWERFUL	
PEARN, William	A.B.	ASIA	
PEARSE, James	A.B.	Pcss CHARLOTTE	
PEARSE, William	Pte. R.M.	Pcss CHARLOTTE	
PEARSON, Andrew	Capt' Forecastle	EDINBURGH	(M) Anchor Type LS & GC
	A.B.	ALBION	Navarino
PEARSON, John.J.	Pte. R.M.	PIQUE	
PEARSON, Joseph	Carp's Mate	TALBOT	
PEARSON, S.B.	Capt' Main Top	RODNEY	
PEARSON, Richard.H.	A.B.	POWERFUL	
PECK, Chamblain	Pte. R.M.	ASIA	
PECK, Charles	Pte. R.M.	HASTINGS	
PECKER, George	Pte. R.M.	CASTOR	
PEDDER, Henry	Pte. R.M.	VANGUARD	
PEDDLE, John	Capt's Steward	STROMBOLI	
PEDLAR, William	Carp's Crew	THUNDERER	
PEECHEY, William	Capt' Main Top	PIQUE	

PEEKE, James	A.B.	PHOENIX	
PEETRAY, Thomas	A.B.	BELLEROPHON	
PEGG, William	Pte. R.M.	HAZARD	
PELLEW, Henry	Carpenter	MEDEA	
PELLEW, John	Gunner. R.M.A.	CYCLOPS	*(May read PELLEN)*
PELLEW, Hon Pownall.J.	Midshipman	GANGES	
PELLY, George	Pte. R.M.	VANGUARD	
PENDERGRASS, William	Ord	IMPLACABLE	
PENFOLD, William	Pte. R.M.	Pcss CHARLOTTE	
PENNINGTON, William	Ord	IMPLACABLE	
PENNY, George.H.	Boy	Pcss CHARLOTTE	
PENNY, Thomas	Boy	CYCLOPS	
PENSON, William	A.B.	HASTINGS	
PENSY, Joseph	Ord	BELLEROPHON	
PENWARN, John	Cooper's Crew	RODNEY	
PERCEY, George	A.B.	POWERFUL	
PERDU, G.	Capt' Main Top	DAPHNE	
PERFITT, Henry	Pte. R.M.	REVENGE	
PERKIN, William	Pte. R.M.	RODNEY	
PERKINS, John	Pte. R.M.	THUNDERER	
PERKS, William	A.B.	GANGES	
PERRIEND, Henry	A.B.	EDINBURGH	
PERRIER, William	Midshipman	GORGON	
PERRIN, Henry.A.	Ord	ASIA	
PERRIN, Richard	Q.M.	PIQUE	
PERRITON, Henry	Armourer	THUNDERER	
PERRY, Charles	Pte. R.M.	CASTOR	
PERRY, John.W.	A.B.	GORGON	
PERRY, Joseph	Ord	HYDRA	
PERRY, Joseph	Ord	PHOENIX	
PERRY, J.T.	Stoker	PHOENIX	
PERRY, Robert	Ord	VANGUARD	
PERRY, William	Ord	BELLEROPHON	
PESCOTT, Luke	Pte. R.M.	HYDRA	
PETERS, James	Pte. R.M.	BELLEROPHON	
PETERS, John	Gunner Ryl Arty	HECATE	
PETERS, Richard	Bosun's Mate	WASP	
PETERS, Thomas	Boy 2nd Class	STROMBOLI	
PETHERICK, William	A.B.	THUNDERER	
PETIT, John	A.B.	CASTOR	
PETIT, William	A.B.	RODNEY	
PETT, George	Pte. R.M.	THUNDERER	
PETT, James	Capt' Fore Top	ASIA	
PETTY, Daniel	Pte. R.M.	VANGUARD	
PETTY, Edward	Q.M.	WASP	
PETTY, Robert	Ord	VANGUARD	
PETTY, William	A.B.	MAGICIENNE	
PEYTON, Lumley.W.	Mate	POWERFUL	
PHELPS, Henry	Mate	POWERFUL	
PHENICK, Vincent	Capt's Cook	PHOENIX	
PHEZE, Richard	A.B.	GANGES	
PHILLIPS, Alexander	Capt's Coxswain	HASTINGS	
	Capt's Coxswain	ASIA	*Navarino*
PHILLIPS, Andrew	Boy 2nd Class	BENBOW	
PHILLIPS, George	Boy	IMPLACABLE	
PHILLIPS, James.F.	Clerk	BENBOW	
PHILLIPS, James.F.	Ord	GANGES	
PHILLIPS, John	A.B.	DAPHNE	
PHILLIPS, John	Pte. R.M.	EDINBURGH	
PHILLIPS, John	A.B.	RODNEY	
PHILLIPS, John	Not Given	TALBOT	*(Alias Simon PASSMORE)*
PHILLIPS, John	Ord	IMPLACABLE	
PHILLIPS, Joseph	Pte. R.M.	REVENGE	
PHILLIPS, Richard	Ord	BELLEROPHON	
PHILLIPS, Samuel	A.B.	THUNDERER	
PHILLIPS, Simon	Ord	VANGUARD	
PHILLIPS, Thomas	Pte. R.M.	HASTINGS	
PHILLIPS, William	A.B.	RODNEY	
PHILLIPS, William	Pte. R.M.	THUNDERER	
PHILLIPS, William	Pte. R.M.	HASTINGS	
PHILP, Henry	Ord	TALBOT	
	Ord	GENOA	*Navarino*
PHILP, John	Pte. R.M.	TALBOT	
PHILPOT, William	Boatswain	ZEBRA	
PHILPOTT, Ozias	Pte. R.M.	REVENGE	
PHIPPARD, Reuben	Capt' Fore Top	RODNEY	
PHIPPS, William.H.	Midshipman	RODNEY	
PHOEBY, John	L.M.	GORGON	
PHYSICK, Thomas	Stoker	MEDEA	
PICKARD, William	Corporal. R.M.	POWERFUL	
PICKFORD, Samuel	Pte. R.M.	CAMBRIDGE	*(May read James)*
PIDCOCK, Thomas	Clerk	MEDEA	
PIDDELL, William	Carpenter	VANGUARD	
PIERCE, James	Pte. R.M.	WASP	
PIERCY, Richard	Bosun's Mate	BENBOW	*(M.L. as PIERCE)*

SYRIA

PIERREPOINT, Joshua	A.B.	BENBOW	
PIGGE, John	A.B.	MEDEA	
PIKE, Edward	Carp's Crew	Pcss CHARLOTTE	
PIKE, James	Pte. R.M.	REVENGE	
PIKE, John	A.B.	REVENGE	
PIKE, William	Pte. R.M.	PIQUE	
PILBROW, John	Pte. R.M.	ASIA	
PILCHER, George	L.M.	IMPLACABLE	
PILCHER, Henry	Ord	ASIA	
PILE, George	Boy	IMPLACABLE	
PILTON, William	Pte. R.M.	RODNEY	
PIM, Richard	Boy	MAGICIENNE	
PIMM, Charles	Pte. R.M.	STROMBOLI	
PINCHER, George	A.B.	BELLEROPHON	
PINE, George	Yeoman Store Rms	PIQUE	
PINE, John	Gunner	IMPLACABLE	
PINHORN, James	Purser	CYCLOPS	
PINHORN, James.C.	Clerk's Asst	CYCLOPS	
PINHORN, William	A.B.	VANGUARD	
PINN, Richard	Pte. R.M.	VESUVIUS	
PINNICK, James	Boy	ASIA	
PINNINGTON, George	Capt' Main Top	ASIA	
PINNOCK, John	Sgt. R.M.	CAMBRIDGE	
PINNOCK, William	Pte. R.M.	PIQUE	
PIPER, William	Ord	ASIA	
PITCHER, William	Pte. R.M.	ASIA	*(May read PITCHES)*
PITMAN, Francis	A.B.	GANGES	*(May read Isaac)*
PITMAN, Timothy	A.B.	EDINBURGH	
PITT, George	Pte. R.M.	THUNDERER	
PITT, James	Pte. R.M.	ASIA	
PITT, John	Pte. R.M.	CAMBRIDGE	
PITT, John	Pte. R.M.	VANGUARD	
PITT, Philip	Boy	HASTINGS	
PITTS, Richard	Pte. R.M.	REVENGE	
PITTS, Richard	Pte. R.M.	STROMBOLI	
PITTS, William	Ord	BENBOW	
PLENTY, Henry	Pte. R.M.	HAZARD	
PLEYDELL, Thomas.B.	1st Lieut. R.M.	BELLEROPHON	
PLIMSOLL, Joseph	Asst Surgeon	EDINBURGH	
PLOUGHMAN, James	A.B.	BENBOW	
PLUMMER, George	Pte. R.M.	CAMBRIDGE	
PLUMMER, John	Carp's Crew	VESUVIUS	
PLUMSTONE, William	A.B.	PIQUE	
POARDIN, William	A.B.	GANGES	
POCOCK, William	Pte. R.M.	VANGUARD	
POKE, George	Pte. R.M.	GORGON	
POLKINGHORNE, William	Q.M.	CAMBRIDGE	
POLLARD, Francis	A.B.	RODNEY	
POLLEXFIN, Samuel	Boy	IMPLACABLE	
POLLINGTON, Henry	Ord	CAMBRIDGE	
POMEROY, Richard	A.B.	MEDEA	
POOK, William.J.	3rd Engineer	PHOENIX	
POOKE, Edward	A.B.	IMPLACABLE	
POOL, Isaac	Bosun's Mate	CASTOR	
POOLE, George	Pte. R.M.	PHOENIX	
POOLE, Samuel	Cook	PIQUE	
	A.B.	PHILOMEL	*Navarino*
POOLEY, Charles	A.B.	BENBOW	
POORE, George	A.B.	DIDO	
POPE, John.W.	Boy	RODNEY	
POPE, Joseph	A.B.	RODNEY	
POPE, William	Pte. R.M.	POWERFUL	
POPHAM, Robert	Boy	RODNEY	
PORTER, James	A.B.	BENBOW	
PORTER, Joseph	Ward Room Cook	Pcss CHARLOTTE	
PORTOLAM, James	A.B.	ASIA	
PORTON, James	Pte. R.M.	Pcss CHARLOTTE	
POSTLE, Charles.J.	Lieut. R.N.	VANGUARD	
POTTER, Peter	L.M.	GANGES	
POTTER, Thomas	A.B.	Pcss CHARLOTTE	
POTTER, William	Corporal. R.M.	EDINBURGH	
POUND, George	Caulker's Mate	STROMBOLI	
POUND, John	A.B.	EDINBURGH	
POUNDS, Henry	A.B.	VANGUARD	
POUNDSFORD, Robert	Corporal. R.M.	THUNDERER	
POVER, Samuel	Color Sgt. R.M.	DAPHNE	
POWE, John	L.M.	THUNDERER	
POWELL, Daniel	A.B.	Pcss CHARLOTTE	
POWELL, George	Boy	PIQUE	
POWELL, James	Pte. R.M.	BELLEROPHON	
POWELL, John	A.B.	PIQUE	
POWELL, Richard.A.	College Mate	HYDRA	
POWELL, Thomas	Capt' of Hold	Pcss CHARLOTTE	*(M) Anchor Type LS & GC*

POWELL, William	Bosun's Yeoman	ASIA	
POWELL, William	Boy	POWERFUL	
POWER, James	Boy	POWERFUL	
POWERS, John	Cooper	PIQUE	
POWERS, Lawrence	A.B.	BELLEROPHON	
POWERS, Samuel	Ord	BELLEROPHON	
POWIS, Thomas	Pte. R.M.	VANGUARD	
PRATT, James	A.B.	CASTOR	
PRATT, Robert	Pte. R.M.	IMPLACABLE	
PRATT, Steven	Pte. R.M.	Pcss CHARLOTTE	
PREATER, Thomas	Capt' of Mast	PIQUE	
PRENTICE, Golden	Pte. R.M.	GANGES	
PRESCOTT, Henry	Pte. R.M.	MEDEA	
PRESCOTT, Thomas	Sgt. R.M.	EDINBURGH	
PRESSLEY, John	A.B.	GANGES	
PRESTON, Joseph	Gunner Ryl Arty	HECATE	
PRESTON, William	Capt' After Guard	BENBOW	
PREVOST, L.L.	Mate	MAGICIENNE	(Initials may read L.D.)
PRIANTE, Edward	A.B.	IMPLACABLE	(M.L. as PREANTER)
PRICE, Charles	A.B.	BENBOW	
PRICE, Charles	Capt' Fore Top	EDINBURGH	
PRICE, Henry	Corporal. R.M.	Pcss CHARLOTTE	
PRICE, Henry	Corporal. R.M.	REVENGE	
PRICE, Henry	A.B.	CASTOR	
PRICE, James	Sgt. R.M.	RODNEY	
PRICE, James	Pte. R.M.	RODNEY	
PRICE, John.A.P.	Mate	THUNDERER	
PRICE, John.E.	Clerk	HYDRA	
PRICE, Robert	A.B.	VANGUARD	
PRIDDEAUX, Joseph	Sailmaker's Mate	POWERFUL	
PRIDHAM, William.W.	Mate	Pcss CHARLOTTE	
PRIME, John	Pte. R.M.	GANGES	
PRIME, Robert	Stoker	MEDEA	
PRIMMER, William	Ord	BELLEROPHON	
PRIN, Richard	Boy	MAGICIENNE	
PRINCE, William	A.B.	BELLEROPHON	
PRINTEY, George	A.B.	CAMBRIDGE	
PRITCHARD, Charles	A.B.	THUNDERER	
PRIVETT, John	A.B.	DIDO	
PROCTOR, Benjamin	Stoker	GORGON	
PROWSE, Thomas	Boy	EDINBURGH	
PRYCE, Edward	Pte. R.M.	PIQUE	
PRYNN, John	A.B.	RODNEY	
	A.B.	ALBION	Navarino
PSAYLA, Publio	A.B.	THUNDERER	
PUDNEY, Samuel	Pte. R.M.	RODNEY	(May read James)
PUFFETT, John	Pte. R.M.	HASTINGS	
PUGH, James	Caulker	WASP	
PUGH, William	Not Given	STROMBOLI	
PULFORD, William	Pte. R.M.	CASTOR	
PULLING, John	A.B.	RODNEY	
PULLING, Thomas	A.B.	MAGICIENNE	
PULLING, Thomas	A.B.	POWERFUL	
PUMPHREY, George	A.B.	THUNDERER	
PUNCH, James	A.B.	BELLEROPHON	
PURCELL, Henry	Boy	STROMBOLI	
PURKIS, Joshua	A.B.	EDINBURGH	
PURSELL, James	Pte. R.M.	PHOENIX	
PURTON, George	Gunner. R.M.A.	GORGON	
PURVISS, Francis.J.	Ord	REVENGE	
PYE, W.H.	Boy 2nd Class	EDINBURGH	(M.L. as William)
PYLE, Matthew	Pte. R.M.	TALBOT	
PYNE, Thomas	A.B.	RODNEY	
QUANT, Samuel	Pte. R.M.	THUNDERER	
QUAYLE, Thomas	A.B.	STROMBOLI	
	A.B.	ALBION	Navarino
QUICK, Thomas	Boy	Pcss CHARLOTTE	
QUIN, Henry	Boy	DIDO	
QUIN, James	Boy	BELLEROPHON	
QUIN, John	Gunner's Mate	DIDO	
QUINN, John	Pte. R.M.	PIQUE	
QUINN, William	Ord	Pcss CHARLOTTE	
QUINTON, George	Carp's Crew	BENBOW	
QUINTON, Robert	Ord	PIQUE	
QUIRKE, David	Pte. R.M.	DAPHNE	
QUITTENDEN, Benjamin	Pte. R.M.	DIDO	
RADDENBURY, George	Pte. R.M.	IMPLACABLE	
RADFORD, John	Boy	CYCLOPS	
RADFORD, Robert	Pte. R.M.	IMPLACABLE	
RAE, James	Q.M.	BENBOW	
RAFFERTY, Morris	Ord	CASTOR	
RAINSFORD, George	Pte. R.M.	THUNDERER	
RALPH, Andrew	A.B.	Pcss CHARLOTTE	
RALPH, George	Gunner Ryl Arty	PIQUE & other vessels	
RALLS, James	Bosun's Mate	Pcss CHARLOTTE	

SYRIA

RAMAGE, Thomas.M.	Clerk	CASTOR	
RANCE, John	Gunner's Mate	GANGES	
RANDALL, George	Capt's Steward	CYCLOPS	
RANDOLPH, Thomas	Capt's Coxswain	CASTOR	
RANKINS, James	Pte. R.M.	CAMBRIDGE	
RANSON, Thomas	Pte. R.M.	CARYSFORT	
RAPLEY, Daniel	Ord	BENBOW	
RAPSAN, John	Not Given	THUNDERER	(May read RAPSAM)
RASCORL, Thomas	Capt' of Hold	CAMBRIDGE	
RATCLIFF, William	Capt' Mizzen Top	Pcss CHARLOTTE	
RATCLIFFE, John	Ord	GANGES	
RATTENBURY, Richard	A.B.	IMPLACABLE	
RATTER, Joseph	Gunner's Mate	MAGICIENNE	
RATTON, W.G. see WRATTON			
RAVENHALL, Richard	Gunner. R.M.A.	MEDEA	
RAWLINGS, George	Pte. R.M.	CAMBRIDGE	
RAWLINGS, Richard	Pte. R.M.	EDINBURGH	
RAWLINGS, Robert	Fifer. R.M.	PIQUE	
RAWLINGS, William	Sick Berth Attdt	DAPHNE	
RAY, David	Boy	HAZARD	
RAY, Joseph	Armourer	IMPLACABLE	
RAY, William	A.B.	CAMBRIDGE	
	Ord	GLASGOW	Navarino
RAY, William	A.B.	HASTINGS	
RAY, William	Pte. R.M.	CAMBRIDGE	
RAYMOND, R.W.	Pte. R.M.	RODNEY	
RAYNER, James	Bosun's Mate	WASP	
READ, Archibald	A.B.	IMPLACABLE	
READ, George	Ord	ASIA	
READ, William.C.	Ord	EDINBURGH	
READER, William	Boy	CAMBRIDGE	
READING, Robert	A.B.	BENBOW	
REALEY, William	Pte. R.M.	Pcss CHARLOTTE	
REARDON, Edward	A.B.	Pcss CHARLOTTE	
REAVES, Henry	Sailmaker's Mate	RODNEY	
REDDAWAY, Henry	Pte. R.M.	RODNEY	
REDDELL, George	Ord	REVENGE	
REDDEM, Thomas	A.B.	POWERFUL	
REDDICK, Peter	Pte. R.M.	POWERFUL	
REDMAN, John	Pte. R.M.	THUNDERER	
	Pte. R.M.	ALBION	Navarino
REDWOOD, Henry	A.B.	IMPLACABLE	
REED, John	Boy	CASTOR	
REED, Joseph	Pte. R.M.	STROMBOLI	
REED, Thomas	A.B.	GANGES	
REED, William	A.B.	THUNDERER	
REED, William	Pte. R.M.	RODNEY	
REEVE, John.M.	Midshipman	REVENGE	
REEVES, E.	Boy	BENBOW	
REEVES, Gabriel	Pte. R.M.	BELLEROPHON	
REEVES, Robert	Pte. R.M.	ASIA	
REEVES, Robert	Boy	BELLEROPHON	
REGAN, Daniel	A.B.	CAMBRIDGE	
REGAN, Dennis	Carp's Crew	Pcss CHARLOTTE	
REGISTER, Samuel	A.B.	RODNEY	
REID, Archibald	Sgt. Ryl Arty	PIQUE & other vessels	
REID, Douglas	Mate	IMPLACABLE	
REID, William	Gunner Ryl Arty	PIQUE & other vessels	
REILEY, Phillip	Ord	ZEBRA	
REILLY, Hugh.A.	Volunteer	RODNEY & HECATE	
REILLY, Patrick	Purser's Steward	POWERFUL	
REILLY, William	A.B.	GANGES	
REMFRY, Arthur	Coxswain Pinnace	IMPLACABLE	
RENDLE, John	Gun Room Steward	THUNDERER	
RENDLE, Thomas	Ord	DAPHNE	
RENDLE, Thomas	Ord	VANGUARD	
RENNIE, Henry	A.B.	BELLEROPHON	
REVE, John	Pte. R.M.	GANGES	
REVELL, William	Ship's Cook	EDINBURGH	
REYNOLDS, Adolphus	Ord	RODNEY	
REYNOLDS, Barrington	Captain. R.N.	GANGES	
	Midshipman	AMAZON	Amazon. 13 Jany 1810
	Midshipman	IMPETUEUX	B.S. 29 Aug 1800
	Commander	HESPER	Java
REYNOLDS, John	Purser's Steward	GORGON	
REYNOLDS, Jonathan	Fifer. R.M.	ASIA	
REYNOLDS, Joseph	Gunner's Mate	CARYSFORT	
REYNOLDS, Louis.R.	Midshipman	DIDO	
REYNOLDS, Richard	Supn Pte. R.M.	WASP	
REYNOLDS, Thomas	Sgt. R.M.	CASTOR	
REYNOLDS, Thomas	Ord	CAMBRIDGE	

REYNOLDS, William	2 borne	CAMBRIDGE	(A.B. & Boy)
REYNOLDS, William	Boy	CAMBRIDGE	Both men applied
REYNOLDS, William	A.B.	BENBOW	
REYNON, Henry	Pte. R.M.	PHOENIX	
REYPERT, James	Boy	CYCLOPS	
RICE, George.W.	Volunteer 1st Cl	MAGICIENNE	
RICE, John	Bosun's Mate	DIDO	
RICE, Thomas	A.B.	HASTINGS	
RICE, William	Ord	HASTINGS	
RICH, Henry	Boy	Pcss CHARLOTTE	
RICHARDS, Charles	A.B.	HYDRA	
RICHARDS, Charles	Clerk	STROMBOLI	
RICHARDS, Christopher	2 borne	HYDRA	(A.B. & Ord)
RICHARDS, George	Pte. R.M.	WASP	
RICHARDS, George	A.B.	DAPHNE	
RICHARDS, George	Pte. R.M.	PIQUE	
RICHARDS, Rev George	Chaplain	VANGUARD	
RICHARDS, George	A.B.	EDINBURGH	
RICHARDS, Henry	A.B.	GANGES	
RICHARDS, James	Coxswain of Launch	BELLEROPHON	
RICHARDS, James	Boy	GORGON	
RICHARDS, John	Boy	BELLEROPHON	
RICHARDS, Joseph	Ord	BENBOW	
RICHARDS, Joseph.J.	Corporal. R.M.	STROMBOLI	
RICHARDS, Thomas	A.B.	THUNDERER	
RICHARDS, William	A.B.	RODNEY	
	Ord	ASIA	Navarino
RICHARDSON, Arthur	A.B.	GORGON	
RICHARDSON, Henry	Ord	THUNDERER	
RICHARDSON, John	Pte. R.M.	HYDRA	
RICHARDSON, John	A.B.	VANGUARD	
RICHARDSON, Thomas	A.B.	ASIA	
RICHARDSON, William	Pte. R.M.	STROMBOLI	
RICHARDSON, William	Ord	BENBOW	
RICHARDSON, William	Pte. R.M.	BELLEROPHON	
RICHMOND, Hugh	Pte. R.M.	ASIA	
RICHMOND, William	Boy	MAGICIENNE	
RICKARD, Edward	Boy 1st Class	RODNEY	
RICKETT, John	Cook	DAPHNE	
RICKETT, Samuel	Pte. R.M.	GANGES	
RICKETTS, Edmund	Ord	CAMBRIDGE	
RICKETTS, Henry	Corporal. R.M.	HAZARD	
RICKCORD, George.P.	Actg Purser	DIDO	
RIDDLE, George	Gunner Ryl Arty	HECATE	
RIDDLE, James	Pte. R.M.	CAMBRIDGE	
RIDDLE, Robert	Pte. R.M.	STROMBOLI	
RIDOUTT, Joseph	Ord	BENBOW	
RIDE, Samuel	Pte. R.M.	ASIA	
RIDLEY, James	A.B.	CAMBRIDGE	
RIDLEY, Thomas	A.B.	DAPHNE	
RIDOUT, John	Carp's Mate	EDINBURGH	
RIGAN, John	A.B.	IMPLACABLE	
RIGGE, Charles.G.	Lieut. R.N.	ZEBRA	
RIGGS, James	A.B.	POWERFUL	
RIGGS, Thomas	Sailmaker's Crew	CARYSFORT	
RIGNEY, William	Pte. R.M.	PIQUE	
RILEY, Stephen	Boy	BENBOW	
RILEY, Thomas	Pte. R.M.	BENBOW	
RING, Thomas.E.	Surgeon	WASP	
RIPPON, John	A.B.	ASIA	G.H. 7013
	A.B.	GENOA	Navarino
RISBY, William	Pte. R.M.	ASIA	
RISBY, William	Pte. R.M.	CAMBRIDGE	
RISEBOROUGH, James	Pte. R.M.	GANGES	
RISK, James.G.	Asst Surgeon	VANGUARD	
RISK, John.E.F.	Mate	THUNDERER	
ROACH, Richard	Ord	THUNDERER	
ROACH, Robert	Ord	RODNEY	
ROBB, John	A.B.	DIDO	
ROBBINS, Richard	Gunner. R.M.A.	PIQUE	
ROBBINS, Thomas	Pte. R.M.	POWERFUL	
ROBE, Frederick.H.	Captain. 87th Regt	HECATE	
ROBERTS, James	Carp's Mate	DAPHNE	
ROBERTS, John	Pte. R.M.	POWERFUL	
ROBERTS, John	Cook	TALBOT	
ROBERTS, John	A.B.	BELLEROPHON	
ROBERTS, John	Ord	VANGUARD	
ROBERTS, Peter	Coxswain Pinnace	REVENGE	
ROBERTS, Richard	Pte. R.M.	BELLEROPHON	
ROBERTS, Thomas	Boy	HECATE	
ROBERTS, Thomas.G.	A.B.	HASTINGS	
ROBERTS, William	A.B.	RODNEY	
ROBERTS, William	Pte. R.M.	REVENGE	
ROBERTS, William	2 borne	MEDEA	(Ord & Boy)
ROBERTSON, David	Pte. R.M.	Pcss CHARLOTTE	

SYRIA

ROBERTSON, Ebenezer	Asst Surgeon	BENBOW	
ROBERTSON, George	Ord	CAMBRIDGE	
ROBERTSON, John	Ord	CASTOR	
ROBERTSON, John	Carp's Crew	EDINBURGH	
ROBERTSON, Robert	Stoker	MEDEA	
ROBINS, Charles	Ord	BENBOW	
ROBINS, John	Pte. R.M.	IMPLACABLE	
ROBINSON, Benjamin	Q.M.	CARYSFORT	
ROBINSON, Charles	Captain. R.M.	HASTINGS	
	2nd Lieut. R.M.	VALIANT	Basque Roads 1809
ROBINSON, Edward	A.B.	REVENGE	
ROBINSON, George	Pte. R.M.	GANGES	
ROBINSON, George	Ord	HASTINGS	
ROBINSON, James	Boy	POWERFUL	
ROBINSON, James	Pte. R.M.	GANGES	
ROBINSON, John	Boatswain	BENBOW	
ROBINSON, John	M.A.A.	DIDO	
ROBINSON, John	A.B.	POWERFUL	
ROBINSON, John	Pte. R.M.	ASIA	
ROBINSON, John	Boy	HASTINGS	
ROBINSON, Joseph	Pte. R.M.	WASP	
ROBINSON, J.H.	Boy 2nd Class	CASTOR	
ROBINSON, Loftus.C.H.	Volunteer 1st Cl	MEDEA	
ROBINSON, Richard	Pte. R.M.	Pcss CHARLOTTE	
ROBINSON, Robert	A.B.	REVENGE	
ROBINSON, Robert	A.B.	IMPLACABLE	
ROBINSON, Robert.S.	Commander	HYDRA	
ROBINSON, Thomas	Gunner Ryl Arty	PIQUE	
ROBINSON, William	Q.M.	BENBOW	(M) Anchor Type LS & GC
	A.B.	CAMBRIAN	Navarino
ROBINSON, William	A.B.	RODNEY	
ROBINSON, William	Boy	HAZARD	
ROBINSON, William	Pte. R.M.	POWERFUL	
ROBLEY, Joseph	Pte. R.M.	VANGUARD	
ROBSON, John	Boy	GANGES	
ROBSON, Thomas	Capt' Fore Top	HAZARD	
ROCH/ROCK, John	Stoker	VESUVIUS	
ROCHESTER, Richard	Carp's Crew	POWERFUL	
ROCKET, Samuel	Boy	PIQUE	
RODD, Henry	Pte. R.M.	CASTOR	
RODD, John.R.	Mate	Pcss CHARLOTTE	
RODERICK, John	A.B.	RODNEY	
RODGERS, Edward	A.B.	RODNEY	
RODMON, George	Boy	REVENGE	
RODNEY, Mortimer.H.	College Mate	TALBOT	
RODWAY, William	Pte. R.M.	THUNDERER	
ROFF, George	Boy	BENBOW	
ROFF, George	A.B.	BENBOW	
ROGAN, William	Pte. R.M.	IMPLACABLE	
ROGERS, Edward	Boy	HAZARD	
ROGERS, Henry	Sailmaker	BENBOW	
ROGERS, Henry.D.	Lieut. R.N.	REVENGE	
ROGERS, James	Boy	POWERFUL	
ROGERS, John	Pte. R.M.	HASTINGS	
ROGERS, John.G.(Senior)	Carp's Crew	IMPLACABLE	
ROGERS, John.G.(Junior)	Boy 2nd Class	IMPLACABLE	
ROGERS, J.R.	Pte. R.M.	ASIA	
ROGERS, Thomas	Pte. R.M.	ASIA	
ROGERS, Thomas	Pte. R.M.	REVENGE	
ROGERS, William	A.B.	ASIA	
ROGERS, William	Ord	TALBOT	
ROLEY, Edward	Pte. R.M.	CAMBRIDGE	
ROLEY, Henry	Pte. R.M.	CAMBRIDGE	
ROLF, Jeremiah	Gunner. R.M.A.	VESUVIUS	
ROLFE, William	Ord	RODNEY	
ROLLINGS, James.H.	Pte. R.M.	STROMBOLI & THUNDERER	
ROLLINS, James	Pte. R.M.	HASTINGS	
	Pte. R.M.	CAMBRIAN	Navarino
RONTER, Edward.B.	Ord	RODNEY	
RONTER, James	Boy	THUNDERER	
ROOKE, John	Boy	VANGUARD	
ROOKLEY, Thomas	Pte. R.M.	RODNEY	
ROOM, John	Sgt. R.M.	BENBOW	
ROONEY, David	Pte. R.M.	ASIA	
ROPER, George	A.B.	RODNEY	
ROPER, John	Pte. R.M.	ASIA	
ROSCOE, James	Pte. R.M.	REVENGE	
ROSCROW, William	Boy	THUNDERER	
ROSE, Hugh	Lieut Colonel	HECATE	
ROSE, John	Pte. R.M.	HASTINGS	
ROSE, John	Gunner's Mate	POWERFUL	
	Boy	DARTMOUTH	Navarino

ROSE, William	Pte. R.M.	THUNDERER	
ROSKELLI, Thomas	Gunner. R.M.A.	RODNEY	
ROSS, David.H.	Volunteer 1st Cl	BENBOW	
ROSS, Charles	Gunner Ryl Arty	PIQUE & other vessels	
ROSS, Edward	Pte. R.M.	DIDO	
ROSS, George	A.B.	BELLEROPHON	
ROSS, George	Capt' Fore Top	REVENGE	
ROSS, H.G.	Lieut. Ryl Arty	HECATE	
ROSS, James	Ropemaker	EDINBURGH	
ROSS, John.F.	Mate	BENBOW	
ROSS, William	Carp's Crew	Pcss CHARLOTTE	
ROSS, William	Ord	BENBOW	
ROUND, Joseph	Pte. R.M.	IMPLACABLE	
ROUNDSFELL, Joseph	Boy	THUNDERER	
ROUSE, George	Boy	Pcss CHARLOTTE	
ROUSE, William	Gunner. Ryl Arty	HECATE	
ROUTER, James	Boy	THUNDERER	
ROW, Thomas	A.B.	THUNDERER	
ROWAN, Henry.S.	Lieut. Ryl Arty	PIQUE & other vessels	
ROWAN, James	Ord	DAPHNE	
ROWE, Charles	Ord	VANGUARD	
ROWE, Charles	Pte. R.M.	RODNEY	
ROWE, Edward	Purser	STROMBOLI	
ROWE, Edward.H.	Actg 2nd Master	DAPHNE	
ROWE, Frederic	Pte. R.M.	IMPLACABLE	
ROWE, George	Carp's Crew	BENBOW	*(May read RAWE)*
ROWE, G.	Ord	GANGES	
ROWE, James	A.B.	BELLEROPHON	
ROWE, John	Ord	RODNEY	
ROWE, John	Pte. R.M.	VESUVIUS	
ROWE, Richard	Capt' Main Top	BENBOW	
ROWE, Robert	Boy	MAGICIENNE	
ROWE, William	Ord	IMPLACABLE	
ROWE, William	A.B.	TALBOT	
ROWELL, William.W.	Pte. R.M.	GANGES	
ROWLAND, Stephen	Pte. R.M.	CAMBRIDGE	
ROWLAND, Thomas	A.B.	BENBOW	
ROWLANDS, John	Ord	HASTINGS	
ROWLEY, Charles.E.	Volunteer 1st Cl	CARYSFORT	
ROWLEY, Henry	Pte. R.M.	HECATE	
ROWLEY, James	Pte. R.M.	THUNDERER	
ROWSE, John	Pte. R.M.	Pcss CHARLOTTE	
ROWSE, Samuel	A.B.	PIQUE	
ROWSELL, George	Corporal. R.M.	IMPLACABLE	
RUDD, Robert	A.B.	Pcss CHARLOTTE	
RUDGE, George	Pte. R.M.	THUNDERER	
RUDGE, George	Pte. R.M.	STROMBOLI	
RUMBLE, George	Pte. R.M.	VANGUARD	
RUMBLE, William	Boy	MAGICIENNE	
RUMBOLD, James	L.M.	THUNDERER	
RUNCIMAN, John	Surgeon	POWERFUL	
	Asst Surgeon	ALBION	*Algiers*
RUNDEL, Edward	Ord	TALBOT	
RUNDELL, John	Gunner's Crew	IMPLACABLE	
RUSHEN, John	Gunner. R.M.A.	GORGON	
RUSKIN, Charles	A.B.	BENBOW	
RUSHMARK, Moses	Pte. R.M.	BELLEROPHON	
RUSSELL, Charles	Pte. R.M.	STROMBOLI	
RUSSELL, Charles	Boy	BENBOW	
RUSSELL, Edward	Q.M.	BENBOW	*(Alias George NORRIS)*
	Boy 3rd Class	St GEORGE	*Copenhagen 1801*
	Boy 3rd Class	BRITANNIA	*Trafalgar*
	A.B.	Qn CHARLOTTE	*Algiers. (M) Anchor Type LS & GC*
RUSSELL, Edward	Sailmaker's Crew	TALBOT	
RUSSELL, James.T.	Master	CYCLOPS	
RUSSELL, John	Lieut. R.N.	STROMBOLI	
RUSSELL, John	A.B.	REVENGE	
RUSSELL, John	Ord	POWERFUL	
RUSSELL, Michael	A.B.	PIQUE	
RUSSELL, Ralph	Pte. R.M.	Pcss CHARLOTTE	
RUSSELL, Solomon	Gunner. R.M.A.	MEDEA	
RUSSELL, William	Boy	REVENGE	
RUSSELL, William	A.B.	BENBOW	
RUSSELL, William	Ord	PIQUE	
RUSSELL, William	Pte. R.M.	RODNEY	
RUTLEDGE, James	A.B.	EDINBURGH	
RUTTER, Joseph	Boy 2nd Class	MAGICIENNE	
RUTTY, John	Ord	RODNEY	
RYAN, James	A.B.	HASTINGS	
RYAN, Robert	Boy	CAMBRIDGE	
RYAN, William	A.B.	THUNDERER	
RYDER, Edward	Carp's Mate	Pcss CHARLOTTE	
RYDER, George	A.B.	IMPLACABLE	

SYRIA

RYDER, Michael	A.B.	THUNDERER	
	Ord	ASIA	Navarino
RYLEY, James	Ord	PHOENIX	
RYMER, Francis	Carp's Crew	HASTINGS	
SABEY, Samuel	Pte. R.M.	ASIA	
SABIN, William	Pte. R.M.	BELLEROPHON	
SABRE, Peter	Corporal. R.M.	CASTOR	(May read SABIE)
SADLER, George	Corporal. R.M.	VANGUARD	
SADLER, Henry	A.B.	Pcss CHARLOTTE	
SAGER, Miles	Color Sgt. R.M.	HASTINGS	
SAINSBURY, Charles	Pte. R.M.	PIQUE	
SAIT, Henry	Boy	CASTOR	(May read SART)
SALIVA, Joseph	Carp's Crew	CARYSFORT	
SALMON, Benjamin	Gunner	HASTINGS	
SALMON, George	Ord	PIQUE	
SALMOND, Robert	Master	HYDRA	
SALTER, William	Bosun's Mate	EDINBURGH	
SALWAYS, Thomas	Boy	GANGES	
SAMPSON, William	Engineer's Boy	HYDRA	
SAMSON, George	Pte. R.M.	REVENGE	
SAMUELS, Richard	Ord	THUNDERER	
SANDERS, E.W.	College Mate	BELLEROPHON	
SANDERS, John	Ord	RODNEY	
SANDERS, Thomas	Ord	BELLEROPHON	
SANDERS, Thomas	Pte. R.M.	REVENGE	
SANDERS, William	A.B.	CARYSFORT	
SANDERSON, John	Mate	PHOENIX	
SANDFORD, Samuel	Pte. R.M.	THUNDERER	
SANDICOMB, Charles	A.B.	EDINBURGH	
SANFORD, John.A.	Volunteer 1st Cl	REVENGE	
SANSON, Charles	A.B.	HASTINGS	
SARGENT, Phillip	Ord	IMPLACABLE	
SATER, William	Ord	MAGICIENNE	
SATTERLEY, Samuel	A.B.	GANGES	
SAUL, James	A.B.	THUNDERER	
SAUNDERS, George	Pte. R.M.	IMPLACABLE	
SAUNDERS, George	Barber	CASTOR	
SAUNDERS, James	Ord	EDINBURGH	
SAUNDERS, John	Boy	CAMBRIDGE	
SAUNDERS, John	2 borne	RODNEY	(A.B. & Ord)
SAUNDERS, Samuel	A.B.	HYDRA	
	A.B.	ALBION	Navarino
SAUNDERS, William	Pte. R.M.	ASIA	
SAUNDERS, William	A.B.	VANGUARD	
SAUNDERS, William	Ord	GANGES	
SAUNDERSON, Charles	Gun Room Steward	PIQUE	
SAVAGE, E.	Pte. R.M.	POWERFUL	
SAVAGE, Mark	A.B.	RODNEY	
SAVAGE, Samuel	Q.M.	THUNDERER	(M) Anchor Type LS & GC
SAVAGE, William	Boy	REVENGE	
SAVELL, Richard	A.B.	PIQUE	
SAVING, James	Pte. R.M.	BELLEROPHON	
SAWYER, Daniel	Capt's Coxswain	MAGICIENNE	
SAXON, James	Ord	IMPLACABLE	
SAXTON, Benjamin	A.B.	RODNEY	
SAXTY, Henry	Pte. R.M.	THUNDERER	
SAYER, Robert.R.	Lieut. R.N.	ASIA	
SAYERS, George	Pte. R.M.	GANGES	
SCAMMELL, Thomas	Pte. R.M.	BELLEROPHON	
SCANLAN, Peter	Pte. R.M.	CARYSFORT	
SCANNELL, Jeremiah	Ord	BENBOW	
SCARD, James	Ord	VANGUARD	
SCARGILL, Henry	A.B.	GANGES	(May read SEARGILL)
SCARROTT, Timothy	Barber	REVENGE	
SCHOMBERG, Charles.F.	Lieut. R.N.	HASTINGS	
SCLATER, Richard	A.B.	HASTINGS	
SCODLEY, S.W.	A.B.	REVENGE	
SCOFFIELD, William	Boy	HASTINGS	
SCOONES, Leonard.C.	Pte. R.M.	GANGES	
SCOTT, Charles.R.	Captain. Staff Corps	HECATE	
SCOTT, Francis	Lieut. R.N.	RODNEY	(M) A of I/AVA & Baltic
SCOTT, George	A.B.	REVENGE	
SCOTT, George	Q.M.	PHOENIX	
SCOTT, Henry	Pte. R.M.	VANGUARD	
SCOTT, John	Gunner Ryl Arty	PIQUE & other vessels	
SCOTT, John	Ord	BELLEROPHON	
SCOTT, John	Ord	THUNDERER	
SCOTT, Robert.J.	Asst Surgeon	GANGES	
SCOTT, Thomas	Ord	REVENGE	
SCOTT, Thomas	Pte. R.M.	GANGES	
SCOTTEN, William	Engineer's Boy	HECATE	
SCOUGALL, Alexander	Pte. R.M.	BELLEROPHON	
SCOVELL, James	Pte. R.M.	EDINBURGH	

SCOWCROFT, James	Sgt. R.M.	PIQUE	
SCREECH, Benjamin.J.	Ord	IMPLACABLE	
SCREECH, James.C.	Capt' Forecastle	THUNDERER	
SCREECH, William	Capt' Main Top	THUNDERER	
SCRIVEN, Joseph	Boy	WASP	
SCROGGS, George	A.B.	Pcss CHARLOTTE	
SEAGREEN, Robert	A.B.	ASIA	
SEAGROVE, Charles	Capt' After Guard	POWERFUL	
	Boy	ASIA	Navarino
SEAL, George	A.B.	Pcss CHARLOTTE	
SEAL, John	A.B.	Pcss CHARLOTTE	
SEALES, Isaac	Boy	ZEBRA	
SEALEY, George	Pte. R.M.	THUNDERER	
SEAPY, Robert	Ord	VANGUARD	
SEARLE, James	Ord	CAMBRIDGE	
SEARLE, Richard	Captain. R.M.	BENBOW	
SEARLE, Robert	Carp's Crew	GANGES	
SEARLE, William.H.	Ord	HAZARD	
SEARLE, William.R.	2nd Lieut. R.M.	BELLEROPHON	
SEATRY, Richard	A.B.	POWERFUL	(M.L. as SETTREE)
SEBEC, George	A.B.	BELLEROPHON	
SECKER, William	Boy	VANGUARD	
SEDGMAN, William	Ord	CAMBRIDGE	
SEDGWICK, Henry.E.	Boy	PIQUE	
SEELING, Henry	Purser's Steward	PIQUE	
SELBY, Henry	Ord	Pcss CHARLOTTE	
SELLERS, John	Pte. R.M.	RODNEY	
SELLERS, Thomas	A.B.	IMPLACABLE	
SELLY, John	A.B.	DIDO	
SELWYN, Frederick.J.A.	Mate	ASIA	
SENCHAN, Robert	Pte. R.M.	GANGES	
SERGEANT, John	A.B.	Pcss CHARLOTTE	
SEWELL, Moses	Corporal. R.M.	EDINBURGH	
SEX, Jonathan	Pte. R.M.	HASTINGS	
SEYMOUR, John	Pte. R.M.	BENBOW	
SHACKINGER, Earnest	Drummer. R.M.	DAPHNE	
SHADWELL, Charles.F.A.	Lieut. R.N.	CASTOR	
SHALE, James	Ord	CAMBRIDGE	
SHANNAHAN, Edward	A.B.	THUNDERER	
SHANNON, James	Pte. R.M.	CAMBRIDGE	
	Pte. R.M.	GENOA	Navarino
SHARMAN, John	Ord	ASIA	
SHARP, Henry	A.B.	GANGES	
SHARP, James	A.B.	Pcss CHARLOTTE	
SHARP, John	A.B.	IMPLACABLE	
SHARP, Levey	Pte. R.M.	GANGES	
SHARP, William	Pte. R.M.	GANGES	
SHAW, John	Ship's Cook	BELLEROPHON	
	A.B.	VICTORIOUS	Victorious with Rivoli
SHAW, William	Gun Room Steward	VESUVIUS	
SHAY, Daniel	Boy	DAPHNE	(Might read STRAY)
SHEA, Henry.D.	Asst Surgeon	ASIA	
SHEA, James	Capt' Main Top	CARYSFORT	
SHEAFF, James	A.B.	CAMBRIDGE	
SHEALE, Thomas	Purser's Steward	HASTINGS	
SHEARMAN, Edward	Pte. R.M.	REVENGE	
SHEARMAN, Thomas	A.B.	CAMBRIDGE	
SHEARS, John.A.	Mate	WASP	
SHEEHAN, James	Capt' of Mast	BENBOW	
SHEEHAN, John	Royal Artillery	HECATE	(? Shoeing Smith)
SHEELER, Benjamin	Carp's Crew	CAMBRIDGE	
SHEEHAN, William	Ord	Pcss CHARLOTTE	
SHELABEER, John	Carp's Crew	RODNEY	
SHELDRAKE, William	Carp's Crew	GANGES	
SHELL, William	Drummer. R.M.	MAGICIENNE	
SHEPHARD, James	A.B.	EDINBURGH	(May read SHEPLAND)
SHEPHARD, James	Boy	POWERFUL	
SHEPHARD, Thomas	Capt' Mizzen Top	GANGES	
SHEPHERD, Charles	Boy	VESUVIUS	
SHEPHERD, Henry	Pte. R.M.	PIQUE	
SHEPHERD, John	M.A.A.	VESUVIUS	
SHEPHERD, John	Gunner Ryl Arty	HECATE	
SHEPHERD, John	Carp's Crew	CAMBRIDGE	
SHEPHERD, Thomas	Pte. R.M.	PIQUE	
SHEPHERD, Thomas	Capt's Cook	TALBOT	(M.L. as SHEPHARD)
SHEPHERD, William	Ord	BENBOW	
SHEPPARD, Jacob	Pte. R.M.	BENBOW	
SHEPPARD, James	Pte. R.M.	DAPHNE	
SHEPPARD, John	A.B.	HASTINGS	
SHEPPARD, John	Carp's Crew	HASTINGS	
SHEPPARD, Nathaniel	Ord	ASIA	
SHEPPARD, Robert	A.B.	HASTINGS	
SHEPPARD, William	Gunner. R.M.A.	HECATE	
SHERBERT, Jeremiah	A.B.	RODNEY	
SHERGOLD, Ambrose	Pte. R.M.	RODNEY	

SYRIA

SHERGOLD, George	Pte. R.M.	BENBOW	
SHERGOLD, James	Pte. R.M.	BELLEROPHON	
SHERGOLD, Thomas.H.	Pte. R.M.	STROMBOLI	
SHERGOULD, Samuel	Pte. R.M.	BENBOW	
SHERIDAN, James	Gunner. Ryl Arty	PIQUE & other vessels	
SHERLEY, Thomas	Ord	VANGUARD	
SHERLOCK, James	A.B.	POWERFUL	
SHERLOCK, James	Pte. R.M.	HASTINGS	
SHERLOCK, William	A.B.	EDINBURGH	
SHERMAN, John	Cooper	BELLEROPHON	
SHERMER, John	Pte. R.M.	Pcss CHARLOTTE	
SHERMON, George	Boy	BELLEROPHON	
SHERRIFF, Thomas	Pte. R.M.	IMPLACABLE	
SHERVILL, Thomas	Corporal. R.M.	BENBOW & CYCLOPS	
SHERWELL, Thomas	Bosun's Mate	MAGICIENNE	
	Boy	DARTMOUTH	*Navarino*
SHEWELL, William	Boy	MAGICIENNE	
SHEWEN, Edward.T.P.	1st Lieut. R.M.	Pcss CHARLOTTE	
SHIELD, Neil	Pte. R.M.	HASTINGS	
SHIELDS, Edward	Gunner	HYDRA	
	A.B.	ROSE	*Navarino*
SHIELDS, Francis	Gunner's Mate	POWERFUL	
SHINN, William	Pte. R.M.	REVENGE	
SHINNOCK, Charles	Stoker	HYDRA	
SHIPCOTT, Thomas	Ord	POWERFUL	*Duplicate issued in 1896*
SHIRLOCK, James	A.B.	RODNEY	
SHORE, Thomas	Boy	MEDEA	
SHORLER, John	Sgt. R.M.	STROMBOLI	
SHORT, James	A.B.	RODNEY	
SHORT, James	Pte. R.M.	IMPLACABLE	
SHORT, John	Gunner Ryl Arty	HECATE	
SHORT, Samuel.F.	Mate	CYCLOPS	
SHORT, William	Q.M.	MEDEA	
SHORT, William	A.B.	TALBOT	
SHORT, William	Pte. R.M.	THUNDERER	
SHORTT, Francis.H.	Mate	CAMBRIDGE	
SHOTTER, Charles	Ord	EDINBURGH	
SHOTTER, William	A.B.	RODNEY	
	Boy	GENOA	*Navarino*
SHOWYER, Thomas	Boy	ASIA	
SHRIMPTON, William	Stoker	STROMBOLI	
SHRUBSOLE, Joseph.J.	Boy	GORGON	
SHUTE, James	Clerk's Asst	GORGON	
SHUTE, William	Gunner	GANGES	
SILLMAN, William	Pte. R.M.	HASTINGS	
SILVESTER, George	A.B.	PIQUE	
SIM, Arthur.J.	A.B.	CAMBRIDGE	
SIMCOCK, Henry	Pte. R.M.	IMPLACABLE	
SIMMONDS, George	Ord	VANGUARD	
SIMMONDS, George	Barber	Pcss CHARLOTTE	(M.L. as SIMMONS)
SIMMONDS, Richard	Clerk	REVENGE	
SIMMONDS, Thomas	A.B.	GANGES	
SIMMONS, James	Q.M.	RODNEY	
SIMMONS, John	Midshipman's Cook	PIQUE	
SIMMONS, John	A.B.	ASIA	
SIMMS, George	Q.M.	VANGUARD	
SIMMS, James	2 borne	IMPREGNABLE	(A.B. & Ord)
SIMMS, John	Pte. R.M.	HASTINGS	
SIMPKINS, John	Pte. R.M.	Pcss CHARLOTTE	
SIMPSON, Charles	A.B.	RODNEY	
SIMPSON, David.J.	Purser	HECATE	
SIMPSON, George	A.B.	EDINBURGH	
SIMPSON, Henry.G.	Midshipman	Pcss CHARLOTTE	
SIMPSON, J.	Mate	ZEBRA	
SIMPSON, John	2 borne	POWERFUL	(Capt' M.T. & A.B.)
SIMS, John	A.B.	CAMBRIDGE	
SIMS, John	Pte. R.M.	EDINBURGH	
SIMS, William	Pte. R.M.	Pcss CHARLOTTE	
SINCLAIR, John	Ord	CASTOR	
SINCLAIR, Robert	Capt' Forecastle	CYCLOPS	
SINEL, Philip	Boy	ASIA	
SINGLE, Thomas	Pte. R.M.	THUNDERER	
SISSONS, Charles	Boy	POWERFUL	
SIXSMITH, John	Boy	THUNDERER	
SIXSMITH, William	Fifer. R.M.	THUNDERER	
SKILLEN, Robert	Boy	Pcss CHARLOTTE	
SKINNARD, John	A.B.	GANGES	
SKINNER, George	Pte. R.M.	VANGUARD	
SKINNER, John	Pte. R.M.	Pcss CHARLOTTE	
SKINNER, Robert	A.B.	DAPHNE	
SKINNER, Thomas	Pte. R.M.	Pcss CHARLOTTE	
SLADE, Henry	A.B.	GANGES	
SLADE, John	Pte. R.M.	IMPLACABLE	

SLADE, John	A.B.	PIQUE	
SLATE, John	Corporal. R.M.	STROMBOLI	
SLAUGHTER, George.F.	Clerk	CARYSFORT	
SLEDGE, William	A.B.	ASIA	(M.L. as SLADE)
SLEE, William	Boy	RODNEY	
SLICKLAND, John.C.	Pte. R.M.	THUNDERER	(Badly written. ? spelling)
SLEEMAN, John	Sapper & Miner	HECATE	
SLIDIVER, John	Purser's Steward	WASP	
SLIGHT, Augustus	Asst Surgeon	WASP	
SLIGHT, Julian.F.	Mate	IMPLACABLE	
SLIGHT, William	Q.M.	DIDO	(M) Anchor Type LS & GC emboldens a piece of Church plate
SLITER, James	Carp's Crew	ASIA	
SLOANE, John	Ord	THUNDERER	
SLOWLEY, W.G.	Boy	EDINBURGH	
SLUMEN, George	A.B.	RODNEY	
SMALL, Henry	A.B.	VANGUARD	
SMALLMAN, William	Pte. R.M.	BENBOW	
SMART, John	Fifer. R.M.	REVENGE	
SMART, Joseph	Fifer. R.M.	POWERFUL	
SMEDLEY, Thomas	Pte. R.M.	WASP	
SMEE, John	Sick Berth Attdt	IMPLACABLE	
SMEE, William	A.B.	VESUVIUS	
SMITH, Andrew	Ord	THUNDERER	
SMITH, Sir Charles	Colonel. R.E.	Pcss CHARLOTTE	
SMITH, Charles	A.B.	IMPLACABLE	
SMITH, Daniel	A.B.	THUNDERER	
SMITH, David	A.B.	REVENGE	
SMITH, David	A.B.	BELLEROPHON	
SMITH, Edward	Pte. R.M.	HECATE	
SMITH, Frederick	Midshipman	ASIA	
SMITH, Frederick	Pte. R.M.	EDINBURGH	
SMITH, George	Pte. R.M.	BELLEROPHON	
SMITH, George	Capt' of Mast	CARYSFORT	
SMITH, George	Bosun's Mate	HASTINGS	
SMITH, George	2 borne	HASTINGS	
SMITH, George	Purser's Steward	REVENGE	
SMITH, George	Pte. R.M.	POWERFUL	
SMITH, George	Pte. R.M.	BENBOW	
SMITH, George (1)	A.B.	Pcss CHARLOTTE	
SMITH, George	A.B.	RODNEY	
SMITH, George	Pte. R.M.	ASIA	
SMITH, Harry	Mate	VANGUARD	
SMITH, Henry	Pte. R.M.	HASTINGS	
SMITH, Henry	Captain. R.M.	BELLEROPHON	
SMITH, Henry	Pte. R.M.	VANGUARD	
SMITH, Henry	Ord	ASIA	
SMITH, Henry	Pte. R.M.	RODNEY	(Alias Wright SMITH)
SMITH, Hugh	Sgt Sapper & Miner	Pcss CHARLOTTE & other vessels	
SMITH, James	Pte. R.M.	HAZARD	
SMITH, James (b)	Surgeon	BENBOW	
SMITH, James	Purser's Steward	ASIA	
	Boy 1st Class	ALBION	Navarino
SMITH, James	A.B.	THUNDERER	
SMITH, James	Ord	IMPLACABLE	
SMITH, James	A.B.	BENBOW	
SMITH, James	Bosun's Mate	DAPHNE	
SMITH, John	Q.M.	EDINBURGH	
SMITH, John	A.B.	TALBOT	
SMITH, John	Q.M.	WASP	
SMITH, John	Gunner. R.M.A.	PIQUE	
SMITH, John	Sailmaker's Mate	GANGES	
SMITH, John	3 borne	GANGES	
SMITH, John	Pte. R.M.	IMPLACABLE	
SMITH, John	Boatswain	POWERFUL	
SMITH, John	Yeoman of Signals	IMPLACABLE	
SMITH, John	Ord	HASTINGS	
SMITH, John	2 borne	CASTOR	
SMITH, John	Corporal. R.M.	ZEBRA	
SMITH, John	5 borne	RODNEY	Three men applied
SMITH, John	A.B.	VANGUARD	
SMITH, John.J.	A.B.	Pcss CHARLOTTE	
SMITH, John.McD	Mate	MAGICIENNE	
SMITH, Joseph	Pte. R.M.	ASIA	
SMITH, Joseph	Boy	TALBOT	
SMITH, Richard	A.B.	REVENGE	
SMITH, Richard	2 Ords borne	VANGUARD	
SMITH, Richard	Pte. R.M.	STROMBOLI	
SMITH, Richard	Capt' Main Top	ASIA	
SMITH, Robert	A.B.	THUNDERER	
SMITH, Samuel	Pte. R.M.	CAMBRIDGE	
SMITH, Samuel	Pte. R.M.	VANGUARD	
SMITH, Samuel	Sgt. R.M.	GANGES	
SMITH, Samuel	Pte. R.M.	BELLEROPHON	

SYRIA

SMITH, Thomas	Pte. R.M.	HAZARD	
SMITH, Thomas	A.B.	HASTINGS	
SMITH, Thomas	Ord	Pcss CHARLOTTE	
SMITH, Thomas	L.M.	HASTINGS	
SMITH, Thomas	Ord	RODNEY	
SMITH, Thomas	Pte. R.M.	HASTINGS	
SMITH, Thomas	L.M.	REVENGE	
SMITH, Thomas	Pte. R.M.	STROMBOLI	
SMITH, Thomas	Ord	RODNEY	
SMITH, Thomas	Ord	VANGUARD	
SMITH, Thomas	Ord	Pcss CHARLOTTE	
SMITH, Thomas.J.	A.B.	THUNDERER	
SMITH, William	Capt' Main Top	THUNDERER	
SMITH, William	Gunner's Crew	PIQUE	
SMITH, William	A.B.	IMPLACABLE	
SMITH, William	Pte. R.M.	BELLEROPHON	
SMITH, William	A.B.	BENBOW	
SMITH, William	3 borne	ALBION	
SMITH, William	Capt' After Guard	CAMBRIDGE	
SMITH, William	A.B.	HECATE	
SMITH, William	Capt' Main Top	DIDO	
SMITH, William	2 borne	IMPLACABLE	
SMITH, William	Q.M.	CASTOR	
SMITH, William	Ord	EDINBURGH	
SMITH, William	Boy	THUNDERER	
SMITH, William	A.B.	ZEBRA	
SMITH, William.J.	Pte. R.M.	DIDO	
SMYHT, Robert	Sgt. R.M.	THUNDERER	
SNADEN, Peter	Pte. R.M.	GANGES	
SNAPE, Michael.J.	Boy 1st Class	EDINBURGH	
SNELL, George	Pte. R.M.	ASIA	
SNELL, John	A.B.	GANGES	(Alias John LOVE)
	Not Given	PRESIDENT	St Sebastian (see note)
SNELLGROVE, George.T.	Pte. R.M.	BENBOW	
SNELLGROVE, Isaac	Pte. R.M.	HAZARD	
SNOOK, John	Capt' Fore Top	MAGICIENNE	
SNOOK, William	A.B.	ZEBRA	
SNOW, William	Carp's Crew	CARYSFORT	
SNOW, William	Pte. R.M.	Pcss CHARLOTTE	
SOBES, John	A.B.	CAMBRIDGE	
SOFFE, Henry	Ord	VANGUARD	
SOLDATO, Antonio	A.B.	HASTINGS	
SOLE, Val.S.	A.B.	EDINBURGH	
SOLMAN, Charles	Boy	THUNDERER	
SOMERVILLE, James	A.B.	RODNEY	
SOMERVILLE, John	Corporal. R.M.	REVENGE	
SOMERVILLE, Rev Philip	Chaplain	BELLEROPHON	
SONE, Charles	A.B.	VANGUARD	
SONE, Henry	A.B.	HASTINGS	
SONE, George	Ord	VANGUARD	
SOP, John	A.B.	CARYSFORT	
SOPER, Thomas	Not Given	BELLEROPHON	
SORLEY, William	A.B.	IMPLACABLE	
SORRELL, George	Pte. R.M.	BELLEROPHON	
SOTHEBY, Edward.S.	Lieut. R.N.	DIDO	
SOUL, George	Pte. R.M.	CAMBRIDGE	
SOUTER, James	Gunner. R.M.A.	GORGON	
SOUTH, William	Stoker	CYCLOPS	
SOUTHCOTE, John	A.B.	REVENGE	
SOUTHERN, Henry	Ord	Pcss CHARLOTTE	
SOUTHEY, Job	Boy	THUNDERER	(Might read John)
SOUTHWOOD, John	Ord	RODNEY	
SOWARD, Edward	Pte. R.M.	ASIA	
SOWERSBY, John	A.B.	GANGES	
SOWTER, James	Carp's Crew	POWERFUL	
SPACKMAN, Young	Pte. R.M.	EDINBURGH	
SPAIN, William	Coxswain of Launch	CASTOR	
SPALDING, Hugh	Gunner	DIDO	
SPALDING, Richard.C.	1st Lieut. R.M.	HASTINGS	
SPANNER, Charles	Carp's Crew	BELLEROPHON	
SPARKAAS, William	Ropemaker	THUNDERER	(Alias SPARKES)
SPARKMAN, James	A.B.	GANGES	
	Boy	CAMBRIAN	Navarino
SPARKS, C or E	Capt' After Guard	Pcss CHARLOTTE	
SPARKS, Edward	Ord	THUNDERER	
SPARKS, John	Q.M.	THUNDERER	
SPARKS, John	A.B.	MAGICIENNE	
SPARKS, Samuel	Pte. R.M.	THUNDERER	
SPARKS, Thomas	Ord	BENBOW	
SPARKS, William	Ord	REVENGE	
SPARROW, James	Pte. R.M.	THUNDERER	
SPARROW, John	Drummer. R.M.	BENBOW	
SPARROW, Thomas	Pte. R.M.	IMPLACABLE	

SPARROWHAWK, George	Ord	REVENGE	
SPATMAN, John	Pte. R.M.	Pcss CHARLOTTE	
SPAWFORTH, John	A.B.	Pcss CHARLOTTE	
SPEED, Arthur.A.	Clerk	ASIA	
SPEED, John	Purser	ASIA	
SPEED, John	Q.M.	STROMBOLI	
SPENCER, Frederick	Boy	WASP	
SPENCER, James	Ord	BENBOW	
SPENCER, Samuel	Ord	BENBOW	
SPENCER, William	Ord	EDINBURGH	
SPENDER, Israel	Pte. R.M.	HASTINGS	
SPERRING, Richard	Carp's Crew	VESUVIUS	
SPETEUI, Joseph	Capt's Cook	GORGON	
SPICELY, George	A.B.	PHOENIX	
SPIERS, William	Pte. R.M.	Pcss CHARLOTTE	
SPIKEMAN, Thomas	Pte. R.M.	VANGUARD	
SPILLER, Robert	Pte. R.M.	Pcss CHARLOTTE	
SPINKS, William.H.	Carp's Crew	MEDEA	
SPITTURI, Joseph	Gun Room Cook	POWERFUL	
SPRATT, Frederick	Pte. R.M.	EDINBURGH	
SPRATT, James	Boy	CYCLOPS	
SPRINGETT, Thomas	A.B.	EDINBURGH	
SPRINGLE, James	Coal Trimmer	HYDRA	
SPROULE, Thomas	A.B.	CAMBRIDGE	(M.L. as SPRULES)
SPURINGEY, John	Pte. R.M.	THUNDERER	
SPURRELL, William	A.B.	IMPLACABLE	
SQUIRE, George.R.	A.B.	Pcss CHARLOTTE	
SQUSE, George	Pte. R.M.	STROMBOLI	
STABB, John	Ropemaker	CYCLOPS	
STACEY, John	Pte. R.M.	IMPLACABLE	
STACEY, Thomas	Supn Pte. R.M.	STROMBOLI	
STACEY, Thomas	Boy	THUNDERER	
STAFFORD, Robert	Fifer. R.M.	GANGES	
STAGG, Edward	A.B.	GANGES	
STAGG, Henry	Ropemaker	BELLEROPHON	
STAMFORTH, Henry	Ord	VANGUARD	
STAMMER, Stephen	Pte. R.M.	Pcss CHARLOTTE	
STANDING, William	Carp's Crew	VANGUARD	
STANES, Thomas	Pte. R.M.	VESUVIUS	
STANFELL, Francis.H.	College Mate	BENBOW	
STANFORD, James	Fifer. R.M.	TALBOT	
STANHOUSE, David	Q.M.	DIDO	
STANLAKE, Thomas	Carp's Mate	Pcss CHARLOTTE	
STANLEY, John	Boatswain	WASP	
STANLEY, John	Carpenter	DIDO	
STANNARD, Samuel	Ord	REVENGE	
STAPLES, Joseph	Gunner. R.M.A.	CYCLOPS	
STAPLETON, Francis	Ord	THUNDERER	
STARES, Thomas	Capt' Main Top	PIQUE	(M) A of I/AVA, SA 1853 Baltic. Vic Wide LS&GC
STARK, John	A.B.	IMPLACABLE	
STARK, William	A.B.	PIQUE	
STARLING, James	Ord	BENBOW	
STARLING, John	Capt' Forecastle	Pcss CHARLOTTE	
STARLING, Stephen	Capt' Fore Top	REVENGE	
STARLING, William	A.B.	MAGICIENNE	
STARR, George.J.	Capt's Clerk	EDINBURGH	
START, Thomas	Pte. R.M.	BELLEROPHON	
STAUNTON, James	A.B.	CAMBRIDGE	
STAUNTON, Patrick	Ord	POWERFUL	
STAUNTON, Samuel	Pte. R.M.	Pcss CHARLOTTE	
St CLAIR, Henry	Boy	HASTINGS	
STEDMAN, James	Pte. R.M.	BENBOW	
STEEL, Charles.D.	Asst Surgeon	CYCLOPS	
STEEL, Daniel	A.B.	ASIA	
STEEL, George	A.B.	POWERFUL	
STEEL, James	Pte. R.M.	EDINBURGH	
STEEL, James	A.B.	Pcss CHARLOTTE	
STEELE, Joseph	Ord	WASP	
STEER, George	L.M.	THUNDERER	
STENTIFORD, Henry	Boy	THUNDERER	
STEERS, John	A.B.	EDINBURGH	(May read SLEERS)
STEPHENS, Benjamin	A.B.	TALBOT	
STEPHENS, George.G.	Ord	REVENGE	
STEPHENS, Henry	Ord	BENBOW	
STEPHENS, John	Carp's Crew	EDINBURGH	
STEPHENS, John	Ord	RODNEY	
STEPHENS, John	Boy	GANGES	
STEPHENS, John	2 borne	VANGUARD	
STEPHENS, Nicholas	A.B.	THUNDERER	
STEPHENS, Samuel	Engineer's Boy	GORGON	
STEPHENS, Thomas	Stoker	PHOENIX	
STEPHENS, William	A.B.	IMPLACABLE	
STEPHENS, William	A.B.	CAMBRIDGE	(Alias WATKINS)
STEPHENS, William.K.	Lieut. R.N.	CARYSFORT	

SYRIA

STEPHENSON, George	Follower of Sir Baldwin Walker. Capt. R.N.		
STEPHENSON, Henry	Drummer. R.M.	POWERFUL	
STEPHENSON, John	A.B.	VESUVIUS	(& as STEVENSON)
STEPHENSON, Joseph	Q.M.	POWERFUL	(& as STEVENSON)
STEVENS, George	Capt's Coxswain	WASP	
	L.M.	ALBION	Navarino
STEVENS, Frederick.H.	Mate	MEDEA	
STEVENS, Henry	A.B.	THUNDERER	
STEVENS, James	A.B.	HASTINGS	
STEVENS, Robert	L.M.	REVENGE	(M.L. as STEPHENS)
STEVENS, William	Capt's Steward	ASIA	
STEVENS, William	Ward Room Stwd	IMPLACABLE	
STEVENSON, Charles	Boy	CAMBRIDGE	
STEVENSON, Henry	Fifer. R.M.	GORGON	
STEVENSON, Joseph	Pte. R.M.	STROMBOLI	
STEVENSON, Joseph	Q.M.	POWERFUL	
STEVENSON, William	Cooper's Crew	IMPLACABLE	
STEWARD, George	Pte. R.M.	BELLEROPHON	
STEWARD, George	Ord	REVENGE	
STEWARD, James	Capt' Fore Top	HAZARD	
STEWARD, William	A.B.	TALBOT	
STEWARD, William	Pte. R.M.	BENBOW	
STEWART, Alexander	Carp's Crew	BENBOW	
STEWART, Daniel	Stoker	CYCLOPS	
STEWART, Henry	Mate	CASTOR	
STEWART, Houston	Captain. R.N.	BENBOW	
STEWART, James.A.	2nd Lieut. R.M.	EDINBURGH	
STEWART, John (b)	Asst Surgeon	BELLEROPHON	
STEWART, John.H.	2nd Lieut. R.M.	REVENGE	
STEWART, Michael	Capt' Forecastle	ZEBRA	
STEWART, Robert	Not Given	REVENGE	
STEWART, William	Pte. R.M.	GANGES	
STEWART, William	A.B.	GANGES	
STEWART, William	Capt' Forecastle	BENBOW	
STEWART, William	Pte. R.M.	POWERFUL	
STEWART, William	Sailmaker's Mate	REVENGE	
STEWART, William.H.	Midshipman	CARYSFORT	
STIDEFORD, John	Carp's Crew	CARYSFORT	
STIDSON, Richard	A.B.	IMPLACABLE	
STIDSTONE, William	A.B.	STROMBOLI	
STILLMAN, Jonathan	Pte. R.M.	HAZARD	
STINTON, Joseph	Pte. R.M.	STROMBOLI	
STIPLING, Thomas	A.B.	CAMBRIDGE	
STIRLING, James	A.B.	BENBOW	
STOCKMAN, George	Ord	HYDRA	
STOCKS, William	Pte. R.M.	POWERFUL	
STOCKTON, Robert	A.B.	POWERFUL	
STOKES, George	Pte. R.M.	VESUVIUS	
STOKES, Henry	Mate	DAPHNE	
STOKES, John	Gunner's Crew	EDINBURGH	
STOKES, John.G.	Pte. R.M.	POWERFUL	
STONE, John	Admiral's Domestic	Pcss CHARLOTTE	
STONE, Joseph	Q.M.	HASTINGS	
STONE, Robert	A.B.	CYCLOPS	
STONE, Samuel	Engineer's Apprentice	PHOENIX	
STONE, William	Ord	THUNDERER	
STONER, Matthew	Boy 2nd Class	HECATE	
STONESHEAD, Abraham	Sailmaker's Crew	GANGES	
STOPFORD, James.J.	Actg Commander	ZEBRA	
STOPFORD, Joshua	Ord	ASIA	
STOPFORD, Sir Robert	Commanding in Chief	Pcss CHARLOTTE	as Admiral
	Captain. R.N.	AQUILON	1 June 1794 (See notes)
	Captain. R.N.	PHAETON	17 June 1795
	Captain. R.N.	SPENCER	St Domingo
	Captain. R.N.	CAESAR	Basque Roads 1809
	Rear Admiral	SCIPION	Java
STOPFORD, Robert.F.	Captain. R.N.	PHOENIX	
STOREY, Benjamen	A.B.	GANGES	
STOUSE, John	A.B.	EDINBURGH	
STOUT, John	Ord	TALBOT	
STRACHAN, Richard	A.B.	EDINBURGH	
STRADLING, William	Pte. R.M.	STROMBOLI	
STRANGE, Richard	L.M.	REVENGE	(Could read Robert)
STRANGE, Thomas	Ord	REVENGE	
STRATTON, Henry	Pte. R.M.	STROMBOLI	
STRAW, Philip	Bombdr. R.M.A.	PIQUE & STROMBOLI	
STRAWN, Thomas	Fifer. R.M.	PIQUE	
STREET, Henry	Ord	RODNEY	(May read Richard)
STREETS, Joseph	A.B.	GANGES	
STREVINS, Henry	A.B.	THUNDERER	

STRICKLAND, George	A.B.	BELLEROPHON	
STRINGER, John	Pte. R.M.	EDINBURGH	
STRINGER, Richard	Pte. R.M.	Pcss CHARLOTTE	
STRIPE, John	Ord	BENBOW	
STRODE, Augustus.C.	Volunteer 1st Cl	BENBOW	
STRODE, Frederick.T.C.	College Mate	HASTINGS	
STRONG, James	A.B.	GANGES	*(M) Anchor Type LS & GC*
STRONG, John	A.B.	DIDO	
STRONG, Robert	A.B.	BENBOW	
STROUD, Henry	Commander	ASIA	
STROUD, Henry	Ord	Pcss CHARLOTTE	
STROUD, John	Ord	THUNDERER	
STROUD, Richard	A.B.	TALBOT	
STRUGNELL, George	A.B.	HASTINGS	
STRUGNELL, John	Carp's Crew	EDINBURGH	
STUART, John.H.	A.B.	BELLEROPHON	
STUART, Thomas	Lieut. R.N.	HAZARD	
STUBBS, Frederick	Pte. R.M.	EDINBURGH	
STUBBS, Robert	Pte. R.M.	RODNEY	
STUBBS, William.H.	Ord	Pcss CHARLOTTE	
STUPART, Frederic	Asst Surgeon	RODNEY	
STUPART, Robert.D.	Mate	GORGON	
STWICH, Thomas	Corporal. R.M.	CAMBRIDGE	
STYLES, William	A.B.	VANGUARD	
STYMAN, Henry	Boy	DIDO	
SUCH, Thomas	Pte. R.M.	VANGUARD	
SUCKLING, Robert.W.	Lieut. R.N.	DIDO	
SULLIVAN, Daniel	A.B.	IMPLACABLE	
SULLIVAN, Denis	Ord	POWERFUL	
SULLIVAN, Denis	Sgt. R.M.	REVENGE	
SULLIVAN, Edward	Boy	CYCLOPS	
SULLIVAN, George	Ord	POWERFUL	
SULLIVAN, John	Carp's Crew	VANGUARD	
SULLIVAN, John	Ord	REVENGE	
SULLIVAN, John	Ord	RODNEY	
SULLIVAN, Patrick	Ord	TALBOT	
SULLIVAN, Patrick	A.B.	POWERFUL	
SULLIVAN, Thomas	A.B.	THUNDERER	
SULLIVAN, Timothy	Ord	ASIA	
SULLIVAN, Timothy	A.B.	THUNDERER	
SULLIVAN, William	Pte. R.M.	HASTINGS	
SUMMERS, Edwin.J.	A.B.	GANGES	
SUMMERS, Henry	Stoker	GORGON	
SUMMERS, John	Carp's Crew	HASTINGS	
SUMMERS, John	A.B.	BELLEROPHON	
SUMMERS, Thomas	A.B.	GANGES	
SUNDERLAND, George.H.C.	Mate	POWERFUL	
SURALL, John	Ord	Pcss CHARLOTTE	
SURGISON, William	Q.M.	BENBOW	
SURRIDGE, Samuel	A.B.	PIQUE	
SURRIDGE, Thomas	Pte. R.M.	IMPLACABLE	
SUTHERLAND, Daniel	Sailmaker's Crew	BENBOW	
SUTTON, Bartholomew	L.M.	CAMBRIDGE	*(Initials may be B.C.)*
SUTTON, Charles	Pte. R.M.	REVENGE	
SUTTON, Edward	A.B.	GANGES	
SUTTON, George	Gunner's Crew	HAZARD	
SUTTON, Jeremiah	Ord	PIQUE	
SUTTON, John	Pte. R.M.	Pcss CHARLOTTE	
SUTTON, Thomas	Pte. R.M.	RODNEY	
SUTTON, William.H.	Ord	BENBOW	
SWAINE/SWAIN, William	Bosun's Mate	VANGUARD	
	L.M.	DARTMOUTH	*Navarino*
SWAINE, Charles	Ord	Pcss CHARLOTTE	
SWAN, Edward	Pte. R.M.	VANGUARD	
SWAN, George	Q.M.	MAGICIENNE	
SWAN, Hare	Ord	Pcss CHARLOTTE	
SWASH, Thomas	Pte. R.M.	REVENGE	
SWEENEY, Denis	Pte. R.M.	REVENGE	
SWEENEY, Edward	A.B.	CASTOR	*(M.L. as SWENE)*
SWEENEY, Thomas	Ord	RODNEY	
SWEET, William	Sgt. R.M.	IMPLACABLE	
SWEETENGHAM, Charles	Ord	Pcss CHARLOTTE	
SWEETLAND, William	Pte. R.M.	RODNEY	
SWEETMAN, Austin	Ord	RODNEY	
SWEETMAN, William	A.B.	REVENGE	
SWENY, John	Boy	BELLEROPHON	
SWIFT, William	2nd Engineer	CYCLOPS	
SWINYARD, John	Bosun's Mate	CARYSFORT	
SYKES, James	Capt' Main Top	WASP	
SYMES, Thomas	L.M.	REVENGE	
SYMMONDS, James	Sgt. R.M.	THUNDERER	
SYMONDS, J.F.A.	Lieut. R.E.	HECATE	
SYMONDS, William	A.B.	CASTOR	
SYMONS, John	2 borne	RODNEY	*(A.B. & Ord)*
TABRAN, William	A.B.	POWERFUL	

SYRIA

TAGLIAVENTO, Cereaca	Pilot	THUNDERER	
TALBOT, George	Pte. R.M.	Pcss CHARLOTTE	
TALBOT, John	Q.M.	BENBOW	
TALBOT, Robert	A.B.	CARYSFORT	
TALBOT, Thomas	Pte. R.M.	REVENGE	
TALL, William	A.B.	IMPLACABLE	
TALLON, Garrett	L.M.	REVENGE	
TANDY, John	Pte. R.M.	RODNEY	(May read TUNDY)
TAMLIN, Philip	Purser's Steward	MEDEA	
TANNER, Henry	Carp's Crew	HAZARD	
TANNER, Thomas	A.B.	DIDO	
TANRANNACK, William	A.B.	BELLEROPHON	
TANSON, William.H.	Pte. R.M.	VANGUARD	
TAPSON, William	A.B.	THUNDERER	
TATCHELL, Andrew	Ord	CARYSFORT	
TATE, F.J.	Boy	POWERFUL	(Initials as squiggles)
TATTERSILL, George	A.B.	ASIA	
TAVERNER, George	Pte. R.M.	BELLEROPHON	
TAYLOR, Alexander	Gunner	TALBOT	
TAYLOR, Alexander	A.B.	BELLEROPHON	
TAYLOR, Allen	Pte. R.M.	BENBOW	
TAYLOR, Andrew	A.B.	GANGES	
TAYLOR, Edward	Bosun's Mate	GANGES	(M) Anchor Type LS & GC
TAYLOR, Edward	Pte. R.M.	REVENGE	
TAYLOR, Edward	Pte. R.M.	STROMBOLI	
TAYLOR, Frederick.F.F.	2nd Master	MAGICIENNE	
	Master's Asst	GLASGOW	Navarino
TAYLOR, George	Ord	BENBOW	
TAYLOR, George	A.B.	DAPHNE	
TAYLOR, Godfrey	Volunteer 1st Cl	CAMBRIDGE	
TAYLOR, Henry	L.M.	REVENGE	
TAYLOR, Henry	Ord	MAGICIENNE	
TAYLOR, Isaac	Pte. R.M.	REVENGE	
TAYLOR, James	A.B.	HASTINGS	(Alias John SHOULDERS) (M) Anchor Type LS & GC
TAYLOR, Jethro	Pte. R.M.	THUNDERER	
TAYLOR, John	Pte. R.M.	BENBOW	
TAYLOR, John	Ord	GANGES	
	Ord	ALBION	Algiers
TAYLOR, John	Ord	EDINBURGH	
TAYLOR, John	Gun Room Steward	IMPLACABLE	
TAYLOR, John	L.M.	REVENGE	
TAYLOR, John	Pte. R.M.	THUNDERER	
TAYLOR, Joseph	Pte. R.M.	POWERFUL	
TAYLOR, Joseph	Ropemaker	HASTINGS	
TAYLOR, J.	Pte. R.M.	HASTINGS	
TAYLOR, J.E.	A.B.	HASTINGS	
TAYLOR, Joseph.N.	A.B.	HASTINGS	
TAYLOR, Richard	A.B.	THUNDERER	
TAYLOR, Richard	Pte. R.M.	Pcss CHARLOTTE	
TAYLOR, Richard	Pte. R.M.	ASIA	
TAYLOR, Robert	A.B.	POWERFUL	
TAYLOR, Robert	Pte. R.M.	ASIA	
TAYLOR, Samuel	Pte. R.M.	WASP	
TAYLOR, Samuel	Pte. R.M.	STROMBOLI	
TAYLOR, Thomas	Pte. R.M.	PIQUE	
TAYLOR, Thomas	Pte. R.M.	POWERFUL	
TAYLOR, Thomas	A.B.	REVENGE	
TAYLOR, William	Pte. R.M.	HASTINGS	
TAYLOR, William	Pte. R.M.	DAPHNE	
TAYLOR, William	Pte. R.M.	STROMBOLI	
TAYLOR, William	Stoker	GORGON	
TAYLOR, William	Sgt. R.M.	VESUVIUS	
TAYLOR, William	A.B.	POWERFUL	
TAYLOR, William.N.	Lieut. R.N.	RODNEY	
TEE, John	Ord	POWERFUL	
TELFER, Thomas.A.	Clerk's Asst	BENBOW	
TEMPEST, John	A.B.	HAZARD	
TENNISON, Lewis	Boy	BENBOW	
TERRELL, James	Pte. R.M.	Pcss CHARLOTTE	
TERRIL, Robert	Gunner's Crew	ASIA	
TERRY, Michael	L.M.	REVENGE	
TEW, Moses	Boy 1st Class	CYCLOPS	
THAW, John	Engineer	STROMBOLI	
THAYER, John	Pte. R.M.	STROMBOLI	
THEOBALD, John	Carp's Mate	PHOENIX	
THEOBALD, William	Carp's Crew	Pcss CHARLOTTE	
THOMAS, David	Pte. R.M.	PIQUE	
THOMAS, Israel	Ord	MAGICIENNE	
THOMAS, James	Capt' Fore Top	Pcss CHARLOTTE	
THOMAS, John	Pte. R.M.	REVENGE	
THOMAS, John	A.B.	EDINBURGH	
THOMAS, John	2 A.Bs borne	RODNEY	

THOMAS, John	A.B.	CAMBRIDGE	
THOMAS, John	2 Ptes R.M. borne	GANGES	
THOMAS, John	Master's Asst	REVENGE	
THOMAS, John	A.B.	GANGES	
THOMAS, John	Ord	BENBOW	
THOMAS, Joseph	A.B.	CAMBRIDGE	
THOMAS, Joseph	A.B.	GANGES	
THOMAS, Martin	A.B.	REVENGE	
THOMAS, Silas	L.M.	REVENGE	
THOMAS, Stephen	Pte. R.M.	BELLEROPHON	
THOMAS, William	Ord	VANGUARD	
THOMAS, William	Corporal. R.M.	RODNEY	
THOMPSELL, William	Gunner's Crew	EDINBURGH	
THOMPSON, Edward	Ord	ASIA	
THOMPSON, George	Capt' Fore Top	WASP	
THOMPSON, George	A.B.	VESUVIUS	
THOMPSON, James	A.B.	Pcss CHARLOTTE	
THOMPSON, James	2 borne	ASIA	*(A.B. & Ord)*
THOMPSON, James	Ord	ASIA	*Both men applied*
THOMPSON, James	Capt' of Mast	EDINBURGH	
THOMPSON, John	3 A.Bs borne	GANGES	*Two men applied*
THOMPSON, John	Boatswain	CYCLOPS	
THOMPSON, John	M.A.A.	STROMBOLI	
THOMPSON, Michael	A.B.	REVENGE	
THOMPSON, Moses	Q.M.	CAMBRIDGE	
THOMPSON, Peter	A.B.	ASIA	
THOMPSON, Richard	Master	VANGUARD	
THOMPSON, Thomas	Capt' Forecastle	STROMBOLI	
THOMPSON, Thomas.P.	Lieut. R.N.	MAGICIENNE	
THOMPSON, William	A.B.	ZEBRA	
THOMPSON, William	A.B.	VANGUARD	
THOMPSON, William	Q.M.	EDINBURGH	*(M) Anchor Type LS & GC*
THOMPSON, Zachariah.J.	Gunner. R.M.A.	CYCLOPS	
THOMSON, Charles	Lieut. R.N.	HASTINGS (P)	
THOMSON, Daniel	Carpenter	HYDRA	
THOMSON, John	Pte. R.M.	ASIA	
THORN, James	Capt's Cook	REVENGE	*(May read THOM)*
THORN, Thomas	Pte. R.M.	POWERFUL	
THORN, William	Capt' Forecastle	WASP	
THORNCROFT, G.	Pte. R.M.	RODNEY	
THORNDYCROFT, John	Color Sgt R.M.	DIDO	
THORNE, George	Purser	BELLEROPHON	
THORNE, Philip	Pte. R.M.	EDINBURGH	
THORP, William	Lieut. R.N.	GORGON	
THORPE, John	Pte. 7th Fusiliers	HECATE	
THORPE, Samuel	Boy	TALBOT	
THORPE, Thomas.J.	Carp's Mate	ASIA	
THRALL, William	Pte. R.M.	EDINBURGH	
THRUM, G	Boy	CYCLOPS	
THRUPP, J.N.	Ord	BELLEROPHON	*(M.L. as TRIPP)*
THURSTON, Edward	A.B.	PIQUE	
TIBBS, Thomas	Boy	GANGES	
TICKELL, James	Capt' of Mast	RODNEY	
TICKNER, George	Ord	MAGICIENNE	
TIERNEY, Charles	Ord	VANGUARD	
TILBERRY, William	Q.M.	POWERFUL	
TILL, George	A.B.	VANGUARD	
TILLEY, George	Gunner	BENBOW	
TILLEY, Robert	Capt' Mizzen Top	VANGUARD	
TILLEY, William	Pte. R.M.	Pcss CHARLOTTE	
TIMMS, T.	A.B.	HASTINGS	
TINDALL, Felix	Ord	BELLEROPHON	
TINGLE, John	Pte. R.M.	GANGES	
TINKER, Isaac	A.B.	RODNEY	
TIPPETT, Joseph	Boy	EDINBURGH	
TIPPLE, John	Ord	BENBOW	
TITMAN, Timothy	A.D.	EDINBURGH	
TOBIAS, Thomas	Q.M.	CAMBRIDGE	
TOBIN, Patrick	A.B.	BELLEROPHON	
TOBREY, James	Yeoman of Signals	Pcss CHARLOTTE	
TODD, Samuel	Boy	DIDO	
TOLLERFIELD, William	Ord	HASTINGS	
TOMEY, Jeremiah	A.B.	HYDRA	
TOMKINS, John	Pte. R.M.	BENBOW	
TOMKYS, Edward	Pte. R.M.	BELLEROPHON	
TOMLINSON, John	A.B.	HASTINGS	
TOMS, James	L.M.	REVENGE	
TOMS, John	Ord	BELLEROPHON	
TONG, Henry	Bosun's Mate	ASIA	
TOOHILL, Daniel	A.B.	CAMBRIDGE	
TOOLE, Francis	Pte. R.M.	Pcss CHARLOTTE	
TOOLE, Luke	A.B.	ASIA	
TOOMEY, John	Ord	POWERFUL	
TOOMEY, John	Boy	ASIA	
TOOMEY, Thomas	L.M.	THUNDERER	

SYRIA

TOOMEY, William	Ord	POWERFUL	
TOOMY, Jeremiah	A.B.	POWERFUL	
TORRINGTON, Edward	Boy	REVENGE	
TORRINGTON, William	Ord	POWERFUL	
TOSSILL, James	Pte. R.M.	CARYSFORT	
TOUT, James	Pte. R.M.	TALBOT	
TOUT, William	Boy	DAPHNE	
TOUTE, George.R.	A.B.	GANGES	
TOVES, John	A.B.	CAMBRIDGE	
TOWER, Arthur	Mate	GANGES	
TOWNER, James	Pte. R.M.	BENBOW	
TOWNING, Charles	Boy 2nd Class	VANGUARD	
TOWNLEY, Charles	A.B.	CARYSFORT	
TOWNSEND, David	Pte. R.M.	EDINBURGH	
TOWNSEND, John	Mate	REVENGE	
TOWNSEND, William	A.B.	GANGES	
TOWSEY, George.W.	Mate	DAPHNE	
TOZER, Edward	Pte. R.M.	TALBOT	
TRACEY, Joseph	A.B.	Pcss CHARLOTTE	
TRANAH, William	Pte. R.M.	REVENGE	
TRATTLE, Edward	Ord	BENBOW	
TREAYS, Samuel	Carp's Crew	VANGUARD	
TREBEL, John	Bosun's Mate	VANGUARD	
TREE, James	Pte. R.M.	CAMBRIDGE	
TREGASKING, John	Sailmaker	REVENGE	*(M) Anchor Type LS & GC*
	Sailmaker	MUTINE	*Algiers*
	Sailmaker	ASIA	*Navarino*
TREGENNIS, William	Sailmaker's Crew	CASTOR	*Badly written. TREQUIMO (?)*
TREHERNE, Barnaby	Pte. R.M.	VANGUARD	
TRELEAR, Nicholas	L.M.	CAMBRIDGE	
TREVAIL, Phillip	Sapper & Miner	HECATE	
TREWEEK, William	Ord	PHOENIX	
TRIGGS, Angel	Boy	BENBOW	
TRIM, Abraham	Pte. R.M.	IMPLACABLE	
TRIM, John	Pte. R.M.	THUNDERER	
TRIMBY, John	Pte. R.M.	POWERFUL	
TRIMNELL, Joseph	Gunner's Mate	GORGON	
TRINES, George	Boy	STROMBOLI	
TRIVES, Robert	A.B.	REVENGE	
TRIVETT, George	Ord	HASTINGS	
TROLLIP, John	Pte. R.M.	EDINBURGH	
TROLLOPE, Henry	Mate	ASIA	
TROOD, Charles	Pte. R.M.	IMPLACABLE	
TROTTER, James	Boy	CAMBRIDGE	
TROUBRIDGE, Edward.N.	Lieut. R.N.	BENBOW	
TRUEBRIDGE, William	Carp's Crew	REVENGE	
TRUEMAN, Thomas.M.	Pte. R.M.	IMPLACABLE	
TRUSCOTT, Henry	A.B.	PIQUE	
TRUSLER, John	A.B.	Pcss CHARLOTTE	
TRUSSWELL, John	Pte. R.M.	GANGES	
TUCKER, Abel	Ord	RODNEY	
TUCKER, Abel	Ord	ASIA	
TUCKER, E.G.H.	Master's Asst	POWERFUL	*Navy List as E.J.H.*
TUCKER, George	Capt' Main Top	GANGES	
TUCKER, James	A.B.	VANGUARD	
TUCKER, Job	Pte. R.M.	Pcss CHARLOTTE & VANGUARD	
TUCKER, Joseph	Pte. R.M.	RODNEY	
TUCKER, J.B.	A.B.	CAMBRIDGE	
TUCKER, Nicholas	A.B.	CASTOR	
TUCKER, Rev William.G.	Chaplain	HASTINGS	
TUCKEY, William	Blacksmith	BELLEROPHON	
	L.M.	ACTIVE	*Lissa*
	L.M.	ACTIVE	*Pelagosa. 29 Novr 1811*
TUGWELL, George	Pte. R.M.	BENBOW	
TULLY, Robert	Pte. R.M.	EDINBURGH	
TUNBRIDGE, William	Pte. R.M.	GANGES	
TUNNEY, William	A.B.	VANGUARD	
TURLEY, Eleazar	Pte. R.M.	GANGES	
TURLEY, Thomas.J.	Ord	BENBOW	
TURNBULL, James	A.B.	EDINBURGH	
	Boy	DARTMOUTH	*Navarino*
TURNBULL, George	Boy	DIDO	
TURNBULL, Thomas	A.B.	Pcss CHARLOTTE	
TURNER, Edward	Ord	Pcss CHARLOTTE	
TURNER, George	A.B.	RODNEY	
TURNER, George	A.B.	GANGES	
TURNER, Henry	A.B.	IMPLACABLE	
TURNER, Henry	Pte. R.M.	CYCLOPS	
TURNER, James	Pte. R.M.	GANGES	
TURNER, James	Coxswain Pinnace	RODNEY	
TURNER, John	Gunner	BENBOW	
TURNER, John	Pte. R.M.	CAMBRIDGE	

TURNER, John	Capt' Main Top	IMPLACABLE	
TURNER, John	Q.M.	POWERFUL	
TURNER, Robert	A.B.	CARYSFORT	
TURNER, Robert	A.B.	CAMBRIDGE	
TURNER, Robert	Gunner. R.M.A.	STROMBOLI	
TURNER, Samuel	Boy	CARYSFORT	
TURNER, Stephen	Ord	CAMBRIDGE	
TURNER, Thomas	Gunner	POWERFUL	
TURNER, Thomas	Addtl Clerk	PIQUE	
TURNER, William	Gunner's Mate	ASIA	
TURNER, William	Pte. R.M.	GANGES	
TURNEY, William	Pte. R.M.	REVENGE	
TURPIN, Robert	Boy	THUNDERER	
TUTT, Edward	Ord	BENBOW	
TWINE, John.G.	A.B.	EDINBURGH	
TWINE, Thomas	Pte. R.M.	Pcss CHARLOTTE	
TWINE, Thomas	Pte. R.M.	STROMBOLI	
TWIST, James	Gunner. R.M.A.	MEDEA	
TWORT, William	Carp's Crew	ZEBRA	
TYLER, E.W.	Sailmaker's Crew	Pcss CHARLOTTE	
TYLER, Samuel	A.B.	GANGES	
	Boy	ASIA	*Navarino*
TYLER, Thomas	Pte. R.M.	DIDO	
TYSON, Wiliam	Boy	TALBOT	
UBSDELL, Joseph	A.B.	TALBOT	
UFFEN, John	A.B.	RODNEY	
UNDERDOWN, John	A.B.	VANGUARD	
UREN, Benjamin	Ord	TALBOT	
URQUHART, John	Surgeon	THUNDERER	
USMAR, Edward.G.	Pte. R.M.	PIQUE	
VALENTINE, John	Pte. R.M.	BENBOW	
VALENTINE, Joseph	Pte. R.M.	CAMBRIDGE	
VANCE, Richard	A.B.	BELLEROPHON	
VANN, John	Ord	CAMBRIDGE	
VANSITTART, Charles.A.	College Midshipman	GANGES	
VARLO, Berney	Lieut. R.M.	CASTOR	
VARLO, Henry	Lieut. R.M.	EDINBURGH	
VARNEY, Thomas	Pte. R.M.	CARYSFORT	
VAUGHAN, George	A.B.	CARYSFORT	
VAUGHAN, John	Boatswain	VANGUARD	
	Boy 3rd Class	MALTA	*Gaieta. 24 July 1815*
VAUGHAN, John	A.B.	BELLEROPHON	
VAUGHAN, William	Pte. R.M.	POWERFUL	
VAUGHAN, William	Stoker	PHOENIX	
VEAL, Stephen	Ord	PIQUE	
VEARY, Thomas	A.B.	STROMBOLI	
VEITCH, Harry.T.	Mate	HASTINGS	
VEITCH, James.R.	Mate	HASTINGS	
VELLER, George	Ward Room Steward	HASTINGS	
VENES, Jesse	Pte. R.M.	Pcss CHARLOTTE	
VENNING, Samuel	Boy	GANGES	
VERNON, Charles	Pte. R.M.	ASIA	
VERNON, Richard	Ord	BENBOW	
VERPUP, John	Not Given	WASP	
VERRELL, Jeremiah	A.B.	BELLEROPHON	
VERRENT, Daniel	Ord	Pcss CHARLOTTE	
VICARY, Joseph	Pte. R.M.	IMPLACABLE	
VICARY, Samuel	Pte. R.M.	THUNDERER	
VICKERS, George	Pte. R.M.	VANGUARD	
VIENNAN, John	Pte. R.M.	PIQUE	
VILE, Benjamin	Sgt. R.M.	TALBOT	
VINCENT, Alfred	A.B.	GANGES	
VINCENT, Edward	Bosun's Mate	BELLEROPHON	
VINCENT, Edward	Pte. R.M.	IMPLACABLE	
VINCENT, John	Pilot	GANGES	
VINCENT, Joseph	Coxswain Launch	GANGES	*(Additional clasp?)*
VINCENT, Robert	Ord	CAMBRIDGE	
VINCENT, William	Capt' Forecastle	POWERFUL	
VINE, James	Boy	RODNEY	
VINE, John	Ord	BELLEROPHON	
VINER, Charles	Pte. R.M.	THUNDERER	
VINES, Matthew	Pte. R.M.	Pcss CHARLOTTE	
VIRGIN, Robert	Pte. R.M.	CAMBRIDGE	
VUTTLE, John	Ord	BELLEROPHON	
VIVYAN, William.W.	Ord	THUNDERER	
VOAK, James	A.B.	EDINBURGH	
VOGWILL, John	Ord	THUNDERER	
VOKES, John	Capt' After Guard	CARYSFORT	
VOKES, William	Stoker	VESUVIUS	
VOLLER, John	Ord	VANGUARD	
VOSPER, Amos	Boy	IMPLACABLE	
VOSPER, John	Boy	RODNEY	
WADDICK, John	Ord	RODNEY	
WADDLEY, Edward	Pte. R.M.	CASTOR	
WAGGONER, Henry	Capt' Fore Top	POWERFUL	

SYRIA

WAIT, Robert	Pte. R.M.	ASIA	
WAITE, John	A.B.	CASTOR	
WAKE, Charles	Midshipman	BENBOW	
WAKEFORD, Henry	Pte. R.M.	VANGUARD	
WAKEHAM, Samuel	Ord	BELLEROPHON	
WAKEHAM, Samuel	Boy	HAZARD	(May read James)
WAKEHAM, James	Ord	MEDEA	
WAKINSHAW, James	Carp's Crew	POWERFUL	
WALDEGRAVE, William	Captain. R.N.	REVENGE	
	Lieut. R.N.	VILLE De PARIS	B.S. 1 Nov 1809
WALDRON, William	A.B.	PHOENIX	
WALE, George.H.	Midshipman	ASIA	
WALKE, John	Pte. R.M.	HASTINGS	
WALKER, Aaron	Pte. R.M.	RODNEY	
WALKER, Sir Baldwin	Captain. R.N.	Commanding Ottoman Navy	
WALKER, Edward	Ord	Pcss CHARLOTTE	
WALKER, Henry	Pte. R.M.	BENBOW	
WALKER, Henry	Carp's Crew	REVENGE	
WALKER, Samuel	Boy	WASP	
WALKER, Stephen	Q.M.	HECATE	
WALKER, William	Pte. R.M.	BENBOW	
WALL, Edward	Carp's Crew	IMPLACABLE	
WALL, George	A.B.	BENBOW	
WALL, Henry	Boy	BENBOW	
WALL, Richard.D.	Purser's Steward	BELLEROPHON	
WALL, Thomas	Pte. R.M.	STROMBOLI	
WALL, William	Pte. R.M.	RODNEY	
WALLACE, John	Ord	VANGUARD	
WALLACE, Peter	Capt' Forecastle	IMPLACABLE	
WALLACE, William	A.B.	REVENGE	(May read Wm.L.)
WALLES, Richard	Pte. R.M.	CAMBRIDGE	
WALLING, James	Pte. R.M.	RODNEY	
WALLIS, John	Pte. R.M.	BENBOW	
	Pte. R.M.	CAMBRIAN	Navarino
WALLOP, Thomas	Pte. R.M.	VANGUARD	
WALLS, William	A.B.	ASIA	
WALMSLEY, James	Gunner's Crew	BELLEROPHON	
WALSH, James	Asst Surgeon	ZEBRA	
WALSH, John	Carp's Crew	VESUVIUS	
WALSH, John	Capt' Fore Top	RODNEY	
WALTER, John	Purser	IMPLACABLE	
WALTERS, John	Pte. R.M.	BENBOW	
WALTERS, Nicholas	Pte. R.M.	GANGES	
WALTON, Charles.J.	Mate	GORGON	
WALTON, John	Pte. R.M.	DIDO	
WANLESS, Joseph	Ord	ASIA	
WANSTALL, George	Q.M.	CASTOR	
WARD, Abraham	Ord	VANGUARD	
WARD, Edward	A.B.	THUNDERER	
WARD, Henry	Ord	Pcss CHARLOTTE	
WARD, James	Carp's Crew	EDINBURGH	
WARD, James.H.	Commander	HECATE	
WARD, John	Paymaster & Purser	PIQUE	
WARD, Joseph	A.B.	THUNDERER	
WARD, Joseph	Sgt. R.M.	CYCLOPS	
WARD, William	Coxswain Launch	IMPLACABLE	
WARD, William	A.B.	ASIA	
WARD, William	A.B.	BELLEROPHON	
WARDEN, Frederick	Commander	MEDEA	
WARE, Edmund	A.B.	REVENGE	
WARE, John	Carp's Crew	HASTINGS	
WARE, William	A.B.	RODNEY	
WAREHAM, Richard	Pte. R.M.	BENBOW	
WARFORD, John	Gunner. R.M.A.	HECATE	
WARLING, J.	Ship's Cook	DAPHNE	
WARMAN, John	Ord	GANGES	
WARN, Richard	A.B.	HYDRA	
WARNE, John	A.B.	Pcss CHARLOTTE	
WARNE, Richard	Boy 2nd Class	BELLEROPHON	
WARNER, Henry	Gunner's Mate	GORGON	
	L.M.	ALBION	Navarino
WARNER, John	Painter	MAGICIENNE	
WARNER, Robert	Ord	RODNEY	
WARRE, Arthur.B.	Volunteer 1st Cl	VANGUARD	
WARREN, Charles	Ship's Corporal	GANGES	
WARREN, Charles.B.	Lieut. R.N.	MAGICIENNE	
	Midshipman	ALBION	Navarino
WARREN, Dennis	Ord	POWERFUL	
WARREN, George	Ord	THUNDERER	
WARREN, Henry	Mate	PIQUE	
WARREN, John	Ord	POWERFUL	

WARREN, John	Caulker	Pcss CHARLOTTE	
	Caulker	GENOA	*Navarino*
WARREN, Joseph	Pte. R.M.	BENBOW	
WARREN, Samuel	Boy	PHOENIX	
WARREN, Thomas	Pte. R.M.	STROMBOLI	
WARREN, Thomas	Pte. R.M.	REVENGE	
WARREN, Thomas	Pte. R.M.	THUNDERER	
WARREN, William	Pte. R.M.	Pcss CHARLOTTE	
WARREN, William	Boy	TALBOT	
WARWELL, William	A.B.	ASIA	
WATCHAM, George	Pte. R.M.	PHOENIX	
WATERHOUSE, William	Pte. R.M.	STROMBOLI	
WATERS, John	L.M.	GANGES	
WATERS, J.	Ord	RODNEY	
WATERS, William	Pte. R.M.	REVENGE	
WATERS, W.B.	Pte. R.M.	STROMBOLI	
WATHEN, Frederic	Ord	THUNDERER	
WATKINS, James	Carp's Crew	GORGON	
WATKINS, Joseph	Sailmaker's Mate	CAMBRIDGE	
WATKINS, Richard	Purser	CASTOR	
WATKINS, Samuel	A.B.	ASIA	
WATKINS, Thomas	Pte. R.M.	MAGICIENNE	
WATSON, Charles	A.B.	MAGICIENNE	
WATSON, Henry	A.B.	EDINBURGH	
	Ord	ALBION	*Algiers*
WATSON, James	Carpenter	ASIA	
	A.B.	VENERABLE	*Venerable. 16 Jany 1814*
WATSON, James	Carp's Crew	VANGUARD	
WATSON, James	Bosun's Mate	ASIA	
WATSON, James.J.	Boy	IMPLACABLE	
WATSON, John	Pte. R.M.	POWERFUL	
WATSON, John (2)	Pte. R.M.	POWERFUL	
WATSON, Joseph	A.B.	GANGES	
WATSON, Peter	Blacksmith	IMPLACABLE	
WATSON, Robert	Sailmaker's Mate	CAMBRIDGE	
WATSON, Thomas	Capt' of Mast	EDINBURGH	
WATSON, William	Boy	BELLEROPHON	
WATSON, William	A.B.	RODNEY	
WATT, Thomas	A.B.	HASTINGS	
WATTON, John	Ord	THUNDERER	
WATTS, Andrew	A.B.	Pcss CHARLOTTE	
WATTS, Charles	Pte. R.M.	IMPLACABLE	
WATTS, John	2 Ptes. R.M. borne	REVENGE	*Both men applied*
WATTS, John	A.B.	POWERFUL	
WATTS, John.T.	Pte. R.M.	EDINBURGH	
WATTS, Joseph	A.B.	ASIA	
WATTS, Joseph	Pte. R.M.	REVENGE	
WATTS, Thomas	Pte. R.M.	GORGON	
WATTS, William	Pte. R.M.	POWERFUL	
WAVENS, Thomas	Pte. R.M.	RODNEY	
WAVENS, Thomas	Pte. R.M.	VESUVIUS	
WAY, George	A.B.	ASIA	
WAYE, John	Ord	GANGES	
WAYE, Thomas	Ord	CAMBRIDGE	
WAYMOUTH, Joseph	Capt' Main Top	THUNDERER	
WEARING, John.W.	2nd Lieut. R.M.	BENBOW	
WEARN, Thomas.P.	Ward Room Steward	BENBOW	
WEATHERHEAD, John	Bosun's Mate	TALBOT	
WEBB, Daniel	Pte. R.M.	RODNEY	
WEBB, George	A.B.	POWERFUL	
WEBB, James	Boy	VANGUARD	
WEBB, Jeremiah	A.B.	MAGICIENNE	
WEBB, John	Master	DAPHNE	
WEBB, John	Pte. R.M.	HYDRA	
WEBB, John	Bosun's Mate	EDINBURGH	
WEBB, John	Pte. R.M.	GANGES	
WEBB, John	Pte. R.M.	RODNEY	
WEBB, John	Ord	CASTOR	
WEBB, Joseph	Ropemaker	DAPHNE	
WEBB, Richard	Ord	IMPLACABLE	
WEBB, Samuel.W.	Asst Surgeon	MEDEA	
WEBB, Thomas	A.B.	CASTOR	
WEBB, William	A.B.	Pcss CHARLOTTE	
WEBB, William	Pte. R.M.	HASTINGS	
WEBBER, John	A.B.	PIQUE	
WEBBER, John	A.B.	CAMBRIDGE	
WEBBER, John	Carp's Crew	ASIA	
WEBBER, Jonah	Pte. R.M.	REVENGE	
WEBBER, Matthew	A.B.	IMPLACABLE	
WEBSTER, Sir Godfrey Bart.	Lieut. R.N.	THUNDERER	
WEBSTER, Samuel	Ord	ASIA	
WEBSTER, Thomas	A.B.	REVENGE	
WEDGE, William	A.B.	HASTINGS	
WEDLOCK, Thomas	A.B.	CAMBRIDGE	
WEDLOCK, Thomas	Boy	CAMBRIDGE	

SYRIA

WEEDON, William	Pte. R.M.	CAMBRIDGE	
WEEKLY, James	Pte. R.M.	CAMBRIDGE	
WEEKS, Francis	Pte. R.M.	REVENGE	
WEEKS, George	Engineer	CYCLOPS	
WEEKS, John	Ord	RODNEY	
WEEKS, John	A.B.	THUNDERER	
WEEKS, Thomas	A.B.	RODNEY	
WEELER, Joseph	Ord	RODNEY	
WEIR, Alexander	Actg Master	IMPLACABLE	
WEIR, George	Boy	GORGON	
WELCH, Charles	Pte. R.M.	STROMBOLI	
WELCH, John	A.B.	Pcss CHARLOTTE	
WELCH, John	A.B.	HASTINGS	
WELCH, Robert.G.	Lieut. R.N.	CAMBRIDGE	
WELCH, William	A.B.	HASTINGS	
WELCH, William	Ord	POWERFUL	
WELHAM, John	Ord	ASIA	
WELLESLEY, George.G.	Lieut. R.N.	CASTOR	
WELLING, Edwin	Pte. R.M.	POWERFUL	
WELLINGTON, Henry.J.	Lieut. R.N.	HAZARD	
WELLINGTON, Peter	Actg Master	STROMBOLI	
WELLMAN, John	Ord	CAMBRIDGE	
WELLS, Edward	A.B.	EDINBURGH	
	Ship's Corporal	DARTMOUTH	*Navarino*
WELLS, Edward	Boy	EDINBURGH	
WELLS, James	A.B.	CAMBRIDGE	
WELLS, James	Pte. R.M.	POWERFUL	
WELLS, Timothy	Ord	THUNDERER	
WELLS, William	Not Given	Not Given	
WELLSFORD, Samuel	Pte. R.M.	THUNDERER	
WELMAN, John	A.B.	RODNEY	
WELSH, E.	Boy	GORGON	
WELSH, George	Pte. R.M.	BENBOW	
WELSH, John	Cooper's Crew	VESUVIUS	
WELSH, Richard	Pte. R.M.	Pcss CHARLOTTE	
WEMYSS, John.M.	Lieut. R.M.A.	CYCLOPS	
WENHAM, Thomas	Ord	ZEBRA	
WENN, Benjamin	Stoker	GORGON	
WEST, Alexander.G.	College Mate	BENBOW	
WEST, Edward	Pte. R.M.	BELLEROPHON	
WEST, Frederic	Pte. R.M.	TALBOT	
WEST, James	A.B.	CASTOR	
WEST, James	Ord	ASIA	
WEST, John	A.B.	HASTINGS	
WEST, John	Boy	ASIA	
WEST, Philip	Pte. R.M.	THUNDERER	
WEST, Samuel	Pte. R.M.	GANGES	
WEST, Thomas	Pte. R.M.	BENBOW	
WEST, Thomas	Pte. R.M.	PIQUE	
WEST, Thomas	Ord	IMPLACABLE	
WEST, William	A.B.	RODNEY	
WEST, William	Surgeon	REVENGE	
WEST, William	Coxswain Launch	CAMBRIDGE	
WEST, William	Pte. R.M.	CAMBRIDGE	
WESTCOTT, Henry	Carp's Mate	THUNDERER	
WESTLAKE, John	A.B.	VANGUARD	
WESTLAKE, Joseph	Corporal. R.M.	WASP	
WESTLAKE, William	Pte. R.M.	WASP	
WESTON, John	Pte. R.M.	STROMBOLI	
WESTON, William	Pte. R.M.	REVENGE	
WEYMAN, William	Pte. R.M.	Pcss CHARLOTTE	
WEYMOUTH, John	A.B.	Pcss CHARLOTTE	
WEYMOUTH, W.	Boy	GANGES	
WHALEBONE, John	Carp's Mate	CASTOR	
WHALING, John	A.B.	PIQUE	
WHARTON, John.A.L.	Mate	PIQUE	
WHARTON, Zechariah	Pte. R.M.	BELLEROPHON	
WHATELY, George	Midshipman	HASTINGS	
WHEATFIELD, John	Pte. R.M.	BELLEROPHON	
WHEATLEY, Joseph	A.B.	REVENGE	
WHEELER, Edward	Ord	EDINBURGH	
WHEELER, Frederick	Pte. R.M.	THUNDERER	
WHEELER, George	A.B.	Pcss CHARLOTTE	
WHEELER, Isaac	A.B.	CAMBRIDGE	
WHEELER, Richard	Boy	CAMBRIDGE	
WHEELER, William	Ord	BENBOW	
WHEELWRIGHT, Thomas	Pte. R.M.	BENBOW	
WHETTEN, Henry	Pte. R.M.	VANGUARD	
WHICKER, Joseph	Ord	BELLEROPHON	
WHIFFEN, John	Pte. R.M.	CAMBRIDGE	
WHILEY, William	Boy	REVENGE	
WHIPPLE. Thomas.G.O'D.	Mate	POWERFUL	
WHIPPS, Thomas	Pte. R.M.	ASIA	

WHITBREAD, R.	Boy	CAMBRIDGE	
WHITCOMBE, Charles.B.	Gun Room Steward	POWERFUL	
WHITCOMBE, Richard	Pte. R.M.	THUNDERER	
WHITCROSS, James.H.	Ord	BENBOW	*(May read as WHITECROSS)*
WHITE, Charles	Boy	POWERFUL	
WHITE, Edward	Pte. R.M.	PIQUE & CARYSFORT	
WHITE, George	2 Ords borne	HASTINGS	
WHITE, George	A.B.	HASTINGS	
WHITE, George	A.B.	DAPHNE	
WHITE, George	Boy	DAPHNE	
WHITE, George.H.P.	Lieut. R.N.	IMPLACABLE	
WHITE, Henry	Pte. R.M.	BELLEROPHON	
WHITE, James	A.B.	HASTINGS	
WHITE, James	A.B.	VANGUARD	
WHITE, James	Armourer	VANGUARD	
WHITE, James	2 borne	ASIA	*(Stoker & Pte. R.M.)*
WHITE, John	Pte. R.M.	HYDRA	
WHITE, John	Q.M.	CASTOR	
WHITE, John	Painter	GANGES	
WHITE, John	Ord	MAGICIENNE	
WHITE, John	Ord	BENBOW	
WHITE, Joseph	Pte. R.M.	PIQUE	
WHITE, Joseph	A.B.	HYDRA	
	Boy	ALBION	*Navarino*
WHITE, Richard.D.	Mate	THUNDERER	
WHITE, Thomas	A.B. & Gunner's Cook	THUNDERER	*One man. Two rates on Roll*
WHITE, Thomas	A.B.	BENBOW	
WHITE, Thomas	Pte. R.M.	Pcss CHARLOTTE	
WHITE, Thomas	Ord	VESUVIUS	
WHITE, Thomas	A.B.	HASTINGS	
WHITE, William	Pte. R.M.	BELLEROPHON	*(Also as WIGHT on Roll)*
WHITE, William	Pte. R.M.	THUNDERER	
WHITE, William	A.B.	VANGUARD	
WHITE, William	Ord	TALBOT	
WHITE, William	Boy	BENBOW	
WHITE, William.W.	Master	GORGON	
WHITEHART, Robert	A.B.	GANGES	
WHITEHORNE, Wiliam	A.B.	POWERFUL	
WHITEHOUSE, James	Corporal. R.M.	Pcss CHARLOTTE	
	Corporal. R.M.	DARTMOUTH	*Navarino*
WHITEHOUSE, William	Pte. R.M.	RODNEY	
WHITELOCK, G.	Boy	CAMBRIDGE	
WHITELOCK, Thomas	Ord	GANGES	
WHITER, George	Boy	CASTOR	
WHITEROD, George	Pte. R.M.	CASTOR	
WHITEWOOD, John	Gunner. R.M.A.	PIQUE	
WHITFORD, Henry	Pte. R.M.	CYCLOPS	
WHITMARSH, Stephen	Capt' of Mast	Pcss CHARLOTTE	
WHITMORE, Robert	A.B.	POWERFUL	
WHITTAKER, Joseph	Pte. R.M.	GANGES	
WHITTAKER, Thomas	Drummer. R.M.	PIQUE	
WHITTING, William	Pte. R.M.	BELLEROPHON	
WHITTINGTON, William	Boy	REVENGE	
WHITTLE, Charles	Ord	REVENGE	
WHITTLE, Thomas	Pte. R.M.	Pcss CHARLOTTE	
WHITTLE, Thomas	Ord	HASTINGS	
WHITWORTH, Charles	Pte. R.M.	HASTINGS	
WHYLOCK, James	Captain. R.M.	STROMBOLI & POWERFUL	*(Acre medal in gold)*
	1st Lieut. R.M.	MERCURY	*Off Rota. 4 April 1808*
WICKENDEN, John	Boy	WASP	
WICKER, Jesse	Boy 1st Class	POWERFUL	
WICKHAM, William	A.B.	THUNDERER	
WICKS, William	Pte. R.M.	ASIA	
WIDDECOMBE, John	A.B.	IMPLACABLE	
WIDDEN, Hugh	A.B.	Pcss CHARLOTTE	
WIEDOCK, Thomas	A.B.	Pcss CHARLOTTE	
WIDYER, William	Pte. R.M.	IMPLACABLE	
WIGLEY, George	Ord	BENBOW	
WIGHT, James	Ord	BENBOW	
WILBRAHAM, Richard	Captain. 7th Fusiliers	HECATE	
WILDISH, William	Carp's Crew	ASIA	
WILCOX, James	Pte. R.M.	POWERFUL	
WILCOX, John	Gunner	PIQUE	
WILCOX, Joseph	Pte. R.M.	BELLEROPHON	
WILCOX, Lewis	Ship's Corporal	PIQUE	*(M) Anchor Type LS & GC*
WILCOX, Thomas	Ord	BELLEROPHON	
WILD, James	Capt' Main Top	REVENGE	
WILDE, Charles	Pte. R.M.	POWERFUL	
WILDS, Edward	Boy	EDINBURGH	
WILES, William	Clerk	THUNDERER	
WILKES, Caleb	Pte. R.M.	EDINBURGH	
WILKINS, Frederick	Ord	Pcss CHARLOTTE	
WILKINS, James	Pte. R.M.	BENBOW	

SYRIA

WILKINS, John	Carp's Crew	HYDRA	
WILKINS, John	A.B.	VANGUARD	
WILKINS, John.C.	A.B.	BELLEROPHON	
WILKINS, Robert.J.	Boy	CASTOR	
WILKINS, Thomas	A.B.	Pcss CHARLOTTE	
WILKINS, William	A.B.	Pcss CHARLOTTE	
WILKINS, William	Pte. R.M.	BENBOW	
WILKINSON, Abraham	Pte. R.M.	CARYSFORT	
WILKINSON, Charles.N.	Asst Surgeon	BENBOW	
WILKINSON, Cornelius	Ord	ASIA	
WILKINSON, Edman	Pte. R.M.	BENBOW	
WILKINSON, William	A.B.	BELLEROPHON	
WILKINSON, William	Gunner	ASIA	
WILKS, John	A.B.	ASIA	
WILLCOCKS, John	Carp's Mate	CYCLOPS	
WILLCOCKS, Joshua	Ord	RODNEY	
WILLCOCKS, Robert	Ropemaker	RODNEY	
WILLCOCKS, Walter	Pte. R.M.	HASTINGS	
WILLES, John	Pte. R.M.	POWERFUL	*(May read WILLIS)*
WILLIAM, William	A.B.	RODNEY	
WILLIAMS, Benjamin	A.B.	GANGES	*(M) Anchor Type LS & GC*
WILLIAMS, Charles	Painter	CARYSFORT	
WILLIAMS, Edward	Master	PHOENIX	
WILLIAMS, Edward	Pte. R.M.	HASTINGS	
WILLIAMS, Edward	Pte. R.M.	REVENGE	
WILLIAMS, Evan	Gunner Ryl Arty	HECATE	
WILLIAMS, Francis	Ord	CAMBRIDGE	
WILLIAMS, George	A.B.	STROMBOLI	
WILLIAMS, George	A.B.	GANGES	
WILLIAMS, George	Q.M.	VESUVIUS	
WILLIAMS, Henry	Ord	VANGUARD	
WILLIAMS, James	Stoker	PHOENIX	
WILLIAMS, James	2 borne	POWERFUL	*(A.B. & Painter)*
WILLIAMS, James	A.B.	CAMBRIDGE	
WILLIAMS, John	A.B.	GANGES	
	A.B.	CAMBRIAN	*Navarino*
WILLIAMS, John	A.B.	POWERFUL	
WILLIAMS, John	Ship's Corporal	REVENGE	
WILLIAMS, John	Ord	PIQUE	
WILLIAMS, John	Pte. R.M.	IMPLACABLE	
WILLIAMS, John	4 borne	IMPLACABLE	
WILLIAMS, John	Pte. R.M.	HECATE	
WILLIAMS, John	A.B.	VANGUARD	
WILLIAMS, John	3 borne	RODNEY	*Two men applied*
WILLIAMS, John	2 A.Bs borne	HASTINGS	*(M) Anchor Type LS & GC*
WILLIAMS, John	A.B.	EDINBURGH	
WILLIAMS, John	Q.M.	BELLEROPHON	G.H. 3013
	A.B.	GLASGOW	*Navarino*
WILLIAMS, John	Gunner Ryl Arty	HECATE	
WILLIAMS, Joseph	Boy	VANGUARD	
WILLIAMS, Malcolm	A.B.	HASTINGS	
WILLIAMS, Nathaniel	Yeoman of Signals	RODNEY	
WILLIAMS, Oliver	Q.M.	IMPLACABLE	
WILLIAMS, Richard	Mate	THUNDERER	
WILLIAMS, Richard	Pte. R.M.	IMPLACABLE	
WILLIAMS, Richard	A.B.	ASIA	
WILLIAMS, Samuel	Ord	BELLEROPHON	
WILLIAMS, Samuel	Q.M.	REVENGE	
WILLIAMS, Thomas	2 Ords borne	RODNEY	*Both men applied*
WILLIAMS, Thomas	Pte. R.M.	MAGICIENNE	
WILLIAMS, Thomas	A.B.	HASTINGS	
WILLIAMS, Thomas	A.B.	IMPLACABLE	
WILLIAMS, Thomas	A.B.	STROMBOLI	
WILLIAMS, William	Boy	CASTOR	
WILLIAMS, William	3 borne	RODNEY	*Two men applied*
WILLIAMS, William	Not Given	RODNEY	
	Not Given	GENOA	*Navarino*
WILLIAMS, William	Capt' Forecastle	REVENGE	
WILLIAMS, William	Capt' After Guard	ASIA	
WILLIAMS, William	Ord	EDINBURGH	
WILLIAMS, William	Ord	THUNDERER	
WILLIAMS, William	Carp's Crew	REVENGE	
WILLIAMS, Woodford.J.	Commander	STROMBOLI	
	College Midshipman	ROSE	*Navarino*
WILLIAMS, Zacharia	Pte. R.M.	BENBOW	
WILLIAMSON, James	L.M.	REVENGE	
WILLIAMSON, John	Capt's Coxswain	CARYSFORT	
	Boy	DARTMOUTH	*Navarino*
WILLIAMSON, Peter	Ord	CASTOR	
WILLIAMSON, William	Gunner's Crew	GANGES	
	Gunner's Crew	ASIA	*Navarino*
WILLIS, George	Pte. R.M.	Pcss CHARLOTTE	
WILLIS, George	Pte. R.M.	STROMBOLI	

WILLIS, William	Pte. R.M.	EDINBURGH	
WILLIS, William	Pte. R.M.	HASTINGS	
WILLISFORD, John	Boy 1st Class	GANGES	
WILLISON, John	Capt' Fore Top	DAPHNE	
WILLMOT, Samuel	Pte. R.M.	REVENGE	
WILLMOTT, William	Stoker	GORGON	
WILLOUGHBY, Samuel	Capt' of Mast	VANGUARD	
WILLS, Frederick	2nd Master	REVENGE	
WILLS, George	Capt' Fore Top	TALBOT	
WILLS, John	Ropemaker	PIQUE	
WILLSON, John	Boy	ASIA	
WILLSON, Thomas	3 borne	Pcss CHARLOTTE	(2 A.Bs & Ord)
WILLSON, William	A.B.	CARYSFORT	
WILLTON, William	Boy	MAGICIENNE	
WILMORE, George	Capt's Coxswain	ZEBRA	
	A.B.	FURY	Algiers
WILMOT, Arthur.P.E.	Lieut. R.N.	POWERFUL	
WILMOT, John	A.B.	HYDRA	
WILMOT, John	Ord	PIQUE	
WILSON, Alexander	Asst Surgeon	WASP	
WILSON, David	Gunner. R.M.A.	PIQUE	
WILSON, George	Master	MEDEA	
	Master's Asst	ALBION	Navarino
WILSON, George	Capt' Main Top	Pcss CHARLOTTE	(Alias David HAWSON)
WILSON, Horatio	Boy	EDINBURGH	
WILSON, James.K.	1st Lieut. R.M.	Pcss CHARLOTTE	
WILSON, Jeffery	Ord	BENBOW	
WILSON, John	Surgeon	VANGUARD	
WILSON, John	A.B.	Pcss CHARLOTTE	
WILSON, Rev Roland	Chaplain	EDINBURGH	
WILSON, Samuel	Pte. R.M.	ASIA	
WILSON, Thomas	Sailmaker	BELLEROPHON	
WILSON, Thomas	Boy	REVENGE	
WILSON, Thomas	Boy	Pcss CHARLOTTE	
WILSON, William	Painter	CARYSFORT	
WILSON, William	A.B.	THUNDERER	
WILSON, William	A.B.	HASTINGS	(M) Anchor Type LS & GC
WILSON, William	Ord	BELLEROPHON	
WIMBLE, James	A.B.	MEDEA	
WINDEBANK, Edward	Ord	BENBOW	
WINDEBANKE, James	Gunner's Mate	ASIA	
WINDLE, John	Boy	Pcss CHARLOTTE	
WINDSOR, George	A.B.	GANGES	
	Gunner's Crew	GLASGOW	Navarino
WINDSOR, Henry	Blacksmith	DAPHNE	
WINDSOR, William	Ord	HASTINGS	(May read WINDSORM)
WINDSOR, William.H.	Boy	Pcss CHARLOTTE	
WINES, William	Pte. R.M.	RODNEY	
WINFIELD, Joseph	Pte. R.M.	VANGUARD	
WINGFIELD, George	Boy	TALBOT	
WINGFIELD, John	Actg Cook	CASTOR	
WINGHAM, Adam	Capt' Fore Top	RODNEY	
WINLO, George.W.	Lieut. R.N.	IMPLACABLE	
WINN, John	Cooper	Pcss CHARLOTTE	
WINNACOTT, Robert	Boy	Pcss CHARLOTTE	
WINSOR, Daniel	A.B.	IMPLACABLE	
WINSOR, William	A.B.	GANGES	
WINSTON, John	Pte. R.M.	POWERFUL	
WINTER, Charles	A.B.	VANGUARD	
WINTHROP, George.T.S.	Midshipman	VESUVIUS	
WINTHROP, Hay.E.S.	Lieut. R.N.	CASTOR	
WINTON, William	Stoker	MEDEA	
WINWOOD, Thomas	A.B.	GANGES	
WISDOM, John	Ord	Pcss CHARLOTTE	
WISDOM, Richard	Boy	BENBOW	
WISE, Benjamin	Pte. R.M.	PIQUE	
WISE, Charles.A.	Volunteer 1st Cl	VESUVIUS	
WISE, George.H.L.	Clerk	DIDO	
WISE, John	Boy	MAGICIENNE	
WISE, William	Pte. R.M.	PIQUE	
WISEMAN, Sir William	Lieut. R.N.	VANGUARD	
WISEMAN, William.H.	Tempy Clerk	Pcss CHARLOTTE	
WITCHER, William	Boy 1st Class	POWERFUL	
WITHERS, John	Boy	VANGUARD	
WITMAN, Robert	A.B.	POWERFUL	
WITTCOMBE, William	Ord	BELLEROPHON	
WITTEREN, William	Capt' After Guard	BENBOW	(Additional clasp?)
WOLFINDEN, George	Pte. R.M.	REVENGE	
WOLSGROVE, Joseph	Sgt. R.M.	BELLEROPHON	
WOOD, Alfred	Boy 2nd Class	PIQUE	
WOOD, Charles.O.	College Mate	BELLEROPHON	
WOOD, David	Q.M.	REVENGE	
WOOD, Edward	Boy	GANGES	
WOOD, Francis	A.B.	RODNEY	
WOOD, Henry	Pte. R.M.	POWERFUL	

SYRIA

WOOD, James	Boy	Pcss CHARLOTTE	
WOOD, James	Capt' Forecastle	IMPLACABLE	
WOOD, John	Cook	CYCLOPS	
WOOD, John	Ord	GANGES	
WOOD, John	Capt' Forecastle	IMPLACABLE	(M) Anchor Type LS & GC
WOOD, John	Pte. R.M.	PIQUE	
WOOD, John	Pte. R.M.	REVENGE	
WOOD, J.P.	Pte. R.M.	STROMBOLI	(Alias PITWOOD)
WOOD, Peter	Ord	ZEBRA	
WOOD, Richard	Volunteer	THUNDERER	
WOOD, Thomas	Boy 2nd Class	GANGES	
WOOD, Thomas	A.B.	Pcss CHARLOTTE	
	L.M.	HECLA	Algiers
WOOD, William	A.B.	REVENGE	
WOOD, William	Mate	MAGICIENNE	
WOODCOCK, R.H.	Ord	EDINBURGH	
WOODFORD, John	Ord	BENBOW	
WOODGER, William	2nd Master	HASTINGS	
WOODHOUSE, Henry	A.B.	EDINBURGH	
WOODHOUSE, Isaac	Carp's Crew	REVENGE	
WOODHOUSE, John	Pte. R.M.	GANGES	
WOODHOUSE, Richard	A.B.	Pcss CHARLOTTE	
WOODLEY, Augustus.J.	Mate	REVENGE	
WOODMAN, James	Gunner	WASP	
WOODMAN, Joseph	Boy 1st Class	ASIA	
WOODROW, Frederick	M.A.A.	CAMBRIDGE	(M) Anchor Type LS & GC
WOODRUFF, Henry	Ord	EDINBURGH	
WOODRUFF, Morris	A.B.	EDINBURGH	(M.L. as WOODRIFFE)
WOODRUFF, William	Ord	REVENGE	
WOODS, James	Bosun's Mate	GANGES	
WOODS, William	A.B.	GORGON	
WOODTHORP, William	Purser's Steward	MAGICIENNE	
WOODWARD, Joseph	Corporal. R.M.	IMPLACABLE	
WOODWARD, Joseph	Pte. R.M.	CAMBRIDGE	
WOODWARD, Thomas	Pte. R.M.	HASTINGS	
WOODWARD, Thomas	Purser	WASP	
WOODYER, Joseph	Pte. R.M.	REVENGE	
WOOLBY, Thomas	A.B.	HASTINGS	
WOOLCOMBE, Walter	Sgt. R.M.	RODNEY	
WOOLDRIDGE, John	Gunner's Crew	IMPLACABLE	
WOOLLETT, John	Ord	CYCLOPS	
WOOLLEY, Joseph	Pte. R.M.	Pcss CHARLOTTE	
WOOLLEY, Joseph	Pte. R.M.	REVENGE	
	Pte. R.M.	GENOA	Navarino
WOOLRIDGE, William	A.B.	BELLEROPHON	
WOOLRIDGE, William	Yeoman of Signals	DAPHNE	
WOOLS, William	Pte. R.M.	HASTINGS	
WOOLVET, Thomas	Coxswain Pinnace	ASIA	
WOOTTEN, Joseph.J.	A.B.	HASTINGS	
WOOTTON, William	Not Given	THUNDERER	
WORKMAN, William	Ord	ASIA	
WORSTER, William	Ord	CAMBRIDGE	
WORTH, Henry.J.	Commander	HASTINGS	(M) A of I/AVA. Liffey
	Midshipman	VENERABLE	Venerable. 16 Jany 1814
WORTH, William	Pte. R.M.	TALBOT	
WORTHY, John	A.B.	CARYSFORT	
WOTTLEY, Thomas	Pte. R.M.	BENBOW	
WRATTON, W.G.	Engineer	GORGON	(Also as RATTON)
WRAY, James	Pte. R.M.	GANGES	
WRIGHT, George	Master	DIDO	
WRIGHT, George	Boy	EDINBURGH	
WRIGHT, Henry	Pte. R.M.	STROMBOLI	
WRIGHT, Henry	Ord	EDINBURGH	
WRIGHT, Henry	Ord	BELLEROPHON	
WRIGHT, James	Armourer	VANGUARD	
WRIGHT, James	Pte. R.M.	PIQUE	
WRIGHT, James	Boy	CASTOR	
WRIGHT, John	Color Sgt. R.M.	BELLEROPHON	
WRIGHT, John	Pte. R.M.	POWERFUL	
WRIGHT, John	Carp's Crew	GANGES	
WRIGHT, John	A.B.	REVENGE	
WRIGHT, Joseph	Ord	CASTOR	
WRIGHT, Philip	Capt of Top	HECATE	
WRIGHT, Richard	A.B.	CAMBRIDGE	
WRIGHT, Sydney.E.	Boy 2nd Class	HASTINGS	
WRIGHT, Thomas	A.B.	IMPLACABLE	
WRIGHT, William	A.B.	POWERFUL	
WRIGHT, William	Pte. R.M.	POWERFUL	
WRIGHT, William	Admiral's Domestic	Pcss CHARLOTTE	
WRIGHT, William	A.B.	Pcss CHARLOTTE	
WRIGHT, William.A.G.	2nd Lieut. R.M.	VANGUARD	
WRIGHTON, Edward	Blacksmith	ASIA	
WRIGHTON, William	Ord	ASIA	

WRITTON, Edward	Boy 1st Class	CARYSFORT	
WURR, Benjamen	Pte. R.M.	POWERFUL	
WYATT, George	Boy	ASIA	
WYATT, John	Boy	REVENGE	
WYATT, William	A.B.	POWERFUL	
WYATT, William	A.B.	VANGUARD	
WYATT, William	A.B.	DAPHNE	
WYBURN, John	A.B.	DAPHNE	*(M) Anchor Type LS&GC (WYBORN)*
WYLES, James	Stoker	VESUVIUS	
WYLES, William	Pte. R.M.	HASTINGS	
WYLIE, William	Q.M.	HASTINGS	
WYLEY, William	Boy	REVENGE	
WYNHALL, Robert	Boy	THUNDERER	
WYPPE, Robert	Pte. R.M.	HECATE	
YARNOLD, Thomas	Pte. R.M.	RODNEY	
YATES, James	Pte. R.M.	Pcss CHARLOTTE	
YATES, John	Pte. R.M.	BENBOW	
YEATES, John.G.	Volunteer 1st Cl	THUNDERER	
YELLAND, George	A.B.	VANGUARD	
YELLAND, William	Q.M.	CARYSFORT	
YEO, Edward	Q.M.	GANGES	
YEO, George	Boy	IMPLACABLE	
YEO, John	Pte. R.M.	IMPLACABLE	
YEOMAN, William	A.B.	HYDRA	
YEOMANS, John	Pte. R.M.	THUNDERER	
YONGE, Frederick.D.	Mate	Pcss CHARLOTTE	
YOULE, William	Ord	CAMBRIDGE	
YOUNG, Benjamin	A.B.	EDINBURGH	
YOUNG, Edward	A.B.	VANGUARD	
YOUNG, Edward	Q.M.	ASIA	
YOUNG, George	Stoker	STROMBOLI	
YOUNG, George	A.B.	CAMBRIDGE	
YOUNG, Henry	Boy	EDINBURGH	
YOUNG, Jacob	Pte. R.M.	BELLEROPHON	
	Pte. R.M.	ALBION	*Navarino*
YOUNG, James	A.B.	BELLEROPHON	
YOUNG, James	Sgt. R.M.	ASIA	
YOUNG, James	Pte. R.M.	THUNDERER	
YOUNG, John	Gunner. R.M.A.	PIQUE	
YOUNG, John (2)	Pte. R.M.	PIQUE	
YOUNG, John	Ord	REVENGE	
YOUNG, Peter	Corporal. R.M.	Pcss CHARLOTTE	
YOUNG, Robert	A.B.	VANGUARD	
YOUNG, Thomas	A.B.	Pcss CHARLOTTE	
YOUNG, William	Ord	BENBOW	
YOUNG, William.A.	Purser's Steward	CARYSFORT	
YOUNG, William.B.	Secretary's Clerk	Pcss CHARLOTTE	
YOUNGHUSBAND, George	A.B.	VANGUARD	
YULE, John	Master	BENBOW	
ZAARO, Gayton	A.B.	THUNDERER	
ZAMITT, Antonio	Gun Room Cook	REVENGE	
	Gun Room Cook	ROSE	*Navarino*
ZEMBY, Frederic	Young Gentleman's Stwd	REVENGE	

ABBREVIATIONS

@	Alias	N.O.R.	Not on ADM 171/1-3 Roll
A of I	Army of India	N' yet F'	Not yet found on M.L.
Acct Gen	Accountant General	(P)	Officer Promoted. Wholly/partially responsible for creation of clasp.
Adm Mid	Admiralty Midshipman		
Aft Gd	After Guard (= Quarter Deck)		
		Pdr.	Powder
Appld	Applied for award	P.O.W.	Prisoner of War
Armr	Armourer	Qtr	Quarter
Asst	Assistant	Q.M.	Quarter Master
Awd	Awarded	Recd & Revd	Received
B.S.	Boat Service		
Ck	Cook	R.M.	Used throughout Roll although 'Royal' prefix did not pre-date 1802
Cmmdg	Commanding		
Dtd	Dated		
Fnd	Found	'Run'	Deserted. Notation could be rescinded ('removed')
F.Top	Fore Top		
F.X.	Forecastle	Secy	Secretary
G.H.	Greenwich Hospital (ADM 73/93)	Slmkr	Sailmaker
		Sly Wnd	Slightly wounded
(G.M.)	Gold Medal Action	Svly Wnd	Severely wounded
I/Cmd	In Command	SLVO	Supernumerary List Victuals only
L.M.	Landsman		
(M)	Additional medal(s)	SLWV	Supn' List Wages & Victuals
M.G.S.	Military General Service	Supn	Supernumerary
M.I.D.	Mention in Despatches	VA-NOR	Verified aboard. Not on Roll
M.A.A.	Master at Arms	Vfd Abd	Verified aboard
M.L.	Muster List/Book (ADM 36/- & 37/-)	Vol or Volt	Volunteer
		W.O.	Warrant Officer
M or Mn.Top	Main Top	Yeo	Yeoman

INDEX

Clasp Title: number awarded	( )	Page	Clasp Title: number awarded	( )	Page
			BOAT SERVICE ACTIONS		
ACHERON 3 Feby 1805	(2)	95	27 Oct 1800	(5)	66
ACRE 30 May 1799	(51)	59	21 July 1801	(7)	93
ALGIERS (27 Augt 1816)	(1328)	275	27 June 1803	(5)	93
AMANTHEA 25 July 1810	(23)	213	4 Nov 1803	(1)	94
AMAZON 13 Jany 1797	(6)	30	4 Feb 1804	(10)	94
AMAZON 13 March 1806	(30)	140	4 June 1805	(10)	96
AMETHYST Wh THETIS			16 July 1806	(52)	142
(10 Nov 1808)	(31)	159	2 Jan 1807	(3)	148
AMETHYST 5 April 1809	(27)	173	21 Jan 1807	(8)	148
ANHOLT 27 March 1811	(40)	222	19 April 1807	(nil)	148
ANN 24 Novr 1807	(nil)	150	13 Feb 1808	(2)	150
ANSE LA BARQUE			10 July 1808	(8)	156
18 Decr 1809	(52)	195	11 Aug 1808	(17)	156
ANSON 23 Augt 1806	(11)	145	28 Nov 1808	(2)	160
ARETHUSA 23 Augt 1806	(17)	144	7 July 1809	(35)	188
ARROW 13 Septr 1799	(2)	61	14 July 1809	(7)	189
ARROW 3 Feby 1805	(8)	95	25 July 1809(a)	(nil)	189
ARROW 6 April 1811	(nil)	222	25 July 1809(b)	(36)	190
ASTRAEA 10 April 1795	(2)	18	27 July 1809	(10)	191
BANDA NEIRA			29 July 1809	(11)	191
(9 Augt 1810)	(68)	213	28 Aug 1809	(15)	191
BASQUE ROADS 1809			1 Nov 1809	(110)	192
(11 April)	(529)	174	13 Dec 1809	(9)	194
BEAVER 31 March 1804	(nil)	94	13 Feb 1810	(20)	209
BLANCHE 4 Jany 1795	(5)	15	1 May 1810	(15)	210
BLANCHE 19 Decr 1796	(4)	29	28 June 1810	(26)	211
BLANCHE 19 July 1806	(22)	144	27 Sep 1810	(36)	216
BOADICEA 18 Septr 1810	(15)	215	4 Nov 1810	(1)	217
			23 Nov 1810	(42)	217
BOAT SERVICE ACTIONS			24 Dec 1810	(6)	218
(Engraved details may differ)			4 May 1811	(10)	223
15 Mar 1793	(1)	1	30 July 1811	(4)	225
17 Mar 1794	(29)	2	2 Aug 1811	(9)	226
29 May 1797	(3)	39	20 Sep 1811	(6)	239
9 June 1799	(4)	60	4 Dec 1811	(19)	241
20 Dec 1799	(3)	62	4 April 1812	(4)	244
29 July 1800	(4)	64	1 & 18 Sep 1812	(21)	247
29 Aug 1800	(25)	65	17 Sep 1812	(11)	248

Clasp Title: number awarded	( )	Page
BOAT SERVICE ACTIONS		
29 Sep 1812	(25)	248
6 Jan 1813	(25)	249
21 Mar 1813	(3)	250
29 April 1813(a)	(2)	250
Ap & May 1813 or		
29 April 1813(b)	(57)	251
2 May 1813	(48)	252
8 April 1814	(24)	265
24 May 1814	(12)	265
3 & 6 Sep 1814	(1)	268
14 Dec 1814	(205)	268
BONNE CITOYENNE Wh		
FURIEUSE (6 July 1809)	(12)	188
BRISEIS 14 Octr 1810	(2)	217
CAMPERDOWN		
(11 Oct 1797)	(298)	40
CAPTURE OF THE		
DESIREE (8 July 1800)	(24)	64
CARRIER 4 Novr 1807	(1)	149
CARYSFORT 29 May 1794	(nil)	2
CASTOR 17 June 1809	(13)	186
CENTAUR 26 Augt 1808	(42)	157
CENTURION 18 Sept 1804	(12)	95
CHEROKEE 10 Jany 1810	(4)	197
CHERUB 28 March 1814	(7)	264
CHILDERS 14 March 1808	(4)	151
COMET 11 Augt 1808	(4)	156
COMUS 15 Augt 1807	(10)	149
CONFIANCE 14 Jany 1809	(8)	161
COPENHAGEN 1801		
(2 April)	(555)	78
COURIER 22 Novr 1799	(3)	62
CRESCENT 20 Octr 1793	(12)	1
CRUIZER 1 Novr 1808	(4)	159
CURACOA (1 Jan 1807)	(62)	146
CYANE 25 & 27 June 1809	(5)	187
CYANE 16 Jany 1814	(7)	261
DIANA 11 Septr 1809	(8)	192
DIDO 24 June 1795	(1)	26
DRYAD 13 June 1796	(6)	28
EGYPT (8 March – 2 Sept 1801)	(618)	66
EMERALD 13 March 1808	(10)	151
ENDYMION Wh		
PRESIDENT		
(15 Jan 1815)	(58)	272
ESPOIR 7 Augt 1798	(1)	56
ESPOIR 25 & 27 June 1809	(5)	188
EUROTAS 25 Feby 1814	(32)	261
FAIRY 5 Feby 1800	(4)	62
FIRM 24 April 1810	(1)	210
FISGARD 20 Octr 1798	(9)	58

Clasp Title: number awarded	( )	Page
GAIETA 24 July 1815	(89)	273
GLUCKSTADT		
5 Jany 1814	(44)	259
GRASSHOPPER		
24 April 1808	(7)	153
GRIFFON 27 March 1812	(3)	244
GROWLER 22 May 1812	(1)	246
GUADALOUPE (28 Jan –		
5 Feb 1810)	(483)	197
GUT OF GIBRALTAR		
12 July 1801	(144)	89
HARPY 5 Feby 1800	(4)	62
HAWKE 18 Augt 1811	(6)	226
HEBRUS WITH		
L'ETOILE		
(27 March 1814)	(40)	262
HORATIO 10 Feby 1809	(13)	173
HUSSAR 17 May 1795	(1)	18
HYDRA 6 Augt 1807	(12)	149
IMPLACABLE		
26 Augt 1808	(44)	158
INDEFATIGABLE		
20 April 1796	(8)	27
INDEFATIGABLE		
13 Jany 1797	(10)	29
ISLE ST MARCOU		
6 May 1798	(3)	47
JAVA (18 Sept 1811)	(665)	226
1 JUNE 1794		
(Howe's Action)	(540)	3
17 JUNE 1795		
(Cornwallis' retreat)	(49)	19
23rd JUNE 1795		
(Bridport's Action)	(182)	20
LAPWING 3 Decr 1796	(2)	28
LION 15 July 1798	(23)	47
LISSA (13 March 1811)	(124)	218
LIVELY 13 March 1795	(6)	15
LOCUST 11 Novr 1811	(2)	239
LONDON 13 March 1806	(27)	141
LOUISA 28 Octr 1807	(1)	149
LOWESTOFFE		
24 June 1795	(6)	26
MALAGA 29 April 1812	(19)	244
14 MARCH 1795		
(Hotham's Action)	(97)	15
MARS 21 April 1798	(26)	46
MARTINIQUE		
(24 Feb 1809)	(486)	161
MINERVE 19 Decr 1796	(4)	29
MOSQUITO 9 June 1795	(nil)	18
NASSAU 22 March 1808	(31)	152

Clasp Title: number awarded	( )	Page	Clasp Title: number awarded	( )	Page
NAVARINO (20 Oct 1827)	(1142)	296	SCHIERMONNIKOOG		
NILE (1 Augt 1798)	(326)	48	12 Aug 1799	(9)	61
NORTHUMBERLAND			SCORPION 31 March 1804	(4)	94
22 May 1812	(63)	245	SCORPION 12 Jany 1810	(8)	197
4 NOVR 1805			SEAHORSE Wh BADERE		
(Strachan's Action)	(296)	126	ZAFFERE (5/6 July 1808)	(32)	155
NYMPHE 18 June 1793	(4)	1	SEALARK 21 July 1812	(4)	247
NYMPHE 8 March 1797	(5)	39	SEINE 20 Augt 1800	(7)	65
12 OCTR 1798			SHANNON Wh		
(Warren's Action)	(78)	56	CHESAPEAKE		
OFF MARDOE 6 July 1812	(47)	246	(1 June 1813)	(42)	253
OFF ROTA 4 April 1808	(19)	153	SIRIUS 17 April 1806	(20)	142
OFF TAMATAVE			SKYLARK 11 Novr 1811	(4)	239
20 May 1811	(87)	223	SOUTHAMPTON		
OFF THE PEARL ROCK			9 June 1796	(8)	28
13 Dec 1808	(16)	160	SPARTAN 3 May 1810	(30)	211
ONYX 1 Jany 1809	(5)	161	SPEEDY 6 Novr 1799	(3)	61
OTTER 18 Septr 1810	(8)	215	SPEEDY 6 May 1801	(7)	89
PASLEY 28 Octr 1801	(4)	93	SPIDER 25 Augt 1795	(1)	26
PELAGOSA 29 Novr 1811	(74)	239	STATELY 22 March 1808	(31)	151
PELICAN 14 Augt 1813	(4)	254	STAUNCH 18 Sepr 1810	(2)	215
PENELOPE 30 March 1800	(11)	63	SUPERIEURE		
PETEREL 21 March 1800	(2)	63	10 Feby 1809	(1)	173
PHOEBE 21 Decr 1797	(5)	46	SURLY 24 April 1810	(1)	210
PHOEBE 19 Feby 1801	(6)	66	SURPRISE WITH		
PHOEBE 28 March 1814	(36)	263	HERMIONE		
PHOENIX 10 Augt 1805	(29)	97	(25 Oct 1799)	(7)	61
PICKLE 3 Jany 1807	(2)	148	SYBILLE 28 Feby 1799	(12)	59
PIQUE 26 March 1806	(8)	141	SYLPH 28 Sepr 1801	(2)	93
POMPEE 17 June 1809	(47)	184	SYLVIA 26 April 1810	(1)	210
PORT SPERGUI			SYRIA (10 Sept –		
17 March 1796	(4)	26	4 Nov 1840)	(6978)	313
RAPID 24 April 1808	(1)	154	TELEGRAPH		
RECRUIT 17 June 1809	(7)	187	18 March 1799	(nil)	59
REDWING 7 May 1808	(7)	154	TERPSICHORE		
REDWING 31 May 1808	(7)	155	13 Octr 1796	(3)	28
ROMNEY 17 June 1794	(2)	15	THE POTOMAC		
ROSARIO 27 March 1812	(7)	243	17 Aug 1814	(108)	266
ROYALIST			THETIS 17 May 1795	(3)	18
May & June 1810	(3)	211	THISTLE 10 Feby 1810	(nil)	209
ROYALIST 29 Decr 1812	(4)	249	THUNDER 9 Octr 1813	(9)	259
ST DOMINGO (6 Feb 1806)	(396)	132	TRAFALGAR		
ST SEBASTIAN			(21 Oct 1805)	(1613)	98
(8 Sept 1813)	(293)	254	UNICORN 8 June 1796	(4)	27
ST VINCENT (14 Feb 1797)	(348)	30	VENERABLE 16 Jany 1814	(42)	260
SAN FIORENZO			VICTORIOUS WITH		
8 Mar 1797	(8)	39	RIVOLI (22 Feb 1812)	(67)	242
SAN FIORENZO			VINCIEGO 30 March 1800	(2)	63
14 Feby 1805	(13)	96	VIPER 26 Decr 1799	(2)	62
SAN FIORENZO			VIRGINIE 19 May 1808	(21)	154
8 March 1808	(18)	150	WEAZEL 22 Feby 1812	(6)	243
SANTA MARGARITTA			WEAZEL 22 April 1813	(8)	250
8 June 1796	(3)	27	WOLVERINE 13 Sepr 1799	(nil)	61
SAPPHO 2 March 1808	(4)	150	ZEBRA 17 March 1794	(2)	2

www.ingramcontent.com/pod-product-compliance
Lightning Source LLC
Chambersburg PA
CBHW080857230426
43663CB00013B/2562